DLA Piper UK LLP Leeds

# HALSBURY'S
# Laws of England

## FIFTH EDITION
## 2017

## Volume 93

This is volume 93 of the Fifth Edition of Halsbury's Laws of England, containing the first part of the title SHIPPING AND MARITIME LAW.

The title SHIPPING AND MARITIME LAW replaces the title of the same name contained in volumes 93 (2008) and 94 (2008). Upon receipt of volumes 93 (2017) and 94 (2017), volumes 93 (2008) and 94 (2008) may be archived.

For a full list of volumes comprised in a current set of Halsbury's Laws of England please see overleaf.

Fifth Edition volumes:

1 (2008), 2 (2017), 3 (2011), 4 (2011), 5 (2013), 6 (2011), 7 (2015), 8 (2015), 9 (2017), 10 (2017), 11 (2015), 12 (2015), 12A (2015), 13 (2017), 14 (2016), 15 (2016), 15A (2016), 16 (2017), 17 (2017), 18 (2009), 19 (2011), 20 (2014), 21 (2016), 22 (2012), 23 (2016), 24 (2010), 25 (2016), 26 (2016), 27 (2015), 28 (2015), 29 (2014), 30 (2012), 31 (2012), 32 (2012), 33 (2013), 34 (2011), 35 (2015), 36 (2015), 37 (2013), 38 (2013), 38A (2013), 39 (2014), 40 (2014), 41 (2014), 41A (2014), 42 (2011), 43 (2011), 44 (2011), 45 (2010), 46 (2010), 47 (2014), 47A (2014), 48 (2015), 49 (2015), 50 (2016), 50A (2016), 51 (2013), 52 (2014), 53 (2014), 54 (2017), 54A (2017), 55 (2012), 56 (2017), 57 (2012), 58 (2014), 58A (2014), 59 (2014), 59A (2014), 60 (2011), 61 (2010), 62 (2016), 63 (2016), 64 (2016), 65 (2015), 66 (2015), 67 (2016), 68 (2016), 69 (2009), 70 (2012), 71 (2013), 72 (2015), 73 (2015), 74 (2011), 75 (2013), 76 (2013), 77 (2016), 78 (2010), 79 (2014), 80 (2013), 81 (2010), 82 (2010), 83 (2010), 84 (2013), 84A (2013), 85 (2012), 86 (2013), 87 (2017), 88 (2012), 88A (2013), 89 (2011), 90 (2011), 91 (2012), 92 (2015), 93 (2017), 94 (2017), 95 (2017), 96 (2012), 97 (2015), 97A (2014), 98 (2013), 99 (2012), 100 (2009), 101 (2009), 102 (2016), 103 (2016), 104 (2014)

Consolidated Index and Tables:

2017 Consolidated Index (A–E), 2017 Consolidated Index (F–O), 2017 Consolidated Index (P–Z), 2018 Consolidated Table of Statutes, 2018 Consolidated Table of Statutory Instruments, 2017 Consolidated Table of Cases (A–G), 2017 Consolidated Table of Cases (H–Q), 2017 Consolidated Table of Cases (R–Z, ECJ Cases)

Updating and ancillary materials:

2017 annual Cumulative Supplement; monthly Noter-up; annual Abridgments 1974–2016

September 2017

# HALSBURY'S
# Laws of England

## Volume 93

2017

 LexisNexis®

Members of the LexisNexis Group worldwide

| | |
|---|---|
| United Kingdom | RELX (UK) Ltd, trading as LexisNexis, 1–3 Strand, London WC2N 5JR and 9–10 St Andrew Square, Edinburgh EH2 2AF |
| Australia | Reed International Books Australia Pty Ltd trading as LexisNexis, Chatswood, New South Wales |
| Austria | LexisNexis Verlag ARD Orac GmbH & Co KG, Vienna |
| Benelux | LexisNexis Benelux, Amsterdam |
| Canada | LexisNexis Canada, Markham, Ontario |
| China | LexisNexis China, Beijing and Shanghai |
| France | LexisNexis SA, Paris |
| Germany | LexisNexis GmbH, Dusseldorf |
| Hong Kong | LexisNexis Hong Kong, Hong Kong |
| India | LexisNexis India, New Delhi |
| Italy | Giuffrè Editore, Milan |
| Japan | LexisNexis Japan, Tokyo |
| Malaysia | Malayan Law Journal Sdn Bhd, Kuala Lumpur |
| New Zealand | LexisNexis New Zealand Ltd, Wellington |
| Singapore | LexisNexis Singapore, Singapore |
| South Africa | LexisNexis, Durban |
| USA | LexisNexis, Dayton, Ohio |

| | |
|---|---|
| FIRST EDITION | *Published in 31 volumes between 1907 and 1917* |
| SECOND EDITION | *Published in 37 volumes between 1931 and 1942* |
| THIRD EDITION | *Published in 43 volumes between 1952 and 1964* |
| FOURTH EDITION | *Published in 56 volumes between 1973 and 1987, with reissues between 1988 and 2008* |
| FIFTH EDITION | *Published between 2008 and 2014, with reissues from 2014* |

© 2017 RELX (UK) Ltd

A CIP Catalogue record for this book is available from the British Library.

ISBN 978-1-4743-0602-7

9 781474 306027

ISBN for the set: 9781405734394
ISBN for this volume: 9781474306027

Typeset by LexisNexis
Printed and bound by CPI Group (UK) Ltd, Croydon, CR0 4YY

Visit LexisNexis at www.lexisnexis.co.uk

## Editor of this Volume

SIMON CADDE, LLB

## Managing Editor

HELEN HALVEY, LLB

# SHIPPING AND MARITIME LAW

## Consultant Editor

ANDREW TETTENBORN, LLB (Cantab),
Professor of Commercial Law,
Institute of International Shipping and Trade Law,
Swansea University;
Barrister (non-practising)

The law stated in this volume is in general that in force on 1 September 2017, although subsequent changes have been included wherever possible.

Any future updating material will be found in the Noter-up and annual Cumulative Supplement to Halsbury's Laws of England.

# TABLE OF CONTENTS

# HOW TO USE HALSBURY'S LAWS OF ENGLAND

## Volumes

Each text volume of Halsbury's Laws of England contains the law on the titles contained in it as at a date stated at the front of the volume (the operative date).

Information contained in Halsbury's Laws of England may be accessed in several ways.

*First, by using the tables of contents.*

Each volume contains both a general Table of Contents, and a specific Table of Contents for each title contained in it. From these tables you will be directed to the relevant part of the work.

**Readers should note that the current arrangement of titles can be found in the Noter-up.**

*Secondly, by using tables of statutes, statutory instruments, cases or other materials.*

If you know the name of the Act, statutory instrument or case with which your research is concerned, you should consult the Consolidated Tables of statutes, cases and so on (published as separate volumes) which will direct you to the relevant volume and paragraph.

(Each individual text volume also includes tables of those materials used as authority in that volume.)

*Thirdly, by using the indexes.*

If you are uncertain of the general subject area of your research, you should go to the Consolidated Index (published as separate volumes) for reference to the relevant volume(s) and paragraph(s).

(Each individual text volume also includes an index to the material contained therein.)

## Updating publications

The text volumes of Halsbury's Laws should be used in conjunction with the annual Cumulative Supplement and the monthly Noter-up.

*The annual Cumulative Supplement*

The Supplement gives details of all changes between the operative date of the text volume and the operative date of the Supplement. It is arranged in the same volume, title and paragraph order as the text volumes. Developments affecting particular points of law are noted to the relevant paragraph(s) of the text volumes.

*For narrative treatment of material noted in the Cumulative Supplement, go to the Annual Abridgment volume for the relevant year.*

### Destination Tables

In certain titles in the annual _Cumulative Supplement_, reference is made to Destination Tables showing the destination of consolidated legislation. Those Destination Tables are to be found either at the end of the titles within the annual _Cumulative Supplement_, or in a separate _Destination Tables_ booklet provided from time to time with the _Cumulative Supplement_.

### The Noter-up

The Noter-up is issued monthly and notes changes since the publication of the annual Cumulative Supplement. Also arranged in the same volume, title and paragraph order as the text volumes, the Noter-up follows the style of the Cumulative Supplement.

_For narrative treatment of material noted in the Noter-up, go to the Annual Abridgment volume for the relevant year._

# REFERENCES AND ABBREVIATIONS

| | |
|---|---|
| ACT | Australian Capital Territory |
| A-G | Attorney General |
| Admin | Administrative Court |
| Admlty | Admiralty Court |
| Adv-Gen | Advocate General |
| affd | affirmed |
| affg | affirming |
| Alta | Alberta |
| App | Appendix |
| art | article |
| Aust | Australia |
| B | Baron |
| BC | British Columbia |
| C | Command Paper (of a series published before 1900) |
| c | chapter number of an Act |
| CA | Court of Appeal |
| CAC | Central Arbitration Committee |
| CA in Ch | Court of Appeal in Chancery |
| CB | Chief Baron |
| CCA | Court of Criminal Appeal |
| CCR | County Court Rules 1981 (as subsequently amended) |
| CCR | Court for Crown Cases Reserved |
| CJEU | Court of Justice of the European Union |
| C-MAC | Courts-Martial Appeal Court |
| CO | Crown Office |
| COD | Crown Office Digest |
| CPR | Civil Procedure Rules |
| Can | Canada |
| Cd | Command Paper (of the series published 1900–18) |
| Cf | compare |
| Ch | Chancery Division |
| ch | chapter |
| cl | clause |
| Cm | Command Paper (of the series published 1986 to date) |
| Cmd | Command Paper (of the series published 1919–56) |
| Cmnd | Command Paper (of the series published 1956–86) |
| Comm | Commercial Court |

| | |
|---|---|
| Comr | Commissioner |
| Court Forms (2nd Edn) | Atkin's Encyclopaedia of Court Forms in Civil Proceedings, 2nd Edn. See note 2 post. |
| CrimPR | Criminal Procedure Rules |
| DC | Divisional Court |
| DPP | Director of Public Prosecutions |
| EAT | Employment Appeal Tribunal |
| EC | European Community |
| ECJ | Court of Justice of the European Community (before the Treaty of Lisbon (OJ C306, 17.12.2007, p 1) came into force on 1 December 2009); European Court of Justice (after the Treaty of Lisbon (OJ C306, 17.12.2007, p 1) came into force on 1 December 2009) |
| EComHR | European Commission of Human Rights |
| ECSC | European Coal and Steel Community |
| ECtHR Rules of Court | Rules of Court of the European Court of Human Rights |
| EEC | European Economic Community |
| EFTA | European Free Trade Association |
| EGC | European General Court |
| EWCA Civ | Official neutral citation for judgments of the Court of Appeal (Civil Division) |
| EWCA Crim | Official neutral citation for judgments of the Court of Appeal (Criminal Division) |
| EWHC | Official neutral citation for judgments of the High Court |
| Edn | Edition |
| Euratom | European Atomic Energy Community |
| EU | European Union |
| Ex Ch | Court of Exchequer Chamber |
| ex p | ex parte |
| Fam | Family Division |
| Fed | Federal |
| Forms & Precedents (5th Edn) | Encyclopaedia of Forms and Precedents other than Court Forms, 5th Edn. See note 2 post |
| GLC | Greater London Council |
| HC | High Court |
| HC | House of Commons |
| HK | Hong Kong |
| HL | House of Lords |
| HMRC | Her Majesty's Revenue and Customs |
| IAT | Immigration Appeal Tribunal |
| ILM | International Legal Materials |

INLR .......................... Immigration and Nationality Law Reports
IRC ........................... Inland Revenue Commissioners
Ind ........................... India
Int Rels....................... International Relations
Ir ............................. Ireland
J ............................. Justice
JA ............................ Judge of Appeal
Kan .......................... Kansas
LA ........................... Lord Advocate
LC ........................... Lord Chancellor
LCC .......................... London County Council
LCJ .......................... Lord Chief Justice
LJ ............................ Lord Justice of Appeal
LoN........................... League of Nations
MR ........................... Master of the Rolls
Man .......................... Manitoba
n............................. note
NB ........................... New Brunswick
NI............................ Northern Ireland
NS ........................... Nova Scotia
NSW.......................... New South Wales
NY........................... New York
NZ........................... New Zealand
OHIM........................ Office for Harmonisation in the Internal Market
OJ............................ The Official Journal of the European Union
 published by the Publications Office of the
 European Union
Ont .......................... Ontario
P............................. President
PC........................... Judicial Committee of the Privy Council
PEI.......................... Prince Edward Island
Pat .......................... Patents Court
q............................. question
QB........................... Queen's Bench Division
QBD......................... Queen's Bench Division of the High Court
Qld .......................... Queensland
Que.......................... Quebec
r............................. rule
RDC.......................... Rural District Council
RPC.......................... Restrictive Practices Court
RSC.......................... Rules of the Supreme Court 1965 (as subsequently
 amended)
reg .......................... regulation
Res........................... Resolution

| | |
|---|---|
| revsd | reversed |
| Rly | Railway |
| s | section |
| SA | South Africa |
| S Aust | South Australia |
| SC | Supreme Court |
| SI | Statutory Instruments published by authority |
| SR & O | Statutory Rules and Orders published by authority |
| SR & O Rev 1904 | Revised Edition comprising all Public and General Statutory Rules and Orders in force on 31 December 1903 |
| SR & O Rev 1948 | Revised Edition comprising all Public and General Statutory Rules and Orders and Statutory Instruments in force on 31 December 1948 |
| SRNI | Statutory Rules of Northern Ireland |
| STI | Simon's Tax Intelligence (1973–1995); Simon's Weekly Tax Intelligence (1996-current) |
| Sask | Saskatchewan |
| Sch | Schedule |
| Sess | Session |
| Sing | Singapore |
| TCC | Technology and Construction Court |
| TS | Treaty Series |
| Tanz | Tanzania |
| Tas | Tasmania |
| UDC | Urban District Council |
| UKHL | Official neutral citation for judgments of the House of Lords |
| UKPC | Official neutral citation for judgments of the Privy Council |
| UN | United Nations |
| V-C | Vice-Chancellor |
| Vict | Victoria |
| W Aust | Western Australia |
| Zimb | Zimbabwe |

NOTE 1. A general list of the abbreviations of law reports and other sources used in this work can be found at the beginning of the Consolidated Table of Cases.

NOTE 2. Where references are made to other publications, the volume number precedes and the page number follows the name of the publication; eg the reference '12 Forms & Precedents (5th Edn) 44' refers to volume 12 of the Encyclopaedia of Forms and Precedents, page 44.

NOTE 3. An English statute is cited by short title or, where there is no short title, by regnal year and chapter number together with the name by which it is commonly known or a description of its subject matter and date. In the case of a foreign statute, the mode of citation generally follows the style of citation in use in the country concerned with the addition, where necessary, of the name of the country in parentheses.

NOTE 4. A statutory instrument is cited by short title, if any, followed by the year and number, or, if unnumbered, the date.

# TABLE OF STATUTES

# TABLE OF STATUTORY INSTRUMENTS

# TABLE OF PROCEDURE

## Civil Procedure

### Civil Procedure Rules 1998, SI 1998/3132 (CPR)

### Practice Directions relating to Civil Procedure

# TABLE OF EUROPEAN UNION LEGISLATION

## Secondary Legislation

### Decisions

### Directives

### Regulations

## Recommendations

# TABLE OF TREATIES AND CONVENTIONS, ETC

# TABLE OF CASES

## C

PARA

PARA

## H

PARA

# I

PARA

PARA

PARA

# W

Decisions of the European Court of Justice are listed below numerically. These decisions
are also included in the preceding alphabetical list.

# SHIPPING AND MARITIME LAW

Vol 93

# 1. INTRODUCTION

## (1) IN GENERAL

### (i) Scope of Title

**1. Private maritime law and the public international law of the sea.** This title sets out the law of England and Wales relating to shipping and maritime matters as applied by the Admiralty Court within its jurisdiction[1], being the relevant private maritime law that applies where the public international law of the sea does not[2]. This title is not concerned with military uses of the sea[3] (nor with the related issue of prize[4]) but with peaceful uses of the sea, which include the domestic jurisdiction over merchant shipping[5] and matters of navigation (including safety and security at sea and the avoidance of collisions)[6]. Hovercraft are also discussed[7]. Although maritime lien[8] and marine salvage[9] are described in this title, marine insurance and carriage by sea generally are not[10]; nor are matters such as the exploitation of the sea and its resources[11], the exploitation of the continental shelf[12] or related matters consequent on man's use of the sea[13]. These subjects are covered elsewhere in the work[14].

1 Ie the Admiralty jurisdiction of the High Court assigned to the Admiralty Court, which includes jurisdiction to hear and determine questions and claims as to the possession, ownership or mortgage of a ship, damage done or received by a ship, salvage, towage, pilotage, supply of goods or materials, wages, disbursements, bottomry and forfeiture or condemnation of a ship, and, with certain exceptions, the jurisdiction of the High Court under the Merchant Shipping Act 1995 (as to which see PARA 15 et seq): see the Senior Courts Act 1981 ss 6(1), 20–24; and PARA 85 et seq. Although the sources of the original maritime law were largely non-statutory, the inherent jurisdiction of the Admiralty Court, and the law that it applies, is now governed largely by statute: see PARA 79 et seq.
2 Because the scope of this title is limited to the municipal law of the United Kingdom, the rules that govern international relations between states in shipping and maritime matters are dealt with elsewhere in this work. Specifically, in relation to the rules that are used to govern the legal status of waters, rights of passage and protection, and criminal and civil jurisdiction, see INTERNATIONAL RELATIONS LAW vol 61 (2010) PARA 121 et seq. This is not to say that the law which is within the cognisance of the Admiralty Court lacks an international aspect, as this is inherent in the subject matter, and is manifest eg in relation to its dealings with non-British ships and with injurious acts committed within its jurisdiction: see PARA 3 et seq. Of course, the United Kingdom is governed also by any international treaties which it has ratified and by the legislation of the European Union: see PARA 7 et seq.
    The law relating to landward waters, ie inland waters and the inland waterways, is also dealt with elsewhere in this work: see WATER AND WATERWAYS vol 100 (2009) PARA 63 et seq. As to the sovereignty of airspace which is superjacent to the sea see AVIATION vol 2 (2017) PARA 703.
3 As to general maritime issues relating to war and neutrality, however, see PARAS 4–6, 1167.
4 As to which see PRIZE.
5 Ie that which is to be found within the relevant parts of the Merchant Shipping Act 1995 and other statutes such as the Shipping and Trading Interests (Protection) Act 1995: see PARA 15 et seq. As to the provisions governing vessels which come within the jurisdiction of the Merchant Shipping Act 1995 see PARA 229 et seq; and as to the crew and crewing requirements under the Merchant Shipping Act 1995 see PARA 423 et seq. As to offences and legal proceedings arising from the application of these statutes see PARA 1073 et seq.
6 As to pilotage and towage see PARA 574 et seq; as to safety and security at sea see PARA 601 et seq; and as to the avoidance of collisions see PARA 690 et seq. As to accident investigations and inquiries see PARA 815 et seq. As to lighthouse authorities see PARA 1017 et seq.
7 See PARA 381 et seq.
8 See PARA 964 et seq.
9 See PARA 849 et seq.
10 As to marine insurance see INSURANCE vol 60 (2011) PARA 238 et seq; and as to carriage by sea see CARRIAGE AND CARRIERS vol 7 (2015) PARA 206 et seq. As the limitation of liability in maritime claims, however, see PARA 992 et seq.

11 As to eg fishing see FISHERIES AND AQUACULTURE vol 51 (2013) PARA 201 et seq. As to marine scientific research see INTERNATIONAL RELATIONS LAW vol 61 (2010) PARA 194.

12 Eg for the purposes of obtaining its fuel and energy reserves (as to which see ENERGY AND CLIMATE CHANGE vol 44 (2011) PARAS 1078 et seq, 1100 et seq, which deal with such matters as offshore workings, offshore storage and installations and submarine pipelines).

13 As to eg marine pollution see ENVIRONMENTAL QUALITY AND PUBLIC HEALTH vol 45 (2010) PARAS 572–575.

14 See notes 10–13.

## (ii) English Private Maritime Law

**2. English maritime law.** Maritime law[1] is not the ordinary municipal law of England and Wales, but is the law which either is binding on the Admiralty Court by statute or has been adopted by the court by decision, tradition and principle[2]. It comprises both the inherent jurisdiction of the former High Court of Admiralty[3], the extent of which jurisdiction is to be deduced from practice or judgments[4], and law derived from statute[5]. Statute law has now superseded to a considerable extent the original maritime law; and the Admiralty jurisdiction of the High Court is largely governed by statute[6].

1  In relation eg to navigation on the high seas beyond the territorial limits of the United Kingdom maritime law was said to be 'those rules of navigation which usually prevail among nations navigating the seas where the collision takes place': *The Zollverein* (1856) Sw 96 at 99 per Dr Lushington. It was this law which was applied by the English Admiralty Court in cases of collision on the high seas, not the law of the ship's flag: see eg *Chartered Mercantile Bank of India, London and China v Netherlands India Steam Navigation Co Ltd* (1883) 10 QBD 521 at 545, 5 Asp MLC 65 at 71, CA, per Lindley LJ. The statement as to the nature of maritime law made in *The Zollverein* was made in reference to the law apart from statute, in particular apart from the effect of the Merchant Shipping Act Amendment Act 1862 s 25 (repealed), which established collision regulations, and s 54 (repealed), which rendered the provisions for limitation of liability applicable to foreign ships. As to the provisions now in force relating to the prevention of collisions see PARA 690 et seq; and as to the provisions now in force relating to the limitation of liability in maritime claims see PARA 992 et seq. The Admiralty Court applied the general rule of the sea to a ship belonging to the Crown to which the merchant shipping legislation did not apply: see *HMS Topaze* (1864) 10 LT 659 at 661; *HMS Supply* (1865) 12 LT 799.

2  See *The Gas Float Whitton No 2* [1896] P 42 at 47, 8 Asp MLC 110 at 111, CA (affd sub nom *Wells v Gas Float Whitton No 2 (Owners)* [1897] AC 337, 8 Asp MLC 272, HL) (a salvage case), citing *The Gaetano and Maria* (1882) 7 PD 137 at 143, 4 Asp MLC 535 at 539, 540, CA; and see PARA 82. The maritime law so adopted has been referred to as part of the common law: see eg *Chartered Mercantile Bank of India, London and China v Netherlands India Steam Navigation Co Ltd* (1883) 10 QBD 521 at 537, 5 Asp MLC 65 at 68, CA, per Lord Esher MR.

3  As to the origin and exercise of the jurisdiction of Admiralty courts see PARA 79 et seq. The inherent jurisdiction of the Admiralty Court is derived from that of the High Court of Admiralty, as extended by the Admiralty Court Act 1840, the Admiralty Court Act 1854 and the Admiralty Court Act 1861 (all now repealed). The principal subjects of jurisdiction left with the Admiralty Court after its conflict with the common law courts were injurious acts committed on the high seas, suits of salvage, suits of possession, cases of hypothecation (since the contract of hypothecation was not recognised by the common law), and cases concerning seamen's wages: see PARA 80.

4  *The Gas Float Whitton No 2* [1896] P 42 at 48, 8 Asp MLC 110 at 111, CA; affd sub nom *Wells v Gas Float Whitton No 2 (Owners)* [1897] AC 337, 8 Asp MLC 272, HL.

5  As to the current merchant shipping legislation see PARA 15 et seq.

6  See the Senior Courts Act 1981 ss 20–24; and PARA 85 et seq.

**3. Extended scope of English jurisdiction.** Maritime law is principally within the cognisance of the Admiralty Court[1] and necessarily has international aspects[2]. The jurisdiction of the Admiralty Court has long extended to foreign ships on the high seas[3], except ships of a foreign sovereign state used for public purposes[4], and to injurious acts committed on the high seas[5].

The rules on jurisdiction which apply in relation to tort can no longer draw a sharp distinction between torts which took place in England and torts which took place outside. The English court has jurisdiction in respect of torts, whether English or foreign, whenever it has jurisdiction in personam over the defendant[6].

1   As to Admiralty jurisdiction and Admiralty courts see PARA 79 et seq. The Admiralty jurisdiction of the High Court is now governed principally by the Senior Courts Act 1981 ss 20–24: see PARA 85 et seq.
    Although the Merchant Shipping Act 1995 s 14 (offences relating to a ship's British connection) (see PARA 1065) applies to things done outside, as well as to things done within, the United Kingdom, criminal jurisdiction over eg crimes committed in whole or in part in a British ship is not within the scope of this title, but is considered elsewhere. It arose out of Admiralty jurisdiction but, if the trial is in England or Wales, would be exercised as part of the general criminal jurisdiction: see CRIMINAL PROCEDURE vol 27 (2015) PARA 11 et seq. Foreigners in a British ship are subject to English criminal jurisdiction: see *R v Keyn* (1876) 2 Ex D 63 at 161 per Cockburn CJ; and CRIMINAL PROCEDURE vol 27 (2015) PARAS 12–13. Similarly, carriage by sea and the principles of English law relating to the sale of goods are not within the scope of this title, even where the goods are to be carried in ships. As to the law relating to charterparties, bills of lading and the carriage of goods by sea see CARRIAGE AND CARRIERS vol 7 (2015) PARA 206 et seq; and as to the general law concerning contracts for the sale of goods see SALE OF GOODS AND SUPPLY OF SERVICES vol 91 (2012) PARA 28 et seq. As to the meaning of 'United Kingdom' see PARA 16 note 3.
2   See eg *The Charkieh* (1873) LR 4 A & E 120 at 122, where Sir R Phillimore said, in relation to the Admiralty Court, that the court administers private international law and has jurisdiction notwithstanding that the parties are foreigners. English maritime law, apart from statute, should be distinguished from the international law administered, subject to statute, in regard to prize: see PRIZE vol 85 (2012) PARA 601 et seq. The instance court of Admiralty was a municipal court, different from a court of Admiralty acting under prize commission: see *The Wild Ranger* (1862) 32 LJPM & A 49 at 56 per Dr Lushington. The term 'instance court' signified the civil court as distinct from the prize court.
3   See eg *The Mali Ivo* (1869) LR 2 A & E 356 (collision); *Chartered Mercantile Bank of India, London and China v Netherlands, India Steam Navigation Co Ltd* (1883) 10 QBD 521 at 537, 545, 5 Asp MLC 65 at 68, 71, CA; *Mersey Docks and Harbour Board v Turner, The Zeta* [1893] AC 468 at 482–486, 7 Asp MLC 369 at 373, 374, HL.
4   See *The Parlement Belge* (1880) 5 PD 197, 4 Asp MLC 234, CA (action in rem); *The Annette, The Dora* [1919] P 105. As to foreign sovereign immunity from process and its waiver see PARA 90 et seq.
5   *The Tubantia* [1924] P 78 at 86, 18 Ll L Rep 158 at 159 (trespass to the possession of a salvor). A distinction must be drawn between civil and criminal jurisdiction. As to Admiralty jurisdiction in relation to torts see CONFLICT OF LAWS vol 19 (2011) PARA 666.
6   See the Private International Law (Miscellaneous Provisions) Act 1995 Pt III (ss 9–15); Parliament and Council Regulation (EC) 864/2007 (OJ L199, 31.7.2007, p 40) ('the Rome II Regulation'); and CONFLICT OF LAWS vol 19 (2011) PARA 647 et seq.

## (iii)  Maritime Issues relating to War and Neutrality

**4.  Requisition of British ships.** In time of war or national emergency, the Crown has a prerogative right to requisition British ships in territorial waters[1]. The requisition of ships and of anything on board ship[2] and the requisition of shipping space were effected during the 1939–45 war under defence regulations[3]; and compensation was payable in accordance with statute[4], there being established a shipping claims tribunal for determining disputes as to the payment of compensation[5].

1   See CONSTITUTIONAL AND ADMINISTRATIVE LAW vol 20 (2014) PARA 547; and see eg the Prerogative Order in Council Requisition of Ships Order 1982 (4 April 1982) (relating to the Falkland Islands conflict).
2   A mere order to discharge a cargo is not necessarily a requisition of the cargo: see *Nicolaou v Minister of War Transport* [1944] 2 All ER 322.
3   See the Defence (General) Regulations 1939, SR & O 1939/927, regs 53, 54 (revoked).
4   See the Compensation (Defence) Act 1939 ss 1(1)(b), 4–6; and ARMED CONFLICT AND EMERGENCY vol 3 (2011) PARA 11.
5   See the Compensation (Defence) Act 1939 s 8(1), (2); and ARMED CONFLICT AND EMERGENCY vol 3 (2011) PARA 11. As to insurance of ships against war risks see INSURANCE vol 60 (2011) PARA 793 et seq.

**5.   Convoys.** In times of war, it has been the custom for cargo vessels to sail in convoy, to lessen the effect of enemy action[1]. As a result, a master of a ship may be placed under a contractual duty to sail in convoy by a term of the contract of carriage[2], express or implied, to that effect[3]. In time of war, ships may become subject to orders of the Defence Council[4], issued with legislative authority, in respect of their movements and navigation generally[5]; and these orders may enjoin obedience to routeing instructions issued by the Defence Council or by a convoy commander[6].

If the master or other person having command of any ship of any of Her Majesty's subjects in convoy with any of Her Majesty's ships of war[7] wilfully disobeys any lawful signal, instruction or command of the convoy commander or without leave deserts the convoy, he is liable on conviction to a fine of any amount or imprisonment for not more than one year[8].

During the 1939–45 war the duty of obedience to convoy orders overrode contrary obligations under the regulations for preventing collisions at sea[9], and the master of a vessel was not, therefore, negligent in not complying with those regulations if he was executing convoy orders[10]. Otherwise, masters of vessels remained bound by the duty of good seamanship and, so far as the circumstances permitted, the duty to take the action prescribed by those regulations to avoid collision[11]. Where the master of a vessel accepts and undertakes the duties of a convoy commander, the owners of his vessel are not liable for damage by consequent collision caused by an act of negligence on the part of the master in the course of performing his duties as convoy commander[12].

1   As to the meaning of 'sailing in convoy' see *Hibbert v Pigou* (1783) 3 Doug KB 224. As to extent and condition of sailing in convoy see further *Jefferies v Legendra* (1691) Carth 216; *Lethulier's Case* (1602) 2 Salk 443; *Gordon v Morley, Campell v Bordieu* (1747) 2 Stra 1265; *Lilly v Ewer* (1779) 1 Doug KB 72; *Smith v Readshaw* (1781) 2 Park's Marine Insurances (8th Edn) 708; *Manning v Gist* (1782) 3 Doug KB 74; *D'Eguino v Bewicke* (1795) 2 Hy Bl 551; *De Garey v Clagget* (1795) 2 Park's Marine Insurances (8th Edn) 708; *Webb v Thomson* (1797) 1 Bos & P 5; *Audley v Duff* (1800) 2 Bos & P 111; *Anderson v Pitcher* (1800) 2 Bos & P 164. As to sailing in or without convoy in relation to marine insurance see *Harrington v Halkeld* (1778) 2 Park's Marine Insurances (8th Edn) 639; and INSURANCE vol 60 (2011) PARAS 319–320.
2   As to contracts of carriage see CARRIAGE AND CARRIERS vol 7 (2015) PARA 206 et seq.
3   See *Philips v Baillie* (1784) 3 Doug KB 374; *Runquist v Ditchell* (1799) 3 Esp 64; *Magalhaens v Busher* (1814) 4 Camp 54.
4   As to the Defence Council see CONSTITUTIONAL AND ADMINISTRATIVE LAW vol 20 (2014) PARA 562.
5   During the 1939–45 war, the Admiralty had power to make navigation orders and a master of a vessel contravening or not complying with such an order was guilty of an offence: see the Defence (General) Regulations 1939, SR & O 1939/927, reg 43 (revoked).
6   For an example of such a navigation order see *The Vernon City* [1942] P 9; affd [1942] P 61, 72 Ll L Rep 223, CA.
7   For these purposes, 'any of Her Majesty's ships of war' includes any hired armed ship or vessel in Her Majesty's service: Naval Prize Act 1864 s 2.
8   Naval Prize Act 1864 s 46 (amended by the Courts Act 1971 s 56(4), Sch 11 Pt IV).
9   As to the current regulations see PARA 690 et seq.
10  *The Vernon City* [1942] P 9; affd [1942] P 61, 72 Ll L Rep 223, CA. See also *Larchbank (Owners) v British Petrol (Owners), The Larchbank* [1943] AC 299 at 305, 74 Ll L Rep 135 at 138, HL, per Lord Wright.
11  *The Scottish Musician* [1942] P 128, 72 Ll L Rep 284; *The FJ Wolfe* [1946] P 91, sub nom *A-G v Anglo-American Oil Co Ltd, The FJ Wolfe* [1946] 1 All ER 359, CA. See also *The Emlyn* [1918] P 67.
12  *The Glaucus and City of Florence* [1948] P 95, 81 Ll L Rep 131. As to the duty of the commander of a naval escort in respect of the navigation of a convoy and the question of his liability for negligence in carrying out that duty see *The Sobieski* [1949] P 313, [1949] 1 All ER 701, 82 Ll L Rep 370, CA (where a failure to take reasonable care made the escort commander liable personally, but this was not a fault in the navigation of his vessel, hence no contribution was ordered).

**6.  Hospital ships.** Hospital ships must in no circumstances be attacked but must be respected and protected at all times: they are subject to control and search by the conflicting parties and must give assistance without distinction of nationality[1].

Hospital ships must have all their exterior surfaces white and one or more dark red crosses must be painted on each side of the hull and on horizontal surfaces; a white flag with a red cross must be flown at the mainmast[2].

1   See ARMED CONFLICT AND EMERGENCY vol 3 (2011) PARA 28.
2   See ARMED CONFLICT AND EMERGENCY vol 3 (2011) PARA 29. As to the restrictions on the use of the red cross emblem and the words 'Red Cross' and 'Geneva Cross' see ARMED CONFLICT AND EMERGENCY vol 3 (2011) PARA 29.

## (2)  CONVENTIONS AND LEGISLATION

### (i)  International Conventions and Organisations

**7.  International Conventions.** Difficulties which might otherwise arise from differences between the law administered by the English Admiralty Court and the law administered by courts of foreign countries, either because of differences in rules of conduct on the high seas adopted in those courts or because of differing statute law, have been lessened or avoided by international Conventions.

Conventions relating to maritime law have been incorporated into English law in one of two ways: by statutory measures whose provisions have the effect of the Convention[1]; or by statutory measures which embody the original text of the Convention itself, usually in a Schedule, with separate changes to be made under English law for the satisfactory operation of the Convention[2]. The former method of incorporation may lead to difficulties or ambiguities in interpretation, whereas the latter method should not[3].

Among the international Conventions are:
(1)    the International Convention relating to the Arrest of Seagoing Ships 1952[4];
(2)    the International Convention on Load Lines 1966[5];
(3)    the International Convention on Tonnage Measurement of Ships 1969[6];
(4)    the Convention on the International Regulations for Preventing Collisions at Sea (COLREGS) 1972[7];
(5)    the International Convention for Safe Containers ('CSC') 1972[8];
(6)    the International Convention for the Safety of Life at Sea ('SOLAS') 1974[9];
(7)    the Convention on Limitation of Liability for Maritime Claims 1976[10];
(8)    the Merchant Shipping (Minimum Standards) Convention 1976[11];
(9)    the Convention on the International Maritime Satellite Organisation ('INMARSAT')[12];
(10)   the International Convention for the Safety of Fishing Vessels 1977[13];
(11)   the International Convention on Standards of Training, Certification and Watchkeeping for Seafarers ('STCW') 1978[14];
(12)   the International Convention on Maritime Search and Rescue 1979[15];
(13)   the Convention for the Suppression of Unlawful Acts against the Safety of Maritime Navigation 1988[16];
(14)   the International Convention on Salvage 1989[17];
(15)   the International Convention on the Removal of Wrecks ('ICRW') 2007[18].

Conventions which govern related activities such as carriage by sea or marine pollution are discussed elsewhere in this work[19].

Relevant measures which bind the United Kingdom arise also from membership of the EU[20].

1 See eg the Merchant Shipping (Load Line) Regulations 1998, SI 1998/2241, which apply the provisions of the International Convention on Load Lines (London, 5 April to 4 July 1966; TS 58 (1968); Cmnd 3708) to all United Kingdom ships which go to sea (with certain exceptions) and to all sea-going foreign ships within United Kingdom waters (see head (2) in the text; and PARA 660 et seq).

2 See eg the Merchant Shipping Act 1995 s 224(1), (2), Sch 11 Pt I (salvage), which incorporates the International Convention on Salvage (London, 28 April 1989; Cm 1526) (see head (14) in the text; and PARA 851 et seq).

3 As to the interpretation of treaties etc see INTERNATIONAL RELATIONS LAW vol 61 (2010) PARA 95 et seq.

4 Ie the International Convention relating to the Arrest of Seagoing Ships 1952 (Brussels, 10 May 1952; Cmd 8954). The Administration of Justice Act 1956 (largely repealed) (see now the Senior Courts Act 1981 Pt II (ss 15–52)) gave effect in English law to the International Convention relating to the Arrest of Seagoing Ships 1952, although the Convention is not mentioned explicitly: see *The Banco* [1971] P 137, [1971] 1 All ER 524, [1971] 1 Lloyd's Rep 49, CA; and PARA 86. The International Convention relating to the Arrest of Seagoing Ships 1952 art 7(2) is implemented by the Civil Jurisdiction and Judgments Act 1982 s 26 which enables the court to retain an arrested ship (or any bail or security given instead) as security for the satisfaction of a judgment of a foreign court which is enforceable in England and Wales, where the ship was arrested in proceedings begun in England and Wales and subsequently stayed or dismissed on jurisdictional grounds: see PARA 86.

5 Ie the International Convention on Load Lines (London, 5 April to 4 July 1966; TS 58 (1968); Cmnd 3708), implemented by the Merchant Shipping (Load Lines) Act 1967 (repealed) (see now the Merchant Shipping (Load Line) Regulations 1998, SI 1998/2241; and note 1).

6 Ie the International Convention on Tonnage Measurement of Ships (London, 23 June to 23 December 1969; TS 50 (1982); Cmnd 8716), implemented by the Merchant Shipping (Tonnage) Regulations 1997, SI 1997/1510 (as to which see PARA 248 et seq).

7 See the International Regulations for Preventing Collisions at Sea (London, 20 October 1972; TS 77 (1977); Cmnd 6962). Vessels to which the Merchant Shipping (Distress Signals and Prevention of Collisions) Regulations 1996, SI 1996/75, apply must comply with the provisions of the International Regulations for Preventing Collisions at Sea 1972: see PARA 690 et seq. See also the International Convention on certain Rules concerning Civil Jurisdiction in matters of Collision 1952 (Brussels, 10 May 1952; Cmd 8954), to which the Administration of Justice Act 1956 (largely repealed) gave effect in English law (see now the Senior Courts Act 1981 Pt II (ss 15–52), especially s 22 (cited in PARA 94); and note 4).

8 Ie the International Convention for Safe Containers (Geneva, 2 December 1972; TS 40 (1979); Cmnd 7535). See PARA 649 et seq.

9 Ie the International Convention for the Safety of Life at Sea 1974 (London, 1 November 1974 to 1 July 1975; TS 46 (1980); Cmnd 7874), with Protocol (London, 1 June 1978 to 1 March 1979; TS 40 (1981); Cmnd 8277). The Convention covers safety measures (see PARA 634 et seq), including matters such as the seaworthiness of vessels (as to which see PARA 602 et seq) and the carriage of goods (as to which see PARA 649 et seq).

10 Ie the Convention on Limitation of Liability for Maritime Claims (London, 1 to 19 November 1976; TS 13 (1990); Cm 955), implemented by the Merchant Shipping Act 1979 s 17, Sch 4 (repealed) (see now the Merchant Shipping Act 1995 Sch 7 Pt I; and PARA 992 et seq).

11 Ie the Merchant Shipping (Minimum Standards) Convention 1976 (ILO No 147) (Cmnd 7183), partly implemented by the Merchant Shipping and Fishing Vessels (Health and Safety at Work) Regulations 1997, SI 1997/2962 (as to which see PARA 626 et seq); and the Merchant Shipping and Fishing Vessels (Health and Safety at Work) (Employment of Young Persons) Regulations 1998, SI 1998/2411 (as to which see PARAS 449, 450).

12 Ie the Convention on the International Maritime Satellite Organisation (INMARSAT) (with Operating Agreement) (London, 3 September 1976; TS 94 (1979); Cmnd 7722).

13 Ie the Torremolinos International Convention for the Safety of Fishing Vessels (London, 1 October 1977 to 13 June 1978; Misc 17 (1978); Cmnd 7252), implemented via the Torremolinos Protocol (Cmnd 3339) relating to the Torremolinos International Convention for the Safety of Fishing Vessels 1977 and the Cape Town Agreement of 2012 on the Implementation of the Provisions of the 1993 Protocol relating to the Torremolinos International Convention for the Safety of Fishing Vessels, 1977. Compliance is provided for by Council Directive (EC) 97/70 of 11 December 1997

(OJ L34, 09.02.1998, p 1) setting up a harmonised safety regime for fishing vessels of 24 metres in length and over, which is implemented in the United Kingdom by the Fishing Vessels (EC Directive on Harmonised Safety Regime) Regulations 1999, SI 1999/2998 (as to which see PARAS 607, 608.

14 Ie the International Convention on Standards of Training, Certification and Watchkeeping for Seafarers 1978 (London, 1 December 1978 to 30 November 1979; TS 50 (1984); Cmnd 9266), implemented by the Merchant Shipping (Standards of Training, Certification and Watchkeeping) Regulations 2015, SI 2015/782 (as to which see PARA 503 et seq).

15 Ie the International Convention on Maritime Search and Rescue (Hamburg, 9 to 27 April 1979; Misc 19 (1980); Cmnd 7994) (see further Council Recommendation (EC) 83/419 (OJ L237, 26.8.83, p 34) on the ratification of or accession to the International Convention on Maritime Search and Rescue 1979; and PARA 14).

16 Ie the Convention for the Suppression of Unlawful Acts against the Safety of Maritime Navigation (Rome, 10 March 1988; TS 64 (1995); Cm 2947); and see the Protocol for the Suppression of Unlawful Acts against the Safety of Fixed Platforms located on the Continental Shelf, supplementary to the Rome Convention (Rome, 10 March 1988; TS 64 (1995); Cm 2947). These Conventions have been implemented in the United Kingdom by the Aviation and Maritime Security Act 1990: see PARA 1147 et seq.

17 Ie the International Convention on Salvage (London, 28 April 1989; Cm 1526), implemented by the Merchant Shipping Act 1995 Sch 11 Pt I: see PARA 851 et seq.

18 Ie the International Convention on the Removal of Wrecks (Nairobi, 18 May 2007; Cm 8243), implemented by the Merchant Shipping Act 1995 Pt 9A (ss 255A–255U): see PARA 923 et seq.

19 The most important are: the International Convention for the Prevention of Pollution from Ships (London, 8 October to 2 November 1973; Misc 26 (1974); Cmnd 5748), with Protocol (London, 1 June 1978 to 31 May 1979; Misc 27 (1978); Cmnd 7347) ('MARPOL') (as to which see ENVIRONMENTAL QUALITY AND PUBLIC HEALTH vol 45 (2010) PARA 4); and the International Convention on Civil Liability for Oil Pollution Damage (Brussels, 29 November 1969 to 31 December 1970; TS 106 (1975); Cmnd 6183) with Protocol (London, 27 November 1992) ('CLC') (as to which see ENVIRONMENTAL QUALITY AND PUBLIC HEALTH vol 45 (2010) PARA 441 et seq). As to conventions relating to arbitration and legal procedure see ARBITRATION vol 2 (2017) PARA 588 et seq; and as to conventions relating to the carriage of goods and passengers by sea see CARRIAGE AND CARRIERS vol 7 (2015) PARAS 372 et seq, 635 et seq. As to the Convention on Facilitation of International Maritime Traffic (London, 9 April 1965; TS 46 (1967); Cmnd 3299 (amended by TS 63 (1972); Cmnd 5006; annex amended by TS 63 (1978); Cmnd 7243) see INTERNATIONAL RELATIONS LAW vol 61 (2010) PARA 121.

20 See PARA 14 et seq.

## 8. United Nations Conference on the Law of the Sea 1958.

On 29 April 1958, four Conventions were adopted, following the first United Nations Conference on the Law of the Sea held from 24 February to 27 April in that year at Geneva, on the following subjects[1]:

(1)  the territorial sea and the contiguous zone[2];
(2)  the high seas[3];
(3)  fishing and conservation of the living resources of the high seas[4]; and
(4)  the continental shelf[5].

There was also an optional Protocol of signature concerning the compulsory settlement of disputes, and nine resolutions were adopted relating to nuclear tests on the high seas, the pollution of the high seas by radioactive materials, the humane killing of marine life and other matters[6].

1  Certain provisions of the 1958 conference were made effective by the Continental Shelf Act 1964 (see INTERNATIONAL RELATIONS LAW vol 61 (2010) PARA 172) and by the Tokyo Convention Act 1967 s 4 (now repealed) (definition of 'piracy').

2  Ie the Convention on the Territorial Sea and the Contiguous Zone (Geneva, 29 April 1958; TS 3 (1965); Cmnd 2511).

3  Ie the Convention on the High Seas (Geneva, 29 April 1958; TS 5 (1963); Cmnd 1929).

4  Ie the Convention on Fishing and Conservation of the Living Resources of the High Seas (Geneva, 29 April to 31 October 1958; TS 39 (1966); Cmnd 3028).

5  Ie the Convention on the Continental Shelf (Geneva, 29 April to 31 October 1958; TS 39 (1964); Cmnd 2422).

6  See note 1.

**9. United Nations Convention on the Law of the Sea 1982.** On 10 December 1982, the United Nations Convention on the Law of the Sea 1982 ('UNCLOS') was adopted at Montego Bay, Jamaica after nine years of work by the Third United Nations Conference on the Law of the Sea[1]. The 1982 Convention entered into force on 16 November 1994, 12 months after the sixtieth instrument of ratification was received[2].

The 1982 Convention lays down a comprehensive regime of law and order in the world's oceans and seas[3], establishing rules governing all uses of the oceans and their resources, including measures relating to:

(1)     the territorial sea and contiguous zone[4];

(2)     straits used for international navigation[5];

(3)     archipelago states[6];

(4)     the exclusive economic zone[7];

(5)     the continental shelf[8];

(6)     the high seas[9];

(7)     regime of islands[10];

(8)     enclosed or semi-enclosed seas[11];

(9)     right of access of land-locked states to and from the sea and freedom of transit[12];

(10)    the Area[13];

(11)    protection and preservation of the marine environment[14];

(12)    marine scientific research[15];

(13)    development and transfer of marine technology[16];

(14)    settlement of disputes[17]; and

(15)    supplementary matters which are contained in annexes to the Convention[18].

The United Kingdom was not an original signatory to the 1982 Convention but became a party to the Convention on 24 August 1997[19].

The 1982 Convention prevails, as between states parties, over the Geneva Conventions on the Law of the Sea of 1958[20].

1   Ie the United Nations Convention on the Law of the Sea (Montego Bay, 10 December 1982 to 9 December 1984; TS 3 Misc 11 (1983); Cmnd 8941) (the 'United Nations Convention on the Law of the Sea 1982').

2   For many states, the conclusion of the Agreement relating to the Implementation of Part XI of the United Nations Convention on the Law of the Sea of 10 December 1982 (New York, 28 July 1994; Misc 44 (1994); Cmnd 2705) (see note 13) provided the condition that allowed the entry into force of United Nations Convention on the Law of the Sea 1982.

3   As to the general introductory provision see the United Nations Convention on the Law of the Sea 1982 Pt I (art 1) (use of terms and scope); as to the general provisions which cover the signatories' general rights and duties under the Convention see Pt XVI (arts 300–304); and as to the provisions which govern the signature, ratification, amendment etc of the Convention see Pt XVII (arts 305–320) (final clauses).

    In order to administer and to enforce the regime established by the United Nations Convention on the Law of the Sea 1982, the following bodies are established thereunder:

    (1)     the International Seabed Authority (see note 13);

    (2)     the International Tribunal for the Law of the Sea (see note 18);

    (3)     the Commission on the Limits of the Continental Shelf (see note 18).

4   Ie the United Nations Convention on the Law of the Sea 1982 Pt II (arts 2–33) which relates to: general provisions (art 2); limits of the territorial sea (arts 3–16); innocent passage in the territorial sea (arts 17–32); and contiguous zone (art 33).

5   Ie the United Nations Convention on the Law of the Sea 1982 Pt III (arts 34–45) which relates to: general provisions (arts 34–36); transit passage (arts 37–44); and innocent passage (art 45).

6   Ie the United Nations Convention on the Law of the Sea 1982 Pt IV (arts 46–54).

7   Ie the United Nations Convention on the Law of the Sea 1982 Pt V (arts 55–75).

8   Ie the United Nations Convention on the Law of the Sea 1982 Pt VI (arts 76–85).

9   Ie the United Nations Convention on the Law of the Sea 1982 Pt VII (arts 86–120) which relates to: general provisions (arts 86–115); and management and conservation of the living resources of the high seas (arts 116–120).

10  Ie the United Nations Convention on the Law of the Sea 1982 Pt VIII (art 121).

11  Ie the United Nations Convention on the Law of the Sea 1982 Pt IX (arts 122, 123).

12  Ie the United Nations Convention on the Law of the Sea 1982 Pt X (arts 124–132).

13  Ie the United Nations Convention on the Law of the Sea 1982 Pt XI (arts 133–191) which relates to: general provisions (arts 133–135); principles governing the Area (arts 136–149); development of resources of the Area (arts 150–155); the Authority (arts 156–185); and settlement of disputes and advisory opinions (arts 186–191). 'Area' means the seabed and ocean floor and subsoil thereof, beyond the limits of national jurisdiction (art 1(1)(1)); and 'Authority' means the International Seabed Authority (art 1(1)(2)). As to the International Sea-Bed Authority see PARA 12. There is also a supplementary Agreement relating to the Implementation of Part XI of the United Nations Convention on the Law of the Sea of 10 December 1982 (New York, 28 July 1994; Misc 44 (1994); Cmnd 2705), which sought a compromise on the controversial provisions on deep seabed mining and significantly alters certain provisions of the United Nations Convention on the Law of the Sea 1982 Pt XI in favour of a more market orientated approach.

14  Ie the United Nations Convention on the Law of the Sea 1982 Pt XII (arts 192–237) which relates to: general provisions (arts 192–196); global and regional co-operation (arts 197–201); technical assistance (arts 202, 203); monitoring and environmental assessment (arts 204–206); international rules and national legislation to prevent, reduce and control pollution of the marine environment (arts 207–212); enforcement (arts 213–222); safeguards (arts 223–233); ice-covered areas (art 234); responsibility and liability (art 235); sovereign immunity (art 236); and obligations under other Conventions on the protection and preservation of the marine environment (art 237).

15  Ie the United Nations Convention on the Law of the Sea 1982 Pt XIII (arts 238–265) which relates to: general provisions (arts 238–241); international co-operation (arts 242–244); conduct and promotion of marine scientific research (arts 245–257); scientific research installations or equipment in the marine environment (arts 258–262); responsibility and liability (art 263); and settlement of disputes and interim measures (arts 264, 265).

16  Ie the United Nations Convention on the Law of the Sea 1982 Pt XIV (arts 266–278) which relates to: general provisions (arts 266–269); international co-operation (arts 270–274); national and regional marine scientific and technological centres (arts 275–277); and co-operation among international organisations (art 278).

17  Ie the United Nations Convention on the Law of the Sea 1982 Pt XV (arts 279–299) which relates to: general provisions and general obligations (arts 279–285); compulsory procedures entailing binding decisions (arts 286–296); and limitations and exceptions to applicability of arts 286–296 (arts 297–299).

18  Ie the United Nations Convention on the Law of the Sea 1982 Annex I (highly migratory species); Annex II (Commission on the Limits of the Continental Shelf); Annex III (basic conditions of prospecting, exploration and exploitation); Annex IV (statute of the Enterprise); Annex V (conciliation); Annex VI (statute of the International Tribunal for the Law of the Sea); Annex VII (arbitration); Annex VIII (special arbitration); Annex IX (participation by international organisations). As to the International Tribunal for the Law of the Sea see PARA 10. The purpose of the Commission on the Limits of the Continental Shelf is to facilitate the implementation of the United Nations Convention on the Law of the Sea 1982 in respect of the establishment of the outer limits of the continental shelf beyond 200 nautical miles from the baselines from which the breadth of the territorial sea is measured (as to which see INTERNATIONAL RELATIONS LAW vol 61 (2010) PARA 123 et seq).

19  See the London Gazette 29 August 1997; and note 2. Prior to the United Kingdom becoming a signatory to the 1982 Convention, certain provisions had been enacted in primary and secondary legislation which gave effect to the 1982 Convention in part: see eg the Merchant Shipping Act 1995 s 129(1) (as to which see ENVIRONMENTAL QUALITY AND PUBLIC HEALTH vol 45 (2010) PARA 362); the Merchant Shipping and Maritime Security Act 1997 s 26, Sch 5 (cited in PARA 1186) and s 28 (cited in PARA 10); the International Sea-Bed Authority (Immunities and Privileges) Order 2000, SI 2000/1815) (cited in PARA 11); and the International Tribunal for the Law of the Sea (Immunities and Privileges) Order 2005, SI 2005/2047) (cited in PARA 10).

20  See the United Nations Convention on the Law of the Sea 1982 Pt XVII art 311(1). As to the Geneva Conventions on the Law of the Sea of 1958, which continue to exist and are not abrogated by the United Nations Convention on the Law of the Sea 1982, see PARA 8.

**10.  International Tribunal for the Law of the Sea.** The International Tribunal for the Law of the Sea (the 'Tribunal') was established in accordance with Annex VI to the United Nations Convention on the Law of the Sea 1982 to deal with the settlement of disputes[1].

The Tribunal has the legal capacities in the United Kingdom of a body corporate[2], and provision is made for the members of the Tribunal to enjoy, when engaged on the business of the Tribunal in the United Kingdom, the like privileges and immunities as are[3] accorded to the head of a diplomatic mission[4]. Provision is also made for the Tribunal to enjoy immunity from suit and legal process[5], and for the Tribunal and its members to be exempted from specified forms of taxation[6].

If in any proceedings a question arises whether a person is or is not entitled to any privilege or immunity by virtue of the above provisions, a certificate issued by or under the authority of the Secretary of State stating any fact relating to that question is conclusive evidence of that fact[7].

1   See the United Nations Convention on the Law of the Sea (Montego Bay, 10 December 1982 to 9 December 1984; TS 3 Misc 11 (1983); Cmnd 8941) (the 'United Nations Convention on the Law of the Sea 1982') Annex VI; and PARA 9. The Tribunal is an international court with its seat in Hamburg and has jurisdiction to hear disputes submitted to it in accordance with the 1982 Convention and all matters specifically provided for in any other agreement which confers jurisdiction on it.
2   International Tribunal for the Law of the Sea (Immunities and Privileges) Order 2005, SI 2005/2047, art 3.
3   Ie in accordance with the 1961 Convention Articles (as to which see INTERNATIONAL RELATIONS LAW vol 61 (2010) PARA 267 et seq): see the International Tribunal for the Law of the Sea (Immunities and Privileges) Order 2005, SI 2005/2047, art 13. For these purposes, '1961 Convention Articles' means the Articles, being certain Articles of the Vienna Convention on Diplomatic Relations (Vienna, 18 April 1961; TS 19 (1965); Cmnd 2565), which are set out in the Diplomatic Privileges Act 1964 s 2(1), Sch 1 (as to which see INTERNATIONAL RELATIONS LAW vol 61 (2010) PARA 265 et seq): see the International Tribunal for the Law of the Sea (Immunities and Privileges) Order 2005, SI 2005/2047, art 2.
4   See the International Tribunal for the Law of the Sea (Immunities and Privileges) Order 2005, SI 2005/2047, art 13.
5   See the International Tribunal for the Law of the Sea (Immunities and Privileges) Order 2005, SI 2005/2047, art 4.
6   See the International Tribunal for the Law of the Sea (Immunities and Privileges) Order 2005, SI 2005/2047, arts 6–12.
7   Merchant Shipping and Maritime Security Act 1997 s 28(6). As to the Secretary of State see PARA 36.

**11.   International Sea-Bed Authority.** The International Sea-Bed Authority was established under the United Nations Convention on the Law of the Sea 1982[1]; and it is the organisation through which States Parties[2] organise and control all activities of exploration for, and exploitation of, the resources of the sea bed and ocean floor and subsoil thereof, beyond the limits of national jurisdiction[3]. The Enterprise is the organ of that Authority which carries out all those activities, as well as the transporting, processing and marketing of minerals recovered from the sea bed and ocean floor and subsoil thereof, beyond the limits of national jurisdiction[4].

The International Sea-Bed Authority and the Enterprise have conferred upon them the legal capacities of a body corporate[5]. Privileges and immunities[6] are also conferred on:

(1)      the Authority[7] and (separately) the Enterprise[8];
(2)      representatives of members of the Authority[9];
(3)      the Secretary-General of the Authority (or any official acting on his behalf during his absence from duty) and the Director-General of the Enterprise[10];
(4)      all officials of the Authority[11]; and

(5)     experts (other than officials of the Authority) performing missions on behalf of the Authority[12].

1   See the United Nations Convention on the Law of the Sea (Montego Bay, 10 December 1982 to 9 December 1984; TS 3 Misc 11 (1983); Cmnd 8941) (the 'United Nations Convention on the Law of the Sea 1982') art 156(1); and PARA 9.
     The relevant provisions of the 1982 Convention which establish the International Seabed Authority and set out how it should function are contained in Pt XI Section 4 (arts 156–185), as follows:
     (1)     Subsection A (General Provisions), covering the establishment of the Authority (art 156); the nature and fundamental principles of the Authority (art 157); and the organs of the Authority (art 158);
     (2)     Subsection B (the Assembly), covering the composition, procedure and voting in and relating to the Assembly (art 159) as well as its powers and functions (art 160);
     (3)     Subsection C (the Council), covering the composition, procedure and voting in and relating to the Council (art 160), its powers and functions (art 161) as well as the establishment of organs of the Council, namely an Economic Planning Commission and a Legal and Technical Commission (arts 162–165).
     (4)     Subsection D (the Secretariat) (arts 166–169);
     (5)     Subsection E (the Enterprise) (art 170);
     (6)     Subsection F (the financial arrangements of the Authority) (arts 171–175);
     (7)     Subsection G (legal status, privileges and immunities of and connected with the Authority) (arts 176–183);
     (8)     Subsection H (suspension of the exercise of rights and privileges of members) (arts 184, 185).
     As to the Sea-Bed Disputes Chamber of the International Tribunal for the Law of the Sea which is the forum designated for the settlement of disputes etc see the United Nations Convention on the Law of the Sea 1982 Pt XI Section 5 (arts 186–191). As to the International Tribunal for the Law of the Sea see PARAS 9–10.
2   For these purposes, 'States Parties' means states which have consented to be bound by the 1982 Convention and for which that Convention is in force: see the United Nations Convention on the Law of the Sea 1982 art 1(2)(1).
3   See the United Nations Convention on the Law of the Sea 1982 art 157(1).
4   See the United Nations Convention on the Law of the Sea 1982 art 170(1).
5   See the International Sea-Bed Authority (Immunities and Privileges) Order 2000, SI 2000/1815, arts 4, 5.
6   Ie in accordance with both the United Nations Convention on the Law of the Sea 1982 and the Protocol on the Privileges and Immunities of the International Seabed Authority (Kingston, 27 March 1998; TS 25 (2004); Cm 6260).
7   See the International Sea-Bed Authority (Immunities and Privileges) Order 2000, SI 2000/1815, arts 6–13.
8   See the International Sea-Bed Authority (Immunities and Privileges) Order 2000, SI 2000/1815, arts 14, 15. Articles 6–12 do not apply to the Enterprise but art 13 (relief, under arrangements made by the Secretary of State, by way of a refund of insurance premium tax and air passenger duty paid in the exercise of official activities) does: see art 14.
9   See the International Sea-Bed Authority (Immunities and Privileges) Order 2000, SI 2000/1815, art 16 (amended by virtue of the British Overseas Territories Act 2002 s 2(3)).
10  See the International Sea-Bed Authority (Immunities and Privileges) Order 2000, SI 2000/1815, art 17 (amended by virtue of the British Overseas Territories Act 2002 s 2(3); and by SI 2006/1075).
11  See the International Sea-Bed Authority (Immunities and Privileges) Order 2000, SI 2000/1815, art 18.
12  See the International Sea-Bed Authority (Immunities and Privileges) Order 2000, SI 2000/1815, art 19 (amended by virtue of the British Overseas Territories Act 2002 s 2(3)).

## 12. The International Maritime Organisation.
The International Maritime Organisation (the 'IMO') was established under a Convention which came into force in 1958[1]. The purposes of the IMO are:
     (1)     to provide machinery for co-operation among governments in the field of governmental regulation and practices relating to technical matters of all kinds affecting shipping engaged in international trade, and to

encourage the general adoption of the highest practicable standards in matters concerning maritime safety, efficiency of navigation and prevention and control of marine pollution from ships[2];

(2)    to encourage the removal of discriminatory action and unnecessary restrictions by governments affecting shipping engaged in international trade so as to promote the availability of shipping services to the commerce of the world without discrimination[3];

(3)    to provide for the consideration by the IMO of matters concerning unfair restrictive practices by shipping concerns[4];

(4)    to provide for the consideration by the IMO of any matters concerning shipping that may be referred to it by any organ or specialised agency of the United Nations[5];

(5)    to provide for the exchange of information among governments on matters under consideration by the IMO[6].

In general, membership of the organisation is open to all states[7]. Decisions are made by a majority vote, each member having one vote[8].

The IMO consists of an assembly, a council, a maritime safety committee, a legal committee, a marine environment protection committee ('MEPC'), a technical co-operation committee, together with such subsidiary organs as the IMO may at any time consider necessary, as well as a secretariat[9].

The headquarters of the IMO are in London[10].

Provision is made to regulate the IMO's relationships and co-operation with the United Nations (including a duty to co-operate with the United Nations' specialised agencies), as well as with intergovernmental organisations and non-governmental organisations[11].

The Convention under which the IMO was established may be amended[12]; and provision is made for the settlement of disputes concerning its interpretation[13].

In the United Kingdom, the IMO has the legal capacity of a body corporate[14]. Privileges and immunities[15] are conferred on:

(a)    the IMO[16];

(b)    representatives of members of the IMO on any of its organs at meetings convened by it[17];

(c)    every person designated by a member of the IMO as its principal permanent representative or acting principal permanent representative to the IMO in the United Kingdom (and on members of their family forming part of their household)[18];

(d)    its officers[19]; and

(e)    experts (other than officers of the IMO) serving on any committee of the IMO or employed on missions on behalf of the IMO[20].

1   See the Convention for the Establishment of the Inter-Governmental Maritime Consultative Organisation (1958) (TS 54 (1958); Cmnd 589) (the 'IMO Convention 1958'). On 22 May 1982, the name of the organisation was changed from the Inter-Governmental Maritime Consultative Organisation to the International Maritime Organisation (the 'IMO').

2   See the IMO Convention 1958 Pt I art 1(a). A further purpose is to deal with administrative and legal matters related to the purposes set out in Pt I art 1: see Pt I art 1(a). On the relation between EU and member state competence as regards the IMO see Case C-45/07 *EC v Greece* [2009] ECR I-701, ECJ.

3   See the IMO Convention 1958 Pt I art 1(b). Assistance and encouragement given by a government for the development of its national shipping and for purposes of security do not in themselves constitute discrimination, provided that such assistance and encouragement is not based on measures designed to restrict the freedom of shipping of all flags to take part in international trade: see Pt I art 1(b).

4   See the IMO Convention 1958 Pt I art 1(c). The purpose set out under head (3) in the text must be conducted in accordance with Pt II (arts 2, 3) (functions), which state that the IMO provides for the drafting of conventions, agreements or other suitable instruments, provides machinery for

consultation among members and exchange of information and facilitates technical co-operation (see Pt II art 2); and that, for matters capable of settlement through the normal processes of international shipping business, the IMO should recommend their resolution in that manner (see Pt II art 3): see Pt I art 1(c).

5 See the IMO Convention 1958 Pt I art 1(d).

6 See the IMO Convention 1958 Pt I art 1(e).

7 See the IMO Convention 1958 Pt III arts 4–10.

8 See the IMO Convention 1958 Pt XIII art 57.

9 See the IMO Convention 1958 Pt IV art 11. As to the constitution and functions of these bodies, and as to finances and rating, see Pts V-XII (arts 15–56).

10 See the IMO Convention 1958 Pt XIV art 58. The site of the headquarters may be changed, if necessary, by a two-thirds' majority vote of the assembly; and the assembly may hold sessions in any place other than the headquarters if the council deems it necessary: see Pt XIV art 58.

11 See the IMO Convention 1958 Pt XV (arts 59–63). The United Nations Convention on the Law of the Sea (Montego Bay, 10 December 1982 to 9 December 1984; TS 3 Misc 11 (1983); Cmnd 8941) (the 'United Nations Convention on the Law of the Sea 1982') (as to which see PARA 9) covers some issues not regulated under IMO treaty instruments eg the jurisdictional power of the coastal state.

12 See the IMO Convention 1958 Pt XVII (arts 66–68).

13 See the IMO Convention 1958 Pt XVIII (arts 69, 70). Questions or disputes over interpretation or application of the Convention are referred to the Assembly and, if they cannot be settled, are referred to the International Court of Justice for an advisory opinion: see Pt XVIII.

14 See the International Maritime Organisation (Immunities and Privileges) Order 2002, SI 2002/1826, arts 4, 5.

15 As to the IMO Convention provisions on legal capacity, privileges and immunities which should be applied by members and by the organisation see the IMO Convention 1958 Pt XVI (arts 64, 65).

16 See the International Maritime Organisation (Immunities and Privileges) Order 2002, SI 2002/1826, arts 6–13.

17 See the International Maritime Organisation (Immunities and Privileges) Order 2002, SI 2002/1826, art 14.

18 See the International Maritime Organisation (Immunities and Privileges) Order 2002, SI 2002/1826, art 15.

19 See the International Maritime Organisation (Immunities and Privileges) Order 2002, SI 2002/1826, arts 16–18.

20 See the International Maritime Organisation (Immunities and Privileges) Order 2002, SI 2002/1826, art 19.

**13. Comité Maritime International.** The Comité Maritime International is a non-governmental not-for-profit international organisation established in Antwerp in 1897, the object of which is to contribute by all appropriate means and activities to the unification of maritime law in all its aspects; to that end it promotes the establishment of national associations of maritime law and co-operates with other international organisations[1]. The domicile of the Comité Maritime International is established in Belgium[2].

The Comité Maritime International consists of national, or multinational, associations of maritime law, the objects of which conform to that of the Comité Maritime International and the membership of which is open to persons, individuals or bodies corporate, who either are involved in maritime activities or are specialists in maritime law[3].

The Assembly of the Comité Maritime International consists of all its members and the members of the Executive Council[4]; and the functions of the Assembly are:

(1)     to elect the officers of the Comité Maritime International[5];

(2)     to elect members of and to suspend or expel members from the Comité Maritime International[6];

(3)     to fix the amounts of subscriptions payable by members to the Comité Maritime International[7];

(4)     to elect auditors[8] and to consider and, if thought fit, approve the accounts and the budget[9];

(5)     to consider reports of the Executive Council and to take decisions on the future activity of the Comité Maritime International[10];

(6)     to approve the convening and decide the agenda of, and ultimately approve resolutions adopted by, international conferences[11];

(7)     to adopt rules governing the expulsion of members[12];

(8)     to adopt rules of procedure not inconsistent with the provisions of the Constitution[13]; and

(9)     to amend the Constitution of the Comité Maritime International[14].

The Comité Maritime International meets in International Conference upon dates and at places approved by the Assembly, for the purpose of discussing and adopting resolutions upon subjects on an agenda likewise approved by the Assembly[15].

1   See the Constitution of the Comité Maritime International (2001) art 1.
2   See the Constitution of the Comité Maritime International (2001) art 2. The Comité Maritime International is domiciled in the City of Antwerp: see art 2.
3   See the Constitution of the Comité Maritime International (2001) art 3(I)(a). As to membership of the Comité Maritime International see art 3(I)(a)–(f); as to expulsion see art 3(II)(a)–(g); and as to the liability of members for obligations of the Comité Maritime International see art 3(III).
4   See the Constitution of the Comité Maritime International (2001) art 4. As to meetings of the Assembly and quorum see art 5; and as to the agenda and voting see art 6. Provision is made for officers of the Comité Maritime International (see Pt III (arts 8–16)) and its Executive Council (see Pt IV (arts 17–19)). As to financial matters and the liability of the Comité Maritime International see arts 22, 23.
5   See the Constitution of the Comité Maritime International (2001) art 7(a).
6   See the Constitution of the Comité Maritime International (2001) art 7(b).
7   See the Constitution of the Comité Maritime International (2001) art 7(c). As to arrears of subscriptions see art 21.
8   See the Constitution of the Comité Maritime International (2001) art 7(d).
9   See the Constitution of the Comité Maritime International (2001) art 7(e).
10  See the Constitution of the Comité Maritime International (2001) art 7(f).
11  See the Constitution of the Comité Maritime International (2001) art 7(g).
12  See the Constitution of the Comité Maritime International (2001) art 7(h).
13  See the Constitution of the Comité Maritime International (2001) art 7(i).
14  See the Constitution of the Comité Maritime International (2001) art 7(l).
15  See the Constitution of the Comité Maritime International (2001) art 20.

## (ii)  EU Legislation

**14.  Shipping- and maritime-related measures of the European Union.** The policy of the then European Community in relation to measures governing international shipping and seaborne trade concentrated initially on encouraging member states to ratify, or to accede to, existing international Conventions, which were often promulgated under the auspices of other multi-national organisations like the United Nations or the International Maritime Organisation[1]. Member states were, however, reluctant to accept a legal obligation to conclude Conventions (generally because they wished to retain competence in the relevant areas for themselves) so Community encouragement began to take the form of Council Recommendations, as follows:

(1)     a Council Recommendation[2] on the ratification of the International Convention for the Safety of Life at Sea 1974 ('SOLAS')[3], the International Convention for the Prevention of Pollution from Ships ('MARPOL')[4], and an International Labour Convention concerning minimum standards in merchant ships[5];

(2)      a Council Recommendation[6] on the ratification of the International Convention on Standards of Training, Certification and Watchkeeping for Seafarers 1978[7];

(3)      a Council Recommendation[8] on the ratification of the Torremolinos International Convention for the Safety of Fishing Vessels[9];

(4)      a Council Recommendation[10] on the ratification of or accession to the International Convention on Maritime Search and Rescue (SAR)[11].

Also of note is a Council Decision[12] on setting up a consultation procedure on relations between member states and third countries in shipping matters and on action relating to such matters in international organisations.

Increasingly, however, European measures have sought to regulate spheres of activity in the area of shipping and maritime law, the main such measures being concerned with:

(a)      pilotage in the North Sea[13];

(b)      medical treatment onboard vessels[14];

(c)      rules and standards for ship inspection and survey organisations and for the relevant activities of maritime administrations[15];

(d)      port state control of shipping[16];

(e)      marine equipment[17];

(f)      the safe operation of regular Ro-Ro ferry and high-speed passenger craft services[18];

(g)      the Agreement on the organisation of working time of seafarers concluded by the European Community Shipowners' Association ('ECSA') and the Federation of Transport Workers' Unions in the European Union ('FST') (as interpreted in accordance with the Maritime Labour Convention ('MLC')[19];

(h)      seafarers' hours of work on board ships calling at Community ports[20];

(i)      training of seafarers[21];

(j)      the accelerated phasing-in of double hull or equivalent design requirements for single hull oil tankers[22];

(k)      the establishment of a European Maritime Safety Agency[23];

(l)      the establishment of a vessel traffic monitoring and information system[24];

(m)      the establishment of a Committee on Safe Seas and the Prevention of Pollution from Ships ('COSS')[25];

(n)      the investigation of accidents[26];

(o)      aspects of the organisation of working time[27];

(p)      ship and port security[28];

(q)      the transfer of cargo and passenger ships between registers within the Community[29];

(r)      the implementation of the International Safety Management Code within the Community[30];

(s)      the application of EU competition law to liner conferences[31];

(t)      the prohibition of organotin compounds on ships[32];

(u)      technical requirements for inland waterway vessels[33];

(v)      compliance with flag state requirements[34]; and

(w)      the insurance of shipowners for maritime claims[35].

1     As to a survey of the international Conventions which apply to shipping and maritime law see PARA 7 et seq. In connection with the relationship between EU law and international maritime conventions see Case C-308/06 *R (on the application of International Association of Independent Tanker Owners (Intertanko)) v Secretary of State for Transport* [2008] ECR I-4057, [2008] 3 CMLR 203, [2008] 2 Lloyd's Rep 260, ECJ; Case C-188/07 *Commune de Mesquer v Total France SA* [2008] ECR I-4501, [2008] 3 CMLR 445, [2008] 2 Lloyd's Rep 672, ECJ.

2  Ie Council Recommendation (EC) 78/584 (OJ L194, 19.7.78, p 17).
3  Ie the International Convention for the Safety of Life at Sea 1974 (London, 1 November 1974 to 1 July 1975; TS 46 (1980); Cmnd 7874), with Protocol (London, 1 June 1978 to 1 March 1979; TS 40 (1981); Cmnd 8277) (as to which see PARA 7). As to implementation see PARA 627.
4  Ie the International Convention for the Prevention of Pollution from Ships (London, 8 October to 2 November 1973; Misc 26 (1974); Cmnd 5748), with Protocol (London, 1 June 1978 to 31 May 1979; Misc 27 (1978); Cmnd 7347): see ENVIRONMENTAL QUALITY AND PUBLIC HEALTH vol 45 (2010) PARA 4. As to pollution see also Council Decision (EC) 2004/246 (OJ L78, 16.3.2004, p 22) authorising the member states to ratify the Protocol of 2003 to the International Convention on the Establishment of an International Fund for Compensation for Oil Pollution Damage 1992.
5  Ie the International Labour Convention No 147 (Geneva, 11 November 1976; TS 22 (1984); Cmnd 9186).
6  Ie Council Recommendation (EC) 79/114 (OJ L33, 8.2.79, p 31).
7  Ie the International Convention on Standards of Training, Certification and Watchkeeping for Seafarers 1978 (London, 1 December 1978 to 30 November 1979; TS 50 (1984); Cmnd 9266) (the 'STCW Convention') (as to which see PARA 7).
8  Ie Council Recommendation (EC) 80/907 (OJ L259, 2.10.80, p 29).
9  Ie the Torremolinos International Convention for the Safety of Fishing Vessels (London, 1 October 1977 to 13 June 1978; Misc 17 (1978); Cmnd 7252) (as to which see PARA 7).
10 Ie Council Recommendation (EC) 83/419 (OJ L237, 26.8.83, p 34).
11 Ie the International Convention on Maritime Search and Rescue (Hamburg, 9 to 27 April 1979; Misc 19 (1980); Cmnd 7994) (as to which see PARA 7).
12 Ie Council Decision (EC) 77/587 (OJ L239, 17.9.77, p 23).
13 See Council Directive (EC) 79/115 (OJ L33, 8.2.79, p 32); and PARA 596.
14 See Council Directive (EC) 92/29 (OJ L113, 30.4.92, p 19) (implemented in the United Kingdom by the Merchant Shipping and Fishing Vessels (Medical Stores) Regulations 1995, SI 1995/1802 (see PARA 498)).
15 See Council Directive (EC) 2009/15 (OJ L131, 28.05.09, p 47) (implemented in the United Kingdom by the Merchant Shipping (Ship Inspection and Survey Organisations) (Revocation) Regulations 2011, SI 2011/3056 (an amending provision); and the Merchant Shipping (High-Speed Craft) Regulations 2004, SI 2004/302 (see PARA 617 et seq).
16 See Parliament and Council Directive (EC) 2009/16 (OJ L131, 28.5.2009, p 57) (implemented in the United Kingdom by the Merchant Shipping (Port State Control) Regulations 2011, SI 2011/2601 (see PARA 678 et seq)). See also Council Directive (EC) 96/40 (OJ L196, 7.8.96, p 8).
17 See Parliament and Council Directive (EU) 2014/90 (OJ L257, 28.2.2014, p 146) (implemented in the United Kingdom by the Merchant Shipping (Marine Equipment) Regulations 1999, SI 1999/1957 (see PARA 638)).
18 See Council Directive (EC) 1999/35 (OJ L138, 1.6.1999, p 1) (implemented in the United Kingdom by the Merchant Shipping (Mandatory Surveys for Ro-Ro Ferry and High Speed Passenger Craft) Regulations 2001, SI 2001/152 (see PARA 606)).
19 See Council Directive (EC) 1999/63 (OJ L167, 2.7.1999, p 33) (implemented in the United Kingdom by the Merchant Shipping (Maritime Labour Convention) (Medical Examination) Regulations 2010, SI 2010/737 (as to which see PARAS 424, 564 et seq) and the Merchant Shipping (Hours of Work) Regulations 2002, SI 2002/2125 (see PARA 511)). As to the Maritime Labour Convention see also Parliament and Council Directive (EC) 2008/13 (OJ L76, 19.3.2008, p 41) (implemented in the United Kingdom by the Merchant Shipping (Maritime Labour Convention) (Minimum Requirements for Seafarers etc) Regulations 2014, SI 2014/1613); and PARA 482 et seq.
20 See Parliament and Council Directive (EC) 1999/95 (OJ L14, 20.01.2000, p 29) (implemented in the United Kingdom by the Merchant Shipping (Hours of Work) Regulations 2002, SI 2002/2125 (see PARA 511).
21 See Parliament and Council Directive (EC) 2008/106 (OJ L323, 3.12.2008, p 33) (implemented in part in the United Kingdom by the Merchant Shipping (Minimum Standards of Safety Communications) Regulations 1997, SI 1997/529 (see PARA 639)).
22 See Parliament and Council Regulation (EU) 530/2012 (OJ L172, 30.6.2012, p 3).
23 See Parliament and Council Regulation (EC) 1406/2002 (OJ L208, 5.8.2002, p 1).
24 See Parliament and Council Directive (EC) 2002/59 (OJ L208, 05.08.2002, p 10) (implemented in the United Kingdom by the Merchant Shipping (Vessel Traffic Monitoring and Reporting Requirements) Regulations 2004, SI 2004/2110 (see PARA 648)).
25 See Parliament and Council Regulation (EC) 2099/2002 (OJ L324, 29.11.2002, p 1).

26 See Parliament and Council Directive (EC) 2009/18 (OJ L131, 28.5.2009, p 114) (implemented in the United Kingdom by the Merchant Shipping (Accident Reporting and Investigation) Regulations 2012, SI 2012/1743) (see PARA 815 et seq)).

27 See Parliament and Council Directive (EC) 2003/88 (OJ L299, 18.11.2003, p 9); and PARAS 511, 515.

28 See Parliament and Council Regulation (EC) 725/2004 (OJ L129, 29.04.2004, p 6). As to implementation in the United Kingdom (in so far as it is necessary) see the Ship and Port Facility (Security) Regulations 2004, SI 2004/1495; and PARA 684 et seq. See also Parliament and Council Directive (EC) 2005/65 (OJ L310, 25.11.2005, p 28) (implemented in the United Kingdom by the Port Security Regulations 2009, SI 2009/2048).

29 See Parliament and Council Regulation (EC) 789/2004 (OJ L138, 30.4.2004, p 19).

30 See Parliament and Council Regulation (EC) 336/2006 (OJ L64, 4.3.2006, p 1) (implemented in the United Kingdom by the Merchant Shipping (International Safety Management (ISM) Code) Regulations 2014, SI 2014/1512).

31 See Council Regulation (EC) 1419/2006 (OJ L269, 28.9.2006, p 1). See also Parliament and Council Regulation (EC) 1490/2007; and PARA 78.

32 See Parliament and Council Regulation (EC) 782/2003 (OJ L115, 9.5.2003, p 1) (implemented in the United Kingdom by the Merchant Shipping (Anti-Fouling Systems) Regulations 2009, SI 2009/2796 (amended by SI 2011/3056; SI 2014/3306).

33 See Parliament and Council Directive (EC) 2006/87 (OJ L389, 30.12.2006, p 1) (implemented in the United Kingdom by the Merchant Shipping (Technical Requirements for Inland Waterway Vessels) Regulations 2010, SI 2010/1075).

34 See Parliament and Council Directive (EC) 2009/21 (OJ L131, 28.5.2009, p 132) (implemented in the United Kingdom by the Merchant Shipping (Flag State Directive) Regulations 2011, SI 2011/2667).

35 See Parliament and Council Directive (EC) 2009/20 (OJ L131, 28.5.2009, p 128).

## (iii) United Kingdom Legislation

### A. EXISTING STATUTE LAW

**15. Principal legislation.** There are two principal consolidating Acts relating to merchant shipping: the Merchant Shipping Act 1995 and the Shipping and Trading Interests (Protection) Act 1995[1].

In addition, there is a considerable body of subordinate legislation made, or having effect as if made, thereunder[2].

1 The Merchant Shipping Act 1995 consolidated the Merchant Shipping Acts 1894 to 1994 (ie the Merchant Shipping Act 1894, the Merchant Shipping Act 1906, the Merchant Shipping Act 1964, the Merchant Shipping (Load Lines) Act 1967, the Merchant Shipping Act 1979, the Merchant Shipping Act 1984, the Merchant Shipping Act 1988, the Merchant Shipping (Registration, etc) Act 1993 and the Merchant Shipping (Salvage and Pollution) Act 1994). The Shipping and Trading Interests (Protection) Act 1995 consolidated certain enactments for the protection of shipping and trading interests.

2 See PARA 37 et seq.

**16. Territorial extent.** The Merchant Shipping Act 1995[1] extends to England and Wales[2], Scotland and Northern Ireland[3]. Her Majesty may by Order in Council direct that any provision of the Merchant Shipping Act 1995 (and instruments made thereunder), with such exceptions, adaptations and modifications (if any) as may be specified in the Order, is to extend to any relevant British possession[4]. Such an Order in Council may make such transitional, incidental or supplementary provision as appears to Her Majesty to be necessary or expedient[5].

Her Majesty may, in relation to any relevant British possession, by Order in Council direct that, with such exceptions, adaptations and modifications, if any, as may be specified in the Order, any of the provisions of the Merchant Shipping Act 1995 are to have effect as if references in them to the United Kingdom included a reference to that possession[6].

Either such Order in Council may[7], in its application to any relevant British possession, provide for such authority in that possession as is specified in the Order to furnish the Secretary of State[8] or the registrar[9] with such information with respect to the registration of ships in that possession under its law as is specified in the Order or as the Secretary of State may from time to time require, and for any such information to be so furnished at such time or times and in such manner as is or are so specified or, as the case may be, as the Secretary of State may so require[10].

1 Ie except for the Merchant Shipping Act 1995 s 18 (provision for regulating registration in relevant British possessions of ships other than small ships and fishing vessels by reference to categories of registries) (see PARA 246) and s 193(5) (prospectively repealed) (general lighthouse authority as respects Gibraltar, the Channel Islands and the Isle of Man) (see PARA 1017): s 315(1).

2 In any Act, unless the contrary intention appears, 'England' means, subject to any alteration of the boundaries of local government areas, the areas consisting of the counties established by the Local Government Act 1972 s 1 (see LOCAL GOVERNMENT vol 69 (2009) PARAS 5, 22), and Greater London and the Isles of Scilly; and 'Wales' means the combined areas of the counties created by s 20 (as originally enacted) (see LOCAL GOVERNMENT vol 69 (2009) PARAS 5, 37), but subject to any alteration made under s 73 (consequential alteration of boundary following alteration of watercourse: see LOCAL GOVERNMENT vol 69 (2009) PARA 90): see the Interpretation Act 1978 s 5, Sch 1 (definition substituted by the Local Government (Wales) Act 1994 s 1(3), Sch 2 para 9). As to local government areas and authorities in England and Wales see LOCAL GOVERNMENT vol 69 (2009) PARA 22 et seq. As to boundary changes see LOCAL GOVERNMENT vol 69 (2009) PARA 54 et seq.

3 Merchant Shipping Act 1995 s 315(1). Without prejudice to s 315(1), the repeals made by the Merchant Shipping Act 1995 do not affect the law in force in any country or territory which is outside the United Kingdom: s 314(3), Sch 14 para 1(1). In particular, the repeal of the Merchant Shipping Act 1894 s 735 does not affect the power of Her Majesty in Council to confirm any legislation made by the legislature of a British possession under s 735 (repealed) as it extends to that possession: Merchant Shipping Act 1995 Sch 14 para 1(2). The provisions of the 1995 Act, including the repeal of any power by Order in Council to extend any enactment to a relevant British possession, or of any enactment which has been so extended, do not extend to any such possession, except in so far as they are extended to that possession by an Order in Council under s 315(2) (see the text and note 4): Sch 14 para 1(3). 'United Kingdom' means Great Britain and Northern Ireland: Interpretation Act 1978 Sch 1. 'Great Britain' means England, Scotland and Wales: Union with Scotland Act 1706, preamble art I; Interpretation Act 1978 s 22(1), Sch 2 para 5(a). In the Merchant Shipping Act 1995, unless the context otherwise requires, 'relevant British possession' means the Isle of Man, any of the Channel Islands and any colony: s 313(1). As to the meaning of 'colony' see STATUTES AND LEGISLATIVE PROCESS vol 96 (2012) PARA 1208. As to the legal status of the Channel Islands and the Isle of Man (neither of which are within the United Kingdom) see COMMONWEALTH vol 13 (2017) PARAS 694–704; and see also CONSTITUTIONAL AND ADMINISTRATIVE LAW vol 20 (2014) PARA 3.

4 Merchant Shipping Act 1995 s 315(2). As to the making of Orders under the Merchant Shipping Act 1995 generally see PARA 39. At the date at which this volume states the law, the following Orders had been made under s 315(2): the Merchant Shipping (Liability and Compensation for Oil Pollution Damage) (Transitional Provisions) (Overseas Territories) Order 1997, SI 1997/2578; the Merchant Shipping (Limitation of Liability for Maritime Claims) (Overseas Territories) Order 1997, SI 1997/2579; the Merchant Shipping (Oil Pollution) (Anguilla) Order 1997, SI 1997/2580; the Merchant Shipping (Oil Pollution) (British Antarctic Territory) Order 1997, SI 1997/2582; the Merchant Shipping (Oil Pollution) (British Indian Ocean Territory) Order 1997, SI 1997/2583; the Merchant Shipping (Oil Pollution) (Falkland Islands) Order 1997, SI 1997/2584; the Merchant Shipping (Oil Pollution) (Pitcairn) Order 1997, SI 1997/2585 (amended by SI 1998/1067); the Merchant Shipping (Salvage Convention) (Overseas Territories) Order 1997, SI 1997/2586; the Merchant Shipping (Oil Pollution) (Sovereign Base Areas) Order 1997, SI 1997/2587 (amended by SI 1998/1068); the Merchant Shipping (Oil Pollution) (South Georgia and the South Sandwich Islands) Order 1997, SI 1997/2588; the Merchant Shipping (Oil Pollution) (Turks and Caicos Islands) Order 1997, SI 1997/2589; the Merchant Shipping (Oil Pollution) (Virgin Islands) Order 1997, SI 1997/2590; the Merchant Shipping (Oil Pollution) (Jersey) Order 1997, SI 1997/2598 (prospectively repealed by SI 2015/1893); the Merchant Shipping (Oil Pollution and General Provisions) (Guernsey) Order 1998, SI 1998/260; the Merchant Shipping (Oil Pollution) (Pitcairn) (Amendment) Order 1998, SI 1998/1067; the Merchant Shipping (Oil Pollution) (Sovereign Base Areas) (Amendment) Order 1998, SI 1998/1068; the Merchant Shipping (Oil Pollution) (Cayman Islands) Order 1998, SI 1998/1261; the Merchant Shipping (Oil Pollution) (Montserrat) Order 1998, SI 1998/1262; the Merchant Shipping (Oil Pollution) (Saint Helena) Order 1998, SI

1998/1263; the Merchant Shipping (Revocation) (Bermuda) Order 2002, SI 2002/3147; the Merchant Shipping (Confirmation of Legislation and Repeals) (Jersey) Order 2004, SI 2004/1284; the Merchant Shipping (Oil Pollution and General Provisions) (Isle of Man) Order 2004, SI 2004/3041; the Merchant Shipping (Oil Pollution) (Gibraltar) Order 2004, SI 2004/3042; and the Overseas Territories (Change of Name) (No 8) Order 2011, SI 2011/2981.

By virtue of the Interpretation Act 1978 s 17(2)(b), the following saved instruments continue in force until superseded by an instrument made under s 315: the Merchant Shipping Safety Convention (Isle of Man) Order 1934, SR & O 1934/1414; the Merchant Shipping Safety Convention (Guernsey) No 1 Order 1935, SR & O 1935/562; the Merchant Shipping Safety Convention (Guernsey) No 2 Order 1935, SR & O 1935/563; the Merchant Shipping Safety Convention (Straits Settlements) No 2 Order 1935, SR & O 1935/716; the Merchant Shipping Safety Convention (Singapore) No 1 Order 1953, SI 1953/1218; the Merchant Shipping Safety Convention (Singapore) No 2 Order 1953, SI 1953/1219; the Oil in Navigable Waters (Guernsey) Order 1966, SI 1966/393; the Oil in Navigable Waters (Isle of Man) Order 1966, SI 1966/394; the Merchant Shipping (Load Lines Certificates) (Various Countries) Order 1968, SI 1968/1110; the Wireless Telegraphy (Channel Islands) Order 1969, SI 1969/1369; the Wireless Telegraphy (Isle of Man) Order 1969, SI 1969/1371; the Merchant Shipping (Oil Pollution) (Belize) Order 1975, SI 1975/2164 (amended by SI 1981/214); the Merchant Shipping (Oil Pollution) (Gilbert Islands) Order 1975, SI 1975/2168; the Merchant Shipping (Oil Pollution) (Seychelles) Order 1975, SI 1975/2172; the Merchant Shipping (Oil Pollution) (Solomon Islands) Order 1975, SI 1975/2173; the Merchant Shipping (Oil Pollution) (Tuvalu) Order 1975, SI 1975/2174; the Merchant Shipping Act 1979 (Guernsey) Order 1980, SI 1980/569; the Merchant Shipping Act 1979 (Belize) Order 1980, SI 1980/1509 (amended by SI 1981/420); the Merchant Shipping Act 1979 (British Virgin Islands) Order 1980, SI 1980/1511 (amended by SI 1981/422); the Merchant Shipping Act 1979 (Cayman Islands) Order 1980, SI 1980/1512 (amended by SI 1981/423); the Merchant Shipping Act 1979 (Falkland Islands) Order 1980, SI 1980/1513 (amended by SI 1981/424); the Merchant Shipping Act 1979 (Montserrat) Order 1980, SI 1980/1515 (amended by SI 1981/426); the Merchant Shipping Act 1979 (Pitcairn) Order 1980, SI 1980/1516 (amended by SI 1981/427); the Merchant Shipping Act 1979 (Saint Helena) Order 1980, SI 1980/1517 (amended by SI 1981/428; SI 2011/2981); the Merchant Shipping Act 1979 (Sovereign Base Areas) 1980, SI 1980/1518 (amended by SI 1981/429); the Merchant Shipping Act 1979 (Turks and Caicos Islands) Order 1980, SI 1980/1519 (amended by SI 1981/430); the Merchant Shipping Act 1979 (Isle of Man) Order 1980, SI 1980/1526; the Merchant Shipping (Oil Pollution) Act 1971 (Guernsey) Order 1981, SI 1981/244; the Merchant Shipping Act 1970 (Guernsey) Order 1981, SI 1981/1809; the Merchant Shipping Act 1979 (Guernsey) Order 1981, SI 1981/1810; the Prevention of Oil Pollution Act 1971 (Overseas Territories) Order 1982, SI 1982/1668; the Merchant Shipping Act 1979 (Isle of Man) Order 1984, SI 1984/1161; the Merchant Shipping (Metrication) (Isle of Man) Order 1984, SI 1984/1164; the Merchant Shipping Acts 1983 and 1984 (Isle of Man) Order 1984, SI 1984/1985; the Merchant Shipping (Distress Signals and Prevention of Collisions) (Guernsey) Order 1986, SI 1986/1163 (amended by SI 1989/2410); the Admiralty Jurisdiction (Gibraltar) Order 1987, SI 1987/1263; the Merchant Shipping Act 1974 (Cayman Islands) Order 1988, SI 1988/789; the Merchant Shipping Act 1970 (Cayman Islands) Order 1988, SI 1988/246; the Merchant Shipping Act 1979 (Cayman Islands) Order 1988, SI 1988/790; the Merchant Shipping (Tonnage) (Overseas Territories) Order 1988, SI 1988/1085; the Merchant Shipping Act 1970 (Overseas Territories) Order 1988, SI 1988/1086; the Merchant Shipping Act 1988 (Cayman Islands) Order 1988, SI 1988/1841; the Merchant Shipping Act 1979 (Guernsey) Order 1988, SI 1988/1851; the Merchant Shipping (Certification of Deck Officers and Marine Engineer Officers) (Guernsey) Order 1988, SI 1988/1991; the Merchant Shipping Act 1988 (Isle of Man) Order 1989, SI 1989/679; the Merchant Shipping Act 1979 (Overseas Territories) Order 1989, SI 1989/2400 (amended by SI 1993/1786); the Merchant Shipping (Distress Signals and Prevention of Collisions) (Guernsey) Order 1989, SI 1989/2410 (amended by SI 1991/763); the Fishing Vessels (Life-Saving Appliances) (Guernsey) Order 1990, SI 1990/2147; the Fishing Vessels (Safety Provisions) (Guernsey) Order 1990, SI 1990/2148; the Merchant Shipping (Safety Convention) (Guernsey) Order 1990, SI 1990/2150; and the Merchant Shipping Act 1988 (Guernsey) Order 1991, SI 1991/2875.

5  Merchant Shipping Act 1995 s 315(4).
6  Merchant Shipping Act 1995 s 315(3).
7  Ie without prejudice to the generality of the Merchant Shipping Act 1995 s 315(4) (see the text and note 5): see s 315(5).
8  As to the Secretary of State see PARA 36.
9  As to the meaning of 'registrar' for these purposes see PARA 254 note 11.
10 Merchant Shipping Act 1995 s 315(5).

B.   APPLICATION OF THE MERCHANT SHIPPING ACT 1995 TO CERTAIN DESCRIPTIONS OF SHIPS
ETC

**17. Non-United Kingdom ships.** The Secretary of State may make regulations[1] specifying any description of non-United Kingdom ships[2] and directing that such of the provisions of the Merchant Shipping Act 1995 and of instruments thereunder[3] as may be specified in the regulations[4]:

(1)    are to extend to non-United Kingdom ships of that description and to masters[5] and seamen[6] employed in them[7]; or

(2)    are to so extend in such circumstances as may be so specified, with such modifications, if any, as may be so specified[8].

Regulations so made may contain such transitional, supplementary and consequential provisions as appear to the Secretary of State to be expedient[9].

1   As to the Secretary of State see PARA 36; and as to his power to make subordinate legislation, including his power to appoint committees for the purpose of advising him when considering the making or alteration of any regulations, see PARA 39.
2   For these purposes, 'non-United Kingdom ships' means ships which are not registered in the United Kingdom: Merchant Shipping Act 1995 s 307(3). As to the meaning of 'ship' see PARA 229; and as to the meaning of 'registered' see PARA 254 note 2.
3   As to which see PARAS 15, 16.
4   Merchant Shipping Act 1995 s 307(1). As to the regulations so made see note 9.
5   As to the meaning of 'master' see PARA 444 note 1.
6   As to the meaning of 'seaman' see PARA 457 note 5.
7   Merchant Shipping Act 1995 s 307(1)(a). As to the regulations so made see note 9.
8   Merchant Shipping Act 1995 s 307(1)(b). As to the regulations so made see note 9.
9   Merchant Shipping Act 1995 s 307(2). In exercise of the power conferred by s 307, the Secretary of State has made the following regulations: the Fishing Vessels (Safety Provisions) (Amendment) Rules 1998, SI 1998/928 (an amending provision); the Merchant Shipping (Crew Accommodation) (Fishing Vessels) (Amendment) Regulations 1998, SI 1998/929 (an amending provision); the Fishing Vessels (Safety of 15–24 Metre Vessels) Regulations 2002, SI 2002/2201 (see FISHERIES AND AQUACULTURE vol 51 (2013) PARA 309); the Merchant Shipping (Boatmasters' Qualifications, Crew and Hours of Work) Regulations 2015, SI 2015/410 (see PARA 502 et seq); and the Merchant Shipping (Standards of Training, Certification and Watchkeeping) Regulations 2015, SI 2015/782 (see PARA 503 et seq). By virtue of the Interpretation Act 1978 s 17(2)(b), the following regulations take effect under the Merchant Shipping Act 1995 s 307 until superseded by an instrument made thereunder: the Merchant Shipping (Crew Accommodation) (Fishing Vessels) Regulations 1975, SI 1975/2220 (see FISHERIES AND AQUACULTURE vol 51 (2013) PARA 310); the Merchant Shipping (Returns of Births and Deaths) Regulations 1979, SI 1979/1577 (see PARA 644); the Merchant Shipping Act 1970 (Unregistered Fishing Vessels) Regulations 1991, SI 1991/1365; the Merchant Shipping Act 1970 (Unregistered Ships) Regulations 1991, SI 1991/1366; and the Merchant Shipping Act 1988 (Unregistered Ships) Regulations 1991, SI 1991/1367.

**18. Meaning of 'qualifying foreign ship'.** For the purposes of the Merchant Shipping Act 1995, 'qualifying foreign ship' means any ship[1] other than a British ship[2] or a ship which is not registered[3] under Part II of the Merchant Shipping Act 1995[4] and which (although not[5] a British ship) is both:

(1)    wholly owned by any of the following persons[6]:
   (a)    British citizens[7];
   (b)    British overseas territories citizens[8];
   (c)    British Overseas citizens[9];
   (d)    persons who under the British Nationality Act 1981 are British subjects[10];
   (e)    persons who are British Nationals (Overseas) within the meaning of the British Nationality Act 1981[11];
   (f)    persons who are British protected persons within the meaning of the British Nationality Act 1981[12]; or
   (g)    bodies corporate incorporated in the United Kingdom or in any relevant British possession[13] and having their principal place of business in the United Kingdom or in any relevant British possession[14]; and

(2)      not registered under the law of a country outside the United Kingdom[15].

1    As to the meaning of 'ship' see PARA 229.
2    Merchant Shipping Act 1995 s 313A(1)(a) (s 313A added by the Merchant Shipping and Maritime
     Security Act 1997 Sch 6 para 20). In the Merchant Shipping Act 1995, unless the context otherwise
     requires, 'qualifying foreign ship' has the meaning given in s 313A: see s 313(1) (definition added
     by the Merchant Shipping and Maritime Security Act 1997 Sch 6 para 19(2)(c)). 'Foreign', in
     relation to a ship, means that it is neither a United Kingdom ship nor a small ship, as defined in
     the Merchant Shipping Act 1995 s 1(2) (see PARA 230), which is a British ship: s 313(1). As to the
     meanings of 'British ship' and 'United Kingdom ship' see PARA 230; and as to the meaning of
     'United Kingdom' see PARA 16 note 3.
3    As to the meaning of 'registered' see PARA 254 note 2.
4    Ie under the Merchant Shipping Act 1995 Pt II (ss 8–23) (see PARA 237 et seq): see s 313A(1)(b)
     (as added: see note 2).
5    Ie by virtue of the Merchant Shipping Act 1995 s 1(1)(d) (see PARA 230): see s 313A(1)(b) (as
     added: see note 2).
6    Merchant Shipping Act 1995 s 313A(1)(b)(i) (as added: see note 2). The text refers to persons
     falling within s 313A(2) (see heads (i) to (vi) in the text): see s 313A(1)(b)(i).
7    Merchant Shipping Act 1995 s 313A(2)(a) (as added: see note 2). For these purposes, 'British
     citizen' has the same meaning as in the British Nationality Act 1981 (see BRITISH NATIONALITY
     vol 4 (2011) PARA 23 et seq): Merchant Shipping Act 1995 s 313(1).
8    Merchant Shipping Act 1995 s 313A(2)(b) (s 313A as added (see note 2); s 313A(2)(b) amended
     by virtue of the British Overseas Territories Act 2002 s 2(3)). For these purposes, 'British overseas
     territories citizen' has the same meaning as in the British Nationality Act 1981 (see BRITISH
     NATIONALITY vol 4 (2011) PARAS 406, 445–458): Merchant Shipping Act 1995 s 313(1)
     (definition added by virtue of the British Overseas Territories Act 2002 s 2(3)).
9    Merchant Shipping Act 1995 s 313A(2)(c) (as added: see note 2). For these purposes, 'British
     Overseas citizen' has the same meaning as in the British Nationality Act 1981 (see BRITISH
     NATIONALITY vol 4 (2011) PARA 459 et seq): Merchant Shipping Act 1995 s 313(1).
10   Merchant Shipping Act 1995 s 313A(2)(d) (as added: see note 2). As to British subjects under the
     British Nationality Act 1981 see BRITISH NATIONALITY vol 4 (2011) PARAS 407, 469–470.
11   Merchant Shipping Act 1995 s 313A(2)(e) (as added: see note 2). As to British Nationals
     (Overseas) within the meaning of the British Nationality Act 1981 see BRITISH NATIONALITY vol
     4 (2011) PARAS 406, 465–467.
12   Merchant Shipping Act 1995 s 313A(2)(f) (as added: see note 2). As to British protected persons
     within the meaning of the British Nationality Act 1981 see BRITISH NATIONALITY vol 4 (2011)
     PARAS 408, 476–480.
13   As to the meaning of 'relevant British possession' see PARA 16 note 3.
14   Merchant Shipping Act 1995 s 313A(2)(g) (as added: see note 2).
15   Merchant Shipping Act 1995 s 313A(1)(b)(ii) (as added: see note 2).

**19.  Government ships.** Subject to any of its other provisions, the Merchant
Shipping Act 1995 does not apply to ships[1] belonging to Her Majesty[2]. However,
Her Majesty may by Order in Council make regulations with respect to the
manner in which government ships[3] may be registered as British ships[4] under Part
II of the Merchant Shipping Act 1995[5]; and the 1995 Act, subject to any
exceptions and modifications which may be made by Order in Council, either
generally or as respects any special class of government ships, applies to
government ships registered in accordance with the Order as if they were
registered in accordance with Part II of the 1995 Act[6].

1    As to the meaning of 'ship' see PARA 229.
2    Merchant Shipping Act 1995 s 308(1).
3    For these purposes, 'government ships' means ships not forming part of Her Majesty's navy which
     belong to Her Majesty, or are held by any person on behalf of or for the benefit of the Crown (and
     for that reason cannot be registered under the Merchant Shipping Act 1995 Pt II (ss 8–23) (as to
     which see PARA 237 et seq)): s 308(4). In the Merchant Shipping Act 1995, unless the context
     otherwise requires, 'government ship' has the meaning given in s 308: see s 313(1). As to the
     meaning of 'registered' see PARA 254 note 2.
4    As to the meaning of 'British ship' see PARA 230.
5    Ie under the Merchant Shipping Act 1995 Pt II (see PARA 237 et seq): see s 308(2).
6    Merchant Shipping Act 1995 s 308(2). Any Order in Council under s 308(2) must be laid before
     Parliament after being made: see s 308(3). As to the making of Orders under the Merchant

Shipping Act 1995 generally see PARA 39. By virtue of the Interpretation Act 1978 s 17(2)(b), the following Orders have effect as if made under the Merchant Shipping Act 1995 s 308(2), (3): Order in Council dated 9 February 1920 (Registration of Ministry of Agriculture and Fisheries Vessels), SR & O 1920/260; Order in Council dated 14 July 1921 (Registration of Board of Trade Vessels), SR & O 1921/1211 (amended by SI 1978/1533); Order in Council dated 8 December 1924 (Registration of Australian Government Vessels), SR & O 1924/1391; Order in Council dated 10 August 1926 (Registration of Straits Settlements Vessels), SR & O 1926/1036; Order in Council dated 5 November 1929 (Registration of Vessels in the Service of the Indian Government), SR & O 1929/986; Order in Council dated 15 May 1930 (Registration of Northern Ireland Government Vessels), SR & O 1930/336; the Merchant Shipping (Registration of New Zealand Government Ships) Order 1946, SR & O 1946/1086; the Merchant Shipping (Registration of Sierra Leone Government Ships) Order 1951, SI 1951/143; the Merchant Shipping (Registration of Federation of Nigeria Government Ships) Order 1957, SI 1957/861; the Merchant Shipping (Registration of Scottish Fishery Cruisers, Research Ships etc) Order 1960, SI 1960/2217 (amended by SI 1972/2001); the Merchant Shipping (Registration of Ships) (Highlands and Islands Shipping Services) Order 1961, SI 1961/1514; the Registration of Government Ships (British Antarctic Territory) Order 1963, SI 1963/1494; the Merchant Shipping (Registration of Colonial Government Ships) Order 1963, SI 1963/1631 (amended by SI 1965/1867; SI 1967/1903; SI 1978/1628; SI 1985/1200); the Merchant Shipping (Registration of Western Australia Government Ships) Order 1964, SI 1964/270; the Merchant Shipping (Ministry of Technology Ships) Order 1966, SI 1966/269; the Merchant Shipping (Registration of Queensland Government Ships) Order 1968, SI 1968/1092; the Merchant Shipping (Registration of South Australian Government Ships) Order 1971, SI 1971/872; the Merchant Shipping (Ministry of Defence Ships) Order 1989, SI 1989/1991 (amended by SI 1992/1293; SI 1992/1294); the Merchant Shipping (Ministry of Defence Commercially Managed Ships) Order 1992, SI 1992/1293; and the Merchant Shipping (Ministry of Defence Yachts) Order 1992, SI 1992/1294.

**20. Ships chartered by demise to the Crown.** If, for the time being[1]:

(1)    a ship[2] is registered[3] in the United Kingdom[4] and is in the service of a government department[5] (the 'relevant department') by reason of a charter by demise to the Crown[6]; and

(2)    there is in force[7] an Order in Council providing for the registration of government ships[8] in the service of the relevant department[9],

then the following statutory provisions, namely:

(a)    the provisions of the Order in Council referred to in head (2) above (excluding those relating to registration under the Order)[10]; and

(b)    the provisions of the Merchant Shipping Act 1995 as they so apply[11],

have the same effect[12] in relation to that ship as they have in relation to a government ship in the service of the relevant department (whether referred to as such or as such a ship registered in pursuance of that Order in Council)[13].

Part II of the Merchant Shipping Act 1995[14] has effect[15] in relation to such a ship in like manner as if it were not, for the purposes of the 1995 Act, a ship belonging to Her Majesty[16]. However, Her Majesty may by Order in Council provide that any such statutory provision[17] specified in the Order[18]:

(i)    does not have effect[19] in relation to such a ship[20]; or

(ii)    is to so have effect in relation to such a ship, but subject to such modifications as are specified in the Order[21].

Any such Order in Council may make such transitional, incidental or supplementary provision as appears to Her Majesty to be necessary or expedient[22].

1   See the Merchant Shipping Act 1995 s 309(1).
2   As to the meaning of 'ship' see PARA 229.
3   As to the meaning of 'registered' see PARA 254 note 2.
4   Merchant Shipping Act 1995 s 309(1)(a)(i). As to the meaning of 'United Kingdom' see PARA 16 note 3.
5   Ie including a Northern Ireland department: see the Merchant Shipping Act 1995 s 309(1)(a)(ii).
6   Merchant Shipping Act 1995 s 309(1)(a)(ii).
7   Ie under the Merchant Shipping Act 1995 s 308(2) (as to which see PARA 19): see s 309(1)(b).
8   As to the meaning of 'government ship' for these purposes see PARA 19 note 3.
9   Merchant Shipping Act 1995 s 309(1)(b).
10  Merchant Shipping Act 1995 s 309(2)(a).

11  Merchant Shipping Act 1995 s 309(2)(b). The text refers to the provisions of the Merchant
    Shipping Act 1995 as they apply by virtue of s 308(2) (as to which see PARA 19) and the Order
    in Council mentioned in head (a) in the text: see s 309(2)(b).
12  Ie subject to the Merchant Shipping Act 1995 s 309(3), (4) (as to which see the text and notes
    14–21): see s 309(2).
13  Merchant Shipping Act 1995 s 309(2). In the application of any provision of the Merchant
    Shipping Act 1995, other than a provision of Pt II (ss 8–23) (as to which see PARA 237 et seq), in
    relation to a ship to which s 309 applies, any reference to the owner of the ship is to be construed
    as a reference to the relevant department: s 309(5).
14  Ie the Merchant Shipping Act 1995 Pt II (as to which see PARA 237 et seq): see s 309(3).
15  Ie subject to the Merchant Shipping Act 1995 s 309(4) (as to which see the text and notes 17–21):
    see s 309(3).
16  Merchant Shipping Act 1995 s 309(3).
17  Ie any statutory provision falling within the Merchant Shipping Act 1995 s 309(2) (see the text and
    notes 10–13) or s 309(3) (see the text and notes 14–16): see s 309(4).
18  Merchant Shipping Act 1995 s 309(4).
19  Ie does not have effect in accordance with the Merchant Shipping Act 1995 s 309(2) (see the text
    and notes 10–13) or s 309(3) (see the text and notes 14–16): see s 309(4)(a).
20  Merchant Shipping Act 1995 s 309(4)(a).
21  Merchant Shipping Act 1995 s 309(4)(b).
22  Merchant Shipping Act 1995 s 309(6). At the date at which this volume states the law, no Order
    in Council had been made under s 309 and none has effect as if so made.

**21.  Hovercraft.** The enactments and instruments with respect to which
provision may be made by Order in Council under the Hovercraft Act 1968[1]
include the Merchant Shipping Act 1995 (except the provisions relating to British
ships[2] and to the registration of ships[3]) and any instrument made thereunder[4].

The provisions of the Merchant Shipping (High Speed Craft) Regulations 2004
apply to certain hovercraft[5].

1  Ie under the Hovercraft Act 1968 s 1(1)(h) (as to which see PARA 382): see the Merchant Shipping
   Act 1995 s 310.
2  Ie the Merchant Shipping Act 1995 Pt I (ss 1–7) (as to which see PARAS 230–235): see s 310.
3  Ie the Merchant Shipping Act 1995 Pt II (ss 8–23) (as to which see PARA 237 et seq): see s 310.
4  Merchant Shipping Act 1995 s 310. As to hovercraft see PARA 381 et seq; and as to the regulation
   of craft to prevent smuggling see PARA 25.
5  Ie the Merchant Shipping (High Speed Craft) Regulations 2004, SI 2004/302, which have been
   made under the Merchant Shipping Act 1995 ss 47, 85, 86 (see PARA 617 et seq).

**22.  Provision made for shipping legislation to apply to structures etc.** The
Secretary of State[1] may by order[2]:

(1)     provide for a shipping provision[3] to apply (with or without
        modification) in relation to specified things which are used, navigated or
        situated wholly or partly in or on water[4];

(2)     provide for a shipping provision not to apply in relation to specified
        things which are used, navigated or situated wholly or partly in or on
        water[5];

(3)     modify a shipping provision in its application in relation to specified
        things which are used, navigated or situated wholly or partly in or on
        water[6].

1  As to the Secretary of State see PARA 36.
2  Railways and Transport Safety Act 2003 s 112(1). As to the making of such orders see s 112(5),
   (7). At the orders made under s 112 see note 4. As to the Secretary of State's power to make
   subordinate legislation see PARA 39.
3  For these purposes, 'shipping provision' means a provision which is made by or by virtue of an Act
   (including the Railways and Transport Safety Act 2003), and is expressed to apply in relation to
   ships, vessels or boats (or a specified class or description of ship, vessel or boat): s 112(2). An order
   under s 112(1) may, in particular, be made in respect of a provision which either confers power to
   legislate, or creates an offence (s 112(3)); and such an order has effect despite (and may amend) any
   provision which forms part of or relates to the shipping provision concerned, and defines 'ship',
   'vessel' or 'boat' or in any other way limits or determines the application of the shipping provision
   concerned (s 112(4)).

4    Railways and Transport Safety Act 2003 s 112(1)(a). An order under s 112(1)(a) may provide for
     the shipping provision not to apply, or to apply with specified modifications, where it would
     conflict with a specified provision or class of provision made by or by virtue of an enactment: see
     s 112(6). In exercise of the power conferred by s 112(1)(a), the Merchant Shipping (Prevention of
     Pollution) (Drilling Rigs and Other Platforms) Order 2005, SI 2005/74, has been made.
     Accordingly, the Merchant Shipping Act 1995 s 128(1)(e) (giving effect to certain international
     agreements which have been ratified by the United Kingdom and which relate to the prevention,
     reduction or control of pollution of the sea or other waters by matter from ships) (see
     ENVIRONMENTAL QUALITY AND PUBLIC HEALTH vol 45 (2010) PARA 360) applies in relation
     to drilling rigs and other platforms which are used, navigated or situated wholly or partly in or on
     water, as it applies in relation to ships: see the Merchant Shipping (Prevention of Pollution)
     (Drilling Rigs and Other Platforms) Order 2005, SI 2005/74, art 2.
5    Railways and Transport Safety Act 2003 s 112(1)(b).
6    Railways and Transport Safety Act 2003 s 112(1)(c). An order under s 112(1)(c) may provide for
     the shipping provision not to apply, or to apply with specified modifications, where it would
     conflict with a specified provision or class of provision made by or by virtue of an enactment: see
     s 112(6).

**23. Fishing vessels.** Special provision is made in the Merchant Shipping Act
1995 relating to fishing vessels[1].

1    See the Merchant Shipping Act 1995 Pt V (ss 109–127). As to the meaning of 'fishing vessel' see
     PARA 230 note 9.

### (iv)  Cognate Law

**24. Reports of craft movement for customs control.** For the purposes of the
statutory prohibitions and restrictions, including duty, on the import and export
of goods and animals[1], reports must be made of every ship arriving at, and
clearance must be obtained of every ship departing from, a port appointed for
those purposes from or to any place outside the United Kingdom[2].

Notification of the arrival of pleasure craft in the United Kingdom from a place
outside the customs territory of the EU or from certain other territories must be
given to an officer of Revenue and Customs as soon as possible after the arrival
of the craft[3].

1    As to such prohibitions generally see ANIMALS vol 2 (2017) PARA 167 et seq; CUSTOMS AND
     EXCISE vol 31 (2012) PARAS 997 et seq, 1025 et seq.
2    See CUSTOMS AND EXCISE vol 31 (2012) PARAS 948 et seq, 997 et seq. As to the meaning of
     'United Kingdom' see PARA 16 note 3. In connection with reporting requirements see also the
     Convention on Facilitation of International Maritime Traffic (London, 9 April 1965; TS 46
     (1967); Cmnd 3299 (amended by TS 63 (1972); Cmnd 5006; annex amended by TS 63 (1978);
     Cmnd 7243); Parliament and Council Directive (EU) 2010/65 (OJ L283, 29.10.2010, p 1) on
     reporting formalities for ships arriving in and/or departing from ports of the member states; and
     INTERNATIONAL RELATIONS LAW vol 61 (2010) PARA 121.
3    See the Pleasure Craft (Arrival and Report) Regulations 1996, SI 1996/1406; and CUSTOMS AND
     EXCISE vol 31 (2012) PARA 950.

**25. Regulation of craft to prevent smuggling.** The Commissioners for Her
Majesty's Revenue and Customs[1] may make general regulations with respect to
small ships[2] and any such regulations may in particular make provision as to the
purposes for which and the limits within which such ships may be used[3]. Different
provision may be made by such regulations for different classes or descriptions of
small ships[4].

The Commissioners may, in respect of any small ship, grant a licence exempting
that ship from all or any of the provisions of any regulations so made[5]; and any
such licence may be granted for such period, for such purposes and subject to such
conditions and restrictions as the Commissioners see fit, and may be revoked at
any time by the Commissioners[6]. Any small ship which, except under and in
accordance with the terms of a licence so granted, is used contrary to any

regulations so made, and any ship granted such a licence which is found not to have that licence on board, is liable to forfeiture[7].

Every boat belonging to a British ship and every other vessel not exceeding 100 tons register, not being a fishing vessel registered under Part II of the Merchant Shipping Act 1995[8], and every hovercraft, must be marked in such manner as the Commissioners may direct; and any such boat, vessel or hovercraft which is not so marked is liable to forfeiture[9].

The Commissioners may make regulations:

(1)    prescribing the procedure for making a report of a ship arriving, or expected to arrive, at a port from any place outside the United Kingdom or carrying any goods brought in that ship from some place outside the United Kingdom and not yet cleared on importation[10];

(2)    prescribing the procedure to be followed by a ship arriving at a port[11].

1    As to the Commissioners for Her Majesty's Revenue and Customs see CUSTOMS AND EXCISE vol 31 (2012) PARA 921 et seq.
2    For these purposes, 'small ships' means ships not exceeding 100 tons register; and hovercraft of whatever size: Customs and Excise Management Act 1979 s 81(1). 'Ship' and 'vessel' include any boat or other vessel whatsoever (and, to the extent provided in s 2, any hovercraft): s 1(1). 'Tons register' means the tons of a ship's net tonnage as ascertained and registered according to the tonnage regulations of the Merchant Shipping Act 1995 (see PARA 248) or, in the case of a ship which is not registered under that Act, ascertained in like manner as if it were to be so registered: Customs and Excise Management Act 1979 s 1(1) (amended by the Merchant Shipping Act 1995 s 314(2), Sch 13 para 53(1), (2)(b)). 'Hovercraft' means a hovercraft within the meaning of the Hovercraft Act 1968 (see PARA 381): Customs and Excise Management Act 1979 s 1(1).
3    Customs and Excise Management Act 1979 s 81(2) (amended by virtue of the Commissioners for Revenue and Customs Act 2005 s 50(1), (2), (7)). At the date at which this volume states the law, no such regulations had been made.
4    Customs and Excise Management Act 1979 s 81(3).
5    Customs and Excise Management Act 1979 s 81(4) (amended by virtue of the Commissioners for Revenue and Customs Act 2005 s 50(1), (2), (7)).
6    Customs and Excise Management Act 1979 s 81(5) (amended by virtue of the Commissioners for Revenue and Customs Act 2005 s 50(1), (2), (7)).
7    Customs and Excise Management Act 1979 s 81(6).
8    Ie the Merchant Shipping Act 1995 Pt II (ss 8–23) (as to which see PARA 237 et seq): see the Customs and Excise Management Act 1979 s 81(7) (amended by the Merchant Shipping Act 1995 Sch 13 para 53(1), (3); and by virtue of the Commissioners for Revenue and Customs Act 2005 s 50(1), (2), (7)).
9    Customs and Excise Management Act 1979 s 81(7) (as amended: see note 8). As to ships' markings see PARA 280 et seq.
10   See the Customs and Excise Management Act 1979 s 35(1), (2), (4); and CUSTOMS AND EXCISE vol 31 (2012) PARA 950. In exercise of the powers conferred by s 35, the Commissioners made the Ship's Report, Importation and Exportation by Sea Regulations 1981, SI 1981/1260 (see CUSTOMS AND EXCISE vol 31 (2012) PARAS 951–952); and the Pleasure Craft (Arrival and Report) Regulations 1996, SI 1996/1406 (see CUSTOMS AND EXCISE vol 31 (2012) PARA 950).
      As to the disclosure and sharing of information which is obtained or held in the exercise of specified powers and relates to passengers or freight on a ship, the crew of a ship, or to voyages (or to such other matters in respect of travel or freight as the Secretary of State and the Treasury may jointly specify by order) and which is obtained or held to the extent that the information is likely to be of use for immigration purposes, police purposes, or Revenue and Customs purposes see the Immigration, Asylum and Nationality Act 2006 ss 36, 37, 39; and IMMIGRATION AND ASYLUM vol 57 (2012) PARAS 147–149.
11   See the Customs and Excise Management Act 1979 s 42(1)(a); and CUSTOMS AND EXCISE vol 31 (2012) PARA 950. In exercise of the powers so conferred, the Commissioners made the Ship's Report, Importation and Exportation by Sea Regulations 1981, SI 1981/1260; and the Pleasure Craft (Arrival and Report) Regulations 1996, SI 1996/1406 (see note 10).

**26. Public health precautions.** The masters of ships arriving in, or departing from, the United Kingdom must observe the regulations for preventing danger to health from, or the spread of infection by means of, those ships; and these requirements are enforced by the port health authorities[1].

Certain statutory obligations in relation to the infestation of food apply to all vessels used for the transport or storage of food; and certain other obligations in relation to the destruction of rats and mice apply to any vessel which is not a sea-going ship[2].

1 See the Public Health (Ships) Regulations 1979, SI 1979/1435; and ENVIRONMENTAL QUALITY AND PUBLIC HEALTH vol 46 (2010) PARA 933 et seq. On unjustified detention on health and safety grounds see *Club Cruise Entertainment and Travelling Services Europe BV v Department for Transport, The Van Gogh* [2008] EWHC 2794 (Comm), [2009] 1 All ER (Comm) 955.
2 See the Prevention of Damage by Pests (Application to Shipping) Order 1951, SI 1951/967; and ENVIRONMENTAL QUALITY AND PUBLIC HEALTH vol 46 (2010) PARA 861 et seq.

**27. Importation of animals by sea.** The importation of animals by any specified vessel may be prohibited by order; and orders may be made securing for animals carried by sea proper food, water and ventilation and protection from unnecessary suffering[1].

1 See ANIMALS vol 2 (2017) PARA 167 et seq.

**28. Births and deaths at sea.** The Secretary of State may make regulations under the Merchant Shipping Act 1995 in relation to births and deaths in ships[1]; and such regulations may require the master of any United Kingdom ship to make a return to a superintendent or proper officer of the birth or death of any person occurring in the ship and the death of any person employed in the ship, wherever occurring outside the United Kingdom, and to notify any such death to such person, if any, as the deceased may have named to him as his next of kin[2].

The Registrar General must preserve any returns made in the marine register book[3].

Similar duties are imposed in relation to births and deaths on board Her Majesty's ships[4] and on hovercraft[5].

1 See the Merchant Shipping Act 1995 s 108; and PARA 644. As to the regulations so made see the Merchant Shipping (Returns of Births and Deaths) Regulations 1979, SI 1979/1577; and PARA 644.
    As to the Secretary of State see PARA 36; and as to his power to make subordinate legislation under the Merchant Shipping Act 1995 see PARA 39.
2 See note 1.
3 See REGISTRATION CONCERNING THE INDIVIDUAL vol 88 (2012) PARA 295.
4 See REGISTRATION CONCERNING THE INDIVIDUAL vol 88 (2012) PARA 301.
5 See PARA 418 et seq.

**29. Control of loading, unloading, coaling etc of ships in docks, harbours, canals etc.** Certain provisions of the Factories Act 1961 apply to the process of loading, unloading or coaling of any ship in any dock, harbour or canal, and to all machinery or plant (including any gangway or ladder used by any person employed to load or unload or coal a ship) used in those processes as if the processes were carried on in a factory and the machinery or plant were machinery or plant in a factory, and the person who carries on those processes were the occupier of a factory[1].

1 See the Factories Act 1961 s 125; and HEALTH AND SAFETY AT WORK vol 52 (2014) PARA 306. See also the Dangerous Substances in Harbour Areas Regulations 1987, SI1987/37; and PORTS AND HARBOURS vol 85 (2012) PARA 101 et seq; and the various health and safety-related regulations made under the Merchant Shipping Act 1995 (see PARA 602 et seq).

**30. Control of work carried out in relation to ships or vessels.** Many of the provisions of the Factories Act 1961 apply to certain work carried out in a harbour or wet dock or in a ship but not to such work done either by the master or crew or during a trial run[1].

1 See the Factories Act 1961 s 126; and HEALTH AND SAFETY AT WORK vol 52 (2014) PARA 306.

**31. Retail of alcohol on vessels etc.** For the purposes of the Licensing Act 2003, an activity is not a licensable activity[1] if it is carried on (inter alia) aboard a hovercraft engaged on a journey, aboard a vessel engaged on an international journey, or at an approved wharf at a designated port or hoverport[2].

1 As to licensable activities for the purposes of the Licensing Act 2003 see LEISURE AND ENTERTAINMENT vol 67 (2016) PARA 33 et seq.
2 See the Licensing Act 2003 s 173; and LEISURE AND ENTERTAINMENT vol 67 (2016) PARA 34.

**32. Ships as goods; marine insurance.** Ships are personal chattels and as such are goods within the meaning of the law relating to the sale of goods[1]. Ships are also goods for the purposes of the statutory controls over mergers[2] and market investigations[3] and for the purposes of enforcing certain consumer legislation[4].

Ships, goods, freight, profits and every lawful marine adventure may be the subject of a contract of marine insurance against maritime perils, the law as to such insurance being codified in the Marine Insurance Act 1906[5].

1 In connection with a contract for the sale of a ship see *Polestar Maritime Ltd v YHM Shipping Co Ltd* [2012] EWCA Civ 153, [2012] 2 All ER (Comm) 447; *Dalmare SpA v Union Maritime Ltd* [2012] EWHC 3537 (Comm), [2013] 2 All ER (Comm) 70, [2013] 1 Lloyd's Rep 509; *Austen v Pearl Motor Yachts Ltd* [2014] EWHC 3544 (Comm), [2014] All ER (D) 04 (Nov); and see generally SALE OF GOODS AND SUPPLY OF SERVICES vol 91 (2012) PARA 31.
2 See the Enterprise Act 2002 Pt 3 (ss 22–130); and COMPETITION vol 18 (2009) PARA 172 et seq.
3 See the Enterprise Act 2002 Pt 4 (ss 131–184); and COMPETITION vol 18 (2009) PARA 276 et seq.
4 See the Enterprise Act 2002 Pt 8 (ss 210–236); and COMPETITION vol 18 (2009) PARA 339 et seq.
5 See INSURANCE vol 60 (2011) PARA 238 et seq. The rules of the common law including the law merchant, save in so far as they are inconsistent with the express provisions of the Marine Insurance Act 1906, continue to apply to contracts of marine insurance: see s 91(2); and INSURANCE vol 60 (2011) PARA 15. In connection with an illegal marine insurance contract see *Islamic Republic of Iran Shipping Lines v Steamship Mutual Underwriting Association (Bermuda) Ltd* [2010] EWHC 2661 (Comm), [2011] 2 All ER (Comm) 609, [2011] 1 Lloyd's Rep 195.

**33. Piracy.** All states who are party to the United Nations Convention on the Law of the Sea 1982[1] must cooperate to the fullest possible extent in the repression of piracy on the high seas or in any other place outside the jurisdiction of any state[2]. The acts which constitute piracy in international law, and their punishment, are considered elsewhere in this work[3].

1 Ie the United Nations Convention on the Law of the Sea (Montego Bay, 10 December 1982 to 9 December 1984; TS 3 Misc 11 (1983); Cmnd 8941) (the 'United Nations Convention on the Law of the Sea 1982') (as to which see PARA 9).
2 See the United Nations Convention on the Law of the Sea 1982 arts 100, 101–103 (which are set out in the Merchant Shipping and Maritime Security Act 1997 s 26(1), Sch 5); and PARA 1186.
3 See INTERNATIONAL RELATIONS LAW vol 61 (2010) PARA 155 et seq.

**34. Powers relating to the prevention of terrorism etc.** The Terrorism Act 2000 confers powers to stop, question and detain persons arriving in or leaving Great Britain[1] or Northern Ireland by ship, to search ships and to require the owners or agents of ships employed to carry passengers for reward and coming to Great Britain from the Republic of Ireland, Northern Ireland or any of the Islands (or going from Great Britain to any other of those places) to arrange for the ships to call at designated ports for the purpose of disembarking or embarking passengers[2].

The Terrorism Act 2000 also confers powers to require the provision of passenger information[3].

1 As to the meaning of 'Great Britain' see PARA 16 note 3.
2 See the Terrorism Act 2000 Sch 7; and POLICE AND INVESTIGATORY POWERS vol 84A (2013) PARA 748 et seq.
3 See the Terrorism Act 2000 Sch 7; and POLICE AND INVESTIGATORY POWERS vol 84A (2013) PARA 755. As to the disclosure and sharing of information which is obtained or held in the exercise of specified powers and relates to passengers or freight on a ship, the crew of a ship, or to voyages (or to such other matters in respect of travel or freight as the Secretary of State and the Treasury

may jointly specify by order) and which is obtained or held to the extent that the information is likely to be of use for immigration purposes, police purposes, or Revenue and Customs purposes see also the Immigration, Asylum and Nationality Act 2006 ss 36, 37, 39; and IMMIGRATION AND ASYLUM vol 57 (2012) PARAS 147–149.

**35. Recreational craft.** Recreational craft must satisfy the essential safety requirements which are applicable to them and must meet certain other safety requirements before they are put on the market, including being put into service[1].

1  See the Recreational Craft Regulations 2004, SI 2004/1464 (implementing Parliament and Council Directive (EU) 2013/53 (OJ L354, 28.12.2013, p 90)); and CONSUMER PROTECTION vol 21 (2016) PARAS 597–598.

# (3) ADMINISTRATION

## (i) The Secretary of State and the Welsh Authorities

**36. The Secretary of State and the Welsh authorities.** Despite the fact that older statutes refer to ministers (occasionally, to specific ministers) or to government departments, the office of Secretary of State is a unified office, and in law each Secretary of State is capable of performing the duties of all or any of the departments[1]. Accordingly, many modern statutes refer simply to the 'Secretary of State' without reference to a particular department or ministry[2].

Many statutory functions vested in a Secretary of State or a Minister of the Crown are transferred so as to be exercisable in relation to Wales[3] by the Welsh Ministers[4]. However, for the purposes of this title, the functions so transferred are limited to functions under the Protection of Wrecks Act 1973[5]. Nor does the legislative competence of the National Assembly for Wales extend to shipping, apart from:

(1)     financial assistance for shipping services to, from or within Wales[6]; and

(2)     regulation of the use of vessels carrying animals for the purposes of protecting human, animal, fish or plant health, animal welfare or the environment[7].

1  See CONSTITUTIONAL AND ADMINISTRATIVE LAW vol 20 (2014) PARA 153.
2  In any enactment, 'Secretary of State' means one of Her Majesty's Principal Secretaries of State: see the Interpretation Act 1978 s 5, Sch 1; and STATUTES AND LEGISLATIVE PROCESS vol 96 (2012) PARA 1209. As to the functions of the Secretary of State under the Merchant Shipping Act 1995 see PARA 37 et seq.
3  As to the meaning of 'Wales' see PARA 16 note 2.
4  See the Government of Wales Act 2006 s 162(1), Sch 11 para 30; and STATUTES AND LEGISLATIVE PROCESS vol 96 (2012) PARA 1033 et seq.
5  Ie the Protection of Wrecks Act 1973 (see PARAS 948, 1166), except s 2 (see PARA 948): see the National Assembly for Wales (Transfer of Functions) Order 1999, SI 1999/672, Sch 1.
6  See the Government of Wales Act 2006 s 108(3)–(5), Sch 7 para 10 (amended by SI 2007/2143; SI 2010/2968); and PARA 66.
7  See the Government of Wales Act 2006 s 108(3)–(5), Sch 7 para 10 (as amended: see note 6).

**37. General functions of the Secretary of State under the Merchant Shipping Act 1995.** Under the Merchant Shipping Act 1995, the Secretary of State[1] continues to have the general superintendence of all matters relating to merchant shipping and seamen[2] and is authorised to carry into execution the provisions of that Act and of all Acts relating to merchant shipping and seamen for the time being in force, except where otherwise provided or so far as relating to revenue[3].

Under the Merchant Shipping Act 1995, the Secretary of State continues also to have the functions of taking, or co-ordinating, measures to prevent, reduce and minimise the effect of, marine pollution[4].

1　As to the Secretary of State see PARA 36.
2　As to the meaning of 'seaman' see PARA 457 note 5.
3　Merchant Shipping Act 1995 s 292(1). The Secretary of State may take any legal proceedings under the Merchant Shipping Act 1995 in the name of any of his officers: s 292(2).
4　See the Merchant Shipping Act 1995 s 293; and ENVIRONMENTAL QUALITY AND PUBLIC HEALTH vol 45 (2010) PARA 58.

**38.　Secretary of State's general power under the Merchant Shipping Act 1995 to dispense.** The Secretary of State[1] may, if he thinks fit, and upon such conditions, if any, as he thinks fit to impose, exempt any ship[2] from any specified requirement of, or prescribed under, the Merchant Shipping Act 1995[3], or dispense with the observance of any such requirement in the case of any ship, if he is satisfied, as respects that requirement, of the following matters[4], namely:

(1)　that the requirement has been substantially complied with in the case of that ship or that compliance with it is unnecessary in the circumstances[5]; and

(2)　that the action taken or provision made as respects the subject matter of the requirement in the case of the ship is as effective as, or more effective than, actual compliance with the requirement[6].

The Secretary of State must annually lay before both Houses of Parliament a special report stating:

(a)　the cases in which he has exercised his powers to dispense[7] during the preceding year[8]; and

(b)　the grounds upon which he has acted in each case[9].

1　As to the Secretary of State see PARA 36.
2　As to the meaning of 'ship' see PARA 229.
3　Ie other than the Merchant Shipping Act 1995 Pt VI Ch II (ss 131–151) (oil pollution) (see ENVIRONMENTAL QUALITY AND PUBLIC HEALTH vol 45 (2010) PARA 425 et seq): see s 294(1).
4　Merchant Shipping Act 1995 s 294(1).
5　Merchant Shipping Act 1995 s 294(2)(a).
6　Merchant Shipping Act 1995 s 294(2)(b).
7　Ie under the Merchant Shipping Act 1995 s 294 (see the text and notes 1–6): see s 294(3)(a).
8　Merchant Shipping Act 1995 s 294(3)(a).
9　Merchant Shipping Act 1995 s 294(3)(b).

**39.　Secretary of State's power to make regulations, orders, rules and directions under the Merchant Shipping Act 1995.** Provision is made in relation to the Secretary of State's power to make regulations, orders, rules and directions under the Merchant Shipping Act 1995[1].

The Secretary of State may, if he thinks fit, appoint committees for the purpose of advising him when considering the making or alteration of any regulations, rules or scales for the purposes[2] of the Merchant Shipping Act 1995[3]. Committees may be so appointed to advise the Secretary of State, particularly as regards any special regulations, rules or scales or generally as regards any class or classes of regulations, rules or scales which the Secretary of State may assign to them[4].

1　See the Merchant Shipping Act 1995 s 306(1)–(3) (amended by the Merchant Shipping and Maritime Security Act 1997 s 29(1), Sch 6 para 18(1)–(4); the Wreck Removal Convention Act 2011 s 1; and SI 1998/2241). Before making the following regulations or rules, namely:
　　(1)　regulations under the Merchant Shipping Act 1995 Pt III (ss 24–84) (masters and seamen) (see PARA 423 et seq) or s 108 (returns of births and deaths in ships) (see PARA 644) or s 130A (waste reception facilities at harbours) (see ENVIRONMENTAL QUALITY AND PUBLIC HEALTH vol 45 (2010) PARA 421); or
　　(2)　rules under Pt V Ch II (ss 121–127) (fishing vessels (safety)) (see PARA 607 et seq),

the Secretary of State must consult with organisations in the United Kingdom appearing to him representative of persons who will be affected by the regulations or rules: s 306(4) (amended by the Merchant Shipping and Maritime Security Act 1997 Sch 6 para 18(1), (5)). As to the meaning of 'United Kingdom' see PARA 16 note 3.

Any direction, notice, order or authorisation under the Merchant Shipping Act 1995 given or made by the Secretary of State must be in writing (s 306(5)); and any power to give a direction includes power to vary or revoke the direction by a subsequent direction (s 306(6)).

Where a person has power under the Merchant Shipping Act 2005 to make subordinate legislation and proposes to exercise that power to make subordinate legislation which refers to an international instrument (ie an international convention or treaty or an instrument made under such a convention or treaty, apart from an EU instrument), the power may be exercised so as to have the effect that the reference to the instrument is construed as a reference to the instrument as modified from time to time and, if the instrument is replaced by another instrument, as a reference to that other instrument ('ambulatory provision'): s 306A(1), (2), (4), (6) (s 306A added by the Deregulation Act 2015 s 106). For these purposes an instrument is modified if omissions, additions or other alterations to the text of the instrument take effect, or supplementary provision made under the instrument takes effect: Merchant Shipping Act 2005 s 306A(3) (as so added). Subordinate legislation which makes ambulatory provision may make provision as to when a modification of an international instrument is to be treated as taking effect for these purposes and when an international instrument is to be treated as having been replaced by another instrument: s 306A(5) (as so added).

2   Ie other than for the purposes of the Merchant Shipping Act 1995 Pt VI Ch II (ss 131–151) (oil pollution) (see ENVIRONMENTAL QUALITY AND PUBLIC HEALTH vol 45 (2010) PARA 425 et seq): see s 301(1).

3   Merchant Shipping Act 1995 s 301(1). A committee so appointed must consist of persons representing the interests principally affected or having special knowledge of the subject matter (s 301(2)); and the Secretary of State must pay to the members of any such committee such travelling and other allowances as the Secretary of State determines with the consent of the Treasury (s 301(3)). As to the Treasury see CONSTITUTIONAL AND ADMINISTRATIVE LAW vol 20 (2014) PARA 262 et seq.

4   Merchant Shipping Act 1995 s 301(4).

## 40. Secretary of State's power to prepare and approve forms required under the Merchant Shipping Act 1995.

The Secretary of State[1] may prepare and approve forms for any book, instrument or paper required under the Merchant Shipping Act 1995, and may alter such forms as he thinks fit[2].

The Secretary of State must cause every such form to be marked with the distinguishing mark of his department and, before finally issuing any form or making any alteration in a form, must cause public notice thereof to be given in such manner as he thinks requisite in order to avoid inconvenience[3].

The Secretary of State must cause such forms to be supplied at offices of Revenue and Customs and at offices of the Department of Transport, free of charge or at such reasonable prices as the Secretary of State may fix, or he may license any persons to print and sell the forms[4].

Every such book, instrument or paper must be made in the form, if any, approved by the Secretary of State, or as near as circumstances permit; and, unless so made, is not admissible in evidence in any civil proceedings on the part of the owner or master[5] of any ship[6].

Every such book, instrument or paper, if made in a form purporting to be the proper form and to be marked with the distinguishing mark[7], is deemed to be in the form required by the Merchant Shipping Act 1995, unless the contrary is proved[8].

If any person prints, sells or uses any document purporting to be a form approved by the Secretary of State knowing that the document is not the form approved for the time being or that the document has not been prepared or issued by the Secretary of State, that person is liable on summary conviction to a fine[9].

1   As to the Secretary of State see PARA 36.

2   Merchant Shipping Act 1995 s 300(1). The provisions of s 300(1)–(5) do not apply where special
    provision is made by the Merchant Shipping Act 1995: s 300(6).
3   Merchant Shipping Act 1995 s 300(2). See note 2.
4   Merchant Shipping Act 1995 s 300(3) (amended by virtue of the Commissioners for Revenue and
    Customs Act 2005 s 50(1), (2), (7)). See note 2.
5   As to the meaning of 'master' see PARA 444 note 1.
6   Merchant Shipping Act 1995 s 300(4). See note 2. As to the meaning of 'ship' see PARA 229.
7   Ie marked in accordance with the Merchant Shipping Act 1995 s 300(2) (see the text and note 3):
    see s 300(5).
8   Merchant Shipping Act 1995 s 300(5). See note 2.
9   See the Merchant Shipping Act 1995 s 300(7); and PARA 1182.

**41.  Secretary of State's power to require returns etc from officers under the Merchant Shipping Act 1995.** All superintendents[1] must make and send to the Secretary of State[2] such returns or reports on any matter relating to British merchant shipping[3] or seamen[4] as he may require[5]. All superintendents must also, when required by the Secretary of State, produce to him or to his officers all official log books[6] and other documents which are delivered to them under the Merchant Shipping Act 1995[7].

All consular officers[8] abroad and all officers of revenue and customs abroad must make and send to the Secretary of State such returns or reports on any matter relating to British merchant shipping or seamen as he may require[9].

All surveyors of ships[10] must make such returns to the Secretary of State as he may require with respect to:

(1)     the build, dimensions, draught, burden, speed and room for fuel of ships surveyed by them[11]; and

(2)     the nature and particulars of machinery and equipment of such ships[12].

The owner, master[13] and engineer of any ship being surveyed must, when required to do so, give to the surveyors all such information and assistance within his power as the surveyors require for the purpose of such returns[14].

1   Ie all mercantile marine superintendents appointed under the Merchant Shipping Act 1995 s 296
    (see PARA 61): see s 313(1).
2   As to the Secretary of State see PARA 36.
3   As British merchant shipping see PARA 229 et seq.
4   As to the meaning of 'seaman' see PARA 457 note 5.
5   Merchant Shipping Act 1995 s 299(1).
6   As to official log books see PARAS 551–552.
7   Merchant Shipping Act 1995 s 299(3). The following duties also are imposed on all
    superintendents, and on all officers of revenue and customs (see the text and notes 8–9), as respects
    all documents which are delivered or transmitted to or retained by them in pursuance of the
    Merchant Shipping Act 1995 (s 298(1) (amended by virtue of the Commissioners for Revenue and
    Customs Act 2005 s 50(1), (2), (7))), namely:
    (1)     they must take charge of the documents and keep them for such time, if any, as may be
            necessary for the purpose of settling any business arising at the place where the
            documents come into their hands, or for any other proper purpose (Merchant Shipping
            Act 1995 s 298(2)); and
    (2)     they must, if required, produce them for any of those purposes, and must then transmit
            them to the Registrar General of Shipping and Seamen (s 298(3)), who must retain
            documents transmitted to him in this way for such period as the Secretary of State may
            direct (s 298(4) (substituted by the Merchant Shipping and Maritime Security Act 1997
            s 23)).
    As from a day to be appointed by the Secretary of State by order under the Merchant Shipping
    Act 1995 s 314(3), Sch 14 para 6(1), s 298 ceases to have effect: see Sch 14 para 6(1), (2).
    However, at the date at which this volume states the law, no such day had been appointed. As to
    the Secretary of State's power to give directions under the Merchant Shipping Act 1995 see
    PARA 39. As to the appointment of officers of Revenue and Customs see CUSTOMS AND EXCISE
    vol 31 (2012) PARA 921 et seq.

Documents transmitted to the Registrar General of Shipping and Seamen under s 298 are admissible in evidence and, when in the custody of the Registrar General of Shipping and Seamen, are open to public inspection: see s 287(1)(e); and PARA 1058. As to the Registrar General of Shipping and Seamen see PARA 62.

8   As to British consular officers see INTERNATIONAL RELATIONS LAW vol 61 (2010) PARA 30.
9   Merchant Shipping Act 1995 s 299(2) (amended by virtue of the Commissioners for Revenue and Customs Act 2005 s 50(1), (2), (7)). As to the duties which are imposed on all officers of revenue and customs as respects all documents which are delivered or transmitted to or retained by them in pursuance of the Merchant Shipping Act 1995 see note 7.
10  As to the meaning of 'surveyor of ships' see PARA 46 note 13; and as to the meaning of 'ship' see PARA 229.
11  Merchant Shipping Act 1995 s 299(4)(a).
12  Merchant Shipping Act 1995 s 299(4)(b).
13  As to the meaning of 'master' see PARA 444 note 1.
14  Merchant Shipping Act 1995 s 299(5). If the owner, master or engineer, on being so required to give any information or assistance, fails without reasonable excuse to give the information or assistance, he is liable on summary conviction to a fine: see s 299(6); and PARA 1179.

## 42. Secretary of State's power to require statistical returns in respect of carriage of goods and passengers by sea.

The Secretary of State[1] may require by notice in writing any person carrying on business or trade in the maritime transport sector[2] to furnish, in such form and manner and within such time as may be specified, such periodical or other returns about cargo, vessel and passenger movement information (including information about the vessel and additional particulars in relation to the transport of containers or ro-ro units)[3] in relation to the carriage of goods and passengers by sea going vessels as may be specified[4].

The failure to furnish returns as so required, or to furnish a false return, is an offence[5].

1   As to the Secretary of State see PARA 36.
2   For these purposes, 'person carrying on business or trade in the maritime transport sector' includes any maritime transport operator and any person who acts as an agent on behalf of a maritime transport operator in relation to a contract for the transport of goods or persons by sea concluded with a shipper or a passenger; and 'maritime transport operator' means any person by whom or on behalf of whom a contract for the transport of goods or persons by sea is concluded with a shipper or a passenger: Statistical Returns (Carriage of Goods and Passengers by Sea) Regulations 1997, SI 1997/2330, reg 2(1).
3   Ie such periodical or other returns about such of the matters set out in the Statistical Returns (Carriage of Goods and Passengers by Sea) Regulations 1997, SI 1997/2330, reg 3, Schedule: see reg 3.
4   Statistical Returns (Carriage of Goods and Passengers by Sea) Regulations 1997, SI 1997/2330, reg 3. The Statistical Returns (Carriage of Goods and Passengers by Sea) Regulations 1997, SI 1997/2330, implement Council Directive (EC) 2009/42 (OJ L141, 6.6.2009, p 29) on statistical returns in respect of carriage of goods and passengers by sea. As to the Secretary of State's power to direct returns as to passengers to be furnished to him by masters of ships see PARA 643.
5   See the Statistical Returns (Carriage of Goods and Passengers by Sea) Regulations 1997, SI 1997/2330, reg 4; and PARA 1122.

## 43. Financial assistance for training.

The Secretary of State[1] may, with the consent of the Treasury[2], give any person or body of persons of any description determined by him[3] financial assistance in respect of expenses incurred or to be incurred by any such person or body in connection with the training (whether in the United Kingdom[4] or elsewhere) of officers and ratings for service in merchant ships[5], including expenses incurred or to be incurred by any such person in connection with his undergoing any such training[6]. Such assistance may be given by way of a grant or a loan or otherwise, and, in giving any such assistance, the Secretary of State may impose such conditions as he thinks fit, including conditions requiring a grant to be repaid in specified circumstances[7].

This power to give financial assistance[8] is without prejudice to any other power of the Secretary of State to give such assistance in connection with any such training[9] (whether in the United Kingdom or elsewhere) of officers and ratings for service in merchant ships[10].

In providing such assistance[11], the Secretary of State must have regard to the maintenance and development of the United Kingdom's merchant fleet and marine related business[12] and for that purpose he must[13]:

(1) keep under review all aspects of that fleet and business[14]; and
(2) seek the advice of those who appear to him to have experience of that fleet or business[15].

1 As to the Secretary of State see PARA 36.
2 As to the Treasury see CONSTITUTIONAL AND ADMINISTRATIVE LAW vol 20 (2014) PARAS 262–265.
3 Ie for the purposes of the Merchant Shipping Act 1995 s 56: see s 56(1).
4 As to the meaning of 'United Kingdom' see PARA 16 note 3.
5 As to the meaning of 'ship' see PARA 229.
6 Merchant Shipping Act 1995 s 56(1).
7 Merchant Shipping Act 1995 s 56(2).
8 Ie the Merchant Shipping Act 1995 s 56: see s 56(3).
9 Ie any such training as is mentioned in the Merchant Shipping Act 1995 s 56(1): see s 56(3).
10 Merchant Shipping Act 1995 s 56(3).
11 Ie in accordance with the Merchant Shipping Act 1995 s 56: see s 56(4) (s 56(4), (5) added by the Merchant Shipping and Maritime Security Act 1997 s 17).
12 For these purposes, 'marine related business' means any trade, business or other activity concerned with the manufacture of, or the provision of goods and services for, or the operation or use of, ships and includes maritime educational establishments, marine classification societies, marine equipment suppliers, marine surveyors, marine and naval architects, marine insurance companies, protection and indemnity clubs, providers of maritime financial or legal services, the operators of ports and harbours and shipbrokers: Merchant Shipping Act 1995 s 56(5) (as added: see note 11).
13 Merchant Shipping Act 1995 s 56(4) (as added: see note 11).
14 Merchant Shipping Act 1995 s 56(4)(a) (as added: see note 11).
15 Merchant Shipping Act 1995 s 56(4)(b) (as added: see note 11).

**44. Financial assistance in respect of crew relief costs.** The Secretary of State[1] may, with the consent of the Treasury[2], give financial assistance to[3]:

(1) the owner of a ship[4] registered[5] in the British Islands[6]; or
(2) any manager of a ship so registered, being either an individual ordinarily resident in the British Islands[7] or a body corporate which is incorporated in the British Islands and has its principal place of business there[8],

in respect of travel and other costs incurred by the owner or manager in connection with members of the ship's crew[9] joining or leaving the ship outside the limited European trading area[10].

If the Secretary of State so determines, eligibility for such assistance[11] is conditional on the fulfilment of such conditions with respect to all or any of the following matters as are specified in his determination[12]:

(a) the nationality of any person in relation to whom any such costs as are mentioned above are incurred[13];
(b) the ordinary residence of any such person[14];
(c) the place, outside the limited European trading area, where any such person joins or leaves his ship[15].

Such assistance[16] may be given by way of a grant or loan or otherwise; and, in giving any such assistance, the Secretary of State may impose such conditions as he thinks fit[17].

1 As to the Secretary of State see PARA 36.
2 As to the Treasury see CONSTITUTIONAL AND ADMINISTRATIVE LAW vol 20 (2014) PARAS 262–265.

3   Merchant Shipping Act 1995 s 76(1).
4   As to the meaning of 'ship' under the Merchant Shipping Act 1995 see PARA 229.
5   As to the meaning of 'registered' for these purposes see PARA 254 note 2.
6   Merchant Shipping Act 1995 s 76(1)(a). As to the meaning of 'British Islands' see STATUTES AND LEGISLATIVE PROCESS vol 96 (2012) PARA 1208.
7   As to ordinary residence see IMMIGRATION AND ASYLUM vol 57 (2012) PARA 140; CONFLICT OF LAWS vol 19 (2011) PARA 359.
8   Merchant Shipping Act 1995 s 76(1)(b).
9   For these purposes, the crew of a ship is to be taken to include the master and other officers of the ship: Merchant Shipping Act 1995 s 76(4)(a). As to the meaning of 'master' see PARA 444 note 1.
10  Merchant Shipping Act 1995 s 76(1). For these purposes, 'limited European trading area' has the same meaning as it has for the purposes of any regulations under s 47 (see PARA 503): s 76(4)(b).
11  Ie financial assistance under the Merchant Shipping Act 1995 s 76: see s 76(2).
12  Merchant Shipping Act 1995 s 76(2).
13  Merchant Shipping Act 1995 s 76(2)(a). The text refers to any such costs as are mentioned in s 76(1) (see the text and notes 1–10): see s 76(2)(a).
14  Merchant Shipping Act 1995 s 76(2)(b).
15  Merchant Shipping Act 1995 s 76(2)(c).
16  Ie financial assistance under the Merchant Shipping Act 1995 s 76: see s 76(3).
17  Merchant Shipping Act 1995 s 76(3).

## (ii) The Admiralty Registrar

**45. The Admiralty Registrar and Registry.** In general, the Admiralty Registrar[1] deals with all applications in Admiralty claims[2] on matters which elsewhere in the Queen's Bench Division would be dealt with on application by a master[3]. However, the Admiralty Court[4] may refer to the Admiralty Registrar any question or issue for his determination (a 'reference') at any stage in a claim[5].

All Admiralty claims must be issued in the Admiralty and Commercial Registry[6], which is the administrative office for the Admiralty Court and the Commercial Court[7].

1   As to the Admiralty Registrar see PARA 140.
2   As to the procedure in Admiralty claims generally see PARA 91 et seq.
3   See PARA 141 et seq. Accordingly, the Admiralty Registrar may refer to a judge any matter which he thinks should properly be decided by a judge: see *Practice Direction—Applications* PD 23A para 1.
4   As to the Admiralty jurisdiction of the High Court see PARA 79 et seq.
5   See *Practice Direction—Admiralty Claims* PD 61 para 13; and PARA 143 et seq. However, the court will not order a reference if it can satisfactorily dispose of the question: see PARA 143.
6   See *Practice Direction—Commercial Court* PD 58 para 2 (which is applied by *Practice Direction—Admiralty Claims* PD 61 para 1); and PARA 143 et seq.
7   See the Admiralty and Commercial Courts Guide (2016) para A2.1. As to the Admiralty and Commercial Courts Guide see PARA 91 note 3.

## (iii) Enforcement Officers and their Powers

### A.   ENFORCEMENT OFFICERS

**46. Appointment of inspectors and surveyors.** The Secretary of State[1] may, if he thinks fit, appoint any person as an inspector[2] to report to him:

(1)   upon the nature and causes of any accident[3] or damage which any ship[4] has or is alleged to have sustained or caused[5];

(2)   whether any requirements, restrictions or prohibitions imposed by or under the Merchant Shipping Act 1995[6] have been complied with or, as the case may be, contravened[7];

(3)   whether the hull and machinery of a ship[8] are sufficient and in good condition[9];

(4)     what measures have been taken to prevent the escape of oil[10] or mixtures containing oil[11].

The Secretary of State may, at such ports[12] as he thinks fit, appoint persons to be surveyors of ships for the purposes of the Merchant Shipping Act 1995 and he may remove any person so appointed[13]. A surveyor of ships may be appointed either as a ship surveyor or as an engineer surveyor or as both[14]; and surveyors of ships may be appointed either generally or for any particular case or purpose[15]. The Secretary of State may also appoint a surveyor general of ships for the United Kingdom[16] and such other officers in connection with the survey of ships and other matters incidental thereto as he thinks fit[17].

The Secretary of State may also appoint persons to be inspectors for the purposes of the statutory provisions relating to improvement notices and prohibition notices[18].

1   As to the Secretary of State see PARA 36.
2   In the Merchant Shipping Act 1995, unless the context otherwise requires, 'departmental inspector' means an inspector appointed under s 256(1): ss 256(9)(a), 313(1). As to the powers of an inspector so appointed see PARA 46; and as to the payment of the salary etc of an inspector see PARA 65. Every inspector appointed under s 256(1) is to be treated as appointed under s 256(6) (see the text and note 18): s 256(7) (amended by the Merchant Shipping and Marine Safety Act 1997 s 29(1), Sch 6 para 15).
    In relation to a vessel, an inspector appointed under the Merchant Shipping Act 1995 s 256 is an 'authorised person' for the purposes of the Licensing Act 2003 Pt 3 (ss 11–59) (see s 13(2); and LEISURE AND ENTERTAINMENT vol 67 (2016) PARA 61) (premises licences) and Pt 4 (ss 60–97) (see s 69(2); and LEISURE AND ENTERTAINMENT vol 67 (2016) PARA 130) (clubs).
3   As to accident investigations and inquiries see PARA 815 et seq.
4   As to the meaning of 'ship' see PARA 229.
5   Merchant Shipping Act 1995 s 256(1)(a).
6   For these purposes, the reference to requirements, restrictions or prohibitions under the Merchant Shipping Act 1995 includes any such requirements, restrictions or prohibitions constituting the terms of any approval, licence, consent or exemption in any document issued thereunder: Merchant Shipping Act 1995 s 256(9).
7   Merchant Shipping Act 1995 s 256(1)(b). See note 13.
8   As to the power to make provision by safety regulations with respect to ships and their machinery and equipment see PARA 602 note 1.
9   Merchant Shipping Act 1995 s 256(1)(c).
10  As to the prevention of oil pollution generally see ENVIRONMENTAL QUALITY AND PUBLIC HEALTH vol 45 (2010) PARA 425 et seq.
11  Merchant Shipping Act 1995 s 256(1)(d). See note 13.
12  In the Merchant Shipping Act 1995, unless the context otherwise requires, 'port' includes place: s 313(1).
13  Merchant Shipping Act 1995 s 256(2). In the Merchant Shipping Act 1995, unless the context otherwise requires, 'surveyor of ships' means a surveyor appointed under s 256(2): ss 256(9)(b), 313(1). Every surveyor of ships is to be treated as a person appointed generally under s 256(1) (see the text and notes 1-11) to report to the Secretary of State in every kind of case falling within s 256(1)(b) (see head (2) in the text) and s 256(1)(d) (see head (4) in the text) in relation to Pt VI Ch II (ss 131–151) (oil pollution) (see ENVIRONMENTAL QUALITY AND PUBLIC HEALTH vol 45 (2010) PARA 425 et seq): s 256(8). As to returns required to be made by surveyors and the giving of information to surveyors see PARA 41; and as to the salaries etc of surveyors of ships see PARA 65.
    In relation to a vessel, a surveyor of ships appointed under the Merchant Shipping Act 1995 s 256 is an 'authorised person' for the purposes of the Licensing Act 2003 Pts 3, 4 (see ss 13(2), 69(2)).
14  Merchant Shipping Act 1995 s 256(3).
15  Merchant Shipping Act 1995 s 256(4).
16  As to the meaning of 'United Kingdom' see PARA 16 note 3.
17  Merchant Shipping Act 1995 s 256(5).
18  Merchant Shipping Act 1995 s 256(6). The text refers to the statutory provisions contained in ss 261–266 (see PARA 51 et seq): see s 256(6).
    Every inspector appointed under s 256(1) (see the text and notes 1-11) is to be treated as appointed under s 256(6): see s 256(7) (as amended: see note 2).

**47. Power to require production of ship's documents.** Powers are conferred by the Merchant Shipping Act 1995[1]:

(1)    to require the owner, master[2] or any of the crew to produce any official log books[3] or other documents relating to the crew or any member of the crew in their possession or control[4];

(2)    to require the master to produce a list of all persons on board his ship[5], and take copies of or extracts from the official log books or other such documents[6];

(3)    to muster the crew[7]; and

(4)    to require the master to appear and give any explanation concerning the ship or her crew or the official log books or documents produced or required to be produced[8].

The powers so conferred[9] are conferred in relation to United Kingdom ships[10] and are available to any of the following officers, namely:

(a)    any Departmental officer[11];

(b)    any commissioned naval officer[12];

(c)    any British consular officer[13];

(d)    the Registrar General of Shipping and Seamen[14] or any person discharging his functions[15];

(e)    any officer of Revenue and Customs[16];

(f)    any superintendent[17],

whenever the officer has reason to suspect that the Merchant Shipping Act 1995 or any law for the time being in force relating to merchant seamen or navigation is not complied with[18].

If any person, on being duly required[19] by an officer to produce a log book or any document, fails without reasonable excuse to produce the log book or document, he is liable on summary conviction to a fine[20].

If any person, on being duly required[21] by any officer:

(i)    to produce a log book or document, refuses to allow the log book or document to be inspected or copied[22];

(ii)    to muster the crew, impedes the muster[23]; or

(iii)    to give any explanation, refuses or neglects to give the explanation or knowingly misleads or deceives the officer[24],

he is liable on summary conviction to a fine[25].

1   Ie conferred by the Merchant Shipping Act 1995 s 257: see s 257(2).
2   As to the meaning of 'master' see PARA 444 note 1.
3   As to official log books see PARAS 551–552.
4   Merchant Shipping Act 1995 s 257(2)(a).
5   As to the meaning of 'ship' see PARA 229.
6   Merchant Shipping Act 1995 s 257(2)(b).
7   Merchant Shipping Act 1995 s 257(2)(c).
8   Merchant Shipping Act 1995 s 257(2)(d).
9   Ie the powers conferred by the Merchant Shipping Act 1995 s 257: see s 257(1).
10  As to the meaning of 'United Kingdom ship' see PARA 230.
11  Merchant Shipping Act 1995 s 257(1)(a). In the Merchant Shipping Act 1995, unless the context otherwise requires, 'departmental officer' means any officer of the Secretary of State discharging functions of his for the purposes of the Merchant Shipping Act 1995: ss 256(9)(c), 313(1). As to the Secretary of State see PARA 36.
12  Merchant Shipping Act 1995 s 257(1)(b). In the Merchant Shipping Act 1995, unless the context otherwise requires, 'commissioned naval officer' means a commissioned officer of Her Majesty's Navy on full pay: s 313(1).
13  Merchant Shipping Act 1995 s 257(1)(c). As to British consular officers see INTERNATIONAL RELATIONS LAW vol 61 (2010) PARA 30.
14  As to the Registrar General of Shipping and Seamen see PARA 62.

15 Merchant Shipping Act 1995 s 257(1)(d).
16 Merchant Shipping Act 1995 s 257(1)(e) (amended by virtue of the Commissioners for Revenue and Customs Act 2005 s 50(1), (2), (7)). As to the appointment of officers of Revenue and Customs see CUSTOMS AND EXCISE vol 31 (2012) PARA 921 et seq.
17 Merchant Shipping Act 1995 s 257(1)(f). As to the meaning of 'superintendent' see PARA 61 note 1.
18 Merchant Shipping Act 1995 s 257(1).
   The powers conferred by s 257 are exercisable by British sea-fisheries officers in relation to fishing boats for the purpose of enforcing the collision regulations made under s 85 (see PARA 715 et seq): see the Sea Fisheries Act 1968 s 8(6); and FISHERIES AND AQUACULTURE vol 51 (2013) PARA 278.
19 Ie duly required under the Merchant Shipping Act 1995 s 257: see s 257(3); and PARA 1175.
20 See the Merchant Shipping Act 1995 s 257(3); and PARA 1175.
21 Ie duly required under the Merchant Shipping Act 1995 s 257: see s 257(4); and PARA 1175.
22 See the Merchant Shipping Act 1995 s 257(4)(a); and PARA 1175.
23 See the Merchant Shipping Act 1995 s 257(4)(b); and PARA 1175.
24 See the Merchant Shipping Act 1995 s 257(4)(c); and PARA 1175.
25 See the Merchant Shipping Act 1995 s 257(4); and PARA 1175.

**48. Powers to inspect ships and their equipment etc.** For the purpose of seeing that the provisions of the Merchant Shipping Act 1995 (other than certain provisions relating to oil pollution[1]) and of regulations and rules so made[2], or specified provisions of the Maritime Labour Convention[3], are complied with, or that the terms of any approval, licence, consent, direction or exemption given by virtue of regulations under the 1995 Act are duly complied with, the following persons, namely[4]:

(1) a surveyor of ships[5];
(2) a superintendent[6];
(3) any person appointed by the Secretary of State[7], either generally or in a particular case, to exercise the powers[8] to inspect ships and their equipment etc[9],

may at all reasonable times go on board a ship in the United Kingdom[10] or in United Kingdom waters[11] and inspect the ship and its equipment or any part thereof, any articles on board and any document carried in the ship in pursuance of the Merchant Shipping Act 1995, in pursuance of regulations or rules made thereunder, or pursuant to the specified provisions of the Maritime Labour Convention[12].

A person exercising these powers[13] to inspect ships and their equipment etc must not unnecessarily detain or delay a ship but may, if he considers it necessary in consequence of an accident[14] or for any other reason, require a ship to be taken into dock for a survey of its hull or machinery[15].

If any person obstructs a person in the exercise of these powers[16], or fails to comply with a requirement made by a person exercising his powers, he is liable on summary conviction to a fine[17].

1 Ie other than the Merchant Shipping Act 1995 ss 131–141, 143–151 (oil pollution) (see ENVIRONMENTAL QUALITY AND PUBLIC HEALTH vol 45 (2010) PARA 425 et seq): see s 258(1) (as amended: see note 3).
2 Ie made under the Merchant Shipping Act 1995, other than ss 131–141, 143–151 (oil pollution): see s 258(1) (as amended: see note 3).
3 Ie for the purpose of checking compliance with the Merchant Shipping (Maritime Labour Convention) (Minimum Requirements for Seafarers etc) Regulations 2014, SI 2014/1613 (as to which see PARA 423). See in particular reg 55 (inspection of non-United Kingdom ships).
4 Merchant Shipping Act 1995 s 258(1) (amended by the Merchant Shipping and Maritime Security Act 1997 ss 9, 29(2), Sch 1 para 4(2), Sch 7 Pt I); Merchant Shipping (Maritime Labour Convention) (Minimum Requirements for Seafarers etc) Regulations 2014, SI 2014/1613, reg 54(1). In those regulations persons referred to in the text are known as a 'relevant inspector' (reg 2(1)), and in the case of a United Kingdom ship (see PARA 423 note 6) are exercisable by a 'proper

officer' (see the Merchant Shipping Act 1995 s 313(1); the Merchant Shipping (Maritime Labour Convention) (Minimum Requirements for Seafarers etc) Regulations 2014, SI 2014/1613, regs 2(1), 54(1); and note 12).

5  Merchant Shipping Act 1995 s 258(1)(a). As to the meaning of 'surveyor of ships' see PARA 46 note 13.

6  Merchant Shipping Act 1995 s 258(1)(b). As to the meaning of 'superintendent' see PARA 61 note 1.

7  As to the Secretary of State see PARA 36.

8  Ie under the Merchant Shipping Act 1995 s 258: see s 258(1)(c).

9  Merchant Shipping Act 1995 s 258(1)(c). As to the meaning of 'ship' see PARA 229.

10  As to the meaning of 'United Kingdom' see PARA 16 note 3.

11  In the Merchant Shipping Act 1995, 'United Kingdom waters' means the sea or other waters within the seaward limits of the territorial sea of the United Kingdom: see s 313(2)(a). See note 11. As to the territorial sea generally see INTERNATIONAL RELATIONS LAW vol 61 (2010) PARA 123.

12  Merchant Shipping Act 1995 s 258(1) (as amended: see note 3); Merchant Shipping (Maritime Labour Convention) (Minimum Requirements for Seafarers etc) Regulations 2014, SI 2014/1613, reg 54(1). Other than in the context of the Merchant Shipping (Maritime Labour Convention) (Minimum Requirements for Seafarers etc) Regulations 2014, SI 2014/1613, the powers conferred by the Merchant Shipping Act 1995 s 258(1) are, if the ship is a United Kingdom ship, also exercisable outside United Kingdom waters and may be so exercised by a proper officer as well as the persons mentioned in heads (1) to (3) in the text: Merchant Shipping Act 1995 s 258(2) (amended by the Merchant Shipping and Maritime Security Act 1997 Sch 1 para 4(4)). In the Merchant Shipping Act 1995, unless the context otherwise requires, 'proper officer' means a consular officer appointed by Her Majesty's government in the United Kingdom and, in relation to a port in a country outside the United Kingdom which is not a foreign country, also any officer exercising in that port functions similar to those of a superintendent; 'consular officer', in relation to a foreign country, means the officer recognised by Her Majesty as a consular officer of that foreign country: s 313(1). As to consular officers in the United Kingdom see INTERNATIONAL RELATIONS LAW vol 61 (2010) PARA 290 et seq. However, the powers conferred by s 258(1), including in the context of its application under the Merchant Shipping (Maritime Labour Convention) (Minimum Requirements for Seafarers etc) Regulations 2014, SI 2014/1613, are not exercisable in relation to a qualifying foreign ship while the ship is exercising the right of innocent passage or the right of transit passage through straits used for international navigation: Merchant Shipping Act 1995 s 258(1A) (added by the Merchant Shipping and Maritime Security Act 1997 Sch 1 para 4(3)); Merchant Shipping (Maritime Labour Convention) (Minimum Requirements for Seafarers etc) Regulations 2014, SI 2014/1613, reg 54(2). As to the meaning of 'port' see PARA 46 note 12; as to the meaning of 'qualifying foreign ship' see PARA 18; as to the meanings of 'right of innocent passage', 'right of transit passage' and 'straits used for international passage' see PARA 69; and as to the meaning of 'United Kingdom ship' see PARA 230. As to innocent passage generally see INTERNATIONAL RELATIONS LAW vol 61 (2010) PARA 133; and as to transit passage generally see INTERNATIONAL RELATIONS LAW vol 61 (2010) PARA 143.

The Merchant Shipping Act 1995 s 258 applies both to the Merchant Shipping and Fishing Vessels (Control of Noise at Work) Regulations 2007, SI 2007/3075, and to the Merchant Shipping and Fishing Vessels (Health and Safety at Work) (Carcinogens and Mutagens) Regulations 2007, SI 2007/3100, as if they were for all purposes made under the Merchant Shipping Act 1995 s 85 (see PARA 602 note 1) and accordingly s 258 applies in relation to government ships: see the Merchant Shipping and Fishing Vessels (Control of Noise at Work) Regulations 2007, SI 2007/3075, reg 19; the Merchant Shipping and Fishing Vessels (Health and Safety at Work) (Carcinogens and Mutagens) Regulations 2007, SI 2007/3100, reg 22; and PARAS 628, 631. As to government ships see PARA 19.

13  Ie powers under the Merchant Shipping Act 1995 s 258, including as applied by the Merchant Shipping (Maritime Labour Convention) (Minimum Requirements for Seafarers etc) Regulations 2014, SI 2014/1613: see the Merchant Shipping Act 1995 s 258(3); and the Merchant Shipping (Maritime Labour Convention) (Minimum Requirements for Seafarers etc) Regulations 2014, SI 2014/1613, reg 54(2).

14  As to accident investigations and inquiries see PARA 815 et seq.

15  Merchant Shipping Act 1995 s 258(3); Merchant Shipping (Maritime Labour Convention) (Minimum Requirements for Seafarers etc) Regulations 2014, SI 2014/1613, reg 54(2).

16  Ie powers under the Merchant Shipping Act 1995 s 258, including as applied by the Merchant Shipping (Maritime Labour Convention) (Minimum Requirements for Seafarers etc) Regulations 2014, SI 2014/1613: see the Merchant Shipping Act 1995 s 258(5); and the Merchant Shipping (Maritime Labour Convention) (Minimum Requirements for Seafarers etc) Regulations 2014, SI 2014/1613, reg 54(2).

17  See the Merchant Shipping Act 1995 s 258(5); and PARA 1176.

**49. Powers of inspectors in relation to premises and ships.** In relation to
any premises in the United Kingdom[1] or any United Kingdom ship[2] wherever it
may be, and any other ship which is present in the United Kingdom or in United
Kingdom waters[3], an inspector[4]:

(1)    may at any reasonable time (or, in a situation which in his opinion is or
may be dangerous, at any time) enter any premises or board any ship if
he has reason to believe that it is necessary for him to do so[5];

(2)    may, on entering any premises by virtue of head (1) above or on
boarding a ship by virtue of head (1) above, take with him any other
person authorised for the purpose by the Secretary of State and any
equipment or materials he requires[6];

(3)    may make such examination and investigation as he considers
necessary[7];

(4)    may give a direction requiring that the premises or ship or any part of
the premises or ship or any thing in the premises or ship or such a part
are to be left undisturbed (whether generally or in particular respects)
for so long as is reasonably necessary for the purposes of any
examination or investigation under head (3) above[8];

(5)    may take such measurements and photographs and make such
recordings as he considers necessary for the purpose of any examination
or investigation under head (3) above[9];

(6)    may take samples of any articles or substances found in the premises or
ship and of the atmosphere in or in the vicinity of the premises or ship[10];

(7)    may, in the case of any article or substance which he finds in the
premises or ship and which appears to him to have caused or to be likely
to cause danger to health or safety, cause it to be dismantled or subjected
to any process or test (but not so as to damage or destroy it unless that
is in the circumstances necessary)[11];

(8)    may, in the case of any such article or substance as is mentioned in head
(7) above, take possession of it and detain it for so long as is necessary
for all or any of the following purposes[12], namely:

(a)    to examine it and do to it anything which he has power to do
under head (7) above[13];

(b)    to ensure that it is not tampered with before his examination of
it is completed[14]; and

(c)    to ensure that it is available for use as evidence in any
proceedings for a statutory offence[15];

(9)    may require any person who he has reasonable cause to believe is able
to give any information relevant to any examination or investigation
under head (3) above[16]:

(a)    to attend at a place and time specified by the inspector[17];

(b)    to answer, in the absence of persons other than any persons
whom the inspector may allow to be present and a person
nominated to be present by the person on whom the requirement
is imposed, such questions as the inspector thinks fit to ask[18]; and

(c)    to sign a declaration of the truth of his answers[19];

(10)    may require the production of, and inspect and take copies of or of any
entry in[20]:

(a)    any books or documents which by virtue of any provision of the
Merchant Shipping Act 1995 are required to be kept[21]; and

(b)    any other books or documents which he considers it necessary
for him to see for the purposes of any examination or
investigation under head (3) above[22];

(11)   may require any person to afford him such facilities and assistance with respect to any matters or things within that person's control or in relation to which that person has responsibilities as the inspector considers are necessary to enable him to exercise any of the powers conferred on him by heads (1) to (10) above[23].

However, nothing in these powers[24] authorises a person unnecessarily to prevent a ship from proceeding on a voyage[25].

A person who:

(i)    intentionally obstructs an inspector in the exercise of any power available to him[26] in relation to premises and ships[27]; or

(ii)   without reasonable excuse does not comply with a requirement duly imposed[28] or prevents another person from complying with such a requirement[29]; or

(iii)  without prejudice to the generality of head (ii) above, makes a statement or signs a declaration which he knows is false, or recklessly makes a statement or signs a declaration which is false, in purported compliance with a requirement duly made[30],

is liable on conviction on indictment to imprisonment for a term not exceeding two years or a fine, or to both, or on summary conviction to a fine[31].

1   Merchant Shipping Act 1995 s 259(1)(a); Merchant Shipping (Maritime Labour Convention) (Minimum Requirements for Seafarers etc) Regulations 2014, SI 2014/1613, reg 54(3). As to the meaning of 'United Kingdom' see PARA 16 note 3.
2   Merchant Shipping Act 1995 s 259(1)(b). As to the ships etc in relation to which the inspection powers apply see PARA 48: this includes any ship to which the Merchant Shipping (Maritime Labour Convention) (Minimum Requirements for Seafarers etc) Regulations 2014, SI 2014/1613, applies (as to which see PARA 423) (reg 54(3)(b)). As to the meaning of 'United Kingdom ship' for the purposes of the Merchant Shipping Act 1995 see PARA 230; and as to the meaning of 'ship' for those purposes see PARA 229. As to the meaning of 'ship' for the purposes of the Merchant Shipping (Maritime Labour Convention) (Minimum Requirements for Seafarers etc) Regulations 2014, SI 2014/1613, see PARA 423 note 2.
3   Merchant Shipping Act 1995 s 259(1). As to the meaning of 'United Kingdom waters' see PARA 48 note 11. As to the exercise of certain powers under s 259(1) see further notes 5, 7, 20.
4   Merchant Shipping Act 1995 s 259(2). The powers conferred by s 259 are available to any Departmental inspector, or any inspector appointed under s 256(6) (see PARA 46), for the purpose of performing his functions: see s 259(1). As to the meaning of 'Departmental inspector' see PARA 46 note 2.
    The powers conferred on a Departmental inspector by s 259 are conferred also on a superintendent or proper officer holding an inquiry under s 272 or an inspection under the Merchant Shipping (Maritime Labour Convention) (Minimum Requirements for Seafarers etc) Regulations 2014, SI 2014/1613: see the Merchant Shipping Act 1995 s 272(2); the Merchant Shipping (Maritime Labour Convention) (Minimum Requirements for Seafarers etc) Regulations 2014, SI 2014/1613, reg 54(1), (2); and PARAS 48, 847. As to the meaning of 'proper officer' see PARA 48 note 12; and as to the meaning of 'superintendent' see PARA 61 note 1.
    The powers conferred on an inspector by s 259 are conferred also on:
    (1)    an arbitrator to whom certain matters are referred in relation to a detention notice issued under s 95 (see PARA 1141) (see s 96(8); and PARA 1142);
    (2)    (with the exception of s 259(3), (4), (6) (see the text and notes 5, 7, 20)) arbitrators to whom certain questions arising in relation to ss 261–263 (see PARAS 51–53) are referred (see s 264(7); and PARA 54);
    (3)    inspectors of marine accidents (see s 267(8); and PARA 815) and certain persons specified in regulations made under s 267 with respect to the investigation of such accidents (see s 267(4)(i); the Merchant Shipping (Accident Reporting and Investigation) Regulations 2005, SI 2005/881, reg 10);
    (4)    a superintendent or proper officer (see the Merchant Shipping Act 1995 s 271(4); and PARA 846);
    (5)    (with the exception of s 259(2)(d)–(h) (see heads (4) to (8) in the text)) an inspector appointed for the purpose of determining whether a fishing vessel is eligible to be registered on Part II of the central register of British ships (see the Merchant Shipping (Registration of Ships) Regulations 1993, SI 1993/3138, reg 16; and PARA 265);

(6)     an arbitrator appointed pursuant to the Merchant Shipping (Port State Control) Regulations 2011, SI 2011/2601, reg 15 (arbitration) applies (see reg 15(10)); and

(7)     an authorised person exercising functions under the Merchant Shipping (Domestic Passenger Ships) (Safety Management Code) Regulations 2001, SI 2001/3209, reg 9 (enforcement) (see PARA 627).

The Merchant Shipping Act 1995 s 259 and s 260 apply both to the Merchant Shipping and Fishing Vessels (Control of Noise at Work) Regulations 2007, SI 2007/3075, and to the Merchant Shipping and Fishing Vessels (Health and Safety at Work) (Carcinogens and Mutagens) Regulations 2007, SI 2007/3100, as if they were for all purposes made under the Merchant Shipping Act 1995 s 85 (see PARA 602 note 1) and accordingly ss 259, 260 apply in relation to government ships: see the Merchant Shipping and Fishing Vessels (Control of Noise at Work) Regulations 2007, SI 2007/3075, reg 19; the Merchant Shipping and Fishing Vessels (Health and Safety at Work) (Carcinogens and Mutagens) Regulations 2007, SI 2007/3100, reg 22; and PARAS 628, 631. As to government ships see PARA 19.

5   Merchant Shipping Act 1995 s 259(2)(a). The powers conferred by s 259(2)(a) are also exercisable, in relation to a ship in a harbour in the United Kingdom, by the harbour master or other persons appointed by the Secretary of State for the purpose, for the purpose of ascertaining the circumstances relating to an alleged discharge of oil or a mixture containing oil from the ship into the harbour: s 259(6). In the Merchant Shipping Act 1995, unless the context otherwise requires, 'harbour' includes estuaries, navigable rivers, piers, jetties and other works in or at which ships can obtain shelter or ship and unship goods or passengers: s 313(1). As to the Secretary of State see PARA 36.

The powers conferred by s 259(2) to inspect premises are also exercisable, for the purposes of Pt VI Ch II (ss 131–151) (oil pollution) (see ENVIRONMENTAL QUALITY AND PUBLIC HEALTH vol 45 (2010) PARA 425 et seq), in relation to any apparatus used for transferring oil: s 259(4). In this context, and in relation to places on land in Northern Ireland and apparatus located in Northern Ireland otherwise than on board ships, see further s 259(5); and the Merchant Shipping (Maritime Labour Convention) (Minimum Requirements for Seafarers etc) Regulations 2014, SI 2014/1613, reg 54(3). See note 4.

6   Merchant Shipping Act 1995 s 259(2)(b). See notes 4, 5.

7   Merchant Shipping Act 1995 s 259(2)(c). See notes 4, 5. The powers conferred by s 259(2)(c) are also exercisable, in relation to a ship in a harbour in the United Kingdom, by the harbour master or other persons appointed by the Secretary of State for the purpose, for the purpose of ascertaining the circumstances relating to an alleged discharge of oil or a mixture containing oil from the ship into the harbour: s 259(6).

8   Merchant Shipping Act 1995 s 259(2)(d). See notes 4, 5.

9   Merchant Shipping Act 1995 s 259(2)(e). See notes 4, 5.

10   Merchant Shipping Act 1995 s 259(2)(f). See notes 4, 5. The Secretary of State may by regulations make provision as to the procedure to be followed in connection with the taking of samples under s 259(2)(f) and provision as to the way in which samples that have been so taken are to be dealt with: s 259(8); Merchant Shipping (Maritime Labour Convention) (Minimum Requirements for Seafarers etc) Regulations 2014, SI 2014/1613, reg 54(4). At the date at which this volume states the law, no such regulations had been made. As to the Secretary of State's power to make regulations generally, and as to his power to appoint committees for the purpose of advising him when considering the making or alteration of any regulations, see PARA 39.

11   Merchant Shipping Act 1995 s 259(2)(g). See notes 4, 5. Where an inspector proposes to exercise the power conferred by s 259(2)(g) in the case of an article or substance found in any premises or ship, he must, if so requested by a person who at the time is present and has responsibilities in relation to the premises or ship, cause anything which is to be done by virtue of that power to be done in the presence of that person unless the inspector considers that its being done in that person's presence would be prejudicial to the safety of that person: s 259(9); Merchant Shipping (Maritime Labour Convention) (Minimum Requirements for Seafarers etc) Regulations 2014, SI 2014/1613, reg 54(3). Before exercising the power conferred by the Merchant Shipping Act 1995 s 259(2)(g), an inspector must consult such persons as appear to him appropriate for the purpose of ascertaining what dangers, if any, there may be in doing anything which he proposes to do under that power: s 259(10); Merchant Shipping (Maritime Labour Convention) (Minimum Requirements for Seafarers etc) Regulations 2014, SI 2014/1613, reg 54(3).

12   Merchant Shipping Act 1995 s 259(2)(h). See notes 4, 5. Where, under the power conferred by s 259(2)(h), an inspector takes possession of any article or substance found in any premises or ship, he must leave there, either with a responsible person or, if that is impracticable, fixed in a conspicuous position, a notice giving particulars of that article or substance sufficient to identify it and stating that he has taken possession of it under that power; and, before taking possession of any such substance under that power, an inspector must, if it is practicable for him to do so, take a sample of the substance and give to a responsible person at the premises or on board the ship a

portion of the sample marked in a manner sufficient to identify it: s 259(11); Merchant Shipping (Maritime Labour Convention) (Minimum Requirements for Seafarers etc) Regulations 2014, SI 2014/1613, reg 54(3). The Secretary of State may by regulations make provision as to the procedure to be followed in connection with the taking of samples under the Merchant Shipping Act 1995 s 259(11) (other than insofar as it is applied by the Merchant Shipping (Maritime Labour Convention) (Minimum Requirements for Seafarers etc) Regulations 2014, SI 2014/1613, reg 54(3)) and provision as to the way in which samples that have been so taken are to be dealt with: Merchant Shipping Act 1995 s 259(8). At the date at which this volume states the law, no such regulations had been made. As to the service of documents under the Merchant Shipping Act 1995 generally see s 291; and PARA 74.

13  Merchant Shipping Act 1995 s 259(2)(h)(i). See notes 4, 5.
14  Merchant Shipping Act 1995 s 259(2)(h)(ii). See notes 4, 5.
15  Merchant Shipping Act 1995 s 259(2)(h)(iii). See notes 4, 5. A 'statutory offence' in this context is any offence under the Merchant Shipping Act 1995 or any instrument made under it (see PARA 1049 et seq) and any offence under the Merchant Shipping (Maritime Labour Convention) (Minimum Requirements for Seafarers etc) Regulations 2014, SI 2014/1613 (see PARA 448 et seq): Merchant Shipping Act 1995 s 259(2)(h)(iii); Merchant Shipping (Maritime Labour Convention) (Minimum Requirements for Seafarers etc) Regulations 2014, SI 2014/1613, reg 54(3)(c).
16  Merchant Shipping Act 1995 s 259(2)(i). See notes 4, 5.
17  Merchant Shipping Act 1995 s 259(2)(i)(i). See notes 4, 5. A person who complies with a requirement imposed on him in pursuance of s 259(2)(i)(i) is entitled to recover from the person who imposed the requirement such sums in respect of the expenses incurred in complying with the requirement as are prescribed by regulations made by the Secretary of State: s 260(3); Merchant Shipping (Maritime Labour Convention) (Minimum Requirements for Seafarers etc) Regulations 2014, SI 2014/1613, reg 54(4). Such regulations may make different provision for different circumstances: Merchant Shipping Act 1995 s 260(4). Any payments so made must be made out of money provided by Parliament: s 260(5). However, at the date at which this volume states the law, no such regulations had been made.
18  Merchant Shipping Act 1995 s 259(2)(i)(ii). See notes 4, 5. No answer given by a person in pursuance of a requirement imposed under s 259(2)(i) is admissible in evidence against that person or the husband or wife of that person in any proceedings except proceedings in pursuance of s 260(1)(c) (see head (iii) in the text) in respect of a statement in or a declaration relating to the answer; and a person nominated as mentioned in s 259(2)(i) is entitled, on the occasion on which the questions there mentioned are asked, to make representations to the inspector on behalf of the person who nominated him: s 259(12); Merchant Shipping (Maritime Labour Convention) (Minimum Requirements for Seafarers etc) Regulations 2014, SI 2014/1613, reg 54(3).
19  Merchant Shipping Act 1995 s 259(2)(i)(iii). See notes 4, 5.
20  Merchant Shipping Act 1995 s 259(2)(j). See notes 4, 5. The powers conferred by s 259(2)(j) are also exercisable, in relation to a ship in a harbour in the United Kingdom, by the harbour master or other persons appointed by the Secretary of State for the purpose, for the purpose of ascertaining the circumstances relating to an alleged discharge of oil or a mixture containing oil from the ship into the harbour: s 259(6).
    The powers conferred by s 259(2) to require the production of any document and copy it include, in relation to oil record books required to be carried under s 142 (see ENVIRONMENTAL QUALITY AND PUBLIC HEALTH vol 45 (2010) PARA 432), power to require the master to certify the copy as a true copy: s 259(3). As to the meaning of 'master' see PARA 444 note 1.
    However, nothing in s 259 is to be taken to compel the production by any person of a document of which he would on grounds of legal professional privilege be entitled to withhold production on an order for discovery in an action in the High Court: s 260(2); Merchant Shipping (Maritime Labour Convention) (Minimum Requirements for Seafarers etc) Regulations 2014, SI 2014/1613, reg 54(3).
21  Merchant Shipping Act 1995 s 259(2)(j)(i). See notes 4, 5.
22  Merchant Shipping Act 1995 s 259(2)(j)(ii). See notes 4, 5.
23  Merchant Shipping Act 1995 s 259(2)(k). See notes 4, 5. A person who complies with a requirement imposed on him in pursuance of s 259(2)(k) is entitled to recover from the person who imposed the requirement such sums in respect of the expenses incurred in complying with the requirement as are prescribed by regulations made by the Secretary of State: s 260(3). Such regulations may make different provision for different circumstances: s 260(4). At the date at which this volume states the law, no such regulations had been made. Any payments so made must be made out of money provided by Parliament: s 260(5).
24  Ie nothing in the Merchant Shipping Act 1995 s 259(1)–(6) (see the text and notes 1–23): see s 259(7); and the Merchant Shipping (Maritime Labour Convention) (Minimum Requirements for Seafarers etc) Regulations 2014, SI 2014/1613, reg 54(3).

25  Merchant Shipping Act 1995 s 259(7); Merchant Shipping (Maritime Labour Convention) (Minimum Requirements for Seafarers etc) Regulations 2014, SI 2014/1613, reg 54(3). See note 4.
26  Ie under the Merchant Shipping Act 1995 s 259 (see the text and notes 1–25): see s 260(1)(a).
27  See the Merchant Shipping Act 1995 s 260(1)(a); and PARA 1177. See note 4.
28  Ie in pursuance of the Merchant Shipping Act 1995 s 259 (see the text and notes 1–25): see s 260(1)(b).
29  See the Merchant Shipping Act 1995 s 260(1)(b); and PARA 1177. See note 4.
30  See the Merchant Shipping Act 1995 s 260(1)(c); and PARA 1177. The text refers to a requirement made in pursuance of s 259(2)(i) (see head (9) in the text): see s 260(1)(c). See notes 4, 18.
31  See the Merchant Shipping Act 1995 s 260(1); and PARA 1177. See note 4.

## 50. Powers to detain ships which do not comply with the Maritime Labour Convention.

Where a relevant inspector[1] has clear grounds for believing that a ship[2] does not comply with the applicable provisions[3] of the Maritime Labour Convention[4] and either the conditions on board are clearly hazardous to the safety, health or security of seafarers[5] or the non-compliance represents a serious breach[6] or the latest in a series of repeated breaches[7], that ship is liable to be detained[8]. Where a relevant inspector has clear grounds for believing that the shipowner[9] has failed to make provision for the repatriation of seafarers[10] in connection with which the Secretary of State has[11] incurred costs[12], and the Secretary of State has requested reimbursement of those costs but has not been reimbursed[13], every ship which is owned by the shipowner is liable to be detained[14].

Where a ship is detained under these provisions and all of the grounds for detention have ceased to apply, a person having power to detain the ship must, at the request of the shipowner or the master of the ship, immediately release the ship:

(1)     if no proceedings for an offence[15] are instituted within the period of seven days beginning with the day on which the ship is detained[16];

(2)     if proceedings for such an offence, having been instituted within that period, are concluded without the shipowner or master of the ship being convicted[17];

(3)     if security is given to the Secretary of State[18] by or on behalf of the shipowner or the master of the ship[19];

(4)     where the shipowner or the master of the ship is convicted of such an offence, if any costs or expenses ordered to be paid by that person, and any fine imposed on that person, have been paid[20]; or

(5)     if the release is ordered by a court or tribunal[21] and any bond or other financial security ordered by such court or tribunal is posted[22].

A ship is liable to be detained if the Secretary of State receives a request from the consul, diplomatic representative or appropriate maritime authorities of another state which has ratified the Maritime Labour Convention that the ship be[23] detained[24], although a ship may not be detained under this provision unless the Secretary of State receives satisfactory evidence that the state has incurred costs[25] in connection with a failure of the shipowner to comply with its legal duties concerning repatriation[26] and a request for reimbursement has been made but those costs have not been reimbursed[27]. Where a ship is so detained and the Secretary of State receives satisfactory evidence that the costs[28] have been reimbursed[29] or a request from the consul, diplomatic representative or appropriate maritime authorities of the relevant State that the ship be released from detention[30], a person having power to detain the ship must immediately release the ship[31].

A person having powers to detain a ship may permit a ship which is liable to be detained under these provisions to proceed to sea for the purpose of proceeding to the nearest appropriate repair yard available[32].

1 As to the meaning of 'relevant inspector' see PARA 48 note 4.
2 As to the meaning of 'ship' in this context see PARA 423 note 2. The power under with the Merchant Shipping (Maritime Labour Convention) (Minimum Requirements for Seafarers etc) Regulations 2014, SI 2014/1613, regs 56, 57 (see the text and notes 3–32) to detain a ship may be exercised as regards a United Kingdom ship wherever it may be, but as regards a ship which is not a United Kingdom ship may only be exercised if the ship in question is in a port or shipyard in the United Kingdom or at an offshore terminal in United Kingdom waters: reg 58(1). As to the meaning of 'United Kingdom ship' in this context see PARA 423 note 6; as to the meaning of 'United Kingdom waters' see PARA 423 note 8. Where a ship other than a United Kingdom ship is detained, the Secretary of State must immediately inform the consul or diplomatic representative of the state whose flag the ship is entitled to fly, or the appropriate maritime authorities of that state, and invite them to send a representative to attend the ship: reg 58(5). As to the Secretary of State see PARA 36.
3 Ie does not comply with the Merchant Shipping (Maritime Labour Convention) (Minimum Requirements for Seafarers etc) Regulations 2014, SI 2014/1613 (as to which see PARA 423).
4 Merchant Shipping (Maritime Labour Convention) (Minimum Requirements for Seafarers etc) Regulations 2014, SI 2014/1613, reg 56(1)(a).
5 Merchant Shipping (Maritime Labour Convention) (Minimum Requirements for Seafarers etc) Regulations 2014, SI 2014/1613, reg 56(1)(b)(i). As to the meaning of 'seafarer' in this context see PARA 423.
6 Ie of the Merchant Shipping (Maritime Labour Convention) (Minimum Requirements for Seafarers etc) Regulations 2014, SI 2014/1613, or the requirements of the Maritime Labour Convention (including the rights of seafarers referred to in Articles III and IV of the Convention which are secured by it).
7 Merchant Shipping (Maritime Labour Convention) (Minimum Requirements for Seafarers etc) Regulations 2014, SI 2014/1613, reg 56(1)(b)(ii).
8 Merchant Shipping (Maritime Labour Convention) (Minimum Requirements for Seafarers etc) Regulations 2014, SI 2014/1613, reg 56(1). Where a ship is liable to be detained under reg 56 or reg 57, the person detaining the ship must serve on the master of the ship a detention notice which states the grounds for the detention and requires the terms of the notice to be complied with until the ship is released by any person mentioned in the Merchant Shipping Act 1995 s 284(1) (see PARA 1190): Merchant Shipping (Maritime Labour Convention) (Minimum Requirements for Seafarers etc) Regulations 2014, SI 2014/1613, reg 58(4).
9 As to the meaning of 'shipowner' in this context see PARA 448 note 4.
10 Ie provision under the Merchant Shipping (Maritime Labour Convention) (Minimum Requirements for Seafarers etc) Regulations 2014, SI 2014/1613, reg 19 (see PARA 540) or reg 22 (see PARA 541).
11 Ie under the Merchant Shipping (Maritime Labour Convention) (Minimum Requirements for Seafarers etc) Regulations 2014, SI 2014/1613, reg 27 (see PARA 540).
12 Merchant Shipping (Maritime Labour Convention) (Minimum Requirements for Seafarers etc) Regulations 2014, SI 2014/1613, reg 56(2)(a).
13 Merchant Shipping (Maritime Labour Convention) (Minimum Requirements for Seafarers etc) Regulations 2014, SI 2014/1613, reg 56(2)(b).
14 Merchant Shipping (Maritime Labour Convention) (Minimum Requirements for Seafarers etc) Regulations 2014, SI 2014/1613, reg 56(2).
15 Ie an offence under the Merchant Shipping (Maritime Labour Convention) (Minimum Requirements for Seafarers etc) Regulations 2014, SI 2014/1613.
16 Merchant Shipping (Maritime Labour Convention) (Minimum Requirements for Seafarers etc) Regulations 2014, SI 2014/1613, reg 56(3)(a).
17 Merchant Shipping (Maritime Labour Convention) (Minimum Requirements for Seafarers etc) Regulations 2014, SI 2014/1613, reg 56(3)(b). The Merchant Shipping Act 1995 s 145 (interpretation of references in s 144 to the institution of proceedings or their conclusion without conviction: see ENVIRONMENTAL QUALITY AND PUBLIC HEALTH vol 45 (2010) PARA 434) applies for the purposes of the Merchant Shipping (Maritime Labour Convention) (Minimum Requirements for Seafarers etc) Regulations 2014, SI 2014/1613, reg 56(3), (4) as if references to the owner of a ship were to the shipowner under the Merchant Shipping (Maritime Labour Convention) (Minimum Requirements for Seafarers etc) Regulations 2014, SI 2014/1613, and references to an offence under the Merchant Shipping Act 1995 s 131 were references to an offence under the Merchant Shipping (Maritime Labour Convention) (Minimum Requirements for Seafarers etc) Regulations 2014, SI 2014/1613: reg 56(6).

18 Ie if either the sum of £30,000 is paid to the Secretary of State by way of security or security which, in the opinion of the Secretary of State, is satisfactory and is for an amount not less than £30,000 is given to the Secretary of State: Merchant Shipping (Maritime Labour Convention) (Minimum Requirements for Seafarers etc) Regulations 2014, SI 2014/1613, reg 56(3)(c)(i), (ii).

19 Merchant Shipping (Maritime Labour Convention) (Minimum Requirements for Seafarers etc) Regulations 2014, SI 2014/1613, reg 56(3)(c). The Secretary of State must repay any sum paid in pursuance of reg 56(3)(c) or release any security so given if no proceedings for an offence under the Merchant Shipping (Maritime Labour Convention) (Minimum Requirements for Seafarers etc) Regulations 2014, SI 2014/1613, are instituted within the period of seven days beginning with the day on which the sum is paid or the security is given (reg 56(4)(a)) or if proceedings for such an offence, having been instituted within that period, are concluded without the shipowner or the master of the ship being convicted (reg 56(4)(b)). Where a sum has been paid, or security has been given, by any person in pursuance of reg 54(3)(c) and the shipowner or the master of the ship is convicted of an offence under the Merchant Shipping (Maritime Labour Convention) (Minimum Requirements for Seafarers etc) Regulations 2014, SI 2014/1613, the sum so paid or the amount made available under the security must be applied first in payment of any costs or expenses ordered by the court to be paid by the shipowner or the master of the ship (reg 56(5)(a)) and next in payment of any fine imposed by the court (reg 56(5)(b)), and any balance must be repaid to the first-mentioned person (reg 56(5)).

20 Merchant Shipping (Maritime Labour Convention) (Minimum Requirements for Seafarers etc) Regulations 2014, SI 2014/1613, reg 56(3)(d).

21 Ie a court or tribunal referred to in the United Nations Convention on the Law of the Sea 1982 (Montego Bay, 10 December 1982 to 9 December 1984; TS 3 Misc 11 (1983); Cmnd 8941) (as to which see PARA 9) art 292.

22 Merchant Shipping (Maritime Labour Convention) (Minimum Requirements for Seafarers etc) Regulations 2014, SI 2014/1613, reg 56(3)(e).

23 Ie pursuant to paragraph 6 of Standard A2.5 of the Convention (power for states to detain or request detention of ships in connection with a shipowner defaulting in its duty to repatriate a seafarer).

24 Merchant Shipping (Maritime Labour Convention) (Minimum Requirements for Seafarers etc) Regulations 2014, SI 2014/1613, reg 57(1).

25 Ie pursuant to paragraph 5 of Standard A2.5 (repatriation) of the Convention.

26 Merchant Shipping (Maritime Labour Convention) (Minimum Requirements for Seafarers etc) Regulations 2014, SI 2014/1613, reg 57(2)(a).

27 Merchant Shipping (Maritime Labour Convention) (Minimum Requirements for Seafarers etc) Regulations 2014, SI 2014/1613, reg 57(2)(b).

28 Ie the costs referred to in the Merchant Shipping (Maritime Labour Convention) (Minimum Requirements for Seafarers etc) Regulations 2014, SI 2014/1613, reg 57(2) (see the text and notes 26–27).

29 Merchant Shipping (Maritime Labour Convention) (Minimum Requirements for Seafarers etc) Regulations 2014, SI 2014/1613, reg 57(3)(a).

30 Merchant Shipping (Maritime Labour Convention) (Minimum Requirements for Seafarers etc) Regulations 2014, SI 2014/1613, reg 57(3)(b).

31 Merchant Shipping (Maritime Labour Convention) (Minimum Requirements for Seafarers etc) Regulations 2014, SI 2014/1613, reg 57(3).

32 Merchant Shipping (Maritime Labour Convention) (Minimum Requirements for Seafarers etc) Regulations 2014, SI 2014/1613, reg 58(2).

C. POWERS IN CONNECTION WITH IMPROVEMENT NOTICES AND PROHIBITION NOTICES

**51. Improvement notices.** If an inspector appointed by the Secretary of State[1] is of the opinion that a person:

(1)     is contravening one or more of the relevant statutory provisions[2]; or

(2)     has contravened one or more of those provisions in circumstances that make it likely that the contravention[3] will continue or be repeated[4],

he may serve on that person a notice (an 'improvement notice')[5].

An improvement notice must:

(a)     state that the inspector is of such opinion, specify the provision or provisions as to which he is of that opinion, and give particulars of the reasons why he is of that opinion[6]; and

(b)     require the person on whom the notice is served to remedy the
        contravention in question or, as the case may be, the matters occasioning
        it within such period as may be specified in the notice[7].

The period specified in pursuance of head (b) above must not expire before the
end of the period within which a notice can be given to the inspector[8] requiring
questions relating to the improvement notice to be referred to arbitration[9].

1   Ie an inspector appointed under the Merchant Shipping Act 1995 s 256(6) (see PARA 46): see s
    261(1). As to the Secretary of State see PARA 38.
2   Merchant Shipping Act 1995 s 261(1)(a). See note 5. For these purposes, 'relevant statutory
    provisions' means:
    (1)     s 43 (see PARA 490), s 44 (see PARA 500), s 46 (see PARA 502), s 47 (see PARA 503),
            s 48 (see PARA 505), s 49, s 50 (see PARA 503), s 51 (see PARA 506), s 52 (see
            PARA 1083), s 53 (see PARA 496), s 54 (see PARA 1084), s 55 (see PARA 449), ss 85, 86
            (see PARA 602 note 1), s 88 (and Sch 2) (see PARA 601), s 99 (see PARA 1145), s 109
            (see PARA 457 note 3), s 115 (see PARA 515), s 116 (see PARA 503 note 21), s 121 (see
            PARA 607), s 122 (see PARA 608), s 123 (see PARA 609), s 124 (see PARA 609), s 125
            (see PARA 610), s 126 (see PARA 611), ss 128–130A (see ENVIRONMENTAL QUALITY
            AND PUBLIC HEALTH vol 45 (2010) PARAS 360, 362, 364, 421), ss 131–151 (see
            ENVIRONMENTAL QUALITY AND PUBLIC HEALTH vol 45 (2010) PARA 425 et seq)
            and s 272 (see PARA 847) (s 261(4)(a) (amended by the Merchant Shipping and
            Maritime Security Act 1997 s 29(1), Sch 6 para 16; SI 1998/2241; and SI 1998/2647));
    (2)     the provisions of any instrument of a legislative character having effect under any of
            those provisions (Merchant Shipping Act 1995 s 261(4)(b)); and
    (3)     the Merchant Shipping (Maritime Labour Convention) (Minimum Requirements for
            Seafarers etc) Regulations 2014, SI 2014/1613 (see PARA 448 et seq) (reg 54(5)).
3   For these purposes, 'contravention' includes failure to comply; and 'failure' includes refusal:
    Merchant Shipping Act 1995 s 313(1).
4   Merchant Shipping Act 1995 s 261(1)(b). See note 5.
5   Merchant Shipping Act 1995 s 261(1). A notice served on a person under s 261 is referred to in
    ss 262–266 (see PARAS 52–55, 1178) as an improvement notice: see s 261(1). As to the service of
    documents under the Merchant Shipping Act 1995 generally see s 291; and PARA 74. As to the
    content and effect of improvement notices see PARA 52; and as to offences arising from the
    contravention of any requirement imposed by an improvement notice see PARA 1178.
        The Merchant Shipping Act 1995 s 261 applies both to the Merchant Shipping and Fishing
    Vessels (Control of Noise at Work) Regulations 2007, SI 2007/3075, and to the Merchant
    Shipping and Fishing Vessels (Health and Safety at Work) (Carcinogens and Mutagens)
    Regulations 2007, SI 2007/3100, as if they were for all purposes made under the Merchant
    Shipping Act 1995 s 85 and accordingly s 261 applies in relation to government ships: see the
    Merchant Shipping and Fishing Vessels (Control of Noise at Work) Regulations 2007, SI
    2007/3075, reg 19; the Merchant Shipping and Fishing Vessels (Health and Safety at Work)
    (Carcinogens and Mutagens) Regulations 2007, SI 2007/3100, reg 22; and PARAS 628, 631. As to
    government ships see PARA 19.
6   Merchant Shipping Act 1995 s 261(2)(a). See note 5.
7   Merchant Shipping Act 1995 s 261(2)(b). See note 5.
8   Ie under the Merchant Shipping Act 1995 s 264 (see PARA 54): see s 261(3). Any notice authorised
    by s 261 to be given to an inspector may be given by delivering it to him or by leaving it at, or
    sending it by post to, his office: see s 291(5); and PARA 74.
9   Merchant Shipping Act 1995 s 261(3). See note 5. As to references to arbitration see PARA 54.

**52. Prohibition notices.** If, as regards any relevant activities[1] which are being
or are likely to be carried on on board any ship[2] by or under the control of any
person, an inspector appointed by the Secretary of State[3] is of the opinion that, as
so carried on or as likely to be so carried on, the activities involve or, as the case
may be, will involve the risk of serious personal injury to any person (whether on
board the ship or not) or serious pollution of any navigable waters, the inspector
may serve on the first-mentioned person a notice (a 'prohibition notice')[4].
    A prohibition notice must:
    (1)     state that the inspector is of such opinion[5];
    (2)     specify the matters which in his opinion give or, as the case may be, will
            give rise to such risk[6];

(3)    where in his opinion any of those matters involve or, as the case may be, will involve a contravention[7] of any of the relevant statutory provisions state that he is of that opinion, specify the provision or provisions as to which he is of that opinion, and give particulars of the reasons why he is of that opinion[8]; and

(4)    direct that the activities to which the notice relates are not to be carried on by or under the control of the person on whom the notice is served[9], or that the ship is not to go to sea[10], (or both of those things) unless the matters specified in the notice in pursuance of head (2) above, and any associated contraventions of any provision so specified in pursuance of head (3) above, have been remedied[11].

A direction contained in a prohibition notice in pursuance of head (4) above takes effect at the end of the period specified in the notice or, if the direction is given in pursuance of head (4)(b) above or the notice so declares, immediately[12].

1    For these purposes, 'relevant activities' means activities to or in relation to which any of the relevant statutory provisions apply or will, if the activities are carried on as mentioned in the Merchant Shipping Act 1995 s 262(1), apply: see s 262(2). As to the meaning of 'relevant statutory provisions' for these purposes see PARA 51 note 2.
2    As to the meaning of 'ship' see PARA 229.
3    Ie an inspector appointed under the Merchant Shipping Act 1995 s 256(6) (see PARA 46): see s 262(1). As to the Secretary of State see PARA 36.
4    Merchant Shipping Act 1995 s 262(1). A notice served on a person under s 262 is referred to in ss 263–266 (see PARAS 53–55, 1178) as a prohibition notice: see s 262(1). As to the service of documents under the Merchant Shipping Act 1995 generally see s 291; and PARA 74. As to the content and effect of prohibition notices see PARA 53; as to compensation in connection with invalid prohibition notices see PARA 55; and as to offences arising from the contravention of any requirement imposed by a prohibition notice see PARA 1178.
        Section 262 applies both to the Merchant Shipping and Fishing Vessels (Control of Noise at Work) Regulations 2007, SI 2007/3075, and to the Merchant Shipping and Fishing Vessels (Health and Safety at Work) (Carcinogens and Mutagens) Regulations 2007, SI 2007/3100, as if they were for all purposes made under the Merchant Shipping Act 1995 s 85 (see PARA 602 note 1) and accordingly s 262 applies in relation to government ships: see the Merchant Shipping and Fishing Vessels (Control of Noise at Work) Regulations 2007, SI 2007/3075, reg 19; the Merchant Shipping and Fishing Vessels (Health and Safety at Work) (Carcinogens and Mutagens) Regulations 2007, SI 2007/3100, reg 22; and PARAS 628, 631. As to government ships see PARA 19.
5    Merchant Shipping Act 1995 s 262(3)(a). See note 4.
6    Merchant Shipping Act 1995 s 262(3)(b). See note 4.
7    As to the meaning of 'contravention' see PARA 51 note 3.
8    Merchant Shipping Act 1995 s 262(3)(c). See note 4.
9    Merchant Shipping Act 1995 s 262(3)(d)(i). See note 4.
10   Merchant Shipping Act 1995 s 262(3)(d)(ii). See note 4.
11   Merchant Shipping Act 1995 s 262(3)(d). See note 4.
12   Merchant Shipping Act 1995 s 262(4). See note 4.

**53.   Contents and effect of notices.** An improvement notice[1] or a prohibition notice[2] may, but need not, include directions as to the measures to be taken to remedy any contravention[3] or matter to which the notice relates; and any such directions may be framed so as to afford the person on whom the notice is served a choice between different ways of remedying the contravention or matter[4].

An improvement notice or a prohibition notice must not direct any measures to be taken to remedy the contravention of any of the relevant statutory provisions[5] that are more onerous than those necessary to secure compliance with that provision[6].

Where an improvement notice or a prohibition notice that is not to take immediate effect has been served:

(1)    the notice may be withdrawn by an inspector at any time before the end of the period specified in it[7]; and

(2)     the period so specified may be extended or further extended by an
        inspector at any time when a reference to arbitration in respect of the
        notice is not pending[8].

1   As to the meaning of 'improvement notice' see PARA 51.
2   As to the meaning of 'prohibition notice' see PARA 52.
3   As to the meaning of 'contravention' see PARA 51 note 3.
4   Merchant Shipping Act 1995 s 263(1). Section 263 applies both to the Merchant Shipping and
    Fishing Vessels (Control of Noise at Work) Regulations 2007, SI 2007/3075, and to the Merchant
    Shipping and Fishing Vessels (Health and Safety at Work) (Carcinogens and Mutagens)
    Regulations 2007, SI 2007/3100, as if they were for all purposes made under the Merchant
    Shipping Act 1995 s 85 (see PARA 602 note 1) and accordingly s 263 applies in relation to
    government ships: see the Merchant Shipping and Fishing Vessels (Control of Noise at Work)
    Regulations 2007, SI 2007/3075, reg 19; the Merchant Shipping and Fishing Vessels (Health and
    Safety at Work) (Carcinogens and Mutagens) Regulations 2007, SI 2007/3100, reg 22; and
    PARAS 628, 631. As to government ships see PARA 19.
5   As to the meaning of 'relevant statutory provisions' for these purposes see PARA 51 note 2.
6   Merchant Shipping Act 1995 s 263(2). See note 4.
7   Merchant Shipping Act 1995 s 263(3)(a). The text refers to such periods as may be specified in the
    notice in pursuance of s 261(2)(b) (see PARA 51) or, as the case may be, s 262(4) (see PARA 52):
    see s 263(3)(a). See note 4.
8   Merchant Shipping Act 1995 s 263(3)(b). The text refers to a reference to arbitration which is not
    pending under s 264 (see PARA 54): see s 263(3)(b). See note 4.

**54. References of notices to arbitration.** Any question:
(1)     as to whether any of the reasons or matters specified in an improvement
        notice[1] or a prohibition notice[2] in connection with any opinion formed
        by the inspector[3] constituted a valid basis for that opinion[4]; or
(2)     as to whether any directions included in such a notice[5] were reasonable[6],
must, if the person on whom the notice was served so requires by a notice given
to the inspector[7] within 21 days from the service of the improvement or
prohibition notice, be referred to a single arbitrator appointed by agreement
between the parties for that question to be decided by him[8].

Where a notice to arbitration is so given by a person[9], then:
(a)     in the case of an improvement notice, the giving of the notice has the
        effect of suspending the operation of the improvement notice until the
        decision of the arbitrator is published to the parties or the reference is
        abandoned by that person[10];
(b)     in the case of a prohibition notice, the giving of the notice has the effect
        of so suspending the operation of the prohibition notice if, but only if,
        on the application of that person the arbitrator so directs, and then only
        from the giving of the direction[11].

Where, on a reference to arbitration[12], the arbitrator decides as respects any
reason, matter or direction to which the reference relates, that in all the
circumstances either:
(i)     the reason or matter did not constitute a valid basis for the inspector's
        opinion[13]; or
(ii)    the direction was unreasonable[14],
he must either cancel the notice or affirm it with such modifications as he may in
the circumstances think fit; and in any other case the arbitrator must affirm the
notice in its original form[15]. However, where any such reference[16] involves the
consideration by the arbitrator of the effects of any particular activities or state of
affairs on the health or safety of any persons, he must not on that reference make
any such decision as is mentioned either in head (i) or head (ii) above except after:

(A) in the case of an improvement notice, affording an opportunity of making oral representations to him with respect to those effects to a member of any such panel of representatives of maritime trade unions as may be appointed by the Secretary of State for these purposes[17]; or

(B) in the case of a prohibition notice, affording an opportunity of making such representations to him to either a representative of a trade union representing persons whose interests it appears to him that the notice was designed to safeguard or a member of any such panel as is referred to in head (A) above, as he thinks appropriate[18]; and

(C) (in either case) considering any representations made to him in pursuance of head (A) or head (B) above[19].

1 Ie specified in an improvement notice in pursuance of the Merchant Shipping Act 1995 s 261(2)(a) (see PARA 51): see s 264(1)(a). As to the meaning of 'improvement notice' see PARA 51.
2 Ie specified in a prohibition notice in pursuance of the Merchant Shipping Act 1995 s 262(3)(b) or s 262(3)(c) (see PARA 52): see s 264(1)(a). As to the meaning of 'prohibition notice' see PARA 52.
3 Ie an inspector appointed by the Secretary of State under the Merchant Shipping Act 1995 s 256(6): see PARA 46. As to the Secretary of State see PARA 36.
4 Merchant Shipping Act 1995 s 264(1)(a).
5 Ie any directions included in pursuance of the Merchant Shipping Act 1995 s 263(1) (see PARA 53): see s 264(1)(b).
6 Merchant Shipping Act 1995 s 264(1)(b).
7 As to the service of documents under the Merchant Shipping Act 1995 generally see s 291; and PARA 74. Any notice authorised by s 264 to be given to an inspector may be given by delivering it to him or by leaving it at, or sending it by post to, his office: see s 291(5); and PARA 74.
8 Merchant Shipping Act 1995 s 264(1). As to references to an arbitrator in Scotland see s 264(8). The provisions of the Arbitration Act 1996 Pt I (ss 1–84) apply to every arbitration under an enactment (a 'statutory arbitration') (see s 94), subject to certain adaptions and exclusions (see ss 95–98); and see ARBITRATION vol 2 (2017) PARA 509 et seq.
    In connection with his functions under the Merchant Shipping Act 1995 s 264, an arbitrator has the powers conferred on an inspector by s 259, other than s 259(3), (4), (6) (see PARA 49): s 264(7). However, a person is not qualified for appointment as an arbitrator under s 264 unless he is:
    (1) a person holding a certificate of competency as a master mariner or as a marine engineer officer class 1, or a person holding a certificate equivalent to any such certificate (s 264(5)(a));
    (2) a naval architect (s 264(5)(b));
    (3) (until a day to be appointed) a person who has a 10 year general qualification within the meaning of the Courts and Legal Services Act 1990 s 71 (see LEGAL PROFESSIONS vol 66 (2015) PARA 540) or (as from that day) a person who satisfies the judicial-appointment eligibility condition on a seven-year basis (Merchant Shipping Act 1995 s 264(5)(c), (6)(a) (s 264(6)(a) prospectively substituted, s 264(6)(b), (c) prospectively amended, by the Tribunals, Courts and Enforcement Act 2007 s 50, Sch 10 Pt 1 para 26(1)–(3)));
    (4) an advocate or solicitor in Scotland of at least 10 (until the appointed day) or seven (as from that day) years' standing (Merchant Shipping Act 1995 s 264(6)(b) (as so prospectively amended)); or
    (5) is a member of the bar of Northern Ireland or a solicitor of the Court of Judicature of Northern Ireland of at least 10 (until the appointed day) or seven (as from that day) years' standing (s 264(6)(c) (as so prospectively amended); amended by the Tribunals, Courts and Enforcement Act 2007 s 50, Sch 10 Pt 1 para 26(1)–(3))); or
    (6) a person with special experience of shipping matters, of the fishing industry or of activities carried on in ports (Merchant Shipping Act 1995 s 264(5)(d)).
    As to the meaning of 'port' see PARA 46 note 12. As to the judicial-appointment eligibility condition see the Tribunals, Courts and Enforcement Act 2007 ss 50–52; and COURTS AND TRIBUNALS vol 24 (2010) PARA 645.
    The Merchant Shipping Act 1995 s 264 applies both to the Merchant Shipping and Fishing Vessels (Control of Noise at Work) Regulations 2007, SI 2007/3075, and to the Merchant Shipping and Fishing Vessels (Health and Safety at Work) (Carcinogens and Mutagens) Regulations 2007, SI 2007/3100, as if they were for all purposes made under the Merchant Shipping Act 1995 s 85 (see PARA 602 note 1) and accordingly s 264 applies in relation to government ships: see the Merchant Shipping and Fishing Vessels (Control of Noise at Work) Regulations 2007, SI 2007/3075, reg 19; the Merchant Shipping and Fishing Vessels (Health and

Safety at Work) (Carcinogens and Mutagens) Regulations 2007, SI 2007/3100, reg 22; and PARAS 628, 631. As to government ships see PARA 19.

9  Ie in accordance with the Merchant Shipping Act 1995 s 264(1) (see the text and notes 1–8): see s 264(2).

10  Merchant Shipping Act 1995 s 264(2)(a).

11  Merchant Shipping Act 1995 s 264(2)(b).

12  Ie a reference under the Merchant Shipping Act 1995 s 264: see s 264(3).

13  Merchant Shipping Act 1995 s 264(3)(a).

14  Merchant Shipping Act 1995 s 264(3)(b).

15  Merchant Shipping Act 1995 s 264(3).

16  Ie a reference under the Merchant Shipping Act 1995 s 264: see s 264(4).

17  Merchant Shipping Act 1995 s 264(4)(a).

18  Merchant Shipping Act 1995 s 264(4)(b).

19  Merchant Shipping Act 1995 s 264(4)(c).

## 55. Compensation in connection with invalid prohibition notices.

If, on a reference to arbitration[1] relating to a prohibition notice[2]:

(1)     the arbitrator[3] decides that any reason or matter did not constitute a valid basis for the inspector's opinion[4]; and

(2)     it appears to him that there were no reasonable grounds for the inspector to form that opinion[5],

the arbitrator may award the person on whom the notice was served such compensation in respect of any loss suffered by him in consequence of the service of the notice as the arbitrator thinks fit[6].

If, on any such reference, the arbitrator decides that any direction included in the notice[7] was unreasonable, the arbitrator may award the person on whom the notice was served such compensation in respect of any loss suffered by him in consequence of the direction as the arbitrator thinks fit[8].

An arbitrator must not, however, award any such compensation[9] in the case of any prohibition notice unless:

(a)     it appears to him that the direction given[10] contained a specific requirement that the ship was not to go to sea[11]; or

(b)     it appears to him that the inspector was of the opinion that there would be such a risk of injury or pollution as is referred to in the notice if the ship went to sea and that the effect of the direction so given[12] was to prohibit the departure of the ship unless the matters, or (as the case may be) the matters and contraventions[13], referred to in the direction were remedied[14].

Any compensation so awarded[15] is payable by the Secretary of State[16].

1  Ie a reference under the Merchant Shipping Act 1995 s 264 (see PARA 54): see s 265(1).

2  Merchant Shipping Act 1995 s 265(1). As to the meaning of 'prohibition notice' see PARA 52.

3  As to the arbitrator see PARA 54 note 8; and as to references to an arbitrator in Scotland see s 265(5).

4  Merchant Shipping Act 1995 s 265(1)(a). The text refers to an inspector appointed by the Secretary of State under the Merchant Shipping Act 1995 s 256(6): see PARA 46. As to the Secretary of State see PARA 36.

5  Merchant Shipping Act 1995 s 265(1)(b). See note 4.

6  Merchant Shipping Act 1995 s 265(1). Section 265 applies both to the Merchant Shipping and Fishing Vessels (Control of Noise at Work) Regulations 2007, SI 2007/3075, and to the Merchant Shipping and Fishing Vessels (Health and Safety at Work) (Carcinogens and Mutagens) Regulations 2007, SI 2007/3100, as if they were for all purposes made under the Merchant Shipping Act 1995 s 85 (see PARA 602 note 1) and accordingly s 265 applies in relation to government ships: see the Merchant Shipping and Fishing Vessels (Control of Noise at Work) Regulations 2007, SI 2007/3075, reg 19; the Merchant Shipping and Fishing Vessels (Health and Safety at Work) (Carcinogens and Mutagens) Regulations 2007, SI 2007/3100, reg 22; and PARAS 628, 631. As to government ships see PARA 19.

7  As to such directions see PARAS 52–53.

8  Merchant Shipping Act 1995 s 265(2).

9  Ie under the Merchant Shipping Act 1995 s 265(1) (see the text and notes 1–6) or s 265(2) (see the text and notes 7–8): see s 265(3).

10  Ie in pursuance of the Merchant Shipping Act 1995 s 262(3)(d) (see PARA 52): see s 265(3)(a).

11  Merchant Shipping Act 1995 s 265(3)(a). The text refers to any such requirement as is mentioned in s 262(3)(d)(ii) (see PARA 52): see s 265(3)(a). As to the meaning of 'ship' see PARA 229.

12  Ie given in pursuance of the Merchant Shipping Act 1995 s 262(3)(d) (see PARA 52): see s 265(3)(b).

13  As to the meaning of 'contravention' see PARA 51 note 3.

14  Merchant Shipping Act 1995 s 265(3)(b).

15  Ie under the Merchant Shipping Act 1995 s 265 (see the text and notes 1–14): see s 265(4).

16  Merchant Shipping Act 1995 s 265(4).

### (iv) Lighthouse Authorities

**56. The Lighthouse Authorities.** There are three General Lighthouse Authorities (GLAs)[1], each with separate geographical responsibilities, namely:

(1)  the Trinity House which is the GLA as respects England and Wales and the adjacent seas and islands[2];

(2)  the Northern Lighthouse Board (Commissioners of Northern Lighthouses) which is the GLA as respects Scotland and the adjacent seas and islands, as well as respects the Isle of Man and the seas adjacent thereto[3]; and

(3)  the Commissioners of Irish Lights who constitute the GLA as respects Northern Ireland and the adjacent seas and islands, as well as the Republic of Ireland[4].

The three GLAs provide, for example, lighthouse services and navigational aids and other aids for the safety of ships[5].

The GLAs are funded exclusively through the General Lighthouse Fund (GLF) which is administered by the Secretary of State[6]. Its income is mainly derived from the payment of general light dues charged predominantly on commercial shipping in the United Kingdom and Ireland (both Northern Ireland and the Republic of Ireland)[7] but the fund is supplemented by a grant from the Irish government.

All lighthouses were automated by 1998, with controls centralised at each GLA's headquarters, and the GLAs have focused since on continuing to reduce costs and on investing inwardly in both depots and ships.

1  As to the lighthouse authorities generally see PARA 1017 et seq.

2  See PARA 1018.

3  See PARA 1019.

4  See PARA 1020.

5  See PARA 1023 et seq.

6  See PARA 1039 et seq.

7  See PARA 1033 et seq.

### (v) Other Bodies and Agencies

**57. The Maritime and Coastguard Agency.** The Maritime and Coastguard Agency ('MCA'), which is an executive agency of the Department for Transport, is responsible throughout the United Kingdom for implementing the government's maritime safety policy[1]. This includes providing Maritime Safety Information ('MSI') to ships at sea (including the broadcast of warnings and forecasts), co-ordinating search and rescue ('SAR') at sea through Her Majesty's Coastguard, and checking that ships (both United Kingdom ships and ships of other flags visiting United Kingdom ports) meet United Kingdom and international safety rules[2].

1   The MCA came into being in 1998 when the Coastguard Agency and Marine Safety Agency ('MSA') merged.
2   As to Her Majesty's Coastguard see PARA 58.

**58. Her Majesty's Coastguard.** Her Majesty's Coastguard consists of such numbers of officers and men as the Secretary of State[1] may with the consent of the Treasury from time to time think fit, and is raised, maintained, equipped and governed by the Secretary of State and employed as a coast-watching force[2]. The management and control of Her Majesty's Coastguard is vested in the Secretary of State[3].

1   As to the Secretary of State for these purposes see the text and notes 3–7.
2   See the Coastguard Act 1925 s 1(1). As to the function of the coastguard in relation to wrecks see PARAS 123, 923 et seq. As to remuneration under the Merchant Shipping Act 1995 for coastguard services especially see PARA 936.
    The Maritime and Coastguard Agency ('MCA') co-ordinates search and rescue ('SAR') at sea through Her Majesty's Coastguard: see PARA 57. There is no duty of care owed by the coastguard to persons in distress in the context of a search and rescue operation: *OLL Ltd v Secretary of State for Transport* [1997] 3 All ER 897.
3   As to the Secretary of State see PARA 36.

**59. Wreck commissioners.** The Lord Chancellor[1] may appoint such number of persons as he thinks fit to be wreck commissioners and may remove any wreck commissioners appointed by him[2].

A wreck commissioner must vacate his office on the day on which he attains the age of 70 years[3].

There must be paid to any wreck commissioner such remuneration, out of money provided by Parliament, as the Lord Chancellor may with the consent of the Treasury determine[4]; and there must be paid to any assessor appointed under the Merchant Shipping Act 1995 such remuneration, out of money provided by Parliament, as the Lord Chancellor may with the consent of the Treasury determine[5].

1   As to the Lord Chancellor see CONSTITUTIONAL AND ADMINISTRATIVE LAW vol 20 (2014) PARA 255 et seq.
2   Merchant Shipping Act 1995 s 297(1). The Lord Chancellor's function under s 297(1) is a protected function for the purposes of the Constitutional Reform Act 2005 s 19: see s 19(5), Sch 7 para 4; and CONSTITUTIONAL AND ADMINISTRATIVE LAW vol 20 (2014) PARA 261. However, any appointment to the office of wreck commissioner in exercise of the function under the Merchant Shipping Act 1995 s 297(1) must be made (by virtue of the Constitutional Reform Act 2005 s 85, Sch 14 Pt 3) in accordance with ss 85–93, 96: see COURTS AND TRIBUNALS vol 24 (2010) PARAS 944–945.
    The Lord Chancellor may remove a wreck commissioner from office only with the concurrence of the Lord Chief Justice of England and Wales or (if the commissioner was appointed to act in Northern Ireland) the Lord Chief Justice of Northern Ireland: Merchant Shipping Act 1995 s 297(3A) (added by the Constitutional Reform Act 2005 s 15(1), Sch 4 Pt 1 para 239). As to the appointment of a person to act as wreck commissioner in Northern Ireland see the Merchant Shipping Act 1995 s 297(3).
    As to the function of the coastguard in relation to wrecks see PARA 923 et seq.
3   Merchant Shipping Act 1995 s 297(2). However, s 297(2) is subject to the Judicial Pensions and Retirement Act 1993 s 26(4)–(6) (power to authorise continuance in office up to the age of 75 years) (see COURTS AND TRIBUNALS vol 24 (2010) PARA 956): see the Merchant Shipping Act 1995 s 297(2).
4   Merchant Shipping Act 1995 s 297(4). As to the Treasury see CONSTITUTIONAL AND ADMINISTRATIVE LAW vol 20 (2014) PARA 262 et seq.
5   Merchant Shipping Act 1995 s 297(5).

**60. The receiver of wreck.** The receiver of wreck investigates the ownership of items found in or on the shores of the sea or any tidal water[1].

1 As to the receiver of wreck see PARA 929. As to the function of the coastguard in relation to wrecks see PARA 923 et seq.

**61. Mercantile marine superintendents.** Under the Merchant Shipping Act 1995, there continue to be officers known as mercantile marine superintendents[1]. They are appointed, and may be removed, by the Secretary of State[2]. Mercantile marine superintendents exercise the functions conferred on superintendents by the Merchant Shipping Act 1995[3].

1 Merchant Shipping Act 1995 s 296(1). In the Merchant Shipping Act 1995, unless the context otherwise requires, 'superintendent' means a mercantile marine superintendent appointed under s 296: s 313(1).
2 Merchant Shipping Act 1995 s 296(2). As to the Secretary of State see PARA 36.
3 Merchant Shipping Act 1995 s 296(3).

**62. Registrar General of Shipping and Seamen.** Under the Merchant Shipping Act 1995, there continues to be an officer known as the Registrar General of Shipping and Seaman[1]. He is appointed, and may be removed, by the Secretary of State[2]; and he must exercise such functions as are conferred on him by the Merchant Shipping Act 1995 and must keep such records and perform such other duties as the Secretary of State may direct[3].

The Secretary of State may appoint and remove persons to perform on behalf of the Registrar General of Shipping and Seamen such of his functions[4] as the Secretary of State or the Registrar General of Shipping and Seamen may direct[5].

1 Merchant Shipping Act 1995 s 295(1).
2 Merchant Shipping Act 1995 s 295(2). As to the Secretary of State see PARA 36.
3 Merchant Shipping Act 1995 s 295(3). As to the Secretary of State's power to give directions under the Merchant Shipping Act 1995 see PARA 39.
4 Ie other than the functions of the Registrar General of Shipping and Seamen as registrar under the Merchant Shipping Act 1995 Pt II (ss 8–23) (see PARA 237 et seq): see s 295(5).
5 Merchant Shipping Act 1995 s 295(4), (5).

### (vi) General Financial Provisions under the Merchant Shipping Act 1995

**63. Power to make regulations prescribing fees.** The Secretary of State[1] may, with the consent of the Treasury[2], make regulations[3] prescribing fees to be charged in respect of either the issue or recording in pursuance of the Merchant Shipping Act 1995 of any certificate, licence or other document, or the doing of any thing in pursuance of that Act[4].

In the case of fees for the measurement of a ship's tonnage[5] the fees may be prescribed as maximum fees[6].

All fees received by the Secretary of State under the Merchant Shipping Act 1995 must be paid into the Consolidated Fund[7].

1 As to the Secretary of State see PARA 36.
2 As to the Treasury see CONSTITUTIONAL AND ADMINISTRATIVE LAW vol 20 (2014) PARA 262 et seq.
3 As to the Secretary of State's power to make subordinate legislation, including his power to appoint committees for the purpose of advising him when considering the making or alteration of any regulations, see PARA 39.
4 Merchant Shipping Act 1995 s 302(1). In exercise of the power so conferred, the Secretary of State has made the Merchant Shipping (Fees) Regulations 2006, SI 2006/2055 (amended by SI 2006/3225; SI 2011/3056; SI 2015/315; SI 2015/410; SI 2015/782); the Merchant Shipping (Fees) Regulations 2015, SI 2015/315; and the Pollution Prevention and Control (Fees) (Miscellaneous Amendments and Other Provisions) Regulations 2015, SI 2015/1431 (amended by SI 2016/529). See also the Merchant Shipping (Boatmasters' Qualifications, Crew and Hours of Work) Regulations 2015, SI 2015/410.

5 As to measurement of tonnage see PARA 248 et seq.
6 Merchant Shipping Act 1995 s 302(2).
7 Merchant Shipping Act 1995 s 302(3). As to payments to be made into the Consolidated Fund under the Merchant Shipping Act 1995 see PARA 64. As to the Consolidated Fund generally see CONSTITUTIONAL AND ADMINISTRATIVE LAW vol 20 (2014) PARA 480.

**64. Payments to be made into the Consolidated Fund.** The following sums must be paid into the Consolidated Fund[1]:

(1)    all fees, charges and expenses payable in respect of the survey and measurement of ships[2];

(2)    any fees received by receivers of wrecks[3];

(3)    any sums received by the Secretary of State under the Merchant Shipping Act 1995 or which are, by any provision of it, required to be paid into the Consolidated Fund[4].

All such fees[5] must be paid at such time and in such manner as the Secretary of State directs[6].

1 Merchant Shipping Act 1995 s 305(1). As to the Consolidated Fund see CONSTITUTIONAL AND ADMINISTRATIVE LAW vol 20 (2014) PARA 480.
2 Merchant Shipping Act 1995 s 305(1)(a). As to the meaning of 'ship' see PARA 229. As to the survey and measurement of ships see PARA 276 et seq.
3 Merchant Shipping Act 1995 s 305(1)(b). As to receivers of wrecks see PARA 929.
4 Merchant Shipping Act 1995 s 305(1)(c).
5 Ie all fees mentioned in the Merchant Shipping Act 1995 s 305: see s 305(2).
6 Merchant Shipping Act 1995 s 305(2). As to the Secretary of State see PARA 36; and as to his power to give directions under the Merchant Shipping Act 1995 see PARA 39.

**65. Expenses charged on money provided by Parliament.** The following expenses and other amounts are payable out of money provided by Parliament:

(1)    the expenses incurred by the Secretary of State[1] under the Merchant Shipping Act 1995[2];

(2)    the salaries, pensions, gratuities and allowances of surveyors of ships[3], Departmental inspectors[4] and superintendents[5];

(3)    the sums required for the contribution from the United Kingdom[6] towards maintaining, in accordance with the Safety Convention[7], a service in the North Atlantic for the study and observation of ice and for the ice patrol[8];

(4)    the expenses of obtaining depositions, reports and returns respecting wrecks and casualties[9];

(5)    such sums as the Secretary of State may in his discretion think fit to pay in respect of claims on account of the proceeds of wreck[10];

(6)    the expenses incurred in respect of receivers of wrecks[11] and the performance of their duties[12];

(7)    such expenses as the Secretary of State directs[13] for:

    (a)    establishing and maintaining on the coasts of the United Kingdom proper lifeboats with the necessary crews and equipment[14];

    (b)    affording assistance towards the preservation of life and property in cases of shipwreck and distress at sea[15]; or

    (c)    rewarding the preservation of life in such cases[16];

(8)    any other amounts which are by virtue of any provision of the Merchant Shipping Act 1995 payable out of money provided by Parliament[17].

1 As to the Secretary of State see PARA 36.
2 Merchant Shipping Act 1995 s 304(1)(a).
3 As to the meaning of 'surveyor of ships' see PARA 46 note 13; and as to the meaning of 'ship' see PARA 229.
4 As to the meaning of 'Departmental inspector' see PARA 46 note 2.
5 Merchant Shipping Act 1995 s 304(1)(b). As to the meaning of 'superintendent' see PARA 61 note 1.
6 As to the meaning of 'United Kingdom' see PARA 16 note 3.

7   For these purposes, 'Safety Convention' means the International Convention for the Safety of Life at Sea 1974 (London, 1 November 1974 to 1 July 1975; TS 46 (1980); Cmnd 7874) (as to which see PARA 7): Merchant Shipping Act 1995 s 304(2).
8   Merchant Shipping Act 1995 s 304(1)(c).
9   Merchant Shipping Act 1995 s 304(1)(d). As to wrecks etc generally see PARAS 122 et seq, 923 et seq.
10  Merchant Shipping Act 1995 s 304(1)(e).
11  As to receivers of wrecks see PARA 929.
12  Merchant Shipping Act 1995 s 304(1)(f).
13  As to the Secretary of State's power to give directions under the Merchant Shipping Act 1995 see PARA 39.
14  Merchant Shipping Act 1995 s 304(1)(g)(i).
15  Merchant Shipping Act 1995 s 304(1)(g)(ii).
16  Merchant Shipping Act 1995 s 304(1)(g)(iii).
17  Merchant Shipping Act 1995 s 304(1)(h).

### (vii) Funding of Maritime Services

**66. In general.** Regulations made by the Secretary of State[1] under the Merchant Shipping Act 1995 in relation to the funding of maritime services[2] may make provision:

(1)     for the Secretary of State to impose charges in order to recover costs incurred by him in connection with his maritime functions[3];

(2)     for charges relating to expenses payable out of the General Lighthouse Fund[4] which may be recoverable otherwise than by the levying of general light dues[5];

(3)     with regard to ships[6] in respect of which charges may be imposed[7];

(4)     with regard to the persons by whom charges are to be paid[8].

Such regulations may impose a charge of a fixed amount or of an amount to be determined in accordance with the regulations, and may impose different charges in relation to ships of different descriptions or in different circumstances[9]. Supplementary provision is made giving powers to require such information as the collecting authority may reasonably require for the purposes of the regulations[10] and with respect to the collection and recovery of charges[11].

The legislative competence of the National Assembly for Wales does not extend to shipping generally, but it does have power to provide financial assistance for shipping services to, from or within Wales[12].

1   As to the Secretary of State see PARA 36.
2   Ie under the Merchant Shipping Act 1995 s 302A, Sch 11A (see PARA 67 et seq): see Sch 11A para 14 (Sch 11A added by the Merchant Shipping and Maritime Security Act 1997 s 13, Sch 2 para 2). Regulations under the Merchant Shipping Act 1995 Sch 11A must be made by the Secretary of State with the consent of the Treasury (Sch 11A para 16(1) (as so added)); and must not be made unless a draft of them has been laid before, and approved by a resolution of, the House of Commons (Sch 11A para 16(2) (as so added)). Such regulations may include such transitional, incidental or supplementary provision as appears to the Secretary of State to be necessary or appropriate: Sch 11A para 14 (as so added). However, at the date at which this volume states the law, no such regulations had been made. As to the Secretary of State's power to make subordinate legislation under the Merchant Shipping Act 1995 generally see PARA 39. As to the Treasury see CONSTITUTIONAL AND ADMINISTRATIVE LAW vol 20 (2014) PARA 262 et seq.
    Any sums received in consequence of regulations under Sch 11A must be paid into the Consolidated Fund: Sch 11A para 15 (as so added). As to payments to be made into the Consolidated Fund under the Merchant Shipping Act 1995 see PARA 64. As to the Consolidated Fund generally see CONSTITUTIONAL AND ADMINISTRATIVE LAW vol 20 (2014) PARA 480.
3   See the Merchant Shipping Act 1995 Sch 11A para 2; and PARA 67. As to the meaning of 'maritime functions' for these purposes see PARA 67.
4   As to the General Lighthouse Fund see PARA 1039 et seq.
5   See the Merchant Shipping Act 1995 Sch 11A paras 3, 12, 13; and PARA 68. For these purposes, 'general light dues' has the same meaning as in Pt VIII (ss 193–223) (as to which see PARA 1033): see Sch 11A para 1 (as added: see note 2).

6  As to the meaning of 'ship' see PARA 229.

7  See the Merchant Shipping Act 1995 Sch 11A para 4; and PARA 69.

8  See the Merchant Shipping Act 1995 Sch 11A para 5; and PARA 70.

9  See the Merchant Shipping Act 1995 Sch 11A para 6; and PARA 71.

10 See the Merchant Shipping Act 1995 Sch 11A para 7; and PARA 72. Supplementary provision is made in relation to the disclosure of information for the purpose of enabling or assisting the Secretary of State to perform his functions under the regulations: see Sch 11A para 8; and PARA 72.

11 See the Merchant Shipping Act 1995 Sch 11A paras 9, 10, 13; and PARAS 68, 73. Supplementary provision is made allowing distress to be levied and for the disposal of any ship, goods, equipment or other thing on which distress is levied in circumstances where the owner or master has failed to pay charges due: see Sch 11A para 11; and PARA 73.

12 See the Government of Wales Act 2006 s 108(3)–(5), Sch 7 para 10; and STATUTES AND LEGISLATIVE PROCESS vol 96 (2012) PARA 1000.

**67. Charges in respect of maritime matters.** Regulations made under the Merchant Shipping Act 1995 in relation to the funding of maritime services[1] may make provision imposing charges for the purpose of recovering the whole or a part of the costs incurred by the Secretary of State[2] in connection with his maritime functions[3]. For these purposes, 'maritime functions' means:

(1)     functions conferred by or under any provision of the Merchant Shipping Act 1995 (apart from the provisions relating to registration[4] and to lighthouse authorities)[5];

(2)     functions under any international agreement[6] relating to the safety of ships, to the prevention of pollution from ships, or to living and working conditions on board ships[7]; and

(3)     other functions relating to the promotion of the safety of ships[8].

1  Ie regulations under the Merchant Shipping Act 1995 s 302A, Sch 11A: see Sch 11A para 2(1) (Sch 11A added by the Merchant Shipping and Maritime Security Act 1997 s 13, Sch 2 para 2). As to the making of regulations under the Merchant Shipping Act 1995 Sch 11A see PARA 66; and as to further provision which may be made by such regulations see PARA 68 et seq. At the date at which this volume states the law, no such regulations had been made.

2  As to the Secretary of State see PARA 36.

3  Merchant Shipping Act 1995 Sch 11A para 2(1) (as added: see note 1).

4  Ie apart from the Merchant Shipping Act 1995 Pt II (ss 8–23) (registration) (as to which see PARA 237 et seq): see Sch 11A para 2(2)(a) (as added: see note 1).

5  Merchant Shipping Act 1995 Sch 11A para 2(2)(a) (as added: see note 1). The text refers to the provisions of Pt VIII (ss 193–223) (lighthouses) (as to which see PARA 1017 et seq): see Sch 11A para 2(2)(a) (as so added).

6  As to international conventions and other agreements see PARA 7 et seq.

7  Merchant Shipping Act 1995 Sch 11A para 2(2)(b) (as added: see note 1).

8  Merchant Shipping Act 1995 Sch 11A para 2(2)(c) (as added: see note 1).

**68. Charges relating to expenses payable out of the General Lighthouse Fund.** If:

(1)     an EU obligation[1]; or

(2)     any international agreement made between any three or more countries including the Republic of Ireland and ratified by the United Kingdom[2],

requires the United Kingdom to provide for any of the costs incurred by General Lighthouse Authorities[3] in respect of lighthouses, buoys and beacons[4] to be recovered otherwise than by means of the levying of general light dues[5], regulations made under the Merchant Shipping Act 1995 in relation to the funding of maritime services[6] may make provision imposing charges for the purposes of recovering all or any part of the costs required to be so recovered[7].

If such regulations make any such provision as to charges for expenses payable out of the General Lighthouse Fund[8], regulations may also[9]:

(a)     provide for payments which, apart from the regulations, would fall to be made out of the General Lighthouse Fund to be made by the Secretary of State[10] out of money provided by Parliament[11];

(b) provide for amounts which, apart from the regulations, would fall to be paid into the General Lighthouse Fund[12] to be paid by the Secretary of State into the Consolidated Fund[13];

(c) provide for the payment out of money provided by Parliament into the General Lighthouse Fund of amounts representing the whole or part of any charges imposed by such regulations[14]; and

(d) make such amendments, repeals or other modifications of any of the provisions of the Merchant Shipping Act 1995 relating to the General Lighthouse Fund or general light dues as appear to the Secretary of State to be necessary or expedient in consequence of, or in connection with, the provision made by virtue of the provisions allowing charges to be imposed by such regulations[15] or head (a), (b) or (c) above[16].

If such regulations confer on General Lighthouse Authorities functions relating to the collection and recovery of charges[17], regulations made in relation to the funding of maritime services[18] may also provide for the making by the Secretary of State to each general lighthouse authority out of money provided by Parliament of payments in respect of expenses incurred by that authority in connection with the collection or recovery of charges[19].

1 Merchant Shipping Act 1995 s 302A, Sch 11A para 3(1)(a) (Sch 11A added by the Merchant Shipping and Maritime Security Act 1997 s 13, Sch 2; Merchant Shipping Act 1995 Sch 11A para 3(1)(a) amended by SI 2011/1043).

2 Merchant Shipping Act 1995 Sch 11A para 3(1)(b) (as added: see note 1). As to the meaning of 'United Kingdom' see PARA 16 note 3. As to international conventions and other agreements see PARA 7 et seq.

3 For these purposes, 'general lighthouse authority' has the same meaning as in the Merchant Shipping Act 1995 Pt VIII (ss 193–223) (as to which see PARA 1017): see Sch 11A para 1 (as added: see note 1).

4 For these purposes, 'buoys and beacons' includes equipment which is intended as an aid to the navigation of ships and, subject to that, expressions used in the Merchant Shipping Act 1995 Sch 11A para 3 and in Pt VIII (see PARA 1017 et seq) have the same meaning as in Pt VIII: see Sch 11A para 3(2) (as added: see note 1). Accordingly, as to the meaning of 'lighthouse' see PARA 1017 note 1.

5 Ie in accordance with the Merchant Shipping Act 1995 s 205 (see PARA 1033), as it has effect on 19 March 1997: see Sch 11A para 3(1) (as added and amended: see note 1). As to the meaning of 'general light dues' for these purposes see PARA 66 note 5.

6 Ie regulations under the Merchant Shipping Act 1995 Sch 11A: see Sch 11A para 3(1) (as added and amended: see note 1). As to the making of regulations under the Merchant Shipping Act 1995 Sch 11A see PARA 66; and as to further provision which may be made by such regulations see PARAS 67, 69 et seq. At the date at which this volume states the law, no such regulations had been made.

7 Merchant Shipping Act 1995 Sch 11A para 3(1) (as added and amended: see note 1).

8 Ie if regulations under the Merchant Shipping Act 1995 Sch 11A make any provision by virtue of Sch 11A para 3 (see the text and notes 1–7): see Sch 11A para 12 (as added: see note 1). As to the General Lighthouse Fund see PARA 1039 et seq.

9 Merchant Shipping Act 1995 Sch 11A para 12 (as added: see note 1).

10 As to the Secretary of State see PARA 36.

11 Merchant Shipping Act 1995 Sch 11A para 12(a) (as added: see note 1).

12 Ie other than general light dues levied in accordance with the Merchant Shipping Act 1995 s 205 (see PARA 1033): see Sch 11A para 12(b) (as added: see note 1).

13 Merchant Shipping Act 1995 Sch 11A para 12(b) (as added: see note 1). As to payments to be made into the Consolidated Fund under the Merchant Shipping Act 1995 see PARA 64. As to the Consolidated Fund generally see CONSTITUTIONAL AND ADMINISTRATIVE LAW vol 20 (2014) PARA 480.

14 Merchant Shipping Act 1995 Sch 11A para 12(c) (as added: see note 1). The text refers to charges imposed by regulations made under Sch 11A by virtue of Sch 11A para 3 (see the text and notes 1–7): see Sch 11A para 12(c) (as so added).

15 Ie charges imposed by regulations made under the Merchant Shipping Act 1995 Sch 11A by virtue of Sch 11A para 3 (see the text and notes 1–7): see Sch 11A para 12(d) (as added: see note 1).

16 Merchant Shipping Act 1995 Sch 11A para 12(d) (as added: see note 1).

17 Ie if regulations under the Merchant Shipping Act 1995 Sch 11A make any provision by virtue of Sch 11A para 9(2) (see PARA 73): see Sch 11A para 13 (as added: see note 1).

18 Ie regulations under the Merchant Shipping Act 1995 Sch 11A: see Sch 11A para 13 (as added: see note 1).

19 Merchant Shipping Act 1995 Sch 11A para 13 (as added: see note 1).

**69. Ships in respect of which charges may be imposed.** Regulations made under the Merchant Shipping Act 1995 in relation to the funding of maritime services[1] may not require a charge to be paid except in respect of:

    (1)     a ship[2] which has entered a port[3] in the United Kingdom[4];

    (2)     a ship which is anchored off a port in the United Kingdom[5]; or

    (3)     a ship which is anchored within 500 metres of an installation[6] which is in United Kingdom waters or a part of the sea specified[7] for purposes which relate to the protection and preservation of the marine environment[8].

Nothing in any such regulations is to be construed as requiring a charge to be paid in respect of a qualifying foreign ship[9] which is exercising the right of innocent passage[10], or the right of transit passage[11] through straits used for international navigation[12], except to the extent that international law allows such a charge to be imposed[13].

Subject to these restrictions[14], the regulations may impose a charge in respect of such description of ship as may be prescribed[15]. In particular:

    (a)     regulations may impose a charge in respect of a ship even though no service has been provided or function exercised in the case of that ship[16]; and

    (b)     regulations may provide that no charge is imposed in respect of a ship which does not exceed a prescribed tonnage or does not exceed a prescribed length[17].

1 Ie regulations under the Merchant Shipping Act 1995 s 302A, Sch 11A: see Sch 11A para 4(1) (Sch 11A added by the Merchant Shipping and Maritime Security Act 1997 s 13, Sch 2 para 2). As to the making of regulations under the Merchant Shipping Act 1995 Sch 11A see PARA 66; and as to further provision which may be made by such regulations see PARAS 67, 68, 70 et seq. At the date at which this volume states the law, no such regulations had been made.

2 As to the meaning of 'ship' see PARA 229.

3 As to the meaning of 'port' see PARA 46 note 12.

4 Merchant Shipping Act 1995 Sch 11A para 4(1)(a) (as added: see note 1). As to the meaning of 'United Kingdom' see PARA 16 note 3.

    For these purposes, the circumstances in which a ship is to be regarded as entering a port in the United Kingdom include circumstances in which the ship enters any United Kingdom waters which are regulated or managed by a harbour authority: see Sch 11A para 4(5) (as so added). In the Merchant Shipping Act 1995, unless the context otherwise requires, 'harbour authority' means, in relation to a harbour, the person who is the statutory harbour authority for the harbour or (if there is no statutory harbour authority for the harbour) the person (if any) who is the proprietor of the harbour or who is entrusted with the function of managing, maintaining or improving the harbour: s 313(1) (definition substituted by the Merchant Shipping and Maritime Security Act 1997 s 29(1), Sch 6 para 19(2)(a)). 'Statutory harbour authority' means, in relation to Great Britain, a harbour authority within the meaning of the Harbours Act 1964 (see PORTS AND HARBOURS vol 85 (2012) PARA 20): Merchant Shipping Act 1995 s 313(1) (definition substituted by the Merchant Shipping and Maritime Security Act 1997 Sch 6 para 19(2)(d)). As to the meaning of 'Great Britain' see PARA 16 note 3; as to the meaning of 'harbour' see PARA 49 note 5; and as to the meaning of 'United Kingdom waters' see PARA 48 note 10.

5 Merchant Shipping Act 1995 Sch 11A para 4(1)(b) (as added: see note 1).

6 For these purposes, 'installation' means an installation which is an offshore installation within the meaning of the Mineral Workings (Offshore Installations) Act 1971 (see ENERGY AND CLIMATE CHANGE vol 44 (2011) PARA 1078 et seq) or is to be taken to be an installation for the purposes of the Petroleum Act 1987 ss 21–23 (safety zones) (see ENERGY AND CLIMATE CHANGE vol 44 (2011) PARA 1084): see the Merchant Shipping Act 1995 Sch 11A para 4(6) (as added: see note 1).

7  Ie a part of the sea specified by virtue of the Merchant Shipping Act 1995 s 129(2)(b) (see ENVIRONMENTAL QUALITY AND PUBLIC HEALTH vol 45 (2010) PARA 362): see Sch 11A para 4(1)(c) (as added: see note 1).

8  Merchant Shipping Act 1995 Sch 11A para 4(1)(c) (as added: see note 1).

9  As to the meaning of 'qualifying foreign ship' see PARA 18.

10  For these purposes, 'right of innocent passage' is to be construed in accordance with the United Nations Convention on the Law of the Sea 1982 (Montego Bay, 10 December 1982 to 9 December 1984; TS 3 Misc 11 (1983); Cmnd 8941) (as to which see PARA 9): see the Merchant Shipping Act 1995 s 313(2A) (added by the Merchant Shipping and Maritime Security Act 1997 Sch 6 para 19(1), (3)). As to innocent passage generally see INTERNATIONAL RELATIONS LAW vol 61 (2010) PARA 133.

11  For these purposes, 'right of transit passage' is to be construed in accordance with the United Nations Convention on the Law of the Sea 1982 (as to which see note 9): see the Merchant Shipping Act 1995 s 313(2A) (as added: see note 10). As to transit passage generally see INTERNATIONAL RELATIONS LAW vol 61 (2010) PARA 143.

12  For these purposes, 'straits used for international navigation' is to be construed in accordance with the United Nations Convention on the Law of the Sea 1982 (see note 10): see the Merchant Shipping Act 1995 s 313(2A) (as added: see note 10).

13  Merchant Shipping Act 1995 Sch 11A para 4(2) (as added: see note 1).

14  Ie subject to the Merchant Shipping Act 1995 Sch 11A para 4(1), (2) (see the text and notes 1–13): see Sch 11A para 4(3) (as added: see note 1).

15  Merchant Shipping Act 1995 Sch 11A para 4(3) (as added: see note 1). For these purposes, 'prescribe' means prescribe by regulations: see Sch 11A para 1 (as so added).

16  Merchant Shipping Act 1995 Sch 11A para 4(4)(a) (as added: see note 1).

17  Merchant Shipping Act 1995 Sch 11A para 4(4)(b) (as added: see note 1).

**70. Persons by whom charges are to be paid.** Regulations made under the Merchant Shipping Act 1995 in relation to the funding of maritime services[1] may not require a charge to be paid in respect of a ship[2] by a person who is not:

(1)      the owner of the ship[3];

(2)      the person registered[4] as the owner of the ship[5];

(3)      the operator of the ship[6];

(4)      the manager of the ship[7];

(5)      the charterer of the ship[8]; or

(6)      the agent of a person mentioned in any of heads (1) to (5) above[9].

Subject to these restrictions[10], charges imposed by the regulations are payable by such persons as may be prescribed[11].

1  Ie regulations under the Merchant Shipping Act 1995 s 302A, Sch 11A: see Sch 11A para 5(1) (Sch 11A added by the Merchant Shipping and Maritime Security Act 1997 s 13, Sch 2 para 2). As to the making of regulations under the Merchant Shipping Act 1995 Sch 11A see PARA 66; and as to further provision which may be made by such regulations see PARAS 67–69, 71 et seq. At the date at which this volume states the law, no such regulations had been made.

2  As to the meaning of 'ship' see PARA 229.

3  Merchant Shipping Act 1995 Sch 11A para 5(1)(a) (as added: see note 1).

4  As to the meaning of 'registered' see PARA 254 note 2.

5  Merchant Shipping Act 1995 Sch 11A para 5(1)(b) (as added: see note 1).

6  Merchant Shipping Act 1995 Sch 11A para 5(1)(c) (as added: see note 1).

7  Merchant Shipping Act 1995 Sch 11A para 5(1)(d) (as added: see note 1).

8  Merchant Shipping Act 1995 Sch 11A para 5(1)(e) (as added: see note 1).

9  Merchant Shipping Act 1995 Sch 11A para 5(1)(f) (as added: see note 1).

10  Ie subject to the Merchant Shipping Act 1995 Sch 11A para 5(1) (see the text and notes 1–9): see Sch 11A para 5(2) (as added: see note 1).

11  Merchant Shipping Act 1995 Sch 11A para 5(2) (as added: see note 1). For these purposes, 'prescribe' means prescribe by regulations: see Sch 11A para 1 (as so added).

**71. Amount of charges.** Regulations made under the Merchant Shipping Act 1995 in relation to the funding of maritime services[1] may impose a charge of a fixed amount or of an amount determined in accordance with the regulations, and may impose different charges in relation to ships[2] of different descriptions or in different circumstances[3].

Such regulations may in particular impose in respect of a ship a charge whose amount depends on[4]:

(1)　　whether action has been or is being taken with a view to enforcing international shipping standards in the case of that ship or with a view to preventing, reducing or minimising the effects of pollution from that ship[5], and (if any such action has been or is being so taken) the nature of the action[6];

(2)　　the tonnage or length of the ship[7].

1　Ie regulations under the Merchant Shipping Act 1995 s 302A, Sch 11A: see Sch 11A para 6(1) (Sch 11A added by the Merchant Shipping and Maritime Security Act 1997 s 13, Sch 2 para 2). As to the making of regulations under the Merchant Shipping Act 1995 Sch 11A see PARA 66; and as to further provision which may be made by such regulations see PARAS 67–70, 72 et seq. At the date at which this volume states the law, no such regulations had been made.
2　As to the meaning of 'ship' see PARA 229.
3　Merchant Shipping Act 1995 Sch 11A para 6(1) (as added: see note 1).
4　Merchant Shipping Act 1995 Sch 11A para 6(2), (3) (as added: see note 1).
5　Merchant Shipping Act 1995 Sch 11A para 6(2)(a) (as added: see note 1).
6　Merchant Shipping Act 1995 Sch 11A para 6(2)(b) (as added: see note 1).
7　Merchant Shipping Act 1995 Sch 11A para 6(3) (as added: see note 1).

## 72. Powers to require information and to disclose information.
Regulations made under the Merchant Shipping Act 1995 in relation to the funding of maritime services[1] may include provision requiring any relevant authority[2] or any person who is or may be liable to pay charges under the regulations in respect of a ship[3] to provide any collecting authority[4] with such information as the collecting authority may reasonably require for the purposes of the regulations[5].

No obligation as to secrecy or other restriction on the disclosure of information, whether imposed by statute or otherwise, prevents a Minister of the Crown[6] or a Northern Ireland department from disclosing:

(1)　　to the Secretary of State[7]; or

(2)　　to a person appointed by the Secretary of State to collect charges under regulations so made in relation to the funding of maritime services[8],

information for the purpose of enabling or assisting the Secretary of State to perform his functions under the regulations[9]. Information so obtained by any person must not be disclosed by him to any other person except where the disclosure is made either to a person falling within head (1) or head (2) above or for the purposes of any legal proceedings arising out of the regulations[10].

1　Ie regulations under the Merchant Shipping Act 1995 s 302A, Sch 11A: see Sch 11A para 7(1) (Sch 11A added by the Merchant Shipping and Maritime Security Act 1997 s 13, Sch 2 para 2). As to the making of regulations under the Merchant Shipping Act 1995 Sch 11A see PARA 66; and as to further provision which may be made by such regulations see PARAS 67–71, 73 et seq. At the date at which this volume states the law, no such regulations had been made.
2　For these purposes, 'relevant authority' means a harbour authority, the Commissioners of Revenue and Customs and a conservancy authority: see the Merchant Shipping Act 1995 Sch 11A para 7(2) (Sch 11A as added (see note 1); Sch 11A para 7(2) amended by virtue of the Commissioners for Revenue and Customs Act 2005 s 50(1), (2), (7)). In the Merchant Shipping Act 1995, unless the context otherwise requires, 'conservancy authority' includes all persons entrusted with the function of conserving, maintaining or improving the navigation of a tidal water, as defined in s 255 (see PARA 923 note 6): s 313(1). As to the meaning of 'harbour authority' see PARA 69 note 4. As to the Commissioners for Revenue and Customs see CUSTOMS AND EXCISE vol 31 (2012) PARA 921 et seq.
3　As to the meaning of 'ship' see PARA 229.
4　For these purposes, 'collecting authority' means the Secretary of State, a Departmental officer and a general lighthouse authority: see the Merchant Shipping Act 1995 Sch 11A para 7(2) (as added:

see note 1). As to the meaning of 'departmental officer' see PARA 47 note 11; and as to the meaning of 'general lighthouse authority' for these purposes see PARA 68 note 3. As to the Secretary of State see PARA 36.

5 Merchant Shipping Act 1995 Sch 11A para 7(1) (as added: see note 1).
6 In the Merchant Shipping Act 1995, unless the context otherwise requires, 'Minister of the Crown' has the same meaning as in the Ministers of the Crown Act 1975 (see CONSTITUTIONAL AND ADMINISTRATIVE LAW vol 20 (2014) PARA 162): Merchant Shipping Act 1995 s 313(1) (definition added by the Merchant Shipping and Maritime Security Act 1997 s 29(1), Sch 6 para 19(1), (2)(b)).
7 Merchant Shipping Act 1995 Sch 11A para 8(1)(a) (as added: see note 1).
8 Merchant Shipping Act 1995 Sch 11A para 8(1)(b) (as added: see note 1). The text refers to regulations made under Sch 11A (see note 1): see Sch 11A para 8(1)(b) (as so added).
9 Merchant Shipping Act 1995 Sch 11A para 8(1) (as added: see note 1).
10 Merchant Shipping Act 1995 Sch 11A para 8(2) (as added: see note 1).

**73. Collection and recovery etc.** Regulations made under the Merchant Shipping Act 1995 in relation to the funding of maritime services[1] may make provision:

(1)     with respect to the collection and recovery of charges, and for charges which fall due under the regulations but which are not paid to carry interest[2];

(2)     for appeals against decisions that charges are due in respect of ships[3];

(3)     for authorising distress to be levied on any ship in respect of which the owner or master[4] has failed to pay charges due under the regulations, and on any goods, equipment or other thing belonging to, or on board, the ship[5];

(4)     for the disposal of any ship, goods, equipment or other thing on which distress is levied in accordance with the regulations[6]; and

(5)     for the imposition and recovery of costs, charges, expenses and fees in connection with anything done under regulations made by virtue of head (3) or (4) above[7].

1 Ie regulations under the Merchant Shipping Act 1995 s 302A, Sch 11A: see Sch 11A para 9(1) (Sch 11A added by the Merchant Shipping and Maritime Security Act 1997 s 13, Sch 2 para 2). As to the making of regulations under the Merchant Shipping Act 1995 Sch 11A see PARA 66; and as to further provision which may be made by such regulations see PARAS 67–72. At the date at which this volume states the law, no such regulations had been made.
2 Merchant Shipping Act 1995 Sch 11A para 9(1) (as added: see note 1). Regulations so made by virtue of Sch 11A para 9(1) may in particular confer on general lighthouse authorities functions relating to the collection and recovery of charges: Sch 11A para 9(2) (as so added). If regulations under the Merchant Shipping Act 1995 Sch 11A make any such provision, such regulations may also provide for the making by the Secretary of State to each general lighthouse authority out of money provided by Parliament of payments in respect of expenses incurred by that authority in connection with the collection or recovery of charges: see Sch 11A para 13; and PARa 68. As to the meaning of 'general lighthouse authority' for these purposes see PARA 68 note 3. As to the Secretary of State see PARA 36.
3 Merchant Shipping Act 1995 Sch 11A para 10 (as added: see note 1). As to the meaning of 'ship' see PARA 229.
4 As to the meaning of 'master' see PARA 444 note 1.
5 Merchant Shipping Act 1995 Sch 11A para 11(a) (as added: see note 1).
6 Merchant Shipping Act 1995 Sch 11A para 11(b) (as added: see note 1).
7 Merchant Shipping Act 1995 Sch 11A para 11(c) (as added: see note 1).

### (viii) Service of Documents under the Merchant Shipping Act 1995

**74. Service of documents.** Any document authorised or required to be served on any person may be served on that person by delivering it to him, by leaving it at his proper address or by sending it by post to him at his proper address[1].

Any such document required to be served on the master[2] of a ship[3] may be served:

(1)		where there is a master, by leaving it for him on board the ship with the person appearing to be in command or charge of the ship[4];

(2)		where there is no master, on the managing owner of the ship or, if there is no managing owner, on any agent of the owner or, where no such agent is known or can be found, by leaving a copy of the document fixed to the mast of the ship[5].

Any document authorised or required to be served on any person may:

(a)		in the case of a body corporate, be served on the secretary or clerk of that body[6];

(b)		in the case of a partnership, be served on a partner or a person having the control or management of the partnership business[7].

Any notice authorised or required by or under the Merchant Shipping Act 1995 provisions relating to the registration of ships in the United Kingdom[8] to be served on the Secretary of State[9] may be served by post[10].

Any notice authorised by the provisions relating to improvement notices and prohibition notices[11] to be given to an inspector[12] may be given by delivering it to him or by leaving it at, or sending it by post to, his office[13].

Any document authorised or required by or under any enactment to be served on the registered[14] owner of a United Kingdom ship[15] is treated as duly served on him if served on such persons, in such circumstances and by such method, as may be specified in registration regulations[16].

The proper address of any person on whom any document is to be served is[17] his last known address[18], except that:

(i)		in the case of a body corporate or its secretary or clerk, it is the address of the registered or principal office of that body[19];

(ii)		in the case of a partnership or a person having the control or management of the partnership business, it is the principal office of the partnership[20];

and, for these purposes, the principal office of a company registered outside the United Kingdom or of a partnership carrying on business outside the United Kingdom is its principal office in the United Kingdom[21].

If the person to be served with any notice has, whether in pursuance of the registration regulations or otherwise, specified an address in the United Kingdom other than his proper address[22] as the one at which he or someone on his behalf will accept notices of the same description as that notice, that address is also treated[23] as his proper address[24].

A letter containing a notice to be served on any person[25] or a notice authorised or required to be served under registration regulations on a representative person[26] is deemed[27] to be properly addressed if it is addressed to that person at the address for the time being recorded in relation to him in the register[28]; and a letter containing any other notice under registration regulations is deemed to be properly addressed if it is addressed to the last known address of the person to be served, whether of his residence or of a place where he carries on business[29].

1	Merchant Shipping Act 1995 s 291(1).
2	As to the meaning of 'master' see PARA 444 note 1.
3	As to the meaning of 'ship' see PARA 229.
4	Merchant Shipping Act 1995 s 291(2)(a).
5	Merchant Shipping Act 1995 s 291(2)(b).
6	Merchant Shipping Act 1995 s 291(3)(a).
7	Merchant Shipping Act 1995 s 291(3)(b).
8	Ie the Merchant Shipping Act 1995 Pt II (ss 8–23) (see PARA 237 et seq): see s 291(4). As to the meaning of 'United Kingdom' see PARA 16 note 3.
9	As to the Secretary of State see PARA 36.

10 Merchant Shipping Act 1995 s 291(4).
11 Ie authorised by the Merchant Shipping Act 1995 s 261 (see PARA 51), s 262 (see PARA 52), s 263 (see PARA 53) or s 264 (see PARA 54): see s 291(5).
12 As to the powers of inspectors appointed under the Merchant Shipping Act 1995 s 256 see PARA 46.
13 Merchant Shipping Act 1995 s 291(5).
14 As to the meaning of 'registered' for these purposes see PARA 254 note 2.
15 As to the meaning of 'United Kingdom ship' see PARA 230.
16 Merchant Shipping Act 1995 s 291(6). As to the meaning of 'registration regulations' see PARA 247.
17 Ie for the purposes of the Merchant Shipping Act 1995 s 291 and of the Interpretation Act 1978 s 7 (service of documents by post) (see STATUTES AND LEGISLATIVE PROCESS vol 96 (2012) PARA 1219) in its application to the Merchant Shipping Act 1995 s 291: see s 291(7).
18 Merchant Shipping Act 1995 s 291(7).
19 Merchant Shipping Act 1995 s 291(7)(a).
20 Merchant Shipping Act 1995 s 291(7)(b).
21 Merchant Shipping Act 1995 s 291(7).
22 Ie within the meaning of the Merchant Shipping Act 1995 s 291(7) (see the text and notes 17–21): see s 291(8).
23 Ie for the purposes of the Merchant Shipping Act 1995 s 291 and of the Interpretation Act 1978 s 7: see the Merchant Shipping Act 1995 s 291(8).
24 Merchant Shipping Act 1995 s 291(8).
25 Ie under the Merchant Shipping Act 1995 s 291(6) (see the text and notes 14–16): see s 291(9).
26 Ie within the meaning of the registration regulations (see PARA 267): see s 291(9).
27 Ie for the purposes of the Interpretation Act 1978 s 7: see the Merchant Shipping Act 1995 s 291(9).
28 Merchant Shipping Act 1995 s 291(9). As to the meaning of 'register' see PARA 254 note 2.
29 Merchant Shipping Act 1995 s 291(9).

# (4) SHIPPING AND TRADING INTERESTS

## (i) Protection of Shipping etc Interests from Foreign Action

**75. Power to regulate the provision of shipping services in the event of foreign action.** The Secretary of State[1] may exercise his powers to regulate the provision of shipping services[2] if he is satisfied that:

(1)      a foreign government[3]; or
(2)      persons purporting to exercise governing authority over any territory outside the United Kingdom[4]; or
(3)      any agency or authority of a foreign government or of such persons[5],

has adopted, or proposes to adopt, measures or practices concerning or affecting any shipping services[6] which:

(a)      are damaging or threaten to damage the shipping or trading interests of the United Kingdom[7]; or
(b)      are damaging or threaten to damage the shipping or trading interests of another state[8],

and if, in the latter case, the Secretary of State is satisfied that such action[9] would be in fulfilment of the obligations of the United Kingdom to that other state or would be appropriate in view of any arrangements made between Her Majesty's government and the government of that other state[10].

The Secretary of State may by order[11] make provision for requiring persons in the United Kingdom carrying on any trade or business to provide the Secretary of State with all such information as he may require for the purpose of enabling him to determine what further action so to take[12] and to ensure compliance with any orders or directions so made or given[13].

The Secretary of State may by order (a 'protective order') provide for[14]:

(i)     regulating the provision of any shipping services and the rates, fares or other amounts which may or must be charged for providing those services[15];

(ii)    regulating[16] the admission and departure of ships to and from the United Kingdom ports[17], the nature of the shipping services they may be used to provide (whether by reference to the cargoes or passengers they may carry or otherwise)[18], and the loading or unloading of cargoes, the embarkation or disembarkation of passengers, or the doing of other things in connection with the provision of any shipping services[19];

(iii)   regulating the making and implementation of agreements (including charterparties) whose subject matter relates directly or indirectly to the provision of any shipping services, and requiring such agreements to be subject to the Secretary of State's approval in such cases as he may specify[20];

(iv)    imposing charges in respect of ships which enter United Kingdom ports in connection with the provision of any shipping services[21];

(v)     imposing, in pursuance of any EU obligation, such tax or duty payable by such persons and in such circumstances as the Secretary of State may specify[22].

Such an order may authorise the Secretary of State to give directions to any person for the purposes of the order[23].

Any order or direction so made or given[24] may be either general or special, and may be subject to such conditions or exceptions as the Secretary of State specifies (including conditions and exceptions operating by reference to the giving or withholding of his approval for any course of action)[25]; and may be in terms that require compliance either generally or only in specified cases[26].

A recital in such an order[27] that the persons who have adopted, or propose to adopt, the measures or practices in question are such persons as are mentioned in head (1), (2), or (3) above is conclusive[28].

A protective order made under either head (iv) or head (v) above is referred to as a 'charging order'[29]; and a charging order may[30]:

(A)    apply to ships of any description specified in the order, and may apply in particular to ships registered in a specified country, or to ships carrying goods or cargoes of a specified description or providing any other specified shipping services[31];

(B)    contain such provisions as appear to the Secretary of State expedient to enable the Commissioners for Revenue and Customs to collect any charge, tax or duty imposed by the order[32]; and

(C)    apply, subject to any modifications or exceptions specified in the order, any of the enactments for the time being in force relating to duties, whether for revenue or customs, chargeable on goods imported into the United Kingdom[33].

Any charge, tax or duty imposed by a charging order may be a fixed amount or an amount depending on the tonnage of the ship and is payable to the Secretary of State[34]. Any sum received by the Secretary of State must be paid into the Consolidated Fund[35].

A charging order is not to be made except with the consent of the Treasury[36].

1   As to the Secretary of State see PARA 36.
2   Ie the powers conferred by the Shipping and Trading Interests (Protection) Act 1995 s 1: see s 1(1). As to the meaning of 'shipping services' see note 6.

3 Shipping and Trading Interests (Protection) Act 1995 s 1(1)(a). For these purposes, 'foreign government' means the government of any state other than the United Kingdom: s 1(9)(a). As to the meaning of 'United Kingdom' see PARA 16 note 3.

4 Shipping and Trading Interests (Protection) Act 1995 s 1(1)(b). See note 5.

5 Shipping and Trading Interests (Protection) Act 1995 s 1(1)(c). For these purposes, references to an agency or authority of a foreign government, or of such persons as are mentioned in s 1(1)(b) (see head (2) in the text), include references to any undertaking appearing to the Secretary of State to be, or to be acting on behalf of, an undertaking which is in effect owned or controlled, directly or indirectly, by a state other than, or by a territory outside, the United Kingdom: s 1(9)(b).

6 For these purposes, 'shipping services' means services provided by means of ships, and includes the carriage of goods or passengers at sea, cable laying, dredging and services provided by offshore support vessels: Shipping and Trading Interests (Protection) Act 1995 s 1(9)(d). For these purposes, 'ship' includes every description of vessel used in navigation: see the Merchant Shipping Act 1995 s 313(1); definition applied by virtue of the Shipping and Trading Interests (Protection) Act 1995 s 9(2). For the purposes of s 1 only, references to ships are to ships of any registration: s 1(9)(e).

7 Shipping and Trading Interests (Protection) Act 1995 s 1(1)(i). In a case falling within s 1(1)(i), a protective order (as to which see the text and notes 14–23) must specify the measures or practices which in the opinion of the Secretary of State are damaging or threaten to damage shipping or trading interests of the United Kingdom: s 1(4). As to the enforcement of such orders see PARA 1180.

8 Shipping and Trading Interests (Protection) Act 1995 s 1(1)(ii).

9 Ie action under the Shipping and Trading Interests (Protection) Act 1995 s 1: see s 1(1).

10 Shipping and Trading Interests (Protection) Act 1995 s 1(1).

11 The power to make an order under the Shipping and Trading Interests (Protection) Act 1995 s 1 is exercisable by statutory instrument (s 1(7)); but, before the Secretary of State makes such an order, he must consult such representatives of the shipping or trading interests of the United Kingdom, and such other persons, as appear to him appropriate (s 1(8)). As to Parliamentary control of such orders see PARA 76. At the date at which this volume states the law, no such order had been made. See note 7.

12 Shipping and Trading Interests (Protection) Act 1995 s 1(2)(a). The text refers to further action to be taken under s 1: see s 1(2)(a).

13 Shipping and Trading Interests (Protection) Act 1995 s 1(2)(b). The text refers to orders or directions made or given under s 1: see s 1(2)(b). As to orders which may authorise the Secretary of State to give directions under s 1 to any person for the purposes of the order see the text and note 23.

An order made under s 1 with the consent of the Commissioners for Revenue and Customs may provide for the enforcement and execution of any order or direction under s 1 by officers of Revenue and Customs: s 3(1) (amended by virtue of the Commissioners for Revenue and Customs Act 2005 s 50(1), (2), (7)). Officers of Revenue and Customs acting under any provision made under the Shipping and Trading Interests (Protection) Act 1995 s 3(1) have power to enter any premises or ship: s 3(2) (amended by virtue of the Commissioners for Revenue and Customs Act 2005 s 50(1), (2), (7)). The Customs and Excise Management Act 1979 s 65 (power to refuse or cancel clearance of a ship or an aircraft: see CUSTOMS AND EXCISE vol 31 (2012) PARA 1021) applies as if the Shipping and Trading Interests (Protection) Act 1995 s 1, s 2 (as to which see the text and notes 30–37) and s 3 were contained in the Customs and Excise Management Act 1979: Shipping and Trading Interests (Protection) Act 1995 s 3(3). As to the Commissioners for Revenue and Customs see CUSTOMS AND EXCISE vol 31 (2012) PARA 921 et seq.

14 Shipping and Trading Interests (Protection) Act 1995 s 1(3). In the Shipping and Trading Interests (Protection) Act 1995, 'protective order' has the meaning given by s 1(3): see s 9(2).

15 Shipping and Trading Interests (Protection) Act 1995 s 1(3)(a).

16 For these purposes, 'regulating', except in relation to rates, fares or other amounts which may or must be charged as mentioned in the Shipping and Trading Interests (Protection) Act 1995 s 1(3)(a) (see head (i) in the text), includes imposing a prohibition: see s 1(3).

17 Shipping and Trading Interests (Protection) Act 1995 s 1(3)(b)(i). For these purposes, 'port' includes place: see the Merchant Shipping Act 1995 s 313(1); definition applied by virtue of the Shipping and Trading Interests (Protection) Act 1995 s 9(2). For the purposes of s 1 only, 'port' includes an offshore terminal; and references to entering or leaving a port include references to using or ceasing to use an offshore terminal: s 1(9)(c).

18 Shipping and Trading Interests (Protection) Act 1995 s 1(3)(b)(ii).

19 Shipping and Trading Interests (Protection) Act 1995 s 1(3)(b)(iii).

20 Shipping and Trading Interests (Protection) Act 1995 s 1(3)(c).

21 Shipping and Trading Interests (Protection) Act 1995 s 1(3)(d). See the text and notes 29–36.

22  Shipping and Trading Interests (Protection) Act 1995 s 1(3)(e) (amended by SI 2011/1043). See the text and notes 29–36.
23  Shipping and Trading Interests (Protection) Act 1995 s 1(5). Any power to give directions conferred by the Shipping and Trading Interests (Protection) Act 1995 includes power to vary or revoke directions so given: s 9(3).
24  Ie any order or direction made or given under the Shipping and Trading Interests (Protection) Act 1995 s 1: see s 1(6).
25  Shipping and Trading Interests (Protection) Act 1995 s 1(6)(a).
26  Shipping and Trading Interests (Protection) Act 1995 s 1(6)(b).
27  Ie an order under the Shipping and Trading Interests (Protection) Act 1995 s 1: see s 1(10).
28  Shipping and Trading Interests (Protection) Act 1995 s 1(10).
29  Shipping and Trading Interests (Protection) Act 1995 s 2(1).
30  Ie without prejudice to the Shipping and Trading Interests (Protection) Act 1995 s 1(6) (see the text and notes 24–26): see s 2(3).
31  Shipping and Trading Interests (Protection) Act 1995 s 2(3)(a).
32  Shipping and Trading Interests (Protection) Act 1995 s 2(3)(b) (amended by virtue of the Commissioners for Revenue and Customs Act 2005 s 50(1), (2), (7)).
33  Shipping and Trading Interests (Protection) Act 1995 s 2(3)(c).
34  Shipping and Trading Interests (Protection) Act 1995 s 2(4). However, no charging order may authorise the Secretary of State to give directions to any person for the purpose of recovering any charge, tax or duty: s 2(2).
35  Shipping and Trading Interests (Protection) Act 1995 s 2(6). As to the Consolidated Fund generally see CONSTITUTIONAL AND ADMINISTRATIVE LAW vol 20 (2014) PARA 480.
36  Shipping and Trading Interests (Protection) Act 1995 s 2(5). As to the Treasury see CONSTITUTIONAL AND ADMINISTRATIVE LAW vol 20 (2014) PARA 262 et seq.

**76.  Parliamentary control of orders to regulate the provision of shipping services in the event of foreign action.** No protective order[1] may be made unless a draft of it has been approved by resolution of each House of Parliament or unless it is declared in the order that it appears to the Secretary of State[2] that by reason of urgency it is necessary to make the order without a draft having been so approved[3]. A protective order made without a draft having been approved by resolution of each House of Parliament ceases to have effect at the expiration of a period of 28 days beginning with the date on which it was made[4] unless before the expiration of that period it has been approved by resolution of each House of Parliament, but without prejudice to anything previously done, or to the making of a new order[5]. However, these restrictions[6] do not apply to a protective order which is made for the purpose only of implementing any EU obligation[7].

An order to regulate the provision of shipping services in the event of foreign action[8] which is not a protective order is subject to annulment in pursuance of a resolution of either House of Parliament[9]. If such an order recites that it is made for the purpose only of implementing any EU obligation[10], or that it is not a protective order, the recital is conclusive[11].

1   As to the meaning of 'protective order' see PARA 75.
2   As to the Secretary of State see PARA 36.
3   Shipping and Trading Interests (Protection) Act 1995 s 4(1).
4   In reckoning for the purposes of the Shipping and Trading Interests (Protection) Act 1995 s 4(2), any period of 28 days, no account is to be taken of any period during which Parliament is dissolved or prorogued or during which both Houses are adjourned for more than four days: see s 4(2).
5   Shipping and Trading Interests (Protection) Act 1995 s 4(2).
6   Ie the provisions of the Shipping and Trading Interests (Protection) Act 1995 s 4(1), (2) (see the text and notes 1–5): see s 4(3) (amended by SI 2011/1043).
7   Shipping and Trading Interests (Protection) Act 1995 s 4(3) (amended by SI 2011/1043).
8   Ie under the Shipping and Trading Interests (Protection) Act 1995 s 1 (see PARA 75): see s 4(4). As to the meaning of 'shipping services' for these purposes see PARA 75 note 6.
9   Shipping and Trading Interests (Protection) Act 1995 s 4(4).
10  Ie recites that it is made as mentioned in the Shipping and Trading Interests (Protection) Act 1995 s 4(3) (see the text and notes 6–7): see s 4(5).
11  Shipping and Trading Interests (Protection) Act 1995 s 4(5).

## (ii) Protection of Coastal Shipping Services

**77. Power to prohibit provision of coastal shipping services which are not British-based.** The Secretary of State[1] may by order[2] provide for the provision of the following shipping services[3] to be prohibited, except where such services are provided from one or more permanent places of business maintained in the British Islands[4]:

(1) the carriage of goods or passengers by sea between ports[5] in the United Kingdom[6] or between a port in the United Kingdom and an offshore installation[7] in United Kingdom controlled waters[8] or between offshore installations in United Kingdom controlled waters[9];

(2) the carriage of passengers by sea on voyages or excursions beginning and ending at the same port in the United Kingdom, other than voyages or excursions which involve calling at any port or ports outside the British Islands, whether passengers disembark there or not[10]; or

(3) shipping services, other than the carriage of goods or passengers by sea, which are provided by means of ships out of ports in the United Kingdom, whether so provided within United Kingdom controlled waters or not, or provided within United Kingdom controlled waters by means of ships operating out of ports outside the United Kingdom[11].

Such an order may make provision:

(a) with respect to the circumstances in which shipping services are to be regarded for the purposes of the order as being provided from one or more permanent places of business maintained in the British Islands[12];

(b) authorising the Secretary of State to issue licences sanctioning the provision of shipping services mentioned in heads (1) to (3) above, notwithstanding that they are not provided as mentioned in head (a) above, in cases where he is satisfied that there is no one willing and able to provide the services in question as mentioned in that head[13];

(c) requiring the payment, in connection with applications for such licences, of fees determined with the approval of the Treasury[14];

(d) exempting any prescribed[15] class or description of shipping services from any prohibition so imposed[16];

(e) authorising the Secretary of State, or a person appointed by him for the purposes, to serve notices requiring the production or furnishing of documents or information appearing to the Secretary of State or any such person to be necessary to enable him to determine such matters as may be prescribed[17];

(f) with respect to the manner of service of notices in pursuance of head (e) above[18].

The provisions of such an order must not discriminate between shipping services provided by different persons on the basis of the place of registration of the ships by means of which the services are provided[19].

1 As to the Secretary of State see PARA 36.
2 The power to make an order under the Shipping and Trading Interests (Protection) Act 1995 s 5 is exercisable by statutory instrument, but no such order may be made unless a draft of it has been laid before and approved by resolution of each House of Parliament: s 5(7). Any such order may make different provision for different circumstances, and may make such transitional, incidental or supplementary provision as appears to the Secretary of State to be necessary or expedient: s 5(4). At the date at which this volume states the law, no such order had been made. As to the enforcement of such orders see PARA 1181.
    The Merchant Shipping Act 1995 s 256(1) (appointment of inspectors) (see PARA 46) has effect in relation to any order under the Shipping and Trading Interests (Protection) Act 1995 s 5 or any licence issued by virtue of s 5(3)(b) (see head (b) in the text), as the Merchant Shipping Act 1995 s 256(1) has effect in relation to any such regulations or licence as is referred to in s 256(1)(b), (9);

but s 259 (see PARA 49) has effect in relation to any inspector appointed by virtue of the Shipping and Trading Interests (Protection) Act 1995 s 5 with the omission of the Merchant Shipping Act 1995 s 259(2)(f)–(h): Shipping and Trading Interests (Protection) Act 1995 s 5(6).

3  For these purposes, 'shipping services' means the carriage of goods or passengers by sea, services provided by offshore support vessels, and such other services provided by means of ships as the Secretary of State may specify in an order under the Shipping and Trading Interests (Protection) Act 1995 s 5: s 5(8). As to the meaning of 'ship' for these purposes see PARA 75 note 6.

4  Shipping and Trading Interests (Protection) Act 1995 s 5(1). As to the meaning of 'British Islands' see STATUTES AND LEGISLATIVE PROCESS vol 96 (2012) PARA 1208.

5  As to the meaning of 'port' see PARA 75 note 17.

6  As to the meaning of 'United Kingdom' see PARA 16 note 3.

7  For these purposes, 'offshore installation' has the same meaning as in the Mineral Workings (Offshore Installations) Act 1971 (see ENERGY AND CLIMATE CHANGE vol 44 (2011) PARA 1078 et seq): Shipping and Trading Interests (Protection) Act 1995 s 5(8).

8  For these purposes, 'United Kingdom controlled waters' means waters within the seaward limits of the territorial sea of the United Kingdom and waters in any area designated under the Continental Shelf Act 1974 s 1(7) (see ENERGY AND CLIMATE CHANGE vol 44 (2011) PARA 1040): Shipping and Trading Interests (Protection) Act 1995 s 5(8). As to the extent of the territorial and non-territorial sea, the baselines used for delimitation, and associated rights see INTERNATIONAL RELATIONS LAW vol 61 (2010) PARA 121 et seq.

9  Shipping and Trading Interests (Protection) Act 1995 s 5(2)(a).

10  Shipping and Trading Interests (Protection) Act 1995 s 5(2)(b).

11  Shipping and Trading Interests (Protection) Act 1995 s 5(2)(c).

12  Shipping and Trading Interests (Protection) Act 1995 s 5(3)(a).

13  Shipping and Trading Interests (Protection) Act 1995 s 5(3)(b).

14  Shipping and Trading Interests (Protection) Act 1995 s 5(3)(c). As to the Treasury see CONSTITUTIONAL AND ADMINISTRATIVE LAW vol 20 (2014) PARA 262 et seq.

15  For these purposes, 'prescribed' means prescribed by an order under the Shipping and Trading Interests (Protection) Act 1995 s 5: s 5(8). See note 2.

16  Shipping and Trading Interests (Protection) Act 1995 s 5(3)(d). The text refers to any prohibition imposed by virtue of s 5(1) (see the text and notes 1–4): see s 5(3)(d).

17  Shipping and Trading Interests (Protection) Act 1995 s 5(3)(e).

18  Shipping and Trading Interests (Protection) Act 1995 s 5(3)(f).

19  Shipping and Trading Interests (Protection) Act 1995 s 5(5).

### (iii)  Liner Conferences

**78. Code of conduct for liner conferences.** The desire of the developing countries to obtain a greater share of the market in liner traffic[1] gave rise to the Convention on a Code of Conduct for Liner Conferences[2], which was negotiated under the auspices of the United Nations Conference on Trade and Development. The Convention lays down rules relating to membership of conferences[3], the participation in the trade[4], internal procedures on conferences[5], availability of conference agreements[6], relations with shippers[7], freight rates[8], miscellaneous matters[9] and the settlement of disputes[10].

Despite the manifest imperfections of the Code, effect is given to it within the EU, albeit with reservations[11].

1  Liner traffic is traffic by merchant ships which provide a regular service on particular routes.

2  Ie the Convention on a Code of Conduct for Liner Conferences (Geneva, 6 April 1974). 'Liner conference' or 'conference' means a group of two or more vessel-operating carriers providing international liner services for the carriage of cargo on a particular route or routes within specified geographical limits and which has an agreement or arrangement within the framework of which they operate under uniform or common freight rates and any other agreed conditions with respect to the provision of liner services: see Ch I (definitions). These other conditions often include conditions as to market sharing. As to the position of liner conferences under EC competition law see PARA 78.

3  See the Code of Conduct for Liner Conferences art 1.

4  See the Code of Conduct for Liner Conferences art 2.

5  See the Code of Conduct for Liner Conferences arts 3–5.

6  See the Code of Conduct for Liner Conferences art 6.

7  See the Code of Conduct for Liner Conferences Ch III (arts 7–11).

8   See the Code of Conduct for Liner Conferences Ch IV (arts 12–17).
9   See the Code of Conduct for Liner Conferences Ch V (arts 18–22).
10  See the Code of Conduct for Liner Conferences Ch VI (arts 23–46).
11  See Council Regulation (EC) 954/79 (OJ L121, 17.5.79, p 1) concerning the ratification by
    Member States of, or their accession to, the United Nations Convention on a Code of Conduct for
    Liner Conferences.

# 2. ADMIRALTY JURISDICTION OF THE HIGH COURT

## (1) THE JURISDICTION

### (i) Outline of the Jurisdiction

**79. Outline of jurisdiction.** The Admiralty Court is part of the Queen's Bench Division[1] and has jurisdiction in all causes and matters assigned by the Senior Courts Act 1981 to that division involving either the exercise of the Admiralty jurisdiction of the High Court[2] or its jurisdiction as a prize court[3]. The Admiralty jurisdiction is invoked by other statutes, most notably the Hovercraft Act 1968[4] and the Merchant Shipping Act 1995[5].

Admiralty claims may be either in rem[6] or in personam (now referred to as 'other claims')[7]. Limitation claims (being the statutory right afforded to shipowners and other persons to limit their liability in connection with a ship or other property) are also heard in the Admiralty Court[8]. Any such proceedings (whatever their exact nature) are subject to the jurisdictional rules now contained in EU legislation[9].

A ship, as well as being liable to arrest as the subject of a claim in rem, may be seized in execution under a writ of control[10] because the ordinary remedies for enforcing a judgment in the High Court[11] are applicable to Admiralty claims.

1 The Administration of Justice Act 1970 abolished the Probate, Divorce and Admiralty Division of the High Court (see s 1(1) (repealed)), and provided for the constitution of the Admiralty Court of the Queen's Bench Division (see s 2(1) (repealed) (see now the Senior Courts Act 1981 s 6(1); and COURTS AND TRIBUNALS vol 24 (2010) PARA 708)). As to the distribution of business between divisions of the High Court see COURTS AND TRIBUNALS vol 24 (2010) PARA 703; and as to the Queen's Bench Division generally see COURTS AND TRIBUNALS vol 24 (2010) PARA 706. The judges of the Admiralty Court are puisne judges of the High Court nominated from time to time to be Admiralty judges: see s 6(2); and COURTS AND TRIBUNALS vol 24 (2010) PARA 708. However, jurisdiction over some questions of assessment of damages and investigation of accounts is exercised by the Admiralty Registrar: *Maid of Kent* (1881) 6 PD 178. As to the Admiralty Registrar see PARA 140. As to the development of the law that is administered in Admiralty see PARA 80 et seq.
2 The Admiralty jurisdiction of the High Court is provided for in the Senior Courts Act 1981 ss 20–24 (see PARA 85 et seq) and is defined by s 20(1) as being:
    (1)    jurisdiction to hear and determine any of the questions and claims mentioned in s 20(2) (see s 20(1)(a); and PARA 93 et seq);
    (2)    jurisdiction in relation to any of the proceedings mentioned in s 20(3) (see s 20(1)(b); and PARAS 91, 180, 194 et seq);
    (3)    any other Admiralty jurisdiction which it had immediately before 1 January 1982 (that is, before the commencement of the Senior Courts Act 1981) (see ss 20(1)(c), 153(2); and PARA 85); and
    (4)    any jurisdiction connected with ships or aircraft which is vested in the High Court apart from s 20 and is for the time being by rules of court made or coming into force after the commencement of the Senior Courts Act 1981 assigned to the Queen's Bench Division and directed by the rules to be exercised by the Admiralty Court (see s 20(1)(d); and PARA 85).
    The Senior Courts Act 1981 ss 20–24 (see PARA 85 et seq) may be extended, with such exceptions, adaptations and modifications as may be specified, to any of the Channel Islands or the Isle of Man by Order in Council: see s 150(1); and PARA 216.
3 See the Senior Courts Act 1981 s 62(2); and PARA 85. As to the High Court's jurisdiction as a prize court see PARA 89; and PRIZE vol 85 (2012) PARA 645 et seq.
4 See the Hovercraft Act 1968; and PARA 87 et seq.
5 Ie in respect of liability for oil pollution: see the Merchant Shipping Act 1995 s 166; and PARA 88. As to merchant shipping and liability for oil pollution generally see ENVIRONMENTAL QUALITY AND PUBLIC HEALTH vol 45 (2010) PARA 348 et seq.
6 As to the commencement of claims in rem see PARA 158 et seq.
7 As to the commencement of claims in personam ('other claims') see PARA 186 et seq.

8   As to limitation claims generally see PARA 194 et seq.
9   As to the rules relating to conflicts of jurisdiction see PARA 95 et seq. As to restrictions on jurisdiction generally see PARA 90.
10  As to writs of control see PARA 208; and CIVIL PROCEDURE vol 12A (2015) PARA 1379 et seq. A person who maliciously, and without reasonable and probable cause, procures the arrest of a ship by Admiralty proceedings is liable to pay damages to the person aggrieved: see *The Strathnaver* (1875) 1 App Cas 58, PC; and TORT vol 97 (2015) PARA 755.
11  As to enforcement generally see CIVIL PROCEDURE vol 12A (2015) PARA 1268 et seq.

## (ii) Origins of Jurisdiction

**80. Origin and conflict with common law courts.** The jurisdiction of the Admiralty Court in respect of offences committed upon the high seas is of ancient origin[1]. As a result of possessing this criminal jurisdiction, the Court of the Lord High Admiral began to hear disputes also in all civil matters connected with the sea[2] and gradually usurped the jurisdiction of the common law courts in matters arising in inland tidal waters, in consequence of which two statutes were passed in the reign of Richard II confining the jurisdiction of the admirals and their deputies to things done upon the sea and in the main streams of great rivers to the seaward side of the bridges[3].

The criminal jurisdiction of the Admiralty as adjusted by these statutes continued until 1537, when it was to a great extent transferred to commissioners of oyer and terminer under the Great Seal, of whom one was the judge of the High Court of Admiralty[4]. All proceedings on indictment for offences within the jurisdiction of the Admiralty of England are now to be brought before the Crown Court[5].

The civil jurisdiction of the Admiralty Court continued within the limits laid down by the statutes of Richard II[6], but its exercise involved the Admiralty Court in a long struggle with the superior courts of common law. The Admiralty Court asserted the highest and fullest jurisdiction over everything which might happen upon the high seas, but it was obliged to give way to the common law courts and ceased to exercise jurisdiction to the full extent which it had formerly claimed[7]. Nevertheless in the reign of William IV it still retained a curtailed jurisdiction which included a number of important subjects[8].

1   Whether or not Admiralty jurisdiction in England took its origin from Saxon times (see 2 Co Litt 260b; Prynne's Animadversions on the 4th Institute 123), by the reign of Edward III the authority of the Crown to administer justice in respect of piracy or spoil and other offences committed upon the sea was undisputed (see *R v Keyn* (1876) 2 ExD 63 at 167 per Cockburn CJ; and see *The Zeta* [1892] P 285 at 300, CA, per Lord Esher MR).
2   See RG Marsden *The Selden Society's Select Pleas of the Court of Admiralty, AD 1390–1602* (1892–1897).
3   13 Ric 2 stat 1 (1389–90) c 5 (repealed by the Civil Procedure Acts Repeal Act 1879, but with a saving of its effect so far as jurisdiction is concerned); Admiralty Jurisdiction Act 1391 (repealed). For a contemporary consideration of the historical development of Admiralty jurisdiction see *The Goring* [1988] AC 831, [1988] 1 All ER 641, HL.
4   See the Offences at Sea Act 1536 (repealed). The jurisdiction of the Admiralty over criminal offences committed at sea was subsequently regulated by the Central Criminal Court Act 1834 s 22 (repealed by the Administration of Justice Act 1964 s 41(8), Sch 5, and replaced by Sch 1 para 5 (repealed)), and the Admiralty Offences Act 1844 (repealed). See also *R v Keyn* (1876) 2 ExD 63 at 66–67; *The Hercules* (1819) 2 Dods 353 at 371.
5   See the Senior Courts Act 1981 s 46; and COURTS AND TRIBUNALS vol 24 (2010) PARA 720. As to the extent of Admiralty jurisdiction in criminal matters see CRIMINAL PROCEDURE vol 27 (2015) PARAS 13–14.
6   See note 3.
7   See *R v City of London Court Judge and Payne* [1892] 1 QB 273 at 292–294, CA, per Lord Esher MR.
8   The subjects included collisions between ships and injurious acts committed on the high seas (see *Mersey Docks and Harbour Board v Turner, The Zeta* [1893] AC 468, 7 Asp MLC 369, HL; *The*

*Tubantia* [1924] P 78, 16 Asp MLC 346), salvage services not rendered within the body of a county (see *The Raft of Timber* (1844) 2 Wm Rob 251; *The Eleanor* (1805) 6 Ch Rob 39), possession of ships where no title was in question (see *The Warrior* (1818) 2 Dods 288), bottomry and respondentia (see *The Atlas* (1827) 2 Hag Adm 48) and claims for seamen's wages where there had been no special contract (see *Opy v Adison* (1693) 12 Mod Rep 38). As to the extent of Admiralty jurisdiction regarding salvage claims see PARA 113 et seq; and regarding bottomry and respondentia see PARA 134.

## 81. Advent of statutory jurisdiction.

The Admiralty Court Act 1840 was passed to improve the practice and extend the jurisdiction of the High Court of Admiralty in England[1]. This was the first of a series of Acts which enlarged or defined the jurisdiction, the latest of which is the Senior Courts Act 1981 as amended by the Merchant Shipping Act 1995. Part II of the Senior Courts Act 1981[2] derives substantially from Part I of the Administration of Justice Act 1956[3], which redefined the Admiralty jurisdiction of the High Court so as, among other things, to give effect by domestic legislation to certain international conventions[4]. In addition to specifying in detail the questions or claims within the Admiralty jurisdiction[5], the Senior Courts Act 1981 expressly preserves any other Admiralty jurisdiction vested in the High Court immediately before its commencement[6].

1 The Admiralty Court Act 1840 was repealed by the Statute Law (Repeals) Act 1969 s 1, Schedule Pt VII.
2 Ie the Senior Courts Act 1981 Pt II (ss 15–52).
3 Ie the Administration of Justice Act 1956 Pt I (ss 1–8) (repealed).
4 As to which see PARA 85.
5 See the Senior Courts Act 1981 s 20(1)(a), (2); and PARA 93 et seq.
6 See the Senior Courts Act 1981 s 20(1)(c); and PARA 85.

## 82. Law administered in Admiralty.

Maritime law[1] is the law developed and administered in the Admiralty Court in exercising both its original jurisdiction[2] and the jurisdiction derived from statute[3]. Outside the special field of prize[4], in times of hostilities there is no maritime law of the world, as distinct from the internal municipal laws of the individual countries, that is capable of giving rise to rights or liabilities enforceable in English courts; but, because of the subject matter and historic derivation from sources common to many maritime nations[5], the internal municipal laws of different countries show greater similarity to one another than is found in law relating to what happens on land[6].

Although maritime law was developed in a separate court in England, its development was nevertheless related to the law being developed in other courts, and the effect of the merger, in 1875, of the High Court of Admiralty with the High Court of Justice[7] was to foster the development of common concepts between the common law courts and the Admiralty Court, which began at least as early as 1840 with the passing of the Admiralty Court Act 1840[8]. Since the mid 19th century, the development of English maritime law has continued to be greatly influenced by changes in concepts of the common law, and to regard it as constituting today a system of law entirely separate from the general law may lead to error[9]. In one sense, maritime law is part of the common law and it has been referred to as such[10]. The maritime law of England and Scotland is the same law and House of Lords or Supreme Court decisions on appeals from Scotland are therefore authoritative in England[11].

1 In relation to navigation upon the high seas beyond the territorial limits of the United Kingdom, it has been said that the maritime law consisted of 'those rules of navigation which usually prevail among nations navigating the seas where the collision takes place': see *The Zollverein* (1856) Sw 96 at 99 per Dr Lushington. This statement was made in reference to the law as it was before the passing of the Merchant Shipping Act Amendment Act 1862 s 25 (repealed), which established collision regulations. Breach by the master of a ship of the collision regulations does not give rise to any statutory presumption of fault: see the Merchant Shipping Act 1995 s 92(3); and PARA 727. However, such breach will be evidence of negligence. For the enactments now in force with regard to the prevention of collisions see s 85; and PARAS 602 note 1, 690 et seq.

2   The original and common law jurisdiction of the court must be ascertained from the continuous practice and the judgments of its judges and from the judgments of the courts at Westminster; the former, in their court, using the law of the Rhodians, of Wisbey, the Hanse towns, of Oleron (incorporated in the 15th Century Black Book of Admiralty), the Digest and French and other ordinances, which, though they are not part of the law of England, contain many valuable principles and statements of marine practice: see *The Gas Float Whitton No 2* [1896] P 42 at 48, 8 Asp MLC 110 at 111, CA, per Lord Esher MR, quoting Abbott's *Law of Merchant Ships and Seamen* (5th Edn) Preface to the 1st Edn xi.

3   See PARAS 81, 85.

4   As to prize law see PRIZE vol 85 (2012) PARA 601 et seq.

5   See note 2.

6   See *The Tojo Maru* [1972] AC 242 at 290–291, [1971] 1 All ER 1110 at 1133, HL, per Lord Diplock.

7   See the Supreme Court of Judicature Act 1873 s 3 (repealed), which came into force on 1 November 1875: Supreme Court of Judicature (Commencement) Act 1874 (repealed).

8   The Admiralty Court Act 1840 was repealed by the Statute Law (Repeals) Act 1969 s 1, Schedule Pt VII: see PARA 81.

9   See *The Tojo Maru* [1972] AC 242 at 291, [1971] 1 All ER 1110 at 1133, HL, per Lord Diplock. See also *Cox v Ergo Versicherung AG* [2014 UKSC 22, [2014] AC 1379, [2014] 2 All ER 926 at [30], per Lord Sumption SCJ.

10  See eg *Chartered Mercantile Bank of India, London and China v Netherlands India Steam Navigation Co Ltd* (1883) 10 QBD 521 at 537, 5 Asp MLC 65 at 68, CA, per Lord Esher MR.

11  *Currie v M'Knight* [1897] AC 97, 8 Asp MLC 193, HL.

**83.  Origin of claims in rem.**  Originally, a suit in Admiralty was commenced by the arrest either of the person of the defendant or of his goods, whether or not the ship or goods in question constituted the subject matter of the offence, the purpose being to make the defendant put up bail or provide a fund for securing compliance with the judgment, if any, when it was obtained against him[1]. The result of the conflict between the Court of Admiralty and the common law courts[2] was that this method of procedure became obsolete[3], but the Admiralty Court succeeded in establishing a right to arrest property which was the subject matter of a dispute, and to enforce its judgments against the property so arrested, on the theory that a maritime lien[4] to the extent of the claim attached to the property from the moment of the creation of such claim. Such a claim became known as an action in rem. The right to enforce a maritime lien by an action in rem was confined to the property by which the damage was caused or in relation to which the claim arose, and was enforceable against the property in the hands of an innocent purchaser[5].

The present law preserves the jurisdiction based upon the maritime lien[6] and extends the right to proceed in rem to many claims which do not give rise to a maritime lien[7]. In addition, in many cases jurisdiction may now be established by the commencement of proceedings against any other ship in the same beneficial ownership as the ship in connection with which the claim arose[8].

1   *The Banco* [1971] P 137 at 150, [1971] 1 All ER 524 at 531, [1971] Lloyd's Rep 49 at 51, CA, per Lord Denning MR, citing Clerk's *Praxis Curiae Admiralitatis* (Simpson Edn, 1743), quoted in *The Dictator* [1892] P 304 at 311, and *the Selden Society's Select Pleas in the Court of Admiralty* vol 1 p lxiii. See also *The Monica S* [1968] P 741 at 749–750, [1967] 3 All ER 740 at 745–746 per Brandon J, where the historical background in respect of statutory rights of action in rem is summarised.

2   As to which see PARA 80.

3   The last instance of personal arrest is said to have been in 1780: see *The Clara* (1855) Sw 1 at 3. See also *The Dictator* [1892] P 304 at 313, 7 Asp MLC 251 at 254.

4   As to maritime liens generally see PARA 964 et seq.

5   *The Ripon City* [1897] P 226 at 241–242, 8 Asp MLC 304 at 311. See also *The Bold Buccleugh* (1852) 7 Moo PCC 267, approved in *Currie v M'Knight* [1897] AC 97 at 106, 8 Asp MLC 193 at 195, HL.

6   See the Senior Courts Act 1981 s 21(3); and PARA 93.

7   See the Senior Courts Act 1981 s 21(2), (4); and PARA 93.

8   See the Senior Courts Act 1981 s 21(4)(b); and PARA 93.

**84.  Origin of claims in personam ('other claims').** The inherent jurisdiction possessed by the Court of Admiralty was exercised not only by proceedings in rem brought to enforce the maritime liens[1] attaching to the res (that is, the subject property of the claim) in each case, but, where the ship was lost or for some other reason could not be arrested, a claimant having a claim cognisable by the court, other than a claim on a bottomry or respondentia bond[2] or to the possession of the ship, might take proceedings in personam against the owners of the property which would have been arrested if the proceedings had been in rem[3]. Subsequently, in 1854, the High Court of Admiralty was empowered by statute to institute proceedings by personal service of a monition upon the owners of the property the subject matter of the dispute, without the necessity of issuing a warrant to arrest the property[4].

A claim in personam may be brought in the High Court in all cases within the Admiralty jurisdiction of that court[5], although the exercise of jurisdiction may be inhibited by the operation of rules of court relating to service of proceedings out of the jurisdiction[6], and in collision and other similar cases the jurisdiction of the court cannot in any event be exercised unless certain special conditions are fulfilled[7].

1   See PARA 83. As to maritime liens generally see PARA 964 et seq.
2   As to the meanings of 'bottomry' and 'respondentia' see PARA 134.
3   *The Volant* (1842) 1 Wm Rob 383. See also *R v City of London Court Judge and Payne* [1892] 1 QB 273 at 307–310, CA, and the cases there cited. It was assumed where the proceedings were by monition (as to which see note 4) that an action in rem was depending so that all rights were tacitly reserved: see *The Trelawney* (1801) 3 Ch Rob 216n; *The Five Steel Barges* (1890) 15 PD 142 at 146; *The Port Victor (cargo ex)* [1901] P 243 at 254, 256, CA.
4   See the Admiralty Court Act 1854 s 13 (repealed). The monition in personam was a form of summons to appear in the action. As to the present practice see PARA 94.
5   See the Senior Courts Act 1981 s 21(1); and PARA 94.
6   As to which see PARA 188.
7   See the Senior Courts Act 1981 s 22; and PARA 94.

### (iii)  Present Jurisdiction

**85.  Jurisdiction under the Senior Courts Act 1981.** The Admiralty Court takes Admiralty business, that is to say causes and matters assigned to the Queen's Bench Division[1] and involving the exercise of either the High Court's Admiralty jurisdiction[2] or its jurisdiction as a prize court[3].

The Admiralty jurisdiction of the High Court of Justice is derived partly from statute and partly from the inherent jurisdiction of the High Court of Admiralty[4]. The Senior Courts Act 1981 lists the specific areas of jurisdiction of the High Court in this regard[5] and includes any such jurisdiction which either it had immediately before 1 January 1982 (that is, before the commencement of the Senior Courts Act 1981)[6], or is connected with ships[7] (or aircraft[8]) and is vested in the High Court and is for the time being assigned by rules of court to the Queen's Bench Division and directed by the rules to be exercised by the Admiralty Court[9]. Although the jurisdiction of the High Court is concerned mainly with questions and claims arising in relation to ships[10], it extends to hovercraft[11] and, in respect of certain questions and claims, also to aircraft[12].

However, nothing in the provisions of the Senior Courts Act 1981 that set out the Admiralty jurisdiction[13]:

(1)      is to be construed as limiting the jurisdiction of the High Court to refuse to entertain an action for wages by the master[14] or a member of the crew of a ship, not being a British ship[15];

(2)     affects the power of a receiver of wreck to detain a ship in respect of a salvage claim[16]; or

(3)     authorises proceedings in rem[17] in respect of any claim against the Crown, or the arrest, detention or sale of any of Her Majesty's ships[18] or Her Majesty's aircraft[19], or[20] Her Majesty's hovercraft[21], or of any cargo or other property belonging to the Crown[22].

1   As to the distribution of business between divisions of the High Court see COURTS AND TRIBUNALS vol 24 (2010) PARA 703; and as to the Queen's Bench Division generally see COURTS AND TRIBUNALS vol 24 (2010) PARA 706.

2   As to the Admiralty jurisdiction of the High Court of Justice see the Senior Courts Act 1981 ss 20–24; and the text and notes 4–22. As to the mode of exercise of this jurisdiction see s 21; and PARAS 93–94. As to foreign aspects of the Admiralty jurisdiction see PARA 86. The Admiralty jurisdiction of the High Court extends also to hovercraft: see PARA 87.

3   Senior Courts Act 1981 s 62(2). As to the High Court's jurisdiction as a prize court see PARA 89.

4   As to the development of the law that is administered in Admiralty see PARA 80 et seq.

5   The Admiralty jurisdiction of the High Court is defined by the Senior Courts Act 1981 s 20(1) as being:

    (1)     jurisdiction to hear and determine any of the questions and claims mentioned in s 20(2) (see s 20(1)(a); and PARA 93 et seq); and

    (2)     jurisdiction in relation to any of the proceedings mentioned in s 20(3) (see s 20(1)(b); and PARAS 91, 180, 194 et seq),

    and includes the areas set out in the text and notes 6–9.

    The jurisdiction established by s 20 creates no new rights of action or maritime liens but extends to all ships whether British or not and whether registered or not and wherever the residence or domicile of their owners may be, and to all claims, wherever arising: see s 20(7)(a), (b); and PARA 86. The areas of jurisdiction so defined must be considered in conjunction with the mode of exercise of that jurisdiction (see s 21; and PARAS 93–94) and the restrictions placed on that jurisdiction (see s 22 (cited in PARA 94); and s 23 (cited in PARA 86)).

6   Senior Courts Act 1981 ss 20(1)(c), 153(2).

    Section 152(4), Sch 7 repealed the Administration of Justice Act 1956 s 1(1), which conferred upon the High Court any other jurisdiction which either was vested in the High Court of Admiralty before 1 November 1875 or was conferred on the High Court as being a court with Admiralty jurisdiction by or under any Act which came into operation on or after that date, and also any other jurisdiction connected with ships or aircraft vested in the High Court which was for the time being assigned by the rules of court to the Queen's Bench Division and directed by the rules to be exercised by the Admiralty Court. In *The Queen of the South* [1968] P 449 at 455, [1968] 1 All ER 1163 at 1168, Brandon J expressed the view (obiter) that the effect of the Administration of Justice Act 1956 s 1(1) was to preserve, independently of, and concurrently with, any jurisdiction conferred by s 1(1)(a)–(s) (repealed), the jurisdiction which was formerly conferred by the Admiralty Court Act 1840, the Admiralty Court Act 1861, the Supreme Court of Judicature Act 1873, the Supreme Court of Judicature Act 1875, and the Supreme Court of Judicature (Consolidation) Act 1925 (all repealed). It seems doubtful, however, whether jurisdiction 'is conferred' within the meaning of the Administration of Justice Act 1956 s 1(1) (repealed), by for example the Supreme Court of Judicature (Consolidation) Act 1925 s 22 (which was repealed by the Administration of Justice Act 1956 ss 7(2), 57(2), Sch 2). The same would apply to the Supreme Court of Judicature Act 1873, which was wholly repealed in 1956. Cf the wording of the Administration of Justice Act 1956 s 1(1) (repealed) in relation to jurisdiction vested in the High Court of Admiralty immediately before the commencement of the Supreme Court of Judicature Act 1873. See also PARA 91.

7   For the purposes of the Senior Courts Act 1981 ss 20–23, unless the context otherwise requires, 'ship' includes any description of vessel used in navigation and, except in the definition of 'port' in s 22(2) (see PARA 94), and in s 24(2)(c) (see head (3) in the text), includes, subject to the Hovercraft Act 1968 s 2(3) (see PARA 383), a hovercraft: Senior Courts Act 1981 s 24(1).

8   As to the application of wreck and salvage law to aircraft see AVIATION vol 2 (2017) PARA 1367; and as to the jurisdiction in civil matters that arises in relation to aircraft or air navigation see AVIATION vol 2 (2017) PARA 1384.

9   Senior Courts Act 1981 s 20(1)(d). As to the procedure that applies to Admiralty claims and to the distribution of business to the Admiralty Court (including rules of court, practice directions and other guidance) see PARA 157 et seq.

10 See the Senior Courts Act 1981 s 20(7); and PARA 86. See also PARAS 87, 110. The Admiralty jurisdiction of the High Court also includes jurisdiction to hear and determine expenses and compensation claims arising from a safety direction made by the Secretary of State: see PARA 677.

11 As to the Admiralty jurisdiction in respect of hovercraft see PARA 87.

12 See the Senior Courts Act 1981 s 20(1)(a), (2)(j) (claims in the nature of salvage in respect of aircraft) (see PARAS 113, 114) and s 20(1)(a), (2)(k), (l) (claims in the nature of towage and pilotage in respect of aircraft) (see PARA 125). For the purposes of ss 20–23, 'towage' and 'pilotage', in relation to an aircraft, mean towage and pilotage while the aircraft is waterborne: see s 24(1); and PARA 93 note 40.

13 Ie nothing in the Senior Courts Act 1981 ss 20–23 (see PARA 85 et seq): see s 24(2).

14 For the purposes of the Senior Courts Act 1981 ss 20–23, unless the context otherwise requires, 'master' has the same meaning as in the Merchant Shipping Act 1995 s 313(1) (see PARA 444 note 1) and accordingly includes every person (except a pilot) having command or charge of a ship: Senior Courts Act 1981 s 24(1) (definition amended by the Merchant Shipping Act 1995 s 314(2), Sch 13 para 59(3)).

15 Senior Courts Act 1981 s 24(2)(a). As to British ships under the Merchant Shipping Act 1995 see PARA 229 et seq.

16 Senior Courts Act 1981 s 24(2)(b) (amended by the Merchant Shipping Act 1995 Sch 13 para 59(3)). The text refers to the power of a receiver of wreck contained in the provisions of the Merchant Shipping Act 1995 s 226 (as to which see PARA 919): see the Senior Courts Act 1981 s 24(2)(b).

17 As to proceedings in rem see PARAS 83 et seq, 92 et seq.

18 For these purposes, 'Her Majesty's ships' has the meaning given by the Crown Proceedings Act 1947 s 38(2) (see CROWN AND CROWN PROCEEDINGS vol 29 (2014) PARA 86): Senior Courts Act 1981 s 24(3).

19 For these purposes, 'Her Majesty's aircraft' has the meaning given by the Crown Proceedings Act 1947 s 38(2) (see CROWN AND CROWN PROCEEDINGS vol 29 (2014) PARA 86): Senior Courts Act 1981 s 24(3).

20 Ie subject to the Hovercraft Act 1968 s 2(3) (see PARA 383): see the Senior Courts Act 1981 s 24(2)(c).

21 For these purposes, 'Her Majesty's hovercraft' means hovercraft belonging to the Crown in right of Her Majesty's Government in the United Kingdom or Her Majesty's Government in Northern Ireland: Senior Courts Act 1981 s 24(3). As to the meaning of 'United Kingdom' see PARA 16 note 3.

22 Senior Courts Act 1981 s 24(2)(c).

**86. Foreign aspects of Admiralty jurisdiction.** The jurisdiction of the Admiralty Court has long extended both to foreign ships on the high seas[1], except ships in the ownership or possession of a foreign sovereign state and used for public purposes[2], and over injurious acts done on the high seas[3]. The Admiralty jurisdiction of the High Court applies[4]:

(1)    in relation to all ships[5] or aircraft[6], whether British or not and whether registered or not and wherever the residence or domicile of their owners may be[7];

(2)    in relation to all claims, wherever arising (including, in the case of cargo or wreck salvage, claims in respect of cargo or wreck found on land)[8]; and

(3)    so far as they relate to mortgages and charges, to all mortgages or charges, whether registered or not and whether legal or equitable, including mortgages and charges created under foreign law[9].

The extent of the jurisdiction is subject to statutory rules governing the mode of exercise of jurisdiction[10] and to restrictions in collision and other similar cases where the claim is in personam[11].

The general jurisdictional provisions contained in Part II of the Senior Courts Act 1981[12] are based, in part at least, on the International Convention relating to the Arrest of Sea-going Ships[13] and the International Convention on certain Rules concerning Civil Jurisdiction in matters of Collision[14], to both of which the United

Kingdom is a signatory[15]. Where the meaning of the Act is not clear, the court may look to the terms of these Conventions to assist in the construction of the Act[16].

1    See eg *The Mali Ivo* (1869) LR 2 A & E 356 (collision); *Chartered Mercantile Bank of India, London and China v Netherlands India Steam Navigation Co Ltd* (1883) 10 QBD 521 at 537, 5 Asp MLC 65 at 68, CA, per Brett LJ, and at 545 and 71 per Lindley LJ; *The Zeta* [1893] AC 468 at 482–486, 7 Asp MLC 369 at 373–374, HL, per Lord Herschell LC.

2    *The Parlement Belge* (1880) 5 PD 197, 4 Asp MLC 234, CA (action in rem); *The Annette, The Dora* [1919] P 105; *Compania Naviera Vascongado v SS Cristina* [1938] AC 485, [1938] 1 All ER 719, 60 Ll L Rep 147, HL; *Spain v The Arantzazu Mendi* [1939] AC 256, [1939] 1 All ER 719, HL. Such vessels cannot be proceeded against or arrested: *The Parlement Belge*; *The Jassy* [1906] P 270, 10 Asp MLC 278. It is not clear what the limits of 'public purposes' are. It has been held that immunity is not lost even if the vessel is employed by a foreign government in ordinary trading for profit: *The Parlement Belge*; *The Porto Alexandre* [1920] P 30, 15 Asp MLC 1, 1 Ll L Rep 191, CA. The trend of more recent cases, however, is to restrict the scope of immunity for state-owned vessels: see *The Philippine Admiral* [1977] AC 373, [1976] 1 All ER 78, PC (immunity lost for state-owned ship used for trading purposes). See also *Thai-Europe Tapioca Service Ltd v Government of Pakistan* [1975] 3 All ER 961, [1975] 1 WLR 1485, CA. State immunity is now governed by the State Immunity Act 1978: see INTERNATIONAL RELATIONS LAW vol 61 (2010) PARA 244 et seq.

3    *The Tubantia* [1924] P 78 at 86, 16 Asp MLC 346 at 350 (trespass to the possession of a salvor). A distinction must be drawn between civil and criminal jurisdiction. As to Admiralty jurisdiction in relation to crime see CRIMINAL PROCEDURE vol 27 (2015) PARAS 13–14; and as to the conflict of laws in relation to torts see CONFLICT OF LAWS vol 19 (2011) PARA 647 et seq.

4    Ie provided that nothing in the Senior Courts Act 1981 s 20(7) (see heads (1) to (3) in the text) is construed as extending the cases in which money or property is recoverable under any of the provisions of the Merchant Shipping Act 1995: Senior Courts Act 1981 s 20(7) proviso (amended by the Merchant Shipping Act 1995 s 314(2), Sch 13 para 59(2)). As to the Admiralty jurisdiction of the High Court of Justice generally see PARA 85. As to the mode of exercise of this jurisdiction see the Senior Courts Act 1981 s 21; and PARAS 93–94.

5    As to the meaning of 'ship' for these purposes see PARA 85 note 7. The Admiralty jurisdiction of the High Court also extends to hovercraft: see PARA 87.

6    The wording of the Senior Courts Act 1981 s 20(7) extends its jurisdiction to all aircraft but only in respect of those claims or questions with regard to which the word 'aircraft' is used in the legislation: see *Re Glider Standard Austria SH 1964* [1965] P 463, [1965] 2 All ER 1022, [1965] 2 Lloyd's Rep 189. It has been held that a flying boat is not a 'ship or vessel' within the meaning of the collision liability clause in a policy of marine insurance: see *Polpen Shipping Co Ltd v Commercial Union Assurance Co Ltd* [1943] KB 161, [1943] 1 All ER 162. See also *Watson v RCA Victor Co Inc* (1934) 50 Ll L Rep 77, where it was held that a seaplane is not a 'ship or vessel' within the meaning of the Merchant Shipping Acts. For the purposes of the Merchant Shipping Act 1995 Pt IX (ss 224–255) (salvage and wreck), 'vessel' includes any ship or boat, or any other description of vessel used in navigation: see s 255(1); and PARA 919 note 5. As to the application of wreck and salvage law to aircraft see AVIATION vol 2 (2017) PARA 1367; and as to the jurisdiction in civil matters that arises in relation to aircraft or air navigation see AVIATION vol 2 (2017) PARA 1384.

7    Senior Courts Act 1981 s 20(7)(a). As to the rules of domicile and residence generally see CONFLICT OF LAWS vol 19 (2011) PARA 336 et seq. See note 4.

8    Senior Courts Act 1981 s 20(7)(b). See note 4. However, the High Court does not have jurisdiction to determine any claim or question certified by the Secretary of State to be a claim or question which, under the Rhine Navigation Convention 1868, falls to be determined in accordance with the provisions of that Convention; and any proceedings to enforce such a claim which are commenced in the High Court must be set aside: Senior Courts Act 1981 s 23. 'Rhine Navigation Convention' means the Convention of the 7 October 1868 as revised by any subsequent Convention (see the Senior Courts Act 1981 s 24(1)), which established Rhine Courts to deal with certain matters of civil and criminal jurisdiction in relation to navigation on the Rhine (see art 33 et seq). A number of shipping and insurance companies have undertaken that they will not seek the Secretary of State's certificate in cases of claims by United Kingdom citizens for death or personal injury, if the ship concerned was British or was insured with one of the companies giving the undertaking: see the written answer of the Minister of Transport in the House of Commons, 599 HC Official Report (5th Series), 5 February 1959, written answers col 125. See also *The Atlantic Star* [1973] QB 364, [1972] 3 All ER 705, [1972] 2 Lloyd's Rep 446, CA (refusal to stay proceedings where incident occurred in foreign territorial waters and defendant ship was served with process in England). In connection with the landward side of Admiralty jurisdiction see

*Barnes v The Charterers of the Motor Vessel (The Snow Bunting)* [2012] 2 Lloyd's Rep 647. As to the Secretary of State see PARA 36. As to the meanings of 'Great Britain' and 'United Kingdom' see PARA 16 note 3.

The Senior Courts Act 1981 Pt II (ss 15–52) follows the terms of the international conventions mentioned in notes 10, 13, which do not apply in cases covered by the Rhine Navigation Convention. As to this and other limitations on the jurisdiction of the Admiralty Court see PARA 90.

9   Senior Courts Act 1981 s 20(7)(c). See note 4. As to claims relating to mortgages and charges see PARA 109.

10  See the Senior Courts Act 1981 s 21; and PARA 93 et seq. See also the International Convention relating to the Arrest of Seagoing Ships 1952 (Brussels, 10 May 1952; Cmd 8954); the International Convention on certain Rules concerning Civil Jurisdiction in Matters of Collision 1952 (Brussels, 10 May 1952; Cmd 8954); and PARAS 85, 95 et seq.

11  See the Senior Courts Act 1981 s 22; and PARA 94.

12  Ie contained in the Senior Courts Act 1981 Pt II.

13  Ie the International Convention relating to the Arrest of Sea-going Ships 1952 (Brussels, 10 May 1952; Cmd 8954) (as to which see PARA 7). As to jurisdictional issues in particular see art 7, especially art 7(2) (security in case of stay), which is implemented in England and Wales by the Civil Jurisdiction and Judgments Act 1982 s 26. Accordingly, where in England and Wales a court stays or dismisses Admiralty proceedings on the ground that the dispute in question should be submitted to the determination of the courts of another part of the United Kingdom or of an overseas country, the court may, if in those proceedings property has been arrested or bail or other security has been given to prevent or obtain release from arrest, order as follows (Civil Jurisdiction and Judgments Act 1982 s 26(1) (amended by the Arbitration Act 1996 s 107(2), Sch 4)):

(1)   that the property arrested be retained as security for the satisfaction of any award or judgment which is given in respect of the dispute in the legal proceedings in favour of which those proceedings are stayed or dismissed, and which is enforceable in England and Wales (Civil Jurisdiction and Judgments Act 1982 s 26(1)(a) (amended by the Arbitration Act 1996 Sch 4)); or

(2)   that the stay or dismissal of those proceedings be conditional on the provision of equivalent security for the satisfaction of any such award or judgment (Civil Jurisdiction and Judgments Act 1982 s 26(1)(b)).

Where a court makes such an order, it may attach such conditions to the order as it thinks fit, in particular conditions with respect to the institution or prosecution of the relevant legal proceedings (s 26(2) (amended by the Arbitration Act 1996 Sch 4)); and, subject to any provision made by rules of court and to any necessary modifications, the same law and practice applies in relation to property retained in pursuance of such an order as would apply if it were held for the purposes of proceedings in that court (Civil Jurisdiction and Judgments Act 1982 s 26(3)). As to the meanings of 'England' and 'Wales' see PARA 16 note 2.

14  Ie the International Convention on certain Rules concerning Civil Jurisdiction in matters of Collision 1952 (Brussels, 10 May 1952; Cmd 8954) (as to which see PARA 7).

15  See *The Andrea Ursula* [1973] QB 265 at 270, [1971] 1 All ER 821 at 825, [1971] 1 Lloyd's Rep 145 at 148 per Brandon J.

16  *The Annie Hay* [1968] P 341, [1968] 1 All ER 657; *The Banco* [1971] P 137, [1971] 1 All ER 524, [1971] 1 Lloyd's Rep 49, CA; and *The Andrea Ursula* [1973] QB 265, [1971] 1 All ER 821, [1971] 1 Lloyd's Rep 145; all following *Salomon v Customs and Excise Comrs* [1967] 2 QB 116, [1966] 3 All ER 871, CA; and *Post Office v Estuary Radio Ltd* [1968] 2 QB 740, [1967] 3 All ER 663, CA.

## 87. Jurisdiction under the Hovercraft Act 1968. Part II of the Senior Courts Act 1981[1] has effect as if references to ships, subject to certain exceptions, included references to hovercraft[2]; but the application of that legislation to hovercraft may be excluded or modified by Order in Council[3].

1   Ie the Senior Courts Act 1981 Pt II (ss 15–52) (see PARAS 79 et seq, 88 et seq).

2   See the Hovercraft Act 1968 s 2(1); and PARA 383. As to the regulation of hovercraft generally see PARA 381 et seq.

Except as otherwise provided by or under the Hovercraft Act 1968 or an enactment passed before 26 July 1968, as from 29 June 1972 a hovercraft must not be treated as a ship, aircraft or motor vehicle for the purposes of any such enactment or any instrument having effect by virtue of any such enactment: see s 4(3); and PARA 381.

3   See the Hovercraft Act 1968 s 2(3); and PARA 383.

**88. Jurisdiction under the Merchant Shipping Act 1995 in respect of liability for damage from oil pollution.** Admiralty jurisdiction in respect of claims for damage done by a ship[1] extends to claims under the Merchant Shipping Act 1995 in respect of:

    (1)    liability incurred for oil pollution damage[2]; or

    (2)    a liability falling on the International Oil Pollution Compensation Funds[3].

1  As to which generally see the Senior Courts Act 1981 s 20(1)(a), (2)(e); and PARA 110 et seq.

2  See the Senior Courts Act 1981 s 20(5)(a); and COURTS AND TRIBUNALS vol 24 (2010) PARA 703. Head (1) in the text refers to liability that may be incurred under the Merchant Shipping Act 1995 Pt VI Ch III (ss 152–171) (see ENVIRONMENTAL QUALITY AND PUBLIC HEALTH vol 45 (2010) PARA 441 et seq). As to the jurisdiction of United Kingdom courts and the registration of foreign judgments under Pt VI Ch III see s 166; and ENVIRONMENTAL QUALITY AND PUBLIC HEALTH vol 45 (2010) PARA 456.

3  See the Senior Courts Act 1981 s 20(5)(b); and COURTS AND TRIBUNALS vol 24 (2010) PARA 703. Head (2) in the text refers to liability that may be incurred under the Merchant Shipping Act 1995 Pt VI Ch IV (ss 172–182C) (see ENVIRONMENTAL QUALITY AND PUBLIC HEALTH vol 45 (2010) PARA 464 et seq). See also *Practice Direction—Admiralty Claims* PD 61 para 11; and PARA 155.

**89. Jurisdiction as a prize court.** The High Court is a prize court[1] and has all such jurisdiction[2] as is conferred on it by the Prize Acts 1864 to 1944[3] and all such other jurisdiction on the high seas and elsewhere as it had as a prize court immediately before 1 January 1982 (that is, before the commencement of the Senior Courts Act 1981)[4].

Appeals from all Admiralty courts in prize cases (including the High Court when acting as a prize court) lie to the Judicial Committee of the Privy Council[5].

1  See generally PRIZE vol 85 (2012) PARA 645 et seq.

2  Ie in accordance with the Senior Courts Act 1981 s 19(2) (general jurisdiction of the High Court) (see COURTS AND TRIBUNALS vol 24 (2010) PARA 700): see s 27.

3  See the Senior Courts Act 1981 s 27(a); and COURTS AND TRIBUNALS vol 24 (2010) PARA 701. In the Prize Acts 1864 to 1944, references to the High Court of Admiralty are by virtue of the Senior Courts Act 1981 s 151(5), Sch 4 para 1 to be construed as references to the High Court: see s 27(a). As to the Prize Acts 1864 to 1944 see PRIZE vol 85 (2012) PARA 603.

4  See the Senior Courts Act 1981 ss 27(b), 153(2); and PRIZE vol 85 (2012) PARA 645.

5  See the Naval Prize Act 1864 s 5; and PRIZE vol 85 (2012) PARA 684. As to the Judicial Committee of the Privy Council see CONSTITUTIONAL AND ADMINISTRATIVE LAW vol 20 (2014) PARA 147.

**90. Restrictions on jurisdiction.** The jurisdiction of the English courts may be excluded or limited in Admiralty matters, or generally, as a result of (for example):

    (1)    conflicts of jurisdiction, and disputes as to the forum in which claims should be heard[1];

    (2)    statutory rules governing the mode of exercise of the jurisdiction[2] and statutory restrictions on the entertainment of actions in collision and other similar cases where the claim is in personam[3];

    (3)    restrictions on the entertainment of claims for wages by the master or a member of the crew of a foreign ship, in cases where the consul in London objects[4];

    (4)    restrictions on the entertainment of claims against the Crown, or the arrest, detention or sale of any of Her Majesty's ships or aircraft, or of any cargo or other property belonging to the Crown[5];

    (5)    the general immunity enjoyed by certain individuals and bodies from the jurisdiction of the English courts[6];

(6)    the general restriction, except by leave of the court and subject to such terms as it may impose, on claims or proceedings against companies or their property in cases where a winding-up order has been made or a provisional liquidator has been appointed in respect of that company[7].

1    The matters mentioned in head (1) in the text are subject to relevant agreements and commitments which are binding on the United Kingdom: see PARA 95 et seq. See also PARA 85. As to the meaning of 'United Kingdom' see PARA 16 note 3.

2    See the Senior Courts Act 1981 s 21; and PARA 93 et seq. See also PARAS 85, 95 et seq.

3    See the Senior Courts Act 1981 s 22; and PARA 94. The power of a receiver of wreck to detain a ship in respect of a salvage claim is also unaffected by the Admiralty jurisdiction of the High Court: see the Senior Courts Act 1981 s 24(2)(b); and PARA 85.

4    See the Consular Relations Act 1968 s 4; and PARA 128. See also the Senior Courts Act 1981 s 24(2)(a); and PARA 85. As to the requirements as to notice to the consul of the foreign state when a foreign ship is arrested see PARA 161.

5    See the Crown Proceedings Act 1947 s 29(1); and PARA 179. See also the Senior Courts Act 1981 s 24(2)(c); and PARA 85.

6    Predominant among the persons mentioned in head (5) in the text are states, and others entitled to plead sovereign or diplomatic immunity, although the nature and extent of the immunity varies according to the identity of the claimant and the nature of the claim brought: see INTERNATIONAL RELATIONS LAW vol 61 (2010) PARA 242 et seq. See also PARA 86. Cf *Bridge Oil Ltd v Owners and/or Demise Charterers of the Ship Giuseppe di Vittorio* (1997) Times, 10 November, [1997] All ER (D) 39, CA, a case in which the Republic of Ukraine as owner of the vessel and a successor state to the former Union of Soviet Socialist Republics was not entitled to claim sovereign immunity to defeat the creditor's claim.

    Similar immunities to those mentioned in head (5) in the text may be conferred upon an international organisation by order made under the International Organisations Act 1968: see INTERNATIONAL RELATIONS LAW vol 61 (2010) PARA 309 et seq.

7    See the Insolvency Act 1986 s 130; and COMPANY AND PARTNERSHIP INSOLVENCY vol 17 (2011) PARA 851. See also the Cross-Border Insolvency Regulations 2006, SI 2006/1030; Parliament and Council Regulation (EU) 2015/848 (OJ L141, 5.6.2015, p 19) on insolvency proceedings; *Aria Inc v Credit Agricole Corporate and Investment Bank* [2014] EWHC 872 (Comm), [2014] All ER (D) 244 (Mar); *Bank of Tokyo-Mitsubishi UFJ Ltd v Owners of the MV Sanko Mineral* [2014] EWHC 3927 (Admlty), [2015[ 2 All ER (Comm) 979; and COMPANY AND PARTNERSHIP INSOLVENCY vol 17 (2011) PARA 1127 et seq. See also, as to insolvency generally, *International Transportation Service Inc v Owners of the Ship 'Convenience Container'* [2006] HKCFI 465, [2006] 2 Lloyd's Rep 556.

## (iv) Procedural Matters

**91. Assignment of business to Admiralty Court.** All jurisdiction vested in the High Court under the Senior Courts Act 1981 belongs to all the divisions alike[1], and all the judges of that court have equal power, authority and jurisdiction[2]. However, the following claims must be started in the Admiralty Court[3]:

(1)    a claim in rem[4]; a claim for damage done by a ship[5]; a claim concerning the ownership of a ship[6]; a claim under the Merchant Shipping Act 1995[7]; a claim for loss of life or personal injury as specified in the Senior Courts Act 1981[8]; a claim by a master or member of a crew for wages[9]; a claim in the nature of towage[10]; or a claim in the nature of pilotage[11];

(2)    a collision claim[12];

(3)    a limitation claim[13]; or

(4)    a salvage claim[14].

Any other Admiralty claim may be started in the Admiralty Court[15].

All proceedings by which any application is made to the High Court under the Merchant Shipping Act 1995 are also taken by the Admiralty Court[16].

The procedural rule that allows the High Court to order proceedings in any Division of the High Court to be transferred to another Division, and allows a judge dealing with claims in a specialist list to order proceedings to be transferred to or from that list[17], applies to claims in the Admiralty Court except that the

Admiralty Court may order the transfer of a claim to the Commercial List[18], to a Mercantile Court[19], to the Mercantile list at the County Court at Central London[20], or to any other appropriate court[21].

1  See the Senior Courts Act 1981 s 5(5); and COURTS AND TRIBUNALS vol 24 (2010) PARA 696. This is without prejudice to the provisions of the Senior Courts Act 1981 relating to the distribution of business in the High Court: see s 5(5). As to the distribution of business between divisions of the High Court see COURTS AND TRIBUNALS vol 24 (2010) PARA 703.

2  See the Senior Courts Act 1981 s 4(3); and COURTS AND TRIBUNALS vol 24 (2010) PARA 695.

3  CPR 61.2(1). For these purposes, 'Admiralty Court' means the Admiralty Court of the Queen's Bench Division of the High Court of Justice (CPR 61.1(2)(b)); and 'Admiralty claim' means a claim within the Admiralty jurisdiction of the High Court as set out in the Senior Courts Act 1981 s 20 (see PARAS 85 et seq, 92 et seq) (CPR 61.1(2)(a)). CPR Pt 61 applies to Admiralty claims (CPR 61.1(1); and see the Admiralty and Commercial Courts Guide (2016) para N1.1) but CPR Pt 58 (Commercial Court) applies to claims in the Admiralty Court where CPR Pt 61 does not provide otherwise (CPR 61.1(3)). Similarly, the practice direction which supplements CPR Pt 58 (ie *Practice Direction—Commercial Court* PD 58) also applies to Admiralty claims except where it is inconsistent with either CPR Pt 61 or *Practice Direction—Admiralty Claims* PD 61: see para 1.1. As to the procedure that governs Admiralty claims, including CPR Pt 61 and *Practice Direction—Admiralty Claims* PD 61, see PARA 157 et seq. As to the practice and procedure that applies in the Commercial Court, including CPR Pt 58 and *Practice Direction—Commercial Court* PD 58, see CIVIL PROCEDURE vol 11 (2015) PARA 170 et seq; COURTS AND TRIBUNALS vol 24 (2010) PARA 708.

   The Admiralty and Commercial Courts Guide is published with the approval of the Lord Chief Justice and the Head of Civil Justice in consultation with the Judges of the Admiralty and Commercial Courts and with the advice and support of the Admiralty Court and Commercial Court Committees: see para A1.2. It is intended to provide guidance about the conduct of proceedings in the Admiralty and Commercial Courts and, within the framework of the Civil Procedure Rules and Practice Directions, to establish the practice to be followed in those courts: see para A1.2; and PARA 157 et seq. As to the Commercial Court Committee see para A3; and as to the Admiralty Court Committee see para N2.

4  CPR 61.2(1)(a)(i). For these purposes, 'claim in rem' means a claim in an admiralty action in rem: CPR 61.1(2)(c). As to claims in rem see PARAS 83 et seq, 92 et seq; and as to the procedure that applies to claims in rem see PARA 158 et seq.

5  CPR 61.2(1)(a)(ii). For these purposes, 'ship' includes any vessel used in navigation: CPR 61.1(2)(k) (as so added). As to claims for damage done by a ship see PARA 110 et seq.

6  CPR 61.2(1)(a)(iii). As to claims concerning the ownership of a ship see PARA 104 et seq.

7  CPR 61.2(1)(a)(iv). Specifically, the Admiralty jurisdiction of the High Court to hear and determine any claim for damage done by a ship (as to which see the Senior Courts Act 1981 s 20(1)(a), (2)(e); and PARA 110 et seq) extends to claims in respect of liability for damage from oil pollution incurred under the Merchant Shipping Act 1995 Pt VI Ch III (ss 152–171) (see the Senior Courts Act 1981 s 20(5)(a); and COURTS AND TRIBUNALS vol 24 (2010) PARA 703) or under the Merchant Shipping Act 1995 Pt VI Ch IV (ss 172–182C) (see the Senior Courts Act 1981 s 20(5)(b); and ENVIRONMENTAL QUALITY AND PUBLIC HEALTH vol 45 (2010) PARA 464 et seq): see PARA 88.

8  CPR 61.2(1)(a)(v). The text refers to a claim that is specified in the Senior Courts Act 1981 s 20(2)(f) (as to which see PARA 112): see CPR 61.2(1)(a)(v).

9  CPR 61.2(1)(a)(vi). As to claims by a master or member of a crew for wages see PARA 127 et seq.

10  CPR 61.2(1)(a)(vii). As to claims in the nature of towage see PARA 125 et seq.

11  CPR 61.2(1)(a)(viii). As to claims in the nature of pilotage see PARA 125 et seq.

12  CPR 61.2(1)(b). For these purposes, 'collision claim' means a claim within the Senior Courts Act 1981 s 20(3)(b) (see PARA 180): see CPR 61.1(2)(d).

13  CPR 61.2(1)(c). For these purposes, 'limitation claim' means a claim under the Merchant Shipping Act 1995 for the limitation of liability in connection with a ship or other property (see PARA 195 et seq): see CPR 61.1(2)(e). See also the Senior Courts Act 1981 s 20(1)(b), (3)(c); and PARA 194.

14  CPR 61.2(1)(d). For these purposes, 'salvage claim' means a claim:

   (1)  for or in the nature of salvage (see PARAS 113, 849 et seq) (CPR 61.1(2)(f)(i));
   (2)  for special compensation under the Merchant Shipping Act 1995 Sch 11 art 14 (ie regarding salvage operations in respect of a vessel which by itself or its cargo threatened damage to the environment) (see PARAS 113, 879) (CPR 61.1(2)(f)(ii));
   (3)  for the apportionment of salvage (as to which see PARAS 113, 119, 902 et seq) (CPR 61.1(2)(f)(iii)); and
   (4)  arising out of or connected with any contract for salvage services (as to which see PARA 113) (CPR 61.1(2)(f)(iv)).

15 CPR 61.2(2).
16 Senior Courts Act 1981 s 20(1)(b), (3)(a) (s 20(3)(a) amended by the Merchant Shipping Act 1995 s 314(2), Sch 13 para 59(2)).
17 Ie CPR 30.5 (as to which see CIVIL PROCEDURE vol 11 (2015) PARA 106): see CPR 61.2(3). As to specialist proceedings see CIVIL PROCEDURE vol 11 (2015) PARA 170 et seq. If a claim is to be in one of the specialist High Court lists, and the High Court is to issue the claim form, the form must state that the claim is to be in one of the specialist lists and also state which list: see CPR 16.3; and CIVIL PROCEDURE vol 11 (2015) PARA 344.
18 CPR 61.2(3)(a). As to the Commercial List see CIVIL PROCEDURE vol 11 (2015) PARA 170 et seq.
19 CPR 61.2(3)(b). As to the Mercantile Courts and business lists see CIVIL PROCEDURE vol 11 (2015) PARA 179.
20 CPR 61.2(3)(c). As to the Mercantile list at the Central London County Court see CIVIL PROCEDURE vol 11 (2015) PARA 179.
21 CPR 61.2(3)(d). See also *NV Bureau Wijsmuller v The Tojo Maru (Owners)* [1968] 2 Lloyd's Rep 436, CA (a salvage case, in which a judge's decision not to order a transfer was reversed on appeal).

## 92. Nature of claims in rem and claims in personam ('other claims').

A claim in rem is a claim against the ship itself[1], but the view that, if the owners of the vessel do not acknowledge service of the claim form in order to defend their property, then no personal liability can be established against them[2] has been questioned[3]. It has been stated that, if the defendant acknowledges service, a claim in rem becomes (or continues also as) a claim in personam[4]; but the Admiralty jurisdiction of the High Court may now in all cases be invoked by a claim in personam, although this is subject to certain restrictions in the case of collision and similar cases, except where the defendant submits or agrees to submit to the jurisdiction of the court[5].

The foundation of a claim in rem is the lien resulting from the personal liability of the owner of the res (that is, the subject property of the claim)[6]. Therefore, a claim in rem cannot be brought to recover damages for injury caused to a ship by the malicious act of the master of the defendant's ship[7], or for damage done at a time when the ship was in the control of third parties by reason of compulsory requisition[8]. On the other hand, in several cases, ships allowed by their owners to be in the possession and control of charterers have been successfully proceeded against to enforce liens which arose whilst the ships were in control of such third parties[9].

The defendant in an Admiralty claim in personam is liable, as in other claims in the High Court, for the full amount of the claimant's proved claim[10]. Equally, in a claim in rem, a defendant who acknowledges service is now liable for the full amount of the judgment[11], even though it exceeds the value of the res or of the bail provided[12]. The right to recovery of damages may, however, be affected by the right of the defendant to the benefit of statutory provisions relating to limitation of liability[13].

1 As to the origin of claims in rem see PARA 83.
2 The traditional view is that, where there has been no acknowledgment of service (formerly entry of appearance) in a claim in rem, the claimant's only remedy is the sale of the arrested res, so that he can neither obtain execution for any unsatisfied balance of his claim, nor claim any remedy such as an order for specific performance against the defendant: see *The Burns* [1907] P 137 at 149, CA (a case decided under the Public Authorities Protection Act 1893 (repealed) limiting the time within which action may be taken against certain persons, and following *The Longford* (1889) 14 PD 34, CA). See also *The Banco* [1971] P 137 at 151, [1971] 1 All ER 524 at 531, [1971] 1 Lloyd's Rep 49 at 52, CA, per Lord Denning MR.
3 See *The Conoco Britannia* [1972] 2 All ER 238 at 245 per Brandon J, where it was said that the point did not, strictly speaking, arise for decision in any of the cases cited in note 2, and, to this extent, has not been decided. See also *Stolt Kestrel BV v Sener Petrol Denizcilik Ticaret AS; CDE SA v Sure Wind Marine Ltd* [2015] EWCA Civ 1035, [2015] All ER (D) 146 (Oct).
4 *The Gemma* [1899] P 285 at 292, CA, per AL Smith LJ. Cf *The Broadmayne* [1916] P 64 at 77, CA, proposing the view that the claim proceeds only as if it were a claim in personam whilst still

retaining the characteristics of a claim in rem. As to the origin of claims in personam (now known as 'other claims') see PARA 84; and as to claims in personam ('other claims') generally see PARA 92 et seq.

After acknowledgment of service in an Admiralty claim in rem, the claim does not lose its in rem character, but proceeds as a hybrid, being both in rem and in personam even though the res may have been released by the court: see *The Maciej Rataj* [1992] 2 Lloyd's Rep 552, CA. See also *The Indian Endurance (No 2), Republic of India v India Steamship Co Ltd* [1998] AC 878, [1997] 4 All ER 380, [1998] 1 Lloyd's Rep 1, HL. See further *The Banco* [1971] P 137 at 151, [1971] 1 All ER 524 at 531, [1971] 1 Lloyd's Rep 49 at 51, CA, per Lord Denning MR; and *The August 8* [1983] 2 AC 450, [1983] 1 Lloyd's Rep 351, PC. It has not yet been decided whether or not, in a claim in rem where the defendant has not acknowledged service, the claimant claiming equitable relief may enforce an order for specific performance or granting an injunction: see *The Conoco Britannia* [1972] 2 All ER 238 at 244–245 per Brandon J. See also *The Nordglimt* [1988] QB 183, [1988] 2 All ER 531, [1987] 2 Lloyd's Rep 470; *The Linda* [1988] 1 Lloyd's Rep 175.

For the purposes of Parliament and Council Regulation (EU) 1215/2012 (OJ L351, 20.12.2012, p 1) on jurisdiction and the recognition and enforcement of judgments in civil and commercial matters ('the 'Brussels I' Regulation') (see CONFLICT OF LAWS vol 19 (2011) PARA 366 et seq), no distinction is drawn between in rem and in personam proceedings: see *The Deichland* [1990] 1 QB 361, [1989] 2 All ER 1066, CA; Case C-406/92 *The Tatry* C [1999] QB 515.

5   See the Senior Courts Act 1981 ss 21, 22; and PARA 94. See *LD Commodities Rice Merchandising LLC v Owners and/or Demise Charterers of the Vessel Styliani Z* [2015] EWHC 3060 (Admlty), [2016] 1 Lloyd's Rep 395 (claim wrongly started in personam).

6   *The Utopia* [1893] AC 492 at 499, PC; *The Castlegate* [1893] AC 38 at 52, HL, per Lord Watson; and see *The Parlement Belge* (1880) 5 PD 197, CA; *The Father Thames* [1979] 2 Lloyd's Rep. 364 (ship liable in rem even though negligence only of bareboat charterer). As to the personal liability of the beneficial owner as a ground of statutory jurisdiction in rem see PARA 93. For a general discussion of maritime liens see PARA 964 et seq.

7   *The Ida* (1860) Lush 6; see also *Currie v M'Knight* [1897] AC 97, 8 Asp MLC 193, HL.

8   *The Sylvan Arrow* [1923] P 220, 16 Asp MLC 244, where the authorities are reviewed by Hill J.

9   *The Ruby Queen* (1861) Lush 266; *The Lemington* (1874) 2 Asp MLC 475; *The Tasmania* (1888) 13 PD 110. The authorities differ as to whether the right to proceed in rem against the ship in the possession and control of charterers arises on the basis that the charterers are deemed to have authority from the owner to subject the ship to the lien (*The Ripon City* [1897] P 226 at 244), or whether the lien arises by reason of the charterers being 'owners' for this purpose (see the remarks of Brandon J in *The Andrea Ursula* [1973] QB 265 at 269–270, [1971] 1 All ER 821 at 824–825, [1971] 1 Lloyd's Rep 145 at 147–148, where the issue is regarded as irrelevant since the Administration of Justice Act 1956). Charterers having possession and control as above are usually described as charterers by demise or bareboat charterers. See also PARA 93.

10   This follows from the unification of jurisdiction and of law on the creation of the High Court by the Supreme Court of Judicature Act 1873 (repealed).

11   *The Dictator* [1892] P 304; *The Joannis Vatis (No 2)* [1922] P 213.

12   *The Dupleix* [1912] P 8, following the view expressed by Jeune J in *The Dictator* [1892] P 304, and approved by the Court of Appeal in *The Gemma* [1899] P 285, CA. In any event, since the Supreme Court of Judicature Consolidation Acts 1873 and 1875, the defendant who acknowledges service renders himself liable to all the remedies enforceable by the High Court of Justice: see *The Joannis Vatis (No 2)* [1922] P 213 at 222 per Duke P. See also *The Indian Endurance (No 2), Republic of India v India Steamship Co Ltd* [1998] AC 878, [1997] 4 All ER 380, [1998] 1 Lloyd's Rep 1, HL. As to the position where the defendant in a claim in rem does not acknowledge service see the text and notes 2–3.

13   As to the statutory right to limit liability and the procedure relating to such claims see PARA 194 et seq.

**93. Claims in rem and the ship or property which is the subject.** The Admiralty jurisdiction of the High Court[1] may be invoked, and an action in rem brought against the ship[2] or property in connection with which any of the following claims or questions arise[3]:

(1)   any claim to the possession of a ship or ownership of a ship or to the ownership of a share in a ship[4];

(2)   any question arising between the co-owners of a ship as to possession, employment or earnings of that ship[5];

(3)   any claim in respect of a mortgage or charge on a ship or any share in a ship[6]; and

(4)     any claim for the forfeiture or condemnation of a ship, or of goods
        which are being or have been carried, or have attempted to be carried,
        in a ship, or for the restoration of a ship or any such goods after seizure,
        or for droits of Admiralty[7].

Where a dispute under a charterparty has gone to arbitration, current case law is
uncertain as to whether a claim in rem may be brought to enforce the award[8].
Jurisdiction exists even though the claimant's purpose in invoking it is simply to
obtain security in arbitration proceedings, but exercise of the power of arrest is
discretionary, not mandatory[9].

The Admiralty jurisdiction of the High Court may be invoked also to hear and
determine a number of other claims[10], as follows:

(a)     any claim for damage done by a ship[11];
(b)     any claim for loss of life or personal injury sustained in consequence of
        any defects in a ship or in her apparel or equipment, or in consequence
        of the wrongful act, neglect or default of certain persons[12], being an act,
        neglect or default in the navigation or management of the ship, in the
        loading, carriage or discharge of goods on, in or from the ship, or in the
        embarkation, carriage or disembarkation of persons on, in or from the
        ship[13];
(c)     any claim for loss of or damage to goods carried in a ship[14];
(d)     any claim arising out of any agreement relating to the carriage of goods
        in a ship or for the use or hire of a ship[15];
(e)     any of the following claims (whether in connection with a ship or an
        aircraft), namely:
        (i)     any claim under the International Convention on Salvage 1989[16];
        (ii)    any claim under any contract for or in relation to salvage
                services[17]; or
        (iii)   any claim in the nature of salvage not falling within head (i) or
                head (ii) above[18];
(f)     any claim in the nature of towage in respect of a ship or an aircraft[19];
(g)     any claim in the nature of pilotage in respect of a ship or aircraft[20];
(h)     any claim in respect of goods or materials supplied to a ship for her
        operation or maintenance[21];
(i)     any claim in respect of the construction, repair or equipment of a ship
        or dock charges or dues[22];
(j)     any claim by a master or member of the crew of a ship for wages
        (including any sum allotted out of wages or adjudged by a
        superintendent to be due by way of wages)[23];
(k)     any claim by a master, shipper, charterer or agent in respect of
        disbursements made on account of a ship[24];
(l)     any claim arising out of an act which is or is claimed to be a general
        average act[25]; and
(m)     any claim arising out of bottomry[26].

However, in the case of any claim falling within heads (a) to (m) above[27], where
the claim arises in connection with a ship[28], and where the person who would be
liable in a claim in personam (the 'relevant person')[29] was, when the cause of
action arose, the owner or charterer of, or in possession or in control of, the
ship[30], the jurisdiction may be invoked by a claim in rem[31] either:

(A)     against that ship (if at the time when the claim is brought the relevant
        person is either the beneficial owner[32] of that ship as respects all the
        shares in it or the charterer of it under a charter by demise)[33]; or

(B)     against any other ship of which, at the time when the claim is brought[34], the relevant person is the beneficial owner as respects all the shares in it[35].

The purpose of this provision is to confer the right to arrest either the ship in respect of which the cause of action is alleged to have arisen or any other ship in the same ownership (that is, against what is generally referred to as a 'sister' ship which is owned by the person who would be liable in a claim in personam)[36]. This right is conferred whether or not the claim in rem gives rise to a maritime lien on the ship mentioned in head (A) above[37]. Where, as regards any such claim falling within heads (a) to (m) above[38], a ship has been served with a claim form or arrested in a claim in rem brought to enforce that claim, no other ship may be served with a claim form or arrested in that or any other claim in rem brought to enforce that claim, but this does not prevent the issue, in respect of any one such claim, of a claim form naming more than one ship or of two or more claim forms each naming a different ship[39].

In the case of a claim in the nature of towage or pilotage in respect of an aircraft[40], a claim in rem may be brought in the High Court against that aircraft if, at the time when the claim is brought, it is beneficially owned by the person who would be liable on the claim in a claim in personam[41].

In any case where there is a maritime lien[42] or other charge[43] on any ship, aircraft or other property for the amount claimed, a claim in rem may be brought in the High Court against that ship, aircraft or property[44]. A maritime lien may be so invoked against the ship, aircraft or other property, even in the hands of an innocent purchaser[45].

Where, in the exercise of its Admiralty jurisdiction, the High Court orders any ship, aircraft or other property to be sold, the court has jurisdiction to hear and determine any question arising as to the title to the proceeds of sale[46].

Nothing in the Crown Proceedings Act 1947 authorises proceedings in rem in respect of any claim against the Crown, or the arrest, detention or sale of any of His Majesty's ships or aircraft, or of any cargo or other property belonging to the Crown, or gives to any person any lien on any such ship, aircraft, cargo or other property[47].

1   As to the Admiralty jurisdiction of the High Court of Justice generally see PARA 85 et seq. The Admiralty jurisdiction of the High Court extends also to hovercraft: see PARA 87.
2   As to the origin of claims in rem see PARA 83; and as to claims in rem generally see PARA 92. As to the meaning of 'ship' for these purposes see PARA 85 note 7.
3   See the Senior Courts Act 1981 s 21(2). As to claims where the right is conferred to arrest either the ship in respect of which the cause of action is alleged to have arisen or any other ship in the same ownership see heads (a) to (m) in the text. As to the procedure that governs Admiralty claims see PARA 157 et seq.
4   See the Senior Courts Act 1981 ss 20(1)(a), (2)(a), 21(2); and PARA 104.
5   See the Senior Courts Act 1981 ss 20(1)(a), (2)(b), 21(2); and PARA 106.
6   See the Senior Courts Act 1981 ss 20(1)(a), (2)(c), 21(2); and PARA 109.
7   See the Senior Courts Act 1981 ss 20(1)(a), (2)(s), 21(2); and PARA 135.
8   See *The Bumbesti* [2000] QB 559, [2000] 2 All ER 692, [1999] 2 Lloyd's Rep 481 (not following *The St Anna* [1983] 2 All ER 691); *The Irina Zharkikh* [2001] 2 Lloyd's Rep 319 at [54] (following *The Bumbesti*); see also *Handytankers AS v Alas (Owners)* [2014] HKCFI 1281, [2015] 1 Lloyd's Rep. 211.
9   See *The Vasso (formerly Andria)* [1984] QB 477, [1984] 1 All ER 1126, CA.
10  See the Senior Courts Act 1981 s 20(1)(a); and PARA 104 et seq. The other claims referred to in the text are those mentioned in s 20(1)(a), (2)(e)–(r) (see heads (a)–(m) in the text): see s 20(1)(a); and PARA 110 et seq.
11  See the Senior Courts Act 1981 s 20(1)(a), (2)(e); and PARA 110. Claims in respect of damage received by a ship (as to which see s 20(1)(a), (2)(d); and PARA 110) no longer give rise to

proceedings in rem, this being the combined effect of s 21(2), (4) (see heads (1) to (4) and heads (a) to (m) in the text), neither of which mentions s 20(1)(a), (2)(d).

12 The persons specified for these purposes are (by virtue of the Senior Courts Act 1981 s 20(1)(a), (2)(f): see PARA 112):
    (1)    the owners, charterers or persons in possession or control of a ship; or
    (2)    the master or crew of a ship, or any other person for whose wrongful acts, neglects or defaults the owners, charterers or persons in possession or control of a ship are responsible.

13 See the Senior Courts Act 1981 s 20(1)(a), (2)(f); and PARA 112.
14 See the Senior Courts Act 1981 s 20(1)(a), (2)(g); and PARA 111.
15 See the Senior Courts Act 1981 s 20(1)(a), (2)(h); and PARA 111. To fall within the provisions, an agreement must have a reasonably direct connection with the carriage of goods in a ship: _Gatoil International Inc v Arkwright-Boston Manufacturers Mutual Insurance Co_ [1985] AC 255, [1985] 1 All ER 129, [1985] 1 Lloyd's Rep 181, HL. See also _Petrofina SA v AOT Ltd, The Maersk Nimrod_ [1992] QB 571, [1991] 3 All ER 161 (agreement relating to carriage of goods in a ship does not cover cifcontract for sale of goods, since carriage of goods by sea was merely one matter to which contract related and was not its central concern).
16 See the Senior Courts Act 1981 s 20(1)(a), (2)(j)(i); and PARAS 113–114. The text refers to the International Convention on Salvage 1989 (London, 28 April 1989; Cm 1526) (as to which see PARA 7) as it has effect under the Merchant Shipping Act 1995 s 224 (as to which see PARAS 851 et seq): see the Senior Courts Act 1981 s 20(6)(a); and PARA 113.
17 See the Senior Courts Act 1981 s 20(1)(a), (2)(j)(ii); and PARAS 113–114.
18 See the Senior Courts Act 1981 s 20(1)(a), (2)(j)(iii); and PARAS 113–114.
19 See the Senior Courts Act 1981 s 20(1)(a), (2)(k); and PARA 125.
20 See the Senior Courts Act 1981 s 20(1)(a), (2)(l); and PARA 125.
21 See the Senior Courts Act 1981 s 20(1)(a), (2)(m); and PARA 126.
22 See the Senior Courts Act 1981 s 20(1)(a), (2)(n); and PARA 126.
23 See the Senior Courts Act 1981 s 20(1)(a), (2)(o); and PARAS 127–130.
24 See the Senior Courts Act 1981 s 20(1)(a), (2)(p); and PARAS 127, 132.
25 See the Senior Courts Act 1981 s 20(1)(a), (2)(q); and PARA 133.
26 See the Senior Courts Act 1981 s 20(1)(a), (2)(r); and PARA 134.
27 Ie any such claim as is mentioned in the Senior Courts Act 1981 s 20(1)(a), (2)(e)–(r) (see heads (a) to (m) in the text): see s 21(4).
28 Senior Courts Act 1981 s 21(4)(a).
29 In determining for the purposes of the Senior Courts Act 1981 s 21(4) whether a person would be liable on an in personam claim, it must be assumed that he has his habitual residence or place of business within England and Wales: s 21(7). As to the meanings of 'England' and 'Wales' see PARA 17 note 2. As to a discussion of habitual residence in European and domestic law see CONFLICT OF LAWS vol 19 (2011) PARA 360. As to a person's place of business see COMPANIES vol 14 (2016) PARA 117. The purpose of the words 'the person who would be liable on the claim in an action in personam' is to identify the person or persons whose ship or ships may be arrested and they do not require the claimant to prove that he has a good cause of action before making an arrest: see _The St Elefterio_ [1957] P 179 at 186, [1957] 2 All ER 374 at 377, [1957] 1 Lloyd's Rep 283 at 287 per Willmer J. See also _The Giuseppe di Vittorio_ [1998] 1 Lloyd's Rep 136, CA; _Bank of Tokyo-Mitsubishi UFJ Ltd v Owners of the MV Sanko Mineral_ [2014] EWHC 3927 (Admlty), [2014] All ER (D) 14 (Dec). As to the origin of claims in personam see PARA 84; and as to claims in personam generally see PARA 92 et seq.
30 Senior Courts Act 1981 s 21(4)(b). See _Aluflet SA v Vinave Empresa de Navegaçao Maritima LDA, The Faial_ [2000] 1 Lloyd's Rep 473; _The Chem Orchid_ [2015] SGHC 50, [2015] 2 Lloyd's Rep 666; _The Catur Samudra_ [2010] SGHCD 18, [2010] 1 Lloyd's Rep 305 (on parallel Singapore provisions); _Chimbusco Pan Nation Petro-Chemical Co Ltd v The Owners and/or Demise Charterers of the Ship or Vessel Decurion_ [2013] HKCA 180; [2013] 2 Lloyd's Rep 407 (on parallel Hong Kong provisions).
31 The claim form may be served effectively upon a ship, and security obtained by the arrest of the ship even in cases where no maritime lien attaches, despite a change in ownership of the vessel between the time of issue of the claim form and service: _The Monica S_ [1968] P 741, [1967] 3 All ER 740; but see the views expressed obiter in _The Banco_ [1971] P 137 at 153, [1971] 1 All ER 524 at 533, [1971] 1 Lloyd's Rep 49 at 53, CA, per Lord Denning MR and at 159, 538 and 57 per Megaw LJ. See also _The Helene Roth_ [1980] QB 273, [1980] 1 All ER 1078, [1980] 1 Lloyd's Rep 477, where the change in ownership of the defendant vessel was held to be no bar to the renewal of the claim form. See also _The Giuseppe di Vittorio_ [1998] 1 Lloyd's Rep 136, CA.
32 'Beneficial owner' has been held to mean a person who lawfully has full possession and control, and to include a charterer by demise: _The Andrea Ursula_ [1973] QB 265, [1971] 1 All ER 821, [1971] 1 Lloyd's Rep 145 (not following _The St Merriel_ [1963] P 247, [1963] 1 All ER 537). This decision was not followed in _The I Congreso del Partido_ [1978] QB 500 at 538–543, [1978] 1 All

ER 1169 at 1201–1204, [1977] 1 Lloyd's Rep 536 at 560–562 per Goff J, where it was held that the phrase 'beneficially owned' did not apply to a demise charterer but has its ordinary meaning of equitable owner. As to beneficial ownership see also *The Nazym Khikmet* [1996] 2 Lloyd's Rep 362, CA. Where the transfer of a vessel (whether British or not) is a sham, the original owner will retain beneficial ownership: *The Tjaskemolen (now named Visvliet)* [1997] 2 Lloyd's Rep 465. See also *The Giuseppe di Vittorio* [1998] 1 Lloyd's Rep 136, CA.

33  Senior Courts Act 1981 s 21(4)(i). The 'relevant person' can be a demise charterer, even in the absence of a consensual agreement between the parties in the nature of a demise charter, if the legal relationship between the parties invests the 'relevant person' with the right of a demise charterer against the owner of the vessel: *The Giuseppe di Vittorio* [1998] 1 Lloyd's Rep 136, CA. A slot charterer of spaces on a container ship for the carriage of goods is capable of coming within the definition of a charterer in the Senior Courts Act 1981 s 21(4)(b), despite the fact that the slot charter gave control of only part of the vessel to the charterer: *The Tychy* [1999] 2 Lloyd's Rep 11, CA. See also *The Giuseppe di Vittorio*.

34  See note 31.

35  Senior Courts Act 1981 s 21(4)(ii).

36  See *The St Elefterio* [1957] P 179 at 185–186, [1957] 2 All ER 374 at 377, [1957] 1 Lloyd's Rep 283 at 287 per Willmer J (discussing the Administration of Justice Act 1956 s 3(4) (now repealed, and re-enacted, by the Senior Courts Act 1981: see now s 21(4)), the Administration of Justice Act 1956 s 3(4) having conferred this right for the first time in England). See also *The Aventicum* [1978] 1 Lloyd's Rep 184 (court empowered by the Administration of Justice Act 1956 s 3(4) (repealed: see now the Senior Courts Act 1981 s 21(4)) to look behind registered owner to determine true beneficial owner); *The Maritime Trader* [1981] 2 Lloyd's Rep 153 (ship owned by wholly-owned subsidiary company not 'beneficially owned' by defendant holding company). *The Maritime Trader* concerned a vertical relationship between a holding company and a subsidiary. The horizontal relationship between 'one-ship companies' was considered in the Court of Appeal in *The Evpo Agnic* [1988] 3 All ER 810, [1988] 1 WLR 1090, [1988] 2 Lloyd's Rep 411, CA. It has been held that the right of arrest under the Senior Courts Act 1981 s 21(4) does not extend to a ship owned by a sister company of the company owning the ship in connection with which the claim arose: see *The Nazym Khikmet* [1996] 2 Lloyd's Rep 362, CA. See also *The Giuseppe di Vittorio* [1998] 1 Lloyd's Rep 136, CA.

37  Senior Courts Act 1981 s 21(4). For a general discussion of maritime liens see PARA 964 et seq.

38  Ie any such claim as is mentioned in the Senior Courts Act 1981 s 20(1)(a), (2)(e)–(r) (see heads (a) to (m) in the text): see s 21(8).

39  Senior Courts Act 1981 s 21(8). See also *The Banco* [1971] P 137, [1971] 1 All ER 524, [1971] 1 Lloyd's Rep 49, CA. A claim form naming more than one vessel must be amended when one vessel has been selected for service of the proceedings by deleting the names of the other vessels: see *The Banco*; and PARA 158. Although the Senior Courts Act 1981 s 21(8) prevents the service of an in rem claim form and arrest of more than one ship in respect of the same claim, where a ship is served with an in rem claim form and arrested in the mistaken belief that it was a ship against which a claim in rem can be brought, this will not bar a subsequent claim against and arrest of a ship against which a claim can properly be brought: *The Stephan J* [1985] 2 Lloyd's Rep 344. The affidavit in support of the application for the second arrest should refer to the previous mistaken arrest and the reasons for it: *The Stephan J*.

40  For the purposes of the Senior Courts Act 1981 ss 20–23, unless the context otherwise requires, 'towage' and 'pilotage', in relation to an aircraft, mean towage and pilotage while the aircraft is waterborne: s 24(1). As to towage and pilotage see PARA 125.

41  Senior Courts Act 1981 s 21(5). In determining for the purpose of s 21(5) whether a person would be liable on a claim in personam, it must be assumed that he has his habitual residence or place of business within England and Wales: s 21(7).

42  The principal claims in respect of which the law recognises maritime liens are bottomry, salvage, wages, master's wages, disbursements and liabilities, and damage done by a ship: see *The Ripon City* [1897] P 226, 8 Asp MLC 304 per Gorrell Barnes J. As to the extent of Admiralty jurisdiction regarding salvage claims see PARA 113 et seq; as to wages and master's wages see PARA 127 et seq; and as to disbursements and liabilities see PARAS 131–132.

43  As to the meaning of 'other charge' (which has been held not to include a repairer's possessory lien) see *The St Merriel* [1963] P 247, [1963] 1 All ER 537, [1963] 1 Lloyd's Rep 63; and *The Acrux* [1965] P 391 at 403, [1965] 1 Lloyd's Rep 565 at 572 per Hewson J.

44  Senior Courts Act 1981 s 21(3). As to the meaning of 'ship' for these purposes see *The Alexander* (1812) 1 Dods 278; *The Silia* [1981] 2 Lloyd's Rep 534.

45  *The Bold Buccleugh* (1852) 7 Moo PCC 267; *Currie v M'Knight* [1897] AC 97, 8 Asp MLC 193, HL; *The Ripon City* [1897] P 226, 9 Asp MLC 304.

46  Senior Courts Act 1981 s 21(6). As to orders for sale see PARA 178.

47 See the Crown Proceedings Act 1947 s 29(1); and PARA 179. As to conversion into a claim in personam when proceedings are commenced inadvertently against Crown property see s 29(2); and PARA 179. See also CROWN AND CROWN PROCEEDINGS vol 29 (2014) PARA 86.

**94. Claims in personam ('other claims').** A claim in personam[1] may be brought in the High Court in all cases that fall within the Admiralty jurisdiction of that court[2], except where a restriction applies[3] in relation to any claim for damage, loss of life or personal injury arising out of[4]:

(1)   a collision between ships[5];

(2)   the carrying out of (or omission to carry out) a manoeuvre in the case of one or more of two or more ships[6]; or

(3)   non-compliance, on the part of one or more of two or more ships, with the collision regulations[7].

The High Court must not entertain any claim in personam to enforce a claim[8] which falls within heads (1) to (3) above unless[9]:

(a)   the defendant has his habitual residence or place of business within England and Wales[10];

(b)   the cause of action arose within inland waters[11] of England and Wales or within the limits of a port[12] of England and Wales[13]; or

(c)   a claim arising out of the same incident or series of incidents is proceeding in the court or has been heard and determined in the court[14].

Nor may the High Court entertain any claim in personam to enforce a claim which falls within heads (1) to (3) above until any proceedings previously brought by the claimant in any court outside England and Wales against the same defendant in respect of the same incidents or series of incidents[15] have been discontinued or otherwise come to an end[16]. The High Court has jurisdiction otherwise[17] to entertain such a claim whenever any of the conditions specified in heads (a) to (c) above is satisfied, and the rules of court relating to the service of process outside the jurisdiction[18] make such provision as may appear to the rule-making authority to be appropriate having regard to this purpose[19].

The restrictions on jurisdiction contained in these provisions[20] do not prevent a claim or a counterclaim which is duly brought in the High Court[21] being transferred, in accordance with the enactments in that behalf[22], to some other court[23].

1   As to the origin of claims in personam see PARA 84.

2   Senior Courts Act 1981 s 21(1). As to the Admiralty jurisdiction of the High Court of Justice generally see PARA 85 et seq. As to the mode of exercise of this jurisdiction see also PARA 93. Where claims are made in personam and the defendant is outside the jurisdiction, the exercise of jurisdiction may be inhibited because permission to serve must be granted in such cases generally: see CPR Pt 6; the Admiralty and Commercial Courts Guide (2016) paras B8.1–B8.3; PARA 188; CIVIL PROCEDURE vol 11 (2015) PARA 263 et seq; CONFLICT OF LAWS vol 19 (2011) PARA 363; and. See also the text and notes 17–23.

   Practice Direction—Admiralty Claims PD 61 para 12 ('other claims') applies to Admiralty claims which, before the coming into force of CPR Pt 61 (ie before 25 March 2002: see the Civil Procedure (Amendment No 5) Rules 2001, SI 2001/4015, r 1), would have been called claims in personam: see *Practice Direction—Admiralty Claims* PD 61 para 12.1; and PARA 186 et seq. As to the procedure that governs Admiralty claims see PARA 157 et seq. As to CPR Pt 61, *Practice Direction—Admiralty Claims* PD 61 and the Admiralty and Commercial Courts Guide generally see PARA 91 note 3.

3   Ie because the jurisdiction conferred by the Senior Courts Act 1981 s 21 (as to which see the text and notes 1–2) is subject to s 22 (as to which see the text and notes 4–23): see s 21(1). For the avoidance of doubt, s 22 applies in relation to the jurisdiction of the High Court not being Admiralty jurisdiction, as well as in relation to its Admiralty jurisdiction: s 22(8).

4   Senior Courts Act 1981 s 22(1).

5   Senior Courts Act 1981 s 22(1)(a). As to the meaning of 'ship' for these purposes see PARA 85 note 7.

6   Senior Courts Act 1981 s 22(1)(b).

7 Senior Courts Act 1981 s 22(1)(c). For the purposes of ss 20–23, unless the context otherwise requires, 'collision regulations' means safety regulations under the Merchant Shipping Act 1995 s 85 (see PARA 602 note 1): Senior Courts Act 1981 s 24(1) (definition amended by the Merchant Shipping Act 1995 s 314(2), Sch 13 para 59(3)).

8 The Senior Courts Act 1981 s 22(2), (3) (see the text and notes 9–16) applies to counterclaims (except counterclaims in proceedings arising out of the same incident or series of incidents) as it applies to claims: s 22(4). Accordingly, in the application of s 22(2), (3) to counterclaims, references to the claimant and defendant are to be construed as references to the claimant on the counterclaim and the defendant to the counterclaim respectively: see s 22(4). However, s 22(2), (3) does not apply to any claim or counterclaim if the defendant submits or has agreed to submit to the jurisdiction of the court: s 22(5).

9 Senior Courts Act 1981 s 22(2). See note 8.

10 Senior Courts Act 1981 s 22(2)(a). See note 8. As to the position of a defendant having an agent in England see *The World Harmony* [1967] P 341, [1965] 2 All ER 139. As to the meanings of 'England' and 'Wales' see PARA 16 note 2. As to a discussion of habitual residence in European and domestic law see CONFLICT OF LAWS vol 19 (2011) PARA 360. As to a person's place of business see COMPANIES vol 14 (2016) PARA 117.

11 For these purposes, 'inland waters' includes any part of the sea adjacent to the coast of the United Kingdom certified by the Secretary of State to be waters falling by international law to be treated as within the territorial sovereignty of Her Majesty apart from the operation of that law in relation to territorial waters: Senior Courts Act 1981 s 22(2). As to the meaning of 'United Kingdom' see PARA 16 note 3. As to the Secretary of State see PARA 36. As to the extent of the territorial and non-territorial sea, the baselines used for delimitation, and associated rights see INTERNATIONAL RELATIONS LAW vol 61 (2010) PARA 121 et seq.

12 For these purposes, 'port' means any port, harbour, river, estuary, haven, dock, canal or other place so long as a person or body of persons is empowered by or under an Act to make charges in respect of ships entering it or using the facilities in it; and 'limits of a port' means the limits as fixed by or under the Act in question or, as the case may be, by the relevant charter or custom: Senior Courts Act 1981 s 22(2). 'Charges' means any charges with the exception of light dues, local light dues and any other charges in respect of lighthouses, buoys or beacons and of charges in respect of pilotage: s 22(2). As to charges in respect of lighthouses etc see PARA 65 et seq. As to harbour charges generally see PORTS AND HARBOURS vol 85 (2012) PARA 68 et seq.

13 Senior Courts Act 1981 s 22(2)(b). See note 8.

14 Senior Courts Act 1981 s 22(2)(c). See note 8.

15 See *The World Harmony* [1967] P 341, [1965] 2 All ER 139 (where proceedings are commenced in different jurisdictions on the same day, they are treated as having been commenced at the same time and neither is previous (or subsequent) to the other).

16 Senior Courts Act 1981 s 22(3). See note 8. See also PARA 101.

17 Ie subject to the Senior Courts Act 1981 s 22(3) (see the text and notes 15–16): see s 22(6).

18 As to service of process outside the jurisdiction see note 2.

19 Senior Courts Act 1981 s 22(6).

20 Ie in the Senior Courts Act 1981 s 22: see s 22(7).

21 Ie brought in accordance with the provisions of the Senior Courts Act 1981 s 22: see s 22(7).

22 As to the provisions relating to transfer of proceedings see PARA 91.

23 Senior Courts Act 1981 s 22(7).

### (v) Conflicts of Jurisdiction

#### A. IN GENERAL

**95. Conflicts of jurisdiction in Admiralty proceedings.** The international nature of maritime affairs, and the right to proceed in rem[1], readily produce conflicts of jurisdiction, and disputes as to the forum in which claims should be heard[2].

Where a claim is brought in personam[3], the position is in general the same as in non-Admiralty proceedings, namely that a defendant who is liable to be served with a claim form (whether within or out of the jurisdiction) is subject to the jurisdiction of the court[4]. No such procedure exists for proceedings brought in rem, which necessarily involve service on a vessel in the territorial waters of the United Kingdom[5]. However, provided that the claim is one which by its nature may be enforced by a claim in rem[6], service on the ship[7] is sufficient to found jurisdiction, even in the absence of any other factor connecting the case with the United Kingdom[8]. Nevertheless, even where jurisdiction has been established by service on the defendant or on the res (that is, the subject property of the claim), the court has inherent power, preserved by statute, to order a stay of proceedings[9].

In cases governed by the Civil Jurisdiction and Judgments Act 1982[10], the court may be obliged to decline jurisdiction[11], although this does not prejudice the right of a claimant to take advantage of particular rules on jurisdiction contained in other international conventions[12]. Further conventions apply, in particular, to:

(1)       claims arising out of the international carriage of passengers by sea[13];

(2)       collisions at sea[14];

(3)       oil pollution by ships[15]; and

(4)       proceedings relating to the remuneration of officers or crew of ships or aircraft[16].

1   As to the origin of claims in rem see PARA 83; and as to claims in rem generally see PARA 92 et seq.

2   See generally CONFLICT OF LAWS.

3   Claims in personam are now referred to as 'other claims': see *Practice Direction—Admiralty Claims* PD 61 para 12.1; and PARA 186 et seq. As to the origin of claims in personam see PARA 84; and as to claims in personam generally see PARA 92 et seq. As to the procedure that governs Admiralty claims see PARA 157 et seq.

4   See CONFLICT OF LAWS vol 19 (2011) PARA 396. As to cases where a court may be may be obliged to decline jurisdiction or to stay proceedings see the text and notes 10–12. The exercise of jurisdiction may be inhibited generally in cases where the defendant is outside the jurisdiction because permission to serve must be granted in such cases: see CPR Pt 6; *Practice Direction—Service out of the Jurisdiction* PD 6B; the Admiralty and Commercial Courts Guide (2016) paras B8.1–B8.3; CIVIL PROCEDURE vol 11 (2015) PARA 263 et seq; CONFLICT OF LAWS vol 19 (2011) PARA 363.

5   As to service of the in rem claim form see PARA 160. An order will not be made for substituted service of an in rem claim form: *The Good Herald* [1987] 1 Lloyd's Rep 236. As to the meaning of 'United Kingdom' see PARA 16 note 3. As to the territorial waters of the United Kingdom see INTERNATIONAL RELATIONS LAW vol 61 (2010) PARA 121 et seq; WATER AND WATERWAYS vol 100 (2009) PARA 31.

6   Ie provided it is a claim as mentioned in the Senior Courts Act 1981 s 20(1)(a), (2)(a)–(c), (e)–(s) (see PARAS 93, 104 et seq), or there is a maritime lien or other charge on the ship (see s 21(2)–(4); and PARA 93).

7   Ie or, in some cases, on a sister ship: see the Senior Courts Act 1981 s 21(4); and PARA 93.

8   See PARA 86.

9   See the Senior Courts Act 1981 s 49(3); the Civil Jurisdiction and Judgments Act 1982 s 49; and CONFLICT OF LAWS vol 19 (2011) PARA 406 et seq. For the circumstances in which a stay may be ordered see PARA 100 et seq. The court also has specific statutory powers under the Arbitration Act 1996 s 9 to stay proceedings brought in breach of an arbitration agreement: see ARBITRATION vol 2 (2017) PARA 522. As to arbitration agreements see PARA 103.

10   The Civil Jurisdiction and Judgments Act 1982 makes provision for Parliament and Council Regulation (EU) 1215/2012 (OJ L351, 20.12.2012, p 1) on jurisdiction and the recognition and enforcement of judgments in civil and commercial matters ('the 'Brussels I' Regulation') and preserves the effect of the Convention on Jurisdiction and Enforcement of Judgments in Civil and Commercial Matters (Lugano, 16 September 1988, OJ L319, 25.11.88, p 9) (the 'Lugano Convention'): see CONFLICT OF LAWS vol 19 (2011) PARA 366 et seq.

11   See PARA 96 et seq. In one sense, the rules of the 'Brussels I' Regulation and of the Lugano Convention, and subordinate legislation relating to them, may be seen as a partial definition or redefinition of whether it is lawful to serve process upon a defendant: see CONFLICT OF LAWS vol 19 (2011) PARA 396.

12   See CONFLICT OF LAWS vol 19 (2011) PARA 402. But the provisions of the Regulation and of the Convention as to lis alibi pendens (see PARA 101) may still operate to prevent the exercise of such jurisdiction: Case C-406/92 *The Tatry (cargo owners) v The Maciej Rataj (owners)* [1994] ECR I-5439, [1995] All ER (EC) 229, ECJ.

13   See the Merchant Shipping Act 1995 s 183(1), which gives effect to the Convention relating to the Carriage of Passengers and their Luggage by Sea (Athens, 13 December 1974; Misc 27 (1975);

Cmnd 6326), as set out in the Merchant Shipping Act 1995 s 183, Sch 6 (see generally CARRIAGE AND CARRIERS vol 7 (2015) PARA 635 et seq).

14 See the Senior Courts Act 1981 s 22 (cited in PARA 94), which is based on the International Convention for the Unification of Certain Rules Concerning Civil Jurisdiction in matters of Collision (Brussels, 10 May 1952; TS 47 (1960); Cmnd 1128) (as to which see PARA 7).

15 See the Merchant Shipping Act 1995 (particularly s 166); and ENVIRONMENTAL QUALITY AND PUBLIC HEALTH vol 45 (2010) PARA 456 et seq.

16 See the Consular Relations Act 1968 s 4, and Orders in Council made thereunder, giving effect to a number of international agreements entered into by the United Kingdom; and see PARA 128. See also INTERNATIONAL RELATIONS LAW vol 61 (2010) PARA 303.

### B. EFFECT OF THE CIVIL JURISDICTION AND JUDGMENTS ACT 1982

## 96. Cases governed by the Civil Jurisdiction and Judgments Act 1982.
The Civil Jurisdiction and Judgments Act 1982 makes provision for the 'Brussels I' Regulation[1] and preserves the effect of the Lugano Convention on Jurisdiction and the Enforcement of Judgments in Civil and Commercial Matters (the 'Lugano Convention')[2]. Accordingly, it assumes fundamental importance in determining the jurisdiction of the court in cases where one or more of the parties is domiciled in a Regulation or contracting state[3], and where the courts of another Regulation or contracting state are already seised of the same or a related matter[4].

However, neither the 'Brussels I' Regulation nor the Lugano Convention contains provisions specifically concerned with maritime matters[5], and no distinction is drawn between Admiralty claims in personam and those in rem[6]. It is assumed that the English courts will apply the Regulation and Convention equally to Admiralty claims in personam and in rem[7].

1 Ie Parliament and Council Regulation (EU) 1215/2012 (OJ L351, 20.12.2012, p 1) on jurisdiction and the recognition and enforcement of judgments in civil and commercial matters: see CONFLICT OF LAWS vol 19 (2011) PARA 366 et seq. The 'Brussels I' Regulation replaced in its entirety the Brussels Convention on Jurisdiction and Enforcement of Judgments in Civil and Commercial Matters (Brussels, 27 September 1968; Cmnd 7395).

2 Ie the Convention on Jurisdiction and Enforcement of Judgments in Civil and Commercial Matters (Lugano, 16 September 1988, OJ L319, 25.11.88, p 9) (the 'Lugano Convention'), which was signed by the United Kingdom on 18 September 1989: see CONFLICT OF LAWS vol 19 (2011) PARA 366 et seq. The Lugano Convention enables European Free Trade Association countries, subject to minor modifications, to join the regime established by the 'Brussels I' Regulation: see CONFLICT OF LAWS vol 19 (2011) PARA 366 et seq. In connection with the extent of the Convention see also *The Deichland* [1990] 1 QB 361, [1989] 2 All ER 1066, CA.

3 As to jurisdiction based on domicile for these purposes see CONFLICT OF LAWS vol 19 (2011) PARA 380 et seq. As to the meanings of 'contracting state' and 'Regulation state' see CONFLICT OF LAWS vol 19 (2011) PARA 366.

4 See CONFLICT OF LAWS vol 19 (2011) PARA 403 et seq.

5 Nevertheless, certain provisions have been held to have the effect of indirectly incorporating into English law the International Convention for the Unification of Certain Rules Relating to the Arrest of Sea-Going Ships (Brussels, 10 May, 1952; Cmd 8954): see *The Nordglimt* [1988] QB 183, [1988] 2 All ER 531, [1987] 2 Lloyd's Rep 470 (overruled on other grounds by the House of Lords in *India (Republic) v India Steamship Co Ltd (Indian Endurance and Indian Grace) (No 2)* [1998] AC 878, [1997] 4 All ER 380, HL); *The Deichland* [1990] 1 QB 361, [1989] 2 All ER 1066, CA; and *The Anna H* [1994] 1 Lloyd's Rep 287; *The Bergen* [1997] 1 Lloyd's Rep 380.

6 Claims in personam are now referred to as 'other claims': see *Practice Direction—Admiralty Claims* PD 61 para 12.1; and PARA 186 et seq. The European Court of Justice has held that, for the purposes of the Brussels Convention (as to which see note 1), the distinction drawn by the law of a contracting state between a claim in rem and a claim in personam (a peculiarly common law distinction not recognised in civil law jurisdictions) is not material: Case C-406/92 *The Maciej Rataj* [1995] All ER (EC) 229, [1995] 1 Lloyd's Rep 302, ECJ. As to the origin of claims in rem see PARA 83; as to the origin of claims in personam see PARA 84; and as to claims in rem and claims in personam generally see PARA 92 et seq. As to the procedure that governs Admiralty claims see PARA 157 et seq.

7 This would be consistent with the reasoning of the Court of Appeal in *The Deichland* [1990] 1 QB 361, [1989] 2 All ER 1066, CA, in which the court's overriding consideration seems to have been to give the words used in the Brussels Convention a broad and purposive construction which

would not be thwarted by peculiar concepts of national law. It is not clear, however, whether the same reasoning would apply to a claim which is truly in rem, when it really is the ship that is being sued. The court may not wish to make any distinctions between claims quasi in rem and claims truly in rem in order to be consistent with the overall scheme and purpose of the 'Brussels I' Regulation and the Lugano Convention, which is to prevent conflicting judgments.

## 97. Claims in rem under the Civil Jurisdiction and Judgments Act 1982.

The 'Brussels I' Regulation[1] and the Lugano Convention[2] are silent on the question of Admiralty proceedings in rem[3], and no guidance is given in the Civil Jurisdiction and Judgments Act 1982 itself[4]. The traditional view was that the defendant in an Admiralty action in rem (now a claim in rem) is the ship itself, and not the owners or other persons interested in it[5]. Although ships are frequently arrested at the same time as being served with proceedings in rem, arrest is normally unnecessary in order to found jurisdiction, for which service alone is sufficient[6]. However, it had been held that special features of English Admiralty law could not affect the interpretation of the predecessor Brussels Convention[7], and that the court's jurisdiction may be contested if the owner of the ship, or other person liable to be adversely affected by the result of the proceedings, is domiciled in another contracting state[8].

Both the 'Brussels I' Regulation and the Lugano Convention provide that they do not affect any other conventions to which the contracting states are or will be parties and which, in relation to particular matters, govern jurisdiction or the recognition or enforcement of judgments[9]. It has been held that these include the International Convention relating to the Arrest of Sea-going Ships 1952 (the 'Brussels Arrest Convention')[10], which makes provision[11] for the courts of a country in which a ship is arrested to have jurisdiction to determine the case on its merits[12]. Consequently, where a ship can be arrested in the United Kingdom in proceedings in rem[13], and is so arrested, the court will retain jurisdiction based upon the arrest, irrespective of the domicile of the shipowner or other person interested in the res (that is, the subject property of the claim)[14]. Another Convention held to be included is the International Convention for the Unification of Certain Rules Concerning Civil Jurisdiction in matters of Collision[15], which goes further than the Brussels Arrest Convention in one important respect: the court will retain jurisdiction if the vessel could have been arrested but was not because bail or other security was furnished[16].

1 See PARA 96 note 1.
2 See PARA 96 note 2.
3 As to the origin of claims in rem see PARA 83; and as to claims in rem generally see PARA 92 et seq. As to the procedure that governs Admiralty claims see PARA 157 et seq.
4 Ie the Civil Jurisdiction and Judgments Act 1982: see PARA 95. Section 26 makes provision regarding security obtained in an Admiralty claim where proceedings are stayed, but otherwise makes no express reference to Admiralty proceedings: see PARA 85.
5 See PARA 92.
6 *The Nautik* [1895] P 121.
7 Ie the Brussels Convention on Jurisdiction and Enforcement of Judgments in Civil and Commercial Matters (Brussels, 27 September 1968; Cmnd 7395), which the 'Brussels I' Regulation has replaced in its entirety: see PARA 96.
8 *The Deichland* [1990] 1 QB 361, [1989] 2 All ER 1066, CA, where it was held that in such circumstances the owner, or other interested person, is 'sued' within the meaning of the Civil Jurisdiction and Judgments Act 1982. As to the meaning of 'contracting state' see CONFLICT OF LAWS vol 19 (2011) PARA 366.
9 See PARA 95.
10 Ie the International Convention for the Unification of Certain Rules Relating to the Arrest of Sea-Going Ships (Brussels, 10 May, 1952; Cmnd 8954) (as to which see PARA 7).
11 Ie by the International Convention Relating to the Arrest of Sea-Going Ships art 7. Although this convention has not been enacted verbatim in the United Kingdom, the Administration of Justice Act 1956 s 3 (repealed) contained provisions enacted for the purpose of giving effect to it, and these

provisions are now re-enacted in similar terms in the Senior Courts Act 1981 s 21 (as to which see PARA 93). See further *The Eschersheim* [1976] 1 All ER 920, [1976] 1 WLR 430, HL.

12 *The Nordglimt* [1988] QB 183, [1988] 2 All ER 531, [1987] 2 Lloyd's Rep 470 (overruled on other grounds in *India (Republic) v India Steamship Co Ltd (Indian Endurance and Indian Grace) (No 2)* [1998] AC 878, [1997] 4 All ER 380, HL); *The Deichland* [1990] 1 QB 361, [1989] 2 All ER 1066, CA; *The Anna H* [1994] 1 Lloyd's Rep 287; *The Bergen* [1997] 1 Lloyd's Rep 380. In establishing jurisdiction over a claim in rem, the Brussels Arrest Convention 1952 requires only that the legal consequences of the detention of a ship are that it becomes security for a maritime claim and not that a claimant's commercial motive has to be to obtain security: *The Anna H*.

See also *Steamship Mutual Underwriting Association (Bermuda) Ltd v Owners of the Cargo Lately Laden on Board the Vessel 'Jutha Rajpruek'* [2003] EWCA Civ 378, (2003) Times, 19 March, sub nom *The Juntha Rajpruek* [2003] 2 Lloyd's Rep 107 (in most jurisdictions subject to the Arrest Convention 1952, jurisdiction was established by arrest of the ship; the fact that the defendant's undertaking was conditional upon cargo owners not arresting the ship inevitably meant that the defendant undertook to accept service in respect of proceedings before courts which had not yet become seized of the action).

13 Ie provided it is a claim as mentioned in the Senior Courts Act 1981 s 20(1)(a), (2)(a)–(c), (e)–(s) (see PARAS 93, 104 et seq), or there is a maritime lien or other charge on the ship (see s 21(2)–(4); and PARA 93).

14 See *The Deichland* [1990] 1 QB 361, [1989] 2 All ER 1066, CA, where the claimant accepted security in lieu of arrest, and the mere fact that the vessel could have been arrested was held insufficient to found jurisdiction.

15 Ie the International Convention for the Unification of Certain Rules Concerning Civil Jurisdiction in matters of Collision (Brussels, 10 May 1952; Cmnd 1128) (as to which see PARA 7).

16 *The Po* [1991] 2 Lloyd's Rep 206, CA.

## 98. Claims in personam under the Civil Jurisdiction and Judgments Act 1982.

Where a claim is brought in personam[1] under the Civil Jurisdiction and Judgments Act 1982[2], the position is in general the same as in non-Admiralty proceedings, namely that a defendant who is liable to be served with a claim form (whether within or out of the jurisdiction) is subject to the jurisdiction of the court[3].

1 Claims in personam are now referred to as 'other claims': see *Practice Direction—Admiralty Claims* PD 61 para 12.1; and PARA 186 et seq. As to the origin of claims in personam see PARA 84; and as to claims in personam generally see PARA 92 et seq. As to the procedure that governs Admiralty claims see PARA 157 et seq.

2 Ie the Civil Jurisdiction and Judgments Act 1982: see PARA 95.

3 See CONFLICT OF LAWS vol 19 (2011) PARA 396 et seq.

## 99. Stay of proceedings under the Civil Jurisdiction and Judgments Act 1982.

The 'Brussels I' Regulation[1] and the Lugano Convention[2] provide that, where proceedings involving the same cause of action and between the same parties are brought in the courts of different Regulation or contracting states[3], any court other than the court first seised must of its own motion stay its proceedings until such time as the jurisdiction of the court first seised is established[4]. Where the jurisdiction of the court first seised is established, any court other than the court first seised must decline jurisdiction in favour of that court[5]. Where 'related actions'[6] are brought in the courts of different Regulation or contracting states, any court other than the court first seised may, while the actions are pending at first instance, stay its proceedings[7].

The above provisions apply irrespective of whether the defendant is domiciled in a Regulation or contracting state[8]. The English court will be 'seised' of proceedings in rem[9] when the claim form is served[10]. This is probably also true for claims in personam[11].

These provisions do not preclude the issue and service on a ship in the United Kingdom of a claim form in rem, and the words 'decline jurisdiction' have been interpreted in this context to mean 'decline to exercise jurisdiction'[12]. However, the European Court of Justice has held that, for the purposes of the Civil Jurisdiction and Judgments Act 1982, the distinction drawn by the law of a

Regulation or contracting state between a claim in rem and a claim in personam is immaterial[13]. Where the parties and cause of action are the same, the court's approach depends solely on which court was first seised of the matter, and questions of forum conveniens[14] have no application[15].

1 See PARA 96 note 1.
2 See PARA 96 note 2.
3 As to the meanings of 'contracting state' and 'Regulation state' see CONFLICT OF LAWS vol 19 (2011) PARA 366.
4 See the 'Brussels I' Regulation art 27; the Lugano Convention art 21; and CONFLICT OF LAWS vol 19 (2011) PARA 404.
5 See the 'Brussels I' Regulation art 27; the Lugano Convention art 21; and CONFLICT OF LAWS vol 19 (2011) PARA 404. These provisions do not apply where a situation is governed by a specialised Convention unless that Convention does not contain provisions regarding proceedings pending in other jurisdictions: Case C-406/92 *The Maciej Rataj* [1995] All ER (EC) 229, [1995] 1 Lloyd's Rep 302, ECJ; applied in *Frans Maas Logistics (UK) Ltd v CDR Trucking BV* [1999] 2 Lloyd's Rep 179, [1999] 1 All ER (Comm) 737.
6 In *Sarrio SA v Kuwait Investment Authority* [1999] 1 AC 32, [1997] 4 All ER 929, [1998] 1 Lloyd's Rep 129, HL, the House of Lords held that in determining whether proceedings were 'related' for the purposes of the Brussels Convention art 22 (see now the 'Brussels I' Regulation art 28; and the Lugano Convention art 22) the court should apply the wide test set out therein, which was designed to cover a range of circumstances, from cases where the matters before the courts were virtually identical to cases where the connection was close enough to make it expedient for them to be heard and determined together.
7 See the 'Brussels I' Regulation art 28; the Lugano Convention art 22; and CONFLICT OF LAWS vol 19 (2011) PARA 405.
8 Case C-351/89 *Overseas Union Insurance Ltd v New Hampshire Insurance Co* [1992] 1 QB 434, [1991] ECR I-3317, ECJ.
9 As to the origin of claims in rem see PARA 83; and as to claims in rem generally see PARA 92 et seq. As to the procedure that governs Admiralty claims see PARA 157 et seq.
10 *The Nord Sea and Freccia Del Nord* [1989] 1 Lloyd's Rep 388.
11 See *Dresser UK Ltd v Falcongate Freight Management Ltd, The Duke of Yare* [1992] QB 502, [1992] 2 All ER 450, CA. The Court of Appeal in this case stated that there might be exceptions to this rule, for example if an exercise of jurisdiction (such as a freezing order) preceded service. However, a differently constituted Court of Appeal in *Neste Chemicals SA v DK Line SA, The Sargasso* [1994] 3 All ER 180, [1994] 2 Lloyd's Rep 6, CA, disapproved the propositions that there might be exceptions to the time of service rule.
    Claims in personam are now referred to as 'other claims': see *Practice Direction—Admiralty Claims* PD 61 para 12.1; and PARA 186 et seq. As to the origin of claims in personam see PARA 84; and as to claims in personam generally see PARA 92 et seq.
12 *The Linda* [1988] 1 Lloyd's Rep 175 at 178 per Sheen J.
13 Case C-406/92 *The Maciej Rataj* [1995] All ER (EC) 229, [1995] 1 Lloyd's Rep 302, ECJ.
14 As to the doctrine of forum non conveniens see PARA 100.
15 *The Linda* [1988] 1 Lloyd's Rep 175 at 179–180 per Sheen J. Nothing in the Civil Jurisdiction and Judgments Act 1982 prevents any court in the United Kingdom from staying, sisting, striking out or dismissing any proceedings before it, on the ground of forum non conveniens or otherwise, where to do so is not inconsistent with the 'Brussels I' Regulation or the Lugano Convention: see the Civil Jurisdiction and Judgments Act 1982 s 49; and CONFLICT OF LAWS vol 19 (2011) PARA 406 et seq.

C. STAY OF PROCEEDINGS UNDER NATIONAL LAW

**100. Forum non conveniens.** Subject to the Civil Jurisdiction and Judgments Act 1982[1], the court may stay proceedings if there is another forum in which the case can be more conveniently tried[2]. Account is taken not only of convenience and expense, but also of other factors, such as the law governing the transaction, which point to the most appropriate or natural forum[3]. In ascertaining the most appropriate forum, the court searches for the country with which the case has its most real and substantial connection[4].

If a foreign court is found to be a more appropriate forum, a stay may still be refused if its effect would be to deprive the claimant of some real and legitimate personal or juridical advantage available to him by suing in England[5]. A common instance of this in Admiralty proceedings is the opportunity for the claimant to secure his claim by the arrest of the vessel in a claim in rem[6]. Other examples from the decided cases are the availability in England of a more generous limitation period[7], a speedier or cheaper trial[8], a more generous measure of damages[9], or a more favourable rule of substantive law[10]. Particular weight may be attached to juridical advantages which do not involve a corresponding disadvantage to the defendant[11]. Normally, however, the court will not compare the quality of justice available in England with that dispensed elsewhere, and allegations that a fair trial would not be obtainable in the foreign jurisdiction must be supported by cogent evidence[12].

Ultimately, the court's task is to weigh the balance of factors both for and against a stay[13], so that even if the claimant can point to a legitimate advantage in suing in England, this will not be decisive if another jurisdiction is clearly the more appropriate forum[14].

1   As to cases which are subject to the Civil Jurisdiction and Judgments Act 1982 see PARA 96.
2   English law on this topic has developed considerably to the point where it is now indistinguishable from the (originally) Scottish legal doctrine of forum non conveniens: *The Abidin Daver* [1984] AC 398 at 411, [1984] 1 All ER 470 at 476, HL, per Lord Diplock; *Spiliada Maritime Corpn v Cansulex Ltd, The Spiliada* [1987] AC 460 at 474, [1986] 3 All ER 843 at 854, HL, per Lord Goff of Chieveley. See also *Re Harrods (Buenos Aires) Ltd* [1992] Ch 72, [1991] 4 All ER 334, CA; and *Ace Insurance SA-NV v Zurich Insurance Co* [2001] EWCA Civ 173, [2001] 1 All ER (Comm) 802, [2001] 1 Lloyd's Rep 618 (affg *Ace Insurance SA-NV v Zurich Insurance Co* [2000] 2 All ER (Comm) 449, [2000] 2 Lloyd's Rep 423), where it was held that the court had jurisdiction to stay on the grounds of forum non conveniens in favour of a non-contracting state even though the defendant was domiciled and correctly sued in a contracting state under the Convention on Jurisdiction and Enforcement of Judgments in Civil and Commercial Matters (Lugano, 16 September 1988, OJ L319, 25.11.88, p 9) (the 'Lugano Convention') (see CONFLICT OF LAWS vol 19 (2011) PARA 366 et seq). As to forum non conveniens see further CONFLICT OF LAWS vol 19 (2011) PARA 407.
3   *Spiliada Maritime Corpn v Cansulex Ltd, The Spiliada* [1987] AC 460 at 474 et seq, [1986] 3 All ER 843 at 854 et seq, HL, per Lord Goff of Chieveley.
4   See *Spiliada Maritime Corpn v Cansulex Ltd, The Spiliada* [1987] AC 460, [1986] 3 All ER 843, HL.
5   See *Rockware Glass Ltd v MacShannon* [1978] AC 795, [1978] 1 All ER 625, HL.
6   See *The Atlantic Star* [1974] AC 436 at 454, [1973] 2 All ER 175 at 182, HL, per Lord Reid; *The Wladyslaw Lokietek* [1978] 2 Lloyd's Rep 520 at 540 per Brandon J; *The El Amria* [1981] 2 Lloyd's Rep 119, CA. This factor may not, however, carry weight if the defendant undertakes to provide equivalent security for the claim, or counterclaim, against him in foreign proceedings: *The Abidin Daver* [1984] AC 398, [1984] 1 All ER 470, HL. As to the origin of claims in rem see PARA 83; and as to claims in rem generally see PARA 92 et seq.
7   *Spiliada Maritime Corpn v Cansulex Ltd, The Spiliada* [1987] AC 460 at 483, [1986] 3 All ER 843 at 860, HL, per Lord Goff of Chieveley. It is otherwise if the claimant has acted unreasonably in allowing the claim to become time-barred in the foreign jurisdiction: see *Spiliada Maritime Corpn v Cansulex Ltd, The Spiliada* at 483 and 860 per Lord Goff of Chieveley.
8   *Rockware Glass Ltd v MacShannon* [1978] AC 795 at 814–815, [1978] 1 All ER 625 at 632–633, HL, per Lord Diplock; *The Jalakrishna* [1983] 2 Lloyd's Rep 628; *The Vishva Ajay* [1989] 2 Lloyd's Rep 558.
9   *The Jalakrishna* [1983] 2 Lloyd's Rep 628. However, the court will not refuse to stay proceedings on the ground that the other forum would limit recovery to a lesser amount than that available in England by applying an alternative convention: see *The Herceg Novi v Ming Galaxy* [1998] 4 All ER 238, [1998] 2 Lloyd's Rep 454, CA; approving *The Kapitan Shvetsov* [1998] 1 Lloyd's Rep 199, CA.
10  *The Atlantic Star* [1974] AC 436 at 468, [1973] 2 All ER 175 at 194, HL, per Lord Wilberforce; *Power Curber International Ltd v National Bank of Kuwait* [1981] 3 All ER 607, [1981] 1 WLR 1233, CA (where it was held that English rules as to choice of law would result in summary judgment for the claimant).
11  *The Efthimis* [1986] 1 Lloyd's Rep 244 (where proceedings in England resulted in all relevant claims being dealt with in one action).

12  *The Abidin Daver* [1984] AC 398, [1984] 1 All ER 470, HL; *The El Amria* [1981] 2 Lloyd's Rep 119, CA.
13  *The Abidin Daver* [1984] AC 398 at 419, [1984] 1 All ER 470 at 482, HL, per Lord Brandon of Oakbrook.
14  See eg *Trendtex Trading Corpn v Crédit Suisse* [1980] QB 629, [1980] 3 All ER 721, CA; affd [1982] AC 679, [1981] 3 All ER 520, HL, where the advantages of wider ranging discovery of documents in England was outweighed by overwhelming connections with Switzerland.

## 101.  Lis alibi pendens.

Subject to the Civil Jurisdiction and Judgments Act 1982[1], the court may intervene to prevent possible injustice where two claims are pending, one in England and the other in a foreign country between the same parties[2].

Where the two claims are begun by different parties, the court may stay the English proceedings on grounds which in principle are those of forum non conveniens[3]. A stay will not necessarily be ordered by reason only that proceedings were instituted first in the foreign jurisdiction[4], or that the refusal of a stay would result in a multiplicity of proceedings[5]. The fact that proceedings are already pending abroad will, however, weigh in the scales in favour of granting a stay, particularly if substantial progress in the foreign proceedings has already been made[6].

Where both claims have been begun by the same party, the court may more readily stay the English proceedings, particularly if it results in no additional advantage to the claimant[7]. Alternatively, the claimant will be required to elect which set of proceedings he wishes to pursue, and if he elects to pursue the proceedings abroad, the English claim will be dismissed and not merely stayed[8]. The court may also grant an injunction restraining the institution[9] or continuance[10] of foreign proceedings.

Whilst the foregoing principles are of general application, the court is specifically precluded by statute from entertaining any claim in personam[11] to enforce a claim for damage, loss of life or personal injury arising out of a collision between ships[12], or out of certain other matters[13], unless any foreign proceedings previously brought by the claimant against the defendant in respect of the same incident or series of incidents have been discontinued or otherwise come to an end[14].

1  As to cases which are subject to the Civil Jurisdiction and Judgments Act 1982 see PARA 96.
2  *Kennedy v Earl of Cassillis* (1818) 2 Swan 313; *McHenry v Lewis* (1882) 22 ChD 397, CA; *Hyman v Helm* (1883) 24 ChD 531, CA. Cf *The Atlantic Star* [1974] AC 436, [1973] 2 All ER 175, HL, where the parties were not identical but similar principles were applied.
3  As to the doctrine of forum non conveniens see PARA 100.
4  *The Coral Isis* [1986] 1 Lloyd's Rep 413.
5  *The Efthimis* [1986] 1 Lloyd's Rep 244, CA.
6  *The Abidin Daver* [1984] AC 398, [1984] 1 All ER 470, HL.
7  *The Atlantic Star* [1974] AC 436, [1973] 2 All ER 175, HL; *McHenry v Lewis* (1882) 22 ChD 397, CA; *Peruvian Guano Co v Bockwoldt* (1883) 23 ChD 225, CA; *Ionian Bank Ltd v Couvreur* [1969] 2 All ER 651, [1969] 1 WLR 781, CA. It is, however, no longer necessary for the proceedings to be vexatious or oppressive: *The Abidin Daver* [1984] AC 398 at 411, [1984] 1 All ER 470 at 476, HL, per Lord Diplock; *Spiliada Maritime Corpn v Cansulex Ltd, The Spiliada* [1987] AC 460 at 474, [1986] 3 All ER 843 at 854, HL, per Lord Goff of Chieveley.
8  *Australian Commercial Research and Development Ltd v ANZ McCaughan Merchant Bank Ltd* [1989] 3 All ER 65.
9  *Lord Portarlington v Soulby* (1834) 3 My & K 104.
10  *Wharton v May* (1799) 5 Ves 27 at 71; *Bushby v Munday* (1821) 5 Madd 297; *Harrison v Gurney* (1821) 2 Jac & W 563; *Beauchamp v Marquess of Huntley* (1822) Jac 546; *Beckford v Kemble* (1822) 1 Sim & St 7; *Lord Portarlington v Soulby* (1834) 3 My & K 104; *Jones v Geddes* (1845) 1 Ph 724; *Carron Iron Co v Maclaren* (1855) 5 HL Cas 416; *Dawkins v Simonetti* (1880) 50 LJP 30, CA; *McHenry v Lewis* (1882) 22 ChD 397, CA; *Hyman v Helm* (1883) 24 ChD 531, CA; *Vardopulo v Vardopulo* (1909) 25 TLR 518, CA; *Heilmann v Falkenstein* (1917) 33 TLR 383;

*Cohen v Rothfield* [1919] 1 KB 410, CA; *Orr-Lewis v Orr-Lewis* [1949] P 347, [1949] 1 All ER 504; *The Soya Margareta* [1960] 2 All ER 756, [1961] 1 WLR 709; *Settlement Corpn v Hochschild* [1966] Ch 10, [1965] 3 All ER 486. The injunction restraining the foreign proceedings is addressed to the claimant in those proceedings, not to the foreign court itself: *Bushby v Munday* (1821) 5 Madd 297; cf *Love v Baker* (1665) 1 Cas in Ch 67. Such relief is, however, only sparingly granted, and will not be ordered unless it would be unconscionable for the claimant to maintain the proceedings abroad: see *Castanho v Brown & Root (UK) Ltd* [1981] AC 557, [1981] 1 All ER 143, [1981] 1 Lloyd's Rep 113, HL; *British Airways Board v Laker Airways Ltd* [1985] AC 58, [1984] 3 All ER 39, HL; cf *Smith Kline & French Laboratories Ltd v Bloch* [1983] 2 All ER 72, [1983] 1 WLR 730, CA.

11　Claims in personam are now referred to as 'other claims': see *Practice Direction—Admiralty Claims* PD 61 para 12.1; and PARA 186 et seq. As to the origin of claims in personam see PARA 84; and as to claims in personam generally see PARA 92 et seq. As to the procedure that governs Admiralty claims see PARA 157 et seq.

12　See the Senior Courts Act 1981 s 22(1)(a); and PARA 94.

13　Ie the carrying out of (or omission to carry out) a manoeuvre in the case of one or more of two or more ships (see the Senior Courts Act 1981 s 22(1)(b); and PARA 94) or non-compliance, on the part of one or more of two or more ships, with the collision regulations (see s 22(1)(c); and PARA 94). As to the meaning of 'collision regulations' for these purposes see PARA 94 note 7.

14　See the Senior Courts Act 1981 s 22(3); and PARA 94.

**102.　Stay of proceedings under a foreign jurisdiction clause.** The court may stay proceedings in England where these are brought in breach of an agreement to refer disputes to the exclusive jurisdiction of a foreign tribunal[1]. The court is not bound to grant a stay but has a discretion whether to do so or not[2]. The conditions material to the exercise of the court's discretion whether to grant a stay or not do not differ in substance from the exercise of the court's discretion upon an application to set aside service of a claim form by reason of such a clause. The factors relevant to the exercise of the discretion are also broadly similar to the criteria considered under the doctrine of forum non conveniens[3]. However, the position is not precisely the same, for it is a prima facie rule that the parties should honour their agreement to refer disputes to the foreign tribunal, and accordingly the burden is on the claimant, or in the case of a counterclaim, on the defendant, to show a strong cause for a stay to be refused[4].

The following matters are relevant in considering the exercise of the discretion to stay[5]:

(1)　the country in which the evidence on the issues of fact is situated, or more readily available, and the effect of that on the relative convenience and expense of a trial as between the English and the foreign courts;

(2)　whether the law of the foreign court applies and, if so, whether it differs from English law in any material respects;

(3)　with what country either party is connected, and how closely;

(4)　whether the defendants genuinely desire trial in the foreign country, or are only seeking procedural advantages; and

(5)　whether the claimants would be prejudiced by having to sue in the foreign court because they would:

(a)　be deprived of security for their claim;

(b)　be unable to enforce any judgment obtained;

(c)　be faced with a time bar not applicable in England; or

(d)　for political, racial, religious or other reasons be unlikely to get a fair trial[5].

1　*The Eleftheria* [1970] P 94, [1969] 2 All ER 641, [1969] 1 Lloyd's Rep 237; *Aratra Potato Co Ltd v Egyptian Navigation Co, The El Amria* [1981] 2 Lloyd's Rep 119, CA. See also *DSV Silo-und Verwalturgsgesellschaft mbH v Sennar (Owners), The Sennar* [1985] 2 All ER 104 at 111, [1985] 1 WLR 490 at 500, [1985] 1 Lloyd's Rep 521 at 527, HL, per Lord Brandon of Oakbrook.

2　See the cases cited in note 1.

3　As to the doctrine of forum non conveniens see PARA 100.

4   *Trendtex Trading Corpn v Crédit Suisse* [1980] QB 629, [1980] 3 All ER 721, CA; affd [1982] AC
    679, [1981] 3 All ER 520, HL.
5   *The Eleftheria* [1970] P 94 at 100, [1969] 2 All ER 641 at 645, [1969] 1 Lloyd's Rep 237 at 242
    per Brandon J; *Aratra Potato Co Ltd v Egyptian Navigation Co, The El Amria* [1981] 2 Lloyd's
    Rep 119, CA. See also *The Chaparral* [1968] 2 Lloyd's Rep 158, CA, and the proceedings in the
    same case in the United States Supreme Court, *The Chaparral* [1972] 2 Lloyd's Rep 315. See also
    CONFLICT OF LAWS vol 19 (2011) PARA 413.
        As to the position where a contract contained an exclusive jurisdiction clause but the Brussels
    Convention on Jurisdiction and Enforcement of Judgments in Civil and Commercial Matters
    (Brussels, 27 September 1968; Cmnd 7395) (see now the 'Brussels I' Regulation; and PARA 96 et
    seq) applied see *Hough v P & O Containers Ltd* [1999] QB 834, [1998] 2 All ER 978; and
    CONFLICT OF LAWS vol 19 (2011) PARA 392.
5   *The Eleftheria* [1970] P 94 at 100, [1969] 2 All ER 641 at 645, [1969] 1 Lloyd's Rep 237 at 242
    per Brandon J; *Aratra Potato Co Ltd v Egyptian Navigation Co, The El Amria* [1981] 2 Lloyd's
    Rep 119, CA. See also *The Chaparral* [1968] 2 Lloyd's Rep 158, CA, and the proceedings in the
    same case in the United States Supreme Court, *The Chaparral* [1972] 2 Lloyd's Rep 315. See also
    CONFLICT OF LAWS vol 19 (2011) PARA 413.
        As to the position where a contract contained an exclusive jurisdiction clause but the Brussels
    Convention on Jurisdiction and Enforcement of Judgments in Civil and Commercial Matters
    (Brussels, 27 September 1968; Cmnd 7395) (see now the 'Brussels I' Regulation; and PARA 96 et
    seq) applied see *Hough v P & O Containers Ltd* [1999] QB 834, [1998] 2 All ER 978; and
    CONFLICT OF LAWS vol 19 (2011) PARA 392.

## 103. Stay of proceedings under an arbitration agreement.

A party to an arbitration agreement[1], against whom legal proceedings are brought, whether by way of a claim or counterclaim, in respect of a matter which under the agreement is to be referred to arbitration may, upon notice to the other parties to the proceedings, apply to the court in which proceedings have been brought to stay the proceedings as far as they concern that matter[2]. The court must[3] grant a stay unless satisfied that the arbitration agreement is null and void[4], inoperative[5], incapable of being performed[6], or if there is not in fact any dispute between the parties[7].

1   For these purposes, 'arbitration agreement' means an agreement to submit to arbitration present
    or future disputes, whether they are contractual or not: see the Arbitration Act 1996 s 6(1); and
    ARBITRATION vol 2 (2017) PARA 513.
2   See the Arbitration Act 1996 s 9(1); and ARBITRATION vol 2 (2017) PARA 522.
3   As from a day to be appointed under the Arbitration Act 1996 s 109(1), s 86 has the effect of
    taking domestic arbitration agreements outside s 9(4) (see the text and notes 4–6), thereby giving
    the court a discretion whether or not to stay the proceedings: see s 86; and ARBITRATION vol 2
    (2017) PARA 522. At the date at which this volume states the law, no such day had been appointed.
    As to the meaning of 'domestic arbitration agreement' for these purposes see s 85(2) (not yet in
    force); and ARBITRATION vol 2 (2017) PARA 522.
4   As to the position where the Hague-Visby Rules apply see *The Hollandia* [1983] 1 AC 565 at
    575–576, [1982] 3 All ER 1141 at 1146–1147, HL, per Lord Diplock. As to the Hague-Visby
    Rules see CARRIAGE AND CARRIERS vol 7 (2015) PARAS 207, 368 et seq.
5   See *The Merak* [1965] P 223 at 239, [1964] 3 All ER 638 at 648–649, [1964] 2 Lloyd's Rep 283
    at 294 per Scarman J (decided under the Arbitration Act 1950 s 4 (repealed)); *Astro Valiente
    Compania Naviera SA v Pakistan Ministry of Food and Agriculture (No 2)* [1982] 1 All ER 823,
    [1982] 1 WLR 1096 (decided under the Arbitration Act 1975; see now the Arbitration Act 1996).
6   See the Arbitration Act 1996 s 9(4); and ARBITRATION vol 2 (2017) PARA 522. The words
    'incapable of being performed' refer only to the question whether an arbitration agreement is
    capable of being performed up to the stage when it results in an award, and do not extend to the
    question whether the party against whom it is made will be capable of satisfying it: see *The Rena K*
    [1979] QB 377, [1979] 1 All ER 397, [1978] 1 Lloyd's Rep 545 (decided under the Arbitration Act
    1975; see now the Arbitration Act 1996).
7   These words appeared in the Arbitration Act 1975 but were omitted from the Arbitration Act
    1996. In *Hayter v Nelson* [1990] 2 Lloyd's Rep 265, it was held that there can be a dispute between
    the parties even though it was clear from the outset that one party was right and the other was
    wrong. The Court of Appeal has held that there will be a dispute until the sums claimed are
    admitted as being due and owing (*Halki Shipping Corpn v Sopex Oils Ltd, The Halki* [1998] 2 All
    ER 23, [1998] 1 WLR 726, [1998] 1 Lloyd's Rep 465, CA) but, in considering a deemed dispute
    clause, the Court of Appeal has held that a dispute persisted after liability was admitted, as the

applicant was entitled to an arbitration award which he could enforce (see *Glencore Grain Ltd v Agros Trading Co Ltd* [1999] 2 All ER (Comm) 288, [1999] 2 Lloyd's Rep 410, CA).

# (2) PARTICULAR SUBJECTS OF JURISDICTION

## (i) Possession or Ownership

**104. Extent of jurisdiction regarding possession or ownership of a ship.**
The Admiralty jurisdiction of the High Court[1] includes jurisdiction to hear and determine any claim relating to the possession or ownership of a ship[2], or to the ownership of any share in a ship[3]. The jurisdiction extends to all ships whether British or not and whether registered or not and wherever the residence or domicile of their owners may be, and to all claims wherever arising (including, in the case of cargo or wreck salvage, claims in respect of cargo or wreck found on land)[4]. This jurisdiction does not extend to aircraft[5].

The jurisdiction to entertain claims for possession is derived from the inherent jurisdiction of the Admiralty Court to take ships or vessels out of the hands of wrongdoers and restore them to the owners[6], and to dispossess masters who ought to be removed[7]. Jurisdiction was originally limited to disputes as to possession alone, for the common law courts declared that where any bona fide claim of ownership was set up as a defence, the Admiralty Court had no jurisdiction to deal with the question of title[8]. To remedy this limitation, a statutory jurisdiction was conferred in 1840 upon the Admiralty Court to decide any question of title to the subject matter of claims for possession[9].

1 As to the Admiralty jurisdiction of the High Court of Justice generally see PARA 85 et seq. As to the mode of exercise of this jurisdiction see the Senior Courts Act 1981 s 21; and PARAS 93–94. The Admiralty jurisdiction of the High Court extends also to hovercraft: see PARA 87.
2 As to the meaning of 'ship' for these purposes see PARA 85 note 7. As to ownership and control of ships generally see PARA 229 et seq.
3 Senior Courts Act 1981 s 20(1)(a), (2)(a). See *Harms Bergung, Transport & Heavylift GmbH & Co KG v Harms Offshore AHT 'Uranus' GmbH & Co KG* [2015] EWHC 1269 (Admlty), [2015[ 2 Lloyd's Rep 175, [2015] All ER (D) 72 (May).
4 See the Senior Courts Act 1981 s 20(7)(a), (b); and PARA 86. Where possession of a foreign ship is sought, although the English court has jurisdiction to entertain the claim, an application to stay the claim on the ground of forum non conveniens is likely to be successful in the absence of some substantial connection with England: see *The Jupiter (No 2)* [1925] P 69, [1925] All ER Rep 203, 21 Ll L Rep 116, CA. As to the doctrine of forum non conveniens see PARA 100. In addition, the court's discretion to refuse to entertain claims for wages by the master or member of the crew of a ship, not being a British ship, is expressly preserved: see the Senior Courts Act 1981 s 24(2)(a); and PARAS 85, 128. As to questions of sovereign immunity see PARAS 86, 90.
5 *Re Glider Standard Austria SH 1964* [1965] P 463, [1965] 2 All ER 1022, [1965] 2 Lloyd's Rep 189.
6 *Re Blanshard* (1823) 2 B & C 244. As to the development of the law that is administered in Admiralty see PARA 80 et seq.
7 *The New Draper* (1802) 4 Ch Rob 287.
8 *The Warrior* (1818) 2 Dods 288.
9 See the Admiralty Court Act 1840 s 4 (repealed by the Supreme Court of Judicature (Consolidation) Act 1925 s 226(1), Sch 6 and replaced by s 22(1)(a)(i), which was itself repealed by the Administration of Justice Act 1956 s 57(2), Sch 2, and replaced by s 1, itself now replaced by the Senior Courts Act 1981 s 20).

**105. Rectification of register.** In a claim for possession or ownership of a British ship[1], the court has power by virtue of its inherent jurisdiction[2] to order the rectification of the register where an incorrect entry has been made with regards to the claimant's title[3], but the court will not rectify the register as against a bona fide purchaser who has taken without notice of some earlier fraud[4]. The court may in a fit case make an order for the delivery up to the persons entitled to the certificate of registry of a British ship[5].

1    As to the jurisdiction of the Admiralty Court regarding the possession or ownership of a ship see PARA 104. As to British ships under the Merchant Shipping Act 1995 see PARA 229 et seq.
2    As to the saving of this jurisdiction see PARA 85.
3    *The Rose* (1873) LR 4 A & E 6; see also *Brond v Broomhall* [1906] 1 KB 571. As to registration of ships generally see PARA 245 et seq.
4    *The Horlock* (1877) 2 PD 243, 3 Asp MLC 421.
5    *The St Olaf* (1877) 2 PD 113; *The Celtic King* [1894] P 175.


### (ii) Co-ownership

**106. Extent of jurisdiction regarding co-ownership.** The Admiralty jurisdiction of the High Court[1] includes jurisdiction to hear and determine any question arising between co-owners of a ship[2] as to possession, employment or earnings of that ship[3]. The jurisdiction extends to all ships, whether British or not and whether registered or not and wherever the residence or domicile of their owners may be, and to all claims wherever arising[4].

The jurisdiction in respect of co-owners includes power to settle any account outstanding and unsettled between the parties in relation to the ship, and to direct that the ship, or any share of the ship, must be sold, and to make such other order as the court thinks fit[5]. In a claim for an account between part-owners, where one of the parties had before the claim parted with all his interest in the ship, the court held that it had jurisdiction to entertain the proceedings and ordered him to give security in respect of the shares he formerly possessed in the ship[6].

1    As to the Admiralty jurisdiction of the High Court of Justice generally see PARA 85 et seq. As to the mode of exercise of this jurisdiction see the Senior Courts Act 1981 s 21; and PARAS 93–94. The Admiralty jurisdiction of the High Court extends also to hovercraft: see PARA 87.
2    As to the meaning of 'ship' for these purposes see PARA 85 note 7. As to ownership and control of ships generally see PARA 229 et seq.
3    Senior Courts Act 1981 s 20(1)(a), (2)(b). See *Harms Bergung, Transport & Heavylift GmbH & Co KG v Harms Offshore AHT 'Uranus' GmbH & Co KG* [2015] EWHC 1269 (Admlty), [2015[ 2 Lloyd's Rep 175, [2015] All ER (D) 72 (May).
4    See the Senior Courts Act 1981 s 20(7)(a), (b); and PARA 86.
5    Senior Courts Act 1981 s 20(4). As to the sale and transfer of ships generally see PARAS 32, 236 et seq.
6    *The Lady of the Lake* (1870) LR 3 A & E 29.


**107. Sale at instance of minority of co-owners.** The sale of a ship or shares in a ship may, in the discretion of the court, be ordered at the instance of a minority of co-owners without the consent of the majority[1]. However, such a minority of co-owners must make out a very strong case to induce the court to make an order for the sale of the whole ship, by which the majority of the co-owners are forced to part with their property whether they like it or not[2].

1    *The Hereward* [1895] P 284; following *The Nelly Schneider* (1878) 3 PD 152. The jurisdiction extends to all ships whether British or not and whether registered or not: see PARA 106.
2    See *The Marion* (1884) 10 PD 4; and *The Hereward* [1895] P 284.


**108. Restraint on dealings with shares.** In the exercise of its jurisdiction over questions of co-ownership[1], the Admiralty Court can restrain the defendant from dealing with the share or shares of a ship registered in England which is the subject of the claim[2].

The High Court also has a specific statutory power, on the application of any interested person, by order to prohibit for a time specified in the order any dealing with a ship or any share in a ship[3], whether the ship is British or not and whether registered or not and wherever the residence or domicile of its owners may be[4].

1  As to the Admiralty jurisdiction of the High Court of Justice in this respect see PARAS 106–107.
2  *The Horlock* (1877) 2 PD 243, 3 Asp MLC 421.
3  See the Merchant Shipping Act 1995 s 16, Sch 1 para6; and PARA 306. It was held in *The Mikado* [1992] 1 Lloyd's Rep 163, that the provision which is now contained in the Merchant Shipping Act 1995 Sch 1 para 6 gave the court original jurisdiction to exercise the power conferred and it did not have to be related to some other cause of action. It was also held that 'interested person' is restricted to a person with a proprietary interest in the ship. See also the Senior Courts Act 1981 s 20(1)(a), (2)(a); and PARA 104. As to the power of the court to order a sale where there has been a transmission of a registered ship or share or shares in such a ship to persons not qualified to own a British ship see the Merchant Shipping Act 1995 Sch 1 para 4; and PARA 306.
4  See the Senior Courts Act 1981 s 20(7)(a); and PARA 86.

### (iii)  Mortgage or Charge

**109.  Extent of jurisdiction regarding claims in respect of a mortgage or charge on a ship.** The Admiralty jurisdiction of the High Court[1] includes jurisdiction to hear and determine any claim in respect of a mortgage or charge[2] on a ship[3] or any share in a ship[4]. This jurisdiction applies[5]:

(1)  in relation to all ships, whether British or not and whether registered or not and wherever the residence or domicile of their owners may be[6];

(2)  in relation to all claims, wherever arising (including, in the case of cargo or wreck salvage, claims in respect of cargo or wreck found on land)[7]; and

(3)  so far as they relate to mortgages and charges, to all mortgages or charges, whether registered or not and whether legal or equitable, including mortgages and charges created under foreign law[8].

1  As to the Admiralty jurisdiction of the High Court of Justice generally see PARA 85 et seq. As to the mode of exercise of this jurisdiction see the Senior Courts Act 1981 s 21; and PARAS 93–94. The Admiralty jurisdiction of the High Court extends also to hovercraft: see PARA 87.
2  For these purposes, the word 'charge' refers to a charge in the nature of a mortgage: see *The St Merriel* [1963] P 247, [1963] 1 All ER 537; *The Acrux* [1965] P 391, [1965] 2 All ER 323.
3  As to the meaning of 'ship' for these purposes see PARA 85 note 7. As to mortgages of ships see generally the Merchant Shipping Act 1995 s 16, Sch 1; and PARAS 318–336.
4  Senior Courts Act 1981 s 20(1)(a), (2)(c).
5  Ie provided that nothing in the Senior Courts Act 1981 s 20(7) (see heads (1) to (3) in the text) is construed as extending the cases in which money or property is recoverable under any of the provisions of the Merchant Shipping Act 1995: see the Senior Courts Act 1981 s 20(7) proviso; and PARA 86.
6  See the Senior Courts Act 1981 s 20(7)(a); and PARA 86.
7  See the Senior Courts Act 1981 s 20(7)(b); and PARA 86.
8  See the Senior Courts Act 1981 s 20(7)(c); and PARA 86.

### (iv)  Damage done by or to a Ship

**110.  Extent of jurisdiction regarding claims for damage done by or to a ship.** The Admiralty jurisdiction of the High Court[1] includes jurisdiction to hear and determine any claim for damage done by a ship[2] and any claim for damage received by a ship[3]. The jurisdiction extends to all ships, whether British or not and whether registered or not and wherever the residence or domicile of their owners may be, and to all claims wherever arising[4].

It is not necessary that there should be actual contact causing damage to establish jurisdiction for damage done by a ship[5]. The jurisdiction has been found to extend to claims for damage caused by a ship's wash[6], for damage done by part of a ship[7], for damage done by a ship to a wreck[8], for expenses of removing a wreck sunk as a result of damage done by another ship[9], and for loss or damage suffered by a ship in negligent salvage operations[10]. Jurisdiction in respect of damage done by a ship also includes claims in respect of statutory liability for damage from oil pollution[11]. Damage received by a ship includes damage caused by a fixed object, such as a pierhead[12].

Claims for loss of or damage to cargo carried on a ship by the fault of another ship may be the subject of an Admiralty claim against the colliding ship[13]. Although a claim against the carrying ship is now within the jurisdiction of the courts[14], the terms of the contract of carriage will generally exclude liability as between the owner of the cargo and the carrying ship[15].

Subject to a statutory exception in respect of certain occurrences involving the carriage of nuclear matter[16], damage done by a ship gives rise to a maritime lien[17].

1   As to the Admiralty jurisdiction of the High Court of Justice generally see PARA 85 et seq. As to the mode of exercise of this jurisdiction see the Senior Courts Act 1981 s 21; and PARAS 93–94. The Admiralty jurisdiction of the High Court extends also to hovercraft: see PARA 87; and see note 17.

2   Senior Courts Act 1981 s 20(1)(a), (2)(e). As to the meaning of 'ship' for these purposes see PARA 85 note 7. A jet ski is not a ship: *Steedman v Schofield* [1992] 2 Lloyd's Rep 163. In the Supreme Court of Judicature (Consolidation) Act 1925 s 22(3) (repealed), the expression 'ship' included any description of vessel used in navigation not propelled by oars. Although it has been held that Admiralty jurisdiction does not include claims arising out of collision between two dumb barges (*Everard v Kendall* (1870) LR 5 CP 428), or two craft solely propelled by oars (*Edwards v Quickenden and Forester* [1939] P 261, 63 Ll L Rep 189, CA), these decisions may now be questioned in the light of the omission of the words 'not propelled by oars' from the Senior Courts Act 1981 s 24(1), and the decision in *Marine Craft Constructors Ltd v Erland Blomqvist (Engineers) Ltd* [1953] 1 Lloyd's Rep 514, where the court emphasised the importance of the purpose for which the craft was being used. The court has jurisdiction in the case of a collision between a dumb barge and a ship: *The Champion* [1934] P 1, 18 Asp MLC 453, 47 Ll L Rep 40. See also *The Queen of the South* [1968] P 449, [1968] 1 All ER 1163, [1968] 1 Lloyd's Rep 182, where motor boats servicing a ship were themselves considered ships. Damage done by deliberately ramming is damage done by a ship: *Fish & Fish Ltd v Sea Shepherd UK* [2011] CSOH 122, 2012 SLT 156.

3   Senior Courts Act 1981 s 20(1)(a), (2)(d).

4   See the Senior Courts Act 1981 s 20(7)(a), (b); and PARA 86. As to the statutory right afforded to shipowners and other persons to limit their liability in connection with a ship or other property see PARA 194 et seq.

5   *The Industrie* (1871) LR 3 A & E 303, 1 Asp MLC 17 (vessel grounding to avoid collision with another vessel); see also *The Miraflores and The Abadesa* [1967] 1 AC 826, [1967] 1 All ER 672, [1967] 1 Lloyd's Rep 191, HL.

6   *The Batavier* (1854) 9 Moo PC 286; *Luxford v Large* (1832) 5 C & P 421; cf *The Royal Eagle* (1950) 84 Ll L Rep 543; and *The Royal Sovereign* (1950) 84 Ll L Rep 549.

7   *The Minerva* [1933] P 224, 18 Asp MLC 426, 46 Ll L Rep 212 (a falling derrick).

8   *The Zelo* [1922] P 9.

9   *The Ella* [1915] P 111; *The Chr Knudsen* [1932] P 153, 18 Asp MLC 347, 43 Ll L Rep 423.

10  *The Jade, The Eschersheim* [1976] 1AllER 920, [1976] 1 WLR 430, HL.

11  See the Merchant Shipping Act 1995 s 166; and PARA 88. As to oil pollution generally see ENVIRONMENTAL QUALITY AND PUBLIC HEALTH vol 45 (2010) PARA 348 et seq.

12  *The Zeta* [1893] AC 468, 7 Asp MLC 369, HL; *The Hoegh Silvercrest* [1962] 1 Lloyd's Rep 9.

13  See the text and notes 1–2.

14  It was held in *The Victoria* (1887) 12 PD 105, 6 Asp MLC 120, that under the Admiralty Court Act 1861 s 12 (repealed), the words 'damage done by a ship' did not extend the jurisdiction of the court to include a claim by owners of cargo against the carrying ship, but this question is academic in the light of the fact that jurisdiction in respect of claims for damage to cargo carried in a ship is now expressly given by the Senior Courts Act 1981 s 20(1)(a), (2)(g) (as to which see PARA 111). Cargo claims against the carrying ship are within Admiralty jurisdiction, but are not 'damage done by a ship': see *The Vinalines Pioneer* [2016] 1 Lloyd's Rep 278 (a decision of the High Court of Singapore).

15  As to exceptions from liability in contracts for carriage of goods by sea see CARRIAGE AND CARRIERS vol 7 (2015) PARAS 266 et seq, 386 et seq.

16  See the Nuclear Installations Act 1965 s 14 (cited in PARA 195; and ENERGY AND CLIMATE CHANGE vol 44 (2011) PARA 901) (any claim in respect of an occurrence which constitutes a breach of a person's duty under the Nuclear Installations Act 1965 does not give rise to any lien or other right in respect of any ship or aircraft).

17 *The Ripon City* [1897] P 226, 8 Asp MLC 304; *The Bold Buccleugh* (1852) 7 Moo PCC 267; *The Veritas* [1901] P 304 at 311, 9 Asp MLC 237 at 241; and see *The Tolten* [1946] P 135, [1946] 2 All ER 372, CA.

Subject to the Hovercraft Act 1968 s 2(3), the law relating to maritime liens applies in relation to hovercraft and property connected with hovercraft as it applies in relation to ships and property connected with ships, and applies notwithstanding that the hovercraft is on land at any relevant time: see s 2(2); and PARA 383.

### (v) Claims relating to Cargo or to Contracts of Carriage or Hire

**111. Extent of jurisdiction regarding claims relating to cargo and carriage.** The Admiralty jurisdiction of the High Court[1] includes jurisdiction to hear and determine:

(1)    any claim for loss of or damage to goods[2] carried in a ship[3]; and
(2)    any claim arising out of any agreement relating to the carriage of goods in a ship or to the use or hire of a ship[4].

The jurisdiction extends to all ships, whether British or not and whether registered or not and wherever the residence or domicile of their owners may be, and to all claims wherever arising[5].

Under head (2) above, the words 'arising out of' should be given the wider meaning of 'connected with' and not the narrower meaning of 'arising under'[6]; and the words 'agreement relating to use or hire of a ship' are not to be given a restricted meaning[7]. The jurisdiction is wide enough to cover claims in tort arising out of any agreement relating to the carriage of goods in a ship[8]. An agreement relating to the use or hire of a ship includes a contract for services rendered by motor boats to a ship where those services involve more than some incidental and minor use of those boats[9]. The words 'use or hire of a ship' are also wide enough to cover the case of the hire of a tug under a towage contract[10]. A claim will only fall within the jurisdiction under head (2) above if the claim arises out of an agreement relating to carriage in a particular vessel, and it does not cover claims relating to carriage in unidentified vessels[11].

Claims in respect of damage to cargo do not, unless they result from damage done by a ship, give rise to a maritime lien[12].

1    As to the Admiralty jurisdiction of the High Court of Justice generally see PARA 85 et seq. As to the mode of exercise of this jurisdiction see the Senior Courts Act 1981 s 21; and PARAS 93–94. The Admiralty jurisdiction of the High Court extends also to hovercraft: see PARA 87.
2    For the purposes of the Senior Courts Act 1981 ss 20–23, unless the context otherwise requires, 'goods' includes baggage: s 24(1).
3    Senior Courts Act 1981 s 20(1)(a), (2)(g). As to the meaning of 'ship' for these purposes see PARA 85 note 7. Jurisdiction under this heading includes examples of claims based on contract as well as on tort arising out of an agreement relating to the carriage of goods in a ship: see *The Fehmarn* [1958] 1 All ER 333, [1958] 1 WLR 159, [1957] 2 Lloyd's Rep 551, CA; *The St Elefterio* [1957] P 179, [1957] 2 All ER 374, [1957] 1 Lloyd's Rep 283; *The Moscanthy* [1971] 1 Lloyd's Rep 37. As to division of loss where two or more vessels are at fault see PARA 771 et seq.
4    Senior Courts Act 1981 s 20(1)(a), (2)(h). The extent of jurisdiction under this heading is the same as that under s 20(1)(a), (2)(g) (see head (1) in the text). See also *Petrofina SA v AOT Ltd, The Maersk Nimrod* [1992] QB 571, [1991] 3 All ER 161, [1991] 1 Lloyd's Rep 269. See further *The Bumbesti* [2000] QB 559, [2000] 2 All ER 692, [1999] 2 Lloyd's Rep 481 (claim arising out of arbitration clause in charterparty not claim arising out of agreement relating to the use or hire of a ship).
5    See the Senior Courts Act 1981 s 20(7)(a), (b); and PARA 86. As to the statutory right afforded to shipowners and other persons to limit their liability in connection with a ship or other property see PARA 194 et seq.
6    See *The Antonis P Lemos* [1985] AC 711, [1985] 1 All ER 695, [1985] 1 Lloyd's Rep 283, HL. Claims for indemnity and contribution under the Civil Liability (Contribution) Act 1978 (as to which see DAMAGES vol 29 (2014) PARA 620 et seq; and TORT vol 97 (2015) PARA 450 et seq) were held to be claims arising out of an agreement for carriage of containers and their contents:

*The Hamburg Star* [1994] 1 Lloyd's Rep 399. The words 'arising out of' are not wide enough to include a claim to enforce an arbitration award, even though the arbitration provision is in a charter party: *The Bumbesti* [2000] QB 559, [2000] 2 All ER 692, [1999] 2 Lloyd's Rep 481. A claim against a guarantor of hire does not 'arise out of' the use or hire of a ship *The Catur Samudra* [2010] SGHCD 18, [2010] 1 Lloyd's Rep 305 (on parallel Singapore provisions).

7   *The Jade, The Eschersheim* [1976] 1 All ER 920, [1976] 1 WLR 430, HL (salvage agreement). A management agreement, which provided that the managers would be solely entitled to enter into charter parties for the owners of the ship they were to manage, was an agreement relating to the use or hire of that ship: *The Stella Nora* [1981] Com LR 200.

8   *The St Elefterio* [1957] P 179, [1957] 2 All ER 374, [1957] 1 Lloyd's Rep 283; approved in *The Antonis P Lemos* [1985] AC 711, [1985] 1 All ER 695, HL. Although there is no need for a contractual nexus between the parties, there must be a reasonably direct connection with the carriage of goods in a ship: *Gatoil International Inc v Arkwright-Boston Manufacturers Mutual Insurance Co* [1985] AC 255, [1985] 1 All ER 129, HL. See also *Bain Clarkson Ltd v The Owners of the Ship, The Sea Friend* [1991] 2 Lloyd's Rep 322.

9   *The Queen of the South* [1968] P 449, [1968] 1 All ER 1163, [1968] 1 Lloyd's Rep 182. As to what may or may not constitute a 'ship' see PARA 110 note 2.

10  See *The Conoco Britannia* [1972] 2 QB 543, [1972] 2 All ER 238, [1972] 1 Lloyd's Rep 342.

11  *The Lloyd Pacifico* [1995] 1 Lloyd's Rep 54.

12  See *The Pieve Superiore* (1874) LR 5 PC 482, 2 Asp MLC 319. Claims against the non-carrying vessel for damage to cargo resulting from collision which give rise to a maritime lien are within the jurisdiction conferred by the Senior Courts Act 1981 s 20(1)(a), (2)(e): see PARA 110. As to the nature of maritime liens generally see PARA 987 et seq.

## (vi) Loss of Life or Personal Injury

**112. Extent of jurisdiction regarding claims for loss of life or personal injury.** The Admiralty jurisdiction of the High Court[1] includes jurisdiction to hear and determine any claim for loss of life[2] or personal injury[3] sustained in consequence of:

    (1)     any defect in a ship[4] or in its apparel or equipment[5]; or

    (2)     in consequence of the wrongful act, neglect or default of[6]:

        (a)     the owners, charterers or persons in possession or control of a ship[7]; or

        (b)     the master[8] or crew of a ship, or any other person for whose wrongful acts, neglects or defaults the owners, charterers or persons in possession or control of a ship are responsible[9].

Jurisdiction under either head (1) or head (2) above requires an act, neglect or default:

    (i)     in the navigation or management of the ship[10];

    (ii)    in the loading, carriage or discharge of goods[11] on, in or from the ship[12]; or

    (iii)   in the embarkation, carriage or disembarkation of persons on, in or from the ship[13].

The jurisdiction extends to all ships, whether British or not and whether registered or not and wherever the residence or domicile of their owners may be, and to all claims wherever arising[14].

1   As to the Admiralty jurisdiction of the High Court of Justice generally see PARA 85 et seq. As to the mode of exercise of this jurisdiction see the Senior Courts Act 1981 s 21; and PARAS 93–94. The Admiralty jurisdiction of the High Court extends also to hovercraft: see PARA 87.

2   Ie a claim under the Fatal Accidents Act 1976: see NEGLIGENCE vol 78 (2010) PARA 24 et seq. It has been held that Admiralty jurisdiction does not extend to a claim for an indemnity in respect of statutory compensation paid for loss of life: *The Molière* [1925] P 27, 16 Asp MLC 470, distinguishing *The Annie* [1909] P 176, 11 Asp MLC 213.

3   As to negligence causing loss, including the joint and several liability of shipowners if two or more vessels are at fault, and as to the right of contribution, see PARA 756 et seq.

4   As to the meaning of 'ship' for these purposes see PARA 85 note 7.

5   Senior Courts Act 1981 s 20(1)(a), (2)(f). The court, on the application of any party to an action to be tried in the Queen's Bench Division, has a discretion to order that the damages be assessed

by a jury (see the Senior Courts Act 1981 s 69; and DAMAGES vol 29 (2014) PARA 638) and provision is made for trial by jury if there is in issue any question or issue of a kind prescribed for these purposes (see *The Kwasind* (1915) 84 LJP 102, CA). However, by the rules of court, save where on a case management conference an order is made for trial with a jury on the ground that there are special reasons, trial is by a judge without a jury, and in practice such assessment is nearly always carried out by the Admiralty Registrar: see PARA 143.

6    Senior Courts Act 1981 s 20(1)(a), (2)(f). The phrase 'wrongful act, neglect or default' derives from the Fatal Accidents Act 1846 s 1 (repealed) (see now the Fatal Accidents Act 1976 s 1; and NEGLIGENCE vol 78 (2010) PARA 25) and covers the breach of a term against negligence in a contract: see *Grein v Imperial Airways Ltd* [1937] 1 KB 50, [1936] 2 All ER 1258, CA; *Quinn v Burch Bros (Builders) Ltd* [1966] 2 QB 370, [1965] 3 All ER 801.

7    Senior Courts Act 1981 s 20(1)(a), (2)(f)(i).

8    As to the meaning of 'master' for these purposes see PARA 85 note 14.

9    Senior Courts Act 1981 s 20(1)(a), (2)(f)(ii).

10   See the Senior Courts Act 1981 s 20(1)(a), (2)(f).

11   As to the meaning of 'goods' for these purposes see PARA 111 note 2.

12   See the Senior Courts Act 1981 s 20(1)(a), (2)(f).

13   See the Senior Courts Act 1981 s 20(1)(a), (2)(f).

14   See the Senior Courts Act 1981 s 20(7)(a), (b); and PARA 86.

## (vii) Salvage

### A. IN GENERAL

**113. Extent of jurisdiction regarding salvage claims.** The Admiralty jurisdiction of the High Court[1] includes jurisdiction to hear and determine any claim:

(1)    under the Salvage Convention 1989[2];

(2)    under any contract for or in relation to salvage services[3]; or

(3)    in the nature of salvage not falling within head (1) or head (2) above[4],

or any corresponding claim in connection with an aircraft[5]. The jurisdiction extends to all ships, whether British or not and whether registered or not and wherever the residence or domicile of their owners may be, and to all claims wherever arising (including, in the case of cargo or wreck salvage, claims in respect of cargo or wreck found on land)[6].

The High Court originally acquired jurisdiction in respect of claims for salvage of property from the inherent jurisdiction of the Admiralty Court[7]. The jurisdiction to award salvage for services in the preservation of life is, except where some property is also salved, entirely statutory[8].

Salvage, whether of property or of life, confers a maritime lien on the property salved[9], but not all claims under this head of jurisdiction will give rise to a maritime lien[10].

1    As to the Admiralty jurisdiction of the High Court of Justice generally see PARA 85 et seq. As to the mode of exercise of this jurisdiction see the Senior Courts Act 1981 s 21; and PARAS 93–94. The Admiralty jurisdiction of the High Court extends also to hovercraft: see PARA 87.

2    Senior Courts Act 1981 s 20(1)(a), (2)(j)(i) (s 20(2)(j) substituted by the Merchant Shipping (Salvage and Pollution) Act 1994 s 1(6), Sch 2 para 6(2)). For these purposes, the 'Salvage Convention 1989' means the International Convention on Salvage 1989 (London, 28 April 1989; Cm 1526) (as to which see PARA 7) as it has effect under the Merchant Shipping Act 1995 s 224 (as to which see PARAS 851 et seq): Senior Courts Act 1981 s 20(6)(a) (s 20(6) substituted by the Merchant Shipping (Salvage and Pollution) Act 1994 Sch 2 para 6(3); Senior Courts Act 1981 s 20(6)(a) amended by the Merchant Shipping Act 1995 s 314(2), Sch 13 para 59(2)(c)).

3    Senior Courts Act 1981 s 20(1)(a), (2)(j)(ii) (as substituted: see note 2). For these purposes, the reference to salvage services includes services rendered in saving life from a ship, and the reference to any claim under any contract for or in relation to salvage services includes any claim arising out of such a contract whether or not arising during the provision of the services: s 20(6)(b) (as substituted: see note 2). As to the meaning of 'ship' for these purposes see PARA 85 note 7. As to salvage generally see PARA 849 et seq.

4    Senior Courts Act 1981 s 20(1)(a), (2)(j)(iii) (as substituted: see note 2).

5   Senior Courts Act 1981 s 20(1)(a), (2)(j) (as substituted: see note 2). The reference to a corresponding claim in connection with an aircraft is a reference to any claim corresponding to any claim in head (1) or in head (2) in the text which is available under the Civil Aviation Act 1982 s 87 (application of law of wreck and salvage to aircraft) (see AVIATION vol 2 (2017) PARA 1367): Senior Courts Act 1981 s 20(6)(c) (as substituted: see note 2). As to salvage in respect of aircraft see PARA 114.
6   See the Senior Courts Act 1981 s 20(7)(a), (b); and PARA 86.
7   As to the development of the law that is administered in Admiralty see PARA 80 et seq.
8   See PARAS 120–121.
9   *The Veritas* [1901] P 304 at 311–312, 9 Asp MLC 237 at 241 per Gorell Barnes J.
10 See, for example, claims for special compensation under the International Convention on Salvage 1989 (London, 28 April 1989; Cm 1526) art 14 (cited in PARA 879) or under the terms of the 'Scopic Clause' (if invoked).

**114. Salvage in respect of aircraft.** The Admiralty jurisdiction of the High Court[1] includes jurisdiction to hear and determine any claim under the Salvage Convention 1989[2] or under any contract for or in relation to salvage services[3]. Any services rendered in assisting, or in saving life[4] from, or in saving the cargo or apparel of, an aircraft in, on or over the sea or any tidal water, or on or over the shores of the sea or any tidal water, are to be deemed to be salvage services in all cases in which they would have been salvage services if they had been rendered in relation to a vessel[5].

Where salvage services are rendered by an aircraft to any property or person, the owner of the aircraft is entitled to the same reward for those services as he would have been entitled to if the aircraft had been a vessel[6].

1   As to the Admiralty jurisdiction of the High Court of Justice generally see PARA 85 et seq. As to the mode of exercise of this jurisdiction see the Senior Courts Act 1981 s 21; and PARAS 93–94. The Admiralty jurisdiction of the High Court extends also to hovercraft: see PARA 87.
2   Ie the International Convention on Salvage 1989 (London, 28 April 1989; Cm 1526) (as to which see PARA 7) as it has effect under the Merchant Shipping Act 1995 s 224 (as to which see PARAS 851 et seq): see the Senior Courts Act 1981 s 20(1)(j)(i), (6)(a); and PARA 113.
3   See the Senior Courts Act 1981 s 20(1)(a), (2)(j)(ii); and PARA 113. The salvage services are those which are available under the Civil Aviation Act 1982 s 87 (see AVIATION vol 2 (2017) PARA 1367): see the Senior Courts Act 1981 s 20(6)(b), (c); and PARA 113. Under the Civil Aviation Act 1982 s 87, Her Majesty may by Order in Council direct that any provisions of any Act for the time being in force which relate to wreck, to salvage of life or property or to the duty of rendering assistance to vessels in distress, with such modifications, if any, as may be specified in the Order, are to apply in relation to aircraft as they apply in relation to vessels: see s 87(4); and AVIATION vol 2 (2017) PARA 1367. For these purposes, any provisions of an Act which relate to vessels laid by or neglected as unfit for sea service are deemed to be provisions relating to wreck (see s 87(5)(a); and AVIATION vol 2 (2017) PARA 1367); and 'Act' includes any local or special Act and any provisions of the Harbours, Docks and Piers Clauses Act 1847, as incorporated with any local or special Act (see PORTS AND HARBOURS vol 85 (2012) PARA 2 et seq), whenever passed (see the Civil Aviation Act 1982 s 87(5)(b); and AVIATION vol 2 (2017) PARA 1367). See also the Aircraft (Wreck and Salvage) Order 1938, SR & O 1938/136 (amended by SI 1964/489), which has effect as if made under the Civil Aviation Act 1982 s 87 by virtue of s 105(3); and AVIATION vol 2 (2017) PARA 1367. As to salvage and wreck see further PARAS 122 et seq, 849 et seq.
4   As to life salvage see PARAS 120–121.
5   See the Civil Aviation Act 1982 s 87(1); and AVIATION vol 2 (2017) PARA 1367. The provisions of s 87(1), (2) have effect notwithstanding that the aircraft concerned is a foreign aircraft and notwithstanding that the services in question are rendered elsewhere than within the limits of the territorial waters adjacent to any part of Her Majesty's dominions: see s 87(3); and AVIATION vol 2 (2017) PARA 1367. As to the extent of the jurisdiction see the Senior Courts Act 1981 s 20(7)(a), (b); and PARA 86. For an example of services to an aircraft see *Watson v RCA Victor Co Inc* (1934) 50 Ll L Rep 77, where, however, jurisdiction under the Air Navigation Act 1920 s 11 (repealed) was restricted to aircraft wrecked within Her Majesty's jurisdiction.
6   See the Civil Aviation Act 1982 s 87(2); and AVIATION vol 2 (2017) PARA 1367. As to the effect of this provision see note 5. For an example of a salvage award for services by an aircraft and her crew see *The American Farmer* (1947) 80 Ll L Rep 672.

## B.	SALVAGE OF PROPERTY

**115. Services for which remuneration is payable.** The High Court[1] has jurisdiction to award salvage remuneration for services rendered to a ship, its cargo or apparel or any other property belonging to it[2]. Salvage remuneration may not, however, be recovered for services rendered to a raft of timber which has not formed part of the cargo of a ship[3], or to a structure afloat on the water, provided for storing gas to be used for lighting a tidal river[4]. There is no jurisdiction to award salvage in respect of services rendered to a vessel in non-tidal waters[5]. The court has power to award interest on a salvage award[6].

1	As to the Admiralty jurisdiction of the High Court of Justice generally see PARA 85 et seq; and as to the Admiralty jurisdiction in relation to salvage etc see PARAS 113–114. As to the common law principles which apply to salvage services see PARA 855 et seq.
2	*Wells v Gas Float Whitton No 2 (Owners)* [1897] AC 337, 8 Asp MLC 272, HL. As to the position regarding aircraft see PARA 114.
3	*The Raft of Timber* (1844) 2 Wm Rob 251.
4	*Wells v Gas Float Whitton No 2 (Owners)* [1897] AC 337, 8 Asp MLC 272, HL. Whether, however, this decision would be applicable to cases where, no owner appearing within a year and a day, similar structures to that in *Wells v Gas Float Whitton No 2 (Owners)* would be the subject of condemnation as droits of Admiralty to the Crown (as to which see PARA 139), may be doubted. Probably in such cases the persons who rendered the salvage services would be held entitled to be rewarded on salvage principles out of the proceeds of the structures salved, as it is questionable that the Crown would be entitled to the droit of Admiralty without any payment to the finders at all. On this point see *Stackpoole v R* (1875) IR 9 Eq 619, CA, where it was held that logs of timber found floating in the sea were droits of Admiralty and not wreck. See also Williams and Bruce's *Admiralty Practice* (3rd Edn) 127n, where many instances of property, other than the property which the House of Lords has declared to be the subject of salvage, are referred to as being salved and condemned as droits of Admiralty after salvage had been paid to the salvors. See also RG Marsden 'Admiralty Droits and Salvage' 15 LQR 353–366.
5	*The Goring* [1988] AC 831, [1988] 1 All ER 641, HL; *The Powstaniec Wielkopolski* [1989] QB 279, [1989] 1 All ER 198, [1989] 1 Lloyd's Rep 58.
6	*The Aldora* [1975] QB 748, [1975] 2 All ER 69.

**116. Persons liable to pay salvage remuneration.** In the absence of agreement to the contrary, the respective owners of different property salved will each be individually liable to the salvor for the amount payable in respect of the salvage to his property and usually the award against each interest will be in proportion to salved values[1]. (This is the position also where the International Convention on Salvage 1989 applies)[2].

Bailees of the property salved, who would have been liable to the owners if the property had been lost, have been held liable in an action in personam to pay the salvor's remuneration[3]. Freight earned or in the course of being earned on the voyage during which the services are rendered will generally be at the risk of shipowner or cargo owner and will contribute to the salvage remuneration as part of the ship or cargo value, as the case may be[4]. It is uncertain whether a claim for salvage lies in respect of voyage freight at the risk of a time charterer, but it seems doubtful[5]. It is generally accepted, but there is no authority on the point, that bunkers owned by time charterers constitute a separate contributory salved interest.

1	*The Mary Pleasants* (1857) Sw 224. The award will be assessed as at the date of termination of the salvage services: *The George Dean* (1857) Sw 290; *The Sunheath* (1925) 22 Ll L Rep 361 at 363 per Bateson J. As to the Admiralty jurisdiction of the High Court in relation to salvage etc see PARAS 113–114.
2	See the International Convention on Salvage 1989 (London, 28 April 1989; Cm 1526) art 13(2); and PARA 878. As to the liability to contribute to salvage remuneration see also PARAS 863, 879 et seq. It is submitted that previous decisions which departed from this general rule, eg where different risks, as distinct from different degrees of risk, were perceived to be involved, are no longer good law: see eg *The Longford* (1881) 6 PD 60; *The Vesta* (1828) 2 Hag Adm 189; and *The Velox* [1906] P 263. See also *The Lista* (1946) 79 Ll L Rep 401.
3	*The Port Victor (cargo ex)* [1901] P 243, CA; *The Five Steel Barges* (1890) 15 PD 142, 6 Asp MLC 580. As to claims in personam see PARA 83 et seq.

4   As to the assessment of the value of freight where the services terminate at an intermediate port see *The Norma* (1860) Lush 124; and *The George Dean* (1857) Sw 290.

5   *Norsk Bjergningskompagni A/S v Owners of the Pantanassa* [1970] P 187, [1970] 1 All ER 848, [1970] 1 Lloyd's Rep 153. As to liability for salvage and the principles upon which the amount of remuneration is determined see also PARA 849 et seq.

**117. Damage caused by salvor.** If by negligence the salvor causes the loss of the property which is the subject of the salvage operation, he will be liable in damages[1]. If in performing the services he negligently causes damage to the salved property, he will be liable in damages even though he has done more good than harm[2]. In assessing the damages, in such circumstances, there must be a deduction of the hypothetical salvage remuneration which would have been awarded but for negligence[3]. The court takes a lenient view of the conduct of salvors and is slow to find them guilty of negligence, as the policy of the law is to encourage the rendering of salvage services, but it will still make such a finding in a proper case[4].

1   See *The Alenquer* [1955] 1 WLR 263; *The Thetis* (1869) LR 2 A & E 365; *The C S Butler* (1874) LR 4 A & E 178. As to the Admiralty jurisdiction of the High Court in relation to salvage etc see PARAS 113–114. As to the degree of care and skill required in salvors see PARA 893; and as to the consequences of negligence found in salvors see PARA 895.

2   *The Tojo Maru* [1972] AC 242, [1971] 1 All ER 1110, [1971] 1 Lloyd's Rep 341, HL. As to the duties of the salvor and of the owner and master see the International Convention on Salvage 1989 (London, 28 April 1989; Cm 1526) art 8 (cited in PARA 856).

3   *The Tojo Maru* [1972] AC 242, [1971] 1 All ER 1110, [1971] 1 Lloyd's Rep 341, HL.

4   *The St Blane* [1974] 1 Lloyd's Rep 557.

**118. Application of salvage law to the Crown.** Subject to certain exceptions[1], the law relating to civil salvage, whether of life or property[2], applies in relation to salvage services in assisting any of Her Majesty's ships[3], or in saving life from any such ship, or in saving any cargo or equipment belonging to Her Majesty in right of her government in the United Kingdom[4], in the same manner as if the ship, cargo or equipment belonged to a private person[5].

Where salvage services are rendered by or on behalf of Her Majesty, whether in right of her government in the United Kingdom or otherwise, Her Majesty is entitled to claim salvage in respect of those services to the same extent as any other salvor, and has the same rights and remedies in respect of those services as any other salvor[6]. Where a ship is requisitioned by the Crown and the terms of requisition do not amount to a demise or sub-demise, it would appear that a claim for salvage should be made by the owners of the ship and not by the Crown[7].

Civil proceedings by the Crown may be instituted either by an authorised government department in its own name, whether that department was or was not[8] authorised to sue, or by the Attorney General[9]. No claim for salvage services by the commander or crew or part of the crew of any of Her Majesty's ships[10] will be finally adjudicated upon without the consent of the Secretary of State[11] to the prosecution of the claim[12]. Any document purporting to give the consent of the Secretary of State for these purposes[13] and to be signed by an officer of the Ministry of Defence is evidence of that consent[14]. If the claim is prosecuted without the required consent[15] the claim must be dismissed with costs[16].

1   Ie subject to the Crown Proceedings Act 1947 s 29 (exclusion of proceedings in rem against the Crown) (see CROWN AND CROWN PROCEEDINGS vol 29 (2014) PARA 86; and PARA 179) so far as it is consistent with the Salvage Convention (as to which see PARA 7): see the Merchant Shipping Act 1995 s 230(1); and PARA 854.

2   Ie except for the Merchant Shipping Act 1995 ss 225–227 (relating to the power of receivers of wreck to value property and to detain and sell property) (as to which see PARAS 919–920): see s 230(1); and PARA 854.

3   For these purposes, 'Her Majesty's ships' has the same meaning as in the Merchant Shipping Act 1995 s 192 (application of shipowners liability to Crown) (see PARA 1015): see s 230(7). As to the meaning of 'ship' for these purposes see PARA 229.

4   As to the meaning of 'United Kingdom' see PARA 16 note 3.
5   See the Merchant Shipping Act 1995 s 230(1); and PARA 854.
6   See the Merchant Shipping Act 1995 s 230(2); and PARA 854.
7   See the definition of 'Her Majesty's ships' in the Merchant Shipping Act 1995 ss 192(2), 230(7) (cited in note 3); and see *The Sarpen* [1916] P 306, CA.
8   Ie whether or not authorised to sue at the commencement of the Crown Proceedings Act 1947 (ie 1 January 1949): see s 17(2); and CROWN AND CROWN PROCEEDINGS vol 29 (2014) PARA 101.
9   See the Crown Proceedings Act 1947 s 17(2); and CROWN AND CROWN PROCEEDINGS vol 29 (2014) PARA 101.
10  For a claim in respect of salvage services by one of Her Majesty's aircraft see *The American Farmer* (1947) 80 Ll L Rep 672.
11  As to the Secretary of State see PARA 36.
12  See the Merchant Shipping Act 1995 s 230(3); and PARA 854. In the case of claims by the commander and crew of one of Her Majesty's ships, no allowance is made for the value of the salving ship (*The Carrie* [1917] P 224; *The Domira* (1913) 29 TLR 557; affd (1914) 30 TLR 521, CA), but the court will take into consideration the responsibility incurred by the officer who takes it upon himself to risk government property (*The Gorliz* (1917) as reported in 119 LT 123; *The Domira* (1914) 30 TLR 521, CA). The mere protection of merchant shipping from hostile attack does not entitle the commander and crew of one of Her Majesty's ships to a salvage award, since such a service is only part of their ordinary duties: *The F D Lambert* [1917] P 232n. Where the risk incurred is no greater than that involved in the performance of their ordinary duties they will not be entitled to a large award: *The Gorliz*. As to the right to salvage arising on the recapture of a neutral ship in the hands of the enemy see *The Svanfos, The Borgila* [1919] P 189.
13  Ie for the purposes of the Merchant Shipping Act 1995 s 230(3) (as to which see the text and notes 10–12): see s 230(4).
14  See the Merchant Shipping Act 1995 s 230(4); and PARA 854.
15  Ie the consent required for the purposes of the Merchant Shipping Act 1995 s 230(3) (as to which see the text and notes 10–12): see s 230(5).
16  See the Merchant Shipping Act 1995 s 230(5); and PARA 854.

**119. Apportionment of salvage remuneration.** A power to apportion amongst the salvors the amount of salvage remuneration was and is incident to the jurisdiction of the Admiralty Court in claims for salvage[1]. Where the aggregate amount of salvage payable in respect of salvage services rendered in United Kingdom waters[2] has been finally determined and exceeds the statutory threshold[3], or where the aggregate amount of salvage payable in respect of salvage services rendered outside United Kingdom waters (of whatever amount) has been finally determined, but where, in either case, any delay or dispute arises as to the apportionment of the amount, the court[4] may cause the amount of salvage to be apportioned among the persons entitled to it in such manner as it thinks just[5]. For the purpose of making that apportionment, the court may:

(1)     appoint any person to carry that apportionment into effect[6];
(2)     compel any person in whose hands or under whose control the amount may be to distribute it or to pay it into court to be dealt with as the court directs[7]; and
(3)     issue such process as it thinks fit[8].

In the case of salvage services rendered by the owners, master and crew of a foreign ship, the apportionment must be in accordance with the law of the flag of that vessel[9].

1   The power is derived from the Merchant Shipping Act 1995 s 229(1)–(3): see the text and notes 2–8. Any decision of the court under s 229 must be made on the basis of the criteria contained in the International Convention on Salvage 1989 (London, 28 April 1989; Cm 1526) art 13 (as to which see PARA 878): see the Merchant Shipping Act 1995 s 229(2); and PARA 903. As to the Admiralty jurisdiction of the High Court in relation to salvage etc see PARAS 113–114.
2   As to the meaning of 'United Kingdom' see PARA 16 note 3; and as to the meaning of 'United Kingdom waters' see PARA 48 note 10.
3   Ie exceeds £5,000: see the Merchant Shipping Act 1995 s 229(1). Where the aggregate amount of salvage payable in respect of salvage services rendered in United Kingdom waters has been finally determined and does not exceed £5,000, but a dispute arises as to the apportionment of the amount among several claimants, the person liable to pay the amount may apply to the receiver for leave to pay it to him: see the Merchant Shipping Act 1995 s 228; and PARA 902.

4   For these purposes, 'court' means the High Court: see the Merchant Shipping Act 1995 s 229(4).
5   See the Merchant Shipping Act 1995 s 229(1); and PARA 903. As to the principles of apportionment see *The Enchantress* (1860) Lush 93; and PARAS 904–905.
6   See the Merchant Shipping Act 1995 s 229(3)(a); and PARA 903.
7   See the Merchant Shipping Act 1995 s 229(3)(b); and PARA 903.
8   See the Merchant Shipping Act 1995 s 229(3)(c); and PARA 903.
9   See the International Convention on Salvage 1989 (London, 28 April 1989; Cm 1526) art 15(2); and PARA 901. This does not extend to wreck found outside United Kingdom territorial waters: *Pierce v Bemis, The Lusitania* [1986] QB 384, [1986] 1 All ER 1011, [1986] 1 Lloyd's Rep 132.

### C.   LIFE SALVAGE

**120.   Nature of life salvage.** Where no property ('res') had been saved and life alone had been preserved from destruction, no suit for a salvage reward could be maintained in the Admiralty Court, one reason being that there could be no proceedings in rem, which was the ancient foundation of the salvage suit[1]. Where, however, both life and property had been saved by one set of salvors, it was and still is the practice to give an enhanced award, the enhancement being a reflection of the value of the services rendered in the saving of life[2]. Statutory provisions were introduced[3] to protect persons who could not be justly compensated because they had saved life only, or very little property[4], but there is still no right of action[5] where no res is saved[6]. Moreover in certain circumstances a salvor may obtain a true life salvage award under the statutory provisions[7] where, even though he himself has rendered no salvage services to ship and cargo[8], some property is preserved[9].

1   *The Fusilier* (1865) Brown & Lush 341 at 344 per Dr Lushington; and see *The Aid* (1822) 1 Hag Adm 83. As to the development of the law that is administered in Admiralty see PARA 80 et seq. As to the common law principles which apply to life salvage see also PARA 864.
2   See *The Johannes* (1860) 1 Lush 182; *The Fusilier* (1865) Brown & Lush 341; *The Willem III* (1871) LR 3 A & E 487, 1 Asp MLC 129; *The Bosworth (No 2)* [1960] 1 All ER 729, [1961] 1 WLR 319, [1960] 1 Lloyd's Rep 173, CA; *The Bosworth (No 3)* [1962] 1 Lloyd's Rep 483. In contrast with the jurisdiction under the Merchant Shipping Act 1995 s 224 (ie the International Convention on Salvage 1989 (London, 28 April 1989; Cm 1526)) (as to which see PARAS 851 et seq), the inherent jurisdiction applies to claims wherever they arise, even in relation to foreign ships: see the Senior Courts Act 1981 s 20(7)(a), (b); and PARA 86.
3   See the Merchant Shipping Act 1854 (repealed and re-enacted in the Merchant Shipping Act 1995 s 224, which gives force of law to the International Convention on Salvage 1989 (London, 28 April 1989; Cm 1526) art 16); and PARA 121.
4   *The Fusilier* (1865) Brown & Lush 341 at 344 per Dr Lushington.
5   See the Merchant Shipping Act 1995 s 224; and the International Convention on Salvage 1989 (London, 28 April 1989; Cm 1526) (cited in PARA 121).
6   *The Renpor* (1883) 8 PD 115, 5 Asp MLC 98, CA.
7   See PARA 121.
8   *The Bosworth (No 3)* [1962] 1 Lloyd's Rep 483.
9   *Nourse v Liverpool Sailing Ship Owners Mutual Protection and Indemnity Association* [1896] 2 QB 16, CA; *The Bosworth (No 2)* [1960] 1 All ER 729, [1961] 1 WLR 319, [1960] 1 Lloyd's Rep 173, CA. See also *The Schiller (cargo ex)* (1877) 2 PD 145, CA, where the property saved was recovered by divers long after the life services were rendered.

**121.   Statutory jurisdiction with respect to life salvage.** A salvor of human life, who has taken part in the services rendered on the occasion of the accident giving rise to salvage, is entitled to a fair share of the payment awarded to the salvor for salving the vessel or other property or preventing or minimising damage to the environment[1]. Where services are rendered wholly or in part in United Kingdom waters[2] in saving life from a vessel of any nationality or elsewhere in saving life from any United Kingdom ship and either the vessel and other property are destroyed[3], or the sum to which the salvor is entitled[4] is less than a reasonable amount for the services rendered in saving life, the Secretary of State[5] may, if he thinks fit, pay to the salvor such sum or, as the case may be, such additional sum as he thinks fit in respect of the services rendered in saving life[6].

1   See the Merchant Shipping Act 1995 s 224; and the International Convention on Salvage 1989 (London, 28 April 1989; Cm 1526) art 16(2). No remuneration is due from persons whose lives are saved, but art 16 does not affect the provisions of national law on this subject: art 16(1). As to the Merchant Shipping Act 1995 s 224 and the International Convention on Salvage 1989 generally see PARAS 851 et seq.
2   As to the meaning of 'United Kingdom waters' under the Merchant Shipping Act 1995 see PARA 48 note 11. The previous legislation (ie the Merchant Shipping Act 1894 s 544 (repealed)) referred to 'British waters', meaning waters within the territorial limits of the United Kingdom, ie in ordinary cases waters within three miles of the coast: see *The Johannes* (1860) 1 Lush 182; *The Leda* (1856) Sw 40 at 43. In respect of a foreign vessel the question whether the services were rendered in British waters or not is one of fact: see *The Willem III* (1871) LR 3 A & E 487, 1 Asp MLC 129; *The Cairo* (1874) LR 4 A & E 184; *The Pacific* [1898] P 170, 8 Asp MLC 422; *The Fulham* [1898] P 206 at 213, 8 Asp MLC 425 at 426–427 (on appeal [1899] P 251, 8 Asp MLC 559, CA); *Jorgensen v Neptune Steam Fishing Co Ltd* 1902 4 F 992, Ct of Sess. For the position with regard to aircraft see PARA 114. In case of doubt, a declaration may be obtained from a responsible minister of the Crown and such declaration is conclusive: *The Fagernes* [1927] P 311, CA; *Sayce v Ameer Ruler Sadig Mohammad Abbasi Bahawalpur State* [1952] 2 QB 390, [1952] 2 All ER 64, CA.
3   It would appear that this covers the case where no property is preserved, as well as where it is subsequently destroyed: see *The Fusilier* (1865) Brown & Lush 341 at 344 per Dr Lushington.
4   Ie under the International Convention on Salvage 1989 (London, 28 April 1989; Cm 1526) art 16(2) (see the text and note 1): see the Merchant Shipping Act 1995 s 224, Sch 11 Pt II para 5.
5   As to the Secretary of State see PARA 36.
6   See the Merchant Shipping Act 1995 Sch 11 Pt II para 5; and PARA 864.

### D.   SALVAGE OF WRECK AND DERELICT

**122. Nature of wreck and derelict.** The Admiralty jurisdiction of the High Court in claims for salvage[1] includes jurisdiction in respect of claims for services rendered in preserving cargo, apparel or wreck[2], including, in the cases of cargo or wreck salvage, claims in respect of cargo or wreck found on land[3]. Furthermore, as part of its inherent jurisdiction, the Admiralty Court recognises as a class of salvage service work done in saving derelict or its contents, and this jurisdiction is not restricted by the locality of the services[4].

The Crown is entitled to all unclaimed wreck found in the United Kingdom[5] or in United Kingdom waters[6], except where the right has been granted to some other person[7]. Wreck includes flotsam, jetsam, lagan and derelict[8] found in or on the shores of the sea or any tidal water[9]. All things found derelict on the sea, including flotsam, jetsam or lagan which have not touched the ground[10] and which are brought within the United Kingdom[11], are prima facie droits of Admiralty but do not become actual droits unless there is no claim to ownership, and until then they are only derelict[12].

1   See the Senior Courts Act 1981 s 20(1)(a), (2)(j); and PARAS 93, 113.
2   See PARAS 123–124.
3   See the Senior Courts Act 1981 s 20(7)(b); and PARA 86.
4   *R (in his Office of Admiralty) v Property Derelict* (1825) 1 Hag Adm 383; *HMS Thetis* (1835) 3 Hag Adm 228; *The Association and The Rhomney* [1970] 2 Lloyd's Rep 59. As to the development of the law that is administered in Admiralty see PARA 80 et seq.
5   As to the meaning of 'United Kingdom' see PARA 16 note 3.
6   As to the meaning of 'United Kingdom waters' under the Merchant Shipping Act 1995 see PARA 48 note 11.
7   See the Merchant Shipping Act 1995 s 241; and PARA 950. This does not extend to wreck found outside United Kingdom territorial waters: *Pierce v Bemis, The Lusitania* [1986] QB 384, [1986] 1 All ER 1011, [1986] 1 Lloyd's Rep 132.
8   As to the meanings of these terms see *Sir Henry Constable's Case* (1601) 5 Co Rep 106a; and PARA 139.
9   See the Merchant Shipping Act 1995 s 255(1); and PARA 923. See also *R v Forty-nine Casks of Brandy* (1836) 3 Hag Adm 257 at 278 per Sir John Nicoll citing Blackstone. For procedures for dealing with wreck see the Merchant Shipping Act 1995 ss 236–240; and PARAS 935–947.

10  *R v Forty-nine Casks of Brandy* (1836) 3 Hag Adm 257; *R v Two Casks of Tallow* (1837) 3 Hag Adm 294.
11  The limits which international right may impose upon any claim under the prerogative of the British Crown to bona vacantia lying on the ocean floor are not clear: see *The Tubantia* [1924] P 78 at 87. As to bona vacantia see CROWN AND CROWN PROCEEDINGS vol 29 (2014) PARA 145 et seq.
12  *HMS Thetis* (1835) 3 Hag Adm 228. As to droits of Admiralty see PARA 139.

**123. Vessels wrecked, stranded or in distress.** The statutory provisions relating to vessels in distress[1] apply in circumstances where a United Kingdom[2] or foreign[3] vessel[4] is wrecked, stranded or in distress at any place on or near the coasts[5] of the United Kingdom or any tidal water[6] within United Kingdom waters[7].

Where any function is conferred on the receiver[8] by any of those provisions relating to vessels in distress[9], that function may be discharged by any officer of revenue and customs or any principal officer of the coastguard[10]. An officer discharging any such functions of the receiver is to be treated, with respect to any goods or articles belonging to a vessel the delivery of which to the receiver is required by any of the statutory provisions relating to wreck[11], as the agent of the receiver[12]. However, an officer discharging such functions is not entitled to any fees payable to receivers; nor is he deprived of any right to salvage[13] to which he would otherwise be entitled[14].

1  Ie the Merchant Shipping Act 1995 ss 232–235 (as to which see PARAS 936–958): see s 231(1); and PARA 936.
2  As to the meaning of 'United Kingdom' see PARA 16 note 3.
3  'Foreign', in relation to a ship, means that it is neither a United Kingdom ship nor a small ship (as defined in the Merchant Shipping Act 1995 s 1(2) (see PARA 230)) which is a British ship: see s 313(1); and PARA 18 note 2. As to the meanings of 'British ship' and 'United Kingdom ship' for these purposes see PARA 230; and as to the meaning of 'ship' see PARA 229.
4  As to the meaning of 'vessel' for the purposes of the Merchant Shipping Act 1995 Pt IX (ss 224–255) (salvage and wreck) see PARA 86 note 6.
5  It has been said that a place 20 miles off the coast was not within these words and that 'nearness' related to the extent of territorial waters: see *The Fulham* [1898] P 206 at 214, 8 Asp MLC 425 at 427 obiter per Gorell Barnes J; affd [1899] P 251, CA.
6  As to the meaning of 'tidal water' for these purposes see PARA 923 note 13.
7  See the Merchant Shipping Act 1995 s 231(1); and PARA 936. As to the meaning of 'United Kingdom waters' under the Merchant Shipping Act 1995 see PARA 48 note 11.
8  As to the meaning of 'receiver' for these purposes see PARA 887 note 4.
9  Ie by any of the Merchant Shipping Act 1995 ss 232–235 (as to which see PARAS 936–958): see s 231(2); and PARA 936.
10  See the Merchant Shipping Act 1995 s 231(2); and PARA 936. As to Her Majesty's Coastguard see PARA 57. As to the appointment of officers of Revenue and Customs see INCOME TAXATION vol 58 (2014) PARA 33.
11  Ie the Merchant Shipping Act 1995 Pt IX Ch II (ss 231–247) (see PARA 936 et seq): see s 231(3). As to the meaning of 'wreck' for these purposes see PARA 923.
12  See the Merchant Shipping Act 1995 s 231(3); and PARA 936.
13  As to the meaning of 'salvage' for these purposes see PARA 849.
14  See the Merchant Shipping Act 1995 s 231(4); and PARA 936.

**124. Wrecked aircraft.** In regard to aircraft, wreck includes any aircraft or any part of an aircraft or any cargo of an aircraft found derelict in or upon the seas surrounding the United Kingdom[1] or the tidal waters of the United Kingdom, or any ports or harbours of the United Kingdom or upon or near the shores of the seas and waters so described[2]. It also includes any aircraft or part of an aircraft or any cargo found or taken into possession outside the United Kingdom and subsequently brought within these limits described[3]. The application to aircraft of provisions relating to wreck includes provisions relating to vessels laid by or unfit for sea service[4].

1  As to the meaning of 'United Kingdom' see PARA 16 note 3.

2   See the Aircraft (Wreck and Salvage) Order 1938, SR & O 1938/136, art 2(b); and AVIATION vol
    2 (2017) PARA 1367. The Aircraft (Wreck and Salvage) Order 1938, SR & O 1938/136, has effect
    as if made under the Civil Aviation Act 1982 s 87 by virtue of s 105(3): see AVIATION vol 2 (2017)
    PARA 1367. See also PARA 114.
3   See the Aircraft (Wreck and Salvage) Order 1938, SR & O 1938/136, art 2(b); and AVIATION vol
    2 (2017) PARA 1367.
4   See the Civil Aviation Act 1982 s 87(5); and AVIATION vol 2 (2017) PARA 1367.

## (viii)  Towage and Pilotage

**125. Extent of jurisdiction regarding claims in the nature of towage or pilotage in respect of a ship or an aircraft.** The Admiralty jurisdiction of the High Court[1] includes jurisdiction to hear and determine any claim in the nature of towage in respect of a ship or an aircraft[2], and any claim in the nature of pilotage in respect of a ship or an aircraft[3]. The jurisdiction extends to all ships, whether British or not and whether registered or not and wherever the residence or domicile of their owners may be, and to all claims wherever arising[4].
A claim in the nature of towage is not confined to actual towage but extends to escorting services by a tug from outside a port into a port[5]. Ordinary towage, that is towage which is only required for expediting the progress of a vessel not in distress[6], is to be distinguished from salvage[7]. Although there is a maritime lien in respect of salvage[8], there is no maritime lien in respect of towage[9]. It is doubtful whether there is a maritime lien in respect of pilotage[10], even though the remuneration of a pilot is similar to wages of master and crew, in respect of which there is a lien[11].

1   As to the Admiralty jurisdiction of the High Court of Justice generally see PARA 85 et seq. As to
    the mode of exercise of this jurisdiction see the Senior Courts Act 1981 s 21; and PARAS 93–94.
    The Admiralty jurisdiction of the High Court extends also to hovercraft: see PARA 87.
2   Senior Courts Act 1981 s 20(1)(a), (2)(k). For the purposes of ss 20–23, 'towage', in relation to an
    aircraft, mean towage while the aircraft is water-borne: see s 24(1); and PARA 93 note 40. See also
    the text and notes 5–7.
3   Senior Courts Act 1981 s 20(1)(a), (2)(l). For the purposes of ss 20–23, 'pilotage', in relation to an
    aircraft, mean pilotage while the aircraft is water-borne: see s 24(1); and PARA 93 note 40.
4   See the Senior Courts Act 1981 s 20(7)(a), (b); and PARA 86.
5   *The Leoborg* [1962] 2 Lloyd's Rep 146.
6   *The Princess Alice* (1849) 3 Wm Rob 138.
7   For the distinction see *Troilus (Cargo Owners) v Gleneagle (Owners, Master and Crew)* [1951]
    AC 820, [1951] 2 All ER 40, [1951] 1 Lloyd's Rep 467, HL. For a case in which towage services
    were held to have developed into salvage services see *The Glenmorven* [1913] P 141.
8   See PARA 113. As to maritime liens generally see PARA 964 et seq.
9   *Westrup v Great Yarmouth Steam Carrying Co* (1889) 43 ChD 241, 6 Asp MLC 443; see also *The
    Henrich Björn* (1886) 11 App Cas 270, 6 Asp MLC 1, HL; but see *La Constancia* (1846) 2 Wm
    Rob 460, 4 Notes of Cases 512 at 521; *The Benares* (1850) 5 LT 185; *The St Lawrence* (1880) 5
    PD 250.
10  *The Clan Grant* (1887) 12 PD 139; *The Ambatielos, The Cephalonia* [1923] P 68, 16 Asp MLC
    120. Pilotage charges imposed by a competent harbour authority are recoverable as a civil debt or
    in any other manner in which ship, passenger and goods dues are recoverable by that authority: see
    the Pilotage Act 1987 s 10(7); and PARA 583. It was held that the previous legislation (giving the
    right to proceed summarily for dues owing) did not prejudice the right, which has always existed,
    to bring a claim in rem for dues, although in general it is advisable to pursue the summary remedy:
    see *The Ambatielos, The Cephalonia* at 75, 122 per Hill J. As to pilotage generally see PARA 574
    et seq. As to harbour authorities see PORTS AND HARBOURS vol 85 (2012) PARA 20.
11  See PARA 127.

## (ix)  Supplies, Repairs and Dock Charges

**126. Extent of jurisdiction regarding supplies, repairs and dock charges.** The Admiralty jurisdiction of the High Court[1] includes jurisdiction to hear and determine any claim in respect of goods[2] and materials supplied to a ship[3] for its operation and maintenance[4], and any claim in respect of the construction, repair or equipment[5] of a ship or in respect of dock charges or dues[6]. The jurisdiction extends to all ships, whether British or not and whether registered or not and wherever the residence or domicile of their owners may be, and to all claims wherever arising[7].

The supply of goods and materials to and the repair of a ship do not confer a maritime lien[8]. The repairer has, however, a common law possessory lien[9].

1    As to the Admiralty jurisdiction of the High Court of Justice generally see PARA 85 et seq. As to the mode of exercise of this jurisdiction see the Senior Courts Act 1981 s 21; and PARAS 93–94. The Admiralty jurisdiction of the High Court extends also to hovercraft: see PARA 87.

2    As to the meaning of 'goods' for these purposes see PARA 111 note 2.

3    As to the meaning of 'ship' for these purposes see PARA 85 note 7.

4    Senior Courts Act 1981 s 20(1)(a), (2)(m). See *Bridge Oil Ltd v Owners and/or Demise Charterers of the Ship Giuseppe di Vittorio* (1997) Times, 10 November, [1997] All ER (D) 39, CA. The supply of crew services comes within the meaning of goods and materials for the purposes of the Senior Courts Act 1981 s 20(1)(a), (2)(m): *Lavington International Ltd v The Nore Challenger and The Nore Commander (Bareboat Charterers)* [2001] 2 All ER (Comm) 667, [2001] 2 Lloyd's Rep 103. Supplies for a ship include a remotely operated vehicle for use from her: see *Re Oceaneering International AG (The Sarah)* [2011] 1 Lloyd's Rep 546.

     The term 'necessaries', used to describe claims similar to the Senior Courts Act 1981 s 20(1)(a), (2)(m) in earlier legislation (see eg the Supreme Court of Judicature (Consolidation) Act 1925 s 22(1)(a)(vii) (repealed)), does not appear in the Senior Courts Act 1981. The jurisdiction under the Administration of Justice Act 1956 s 1(1) (repealed) was no narrower, however, than the old jurisdiction in respect of necessaries (see *The Fairport (No 5)* [1967] 2 Lloyd's Rep 162, in which it was held that money lent for the purchase of supplies could be recovered under the Administration of Justice Act 1956 s 1(1)(m) (repealed)), and the existing jurisdiction is maintained by the Senior Courts Act 1981 s 20(1)(c) (see PARA 85). The question whether the supply of services could be brought under the Administration of Justice Act 1956 s 1(1)(m) (now the Senior Courts Act 1981 s 20(1)(a), (2)(m)) was raised, but not decided, in *The Queen of the South* [1968] P 449, [1968] 1 All ER 1163, [1968] 1 Lloyd's Rep 182, where Brandon J at 455, 1168, 188, respectively, suggested that the effect of the 'sweeping-up' provision at the end of the Administration of Justice Act 1956 s 1(1) (now the Senior Courts Act 1981 s 20(1)(c), (d): see PARA 85) is to preserve to the court, independently of, and concurrently with, any jurisdiction specifically conferred by the lettered paragraphs of the Administration of Justice Act 1956 s 1(1) (now the Senior Courts Act 1981 s 20(1)(a), (2)) over claims for, inter alia, necessaries, the same jurisdiction as was formerly conferred by the repealed enactments. For a definition of 'necessaries' see *The Riga* (1872) LR 3 A & E 516, 1 Asp MLC 246. See also *The River Rima* [1987] 3 All ER 1, CA; affd [1988] 2 All ER 641, [1988] 1 WLR 758, [1988] 2 Lloyd's Rep 193, HL (leased cargo containers not goods supplied to a ship for her operation).

5    Although fuel is not included in the term 'equipment', it is clearly material supplied to a ship for her operation: see *The D'Vora* [1952] 2 All ER 1127, [1953] 1 WLR 34, [1952] 2 Lloyd's Rep 404. A classification certificate has been held to be 'equipment': *The Stinne Peter* (1986, unreported).

6    Senior Courts Act 1981 s 20(1)(a), (2)(n).

7    See the Senior Courts Act 1981 s 20(7)(a), (b); and PARA 86.

8    *The Two Ellens* (1872) LR 4 PC 161; *The Henrich Björn* (1886) 11 App Cas 270, 6 Asp MLC 1, HL; *The Cella* (1888) 13 PD 82, CA; *The James W Elwell* [1921] P 351. As to the security obtained by arrest in proceedings in rem see *The Cella*; *The James W Elwell*; *The Zafiro* [1960] P 1, [1959] 2 All ER 537. As to maritime liens generally see PARA 964 et seq.

9    *The Tergeste* [1903] P 26; *The St Merriel* [1963] P 247, [1963] 1 All ER 537. As to possessory liens generally see LIEN vol 68 (2016) PARAS 802, 820 et seq.

## (x) Wages and Disbursements

**127. Extent of jurisdiction regarding wages and master's disbursements.** The Admiralty jurisdiction of the High Court[1] includes jurisdiction to hear and determine any claim by a master[2] or member of a crew of a ship[3] for wages (including any sum allotted out of wages or adjudged by a superintendent to be due by way of wages)[4]; and any claim by the master of a ship in respect of disbursements made on account of a ship[5]. The jurisdiction extends to all ships, whether British or not and whether registered or not and wherever the residence or domicile of their owners may be, and to all claims wherever arising[6].

There is a maritime lien in respect of seamen's wages[7], and the master of a ship has the same lien for his remuneration and all disbursements or liabilities properly made or incurred by him on account of the ship[8].

1    As to the Admiralty jurisdiction of the High Court of Justice generally see PARA 85 et seq. As to the mode of exercise of this jurisdiction see the Senior Courts Act 1981 s 21; and PARAS 93–94. The Admiralty jurisdiction of the High Court extends also to hovercraft: see PARA 87.

2    As to the meaning of 'master' for these purposes see PARA 85 note 14.

3    As to the meaning of 'ship' for these purposes see PARA 85 note 7. As to foreign ships see PARA 128.

4    Senior Courts Act 1981 s 20(1)(a), (2)(o). The text refers to a mercantile marine superintendent appointed under the Merchant Shipping Act 1995 s 296 (see PARA 61) to whom any dispute relating to the amount payable to a seaman employed under a crew agreement may be submitted for decision: see ss 33, 313(1); and PARA 486. As to amounts recoverable as wages see PARA 130.

5    Senior Courts Act 1981 s 20(1)(a), (2)(p). As to the sums that may be recovered as master's disbursements see PARA 131; and as to disbursements by persons other than a master see PARA 132.

6    See the Senior Courts Act 1981 s 20(7)(a), (b); and PARA 86.

7    The Sydney Cove (1815) 2 Dods 11; The Nymph (1856) Sw 86. The maritime lien in respect of wages due under an ordinary mariner's contract appears always to have existed; it would seem that the effect of the Admiralty Court Act 1861 s 10 (repealed) was to extend the jurisdiction, but not the maritime lien, to cases where wages are due under a special contract: see The Sara (1889) 14 App Cas 209, 6 Asp MLC 413, HL. In The British Trade [1924] P 104, 16 Asp MLC 296, it was conceded that wages under a special contract, so far as earned on board, conferred a maritime lien, but it was decided that the lien did not extend to damages for breach of a service contract; cf The Halcyon Skies [1977] QB 14, [1976] 1 All ER 856 (maritime lien in respect of pension fund contributions). The requirement that the wages be 'earned on board' is no longer relevant to the jurisdiction under the Senior Courts Act 1981, but would seem still to be the test as respects the lien. There will be no lien in respect of severance pay: see The Tacoma City [1991] 1 Lloyd's Rep 330, CA. The scope of the master's lien for wages will be the same as that of a seaman: The Ever Success [1999] 1 Lloyd's Rep 824. The maritime lien will extend to any wages paid via an agency to seamens' dependants: The Turiddu [2000] ICR 354, [1999] 2 Lloyd's Rep 401, CA. A seaman's lien is not capable of being renounced by any agreement: see the Merchant Shipping Act 1995 s 39; and PARA 479. As to the priority ranking of wages claims as a maritime lien see The Ruta [2000] ICR 1024 at 1028, [2000] 1 Lloyd's Rep 359 at 361 per Steel J. As to maritime liens generally see PARA 964 et seq.

8    See the Merchant Shipping Act 1995 s 41; and PARA 480. As to the limits of the lien for disbursements see The Castlegate [1893] AC 38, 7 Asp MLC 284, HL. A volunteer who pays the wages of the master and crew without the sanction of the court does not acquire by subrogation or otherwise the rights of the master and crew as regards the recovery of those wages: see The Leoborg (No 2) [1964] 1 Lloyd's Rep 380; following The Petone [1917] P 198 at 208 per Hill J. Payment may, however, be made with the leave of the court, and the payer be subrogated to those rights: see Sameiet Stavos (OH Meling Rederi) v The Berostar (Owners) [1970] 2 Lloyd's Rep 403.

## 128.    Special position of foreign ships.

The Admiralty jurisdiction of the High Court[1] includes jurisdiction to hear and determine claims for wages by the master[2] or a member of the crew of a foreign ship[3], and nothing in the statutory provisions which confer such jurisdiction[4] is to be construed as limiting the jurisdiction of the High Court to refuse to entertain such a claim[5].

Notice of such claims must be sent to the consul in London (if there is one) of the state concerned[6] and in certain cases the claim may not proceed if the consul objects[7].

1    As to the Admiralty jurisdiction of the High Court of Justice generally see PARA 85 et seq. As to the mode of exercise of this jurisdiction see the Senior Courts Act 1981 s 21; and PARAS 93–94. The Admiralty jurisdiction of the High Court extends also to hovercraft: see PARA 87.

2    As to the meaning of 'master' for these purposes see PARA 85 note 14.

3    See the Senior Courts Act 1981 s 20(1)(a), (2)(o); and PARA 127. See also The Tagus [1903] P 44, 9 Asp MLC 371. As to the meaning of 'ship' for these purposes see PARA 85 note 7.

4    Ie nothing in the Senior Courts Act 1981 ss 20–23 (see PARA 85 et seq): see s 24(2).

5   See the Senior Courts Act 1981 s 24(2)(a); and PARA 85. For cases on the exercise of the discretion
    see *The Nina* (1867) LR 2 PC 38; *The Leon XIII* (1883) 8 PD 121, 5 Asp MLC 73, CA.
6   As to the requirements to send such notice see PARA 161. Any statement made by the consul as to
    the desirability or otherwise of the claim being tried in England will be considered as a factor
    relevant to the exercise of the court's discretion, but the consul has no power of veto save as stated
    in the text and note 7: see the cases cited in note 5; and *The Octavie* (1863) Brown & Lush 215,
    33 LJPM & A 115.
7   See the Consular Relations Act 1968 ss 4, 16 (and Orders in Council made thereunder, which give
    effect to a number of international agreements entered into by the United Kingdom); and
    INTERNATIONAL RELATIONS LAW vol 61 (2010) PARA 303.

**129.  Time limit for proceedings.** Claims for wages in the Admiralty Court[1]
must be brought within six years from the date on which the cause of action
accrued[2].

1   As to which see PARA 127 et seq.
2   Ie under the general requirement that an action to recover any sum recoverable by virtue of any
    enactment is not to be brought after the time stated in the text: see the Limitation Act 1980 s 9(1);
    and LIMITATION PERIODS vol 68 (2016) PARA 1005. As to restrictions generally limiting the
    time within which claims must be brought within the Admiralty jurisdiction of the High Courts see
    PARA 151 et seq.

**130.  What sums may be recovered as wages.** The Admiralty jurisdiction of
the High Court in respect of wages[1] includes a claim for any sum allotted out of
wages or adjudged by a superintendent[2] to be due by way of wages[3].
    Contributions to a foreign seaman's union and insurance fund, which were
deductions made by the master from crew's wages, have been held to be
recoverable as wages where the claim was made by the master[4]. The cost of
repatriation, contributions in respect of foreign income tax and even stamp duty
on insurance contributions have been recovered by the master[5].
    Judgment in a claim for wages may include wages which have accrued since the
date of the issue of the claim form[6]. A claim by a member of the crew of a ship for
damages for wrongful dismissal can be maintained by him in a claim for wages[7].
The court may order that all or any part of the wages claimed have been forfeited
for desertion, misconduct or other offences[8].

1   Ie under the Senior Courts Act 1981 s 20(1)(a), (2)(o): see PARA 127. As to the Admiralty
    jurisdiction of the High Court of Justice generally see PARA 85 et seq. As to the mode of exercise
    of this jurisdiction see the Senior Courts Act 1981 s 21; and PARAS 93–94. The Admiralty
    jurisdiction of the High Court extends also to hovercraft: see PARA 87.
2   Ie a mercantile marine superintendent appointed under the Merchant Shipping Act 1995 s 296 (see
    PARA 61) to whom any dispute relating to the amount payable to a seaman employed under a crew
    agreement may be submitted for decision: see ss 33, 313(1); and PARA 486.
3   See the Senior Courts Act 1981 s 20(1)(a), (2)(o); and PARA 127. Seamen's wages are dealt with
    by the Merchant Shipping Act 1995 ss 30–40 (see PARA 484 et seq) and include interest on unpaid
    wages: see s 30(3) (seaman employed under a crew agreement) (cited in PARA 484); and s 35
    (master or person employed otherwise than under a crew agreement) (cited in PARA 475).
4   *The Fairport (No 3)* [1966] 2 Lloyd's Rep 253; *The Westport (No 4)* [1968] 2 Lloyd's Rep 559;
    but such items are not recoverable by a third party with no authority from the master or crew: see
    *The Acrux* [1965] P 391, [1965] 2 All ER 323, [1965] 1 Lloyd's Rep 565. As to payment of wages
    by third parties see PARA 127 note 8. See also *The Halcyon Skies* [1977] QB 14, [1976] 1 All ER
    856 (contributions to pension fund recoverable as wages).
5   *The Westport (No 4)* [1968] 2 Lloyd's Rep 559.
6   *The Fairport* [1967] P 167, [1966] 2 All ER 1026, [1966] 2 Lloyd's Rep 7.
7   *The Great Eastern* (1867) LR 1 A & E 384. An order made by a duly constituted naval court
    dismissing a seaman with forfeiture of his wages is a bar to a subsequent claim by a seaman for
    wrongful dismissal: *Hutton v Ras Steam Shipping Co Ltd* [1907] 1 KB 834, 10 Asp ML 386, CA.
8   See *The MacLeod* (1880) 5 PD 254; *The Fairport* (1884) 10 PD 13, 5 Asp MLC 348. As to
    deductions from wages and loss of right to wages see the Merchant Shipping Act 1995 ss 32, 38(3),
    40; and PARA 470 et seq.

**131.  What sums may be recovered as master's disbursements.**
Disbursements made by the master of a ship to be recoverable must be properly

incurred by him on account of the ship in the ordinary course of his employment, and in his capacity as master[1]. They must be within his implied authority from the owners[2], and do not include disbursements made by him for purposes for which the charterers ought to have made provision[3].

1 _The Ripon City_ [1897] P 226, 8 Asp MLC 304. See also the Merchant Shipping Act 1995 s 41 (cited in PARA 480); and PARA 971.
2 _The Turgot_ (1886) 11 PD 21, 5 Asp MLC 548; _The Ripon City_ [1897] P 226, 8 Asp MLC 304.
3 _The Turgot_ (1886) 11 PD 21, 5 Asp MLC 548; _The Castlegate_ [1893] AC 38 at 47. A collateral liability undertaken by the master on a debt of the owner is not a disbursement: _The Orienta_ [1895] P 49, 7 Asp MLC 529, CA.

**132. Disbursements made by a shipper, charterer, or agent on account of a ship.** The Admiralty jurisdiction of the High Court in respect of wages[1] includes jurisdiction to hear and determine any claim by a shipper, charterer or agent[2] in respect of disbursements made on account of a ship[3]. The jurisdiction extends to all ships, whether British or not and whether registered or not and wherever the residence or domicile of their owners may be, and to all claims wherever arising[4].

Such claims do not confer a maritime lien[5].

1 Ie under the Senior Courts Act 1981 s 20(1)(a), (2)(p): see PARA 127. As to the Admiralty jurisdiction of the High Court of Justice generally see PARA 85 et seq. As to the mode of exercise of this jurisdiction see the Senior Courts Act 1981 s 21; and PARAS 93–94. The Admiralty jurisdiction of the High Court extends also to hovercraft: see PARA 87.
2 A ship's agent may include a fee for his services in his claim in respect of disbursements made on account of a ship: _The Westport (No 3)_ [1966] 1 Lloyd's Rep 342. However, the disbursements made must relate to an identified ship: see _The Lloyd Pacifico_ [1995] 1 Lloyd's Rep 54. 'Agent' does not include an insurance broker: _Bain Clarkson Ltd v Owners of Sea Friends_ [1991] 2 Lloyd's Rep 322, CA.
3 Senior Courts Act 1981 s 20(1)(a), (2)(p). As to the meaning of 'ship' for these purposes see PARA 85 note 7. For the position with regard to arrest by shipbrokers and agents in respect of necessary disbursements after notice of impending winding up is given see _The Zafiro_ [1960] P 1, [1959] 2 All ER 537.
4 See the Senior Courts Act 1981 s 20(7)(a), (b); and PARA 86.
5 See _The Zafiro_ [1960] P 1, [1959] 2 All ER 537. An insurance premium is not a disbursement on account of a ship see _Bain Clarkson Ltd v Owners of Sea Friends_ [1991] 2 Lloyd's Rep 322, CA. As to maritime liens generally see PARA 964 et seq.

### (xi) General Average

**133. Extent of jurisdiction regarding a general average act.** The Admiralty jurisdiction of the High Court[1] includes jurisdiction to hear and determine any claim arising out of an act which is or is claimed to be a general average act[2]. The jurisdiction extends to all ships, whether British or not and whether registered or not and wherever the residence or domicile of their owners may be, and to all claims wherever arising[3].

The shipowner has a lien for general average on the cargo for its contribution and may require, before he parts with the cargo, security for the due payment of general average, whether the claim is on his own behalf or on behalf of other cargo owners[4]. The shipowner also has the right to enforce contribution by bringing proceedings[5]; this right is shared by any other person claiming contribution[6].

1 As to the Admiralty jurisdiction of the High Court of Justice generally see PARA 85 et seq. As to the mode of exercise of this jurisdiction see the Senior Courts Act 1981 s 21; and PARAS 93–94. The Admiralty jurisdiction of the High Court extends also to hovercraft: see PARA 87.
2 Senior Courts Act 1981 s 20(1)(a), (2)(q). A general average act occurs when any extraordinary sacrifice or expenditure is voluntarily and reasonably made or incurred in time of peril for the purpose of preserving the property imperilled (that is ship and cargo) in the common adventure:

see the Marine Insurance Act 1906 s 66(2); and INSURANCE vol 60 (2011) PARAS 386–387. See also *Birkley v Presgrave* (1801) 1 East 220; and CARRIAGE AND CARRIERS vol 7 (2015) PARA 606.

 It is usual for contracts for the carriage of goods by sea to provide for the adjustment of general average according to the York-Antwerp Rules 1974, a voluntary international code on the subject which differs in a number of respects from the rules of the maritime law. For those rules see INSURANCE vol 60 (2011) PARA 392 et seq. It has been held that, where the contract of affreightment incorporates the York-Antwerp Rules, the rights and obligations of parties to the adventure in relation to general average are contractual: see *The Astraea* [1971] 2 Lloyd's Rep 494, following *Milburn & Co v Jamaica Fruit Importing and Trading Co of London* [1900] 2 QB 540, 9 Asp MLC 122, CA; *Goulandris Bros Ltd v B Goldman & Sons Ltd* [1958] 1 QB 74, [1957] 3 All ER 100, [1957] 2 Lloyd's Rep 207.

3 See the Senior Courts Act 1981 s 20(7)(a), (b); and PARA 86.
4 *Crooks v Allan* (1879) 5 QBD 38, 4 Asp MLC 216.
5 *Anderson v Ocean Steamship Co* (1884) 10 App Cas 107, 5 Asp MLC 401, HL.
6 *Dobson v Wilson* (1813) 3 Camp 480 (cargo); *Morrison Steam Ship Co Ltd v SS Greystoke Castle (Cargo Owners)* [1947] AC 265 at 312, [1946] 2 All ER 696 at 718–719, HL, per Lord Uthwatt (cargo); *Pirie & Co v Middle Dock Co* (1881) 44 LT 426, 4 Asp MLC 388 (freight).

## (xii) Bottomry

**134. Extent of jurisdiction regarding claims arising out of bottomry.** The Admiralty jurisdiction of the High Court[1] includes jurisdiction to hear and determine any claim arising out of bottomry[2]. Claims of bottomry (and respondentia[3]) are brought for the purpose of enforcing bottomry bonds[4], which are contracts in the nature of mortgage of a ship or cargo on which the owner, or master acting for the owner[5], borrows money in circumstances of unforeseen necessity or in case of distress to enable him to repair the ship or to pay for the repairs and dispatch of the vessel for the completion of her voyage[6], and pledges the ship or cargo *pars pro tota* for repayment[7]. If the ship is lost in the course of the voyage the lender on the bottomry bond loses his money unless the terms of the bond otherwise provide; but if the ship arrives safe, then he may recover the loan, with interest, which is sometimes called 'maritime interest' and may be in proportion to the risks of the voyage[8].

 The jurisdiction in respect of claims arising out of bottomry[9] extends to all ships, whether British or not and whether registered or not and wherever the residence or domicile of their owners may be, and to all claims wherever arising[10].

 There is a maritime lien in respect of bottomry[11].

 As long ago as 1926 bottomry bonds were uncommon[12]; today they are obsolete in practice.

1 As to the Admiralty jurisdiction of the High Court of Justice generally see PARA 85 et seq. As to the mode of exercise of this jurisdiction see the Senior Courts Act 1981 s 21; and PARAS 93–94. The Admiralty jurisdiction of the High Court extends also to hovercraft: see PARA 87.
2 Senior Courts Act 1981 s 20(1)(a), (2)(r). As to what constitutes bottomry see the text and notes 3–8; and as to the master's authority to hypothecate the ship and freight by a contract of bottomry see PARA 435.
3 Respondentia is the proper technical term where the cargo alone is hypothecated: see PARA 435.
4 See *The Sultan (cargo ex)* (1859) Sw 504 at 510 per Dr Lushington. It is suggested that claims arising out of bottomry for the purposes mentioned in the text include claims on any instruments used to effect bottomry, whether bonds, bills or otherwise.
5 See *The Gratitudine* (1801) 3 Ch Rob 240.
6 See *Soares v Rahn, The Prince of Saxe Coburg* (1839) 3 Moo PCC 1. The necessity for the loan is essential to the validity of a bottomry bond, and must be proved in any claim on the bond: *The Karnak* (1868) LR 2 A & E 289 (on appeal (1869) LR 2 PC 505); *The St George* [1926] P 217.
7 A bottomry bond is to be distinguished from a loan on the personal credit of the owner or master: see *The Rhadamanthe* (1813) 1 Dods 201; *The Haabet* [1899] P 295; *The St George* [1926] P 217. As to the particulars which should be contained in a valid instrument of bottomry see *The James W Elwell* [1921] P 351.

8   See *The Atlas* (1827) 2 Hag Adm 48 at 53. Maritime risk (ie the condition that payment is
    conditional upon safe arrival) is an essential feature of a bottomry bond: *The Indomitable* (1859)
    Sw 446. Maritime interest is not essential: *The Haabet* [1899] P 295.
9   Ie the jurisdiction set out in the Senior Courts Act 1981 s 20(1)(a), (2)(r) (see the text and notes
    1–2).
10  See the Senior Courts Act 1981 s 20(7)(a), (b); and PARA 86.
11  *The Ripon City* [1897] P 226. As to maritime liens generally see PARA 964 et seq.
12  See *The St George* [1926] P 217 at 229 per Lord Merrivale P.

## (xiii)  Forfeiture, Condemnation and Restoration of Ship or Goods

**135.  Extent of jurisdiction in respect of forfeiture, condemnation and restoration.** The Admiralty jurisdiction of the High Court[1] includes jurisdiction to hear and determine any claim for the forfeiture or condemnation of a ship or of goods which are being or have been carried, or have been attempted to be carried, in a ship, or for the restoration of a ship or any such goods after seizure[2]. The jurisdiction extends to all ships, whether British or not and whether registered or not and wherever the residence or domicile of their owners may be, and to all claims wherever arising[3].

As the court has jurisdiction in respect of any claim for forfeiture or condemnation of a ship or goods, it may grant a declaration in respect of the proceeds of sale of a ship held by the Admiralty Marshal[4].

1   As to the Admiralty jurisdiction of the High Court of Justice generally see PARA 85 et seq; and see
    especially PARA 85, where the preservation of the inherent, together with the statutory, jurisdiction
    of the High Court is discussed. As to the mode of exercise of this jurisdiction see the Senior Courts
    Act 1981 s 21; and PARAS 93–94. The Admiralty jurisdiction of the High Court extends also to
    hovercraft: see PARA 87.
2   Senior Courts Act 1981 s 20(1)(a), (2)(s).
3   See the Senior Courts Act 1981 s 20(7)(a), (b); and PARA 86.
4   *The Skylark* [1965] P 474, [1965] 3 All ER 380. As to the Admiralty Marshal see PARA 160 note 6.

**136.  Forfeiture of ship under the Merchant Shipping Act 1995.** The Merchant Shipping Act 1995 provides for proceedings on forfeiture[1] where any ship[2] either wholly or as to any share in it becomes subject to forfeiture[3] under the provisions of that Act, which relate to: (1) causing a ship which is not a British ship to appear to be a British ship[4]; (2) concealing the nationality of a British ship[5]; and (3) sale of a ship where transmitted to a person not qualified to own a British ship[6].

1   See the Merchant Shipping Act 1995 s 7; and PARA 235.
2   As to the meaning of 'ship' for these purposes see PARA 229.
3   See the Merchant Shipping Act 1995 s 7; and PARA 235. It would appear that the wording of s 7
    is intended to protect the interest of a bona fide purchaser, who formerly had no title as against the
    Crown: see *The Annandale* (1877) 2 PD 218, CA, decided under the Merchant Shipping Act 1854
    s 103 (repealed).
4   See the Merchant Shipping Act 1995 s 3(1) (cited in PARA 1062), s 15 (cited in PARA 1066). As
    to the meaning of 'British ship' for these purposes see PARA 229.
5   See the Merchant Shipping Act 1995 s 3(4) (cited in PARA 1062). See also *The Sceptre* (1876) 3
    Asp MLC 269; and *The Annendale* (1877) 2 PD 218. Specific provisions deal with penalties for the
    improper use of British national colours and the forfeiture of colours improperly displayed: see the
    Merchant Shipping Act 1995 s 4 (cited in PARA 1063). The jurisdiction under s 4, in so far as it
    is not covered by the Senior Courts Act 1981 s 20(1)(a), (2)(s) (Admiralty jurisdiction in respect
    of forfeiture etc) (see PARA 135), is preserved by s 20(1)(c) (see PARA 85), being an ancient
    jurisdiction of the Court of Admiralty: see *R v Ewen* (1856) 2 Jur NS 454; and see further
    PARA 1063.
6   See the Merchant Shipping Act 1995 s 16, Sch 1 para4(4) (cited in PARA 306); and *The Millicent*
    [1891] WN 162.

**137.  Forfeiture of dangerous goods under the Merchant Shipping Act 1995.** Under the Merchant Shipping Act 1995, the High Court may condemn as forfeited any dangerous goods[1] sent or carried, or attempted to be sent or carried, on board any vessel, British or foreign[2], without being properly marked, or without a written notice having been given of the description of the goods, or under a false description or with a false description of the sender or carrier[3].

1  For these purposes, 'dangerous goods' means goods designated as dangerous goods by safety regulations under the Merchant Shipping Act 1995: see s 87(5); and PARA 645.
2  For these purposes, 'foreign', in relation to a ship, means that it is neither a United Kingdom ship nor a small ship (as defined in the Merchant Shipping Act 1995 s 1(2) (see PARA 230)) which is a British ship: see s 313(1); and PARA 18 note 2. As to the meanings of 'British ship' and 'United Kingdom ship' for these purposes see PARA 230; as to the meaning of 'ship' see PARA 229; and as to the meaning of 'United Kingdom' see PARA 16 note 3.
3  See the Merchant Shipping Act 1995 s 87; and PARA 645. See also the Senior Courts Act 1981 s 20(1)(a), (2)(s); and PARA 135. See also, as to the rights of shipowners with respect to dangerous goods, CARRIAGE AND CARRIERS vol 7 (2015) PARAS 261, 385, 437.

**138. Cases under the Foreign Enlistment Act 1870.** All proceedings for the condemnation and forfeiture of a ship, or ship and equipment, or arms and munitions of war, in pursuance of the Foreign Enlistment Act 1870[1], are directed to be taken in the Court of Admiralty, and not in any other court[2], and accordingly now fall within the Admiralty jurisdiction of the High Court[3]. In such cases, in addition to any power granted by that Act, the Court of Admiralty has all powers over a ship or any other matter brought before it which it has in the case of a ship or matter brought before it in the exercise of its ordinary jurisdiction[4].

1  Ships built or equipped without authority for a foreign naval service where the foreign state is at war with a friendly state, and ships fitted out for expeditions against a friendly state are liable to forfeiture under the Foreign Enlistment Act 1870: see ss 8, 11; and ARMED CONFLICT AND EMERGENCY vol 3 (2011) PARAS 13–14.
2  See the Foreign Enlistment Act 1870 s 19.
3  See the Senior Courts Act 1981 s 20(1)(a), (2)(s); and PARA 135.
4  See the Foreign Enlistment Act 1870 s 19.

## (xiv) Droits of Admiralty

**139. Extent of jurisdiction.** The Admiralty jurisdiction of the High Court[1] includes jurisdiction to hear and determine any claim, on behalf of the Crown, for droits of Admiralty[2]. The jurisdiction extends to all claims wherever arising[3]. Things found derelict[4] on the sea, including flotsam[5], jetsam[6] or lagan[7] which, if they have not touched the ground, are Admiralty droits[8]. Such things must be returned to their true owner, if he appears in time; if not, they must be condemned as droits[9]. Property found in the possession of convicted pirates and clearly belonging to them is also included in the term droits of Admiralty, but not property in the possession of pirates but belonging to others[10]. Remuneration in the nature of salvage is also payable to the captors of royal fish (whales and sturgeons, which are droits of Admiralty[11]), and is recoverable in an Admiralty claim of salvage[12].

As there is a statutory procedure under the Merchant Shipping Act 1995 for dealing with wreck (which for this purpose includes jetsam, flotsam, lagan and derelict[13]) and a statutory method of dealing with disputes as to title to wreck[14] summarily, in most cases little occasion arises for the exercise of the jurisdiction of the High Court under this head. The Crown's right to claim wreck does not extend to unclaimed wreck found outside United Kingdom territorial waters[15].

1  As to the Admiralty jurisdiction of the High Court of Justice generally see PARA 85 et seq. As to the mode of exercise of this jurisdiction see the Senior Courts Act 1981 s 21; and PARAS 93–94. The Admiralty jurisdiction of the High Court extends also to hovercraft: see PARA 87.
2  See the Senior Courts Act 1981 s 20(1)(a), (2)(s). As to when prize is a droit of Admiralty see PRIZE vol 85 (2012) PARA 603; and as to the distinction in time of war between droits of Admiralty and droits of the Crown see PRIZE vol 85 (2012) PARAS 602–604.

3   See the Senior Courts Act 1981 s 20(7)(b); and PARA 86.
4   As to the meaning of 'derelict' see *HMS Thetis* (1835) 3 Hag Adm 228; *The Tubantia* [1924] P 78
    at 87–88; *The Association and The Rhomney* [1970] 2 Lloyd's Rep 59. See also *Pierce v Bemis,
    The Lusitania* [1986] QB 384, [1986] 1 All ER 1011, [1986] 1 Lloyd's Rep 132.
5   'Flotsam' are goods which float when a ship is sunk: see *Sir Henry Constable's Case* (1601) 5 Co
    Rep 106a; *The Gas Float Whitton (No 2)* [1896] P 42 at 51, CA.
6   'Jetsam' are goods thrown into the sea to lighten a ship which nevertheless sinks: see *Sir Henry
    Constable's Case* (1601) 5 Co Rep 106a.
7   'Lagan' (or 'ligan') are goods heavier than water (buoyed so that they will not sink) cast into the
    sea from a ship which perishes: see *Sir Henry Constable's Case* (1601) 5 Co Rep 106a.
8   *R v Forty-nine Casks of Brandy* (1836) 3 Hag Adm 257.
9   *R v Property Derelict* (1825) 1 Hag Adm 383.
10  *The Panda* (1842) 1 Wm Rob 423. The Admiralty jurisdiction of the High Court extends to the
    condemnation as droits of Admiralty of ships, goods and other property taken from pirates by Her
    Majesty's ships or the restoration of such goods and property to the owner on payment of
    one-eighth of the value of the property by way of salvage remuneration: see the Piracy Act 1850
    s 5 (amended by the Statute Law Revision Act 1875; and the Statute Law Revision Act 1891).
11  See the statute Prerogativa Regis (temp incert), c 13; *Cinque Ports (Lord Warden) v R* (1831) 2
    Hag Adm 438.
12  *Cinque Ports (Lord Warden) v R* (1831) 2 Hag Adm 438 at 441.
13  See the Merchant Shipping Act 1995 ss 236–240; and PARAS 935–947. As to the meaning of
    'wreck' under the Merchant Shipping Act 1995 see PARA 923.
14  See the Merchant Shipping Act 1995 ss 241–244; and PARAS 950–952.
15  See *Pierce v Bemis, The Lusitania* [1986] QB 384, [1986] 1 All ER 1011, [1986] 1 Lloyd's Rep
    132. As to the meaning of 'United Kingdom' see PARA 16 note 3. As to what constitute the
    territorial waters of the United Kingdom see INTERNATIONAL RELATIONS LAW vol 61 (2010)
    PARA 121 et seq; WATER AND WATERWAYS vol 100 (2009) PARA 31.

# (3) PRACTICE OF THE HIGH COURT

## (i) The Admiralty Registrar

### A.   THE ADMIRALTY REGISTRAR AND REGISTRY

**140.   The Admiralty Registrar.** The Admiralty Registrar is a Queen's Bench
Division Master[1] and a senior officer of the Admiralty and Commercial Registry[2].
In order to qualify for appointment as an Admiralty Registrar, a person must have
a seven year general qualification[3].

The Admiralty Registrar has responsibility for Admiralty claims[4] and has all
the powers of the Admiralty judge except where a rule or practice direction
provides otherwise[5]. Although much of the practice that applies in the Admiralty
Court is the same as that which applies in the Commercial Court[6], one significant
area of difference is that many interim applications are heard by the Admiralty
Registrar[7].

1   See CPR 61.1(2)(l), which defines 'Registrar' for the purposes of CPR Pt 61 as the Queen's Bench
    Division Master with responsibility for Admiralty claims. As to the meaning of 'Admiralty claim'
    for these purposes, and as to the application of CPR Pt 61, see PARA 91 note 3. As to Queen's
    Bench Masters generally see COURTS AND TRIBUNALS vol 24 (2010) PARA 742.
2   As to the Admiralty and Commercial Registry see PARA 142. There was a Registrar attached to the
    old High Court of Admiralty and his office was preserved by the Supreme Court of Judicature Act
    1873 s 77 (repealed).
3   See the Senior Courts Act 1981 s 88, Sch II Pt II; and COURTS AND TRIBUNALS vol 24 (2010)
    PARA 748. As to when a person has a 'general qualification' see the Courts and Legal Services Act
    1990 s 71(3); and LEGAL PROFESSIONS vol 65 (2015) PARA 540. The Admiralty Registrar is
    barred from legal practice: see the Courts and Legal Services Act 1990 s 75, Sch 11; and COURTS
    AND TRIBUNALS vol 24 (2010) PARA 748.
4   See note 1.

5 CPR 61.1(4). As to the procedure that governs Admiralty claims, including CPR Pt 61 and *Practice Direction—Admiralty Claims* PD 61, see PARA 157 et seq. CPR Pt 58 (Commercial Court) applies to claims in the Admiralty Court where CPR Pt 61 does not provide otherwise (see CPR 61.1(3); and PARA 91 note 3); and the practice direction which supplements CPR Pt 58 (ie *Practice Direction—Commercial Court* PD 58) also applies to Admiralty claims except where it is inconsistent with either CPR Pt 61 or *Practice Direction—Admiralty Claims* PD 61 (see para 1.1; and PARA 91 note 3). As to the practice and procedure that applies in the Commercial Court, including CPR Pt 58 and *Practice Direction—Commercial Court* PD 58, see CIVIL PROCEDURE vol 11 (2015) PARA 170 et seq; COURTS AND TRIBUNALS vol 24 (2010) PARA 708.

6 See note 5.

7 See the Admiralty and Commercial Courts Guide (2016) para N1.3. As to interim applications in the Admiralty Court see PARA 204. The Admiralty and Commercial Courts Guide provides additional guidance about the conduct of proceedings in the Admiralty and Commercial Courts and, within the framework of the Civil Procedure Rules and the associated Practice Directions, establishes the practice to be followed in those courts: see para A1.2; and PARA 157 et seq.

## 141. General jurisdiction of the Admiralty Registrar.

In general, the Admiralty Registrar[1] deals with all applications in Admiralty claims[2] on matters which elsewhere in the Queen's Bench Division would be dealt with on application by a Master[3]. In addition to the power of the Admiralty Registrar to hear references[4], he has the power as a judge of the Queen's Bench Division to transact all such business and exercise all such authority and jurisdiction as under the Senior Courts Act 1981 may generally be transacted and exercised by a Queen's Bench Division judge in private[5].

Appeal from an order or decision of the Admiralty Registrar lies to a single judge of the High Court[6].

1 As to the Admiralty Registrar see PARA 140.

2 As to the meaning of 'Admiralty claim' for the purposes of CPR Pt 61 see PARA 91 note 3. As to CPR Pt 61 see further note 5.

3 See PARA 140. A Master may refer to a judge any matter which he thinks should properly be decided by a judge, and the judge may either dispose of the matter or refer it back to the Master: see *Practice Direction—Applications* PD 23A para 1; and CIVIL PROCEDURE vol 12 (2015) PARA 557.

4 As to matters that may be referred to the Admiralty Registrar see PARA 143 et seq.

5 See the Senior Courts Act 1981 s 61(1), Sch 1 para 2; and COURTS AND TRIBUNALS vol 24 (2010) PARA 708. The Admiralty Registrar also has the procedural powers conferred on him by the Civil Procedure Rules: see especially CPR Pt 61; and *Practice Direction—Admiralty Claims* PD 61 (cited in PARA 157 et seq). CPR Pt 58 (Commercial Court) applies to claims in the Admiralty Court where CPR Pt 61 does not provide otherwise (see CPR 61.1(3); and PARA 91 note 3); and the practice direction which supplements CPR Pt 58 (ie *Practice Direction—Commercial Court* PD 58) also applies to Admiralty claims except where it is inconsistent with either CPR Pt 61 or *Practice Direction—Admiralty Claims* PD 61 (see para 1.1; and PARA 91 note 3). As to the practice and procedure that applies in the Commercial Court, including CPR Pt 58 and *Practice Direction—Commercial Court* PD 58, see CIVIL PROCEDURE vol 11 (2015) PARA 170; COURTS AND TRIBUNALS vol 24 (2010) PARA 708.

6 See *Practice Direction—Appeals* PD 52A para 3.5; and CIVIL PROCEDURE vol 12A (2015) PARA 1515. As to objections to a decision of the Admiralty Registrar following a reference see PARA 149.

## 142. Admiralty and Commercial Registry.

The Admiralty and Commercial Registry is the administrative office for the Admiralty Court[1], to which all Admiralty claims[2] are (or, in certain cases, may be) assigned[3]. Applications made for Admiralty claims together with the requisite documents may be posted to the Admiralty and Commercial Registry[4].

Except for orders made by the court on its own initiative and unless the court orders otherwise, every judgment or order made in Admiralty proceedings will be drawn up by the parties[5].

1 See the Admiralty and Commercial Courts Guide (2016) para A2.

2 As to the meaning of 'Admiralty claim' for the purposes of CPR Pt 61 see PARA 91 note 3. As to CPR Pt 61 see note 3.

3   As to the assignment of business to the Admiralty Court see CPR 61.2(1), (2); and PARA 91. As
    to the procedure that governs Admiralty claims, including CPR Pt 61 and *Practice
    Direction—Admiralty Claims* PD 61, see PARAS 140 note 5, 157 et seq.
4   See the Admiralty and Commercial Courts Guide (2016) para N12.1. In addition to the classes of
    business for which the use of postal facilities is permitted by the Civil Procedure Rules or by the
    Admiralty and Commercial Courts Guide, the filing of requests for cautions against arrest and of
    collision statements of case is also permitted in Admiralty matters: see the Admiralty and
    Commercial Courts Guide (2016) para N12.2. As to the issue of documents when the Registry is
    closed see para N7. As to requests for cautions against arrest see PARA 166; and as to collision
    statements of case see PARA 182 et seq.
        A party to any proceedings may, unless the court orders otherwise, obtain from the records of
    the court (as well as other court documents that are specified) a copy of any claim form or other
    statement of case together with any documents filed with or attached to or intended by the
    claimant to be served with such claim form: see CPR 5.4B(1); and CIVIL PROCEDURE vol 11
    (2015) PARA 67. A party to proceedings also may, if the court gives permission, obtain from the
    records of the court a copy of any other document filed by a party or communication between the
    court and a party or another person: see CPR 5.4B(2); and CIVIL PROCEDURE vol 11 (2015)
    PARA 67.
5   See CPR 58.15; *Practice Direction—Commercial Court* PD 58 para 14.2; and CIVIL PROCEDURE
    vol 11 (2015) PARA 177.

### B.   REFERENCES TO THE REGISTRAR

**143. References to the Admiralty Registrar.** The Admiralty Court[1] may at
any stage in a claim[2] refer any question or issue for determination by the
Admiralty Registrar[3] (a 'reference')[4]. For a reference to be valid, it is necessary to
have an order for reference, which can be an order of the court, an order made
following the parties' agreement, or as a term of a decree for limitation. The court
will not order a reference if it can satisfactorily dispose of the question[5].

In collision claims[6], it is usual for liability to be tried first and for the assessment
of damages and interest to be referred to the Admiralty Registrar[7]. The following
matters are normally also referred to the Admiralty Registrar: questions as to
consequential damage in general[8]; the assessment of damage to cargo; the
assessment of damages in salvage claims when damage has been done to the salved
or salving vessel in the course of the services[9]; the investigation of accounts, for
example in claims for goods or materials, or for repairs or disbursements and in
wages and mortgage claims[10]; the assessment of damages in respect of loss of life
and personal injuries[11]; in limitation claims[12], the determination, after a decree
limiting the claimant's liability has been made in court, of the right of the
claimants to share in the fund, and the amounts due to each of them out of that
fund[13]; and the decision as to which claimants for salvage are entitled to
preferential treatment[14].

In modern practice, the Admiralty Registrar decides questions without the
assistance of merchants, but he may be assisted by a nautical assessor or assessors
if questions of navigation or seamanship, or both, may arise on the reference[15].

1   As to the meaning of the 'Admiralty Court' for these purposes see PARA 91 note 3.
2   Ie an 'Admiralty claim': see PARA 91 note 3. As to the assignment of business to the Admiralty
    Court see CPR 61.2(1), (2); and PARA 91. As to the procedure that governs Admiralty claims,
    including CPR Pt 61 and *Practice Direction—Admiralty Claims* PD 61, see PARAS 140 note 5, 157
    et seq.
3   As to the Admiralty Registrar see PARA 140.
4   *Practice Direction—Admiralty Claims* PD 61 para 13.1. The general practice pre-dates the
    Judicature Acts: see eg *The Empress Eugenie* (1860) Lush 138; *The Lemuella* (1860) Lush 147;
    *The Princess Helena* (1861) Lush 190. See also *The Gertrude* (1888) 13 PD 105, CA (interest on
    damages was properly awarded by the registrar; the parties, having proceeded on the
    understanding that the Admiralty practice should apply, had impliedly consented to abide by such
    practice).
5   For an example where the issue of damages is straightforward see *The Eléonore* (1863) Brown &
    Lush 185.

6 As to collision claims see PARA 180 et seq.

7 See the Admiralty and Commercial Courts Guide (2016) para N10.1. If both vessels are damaged and found partly to blame, two references, one in respect of the claim of the claimant and the other in respect of the claim of the defendant, may be necessary.

There is no hard and fast rule as to the dividing line between questions of liability and questions of damages; accordingly such questions as to whether certain consequential loss was or was not caused by the act of the defendant may either be determined by the court or included in the reference to the Registrar: see *The Maid of Kent* (1881) 6 PD 178; *The Guildford* as reported in [1956] 2 All ER 915 at 917, [1956] 2 Lloyd's Rep 74 at 82 per Lord Merriman. See also *SS Singleton Abbey v SS Paludina* [1927] AC 16, HL; and *The Argonaftis* [1989] 2 Lloyd's Rep 487 (claimants obtained judgment on liability for collision damage; issue as to the amount of damages which they were entitled to recover was referred to the Admiralty Registrar). Which of these courses is to be adopted may be decided at the case management conference: see *The Guildford*. As to the case management conference see PARA 204.

8 See *The Maid of Kent* (1881) 6 PD 178 (questions of remoteness and contributory negligence); *Carlsholm v Calliope, The Calliope* [1970] P 172, [1970] 1 All ER 624, [1970] 1 Lloyd's Rep 84. In *The Guildford* [1956] 2 All ER 915, [1956] 2 Lloyd's Rep 74 and *The Lucile Bloomfield* [1967] 2 Lloyd's Rep 308 the matter was dealt with at trial rather than by reference. If the parties desire that such matters be decided by the judge, this should be raised at the case management conference.

9 *The Dwina* [1892] P 58. As to the extent of Admiralty jurisdiction regarding salvage claims see PARA 113 et seq.

10 Generally where the Admiralty Court refers an account, inquiry or enforcement, it will usually refer the matter to the Admiralty Registrar: see the Admiralty and Commercial Courts Guide (2016) para N10.2.

11 *Wilkinson v Liverpool and Glasgow Salvage Association, The Fremantle* [1954] 2 Lloyd's Rep 20; and see *Mortiboys v Skinner, The Devonshire Maid* [1952] 2 Lloyd's Rep 95 (loss of life, personal injuries in a collision); *The St Chad (No 2)* [1962] 2 Lloyd's Rep 347 (assessment of damages against employers). See also *The Medina* (1876) 1 PD 272 (inequitable agreement regarding award for life salvage).

12 As to limitation claims see PARA 194 et seq.

13 As to the distribution of the limitation fund see PARA 201.

14 *The Nicolaou Georgios* [1952] 2 Lloyd's Rep 215.

15 As to the role of assessors generally see PARA 205.

**144. Filing of claim on a reference and of a defence to the claim.** Where a reference to the Admiralty Registrar[1] has been ordered[2], unless the court[3] orders otherwise:

(1)     the claimant must (if particulars of claim have not already been served) file and serve particulars of claim on all other parties within 14 days after the date of the order[4]; and

(2)     any party opposing the claim must file a defence to the claim within 14 days after service of the particulars of claim on him[5].

1 As to the Admiralty Registrar see PARA 140.

2 As to references made to the Admiralty Registrar see PARA 143.

3 Ie the Admiralty Court: see PARA 91 note 3.

4 *Practice Direction—Admiralty Claims* PD 61 para 13.2. As to the filing of documents with the Admiralty and Commercial Registry see PARA 142. As to the procedure that governs Admiralty claims, including CPR Pt 61 and *Practice Direction—Admiralty Claims* PD 61, see PARAS 140 note 5, 157 et seq.

5 *Practice Direction—Admiralty Claims* PD 61 para 13.2.

**145. Requirement for case management conference on a reference.** Where a reference to the Admiralty Registrar[1] has been ordered[2], within seven days of the filing of the defence[3], the claimant must apply for an appointment before the Registrar for a case management conference[4].

1 As to the Admiralty Registrar see PARA 140.

2 As to references made to the Admiralty Registrar see PARA 143.

3 See PARA 144.

4 *Practice Direction—Admiralty Claims* PD 61 para 13.3. As to the case management conference generally see PARA 204. Where necessary, disclosure will be ordered, to be complied with before the hearing of the reference: see *The Pacuare* [1912] P 179, CA (in a total loss claimant required

to produce his books with a view to ascertaining the value of the lost vessel). As to the procedure that governs Admiralty claims, including CPR Pt 61 and *Practice Direction—Admiralty Claims* PD 61, see PARAS 140 note 5, 157 et seq.

**146. Evidence and interim matters.** The practice and procedure of the Commercial Court[1] should, except where inapplicable, be followed in Admiralty proceedings, subject to any Admiralty practice direction and to any order that may be made in an individual case[2].

The ordinary rules of evidence apply on the hearing of a reference but are frequently in practice, by agreement between the parties, relaxed in order to save time and expense[3].

In practice, if any question of seamanship or nautical skill is likely to arise at the reference, a nautical assessor will usually attend[4].

1 As to the practice and procedure that applies in the Commercial Court, including CPR Pt 58 and *Practice Direction—Commercial Court* PD 58, see CIVIL PROCEDURE vol 11 (2015) PARA 170; and COURTS AND TRIBUNALS vol 24 (2010) PARA 708. See also note 2.
2 As to the procedure that governs Admiralty claims, including CPR Pt 61 and *Practice Direction—Admiralty Claims* PD 61, see PARAS 140 note 5, 157 et seq.
3 As to evidence for a hearing in the Admiralty and Commercial Courts see generally the Admiralty and Commercial Courts Guide (2016) Pt H; and as to conduct of the hearing itself see generally Pt J (paras J1–J13). See also PARA 204.
4 As to nautical assessors see PARA 205.

**147. Hearing of reference and decision.** The hearing of a reference made to the Admiralty Registrar[1] proceeds in open court. The Admiralty Registrar, when sitting with merchants and nautical assessors[2], who are assumed to have wide experience in maritime matters, is not bound to accept the evidence of expert witnesses even though the evidence is all one way[3]. Where the decision is as to damages, it shows in a schedule in parallel columns the items claimed and those allowed, and from what period and at what rate interest will run[4].

The Admiralty Registrar's decision will be in writing. The Admiralty Registrar may refer a matter to a judge for decision, either on any particular point arising in the course of the proceedings at the reference, or as to questions involved in the reference generally[5]. The judge may either dispose of the matter or refer it back to the Admiralty Registrar with such directions as he thinks fit[6].

1 As to the Admiralty Registrar see PARA 140; and as to references made to the Admiralty Registrar see PARA 143.
2 As to nautical assessors see PARA 205.
3 *The Steadfast* (1922) 39 TLR 96. Merchants are not usually in practice called upon; cf the position as respects nautical assessors: see PARAS 143, 205.
4 As to interest on damages see *The Joannis Vatis (No 2)* [1922] P 213; *The Aizkarai Mendi* [1938] P 263, [1938] 3 All ER 483, 61 Ll L Rep 274 (life claims); *The Napier Star* [1933] P 136, 45 Ll L Rep 139 (future repairs); *The Kong Magnus* [1891] P 223 (payment despite considerable lapse of time); *The Crispin* (1929) 35 Ll L Rep 197, CA (Registrar's discretion to disallow interest where undue delay); *The Berwickshire* [1950] P 204, [1950] 1 All ER 699 (delay due to war); *The Nassau* [1965] 1 Lloyd's Rep 236 (delay in bringing action to trial); see also *Jefford v Gee* [1970] 2 QB 130, [1970] 1 All ER 1202, [1970] 1 Lloyd's Rep 107, CA (consideration generally of interest in personal injury and Fatal Accidents Act cases; modified by the Court of Appeal in *Birkett v Hayes* [1982] 2 All ER 710, [1982] 1 WLR 816, CA); *The Funabashi* [1972] 2 All ER 181, [1972] 1 WLR 666, [1972] 1 Lloyd's Rep 371 (decision in *Jefford v Gee* applicable to limitation fund cases).
5 See *Practice Direction—Applications* PD 23A para 1; CIVIL PROCEDURE vol 12 (2015) PARA 557; and PARA 141. See also *The John Bellamy* (1870) LR 3 A & E 129; *The Parisian* (1887) 13 PD 16; *The Immacolata Concezione* (1883) 9 PD 37.
6 See *Practice Direction—Applications* PD 23A para 1; CIVIL PROCEDURE vol 12 (2015) PARA 557; and PARA 141.

**148. Costs.** On a reference made to the Admiralty Registrar[1], the Registrar himself may decide whether any (and what part) of the costs are payable by one party to another, the amount of those costs, and when they are to be paid, the allowance or disallowance of these costs being wholly discretionary[2]. Such costs do not depend in any way on how the costs of the claim are to be borne, but are in the discretion of the court as the costs of a new litigation[3].

Each instance is decided on its own merits[4]. Usually, the claimant will be awarded his costs of the reference if he recovers the major part of the sum claimed; however, where an offer has been made and the amount awarded in the reference is less, the party making the offer will usually be entitled to his costs after the date of the offer[5].

In relation to the costs of reference in a limitation claim[6], normally the limiting party pays the claimants' costs of proving their claims and investigating the claims of other parties interested in the limitation fund[7] where this results in reducing the costs of the reference, but not where excessive claims have been submitted[8].

Where claimants against a limitation fund dispute issues between them, the costs of such issues will normally be awarded as between them and follow the event rather than being ordered to be paid by the limiting party[9].

1   As to the Admiralty Registrar see PARA 140; and as to references made to the Admiralty Registrar see PARA 143.
2   See the Senior Courts Act 1981 s 51; CPR 44.3; and CIVIL PROCEDURE vol 12A (2015) PARAS 1684, 1698. See *Aiden Shipping Ltd v Interbulk Ltd* [1986] AC 965, [1986] 2 All ER 409, HL (width of court's discretionary powers).
3   *The Consett* (1880) 5 PD 77, CA; *The Friedeberg* (1885) 10 PD 112, CA. Where two vessels are held to blame in a collision claim, the costs in the reference of each claimant are dealt with on the basis of the reference being a separate proceeding from the claim: see *The Consett*. As to failure to give notice of survey see *The Solace (No 2)* (1936) 55 Ll L Rep 201. As to collision claims see PARA 180 et seq.
4   As to the principles to be applied in relation to costs see CPR 44.3; and CIVIL PROCEDURE vol 12A (2015) PARA 1701.
5   See CPR Pt 36; and CIVIL PROCEDURE vol 12A (2015) PARA 1653 et seq.
6   As to limitation claims see PARA 194 et seq.
7   As to the limitation fund see PARA 196.
8   *The Rijnstroom* (1899) 8 Asp MLC 538.
9   *The Empusa* (1879) 5 PD 6; *African Steam Navigation Co v Swanzy* (1856) 25 LJ Ch 870; *The Expert* (1877) 3 Asp MLC 381; *The Empusa* (1879) 4 Asp MLC 185.

## 149. Appeal against the Admiralty Registrar's decision on the reference.

In accordance with the usual rules on appeals, the court, in an appeal against a decision of the Admiralty Registrar on a reference made to him[1], has power to order that it receives evidence which was not before the Admiralty Registrar and may draw any inference of fact which it considers justified on any of the evidence before it[2]. No objection may be taken on the appeal to any item which was not contested at the reference[3].

The court attaches great weight to the experience of the Admiralty Registrar and will not interfere with the decision on a question of quantum unless there is an error of principle, or an obvious mistake in calculation, or a clear misunderstanding of evidence on a material point[4].

1   As to the Admiralty Registrar see PARA 140; and as to references made to the Admiralty Registrar see PARA 143. For examples of an appeal from a reference see *The Gilbert Rowe* [1997] 2 Lloyd's Rep 218; and see *The Kumanovo and Massira* [1998] 2 Lloyd's Rep 301 (cited in note 4).
2   See CPR 52.21(2), (4); and CIVIL PROCEDURE vol 12A (2015) PARA 1535. Additional evidence may be allowed if the judge is satisfied that the evidence could not reasonably have been produced at the reference by proper diligence and application: see *The Flying Fish* (1865) 3 Moo PCCNS 77; *The Thuringia* (1871) 41 LJ Adm 20, 1 Asp MLC 166.
3   *The Princess Helena* (1861) Lush 190. See also CPR 52.21(5); and CIVIL PROCEDURE vol 12A (2015) PARA 1535.
4   *The Amerika* [1914] P 167, CA (affd sub nom *Admiralty Comrs v SS Amerika* [1917] AC 38, HL); *The Apsleyhall* (1924) 19 Ll L Rep 227, CA; *The St Charles* (1927) 138 LT 456, CA; *The Queen Mary* [1950] P 240 at 245, [1950] 2 All ER 22 at 24, 83 Ll L Rep 415 at 421 per Hodson J (life claims). See also *The Steadfast* (1922) 39 TLR 96 (where the court refused to interfere, even though

the report of the Registrar was at variance with the evidence); *The Aizkarai Mendi* [1938] P 263, [1938] 3 All ER 483 (life claims); and *The Kumanovo and Massira* [1998] 2 Lloyd's Rep 301 (the court would not lightly interfere with the decision of the Registrar where and to the extent that his decision properly depended upon his view of any witness whom he had seen examined and cross-examined).

**150. Order on appeal.** Instead of merely allowing the appeal against a decision of the Admiralty Registrar on a reference made to him[1], or varying that decision, the court may refer the decision back to the Registrar and direct him to make a further decision, either on the case generally, or on any special point[2]. It appears that the order made by the court on the objection application is a final decision and an appeal against the court's consideration of the reference lies to the Court of Appeal in the usual way[3].

1 As to the Admiralty Registrar see PARA 140; and as to references made to the Admiralty Registrar see PARA 143.
2 See *Practice Direction—Applications* PD 23A para 1; CIVIL PROCEDURE vol 12 (2015) PARA 557; and PARA 141. See also *The Minnetonka* [1904] P 202 at 210 per Bucknill J; revsd on another point [1905] P 206, CA.
3 See *Practice Direction—Appeals* PD 52A paras 3.1–3.9; and CIVIL PROCEDURE vol 12A (2015) PARA 1515 et seq. As to appeals from the High Court's consideration of the Registrar's decision on a reference see PARA 218 et seq.

## (ii) Limitation of Time for Admiralty Claims

**151. Claims in rem generally.** The general restrictions limiting the time within which claims founded on contract or on tort must be brought[1] apply to any cause of action within the Admiralty jurisdiction of the High Court[2] as they apply to any other cause of action[3]. A special statutory restriction applies, however, in respect of certain causes of action enforceable in rem[4].

1 See the Limitation Act 1980 s 2 (tort) (cited in LIMITATION PERIODS vol 68 (2016) PARAS 952, 979), and s 5 (contract) (cited in LIMITATION PERIODS vol 68 (2016) PARAS 952, 956).
2 As to the practice of the High Court when exercising its Admiralty jurisdiction see PARA 158 et seq.
3 See LIMITATION PERIODS.
4 See the Merchant Shipping Act 1995 s 190 (time limit for proceedings against owners of ships) (cited in PARAS 152, 1013); and the Carriage of Goods by Sea Act 1971 (cited in PARA 156), which applies the Hague-Visby Rules (as to which see CARRIAGE AND CARRIERS vol 7 (2015) PARAS 207, 368 et seq). As to claims in rem see PARA 158 et seq.

**152. Claims against owners or ship for damage, loss, personal injury or death.** No proceedings may be brought[1] to enforce any claim[2] or lien against a ship[3] or its owners[4] in respect of any damage or loss caused by the fault[5] of that ship to another ship, its cargo or freight, or any property on board it, or damages for loss of life or personal injuries suffered by any person on board it other than passengers[6], the extent of fault being immaterial[7], unless brought within two years[8] of the date when the damage or loss was caused or the loss of life or injury was suffered[9]. This provision applies to proceedings against a sister ship[10]. The Crown is bound by these provisions, which apply to Her Majesty's ships[11] as to other ships[12].

Any claim for damages arising out of the death of, or personal injury to, a passenger or for the loss of, or damage to, luggage is time-barred after a period of two years from, in the case of personal injury, the date when disembarkation took place or ought to have taken place, or if death occurred after that date, from the date of death, provided the period does not exceed three years from the disembarkation[13]. The law of the court seized of the case governs the grounds of suspension and interruption of limitation periods; but the period of limitation may be extended by a declaration of the carrier or by agreement of the parties after the cause of action has arisen provided the declaration or agreement is in writing[14].

1   The protection afforded by statute is not waived by acknowledging service of a claim form: see *The Llandovery Castle* [1920] P 119; *The Alnwick* [1965] P 357, [1965] 2 All ER 569, [1965] 1 Lloyd's Rep 320, CA. See note 9.

2   The limitation applies to counterclaims and cross-claims: *The Fairplay XIV* [1939] P 57, 65 Ll L Rep 108. See also *The Gniezno* [1968] P 418, [1967] 2 All ER 738, [1967] 1 Lloyd's Rep 441. A decree of limitation of liability does not override the two year period and rival claimants are therefore entitled to object to claims of persons who have not commenced proceedings within the statutory period, but, where limitation decrees are made, this may be a good reason for not issuing a claim form, so that in general an extension of time will be granted: see *The Disperser* [1920] P 228 at 235, 15 Asp MLC 112 at 114 per Hill J. See note 9. As to the court's discretion to extend the time see PARA 153.

3   As to the meaning of 'ship' for these purposes see PARA 229. This includes hovercraft: see the Hovercraft (Civil Liability) Order 1986, SI 1986/1305, art 7 (and see note 9). In *Steedman v Schofield* [1992] 2 Lloyd's Rep 163, a claim for damages against the operator of a jet ski was held not to be time-barred by the Maritime Conventions Act 1911 s 8 (repealed) (see now the Merchant Shipping Act 1995 s 190; but see note 9). This case would probably be decided similarly under the Merchant Shipping Act 1995 s 190 (see PARA 1013).

4   For this purpose, 'owners' includes any person responsible for the fault of the vessel, and charterers are to be substituted for owners where the owners are not responsible for navigation and management: see *HMS Archer* [1919] P 1; *The Sobieski* [1949] P 313, [1949] 1 All ER 701, CA. See note 9.

5   'Fault' includes fault in the management of the ship: *John Franetovich & Co v Ministry of Defence, The Norwhale* [1975] QB 589, [1975] 1 Lloyd's Rep 610. See note 9.

6   Passenger claims will be governed by the Convention relating to the Carriage of Passengers and their Luggage by Sea (Athens, 13 December 1974; TS 40 (1987); Cm 202) (the 'Athens Convention') art 16: see the text and note 13.

7   These words apply only to claims in respect of damage or loss to cargo or property, or loss of life or personal injury, arising on board a ship which lie against another ship. Claims which arise on board a ship and which lie against owners of that ship, are not affected by this provision as to limitation: *The Niceto de Larringa* [1966] P 80, [1965] 2 All ER 930. See note 9.

8   The Merchant Shipping Act 1995 is complied with if the claim form is issued within two years, even though it is not served: see *The Espanoleto* [1920] P 223, 15 Asp MLC 287. See note 9. In connection with the two-year period and agreements between the parties see *Gold Shipping Navigation Co SA v Lulu Maritime Ltd* [2009] EWHC 1365 (Admlty), [2010] 2 All ER (Comm) 64, [2009] 2 Lloyd's Rep 484.

9   See the Merchant Shipping Act 1995 s 190(1)–(3); *Stolt Kestrel BV v Sener Petrol Denizcilik Ticaret AS; CDE SA v Sure Wind Marine Ltd* [2015] EWCA Civ 1035, [2015] All ER (D) 146 (Oct); *Owners of the Ship Theresa Libra v Owners of the Ship MSC Pamela* [2013] EWHC 2792 (Admlty), [2013] 2 Lloyd's Rep 596; and PARA 1013. The Merchant Shipping Act 1995 s 190 is derived from the Maritime Conventions Act 1911 s 8 (repealed), although there are significant differences. In particular, the earlier provision did not specify that the extent of fault was immaterial. The cases cited in notes 1–8, which were all based on the Maritime Conventions Act 1911 s 8 (repealed) should, therefore, be treated with some caution when interpreting provisions of the Merchant Shipping Act 1995 s 190.

10 See *The Preveze* [1973] 1 Lloyd's Rep 202 (which considered the Administration of Justice Act 1956: see now the Senior Courts Act 1981 ss 20, 21(4) (see PARA 93)).

11 As to the meaning of 'Her Majesty's ships' see the Crown Proceedings Act 1947 s 38(2); and CROWN AND CROWN PROCEEDINGS vol 29 (2014) PARA 86.

12 See the Merchant Shipping Act 1995 s 192; and PARA 1015.

13 See the Athens Convention art 16 (as to which see CARRIAGE AND CARRIERS vol 7 (2015) PARA 635 et seq) given the force of law by the Merchant Shipping Act 1995 s 183(1), Sch 6 Pt I. This article applies to arbitral proceedings as it applies to a claim: see s 183(2), Sch 6 Pt II para 7; and CARRIAGE AND CARRIERS vol 7 (2015) PARA 648. These provisions are not affected by the Limitation Act 1980 s 33 (discretionary exclusion of time limit for claims in respect of personal injury or death) (see LIMITATION PERIODS vol 68 (2016) PARAS 1001–1002; and *Higham v Stena Sealink Ltd* [1996] 3 All ER 660, [1996] 1 WLR 1107, CA).

14 See note 13.

## 153. Extension of period for claims against owners or ship.
Any court having jurisdiction to deal with proceedings to enforce a claim or lien against a

ship[1] or its owners for damage, loss, personal injury or death[2] may extend the period of limitation that applies, in accordance with rules of court[3], to such extent and on such conditions as it thinks fit[4]. If satisfied that there has not within the period been any reasonable opportunity of arresting the defendant vessel within the jurisdiction of the court, or within the territorial waters of the country to which the claimant's ship belongs or in which the claimant resides or has his principal place of business, the court is bound to extend the period so as to give such reasonable opportunity[5].

1   As to the meaning of 'ship' for these purposes see PARA 229. This includes hovercraft: see PARA 152 note 3.
2   See PARA 152.
3   Although no rules have been made under the Merchant Shipping Act 1995 s 190 (see PARAS 152, 1013), it is thought that the court's discretion is not thereby affected. This was the position under the Maritime Conventions Act 1911 (repealed): see *HMS Archer* [1919] P 1.
4   See the Merchant Shipping Act 1995 s 190(5); and PARA 1013. In an application for an extension of time there is a two stage test: the court must first consider the question of fact as to whether good reason for the extension has been demonstrated by the claimants and only if the claimant has established good reason should the court proceed to exercise its discretion, taking into account the balance of hardship, as to whether such an extension should be granted: *The Al Tabith and The Alanfushi* [1995] 2 Lloyd's Rep 336, CA (distinguishing *The Zirje* [1989] 1 Lloyd's Rep 493). Mere oversight on the part of the claimant in failing to protect the time limit was not a good reason: *The Al Tabith and The Alanfushi*. There is much case law under the Maritime Conventions Act 1911 (repealed) as to how the discretion is to be exercised but these decisions all need now to be considered in light of the two stage test in *The Al Tabith and The Alanfushi*. See also PARA 152 note 9. The exercise of the discretion ought not to be interfered with except on substantial grounds: *The Arraiz* (1924) 132 LT 715, 16 Asp MLC 451, CA. The claim will be allowed to proceed if satisfactory grounds are shown for the delay (*The Cambric* [1912] WN 272), but the party who wishes to have time extended must show substantial reasons why the other party should be deprived of the right to limitation of action which the law gives (see *The Kashmir* [1923] P 85 at 89, 16 Asp MLC 81 at 83, CA). The discretion has been exercised where the claimant was induced by correspondence with the defendants' solicitors to delay whilst awaiting settlement of liability in the collision action arising from the same incident: *The Vadne* [1959] 2 Lloyd's Rep 480. In the exercise of its discretion, the court has allowed a statement of claim in a salvage action to be amended to include allegations of further services arising out of the same occurrence: *The Katcher I* [1969] P 65, [1968] 3 All ER 344, [1968] 2 Lloyd's Rep 232. As to the exercise of discretion see also *The Alnwick* [1965] P 357, [1965] 2 All ER 569, [1965] 1 Lloyd's Rep 320, CA; *The Disperser* [1920] P 228, 15 Asp MLC 112. Applications for an extension have been dismissed where the delay was due to difficulty in ascertaining the amount of the claim (*The James Westoll* [1923] P 94n, 16 Asp MLC 453n, CA), where agreement had been reached on liability but there was no binding agreement to waive the time limit and there was undue delay (*The Sauria and The Trent* [1957] 1 Lloyd's Rep 396, CA), where the claimant was ignorant that she had a claim (*The Kashmir*), where a deliberate decision was taken not to start proceedings (*The Lu Shan* [1991] 2 Lloyd's Rep 386), where unsuccessful proceedings were first taken against another ship (*The PLM 8* [1920] P 236, 15 Asp MLC 51), where the institution of proceedings was postponed while diplomatic representations were made (*HMS Archer* [1919] P 1), where owners elected not to sue in the United Kingdom and let time run out (*The Nedenes* (1925) 23 Ll L Rep 57), where the matter had been allowed to go to sleep and any claim by the defendant against third parties was also statute barred (*The Hesselmorr, The Sergeant* [1951] 1 Lloyd's Rep 146) and where proceedings were not allowed to run while the parties were in negotiations (see *The Albany and The Marie Josaine* [1983] 2 Lloyd's Rep 195; and see *The Mouna* [1991] 2 Lloyd's Rep 221, CA). See also *Gold Shipping Navigation Co SA v Lulu Maritime Ltd* [2009] EWHC 1365 (Admlty), [2010] 2 All ER (Comm) 64, [2009] 2 Lloyd's Rep 484; *Stolt Kestrel BV v Sener Petrol Denizcilik Ticaret AS; CDE SA v Sure Wind Marine Ltd* [2015] EWCA Civ 1035, [2015] All ER (D) 146 (Oct).
5   See the Merchant Shipping Act 1995 s 190(6); and PARA 1013. The test of whether there has been any reasonable opportunity to arrest a vessel is to be determined objectively, without regard to whether steps have actually been taken in an attempt to arrest in a particular jurisdiction: *Santos v Owners of the Baltic Carrier* [2001] 1 Lloyd's Rep 689. A period of ten days during which a ship is under requisition has been held not to constitute reasonable opportunity: *The Largo Law* (1920) 123 LT 560. The Merchant Shipping Act 1995 s 190 has no application to cases in which the defendant vessel is permanently immune from arrest: see *HMS Archer* [1919] P 1.

## 154. Claims under the Salvage Convention 1989.

Any claim relating to payment under the International Convention on Salvage[1] is time-barred if judicial or arbitral proceedings have not been instituted within a period of two years, the limitation period commencing on the day on which the salvage operations are terminated[2]. The person against whom a claim is made may at any time during the running of the limitation period extend that period by a declaration to the claimant and this period may in the like manner be further extended[3]. A claim for indemnity by a person liable may be instituted even after the expiration of the limitation period so provided, if brought within the time allowed by the law of the state where proceedings are instituted[4].

1   See the International Convention on Salvage (London, 28 April 1989; Misc 8 (1991); Cm 1526); the Merchant Shipping Act 1995 s 224(1), Sch 11 Pt I; and PARA 851 et seq. As to salvage see also PARA 115 et seq.
2   See the International Convention on Salvage art 23(1); and PARA 918. Article 23 suggests that the date the final salvage service was performed will be the relevant date from which the time limit will be calculable.
3   See the International Convention on Salvage art 23(2); and PARA 918. The extension of the time limit under art 23(2) is only available where a declaration is made to the salvor; the court has no discretion to extend the time limit.
4   See the International Convention on Salvage art 23(3); and PARA 918. The test as to when proceedings have been commenced is determined according to the lex fori: see *Dresser UK Ltd v Falcongate Freight Management Ltd* [1992] QB 502, [1992] 2 All ER 450, CA; and PARA 99. As to the lex fori see CONFLICT OF LAWS vol 19 (2011) PARA 313.

**155.  Claims for liability in respect of oil pollution.** No proceedings to enforce a claim in respect of a liability for oil pollution[1] may be entertained by any court in the United Kingdom[2] unless the proceedings are commenced not later than three years after the claim arose or, in cases where the damage occurs after the incident, not later than six years after the occurrence or first of the occurrences resulting in the discharge or escape[3], or, as the case may be, in the relevant threat of contamination[4], by reason of which the liability was incurred[5].

No proceedings to enforce a claim against the International Fund established by the International Convention on the Establishment of an International Fund for Compensation for Oil Pollution Damage[6] may be entertained by a court in the United Kingdom unless the proceedings are commenced or a third party notice[7] of proceedings to enforce a claim against the owner or his guarantor in respect of same damage is given to the fund, not later than three years after the damage occurred[8]. In cases where the damage occurs after an incident takes place the claim must be brought within six years of the occurrence or first of the occurrences resulting in the discharge or escape, or, as the case may be, in the relevant threat of contamination, by reason of which the claim against the fund arose[9]. These provisions apply (with appropriate modification) in relation to claims against the Supplementary Fund as they apply in relation to claims against the International Fund[10].

1   Ie under the Merchant Shipping Act 1995 ss 153–154 (as to which see ENVIRONMENTAL QUALITY AND PUBLIC HEALTH vol 45 (2010) PARAS 453–454): see s 162.
2   As to the meaning of 'United Kingdom' see PARA 16 note 3.
3   As to the meanings of 'discharge' and 'escape' for these purposes see ENVIRONMENTAL QUALITY AND PUBLIC HEALTH vol 45 (2010) PARA 443.
4   As to the meaning of 'contamination' for these purposes see ENVIRONMENTAL QUALITY AND PUBLIC HEALTH vol 45 (2010) PARA 443.
5   See the Merchant Shipping Act 1995 s 162; and ENVIRONMENTAL QUALITY AND PUBLIC HEALTH vol 45 (2010) PARA 452.
6   Ie the International Convention on the Establishment of an International Fund for Compensation for Oil Pollution Damage (Brussels, 18 December 1971; TS 95 (1978); Cmnd 7383). The text refers to the International Fund: see the Merchant Shipping Act 1995 Pt VI Ch IV (ss 172–182); and ENVIRONMENTAL QUALITY AND PUBLIC HEALTH vol 45 (2010) PARA 459 et seq.
7   As to the meaning of 'third party notice' for these purposes see the Merchant Shipping Act 1995 s 177(2), (3); and ENVIRONMENTAL QUALITY AND PUBLIC HEALTH vol 45 (2010) PARA 468. Third party notices have been replaced by additional claims: see CPR Pt 20; and CIVIL PROCEDURE vol 11 (2015) PARA 367 et seq.

8   See the Merchant Shipping Act 1995 s 178(1); and ENVIRONMENTAL QUALITY AND PUBLIC
    HEALTH vol 45 (2010) PARA 469. For the purposes of s 177 (see ENVIRONMENTAL QUALITY
    AND PUBLIC HEALTH vol 45 (2010) PARA 468), any party to a claim against an owner or
    guarantor in respect of liability under s 153 (see ENVIRONMENTAL QUALITY AND PUBLIC
    HEALTH vol 45 (2010) PARA 443) may give the fund notice of the proceedings by that person
    serving a notice in writing on the fund together with a copy of the claim form and copies of the
    statements of case (if any) served in the claim: see *Practice Direction—Admiralty Claims* PD 61
    para 11.1; and ENVIRONMENTAL QUALITY AND PUBLIC HEALTH vol 45 (2010) PARA 459 et
    seq. Notice given to the Fund under para 11.1 is deemed to have been given to the supplementary
    fund: see *Practice Direction—Admiralty Claims* PD 61 para 11.2; and ENVIRONMENTAL
    QUALITY AND PUBLIC HEALTH vol 45 (2010) PARA 459 et seq. The fund (or supplementary
    fund) may intervene in any claim to which para 11.1 applies, whether or not served with the notice,
    by serving notice of intervention on the owner, guarantor and the court: see *Practice
    Direction—Admiralty Claims* PD 61 para 11.3; and ENVIRONMENTAL QUALITY AND PUBLIC
    HEALTH vol 45 (2010) PARA 459 et seq. Where a judgment is given against the fund in any claim
    under the Merchant Shipping Act 1995 s 175 (see ENVIRONMENTAL QUALITY AND PUBLIC
    HEALTH vol 45 (2010) PARA 464) or against the supplementary fund in any claim under s 176A
    (see ENVIRONMENTAL QUALITY AND PUBLIC HEALTH vol 45 (2010) PARA 466), the Admiralty
    Registrar will arrange for a stamped copy of the judgment to be sent to the fund (or supplementary
    fund) by post: see *Practice Direction—Admiralty Claims* PD 61 para 11.4; and ENVIRONMENTAL
    QUALITY AND PUBLIC HEALTH vol 45 (2010) PARA 459 et seq). Notice by the fund (or
    supplementary fund) to the Admiralty Registrar of the matters set out in the Merchant Shipping
    Act 1995 s 176(3)(b) in any claim under s 175 (see ENVIRONMENTAL QUALITY AND PUBLIC
    HEALTH vol 45 (2010) PARA 464) and the corresponding provision of s 176B(2)(b) in any claim
    under s 176A (see ENVIRONMENTAL QUALITY AND PUBLIC HEALTH vol 45 (2010) PARA 466)
    must be in writing and sent to the court: see *Practice Direction—Admiralty Claims* PD 61 para
    11.4; and ENVIRONMENTAL QUALITY AND PUBLIC HEALTH vol 45 (2010) PARA 459 et seq. As
    to the Admiralty Registrar see PARA 140.
9   See the Merchant Shipping Act 1995 s 178(2); and ENVIRONMENTAL QUALITY AND PUBLIC
    HEALTH vol 45 (2010) PARAS 453–454.
10  See the Merchant Shipping Act 1995 s 178(3), (4); and ENVIRONMENTAL QUALITY AND PUBLIC
    HEALTH vol 45 (2010) PARAS 453–454. As to the Supplementary Fund see ENVIRONMENTAL
    QUALITY AND PUBLIC HEALTH vol 45 (2010) PARAS 453–454.

**156. Claims on contracts for carriage of goods.** In the case of contracts for
the carriage of goods by sea to which the Hague Rules or the Hague-Visby Rules
apply[1], the carrier and the ship are discharged from all liability in respect of loss
or damage unless suit is brought[2] within one year[3] after delivery of the goods or
the date when the goods should have been delivered[4].

1   As to the Hague-Visby Rules see CARRIAGE AND CARRIERS vol 7 (2015) PARAS 207, 368 et seq.
2   It has been held that the words 'suit is brought' in this context include the commencement of
    arbitration proceedings: see *The Merak* [1965] P 223 at 261, [1965] 1 All ER 230 at 240, CA, per
    Russell LJ. The words refer to the bringing of the suit in the proceedings before the court and not
    the bringing of some other proceedings before a court in another jurisdiction: see *Compagnia
    Colombiana de Seguros v Pacific Steam Navigation Co* [1965] 1 QB 101, [1964] 1 All ER 216,
    where other proceedings had been brought in New York within time but by the wrong party; see
    also Parker LJ's comments on this decision in *Hispanica de Petroleos SA v Vencedora Oceanica
    Navegacion SA, The Kapetan Markos* [1986] 1 Lloyd's Rep 211 at 231, CA, per Parker LJ; and
    *The Nordglimt* [1988] QB 183, [1988] 2 All ER 531, [1987] 2 Lloyd's Rep 470 (since overruled
    on other grounds by the House of Lords in *Republic of India v India Steamship Co Ltd (No 2)*
    [1998] AC 878, [1997] 4 All ER 380, HL). If the claimants have no title to sue at the date of
    bringing the proceedings, the defect cannot be cured by assignment of title to them after the time
    limit has expired: see *Associated Herring Merchants v Reitsma* 1958 SLT 57, Sh Ct.
3   Under an agreement known as the Gold Clause Agreement, entered into between British
    shipowners and underwriters, the year's time limit under the Carriage of Goods by Sea Act 1924
    was in practice generally extended to two years. This agreement continues to be effective under the
    Carriage of Goods by Sea Act 1971.
4   See the Hague-Visby Rules art III r 6; and CARRIAGE AND CARRIERS vol 7 (2015) PARA 401. An
    extension to the period of one year may be authorised if the parties so agree after the cause of
    action has arisen: see Schedule art III r 6; and CARRIAGE AND CARRIERS vol 7 (2015) PARA 401.
    It has been held by the United States District Court that 'delivery of the goods' is not synonymous
    with discharge: see *American Hoesch Inc and Riblet Products Inc v SS Aubade etc and Maritime*

*Commercial Corpn Inc* [1971] 2 Lloyd's Rep 423. The rule does not bar defences: see *Goulandris Bros Ltd v B Goldman & Sons Ltd* [1958] 1 QB 74, [1957] 3 All ER 100, where a cargo owner's defence to a shipowner's claim for a general average contribution, on the ground that the ship was unseaworthy or that the shipowner did not exercise due diligence to make her seaworthy, was held not to be barred.

An action for indemnity against a third person may be brought even after the expiration of the year provided for in the Carriage of Goods by Sea Act 1971 Schedule art III para 6 if brought within the time allowed by the law of the court seized of the case and so long as the time allowed is not less than three months (commencing from the day when the person bringing such action for indemnity has settled the claim or has been served with process in the action against himself): see Schedule art III r 6bis; and CARRIAGE AND CARRIERS vol 7 (2015) PARAS 401–402.

## (iii) Admiralty Claims except Limitation Claims

### A.   IN GENERAL

**157. Outline of procedure in Admiralty claims.** Proceedings in the Admiralty Court are governed by the Civil Procedure Rules ('CPR') and Practice Directions[1]. The specific procedure that applies for the purposes of making an Admiralty claim differs according to the specific nature of the claim, as follows:

(1)      a claim in personam (an 'other claim') commences and proceeds under the CPR as if it were a claim proceeding in the Commercial List[2];

(2)      a claim in rem proceeds differently from other claims in its early stages[3];

(3)      subject to the preparation of a collision statement of case[4], a collision claim commenced in rem proceeds generally as under head (2) above[5] but where a collision claim is not commenced in rem it proceeds generally as under head (1) above[6].

The procedure governing the early stages of a limitation claim differs significantly from the analogous stages of other claims[7].

1   As to the procedure that governs Admiralty claims, including CPR Pt 61 and *Practice Direction—Admiralty Claims* PD 61, see PARAS 140 note 5. As to the meanings of 'Admiralty claim' and 'Admiralty Court' for these purposes see PARA 91 note 3. As to the assignment of business to the Admiralty Court see CPR 61.2(1), (2); and PARA 91.
    The Admiralty and Commercial Courts Guide is published with the approval of the Lord Chief Justice and the Head of Civil Justice in consultation with the Judges of the Admiralty and Commercial Courts and with the advice and support of the Admiralty Court and Commercial Court Users Committees, and is intended to provide guidance about the conduct of proceedings in the Admiralty and Commercial Courts and, within the framework of the Civil Procedure Rules and Practice Directions, to establish the practice to be followed in those courts: see the Admiralty and Commercial Courts Guide (2016) para A1.2. The Guide must be followed in the Admiralty Court unless the content of CPR Pt 61, its associated practice direction, or the terms of the Admiralty and Commercial Courts Guide paras N1–N14 require otherwise: see para N1.2. As to the Admiralty and Commercial Courts Guide see PARA 91 note 3.
2   Ie in accordance with CPR Pt 58 (as to which see CIVIL PROCEDURE vol 11 (2015) PARA 170 et seq): see the Admiralty and Commercial Courts Guide (2016) paras B1–B13, C1–C5, N3.1. *Practice Direction—Admiralty Claims* PD 61 para 12 ('other claims') applies to Admiralty claims which, before the coming into force of CPR Pt 61 (ie before 25 March 2002: see the Civil Procedure (Amendment No 5) Rules 2001, SI 2001/4015, r 1), would have been called claims in personam: see *Practice Direction—Admiralty Claims* PD 61 para 12.1; and PARA 186 et seq.
3   See the Admiralty and Commercial Courts Guide (2016) para N4.1. The procedure is governed generally by CPR 61.3 and *Practice Direction—Admiralty Claims* PD 61 para 3.1-3.11 (as to which see PARA 158 et seq): see the Admiralty and Commercial Courts Guide (2016) paras N3.1, N4.1. As to the meaning of 'claim in rem' for these purposes see PARA 91 note 4.
4   As to which see PARA 182 et seq.
5   See the Admiralty and Commercial Courts Guide (2016) paras N3.1, N5.1. Accordingly, the procedure is governed generally by CPR 61.3 and *Practice Direction—Admiralty Claims* PD 61 paras 3.1-3.11 but subject to CPR 61.4 and *Practice Direction—Admiralty Claims* PD 61 para 4.1-4.5 (as to which see PARA 182 et seq): see the Admiralty and Commercial Courts Guide (2016) paras N4.1, N5.1. As to the meaning of 'collision claim' for these purposes see PARA 91 note 12.
6   See the Admiralty and Commercial Courts Guide (2016) paras N3.1, N5.2. Accordingly, the procedure is governed generally by CPR Pt 58 but subject to CPR 61.4 and *Practice*

*Direction—Admiralty Claims* PD 61 paras 4.1-4.5 (as to which see PARA 182 et seq): see the Admiralty and Commercial Courts Guide (2016) para N5.2.

7    See the Admiralty and Commercial Courts Guide paras (2016) paras N3.1, N6.1. The procedure is contained in CPR 61.11 and *Practice Direction—Admiralty Claims* PD 61 para 10.1 (as to which see PARA 194 et seq): see the Admiralty and Commercial Courts Guide (2016) para N6.1. As to the meaning of 'limitation claim' for these purposes see PARA 91 note 13.

### B.   COMMENCEMENT OF CLAIMS

### (A)   *Commencement of Claims in rem*

#### (a)   The in rem Claim Form

**158.   Issue and form of in rem claim form.** An Admiralty claim in rem[1] is started by the issue of an in rem claim form[2]. The claimant in a claim in rem may be named or may be described (but if not named in the claim form must identify himself by name if requested to do so by any other party)[3]. The defendant must be described in the claim form[4]. As in other proceedings, the claim form must contain a concise statement of the nature of the claim and must specify the remedy sought by the claimant[5]. Applications made for any Admiralty claim, together with the requisite documents, may be posted to the Admiralty and Commercial Registry[6].

The Admiralty Registrar[7] must, after a claim form is issued, issue a direction in writing stating:

(1)    whether the claim should remain in the Admiralty Court or should be transferred to another court[8]; and

(2)    if the claim is to remain in the Admiralty Court, whether it should be dealt with by the Admiralty judge or by the Registrar, and whether the trial will be in London or elsewhere[9].

Once a ship has been served with a claim form, or arrested in a claim in rem brought to enforce the claim being made, no other ship may be served with a claim form or arrested in that or any other claim in rem brought to enforce that claim[10].

1    As to the origin of claims in rem see PARA 83; and as to the jurisdiction of the Admiralty Court in relation to claims in rem see PARA 92 et seq. As to the commencement of claims in personam see PARAS 186–188.
    CPR 61.3 applies to an Admiralty claim in rem: see CPR 61.3(1). As to the procedure that governs Admiralty claims, including CPR Pt 61 and *Practice Direction—Admiralty Claims* PD 61, see PARA 140 note 5. As to the meanings of 'Admiralty claim' and 'Admiralty Court' for these purposes see PARA 91 note 3. As to the assignment of business to the Admiralty Court see CPR 61.2(1), (2); and PARA 91.

2    CPR 61.3(2). The details concerning the issue of an in rem claim form are set out in *Practice Direction—Admiralty Claims* PD 61 para 3: see CPR 61.3(2). A claim form in rem must be in Form ADM1 (Claim Form (Admiralty claim in rem)): see *Practice Direction—Admiralty Claims* PD 61 para 3.1. The procedure set out in the Admiralty and Commercial Courts Guide (2016) paras B4.3 (statement of value), B4.7–B4.11 (statement of truth, trial without service, interest), B7.4–B7.6 (applications for extension of time and certificate of service), C1.1–C1.6, C1.8, C2.1(ii)–C5.4 (form, content, serving and filing) apply to collision claims commenced in rem: see para N4.2. See also Apps 3, 4. As to the Admiralty and Commercial Courts Guide see PARAS 91 note 3, 157 note 1.

3    *Practice Direction—Admiralty Claims* PD 61 para 3.2.

4    *Practice Direction—Admiralty Claims* PD 61 para 3.3. If, after the issue of the form, a ship has been sold to a new owner, the new owner of the ship is a 'person interested' in the ship within the meaning of CPR 61.8(7) (as to which see PARA 169). In such circumstances, the correct procedure is for those who were the owners of the ship at the time when the claim form was issued to acknowledge service, and for the new owner to apply to be made a party to the claim under CPR 61.8(7). That rule, for example, provides the court with jurisdiction to allow a person who has no formal interest in property to be arrested to intervene if the arrest will cause serious hardship, difficulty or danger: see *The Mardina Merchant* [1974] 3 All ER 749, [1975] 1 WLR 147; *The Mawan now named Mara* [1988] 2 Lloyd's Rep 459.

In cases where the claimant contemplates a 'sister ship' claim (as to which see PARA 93), the claim form may, when issued, name not only the offending ship but also all the other ships which are at that time in the defendants' ownership: see the Senior Courts Act 1981 s 21(4), (8); and PARA 93. However, this provision does not give the claimants the right to arrest a ship which was a ship owned by a sister company of the owning company of the particular ship involved in the claim unless the claimants are able to prove that beneficial ownership of all the shares in it lies in the hands of the same defendant: see s 21(4)(ii) (cited in PARA 93); and *The Evpo Agnic* [1988] 3 All ER 810, [1988] 1 WLR 1090, CA; *The Nazym Khikmet* [1996] 2 Lloyd's Rep 362, CA. The claim form must subsequently be amended by the striking out of all the names except the one chosen for the service of the claim form: see the Senior Courts Act 1981 s 21(8) (which gives statutory effect to the ruling in *The Banco* [1971] P 137, [1971] 1 All ER 524, [1971] 1 Lloyd's Rep 49, CA) (cited in PARA 93); and see *The Nord Sea and Freccia del Nord* [1989] 1 Lloyd's Rep 388 at 391 per Sheen J. As to the further requirements to be complied with before a sister ship is arrested see PARA 161. For the conditions for the renewal of a claim form in a sister ship claim see *The Berny* [1979] QB 80, [1978] 1 All ER 1065, [1977] 2 Lloyd's Rep 533; *The Helene Roth* [1980] QB 273, [1980] 1 All ER 1078, [1980] 1 Lloyd's Rep 477.

5    See CPR 16.2; and CIVIL PROCEDURE vol 11 (2015) PARA 343. As to service see PARA 160.

   Subject to CPR 61.4 (special provisions relating to collision claims) (see PARA 181 et seq), the particulars of claim must be contained in or served with the claim form or be served on the defendant by the claimant within 75 days after service of the claim form: CPR 61.3(3). It is important that the defendant is made aware from the claim form itself on whose behalf it has been issued, and that the incident giving rise to the claim is identified: see *The Tuyuti* [1984] 2 Lloyd's Rep 51 at 52–53 per Sheen J; *The Jangmi* [1988] 2 Lloyd's Rep 462. In the case of a collision claim, the claim form need not contain or be followed by particulars of claim and CPR 7.4 (particulars of claim generally) (as to which see CIVIL PROCEDURE vol 11 (2015) PARA 145) does not apply: see CPR 61.4(2); and PARA 181. As to the meaning of 'collision claim' see PARA 91 note 12.

6    As to the Admiralty and Commercial Registry and its functions see PARA 142.

7    As to the Admiralty Registrar see PARA 140.

8    *Practice Direction—Admiralty Claims* PD 61 para 2.1. In making these directions, the Admiralty Registrar must have regard both to the nature of the issues and the sums in dispute and the criteria set out in CPR 26.8 (ie the general rule for allocation) (see CIVIL PROCEDURE vol 11 (2015) PARA 208) in so far as they are applicable: *Practice Direction—Admiralty Claims* PD 61 para 2.2. As to case management in the Admiralty and Commercial Courts generally see PARA 204.

9    *Practice Direction—Admiralty Claims* PD 61 para 2.1. See note 8. Where the Admiralty Registrar directs that the claim should be dealt with by the Admiralty judge, case management directions will be given and any case management conference or pre-trial review will be heard by the Admiralty judge: *Practice Direction—Admiralty Claims* PD 61 para 2.3.

10   See the Senior Courts Act 1981 s 21(8); and PARA 93. However, when a ship has been arrested in the mistaken belief that it was a sister ship (as to which see note 4), another sister ship may be arrested, provided that the documentation in support of the second arrest refers to the previous mistaken arrest and the reasons for it: *The Stephan J* [1985] 2 Lloyd's Rep 344; *The Pioneer Container* [1989] HKLR 465.

**159.  Right of owners of ship or cargo to sue as such.** By the practice of the Admiralty Court[1], the owners of a ship or cargo may sue as such, and this practice is in no way affected by the enabling provisions in the Civil Procedure Rules relating to parties to claims in rem[2], or to the joining of parties to existing proceedings[3]. The claimants to a claim in rem if not named in the in rem claim form must identify themselves by name on the request of any other party[4].

1    As to the procedure that governs Admiralty claims, including CPR Pt 61 and *Practice Direction—Admiralty Claims* PD 61, see PARAS 140 note 5. As to the meanings of 'Admiralty claim' and 'Admiralty Court' for these purposes see PARA 91 note 3. As to the assignment of business to the Admiralty Court see CPR 61.2(1), (2); and PARA 91.

2    See *Practice Direction—Admiralty Claims* PD 61 para 3.2 (cited in PARA 158); and *The Assunta* [1902] P 150.

3    As to the addition and substitution of parties, representative parties, and group litigation generally see CPR Pt 19; and CIVIL PROCEDURE vol 11 (2015) PARA 480 et seq. See also *The Maréchal Suchet* [1896] P 233; and *Marlborough Hill v Cowan & Sons* [1921] 1 AC 444, PC (where the owners of a number of parcels of cargo were joined as claimants on one claim).

4    See *Practice Direction—Admiralty Claims* PD 61 para 3.2 (cited in PARA 158). See also *The Whilelmine (Wilhelmine)* (1842) 1 Wm Rob 335 at 337; *The Euxine* (1871) LR 4 PC 8.

**160.  Service of the in rem claim form.** The in rem claim form, which may be served by the claimant's solicitor or any person on his behalf, should be served as soon as possible after it has been issued[1]. In practice, a convenient opportunity for service on property occurs at the same time as the Admiralty Marshal or substitute enters into possession under a warrant[2]. An order for service by an alternative method is inappropriate to an in rem claim form[3].

Service of a claim form in rem may be made in one of the following ways:

(1)	on the property against which the claim in rem is brought by fixing a copy of the claim form on the outside of the property proceeded against in a position which may reasonably be expected to be seen[4];

(2)	if the property to be served is in the custody of a person who will not permit access to it, by leaving a copy of the claim form with that person[5];

(3)	where the property has been sold by the Marshal[6], by filing the claim form at the court[7];

(4)	where there is a notice against arrest[8], on the person named in the notice as being authorised to accept service[9];

(5)	on any solicitor authorised to accept service[10];

(6)	in accordance with any agreement providing for service of proceedings[11]; or

(7)	in any other manner as the court may direct as allowed for under the Civil Procedure Rules[12] provided that the property against which the claim is brought (or part of it) is within the jurisdiction of the court[13].

Accordingly, unless it is served in one of the ways permitted by the Civil Procedure Rules[14], or where the defendant acknowledges service of the claim form[15], the form, or a copy of it, must be served on the property against which the claim is brought[16], except where that property is freight or where that property has been sold by the Admiralty Marshal[17].

In claims where the property is to be arrested, or in claims where the property is already under arrest in current proceedings, the Marshal will serve the in rem claim form if the claimant requests the court to do so[18]. In all other cases, in rem claim forms must be served by the claimant[19].

Service of the claim form on a ship, freight or cargo is effected in one of the ways specified in the Civil Procedure Rules[20]. Service of the claim form must be made within the jurisdiction[21], in accordance with the practice direction[22], and within 12 months after the date of issue[23]. If the claim form is amended[24], which in a fit case may be done even after judgment[25], the amended claim form must be served in the same way as an original claim form[26].

Any person who pays the prescribed fee may, during office hours, search for, inspect and take a copy of any claim form in rem whether or not it has been served[27].

Where there has been default in acknowledgment of service, the time for judgment in the claim is 14 days from the date of the service of the claim form[28].

1	As to the issue and form of an in rem claim form see PARA 158. As to the service of in rem claim forms see the text and notes 2–26. In certain circumstances, the Admiralty Marshal will effect service of the in rem claim form and where he has so agreed an undertaking (usually given by a solicitor) to pay on demand all expenses incurred by the Admiralty Marshal or his substitute in respect of the service of the claim form will normally be required: see the text and notes 18–19; and as to undertakings see PARA 162.

	CPR 61.3 applies to an Admiralty claim in rem: see CPR 61.3(1). As to the procedure that governs Admiralty claims, including CPR Pt 61 and *Practice Direction—Admiralty Claims* PD 61, see PARAS 140 note 5. As to the meanings of 'Admiralty claim' and 'Admiralty Court' for these purposes see PARA 91 note 3. As to the assignment of business to the Admiralty Court see CPR 61.2(1), (2); and PARA 91.

2	As to arrested property see PARA 164.

3   *The Good Herald* [1987] 1 Lloyd's Rep 236. This is because the property against which the claim
    is issued cannot be arrested unless that property is within the jurisdiction and can be served with
    the claim: see CPR 6.8 (cited in CIVIL PROCEDURE vol 11 (2015) PARA 249). It is not established
    whether CPR 6.9 (cited in CIVIL PROCEDURE vol 11 (2015) PARA 259), which allows the court
    to dispense with service altogether in appropriate cases, may be applied to in rem claim forms.
4   *Practice Direction—Admiralty Claims* PD 61 para 3.6(1)(a). Where the property is freight, service
    may be made either on the cargo in respect of which the freight was earned or on the ship upon
    which that cargo was carried: *Practice Direction—Admiralty Claims* PD 61 para 3.6(1)(b).
5   *Practice Direction—Admiralty Claims* PD 61 para 3.6(2).
6   As to sales by the Admiralty Marshal see PARA 178. For the purposes of CPR Pt 61, references to
    'Marshal' mean the Admiralty Marshal: see CPR 61.1(2)(j).
7   *Practice Direction—Admiralty Claims* PD 61 para 3.6(3). The claim form is deemed to have been
    duly served on the day on which the copy was filed. In this instance, part of the proceeds of sale
    must still be in court: *The Optima* (1905) 74 LJP 94; *The Fornjot* (1907) 24 TLR 26. As to the
    filing of claims with the Admiralty and Commercial Registry see PARA 142.
8   As to cautions against arrest see PARAS 166–167.
9   *Practice Direction—Admiralty Claims* PD 61 para 3.6(4).
10  *Practice Direction—Admiralty Claims* PD 61 para 3.6(5).
11  *Practice Direction—Admiralty Claims* PD 61 para 3.6(6).
12  Ie under CPR 6.17 (see CIVIL PROCEDURE vol 11 (2015) PARA 260): see *Practice
    Direction—Admiralty Claims* PD 61 para 3.6(7).
13  *Practice Direction—Admiralty Claims* PD 61 para 3.6(7). As to the jurisdiction of the court see
    PARA 85 et seq.
14  Ie by *Practice Direction—Admiralty Claims* PD 61 para 3.6 (see heads (1)–(7) in the text).
15  See CPR 61.3(6); and PARA 168. The protection afforded by the Maritime Conventions Act 1911
    s 8 (repealed) (see now the Merchant Shipping Act 1995 s 190; and PARA 1013), restricting
    proceedings after the lapse of two years, is not waived by acknowledgment of service: see
    PARA 152. A defendant who files an acknowledgment of service to an in rem claim form does not
    by doing so lose any right that he may have to dispute the court's jurisdiction: *Practice
    Direction—Admiralty Claims* PD 61 para 3.11. As to acknowledgment of service in general see
    CPR 10.1 (cited in CIVIL PROCEDURE vol 11 (2015) PARA 311); and the Admiralty and
    Commercial Courts Guide (2016) para B9. As to the procedure for disputing the court's
    jurisdiction generally see CPR Pt 11 (cited in CIVIL PROCEDURE vol 11 (2015) PARA 339); and
    the Admiralty and Commercial Courts Guide (2016) para B10. As to the Admiralty and
    Commercial Courts Guide see PARAS 91 note 3, 157 note 1.
16  Where the claim is issued against two or more ships, it must be served on one only: *The Banco*
    [1971] P 137 at 145, [1971] 1 All ER 524 at 529, [1971] 1 Lloyd's Rep 49 at 50, CA, per Lane J.
    A change in ownership of the defendant vessel subsequent to issue of the claim form is no bar to
    service thereof: see *The Monica S* [1968] P 741, [1967] 3 All ER 740 (but cf the reasoning of the
    majority of the Court of Appeal in *The Banco*). See also *The Helene Roth* [1980] QB 273, [1980]
    1 All ER 1078, [1980] 1 Lloyd's Rep 477 (where a change in ownership of the defendant vessel was
    held to be no bar to renewal of the claim). If one ship is arrested in the mistaken belief that it is
    a sister ship, another ship may be arrested, provided that the affidavit in support of the application
    for the second arrest refers to the previous mistaken arrest and the reasons for it: *The Stephan J*
    [1985] 2 Lloyd's Rep 344.
17  See *Practice Direction—Admiralty Claims* PD 61 para 3.6 (see heads (1)–(7) in the text).
18  *Practice Direction—Admiralty Claims* PD 61 para 3.7.
19  *Practice Direction—Admiralty Claims* PD 61 para 3.8.
20  See *Practice Direction—Admiralty Claims* PD 61 para 3.6 (see heads (1)–(7) in the text).
21  Service must be made within the jurisdiction because the court will be seised of the in rem claim
    form from either the time the claim form is served, or from the time of the ship's arrest, whichever
    is earlier. The court cannot have in rem jurisdiction over a ship which does not come within the
    territorial waters of England and Wales: *The Nord Sea and Freccia del Nord* [1989] 1 Lloyd's Rep
    388. As to the territorial jurisdiction of the Supreme Court see PARAS 187, 188.
        The service of an in rem claim form upon property within the jurisdiction of the court is notice
    to all the world of the claim indorsed upon the claim form; hence the importance of complying
    with the proper mode of service: see *The Prins Bernhard* [1964] P 117 at 131, [1963] 3 All ER 735
    at 745, [1963] 2 Lloyd's Rep 236 at 247 per Hewson J. Where, therefore, after the service of the
    claim form in rem, but before a warrant of arrest issued in the proceedings had been served, a
    foreign vessel proceeded against had left the jurisdiction without the owners appearing, on the
    action coming on for hearing as a default cause, the court ruled in favour of the claimants and
    awarded them their costs: *The Nautik* [1895] P 121. As to warrants of arrest see PARAS 161–165.
22  Ie *Practice Direction—Admiralty Claims* PD 61 para 3 (see note 1): see CPR 61.3(5).

23  CPR 61.3(5). CPR 7.5 (requirement for service of a claim form) (see CIVIL PROCEDURE vol 11 (2015) PARA 144) and CPR 7.6 (extension of time for serving a claim form) (see CIVIL PROCEDURE vol 11 (2015) PARA 147) are modified accordingly: see CPR 61.3(5). As to the Civil Procedure Rules that allow the calculation of any period of time for doing any act which is specified by the rules, by a practice direction or by a judgment or order of the court see CPR 2.8, CPR 2.9; and CIVIL PROCEDURE vol 11 (2015) PARAS 121, 122.

24  Ie under CPR Pt 17 (see CIVIL PROCEDURE vol 11 (2015) PARAS 357–360).

25  *The Dictator* [1892] P 64.

26  *The Cassiopeia* (1879) 4 PD 188, CA. As to amendments made to statements of case with the court's permission see CPR 17.3(1); and CIVIL PROCEDURE vol 11 (2015) PARA 359.

27  *Practice Direction—Admiralty Claims* PD 61 para 3.12. As to the supply of documents from court records generally see CPR 5.4; and CIVIL PROCEDURE vol 11 (2015) PARA 67. As to the payment of fees prescribed to be taken in the Supreme Court see the Civil Proceedings Fees Order 2008, SI 2008/1053; and CIVIL PROCEDURE vol 11 (2015) PARA 68.

28  As to acknowledgment of service see CPR 61.3(4); *Practice Direction—Admiralty Claims* PD 61 paras 3.4, 3.9, 3.11; and PARA 168. As to judgments in default generally see CPR Pt 12 (cited in CIVIL PROCEDURE vol 12 (2015) PARA 535 et seq) and CPR 10.2 (cited in CIVIL PROCEDURE vol 11 (2015) PARA 313).

### (b)    Warrant of Arrest

**161. Application for and issue of warrant of arrest.** In a claim in rem[1], the claimant and a judgment creditor may apply to have the property proceeded against arrested[2] by the Admiralty Court[3]. An application for arrest must contain an undertaking to pay all fees and expenses incurred or to be incurred[4] and must be accompanied by a declaration in support[5]. When the court receives an application for arrest that complies with the Civil Procedure Rules and the practice direction, it will issue an arrest warrant[6]. Any party making an application for arrest must request a search to be made in the Register[7] before the warrant is issued in order to determine whether there is a caution against arrest in force with respect to that property[8], and file a declaration in the required form[9]. The declaration so required[10] must be verified by a statement of truth[11] and must state:

(1)    in every claim:
    (a)    the nature of the claim or counterclaim and that it has not been satisfied and if it arises in connection with a ship, the name of that ship[12];
    (b)    the nature of the property to be arrested and, if the property is a ship, the name of the ship and her port of registry[13]; and
    (c)    the amount of the security sought, if any[14].

(2)    in a claim against a ship (or a sister ship) over which the court has jurisdiction[15]:
    (a)    the name of the person who would be liable on the claim if it were not commenced in rem[16];
    (b)    that the person referred to in head (2)(a) above was, when the right to bring the claim arose, either the owner (or charterer) of, or in possession or in control of, the ship in connection with which the claim arose[17]; and
    (c)    that at the time the claim form was issued the person referred to in head (2)(a) above was either the beneficial owner of all the shares in the ship in respect of which the warrant is required or the charterer of it under a charter by demise[18];

(3)    where a warrant of arrest may not be issued against a ship owned by a state where by any convention or treaty, the United Kingdom[19] has undertaken to minimise the possibility of arrest of ships of that state until notice has been served on a consular officer[20] at the consular office of that state in London or the port at which it is intended to arrest the ship[21], that the relevant notice has been served[22];

(4)     where a warrant of arrest may not be issued in a claim in rem against a foreign ship belonging to a port of a state in respect of which an order in council has been made[23], until the expiration of two weeks from appropriate notice to the consul[24], that the relevant notice has been sent[25]; and

(5)     in the case of a claim in respect of liability for oil pollution caused by tankers[26], the facts relied on as establishing that the court is not[27] prevented from considering the claim[28].

It is permissible and proper[29] that there should be an arrest of a vessel in one jurisdiction in support of a determination of the merits of a dispute by a court of competent jurisdiction in another contracting or regulation state[30] and to provide security for the satisfaction of the judgment given by that court[31]. Likewise, if an arbitration[32] has been commenced and the claimants in the arbitration have not obtained security for any possible award in the arbitration, they may quite properly issue an in rem claim form if they know that a ship belonging to the respondents in the arbitration is coming within the jurisdiction and may arrest that ship in order to obtain security[33].

No warrant of arrest will be issued against a ship owned by a state where, by any convention or treaty, the United Kingdom has undertaken to minimise the possibility of arrest of ships of that state until notice[34] has been served on a consular officer at the consular office of that state in London or the port at which it is intended to arrest the ship[35] and a copy of that notice is attached to any declaration that has been filed with the application[36]. Except with the permission of the court or where notice has been given to the consular officer[37], a warrant of arrest must not be issued in a claim in rem against a foreign ship belonging to a port of a state in respect of which an order in council has been made[38] until the expiration of two weeks from appropriate notice to the consul[39].

Where in respect of an in rem claim over which the court has jurisdiction[40], a ship has been served with a claim form or arrested in a claim in rem brought to enforce that claim, no other ship may be served with a claim form or arrested in that or any other claim in rem brought to enforce that claim; but this does not prevent the issue, in respect of any one such claim, of a claim form naming more than one ship or of two or more claim forms each naming a different ship[41].

1   As to the origin of claims in rem see PARA 83; and as to the jurisdiction of the Admiralty Court in relation to claims in rem see PARA 92 et seq. As to the issue of an in rem claim form see PARA 158 et seq.
        As to the procedure that governs Admiralty claims, including CPR Pt 61 and *Practice Direction—Admiralty Claims* PD 61, see PARAS 140 note 5. As to the meanings of 'Admiralty claim' and 'Admiralty Court' for these purposes see PARA 91 note 3. As to the assignment of business to the Admiralty Court see CPR 61.2(1), (2); and PARA 91.
2   There must be a tangible res in existence, and thus a warrant cannot be issued for the arrest of freight apart from a ship or some cargo, nor can freight collected and paid into a bank be arrested: *The Kaleten* (1914) 30 TLR 572.
3   CPR 61.5(1). The practice direction (ie *Practice Direction—Admiralty Claims* PD 61: see note 1) sets out the procedure for applying for arrest: CPR 61.5(2). As to the filing of documents with the Admiralty and Commercial Registry see PARA 142.
4   Ie the application must be in Form ADM4 (Application and undertaking for arrest and custody): see *Practice Direction—Admiralty Claims* PD 61 para 5.1(1).
5   Ie the application must be accompanied by a declaration in Form ADM5 (Declaration in support of application for warrant of arrest): see *Practice Direction—Admiralty Claims* PD 61 para 5.1(2).
6   *Practice Direction—Admiralty Claims* PD 61 para 5.2. There are now no special provisions applicable to warrants for arrest where there is a claim arising out of bottomry (as to which see PARA 134), but it should be noted that no such claim has been made in the High Court for many years. It should also be noted that a warrant of arrest may not be issued as of right in the case of property in respect of which the beneficial ownership has, since the issue of the claim form, changed as a result of a sale or disposal by any court in any jurisdiction exercising Admiralty

jurisdiction in rem: see CPR 61.5(4). For the circumstances in which the warrant is intended to be issued as of right (ie so long as the statutory requirements are complied with) see also *The Varna* [1993] 2 Lloyd's Rep 253, CA.

7   For the purposes of CPR Pt 61, 'Register' means the Register of cautions against arrest and release which is open to inspection as provided by the practice direction: see CPR 61.1(2)(i). As to cautions against arrest see PARAS 166–167.

8   CPR 61.5(3)(a).

9   CPR 61.5(3)(b). The declaration must be in the form set out in the practice direction (ie *Practice Direction—Admiralty Claims* PD 61: see note 1): see CPR 61.5(3)(b). As to the statements that must be made in the declaration see heads (1) to (5) in the text; and see note 5.

10  Ie by CPR 61.5(3)(b) (see the text and note 9): see *Practice Direction—Admiralty Claims* PD 61 para 5.3.

11  It is the duty of the deponent to correct promptly and frankly any statements in the statement of truth that are false or misleading: *The Nordglimt* [1988] QB 183, [1988] 2 All ER 531, [1987] 2 Lloyd's Rep 470. See also *The Vasso (formerly Andria)* [1984] QB 477, [1984] 1 All ER 1126, CA; and PARA 93.

12  *Practice Direction—Admiralty Claims* PD 61 para 5.3(1)(a).

13  *Practice Direction—Admiralty Claims* PD 61 para 5.3(1)(b).

14  *Practice Direction—Admiralty Claims* PD 61 para 5.3(1)(c).

15  Ie by virtue of the Senior Courts Act 1981 s 21(4) (see PARA 93): see *Practice Direction—Admiralty Claims* PD 61 para 5.3(2). It should be noted that under the Senior Courts Act 1981 s 21(4) the claimant does not have the right to arrest a ship which was a ship owned by a sister company of the owning company of 'the particular ship': *The Evpo Agnic* [1988] 3 All ER 810, [1988] 1 WLR 1090, [1988] 2 Lloyd's Rep 411, CA.

16  *Practice Direction—Admiralty Claims* PD 61 para 5.3(2)(a).

17  *Practice Direction—Admiralty Claims* PD 61 para 5.3(2)(b).

18  *Practice Direction—Admiralty Claims* PD 61 para 5.3(2)(c).

19  As to the meaning of 'United Kingdom' see PARA 16 note 3.

20  As to consular officers in the United Kingdom see INTERNATIONAL RELATIONS LAW vol 61 (2010) PARA 290 et seq.

21  Ie in a case set out in CPR 61.5(5) (see the text and notes 34–36): see *Practice Direction—Admiralty Claims* PD 61 para 5.3(3).

22  *Practice Direction—Admiralty Claims* PD 61 para 5.3(3).

23  Ie under the Consular Relations Act 1968 s 4 (the Orders in Council made thereunder giving effect to a number of international agreements entered into by the United Kingdom: see PARA 128; and INTERNATIONAL RELATIONS LAW vol 61 (2010) PARA 303): see *Practice Direction—Admiralty Claims* PD 61 para 5.3(3).

24  Ie in a case set out in CPR 61.5(6) (see the text and notes 37–39): see *Practice Direction—Admiralty Claims* PD 61 para 5.3(3). As to the Civil Procedure Rules that allow the calculation of any period of time for doing any act which is specified by the rules, by a practice direction or by a judgment or order of the court see CPR 2.8, CPR 2.9; and CIVIL PROCEDURE vol 11 (2015) PARAS 121, 122.

25  *Practice Direction—Admiralty Claims* PD 61 para 5.3(3).

26  Ie liability incurred under the Merchant Shipping Act 1995 s 153 (see ENVIRONMENTAL QUALITY AND PUBLIC HEALTH vol 45 (2010) PARA 443): see *Practice Direction—Admiralty Claims* PD 61 para 5.3(4).

27  Ie by reason of the Merchant Shipping Act 1995 s 166(2) (see ENVIRONMENTAL QUALITY AND PUBLIC HEALTH vol 45 (2010) PARA 456): see *Practice Direction—Admiralty Claims* PD 61 para 5.3(4).

28  *Practice Direction—Admiralty Claims* PD 61 para 5.3(4).

29  Ie under the Civil Jurisdiction and Judgments Act 1982 (and the provisions to which that Act gives force) (see PARA 96).

30  See PARA 96.

31  *The Nordglimt* [1988] QB 183, [1988] 2 All ER 531, [1987] 2 Lloyd's Rep 470.

32  As to arbitration agreements see PARA 103.

33  *The Jalamatsya* [1987] 2 Lloyd's Rep 164 (considering the Civil Jurisdiction and Judgments Act 1982 s 26 (as to which see PARA 86)); *The Vasso (formerly Andria)* [1984] QB 477, [1984] 1 All ER 1126, [1984] 1 Lloyd's Rep 235.

34  Ie notice in the form set out in the practice direction, *Practice Direction—Admiralty Claims* PD 61: see CPR 61.5(5)(a). Accordingly, the notice required by CPR 61.5(5)(a) must be in Form ADM6 (Notice to Consular Officer of intention to apply for warrant of arrest): *Practice Direction—Admiralty Claims* PD 61 para 5.4.

35  CPR 61.5(5)(a).

36  CPR 61.5(5)(b). The text refers to any declaration under CPR 61.5(3)(b) (see the text and note 9): see CPR 61.5(5)(b).
37  Ie under CPR 61.5(5) (see the text and notes 34–36): see CPR 61.5(6).
38  Ie under the Consular Relations Act 1968 s 4 (the Orders in Council made thereunder giving effect to a number of international agreements entered into by the United Kingdom: see PARA 128; and INTERNATIONAL RELATIONS LAW vol 61 (2010) PARA 303): see CPR 61.5(6) (as added: see note 3).
39  CPR 61.5(6).
40  Ie by virtue of the Senior Courts Act 1981 ss 20(2)(e)–(r), 21(4) (see PARAS 93, 110 et seq).
41  See the Senior Courts Act 1981 s 21(8); and PARA 93.

**162.   Execution of warrant of arrest.** A warrant of arrest[1] must be executed within the jurisdiction[2]. A warrant of arrest is valid for 12 months but may only be executed if the claim form has been served or remains valid for service at the date of execution[3]. The arrest of property may only be effected by the Admiralty Marshal or his substitute[4]; and the warrant will not be executed without a written undertaking to pay the Marshal's fees and expenses incurred, or to be incurred, by him or on his behalf in respect of the arrest, or endeavours to arrest, the property[5]. The detainer of a vessel or other property in consequence of directions sent by fax is not unusual, and the disregard of a notice by telegram from the Admiralty Marshal that a warrant has been issued against property and that the property is not to be removed is a contempt of court[6].

1  As to applications for and the issue of a warrant of arrest see PARA 161.
    As to the procedure that governs Admiralty claims, including CPR Pt 61 and *Practice Direction—Admiralty Claims* PD 61, see PARAS 140 note 5. As to the meanings of 'Admiralty claim' and 'Admiralty Court' for these purposes see PARA 91 note 3. As to the assignment of business to the Admiralty Court see CPR 61.2(1), (2); and PARA 91.
2  This limitation has always been fundamental to Admiralty procedure in rem: see eg *The Banco* [1971] P 137 at 150, [1971] 1 All ER 524 at 531, [1971] 1 Lloyd's Rep 49 at 51, CA, per Lord Denning MR. As to the Admiralty jurisdiction of the High Court see PARA 85 et seq.
3  CPR 61.5(7). As to the Civil Procedure Rules that allow the calculation of any period of time for doing any act which is specified by the rules, by a practice direction or by a judgment or order of the court see CPR 2.8, CPR 2.9; and CIVIL PROCEDURE vol 11 (2015) PARAS 121, 122.
4  CPR 61.5(8). As to the Admiralty Marshal see PARA 160 note 6. For a note on current procedures for the arrest of a ship see *The Johnny Two* [1992] 2 Lloyd's Rep 257 at 260 per Sheen J. Officers of Revenue and Customs act as the Admiralty Marshal's substitutes at outlying ports. As to the appointment of officers of Revenue and Customs see INCOME TAXATION vol 58 (2014) PARA 33 et seq.
5  The undertaking forms part of the application to arrest in Form ADM4 (Application and undertaking for arrest and custody): see PARA 161. Where, in CPR 61 or in *Practice Direction—Admiralty Claims* PD 61, any undertaking to the Marshal is required it must be given in writing and to his satisfaction or in accordance with such other arrangements as he may require: *Practice Direction—Admiralty Claims* PD 61 para 14.1. Where any party is dissatisfied with a direction given by the Marshal in this respect he may apply to the Admiralty Registrar for a ruling: *Practice Direction—Admiralty Claims* PD 61 para 14.2. As to the Admiralty Registrar see PARA 140.
    As to recovery of expenses from the proceeds of sale paid to the Marshal by an arresting party see *The Falcon* [1981] 1 Lloyd's Rep 13. The marshal's expenses of maintaining the arrest from the time of lodgment of a commission of appraisement and sale and the expenses of the sale are payable in the first instance by the party lodging the commission: *The Falcon*. As to liability for the expenses of second and subsequent arrests see *The Falcon*.
6  *The Seraglio* (1885) 10 PD 120; *The Jarlinn* [1965] 3 All ER 36, [1965] 1 WLR 1098, [1965] 2 Lloyd's Rep 191. As to the mode of service of a warrant of arrest etc see also PARA 163.

**163.   Mode of effecting service of warrant of arrest etc.** Warrants of arrest or in rem claim forms[1], because of the urgency associated with them, may be served on Sundays and other non-working days as required[2]. Service of either an in rem claim form or a warrant[3], if the property to be arrested is a ship, freight, or cargo on board, must be effected by affixing a copy on the outside of the property proceeded against in a position which may reasonably be expected to be seen[4]. If it is not reasonably practicable in the case of a warrant to serve the warrant itself, the property may be arrested by service of a notice of issue of the warrant on the property[5] or by giving notice to those in charge of the property[6]. A ship may be arrested even when the sheriff is in possession, as the seizure by the sheriff can only be subject to any maritime liens with which the ship is incumbered[7].

1	As to in rem claim forms see PARA 158 et seq; and as to applications for and the issue and execution of a warrant of arrest see PARAS 161–162.
	As to the procedure that governs Admiralty claims, including CPR Pt 61 and *Practice Direction—Admiralty Claims* PD 61, see PARA 140 note 5. As to the meanings of 'Admiralty claim' and 'Admiralty Court' for these purposes see PARA 91 note 3. As to the assignment of business to the Admiralty Court see CPR 61.2(1), (2); and PARA 91.
2	As to service of the in rem claim form see PARA 160; and as to service of a warrant see PARAS 161–162. For details of when service is deemed to take place generally see CPR 6.7; and CIVIL PROCEDURE vol 11 (2015) PARA 257.
3	Property is arrested by service on it of an arrest warrant in Form ADM9 (warrant of arrest): see *Practice Direction—Admiralty Claims* PD 61 para 5.5(1).
4	See *Practice Direction—Admiralty Claims* PD 61 paras 3.6(1), 5.5(1); and CPR 61.8(1) (cited in PARA 164). A warrant against freight may be executed by service on the cargo or on the ship: see *Practice Direction—Admiralty Claims* PD 61 paras 3.6(1)(b), 5.5(1). However, where neither ship nor cargo can be arrested, a warrant cannot be issued for the arrest of freight only: *The Kaleten* (1914) 30 TLR 572 (service of warrant for arrest of freight on a clerk of the shipowner's agent held to be bad).
	These methods of service are mandatory and service will be set aside if there is a substantial failure to carry out the proper procedure: *The Prins Bernhard* [1964] P 117, [1963] 3 All ER 735, [1963] 2 Lloyd's Rep 236. Minor irregularities may, however, be condoned: *The Sullivar* [1965] 2 Lloyd's Rep 350.
5	Ie in the manner set out in *Practice Direction—Admiralty Claims* PD 61 para 3.6(1) (see the text and note 4; and PARA 160): see para 5.5(2).
6	See *Practice Direction—Admiralty Claims* PD 61 para 5.5(2). See note 3.
7	*The James W Elwell* [1921] P 351. As to maritime liens generally see PARA 964 et seq.

### 164. Custody of arrested property.

Property under arrest[1] may not be moved without an order of the Admiralty Court and the property may be immobilised or otherwise prevented from sailing in such manner as the Admiralty Marshal[2] may consider is appropriate[3]. Where property is under arrest, an in rem claim form[4] may be served upon it and, in addition, it may be arrested by any other person claiming to have an in rem claim against it[5].

A ship-keeper may be put in possession under the authority of the Admiralty Marshal during the time a ship is under arrest, and any person breaking the arrest or interfering with the property whilst it is under arrest is guilty of a contempt of court and liable to committal or a fine[6]. By the mere arrest of a ship the Marshal gains custody and not possession; subject to his control of the custody all possessory rights which previously existed continue to exist, including all the remedies which are based on possession[7].

1	As to applications for, and the service and execution of, a warrant of arrest see PARAS 161–163.
	As to the procedure that governs Admiralty claims, including CPR Pt 61 and *Practice Direction—Admiralty Claims* PD 61, see PARAS 140 note 5. As to the meanings of 'Admiralty claim' and 'Admiralty Court' for these purposes see PARA 91 note 3. As to the assignment of business to the Admiralty Court see CPR 61.2(1), (2); and PARA 91.
2	As to the Admiralty Marshal see PARA 160 note 6.
3	CPR 61.5(9). When property is arrested, the Admiralty Registrar will issue standard directions in Form ADM10 (Standard Directions to the Admiralty Marshal): *Practice Direction—Admiralty Claims* PD 61 para 5.6. As to the Admiralty Registrar see PARA 140. As to release and other dealings with arrested property see further PARA 173 et seq. As to liability for the cost of maintaining a ship see *The Falcon* [1981] 1 Lloyd's Rep 13.
4	As to in rem claim forms see PARA 158 et seq.
5	CPR 61.8(1).
6	*The Harmonie* (1841) 1 Wm Rob 179; *The Mathesis* (1844) 2 Wm Rob 286 at 288; *The Bure* (1850) 14 Jur 1123; *The Armenian* (20 March 1874, unreported), Admiralty Court; *The Seraglio* (1885) 10 PD 120; *The Jarlinn* [1965] 3 All ER 36, [1965] 1 WLR 1098, [1965] 2 Lloyd's Rep 191; *The Jarvis Brake* [1976] 2 All ER 886, [1976] 2 Lloyd's Rep 320; *The Merdeka* [1982] 1

Lloyd's Rep 401. In the last case, a master who broke arrest was not committed to prison but was fined. However, the judge indicated that in a proper case the court would be prepared to commit to prison a master who breaks arrest. Forcible exclusion of the master whilst the ship is in the custody of the Admiralty Marshal is a contempt of court: *The Abodi Mendi* [1939] P 178, [1939] 1 All ER 701, 63 Ll L Rep 100, CA.

7    *Spain v The Arantzazu Mendi* [1939] AC 256, [1939] 1 All ER 719, HL; *The Queen of the South* [1968] P 449 (exercise of a statutory right of detention).

## 165.    Forgoing of service where undertakings are made by solicitor.

Where the solicitor of the defendant agrees to accept service and undertakes to provide security, no service on the property of the in rem claim form or warrant is required[1]. Where a solicitor fails to comply with his written undertaking to acknowledge service of the claim form, or provide security, he is liable to committal[2] and the undertaking remains binding though no claim form has been issued[3]. The undertaking once given cannot be withdrawn on offering the ship, within the jurisdiction, for arrest, nor do the claimants, by arresting the ship under such circumstances, forfeit their rights under the undertaking[4], and the fact that the undertaking has been given by the solicitor under a mistake as to his authority is no reason for setting it aside[5]. The value of the ship for the purpose of security in pursuance of the undertaking must be ascertained as at the date of the undertaking[6].

1    It is submitted that the practice described in the text, which was formerly governed by RSC Ord 75 r 9, seems to be observed still, although the rule has been revoked and there is no direct replacement provision in the Civil Procedure Rules. (As to service under the CPR generally see CIVIL PROCEDURE vol 11 (2015) PARA 244 et seq). As to service of the in rem claim form see PARA 160; and as to service of a warrant of arrest see PARA 163. As regards arrest, the situation is analogous to that which arises upon the entry of a caution against release: see PARA 167. As to undertakings in Admiralty proceedings generally see PARA 162.
2    See *The Anna and Bertha* (1891) 64 LT 332; and cf *Re Kerly, Son and Verden* [1901] 1 Ch 467, CA. For the practice on committal see CONTEMPT OF COURT vol 22 (2012) PARA 95 et seq.
3    *The Ring* [1931] P 58.
4    *The Borre* [1921] P 390.
5    *The Gertrud* (1927) 138 LT 239.
6    See *The Borre* [1921] P 390 (bail).

### (c)    Caution against Arrest

## 166.    Entry of caution against arrest.

Any person may file[1] a request for a caution against arrest[2], which must be in the prescribed form[3]. When a request is filed in this way, the court will enter the caution in the Register[4] if the request is duly completed[5] and if:

(1)    the person filing the request undertakes to file an acknowledgment of service and to give sufficient security to satisfy the claim with interest and costs[6]; or

(2)    where the person filing the request has constituted a limitation fund[7], he states that such a fund has been constituted and he undertakes that the claimant will acknowledge service of the claim form by which any claim may be begun against the property described in the request[8].

The entry of a caution against arrest is not treated as a submission to the jurisdiction of the English Court[9].

A caution against arrest is valid for 12 months after the date it is entered in the Register[10]; but may be renewed for a further 12 months by filing a further request[11].

1    As to the filing of documents in the Admiralty and Commercial Registry see PARA 142.
2    CPR 61.7(1). As to the procedure that governs Admiralty claims, including CPR Pt 61 and *Practice Direction—Admiralty Claims* PD 61, see PARAS 140 note 5. As to the meanings of 'Admiralty claim' and 'Admiralty Court' for these purposes see PARA 91 note 3. As to the assignment of business to the Admiralty Court see CPR 61.2(1), (2); and PARA 91.

3　See *Practice Direction—Admiralty Claims* PD 61 para 6.2. Accordingly, the request must be in Form ADM7 (Request for caution against arrest): see *Practice Direction—Admiralty Claims* PD 61 para 6.2. See also the text and notes 5–8.

4　See CPR 61.7(2); *Practice Direction—Admiralty Claims* PD 61 para 6.3. As to the meaning of 'Register' for these purposes see PARA 161 note 7. The Register is open for inspection when the Admiralty and Commercial Registry is open: *Practice Direction—Admiralty Claims* PD 61 para 6.4. A caution entered in the Register under CPR 61.7 is known as a 'caution against arrest' for the purposes of CPR Pt 61: CPR 61.1(2)(g).

5　Ie if the request is in the form set out in the practice direction (ie *Practice Direction—Admiralty Claims* PD 61: see note 2): see CPR 61.7(2).

6　CPR 61.7(2)(a).

7　Ie in accordance with the Convention on Limitation of Liability for Maritime Claims (London, 1 to 19 November 1976; Misc 31 (1978); Cmnd 7035) art 11 (see PARA 1003): see CPR 61.7(2)(b). See also PARA 176.

8　CPR 61.7(2)(b).

9　*Practice Direction—Admiralty Claims* PD 61 para 6.1.

10　CPR 61.7(3)(a). As to the withdrawal of cautions see PARA 175.

11　CPR 61.7(3)(b). The provisions of CPR 61.7(1), (2) (see the text and notes 1–8) apply to a further request under CPR 61.7(3)(b): CPR 61.7(4).

**167. Effect of caution against arrest.** The entry in the Register[1] of a caution against arrest[2] does not prevent the arrest of the subject property but, in such a case, the Admiralty Court[3] may order that the arrest be discharged[4] and that the party procuring the arrest pays compensation to the owner of or other persons interested in the property arrested[5].

A solicitor, by signing a request for a caution without qualification[6], renders himself personally liable to perform the undertaking contained therein, and where such an undertaking has been given the claimant is entitled to have a reasonable opportunity of seeing whether he ought to accept it or not; if it is not a satisfactory undertaking, or for any other good and sufficient reason he does not accept it, he will not be condemned in costs and damages for taking out a warrant for arrest[7]. A preliminary search in order to determine whether there is a caution against arrest in force with respect to the subject property is thus advisable in the interest of the claimant in addition to being compulsory before an arrest is made[8].

1　As to the meaning of 'Register' for these purposes see PARA 161 note 7.

2　As to the entry of a caution against arrest see PARA 166.

3　As to the meaning of 'Admiralty Court' for these purposes see PARA 91 note 3. As to the procedure that governs Admiralty claims, including CPR Pt 61 and *Practice Direction—Admiralty Claims* PD 61, see PARAS 140 note 5. As to the meaning of 'Admiralty claim' for these purposes see PARA 91 note 3.

4　CPR 61.7(5)(a).

5　CPR 61.7(5)(b). See also *The Crimdon* [1900] P 171; and the text and notes 6–7. As to the liability in tort for the malicious arrest of a ship see *The Strathnaver* (1875) 1 App Cas 58, PC; and TORT vol 97 (2015) PARA 755. As to a case of wrongful arrest see *Gulf Azov Shipping Co Ltd v Chief Humphrey Irikefe Idisi* [2001] EWCA Civ 505, [2001] 2 All ER (Comm) 673, [2001] 1 Lloyd's Rep 727 (on the facts, the vessel had been detained by the defendants and that detention was wholly improper and lasted for an unconscionable time; it was clear that there was no objective justification for the amount claimed).

6　Ie in Form ADM7 (Request for caution against arrest) (see PARA 166).

7　*The Crimdon* [1900] P 171; cf PARA 165.

8　See CPR 61.5(3); and PARA 161.

### (d)　Acknowledgment of Service

**168. Acknowledgment of service of claim form in rem.** If the defendant to an Admiralty claim in rem[1] wishes to contest the proceedings, either on the merits or on a point of jurisdiction[2] or irregularity, he is required in all cases to acknowledge service of the in rem claim form[3]. A defendant who files an acknowledgment of service to an in rem claim does not lose any right he may have to dispute the jurisdiction of the court[4].

After the acknowledgment of service has been filed, the claim will follow the procedure applicable to a claim proceeding in the Commercial List[5] except that the claimant is allowed 75 days to serve the particulars of claim[6].

If the defendant fails to acknowledge service within the prescribed time, the claimant may apply for judgment in default of notice of intention to defend[7].

1  As to in rem claims see PARA 158 et seq. As to the procedure that governs Admiralty claims, including CPR Pt 61 and *Practice Direction—Admiralty Claims* PD 61, see PARA 140 note 5. As to the meanings of 'Admiralty claim' and 'Admiralty Court' for these purposes see PARA 91 note 3. As to the assignment of business to the Admiralty Court see CPR 61.2(1), (2); and PARA 91.
2  See eg *The Sydney Express* [1988] 2 Lloyd's Rep 257.
3  An acknowledgment of service must be filed in every in rem claim within 14 days after service of the claim form: CPR 61.3(4). This period applies irrespective of whether the claim form contains particulars of claim: see *Practice Direction—Admiralty Claims* PD 61 para 3.5. As to service of the in rem claim form see PARA 160. For details of when service is deemed to take place generally see CPR 6.7; and CIVIL PROCEDURE vol 11 (2015) PARA 257. As to the Civil Procedure Rules that allow the calculation of any period of time for doing any act which is specified by the rules, by a practice direction or by a judgment or order of the court see CPR 2.8, CPR 2.9; and CIVIL PROCEDURE vol 11 (2015) PARAS 121, 122.
   The acknowledgment of service must be in Form ADM2 (Acknowledgment of service) and the person who acknowledges service must identify himself by name therein: *Practice Direction—Admiralty Claims* PD 61 para 3.4. If an in rem claim form has been issued (whether served or not), any person who wishes to defend the claim may file an acknowledgment of service: CPR 61.3(6).
4  *Practice Direction—Admiralty Claims* PD 61 para 3.11. As to acknowledgment of service in general see CPR 10.1; and CIVIL PROCEDURE vol 11 (2015) PARA 311. As to the procedure for disputing the court's jurisdiction generally see CPR Pt 11; and CIVIL PROCEDURE vol 11 (2015) PARA 339. See also PARA 160. As to the filing of documents with the Admiralty and Commercial Registry see PARA 142.
5  As to which see note 1.
6  *Practice Direction—Admiralty Claims* PD 61 para 3.10.
7  See CPR 61.9; and PARA 190 et seq. As to judgments in default generally see CPR Pt 12 (cited in CIVIL PROCEDURE vol 12 (2015) PARA 535 et seq) and CPR 10.2 (cited in CIVIL PROCEDURE vol 11 (2015) PARA 313). As to undertakings to acknowledge service see PARA 165.

## 169. Persons who may acknowledge service of claim form in rem.

An acknowledgment of service must be filed in every in rem claim[1] and the person who acknowledges service must identify himself in it by name[2]. Where the defendants are described and not named on the claim form (for example as 'The Owners of the Ship X'), any acknowledgment of service, in addition to stating that description which appears on the claim form, must also state the full names of the persons acknowledging service and the nature of their ownership[3]. Any person interested in property under arrest (or in the proceeds of sale of such property), or whose interests are affected by any order sought or made, may be made a party to any claim in rem against the property or proceeds of sale[4]. Examples of persons having an interest are mortgagees[5], trustees in bankruptcy[6], underwriters who have accepted abandonment[7], charterers[8], persons who have possessory liens[9], or competing maritime liens[10], owners who have purchased the property against which the claim is brought since the date of the issue of the in rem claim form[11], and generally persons who are claimants in other claims in rem against the same property[12]. If, however, the intervention is unnecessary to protect the intervener's rights he will be refused his costs[13]. Persons who intervene in order to defend the claim cannot set up defences which are not open to the owner of the property[14].

1  As to in rem claims see PARA 158 et seq; and as to acknowledgment of service of claim forms in rem see PARA 168. As to the filing of documents with the Admiralty and Commercial Registry see PARA 142.
   As to the procedure that governs Admiralty claims, including CPR Pt 61 and *Practice Direction—Admiralty Claims* PD 61, see PARAS 140 note 5. As to the meanings of 'Admiralty claim' and 'Admiralty Court' for these purposes see PARA 91 note 3. As to the assignment of business to the Admiralty Court see CPR 61.2(1), (2); and PARA 91.

2   See CPR 61.3(4); *Practice Direction—Admiralty Claims* PD 61 para 3.4; and PARA 168.
3   *Practice Direction—Admiralty Claims* PD 61 para 3.9. A defendant may acknowledge service voluntarily even though the claim form has not been served: see CPR 61.3(6); and PARA 168. See also *The Gniezno* [1968] P 418, [1967] 2 All ER 738, [1967] 1 Lloyd's Rep 441. If the claim form is served on a ship which has been sold since the date of issue of the claim form, the correct procedure is for those who were the owners of the ship at the time when the claim form was issued to acknowledge service; the new owners should make an application for leave to intervene in the claim under CPR 61.8(7) (as to which see the text and note 4): see *The Mawan now named Mara* [1988] 2 Lloyd's Rep 459.
4   CPR 61.8(7). See also PARA 173. These provisions are designed to allow those who have substantial interests in the res ('the property') to intervene, as their interests may otherwise be adversely affected by the claim. The rights of the interveners are limited to the protection of their interests in the property; interveners therefore will not be allowed to raise issues which are ancillary to that purpose: *The Lord Strathcona* [1925] P 143; *The Byzantion* (1922) 127 LT 756, 16 Asp MLC 19. Any party who wishes to resist an application for payment out must either intervene or enter a caution: *The Eva* [1921] P 454. As to cautions see PARAS 166–167. Parties who intervene in order to postpone the sale of the ship may be ordered to give security, which may be increased even after judgment: *The Lord Strathcona (No 2)* [1926] P 18. As to the provision of security see PARAS 171–172. Even where a party has no interest in the res ('the property') under arrest, there is an inherent jurisdiction to grant leave to intervene where justice requires to prevent serious hardship to that party: *The Mardina Merchant* [1974] 3 All ER 749, [1975] 1 WLR 147. As to the addition and substitution of parties, representative parties, and group litigation generally see CPR Pt 19; and CIVIL PROCEDURE vol 11 (2015) PARA 480 et seq.
5   *The Regina del Mare* (1864) Brown & Lush 315 at 316; *The Orienta* [1895] P 49, CA; *The Tagus* [1903] P 44.
6   See *The Riga* (1872) LR 3 A & E 516.
7   Underwriters who have not accepted an abandonment have been allowed to intervene on giving security for costs: see *The Regina del Mare* (1864) Brown & Lush 315.
8   *The Lord Strathcona* [1925] P 143 at 150.
9   *The Immacolata Concezione* (1882) 8 PD 34 at 36; *The Queen of the South* [1968] P 449, [1968] 1 All ER 1163, [1968] 1 Lloyd's Rep 182.
10  See eg *The Linda Flor* (1857) Sw 309; *The Veritas* [1901] P 304 at 308. As to maritime liens generally see PARA 964 et seq.
11  *The Mawan now named Mara* [1988] 2 Lloyd's Rep 459.
12  *The Two Ellens* (1871) LR 3 A & E 345 at 355; *The Chioggia* [1898] P 1 at 3.
13  *The Athenic* [1932] WN 10, 48 TLR 158, 42 Ll L Rep 7.
14  *The Byzantion* (1922) 127 LT 756, 16 Asp MLC 19.

**170. Late acknowledgment of service of claim form in rem.** If a defendant acknowledges service of a claim form in rem[1] at any time after the time limited by the rules for acknowledging service (that is, 14 days after the service of the in rem claim form including the day of service[2]), he is not, unless the court otherwise orders, entitled to any further time for delivering his defence or for any other purpose than if he had acknowledged service within that time[3].

1   As to in rem claims see PARA 158 et seq; and as to acknowledgment of service of claim forms in rem see PARAS 168–169. As to the procedure that governs Admiralty claims, including CPR Pt 61 and *Practice Direction—Admiralty Claims* PD 61, see PARAS 140 note 5. As to the meanings of 'Admiralty claim' and 'Admiralty Court' for these purposes see PARA 91 note 3. As to the assignment of business to the Admiralty Court see CPR 61.2(1), (2); and PARA 91.
2   See CPR 61.3(4); and PARA 168. As to the Civil Procedure Rules that allow the calculation of any period of time for doing any act which is specified by the rules, by a practice direction or by a judgment or order of the court see CPR 2.8, CPR 2.9; and CIVIL PROCEDURE vol 11 (2015) PARAS 121, 122. As to acknowledgment of service in general see CPR Pt 10 (cited in CIVIL PROCEDURE vol 11 (2015) PARAS 311, 313); and the Admiralty and Commercial Courts Guide (2016) para B9. As to the Admiralty and Commercial Courts Guide see PARAS 91 note 3, 157 note 1.
3   See CPR Pt 3; and CIVIL PROCEDURE vol 12 (2015) PARA 507 et seq.

(e)     Provision of Security

**171. Introduction.** The usual step following an acknowledgment of service in a claim in rem[1] is for the owner of the property arrested to procure its release[2] by giving security for the claimant's claim[3]. This may be done:

(1)      by paying the amount of the claimant's claim into court[4];
(2)      by providing security in a sufficient amount[5]; or
(3)      by furnishing a guarantee acceptable to the claimant[6].
The third method is the most common in practice.

1    As to acknowledgment of service of a claim form in rem see PARAS 168–170.
2    For the procedure relating to release see PARAS 173–176.
3    It is submitted that the provisions with regard to caution against arrest or release, releases, security, payment into court and guarantees in lieu of bail apply equally to arrests at the instance of defendants as to arrests at the instance of claimants. This practice was formerly governed by RSC Ord 75 rr 5(1), 6(1), 14(1) and it appears that the practice is still being observed, although the rule has been revoked and there is no direct replacement provision in the Civil Procedure Rules.
4    Money paid into court as security must, in proceedings taking place in London, be paid into the Court Funds Office and such payment is subject to the Court Funds Rules 2011, SI 2011/1734: see CIVIL PROCEDURE vol 11 (2015) PARA 69 et seq. See also *The Markland* (1871) LR 3 A & E 340 at 344; *The Fairport (No 4)* [1967] 2 All ER 914n, [1967] 1 WLR 964, [1967] 1 Lloyd's Rep 602.
5    See PARA 172.
6    In practice, a guarantee or undertaking by a bank, insurance company, protection and indemnity association, or other guarantor satisfactory to the claimant, to pay any amount found to be due from the defendant and not paid by him is usually accepted in lieu of payment into court. In particular, the existence of the guarantee protects the ship against further arrest, for the purpose of obtaining further security in connection with the same cause of action, unless the arresting party has good reason to consider the guarantee insufficient or inoperative: see *The Christiansborg* (1885) 10 PD 141, CA; *The Hartlepool* (1950) 84 Ll L Rep 145; *Westminster Bank Ltd v West of England Steamship Owners' Protection and Indemnity Association Ltd* (1933) 46 Ll L Rep 101; *The Tjaskemolen (No 2)* [1997] 2 Lloyd's Rep 476.

**172. Security given to obtain release or to prevent arrest of property.**
Where an in rem claim form has been issued[1] and security sought, any person who has filed an acknowledgment of service[2] may apply to the Admiralty Court for an order specifying the amount and form of security to be provided[3].

Where, in relation to a claim in rem, security has been given either to obtain the release of property under arrest or to prevent the arrest of property[4], the court may order:

(1)      that the amount of security be reduced (and the court may stay the claim until the order is complied with)[5]; or

(2)      that the claimant be permitted to arrest[6] or re-arrest the property proceeded against in order to obtain further security[7],

provided that the total security to be so provided does not exceed the value of the property at the time of the original arrest or (if the property was not arrested) at the time security was first given[8].

1    As to in rem claims see PARA 158 et seq. As to the procedure that governs Admiralty claims, including CPR Pt 61 and *Practice Direction—Admiralty Claims* PD 61, see PARAS 140 note 5. As to the meanings of 'Admiralty claim' and 'Admiralty Court' for these purposes see PARA 91 note 3. As to the assignment of business to the Admiralty Court see CPR 61.2(1), (2); and PARA 91.
2    As to acknowledgment of service of a claim form in rem see PARAS 168–170.
3    CPR 61.5(10) (CPR Pt 61 added by SI 2001/4015). Historically, the provision of bail as security in Admiralty proceedings was known but this practice has been, and is expected to be, a rarity. Be that as it may, as to the form of bail bond see *The Bulgaria* [1964] 2 Lloyd's Rep 524 (bond expressly reserving the defendant's right to seek to set aside the claim on grounds of sovereign immunity was allowed); and *The Cap Bon* [1967] 1 Lloyd's Rep 543 (form cannot be so altered as to cover a purpose which is not the purpose of Admiralty proceedings in rem). As to the amount, effect and costs of bail see *The Moschanthy* [1971] 1 Lloyd's Rep 37; *The Tribels* [1985] 1 Lloyd's Rep 128 (claim for salvage); *The Russland* [1924] P 55 (number of claims against a ship in respect of which bail has been provided to answer one claim only); *The Roberta* [1938] P 1, CA (third party proceedings); *The Point Breeze* [1928] P 135 (appraisement to ascertain the value of the property). See also *The Joannis Vatis (No 2)* [1922] P 213; and *The Tjaskemolen (No 2)* [1997] 2 Lloyd's Rep 476 (provision of further security). A claimant who has insisted upon bail in an excessive sum may be ordered to pay the additional costs incurred as a result: *The Princesse Marie José* (1913) 109 LT 326; *The George Gordon* (1884) 9 PD 46; *The Chieftain* (1863) 32 LJPM &

A 106; *The Polo II* [1977] 2 Lloyd's Rep 115. As to the amount of bail in collision claims see *The Duchesse de Brabant* (1857) Sw 264; *The Sisters* (1875) 32 LT 837; *The Charlotte* [1920] P 78; *The Norwalk Victory* (1949) 82 Ll L Rep 539.

4  See CPR 61.6(1) (as added: see note 3).
5  CPR 61.6(2)(a) (as added: see note 3). Where the Admiralty Court orders a stay of any claim in rem, any property under arrest in the claim remains under arrest, and any security representing the property remains in force, unless the court otherwise orders: CPR 61.12 (as so added).
6  As to arrest see PARA 161 et seq.
7  CPR 61.6(2)(b) (as added: see note 3).
8  CPR 61.6(3) (as added: see note 3).

## (f)  Dealings with Arrested Property

**173. Removal of property under arrest.** If it is necessary for measures to be taken with respect to property which is under arrest pursuant to an Admiralty claim in rem[1], for instance if it is necessary to remove the property to another place than that at which it was arrested, or for cargo to be unloaded from a ship under arrest, the Admiralty Marshal[2] or other interested party must apply to the court for directions[3]. The need for such an order is often avoided by the issue of an 'omnibus' order by the Admiralty Registrar[4] at the time of the arrest, which normally sets out various measures with respect to the custody of the ship[5]. The Admiralty Marshal will not insure property under arrest for the benefit of parties at any time during the period of arrest (whether before or after the lodging of an application for sale, if any)[6].

Where a ship is not under arrest (but cargo on board her is) or where a ship is under arrest (but cargo on board her is not), and persons interested in the ship or cargo wish to discharge the cargo, they may, without being made parties to the proceedings, request the Admiralty Marshal to authorise steps to discharge the cargo[7]. If the Admiralty Marshal considers such a request reasonable, and if the applicant gives an undertaking in writing acceptable to the Admiralty Marshal to pay his fees, and to pay all expenses to be incurred by him or on his behalf, on demand, the Admiralty Marshal will apply to the court for an order to permit the discharge of the cargo[8]. Where those persons interested in the ship or cargo are unable or unwilling to give such an undertaking, they may be made parties to the claim, and they may apply to the court for an order for discharge of the cargo and for directions as to the fees and expenses of the Admiralty Marshal with regard to the discharge and storage of the cargo[9].

1  As to Admiralty claims in rem see PARA 158 et seq; and as to arrest see PARA 161 et seq. As to the procedure that governs Admiralty claims, including CPR Pt 61 and *Practice Direction—Admiralty Claims* PD 61, see PARAS 140 note 5. As to the meanings of 'Admiralty claim' and 'Admiralty Court' for these purposes see PARA 91 note 3. As to the assignment of business to the Admiralty Court see CPR 61.2(1), (2); and PARA 91.
2  As to the Admiralty Marshal see PARA 160 note 6.
3  See CPR 61.5(9); and PARA 164. As to payment of dock dues by the Admiralty Marshal see *The Queen of the South* [1968] P 449, [1968] 1 All ER 1163, [1968] 1 Lloyd's Rep 182; *The Freightline One* [1986] 1 Lloyd's Rep 266. The same procedure will apply in respect of light dues but not in respect of mooring charges: see *R v Carrick District Council, ex p Prankerd, The Winnie Rigg* [1999] QB 1119, [1998] 2 Lloyd's Rep 675.
4  As to the Admiralty Registrar see PARA 140.
5  See *Practice Direction—Admiralty Claims* PD 61 para 5.6; and PARA 164. When property is arrested, the Admiralty Registrar will issue standard directions in Form ADM10 (Standard Directions to the Admiralty Marshal): see *Practice Direction—Admiralty Claims* PD 61 para 5.6; and PARA 164.
6  See *Practice Direction—Admiralty Claims* PD 61 para 5.7; and Admiralty and Commercial Courts Guide (2016) para N13.1. As to sale see PARA 178. The Admiralty Marshal will, however, use his best endeavours (but without any legal liability for failure to do so) to advise all parties known to him as being on the record in claims in rem against the arrested property, including those who have filed cautions against the release of that property, before any such property moves or is moved beyond the area covered by the usual port risks policy: Admiralty and Commercial Courts Guide

(2016) para N13.2. The usual port risks policy provides, among other things, for a ship to be moved or towed from one berth to another up to a distance of 5 miles within the port where she is lying: Admiralty and Commercial Courts Guide (2016) para N13.3. The Guide also draws the attention of practitioners to the necessity of considering questions of insuring against port risks for the amount of their clients' interest in any property arrested in an Admiralty claim and the inclusion in any policy of a 'Held Covered' clause in case the ship moves or is moved outside the area covered by the usual port risks policy: see the Admiralty and Commercial Courts Guide (2016) para N13.3. As to the Admiralty and Commercial Courts Guide see PARAS 91 note 3, 157 note 1.

7   CPR 61.8(8). There is a general principle that cargo owners must pay for the removal of their own cargo from an arrested ship and that such cost should not be met from the sale of the ship by the Admiralty Marshal: *The Jogoo* [1981] 3 All ER 634, [1981] 1 WLR 1376, [1981] 1 Lloyd's Rep 513.
8   CPR 61.8(9).
9   CPR 61.8(10). For an order for renewal under the court's inherent jurisdiction to prevent hardship see *The Mardina Merchant* [1974] 3 All ER 749, [1954] 1 WLR 147; *Kleinwort Benson Ltd v Sherakte Sahami Sakht, The Myrto (No 2)* [1984] 2 Lloyd's Rep 341.

## 174. Release where there is a caution against release or payment out.

Any person who claims to have an in rem[1] right against any property under arrest pursuant to an Admiralty claim in rem[2], and who wishes to be given notice of any application to the court in respect of that property or its proceeds of sale[3], may file a request for a caution against release[4]. When such a request is filed, a caution against release will be entered in the Register[5].

A search for cautions must be made before a release is issued[6] and, if there is a caution in force, release may not be issued unless at the time of the issue of the release the property is sold by the Admiralty Court, or unless the court orders release[7].

Where the release of any property under arrest is delayed by the entry of a caution against release[8], any person having an interest in the property may apply for an order requiring the person who entered the caution to pay damages for losses suffered by the applicant because of the delay[9]. However, the court may not make such an order if it is satisfied that there was good reason both to request the entry of, and to maintain, the caution[10]. An objection to the sufficiency of security[11] which afterwards was shown to be groundless has been held not to be a sufficient reason for entering a caution against release[12].

1   As to Admiralty claims in rem see PARA 158 et seq. As to the procedure that governs Admiralty claims, including CPR Pt 61 and *Practice Direction—Admiralty Claims* PD 61, see PARAS 140 note 5. As to the meanings of 'Admiralty claim' and 'Admiralty Court' for these purposes see PARA 91 note 3. As to the assignment of business to the Admiralty Court see CPR 61.2(1), (2); and PARA 91.
2   As to arrest see PARA 161 et seq.
3   As to sale see PARA 178.
4   CPR 61.8(2). The request for a caution against release must be in the form set out in the practice direction (ie *Practice Direction—Admiralty Claims* PD 61: see note 1): see CPR 61.8(2). Accordingly, the request for a caution against release must be in Form ADM11 (Request for caution against release): *Practice Direction—Admiralty Claims* PD 61 para 7.1. As to the filing of documents in the Admiralty and Commercial Registry, and as to the Admiralty and Commercial Registry itself, see PARA 142. As to the procedure to be followed when a request for a caution against release must be filed but the Registry is closed see the Admiralty and Commercial Courts Guide (2016) para N7.4–7.10. As to the Admiralty and Commercial Courts Guide generally see PARAS 91 note 3, 157 note 1.
5   CPR 61.8(3); *Practice Direction—Admiralty Claims* PD 61 para 7.2. As to the meaning of 'Register' for these purposes see PARA 161 note 7. The Register is open for inspection when the Admiralty and Commercial Registry is open: *Practice Direction—Admiralty Claims* PD 61 para 7.3. A caution entered in the Register under CPR 61.8 is known as a 'caution against release' for the purposes of CPR Pt 61: CPR 61.1(2)(h).
6   This is because normally all persons who have entered cautions against release must give consent to any release: see CPR 61.8(4); and PARA 175.
7   See CPR 61.8(4); and PARA 175.
8   Ie under CPR 61.8 (see PARA 164 et seq): see CPR 61.8(5).

9   CPR 61.8(5).
10  CPR 61.8(6).
11  As to the provision of security see PARAS 171–172.
12  *The Don Ricardo* (1880) 5 PD 121.

**175. Obtaining release from arrest.** Property will be released from arrest[1] if:

(1)    it is sold[2] by the Admiralty Court[3];
(2)    the Admiralty Court orders release[4] on an application made by any party[5];
(3)    the arresting party and all persons who have entered cautions against release[6] file a request for release[7]; or
(4)    any party files a request for release[8] (which contains an undertaking to pay the fees of, and all expenses incurred by, the Admiralty Marshal[9]) and that party consents to the release of the arresting party and all persons who have entered cautions against release[10].

Any request for the withdrawal of a caution against release must be in the prescribed form[11].

1    Ie pursuant to an Admiralty claim in rem. As to Admiralty claims in rem see PARA 158 et seq; and as to arrest see PARA 161 et seq. As to the procedure that governs Admiralty claims, including CPR Pt 61 and *Practice Direction—Admiralty Claims* PD 61, see PARA 140 note 5. As to the meanings of 'Admiralty claim' and 'Admiralty Court' for these purposes see PARA 91 note 3. As to the assignment of business to the Admiralty Court see CPR 61.2(1), (2); and PARA 91.
2    As to sale see PARA 178.
3    CPR 61.8(4)(a).
4    The court has a discretion to order release and may consider factors such as the convenience of the parties and the risk of deterioration of the vessel: see *The Gay Tucan* [1968] 3 All ER 819, [1969] 1 WLR 163, [1968] 2 Lloyd's Rep 425. The court may order a release even if there is a caution against release: see PARA 174.
     In *The Golden Trader* [1975] QB 348, [1974] 2 All ER 686, where the proceedings had been stayed under the Arbitration Act 1950 s 4(2) (repealed: see now the Arbitration Act 1996 s 9 (power to stay proceedings brought in breach of an arbitration agreement) (see ARBITRATION vol 2 (2017) PARA 522)), an order for release was made. On the application for the release of a vessel held as security for a claim in arbitration, the court will only order the release on the provision of sufficient security to cover the amount of the claim, plus interest and costs: *The Bazias 3* [1993] QB 673, [1993] 2 All ER 964, CA. In *The Rena K* [1979] QB 377, [1979] 1 All ER 397, an order was made but alternative security had to be provided because the stay was unlikely to be the end of the matter. In *The Tuyuti* [1984] QB 838, [1984] 2 All ER 545, CA, the arrest was continued, as it was shown that any arbitration award made was unlikely to be satisfied.
     Under the Civil Jurisdiction and Judgments Act 1982 s 26 (see PARA 96), the court is at liberty if it thinks it appropriate to order the security to be preserved and made available to meet a judgment in foreign proceedings: *The Nordglimt* [1988] QB 183, [1988] 2 All ER 531, [1987] 2 Lloyd's Rep 470. For cases under the Merchant Shipping Act 1995 s 185, Sch 7 (releases where security previously given) see PARA 176.
5    CPR 61.8(4)(b).
6    As to cautions against release see PARA 174.
7    CPR 61.8(4)(c). The request for release must be in the form set out in the practice direction (ie *Practice Direction—Admiralty Claims* PD 61: see note 1): see CPR 61.8(4)(c). Accordingly, the request for release under CPR 61.8(4)(c) must be in Form ADM12 (Request and undertaking for release): *Practice Direction—Admiralty Claims* PD 61 para 7.4. As to the filing of documents in the Admiralty and Commercial Registry, and as to the Admiralty and Commercial Registry itself, see PARA 142. As to the procedure to be followed in relation to release from arrest when the Registry is closed see the Admiralty and Commercial Courts Guide (2016) paras N11.1–11.4. As to the Admiralty and Commercial Courts Guide generally see PARAS 91 note 3, 157 note 1.
8    Ie in the form set out in *Practice Direction—Admiralty Claims* PD 61: see CPR 61.8(4)(d). Accordingly, the request for release under CPR 61.8(4)(d) must be in Form ADM12 (Request and undertaking for release): *Practice Direction—Admiralty Claims* PD 61 para 7.4. See note 7.
9    See CPR 61.8(4)(d); and Form ADM12 (Request and undertaking for release). As to the Admiralty Marshal see PARA 160 note 6. Where, in CPR 61 or in *Practice Direction—Admiralty Claims* PD 61, any undertaking to the Marshal is required it must be given in writing and to his satisfaction or in accordance with such other arrangements as he may require: *Practice Direction—Admiralty Claims* PD 61 para 14.1. Where any party is dissatisfied with a direction given by the Marshal in this respect he may apply to the Admiralty Registrar for a ruling: *Practice Direction—Admiralty Claims* PD 61 para 14.2. As to the Admiralty Registrar see PARA 140. As to recovery from the

proceeds of sale of sums paid to the Admiralty Marshal by an arresting party see *The Falcon* [1981] 1 Lloyd's Rep 13; *The World Star* [1987] 1 Lloyd's Rep 452.

10 CPR 61.8(4)(d).

11 *Practice Direction—Admiralty Claims* PD 61 para 7.5. Any request for the withdrawal of a caution against release must be in Form ADM12A (Request for withdrawal of caution against release): see *Practice Direction—Admiralty Claims* PD 61 para 7.5.

## 176. Release where security previously given.

Where a ship[1] or other property is arrested[2] within the jurisdiction of any state which is a party to the Convention on Limitation of Liability for Maritime Claims[3], and a limitation fund has been constituted[4] by the person alleged to be liable for the claim in respect of which the arrest is made, or security has been given to prevent, or obtain release from, arrest, the court or other competent authority of such state may order release of the ship or other property[5]. Such release must be ordered if the limitation fund has been constituted:

(1)      at the port where the occurrence took place, or if it took place out of port, at the first port of call thereafter[6];

(2)      in respect of claims for loss of life or personal injury at the port of disembarkation[7];

(3)      in respect of damage to cargo at the port of discharge[8]; or

(4)      in the state where the arrest is made[9].

Where a release is so ordered, the applicant is deemed to have submitted to the jurisdiction of the court to adjudicate on the claim for which the ship or property was arrested[10].

Where a limitation fund has been constituted, any person having made a claim against the fund is barred from exercising any right in respect of such a claim against any other assets of a person by or on whose behalf the fund has been constituted[11].

The above rules apply only if the claimant may bring a claim against the limitation fund before the court administering that fund and the fund is actually available and freely transferable in respect of that claim[12].

1    As to the meaning of 'ship' for these purposes see PARA 229.

2    Ie pursuant to an Admiralty claim in rem. As to Admiralty claims in rem see PARA 158 et seq; and as to arrest see PARA 161 et seq. As to the procedure that governs Admiralty claims, including CPR Pt 61 and *Practice Direction—Admiralty Claims* PD 61, see PARA 140 note 5. As to the meanings of 'Admiralty claim' and 'Admiralty Court' for these purposes see PARA 91 note 3. As to the assignment of business to the Admiralty Court see CPR 61.2(1), (2); and PARA 91.

3    Ie the Convention on Limitation of Liability for Maritime Claims (London, 1 to 19 November 1976; Misc 31 (1978); Cmnd 7035), implemented by the Merchant Shipping Act 1979 s 17, Sch 4 (repealed) (see now the Merchant Shipping Act 1995 s 185(1), Sch 7 Pt I; and PARA 992 et seq). An Order in Council made for the purposes of Sch 7 Pt II para 13 and declaring that any state specified in the Order is a party to the Convention on Limitation of Liability for Maritime Claims is, subject to the provisions of any subsequent Order made for those purposes, conclusive evidence that the state is a party to the Convention (Merchant Shipping Act 1995 Sch 7 Pt II para 13 (substituted by SI 1998/1258)); at the date at which this volume states the law no such Order had effect.

4    Ie pursuant to the Merchant Shipping Act 1995 Sch 7 Pt I art 11 (as to which see PARA 1003): see Sch 7 Pt I art 13 para 2; and PARA 1005.

5    See the Merchant Shipping Act 1995 Sch 7 Pt I art 13 para 2; and PARA 1005. The power of the court is discretionary, but should be exercised unless there are substantial reasons to the contrary: *The Putbus* [1969] P 136 at 151, [1969] 2 All ER 676 at 680, [1969] 1 Lloyd's Rep 253 at 257, CA, per Lord Denning MR. It has been suggested that this power does not apply until a limitation decree is actually granted: *Bouygues Offshore SA v Caspian Shipping Co (Nos 1, 3, 4 and 5)* [1998] 2 Lloyd's Rep 461 at 473, CA, obiter per Sir John Knox. However, see *The Bowbelle* [1990] 3 All ER 476, [1990] 1 WLR 1330. As to limitation decrees see PARA 198 et seq.

6    See the Merchant Shipping Act 1995 Sch 7 Pt I art 13 para 2(a); and PARA 1005.

7    See the Merchant Shipping Act 1995 Sch 7 Pt I art 13 para 2(b); and PARA 1005.

8    See the Merchant Shipping Act 1995 Sch 7 Pt I art 13 para 2(c); and PARA 1005.

9    See the Merchant Shipping Act 1995 Sch 7 Pt I art 13 para 2(d); and PARA 1005.

10 See the Merchant Shipping Act 1995 Sch 7 Pt II para 10; and PARA 1005.

11 See the Merchant Shipping Act 1995 Sch 7 Pt I art 13 para 1; and PARA 1005.
12 See the Merchant Shipping Act 1995 Sch 7 Pt I art 13 para 3; and PARA 1005.

**177. Statement of value and appraisement.** In cases where the value of the arrested property is important[1], the value of the property should be agreed or a statement of value obtained from a relevant person before release[2]. If it is not possible to agree the value or to obtain such a statement, an application for the property's appraisement may be made to the court[3]. Without previous challenge, the statement normally cannot be contradicted by evidence at the hearing, nor is the deponent allowed to be cross-examined on it[4]. If the claimant considers the stated value to be incorrect, his proper course is to enter a caution against release[5] and obtain an order from the judge or the Admiralty Registrar for an appraisement by the Admiralty Marshal to ascertain the correct value[6]. Normally, an appraisement by the Admiralty Marshal or his substitute is conclusive[7], but if there appear to be special reasons for so doing, the judge may direct a further appraisement or may himself vary the appraised value at the hearing[8]. The costs of the appraisement are in the discretion of the court, but where the appraised value is considerably more than the value given in the statement of value, the costs of the appraisement are usually ordered to be borne by the defendants[9].

1 Eg where cargo has been arrested for freight only, and in salvage claims. As to arrest see PARA 161 et seq; and as to the extent of Admiralty jurisdiction regarding salvage claims see PARA 113 et seq.
2 The statement should not be made on information and belief, but by a person having actual knowledge of the value: see *The Orangemoor* (1915) 31 TLR 190.
3 An application for an order for the appraisement of a ship may be made in a claim in rem at any stage by any party: see CPR 61.10(1); and PARA 178.
4 *The Hanna* (1877) 3 Asp MLC 505. A bona fide mistake can, however, be rectified even after decree: *The James Armstrong* (1875) LR 4 A & E 380, 3 Asp MLC 46.
5 As to cautions against release see PARA 174.
6 As to the Admiralty Marshal see PARA 160 note 6; and as to the Admiralty Registrar see PARA 140. An order for appraisement, as opposed to an order for appraisement and sale (as to which see PARA 178 et seq), is rare; in practice, values are agreed between the solicitors for the parties without the need for an order for appraisement or even a statement of value. In *The Gay Tucan* [1968] 3 All ER 819, [1969] 1 WLR 163, [1968] 2 Lloyd's Rep 245, however, the release of a yacht was ordered in a possession action subject to bail being given for the value which was to be determined by appraisement.
7 *The San Onofre* [1917] P 96 (where it was held that the Marshal's valuation, based on the ship's market value, was properly reached, the contractual relations between owners and charterers being immaterial for purposes of appraisement); but see *The Castor* [1932] P 142, where it was held that the earning power under a charterparty should be taken into account.
8 *The Venus (cargo ex)* (1866) LR 1 A & E 50; *The Georg* [1894] P 330; *The Hohenzollern* [1906] P 339; and see *The Castor* [1932] P 142.
9 *The Paul* (1866) LR 1 A & E 57.

(g) Survey, Appraisement or Sale of Ship subject to a Claim in rem

**178. Appraisement and sale of ship by court.** An application for an order for the survey, appraisement or sale of a ship may be made in a claim in rem[1] at any stage by any party[2]. If the court makes an order for sale[3], it may set a time within which notice of claims against the proceeds of sale must be filed and the time and manner in which such notice must be advertised[4]. Any party with a judgment against the property or proceeds of sale may at any time after such a time[5] apply to the court for the determination of priorities[6]. Unless the Admiralty judge orders otherwise, a determination of priorities may only be made by the Admiralty judge[7].

Any application to the court concerning either the sale of the property under arrest or the proceeds of sale of property sold by the court must be heard in public and the application notice must be served on all parties to the claim, all persons who have requested cautions against release[8] with regard to the property or the proceeds of sale, and the Admiralty Marshal[9].

Payment out of the proceeds of sale will be made only to judgment creditors and either in accordance with the determination of priorities or as the court orders[10]. So long as a fund remains in court, it is the court's duty to see that it is paid to the proper recipients; thus an order for priorities may be varied at any time before payment out, on application by an interested party[11]. Payment out may nevertheless be ordered, even if other claimants are known to exist, if they have delayed excessively in establishing their claims[12].

1   As to Admiralty claims in rem see PARA 158 et seq; and as to arrest see PARA 161 et seq. As to the procedure that governs Admiralty claims, including CPR Pt 61 and *Practice Direction—Admiralty Claims* PD 61, see PARA 140 note 5. In some circumstances a private sale may be allowed: see *Bank of Scotland Plc v The Owners of the M/V Union Gold* [2013] EWHC 1396 (Admlty), [2013] 2 Lloyd's Rep 596. In connection with preliminary sale see *The Star Viking* [2015] NIQB 70. As to the meanings of 'Admiralty claim' and 'Admiralty Court' for these purposes see PARA 91 note 3. As to the assignment of business to the Admiralty Court see CPR 61.2(1), (2); and PARA 91.

2   CPR 61.10(1). See *The Kathleen* (1874) LR 4 A & E 269 at 271; *The Hercules* (1885) 11 PD 10; *The Westport* [1965] 2 All ER 167, [1965] 1 WLR 796, [1965] 1 Lloyd's Rep 547. See also *The Myrto* [1977] 2 Lloyd's Rep 243 (order made owing to the expense of a prolonged arrest); and *Hobbs, Savill & Co Ltd v The Vasilia (Owners), Albaran Bay Corpn* [1972] 1 Lloyd's Rep 51 (permission was given to mortgagees to pay the master and crew for repatriation to enable the sale of the ship). As to liability for costs of discharging cargo not subject to order for sale see *The Myrto* [1978] 1 Lloyd's Rep 11, CA; *The Jogoo* [1981] 3 All ER 634, [1981] 1 WLR 1376, [1981] 1 Lloyd's Rep 513; *The Myrto (No 2)* [1984] 2 Lloyd's Rep 341. As to statements of value that may be agreed before release see PARA 177.

3   Unless the court orders otherwise, an order for sale must be in Form ADM14 (Order for sale of a ship): *Practice Direction—Admiralty Claims* PD 61 para 9.2. An order for sale before judgment may only be made by the Admiralty judge: *Practice Direction—Admiralty Claims* PD 61 para 9.3. As to Admiralty judges see PARA 140.

    The Admiralty Marshal may choose one or more experienced persons to appraise the vessel and certify its true value in writing: see Form ADM14 para (2). He must sell the vessel for the highest price that can be obtained for it but he must not sell for less than the certified appraised value without an order of court: see Form ADM14 para (3). On completion of the sale the Marshal must pay the proceeds of sale into court and must countersign and file a certificate of value together with an account of his fees and expenses: see Form ADM14 paras (4), (5). Permission of the court should be obtained if any unusual item of expenditure is to be charged: see *The Westport (No 2)* [1965] 2 All ER 447, [1965] 1 WLR 871 (repairs needed to put ship in working order); *The Queen of the South* [1968] P 449, [1968] 1 All ER 1163, [1968] 1 Lloyd's Rep 182 (dock dues). As to payment of fees for a survey carried out by a classification society see *The Honshu Gloria* [1986] 2 Lloyd's Rep 63. As to the Admiralty Marshal see PARA 160 note 6.

    The Admiralty Marshal may, if he thinks fit, offer for sale and sell the property for a price in a foreign currency: *The Halcyon the Great* [1975] 1 All ER 882, [1975] 1 WLR 515. When proceeds of sale are paid into court by the Admiralty Marshal, and such proceeds are in a foreign currency, the funds must be placed on one day call interest bearing account unless the court orders otherwise: *Practice Direction—Admiralty Claims* PD 61 para 9.5. Unless made at the same time as an application for sale (or other prior application) an application to place foreign currency on longer term deposit may be made to the Admiralty Registrar: *Practice Direction—Admiralty Claims* PD 61 para 9.6. Notice of the placement of foreign currency in an interest bearing account must be given to all parties interested in the fund by the party who made the application under para 9.6: *Practice Direction—Admiralty Claims* PD 61 para 9.7. Any interested party who wishes to object to the mode of investment of foreign currency paid into court may apply to the Registrar for directions: *Practice Direction—Admiralty Claims* PD 61 para 9.8. As to the Admiralty Registrar see PARA 140.

4   CPR 61.10(2). As to the filing of documents with the Admiralty and Commercial Registry see PARA 142. All claims against the property are transferred to the fund in court: see *The Queen of the South* [1968] P 449, [1968] 1 All ER 1163, [1968] 1 Lloyd's Rep 182. It seems, however, that this cannot apply to a dock authority's statutory right of retention for dock dues: *The Emilie Millon* [1905] 2 KB 817, CA; *The Queen of the South*. See also *The Freightline One* [1986] 1 Lloyd's Rep 266.

5   Ie the time referred to in CPR 61.10(2) (see the text and notes 3–4): see CPR 61.10(3).

6   CPR 61.10(3). An application notice under CPR 61.10(3) must be served on all persons who have filed a claim against the property: CPR 61.10(4). In cases in which property has been arrested or there is a fund in court, it is usual for any judgment in favour of a claimant to be expressed to be

without prejudice to other claims against the vessel, and reserving all questions as to the priority of such claims: see *The Africano* [1894] P 141 at 150 per Sir Francis H Jeune. The application to the court for the determination of priorities may be dealt with at the same time as an application for payment out: *The Westport (No 4)* [1968] 2 Lloyd's Rep 559. As to claims which the claimant is entitled to bring in priority to all other claims on the fund see *The World Star* [1987] 1 Lloyd's Rep 452. See also *The Jogoo* [1981] 3 All ER 634, [1981] 1 WLR 1376, [1981] 1 Lloyd's Rep 513. As to priority between master and crew see *The Royal Wells* [1985] QB 86, [1984] 3 All ER 193, [1984] 2 Lloyd's Rep 255. As to subrogation of the mortgagees to the rights and priorities of the crew see *The Berostar* [1970] 2 Lloyd's Rep 403; *Hobbs, Savill & Co Ltd v The Vasilia (Owners), Albaran Bay Corpn* [1972] 1 Lloyd's Rep 51. As to recovery of the costs of the arrest as a first priority charge see *The Falcon* [1981] 1 Lloyd's Rep 13.

7   *Practice Direction—Admiralty Claims* PD 61 para 9.4.
8   As to the entry of a caution against arrest see PARA 166.
9   *Practice Direction—Admiralty Claims* PD 61 para 9.1.
10   CPR 61.10(5).
11   *The Fairport (No 4)* [1967] 2 All ER 914n, [1967] 1 WLR 964, [1967] 1 Lloyd's Rep 602.
12   *The Leoborg (No 2)* [1963] 2 Lloyd's Rep 268 and 441.


(h)   Claims in rem etc against the Crown

**179.   Proceedings against the Crown.** Nothing in the Crown Proceedings Act 1947[1] authorises proceedings in rem[2] in respect of any claim against the Crown, or the arrest[3], detention or sale of any of Her Majesty's ships or aircraft[4], or of any cargo or other property belonging to the Crown[5]. Nor does anything in the Crown Proceedings Act 1947 give to any person any lien on such ships, aircraft, cargo or property[6].

Where proceedings in rem have been instituted in the High Court or in the county court against any such ship, aircraft, cargo or other property, the court may, if satisfied, either on an application by the claimant or an application by the Crown, that the proceedings were so instituted by the claimant in the reasonable belief that the ship, aircraft, cargo or other property did not belong to the Crown, order that the proceedings be treated as if they were in personam duly instituted against the Crown in accordance with the Crown Proceedings Act 1947, or duly instituted against any other person whom the court regards as the proper person to be sued in the circumstances, and that the proceedings must continue accordingly[7].

1   As to the Crown Proceedings Act 1947 generally see CONSTITUTIONAL AND ADMINISTRATIVE LAW vol 20 (2014) PARA 191; and CROWN AND CROWN PROCEEDINGS vol 29 (2014) PARA 85 et seq.
2   As to Admiralty claims in rem see PARA 158 et seq.
3   As to arrest see PARA 161 et seq.
4   As to the meanings of 'Her Majesty's ships' and 'Her Majesty's aircraft' see the Crown Proceedings Act 1947 s 38; and CROWN AND CROWN PROCEEDINGS vol 29 (2014) PARA 86.
5   Crown Proceedings Act 1947 s 29(1). See also the Senior Courts Act 1981 s 24(2)(c); and PARA 85.
6   Crown Proceedings Act 1947 s 29(1). As to maritime liens generally see PARA 964 et seq.
7   Crown Proceedings Act 1947 s 29(2) (amended by the Crime and Courts Act 2013 Sch 9 para 20). Such an order as is mentioned in the text may be on such terms as the court thinks just, and such consequential orders may be made as the court thinks expedient: Crown Proceedings Act 1947 s 29(2). As to Admiralty claims in personam ('other claims') generally see PARA 186 et seq.


(B)   *Commencement of Collision Claims*


(a)   The Claim Form and Service

**180.   Jurisdiction of the court in relation to a collision claim.** The Admiralty jurisdiction of the High Court[1] includes jurisdiction in relation to any action to enforce a claim for damage, loss of life or personal injury arising out of[2]:

(1)     a collision between ships[3]; or
(2)     the carrying out of or omission to carry out a manoeuvre in the case of one or more of two or more ships[4]; or
(3)     non-compliance, on the part of one or more of two or more ships, with the collision regulations[5].

The court is specifically precluded by statute from entertaining any claim in personam[6] under heads (1) to (3) above unless some connection can be established between the claim and England or Wales[7] and unless any foreign proceedings previously brought by the claimant against the defendant in respect of the same incident or series of incidents have been discontinued or otherwise come to an end[8].

A party who wishes to dispute the court's jurisdiction in any claim under heads (1) to (3) above (a 'collision claim')[9] must make an application[10] within two months after filing his acknowledgment of service[11].

1   As to the Admiralty jurisdiction of the High Court of Justice generally see PARA 85 et seq. As to the mode of exercise of this jurisdiction see the Senior Courts Act 1981 s 21; and PARAS 93–94. The Admiralty jurisdiction of the High Court extends also to hovercraft: see PARA 87.
2   Senior Courts Act 1981 s 20(1)(b), (3)(b). As to the procedure that governs Admiralty claims, including CPR Pt 61 and *Practice Direction—Admiralty Claims* PD 61, see PARAS 140 note 5. As to the meanings of 'Admiralty claim' and 'Admiralty Court' for these purposes see PARA 91 note 3. As to the assignment of business to the Admiralty Court see CPR 61.2(1), (2); and PARA 91.
3   Senior Courts Act 1981 s 20(1)(b), (3)(b)(i). As to the meaning of 'ship' for these purposes see PARA 85 note 7.
4   Senior Courts Act 1981 s 20(1)(b), (3)(b)(ii).
5   Senior Courts Act 1981 s 20(1)(b), (3)(b)(iii). As to the meaning of 'collision regulations' for these purposes see PARA 94 note 7.
6   Claims in personam are now referred to as 'other claims': see *Practice Direction—Admiralty Claims* PD 61 para 12.1; and PARA 186 et seq. As to the origin of claims in personam see PARA 84; and as to claims in personam generally see PARA 92 et seq.
7   As to the meanings of 'England' and 'Wales' see PARA 16 note 2.
8   See the Senior Courts Act 1981 s 22(1), (3); and PARA 94.
9   As to the meaning of 'collision claim' for these purposes see PARA 91 note 12. CPR 61.4 applies to collision claims: CPR 61.4(1).
10  Ie under CPR Pt 11 (as to which see CIVIL PROCEDURE vol 11 (2015) PARA 339): see CPR 61.4(4).
11  CPR 61.4(4). As to acknowledgment of service in collision claims see PARA 181.

## 181.   The claim form and acknowledgment of service in collision claims.
A collision claim[1] is begun by issuing a claim form which need not contain or be followed by particulars of claim[2]. However, an acknowledgment of service must be filed[3].

A claim form in a collision claim may not be served out of the jurisdiction unless:
(1)     it is an action in personam to enforce a claim to which the relevant provisions of the Senior Courts Act 1981 apply[4]; or
(2)     the defendant has submitted to (or agreed to submit to) the jurisdiction of the court[5],

and the court gives permission[6]. Where permission to serve a claim form out of the jurisdiction is given, the court will specify the period within which the defendant may file an acknowledgment of service and, where appropriate, a collision statement of case[7].

1   As to the meaning of 'collision claim' for these purposes see PARA 91 note 12. CPR 61.4 applies to collision claims: CPR 61.4(1). As to the procedure that governs Admiralty claims, including CPR Pt 61 and *Practice Direction—Admiralty Claims* PD 61, see PARA 140 note 5. As to the meanings of 'Admiralty claim' and 'Admiralty Court' for these purposes see PARA 91 note 3. As to the assignment of business to the Admiralty Court see CPR 61.2(1), (2); and PARA 91.

2    CPR 61.4(2). Accordingly, CPR 7.4 (particulars of claim) (see CIVIL PROCEDURE vol 11 (2015) PARA 145) does not apply to collision claims: see CPR 61.4(2). The procedure set out in the Admiralty and Commercial Courts Guide (2016) paras B4.3 (statement of value), B4.7–B4.11 (statement of truth, trial without service, interest), B7.4–B7.6 (applications for extension of time and certificate of service), C1.1–C1.6, C1.8, C2.1(ii)–C5.4 (form, content, serving and filing) apply to collision claims commenced in rem: see para N4.2, N5.1. Where a collision claim is not commenced in rem, the general procedure applicable to claims proceeding in the Commercial List (ie paras B1.1–B13.5) applies: see para N5.2. As to the Admiralty and Commercial Courts Guide see PARAS 91 note 3, 157 note 1.

3    CPR 61.4(3). As to the filing of documents with the Admiralty and Commercial Registry see PARA 142.

4    Ie unless the case falls within the Senior Courts Act 1981 s 22(2)(a)–(c) (as to which see PARA 94): see CPR 61.4(7)(a).

5    CPR 61.4(7)(b).

6    CPR 61.4(7). The court must give permission as mentioned in the text in accordance with CPR Pt 6 Section IV (CPR 6.30–6.47) (as to which see CIVIL PROCEDURE vol 11 (2015) PARA 261 et seq): see CPR 61.4(7). Service of a claim form out of the jurisdiction in a collision claim (other than a claim in rem) is permitted in the circumstances identified in CPR 61.4(7) only and the procedure set out in the Admiralty and Commercial Courts Guide (2016) App 15 (Service out of the jurisdiction: related practice) should be adapted accordingly: Admiralty and Commercial Courts Guide (2016) para N5.3.

7    CPR 61.4(8). As to collision statements of case see PARA 182 et seq. Before the coming into force of CPR Pt 61 (ie before 25 March 2002: see the Civil Procedure (Amendment No 5) Rules 2001, SI 2001/4015, r 1), a collision statement of case was known as a preliminary act and the law relating to preliminary acts continues to apply to collision statements of case: *Practice Direction—Admiralty Claims* PD 61 para 4.5; Admiralty and Commercial Courts Guide (2016) para N5.4. The preparation and filing by the parties of a collision statement of case is a particular feature of a collision action: see the Admiralty and Commercial Courts Guide (2016) para N5.4.

## (b)   Collision Statement of Case

**182. Filing a collision statement of case.** In any collision claim[1], every party must, within two months after the defendant files the acknowledgment of service[2] or (where the defendant makes an application disputing the jurisdiction or the exercise by the court of its jurisdiction)[3] within two months after the defendant files the further acknowledgment of service, file at the court a completed collision statement of case[4]. When he files his collision statement of case, each party must give notice to every other party that he has done so[5]; and, within 14 days after the last collision statement of case is filed, each party must serve a copy of his collision statement of case on every other party[6].

1    Ie except in the case of a collision between a ship and a landing stage: see *The Craighall* [1910] P 207, CA. As to the meaning of 'collision claim' for these purposes see PARA 91 note 12. CPR 61.4 applies to collision claims: CPR 61.4(1). As to the procedure that governs Admiralty claims, including CPR Pt 61 and *Practice Direction—Admiralty Claims* PD 61, see PARA 140 note 5. As to the meanings of 'Admiralty claim' and 'Admiralty Court' for these purposes see PARA 91 note 3. As to the assignment of business to the Admiralty Court see CPR 61.2(1), (2); and PARA 91.

2    As to acknowledgment of service in collision claims see PARA 181.

3    Ie under CPR Pt 11 (as to which see CIVIL PROCEDURE vol 11 (2015) PARA 339): see CPR 61.4(5).

4    CPR 61.4(5). As to the filing of documents in the Admiralty and Commercial Registry see PARA 142. The completed collision statement of case must be in the form specified in the practice direction (ie *Practice Direction—Admiralty Claims* PD 61: see note 1): see CPR 61.4(5). Accordingly, a collision statement of case must be in Form ADM3 (Collision statement of case): *Practice Direction—Admiralty Claims* PD 61 para 4.1. As to the contents required of a collision statement of case see PARA 183. As to the court's discretion, using its general powers of management, to dispense with collision statements of case see PARA 184; and as to the effect of default in filing a collision statement of case see PARA 192.

5    *Practice Direction—Admiralty Claims* PD 61 para 4.3.

6    *Practice Direction—Admiralty Claims* PD 61 para 4.4.

**183. Contents of collision statement of case.** A collision statement of case[1] must be in the required form[2] and be verified by a statement of truth[3].

Accordingly, a collision statement of case must contain answers to the following questions[4]:

(1)    the names of the ships which came into collision and their ports of registry[5];

(2)    the length, breadth, gross tonnage, horsepower and draught at the material time of the ship, and the nature and tonnage of any cargo carried by the ship[6];

(3)    the date and time (including the time zone) of the collision[7];

(4)    the place of the collision[8];

(5)    the direction and force of the wind[9];

(6)    the state of the weather[10];

(7)    the state, direction and force of the tidal or other current[11];

(8)    the position, the course steered and speed through the water of the ship when the other ship was first seen or immediately before any measures were taken with reference to her presence, whichever was the earlier[12];

(9)    the lights or shapes, if any, carried by the ship[13];

(10)   the distance and bearing of the other ship if and when her echo was first observed by radar[14]; and the distance, bearing and approximate heading of the other ship when first seen[15];

(11)   what light or shape or combination of lights or shapes, if any, of the other ship was first seen[16];

(12)   what other lights or shapes or combinations of lights or shapes, if any, of the other ship were subsequently seen before the collision, and when[17];

(13)   what alterations, if any, were made to the course and speed of the ship after the earlier of the two times referred to in head (8) above up to the time of the collision, and when, and what measures, if any, other than alterations of course or speed, were taken to avoid the collision, and when[18];

(14)   the heading of the ship, the parts of each ship which first came into contact and the approximate angle between the two ships at the moment of contact[19];

(15)   what sound signals, if any, were given, and when[20];

(16)   what sound signals, if any, were heard from the other ship, and when[21].

The collision statement of case must also contain a statement of any other facts or matters upon which the party filing the collision statement of case relies, a statement of all allegations of negligence or other fault on which the party filing the collision statement of case relies, and a statement of the remedy which the party filing the collision statement of case claims[22].

1    As to the requirement to file a collision statement of case see PARA 182.

2    Ie in the form set out in the practice direction (ie *Practice Direction—Admiralty Claims* PD 61): see CPR 61.4(6). Accordingly, a collision statement of case must be in Form ADM3 (Collision statement of case) and must contain the answers and statements specified in *Practice Direction—Admiralty Claims* PD 61 para 4.2 (as to which see the text and notes 4–22): see *Practice Direction—Admiralty Claims* PD 61 paras 4.1, 4.2.
     CPR 61.4 applies to collision claims: CPR 61.4(1). As to the procedure that governs Admiralty claims, including CPR Pt 61 and *Practice Direction—Admiralty Claims* PD 61, see PARA 140 note 5. As to the meanings of 'Admiralty claim' and 'Admiralty Court' for these purposes see PARA 91 note 3. As to the assignment of business to the Admiralty Court see CPR 61.2(1), (2); and PARA 91.

3    CPR 61.4(6). Form ADM3 (Collision statement of case) (as to which see note 4) contains a pro forma statement of truth: see Form ADM3 (Collision statement of case). As to statements of truth generally see CPR Pt 22; and CIVIL PROCEDURE vol 11 (2015) PARA 363 et seq.
     A statement of truth in a collision statement of case is a formal admission binding on the party making it and can only be departed from with the special leave of the court: see *The Seacombe, The Devonshire* [1912] P 21 at 59, CA, per Fletcher Moulton LJ; affd [1912] AC 634, HL (but the question of collision statements of case was not considered there). See also *The Lady Belle* [1933]

P 275. Unless leave is given to admit evidence not in accordance with the collision statement of case, the court may hold the party to the statements in the collision statement of case: see *The Semiramis* [1952] 2 Lloyd's Rep 86 at 93.

4  *Practice Direction—Admiralty Claims* PD 61 para 4.2(1). The text refers to questions that are set out in Form ADM3 (Collision statement of case) Pt 1: see *Practice Direction—Admiralty Claims* PD 61 para 4.2(1). Every party is required, so far as it is able, to provide full and complete answers to the questions contained in Form ADM3 (Collision statement of case) Pt 1, and the answers should descend to a reasonable level of particularity: Admiralty and Commercial Courts Guide (2016) para N5.6. If some of the required information is outside the party's knowledge, he must file the best collision statement of case that he can: *The El Oso* (1925) 133 LT 269; *The Graingers No 4* [1964] 3 All ER 705, [1964] 1 WLR 1474, [1964] 2 Lloyd's Rep 415. The answers to the questions contained in Form ADM3 (Collision statement of case) Pt 1 are treated as admissions made by the party answering the questions and leave to amend such answers will be granted only in exceptional circumstances: Admiralty and Commercial Courts Guide (2016) para N5.7. However, a party who files a defective collision statement of case may be ordered to amend it: *The Godiva* (1886) 11 PD 20. As to the principles applicable to the amendment of a collision statement of case see *The Topaz* [2003] EWHC 320 (Admlty) at [13], [2003] 2 Lloyd's Rep 19 at [13] per Gross J; and the Admiralty and Commercial Courts Guide (2016) para N5.7. As to the Admiralty and Commercial Courts Guide generally see PARAS 91 note 3, 157 note 1.

5  *Practice Direction—Admiralty Claims* PD 61 para 4.2(1), Form ADM3 Pt 1 art 1.
6  *Practice Direction—Admiralty Claims* PD 61 para 4.2(1), Form ADM3 Pt 1 art 2.
7  *Practice Direction—Admiralty Claims* PD 61 para 4.2(1), Form ADM3 Pt 1 art 3.
8  *Practice Direction—Admiralty Claims* PD 61 para 4.2(1), Form ADM3 Pt 1 art 4.
9  *Practice Direction—Admiralty Claims* PD 61 para 4.2(1), Form ADM3 Pt 1 art 5.
10 *Practice Direction—Admiralty Claims* PD 61 para 4.2(1), Form ADM3 Pt 1 art 6.
11 *Practice Direction—Admiralty Claims* PD 61 para 4.2(1), Form ADM3 Pt 1 art 7.
12 *Practice Direction—Admiralty Claims* PD 61 para 4.2(1), Form ADM3 Pt 1 art 8. Where a vessel was at anchor, the heading of the vessel should be stated: *The Macroom* (1927) 137 LT 418; *The Erna* (1927) 27 Ll L Rep 170.
13 *Practice Direction—Admiralty Claims* PD 61 para 4.2(1), Form ADM3 Pt 1 art 9.
14 *Practice Direction—Admiralty Claims* PD 61 para 4.2(1), Form ADM3 Pt 1 art 10(a).
15 *Practice Direction—Admiralty Claims* PD 61 para 4.2(1), Form ADM3 Pt 1 art 10(b).
16 *Practice Direction—Admiralty Claims* PD 61 para 4.2(1), Form ADM3 Pt 1 art 11.
17 *Practice Direction—Admiralty Claims* PD 61 para 4.2(1), Form ADM3 Pt 1 art 12. Every change in the combination of lights seen should be mentioned: *The Monica* [1912] P 147.
18 *Practice Direction—Admiralty Claims* PD 61 para 4.2(1), Form ADM3 Pt 1 art 13.
19 *Practice Direction—Admiralty Claims* PD 61 para 4.2(1), Form ADM3 Pt 1 art 14.
20 *Practice Direction—Admiralty Claims* PD 61 para 4.2(1), Form ADM3 Pt 1 art 15.
21 *Practice Direction—Admiralty Claims* PD 61 para 4.2(1), Form ADM3 Pt 1 art 16.
22 *Practice Direction—Admiralty Claims* PD 61 para 4.2(2); Form ADM3 Pt 2. The wording of Form ADM3 Pt 2 varies slightly in that a statement of 'the relief or remedy which the party filing the collision statement of case claims' is specified and a statement must be included to the effect that the information in Form ADM3 (Collision statement of case) Pt 1 is incorporated in Form ADM3 (Collision statement of case) Pt 2: see Form ADM3 (Collision statement of case) Pt 2. The provisions of the Admiralty and Commercial Courts Guide (2016) App 4 (statements of case) apply to Form ADM3 Pt 2 (but not to Form ADM3 Pt 1): Admiralty and Commercial Courts Guide (2016) para N5.5.

### 184. Power of court to dispense with collision statement of case.

The obligation to file a collision statement of case[1] lies not only on parties who are the owners or operators of the colliding vessels, but also upon all other parties involved in collision claims, such as a widow making a fatal accident claim[2] or a dock authority whose acts are alleged to be a cause of the collision[3]. Although, in the exercise of the court's general discretionary power, such other parties may be excused from the obligation[4], the power is one which the court exercises only in exceptional circumstances[5]. The principle of mutuality applies, so that, if one party is excused, other parties will usually not be required to file a collision statement of case[6].

1  As to the requirement to file a collision statement of case see PARA 182.
2  *Webster v Manchester, Sheffield and Lincolnshire Rly Co* [1884] WN 1, 5 Asp MLC 256n. See also *The El Oso* (1925) 133 LT 269 at 271.
3  *The Beaverford* [1960] 3 All ER 612, [1961] 1 WLR 793, [1960] 2 Lloyd's Rep 216.

4   As to the court's general powers of management in this regard see CPR 3.1(2)(m); and CIVIL
    PROCEDURE vol 12 (2015) PARA 507. See also *The John Boyne* (1877) 36 LT 29, 3 Asp MLC
    341; *Armstrong v Gaselee* (1889) 22 QBD 250, 6 Asp MLC 353 (but note the comments on the
    headnote to that case in *The El Oso* (1925) 133 LT 269).
5   *The Beaverford* [1960] 3 All ER 612, [1961] 1 WLR 793, [1960] 2 Lloyd's Rep 216; *The
    Graingers No 4* [1964] 3 All ER 705, [1964] 1 WLR 1474, [1964] 2 Lloyd's Rep 415 (defendant
    who denied that any collision had occurred not excused).
6   *The El Oso* (1925) 133 LT 269; *The Grainger's No 4* [1964] 3 All ER 705, [1964] 1 WLR 1474,
    [1964] 2 Lloyd's Rep 415. A co-defendant in a multiple collision case cannot be compelled to file
    a collision statement of case except at the instance of the claimant, after the claimant has filed his
    act against that defendant: see *The Carlston, The Balcombe* [1926] P 82.

### (c)   Stay of Proceedings in Collision Claims in rem

**185.  Stay of proceedings in collision claims pending security for
counterclaim.** Where, in a collision claim[1] in rem, (the 'original claim'):
(1)     either a Part 20 claim[2], or a cross claim in rem[3] arising out of the same
        collision or occurrence is made[4]; and
(2)     the party bringing the original claim has caused the arrest[5] of a ship or
        has obtained security[6] in order to prevent such arrest[7], and the party
        bringing the Part 20 claim or cross claim is unable to arrest a ship or
        otherwise to obtain security[8],
then the party bringing the Part 20 claim or cross claim may apply to the
Admiralty Court to stay the original claim until sufficient security is given to
satisfy any judgment that may be given in favour of that party[9].

1   As to the meaning of 'collision claim' for these purposes see PARA 91 note 12. CPR 61.4 applies
    to collision claims: CPR 61.4(1). As to the procedure that governs Admiralty claims, including
    CPR Pt 61 and *Practice Direction—Admiralty Claims* PD 61, see PARA 140 note 5. As to the
    meanings of 'Admiralty claim' and 'Admiralty Court' for these purposes see PARA 91 note 3. As
    to the assignment of business to the Admiralty Court see CPR 61.2(1), (2); and PARA 91.
2   CPR 61.4(9)(a)(i). As to 'Part 20 claims' in general see CPR 20.2; and CIVIL PROCEDURE vol 11
    (2015) PARA 367 et seq.
3   CPR 61.4(9)(a)(ii).
4   CPR 61.4(9)(a).
5   As to arrest see PARA 161 et seq.
6   As to the provision of security see PARA 171 et seq.
7   CPR 61.4(9)(b)(i).
8   CPR 61.4(9)(b)(ii).
9   CPR 61.4(9).

### (C)   Commencement of Claims in personam ('Other Claims')

**186.  Admiralty claims in personam to proceed generally in accordance
with Commercial Court practice.** All Admiralty claims in personam[1] proceed
in accordance with the practice and procedure of the Commercial Court[2], except
for certain requirements that are imposed in relation to the claim form[3] and the
filing of a defence[4], and subject to the provisions relating to limitation claims[5] and
to collision claims[6].

1   As to the origin of claims in personam see PARA 84; and as to claims in personam generally see
    PARA 92 et seq. *Practice Direction—Admiralty Claims* PD 61 para 12 ('other claims') applies to
    Admiralty claims which, before the coming into force of CPR Pt 61 (ie before 25 March 2002: see
    the Civil Procedure (Amendment No 5) Rules 2001, SI 2001/4015, r 1), would have been called
    claims in personam: *Practice Direction—Admiralty Claims* PD 61 para 12.1. As to the procedure
    that governs Admiralty claims, including CPR Pt 61 and *Practice Direction—Admiralty Claims* PD
    61, see PARAS 140 note 5. As to the meanings of 'Admiralty claim' and 'Admiralty Court' for these
    purposes see PARA 91 note 3. As to the assignment of business to the Admiralty Court see CPR
    61.2(1), (2); and PARA 91.
2   *Practice Direction—Admiralty Claims* PD 61 para 12.2. Accordingly, an Admiralty claim in
    personam will proceed in accordance with CPR Pt 58 (as to which see CIVIL PROCEDURE vol 11

(2015) PARA 170 et seq): see *Practice Direction—Admiralty Claims* PD 61 para 12.2. See also the Admiralty and Commercial Courts Guide (2016) paras B1–B13, C1–C5.4, N3.1. As to the Admiralty and Commercial Courts Guide see PARAS 91 note 3, 157 note 1.

3  As to which see PARAS 187–188.

4  As to which see PARA 189.

5  Ie subject to the provisions of CPR Pt 61 and *Practice Direction—Admiralty Claims* PD 61 relating to limitation claims (as to which see PARA 194 et seq): see *Practice Direction—Admiralty Claims* PD 61 para 12.1.

6  *Practice Direction—Admiralty Claims* PD 61 para 12.1. The text refers to the provisions relating to collision claims which are contained in CPR Pt 61 and *Practice Direction—Admiralty Claims* PD 61 (as to which see PARA 180 et seq): see *Practice Direction—Admiralty Claims* PD 61 para 12.1.

**187. Service of claim form and acknowledgment of service where claim is in personam.** An Admiralty claim in personam[1] must be in the prescribed form[2]. The claimant may be named or may be described in the claim form, but if not named there he must identify himself by name if requested to do so by any other party[3]. The defendant must also be named in the claim form[4].

An Admiralty claim in personam must be served by the claimant[5]. Service within the jurisdiction[6] is governed by the general rules applicable in other proceedings[7], and acknowledgment of service is given in accordance with the general practice and procedure of the Commercial Court[8].

1  Except for certain requirements that are imposed in relation to the claim form (see also PARA 188) and the filing of a defence (see PARA 189), all Admiralty claims in personam proceed in accordance with the practice and procedure of the Commercial Court: see PARA 186. As to the origin of claims in personam see PARA 84; and as to claims in personam generally see PARA 92 et seq. *Practice Direction—Admiralty Claims* PD 61 para 12 ('other claims') applies to Admiralty claims which, before the coming into force of CPR Pt 61 (ie before 25 March 2002: see the Civil Procedure (Amendment No 5) Rules 2001, SI 2001/4015, r 1), would have been called claims in personam: see *Practice Direction—Admiralty Claims* PD 61 para 12.1; and PARA 186 note 1.

As to the procedure that governs Admiralty claims, including CPR Pt 61 and *Practice Direction—Admiralty Claims* PD 61, see PARA 140 note 5. As to the meanings of 'Admiralty claim' and 'Admiralty Court' for these purposes see PARA 91 note 3. As to the assignment of business to the Admiralty Court see CPR 61.2(1), (2); and PARA 91.

2  *Practice Direction—Admiralty Claims* PD 61 para 12.3. Accordingly, the claim form must be in Form ADM1A (Claim Form (Admiralty claim)): see *Practice Direction—Admiralty Claims* PD 61 para 12.3.

3  *Practice Direction—Admiralty Claims* PD 61 para 12.4.

4  *Practice Direction—Admiralty Claims* PD 61 para 12.5.

5  *Practice Direction—Admiralty Claims* PD 61 para 12.3.

6  As to service out of jurisdiction see PARA 188. Vessels of the Royal Navy are deemed to be within the jurisdiction wherever they may actually be: *Seagrove v Parks* [1891] 1 QB 551, DC.

7  For the rules about service generally see CPR Pt 6; and CIVIL PROCEDURE vol 11 (2015) PARA 244 et seq. The rules in CPR Pt 6 apply to service of documents except where any other enactment, a rule in another Part of the rules or a Practice Direction makes a different provision or where the court orders otherwise: see CPR 6.1; and CIVIL PROCEDURE vol 11 (2015) PARA 244. See also the Admiralty and Commercial Courts Guide (2016) paras B7.1–B7.6, N7.1–7.3. As to the Admiralty and Commercial Courts Guide see PARAS 91 note 3, 157 note 1.

8  See the Admiralty and Commercial Courts Guide (2016) para B9.1–B9.4; and see CPR 58.6 (as to which see CIVIL PROCEDURE vol 11 (2015) PARA 171).

**188. Service out of jurisdiction of claim form where claim is in personam.** The general rules governing service out of the jurisdiction[1] apply equally to Admiralty claims in personam[2].

Before issuing a claim form or seeking permission to serve out of the jurisdiction, it is necessary to consider whether the jurisdiction of the English courts is affected by the Civil Jurisdiction and Judgments Act 1982[3]. Where each claim in the claim form is a claim which the Court has by virtue of the Civil Jurisdiction and Judgments Act 1982 power to hear and determine, service of the claim form out of the jurisdiction may be effected without permission provided that the procedural requirements are satisfied[4] and provided that the claim form is endorsed before issue with a statement that the court has power under the Act to hear and determine the claim against the defendant, and that no proceedings involving the same claim are pending between the parties in Scotland, Northern Ireland or another contracting or Regulation state[5].

In cases where permission is required[6], the general rules as to that mode of service apply[7]. Of most obvious relevance is the rule that permission to serve is required where the claim either is in the nature of salvage (and any part of the services took place within the jurisdiction)[8] or is being made to enforce a claim under the Merchant Shipping Act 1995[9]. However, other rules of relevance in this context relate to cases where the claim is in respect of a tort committed within the jurisdiction[10], where any person outside the jurisdiction is a necessary or proper party to a claim properly brought against some other person duly served within the jurisdiction[11], and where the claim is brought in respect of a contract which was either made within the jurisdiction, or made by or through an agent trading or residing within the jurisdiction, or is by its terms, or by implication, governed by English law[12]. Where the applicant fails to show that his claim has a reasonable prospect of success, permission will not be granted for service out of the jurisdiction against another party; where there is a substantial question of fact in issue permission should be given; and where there is an exceptionally difficult and doubtful point of law permission may be given[13].

1   Ie CPR 6.17–31: see CIVIL PROCEDURE vol 11 (2015) PARAS 263, 265 et seq. See also *Practice Direction—Service out of the Jurisdiction* (2001) PD 6B; and Council Regulation (EC) 1393/2007 (OJ L324, 10.12.2007, p 79), the text of which is annexed thereto.

2   See the Admiralty and Commercial Courts Guide (2016) para B8.1–B8.3, App 15. Acknowledgment of service is given in accordance with the general practice and procedure of the Commercial Court: see the Admiralty and Commercial Courts Guide (2016) para B9; and CPR 58.6 (as to which see CIVIL PROCEDURE vol 11 (2015) PARA 171). As to the Admiralty and Commercial Courts Guide see PARAS 91 note 3, 157 note 1.

     Except for certain requirements that are imposed in relation to the claim form (see also PARA 187) and the filing of a defence (see PARA 189), all Admiralty claims in personam proceed in accordance with the practice and procedure of the Commercial Court: see PARA 186. As to the origin of claims in personam see PARA 84; and as to claims in personam generally see PARA 92 et seq. *Practice Direction—Admiralty Claims* PD 61 para 12 ('other claims') applies to Admiralty claims which, before the coming into force of CPR Pt 61 (ie before 25 March 2002: see the Civil Procedure (Amendment No 5) Rules 2001, SI 2001/4015, r 1), would have been called claims in personam: see *Practice Direction—Admiralty Claims* PD 61 para 12.1; and PARA 186 note 1. As to the procedure that governs Admiralty claims, including CPR Pt 61 and *Practice Direction—Admiralty Claims* PD 61, see PARA 140 note 5. As to the meanings of 'Admiralty claim' and 'Admiralty Court' for these purposes see PARA 91 note 3. As to the assignment of business to the Admiralty Court see CPR 61.2(1), (2); and PARA 91.

3   As to cases under the Civil Jurisdiction and Judgments Act 1982 see PARAS 96–99.

4   Ie the requirements of CPR 6.19: see CIVIL PROCEDURE vol 11 (2015) PARAS 265, 266.

5   See the Admiralty and Commercial Courts Guide (2016) App 15 para 1. As to the meanings of 'contracting state' and 'Regulation state' see CONFLICT OF LAWS vol 19 (2011) PARA 366.

6   Ie where cases fall within CPR 6.20: see CIVIL PROCEDURE vol 11 (2015) PARA 267.

7   See CPR 6.20; and CIVIL PROCEDURE vol 11 (2015) PARA 267.

8   As to salvage claims generally see PARAS 113 et seq, 849 et seq.

9   See *Practice Direction—Service out of the Jurisdiction* (2001) PD 6B para 3.1(19); and CIVIL PROCEDURE vol 11 (2015) PARAS 267, 285. The text refers to enforcement of a claim under the Merchant Shipping Act 1995 s 153, s 154 or s 175 (oil pollution) (see ENVIRONMENTAL QUALITY AND PUBLIC HEALTH vol 45 (2010) PARAS 443–444): see *Practice Direction—Service out of the Jurisdiction* (2001) PD 6B para 3.1(19)(b); and CIVIL PROCEDURE vol 11 (2015) PARA 285.

10   See *Practice Direction—Service out of the Jurisdiction* (2001) PD 6B para 3.1(9); and CIVIL PROCEDURE vol 11 (2015) PARAS 267, 274.

11   See *Practice Direction—Service out of the Jurisdiction* (2001) PD 6B para 3.1(3); and CIVIL PROCEDURE vol 11 (2015) PARAS 267, 270.

12 See *Practice Direction—Service out of the Jurisdiction* (2001) PD 6B para 3.1(6); and CIVIL PROCEDURE vol 11 (2015) PARAS 267, 273.
13 *The Brabo* [1949] AC 326, [1949] 1 All ER 294, HL.

C.    PROCEDURE FOLLOWING SERVICE

(A)    *Particulars of Claim, Defence and Reply*

**189.  Particulars of claim etc.** For the purposes of an Admiralty claim in rem[1], a collision claim[2] and an Admiralty claim in personam[3], the general practice and procedure of the Commercial Court[4] governs:

(1)    the form, content, serving and filing of particulars of claim[5];
(2)    the form, content, serving and filing of a defence[6];
(3)    the form, content, serving and filing of a reply[7]; and
(4)    amendments made to a statement of case[8].

A party may be ordered to supply further information to support any claim[9].

A counterclaim must be raised by a proceeding recognised by the rules of court for the purpose[10], and it follows that unless he arrests the claimant's vessel, a defendant cannot set up a counterclaim before he has received the claimant's statement of case[11].

However, the court may order (either before or after the issue of a claim form) that the case is to proceed without the filing or service of particulars of claim or defence or of any other statement of case[12].

1    As to the origin of claims in rem see PARA 83; as to the jurisdiction of the Admiralty Court in relation to claims in rem see PARA 92 et seq; and as to commencing such a claim see PARA 158 et seq.
2    As to the meaning of 'collision claim' for these purposes see PARA 91 note 12. As to the jurisdiction of the Admiralty Court in relation to collision claims see PARA 180; and as to commencing such a claim see PARA 181 et seq.
3    As to the origin of claims in personam see PARA 84; as to claims in personam generally see PARA 92 et seq; and as to commencing such a claim see PARA 186 et seq.
4    As to the practice and procedure that applies in the Commercial Court, including CPR Pt 58 and *Practice Direction—Commercial Court* PD 58, see CIVIL PROCEDURE vol 11 (2015) PARA 170 et seq. CPR Pt 58 (Commercial Court) applies generally to claims in the Admiralty Court where CPR Pt 61 does not provide otherwise (see CPR 61.1(3); and PARA 91 note 3); and the practice direction which supplements CPR Pt 58 (ie *Practice Direction—Commercial Court* PD 58) also applies to Admiralty claims except where it is inconsistent with either CPR Pt 61 or *Practice Direction—Admiralty Claims* PD 61 (see para 1.1; and PARA 91 note 3). As to the procedure that governs Admiralty claims, including CPR Pt 61 and *Practice Direction—Admiralty Claims* PD 61, see PARA 140 note 5. As to the meanings of 'Admiralty claim' and 'Admiralty Court' for these purposes see PARA 91 note 3. As to the assignment of business to the Admiralty Court see CPR 61.2(1), (2); and PARA 91.
5    See the Admiralty and Commercial Courts Guide (2016) paras C1–C2; and see further paras N3.1, N4.2–4.3, N5.1). As to the Admiralty and Commercial Courts Guide see PARAS 91 note 3, 157 note 1. As to the filing of documents with the Admiralty and Commercial Registry see PARA 142.
6    See the Admiralty and Commercial Courts Guide (2016) paras C1, C3. Any person who files a defence to a claim in personam must identify himself by name in the defence: *Practice Direction—Admiralty Claims* PD 61 para 12.6.
     If a defendant wishes to raise a limitation of liability defence under the Merchant Shipping Act 1995 s 185 (as to which see PARA 195), this ought to be pleaded as a defence when there is only one claim made or apprehended: see *The Mekhanik Evgrafof and Ivan Derbenev (No 2)* [1988] 1 Lloyd's Rep 330. In a salvage claim (as to which see PARA 113 et seq, and generally see PARA 849 et seq) where the defendant admits by his defence the facts alleged in the particulars of claim but challenges the inferences to be drawn from them, the claimant will not be allowed to call evidence as to the facts. The claimant may, however, put in the log of the defendant's vessel in support of the inference that the vessel was in danger: *The Woodarra* (1921) 38 TLR 160; followed in *The Cornish Rose* [1936] P 174, [1936] 2 All ER 805. Notice of intention to tender the log should be given to the other party so that he may be prepared with any other admissible document directed to the same issue: *The Cornish Rose*. See also *The Buteshire* [1909] P 170 (application for leave to put in the defendants' log in similar circumstances was refused); and *The Sandefjord* [1953] 2 Lloyd's Rep 789 (logs were admitted and a pilot who claimed for his personal services was allowed to give evidence).

    The defence of tender before claim is rarely encountered in Admiralty proceedings but see *Davys v Richardson* (1888) 21 QBD 202, CA; and *The Slaney* [1951] 2 Lloyd's Rep 538 at 544–545 per Lord Merriman (tender before action of specified sum due under a towage contract).

7  See the Admiralty and Commercial Courts Guide (2016) paras C1, C4. See also Form ADM1C (Notes for defendant on replying to an admiralty claim form).

8  See the Admiralty and Commercial Courts Guide (2016) para C5. An amendment may introduce a new cause of action, even after a period of limitation has expired, if the court thinks it just to allow the amendment and the new cause of action arises out of the same facts, or substantially the same facts: see CPR 17.4; and CIVIL PROCEDURE vol 11 (2015) PARA 360. For the application of these rules to a salvage case see *The Katcher I* [1969] P 65, [1968] 3 All ER 344, [1968] 1 Lloyd's Rep 232.

9  Parties have been ordered to supply particulars of allegations as to defects in a vessel (*The Rory* (1882) 7 PD 117, CA), negligent navigation (*The Kanawha* (1913) 108 LT 433) and salvage services (*The Isis* (1883) 8 PD 227).

10  *The Gniezno* [1968] P 418, [1967] 2 All ER 738, [1967] 1 Lloyd's Rep 441. See also *The Saxicava* [1924] P 131, CA; *Impex Transport Aktieselskabet v AG Thames Holdings Ltd* [1982] 1 All ER 897, [1981] 1 WLR 1547, [1981] 2 Lloyd's Rep 566. Furthermore, limitation claims may only be brought by way of counterclaim with permission of the Admiralty Court: see PARA 196.

11  A warrant of arrest may be issued in connection with a counterclaim at any time after the claimant's claim form has been issued: see PARA 161. See also *The Gniezno* [1968] P 418, [1967] 2 All ER 738, [1967] 1 Lloyd's Rep 441. The defendant may at any time issue a claim of his own and thus commence a separate cross claim instead of a counterclaim. It is advisable to proceed by cross claim rather than to rely on the counterclaim procedure if the expiry of a time limit is imminent when proceedings are begun: see *The Fairplay XIV* [1939] P 57 at 61, 62 Ll L Rep 108 at 110 per Sir Boyd Merriman.

    Further proceedings on the counterclaim are generally similar to those in the original claim. In certain circumstances, the person bringing the counterclaim may apply to the court to stay the original claim: see CPR 61.4(9); and PARA 185. A defendant in a claim in rem may set up a counterclaim in personam: *The Clutha* (1876) 45 LJP 108; *The Newbattle* (1885) 10 PD 33, CA. The court has refused to strike out a counterclaim as embarrassing, although the claimants were foreigners who could not have been served with a summons, and the counterclaim could, if the claimants had so chosen, have been tried by a jury: *The Cheapside* [1904] P 339, CA. It is thought that this decision is unaffected by the requirements of the Senior Courts Act 1981 ss 20(2), 22 as the commencement of the original claim by the claimant is a submission to the jurisdiction which satisfies s 22(5) (see PARA 94). It appears that a counterclaim may be entertained by the court notwithstanding that it is not within the Admiralty jurisdiction of the High Court, as all jurisdiction vested in the High Court belongs to all the divisions alike: see the Senior Courts Act 1981 s 5(5); and COURTS AND TRIBUNALS vol 24 (2010) PARA 696. See also PARA 91. But note, however, that under the Civil Jurisdiction and Judgments Act 1982 s 2(2), Sch 1 art 6(3), in relation to a claimant domiciled in a contracting or Regulation state, the counterclaim must arise from the same contract or facts on which the original claim was based, in the court in which the original claim is pending (see PARA 96).

12  See the Admiralty and Commercial Courts Guide (2016) para B4.8; and CPR 58.11 (cited in CIVIL PROCEDURE vol 11 (2015) PARA 173), although it is stated therein that the facility described in the text is to be used with caution.

### (B)    Judgment in Default

**190. Judgment in default in claim in rem.** In an Admiralty claim in rem[1] (other than a collision claim)[2] the claimant may obtain judgment in default of:

    (1)     an acknowledgment of service, but only if the defendant has not filed an acknowledgment of service and the time for doing so[3] has expired[4]; and

    (2)     a defence, but only if a defence has not been filed and the relevant time limit for doing so has expired[5].

An application for judgment in default[6] in an in rem claim must be made by filing an application notice[7], a certificate proving service of the claim form, and evidence proving the claim to the satisfaction of the court[8]. An application notice seeking judgment in default and, unless the court orders otherwise, all evidence in support, must be served on all persons who have entered cautions against release on the Register[9].

The Admiralty Court may set aside or vary any judgment entered in pursuance of these provisions[10]. If, on the hearing of the application, the court is satisfied that the claim is well founded, it may give judgment for the claim, with or without a reference to the Admiralty Registrar[11] or district registrar, and may, at the same time, order the property against which the claim is brought to be appraised and sold[12] and the proceeds paid into court, or may make such order as it deems just in the circumstances[13].

The decree in favour of the claimant's claim will usually be made without prejudice to other claims against the property, and reserving all questions as to the priority of such claims[14].

1	As to the origin of claims in rem see PARA 83; as to the jurisdiction of the Admiralty Court in relation to claims in rem see PARA 92 et seq; and as to commencing such a claim see PARA 158 et seq. As to the procedure that governs Admiralty claims, including CPR Pt 61 and *Practice Direction—Admiralty Claims* PD 61, see PARA 140 note 5. As to the meanings of 'Admiralty claim' and 'Admiralty Court' for these purposes see PARA 91 note 3. As to the assignment of business to the Admiralty Court see CPR 61.2(1), (2); and PARA 91.

2	As to the meaning of 'collision claim' for these purposes see PARA 91 note 12. As to judgment in default of filing a collision statement of case see PARA 192.

3	Ie as set out in CPR 61.3(4) (acknowledgment of service) (see PARA 168): see CPR 61.9(1)(a).

4	CPR 61.9(1)(a).

5	CPR 61.9(1)(b). As to the form, content, serving and filing of a defence see PARA 189. In such a case, judgment may be against the defendant personally, as well as against the property (the res): see *The Deichland* [1988] 2 Lloyd's Rep 454.

6	Ie under CPR 61.9(1) (see the text and notes 1–5): see CPR 6.19(3).

7	Ie as set out in the practice direction (*Practice Direction—Admiralty Claims* PD 61: see note 1): see CPR 61.9(3)(a). Accordingly, an application notice for judgment in default must be in Form ADM13 (Application for judgment in default): see CPR 6.19(3); *Practice Direction—Admiralty Claims* PD 61 para 8.1. As to the filing of documents in the Admiralty and Commercial Registry see PARA 142.

8	CPR 61.9(3).

9	CPR 61.9(4). As to the meaning of 'Register' for these purposes see PARA 161 note 7. As to the entry of a caution against arrest see PARA 166.

10	CPR 61.9(5). As to the proper test under CPR 61.9(5) for the setting aside of a judgment in default entered under CPR Pt 61 see *Humber Boat Works Ltd v Owners of MV 'Selby Paradigm'* [2004] EWHC 1804 (Admlty) at [29], [2004] 2 Lloyd's Rep 714 at [29], [2004] All ER (D) 71 (Aug) at [29]. See also *The Gulf Venture* [1986] 1 Lloyd's Rep 130n, where judgment was set aside on application by a party with a direct financial interest in the outcome of the litigation. It is not necessary for the defendant to have acknowledged service of the claim form when applying to set aside a judgment given in default: *The Ruben Martinez Villena* [1987] 2 Lloyd's Rep 621.

11	As to the Admiralty Registrar see PARA 140.

12	As to appraisement and sale see PARA 178.

13	Judgment in this case is against the property only, which will normally be under arrest. For a discussion of whether, in a case where the defendant has not acknowledged service in a claim in rem, the claimant is limited to the value of the property (the res), and has no further rights to issue the ordinary forms of execution see *The Conoco Britannia* [1972] 2 QB 543 at 554–555, [1972] 2 All ER 238 at 245, [1972] 1 Lloyd's Rep 342 at 347 per Brandon J.

14	*The Africano* [1894] P 141 at 150. See also PARA 207.

**191. Judgment against party in claim in rem where notice of arrest has been entered.** The claimant in an Admiralty claim in rem[1] may apply to the court for judgment against a party at whose instance a notice against arrest was entered[2], where:

(1)	the claim form has been served on that party[3];

(2)	the sum claimed in the claim form does not exceed the amount specified in the undertaking[4] given by that party[5]; and

(3)	that party has not fulfilled that undertaking within 14 days after service on him of the claim form[6].

If the court is satisfied that the claim is well founded, it may give judgment for the amount which appears to it to be due, and enforce payment by committal of the party on whose behalf the caution has been entered, and by arrest of the property (if it is at the time, or subsequently comes, within the jurisdiction of the court)[7].

1   As to the origin of claims in rem see PARA 83; as to the jurisdiction of the Admiralty Court in relation to claims in rem see PARA 92 et seq; and as to commencing such a claim see PARA 158 et seq. As to the procedure that governs Admiralty claims, including CPR Pt 61 and *Practice Direction—Admiralty Claims* PD 61, see PARA 140 note 5. As to the meanings of 'Admiralty claim' and 'Admiralty Court' for these purposes see PARA 91 note 3. As to the assignment of business to the Admiralty Court see CPR 61.2(1), (2); and PARA 91.
2   CPR 61.9(6). As to entering a caution against arrest see PARAS 166–167.
3   CPR 61.9(6)(a).
4   Ie the undertaking made in accordance with CPR 61.7(2)(a) (see PARA 166): see CPR 61.9(6)(b).
5   CPR 61.9(6)(b).
6   CPR 61.9(6)(c).
7   It is submitted that the practice described in the text, which was formerly governed by RSC Ord 75 r 21, seems to be observed still, although the rule has been revoked and there is no direct replacement provision in the Civil Procedure Rules.

## 192. Judgment in default of filing a collision statement of case.

In the case of a collision claim[1], a party who has filed a collision statement of case[2] within the time specified[3] may obtain judgment in default of a collision statement of case[4], but only if the party against whom judgment is sought has not filed a collision statement of case[5] and the time for doing so[6] has expired[7].

An application for judgment in default[8] in a collision claim in rem must be made by filing an application notice[9], a certificate proving service of the claim form, and evidence proving the claim to the satisfaction of the court[10]. Any other claim[11] must be made in accordance with the general provisions relating to judgments in default[12] with any necessary modifications[13]. An application notice seeking judgment in default and, unless the court orders otherwise, all evidence in support, must be served on all persons who have entered cautions against release on the Register[14].

The Admiralty Court may set aside or vary any judgment entered in pursuance of these provisions[15].

1   As to the meaning of 'collision claim' for these purposes see PARA 91 note 12. As to judgment in default in claims in rem generally see PARA 190. As to the procedure that governs Admiralty claims, including CPR Pt 61 and *Practice Direction—Admiralty Claims* PD 61, see PARA 140 note 5. As to the meanings of 'Admiralty claim' and 'Admiralty Court' for these purposes see PARA 91 note 3. As to the assignment of business to the Admiralty Court see CPR 61.2(1), (2); and PARA 91.
2   As to collision statements of case see PARA 182 et seq. As to the filing of documents in the Admiralty and Commercial Registry see PARA 142.
3   Ie the time specified by CPR 61.4(5) (see PARA 182): see CPR 61.9(2).
4   CPR 61.9(2).
5   CPR 61.9(2)(a).
6   Ie as set out in CPR 61.4(5) (see PARA 182): see CPR 61.9(2)(b).
7   CPR 61.9(2)(b).
8   Ie under CPR 61.9(2) (see the text and notes 1–7): see CPR 61.9(3).
9   Ie as set out in the practice direction (*Practice Direction—Admiralty Claims* PD 61: see note 1): see CPR 61.9(3)(a). Accordingly, an application notice for judgment in default must be in Form ADM13 (Application for judgment in default): see CPR 6.19(3); *Practice Direction—Admiralty Claims* PD 61 para 8.1.
10  CPR 61.9(3).
11  *Practice Direction—Admiralty Claims* PD 61 para 12 ('other claims') applies to Admiralty claims which, before the coming into force of CPR Pt 61 (ie before 25 March 2002: see the Civil Procedure (Amendment No 5) Rules 2001, SI 2001/4015, r 1), would have been called claims in personam: see *Practice Direction—Admiralty Claims* PD 61 para 12.1; and PARA 186 et seq. As to the conditions to be met by collision claims before they may be made in personam see PARAS 180–181.
12  As to judgments in default generally see CPR Pt 12 (cited in CIVIL PROCEDURE vol 12 (2015) PARA 535 et seq) and CPR 10.2 (cited in CIVIL PROCEDURE vol 11 (2015) PARA 313).

13  CPR 61.9(3)(b).
14  CPR 61.9(4). As to the meaning of 'Register' for these purposes see PARA 161 note 7. As to the
    entry of a caution against arrest see PARA 166. See also the cases cited in PARA 190.
15  CPR 61.9(5). See also the cases cited in PARA 190.

**193. Judgment in default where the claim is made in personam.** All
Admiralty claims in personam[1] proceed in accordance with the practice and
procedure of the Commercial Court[2], except for certain requirements that are
imposed in relation to the claim form[3] and the filing of a defence[4], and subject to
the provisions relating to limitation claims[5] and to collision claims[6]. Accordingly,
the procedure for obtaining judgment in default in such cases is dealt with
elsewhere[7].

1   As to the origin of claims in personam see PARA 84; and as to claims in personam generally see
    PARA 92 et seq. *Practice Direction—Admiralty Claims* PD 61 para 12 ('other claims') applies to
    Admiralty claims which, before the coming into force of CPR Pt 61 (ie before 25 March 2002: see
    the Civil Procedure (Amendment No 5) Rules 2001, SI 2001/4015, r 1), would have been called
    claims in personam: see *Practice Direction—Admiralty Claims* PD 61 para 12.1; and PARA 186.
    As to CPR Pt 61 and *Practice Direction—Admiralty Claims* PD 61 see note 2.
2   See *Practice Direction—Admiralty Claims* PD 61 para 12.2; and PARA 186. Accordingly, an
    Admiralty claim in personam will proceed in accordance with CPR Pt 58 (as to which see CIVIL
    PROCEDURE vol 11 (2015) PARA 170 et seq): see *Practice Direction—Admiralty Claims* PD 61
    para 12.2. See also the Admiralty and Commercial Courts Guide (2016) paras B1–B13, N3.1. As
    to the Admiralty and Commercial Courts Guide see PARAS 91 note 3, 157 note 1. As to the
    procedure that governs Admiralty claims, including CPR Pt 61 and *Practice Direction—Admiralty
    Claims* PD 61, see PARA 140 note 5. As to the assignment of business to the Admiralty Court see
    CPR 61.2(1), (2); and PARA 91.
3   As to which see PARAS 187–188.
4   As to which see PARA 189.
5   Ie subject to the provisions of CPR Pt 61 and *Practice Direction—Admiralty Claims* PD 61 relating
    to limitation claims (as to which see PARA 194 et seq): see *Practice Direction—Admiralty Claims*
    PD 61 para 12.1; and PARA 186.
6   See *Practice Direction—Admiralty Claims* PD 61 para 12.1; and PARA 186. The text refers to the
    provisions relating to collision claims which are contained in CPR Pt 61 and *Practice
    Direction—Admiralty Claims* PD 61 (as to which see PARA 180 et seq): see *Practice
    Direction—Admiralty Claims* PD 61 para 12.1; and PARA 186.
7   Default judgment is governed by CPR Pt 12 and *Practice Direction—Default Judgment* PD 12
    (cited in CIVIL PROCEDURE vol 12 (2015) PARA 535 et seq): see the Admiralty and Commercial
    Courts Guide (2016) para B11. See also CPR 10.2; and CIVIL PROCEDURE vol 11 (2015)
    PARA 313.

### (iv) Limitation Claims

#### A.   RIGHT TO LIMIT LIABILITY

**194. Jurisdiction of the court in relation to limitation claims.** The
Admiralty jurisdiction of the High Court[1] includes jurisdiction in relation to any
action by shipowners or other persons under the Merchant Shipping Act 1995 for
the limitation of the amount of their liability in connection with a ship[2] or other
property[3]. Every claim in the exercise of that right, known as a limitation claim[4],
must be started in the Admiralty Court[5].

Special provisions apply to such claims[6], relating for example to parties,
procedure, and payment into court[7]. The court must distribute among the
claimants[8] the amounts of their established claims, whether or not a limitation
fund[9] has been constituted[10]. The court has power, and in some circumstances an
obligation, to release a ship or property arrested or attached, where a limitation
fund has been constituted[11].

1   As to the Admiralty jurisdiction of the High Court of Justice generally see PARA 85 et seq. As to
    the mode of exercise of this jurisdiction see the Senior Courts Act 1981 s 21; and PARAS 93–94.
    The Admiralty jurisdiction of the High Court extends also to hovercraft: see PARA 87.

2   As to the meaning of 'ship' for these purposes see PARA 85 note 7.
3   Senior Courts Act 1981 s 20(1)(b), (3)(c). The right of limitation under the Merchant Shipping Act
    1995 referred to in the text derives from s 185(1), Sch 7, which implements the Convention on
    Limitation of Liability for Maritime Claims (London, 1 to 19 November 1976; Misc 31 (1978);
    Cmnd 7035) (as to which see PARA 7): see PARAS 195, 992 et seq.
4   As to the meaning of 'limitation claim' for these purposes see PARA 91 note 13.
5   See CPR 61.2(1)(c); and PARA 91. As to the procedure that governs Admiralty claims, including
    CPR Pt 61 and *Practice Direction—Admiralty Claims* PD 61, see PARA 140 note 5. As to the
    meanings of 'Admiralty claim' and 'Admiralty Court' for these purposes see PARA 91 note 3. As
    to the assignment of business to the Admiralty Court see CPR 61.2(1), (2); and PARA 91.
6   The procedure governing the early stages of a limitation claim differs significantly from the
    analogous stages of other claims: see the Admiralty and Commercial Courts Guide (2016) paras
    N3.1, N6.1; and PARA 196. The procedure is contained in CPR 61.11 and *Practice
    Direction—Admiralty Claims* PD 61 para 10 (as to which see PARA 196 et seq): see the Admiralty
    and Commercial Courts Guide (2016) para N6.1. As to the procedure in other Admiralty claims
    see PARA 157 et seq. As to the Admiralty and Commercial Courts Guide see PARAS 91 note 3, 157
    note 1.
7   See CPR 61.11; *Practice Direction—Admiralty Claims* PD 61 para 10; and PARA 196 et seq.
8   The claimants may include the Crown: see *The Zoe* (1886) 11 PD 72.
9   As to the limitation fund see the Merchant Shipping Act 1995 s 185(1), Sch 7 Pt I art 11; CPR
    61.11(18), (19); *Practice Direction—Admiralty Claims* PD 61 para 10.9–10.14; and PARA 195 et
    seq.
10  See the Merchant Shipping Act 1995 Sch 7 Pt I arts 10–12; and PARAS 1002–1004.
11  As to the release of a ship from arrest where security is previously given under the Convention on
    Limitation of Liability for Maritime Claims 1976 see PARA 176.

### 195. Limitation of liability under the Merchant Shipping Act 1995.

Shipowners and certain other persons have a statutory right to limit their
liability[1]. In exercise of this right, the claimant, normally the owner[2] of a ship[3],
seeks a decree by which his liability in respect of claims arising out of an
occurrence is limited to an amount[4] based upon the tonnage of the ship[5]. A decree
of limitation will be denied if it is proved that the loss resulted from the claimant's
personal act or omission, committed with the intent to cause such loss, or
recklessly and with knowledge that such loss would probably result[6].

Liability may be limited in respect of claims, whatever the basis of liability may
be, for:

(1)     claims in respect of loss of life or personal injury or loss of or damage
        to property (including damage to harbour works, basins and waterways
        and aids to navigation), occurring on board or in direct connection with
        the operation of the ship or with salvage operations, and consequential
        loss resulting from this[7];

(2)     claims in respect of loss resulting from delay in the carriage by sea of
        cargo, passengers or their luggage[8];

(3)     claims in respect of other loss resulting from infringement of rights other
        than contractual rights, occurring in direct connection with the
        operation of the ship or salvage operations[9];

(4)     claims in respect of the raising, removal, destruction or the rendering
        harmless of a ship which is sunk, wrecked, stranded or abandoned,
        including anything that is or has been on board such ship[10];

(5)     claims in respect of the removal, destruction or the rendering harmless
        of the cargo of the ship[11]; and

(6)     claims of a person other than the person liable in respect of measures
        taken in order to avert or minimise loss for which the person liable may
        limit his liability, and further loss caused by such measures[12].

These claims are subject to limitation of liability even if brought by way of
recourse or for indemnity under a contract. However, claims of the types in heads

(4), (5) and (6) above are subject to limitation of liability to the extent that they relate to a contract of remuneration under a contract with the person liable[13].

The right to limit liability extends also to salvors[14] and to insurers of liability for claims subject to the general limits of liability[15]. The liability of a shipowner includes liability in a claim brought against the vessel itself[16].

1  See the Merchant Shipping Act 1995 s 185(1), Sch 7 Pt I art 1; and PARA 993. As to the persons on whom the right mentioned in the text is conferred see also the text and notes 14–16. In relation to oil pollution, the owner of a ship is permitted to limit liability incurred under s 153: see s 157(1); and ENVIRONMENTAL QUALITY AND PUBLIC HEALTH vol 45 (2010) PARA 447. The statutory limitation right may be waived: see *Bahamas Oil Refining Company International Ltd v Owners of the Cape Bari Tankschiffahrts GMBH & Co KG (Bahamas)* [2016] UKPC 20.

   For a discussion of the substantive law in relation to limitation of liability of shipowners and others see PARA 992 et seq; and as to the special provisions concerning procedure in proceedings to limit liability see PARA 194 et seq. These provisions do not apply to aircraft.

   As to the exclusion of claims in respect of occurrences involving nuclear matter see the Nuclear Installations Act 1965 s 14; and ENERGY AND CLIMATE CHANGE vol 44 (2011) PARA 901.

2  As to the meaning of 'shipowner' for these purposes see PARA 993 note 2.
3  As to the meaning of 'ship' for these purposes see PARA 992 note 5.
4  As to the calculation of the limit of liability see PARA 998 et seq.
5  As to the procedure for obtaining a decree see PARA 198 et seq. The tonnage is ascertained as directed by statute: see PARA 998 note 14. As to what amounts to an 'occurrence' see *Strong Wise Ltd v Esso Australia Resources Pty Ltd (The APL Sydney)* [2010] FCA 240, [2010] 2 Lloyd's Rep 555.
6  See the Merchant Shipping Act 1995 Sch 7 Pt I art 4; and PARA 996. Once the shipowner has proven that the claims in respect of which limitation is sought fell within Sch 7 Pt I art 2(1) (see the text and notes 7–12), the burden of proving that the shipowner is not entitled, pursuant to art 4, to limit his liability, falls on those opposing the shipowner's right to limit. This burden of proof will ordinarily lead to a costs order against those who unsuccessfully oppose a shipowner's right to limit: see *The Capitan San Luis* [1994] QB 465, [1994] 1 All ER 1016.
7  See the Merchant Shipping Act 1995 Sch 7 Pt I art 2(1)(a); and PARA 994.
8  See the Merchant Shipping Act 1995 Sch 7 Pt I art 2(1)(b); and PARA 994.
9  See the Merchant Shipping Act 1995 Sch 7 Pt I art 2(1)(c); and PARA 994.
10 See the Merchant Shipping Act 1995 Sch 7 Pt I art 2(1)(d); and PARA 994. The United Kingdom has made a reservation in respect of the Convention on Limitation of Liability for Maritime Claims (London, 1–19 November 1976; TS 13 Cm 955) art 2(1)(d) (ie the Merchant Shipping Act 1995 Sch 7 Pt I art 2(1)(d)); consequently, liability for the cost of wreck removal remains unlimited in so far as the operation is performed pursuant to statutory powers: see Sch 7 Pt II para 3; and PARA 858.
11 See the Merchant Shipping Act 1995 Sch 7 Pt I art 2(1)(e); and PARA 994.
12 See the Merchant Shipping Act 1995 Sch 7 Pt I art 2(1)(f); and PARA 994.
13 See the Merchant Shipping Act 1995 Sch 7 Pt I art 2(2); and PARA 994.
14 Ie as defined in the Merchant Shipping Act 1995 Sch 7 Pt I: see Sch 7 Pt I art 1 para 1; and PARA 993 note 3.
15 See the Merchant Shipping Act 1995 Sch 7 Pt I art 1(6); and PARA 993. As to a similar provision in the context of pollution claims see s 165(3); and ENVIRONMENTAL QUALITY AND PUBLIC HEALTH vol 45 (2010) PARA 455.
16 See the Merchant Shipping Act 1995 Sch 7 Pt I art 1(5); and PARA 993. Thus a shipowner who would be liable in a claim in personam may still enjoy the benefit of limitation of liability even if the claim is brought against the ship in rem. The position would appear to be the same even if the shipowner is not liable in personam, but a claim is brought against his ship in rem. As to Admiralty claims in rem see PARA 158 et seq; and as to Admiralty claims made in personam see PARA 186 et seq.

B.    LIMITATION PROCEEDINGS

**196. Commencement of limitation proceedings.** Limitation of liability may always be raised by way of defence in an Admiralty claim already commenced[1]. A limitation claim for a restricted decree may be brought by counterclaim[2], but a limitation claim for a general decree may only be brought by counterclaim with the permission of the Admiralty Court[3]. Normally, however, a limitation claim is one in which a person faced by two or more actual or potential claims arising out of an occurrence, takes the initiative and invokes the court's special statutory powers[4]. A claim is started by the issue of a limitation claim form[5]. The claimant and at least one defendant must be named in the claim form, but all other defendants may be merely described[6].

The claimant may constitute a limitation fund[7] by making a payment into court[8], which, to be established, must be the sterling equivalent of the number of special drawing rights to which he claims to be entitled to limit his liability under the Merchant Shipping Act 1995 together with interest on that sum from the date of the occurrence giving rise to his liability to the date of payment into court[9]. On making any such payment into court, the claimant must give notice of it in writing to every named defendant, specifying the date of the payment in, the amount paid in, the amount of interest included, the rate of such interest, and the period to which it relates[10]. Money paid into court in this way[11] must not be paid out except under an order of the court[12].

1   This is the effect of *Practice Direction—Admiralty Claims* PD 61 para 10.18, which provides that nothing in CPR 61.11 prevents limitation being relied on by way of defence. Any decision in favour of the defendant in such a case is binding only upon the claimant. Cf the procedure for making a limitation decree binding upon the whole world: see PARA 199. CPR 61.11 applies to limitation claims: CPR 61.11(1). As to the meaning of 'limitation claim' for these purposes see PARA 91 note 13. The procedure governing the early stages of a limitation claim, contained in CPR 61.11 and *Practice Direction—Admiralty Claims* PD 61 para 10.1, differs significantly from the procedure relating to other claims: see the Admiralty and Commercial Courts Guide (2016) para N6.1. As to the Admiralty and Commercial Courts Guide see PARAS 91 note 3, 157 note 1. As to the procedure that governs Admiralty claims, including CPR Pt 61 and *Practice Direction—Admiralty Claims* PD 61, see PARA 140 note 5. As to the meanings of 'Admiralty claim' and 'Admiralty Court' for these purposes see PARA 91 note 3. As to the assignment of business to the Admiralty Court see CPR 61.2(1), (2); and PARA 91. As to the jurisdiction of the court in relation to limitation claims see PARAS 194–195. As to the right to obtain release of an arrested ship in certain cases where limitation applies and security has been given see PARA 176.

2   CPR 61.11(22)(a). As to restricted limitation decrees see CPR 61.11(10); and PARA 198. See also *Yuille v B & B Fisheries Ltd, The Radiant* [1958] 2 Lloyd's Rep 596 (counterclaim for limitation).

3   CPR 61.11(22)(b). As to general limitation decrees see CPR 61.11(11); and PARA 198.

4   Ie under the Merchant Shipping Act 1995 s 185, Sch 7: see PARA 195. A limitation claim can be commenced without liability first being admitted or established: see *Bouygues Offshore SA v Caspian Shipping Co (No 1, 3, 4 and 5)* [1998] 2 Lloyd's Rep 461, CA. As to the possibility of commencing a limitation claim after an award of damages has been made see *The Penelope II* [1979] 2 Lloyd's Rep 42 (on appeal [1980] 2 Lloyd's Rep 17, CA); *The Mekhanik Evgrafov and Ivan Derbenev (No 2)* [1988] 1 Lloyd's Rep 330; although quaere whether this option would still be available under the Merchant Shipping Act 1995: see *The Mekhanik Evgrafov and Ivan Derbenev* at 335 per Sheen J.

5   CPR 61.11(2). The limitation claim form must be as set out in the practice direction (ie *Practice Direction—Admiralty Claims* PD 61: see note 1): see CPR 61.11(2). Accordingly, the claim form in a limitation claim must be in Form ADM15 (Claim Form (Admiralty limitation claim)): *Practice Direction—Admiralty Claims* PD 61 para 10.1(1). The limitation claim form must be accompanied by a declaration setting out the facts upon which the claimant relies and stating the names and addresses (if known) of all persons who, to the knowledge of the claimant, have claims against him in respect of the occurrence to which the claim relates (other than named defendants), and the declaration must be verified by a statement of truth: *Practice Direction—Admiralty Claims* PD 61 para 10.1(2).

6   CPR 61.11(3).

7   A limitation fund may be established before or after a limitation claim has been started: CPR 61.11(19). However, if a limitation claim is not commenced within 75 days after the date the fund was established, the fund will lapse and all money in court (including any interest accrued) will be repaid to the person who made the payment into court: CPR 61.11(20). The fact that a limitation fund has lapsed in this way under CPR 61.11(20) does not prevent the establishment of a new fund: *Practice Direction—Admiralty Claims* PD 61 para 10.9. Neither the constitution of a limitation fund nor the ability to constitute a fund is a pre-condition to a court having jurisdiction: see *Seismic Shipping Inc v Total E & P UK plc, The Western Regent* [2005] EWCA Civ 985 at [20]–[23], [2005] 2 All ER (Comm) 515 at [20]–[23], [2005] 2 Lloyd's Rep 359 at [20]–[23] per Clarke LJ. A guarantee can constitute a limitation fund: see *Kairos Shipping Ltd v Enka & Co LLC; The Atlantik Confidence* [2014] EWCA Civ 217, [2014] 1 Lloyd's Rep 586.

8    CPR 61.11(18). As to the amount to which the claimant is allowed to limit his liability see the
     Merchant Shipping Act 1995 Sch 7 Pt I arts 6–8; and PARA 998 et seq.
9    *Practice Direction—Admiralty Claims* PD 61 para 10.10. Where the claimant does not know the
     sterling equivalent of the number of special drawing rights referred to in the text on the date of
     payment into court, he may calculate the figure on the basis of the latest available published
     sterling equivalent of a special drawing right as fixed by the International Monetary Fund: *Practice
     Direction—Admiralty Claims* PD 61 para 10.11(1). In the event of the sterling equivalent of a
     special drawing right on the date of payment into court being different from that used for
     calculating the amount of that payment into court, the claimant may make up any deficiency by
     making a further payment into court which, if made within 14 days after the payment into court,
     will be treated, except for the purpose of the rules relating to the accrual of interest on money paid
     into court, as if made on the date of that payment into court (*Practice Direction—Admiralty
     Claims* PD 61 para 10.11(2)(a)); or he may apply to the court for payment out of any excess
     amount (together with any interest accrued) paid into court (*Practice Direction—Admiralty
     Claims* PD 61 para 10.11(2)(b)). Such an application under para 10.11(2)(b) may be made without
     notice to any party; and must be supported by evidence proving, to the satisfaction of the court,
     the sterling equivalent of the appropriate number of special drawing rights on the date of payment
     into court: *Practice Direction—Admiralty Claims* PD 61 para 10.12.
10   *Practice Direction—Admiralty Claims* PD 61 para 10.13(1). The claimant must also give notice in
     writing to every named defendant of any excess amount (and interest) paid out to him under para
     10.11(2)(b) (see note 9): *Practice Direction—Admiralty Claims* PD 61 para 10.13(2).
11   Ie under CPR 61.11(18) (see the text and notes 7–10): see CPR 61.11(21).
12   CPR 61.11(21).

## 197. Service of the limitation claim form and acknowledgment. A
limitation claim form[1] must be served on all named defendants, and any other
defendant who requests service upon him, and it may be served on any other
defendant[2]. Every defendant upon whom a limitation claim form is served must
either:

(1)    within 28 days of service, file a defence to the limitation claim[3], or file
       a notice that he admits the claimant's right to limit liability[4]; or
(2)    if he wishes to dispute the court's jurisdiction, or wishes to argue that
       the court should not exercise its jurisdiction, file within 14 days of
       service or (if the limitation claim form is served out of the jurisdiction)
       within the time specified[5] file an acknowledgment of service[6].

However, generally, an acknowledgment of service is not required[7].

1    A limitation claim is started by the issue of a limitation claim form: see PARA 196. CPR 61.11
     applies to limitation claims: CPR 61.11(1). As to the meaning of 'limitation claim' for these
     purposes see PARA 91 note 13. The procedure governing the early stages of a limitation claim,
     contained in CPR 61.11 and *Practice Direction—Admiralty Claims* PD 61 para 10.1, differs
     significantly from the procedure relating to other claims: see the Admiralty and Commercial
     Courts Guide (2016) para N6.1. As to the Admiralty and Commercial Courts Guide see PARAS 91
     note 3, 157 note 1. As to the procedure that governs Admiralty claims, including CPR Pt 61 and
     *Practice Direction—Admiralty Claims* PD 61, see PARA 140 note 5. As to the meanings of
     'Admiralty claim' and 'Admiralty Court' for these purposes see PARA 91 note 3. As to the
     assignment of business to the Admiralty Court see CPR 61.2(1), (2); and PARA 91. As to the
     jurisdiction of the court in relation to limitation claims see PARAS 194–195. As to the right to
     obtain release of an arrested ship in certain cases where limitation applies and security has been
     given see PARA 176.
2    CPR 61.11(4). See also Form ADM15B (Notes for defendant (Admiralty limitation claim)). The
     claim form may not be served out of the jurisdiction unless the case falls within the Senior Courts
     Act 1981 s 22(2)(a)–(c) (claims in personam) (see PARA 94), or unless the defendant has submitted
     or agreed to submit to the jurisdiction of the court, or unless the Admiralty Court has jurisdiction
     over the claim under any applicable Convention: CPR 61.11(5). As to 'any applicable Convention'
     that may affect jurisdiction see the Civil Jurisdiction and Judgments Act 1982; and PARA 95 et seq.
     The court must give permission for service out of the jurisdiction in accordance with CPR Pt 6
     Section III (CPR 6.17–6.31) (as to which see CIVIL PROCEDURE vol 11 (2015) PARAS 263, 265
     et seq): see CPR 61.11(5). Service of a limitation claim form out of the jurisdiction is permitted in
     the circumstances identified in CPR 61.11(5) only and the procedure set out in the Admiralty and
     Commercial Courts Guide (2016) App 15 (Service out of the jurisdiction: related practice) should
     be adapted accordingly: Admiralty and Commercial Courts Guide (2016) para N6.2. As to the

possible scope of CPR 61.11(5) see *ICL Shipping Ltd v Chin Tai Steel Enterprise Co Ltd, The ICL Vikraman* [2003] EWHC 2320 (Comm) at [58]–[65], [2004] 1 All ER (Comm) 246 at [58]–[65], [2004] 1 Lloyd's Rep 21 at [58]–[65].

3   A defence to a limitation claim must be in Form ADM16A (Defence to Admiralty limitation claim): *Practice Direction—Admiralty Claims* PD 61 para 10.2. As to the filing of documents with the Admiralty and Commercial Registry see PARA 142.

4   CPR 61.11(7)(a). A notice admitting the claimant's right to limit liability in a limitation claim must be in Form ADM16 (Notice of admission of right of claimant to limit liability): *Practice Direction—Admiralty Claims* PD 61 para 10.3.

5   Ie the time specified in CPR 6.22 (as to which see CIVIL PROCEDURE vol 11 (2015) PARA 312): see CPR 61.11(7)(b).

6   CPR 61.11(7)(b). The acknowledgment of service must be as set out in the practice direction (ie *Practice Direction—Admiralty Claims* PD 61: see note 1): see CPR 61.11(7)(b). Accordingly, the acknowledgment of service in a limitation claim must be in Form ADM16B (Acknowledgment of Service (Admiralty limitation claim)): *Practice Direction—Admiralty Claims* PD 61 para 10.4. If a defendant files an acknowledgment of service under CPR 61.11(7)(b), he is treated as having accepted that the court has jurisdiction to hear the claim unless he applies under CPR Pt 11 (procedure for disputing the court's jurisdiction) (see CIVIL PROCEDURE vol 11 (2015) PARA 339) within 14 days after filing the acknowledgment of service: CPR 61.11(8).

7   CPR 61.11(6).

## 198. Obtaining a restricted or general limitation decree.

Where, in a limitation claim[1], one or more named defendants admits the right to limit[2], the claimant may apply for a restricted limitation decree[3]. The court will then issue a restricted limitation decree[4] limiting liability only against such named defendants who have admitted the claimant's right to limit liability[5]. A restricted limitation decree may be obtained against any named defendant who fails to file a defence within the time specified for doing so and need not be advertised, although a copy must be served on the defendants to whom it applies[6].

Where all the defendants upon whom the claim form has been served admit the claimant's right to limit liability, the claimant may apply to the Admiralty Registrar for a general limitation decree[7] and the court will issue a limitation decree[8].

In circumstances where one or more of the defendants upon whom the claim form has been served do not admit the claimant's right to limit, the claimant also may apply for a general limitation decree[9]. Where, in this way, the right to limit is not admitted and the claimant seeks a general limitation decree[10], the claimant must, within seven days of the date of the filing of the defence of the named defendant last served or the expiry of the time for doing so, apply for an appointment before the Admiralty Registrar for a case management conference[11].

1   As to the meaning of 'limitation claim' for these purposes see PARA 91 note 13. CPR 61.11 applies to limitation claims: CPR 61.11(1). As to the procedure that governs Admiralty claims, including CPR Pt 61 and *Practice Direction—Admiralty Claims* PD 61, see PARA 140 note 5. As to the practice and procedure that applies in the Commercial Court, including CPR Pt 58 and *Practice Direction—Commercial Court* PD 58, see CIVIL PROCEDURE vol 11 (2015) PARA 170 et seq; COURTS AND TRIBUNALS vol 24 (2010) PARA 708. As to the meanings of 'Admiralty claim' and 'Admiralty Court' for these purposes see PARA 91 note 3. As to the assignment of business to the Admiralty Court see CPR 61.2(1), (2); and PARA 91. As to the jurisdiction of the court in relation to limitation claims see PARAS 194–195. As to the right to obtain release of an arrested ship in certain cases where limitation applies and security has been given see PARA 176.

2   This is one of the permitted responses to service of a limitation claim form: see PARA 197.

3   CPR 61.11(9). The application for a restricted limitation decree must be in the form set out in the practice direction (ie *Practice Direction—Admiralty Claims* PD 61: see note 1): see CPR 61.11(9)(a). Accordingly, an application for a restricted limitation decree must be in Form ADM17 (Application for restricted limitation decree): *Practice Direction—Admiralty Claims* PD 61 para 10.5.

4   Ie in the form set out in the practice direction (ie *Practice Direction—Admiralty Claims* PD 61: see note 1): see CPR 61.11(9)(b). Accordingly, the decree issued by the court on an application for a restricted limitation decree must be in Form ADM18 (Restricted limitation decree): *Practice Direction—Admiralty Claims* PD 61 para 10.5.

5　CPR 61.11(9)(b).

6　CPR 61.11(10).

7　Ie in the form set out in the practice direction (ie *Practice Direction—Admiralty Claims* PD 61: see note 1): see CPR 61.11(11). Accordingly, an application for a general limitation decree must be in Form ADM17A (Application for general limitation decree): *Practice Direction—Admiralty Claims* PD 61 para 10.6.

8　CPR 61.11(11). As to the form of a general limitation decree see Form ADM19 (General limitation decree).

9　CPR 61.11(12). The application mentioned in the text must be in the form set out in the practice direction (ie *Practice Direction—Admiralty Claims* PD 61: see note 1): see CPR 61.11(12). Accordingly, an application for a general limitation decree must be in Form ADM17A (Application for general limitation decree): *Practice Direction—Admiralty Claims* PD 61 para 10.6. On an application under CPR 61.11(12), the Admiralty Registrar may either grant a general limitation decree, or (if he does not grant a decree) order service of a defence, order disclosure by the claimant, or make such other case management directions as may be appropriate: *Practice Direction—Admiralty Claims* PD 61 para 10.8. As to the Admiralty Registrar see PARA 140.

10　Ie in Form ADM17A (Application for general limitation decree): see *Practice Direction—Admiralty Claims* PD 61 para 10.7.

11　*Practice Direction—Admiralty Claims* PD 61 para 10.7.

## 199. Effect of granting limitation decree.

When a limitation decree is granted[1], the Admiralty Court[2]:

(1)　may order that any proceedings relating to any claim arising out of the occurrence be stayed[3];

(2)　may order the claimant to establish a limitation fund[4], if one has not been established, or make such other arrangements for payment of claims against which liability is limited[5];

(3)　may, if the decree is a restricted limitation decree, distribute the limitation fund[6]; and

(4)　must, if the decree is a general limitation decree, give directions as to the advertisement of the decree and set a time within which notice of claims against the fund must be filed or an application made to set aside the decree[7].

When the court grants a general limitation decree, the claimant must advertise it in such manner and within such time as the court directs, and file both a declaration that the decree has been advertised as so directed, and copies of the advertisements[8].

If no decree limiting liability is made by the Admiralty Registrar, statements of case are delivered in limitation claims as in other Admiralty claims in personam[9].

1　As to obtaining a restricted or general limitation decree see PARA 198.

2　As to the meaning of 'Admiralty Court' for these purposes see PARA 91 note 3. As to the assignment of business to the Admiralty Court see CPR 61.2(1), (2); and PARA 91. As to the procedure that governs Admiralty claims, including CPR Pt 61 and *Practice Direction—Admiralty Claims* PD 61, see PARA 140 note 5. As to the practice and procedure that applies in the Commercial Court, including CPR Pt 58 and *Practice Direction—Commercial Court* PD 58, CIVIL PROCEDURE vol 11 (2015) PARA 170 et seq; COURTS AND TRIBUNALS vol 24 (2010) PARA 708. As to the meaning of 'Admiralty claim' for these purposes see PARA 91 note 3. As to the jurisdiction of the court in relation to limitation claims see PARAS 194–195. As to the right to obtain release of an arrested ship in certain cases where limitation applies and security has been given see PARA 176.

3　CPR 61.11(13)(a)(i).

4　As to the establishment and constitution of a limitation fund see PARA 196.

5　CPR 61.11(13)(a)(ii). Neither the constitution of a limitation fund nor the ability to constitute a fund is a pre-condition to either a court having jurisdiction or the grant of a limitation decree: see *Seismic Shipping Inc v Total E&P UK plc, The Western Regent* [2005] EWCA Civ 985 at [20]–[23], [2005] 2 All ER (Comm) 515 at [20]–[23], [2005] 2 Lloyd's Rep 359 at [20]–[23] per Clarke LJ.

6　CPR 61.11(13)(a)(iii). As to the distribution of the limitation fund see PARA 201.

7　CPR 61.11(13)(b). A claim against the fund must be in Form ADM20 (Defendant's claim in a limitation action): *Practice Direction—Admiralty Claims* PD 61 para 10.14. As to proceedings to set aside general limitation decree see PARA 200. The court always has a discretion to extend the time fixed by the limitation decree: *The Kronprinz Olav* [1921] P 52, CA. Usually, the fact that limitation proceedings are pending is a good ground for the exercise of the court's discretion to extend the time: see *The Disperser* [1920] P 228.

8    CPR 61.11(14).

9    As to Admiralty claims in personam see PARA 186 et seq. As to the delivery of statements of case generally see CPR Pt 6; and CIVIL PROCEDURE vol 11 (2015) PARA 316 et seq.

## 200. Proceedings to set aside general limitation decree.

Any person other than a defendant on whom a limitation claim form has been served[1] may apply to the Admiralty Court within the time fixed in the decree to have a general limitation decree set aside[2]. Any such application must be supported by a declaration stating that the applicant has a claim against the claimant arising out of the occurrence, and setting out grounds for contending that the claimant is not entitled to the decree obtained, either in the amount of limitation or at all[3]. No later than seven days after the time for filing claims or declarations, the Admiralty Registrar[4] will fix a date for a case management conference at which directions will be given for the further conduct of the proceedings[5].

1    As to service of a limitation claim form see PARA 197. As to the meaning of 'limitation claim' for these purposes see PARA 91 note 13. CPR 61.11 applies to limitation claims: CPR 61.11(1). As to the procedure that governs Admiralty claims, including CPR Pt 61 and *Practice Direction—Admiralty Claims* PD 61, see PARA 140 note 5. As to the meanings of 'Admiralty claim' and 'Admiralty Court' for these purposes see PARA 91 note 3. As to the assignment of business to the Admiralty Court see CPR 61.2(1), (2); and PARA 91. As to the jurisdiction of the court in relation to limitation claims see PARAS 194–195. As to the right to obtain release of an arrested ship in certain cases where limitation applies and security has been given see PARA 176.

2    CPR 61.11(16). As to the time fixed in the decree see PARA 199.

3    CPR 61.11(17).

4    As to the Admiralty Registrar see PARA 140.

5    *Practice Direction—Admiralty Claims* PD 61 para 10.17.

## 201. Distribution of limitation fund.

No later than the time set in the limitation decree for filing claims[1], each of the defendants who wishes to assert a claim must file and serve his statement of case on both the limiting party and all other defendants (except where the court orders otherwise)[2]. No later than seven days after the time for filing claims or declarations, the Admiralty Registrar[3] will fix a date for a case management conference at which directions will be given for the further conduct of the proceedings[4].

Unless any proceedings are commenced in due time to set aside the decree[5], the limitation fund[6] will be distributed among the parties who have filed valid claims in proportion to their established claims against the fund[7] at a reference, usually directed by the decree, to the Admiralty Registrar[8].

1    As to obtaining a restricted or general limitation decree see PARA 198; and as to the time fixed in the decree see PARA 199. As to the jurisdiction of the court in relation to limitation claims see PARAS 194–195.

2    CPR 61.11(15). A claim against the fund must be in Form ADM20 (Defendant's claim in a limitation action): *Practice Direction—Admiralty Claims* PD 61 para 10.14. A defendant's statement of case filed and served in accordance with CPR 61.11(15) must contain particulars of the defendant's claim: *Practice Direction—Admiralty Claims* PD 61 para 10.15. Any defendant who is unable to file and serve a statement of case in accordance with CPR 61.11(15) and *Practice Direction—Admiralty Claims* PD 61 para 10.15 must file a declaration, verified by a statement of truth, in Form ADM21 (Declaration as to inability of a defendant to file and serve statement of case under a decree of limitation) stating the reason for his inability: *Practice Direction—Admiralty Claims* PD 61 para 10.16. As to the filing of documents with the Admiralty and Commercial Registry see PARA 142.

3    As to the Admiralty Registrar see PARA 140.

4    *Practice Direction—Admiralty Claims* PD 61 para 10.17. These directions may be given in respect of each individual claim and as between defendants eg if any defendant disputes the merits or amount of another defendant's claim. Rival defendants are opposite parties in the litigation, and as such may administer requests for further information and obtain disclosure from each other: *The Nedenes* (1924) 41 TLR 243.

5  As to proceedings to set aside a general limitation decree see PARA 200.

6  As to the establishment and constitution of a limitation fund see PARA 196.

7  No lien or other right in respect of any ship or property affects the proportions in which the fund is divided: see the Merchant Shipping Act 1995 s 185, Sch 7 Pt II para 9; and PARA 1004. This is intended to override the decision in *The Countess* [1923] AC 345, HL, in which the House of Lords held that if one claimant had a possessory lien over the ship, effect had to be given to the superior right even if the effect was to deprive other claimants of their right of recovery against the limitation fund. Interest on sums due is included in the damages for the purposes of limitation: see *The Joannis Vatis (No 2)* [1922] P 213.

8  See PARAS 143, 199. The reference is obligatory except in cases where there is only one claimant against the fund or all claimants are represented by the same solicitor. In these cases, an application notice for payment out is sufficient: see PARA 203. As to references to the Registrar see PARA 143.

**202. Repayment to claimant.** Where there are loss of life claims, and the statutory amount[1] has all been paid into court, but some of the loss of life claimants fail to come in and enter their claims until after the time appointed for claims to be filed, even though the period of two years has not elapsed within which, under the Merchant Shipping Act 1995[2], proceedings in respect of such a claim could be commenced, the court may order that the balance of the limitation fund[3] which remains in court after all the loss of life claimants who have entered claims in due time have been paid, is to be paid back to the claimants. The claimants who have not entered their claims in time being thus excluded from any share in the limited amount[4].

1  As to the calculation of the limit of liability see PARAS 195, 998 et seq.

2  Ie under the Merchant Shipping Act 1995 s 185, Sch 7: see PARA 196.

3  As to the establishment and constitution of a limitation fund see PARA 196.

4  See *The Alma* [1903] P 55. At the time of that decision, the Maritime Conventions Act 1911 (the forerunner to the Merchant Shipping Act 1995 Sch 7) had not been passed, but the court made an order for payment of the balance of the limitation fund to the claimants, although the period of one year prescribed by the Fatal Accidents Act 1846 (now repealed) had not elapsed. It is presumed that the same principles would apply now that the period has been extended by the Merchant Shipping Act 1995. The same principles apparently apply in respect of claims for damage to property, if the general fund exceeds the total of such claims made in time: see *The Alma* at 60 per Jeune P.

## (v) Trial of Admiralty Claims and Post-trial Proceedings

### A.  OFFERS TO SETTLE

**203. Offers to settle and their effect.** The practice as to making an offer to settle proceedings, and a corresponding payment into court (where required) in an Admiralty claim is, in general, similar to the practice applying to proceedings for debt or damages in other claims[1].

However, where a party to a claim to establish liability for a collision claim[2] (other than a claim for loss of life or personal injury)[3]:

(1)  makes an offer to settle[4] not less than 21 days before the start of the trial[5];

(2)  that offer is not accepted[6]; and

(3)  the maker of the offer obtains at trial an apportionment equal to or more favourable than his offer[7],

the parties will, unless the court considers it unjust, be entitled to the following costs[8]:

(a)  the maker of the offer will be entitled to all his costs from 21 days after the offer was made[9], and his costs before then in the percentage to which he would have been entitled had the offer been accepted[10]; and

(b)      all other parties to whom the offer was made will be entitled to their costs up to 21 days after the offer was made in the percentage to which they would have been entitled had the offer been accepted[11]; but will not be entitled to their costs thereafter[12].

1   As to offers to settle and payments into court generally see CPR Pt 36; and CIVIL PROCEDURE vol 12A (2015) PARA 1653 et seq. See also *The Hudson Bay* [1957] 2 Lloyd's Rep 506 (open offer to refer only to the proportionate liability which the offeror was prepared to bear by way of settlement).

2   As to the meaning of 'collision claim' for these purposes see PARA 91 note 12. As to the procedure that governs Admiralty claims generally, including CPR Pt 61 and *Practice Direction—Admiralty Claims* PD 61, see PARA 91 et seq. CPR Pt 58 (Commercial Court) applies generally to claims in the Admiralty Court where CPR Pt 61 does not provide otherwise (see CPR 61.1(3); and PARA 91 note 3); and the practice direction which supplements CPR Pt 58 (ie *Practice Direction—Commercial Court* PD 58) also applies to Admiralty claims except where it is inconsistent with either CPR Pt 61 or *Practice Direction—Admiralty Claims* PD 61 (see para 1.1; and PARA 91 note 3). As to the practice and procedure that applies in the Commercial Court, including CPR Pt 58 and *Practice Direction—Commercial Court* PD 58, see CIVIL PROCEDURE vol 11 (2015) PARA 170 et seq; COURTS AND TRIBUNALS vol 24 (2010) PARA 708. As to the meanings of 'Admiralty claim' and 'Admiralty Court' for these purposes see PARA 91 note 3. As to the assignment of business to the Admiralty Court see CPR 61.2(1), (2); and PARA 91.

3   CPR 61.4(10).

4   Ie in the form set out in CPR 61.4(12): see CPR 61.4(10)(a). Accordingly, an offer under CPR 61.4(10) must be in writing and must contain:
    (1)    an offer to settle liability at stated percentages (CPR 61.4(12)(a) (as so added));
    (2)    an offer to pay costs in accordance with the same percentages (CPR 61.4(12)(b) (as so added));
    (3)    a term that the offer remain open for 21 days after the date it is made (CPR 61.4(12)(c) (as so added)); and
    (4)    a term that, unless the court orders otherwise, on expiry of that period the offer remains open on the same terms except that the offeree should pay all the costs from that date until acceptance (CPR 61.4(12)(d) (as so added)).

5   CPR 61.4(10)(a).

6   CPR 61.4(10)(b).

7   CPR 61.4(10)(c).

8   CPR 61.4(11). As to the entitlement to costs under CPR 61.4(10)–(12) see *Samco Europe v MSC Prestige* [2011] EWHC 1656 (Admlty), [2012] BLR 267 (applying in particular *Trustees of Stokes Pension Fund v Western Power Distribution (South West) plc* [2005] EWCA Civ 854, [2005] 3 All ER 775, [2005] 1 WLR 3595, and *Bristol and West Building Society v Evans Bullock* (5 February 1996, unreported), CA).

9   CPR 61.4(11)(a)(i).

10   CPR 61.4(10)(a)(ii).

11   CPR 61.4(11)(b)(i).

12   CPR 61.4(10)(b)(ii).

### B.    GENERAL PROCEDURE RELATING TO TRIAL

**204. General procedure in the Admiralty Court relating to trial.** For the purposes of an Admiralty claim in rem[1], a collision claim[2], an Admiralty claim in personam[3] and a limitation claim[4], the general practice and procedure of the Commercial Court[5] governs:

    (1)     case management (with certain modifications made in relation to each type of claim)[6];
    (2)     disclosure[7];
    (3)     applications[8];
    (4)     the use of alternative dispute resolution ('ADR')[9];
    (5)     evidence for trial[10];
    (6)     conduct of the trial itself[11];
    (7)     after trial proceedings[12];
    (8)     multi-party disputes[13];
    (9)     litigants in person[14];
    (10)    arbitration[15].

The awarding of costs in Admiralty proceedings is in the unfettered discretion of the Admiralty Court or the Admiralty Registrar, as the case may be[16].

1 As to the origin of claims in rem see PARA 83; as to the jurisdiction of the Admiralty Court in relation to claims in rem see PARA 92 et seq; and as to commencing such a claim see PARA 158 et seq.

2 As to the meaning of 'collision claim' for these purposes see PARA 91 note 12. As to the jurisdiction of the Admiralty Court in relation to collision claims see PARA 180; and as to commencing such a claim see PARA 181 et seq.

3 As to the origin of claims in personam see PARA 84; as to claims in personam generally see PARA 92 et seq; and as to commencing such a claim see PARA 186 et seq.

4 As to limitation claims see PARA 194 et seq.

5 As to the practice and procedure that applies in the Commercial Court, including CPR Pt 58 and *Practice Direction—Commercial Court* PD 58, see CIVIL PROCEDURE vol 11 (2015) PARA 170 et seq; COURTS AND TRIBUNALS vol 24 (2010) PARA 708. CPR Pt 58 (Commercial Court) applies generally to claims in the Admiralty Court where CPR Pt 61 does not provide otherwise (see CPR 61.1(3); and PARA 91 note 3); and the practice direction which supplements CPR Pt 58 (ie *Practice Direction—Commercial Court* PD 58) also applies to Admiralty claims except where it is inconsistent with either CPR Pt 61 or *Practice Direction—Admiralty Claims* PD 61 (see para 1.1; and PARA 91 note 3). As to the procedure that governs Admiralty claims generally, including CPR Pt 61 and *Practice Direction—Admiralty Claims* PD 61, see PARA 91 et seq. As to the meanings of 'Admiralty claim' and 'Admiralty Court' for these purposes see PARA 91 note 3. As to the assignment of business to the Admiralty Court see CPR 61.2(1), (2); and PARA 91.

Pre-trial matters in the Admiralty and Commercial Courts are usually dealt with by the judges of those courts: see *Practice Direction—Commercial Court* PD 58 para 1.2; the Admiralty and Commercial Courts Guide (2016) para A1.5; and CIVIL PROCEDURE vol 11 (2015) PARA 170. However, one significant area of difference between practice in the Commercial Court and practice in the Admiralty Court is that many interlocutory applications are heard by the Admiralty Registrar who has all the powers of the Admiralty judge save as provided otherwise: see CPR 61.1(4); the Admiralty and Commercial Courts Guide (2016) para N1.3; and PARA 140. As to the Admiralty and Commercial Courts Guide see PARAS 91 note 3, 157 note 1. As to the Admiralty Registrar see PARA 140.

6 As to the general practice and procedure of the Commercial Court in this regard see the Admiralty and Commercial Courts Guide (2016) paras D1–D19, App 6; and CIVIL PROCEDURE vol 11 (2015) PARA 173. The case management provisions of the Admiralty and Commercial Courts Guide apply to Admiralty claims save that:

   (1)    in Admiralty claims, the case management provisions are supplemented by the provisions of *Practice Direction—Admiralty Claims* PD 61 para 2 (as to which see PARA 158) which make provision for the early classification and streaming of cases (see the Admiralty and Commercial Courts Guide (2016) para N8.1(i));

   (2)    in a collision case, the claimant should apply for a case management conference within seven days after the last collision statement of case is filed (see the Admiralty and Commercial Courts Guide (2016) para N8.1(ii));

   (3)    in a limitation claim, *Practice Direction—Admiralty Claims* PD 61 para 10.7 applies (as to which see PARA 198) so that where the right to limit is not admitted and the claimant seeks a general limitation decree, the claimant must, within seven days after the date of the filing of the defence of the defendant last served or the expiry of the time for doing so, apply to the Admiralty Registrar for a case management conference (see the Admiralty and Commercial Courts Guide (2016) para N8.1(iii));

   (4)    in a collision claim or a limitation claim, a mandatory case management conference will normally take place on the first available date five weeks after the date when the claimant is required to take steps to fix a date for the case management conference (see the Admiralty and Commercial Courts Guide (2016) para N8.1(iv));

   (5)    in a limitation claim, case management directions are initially given by the Registrar (see *Practice Direction—Admiralty Claims* PD 61 para 10.8 (cited in PARA 198); and the Admiralty and Commercial Courts Guide (2016) para N8.1(v));

   (6)    in the Admiralty Court, the Case Management Information Sheet should be used in the form given in the Admiralty and Commercial Courts Guide (2016) App 6 but with the inclusion of additional questions that are cited in para N8.1(vi) (see para N8.1(vi)).

As to the filing of documents with the Admiralty and Commercial Registry see PARA 142.

It is usual to consolidate pending claims of salvage against the same property (see *The Strathgarry* [1895] P 264); and the conduct of consolidated salvage claims is usually given to the principal salvor. See also the observations of Hill J in *The Creteforest* [1920] P 111 at 116–117; and the decision as to costs in *The Macgregor Laird* [1953] 2 Lloyd's Rep 259 at 268 per Willmer J. Permission for separate representation may be given, but it does not necessarily follow that the costs of separate representation will be allowed: *The Longford* (1881) 6 PD 60 at 67.

Co-claimants in salvage cases are frequently allowed separate representation and separate costs: see eg *The Bosworth (No 2)* [1960] 1 All ER 729, [1961] 1 WLR 319, [1960] 1 Lloyd's Rep 173, CA. Consolidation may be ordered by the court in its discretion without the consent and notwithstanding the objection of the parties (see *The Strathgarry*), and if it becomes expedient after judgment has been delivered the court will make an order that the claims should proceed separately thereafter as originally instituted (see *The Helen R Cooper* (1871) LR 3 A & E 339).

As to the appropriate approach in the Commercial Court and the Admiralty Court to the jurisdiction to strike out, either under CPR 3.4(2) (as to which see CIVIL PROCEDURE vol 12 (2015) PARA 516) or under the inherent jurisdiction of the court, a damage to cargo and short delivery claim which has proceeded to trial and is therefore likely to be uneconomic see *Amgulf Polymers & Chemicals Ltd v The Owners and/or Demise Charterers of MV Athinoula* [2001] 2 All ER (Comm) 821.

7   As to the general practice and procedure of the Commercial Court in this regard see the Admiralty and Commercial Courts Guide (2016) paras E1–E5, Apps 8–10; and CIVIL PROCEDURE vol 11 (2015) PARA 174. In Admiralty cases, the court may decline to order further information if it will affect the conduct of the proceedings. For instance, in claims of damage, the collision statements of case (as to which see PARA 182 et seq) afford the information which would otherwise be furnished by further information: see *The Biola* (1876) 34 LT 185; *The Isle of Cyprus* (1890) 15 PD 134; *The Bernard* [1905] WN 73. Where, however, one ship is lost with all, or most of, her crew, or one or other of the parties is for any reason unable to offer satisfactory evidence, further information may be allowed: see *The Radnorshire* (1880) 5 PD 172.

Where the authenticity of any document disclosed to a party is not admitted, that party must serve notice that the document must be proved at trial in accordance with CPR 32.19 (see CIVIL PROCEDURE vol 12 (2015) PARA 711), which provides that such notice must be served by the latest date for serving witness statements or within seven days of disclosure of the document (whichever is later): see the Admiralty and Commercial Courts Guide (2016) para N9.2(a). Where, apart from the authenticity of the document itself, the date upon which a document or an entry in it is stated to have been made or the person by whom the document states that it or any entry in it was made or any other feature of the document is to be challenged at the trial on grounds which may require a witness to be called at the trial to support the contents of the document, such challenge must be raised in good time in advance of the trial to enable such witness or witnesses to be called, and the grounds of challenge must be explicitly identified in the skeleton argument or outline submissions in advance of the trial: see the Admiralty and Commercial Courts Guide (2016) para N9.2(b). Where, due to the late disclosure of a document it or its contents or character cannot practicably be challenged within the time limits prescribed in the Admiralty and Commercial Courts Guide (2016) para N9.2(a) or N9.2(b), the challenge may only be raised with the permission of the court and having regard to the Overriding Objective (ie CPR 1.1, as to which see CIVIL PROCEDURE vol 12 (2015) PARA 504): see the Admiralty and Commercial Courts Guide (2016) para N9.2(c). As to summonses used merely to obtain documents and prove their authenticity see *Khanna v Lovell White Durrant* [1994] 4 All ER 267, [1995] 1 WLR 121.

8   As to the general practice and procedure of the Commercial Court in this regard see the Admiralty and Commercial Courts Guide (2016) paras F1–F16, App 5; and CIVIL PROCEDURE vol 11 (2015) PARA 175.

9   As to the general practice and procedure of the Commercial Court in this regard see the Admiralty and Commercial Courts Guide (2016) paras G1–G2, App 7; and CIVIL PROCEDURE vol 11 (2015) PARAS 170, 75.

10 As to the general practice and procedure of the Commercial Court in this regard see the Admiralty and Commercial Courts Guide (2016) paras H1–H4, App 11; and CIVIL PROCEDURE vol 11 (2015) PARA 176.

In collision claims, the Admiralty and Commercial Courts Guide (2016) para H1.5 and App 8 (Standard pre-trial Timetable) (see note 7) are subject to the proviso that experience has shown that it is usually desirable for the main elements of a witness's evidence in chief to be adduced orally: see para N9.1. As to evidence in cases where a collision statement of case must be filed (as to which see PARA 182 et seq) see further *Fisher v CHT Ltd* [1965] 2 All ER 601, [1965] 1 WLR 1093 (on appeal on another point [1966] 2 QB 475, [1966] 1 All ER 88, CA). As to the weight to be attached generally to evidence in statements where the facts are contested and there is also oral evidence see *The Scarcity, The Daniel M* [1967] 2 Lloyd's Rep 498 at 508 per Brandon J. As to the role of assessors in collision claims and other cases involving issues of navigation and seamanship see PARA 205.

Whether it is more reasonable to examine a witness beforehand or to detain him ashore pending the trial depends on the circumstances of each case, but the costs judge has a discretion to disallow the cost of detaining a witness ashore, if he might conveniently have been examined beforehand: see *The Ibis VI* [1921] P 255, CA. The question whether evidence should be permitted to be taken abroad is to be decided by the court in its discretion; for the principles which are applied see *Berdan v Greenwood* (1880) 20 ChD 764n, CA. The court is apt to look most favourably on the application of a defendant resident abroad, who has not chosen an English forum (see *Ross v Woodford* [1894] 1 Ch 38; *New v Burns* (1894) 64 LJQB 104, CA) and least favourably upon the application of a claimant for evidence to be taken abroad (*Ross v Woodford*; *Coch v Allcock* (1888) 21 QBD 178, CA; *Emanuel v Soltykoff* (1892) 8 TLR 331, CA).

The court has a wide discretion to admit statements notwithstanding failure to comply with the rules: see *The Ferdinand Retzlaff* [1972] 2 Lloyd's Rep 120 at 126.

11 As to the general practice and procedure of the Commercial Court in this regard see the Admiralty and Commercial Courts Guide (2016) paras J1–J14, Apps 12–14; and CIVIL PROCEDURE vol 11 (2015) PARA 176. See also the Admiralty and Commercial Courts Guide (2016) paras N10.1, N10.2; and PARA 143.

In collision claims, the skeleton argument of each party must be accompanied by a plot or plots of that party's case or alternative cases as to the navigation of vessels during and leading to the collision; and all plots must contain a sufficient indication of the assumptions used in the preparation of the plot: see the Admiralty and Commercial Courts Guide (2016) para N9.3.

12 As to the general practice and procedure of the Commercial Court in this regard see the Admiralty and Commercial Courts Guide (2016) paras K1–K4. As to offers to settle and their effect on costs see PARA 203. As to appraisement and sale of a ship by the court (either before or after judgment) see PARA 178. As to the scope for a rehearing see PARA 206.

13 As to the general practice and procedure of the Commercial Court in this regard see the Admiralty and Commercial Courts Guide (2016) paras L1–L2; and CIVIL PROCEDURE vol 11 (2015) PARA 176.

14 As to the general practice and procedure of the Commercial Court in this regard see the Admiralty and Commercial Courts Guide (2016) paras M1–M3; and CIVIL PROCEDURE vol 11 (2015) PARA 176.

15 As to the general practice and procedure of the Commercial Court in this regard see the Admiralty and Commercial Courts Guide (2016) paras O1–O20; and CIVIL PROCEDURE vol 11 (2015) PARA 178.

16 See the Senior Courts Act 1981 s 51; CPR Pt 44; and CIVIL PROCEDURE vol 12A (2015) PARA 1684 et seq. See also the Admiralty and Commercial Courts Guide (2016) App 16 (Security for Costs). As to the extent of the discretion regarding the awarding of costs see *Aiden Shipping Co Ltd v Interbulk Ltd* [1986] AC 965, [1986] 2 All ER 409, HL. When exercising its discretion in favour of the party incurring the costs, the court must be satisfied that the costs have been incurred for the preservation or enhancement of the fund as a whole rather than solely for one party's benefit: *Festive Holidays Ltd v The Demise Charterers of the ship 'Ocean Glory 1'* [2002] 1 Lloyd's Rep 679, [2001] All ER (D) 344 (Nov). See also *The Young Sid* [1929] P 190, CA (costs of partially successful appeal); *The Capitan San Luis* [1994] QB 465, [1994] 1 All ER 1016 (limitation of liability proceedings).

Where the defendant's vessel was pronounced alone to blame in an action of damage, the defendant was usually ordered to pay all the costs of the proceedings. Similarly, where there was a counterclaim in an action of damage and the vessel was found to be alone to blame, the claimant generally bore the whole costs. In actions where neither party admitted negligence and both the vessels were found to blame in equal degrees, the court usually made no order as to costs, leaving each party to bear his own. See, however, *The Lucile Bloomfield* [1966] 3 All ER 294n, [1966] 1 WLR 1525 (costs not further considered on appeal [1967] 2 All ER 633n, [1967] 1 WLR 697n, CA), where on a finding of equal blame the defendants were ordered to pay half the claimant's costs because no counterclaim had been pursued by the defendants in the jurisdiction. Cf *The Ek* [1966] 1 Lloyd's Rep 440.

When, under the Maritime Conventions Act 1911 (repealed) (see now the Merchant Shipping Act 1995 s 185, Sch 7; and PARA 195 et seq), blame was apportioned in unequal degrees, the court took into account the circumstances of each particular case in exercising its discretion as to costs and had regard to the fact that one party had succeeded more than the other on the question of liability: see *The Modica* [1926] P 72 at 79–80 per Hill J; *The Osprey* [1967] 1 Lloyd's Rep 76 at 94 per Brandon J; followed in *The Bonifaz* [1967] 1 Lloyd's Rep 321. There is no rule that where the blame is unequally divided the costs must be divided in the same proportion: *The Modica*; *The Salabangka* [1943] P 13. If a special order as to costs is made, it has generally taken the form of ordering one party to pay a certain proportion of the other party's costs: *The Robert Koeppen* [1926] P 81n (claimants 25% to blame, defendants 75%; defendants ordered to pay 50% of claimants' costs); *The Osprey* (claimants to blame for 60%, defendants 40%; claimants ordered to pay 20% of defendants' costs). In making its award as to costs, the court may also take into account factors such as alterations of log-books, failure properly to complete the collision statement of case, or untruthfulness of witnesses: *The Lord Northcliffe* (1926) 24 Ll L Rep 187; *The Levante* (1927) 28 Ll L Rep 42; *The El Uruguayo* (1928) 30 Ll L Rep 118; *The Samurai* (1945) 78 Ll L Rep 546; *The Pulkovo and The Oden* [1989] 1 Lloyd's Rep 280. As to the effect of an offer by letter before trial to settle on a percentage of blame basis see *The Hudson Bay* [1957] 2 Lloyd's Rep 506; *The British Patrol* [1968] 1 Lloyd's Rep 117, CA. See also *The Toni* [1974] 1 Lloyd's Rep 489, CA; *The Pulkovo and the Oden*.

Where there had been no negligence on the part of either party and both the claim and counterclaim have been dismissed, it being a mere accident that one party was claimant and the other defendant, usually no order was made as to costs: see *The Dolabella* (1944) 77 Ll L Rep 292; *The Hoyanger* (1946) 79 Ll L Rep 284. If, however, there would have been no litigation had the claimants not issued proceedings, judgment was given for the defendants on the claim with costs, and for the claimants on the counterclaim with costs: *The Cardiff Hall* [1918] P 56. Where no counterclaim was made the action was usually dismissed with costs: *The Llanover* (1944) 77 Ll L Rep 198; *The Luhesand* [1955] 2 Lloyd's Rep 203.

In cases of damage following compulsory pilotage, if the defendants raise a defence both on the merits and on the ground of compulsory pilotage without setting up a counterclaim, and the suit was dismissed by reason of the defence of compulsory pilotage having succeeded, usually no costs were given on either side: see *The Daioz* (1877) 3 Asp MLC 477, CA; *The Winestead* [1895] P 170 at 175 per Bruce J; *The Mercedes de Larrinaga* [1904] P 215 at 235 per Gorell Barnes J; *The Ophelia* [1914] P 46, CA; and see PARA 222. Where the sole issue to be decided was compulsory pilotage, the party succeeding on that issue was usually held entitled to the costs of the action: see *The Oakfield* (1886) 11 PD 34 at 37; *The Ophelia*. The defence of compulsory pilotage was abolished by the Pilotage Act 1913 s 15 (repealed) (see now the Pilotage Act 1987 s 16; and PARA 589), and cannot now arise except in rare instances. Although it is probable that effect would be given to s 16 in the case of a collision occurring on the high seas, compulsory pilotage is still a good defence in the case of a collision occurring in the territorial waters of a country by whose laws that defence has not been abolished: see *The Arum* [1921] P 12; *The Waziristan* [1953] 2 All ER 1213, [1953] 1 WLR 1446, [1953] 2 Lloyd's Rep 361; and see PARA 580 et seq.

Where a claimant sued two defendants and succeeded against only one, and the defendants each threw the blame on the other the court ordered the unsuccessful defendant to pay the costs incurred by the claimant and by the successful defendant to each of them direct: see *The Esrom and The Hopper Wills No 66* [1914] WN 81. See also *The River Lagan* (1888) 57 LJP 28; *The Mystery* [1902] P 115, DC; *The Eland and The Monte Urquiola* [1969] 2 Lloyd's Rep 328. For an example of an order of costs in an action where blame was apportioned among three vessels see *The Miraflores and The Abadesa* [1965] 2 Lloyd's Rep 254 (revsd on the question of liability, [1966] P 18, [1966] 1 All ER 553, [1966] 1 Lloyd's Rep 97, CA; affd [1967] 1 AC 826, [1967] 1 All ER 672, [1967] 1 Lloyd's Rep 191, HL). See also *The Quickstep* (1890) 15 PD 196, DC, where the claimants and one of the defendants were held to blame and the successful defendant obtained an order for costs against the claimants. Where the respective defendants did not mutually blame each other, but the claimant, being in reasonable doubt as to which to sue, sued both and succeeded against only one, the court ordered the claimant to pay the costs of the successful defendant, at the same time giving him permission to add such costs to his costs against the unsuccessful defendant: see *The Svein Jarl* (1923) 129 LT 255; *The Thames III and The KBS* (1928) 166 LT Jo 52. Alternatively, the court has made a direct order. The order made is a matter of the judge's discretion: see *Hong v A and R Brown Ltd* [1948] 1 KB 515, [1948] 1 All ER 185, CA. As to the position in relation to co-defendants see generally CPR Pt 20; and CIVIL PROCEDURE vol 11 (2015) PARA 367 et seq. In such a case the proper course is to join both defendants on one claim form, and the claimant is not allowed the extra costs incurred by bringing separate claims against them: see *The Svein Jarl*. See also *The WH Randall* [1928] P 41, CA. Where, however, the unsuccessful defendant did nothing to induce the claimant to sue the successful defendant, and there was nothing in the circumstances of the case to prompt the claimant to sue the successful defendant, the claimant was ordered to pay the latter's costs without any right to receive them from the unsuccessful defendant: see *The Theodoros, The Blidensol* [1923] P 26 at 30 per Hill J. The same considerations applied where counterclaims were brought against more than one party: see *The Svein Jarl*.

Where an award of salvage was made in an action of salvage (see PARA 113 et seq) in which no payment into court had been made, the usual practice where the salvors had not been guilty of any misconduct was for the claimants to have all the costs of the action: see *The Dwina* [1892] P 58 at 64; *The Rialto* [1891] P 175 at 179 per Butt J. See also *Hatton v Akt Durban Hausen* 1919 SC 154, where the costs of arresting the defendants' vessel were allowed, even though the subsequent proceedings were brought in personam. For an example of a case involving co-claimants, some of whom were successful see *The Southwark* [1962] 2 Lloyd's Rep 62. As to the effect of payments into court and of open offers see PARA 203. Even where no salvage was awarded, the practice of the old Court of Admiralty was to award no costs, or only a nominal sum, to the defendants, if it considered that the action was brought in good faith: see *The Henrietta* (1837) 3 Hag Adm 345n; *The Little Joe* (1860) Lush 88. It is suggested that this is one of the old rules as to costs which have been obsolete since the Judicature Acts: see *The Monkseaton* (1889) 14 PD 51, CA. When, however, salvors have been guilty of misconduct and for that reason there has been a forfeiture of salvage, they have been condemned in costs: see *The Capella* [1892] P 70; *The Yan-Yean* (1883) 8 PD 147 at 150 per Sir James Hannon. For an example of special orders as to costs made in a case involving a salvage claim and a counterclaim for negligent damage, both partially successful see *The Tojo Maru* [1970] P 21 at 50, [1969] 2 All ER 155 at 173, [1969] 1

Lloyd's Rep 133 at 149 per Willmer LJ (on appeal [1970] P 21 at 77, [1969] 3 All ER 1179 at 1195–1196, [1969] 2 Lloyd's Rep 193 at 214–215, CA, per Karminski LJ; costs not further considered in the House of Lords [1972] AC 242, [1971] 1 All ER 1110, [1971] 1 Lloyd's Rep 341, HL).

When salvage services have been rendered to ship and cargo and salvage has been awarded against both, the owners of the salved ship and of the cargo have usually contributed to the costs in proportion to the values on which the award is made, but this has been said to be without prejudice to the salvor's right to recover the whole from either: see *The Elton* [1891] P 265 at 271 per Jeune J.

**205. Assessors.** In collision claims[1] and other cases involving issues of navigation and seamanship, the Admiralty Court may sit with assessors[2]. Nautical assessors and Elder Brethren of Trinity House only advise the court on matters of nautical skill on which information is desired, and it is the duty of the court, having received that information, to exercise its own judgment, and decide the case before it on its own responsibility[3]. Before an Admiralty judge decides whether to accept the evidence of a nautical assessor, the evidence should be put to counsel so that appropriate submissions can be made[4].

The parties are not permitted to call expert evidence on such matters, unless the court orders otherwise[5], and they are reminded of the practice with regard to the disclosure of any answers to the court's questions and the opportunity for comment on them[6].

1  As to the meaning of 'collision claim' for these purposes see PARA 91 note 12. As to the procedure that governs Admiralty claims, including CPR Pt 61 and *Practice Direction—Admiralty Claims* PD 61, see PARA 140 note 5. As to the meanings of 'Admiralty claim' and 'Admiralty Court' for these purposes see PARA 91 note 3. As to the assignment of business to the Admiralty Court see CPR 61.2(1), (2); and PARA 91.

2  CPR 61.13; and see the Admiralty and Commercial Courts Guide (2016) para N14.1. The assessor will normally be asked to assist the court by preparing a report, and by attending the trial and advising the court, on certain matters in dispute in the proceedings: see CPR 35.15(3); and CIVIL PROCEDURE vol 12 (2015) PARA 921. As to assessors in general see also the Senior Courts Act 1981 s 70 (assessors and scientific advisers); CPR 35.15; and CIVIL PROCEDURE vol 12 (2015) PARA 921. See also *Ahmed v Governing Body of the University of Oxford* [2002] EWCA Civ 1907 at [20], [2003] 1 All ER 915 at [20], [2003] 1 WLR 995 at [20], obiter, per Waller LJ. For an example of appointment of a Trinity Master in a case in the Commercial Court of the Queen's Bench Division see *Southport Corpn v Esso Petroleum Co Ltd* [1953] 2 All ER 1204, [1953] 3 WLR 773; affd sub nom *Esso Petroleum Co Ltd v Southport Corpn* [1956] AC 218, [1955] 3 All ER 864, HL.

3  *The Magna Charta* (1871) 1 Asp MLC 153, 25 LT 512, PC; *The Beryl* (1884) 9 PD 137 at 141, CA; *The Duke of Buccleuch* (1889) 15 PD 86 at 95, CA (affd [1891] AC 310, HL); *The Gannet* [1900] AC 234 at 235–236, HL, per Earl of Halsbury LC; *The City of Berlin* [1908] P 110 at 118, CA; *Cambo Shipping Co Ltd v Dampskibsselskabet Magnus* 1920 SC 26; *The Australia* [1927] AC 145, HL; *SS Melanie (Owners) v SS San Onofre (Owners)* (1919) [1927] AC 162n, HL; *SS Artemisia (Owners) v SS Douglas (Owners)* (1925) [1927] AC 164n, HL. If the court is unable to decide whether the advice received from the nautical assessors is sound, the point is not proven, and the loss falls on the party bearing the burden of proof: *The Australia* at 153 per Lord Sumner.

4  *Owners of Bow Spring v Owners of Manzanillo II* [2004] EWCA Civ 1007, [2005] 1 All ER (Comm) 53n, [2005] 1 WLR 144, [2005] 1 Lloyd's Rep 1. The Admiralty Court has set out guidelines concerning the use of nautical assessors in collision actions so as to ensure compliance with the right to a fair and public hearing: see *Global Mariner v Atlantic Crusader* [2005] EWHC 380 (Admlty) at [12]–[17], [2005] 2 All ER (Comm) 389 at [12]–[17], [2005] 1 Lloyd's Rep 699 at [12]–[17] per Gross J, applying *Owners of Bow Spring v Owners of Manzanillo II*; and see note 6.

5  CPR 61.13; and see the Admiralty and Commercial Courts Guide (2016) para N14.1. As to the court's discretion as regards expert evidence generally see CPR 32.1 (cited in CIVIL PROCEDURE vol 12 (2015) PARA 510). See also *The Gazelle* (1842) 1 Wm Rob 471; *The Sir Robert Peel* (1880) 4 Asp MLC 321, CA; *The Kirby Hall* (1883) 8 PD 71 at 75.

6  See the Admiralty and Commercial Courts Guide (2016) para N14.2. The text refers to the guidance with regard to the disclosure of answers to the court's questions and the opportunity for comment on them as set out by Gross J in *Global Mariner v Atlantic Crusader* [2005] EWHC 380 (Admlty), [2005] 2 All ER (Comm) 389, [2005] 1 Lloyd's Rep 699 (cited in note 4): see the Admiralty and Commercial Courts Guide (2016) para N14.2.

**206. Rehearing.** It is well settled that the High Court possesses a power, which will be exercised in a fit case, to rehear Admiralty claims where a mistake is proved to have been made on the first hearing; but this power will only be exercised rarely and with great caution[1].

1 *The Monarch* (1839) 1 Wm Rob 21; *The James Armstrong* (1875) LR 4 A & E 380; *The Georg* [1894] P 330 at 333.

### C. PAYMENTS AND ENFORCEMENT

**207. Payment of money found due.** Where the amount of the liability of the defendants, or of claimants against whom a counterclaim has been substantiated, is ascertained[1] either by the Admiralty Registrar[2], or by virtue of the amount of the principal sum due being specified in the order of the court, the person entitled to receive the amount may, if the proceeds of a ship or cargo are in court or their value has been paid into court, obtain an order directing the amount found due to him to be paid to him, or on his written authority to his solicitor[3]. Where there is more than one claimant it is the duty of the court to see that all persons who have a claim on the fund share in its distribution[4]. If the claim is one for damage, and there are claims both for loss of life and for damage to property, the fund will be distributed pro rata among the various claimants unless the defendants take proceedings to limit their liability[5].

If there have been cross-claims of damage in which both vessels have been held to blame, or proceedings where both claim and counterclaim have succeeded, the amount due will be the amount of the balance, if any, which is found due after the amounts due to the claimants in the cross-claims, or to the claimants and defendants in cases where there are counterclaims, have been set off against each other[6].

1 Where a wrong in respect of which the claim or counterclaim is made involves an expenditure in a foreign currency, the proper rate of exchange for ascertaining the amount payable in English currency is the rate prevailing at the date of the wrong: *SS Celia v SS Volturno* [1921] 2 AC 544, HL; *The Baarn* [1933] P 251, CA. In appropriate cases judgment may be given in a foreign currency: see *The Despina R* [1979] AC 685, [1979] 1 All ER 421, HL, applied in *The Lash Atlantico* [1987] 2 Lloyd's Rep 114, CA; *The Transoceanica Francesca and Nicos V* [1987] 2 Lloyd's Rep 155. In a salvage case, the relevant date for conversion is the date of the services, even though the parties are all foreigners and sterling has been devalued between that date and the date of judgment: *The Teh Hu* [1970] P 106, [1969] 3 All ER 1200, [1969] 2 Lloyd's Rep 365, CA. As to the extent of Admiralty jurisdiction regarding salvage claims see PARA 113 et seq.
2 As to the Admiralty Registrar see PARA 140; and as to references to the Admiralty Registrar PARA 143.
3 See PARA 203.
4 See *The Joannis Vatis* [1922] P 92, CA, where shipowners, suing for themselves and as bailees of the cargo, recovered judgment for the full amount of damage to their vessel and to the cargo, and the cargo-owners, although they had not assented to the action, were held entitled to share in the fund. As to cautions against payment out see PARA 174.
5 *Canadian Pacific Rly Co v SS Storstad* [1920] AC 397, PC.
6 See *The Khedive* (1882) 7 App Cas 795, HL.

**208. Execution by writ of control.** The ordinary remedies for enforcing a judgment in the High Court are applicable to Admiralty claims[1]. Thus writs of control are issued when necessary to recover the amount, including costs, due under the judgment in a claim in personam[2]. In the case of a claim in rem[3], where the defendant has acknowledged service and judgment has been pronounced against him, the claimant is entitled, in the absence of any limitation of liability[4], to a writ of control on the ship released on bail, or on any other property belonging to the defendant, in respect of his claim and costs, or the balance if part payment has been made[5].

1 As to enforcement generally see CIVIL PROCEDURE vol 12A (2015) PARA 1268 et seq.
2 As to writs of control generally see CIVIL PROCEDURE vol 12A (2015) PARA 1379 et seq.

3 As to the origin of claims in rem see PARA 83; as to the jurisdiction of the Admiralty Court in relation to claims in rem see PARA 92 et seq; and as to commencing such a claim see PARA 158 et seq.

4 As to limitation of liability see PARA 194 et seq.

5 See *The Gemma* [1899] P 285, CA; followed in *The Dupleix* [1912] P 8. As to remedies available in the case of judgment in default see PARA 190. As to arrest after damages have been awarded see *The Alletta* [1974] 1 Lloyd's Rep 40; not followed in *The Daien Maru No 18* [1986] 1 Lloyd's Rep 387, Singapore HC.

# (4) OTHER COURTS HAVING ADMIRALTY JURISDICTION

## (i) County Court

**209. Former jurisdiction of the county courts.** The Admiralty jurisdiction of the county courts[1] was abolished with effect from 26 April 1999[2] and all Admiralty proceedings commenced thereafter must be commenced in the High Court[3].

1 As to the jurisdiction of the county courts generally see COURTS AND TRIBUNALS vol 24 (2010) PARA 767 et seq.

2 See the Civil Courts (Amendment) (No 2) Order 1999, SI 1999/1011 (amending the Civil Courts Order 1983, SI 1983/713 (revoked)).

3 As to the jurisdiction of the High Court generally see COURTS AND TRIBUNALS vol 24 (2010) PARA 699 et seq. As to the assignment of business to the Admiralty Court see CPR 61.2(1), (2); and PARA 91. As to the procedure that governs Admiralty claims, including CPR Pt 61 and *Practice Direction—Admiralty Claims* PD 61, see PARA 91 et seq. As to the meanings of 'Admiralty claim' and 'Admiralty Court' for these purposes see PARA 91 note 3.

## (ii) Court of Admiralty of the Cinque Ports

**210. Jurisdiction of the Court of Admiralty of the Cinque Ports.** The Confederation of the Cinque Ports originally comprised the five ports of Hastings, Romney, Hythe, Dover and Sandwich, although other ports have been admitted over the years either as corporate members (also known as corporate limbs) or as non-corporate members (also known as non-corporate limbs)[1].

The Court of Admiralty of the Cinque Ports is presided over by the Judge Official and the Commissary of the Court of Admiralty of the Cinque Ports, but its role today is primarily ceremonial, no cases having been heard by it for many years[2]. The court has inherent jurisdiction to hear a number of Admiralty disputes[3], and additional statutory jurisdiction to hear salvage disputes on appeal from the Salvage Commissioners of the Cinque Ports[4]. In the absence of the parties' consent, the court sat in St James's Church at Dover, but the court may exercise its jurisdiction within the boundaries of jurisdiction of the Lord Warden of the Cinque Ports[5].

1 The continuance of the Confederation of the Cinque Ports is unaffected by the local government areas established by the Local Government Act 1972 Pt I (ss 1–19) (as to which see LOCAL GOVERNMENT vol 69 (2009) PARA 5 et seq) (see s 271(3)); and the Secretary of State or any appropriate Minister may at any time by order under s 254(1) make provision for securing the continued discharge of functions in relation to the Confederation of the Cinque Ports and its courts (including so far as is necessary for that purpose, provision for the constitution of a body to replace any existing corporation), for appropriating property or providing funds for the discharge of such functions, and otherwise for securing that anything required or authorised to be done by, to or in relation to the Confederation or any of its courts may continue to be done (s 254(2)(i); and see LOCAL GOVERNMENT vol 69 (2009) PARA 6).

2 See 4 Hasted's History of Kent 118.

3 The court has same inherent jurisdiction as the High Court of Admiralty possessed before the commencement of the Supreme Court of Judicature Act 1873. As to that inherent jurisdiction see

PARA 80 et seq. As to the jurisdiction and rights in respect of royal fish as droits of the Lord Warden see *Cinque Ports (Lord Warden) v R* (1831) 2 Hag Adm 438. As to royal fish see CROWN AND CROWN PROCEEDINGS vol 29 (2014) PARA 143. As to droits of Admiralty see PARA 139.
4   See the Cinque Ports Act 1821 s 4 (amended by the Statute Law Revision Act 1888; and the Statute Law (Repeals) Act 1993). As to the duties and jurisdiction of the Cinque Ports Salvage Commissioners see PARA 211. Nothing in the Merchant Shipping Act 1995 Pt IX (ss 224–255) (salvage and wreck) (as to which see PARA 849 et seq) prejudices or affects any jurisdiction or powers of Lord Warden or any officers of the Cinque ports or of any court of those ports or of any court having concurrent jurisdiction within the boundaries of those ports; and disputes as to salvage arising without those boundaries must be determined, subject to the International Convention on Salvage (London, 28 April 1989; Misc 8 (1991); Cm 1526), as set out in the Merchant Shipping Act 1995 s 224(1), Sch 11 Pt I (see PARA 851 et seq), in the manner in which they have been hitherto determined: s 314, Sch 14 para 11.
5   As to these boundaries see the Cinque Ports Act 1821 s 18 (amended by the Statute Law Revision Act 1888).

## 211. Duties and jurisdiction of the Cinque Ports Salvage Commissioners.
The Cinque Ports Salvage Commissioners are appointed by the Lord Warden of the Cinque Ports[1], or by the person who is Deputy Warden of the Cinque Ports and Lieutenant of Dover Castle[2]. The Cinque Ports Act 1821, under which such commissioners are appointed, defines the boundaries of the cinque ports to seawards and on the coast[3], and enables the commissioners to determine questions arising as to the salvage of anchors and chain cables found at sea or supplied to ships, and as to salvage services rendered generally to ships within the jurisdiction of the Cinque Ports, and to goods which have been wrecked or stranded within that jurisdiction, provided that the master or owner of the salved ship or the owners of the salved goods, or his or their agents, are present[4].

1   See the Cinque Ports Act 1821 s 1 (amended by the Statute Law (Repeals) Act 1993).
2   The person who is Deputy Warden of the Cinque Ports may exercise any power conferred by the Cinque Ports Act 1821 on the Lord Warden: see s 5A (added by the Statute Law (Repeals) Act 1993 s 1(2), Sch 2 Pt II para 10).
3   As to these boundaries see the Cinque Ports Act 1821 s 18 (amended by the Statute Law Revision Act 1888).
4   See the Cinque Ports Act 1821 ss 1, 2 (both amended by the Statute Law (Repeals) Act 1993). Although this power of the Lord Warden is obsolete, it has been saved in the Merchant Shipping Act 1995 s 314, Sch 14 para 11 (as to which see PARA 210 note 4).

## 212. Appeal from an award of the Cinque Ports salvage commissioners.
An appeal from the determination by the Cinque Ports salvage commissioners of any salvage disputes may, within eight days after the award of salvage is made, be brought either to the Court of Admiralty of the Cinque Ports or to the Admiralty Court of the High Court of Justice[1]. The proceedings must be commenced within 20 days, and the property in respect of the salving of which the award was made may be released on security being given in double the amount of the award[2].

1   See the Cinque Ports Act 1821 s 4 (amended by the Statute Law Revision Act 1888; and the Statute Law (Repeals) Act 1993). See also the Senior Courts Act 1981 s 61(1), Sch 1 para 2; and COURTS AND TRIBUNALS vol 24 (2010) PARA 706. As to the jurisdiction of the High Court generally see COURTS AND TRIBUNALS vol 24 (2010) PARA 699 et seq. As to the assignment of business to the Admiralty Court see CPR 61.2(1), (2); and PARA 91.
2   See the Cinque Ports Act 1821 s 4 (as amended: see note 1). An appeal from the commissioners' award is in the nature of a rehearing rather than an appeal, and it is obligatory on the court to allow a restatement of the case and to admit fresh evidence. The court will, however, in the exercise of its discretion as to costs, discourage the giving of fresh evidence unwarrantably: see *The Caledonia* (1869) LR 4 A & E 11. For further proceedings in appeals from the commissioners see also *The Annette* (1873) LR 4 A & E 9.

## 213. Appeal from the Court of Admiralty of the Cinque Ports.
An appeal lies to the Queen in Council, and any such appeal would be referred to the Judicial Committee of the Privy Council[1].

1   See the Judicial Committee Act 1833 s 3; and COURTS AND TRIBUNALS vol 24 (2010) PARAS 675, 681. See, for an instance of such an appeal, *The Clarisse* (1856) 12 Moo PCC 340.

### (iii)  Other Admiralty Courts

**214.  Former local courts of Admiralty.** Many of the seaport boroughs had in their charters a grant of a court of Admiralty[1], but in 1835 all local courts, except that of the Cinque Ports[2], were deprived of any Admiralty jurisdiction they might have[3]. Certain titular and honorific rights, however, still appear to survive. For instance, the mayor of Southampton has a silver oar as *insigne* of a titular admiralty, and is entitled to receive the first visit from foreign men-of-war visiting the port, and the mayors of some other ports have a similar privilege.

1   Some maritime towns had from a very early period courts of the seaport, which administered the law maritime. Disputes as to jurisdiction arose between the Admiral's court and these courts, which led to two statutes (13 Ric 2 stat 1 c 5 (1389–90) (repealed); and the Admiralty Jurisdiction Act 1391 (repealed)) defining and restricting the jurisdiction of the Admiral: see Carter's History of the English Courts (5th Edn) 103.

2   As to which see PARA 210.

3   See the Municipal Corporations Act 1835 s 108 (repealed). By virtue of local legislation, the Liverpool Court of Passage continued to have Admiralty jurisdiction until its abolition by the Courts Act 1971 s 43 (repealed). Pending proceedings were then transferred to the Liverpool county court. The Mayor's and City of London Court was an Admiralty county court until the Admiralty jurisdiction of the county courts was abolished (as to which see PARA 209).

**215.  Courts of the Vice-Admirals of the coast.** The sea coast of England and Wales is divided into 19 districts, for each of which a Vice-Admiral of the coast may be appointed[1]. Vice-Admirals of the coast represent the Lord High Admiral, or the Lords Commissioners for executing that office, in his capacity so far as it was not concerned with the navy. They are appointed by letters patent under the Great Seal, and the appointment is *durante bene placito*[2]. The jurisdiction extends up to high-water mark and to the first bridges towards the sea on rivers, and is exercisable by a judge[3]. The patent of the Vice-Admiral empowers him to appoint his own officers, excepting, however, the judge, Registrar and marshal of his Vice-Admiralty Court. These excepted officers are appointed by letters patent, but there are none in existence at the present time, and, consequently, although the jurisdiction of these courts of Vice-Admiralty over causes of action arising in the jurisdiction has never been abolished by statute, there is now no means of executing it. There is no jurisdiction as to wreck.

1   These districts are:
    (1)   Northumberland, Durham, and York;
    (2)   Lincoln;
    (3)   Norfolk;
    (4)   Suffolk;
    (5)   Essex;
    (6)   Kent
    (7)   Sussex
    (8)   Hampshire
    (9)   Dorset
    (10)  Devon
    (11)  South Cornwall
    (12)  North Cornwall
    (13)  Somerset
    (14)  Gloucester
    (15)  South Wales;
    (16)  North Wales;
    (17)  Chester;
    (18)  Lancaster; and
    (19)  Westmorland and Cumberland.

2   The form of patent is printed in *Baker's Vice-Admiral of the Coast* 50 et seq, where the jurisdiction exercised by the court is stated. As to the Great Seal see CONSTITUTIONAL AND ADMINISTRATIVE LAW vol 20 (2014) PARAS 583, 593 et seq.

3   By an order of a committee of the Lords and Commons, 1635, the judge was to be a discreet and learned man in the civil laws dwelling or resorting within the circuit of his office, or for want of

a civilian one learned in the common laws of the realm dwelling within the same circuit. In 1663 the Duke of York (afterwards James II), the then Lord High Admiral, issued instructions to the judge of the Court of Admiralty and to the Vice-Admirals, by which the powers and duties of those officers were regulated. Under these the whole of the judicial powers was directed to be exercised by the judge, but the levying and receiving the perquisites of the office or droits of Admiralty remained with the Vice-Admirals. These instructions did not apparently interfere with the jurisdiction of the judges of the Vice-Admiralty Courts, as these judges continued to be appointed. The patents confer no jurisdiction in prize matters (as to which see further PRIZE). See further *Baker's Vice-Admiral of the Coast* 69.

## 216. Jersey, Guernsey and the Isle of Man. The Royal Courts of Jersey and Guernsey and the Admiralty Court of the Isle of Man have an Admiralty jurisdiction[1].

1   The statutory provisions which confer Admiralty jurisdiction, ie the Senior Courts Act 1981 ss 20–24 (as to which see PARA 85 et seq), may be extended, with such exceptions, adaptations and modifications as may be specified, to any of the Channel Islands or the Isle of Man by Order in Council: see s 150(1).
    Accordingly, the Admiralty Jurisdiction (Guernsey) Order 1993, SI 1993/2664, extends the Admiralty jurisdiction of the High Court to the whole of the Bailiwick of Guernsey (Guernsey, Alderney, Herm, Jethou and Sark) and the territorial waters adjacent thereto. However, at the date at which this volume states the law, no order has been made in respect of Jersey. It would appear that the Royal Court of Jersey probably has jurisdiction over all matters arising within the island: see *Re Jersey Jurats* (1866) LR 1 PC 94, although the exact extent of Admiralty jurisdiction is unclear. Similarly, no order has been made in respect of the Isle of Man, but its jurisdiction is almost identical with that of the Admiralty Court of the High Court of Justice: see *Roscoe's Admiralty Practice* (5th Edn) 35, 36.

## 217. Colonial Courts of Admiralty. The Colonial Courts of Admiralty have taken the place of the Vice-Admiralty Courts in British possessions[1]. The jurisdiction of these courts may be more restrictive than the Admiralty jurisdiction of the High Court[2]. The judgments of a Colonial Court of Admiralty are subject to the same local rights of appeal as they would have been if pronounced by the court in the exercise of its ordinary civil jurisdiction[3]. There is an ultimate appeal as of right without special permission to Her Majesty in Council[4] from a judgment of any court in a British possession in the exercise of the jurisdiction conferred by the Colonial Courts of Admiralty Act 1890[5]. Permission of the Privy Council to appeal is necessary if the petition of appeal has not been lodged within the time prescribed by the rules, or, if no time is so prescribed, within six months from the date of the judgment appealed against[6].

1   As to the origin and jurisdiction of the Colonial Courts see the Colonial Courts of Admiralty Act 1890 s 2; and COMMONWEALTH vol 13 (2017) PARA 742.
2   In *The Yuri Maru; The Woron* [1927] AC 906, PC, the Privy Council held that the jurisdiction conferred by the Colonial Courts of Admiralty Act 1890 was that jurisdiction existing at the time the Act came into force. Under the Senior Courts Act 1981, Her Majesty may by order in council direct, either generally or in relation to particular courts or territories, that the Colonial Courts of Admiralty Act 1890 is to have effect in any British possession: see s 150(2). Accordingly, see the Admiralty Jurisdiction (British Indian Ocean Territory) Order 1984, SI 1984/540; and the Admiralty Jurisdiction (Gibraltar) Order 1987, SI 1987/1263. As to orders made under an equivalent provision of the Administration of Justice Act 1956, which by virtue of the Interpretation Act 1978 s 17(2)(b) have effect as if made under the Senior Courts Act 1981 s 150(2), see the Admiralty Jurisdiction (Virgin Islands) Order in Council 1961, SI 1961/2033; the Admiralty Jurisdiction (Cayman Islands) Order 1964, SI 1964/922; the Admiralty Jurisdiction (Turks and Caicos Islands) Order 1965, SI 1965/1529; the Admiralty Jurisdiction (Falkland Islands) Order 1966, SI 1966/686; the Admiralty Jurisdiction (Montserrat) Order 1968, SI 1968/1647; the Admiralty Jurisdiction (St Helena and its Dependencies) Order 1969, SI 1969/858; and the Admiralty Jurisdiction (Bermuda) Order 1974, SI 1974/2148.
3   See the Colonial Courts of Admiralty Act 1890 s 5; and see COMMONWEALTH vol 13 (2017) PARA 742.
4   See the Colonial Courts of Admiralty Act 1890 s 6; and see COMMONWEALTH vol 13 (2017) PARA 742.

5   See the Colonial Courts of Admiralty Act 1890 s 6(1) (cited in COMMONWEALTH vol 13 (2017) PARA 742); *Richelieu and Ontario Navigation Co v SS Cape Breton* [1907] AC 112, PC.
6   See the Colonial Courts of Admiralty Act 1890 s 6(2); and see COMMONWEALTH vol 13 (2017) PARA 742.

# (5) APPEALS

## (i) Appeals from the High Court

### A.   JURISDICTION AND PRELIMINARY PROCEEDINGS

**218.  Application of general law to Admiralty appeals.** Admiralty cases are subject to the same provisions as other cases with regard to the making of applications to appeal from the High Court[1] to the Court of Appeal[2] or to the Supreme Court[3].

1   As to the jurisdiction of the High Court generally see COURTS AND TRIBUNALS vol 24 (2010) PARA 699 et seq. As to the Admiralty jurisdiction of the High Court and the assignment of business to the Admiralty Court see CPR 61.2(1), (2); and PARA 91.
2   As to the provision made for procedure on appeals to the Court of Appeal see CIVIL PROCEDURE vol 12A (2015) PARA 1559 et seq.
3   As to the provision made for procedure on appeals to the Supreme Court see CIVIL PROCEDURE vol 12A (2015) PARA 1584 et seq. As to stay pending appeal to the Supreme Court see *The Ratata* [1897] P 118 at 131.

**219.  Security for costs in appeal from Admiralty claim in rem.** Where the claim in relation to which an appeal is made is an Admiralty claim in rem[1], it is not the usual practice for an appellant who has furnished security[2] in the court below, and so obtained there the release of the property proceeded against, to be required to give security for the costs of the appeal[3]. However, the Court of Appeal has a general power to order security for costs, under special circumstances[4].

1   As to claims in rem see PARA 158 et seq.
2   As to methods of furnishing security in Admiralty claims see PARA 171 et seq.
3   *The Victoria* (1876) 1 PD 280, CA. It is the practice to take into account the costs of a potential appeal when fixing the original demand for security.
4   See CPR 25.15; and CIVIL PROCEDURE vol 12 (2015) PARA 620.

### B.   HEARING AND DECISION

**220.  Principles governing hearing of Admiralty appeal.** The power of receiving additional evidence in its discretion in Admiralty appeals was transferred to the Court of Appeal together with the rest of the jurisdiction over such appeals formerly possessed by the Judicial Committee of the Privy Council[1].

When the Court of Appeal is assisted by nautical assessors, who may advise the court on issues of navigation and seamanship in collision cases[2], it will not generally allow additional evidence to be called on matters of nautical knowledge and skill[3]. As in the case of the court of first instance, it is the duty of the Court of Appeal, having received the advice of the assessors, to exercise its own judgment[4] and, if the advice of the assessors in the Court of Appeal differs from that of those in the court of first instance, the Court of Appeal must make its own choice as to which advice it will follow[5]. It is desirable that questions submitted by the Court of Appeal to its assessors should be in writing[6].

Where there has been a conflict of evidence in the court below, the Court of Appeal must decide, as in other cases, whether the conclusion reached by the judge appealed from is the proper one, but will attach great weight to his view of the evidence owing to the fact that the witnesses were examined before him, and he saw their demeanour and manner of giving evidence[7].

Where in a claim for damage by collision the judge in the court of first instance has found both vessels to blame and, in accordance with the Merchant Shipping Act 1995[8], has apportioned the blame between them, the Court of Appeal, if it agrees with the judge on the facts, will not lightly interfere with his apportionment of blame. If, however, the Court of Appeal takes a different view of the facts, it is bound to review the apportionment[9].

1  See *The Scindia* (1866) LR 1 PC 241; the Judicial Committee Act 1833; the Judicial Committee Act 1843; the Senior Courts Act 1981 s 15(2); and CIVIL PROCEDURE vol 12A (2015) PARA 1559 et seq. As to the general procedure that applies to the hearing of appeals see CPR 52.11; and CIVIL PROCEDURE vol 12A (2015) PARA 1530.
2  As to the role of assessors generally see PARA 205.
3  *The Assyrian* (1890) 6 Asp MLC 525, CA. See, however, *The Antares II and Victory* [1996] 2 Lloyd's Rep 482 where the Admiralty Court stated that although it had been long established that when the court was assisted by nautical assessors expert evidence on matters of navigation and seamanship might not be adduced, the rule did not appear to be absolute.
4  *The Gannet* [1900] AC 234, HL; *The Australia* [1927] AC 145, HL; *The Tovarisch* [1930] P 1 at 7, CA, per Scrutton LJ; *The Otranto* [1930] P 110 at 133, CA, per Lawrence LJ.
5  *The Fina Canada* [1962] 2 Lloyd's Rep 445, CA; *Saul v Saint Andrew's Steam Fishing Co Ltd, The St Chad* [1965] 2 Lloyd's Rep 1, CA; *The Sobieski* (1949) 82 Ll L Rep 370; *The Miraflores and the Abadesa* [1966] 1 Lloyd's Rep 97 (Willmer LJ dissenting, revsd sub nom *Miraflores (Owners) v George Livanos (Owners)* [1967] 1 AC 826, HL); *Hattersley & Sons Ltd v George Hodgson Ltd* (1905) 21 TLR 178, CA (Court of Appeal may consider the opinion and reasons of the assessor which were given to the trial judge). However, the parties to the appeal are not entitled to copies of the opinion and reasons of the assessors given to the trial judge: *The Banshee* (1887) 56 LT 725, CA.
6  *SS Melanie (Owners) v SS San Onofre (Owners)* [1927] AC 162n at 164, HL, per Lord Birkenhead LC.
7  *SS Hontestroom v SS Sagaporack* [1927] AC 37, HL. See also *The Glannibanta* (1876) 1 PD 283, CA; *The Sisters* (1876) 1 PD 117, CA; *The Singapore and The Hebe* (1866) LR 1 PC 378. A judge must not, however, be taken, in preferring the witnesses on one side to those on the other, to be treating all the evidence on one side as exact and all the evidence on the other as necessarily and deliberately untruthful: *The Eurymedon* (1942) 73 Ll L Rep 217 at 225, HL, per Lord Merriman.
8  Ie in accordance with the Merchant Shipping Act 1995 ss 187–189 (multiple fault) (see PARAS 1010–1012).
9  There needs to have been some error of law shown, some misapprehension of a vital factor or some other exceptional reason to revise the apportionment: see *The Umtali* (1938) 160 LT 114, HL; *The Macgregor* [1943] AC 197, [1943] 1 All ER 33, HL; *The Karamea* [1921] P 76, CA (affd sub nom *SS Haugland v SS Karamea* [1922] 1 AC 68, HL). See also *The Clara Camus* (1925) 134 LT 50, CA (revsd (1926) 136 LT 291, HL, but the point referred to in the text was not dealt with); *The British Aviator* [1965] 1 Lloyd's Rep 271, CA; *The Miraflores and the Abadesa* [1966] P 18, [1966] 1 All ER 553, CA; revsd [1967] 1 AC 826, [1967] 1 All ER 672, [1967] 1 Lloyd's Rep 191, HL; *The Almizar* [1970] 1 Lloyd's Rep 67, CA (on appeal [1971] 2 Lloyd's Rep 290, HL); *The Anneliese* [1970] 2 All ER 29n, [1970] 1 Lloyd's Rep 355, CA; *The Statue of Liberty* [1970] 2 Lloyd's Rep 151, CA (on appeal [1971] 2 Lloyd's Rep 277, HL). See also the principles laid down in *The Savina* [1976] 2 Lloyd's Rep 123, HL.

## 221. References to the Admiralty Registrar.

The Court of Appeal has discretionary power to refer any question arising in an appeal to the Admiralty Registrar[1], either alone or assisted by one or more merchants or other assessors[2]. A reference ordered by the Court of Appeal will be dealt with in the same way as a reference ordered by the High Court[3]. The Registrar's decision on the reference may come before the Court of Appeal by way of an appeal against the High Court's consideration of the Registrar's decision[4] but, in such a case, the Court of Appeal will not lightly depart from the Registrar's assessment and may restore it if satisfied that the judge has interfered on inadequate grounds[5].

1  As to the Admiralty Registrar see PARA 140; and as to references to the Admiralty Registrar see PARA 143.

2 See the Judicial Committee Act 1833 s 17; the Senior Courts Act 1981 s 15(2) (see CIVIL PROCEDURE vol 12A (2015) PARA 1550); and *The Flying Fish* (1865) 3 Moo PCCNS 77 at 91 per Lord Chelmsford. It is not the modern practice to appoint merchants or other assessors in the circumstances mentioned in the text; but as to nautical assessors, who may advise the court on issues of navigation and seamanship in collision cases, see PARA 205.
3 As to the raising of a reference by the High Court see *Practice Direction—Admiralty Claims* PD 61 para 13; and PARA 143 et seq.
4 As to appeals against the Admiralty Registrar's decision see PARA 149.
5 *The Amerika* [1914] P 167, CA.

**222. Costs of Admiralty appeal.** The costs of an appeal, like the costs of an Admiralty claim, are in the unfettered discretion of the court[1]. This discretion must be exercised judicially but, in general, costs follow the event. Thus where the Court of Appeal in a collision claim affirms the apportionment of blame made by the court below the appellant will usually be condemned in the costs of the appeal[2]. Where a party succeeds on the appeal, he will be awarded his costs of the appeal, and this is so even in cases where the success consists only in the fact that degrees of blame found by the court below have been readjusted on appeal[3]. As regards the costs of the court below, the Court of Appeal will generally order the costs to be apportioned in accordance with the apportionment of blame found by the Court of Appeal[4]. The rule of practice has been followed in the Court of Appeal that, where the appellants succeed on the ground of compulsory pilotage, no costs will be given[5].

1 *The Young Sid* [1929] P 190, CA, following the decision of the House of Lords in *Donald Campbell & Co Ltd v Pollak* [1927] AC 732, HL. As to costs in Admiralty proceedings in the High Court proceedings see PARA 204.
2 *The Hector* (1883) 8 PD 218, CA, per Bowen LJ; *The City of Manchester* (1880) 5 PD 221, CA; *The Alida Gorthno* [1956] 1 Lloyd's Rep 567, CA; *The Lucile Bloomfield* [1967] 2 All ER 633n, [1967] 1 WLR 697n, [1967] 1 Lloyd's Rep 341, CA. Where an appeal and cross-appeal are dismissed with costs, the principle of no apportionment laid down as to claim and counterclaim cases in *Medway Oil and Storage Co v Continental Contractors Ltd* [1929] AC 88, HL, has been applied: see *The Stentor* [1934] P 133, CA.
3 *The Young Sid* [1929] P 109 (affd at [1929] P 190, CA); *The Fina Canada* [1962] 2 Lloyd's Rep 445, CA; *The British Aviator* [1965] 1 Lloyd's Rep 271, CA; *The British Patrol* [1968] 1 Lloyd's Rep 117, CA; *The Almizar* [1970] 1 Lloyd's Rep 67, CA.
4 As to the effect of an open offer on award of costs on appeal see *The British Patrol* [1968] 1 Lloyd's Rep 117, CA; *The Almizar* [1970] 1 Lloyd's Rep 67, CA; and see PARA 203.
5 See *The Daioz* (1877) 3 Asp MLC 477, CA. As to compulsory pilotage see PARA 580.

### (ii) Appeals from Inferior Courts

**223. Appeals to the Divisional Court of the Queen's Bench Division.** The Divisional Court of the Queen's Bench Division[1] sits to hear statutory shipping casualty rehearings and appeals under the Merchant Shipping Act 1995[2].

1 As to the divisions of the High Court generally see COURTS AND TRIBUNALS vol 24 (2010) PARA 695. As to matters assigned to a Divisional Court of the Queen's Bench Division see CIVIL PROCEDURE vol 12A (2015) PARA 1557.
2 The divisional court's general jurisdiction to hear appeals is rarely invoked in Admiralty matters. However, the Secretary of State may order a case to be reheard in part or wholly if new and important evidence which could not be produced either at a shipping inquiry or at a formal investigation has been discovered, or if there appear to be other grounds for suspecting that a miscarriage of justice may have occurred: see the Merchant Shipping Act 1995 s 64(1) (see PARA 537), s 269(1) (see PARA 844). See also PARA 224 et seq. Such rehearings were ordered following the discovery and surveying of wrecks in the case of *The MV Derbyshire* (see the Report of the re-opened formal investigation into the loss of the MV Derbyshire, 8 November 2000) and in the case of *The Gaul* (see the Department of the Environment, Transport and the Regions Marine Accident Investigation Branch, Marine Accident Report 4/99, Report on the Underwater Survey of the Stern Trawler GAUL H.243 and the supporting Model Experiments, August 1998–January 1999). See also *Rutberg v Williams* [1962] 1 QB 12, [1961] 2 All ER 649, DC (appeal from magistrates as to fine imposed under the Merchant Shipping (Safety and Load Line Conventions) Act 1932 s 44 (repealed)); and *Babbs v Press* [1971] 3 All ER 654, [1971] 1 WLR

1739, [1971] 2 Lloyd's Rep 383, DC (appeal from magistrates dismissing charge brought against licensed waterman under the Pilotage Act 1913 s 30(3) (repealed)).

**224. Appeals to the Divisional Court in relation to statutory marine investigations or inquiries and rehearings.** Appeals from a formal investigation into a shipping accident[1], or from an inquiry under the Merchant Shipping Act 1995 into the fitness or conduct of a master, mate or engineer[2], lie to the Divisional Court of the Queen's Bench Division (if the decision has been given in England[3] or by a naval court) in cases where the person holding the inquiry or investigation (as the case may be) has decided to cancel or suspend the certificate of any person or found any person at fault, and if no application has been made for a re-hearing by order of the Secretary of State[4], or if such an application has been refused[5].

Under the Merchant Shipping Act 1995, the Secretary of State may order that a rehearing of an inquiry into the fitness or conduct of an officer[6] or of a seaman other than an officer[7], or from a formal investigation into a shipping casualty[8], is to take place either before the persons who held the first hearing, or before a wreck commissioner[9] or the High Court[10]. This provision will only apply where the initial inquiry or investigation was held in England, Wales or Northern Ireland[11]. A rehearing must be ordered by the Secretary of State under the Merchant Shipping Act 1995 if new and important evidence which could not be produced at the shipping inquiry or investigation has been discovered, or if there appear to the Secretary of State to be other grounds for suspecting that a miscarriage of justice may have occurred[12]. In a case where at the inquiry or investigation either a person's certificate has been cancelled or suspended or he has been found at fault, then, if an application has not been made to the Secretary of State to order a rehearing, or if one has been made but has been refused, that person, or any other interested person who appeared at the inquiry or investigation, may appeal to the High Court[13].

1 As to which see the Merchant Shipping Act 1995 s 268 (formal investigation into marine accidents); and PARA 830.
2 As to which see the Merchant Shipping Act 1995 s 61 (inquiries as to fitness or conduct of an officer); and PARA 524.
3 As to the meaning of 'England' see PARA 16 note 2.
4 As to such applications see the Merchant Shipping Act 1995 s 64 (appeal from inquiry into fitness or conduct of officer) (see PARA 537), s 269 (appeal from formal investigation into marine accidents) (see PARA 844); and see PARA 227. As to the Secretary of State for these purposes see PARA 36.
5 See the Merchant Shipping Act 1995 s 64(4) (appeal from inquiry into fitness or conduct of officer) (cited in PARA 537), s 269(4) (appeal from formal investigation into marine accidents) (cited in PARA 844). For examples of such appeals see *The City of Lincoln* (1947) 80 Ll L Rep 692, DC; *The Corchester* [1957] P 84, [1956] 3 All ER 878, DC; *The Seistan* [1960] 1 All ER 32, [1960] 1 WLR 186, DC.
  Where on any investigation or inquiry into a shipping casualty the court finds that the casualty has been caused or contributed to by the wrongful act or default of any person, and an application for a rehearing has not been made or has been made and refused, the owner of the ship, or any other person having an interest in the investigation or inquiry who has appeared at the hearing and is affected by the decision of the court, has the same right of appeal against the decision as a master has against a decision with respect to the cancellation or suspension of his certificate: see the Merchant Shipping Act 1995 ss 64(4), 269(4), concerning appeals by 'interested parties'. A master who has been censured, but whose certificate has not been cancelled or suspended, has a right of appeal as 'a person having an interest' in the inquiry.
6 Ie an inquiry held under the Merchant Shipping Act 1995 s 61 (as to which see PARA 524): see s 64(1). A rehearing and an application made under s 61 are treated as an appeal for the purposes of *Practice Direction—Appeals* PD 52 para 22.2 (as to which see PARA 225): see para 22.2(1); and PARA 225.
7 Ie held under the Merchant Shipping Act 1995 s 63 (as to which see PARA 530): see s 64(1).

8　Ie where a formal investigation has been held under the Merchant Shipping Act 1995 s 268 (as to which see PARA 830): see s 269(1).
9　As to wreck commissioners see PARA 59.
10　See the Merchant Shipping Act 1995 s 64(1), (2) (cited in PARA 537), s 269(1), (2) (cited in PARA 844). Rules of court made for the purpose of rehearings under s 64 or under s 269 which are held by the High Court, or of appeals to the High Court, may require the court, subject to such exceptions, if any, as the rules allow, to hold such a rehearing or hear such an appeal with the assistance of one or more assessors: see s 65(2) (cited in PARA 525 note 2), s 270(2) (cited in PARA 831). As to the conduct of rehearings see PARA 225 et seq. As to nautical assessors, who may advise the court on issues of navigation and seamanship in collision cases, see PARA 205.
11　See the Merchant Shipping Act 1995 s 64(2) (cited in PARA 537), s 269(2) (cited in PARA 844). As to the meaning of 'Wales' see PARA 16 note 2.
12　See the Merchant Shipping Act 1995 s 64(1) (cited in PARA 537), s 269(1) (cited in PARA 844).
13　See the Merchant Shipping Act 1995 s 64(4) (cited in PARA 537), s 269(4) (cited in PARA 844). Rules of court may provide for assessors to assist at the hearing: see note 10.

## 225. Procedure on appeal to the Divisional Court.

In relation to appeals made to the Divisional Court under the Merchant Shipping Act 1995[1], the standard practice and procedure applies generally regarding the court's powers[2] and the conduct of the hearing[3]. However, aside from an appeal notice[4], the appellant also must file any report to the Secretary of State[5] containing the decision from which the appeal is brought[6]; and, where a re-hearing by the Divisional Court is ordered under the Merchant Shipping Act 1995[7], the Secretary of State must give reasonable notice to parties whom he considers to be affected by the re-hearing[8].

The Divisional Court may, in special circumstances, order that security must be given for the costs of the appeal[9].

1　As to appeals from marine investigations or inquiries and rehearings under the Merchant Shipping Act 1995 see PARA 224. As to the divisions of the High Court generally see COURTS AND TRIBUNALS vol 24 (2010) PARA 695 et seq. As to matters assigned to a Divisional Court of the Queen's Bench Division see CIVIL PROCEDURE vol 12A (2015) PARA 1557.
2　See CPR 52.10; and CIVIL PROCEDURE vol 12A (2015) PARA 1529.
3　See CPR 52.11; and CIVIL PROCEDURE vol 12A (2015) PARA 1530.
4　As to the appellant's notice and appealing in general see CIVIL PROCEDURE vol 12A (2015) PARA 1514 et seq.
5　As to the Secretary of State for these purposes see PARA 36.
6　*Practice Direction—Statutory Appeals and Appeals which are subject to Special Provision* PD 52D para 25.1(2). *Practice Direction—Statutory Appeals and Appeals which are subject to Special Provision* PD 52D para 25 applies to appeals under the Merchant Shipping Act 1995 and for this purpose a re-hearing and an application under s 61 (as to which see PARA 511) are treated as appeals: *Practice Direction—Statutory Appeals and Appeals which are subject to Special Provision* PD 52D para 25.1(1).
7　Ie under the Merchant Shipping Act 1995 s 64 (cited in PARA 523) or s 269 (cited in PARA 871): see *Practice Direction—Statutory Appeals and Appeals which are subject to Special Provision* PD 52D para 25.1(3). See also PARA 224.
8　*Practice Direction—Statutory Appeals and Appeals which are subject to Special Provision* PD 52D para 25.1(3).
9　See CPR 25.15; and CIVIL PROCEDURE vol 12 (2015) PARA 620.

## 226. Further appeal from the Divisional Court.

Appeal lies to the Court of Appeal from a decision of a Divisional Court, but the permission of the Divisional Court or the Court of Appeal is required in the case of the determination by a Divisional Court of an appeal to the High Court[1].

Subject to specified conditions[2], an appeal may be brought direct to the Supreme Court from a decision of a Divisional Court[3].

1　See CPR Pt 52; *Practice Direction—Appeals* PD 52A para 4.7; and CIVIL PROCEDURE vol 12A (2015) PARA 1542.
2　See the Administration of Justice Act 1969 ss 12, 13, 15; CIVIL PROCEDURE vol 12A (2015) PARA 1585; COURTS AND TRIBUNALS vol 24 (2010) PARA 659.
3　See the Administration of Justice Act 1969 s 12(2)(c); CIVIL PROCEDURE vol 12A (2015) PARA 1585; COURTS AND TRIBUNALS vol 24 (2010) PARA 659.

**227. Rehearing at the instance of the Secretary of State.** A rehearing of a shipping inquiry or investigation[1] may be ordered by the Secretary of State[2] to be heard by the person who held it, by a wreck commissioner[3] or by a Divisional Court of the Queen's Bench Division[4].

1　As to which see the Merchant Shipping Act 1995 s 61 (inquiries as to fitness or conduct of an officer) (cited in PARA 524), s 268 (formal investigation into marine accidents) (cited in PARA 830). See also PARA 224.

2　As to the Secretary of State for these purposes see PARA 36.

3　As to wreck commissioners see PARA 59.

4　See the Merchant Shipping Act 1995 s 64(2) (cited in PARA 537), s 269(2) (cited in PARA 844). As to the procedure on a rehearing see s 65 (regarding inquiries) (cited in PARA 525) and s 270 (regarding formal investigations) (cited in PARA 831).

　　As to the divisions of the High Court generally see COURTS AND TRIBUNALS vol 24 (2010) PARA 695. As to matters assigned to a Divisional Court of the Queen's Bench Division see CIVIL PROCEDURE vol 12A (2015) PARA 1557.

### (iii) Pilotage Appeals

**228. Pilotage appeals.** Certain county courts and stipendiary magistrates formerly had power to hear appeals by pilots in certain cases against decisions of pilotage authorities (for example, in connection with pilots' licences) but this jurisdiction no longer exists[1]. Under the Pilotage Act 1987, which deregulates the pilot service and puts in its place a system administered by harbour authorities, the licensing of pilots is a matter for the competent harbour authorities[2].

1　See the Pilotage Act 1983 s 26 (repealed by the Pilotage Act 1987 s 32(5), Sch 3).

2　See the Pilotage Act 1987 s 3; and PARA 577. As to statutory harbour authorities see PORTS AND HARBOURS vol 85 (2012) PARA 20.

# 3. MERCHANT SHIPS

## (1) BRITISH SHIPS

**229. Meaning of 'ship' for the purposes of the Merchant Shipping Act 1995.** For the purposes of the Merchant Shipping Act 1995, unless the context otherwise requires, 'ship' includes every description of vessel used in navigation[1]. Whether a vessel comes within that meaning of a ship depends on the facts of each case; the statutory definition is intended to enlarge the meaning of 'ship'[2]. To be a 'ship' for the purposes of the merchant shipping legislation[3], a vessel must be used in navigable waters, either inland or at sea[4], and, although she must be constructed for navigation[5], it is not necessary to the definition that she should be able to navigate under her own power[6]. The presence of a rudder and the manning of the vessel with a crew are important as showing that a vessel is a ship[7], but the absence of either does not mean that a vessel is not a ship[8]. The purpose for which a vessel has been and is being used is also material when considering whether she is used in navigation[9].

The Secretary of State[10] may by order:

(1)     provide for a shipping provision[11] to apply (with or without modification) in relation to specified things which are used, navigated or situated wholly or partly in or on water[12];

(2)     provide for a shipping provision not to apply in relation to specified things which are used, navigated or situated wholly or partly in or on water[13];

(3)     modify a shipping provision in its application in relation to specified things which are used, navigated or situated wholly or partly in or on water[14].

1   Merchant Shipping Act 1995 s 313(1). See *Everard v Kendall* (1870) LR 5 CP 428 (collision between barges propelled by oars); *Ex p Ferguson* (1871) LR 6 QB 280 (fishing coble using oars to get out to sea and sails thereafter held to be a ship); *The CS Butler* (1874) LR 4 A & E 238, 2 Asp MLC 408 (lighter propelled by sails and oars on Thames held not to be a ship); *Edwards v Quickenden and Forester* [1939] P 261, 63 Ll L Rep 189 (craft propelled by oars held not to be a vessel); *Clark (Inspector of Taxes) v Perks* [2001] EWCA Civ 1228, [2001] 2 Lloyd's Rep 431, [2001] STC 1254 (jack-up drilling rig with floating hull and retractable legs held to be a ship); *R v Goodwin* [2005] EWCA Crim 3184, [2006] 2 All ER 519, [2006] 1 Lloyd's Rep. 432 (jetski not a vessel 'used in navigation').

    The question appears to be still open whether the use to which the vessel is being put at the time of the collision or the use to which the vessel has been put is the determining factor in deciding whether a vessel is propelled by oars: see *The Champion* [1934] P 1, 47 Ll L Rep 40, DC. It would appear that either may be the determining factor in deciding whether a vessel is used in navigation: see the text and note 9.

2   *The Mac* (1882) 7 PD 126, 4 Asp MLC 555, CA.

3   Ie for the purposes of the Merchant Shipping Act 1995 s 313(1) (see the text and note 1). The cases cited in notes 4–9 were all decided under predecessor merchant shipping legislation.

4   *Southport Corpn v Morriss* [1893] 1 QB 359, DC (electric launch exclusively used for pleasure trips on artificial lake not used in navigation); *Corbett v Pearce* [1904] 2 KB 422, DC (sprit-sail barge used on tidal waters is used in navigation); *Weeks v Ross* [1913] 2 KB 229, 12 Asp MLC 307, DC (motor boat on river used in navigation); and see *The Mac* (1882) 7 PD 126 at 131, 4 Asp MLC 555 at 558, CA, per Cotton LJ.

5   *The Mac* (1882) 7 PD 126, 4 Asp MLC 555, CA; *Wells v Gas Float Whitton No 2 (Owners)* [1897] AC 337, 8 Asp MLC 272, HL; *The Blow Boat* [1912] P 217; *Polpen Shipping Co Ltd v Commercial Union Assurance Co Ltd* [1943] KB 161, [1943] 1 All ER 162; *Marine Craft Constructors Ltd v Erland Blomquist (Engineers) Ltd* [1953] 1 Lloyd's Rep 514.

6   *The Mac* (1882) 7 PD 126, 4 Asp MLC 555, CA; *The Mudlark* [1911] P 116; *The Harlow* [1922] P 175, 15 Asp MLC 498.

7   See the cases cited in note 6.

8	*The St Machar* (1939) 65 Ll L Rep 119; *Cook v Dredging and Construction Co Ltd* [1958] 1 Lloyd's Rep 334.
9	*European and Australian Royal Mail Co Ltd v Peninsular and Oriental Steam Navigation Co* (1866) 14 LT 704 (a vessel used as a coal hulk for four years); *The Mac* (1882) 7 PD 126, 4 Asp MLC 555, CA; *Wells v Gas Float Whitton No 2 (Owners)* [1897] AC 337, 8 Asp MLC 272, HL (moored beacon); *The Harlow* [1922] P 175, 15 Asp MLC 498 (barges used in tow of tugs in carriage of goods on the Thames); *Marine Craft Constructors Ltd v Erland Blomquist Engineers Ltd* [1953] 1 Lloyd's Rep 514 (crane pontoon, stripped of its crane, and temporarily adapted for carrying goods in tow of tug).
10	As to the Secretary of State for these purposes see PARA 36.
11	For these purposes, 'shipping provision' means a provision which is made by or by virtue of an Act (including the Railways and Transport Safety Act 2003), and is expressed to apply in relation to ships, vessels or boats (or a specified class or description of ship, vessel or boat): see s 112(2); and PARA 22.
12	See the Railways and Transport Safety Act 2003 s 112(1)(a); and PARA 22. In exercise of the power conferred by s 112(1)(a), the Merchant Shipping (Prevention of Pollution) (Drilling Rigs and Other Platforms) Order 2005, SI 2005/74, has been made.
13	See the Railways and Transport Safety Act 2003 s 112(1)(b); and PARA 22.
14	See the Railways and Transport Safety Act 2003 s 112(1)(c); and PARA 22.

## 230. Meanings of 'British ship', 'United Kingdom fishing vessel' and 'United Kingdom ship'. A ship[1] is a 'British ship' if:

(1)	the ship is registered[2] in the United Kingdom[3] under Part II of the Merchant Shipping Act 1995[4]; or

(2)	the ship is, as a government ship[5], registered in the United Kingdom in pursuance of an Order in Council[6]; or

(3)	the ship is registered under the law of a relevant British possession[7]; or

(4)	the ship is a small ship[8] other than a fishing vessel[9] and is not registered under Part II of the Merchant Shipping Act 1995[10], but is wholly owned by qualified owners[11] and is not registered under the law of a country outside the United Kingdom[12].

A ship is a 'United Kingdom ship' for the purposes of the Merchant Shipping Act 1995[13] if the ship is registered in the United Kingdom under Part II of the 1995 Act[14]; and 'United Kingdom fishing vessel' has[15] a corresponding meaning[16].

1	As to the meaning of 'ship' see PARA 229.
2	As to the meaning of 'registered' for these purposes see PARA 254 note 2.
3	As to the meaning of 'United Kingdom' see PARA 16 note 3.
4	Merchant Shipping Act 1995 s 1(1)(a). The text refers to registration under Pt II (ss 8–23) (see PARA 245 et seq): see s 1(1)(a).
5	As to the meaning of 'government ships' see PARA 19 note 3.
6	Merchant Shipping Act 1995 s 1(1)(b). The text refers to registration in pursuance of an Order in Council under s 308 (see PARA 19): see s 1(1)(b).
7	Merchant Shipping Act 1995 s 1(1)(c). As to the meaning of 'relevant British possession' for these purposes see PARA 16 note 3.
8	For these purposes, 'small ship' means a ship less than 24 metres in length ('length' having the same meaning as in the tonnage regulations): Merchant Shipping Act 1995 s 1(2). As to the meaning of 'tonnage regulations' see PARA 248.
9	In the Merchant Shipping Act 1995, unless the context otherwise requires, 'fishing vessel' means a vessel for the time being used (or, in the context of an application for registration, intended to be used) for, or in connection with, fishing for sea fish other than a vessel used (or intended to be used) for fishing otherwise than for profit; and for these purposes, 'sea fish' includes shellfish, salmon and migratory trout, as defined by the Fisheries Act 1981 s 44 (see FISHERIES AND AQUACULTURE vol 51 (2013) PARA 219): Merchant Shipping Act 1995 s 313(1). A vessel for the time being used (or intended to be used) wholly for the purpose of conveying persons wishing to fish for pleasure is not a fishing vessel: s 313(3).
10	Merchant Shipping Act 1995 s 1(1)(d)(i). The text refers to registration under Pt II (see PARA 245 et seq): see s 1(1)(d)(i).
11	Merchant Shipping Act 1995 s 1(1)(d)(ii). For these purposes, 'qualified owners' means persons of such description qualified to own British ships as is prescribed by regulations made by the Secretary of State for these purposes: Merchant Shipping Act 1995 s 1(2). As to the Secretary of State see

PARA 36; and as to his power to make subordinate legislation under the Merchant Shipping Act 1995 see PARA 39. At the date at which this volume states the law, no such regulations had been made and none have effect as if so made.

> Be that as it may, in the Merchant Shipping Act 1995, except for s 9 (see PARA 245), and in any other enactment applicable to British ships or ships registered under that Act, any reference, however phrased, to the owner of a British ship, a United Kingdom ship (as to which see the text and notes 12–14) or a ship registered in the United Kingdom, means, in relation to a bareboat charter ship, the person registered as the charterer: see the Merchant Shipping (Modification of Enactments) (Bareboat Charter Ships) Order 1994, SI 1994/774, arts 2, 3 (made under the Merchant Shipping Act 1995 s 17(8): see PARA 357).

12 Merchant Shipping Act 1995 s 1(1)(d)(iii).
13 Ie except the Merchant Shipping Act 1995 s 85 (safety and health on ships) (see PARA 602 note 1) and s 144(3) (notification that a ship other than a United Kingdom ship has been detained for oil pollution offences) (see ENVIRONMENTAL QUALITY AND PUBLIC HEALTH vol 45 (2010) PARA 434): see s 1(3).
14 Merchant Shipping Act 1995 s 1(3). The text refers to registration under Pt II (see PARA 245 et seq): see s 1(1)(3).
15 Ie in the Merchant Shipping Act 1995 Pt V (ss 109–127) (fishing vessels): see s 1(3).
16 Merchant Shipping Act 1995 s 1(3).

**231. British flag.** The flag which every British ship[1] (other than a government ship[2]) is entitled to fly is the red ensign (without any defacement or modification) and[3] no other colours[4]. The following are, however, also proper national colours, that is to say:

(1)     any colours allowed to be worn in pursuance of a warrant from Her Majesty or from the Secretary of State[5];

(2)     in the case of British ships registered[6] in a relevant British possession[7], any colours consisting of the red ensign defaced or modified whose adoption for ships registered in that possession is authorised or confirmed by Her Majesty by Order in Council[8].

Any Order under head (2) above must be laid before Parliament after being made[9].

1  As to the meaning of 'British ship' see PARA 230; and as to the meaning of 'ship' see PARA 229.
2  The Merchant Shipping Act 1995 s 2(1) does not apply to government ships: s 2(2). As to the meaning of 'government ships' see PARA 19 note 3.
3  Ie subject to the Merchant Shipping Act 1995 s 2(2) (see note 2) and s 2(3) (as to which see the text and notes 5–8): see s 2(1).
4  Merchant Shipping Act 1995 s 2(1). As to the duty to show the British flag see PARA 232; and as to the duty to declare the national character of a ship see PARA 233. As to offences relating to the British character of ships see PARA 1062; and as to the penalty for carrying improper colours see PARA 1063.
5  Merchant Shipping Act 1995 s 2(3)(a). As to the Secretary of State see PARA 36.
6  As to the meaning of 'registered' for these purposes see PARA 254 note 2.
7  As to the meaning of 'relevant British possession' for these purposes see PARA 16 note 3.
8  Merchant Shipping Act 1995 s 2(3)(b). As to the making of orders under head (2) in the text, and as to the orders so made, see the text and note 9.
9  Merchant Shipping Act 1995 s 2(4). As to the making of Orders under the Merchant Shipping Act 1995 generally see PARA 39. In exercise of the power conferred by s 2(3)(b), Her Majesty has made:
    (1)     the Merchant Shipping (Gibraltar Colours) Order 1996, SI 1996/281, whereby the adoption for the purposes of the Merchant Shipping Act 1995 s 2(3)(b) as proper colours for ships registered in Gibraltar of the red ensign defaced with the arms of Gibraltar was authorised (Merchant Shipping (Gibraltar Colours) Order 1996, SI 1996/281, art 2(1)), the positioning and proportions of the defacement to be in accordance with art 2(2), Schedule (art 2(2)); and
    (2)     the Merchant Shipping (Falkland Islands Colours) Order 1998, SI 1998/3147, whereby the adoption for the purpose of the Merchant Shipping Act 1995 s 2(3)(b) as proper colours for ships registered in the Falkland Islands of the red ensign defaced with the arms of the Falkland Islands was authorised (Merchant Shipping (Falkland Islands Colours) Order 1998, SI 1998/3147, art 2(1)), the positioning and proportions of the defacement to be in accordance with the illustration in art 2(2), Schedule (art 2(2)).

**232. Duty to show British flag.** A British ship[1], other than a fishing vessel[2], must hoist the red ensign or other proper national colours[3] in the following circumstances[4]:

(1)	on a signal being made to the ship by one of Her Majesty's ships, including any ship under the command of a commissioned naval officer[5]; and

(2)	on entering or leaving any foreign port[6]; and

(3)	in the case of ships of 50 or more tons gross tonnage[7], on entering or leaving any British port[8].

1	As to the meaning of 'British ship' see PARA 230; and as to the meaning of 'ship' see PARA 229.
2	As to the meaning of 'fishing vessel' see PARA 230 note 9.
3	As to the colours which every British ship (other than a government ship) is entitled to fly see PARA 231.
4	Merchant Shipping Act 1995 s 5(1).
5	Merchant Shipping Act 1995 s 5(1)(a). As to the meaning of 'commissioned naval officer' see PARA 47 note 12.
6	Merchant Shipping Act 1995 s 5(1)(b). As to the meaning of 'port' for these purposes see PARA 46 note 12.
7	However, head (3) in the text does not apply to a small ship, as defined in the Merchant Shipping Act 1995 s1(2) (see PARA 230 note 8), registered under Pt II (ss 8–23) (see PARA 245 et seq): s 5(2). As to the meaning of 'registered' for these purposes see PARA 254 note 2.
8	Merchant Shipping Act 1995 s 5(1)(c).

**233. Duty to declare national character of ship.** An officer of Revenue and Customs[1] must not grant a clearance or transire[2] for any ship[3] until the master[4] of such ship has declared to that officer the name of the nation to which he claims that the ship belongs; and that officer must thereupon enter that name on the clearance or transire[5].

If a ship attempts to proceed to sea without such clearance or transire, the ship may be detained until the declaration is made[6].

1	As to the appointment of officers of Revenue and Customs see INCOME TAXATION vol 58 (2014) PARA 33.
2	A transire is a warrant from the custom-house to let goods pass: see CUSTOMS AND EXCISE vol 31 (2012) PARA 1061.
3	As to the meaning of 'ship' for these purposes see PARA 229.
4	As to the meaning of 'master' for these purposes see PARA 444 note 1.
5	Merchant Shipping Act 1995 s 6(1) (amended by virtue of the Commissioners for Revenue and Customs Act 2005 s 50(1), (2), (7)).
6	Merchant Shipping Act 1995 s 6(2). As to enforcing the detention of a ship see PARA 1190.

**234. Ensigns and mooring.** By Admiralty warrant, yachts belonging to members of the Royal Yacht Squadron are permitted on certain terms to carry the white ensign as worn in Her Majesty's navy[1], and, in the case of other privileged clubs, it is either the blue ensign of Her Majesty's fleet, with or without a device, or the red ensign with the distinctive marks on its fly[2]. These privileges are in each case granted by individual warrant, and, in order to be eligible to wear such an ensign, a vessel must be registered, and must continue to belong to the individual to whom the warrant was granted, and the owner must continue as a member of the privileged club to which he belonged at the time of obtaining the warrant. Further, the owner must be on board the yacht, or in effective control of her, when she is in harbour or at anchor near the shore, and the yacht must never be used for any commercial purpose.

Yacht owners who possess Admiralty warrants are allowed the privilege of mooring at government buoys, at naval dockyard ports in the United Kingdom, as a matter of courtesy and at the discretion of the harbour master.

1	This privilege does not confer on the yacht the status of one of Her Majesty's ships: see *HMS Glatton* [1923] P 215.

2 For an illustrated list of yacht club flags see Lloyd's Register of Yachts. As to the use of the white, blue and red ensigns generally see CROWN AND CROWN PROCEEDINGS vol 29 (2014) PARA 48.

**235. Proceedings on forfeiture of a ship.** Where any ship[1] has either wholly or as to any share in it become liable to forfeiture[2], any commissioned naval[3] or military officer[4], or any person appointed by the Secretary of State[5] for the purpose, may seize and detain the ship and bring the ship for adjudication before the court[6].

Where a ship is so subject to adjudication, the court may adjudge the ship and her equipment to be forfeited to Her Majesty and make such order in the case as seems just[7].

No officer or person bringing such proceedings is liable in damages in respect of the seizure or detention of the ship, notwithstanding that the ship has not been proceeded against or, if proceeded against, adjudicated not liable to forfeiture, if the court is satisfied that there were reasonable grounds for the seizure or detention[8]. If the court is not so satisfied, the court may award costs and damages to the party aggrieved and make such other order as the court thinks just[9].

1 As to the meaning of 'ship' for these purposes see PARA 229.
2 Ie under the Merchant Shipping Act 1995 Pt I (ss 1–7) (see PARAS 230 et seq, 1062, 1063): see s 7(1).
3 As to the meaning of 'commissioned naval officer' see PARA 47 note 12.
4 For these purposes, 'commissioned military officer' means a commissioned officer in Her Majesty's land forces on full pay: Merchant Shipping Act 1995 s 313(1). As to the issue of commissions in Her Majesty's land forces see ARMED FORCES vol 3 (2011) PARA 456.
5 As to the Secretary of State see PARA 36.
6 Merchant Shipping Act 1995 s 7(1). For these purposes, 'court' means the High Court: s 7(5). As to the jurisdiction of the High Court generally see COURTS AND TRIBUNALS vol 24 (2010) PARA 699 et seq.
7 Merchant Shipping Act 1995 s 7(2).
8 Merchant Shipping Act 1995 s 7(3). A seizure will not as a rule be deemed unreasonable if made in good faith: see *The Evangelismos* (1858) Sw 378, PC; *Wilson v R* (1866) LR 1 PC 405; *Burns v Nowell* (1880) 5 QBD 444, 4 Asp MLC 323, CA. The circumstances may be such that an application by the British shareholders for relief will be refused: *The Polzeath* [1916] P 117; affd [1916] P 241, 13 Asp MLC 595, CA.
9 Merchant Shipping Act 1995 s 7(4).

# (2) OWNERSHIP

## (i) Acquisition of Ownership

**236. Methods of acquisition.** Ownership in a British ship[1] or share in her may be acquired in any of three ways: (1) by transfer from a person entitled to transfer[2]; (2) by transmission; or (3) by building.

Acquisition by transfer and transmission have been the subject of statutory enactment[3]; acquisition by building is governed by common law[4].

1 As to the meaning of 'British ship' see PARA 230.
2 A ship is not like an ordinary chattel which passes by delivery. A ship is a personal chattel; and specific performance of a contract to sell a ship may be decreed: *Behnke v Bede Shipping Co* [1927] 1 KB 649, 17 Asp MLC 222. See also *The Bineta, Dalby v Bineta (Owners)* [1966] 3 All ER 1007n, [1967] 1 WLR 121, [1966] 2 Lloyd's Rep 419 (sale of yacht).
3 As to transfer and transmission of ships generally see PARA 306 et seq; and as to transfer to the sheriff where execution is levied on a ship or share see *Harley v Harley* (1860) 11 I Ch R 451; *Chasteauneuf v Capeyron* (1882) 7 App Cas 127, 4 Asp MLC 489, PC.
4 As to the law relating to the passing of property in regard to the building of ships see SALE OF GOODS AND SUPPLY OF SERVICES vol 91 (2012) PARA 128; *Sir James Laing & Sons Ltd v Barclay, Curle & Co Ltd* [1908] AC 35, 10 Asp MLC 583, HL; *Re Blyth Shipbuilding and Dry*

Docks Co Ltd, *Forster v Blyth Shipbuilding and Dry Docks Co Ltd* [1926] Ch 494, CA; cf
*McDougall v Aeromarine of Emsworth Ltd* [1958] 3 All ER 431, [1958] 1 WLR 1126, [1958] 2
Lloyd's Rep 345.

## (ii) Rights of Ownership

**237. Powers of registered owner of a ship.** Subject to any rights and powers
appearing from the register[1] to be vested in any other person, the registered owner
of a ship[2] or of a share in a ship has power absolutely to dispose of it provided that
the disposal is made in accordance with the private law provisions for registered
ships[3] and registration regulations[4]. This is not to be taken to imply that interests
arising under contract or other equitable interests cannot subsist in relation to a
ship or a share in a ship; and such interests may be enforced by or against owners
and mortgagees of ships in respect of their interest in the ship or share in the same
manner as in respect of any other personal property[5].

The registered owner of a ship or of a share in a ship has power to give effectual
receipts for any money paid or advanced by way of consideration on any disposal
of the ship or share[6].

Any document authorised or required by or under any enactment to be served
on the registered owner of a United Kingdom ship[7] is to be treated as duly served
on him if served on such persons, in such circumstances and by such method, as
may be specified in registration regulations[8].

1  As to the meaning of 'register' see PARA 254 note 2.
2  As to the meaning of 'ship' see PARA 229.
3  For the purposes of the Merchant Shipping Act 1995 Pt II (ss 8–23), 'the private law provisions for
   registered ships' means the provisions of s 16(1), Sch 1 (as to which see PARAS 306, 318, 321,
   323–324, 328, 335) and registration provisions made for the purposes of Sch 1 or the provisions
   of registration regulations made under s 10(4)(a) (as to which see PARA 247): s 16(6). As to the
   application of Sch 1 see PARA 252. As to the meaning of 'registration regulations' see PARA 247.
4  Merchant Shipping Act 1995 Sch 1 para 1(1).
5  Merchant Shipping Act 1995 Sch 1 para 1(2).
6  Merchant Shipping Act 1995 Sch 1 para 1(3).
7  As to the meaning of 'United Kingdom ship' see PARA 230.
8  Merchant Shipping Act 1995 s 291(6). As to the service of documents under the Merchant
   Shipping Act 1995 generally see s 291; and PARA 74.

**238. Managing owner.** Part owners sometimes delegate authority in respect of
the managing of the ship to one of their number, who is known as the managing
owner[1]. The managing owner is agent for all the other owners[2], with power to do
what is necessary to enable the ship to prosecute her voyage and to earn freight[3].

1  The term 'managing owner' is used in the Merchant Shipping (Registration of Ships) Regulations
   1993, SI 1993/3138, reg 23 (appointment of managing owner where ship has more than one
   owner) (as to which see PARA 271) and in reg 34 (verification of details and marks) (see
   PARA 287), but it is not defined. It is a commercial and not a legal expression: see *Frazer v
   Cuthbertson* (1880) 6 QBD 93 at 98 per Bowen J. A person who is not a part owner may exercise
   the functions of a managing owner, in which case he is known as a 'ship's husband'.
2  *The Ida* (1886) 6 Asp MLC 21 (managing owner received contributions from one part owner as
   agent for all the rest).
3  As to the general powers of a managing owner in regard to the working of the ship and the
   ordering of the necessary supplies and repairs see *Card v Hope* (1824) 2 B & C 661; *Thompson
   v Finden* (1829) 4 C & P 158; *Green v Briggs* (1848) 6 Hare 395; *Darby v Baines* (1851) 9 Hare
   369; *Whitwell v Perrin* (1858) 4 CBNS 412; *Ritchie v Couper* (1860) 28 Beav 344; *Barker v
   Highley* (1863) 15 CBNS 27; *Vanner v Frost* (1870) 39 LJ Ch 626; *The Huntsman* [1894] P 214,
   7 Asp MLC 431. See also *Sims v Brittain* (1832) 4 B & Ad 375 (rights of part owners against
   agents appointed by managing owners); *Steele & Co v Dixon* (1876) 3 R 1003 (no authority to
   order structural alterations); *Swanston v Lishman* (1881) 4 Asp MLC 450, CA (practice as to
   discovery where managing owner is a member of a firm); *The Charles Jackson* (1885) 5 Asp MLC
   399 (claims by managing owner to recover sums he had not paid allowed in settlement of accounts
   with other co-owners, but subject to stay of execution until such co-owners protected against

claims of third persons in respect of those sums); *The Meredith* (1885) 10 PD 69, 5 Asp MLC 400 (right to reasonable remuneration); *The Bellcairn* (1886) 5 Asp MLC 582 (authority to take legal proceedings); *Ocean Iron Steamship Insurance Association Ltd v Leslie* (1887) 6 Asp MLC 226 (authority to make co-owners liable for calls in a mutual insurance association); *Williamson v Hine* [1891] 1 Ch 390, sub nom *Williamson v Hine Bros* 6 Asp MLC 559 (apart from special agreement a shipbroker who is also managing owner, receiving as such a fixed remuneration and whose duties include procuring charters and freights, cannot as shipbroker make extra profit for himself by commission or brokerage for obtaining charters and freights); *The Mount Vernon* (1891) 7 Asp MLC 32 (managing owner must account within reasonable time); *Nicol v Hennessy* (1896) 1 Com Cas 410 (managing owner selling shares in a ship which do not belong to him impliedly covenants to pay actual value of shares to the true owner); *Doeg v Trist* (1897) 2 Com Cas 153 (ship's husband cannot delegate his authority without sanction of owners, or pledge their credit unnecessarily).

**239. Distribution of profits.** Profits are distributed in accordance with any agreement between part owners, or in accordance with the interest of each partner in the ship[1]. Before profits are distributed, the sum earned by the ship must be applied to meet expenses[2]; and no partner is entitled to a share of the profits unless he has contributed his proper share of the capital[3]. A purchaser of a share in a ship which is at the time of the purchase engaged on a voyage is entitled to a share of the freight earned on that voyage, but is liable for a share of the expenses of earning it[4].

1 See the cases cited in PARA 238 note 3. A part owner may in certain circumstances be entitled to sue for his share of profits, even though they accrue from an illegal voyage: *Sharp v Taylor* (1849) 2 Ph 801 (but dicta in that case were doubted in *Sykes v Beadon* (1879) 11 ChD 170 at 195, 196 per Jessel MR). As to the liabilities of part owners see PARA 244.
2 *Green v Briggs* (1848) 6 Hare 395. These include wages (*Lindsay v Gibbs* (1859) 3 De G & J 690), and in some cases insurance (*Ogle v Wrangham* (1790) cited in Abbott's Law of Merchant Ships and Seamen (14th Edn) 130; *Hooper v Lusby* (1814) 4 Camp 66). As to the liability of the shipowner for wages see PARA 243.
3 *Green v Briggs* (1848) 6 Hare 395. Money spent on repairs by one partner is to be treated as capital: *Green v Briggs*.
4 *The Vindobala* (1889) 14 PD 50, 6 Asp MLC 376, CA. A purchaser is not liable where the seller is not in a position to complete the transfer of the ship: *The Bonnie Kate* (1887) 6 Asp MLC 149. As to the transfer of ships generally see PARA 306 et seq.

**240. Control of ship.** The right to the possession and control of the ship lies with the majority owners. Where the majority owners desire to send the ship on a particular voyage, but she is in the possession of a dissenting minority, the majority owners may arrest the ship and obtain from the court[1] a decree of possession, so that they may be enabled to employ the ship as they wish[2].

Similarly, where the minority owners object to the voyage on which it is proposed the ship shall be sent, they may arrest her and sue for an order that she be restrained[3] from pursuing the voyage[4].

In either of these cases, before the majority owners are permitted to send the ship on the desired voyage, they will be compelled to give security for the safe return of the vessel[5].

Where the minority owners object to the prosecution of a particular voyage, they are not obliged to contribute to the expenses of the voyage, but conversely will not be entitled to any of the profits[6].

1 As to the court's powers in its dealings with the ownership of vessels see also PARA 94. The court will require persons seeking to dispossess others to prove their title to a majority of shares: *The Valiant* (1839) 1 Wm Rob 64; *The Victoria* (1859) Sw 408.
2 *The New Draper* (1802) 4 Ch Rob 287; *The Kent* (1862) Lush 495.
3 As to the court's powers to restrain dealings at the instance of minority co-owners see PARA 107.
4 *The Talca* (1880) 5 PD 169, 4 Asp MLC 226; *The England* (1886) 12 PD 32, 6 Asp MLC 140. The court does not interfere to alter the possession of the ship unless such an alteration is sought by the majority of the owners: *The Egyptienne* (1825) 1 Hag Adm 346n; *The Elizabeth and Jane* (1841) 1 Wm Rob 278. The right to arrest is not affected by the fact that the charterparty under which the ship is about to sail was negotiated by the ship's husband appointed by the whole of the

owners: *The Talca*; *The England*. The authority to charter the ship must, however, have been withdrawn from the managing owner before the charterparty was entered into: *The Vindobala* (1889) 14 PD 50, 6 Asp MLC 376, CA. A foreign vessel may not be arrested at the suit of an English part owner, except possibly where the law of the foreign country is the same as that of England: *The Keroula* (1886) 11 PD 92, 6 Asp MLC 23. The court does not enter upon questions of ownership of a foreign ship where foreigners are alone concerned, unless by consent of the parties or upon the intervention of the representative of a foreign state: *The Johan and Siegmund* (1810) Edw 241; *The See Reuter* (1811) 1 Dods 22; *The Evangelistria* (1876) 2 PD 241, 3 Asp MLC 264; *The Agincourt* (1877) 2 PD 239; *The Annette, The Dora* [1919] P 105. A mortgagee of a ship or share cannot as such bring a restraint action: *The Innisfallen* (1866) LR 1 A & E 72. An equitable owner may probably do so: *Von Freeden v Hull* (1907) 10 Asp MLC 247 (revsd on appeal 10 Asp MLC 394, CA). A master cannot now be regarded as having possession of the ship and cargo as a bailee: *The Jupiter (No 3)* [1927] P 122 (affd [1927] P 250, 17 Asp MLC 250, CA). As to the position of mortgagees see PARA 327 et seq.

5	*The Apollo* (1824) 1 Hag Adm 306. The giving of a bail bond does not prevent the majority owners from subsequently disputing the right of the minority owners to have arrested the vessel: *The Keroula* (1886) 11 PD 92, 6 Asp MLC 23. The amount of the security given must bear the same relation to the value of the vessel as does the number of shares held by the minority owners to the whole number of shares in the ship: *The Cawdor* (1898) 8 Asp MLC 475; and see *The Robert Dickinson* (1884) 10 PD 15, 5 Asp MLC 341. The minority owners may not rearrest until the ship has returned to the port to which her safe return is pledged: *The Regalia* (1884) 5 Asp MLC 338. The sureties will be released after a reasonable time: *The Vivienne* (1887) 12 PD 185, 6 Asp MLC 178.

6	*The England* (1886) 12 PD 32, 6 Asp MLC 140; *The Cawdor* (1898) 8 Asp MLC 475.

## 241. Court order for sale of ship.

In certain cases the court will order the sale of the ship, but a strong case must be made out even by majority owners, while the court will be extremely reluctant to make such an order at the instance of minority owners[1]. In a proper case, however, the court will order a sale at the instance of minority owners[2].

In proper cases the court may order an account to be taken between co-owners[3].

1	*The Nelly Schneider* (1878) 3 PD 152, 4 Asp MLC 54; *The Marion* (1884) 10 PD 4, 5 Asp MLC 339. See also PARA 107.
2	*The Hereward* [1895] P 284, 8 Asp MLC 22 (where the majority owners had changed the character of the ownership by transferring the shares to a limited company). The dictum of Bruce J in this case that the majority had no right thus to change the character of the ownership was criticised by Gorell Barnes J in *The Loughborough* (1904) Shipping Gazette, 20 December.
3	As to the court's power to order accounts and sale see the Senior Courts Act 1981 s 20(2)(b), (4) and PARA 106. The court has ordered accounts to be taken of transactions taking place before this jurisdiction was conferred on it by the Admiralty Court Act 1861 s 8 (repealed) (*The Idas* (1863) Brown & Lush 65); and between a part owner and one who had ceased to be a part owner by selling his share (*The Lady of the Lake* (1870) LR 3 A & E 29). The court has also ordered the earnings of the ship in the hands of third persons to be brought into court pending the settlement of a dispute: *The Meggie* (1866) LR 1 A & E 77.

### (iii) Liabilities

## 242. Liability on bills of lading.

The general rule is that prima facie a bill of lading signed by the master is signed by him as the employee or agent of the shipowner, and the owner is liable on such bills of lading[1]. A mere reference in bills of lading to a charterparty which contains a clause that the master should be the employee of the charterer does not amount to notice to the holders of such bills that the master is not the owner's employee[2]. The owner is not, however, liable on bills of lading signed by a master who is not his employee and who has no authority to pledge his credit, even though the shipper has no notice of the charterparty[3].

1	*Manchester Trust v Furness* [1895] 2 QB 539 at 543, 8 Asp MLC 57 at 60, CA, per Lindley LJ. See also *Steel v Lester and Lilee* (1877) 3 CPD 121, 3 Asp MLC 537; and CARRIAGE AND CARRIERS vol 7 (2015) PARA 329 et seq. As to the liability of a shipowner on bills of lading signed

on his behalf by a charterer see *Homburg Houtimport BV v Agrosin Private Ltd, The Starsin* [2003] UKHL 12, [2004] 1 AC 715, [2003] 1 All ER (Comm) 625.
2   *Manchester Trust v Furness* [1895] 2 QB 539, 8 Asp MLC 57, CA.
3   *Baumwoll Manufactur von Carl Scheibler v Furness* [1893] AC 8, 7 Asp MLC 263, HL; cf *Associated Portland Cement Manufacturers (1910) Ltd v Ashton* [1915] 2 KB 1, 13 Asp MLC 40, CA (where a co-owner of a ship took one-third of the gross profits and provided for upkeep and insurance while the master took two-thirds, out of which he paid the crew's wages, bought the ship's provisions, and met the expenses of the voyage; it was held that a charterparty made by the master was made by him as agent of the owner). As to the authority and liability of the master generally see PARA 429 et seq; and as to charterparties and bills of lading generally see CARRIAGE AND CARRIERS vol 7 (2015) PARAS 209 et seq, 314 et seq.

## 243.   Liability for wages.

The owner of a ship is liable for seamen's wages, even though the seamen have in fact been engaged by a master who is the charterer's employee[1]. Where, however, a ship is chartered by demise, the owner is not liable in respect of an allotment note drawn by the master on the charterer[2].

1   See *Re Great Eastern Steamship Co, Williams' Claim* (1885) 5 Asp MLC 511. The decision in this case only refers to the case of seamen discharged before the ship sailed, there having been no written agreement, but it is submitted that the principle may be applied in other circumstances. As to seamen's wages generally see PARA 470 et seq.
2   *Meiklereid v West* (1876) 1 QBD 428, 3 Asp MLC 129, DC; cf the liability on bills of lading (as to which see PARA 242). As to allotment notes see PARAS 476, 477. As to charterparties by demise see CARRIAGE AND CARRIERS vol 7 (2015) PARA 211. In the case of a charterparty not amounting to a demise, where the master is the charterer's employee, it seems that the owner is not liable on bills of lading signed by the master, but is still liable for the seamen's wages.

## 244.   Liability as between part owners.

Persons owning shares in a ship are tenants in common[1]. They may or may not be partners also[2]; and, whether they are or are not in fact partners, they may for certain purposes be treated as such[3]. An agreement between part owners relating to the employment of the ship, as opposed to her ownership, renders them partners in all matters relating to the employment so agreed upon[4].

A part owner is not bound in respect of liabilities incurred by another part owner in regard to the ship, unless he has given authority[5] to the other to contract liabilities on his behalf or has held out the other as having that authority[6], or has ratified the specific acts of the other[7] which have given rise to liability[8].

1   *Ex p Young* (1813) 2 Rose 78n; *R v Collector of Customs, Liverpool* (1813) 2 M & S 223; *Re Nicholson, ex p Harrison* (1814) 2 Rose 76; *Helme v Smith* (1831) 7 Bing 709; *Re Drury and Hudson, ex p Leslie* (1833) 3 LJ Bcy 4; *Green v Briggs* (1848) 6 Hare 395; *Frazer v Cuthbertson* (1880) 6 QBD 93.
2   *Helme v Smith* (1831) 7 Bing 709; *Brodie v Howard* (1855) 17 CB 109. Persons may also be joint owners of a share: see *Ex p Jones* (1816) 4 M & S 450. As to joint ownership giving rise to a partnership see PARTNERSHIP vol 79 (2014) PARAS 9–12.
3   Eg in regard to statutes of limitation, such statutes do not run between co-owners while the co-ownership exists, the existence of co-ownership being in each case a question of fact: *The Pongola* (1895) 8 Asp MLC 89.
4   *Holderness v Shackels* (1828) 8 B & C 612; *Helme v Smith* (1831) 7 Bing 709; *Green v Briggs* (1848) 6 Hare 395.
5   Agency is a question of fact: *Chappell v Bray* (1860) 6 H & N 145.
6   *Frazer v Cuthbertson* (1880) 6 QBD 93. A registered owner will not be bound by the acts of a part owner merely because the latter appears on the register as a managing owner: *Frazer v Cuthbertson* at 98, 99. As to managing owners see PARA 238. Where a part owner has once constituted another his agent for the management of the ship, he must, if he desires to withdraw such authority, do so in some effectual manner: *The Vindobala* (1889) 14 PD 50, 6 Asp MLC 376, CA; *Von Freeden v Hull* (1907) 10 Asp MLC 247 at 394, CA. As to the power of one part owner to recover expenses of insurance from another see *Ogle v Wrangham* (1790) cited in *Abbott's Law of Merchant Ships and Seamen* (14th Edn) 130; *Hooper v Lusby* (1814) 4 Camp 66. See also *Ocean Iron Steamship Insurance Association Ltd v Leslie* (1887) 6 Asp MLC 226. As to mutual insurance associations see INSURANCE vol 60 (2011) PARAS 467–472.
7   *Keay v Fenwick* (1876) 1 CPD 745, CA.
8   *Brodie v Howard* (1855) 17 CB 109 (repairs).

# (3) THE REGISTER AND REGISTRATION

## (i) Registration: In general

### A. ENTITLEMENT TO REGISTER

**245. Basic registration provisions.** A ship[1] is entitled to be registered[2] if:

(1)     it is owned, to the prescribed extent[3], by persons qualified to own British ships[4]; and

(2)     such other conditions are satisfied as are prescribed[5] to secure that, taken in conjunction with the requisite ownership, only ships having a British connection are registered[6],

and any application for registration is duly made[7].

The registrar[8] may nevertheless, if registration regulations so provide, refuse to register or terminate the registration of a ship if, having regard to any relevant requirements of the Merchant Shipping Act 1995[9], he considers it would be inappropriate for the ship to be or, as the case may be, to remain registered[10].

However, the registrar may, if registration regulations so provide, register a fishing vessel[11], notwithstanding that the requirement of head (1) above is not satisfied in relation to a particular owner of a share in the vessel if the vessel otherwise has a British connection[12].

Where a ship becomes registered at a time when it is already registered under the law of a country other than the United Kingdom[13], the owner of the ship must take all reasonable steps to secure the termination of the ship's registration under the law of that country[14]; but this provision does not apply to a ship which becomes registered on a transfer of registration to the register[15] from a relevant British possession[16]. Any person who contravenes[17] this provision[18] commits an offence[19].

1   As to the meaning of 'ship' see PARA 229.
2   As to the meaning of 'registered' for these purposes see PARA 254 note 2.
3   It is for registration regulations:
    (1)     to determine the persons who are qualified to be owners of British ships, or British ships of any class or description, and to prescribe the extent of the ownership required for compliance with the Merchant Shipping Act 1995 s 9(1)(a) (see head (1) in the text) (s 9(2)(a));
    (2)     to prescribe other requirements designed to secure that, taken in conjunction with the requisite ownership, only ships having a British connection are registered (s 9(2)(b)).
  For the purposes of Pt II (ss 8–23), references to a ship's having a British connection are references to compliance with the conditions of entitlement imposed by s 9(1)(a), (b) (see heads (1) and (2) in the text); and 'declaration of British connection' is to be construed accordingly: s 9(9). As to the meaning of 'British ship' see PARA 230. As to the registration regulations see PARA 247.
4   Merchant Shipping Act 1995 s 9(1)(a). As to the meaning of 'qualified owners' see PARA 230 note 11. Where, for the purposes of any enactment, the question arises whether a ship is owned by persons qualified to own British ships, the question is to be determined by reference to the registration regulations under s 9(2)(a) (see note 3 head (1)): s 23(2).
5   Ie under the Merchant Shipping Act 1995 s 9(2)(b) (see note 3 head (2)): see s 9(1)(b).
6   Merchant Shipping Act 1995 s 9(1)(b), (2)(b).
7   Merchant Shipping Act 1995 s 9(1). As to applications for registration see PARA 269 et seq. Any reference in an enactment in any other Act, not amended by Sch 13, or in any instrument made under any other Act to the registration of a ship, or fishing vessel, under the Merchant Shipping Act 1894 Pt I (ss 1–91) (repealed), the Merchant Shipping Act 1983 s 5 (repealed), the Merchant Shipping Act 1988 s 13 (repealed) or the Merchant Shipping (Registration, etc) Act 1993 s 1 (repealed) is to be construed, unless the context otherwise requires, as, or as including, a reference to registration under the Merchant Shipping Act 1995 Pt II (ss 8–23); and connected phrases are to be construed accordingly: Sch 14 para 2.
8   As to the meaning of 'registrar' for these purposes see PARA 254 note 11.

9  For these purposes, 'the relevant requirements of the Merchant Shipping Act 1995' means the requirements of that Act, including requirements falling to be complied with after registration, relating to:
    (1)    the condition of ships or their equipment, so far as relevant to their safety or any risk of pollution (s 9(8)(a)); and
    (2)    the safety, health and welfare of persons employed or engaged in them (s 9(8)(b)).
10  Merchant Shipping Act 1995 s 9(3).
11  As to the meaning of 'fishing vessel' see PARA 230 note 9. As to offences in relation to fishing vessels not registered under the Merchant Shipping Act 1995 see PARA 1066.
12  Merchant Shipping Act 1995 s 9(4).
13  As to the meaning of 'United Kingdom' see PARA 16 note 3.
14  Merchant Shipping Act 1995 s 9(5).
15  As to the meaning of 'register' see PARA 254 note 2.
16  Merchant Shipping Act 1995 s 9(6). As to the meaning of 'relevant British possession' for these purposes see PARA 16 note 3.
17  As to the meaning of 'contravention' see PARA 51 note 3.
18  Ie the Merchant Shipping Act 1995 s 9(5) (see the text and notes 13–14): see s 9(7).
19  See the Merchant Shipping Act 1995 s 9(7); and PARA 1064.

## 246. Regulation of registration in British possessions by reference to categories of registries.

Her Majesty may by Order in Council make provision for regulating the registration in relevant British possessions[1] of ships[2] other than small ships[3] and fishing vessels[4] by reference to categories of registries established by the Order[5].

Any such Order may:

(1)    establish different categories of registries to which different restrictions on the registration of ships in such possessions apply, being restrictions framed by reference to:
    (a)    ships' tonnage[6];
    (b)    types of ships[7];
    (c)    any other specified matter[8]; or
    (d)    any combination of matters falling within one or more of heads (a) to (c) above[9],

(2)    as well as a category of registries to which no such restriction applies[10];

(3)    assign any relevant British possession to such one of the categories so established as appears to Her Majesty to be appropriate[11];

(4)    provide that, where a relevant British possession has been assigned to a category to which any such restriction on registration as is mentioned in head (1) above applies, no ship covered by that restriction is to be registered under the law of that possession[12];

(5)    specify circumstances in which ships may be exempted from any provision made by virtue of head (3) above[13].

1  As to the meaning of 'relevant British possession' for these purposes see PARA 16 note 3.
2  As to the meaning of 'ship' see PARA 229.
3  For these purposes, 'small ship' has the meaning given by the Merchant Shipping Act 1995 s 1(2) (see PARA 230 note 8): s 18(5).
4  As to the meaning of 'fishing vessel' see PARA 230 note 9. As to offences in relation to fishing vessels not registered under the Merchant Shipping Act 1995 see PARA 1066.
5  Merchant Shipping Act 1995 s 18(1). An Order in Council under s 18 may make such transitional, incidental or supplementary provision as appears to Her Majesty to be necessary or expedient: s 18(4). In exercise of the powers conferred by s 18, Her Majesty has made the Merchant Shipping (Categorisation of Registries of Relevant British Possessions) Order 2003, SI 2003/1248.
6  Merchant Shipping Act 1995 s 18(2)(a)(i).
7  Merchant Shipping Act 1995 s 18(2)(a)(ii).
8  Merchant Shipping Act 1995 s 18(2)(a)(iii).
9  Merchant Shipping Act 1995 s 18(2)(a)(iv).
10  Merchant Shipping Act 1995 s 18(2)(a).
11  Merchant Shipping Act 1995 s 18(2)(b).

12 Merchant Shipping Act 1995 s 18(2)(c). Any provision made by virtue of s 18(2)(c) must be expressed to be without prejudice to the operation of any provision for the time being in force under the law of any such possession as is mentioned in s 18(2)(c) by virtue of which the registration of ships in that possession is, or may be, further restricted: s 18(3).
13 Merchant Shipping Act 1995 s 18(2)(d).

B.    REGISTRATION REGULATIONS

**247.   Power to make registration regulations.** The Secretary of State[1] must by regulations ('registration regulations') make provision for and in connection with the registration of ships[2] as British ships[3]. Without prejudice to the generality of this provision, registration regulations may in particular make provision with respect to any of the following matters:

(1)     the persons by whom and the manner in which applications in connection with registration are to be made[4];

(2)     the information and evidence (including declarations of British connection[5]) to be provided in connection with such applications and such supplementary information or evidence as may be required by any specified authority[6];

(3)     the shares in the property in, and the numbers of owners (including joint owners) of, a ship permitted for the purposes of registration and the persons required or permitted to be registered[7] in respect of a ship or to be so registered in specified circumstances[8];

(4)     the issue of certificates (including provisional certificates) of registration, their production and surrender[9];

(5)     restricting and regulating the names of ships registered or to be registered[10];

(6)     the marking of ships registered or to be registered, including marks for identifying the port[11] to which a ship is to be treated as belonging[12];

(7)     the period for which registration is to remain effective without renewal[13];

(8)     the production to the registrar[14] of declarations of British connection or other information relating thereto, as respects registered ships, at specified intervals or at his request[15];

(9)     the survey and inspection of ships registered or to be registered and the recording of their tonnage as ascertained, or reascertained, under the tonnage regulations[16];

(10)    the refusal, suspension and termination of registration in specified circumstances[17];

(11)    matters arising out of the expiration, suspension or termination of registration, including the removal of marks and the cancellation of certificates[18];

(12)    the charging of fees in connection with registration or registered ships[19];

(13)    the transfer of the registration of ships to and from the register[20] from and to registers or corresponding records in countries other than the United Kingdom[21];

(14)    inspection of the register[22];

(15)    any other matter which is authorised or required by the provisions relating to the registration of ships[23] to be prescribed in registration regulations[24].

However, no provision determining, or providing for determining, the fees to be charged or prescribing any arrangements for their determination by other persons may be made without the approval of the Treasury[25].

Registration regulations may:

(a)     make different provision for different classes or descriptions of ships and for different circumstances[26];

(b)    without prejudice to head (a) above, make provision for the granting of exemptions or dispensations by the Secretary of State from specified requirements of the regulations, subject to such conditions, if any, as he thinks fit to impose[27]; and

(c)    make such transitional, incidental or supplementary provision as appears to the Secretary of State to be necessary or expedient, including provision authorising investigations and conferring powers of inspection for verifying the British connection of a ship[28].

Registration regulations:

(i)    may make provision for the registration of any class or description of ships to be such as to exclude the application of the private law provisions for registered ships[29] and, if they do, may regulate the transfer, transmission or mortgaging of ships of the class or description so excluded[30];

(ii)    may make provision for any matter which is authorised or required by those provisions to be prescribed by registration regulations[31]; and

(iii)    must make provision precluding notice of any trust being entered in the register or being receivable by the registrar except as respects specified classes or descriptions of ships or in specified circumstances[32].

Registration regulations may:

(A)    create offences subject to the limitation that no offence is to be punishable with imprisonment or punishable on summary conviction with a fine[33];

(B)    provide for the approval of forms by the Secretary of State and for the discharge of specified functions by specified authorities or persons[34];

(C)    provide for any of their provisions to extend to places outside the United Kingdom[35];

(D)    provide that any reference in any other Act or in any instrument made under any other Act to the port of registry or the port to which a ship belongs is to be construed as a reference to the port identified by the marks required for the purpose by registration regulations[36].

Any document purporting to be a copy of any information contained in an entry in the register and to be certified as a true copy by the registrar is evidence of the matters stated in the document[37].

1  As to the Secretary of State see PARA 36.
2  As to the meaning of 'ship' see PARA 229.
3  Merchant Shipping Act 1995 s 10(1). As to the meaning of 'British ship' see PARA 230. At the date at which this volume states the law, no such regulations had been made under s 10(1) but, by virtue of the Interpretation Act 1978 s 17(2)(b), the Merchant Shipping (Registration of Ships) Regulations 1993, SI 1993/3138 (as to which see PARA 255 et seq) have effect as if so made. As to the Secretary of State's power to make regulations under the Merchant Shipping Act 1995 generally see PARA 39.
4  Merchant Shipping Act 1995 s 10(2)(a).
5  As to the meaning of 'declaration of British connection' see PARA 245 note 3.
6  Merchant Shipping Act 1995 s 10(2)(b). Any notice authorised or required by or under Pt II (ss 8–23) (see PARAS 245 et seq, 248 et seq) to be served on the Secretary of State may be served by post: s 291(4). As to the service of documents under the Merchant Shipping Act 1995 generally see s 291; and PARA 74.
7  As to the meaning of 'registered' for these purposes see PARA 254 note 2.
8  Merchant Shipping Act 1995 s 10(2)(c).
9  Merchant Shipping Act 1995 s 10(2)(d).
10  Merchant Shipping Act 1995 s 10(2)(e).
11  As to the meaning of 'port' see PARA 46 note 12.
12  Merchant Shipping Act 1995 s 10(2)(f).
13  Merchant Shipping Act 1995 s 10(2)(g).

14 As to the meaning of 'registrar' see PARA 254 note 11.
15 Merchant Shipping Act 1995 s 10(2)(h).
16 Merchant Shipping Act 1995 s 10(2)(i). As to the tonnage regulations see PARA 248.
17 Merchant Shipping Act 1995 s 10(2)(j).
18 Merchant Shipping Act 1995 s 10(2)(k).
19 Merchant Shipping Act 1995 s 10(2)(l).
20 As to the meaning of 'register' for these purposes see PARA 254 note 2.
21 Merchant Shipping Act 1995 s 10(2)(m). As to the meaning of 'United Kingdom' see PARA 16 note 3.
22 Merchant Shipping Act 1995 s 10(2)(n).
23 Ie by the Merchant Shipping Act 1995 Pt II (see PARAS 245 et seq, 248 et seq): see s 10(2)(o).
24 Merchant Shipping Act 1995 s 10(2)(o).
25 Merchant Shipping Act 1995 s 10(2). As to the Treasury see CONSTITUTIONAL AND ADMINISTRATIVE LAW vol 20 (2014) PARAS 262–265.
26 Merchant Shipping Act 1995 s 10(3)(a).
27 Merchant Shipping Act 1995 s 10(3)(b).
28 Merchant Shipping Act 1995 s 10(3)(c).
29 As to the meaning of 'the private law provisions for registered ships' for these purposes see PARA 237 note 3.
30 Merchant Shipping Act 1995 s 10(4)(a).
31 Merchant Shipping Act 1995 s 10(4)(b).
32 Merchant Shipping Act 1995 s 10(4)(c).
33 Merchant Shipping Act 1995 s 10(5). As to the powers of magistrates' courts to issue fines on summary conviction see SENTENCING vol 92 (2015) PARA 176. As to the prosecution of offences generally, see PARA 1049.
34 Merchant Shipping Act 1995 s 10(6).
35 Merchant Shipping Act 1995 s 10(7).
36 Merchant Shipping Act 1995 s 10(9).
37 Merchant Shipping Act 1995 s 10(8).

### C. THE TONNAGE REGULATIONS

**248. Tonnage regulations.** The tonnage of any ship[1] to be registered under Part II of the Merchant Shipping Act 1995[2] must be ascertained in accordance with regulations ('tonnage regulations') made by the Secretary of State[3].

Tonnage regulations may:

(1)     make different provisions for different descriptions of ships or for the same description of ships in different circumstances[4];

(2)     make any regulation dependent on compliance with such conditions, to be evidenced in such manner, as may be specified in the regulations[5];

(3)     prohibit or restrict the carriage of goods or stores in spaces not included in the registered tonnage and may provide for making the master[6] and the owner each liable to a fine[7] where such a prohibition or restriction is contravened[8].

Tonnage regulations may make provision:

(a)     for assigning to a ship, either instead of or as an alternative to the tonnage ascertained in accordance with the other provisions of the regulations, a lower tonnage applicable where the ship is not loaded to the full depth to which it can safely be loaded[9];

(b)     for indicating on the ship, by such mark as may be specified in the regulations, that such a lower tonnage has been assigned to it[10]; and

(c)     where the lower tonnage has been assigned to it as an alternative, for indicating on the ship the depth to which the ship may be loaded for the lower tonnage to be applicable[11].

Tonnage regulations may:

(i)     provide for the measurement and survey of ships to be undertaken, in
        such circumstances as may be specified in the regulations, by persons
        appointed by such organisations as may be authorised for the purpose
        by the Secretary of State[12];

(ii)    provide for the issue, by the Secretary of State or by persons appointed
        by such organisations as may be authorised for the purpose by the
        Secretary of State, of certificates of the registered tonnage of any ship or
        of the tonnage which is to be taken for any purpose specified in the
        regulations as the tonnage of a ship not registered in the United
        Kingdom[13], and for the cancellation and delivery up of such certificates
        in such circumstances as may be prescribed by the regulations[14].

Regulations requiring the delivery up of any certificate may make a failure to
comply with the requirement an offence punishable on summary conviction with
a fine[15].

1  As to the meaning of 'ship' see PARA 229.
2  Ie under the Merchant Shipping Act 1995 Pt II (ss 8–23) (see PARAS 245 et seq, 249 et seq): see
   s 19(1). As to the meaning of 'registered' for these purposes see PARA 254 note 2.
3  Merchant Shipping Act 1995 s 19(1). As to the Secretary of State see PARA 36. As to the
   regulations so made under s 19(1) see the Merchant Shipping (Tonnage) Regulations 1997, SI
   1997/1510. By virtue of the Interpretation Act 1978 s 17(2)(b), the Merchant Shipping (Increased
   Penalties) Regulations 1979, SI 1979/1519 (an amending provision) also has effect as if made
   under the Merchant Shipping Act 1995 s 19. As to the Secretary of State's power to make
   regulations under the Merchant Shipping Act 1995 generally see PARA 39.
4  Merchant Shipping Act 1995 s 19(2)(a).
5  Merchant Shipping Act 1995 s 19(2)(b).
6  As to the meaning of 'master' see PARA 444 note 1.
7  As to the powers of magistrates' courts to issue fines on summary conviction see SENTENCING vol
   92 (2015) PARA 176. As to the prosecution of offences generally, see PARA 1049 et seq.
8  Merchant Shipping Act 1995 s 19(2)(c). As to the meaning of 'contravention' see PARA 51 note 3.
9  Merchant Shipping Act 1995 s 19(3)(a).
10 Merchant Shipping Act 1995 s 19(3)(b).
11 Merchant Shipping Act 1995 s 19(3)(c).
12 Merchant Shipping Act 1995 s 19(4).
13 As to the meaning of 'United Kingdom' see PARA 16 note 3.
14 Merchant Shipping Act 1995 s 19(5). As to the Secretary of State's power to make regulations
   prescribing fees to be charged in respect of the issue or recording of any certificate, licence or other
   document see PARA 63.
15 Merchant Shipping Act 1995 s 19(6).

**249.  Tonnage ascertained for registration to be tonnage of ship.** When the
tonnage of any ship[1] has been ascertained and registered in accordance with the
tonnage regulations[2], that tonnage is to be treated as the tonnage of the ship
except so far as registration regulations[3] provide, in specified circumstances, for
the ship to be remeasured and the register[4] amended accordingly[5].

1  As to the meaning of 'ship' see PARA 229.
2  As to the meaning of 'tonnage regulations' see PARA 248.
3  As to the meaning of 'registration regulations' see PARA 247.
4  As to the meaning of 'register' for these purposes see PARA 254 note 2.
5  Merchant Shipping Act 1995 s 11. As to the tonnage of ships of foreign countries adopting the
   tonnage regulations see PARA 250.

**250.  Tonnage of ships of foreign countries adopting the tonnage
regulations.** Her Majesty may by Order in Council make such provision in
relation to the ships[1] of a foreign country as is authorised in the following way[2]
where it appears to Her that the tonnage regulations[3] have been adopted by the
foreign country and are in force there[4].

Such an Order may order that the ships of the foreign country must, without
being remeasured in the United Kingdom[5], be treated as being of the tonnage

denoted by their certificates of registration or other national papers, to the same extent, and for the same purposes as the tonnage denoted in the certificate of registration of a United Kingdom ship[6] is treated as being the tonnage of that ship[7].

Where such an Order is in force in relation to the ships of any country, any space shown in the ship's certificate of registration or other national papers as deducted from the tonnage is to be treated, if a similar deduction in the case of a United Kingdom ship depends on compliance with any conditions or on the compliance being evidenced in any manner, as complying with those conditions and as being so evidenced, unless a surveyor of ships[8] certifies to the Secretary of State[9] that the construction and equipment of the ship as respects that space do not come up to the standard which would be required if the ship were a United Kingdom ship[10].

Any such Order may operate for a limited time and may be subject to such conditions and qualifications, if any, as Her Majesty may consider expedient[11].

If it appears to Her Majesty that the tonnage of any foreign[12] ship, as measured by the rules of the country to which the ship belongs, materially differs from what it would be under the tonnage regulations, Her Majesty may by Order in Council order that[13] any of the ships of that country may, for all or any of the purposes of the Merchant Shipping Act 1995, be remeasured in accordance with the tonnage regulations[14].

1   As to the meaning of 'ship' see PARA 229.
2   Ie as is authorised by the Merchant Shipping Act 1995 s 12: see s 12(1).
3   As to the meaning of 'tonnage regulations' see PARA 248.
4   Merchant Shipping Act 1995 s 12(1). At the date at which this volume states the law, no such Order in Council had been made.
5   As to the meaning of 'United Kingdom' see PARA 16 note 3.
6   As to the meaning of 'United Kingdom ship' see PARA 230. As to certificates of registration under the Merchant Shipping Act 1995 see PARA 298 et seq.
7   Merchant Shipping Act 1995 s 12(2).
8   As to the meaning of 'surveyor of ships' see PARA 46 note 13.
9   As to the Secretary of State see PARA 36.
10  Merchant Shipping Act 1995 s 12(3).
11  Merchant Shipping Act 1995 s 12(4).
12  As to the meaning of 'foreign', in relation to a ship, see PARA 18 note 2.
13  Ie notwithstanding any Order in Council in force under the Merchant Shipping Act 1995 s 12: see s 12(5).
14  Merchant Shipping Act 1995 s 12(5).

D.   DISCLOSURE OF INFORMATION

**251. Disclosure of information relating to registration by other government departments.** No obligation as to secrecy or other restriction on the disclosure of information, whether imposed by statute or otherwise, precludes any of the following persons[1], namely:

(1)    the national authority responsible for fisheries[2];
(2)    the Commissioners of Revenue and Customs[3]; and
(3)    an authorised officer of any of the persons falling within head (1) or head (2) above[4],

from disclosing to the Secretary of State[5], or to the registrar[6], or to an authorised officer of the Secretary of State[7], information for the purpose of assisting the Secretary of State in the performance of his functions relating to the registration of ships[8].

Information so obtained by any person must not be disclosed by him to any other person except where the disclosure is made:

(a) to a person to whom the information could have been duly disclosed[9] by any of the persons mentioned in heads (1) to (3) above[10]; or

(b) for the purposes of any legal proceedings arising out of the provisions relating to the registration of ships[11].

1 Merchant Shipping Act 1995 s 21(1).
2 Merchant Shipping Act 1995 s 21(1), (2)(a). The text refers to the Minister of Agriculture, Fisheries and Food: see s 21(2)(a). However, powers and functions in respect of fisheries are now exercised in England by the Secretary of State or, in Wales, by the Welsh Ministers (although certain functions are exercised jointly by the Secretary of State and the Welsh Ministers): see FISHERIES AND AQUACULTURE vol 51 (2013) PARA 427. As to the meanings of 'England' and 'Wales' see PARA 16 note 2. As to the Welsh Ministers see PARA 36. Provision is made also in relation to responsibilities for sea fishing in Scotland and Northern Ireland: see s 21(1), (2)(b), (c).
3 Merchant Shipping Act 1995 s 21(1), (2)(d) (s 21(2)(d) amended by virtue of the Commissioners for Revenue and Customs Act 2005 s 50(1), (2), (7)). As to the Commissioners for Revenue and Customs see INCOME TAXATION vol 58 (2014) PARA 33.
4 Merchant Shipping Act 1995 s 21(1), (2)(e). The text refers to an authorised officer of any of the persons falling within s 21(2)(a)–(d) (as to s 21(2)(b), (c) see note 2): see s 21(2)(e).
5 Merchant Shipping Act 1995 s 21(1)(a).
6 Merchant Shipping Act 1995 s 21(1)(b). As to the meaning of 'registrar' see PARA 254 note 11.
7 Merchant Shipping Act 1995 s 21(1)(c).
8 Merchant Shipping Act 1995 s 21(1). The text refers to the Secretary of State's functions under Pt II (ss 8–23) (see PARAS 245 et seq, 252 et seq): see s 21(1).
9 Ie in accordance with the Merchant Shipping Act 1995 s 21(1) (see the text and notes 1–8): see s 21(3)(a).
10 Merchant Shipping Act 1995 s 21(3)(a).
11 Merchant Shipping Act 1995 s 21(3)(b). The text refers to any legal proceedings arising out of Pt II: see s 21(3)(b). As to offences and legal proceedings arising out of the Merchant Shipping Act 1995 generally see PARA 1049 et seq.

### E. PRIVATE LAW PROVISIONS

**252. Private law provisions for registered ships and liability as owner.** The statutory provisions which make provision relating to the title to, and the registration of mortgages over, ships[1] have effect[2], but they do not apply in relation to ships which are excluded from their application by registration regulations[3].

Where any person is beneficially interested, otherwise than as mortgagee, in any ship or share in a ship registered[4] in the name of some other person as owner, the person so interested is liable, as well as the registered owner, to any pecuniary penalties imposed by or under the Merchant Shipping Act 1995 or any other Act on the owners of registered ships[5].

Where the registration of any ship terminates by virtue of any provision of the registration regulations, the termination of that registration does not affect any entry made in the register[6] so far as relating to any undischarged registered mortgage[7] of that ship or of any share in it[8].

1 Ie the Merchant Shipping Act 1995 s 16(1), Sch 1 (as to which see PARAS 237, 306, 318, 321, 323, 324, 328, 333, 335): see s 16(1). As to the meaning of 'ship' see PARA 229.
2 Merchant Shipping Act 1995 s 16(1).
3 Merchant Shipping Act 1995 s 16(2). The text refers to ships excluded from the application of Sch 1 by virtue of registration regulations under s 10(4)(a) (see PARA 247): see s 16(2). The provisions of Sch 1 do not apply to small ships (see the Merchant Shipping (Registration of Ships) Regulations 1993, SI 1993/3138, reg 91; and PARA 347) or to ships bareboat chartered-in by British charterers (see the Merchant Shipping Act 1995 s 17(7); and PARA 357). As to the meaning of 'registration regulations' see PARA 247.
4 As to the meaning of 'registered' for these purposes see PARA 254 note 2.
5 Merchant Shipping Act 1995 s 16(3).
6 As to the meaning of 'register' for these purposes see PARA 254 note 2.

7 For these purposes, 'registered mortgage' has the same meaning as in the Merchant Shipping Act 1995 Sch 1 (see PARA 318 note 5): s 16(5).
8 Merchant Shipping Act 1995 s 16(4).

F. PROCEEDINGS ON FORFEITURE

**253. Proceedings on forfeiture of ships.** The provisions under the Merchant Shipping Act 1995 which relate to proceedings on forfeiture of a ship under the provisions relating to British ships[1] apply in relation to ships or shares in ships which become liable to forfeiture under the provisions relating to registration[2] as they apply in relation to ships or shares in ships which become liable to forfeiture under the provisions relating to British ships[3].

1 Ie the Merchant Shipping Act 1995 s 7 (see PARA 235) (which applies to ships liable to forfeiture under Pt I (ss 1–7) (see PARA 230 et seq)): see s 20. As to the meaning of 'ship' see PARA 229; and as to the meaning of 'British ship' see PARA 230.
2 Ie under the Merchant Shipping Act 1995 Pt II (ss 8–23) (see PARA 245 et seq): see s 20.
3 Merchant Shipping Act 1995 s 20. The text refers to ships which become liable to forfeiture under Pt I: see s 20.

(ii) The Register of British Ships in the United Kingdom

**254. Central register of British ships.** There continues to be a register of British ships[1] for all registrations of ships in the United Kingdom[2]. The register must:
(1) be so constituted as to distinguish, in a separate part, registrations of fishing vessels[3] and may be otherwise divided into parts so as to distinguish between classes or descriptions of ships[4];
(2) be maintained in accordance with registration regulations[5] and the private law provisions for registered ships[6] and any directions of a general nature given to the registrar[7] by the Secretary of State[8]; and
(3) be available for public inspection[9].
The register must be maintained by the Registrar General of Shipping and Seamen[10] as registrar[11], although the Secretary of State may designate any person to discharge, on behalf of the registrar, all his functions or such of them as the Secretary of State may direct[12]. The Secretary of State also may give to the registrar directions of a general nature as to the discharge of any of his functions[13].

1 As to the meaning of 'British ship' see PARA 230; and as to the meaning of 'ship' see PARA 229.
2 Merchant Shipping Act 1995 s 8(1). For the purposes of Pt II (ss 8–23), 'register' means the register of British ships maintained for the United Kingdom under s 8; and 'registered', except with reference to the law of another country, is to be construed accordingly: s 23(1). As to the meaning of 'United Kingdom' see PARA 16 note 3.
   The central register was established under the Merchant Shipping (Registration, etc) Act 1993 s 1(1) (repealed) and replaced the three then existing registers maintained under the Merchant Shipping Act 1894 Pt I (ss 1–91) (repealed), the Merchant Shipping Act 1983 s 5 (repealed) and the Merchant Shipping Act 1988 s 13 (repealed): see the Merchant Shipping (Registration, etc) Act 1993 s 1(7) (repealed). Those three registers closed on 21 March 1994 and all registrations in those registers in force on that day became registrations in the new register: see s 1(7) (repealed); the Merchant Shipping (Registration, etc) Act 1993 (Commencement No 1 and Transitional Provisions) Order 1993, SI 1993/3137, art 3(1).
   The Secretary of State may by order make such amendments of any local Act or instrument so far as it provides for the registration of ships in local registers as appear to him to be appropriate in view of the provisions made for the register mentioned in the Merchant Shipping Act 1995 s 8: s 314(4). At the date at which this volume states the law, no such order had been made and none has effect as if so made. As to the Secretary of State see PARA 36; and as to his power to make subordinate legislation under the Merchant Shipping Act 1995 see PARA 39.
3 As to the meaning of 'fishing vessel' see PARA 230 note 9.
4 Merchant Shipping Act 1995 s 8(5).
5 As to the meaning of 'registration regulations' see PARA 247.

6   As to the meaning of 'the private law provisions for registered ships' see PARA 237 note 3.
7   Ie under the Merchant Shipping Act 1995 s 8(4) (see the text and note 13): see s 8(6). As to the registrar see note 11.
8   Merchant Shipping Act 1995 s 8(6).
9   Merchant Shipping Act 1995 s 8(7). As to inspection of copies of documents which are open to public inspection see PARA 1060.
10 As to the Registrar General of Shipping and Seamen see PARA 62.
11 Merchant Shipping Act 1995 s 8(2). For the purposes of Pt II, 'registrar' means the Registrar General of Shipping and Seamen in his capacity as registrar or, as respects functions of his being discharged by another authority or person, that authority or person: s 23(1).
12 Merchant Shipping Act 1995 s 8(3).
13 Merchant Shipping Act 1995 s 8(4). As to the Secretary of State's power to give directions see PARA 39.

**255. The register.** The register[1] maintained by the registrar[2] is divided into the following parts[3]:

(1)      Part I for ships[4], owned by qualified persons[5], which are not fishing vessels or registered on that Part which is restricted to small ships[6];

(2)      Part II for fishing vessels[7];

(3)      Part III for small ships[8]; and

(4)      Part IV for ships which are bareboat charter ships[9].

No ship, including a small ship, may be registered on more than one Part of the register at any one time[10].

Entries in the register must be made in accordance with the following provisions:

(a)      the property in a ship must be divided into 64 shares[11];

(b)      subject to the statutory provisions[12] with respect to joint owners or owners by transmission, not more than 64 persons are entitled to be registered at the same time as owners[13] of any one ship, but this does not affect the beneficial title of any persons represented by or claiming under or through any registered owner or joint owner[14];

(c)      a person is not entitled to be registered as owner of a part of a share, but any number of persons not exceeding five may be registered as joint owners of a ship or of any share or shares in a ship[15];

(d)      joint owners are to be considered as constituting one person only as regards the persons entitled to be registered, and are not entitled to dispose in severalty of any interest in a ship, or in any share in a ship in respect of which they are registered[16].

The registrar is entitled to amend the register where a clerical error has occurred, or sufficient evidence is produced to satisfy him that the entry is incorrect, and, on making the amendment, he must issue a new certificate of registry[17], if necessary[18].

The register may consist of both paper and computerised records and such other records as the Secretary of State may consider to be expedient[19].

Any person is entitled:

(i)      on application to the registrar, to obtain a transcript, certified by an authorised officer, of the entries in the register[20]; and

(ii)      during the official opening hours of the General Registry of Shipping and Seamen, on request to inspect the entries in the register[21].

1   For these purposes, 'register' means the register of British ships established under the Merchant Shipping Act 1995 s 8 (see PARA 254): Merchant Shipping (Registration of Ships) Regulations 1993, SI 1993/3138, reg 1(2); Interpretation Act 1978 s 17(2)(b).
2   Ie in accordance with the Merchant Shipping Act 1995 s 8(1), (2) (see PARA 254): see the Merchant Shipping (Registration of Ships) Regulations 1993, SI 1993/3138, reg 2(1); Interpretation Act 1978 s 17(2)(b). For these purposes, 'registrar' means the person described as 'registrar' in the

Merchant Shipping Act 1995 s 23(1) (see PARA 254 note 11): Merchant Shipping (Registration of Ships) Regulations 1993, SI 1993/3138, reg 1(2); Interpretation Act 1978 s 17(2)(b).

3    Merchant Shipping (Registration of Ships) Regulations 1993, SI 1993/3138, reg 2(1). The registrar may, in certain circumstances, transfer the registration of a ship from one Part of the register to a different Part: see reg 72A; and PARA 343.

4    For these purposes, unless the context otherwise requires, 'ship' includes a fishing vessel (see head (2) in the text) but does not include a small ship (see head (3) in the text) or a bareboat charter ship (see head (4) in the text) except for the purposes of the Merchant Shipping (Registration of Ships) Regulations 1993, SI 1993/3138, Pt XII (regs 101–113A) (miscellaneous provisions) (see PARAS 317, 368 et seq) and Pt XIII (reg 114) (offences) (see PARAS 1067–1071): reg 1(2).

5    Ie in accordance with the Merchant Shipping (Registration of Ships) Regulations 1993, SI 1993/3138: see reg 2(1)(a). As to persons qualified to be owners of ships to be registered on Part I of the register see PARA 258.

6    Merchant Shipping (Registration of Ships) Regulations 1993, SI 1993/3138, reg 2(1)(a). For these purposes, 'small ship' means a ship which is less than 24 metres in overall length and is (or is applying to be) registered under Pt XI (regs 88–100) (registration of small ships) (see PARA 344 et seq): reg 1(2). 'Overall length' has the same meaning as 'length overall' in the Merchant Shipping (Tonnage) Regulations 1997, SI 1997/1510 (see PARA 248): Merchant Shipping (Registration of Ships) Regulations 1993, SI 1993/3138, reg 1(2) (definition substituted by SI 1998/1915).

7    Merchant Shipping (Registration of Ships) Regulations 1993, SI 1993/3138, reg 2(1)(b). For these purposes, 'fishing vessel' means a vessel within the meaning of the Merchant Shipping Act 1995 s 313(1) (see PARA 230 note 9): Merchant Shipping (Registration of Ships) Regulations 1993, SI 1993/3138, reg 1(2); Interpretation Act 1978 s 17(2)(b). As to the status of any Part II certificate under sea fisheries legislation see PARA 377.

8    Merchant Shipping (Registration of Ships) Regulations 1993, SI 1993/3138, reg 2(1)(c).

9    Merchant Shipping (Registration of Ships) Regulations 1993, SI 1993/3138, reg 2(1)(d). For these purposes, 'bareboat charter ship' means a ship registered under the Merchant Shipping Act 1995 s 17 (see PARA 357): Merchant Shipping (Registration of Ships) Regulations 1993, SI 1993/3138, reg 1(2); Interpretation Act 1978 s 17(2)(b).

10   Merchant Shipping (Registration of Ships) Regulations 1993, SI 1993/3138, reg 5.

11   Merchant Shipping (Registration of Ships) Regulations 1993, SI 1993/3138, reg 2(5)(a).

12   Ie the provisions of the Merchant Shipping Act 1995 and of the Merchant Shipping (Registration of Ships) Regulations 1993, SI 1993/3138: see reg 2(5)(b).

13   For these purposes, 'owner' means, in relation to a ship or share in a ship, the person owning the ship or, as the case may be, a share in the ship, whether or not registered as owner: Merchant Shipping (Registration of Ships) Regulations 1993, SI 1993/3138, reg 1(2). However, in the Merchant Shipping Act 1995, except for s 9 (see PARA 245), and in any other enactment applicable to British ships or ships registered under that Act, any reference, however phrased, to the owner of a British ship, a United Kingdom ship or a ship registered in the United Kingdom (as to which see PARA 230), means, in relation to a bareboat charter ship, the person registered as the charterer: see the Merchant Shipping (Modification of Enactments) (Bareboat Charter Ships) Order 1994, SI 1994/774, arts 2, 3.

14   Merchant Shipping (Registration of Ships) Regulations 1993, SI 1993/3138, reg 2(5)(b).

15   Merchant Shipping (Registration of Ships) Regulations 1993, SI 1993/3138, reg 2(5)(c).

16   Merchant Shipping (Registration of Ships) Regulations 1993, SI 1993/3138, reg 2(5)(d).

17   For these purposes, 'certificate of registry' means a certificate of registration which is issued to a ship which is registered under the Merchant Shipping Act 1995 and includes a certificate of bareboat charter, unless the context otherwise requires: Merchant Shipping (Registration of Ships) Regulations 1993, SI 1993/3138, reg 1(2); Interpretation Act 1978 s 17(2)(b). 'Certificate of bareboat charter' means a certificate of registration issued to a ship which is registered under the Merchant Shipping Act 1995 s 17 (see PARA 357): Merchant Shipping (Registration of Ships) Regulations 1993, SI 1993/3138, reg 1(2); Interpretation Act 1978 s 17(2)(b). As to offences in connection with certificates of registry see PARA 1070 et seq.

18   Merchant Shipping (Registration of Ships) Regulations 1993, SI 1993/3138, reg 2(6).

19   Merchant Shipping (Registration of Ships) Regulations 1993, SI 1993/3138, reg 2(2). As to the Secretary of State see PARA 36.

20   Merchant Shipping (Registration of Ships) Regulations 1993, SI 1993/3138, reg 2(3).

21   Merchant Shipping (Registration of Ships) Regulations 1993, SI 1993/3138, reg 2(4).

## 256.   Simple and full registration of fishing vessels, and changing from full to simple mode. Registration on Part II of the register[1] is of two kinds[2]:

(1)     registration of vessels to which the statutory provisions relating to transfers by bill of sale and the registration of mortgages[3] do not apply ('simple registration')[4]; and

(2)     registration of vessels to which those provisions do apply ('full registration')[5].

A fishing vessel which has once been registered with full registration may not thereafter be registered with simple registration unless[6]:

(a)     it is not subject to a registered mortgage[7];

(b)     the vessel has in the meantime been registered outside the United Kingdom[8]; and

(c)     the registrar[9] consents[10].

1   Ie Part II for fishing vessels: see the Merchant Shipping (Registration of Ships) Regulations 1993, SI 1993/3138, reg 2(1)(b); and PARA 255. As to the meaning of 'fishing vessel' for these purposes see PARA 255 note 7; and as to the meaning of 'register' for these purposes see PARA 255 note 1. As to the status of any Part II certificate under sea fisheries legislation see PARA 377.
2   Merchant Shipping (Registration of Ships) Regulations 1993, SI 1993/3138, reg 3.
3   Ie the Merchant Shipping Act 1995 s 16(1), Sch 1 (see PARAS 237, 306, 318, 321, 323–324, 328, 333, 335): see the Merchant Shipping (Registration of Ships) Regulations 1993, SI 1993/3138, reg 3; Interpretation Act 1978 s 17(2)(b).
4   Merchant Shipping (Registration of Ships) Regulations 1993, SI 1993/3138, reg 3(a); Interpretation Act 1978 s 17(2)(b).
5   Merchant Shipping (Registration of Ships) Regulations 1993, SI 1993/3138, reg 3(b); Interpretation Act 1978 s 17(2)(b).
6   Merchant Shipping (Registration of Ships) Regulations 1993, SI 1993/3138, reg 4.
7   Merchant Shipping (Registration of Ships) Regulations 1993, SI 1993/3138, reg 4(a).
8   Merchant Shipping (Registration of Ships) Regulations 1993, SI 1993/3138, reg 4(b). As to the meaning of 'United Kingdom' see PARA 16 note 3.
9   As to the meaning of 'registrar' for these purposes see PARA 255 note 2.
10  Merchant Shipping (Registration of Ships) Regulations 1993, SI 1993/3138, reg 4(c).

**257.   Trusts not to be entered.** No trust, express, implied or constructive may be registered by the registrar[1]; but, where on the bankruptcy of a registered owner[2] or mortgagee his title is transmitted to his trustee in bankruptcy, that person, if a qualified person[3], may be registered as the owner or mortgagee of a British ship[4] or share in a ship[5].

1   Merchant Shipping (Registration of Ships) Regulations 1993, SI 1993/3138, reg 6(1). As to the meaning of 'registrar' for these purposes see PARA 255 note 2.
2   As to the meaning of 'owner' for these purposes see PARA 255 note 13.
3   As to persons qualified to be owners of ships to be registered on Part I of the register see PARA 258.
4   As to the meaning of 'ship' for these purposes see PARA 255 note 4. As to the meaning of 'British ship' under the Merchant Shipping Act 1995 see PARA 230.
5   Merchant Shipping (Registration of Ships) Regulations 1993, SI 1993/3138, reg 6(2).

### (iii)   Qualification and Entitlement for Registration on Part I of the Register

**258.   Persons qualified to be owners of ships to be registered on Part I of the register.** The following persons are qualified to be the owners[1] of ships[2] which are registered on Part I of the register[3]:

(1)     British citizens[4] or non-United Kingdom[5] nationals exercising their right of freedom of movement of workers or right of establishment[6];

(2)     British overseas territories citizens[7];

(3)     British Overseas citizens[8];

(4)     persons who under the British Nationality Act 1981 are British subjects[9];

(5)     persons who are British Nationals (Overseas)[10];

(6)     bodies corporate incorporated in an EEA State[11];

(7)    bodies corporate incorporated in any relevant British possession[12] and having their principal place of business in the United Kingdom or in any such possession[13]; and

(8)    European Economic Interest Groupings duly formed[14] and registered in the United Kingdom[15].

A person who is not so qualified to be the owner of a ship registered on Part I of the register may nevertheless be one of the owners of such a ship if[16]:

(a)    a majority interest in the ship[17] is owned by persons who are so qualified[18]; and

(b)    the ship is registered on Part I of the register[19].

1    As to the meaning of 'owner' for these purposes see PARA 255 note 13.
2    As to the meaning of 'ship' for these purposes see PARA 255 note 4.
3    Merchant Shipping (Registration of Ships) Regulations 1993, SI 1993/3138, reg 7(1). As to the meaning of 'register' for these purposes see PARA 255 note 1. Part I of the register, as mentioned in the text, is for ships, owned by qualified persons, which are not fishing vessels or registered on that Part which is restricted to small ships: see the Merchant Shipping (Registration of Ships) Regulations 1993, SI 1993/3138, reg 2(1)(a); and PARA 255. As to the meaning of 'fishing vessel' for these purposes see PARA 255 note 7; and as to the meaning of 'small ship' for these purposes see PARA 255 note 6.
4    Merchant Shipping (Registration of Ships) Regulations 1993, SI 1993/3138, reg 7(1)(a)(i) (reg 7(1)(a) substituted by SI 1998/2976). As to the meaning of 'British citizen' see BRITISH NATIONALITY vol 4 (2011) PARA 421 et seq.
5    As to the meaning of 'United Kingdom' see PARA 16 note 3.
6    Merchant Shipping (Registration of Ships) Regulations 1993, SI 1993/3138, reg 7(1)(a)(ii) (as substituted: see note 4). For these purposes, 'non-United Kingdom nationals exercising their right of freedom of movement of workers or right of establishment' means (by virtue of reg 1(2) (definition added by SI 1998/2976; amended by SI 2012/1809) persons who are either:
    (1)    nationals of a member state other than the United Kingdom exercising in the United Kingdom their rights under the Treaty on the Functioning of the European Union (Rome, 25 March 1957; TS 1 (1973); Cmnd 5179) art 45 (see EUROPEAN UNION vol 47A (2014) PARA 302) or art 49 (see EUROPEAN UNION vol 47A (2014) PARA 303), as the case may be; or
    (2)    nationals of a state, other than a member state, which a Contracting Party to the EEA Agreement exercising in the United Kingdom their rights under the EEA Agreement art 28 or art 31.
    'EEA Agreement' means the Agreement on the European Economic Area (Oporto, 2 May 1992; EC 7 (1992); Cm 2183) as adjusted by the Protocol (Brussels, 17 March 1993; EC 2 (1993); Cm 2183): see the Merchant Shipping (Registration of Ships) Regulations 1993, SI 1993/3138, reg 1(2) (definition added by SI 1998/2976).
7    Merchant Shipping (Registration of Ships) Regulations 1993, SI 1993/3138, reg 7(1)(b) (amended by virtue of the British Overseas Territories Act 2002 s 2(3)). As to the meaning of 'British overseas territories citizen' see BRITISH NATIONALITY vol 4 (2011) PARAS 406, 445–458.
8    Merchant Shipping (Registration of Ships) Regulations 1993, SI 1993/3138, reg 7(1)(c). As to the meaning of 'British Overseas citizen' see BRITISH NATIONALITY vol 4 (2011) PARA 459 et seq.
9    Merchant Shipping (Registration of Ships) Regulations 1993, SI 1993/3138, reg 7(1)(d). As to British subjects under the British Nationality Act 1981 see BRITISH NATIONALITY vol 4 (2011) PARAS 407, 469–474.
10    Merchant Shipping (Registration of Ships) Regulations 1993, SI 1993/3138, reg 7(1)(e); Interpretation Act 1978 s 17(2)(b). As to British Nationals (Overseas) within the meaning of the British Nationality Act 1981 see BRITISH NATIONALITY vol 4 (2011) PARAS 406, 465–467.
11    Merchant Shipping (Registration of Ships) Regulations 1993, SI 1993/3138, reg 7(1)(f) (amended by SI 1998/2976). For these purposes, 'EEA State' means a state which is a Contracting Party to the EEA Agreement (as to which see note 6): see the Merchant Shipping (Registration of Ships) Regulations 1993, SI 1993/3138, reg 1(2) (definition added by SI 1998/2976).
12    As to the meaning of 'relevant British possession' under the Merchant Shipping Act 1995 see PARA 16 note 3.
13    Merchant Shipping (Registration of Ships) Regulations 1993, SI 1993/3138, reg 7(1)(g). As to a person's place of business see COMPANIES vol 14 (2016) PARA 117.
14    Ie being groups formed in pursuance of Council Regulation (EC) 2137/85 (OJ L199, 31.7.1985, p 1) art 1: see the Merchant Shipping (Registration of Ships) Regulations 1993, SI 1993/3138, reg

7(1)(h). Council Regulation (EC) 2137/85 is implemented in the United Kingdom by the European Economic Interest Grouping Regulations 1989, SI 1989/638 (as to which see COMPANIES vol 15A (2016) PARAS 1823–1824).

15 Merchant Shipping (Registration of Ships) Regulations 1993, SI 1993/3138, reg 7(1)(h).

16 Merchant Shipping (Registration of Ships) Regulations 1993, SI 1993/3138, reg 7(2) (amended by SI 1994/541).

17 Ie within the meaning of the Merchant Shipping (Registration of Ships) Regulations 1993, SI 1993/3138, reg 8 (British connection and majority interest) (see PARA 259): see reg 7(2)(a) (amended by SI 1994/541).

18 Merchant Shipping (Registration of Ships) Regulations 1993, SI 1993/3138, reg 7(2)(a) (as amended: see note 17).

19 Merchant Shipping (Registration of Ships) Regulations 1993, SI 1993/3138, reg 7(2)(b).

**259. British connection and majority interest in the ship.** A ship[1] is entitled to be registered on Part I of the register[2] if a majority interest in the ship is owned by one or more persons[3] qualified[4] to be so registered[5].

Where a majority interest in a ship is owned by persons qualified[6] by reason of being:

(1)     British citizens[7] or non-United Kingdom[8] nationals exercising their right of freedom of movement of workers or right of establishment[9];

(2)     British overseas territories citizens[10];

(3)     persons who are British Nationals (Overseas)[11];

(4)     bodies corporate incorporated in an EEA State[12];

(5)     European Economic Interest Groupings duly formed[13] and registered in the United Kingdom[14],

the ship may be registered only if that person or, as the case may be, any of those persons is resident in the United Kingdom[15]. Where this condition[16] is not satisfied, the ship may be registered only if a representative person is appointed in relation to the ship[17].

Where the majority interest is owned by persons one or more of whom are persons who are qualified[18] by reason of being:

(a)     British Overseas citizens[19] or persons who under the British Nationality Act 1981 are British subjects[20], the ship may be registered only if that person or, as the case may be, any of those persons is resident in the United Kingdom or, where that condition is not satisfied, if the Secretary of State[21] furnishes a declaration that he consents to the ship being registered, and, in addition, a representative person is appointed in relation to the ship[22];

(b)     bodies corporate incorporated in any relevant British possession[23] and having their principal place of business in the United Kingdom or in any such possession, the ship may be registered only if the body corporate has a place of business in the United Kingdom or, where that condition is not satisfied, if a representative person is appointed in relation to the ship[24].

Where the majority interest is owned by the following persons[25]:

(i)     one or more persons who are qualified by reason of being British citizens or non-United Kingdom nationals exercising their right of freedom of movement of workers or right of establishment[26], or being British overseas territories citizens[27], or being persons who are British Nationals (Overseas)[28], or being bodies corporate incorporated in an EEA State[29], or being European Economic Interest Groupings duly formed and registered in the United Kingdom[30];

(ii)     one or more persons qualified by reason of being British Overseas citizens[31] or persons who under the British Nationality Act 1981 are British subjects[32]; or

(iii)    one or more persons qualified by reason of being bodies corporate incorporated in any relevant British possession and having their principal place of business in the United Kingdom or in any such possession[33],

the ship must only be registered[34] if any of those persons is resident in the United Kingdom[35] or, where that condition is not satisfied, if a representative person is appointed in relation to the ship[36].

1    As to the meaning of 'ship' for these purposes see PARA 255 note 4.
2    As to the meaning of 'register' for these purposes see PARA 255 note 1. Part I of the register, as mentioned in the text, is for ships, owned by qualified persons, which are not fishing vessels or registered on that Part which is restricted to small ships: see the Merchant Shipping (Registration of Ships) Regulations 1993, SI 1993/3138, reg 2(1)(a); and PARA 255. As to the meaning of 'fishing vessel' for these purposes see PARA 255 note 7; and as to the meaning of 'small ship' for these purposes see PARA 255 note 6.
3    For these purposes, one or more persons is or are to be treated as owning a majority interest in a ship if there is vested in that person or in those persons, taken together, the legal title to 33 or more shares in the ship, there being left out of account for this purpose any share in which any beneficial interest is owned by a person who is not entitled to be an owner of a British ship: Merchant Shipping (Registration of Ships) Regulations 1993, SI 1993/3138, reg 9(a). As to the meaning of 'owner' for these purposes see PARA 255 note 13. As to the meaning of 'British ship' under the Merchant Shipping Act 1995 see PARA 230.
4    Ie under the Merchant Shipping (Registration of Ships) Regulations 1993, SI 1993/3138, reg 7(1) (see PARA 258): see reg 8(1) (amended by SI 1994/541).
5    Merchant Shipping (Registration of Ships) Regulations 1993, SI 1993/3138, reg 8(1) (as amended: see note 4). Regulation 8(1) is subject to reg 36(4) (refusal of registration) (see PARA 289) and reg 8(2)–(5) (see the text and notes 6–36): reg 8(1) (as so amended).
6    Ie qualified by reason of the Merchant Shipping (Registration of Ships) Regulations 1993, SI 1993/3138, reg 7(1)(a), (b), (e), (f) or (h) (as to which see heads (1) to (5) in the text; and PARA 258): see reg 8(2) (amended by SI 1994/541).
7    As to the meaning of 'British citizen' see BRITISH NATIONALITY vol 4 (2011) PARA 421 et seq.
8    As to the meaning of 'United Kingdom' see PARA 16 note 3.
9    Merchant Shipping (Registration of Ships) Regulations 1993, SI 1993/3138, reg 7(1)(a) (substituted by SI 1998/2976); Merchant Shipping (Registration of Ships) Regulations 1993, SI 1993/3138, reg 8(2) (as amended: see note 6). As to the meaning of 'non-United Kingdom nationals exercising their right of freedom of movement of workers or right of establishment' see PARA 258 note 6.
10   Merchant Shipping (Registration of Ships) Regulations 1993, SI 1993/3138, reg 7(1)(b) (amended by virtue of the British Overseas Territories Act 2002 s 2(3)); Merchant Shipping (Registration of Ships) Regulations 1993, SI 1993/3138, reg 8(2) (as amended: see note 6). As to the meaning of 'British overseas territories citizen' see BRITISH NATIONALITY vol 4 (2011) PARAS 406, 445–458.
11   Merchant Shipping (Registration of Ships) Regulations 1993, SI 1993/3138, reg 7(1)(e); Interpretation Act 1978 s 17(2)(b); Merchant Shipping (Registration of Ships) Regulations 1993, SI 1993/3138, reg 8(2) (as amended: see note 6). As to British Nationals (Overseas) within the meaning of the British Nationality Act 1981 see BRITISH NATIONALITY vol 4 (2011) PARAS 406, 465–367.
12   Merchant Shipping (Registration of Ships) Regulations 1993, SI 1993/3138, reg 7(1)(f) (amended by SI 1998/2976); Merchant Shipping (Registration of Ships) Regulations 1993, SI 1993/3138, reg 8(2) (as amended: see note 6). As to the meaning of 'EEA State' for these purposes see PARA 258 note 11.
13   Ie being groups formed in pursuance of Council Regulation (EC) 2137/85 (OJ L199, 31.7.1985, p 1) art 1: see the Merchant Shipping (Registration of Ships) Regulations 1993, SI 1993/3138, regs 7(1)(h), 8(2) (reg 8(2) as amended: see note 6). Council Regulation (EC) 2137/85 is implemented in the United Kingdom by the European Economic Interest Grouping Regulations 1989, SI 1989/638 (as to which see COMPANIES vol 15A (2016) PARAS 1823–1824).
14   Merchant Shipping (Registration of Ships) Regulations 1993, SI 1993/3138, regs 7(1)(h), 8(2) (reg 8(2) as amended: see note 6). For these purposes, a body corporate is treated as resident in the United Kingdom if, being a body incorporated in a member state, it has a place of business in the United Kingdom: reg 9(b).

15 Merchant Shipping (Registration of Ships) Regulations 1993, SI 1993/3138, reg 8(2) (as amended: see note 6). As to the rules of domicile and residence generally see CONFLICT OF LAWS vol 19 (2011) PARA 336 et seq.

16 Ie the condition in the Merchant Shipping (Registration of Ships) Regulations 1993, SI 1993/3138, reg 8(2) (see the text and notes 6–15): see reg 8(3).

17 Merchant Shipping (Registration of Ships) Regulations 1993, SI 1993/3138, regs 7(1)(h), 8(3). The text refers to the appointment of representative persons in relation to the ship under Pt V (regs 18, 19) (see PARAS 267–268): see reg 8(3).

18 Ie qualified by reason of the Merchant Shipping (Registration of Ships) Regulations 1993, SI 1993/3138, reg 7(1)(c) or reg 7(1)(d) or, as the case may be, reg 7(1)(g) (as to which see heads (a) and (b) in the text; and PARA 258): see reg 8(4) (amended by SI 1994/541).

19 Merchant Shipping (Registration of Ships) Regulations 1993, SI 1993/3138, regs 7(1)(c), 8(4)(a). As to the meaning of 'British Overseas citizen' see BRITISH NATIONALITY vol 4 (2011) PARA 459 et seq.

20 Merchant Shipping (Registration of Ships) Regulations 1993, SI 1993/3138, regs 7(1)(d), 8(4)(a). As to British subjects under the British Nationality Act 1981 see BRITISH NATIONALITY vol 4 (2011) PARAS 407, 469–474.

21 As to the Secretary of State see PARA 36.

22 Merchant Shipping (Registration of Ships) Regulations 1993, SI 1993/3138, reg 8(4)(a).

23 As to the meaning of 'relevant British possession' under the Merchant Shipping Act 1995 see PARA 16 note 3.

24 Merchant Shipping (Registration of Ships) Regulations 1993, SI 1993/3138, regs 7(1)(g), 8(4)(b). As to a person's place of business see COMPANIES vol 14 (2016) PARA 117.

25 Merchant Shipping (Registration of Ships) Regulations 1993, SI 1993/3138, reg 8(5) (amended by SI 1994/541).

26 Ie qualified by reason of the Merchant Shipping (Registration of Ships) Regulations 1993, SI 1993/3138, reg 7(1)(a) (as to which see head (1) in the text; and PARA 258): see reg 8(5)(a).

27 Ie qualified by reason of the Merchant Shipping (Registration of Ships) Regulations 1993, SI 1993/3138, reg 7(1)(b) (as to which see head (2) in the text; and PARA 258): see reg 8(5)(a).

28 Ie qualified by reason of the Merchant Shipping (Registration of Ships) Regulations 1993, SI 1993/3138, reg 7(1)(e) (as to which see head (3) in the text; and PARA 258): see reg 8(5)(a).

29 Ie qualified by reason of the Merchant Shipping (Registration of Ships) Regulations 1993, SI 1993/3138, reg 7(1)(f) (as to which see head (4) in the text; and PARA 258): see reg 8(5)(a).

30 Ie qualified by reason of the Merchant Shipping (Registration of Ships) Regulations 1993, SI 1993/3138, reg 7(1)(h) (as to which see head (5) in the text; and PARA 258): see reg 8(5)(a).

31 Ie qualified by reason of the Merchant Shipping (Registration of Ships) Regulations 1993, SI 1993/3138, reg 7(1)(c) (as to which see head (a) in the text; and PARA 258): see reg 8(5)(b).

32 Ie qualified by reason of the Merchant Shipping (Registration of Ships) Regulations 1993, SI 1993/3138, reg 7(1)(d) (as to which see head (a) in the text; and PARA 258): see reg 8(5)(b).

33 Ie qualified by reason of the Merchant Shipping (Registration of Ships) Regulations 1993, SI 1993/3138, reg 7(1)(g) (as to which see head (b) in the text; and PARA 258): see reg 8(5)(c).

34 Merchant Shipping (Registration of Ships) Regulations 1993, SI 1993/3138, reg 8(5) (as amended: see note 25).

35 Merchant Shipping (Registration of Ships) Regulations 1993, SI 1993/3138, reg 8(5)(i).

36 Merchant Shipping (Registration of Ships) Regulations 1993, SI 1993/3138, reg 8(5)(ii).

## 260. Government ships not required to be registered on Part I of the register.

Nothing in the provisions relating to qualification and entitlement for registration on Part I of the register[1] applies to a government ship[2].

1 Ie nothing in the Merchant Shipping (Registration of Ships) Regulations 1993, SI 1993/3138, Pt III (regs 7–11) (see PARAS 258–261): see reg 10. As to the meaning of 'register' for these purposes see PARA 255 note 1. Part I of the register, as mentioned in the text, is for ships, owned by qualified persons, which are not fishing vessels or registered on that Part which is restricted to small ships: see the Merchant Shipping (Registration of Ships) Regulations 1993, SI 1993/3138, reg 2(1)(a); and PARA 255. As to the meaning of 'fishing vessel' for these purposes see PARA 255 note 7; as to the meaning of 'ship' see PARA 255 note 4; and as to the meaning of 'small ship' for these purposes see PARA 255 note 6.

2 Merchant Shipping (Registration of Ships) Regulations 1993, SI 1993/3138, reg 10. The text refers to government ships, being ships to which the Merchant Shipping Act 1995 s 308(2), (4) (see PARA 19) applies: see the Merchant Shipping (Registration of Ships) Regulations 1993, SI 1993/3138, reg 10; Interpretation Act 1978 s 17(2)(b).

## 261. Fishing vessels not allowed to be registered on Part I of the register.

A fishing vessel[1] may not be registered on Part I of the register[2].

1   As to the meaning of 'fishing vessel' for these purposes see PARA 255 note 7.
2   Merchant Shipping (Registration of Ships) Regulations 1993, SI 1993/3138, reg 11. As to the
    meaning of 'register' for these purposes see PARA 255 note 1. Part I of the register, as mentioned
    in the text, is for ships, owned by qualified persons, which are not fishing vessels or registered on
    that Part which is restricted to small ships: see the Merchant Shipping (Registration of Ships)
    Regulations 1993, SI 1993/3138, reg 2(1)(a); and PARA 255. As to the meaning of 'ship' see
    PARA 255 note 4; and as to the meaning of 'small ship' for these purposes see PARA 255 note 6.

### (iv) Qualification and Entitlement for Registration on Part II of the Register

**262. Eligibility.** The following persons are qualified to be the owners[1] of fishing
vessels[2] which are to be registered on Part II of the register[3]:

(1)     British citizens[4] or non-United Kingdom[5] nationals exercising their right
        of freedom of movement of workers or right of establishment[6];
(2)     bodies corporate incorporated in an EEA State[7] with a place of business
        in the United Kingdom[8];
(3)     European Economic Interest Groupings duly formed[9] and registered in
        the United Kingdom[10];
(4)     a local authority in the United Kingdom[11].

A ship[12] is entitled[13] to be registered only if the legal and beneficial title of the
vessel are vested wholly in one or more of the persons qualified[14] to be owners of
a British fishing vessel[15].

Where any share in a vessel is beneficially owned jointly by persons not all of
whom are qualified[16] to be the owners of a British fishing vessel, the whole of the
share is treated[17] as beneficially owned by persons who are not so qualified[18].

1   As to the meaning of 'owner' for these purposes see PARA 255 note 13.
2   As to the meaning of 'fishing vessel' for these purposes see PARA 255 note 7.
3   Merchant Shipping (Registration of Ships) Regulations 1993, SI 1993/3138, reg 12. As to the
    meaning of 'register' for these purposes see PARA 255 note 1. Part II of the register, as mentioned
    in the text, is for fishing vessels: see the Merchant Shipping (Registration of Ships) Regulations
    1993, SI 1993/3138, reg 2(1)(b); and PARA 255. As to the status of any Part II certificate under sea
    fisheries legislation see PARA 377.
4   As to the meaning of 'British citizen' see BRITISH NATIONALITY vol 4 (2011) PARA 421 et seq.
5   As to the meaning of 'United Kingdom' see PARA 16 note 3.
6   Merchant Shipping (Registration of Ships) Regulations 1993, SI 1993/3138, reg 12(a) (substituted
    by SI 1998/2976). As to the meaning of 'non-United Kingdom nationals exercising their right of
    freedom of movement of workers or right of establishment' see PARA 258 note 6.
7   As to the meaning of 'EEA State' for these purposes see PARA 258 note 11.
8   Merchant Shipping (Registration of Ships) Regulations 1993, SI 1993/3138, reg 12(b) (amended
    by SI 1998/2976). As to a person's place of business see COMPANIES vol 14 (2016) PARA 117.
9   Ie being groups formed in pursuance of Council Regulation (EC) 2137/85 (OJ L199, 31.7.1985,
    p 1) art 1: see the Merchant Shipping (Registration of Ships) Regulations 1993, SI 1993/3138, reg
    12(c). Council Regulation (EC) 2137/85 is implemented in the United Kingdom by the European
    Economic Interest Grouping Regulations 1989, SI 1989/638 (as to which see COMPANIES vol 15A
    (2016) PARAS 1823–1824).
10  Merchant Shipping (Registration of Ships) Regulations 1993, SI 1993/3138, reg 12(c).
11  Merchant Shipping (Registration of Ships) Regulations 1993, SI 1993/3138, reg 12(d). As to local
    authorities in England and Wales see LOCAL GOVERNMENT vol 69 (2009) PARA 22 et seq.
12  As to the meaning of 'ship' see PARA 255 note 4.
13  Ie subject to the Merchant Shipping (Registration of Ships) Regulations 1993, SI 1993/3138, reg
    14 (British connection and representative persons for fishing vessels) (see PARA 263), reg 15
    (dispensations) (see PARA 264) and reg 36(2)–(4) (registration and refusal of registration of a ship)
    (see PARA 289): see the Merchant Shipping (Registration of Ships) Regulations 1993, SI
    1993/3138, reg 13(1).
14  Ie by virtue of the Merchant Shipping (Registration of Ships) Regulations 1993, SI 1993/3138, reg
    12 (see the text and notes 1–11): see reg 13(1).

15 Merchant Shipping (Registration of Ships) Regulations 1993, SI 1993/3138, reg 13(1). In the Merchant Shipping (Registration of Ships) Regulations 1993, SI 1993/3138, unless the context otherwise requires, 'beneficial ownership' is to be determined by reference to every beneficial interest in that vessel, however arising (whether held by trustee or nominee or arising under a contract or otherwise), other than an interest held by any person as mortgagee: reg 1(2).
16 Ie by virtue of the Merchant Shipping (Registration of Ships) Regulations 1993, SI 1993/3138, reg 12 (see the text and notes 1–11): see reg 13(2).
17 Ie for the purposes of the Merchant Shipping (Registration of Ships) Regulations 1993, SI 1993/3138, Pt IV (regs 12–17) (see also PARA 262 et seq): see reg 13(2).
18 Merchant Shipping (Registration of Ships) Regulations 1993, SI 1993/3138, reg 13(2).

**263. British connection and representative persons for fishing vessels.** A fishing vessel[1] may not[2] be registered on Part II of the register[3] unless[4]:

(1)    it is managed, and its operations controlled and directed, from within the United Kingdom[5]; and

(2)    any charterer, manager or operator of the vessel is a person qualified[6] to be the owner[7] of a British fishing vessel[8].

Where:

(a)    the requirements as to entitlement to be registered[9] are satisfied with respect to a fishing vessel[10]; but

(b)    the legal title to the vessel is vested wholly in one or more qualified persons who is or, as the case may be, each of whom is, an individual not resident in the United Kingdom[11],

the vessel is only eligible to be registered as a fishing vessel if a representative person is appointed in relation to the vessel[12].

1  As to the meaning of 'fishing vessel' for these purposes see PARA 255 note 7.
2  Ie notwithstanding that the requirements specified in the Merchant Shipping (Registration of Ships) Regulations 1993, SI 1993/3138, reg 13 (see PARA 262) are satisfied: see reg 14(1).
3  As to the meaning of 'register' for these purposes see PARA 255 note 1. Part II of the register, as mentioned in the text, is for fishing vessels: see the Merchant Shipping (Registration of Ships) Regulations 1993, SI 1993/3138, reg 2(1)(b); and PARA 255. As to the status of any Part II certificate under sea fisheries legislation see PARA 377.
4  Merchant Shipping (Registration of Ships) Regulations 1993, SI 1993/3138, reg 14(1).
5  Merchant Shipping (Registration of Ships) Regulations 1993, SI 1993/3138, reg 14(1)(a). As to the meaning of 'United Kingdom' see PARA 16 note 3.
6  Ie by virtue of the Merchant Shipping (Registration of Ships) Regulations 1993, SI 1993/3138, reg 12 (see PARA 262): see reg 14(1)(b).
7  As to the meaning of 'owner' for these purposes see PARA 255 note 13.
8  Merchant Shipping (Registration of Ships) Regulations 1993, SI 1993/3138, reg 14(1)(b).
9  Ie the requirements specified in the Merchant Shipping (Registration of Ships) Regulations 1993, SI 1993/3138, reg 13 (see PARA 262): see reg 14(2)(a).
10 Merchant Shipping (Registration of Ships) Regulations 1993, SI 1993/3138, reg 14(2)(a).
11 Merchant Shipping (Registration of Ships) Regulations 1993, SI 1993/3138, reg 14(2)(b). As to the rules of domicile and residence generally see CONFLICT OF LAWS vol 19 (2011) PARA 336 et seq.
12 Merchant Shipping (Registration of Ships) Regulations 1993, SI 1993/3138, reg 14(2). The text refers to the appointment of a representative person in relation to the vessel under Pt V (regs 18, 19) (see PARAS 267–268): see reg 14(2).

**264. Dispensations.** Where, in the case of any fishing vessel[1], the Secretary of State[2] is satisfied that[3]:

(1)    a fishing vessel would be eligible to be registered on Part II of the register[4] but for the fact that any particular individual or, as the case may be, each of a number of particular individuals, is not a British citizen[5] or a national of a member state other than the United Kingdom, and is accordingly not a qualified person[6]; and

(2)    it would be appropriate to dispense with the requirement of British citizenship or nationality of such a member state in the case of that individual or those individuals, in view of the length of time he has or they have resided in the United Kingdom and have been involved in the fishing industry of the United Kingdom[7],

the Secretary of State may determine that that requirement should be so dispensed with[8].

If he does so, the vessel is treated, so long as head (1) above applies to it and so long as any such determination remains in force, for the purposes of registration on Part II of the register as being eligible to be registered as a British fishing vessel[9].

1 As to the meaning of 'fishing vessel' for these purposes see PARA 255 note 7.
2 As to the Secretary of State see PARA 36.
3 Merchant Shipping (Registration of Ships) Regulations 1993, SI 1993/3138, reg 15(1).
4 As to the meaning of 'register' for these purposes see PARA 255 note 1. Part II of the register, as mentioned in the text, is for fishing vessels: see the Merchant Shipping (Registration of Ships) Regulations 1993, SI 1993/3138, reg 2(1)(b); and PARA 255.
5 As to the meaning of 'British citizen' see BRITISH NATIONALITY vol 4 (2011) PARA 421 et seq.
6 Merchant Shipping (Registration of Ships) Regulations 1993, SI 1993/3138, reg 15(1)(a).
7 Merchant Shipping (Registration of Ships) Regulations 1993, SI 1993/3138, reg 15(1)(b).
8 Merchant Shipping (Registration of Ships) Regulations 1993, SI 1993/3138, reg 15(1).
9 Merchant Shipping (Registration of Ships) Regulations 1993, SI 1993/3138, reg 15(1). As to the status of any Part II certificate under sea fisheries legislation see PARA 377.

**265. Appointment of inspectors.** For the purpose of determining whether a fishing vessel[1] is eligible to be registered on Part II of the register[2], the Secretary of State[3] may appoint a person to investigate the eligibility of the vessel to be so registered and to make a report of his conclusions to the Secretary of State[4]. Any person so appointed has the powers, for the purpose of conducting the investigation, conferred on an inspector by the Merchant Shipping Act 1995[5].

1 As to the meaning of 'fishing vessel' for these purposes see PARA 255 note 7.
2 As to the meaning of 'register' for these purposes see PARA 255 note 1. Part II of the register, as mentioned in the text, is for fishing vessels: see the Merchant Shipping (Registration of Ships) Regulations 1993, SI 1993/3138, reg 2(1)(b); and PARA 255.
3 As to the Secretary of State see PARA 36.
4 Merchant Shipping (Registration of Ships) Regulations 1993, SI 1993/3138, reg 16.
5 Merchant Shipping (Registration of Ships) Regulations 1993, SI 1993/3138, reg 16; Interpretation Act 1978 s 17(2)(b). The text refers to the powers conferred on an inspector by the Merchant Shipping Act 1995 s 259 (other than s 259(2)(d)–(h)) (see PARA 49): see the Merchant Shipping (Registration of Ships) Regulations 1993, SI 1993/3138, reg 16; Interpretation Act 1978 s 17(2)(b).

**266. Exemptions.** The provisions of the Merchant Shipping Act 1995 which relate to the registration of fishing vessels[1] do not apply to[2]:
(1) salmon cobles[3];
(2) vessels which are ten metres overall length and under and which are not propelled by use of an engine[4]; and
(3) vessels which are ten metres overall length and under which are used to fish for only common eels (Anguila anguilla)[5].

1 Ie the Merchant Shipping Act 1995 s 15(1) (see PARA 1066), under which the Merchant Shipping (Registration of Ships) Regulations 1993, SI 1993/3138, have effect: see reg 17; Interpretation Act 1978 s 17(2)(b).
2 Merchant Shipping (Registration of Ships) Regulations 1993, SI 1993/3138, reg 17.
3 Merchant Shipping (Registration of Ships) Regulations 1993, SI 1993/3138, reg 17(a). For these purposes, 'salmon coble' means a vessel under ten metres in overall length used for fishing for profit only in connection with the private rights of fishing for salmon or migratory trout: reg 1(2). As to the meaning of 'overall length' see PARA 255 note 6.
4 Merchant Shipping (Registration of Ships) Regulations 1993, SI 1993/3138, reg 17(b).
5 Merchant Shipping (Registration of Ships) Regulations 1993, SI 1993/3138, reg 17(c).

## (v) Appointment of Representative Persons

**267. Appointment of representative persons.** Where the entitlement of any ship[1] to be registered is conditional upon the appointment of a representative person[2], the owner[3] of the ship must[4]:

(1)      before applying for the ship to be registered, appoint an individual or body corporate satisfying the requirements set out in heads (a) and (b) below to be the representative person[5]; and

(2)      ensure that, so long as the ship remains registered, an individual or body corporate satisfying those requirements will be so appointed[6].

A representative person is either:

(a)      an individual resident in the United Kingdom[7]; or

(b)      a body corporate incorporated in a member state and having a place of business in the United Kingdom[8].

The appointment of the representative person must be made in a form approved by the Secretary of State[9] and must contain the name and the address of the representative person[10].

The owner of any ship in relation to which any representative person is for the time being appointed under these provisions must:

(i)      on applying for the ship to be registered, send to the registrar[11] the required appointment[12];

(ii)      in the event of any change in the identity, or in the address, of the representative person, notify the registrar of the relevant change within seven days of the change occurring[13];

and the registrar must record the new particulars in the register[14].

1    As to the meaning of 'ship' see PARA 255 note 4.
2    See eg the Merchant Shipping (Registration of Ships) Regulations 1993, SI 1993/3138, reg 8(3) (cited in PARA 259); and the Merchant Shipping (Registration of Ships) Regulations 1993, SI 1993/3138, reg 14(2) (cited in PARA 263).
3    As to the meaning of 'owner' for these purposes see PARA 255 note 13.
4    Merchant Shipping (Registration of Ships) Regulations 1993, SI 1993/3138, reg 18(1).
5    Merchant Shipping (Registration of Ships) Regulations 1993, SI 1993/3138, reg 18(1)(a).
6    Merchant Shipping (Registration of Ships) Regulations 1993, SI 1993/3138, reg 18(1)(b).
7    Merchant Shipping (Registration of Ships) Regulations 1993, SI 1993/3138, reg 18(2)(a). As to the meaning of 'United Kingdom' see PARA 16 note 3. As to the rules of domicile and residence generally see CONFLICT OF LAWS vol 19 (2011) PARA 336 et seq.
8    Merchant Shipping (Registration of Ships) Regulations 1993, SI 1993/3138, reg 18(2)(b). As to a person's place of business see COMPANIES vol 14 (2016) PARA 117.
9    As to the Secretary of State see PARA 36.
10   Merchant Shipping (Registration of Ships) Regulations 1993, SI 1993/3138, reg 18(3).
11   As to the meaning of 'registrar' see PARA 255 note 2.
12   Merchant Shipping (Registration of Ships) Regulations 1993, SI 1993/3138, reg 18(4)(a). The text refers to the appointment required by reg 18(3) (see the text and notes 10–11): see reg 18(4)(a).
13   Merchant Shipping (Registration of Ships) Regulations 1993, SI 1993/3138, reg 18(4)(b).
14   Merchant Shipping (Registration of Ships) Regulations 1993, SI 1993/3138, reg 18(4). As to the meaning of 'register' for these purposes see PARA 255 note 1.

**268. Service on representative persons.** Any document required or authorised to be served by or under the Merchant Shipping Act 1995[1] or required or authorised, by virtue of any statutory provision, to be served for the purpose of the institution of, or otherwise in connection with, proceedings for an offence under the 1995 Act[2], or under any instrument in force under that Act, on the owner[3] of a ship[4] is treated as duly served on him if[5]:

(1)      delivered to any representative person for the time being appointed[6]; or

(2)      sent to any such person by post at the address notified, or, as the case may be, last notified, to the registrar[7] in relation to that person[8]; or

(3)    left for any such person at that address[9].

1   As to the service of documents under the Merchant Shipping Act 1995 generally see s 291; and
    PARA 74.
2   As to offences and legal proceedings arising out of the Merchant Shipping Act 1995 generally see
    PARA 1049 et seq.
3   As to the meaning of 'owner' for these purposes see PARA 255 note 13.
4   As to the meaning of 'ship' see PARA 255 note 4.
5   Merchant Shipping (Registration of Ships) Regulations 1993, SI 1993/3138, reg 19; Interpretation
    Act 1978 s 17(2)(b).
6   Merchant Shipping (Registration of Ships) Regulations 1993, SI 1993/3138, reg 19(a). As to the
    appointment of representative persons see PARA 267.
7   Ie under the Merchant Shipping (Registration of Ships) Regulations 1993, SI 1993/3138, reg 18(4)
    (see PARA 267): see reg 19(b). As to the meaning of 'registrar' see PARA 255 note 2.
8   Merchant Shipping (Registration of Ships) Regulations 1993, SI 1993/3138, reg 19(b).
9   Merchant Shipping (Registration of Ships) Regulations 1993, SI 1993/3138, reg 19(c).

### (vi)  Registration

#### A.    APPLICATION FOR REGISTRATION

**269.   Form of application.** Every application for registration[1] must be made to
the registrar[2] at the General Registry of Shipping and Seamen[3]. Applications in
respect of fishing vessels[4] may also be made through a local office[5].

The application must be made in a form approved by the Secretary of State[6]
and must contain the name and address of the applicant and sufficient
information to enable the ship to be identified[7].

1   Ie made under the Merchant Shipping (Registration of Ships) Regulations 1993, SI 1993/3138: see
    reg 20(1) (amended by SI 1998/2976). For these purposes, 'application for registration' includes,
    except where otherwise stated: application for registration of a ship or share in a ship; application
    for registration of a small ship; application for re-registration of the same; and application for the
    registration of a transfer or transmission of a ship or a share in a ship; but not application for
    renewal of registration: Merchant Shipping (Registration of Ships) Regulations 1993, SI
    1993/3138, reg 1(2). As to the meaning of 'ship' see PARA 255 note 4; and as to the meaning of
    'small ship' for these purposes see PARA 255 note 6.
2   As to the meaning of 'registrar' see PARA 255 note 2.
3   Merchant Shipping (Registration of Ships) Regulations 1993, SI 1993/3138, reg 20(1) (as
    amended: see note 1).
4   As to the meaning of 'fishing vessel' for these purposes see PARA 255 note 7.
5   Merchant Shipping (Registration of Ships) Regulations 1993, SI 1993/3138, reg 20(1) (as
    amended: see note 1). For these purposes, 'local office' means an office listed in the list published
    by the Department of Transport and entitled 'List of Local Offices for Fishing Vessels
    Registration': see reg 1(2).
6   As to the Secretary of State see PARA 36.
7   Merchant Shipping (Registration of Ships) Regulations 1993, SI 1993/3138, reg 20(2). As to the
    requirement to supply supplementary information or evidence where that provided on an
    application for registration is judged to be either not correct or insufficient see PARA 372.

**270.   The applicant.** Every application for registration[1] must be made[2]:
(1)    in the case of individuals, by some one or more of the individuals
       registered or requiring to be registered as owners[3] or by his or their
       agent[4]; or
(2)    in the case of a body corporate, by a duly authorised officer of that body
       corporate, or by its agent[5]; or
(3)    in the case of a European Economic Interest Group[6], by a duly
       authorised officer of that group, or by its agent[7].

1   Ie made under the Merchant Shipping (Registration of Ships) Regulations 1993, SI 1993/3138: see
    reg 21. As to the meaning of 'application for registration' see PARA 269 note 1.
2   Merchant Shipping (Registration of Ships) Regulations 1993, SI 1993/3138, reg 21(1).
3   As to the meaning of 'owner' for these purposes see PARA 255 note 13.

4  Merchant Shipping (Registration of Ships) Regulations 1993, SI 1993/3138, reg 21(1)(a).
5  Merchant Shipping (Registration of Ships) Regulations 1993, SI 1993/3138, reg 21(1)(b).
6  As to European Economic Interest Groups see COMPANIES vol 15A (2016) PARAS 1823–1824.
7  Merchant Shipping (Registration of Ships) Regulations 1993, SI 1993/3138, reg 21(1)(c).

**271. Appointment of managing owner where ship has more than one owner.** Where application for registration[1] is made in respect of a ship[2] which has more than one owner[3] (or whose shares are owned by more than one owner) and no representative person has been appointed[4], one of those owners who is resident in the United Kingdom[5] must be nominated as the managing owner; and the register[6] must be marked accordingly and all correspondence must be sent to that person at the address recorded in the register in respect of that owner[7].

Where the owners determine that a different managing owner should be appointed, the registrar[8] must be notified in writing and the register noted accordingly[9].

Any document required or authorised to be served, by or under the Merchant Shipping Act 1995[10] or required or authorised, by virtue of any statutory provision, to be served for the purpose of the institution of, or otherwise in connection with, proceedings for an offence under the 1995 Act[11], or under any instrument in force under that Act, on the owner of a ship is to be treated as duly served on him if[12]:

(1)   delivered to the managing owner[13];
(2)   sent to the managing owner by post at the address notified (or, as the case may be, last notified) to the registrar[14] in relation to that person[15]; or
(3)   left for the managing owner at that address[16].

1  As to the meaning of 'application for registration' see PARA 269 note 1.
2  As to the meaning of 'ship' for these purposes see PARA 255 note 4.
3  As to the meaning of 'owner' for these purposes see PARA 255 note 13.
4  Ie under the Merchant Shipping (Registration of Ships) Regulations 1993, SI 1993/3138, Pt V (regs 18, 19) (see PARAS 267–268): see reg 23(1).
5  As to the meaning of 'United Kingdom' see PARA 16 note 3. As to the rules of domicile and residence generally see CONFLICT OF LAWS vol 19 (2011) PARA 336 et seq.
6  As to the meaning of 'register' for these purposes see PARA 255 note 1.
7  Merchant Shipping (Registration of Ships) Regulations 1993, SI 1993/3138, reg 23(1).
8  As to the meaning of 'registrar' see PARA 255 note 2.
9  Merchant Shipping (Registration of Ships) Regulations 1993, SI 1993/3138, reg 23(2).
10 As to the service of documents under the Merchant Shipping Act 1995 generally see s 291; and PARA 74.
11 As to offences and legal proceedings arising out of the Merchant Shipping Act 1995 generally see PARA 1049 et seq.
12 Merchant Shipping (Registration of Ships) Regulations 1993, SI 1993/3138, reg 23(3).
13 Merchant Shipping (Registration of Ships) Regulations 1993, SI 1993/3138, reg 23(3)(a).
14 Ie under the Merchant Shipping (Registration of Ships) Regulations 1993, SI 1993/3138, reg 23(1) or reg 23(2) (see the text and notes 1–9): see reg 23(3)(b).
15 Merchant Shipping (Registration of Ships) Regulations 1993, SI 1993/3138, reg 23(3)(b).
16 Merchant Shipping (Registration of Ships) Regulations 1993, SI 1993/3138, reg 23(3)(c).

**272. Supplementary requirements for application for registration.** Every application for registration[1] must be supported by a declaration of eligibility[2] which must be in a form approved by the Secretary of State[3] and must include[4]:

(1)   a declaration of British connection[5];
(2)   a declaration of ownership by every owner[6] setting out his qualification to own a British ship[7];
(3)   a statement of the number of shares in the ship the legal title of which is vested in each owner whether alone or jointly with any other person or persons[8]; and

(4) in respect of an application to register a fishing vessel[9], a statement of the beneficial ownership[10] of any share which is not beneficially owned by its legal owner[11].

Every application for registration of a ship which has, immediately prior to the application, been registered on any other register[12] must be accompanied by a certified extract from that register in respect of that ship[13].

Every application for registration of a fishing vessel on Part II of the register[14] must state whether the application is for full[15] or simple[16] registration[17].

1 As to the meaning of 'application for registration' see PARA 269 note 1.
2 For these purposes, 'declaration of eligibility' means a declaration which complies with the Merchant Shipping (Registration of Ships) Regulations 1993, SI 1993/3138, reg 22(1): reg 1(2). As to the power to dispense with declarations or other evidence otherwise required under the Merchant Shipping (Registration of Ships) Regulations 1993, SI 1993/3138, see PARA 371.
3 As to the Secretary of State see PARA 36.
4 Merchant Shipping (Registration of Ships) Regulations 1993, SI 1993/3138, reg 22(1) (amended by SI 1994/541). The Merchant Shipping (Registration of Ships) Regulations 1993, SI 1993/3138, reg 22(1) is subject to reg 25 (declaration of intent) (see PARA 274): reg 22(1) (as so amended). As to offences in connection with applications see PARA 1070. As to the requirement to supply supplementary information or evidence where that provided on an application for registration is judged to be either not correct or insufficient see PARA 372.
5 Merchant Shipping (Registration of Ships) Regulations 1993, SI 1993/3138, reg 22(1)(a). As to the meaning of 'declaration of British connection' under the Merchant Shipping Act 1995 see PARA 245 note 3.
6 As to the meaning of 'owner' for these purposes see PARA 255 note 13.
7 Merchant Shipping (Registration of Ships) Regulations 1993, SI 1993/3138, reg 22(1)(b). As to the meaning of 'ship' for these purposes see PARA 255 note 4. As to the meaning of 'British ship' under the Merchant Shipping Act 1995 see PARA 230.
8 Merchant Shipping (Registration of Ships) Regulations 1993, SI 1993/3138, reg 22(1)(c).
9 As to the meaning of 'fishing vessel' for these purposes see PARA 255 note 7.
10 As to the meaning of 'beneficial ownership' for these purposes see PARA 262 note 15.
11 Merchant Shipping (Registration of Ships) Regulations 1993, SI 1993/3138, reg 22(1)(d).
12 Ie a register other than the central register of British ships (as to the meaning of which see PARA 255 note 1).
13 Merchant Shipping (Registration of Ships) Regulations 1993, SI 1993/3138, reg 22(2).
14 Part II of the register is for fishing vessels only: see the Merchant Shipping (Registration of Ships) Regulations 1993, SI 1993/3138, reg 2(1)(b); and PARA 255. As to the status of any Part II certificate under sea fisheries legislation see PARA 377.
15 As to the meaning of 'full registration' see PARA 256.
16 As to the meaning of 'simple registration' see PARA 256.
17 Merchant Shipping (Registration of Ships) Regulations 1993, SI 1993/3138, reg 22(3).

## 273. Supplementary requirements for applications by bodies corporate.

Where application for registration[1] is made on behalf of a body corporate, the application must be accompanied by[2]:

(1) if it is a company registered in the United Kingdom[3], a copy of its certificate of incorporation, and, in the case of a company which has changed its name since incorporation, its certificates of change of name[4]; or

(2) if it is a company incorporated in a member state other than the United Kingdom or a company incorporated in any relevant British possession[5], proof in accordance with the laws of the country of its incorporation that the company is an incorporated company[6];

(3) if it is a company, other than a company incorporated in the United Kingdom, with a place of business in the United Kingdom, a certificate from the registrar of companies in England and Wales[7], the registrar of Scottish companies[8] or the registrar of Northern Ireland companies[9] that the company is registered with him as an oversea company[10]; and

(4)      if it is a body corporate incorporated by virtue of an Act of Parliament, a Charter granted by Her Majesty, or an Act of Ordinance of a relevant British possession, proof, sufficient to satisfy the registrar[11], of its incorporation[12].

1   As to the meaning of 'application for registration' see PARA 269 note 1.
2   Merchant Shipping (Registration of Ships) Regulations 1993, SI 1993/3138, reg 24. As to the requirement to supply supplementary information or evidence where that provided on an application for registration is judged to be either not correct or insufficient see PARA 372.
3   As to the meaning of 'United Kingdom' see PARA 16 note 3.
4   Merchant Shipping (Registration of Ships) Regulations 1993, SI 1993/3138, reg 24(a). As to companies and their incorporation etc see COMPANIES vol 14 (2016) PARA 114 et seq.
5   As to the meaning of 'relevant British possession' under the Merchant Shipping Act 1995 see PARA 16 note 3.
6   Merchant Shipping (Registration of Ships) Regulations 1993, SI 1993/3138, reg 24(b).
7   As to the registrar of companies see COMPANIES vol 14 (2016) PARA 126 et seq. As to the meanings of 'England' and 'Wales' see PARA 16 note 2.
8   As to companies in Scotland see COMPANIES vol 14 (2016) PARA 26.
9   As to companies in Northern Ireland see COMPANIES vol 14 (2016) PARA 26.
10  Merchant Shipping (Registration of Ships) Regulations 1993, SI 1993/3138, reg 24(c). As to oversea companies see COMPANIES vol 15A (2016) PARA 2013 et seq. As to a person's place of business see COMPANIES vol 14 (2016) PARA 117.
11  As to the meaning of 'registrar' see PARA 255 note 2.
12  Merchant Shipping (Registration of Ships) Regulations 1993, SI 1993/3138, reg 24(d) (amended by SI 1994/541).

**274. Declaration of intent.** Where, at the time when the application for registration[1] is made, the ownership of a ship[2] has not yet passed (or fully passed) to the persons who are to be its owners[3] when it is registered, the application must be accompanied by a declaration of intent instead of a declaration of eligibility[4]. The declaration of intent must consist of: (1) a draft declaration of eligibility setting out particulars of ownership of the ship as they are intended to be when the ship is registered[5]; and (2) a declaration that the ownership of the ship will, at the time when registration occurs, be as stated in the draft declaration of eligibility[6].

Where an application for registration is accompanied by a declaration of intent and not by a declaration of eligibility, a duly completed declaration of eligibility must be submitted to the registrar[7] prior to registration[8].

1   As to the meaning of 'application for registration' see PARA 269 note 1.
2   As to the meaning of 'ship' for these purposes see PARA 255 note 4.
3   As to the meaning of 'owner' for these purposes see PARA 255 note 13.
4   Merchant Shipping (Registration of Ships) Regulations 1993, SI 1993/3138, reg 25. As to the meaning of 'declaration of eligibility' see PARA 272 note 2. As to the power to dispense with declarations or other evidence otherwise required under the Merchant Shipping (Registration of Ships) Regulations 1993, SI 1993/3138, see PARA 371.
5   Merchant Shipping (Registration of Ships) Regulations 1993, SI 1993/3138, reg 26(a).
6   Merchant Shipping (Registration of Ships) Regulations 1993, SI 1993/3138, reg 26(b).
7   As to the meaning of 'registrar' see PARA 255 note 2.
8   Merchant Shipping (Registration of Ships) Regulations 1993, SI 1993/3138, reg 27.

**275. Evidence required to support registration.** An application to register a ship[1] (other than an application in respect of a fishing vessel[2] requiring simple registration[3]) must be supported by the following evidence of title[4]:
(1)      in the case of a new ship, the builder's certificate[5];
(2)      in the case of a ship which is not new:
      (a)      in respect of a pleasure vessel[6], a previous bill or bills of sale showing the ownership of the ship for at least five years before the application is made or, if the ship has been registered with a full registration at any time within the last five years, a bill or bills of sale evidencing all transfers of ownership during the period since it was so registered[7];

    (b)    in respect of a fishing vessel, a previous bill or bills of sale showing the ownership of the vessel for at least three years before the application is made, or, if the ship has been registered with full registration[8] at any time within the last three years, a bill or bills of sale evidencing all transfers of ownership during the period since it was so registered, or evidence that the vessel has been for at least three years continuously registered as a British fishing vessel with simple registration in the names of the owners[9] applying to be registered and remains so registered[10]; or

    (c)    in respect of a ship other than a pleasure vessel or a fishing vessel, one bill of sale showing the most recent transfer of ownership[11];

(3)    where the evidence required by head (1) or head (2) above is not available, other evidence of title satisfactory to the registrar[12].

Where such an application is made to register a fishing vessel (whether new or second hand)[13], the applicant must submit details of the maximum continuous engine power[14] and, where an engine is permanently de-rated, the modification explanation[15]. Any owner who contravenes this requirement is guilty of an offence[16].

1  As to the meaning of 'ship' for these purposes see PARA 255 note 4. As to the meaning of 'application for registration' see PARA 269 note 1.

2  As to the meaning of 'fishing vessel' for these purposes see PARA 255 note 7.

3  As to the meaning of 'simple registration' see PARA 256.

4  Merchant Shipping (Registration of Ships) Regulations 1993, SI 1993/3138, reg 28(1) (amended by SI 1998/2976; renumbered by SI 1999/3206).

5  Merchant Shipping (Registration of Ships) Regulations 1993, SI 1993/3138, reg 28(1)(a) (reg 28(1) as renumbered: see note 4). For these purposes, 'builder's certificate' means a certificate signed by the builder of the ship and containing a true account of the proper denomination and of the tonnage of the ship, as estimated by him, and of the date and place where the ship was built, and of the name of the person, if any, for whom the ship was built, or the name of the person to whom it was delivered: reg 1(2).

6  For these purposes, 'pleasure vessel' means a pleasure vessel as defined in the Merchant Shipping (Vessels in Commercial Use for Sport or Pleasure) Regulations 1998, SI 1998/2771, reg 2 (see PARA 612): Merchant Shipping (Registration of Ships) Regulations 1993, SI 1993/3138, reg 1(2) (definition substituted by SI 1999/3206).

7  Merchant Shipping (Registration of Ships) Regulations 1993, SI 1993/3138, reg 28(1)(b)(i) (reg 28(1) as renumbered (see note 4); reg 28(1)(b)(i) amended by SI 1999/3206).

8  As to the meaning of 'full registration' see PARA 256.

9  As to the meaning of 'owner' for these purposes see PARA 255 note 13.

10  Merchant Shipping (Registration of Ships) Regulations 1993, SI 1993/3138, reg 28(1)(b)(ii) (reg 28(1) as renumbered (see note 4); reg 28(1)(b)(ii) amended by SI 1999/3206).

11  Merchant Shipping (Registration of Ships) Regulations 1993, SI 1993/3138, reg 28(1)(b)(iii) (reg 28(1) as renumbered (see note 4); reg 28(1)(b)(iii) added by SI 1999/3206). Where a ship has entered the register by virtue of the Merchant Shipping (Registration of Ships) Regulations 1993, SI 1993/3138, reg 28(1)(b)(iii) and subsequently becomes a pleasure vessel or a fishing vessel, the owner must then provide the title evidence required under reg 28(1)(b)(i) (see head (2)(a) in the text) or under reg 28(1)(b)(ii) (see head (2)(b) in the text) respectively or under reg 28(1)(c) (see head (3) in the text) for the ship to remain eligible to be registered: reg 28(2) (added by SI 1999/3206). As to the meaning of 'register' for these purposes see PARA 255 note 1.

12  Merchant Shipping (Registration of Ships) Regulations 1993, SI 1993/3138, reg 28(1)(c) (reg 28(1) as renumbered (see note 4); reg 28(1)(c) amended by SI 1999/3206). As to the meaning of 'registrar' see PARA 255 note 2.

13  Merchant Shipping (Registration of Ships) Regulations 1993, SI 1993/3138, reg 29A(1)(a) (regs 29A, 29B added by SI 1999/3206).

14  Merchant Shipping (Registration of Ships) Regulations 1993, SI 1993/3138, reg 29A(2)(a) (as added: see note 13). The text refers to details of the maximum continuous engine power, determined in accordance with Council Regulation (EC) 2930/86 of 22 September 1986 defining characteristics for fishing vessels (OJ L274, 25.9.1986, p 1) art 5: see the Merchant Shipping (Registration of Ships) Regulations 1993, SI 1993/3138, reg 29A(2)(a) (as so added). For these purposes, 'maximum continuous engine power' has the same meaning as 'engine power' in Council Regulation (EC) 2930/86 art 5.1 (defining characteristics for fishing vessels): Merchant Shipping

(Registration of Ships) Regulations 1993, SI 1993/3138, reg 1(2) (definition added by SI 1999/3206). Where the registrar is not satisfied that the engine power details notified to him, or recorded, for any fishing vessel are correct, he may require the owner to have the engine power measured in accordance with Council Regulation (EC) 2930/86 art 5: Merchant Shipping (Registration of Ships) Regulations 1993, SI 1993/3138, reg 29B (as so added).

15 Merchant Shipping (Registration of Ships) Regulations 1993, SI 1993/3138, reg 29A(2)(b) (as added: see note 13). The Merchant Shipping (Registration of Ships) Regulations 1993, SI 1993/3138, reg 1(2) (definitions added by SI 1999/3206) provides that for these purposes, 'modification explanation' means the clear explanation, referred to in Commission Regulation (EC) 1381/87 of 20 May 1987 establishing detailed rules concerning the marking and documentation of fishing vessels (OJ L132, 21.5.1987, p 9) art 3.3, of the method by which any modification of engine power has been carried out; and 'permanently de-rated engine power' means a modification of the maximum continuous engine power referred to in art 3.3. Commission Regulation (EC) 1381/87 has been repealed by Commission Implementing Regulation (EU) 404/2011 of 8 April 2011 (OJ L112, 30.4.2011, p 1) laying down detailed rules for the implementation of Council Regulation (EC) 1224/2009 (OJ L343, 22.12.2009. p 1) establishing a Community control system for ensuring compliance with the rules of the Common Fisheries Policy, which has not directly replaced Commission Regulation (EC) 1381/87 art 3.3: see, however, as to the certification and verification of engine power Commission Implementing Regulation (EU) 404/2011 arts 61–63.

16 See the Merchant Shipping (Registration of Ships) Regulations 1993, SI 1993/3138, reg 29A(3); and PARA 1067.

### B. SURVEY AND MEASUREMENT

**276. Survey and measurement of ship.** Every ship[1], other than certain fishing vessels[2], must before registration be surveyed by a surveyor of ships[3] and her tonnage ascertained in accordance with the tonnage regulations[4].

Certain fishing vessels[5] must before registration be measured by an authorised measurer[6] and her tonnage calculated in accordance with the tonnage regulations made under the Merchant Shipping Act 1995[7].

After survey or measurement, the surveyor or measurer must issue a certificate specifying the ship's tonnage and build and such other particulars describing the identity of the ship as may be required by the Secretary of State[8]. The certificate must be delivered to the registrar[9] before the ship may be registered[10].

A ship which is being registered for the first time which has been surveyed or measured and its tonnage ascertained within the previous 12 months, or which is being re-registered within 12 months of its registration on the register[11] ceasing, is not required to be surveyed or measured (or its tonnage ascertained) again[12] if a declaration is made by the owners[13] confirming that the survey or measurement and tonnage details have not changed from those previously provided to the registrar[14].

1 As to the meaning of 'ship' for these purposes see PARA 255 note 4.
2 Ie other than a fishing vessel less than 24 metres in length to which the Merchant Shipping (Tonnage) Regulations 1997, SI 1997/1510, Pt IIA (regs 12A–12E) (measurement of smaller fishing vessels) (see PARA 248) does not apply: see the Merchant Shipping (Registration of Ships) Regulations 1993, SI 1993/3138, reg 29(1) (amended by SI 1998/1915; SI 1999/3206). 'Length' in the Merchant Shipping (Registration of Ships) Regulations 1993, SI 1993/3138, reg 29 has the same meaning as in the Tonnage Regulations: Merchant Shipping (Registration of Ships) Regulations 1993, SI 1993/3138, reg 1(2) (definition added by SI 1998/1915). 'Tonnage regulations' means the Merchant Shipping (Tonnage) Regulations 1997, SI 1997/1510 (as to which see PARA 248): Merchant Shipping (Registration of Ships) Regulations 1993, SI 1993/3138, reg 1(2) (definition added by SI 1998/1915). As to the meaning of 'fishing vessel' for these purposes see PARA 255 note 7. See the text and notes 5–7.
3 For these purposes, 'surveyor of ships' means a marine surveyor nominated by the Secretary of State to undertake the surveys required by the Merchant Shipping (Registration of Ships) Regulations 1993, SI 1993/3138, and includes any marine surveyor of the Department of Transport: reg 1(2). As to the Secretary of State see PARA 36.

4   Merchant Shipping (Registration of Ships) Regulations 1993, SI 1993/3138, reg 29(1) (as amended: see note 2). Regulation 29(1) is subject to reg 29A (as to which see PARAS 275, 313–314, 1067): reg 29(1) (as so amended).
5   Ie a fishing vessel of less than 24 metres other than a fishing vessel to which the Merchant Shipping (Tonnage) Regulations 1997, SI 1997/1510, Pt IIA applies: see the Merchant Shipping (Registration of Ships) Regulations 1993, SI 1993/3138, reg 29(2) (amended by SI 1998/1915; SI 1999/3206).
6   For these purposes, 'authorised measurer' means the Secretary of State or any person authorised under the Merchant Shipping (Tonnage) Regulations 1997, SI 1997/1510, or the Merchant Shipping (Fishing Vessels –Tonnage) Regulations 1988, SI 1988/1909 (see PARA 248) to carry out the measurement of ships for the purposes of those regulations: Merchant Shipping (Registration of Ships) Regulations 1993, SI 1993/3138, reg 1(2); Interpretation Act 1978 s 17(2)(b).
7   Merchant Shipping (Registration of Ships) Regulations 1993, SI 1993/3138, reg 29(2) (as amended: see note 5). As to the tonnage regulations made under the Merchant Shipping Act 1995 see PARA 248. The Merchant Shipping (Registration of Ships) Regulations 1993, SI 1993/3138, reg 29(2) is subject to reg 29A: reg 29(2) (as so amended).
8   Merchant Shipping (Registration of Ships) Regulations 1993, SI 1993/3138, reg 29(3).
9   As to the meaning of 'registrar' see PARA 255 note 2.
10  Merchant Shipping (Registration of Ships) Regulations 1993, SI 1993/3138, reg 29(3).
11  As to the meaning of 'register' for these purposes see PARA 255 note 1.
12  Ie in accordance with the Merchant Shipping (Registration of Ships) Regulations 1993, SI 1993/3138, reg 29(1), (2) (see the text and notes 1–7): see reg 29(4) (reg 29(4), (5) added by SI 1998/2976).
13  As to the meaning of 'owner' for these purposes see PARA 255 note 13.
14  Merchant Shipping (Registration of Ships) Regulations 1993, SI 1993/3138, reg 29(4) (as added: see note 12). The registrar may, if he thinks it appropriate, direct that an authorised measurer or surveyor provides such a declaration: reg 29(5) (as so added). As to the power to dispense with declarations or other evidence otherwise required under the Merchant Shipping (Registration of Ships) Regulations 1993, SI 1993/3138, see PARA 371.

### C.   NAMES

**277.   Ship's proposed name.** On making an application for registration[1] of a ship[2], the applicant must propose a name by which the ship is to be called[3].

A ship may not be described by any name other than its registered name[4]; and a change may not be made in a registered ship's name without the prior written permission of the registrar[5].

1   As to the meaning of 'application for registration' see PARA 269 note 1.
2   As to the meaning of 'ship' for these purposes see PARA 255 note 4.
3   Merchant Shipping (Registration of Ships) Regulations 1993, SI 1993/3138, reg 30(1). As to the approval of names see reg 30(2), Sch 1; and PARA 278.
4   Merchant Shipping (Registration of Ships) Regulations 1993, SI 1993/3138, reg 30(3).
5   Merchant Shipping (Registration of Ships) Regulations 1993, SI 1993/3138, reg 30(4). As to the meaning of 'registrar' see PARA 255 note 2.

**278.   Approval of names.** Every application to the registrar[1] to approve a name for a ship[2] must specify a name which is in Roman letters; any numerals must be in Roman or Arabic numerals[3].

In respect of an application to register a ship (other than a fishing vessel[4]) on Part I or IV of the register[5], the registrar must not approve the proposed name if it is[6]:

(1)     already the name of a registered British ship[7]; or
(2)     a name so similar to that of a registered British ship as to be calculated to deceive or likely to confuse[8];
(3)     a name which may be confused with a distress signal[9];
(4)     a name which is prefixed by any letters or name which could be taken to indicate a type of ship or any other word, prefix or suffix which might cause confusion as to the name of the ship[10].

In respect of an application to register a fishing vessel on Part II or IV of the register, the registrar must not approve the proposed name if it is[11]:

(a)   already the name of a vessel in its port of choice[12]; or

(b)   a name so similar to that of a registered British fishing vessel[13] in its port of choice as to be calculated to deceive or likely to confuse[14];

(c)   a name which may be confused with a distress signal[15];

(d)   a name which is prefixed by any letters or name which could be taken to indicate a type of ship or any other word, prefix or suffix which might cause confusion as to the name of the ship[16].

If the registrar is satisfied that a name does not fall within heads (1) to (4) above or heads (a) to (d) above, he must notify the applicant in writing that the name is approved and that the ship may be registered with that name[17]. However, notwithstanding that the registrar is so satisfied as to the proposed name, he may refuse to approve a name which might cause offence or embarrassment or which has a clear and direct connection with the Royal family[18].

Any approval so given by the registrar is valid only for the period of three months beginning with the date it is notified to the applicant[19]. If the registrar is not so satisfied, he must notify the applicant accordingly[20].

The registrar may allow the reservation of a ship's name or designation for a period of ten years[21] if he is satisfied that[22]:

(i)   the ship is intended to replace another of the same name which is to be registered within ten years of the date of the application[23]; and

(ii)   the applicant is the owner[24] of a registered ship with the same name as that which is to be reserved and its British registration will be closed before the registration of the new vessel[25]; or

(iii)   the applicant is the owner of a registered ship with the same name as that which is to be reserved and it will be sold before the registration of the new vessel on condition that it changes its name and that its name is so changed[26].

Applications for such a reservation must be accompanied by a full statement of the circumstances of the case[27].

Where a ship having once been registered has ceased to be registered, no person (unless ignorant of the previous registration, proof whereof will lie on him) may apply for registration of the ship other than by the name by which it was previously registered except with the written permission of the registrar[28].

1   As to the meaning of 'registrar' see PARA 255 note 2.

2   As to the meaning of 'ship' for these purposes see PARA 255 note 4.

3   Merchant Shipping (Registration of Ships) Regulations 1993, SI 1993/3138, reg 30(2), Sch 1 para 1 (amended by SI 1994/541). The Merchant Shipping (Registration of Ships) Regulations 1993, SI 1993/3138, Sch 1 is applied also for the purposes of reg 52 (change of name) (as to which see PARA 315), reg 72 (transfer of registration from relevant British possession) (as to which see PARA 342) and reg 78 (application for registration of a bareboat charter ship) (as to which see PARA 361).

4   As to the meaning of 'fishing vessel' for these purposes see PARA 255 note 7. See the text and notes 11–16.

5   As to the meaning of 'register' for these purposes see PARA 255 note 1. Part I of the register, as mentioned in the text, is for ships, owned by qualified persons, which are not fishing vessels or registered on that Part which is restricted to small ships: see the Merchant Shipping (Registration of Ships) Regulations 1993, SI 1993/3138, reg 2(1)(a); and PARA 255. Part IV of the register is for ships which are bareboat charter ships: see reg 2(1)(d); and PARA 255. As to the meaning of 'bareboat charter ship' see PARA 255 note 9; and as to the meaning of 'small ship' for these purposes see PARA 255 note 6.

6   Merchant Shipping (Registration of Ships) Regulations 1993, SI 1993/3138, Sch 1 para 2.

7   Merchant Shipping (Registration of Ships) Regulations 1993, SI 1993/3138, Sch 1 para 2(a). As to the meaning of 'British ship' under the Merchant Shipping Act 1995 see PARA 230.

8   Merchant Shipping (Registration of Ships) Regulations 1993, SI 1993/3138, Sch 1 para 2(b).

9   Merchant Shipping (Registration of Ships) Regulations 1993, SI 1993/3138, Sch 1 para 2(c).

10 Merchant Shipping (Registration of Ships) Regulations 1993, SI 1993/3138, Sch 1 para 2(d).
11 Merchant Shipping (Registration of Ships) Regulations 1993, SI 1993/3138, Sch 1 para 3.
12 Merchant Shipping (Registration of Ships) Regulations 1993, SI 1993/3138, Sch 1 para 3(a). For these purposes, 'port of choice' means a port listed in reg 31(1), Sch 2 (as to which see PARA 279) which an applicant chooses as a port to be marked on his ship: reg 1(2) (definition amended by SI 1999/3206).
13 As to the meaning of 'British fishing vessel' under the Merchant Shipping Act 1995 see PARA 230.
14 Merchant Shipping (Registration of Ships) Regulations 1993, SI 1993/3138, Sch 1 para 3(b).
15 Merchant Shipping (Registration of Ships) Regulations 1993, SI 1993/3138, Sch 1 para 3(c).
16 Merchant Shipping (Registration of Ships) Regulations 1993, SI 1993/3138, Sch 1 para 3(d).
17 Merchant Shipping (Registration of Ships) Regulations 1993, SI 1993/3138, Sch 1 para 4.
18 Merchant Shipping (Registration of Ships) Regulations 1993, SI 1993/3138, Sch 1 para 5.
19 Merchant Shipping (Registration of Ships) Regulations 1993, SI 1993/3138, Sch 1 para 6.
20 Merchant Shipping (Registration of Ships) Regulations 1993, SI 1993/3138, Sch 1 para 7.
21 Ie notwithstanding the Merchant Shipping (Registration of Ships) Regulations 1993, SI 1993/3138, Sch 1 para 6 (see the text and note 19): see Sch 1 para 8.
22 Merchant Shipping (Registration of Ships) Regulations 1993, SI 1993/3138, Sch 1 para 8.
23 Merchant Shipping (Registration of Ships) Regulations 1993, SI 1993/3138, Sch 1 para 8(a).
24 As to the meaning of 'owner' for these purposes see PARA 255 note 13.
25 Merchant Shipping (Registration of Ships) Regulations 1993, SI 1993/3138, Sch 1 para 8(b).
26 Merchant Shipping (Registration of Ships) Regulations 1993, SI 1993/3138, Sch 1 para 8(c).
27 Merchant Shipping (Registration of Ships) Regulations 1993, SI 1993/3138, Sch 1 para 9.
28 Merchant Shipping (Registration of Ships) Regulations 1993, SI 1993/3138, Sch 1 para 10.

D.    OFFICIAL NUMBER AND PORT OF CHOICE

**279. Allocation of official number and port of choice.** On making an application for registration[1] of a ship[2], the applicant must specify one of the listed ports[3] which it is intended shall be the ship's port of choice[4].

On receipt of an application for registration of a ship for the first time, the registrar[5], if he is satisfied that that ship is eligible to be registered, must[6]:

(1)    allocate to the ship a register number ('official number')[7];
(2)    in the case of a fishing vessel, allocate a port number[8],
and must issue a carving and marking note[9].

The registrar may, on request by a classification society[10], allocate an official number to a ship notwithstanding that he is not yet satisfied as to its eligibility[11]. Where a ship has had a number so allocated and that number has been carved into the ship's beam but the ship is not accepted as being eligible for registration, the number must be permanently defaced and a certificate to that effect provided by the classification society to the registrar[12].

1  As to the meaning of 'application for registration' see PARA 269 note 1.
2  As to the meaning of 'ship' for these purposes see PARA 255 note 4.
3  Ie one of the ports listed in the Merchant Shipping (Registration of Ships) Regulations 1993, SI 1993/3138, reg 31(1), Sch 2 Pt 1 or Pt 2, as is appropriate: see reg 31(1). The ports of choice for ships to be registered on Part I of the register are: Aberdeen; Aberystwyth; Alloa; Arbroath; Ardrossan; Ayr; Banff; Barnstaple; Barrow; Beaumaris; Belfast; Berwick-on-Tweed; Bideford; Blyth; Borrowstoness; Boston; Bridgwater; Bristol; Brixham; Buckie; Burntisland; Caernarvon; Campbeltown; Cardiff; Cardigan; Chester; Colchester; Coleraine; Cowes; Dartmouth; Dover; Dumfries; Dundee; Exeter; Falmouth; Faversham; Felixstowe; Fishguard; Fleetwood; Folkestone; Fowey; Fraserburgh; Glasgow; Gloucester; Goole; Grangemouth; Granton; Great Yarmouth; Greenock; Grimsby; Hartlepool; Hartlepool West; Harwich; Hull; Inverness; Ipswich; Irvine; King's Lynn; Kircaldy; Kirkwall; Lancaster; Leith; Lerwick; Littlehampton; Liverpool; Llanelli; London; Londonderry; Lowestoft; Maldon; Manchester; Maryport; Methil; Middlesbrough; Milford Haven; Montrose; Newcastle; Newhaven; Newport; Newry; North Shields; Padstow; Penzance; Peterhead; Plymouth; Poole; Portland; Port Talbot; Portsmouth; Preston; Ramsgate; Rochester; Runcorn; Rye; Salcombe; Scarborough; Scilly; Shoreham; South Shields; Southampton; St Ives; Stockton; Stornoway; Stranraer; Sunderland; Swansea; Teignmouth; Troon; Truro; Weymouth; Whitby; Whitehaven; Wick; Wigtown; Wisbech; and Workington: Sch 2 Pt 1 (amended by SI 1998/2976). As to the meaning of 'port of choice' see PARA 278 note 12. As to the meaning of 'register' for these purposes see PARA 255 note 1. Part I of the register is for ships,

owned by qualified persons, which are not fishing vessels or registered on that Part which is restricted to small ships: see the Merchant Shipping (Registration of Ships) Regulations 1993, SI 1993/3138, reg 2(1)(a); and PARA 255. As to the meaning of 'fishing vessel' for these purposes see PARA 255 note 7; and as to the meaning of 'small ship' for these purposes see PARA 255 note 6.

The ports for ships to be registered on Part II of the register (fishing vessels), the port letters appearing in parentheses, are: Aberdeen (A); Aberystwyth (AB); Alloa (AA); Arbroath (AH); Ardrossan (AD); Ayr (AR); Ballantrae (BA); Banff (BF); Barnstaple (BE); Barrow (BW); Beaumaris (BS); Belfast (B); Berwick-on-Tweed (BK); Bideford (BD); Blyth (BH); Borrowstoness (BO); Boston (BN); Bridgwater (BR); Bristol (BL); Brixham (BM); Broadford (BRD); Buckie (BCK); Burntisland (BU); Caernarvon (CO); Campbeltown (CN); Cardiff (CF); Cardigan (CA); Carlisle (CL); Castlebay, Barra (CY); Chester (CH); Colchester (CK); Coleraine (CE); Cowes (CS); Dartmouth (DH); Dover (DR); Dumfries (DS); Dundee (DE); Exeter (E); Falmouth (FH); Faversham (F); Fleetwood (FD); Folkestone (FE); Fowey (FY); Fraserburgh (FR); Glasgow (GW); Gloucester (GR); Goole (GE); Grangemouth (GH); Granton (GN); Great Yarmouth (YH); Greenock (GK); Grimsby (GY); Hartlepool (HL); Harwich (HH); Hull (H); Inverness (INS); Ipswich (IH); Irvine (IE); King's Lynn (LN); Kircaldy (KY); Kirkwall (K); Lancaster (LR); Leith (LH); Lerwick (LK); Littlehampton (LI); Liverpool (LL); Llanelli (LA); London (LO); Londonderry (LY); Lowestoft (LT); Maldon (MN); Manchester (MR); Maryport (MT); Methil (ML); Middlesbrough (MH); Milford Haven (M); Montrose (ME); Newcastle (NE); Newhaven (NN); Newport, Gwent (NT); Newry (N); Oban (OB); Padstow (PW); Penzance (PZ); Peterhead (PD); Plymouth (PH); Poole (PE); Portland (PO); Portsmouth (P); Port Talbot (PT); Preston (PN); Ramsgate (R); Rochester (RR); Rothesay (RO); Runcorn (RN); Rye (RX); St Ives (SS); Salcombe (SE); Scarborough (SH); Scilly (SC); Shields, North (SN); Shields, South (SSS); Shoreham (SM); Southampton (SU); Stockton (ST); Stornoway (SY); Stranraer (SR); Sunderland (SD); Swansea (SA); Tarbert, Loch Fyne (TT); Teignmouth (TH); Troon (TN); Truro (TO); Ullapool (UL); Weymouth (WH); Whitby (WY); Wick (WK); Wigtown (WN); Whitehaven (WA); Wisbech (WI); and Workington (WO): Sch 2 Pt 2 (amended by SI 1999/3206). 'Port letters' means the letters for the port of choice: Merchant Shipping (Registration of Ships) Regulations 1993, SI 1993/3138, reg 1(2) (definition substituted by SI 1999/3206). Part II of the register is reserved for fishing vessels: see the Merchant Shipping (Registration of Ships) Regulations 1993, SI 1993/3138, reg 2(1)(b); and PARA 255. As to the status of any Part II certificate under sea fisheries legislation see PARA 377.

The provisions of Sch 2 are applied also for the purposes of reg 72 (transfer of registration from relevant British possession) (as to which see PARA 342) and reg 79 (allocation to bareboat charter ship of port of choice and port numbers) (as to which see PARA 362).

4 Merchant Shipping (Registration of Ships) Regulations 1993, SI 1993/3138, reg 31(1). Any reference in any Act other than the Merchant Shipping Act 1995 or in any other instrument made under any such other Act to the port of registration of the ship or the port to which the ship belongs is to be construed as a reference to the port of choice required to be marked by the Merchant Shipping (Registration of Ships) Regulations 1993, SI 1993/3138, reg 31, reg 53 (see PARA 316), reg 72 (see PARA 342) or reg 79 (see PARA 362): reg 122; Interpretation Act 1978 s 17(2)(b).

5 As to the meaning of 'registrar' see PARA 255 note 2.

6 Merchant Shipping (Registration of Ships) Regulations 1993, SI 1993/3138, reg 31(2).

7 Merchant Shipping (Registration of Ships) Regulations 1993, SI 1993/3138, reg 31(2)(a).

8 Merchant Shipping (Registration of Ships) Regulations 1993, SI 1993/3138, reg 31(2)(b) (substituted by SI 1999/3206). Accordingly, for these purposes, 'port number' means the number allocated for a fishing vessel within its port of choice under the Merchant Shipping (Registration of Ships) Regulations 1993, SI 1993/3138, reg 31(2)(b), reg 53(2) (see PARA 316) or reg 79(2)(a) (see PARA 362): reg 1(2) (definition added by SI 1999/3206).

9 Merchant Shipping (Registration of Ships) Regulations 1993, SI 1993/3138, reg 31(2).

10 For these purposes, 'classification society' means a person authorised to act as a 'certifying authority' for the purposes of the Merchant Shipping (Tonnage) Regulations 1997, SI 1997/1510 (as to which see PARA 248): Merchant Shipping (Registration of Ships) Regulations 1993, SI 1993/3138, reg 1(2); Interpretation Act 1978 s 17(2)(b).

11 Merchant Shipping (Registration of Ships) Regulations 1993, SI 1993/3138, reg 31(3).

12 Merchant Shipping (Registration of Ships) Regulations 1993, SI 1993/3138, reg 31(4).

### E.   CARVING AND MARKING

**280. Carving and marking of ship on first registration.** On receipt of a carving and marking note on first registration[1], the owner[2] must:

(1)    if the ship[3] has not already been surveyed or measured[4], cause it to be so surveyed or measured[5];

(2)    cause the ship to be carved and marked[6];

(3)    where required by the provisions which govern the inspection of marks[7], cause the ship's carving and marking to be inspected by an inspector of marks[8].

1  See PARA 279.
2  As to the meaning of 'owner' for these purposes see PARA 255 note 13.
3  As to the meaning of 'ship' for these purposes see PARA 255 note 4.
4  Ie as required by the Merchant Shipping (Registration of Ships) Regulations 1993, SI 1993/3138, reg 29 (as to which see PARA 276): see reg 32(a).
5  Merchant Shipping (Registration of Ships) Regulations 1993, SI 1993/3138, reg 32(a).
6  Merchant Shipping (Registration of Ships) Regulations 1993, SI 1993/3138, reg 32(b). The text refers to the ship being carved and marked in accordance with reg 32(b), Sch 3 (as to which see PARA 281): see reg 32(b). The provisions of Sch 3 are applied also for the purposes of reg 34 (verification) (as to which see PARA 287), reg 54 (change of name) (as to which see PARA 315) and reg 80 (marking of bareboat charter ship) (as to which see PARA 363).
7  Ie where required by the Merchant Shipping (Registration of Ships) Regulations 1993, SI 1993/3138, reg 33 (as to which see PARA 286): see reg 32(c).
8  Merchant Shipping (Registration of Ships) Regulations 1993, SI 1993/3138, reg 32(c). For these purposes, 'inspector of marks' means an authorised measurer or any person authorised by the Secretary of State to verify the carving and marking of a ship under the Merchant Shipping (Registration of Ships) Regulations 1993, SI 1993/3138: reg 1(2). As to the meaning of 'authorised measurer' see PARA 276 note 6. As to the Secretary of State see PARA 36.

**281.  General requirements relating to carving and marking of ship.** Every ship[1] is required, before it may be registered, to be marked permanently and conspicuously to the satisfaction of the registrar[2] in accordance with the provisions which govern the carving and marking of ships[3].

The Secretary of State[4] may exempt any class of ship from all or any of the requirements relating to carving and marking[5], subject to such conditions, if any, as he thinks fit[6].

The name of a ship[7] must be marked in Roman letters and any numerals must be in Roman or Arabic numerals[8].

1  As to the meaning of 'ship' for these purposes see PARA 255 note 4.
2  As to the meaning of 'registrar' see PARA 255 note 2.
3  Merchant Shipping (Registration of Ships) Regulations 1993, SI 1993/3138, reg 32, Sch 3 para 1. The text refers to the provisions governing the carving and marking of ships which are contained in Sch 3 (see also PARA 282 et seq): see Sch 3 para 1. As to offences in connection with a ship's registration marks see PARA 1069.
4  As to the Secretary of State see PARA 36.
5  Ie from the Merchant Shipping (Registration of Ships) Regulations 1993, SI 1993/3138, Sch 3: see Sch 3 para 2.
6  Merchant Shipping (Registration of Ships) Regulations 1993, SI 1993/3138, Sch 3 para 2.
7  As to the proposal and approval of a ship's name see PARAS 277, 278.
8  Merchant Shipping (Registration of Ships) Regulations 1993, SI 1993/3138, Sch 3 para 7 (amended by SI 1998/2976).

**282.  How ships other than fishing vessels and certain pleasure vessels are to be marked.** Subject to any exemption in respect of that class of ship[1], a ship other than a fishing vessel[2], or a pleasure vessel[3] which is under 24 metres[4], is to be marked as follows[5]:
(1)    its name[6] must be marked on each of its bows, and its name and its port of choice[7] must be marked on its stern[8];
(2)    the marking is to be on a dark ground in white or yellow letters, or on a light ground in black letters, the letters being not less than ten centimetres high and of proportional breadth[9]; and

(3)     its official number[10] and the number denoting its registered tonnage[11] must be cut on its main beam or, if that is not possible, marked or fixed thereon in the manner prescribed[12] for pleasure vessels under 24 metres[13].

1   As to the Secretary of State's power to exempt any class of ship see PARA 281. As to the meaning of 'ship' for these purposes see PARA 255 note 4.
2   Merchant Shipping (Registration of Ships) Regulations 1993, SI 1993/3138, reg 32, Sch 3 para 3(a). As to the meaning of 'fishing vessel' for these purposes see PARA 255 note 7.
3   As to the meaning of 'pleasure vessel' for these purposes see PARA 275 note 6.
4   Merchant Shipping (Registration of Ships) Regulations 1993, SI 1993/3138, Sch 3 para 3(b).
5   Merchant Shipping (Registration of Ships) Regulations 1993, SI 1993/3138, Sch 3 para 3. As to offences in connection with a ship's registration marks see PARA 1069.
6   As to the proposal and approval of a ship's name see PARAS 277, 278.
7   As to the meaning of 'port of choice' see PARA 278 note 12. As to the allocation of port of choice see PARA 279.
8   Merchant Shipping (Registration of Ships) Regulations 1993, SI 1993/3138, Sch 3 para 3(i).
9   Merchant Shipping (Registration of Ships) Regulations 1993, SI 1993/3138, Sch 3 para 3(ii).
10  As to the allocation of a ship's official number see PARA 279.
11  As to the ascertainment and certification of tonnage for registration purposes see PARA 276.
12  Ie the manner prescribed in the Merchant Shipping (Registration of Ships) Regulations 1993, SI 1993/3138, Sch 3 para 4(a) (see PARA 283): see Sch 3 para 3(iii).
13  Merchant Shipping (Registration of Ships) Regulations 1993, SI 1993/3138, Sch 3 para 3(iii).

## 283. How pleasure vessels under twenty-four metres in length are to be marked.
A pleasure vessel[1] which is under 24 metres in length is to be marked as follows[2]:

(1)     the official number[3] and registered tonnage[4] are:
   (a)     to be marked on the main beam or, if there is no main beam, on a readily accessible visible permanent part of the structure of the pleasure vessel either by cutting in, centre punching or raised lettering[5]; or
   (b)     to be engraved on plates of metal, wood or plastic, secured to the main beam (or, if there is no main beam, to a readily accessible permanent part of the structure) with rivets, through bolts with the ends clenched, or screws with the slots removed[6];

(2)     the name[7] and port of choice[8], unless an exempted ship[9], are to be marked on a conspicuous and permanent part of the stern on a dark ground in white or yellow letters, or on a light ground in black letters, the letters being not less than five centimetres high and of proportionate breadth, or, where this is not possible, by the alternative methods given as follows[10]:
   (a)     by engraving on plates of metal or of plastic or by cutting in on a shaped wooden chock; where a shaped wooden chock is used, it should be secured to the hull through bolts, the ends being clenched[11];
   (b)     by individual glass reinforced plastic letters and numbers approximately two millimetres in thickness, these to be fixed to the hull with epoxy adhesive, and painted with suitable paint and coated with translucent epoxy resin[12]; or
   (c)     where metal or plastic plates have been used, these must be fixed by the use of epoxy adhesives; metal or plastic plates secured by adhesives should be coated with translucent epoxy resin after they have been fixed in position[13].

1   As to the meaning of 'pleasure vessel' for these purposes see PARA 275 note 6.
2   Merchant Shipping (Registration of Ships) Regulations 1993, SI 1993/3138, reg 32, Sch 3 para 4. As to offences in connection with a ship's registration marks see PARA 1069.
3   As to the allocation of a ship's official number see PARA 279.
4   As to the ascertainment and certification of tonnage for registration purposes see PARA 276.

5 Merchant Shipping (Registration of Ships) Regulations 1993, SI 1993/3138, Sch 3 para 4(a)(i).
6 Merchant Shipping (Registration of Ships) Regulations 1993, SI 1993/3138, Sch 3 para 4(a)(ii).
7 As to the proposal and approval of a ship's name see PARAS 277, 278.
8 As to the meaning of 'port of choice' see PARA 278 note 12. As to the allocation of port of choice see PARA 279.
9 As to the Secretary of State's power to exempt any class of ship see PARA 281.
10 Merchant Shipping (Registration of Ships) Regulations 1993, SI 1993/3138, Sch 3 para 4(b).
11 Merchant Shipping (Registration of Ships) Regulations 1993, SI 1993/3138, Sch 3 para 4(b)(i).
12 Merchant Shipping (Registration of Ships) Regulations 1993, SI 1993/3138, Sch 3 para 4(b)(ii).
13 Merchant Shipping (Registration of Ships) Regulations 1993, SI 1993/3138, Sch 3 para 4(b)(iii).

**284. How fishing vessels are to be marked.** A fishing vessel[1] is to be marked as follows[2]:

(1) the name of the vessel[3] and the port of choice[4] must be painted in white on a black background or in black on a white background outside the stern of the boat in letters which must not be less than eight centimetres in height and 1.5 centimetres in breadth[5]; and

(2) the port letters[6] and the port number[7] must be painted or displayed on both sides of the bow and on each quarter, as high above the water as possible so as to be clearly visible from the sea and the air, in white on a black background or black on a white background[8];

(3) for vessels not over 17 metres in length, the height of the port letters and port number must be at least 25 centimetres with a line thickness of at least four centimetres[9];

(4) for vessels over 17 metres in length, the height of the port letters and port number must be at least 45 centimetres with a line thickness of at least six centimetres[10];

(5) the port letters and port number must in addition be painted or displayed on the wheel house top or some other prominent horizontal surface[11];

(6) the vessel's official number[12] must be carved into the main beam of the vessel or, if that is not possible, marked or fixed thereon in the manner prescribed[13] for pleasure vessels under 24 metres in length[14].

1 As to the meaning of 'fishing vessel' for these purposes see PARA 255 note 7.
2 Merchant Shipping (Registration of Ships) Regulations 1993, SI 1993/3138, reg 32, Sch 3 para 5. As to offences in connection with a ship's registration marks see PARA 1069.
3 As to the proposal and approval of a ship's name see PARAS 277–278.
4 As to the meaning of 'port of choice' see PARA 278 note 12. As to the allocation of port of choice see PARA 279.
5 Merchant Shipping (Registration of Ships) Regulations 1993, SI 1993/3138, Sch 3 para 5(a).
6 As to the meaning of 'port letters' see PARA 279 note 3.
7 As to the meaning of 'port number' see PARA 279 note 8.
8 Merchant Shipping (Registration of Ships) Regulations 1993, SI 1993/3138, Sch 3 para 5(b) (amended by SI 1999/3206).
9 Merchant Shipping (Registration of Ships) Regulations 1993, SI 1993/3138, Sch 3 para 5(c) (amended by SI 1999/3206).
10 Merchant Shipping (Registration of Ships) Regulations 1993, SI 1993/3138, Sch 3 para 5(d) (amended by SI 1999/3206).
11 Merchant Shipping (Registration of Ships) Regulations 1993, SI 1993/3138, Sch 3 para 5(e) (amended by SI 1999/3206).
12 As to the allocation of a ship's official number see PARA 279.
13 Ie the manner prescribed in the Merchant Shipping (Registration of Ships) Regulations 1993, SI 1993/3138, Sch 3 para 4(a) (see PARA 283): see Sch 3 para 5(f).
14 Merchant Shipping (Registration of Ships) Regulations 1993, SI 1993/3138, Sch 3 para 5(f).

**285. Marking of ship's draught.** A scale of decimetres, or metres and decimetres, denoting a draught of water must be marked on a ship[1], other than an exempted ship[2], on each side of its stem and its stern post, as follows[3]:

(1) in figures in two-decimetre intervals, if the scale is in decimetres[4]; and

(2)    in figures at each metre interval and at intervening two-decimetre intervals, if the scale is in metres and decimetres[5],

the capital letter 'M' being placed after each metre figure; the top figure of the scale showing both the metre and (except where it marks a full metre interval) the decimetre figure; the lower line of the figures, or figures and letters, as the case may be, coinciding with the draught line denoted thereby; the figures and letters being not less than one decimetre in length and being marked by being cut in and painted white or yellow on a dark ground, or in any such other way as the Secretary of State approves[6].

1   As to the meaning of 'ship' for these purposes see PARA 255 note 4.
2   As to the Secretary of State's power to exempt any class of ship see PARA 281. As to the Secretary of State see PARA 36.
3   Merchant Shipping (Registration of Ships) Regulations 1993, SI 1993/3138, reg 32, Sch 3 para 6. As to offences in connection with a ship's registration marks see PARA 1069.
4   Merchant Shipping (Registration of Ships) Regulations 1993, SI 1993/3138, Sch 3 para 6(a).
5   Merchant Shipping (Registration of Ships) Regulations 1993, SI 1993/3138, Sch 3 para 6(b).
6   Merchant Shipping (Registration of Ships) Regulations 1993, SI 1993/3138, Sch 3 para 6.

**286. Inspection of marks.** In respect of a ship[1], other than a pleasure vessel[2] which is under 24 metres in length, an inspector of marks[3] must satisfy himself that the ship has been duly carved and marked[4] and, when so satisfied, must complete the carving and marking note and return it to the registrar[5]. In respect of a fishing vessel[6], the carving and marking note may also be returned to the local office[7].

In respect of a pleasure vessel which is under 24 metres in length, the owner[8] must certify that the ship has been duly carved and marked[9] and return the certified carving and marking note to the registrar[10].

1   As to the meaning of 'ship' for these purposes see PARA 255 note 4.
2   As to the meaning of 'pleasure vessel' for these purposes see PARA 275 note 6.
3   As to the meaning of 'inspector of marks' see PARA 280 note 8.
4   Ie carved and marked in accordance with the Merchant Shipping (Registration of Ships) Regulations 1993, SI 1993/3138, reg 32(b), Sch 3 (as to which see PARA 281 et seq): see reg 33(1).
5   Merchant Shipping (Registration of Ships) Regulations 1993, SI 1993/3138, reg 33(1). As to the meaning of 'registrar' see PARA 255 note 2. As to the issue of a carving and marking note on first registration see PARA 279. As to offences in connection with a ship's marks see PARA 1069.
6   As to the meaning of 'fishing vessel' for these purposes see PARA 255 note 7.
7   Merchant Shipping (Registration of Ships) Regulations 1993, SI 1993/3138, reg 33(1). As to the meaning of 'local office' see PARA 269 note 5.
8   As to the meaning of 'owner' for these purposes see PARA 255 note 13.
9   Ie carved and marked in accordance with the Merchant Shipping (Registration of Ships) Regulations 1993, SI 1993/3138, reg 32(b), Sch 3 (as to which see PARA 281 et seq): see reg 33(2).
10  Merchant Shipping (Registration of Ships) Regulations 1993, SI 1993/3138, reg 33(2).

**287. Verification of measurement and carving and marking.** If the registrar[1] is not satisfied:
(1)    that the particulars of the measurement and tonnage of the ship[2] or such other particulars describing the identity of the ship, as have been required by the Secretary of State[3], furnished to him are correct[4]; or
(2)    that the ship is carved and marked in the required manner[5],

he may direct the owner[6] to have the measurement or other details and/or carving or marking of the vessel verified by an authorised measurer[7] or inspector of marks[8], as appropriate[9].

If the owner fails to comply with the direction of the registrar, the registrar may:
(a)    if the ship is not registered, refuse it registration until his direction has been complied with[10]; or

(b)    if the ship is registered, serve notice on the owner or managing owner[11] or any charterer, manager or operator of the ship requiring him to produce evidence within 30 days sufficient to satisfy him that the particulars of the measurement and tonnage are, or that the marking of the ship is, correct[12].

If, at the expiry of that period of 30 days, the registrar is not so satisfied, he may:

(i)    extend the notice and ask for further information[13]; or

(ii)   serve a final notice which closes the ship's registration, such closure to be effected seven days after the service of that notice[14].

Where a ship's registration is so closed, the owner of the ship must forthwith surrender its certificate of registry[15].

Where the registrar serves such a notice on the owner of a ship in respect of which a mortgage is registered, he must send a copy of that notice to the mortgagee at the address recorded in the register[16] for the mortgagee[17].

1   As to the meaning of 'registrar' see PARA 255 note 2.
2   As to the meaning of 'ship' for these purposes see PARA 255 note 4.
3   As to the Secretary of State see PARA 36.
4   Merchant Shipping (Registration of Ships) Regulations 1993, SI 1993/3138, reg 34(1)(a) (amended by SI 1998/2976).
5   Merchant Shipping (Registration of Ships) Regulations 1993, SI 1993/3138, reg 34(1)(b). The text refers to carving and marking in the manner required by reg 32(b), Sch 3 (as to which see PARA 281 et seq): see reg 34(1)(b).
6   As to the meaning of 'owner' for these purposes see PARA 255 note 13.
7   As to the meaning of 'authorised measurer' see PARA 276 note 6.
8   As to the meaning of 'inspector of marks' see PARA 280 note 8.
9   Merchant Shipping (Registration of Ships) Regulations 1993, SI 1993/3138, reg 34(1) (amended by SI 1998/2976). As to offences in connection with a ship's marks see PARA 1069.
10  Merchant Shipping (Registration of Ships) Regulations 1993, SI 1993/3138, reg 34(2)(a).
11  The term 'managing owner' is used in the Merchant Shipping (Registration of Ships) Regulations 1993, SI 1993/3138, reg 23 (appointment of managing owner where ship has more than one owner) (as to which see PARA 271), as well as in reg 34, but it is not defined; however, see PARA 238.
12  Merchant Shipping (Registration of Ships) Regulations 1993, SI 1993/3138, reg 34(2)(b).
13  Merchant Shipping (Registration of Ships) Regulations 1993, SI 1993/3138, reg 34(3)(a).
14  Merchant Shipping (Registration of Ships) Regulations 1993, SI 1993/3138, reg 34(3)(b).
15  Merchant Shipping (Registration of Ships) Regulations 1993, SI 1993/3138, reg 34(4). As to the meaning of 'certificate of registry' see PARA 255 note 17.
16  As to the meaning of 'register' see PARA 255 note 1.
17  Merchant Shipping (Registration of Ships) Regulations 1993, SI 1993/3138, reg 34(5).

**288. Cancellation of carving and marking note.** If a carving and marking note duly issued[1] is not duly completed and returned to the registrar[2] within three months of its issue, the registrar may cancel it and the application is to be treated as having been withdrawn[3].

1   Ie under the Merchant Shipping (Registration of Ships) Regulations 1993, SI 1993/3138, reg 31 (as to which see PARA 279): see reg 35.
2   As to the meaning of 'registrar' see PARA 255 note 2.
3   Merchant Shipping (Registration of Ships) Regulations 1993, SI 1993/3138, reg 35.

F.    COMPLETION OF REGISTRATION

**289. Registration and refusal of registration of a ship.** Where a registrar[1] is satisfied in respect of an application that[2]:

(1)    the ship[3] is eligible to be registered as a British ship[4]; and

(2)    the ship has been duly carved and marked[5] and that the appropriate survey or measuring certificate has been provided[6]; and

(3)    the particulars of the ship furnished to him are correct[7]; and

(4)    title to the ship has been adequately proved, where necessary[8]; and
(5)    the relevant requirements imposed by the statutory provisions
        governing the registration of ships[9] have been complied with[10],
he must register the ship by entering in the register[11] the prescribed particulars[12]
of the ship and its owners[13]. If the registrar is not so satisfied, he must[14] refuse the
application[15].

The registrar may refuse to register any fishing vessel[16] if he is not satisfied that
there is in force as respects the vessel any certificate required to be so in force[17] by
the Merchant Shipping Act 1995[18].

The registrar must refuse to register any vessel intending to fish in Community
waters if that vessel has received a decommissioning grant or any other financial
assistance from the European Commission or a member state on condition that it
refrains from fishing in those waters or has been withdrawn from fishing as a
condition of an award of a construction grant to another boat[19].

Notwithstanding that a ship is otherwise entitled to be registered, the registrar
may refuse to register it if, taking into account any requirement of the Merchant
Shipping Act 1995, including any instrument made thereunder, relating to the
condition of the ship or its equipment so far as it is relevant to its safety or to any
risk of pollution or to the safety, health and welfare of persons employed or
engaged in any capacity on board the ship, he considers that it would be
inappropriate for the ship to be registered[20].

1  As to the meaning of 'registrar' see PARA 255 note 2.
2  Merchant Shipping (Registration of Ships) Regulations 1993, SI 1993/3138, reg 36(1).
3  As to the meaning of 'ship' for these purposes see PARA 255 note 4.
4  Merchant Shipping (Registration of Ships) Regulations 1993, SI 1993/3138, reg 36(1)(a). As to the
    meaning of 'British ship' under the Merchant Shipping Act 1995 see PARA 230.
5  As to the carving and marking of a ship on first registration see PARA 280 et seq.
6  Merchant Shipping (Registration of Ships) Regulations 1993, SI 1993/3138, reg 36(1)(b). As to the
    survey and measurement of ships see PARA 276 et seq.
7  Merchant Shipping (Registration of Ships) Regulations 1993, SI 1993/3138, reg 36(1)(c).
8  Merchant Shipping (Registration of Ships) Regulations 1993, SI 1993/3138, reg 36(1)(d).
9  Ie the relevant requirements of the Merchant Shipping (Registration of Ships) Regulations 1993,
    SI 1993/3138 (see PARAS 255 et seq, 290 et seq): see reg 36(1)(e).
10 Merchant Shipping (Registration of Ships) Regulations 1993, SI 1993/3138, reg 36(1)(e).
11 As to the meaning of 'register' for these purposes see PARA 255 note 1.
12 Ie the particulars specified in the Merchant Shipping (Registration of Ships) Regulations 1993, SI
    1993/3138, reg 36(1), Sch 4 (see PARA 290 et seq): see reg 36(1). The provisions of Sch 4 are
    applied also for the purposes of reg 82 (registration of bareboat charter ships) (as to which see
    PARA 364).
13 Merchant Shipping (Registration of Ships) Regulations 1993, SI 1993/3138, reg 36(1). As to the
    meaning of 'owner' for these purposes see PARA 255 note 13.
14 Ie subject to the Merchant Shipping (Registration of Ships) Regulations 1993, SI 1993/3138, reg
    106 (requirement for supplementary information) (see PARA 372): see reg 36(4).
15 Merchant Shipping (Registration of Ships) Regulations 1993, SI 1993/3138, reg 36(4).
16 As to the meaning of 'fishing vessel' for these purposes see PARA 255 note 7.
17 Ie by virtue of the Merchant Shipping Act 1995 s 125 (see PARA 610): see reg 36(2); Interpretation
    Act 1978 s 17(2)(b).
18 Merchant Shipping (Registration of Ships) Regulations 1993, SI 1993/3138, reg 36(2);
    Interpretation Act 1978 s 17(2)(b).
19 Merchant Shipping (Registration of Ships) Regulations 1993, SI 1993/3138, reg 36(3).
20 Merchant Shipping (Registration of Ships) Regulations 1993, SI 1993/3138, reg 36(5);
    Interpretation Act 1978 s 17(2)(b).

**290. Particulars of owners who are individuals.** The following information
is to be registered about each owner[1] of a ship[2] who is an individual[3]:
(1)    surname, forename and title[4];
(2)    address[5];
(3)    nationality[6];

 (4) number of shares owned by him and, if held jointly, with whom the shares are held[7];

 (5) the name of the managing owner[8].

1 As to the meaning of 'owner' for these purposes see PARA 255 note 13.
2 As to the meaning of 'ship' for these purposes see PARA 255 note 4.
3 Merchant Shipping (Registration of Ships) Regulations 1993, SI 1993/3138, reg 36(1), Sch 4 para 1.
4 Merchant Shipping (Registration of Ships) Regulations 1993, SI 1993/3138, Sch 4 para 1(a).
5 Merchant Shipping (Registration of Ships) Regulations 1993, SI 1993/3138, Sch 4 para 1(b).
6 Merchant Shipping (Registration of Ships) Regulations 1993, SI 1993/3138, Sch 4 para 1(c).
7 Merchant Shipping (Registration of Ships) Regulations 1993, SI 1993/3138, Sch 4 para 1(d).
8 Merchant Shipping (Registration of Ships) Regulations 1993, SI 1993/3138, Sch 4 para 1(e). The term 'managing owner' is used in reg 23 (appointment of managing owner where ship has more than one owner) (as to which see PARA 271), as well as in reg 34, but it is not defined; however, see PARA 238.

**291. Particulars of owners who are bodies corporate.** The following information is to be registered about each owner[1] of a ship[2] which is a body corporate[3]:

 (1) name of owner[4];

 (2) the address of its registered office[5];

 (3) country of incorporation[6];

 (4) where it is a body corporate incorporated in the United Kingdom[7] or in a relevant British possession[8], its principal place of business[9];

 (5) where it is a body corporate incorporated in a member state other than the United Kingdom, its place of business in the United Kingdom[10];

 (6) number of shares owned by the company and, if held jointly, with whom the shares are held[11].

1 As to the meaning of 'owner' for these purposes see PARA 255 note 13.
2 As to the meaning of 'ship' for these purposes see PARA 255 note 4.
3 Merchant Shipping (Registration of Ships) Regulations 1993, SI 1993/3138, reg 36(1), Sch 4 para 2.
4 Merchant Shipping (Registration of Ships) Regulations 1993, SI 1993/3138, Sch 4 para 2(a).
5 Merchant Shipping (Registration of Ships) Regulations 1993, SI 1993/3138, Sch 4 para 2(b).
6 Merchant Shipping (Registration of Ships) Regulations 1993, SI 1993/3138, Sch 4 para 2(c).
7 As to the meaning of 'United Kingdom' see PARA 16 note 3. As to companies and their incorporation etc in England and Wales see COMPANIES vol 14 (2016) PARA 114 et seq.
8 As to the meaning of 'relevant British possession' under the Merchant Shipping Act 1995 see PARA 16 note 3.
9 Merchant Shipping (Registration of Ships) Regulations 1993, SI 1993/3138, Sch 4 para 2(d). As to a person's place of business see COMPANIES vol 14 (2016) PARA 117.
10 Merchant Shipping (Registration of Ships) Regulations 1993, SI 1993/3138, Sch 4 para 2(e).
11 Merchant Shipping (Registration of Ships) Regulations 1993, SI 1993/3138, Sch 4 para 2(f).

**292. Particulars of owners who are representative persons or charterers of fishing vessels.** The following information is to be registered about:

 (1) any representative person appointed in relation to a ship[1]; and

 (2) in respect of fishing vessels[2], any charterer[3], namely:

  (a) the full name of the individual or body corporate[4];

  (b) the address of the individual or the place of business in the United Kingdom[5] of the body corporate[6].

1 Merchant Shipping (Registration of Ships) Regulations 1993, SI 1993/3138, reg 36(1), Sch 4 para 3(a). As to the appointment of representative persons in relation to a ship see Pt V (regs 18, 19); and PARAS 267–268. As to the meaning of 'ship' for these purposes see PARA 255 note 4.
2 As to the meaning of 'fishing vessel' for these purposes see PARA 255 note 7.
3 Merchant Shipping (Registration of Ships) Regulations 1993, SI 1993/3138, Sch 4 para 3(b).
4 Merchant Shipping (Registration of Ships) Regulations 1993, SI 1993/3138, Sch 4 para 3(b)(i).
5 As to the meaning of 'United Kingdom' see PARA 16 note 3. As to a person's place of business see COMPANIES vol 14 (2016) PARA 117.
6 Merchant Shipping (Registration of Ships) Regulations 1993, SI 1993/3138, Sch 4 para 3(b)(ii).

**293. Particulars to be registered about ships.** The following information is to be registered about ships[1] registered or to be registered on Part I of the register[2]:
(1)     name[3];
(2)     either the IMO number[4] or the International Standards Organisation Hull Identification Number ('HIN'), as appropriate[5];
(3)     radio call sign[6];
(4)     port of choice[7];
(5)     official number[8];
(6)     year of build[9];
(7)     method of propulsion, for example whether sail, steam, motor or dumb[10];
(8)     where built[11];
(9)     name and address of builders[12];
(10)    date keel laid/when built[13];
(11)    length (metric units)[14];
(12)    breadth (metric units)[15];
(13)    depth (metric units)[16];
(14)    type of ship, for example dry cargo, oil tanker, passenger, bulk carrier[17];
(15)    material used to construct hull[18];
(16)    such of the following tonnages as are specified in the certificate of survey: gross, net and registered[19];
(17)    make and model of engine or engines[20];
(18)    total power of engines in kilowatts[21].

1   As to the meaning of 'ship' for these purposes see PARA 255 note 4.
2   Merchant Shipping (Registration of Ships) Regulations 1993, SI 1993/3138, reg 36(1), Sch 4 para 4. As to the meaning of 'register' for these purposes see PARA 255 note 1. Part I of the register, as mentioned in the text, is for ships, owned by qualified persons, which are not fishing vessels or registered on that Part which is restricted to small ships: see reg 2(1)(a); and PARA 255. As to the meaning of 'fishing vessel' for these purposes see PARA 255 note 7; and as to the meaning of 'small ship' for these purposes see PARA 255 note 6.
3   Merchant Shipping (Registration of Ships) Regulations 1993, SI 1993/3138, Sch 4 para 4(a). As to the proposal and approval of a ship's name see PARAS 277, 278.
4   'IMO number' is not defined for the purposes of the Merchant Shipping (Registration of Ships) Regulations 1993, SI 1993/3138. However, under the Tonnage Tax (Training Requirement) Regulations 2000, SI 2000/2129, the IMO number is the number assigned to the ship in accordance with Resolution A.600(15) of 19 November 1987 of the International Maritime Organisation: see reg 2; and INCOME TAXATION vol 59 (2014) PARA 1993. As to the International Maritime Organisation see PARA 12.
5   Merchant Shipping (Registration of Ships) Regulations 1993, SI 1993/3138, Sch 4 para 4(b) (substituted by SI 1998/2976).
6   Merchant Shipping (Registration of Ships) Regulations 1993, SI 1993/3138, Sch 4 para 4(c).
7   Merchant Shipping (Registration of Ships) Regulations 1993, SI 1993/3138, Sch 4 para 4(d). As to the meaning of 'port of choice' see PARA 278 note 12. As to the allocation of port of choice see PARA 279.
8   Merchant Shipping (Registration of Ships) Regulations 1993, SI 1993/3138, Sch 4 para 4(e). As to the allocation of a ship's official number see PARA 279.
9   Merchant Shipping (Registration of Ships) Regulations 1993, SI 1993/3138, Sch 4 para 4(f).
10  Merchant Shipping (Registration of Ships) Regulations 1993, SI 1993/3138, Sch 4 para 4(g).
11  Merchant Shipping (Registration of Ships) Regulations 1993, SI 1993/3138, Sch 4 para 4(h).
12  Merchant Shipping (Registration of Ships) Regulations 1993, SI 1993/3138, Sch 4 para 4(i).
13  Merchant Shipping (Registration of Ships) Regulations 1993, SI 1993/3138, Sch 4 para 4(j).
14  Merchant Shipping (Registration of Ships) Regulations 1993, SI 1993/3138, Sch 4 para 4(k).
15  Merchant Shipping (Registration of Ships) Regulations 1993, SI 1993/3138, Sch 4 para 4(l).
16  Merchant Shipping (Registration of Ships) Regulations 1993, SI 1993/3138, Sch 4 para 4(m).
17  Merchant Shipping (Registration of Ships) Regulations 1993, SI 1993/3138, Sch 4 para 4(n).
18  Merchant Shipping (Registration of Ships) Regulations 1993, SI 1993/3138, Sch 4 para 4(o).
19  Merchant Shipping (Registration of Ships) Regulations 1993, SI 1993/3138, Sch 4 para 4(p) (Sch 4 para 4(p) substituted for Sch 4 para 4(p)–(r) as originally enacted by SI 1998/2976). As to the survey and measurement of ships, including the ascertainment and certification of tonnage for registration purposes, see PARA 276.

20 Merchant Shipping (Registration of Ships) Regulations 1993, SI 1993/3138, Sch 4 para 4(s).
21 Merchant Shipping (Registration of Ships) Regulations 1993, SI 1993/3138, Sch 4 para 4(t).

**294. Particulars to be registered about fishing vessels.** The following information is to be registered about fishing vessels[1] registered or to be registered on Part II of the register[2]:

   (1)    official number[3] and EC number[4];
   (2)    IMO number[5];
   (3)    port letters[6] and port number[7];
   (4)    name[8];
   (5)    radio call sign[9];
   (6)    whether full[10] or simple[11] registration[12];
   (7)    material used to construct hull[13];
   (8)    name of builder[14];
   (9)    year of build[15];
   (10)   place and country of build[16];
   (11)   date of entry into service[17];
   (12)   overall length (metric units)[18];
   (13)   registered length (metric units)[19];
   (14)   breadth (metric units)[20];
   (15)   depth (metric units)[21];
   (16)   gross tonnage[22];
   (17)   net tonnage[23];
   (18)   maximum continuous engine power[24] in kilowatts, or, if the owner[25] notifies the registrar[26] of a modification, permanently de-rated engine power[27] in kilowatts[28];
   (19)   make and model of engine[29];
   (20)   number of cylinders[30];
   (21)   number of engines[31];
   (22)   number of revolutions per minute[32];
   (23)   modification explanation[33].

1 As to the meaning of 'fishing vessel' for these purposes see PARA 255 note 7.
2 Merchant Shipping (Registration of Ships) Regulations 1993, SI 1993/3138, reg 36(1), Sch 4 para 5. Part II of the register, as mentioned in the text, is reserved for fishing vessels: see reg 2(1)(b); and PARA 255. As to the meaning of 'register' see PARA 255 note 1. As to the status of any Part II certificate under sea fisheries legislation see PARA 377.
3 As to the allocation of a ship's official number see PARA 279.
4 Merchant Shipping (Registration of Ships) Regulations 1993, SI 1993/3138, Sch 4 para 5(a).
5 Merchant Shipping (Registration of Ships) Regulations 1993, SI 1993/3138, Sch 4 para 5(b). As to the IMO number see PARA 293 note 4.
6 As to the meaning of 'port letters' see PARA 279 note 3.
7 Merchant Shipping (Registration of Ships) Regulations 1993, SI 1993/3138, Sch 4 para 5(c) (amended by SI 1999/3206). As to the meaning of 'port number' see PARA 279 note 8.
8 Merchant Shipping (Registration of Ships) Regulations 1993, SI 1993/3138, Sch 4 para 5(d). As to the proposal and approval of a ship's name see PARAS 277, 278.
9 Merchant Shipping (Registration of Ships) Regulations 1993, SI 1993/3138, Sch 4 para 5(e).
10 As to the meaning of 'full registration' see PARA 256.
11 As to the meaning of 'simple registration' see PARA 256.
12 Merchant Shipping (Registration of Ships) Regulations 1993, SI 1993/3138, Sch 4 para 5(f).
13 Merchant Shipping (Registration of Ships) Regulations 1993, SI 1993/3138, Sch 4 para 5(g).
14 Merchant Shipping (Registration of Ships) Regulations 1993, SI 1993/3138, Sch 4 para 5(h).
15 Merchant Shipping (Registration of Ships) Regulations 1993, SI 1993/3138, Sch 4 para 5(i).
16 Merchant Shipping (Registration of Ships) Regulations 1993, SI 1993/3138, Sch 4 para 5(j).
17 Merchant Shipping (Registration of Ships) Regulations 1993, SI 1993/3138, Sch 4 para 5(k).
18 Merchant Shipping (Registration of Ships) Regulations 1993, SI 1993/3138, Sch 4 para 5(l).
19 Merchant Shipping (Registration of Ships) Regulations 1993, SI 1993/3138, Sch 4 para 5(m).
20 Merchant Shipping (Registration of Ships) Regulations 1993, SI 1993/3138, Sch 4 para 5(n).
21 Merchant Shipping (Registration of Ships) Regulations 1993, SI 1993/3138, Sch 4 para 5(o).

22 Merchant Shipping (Registration of Ships) Regulations 1993, SI 1993/3138, Sch 4 para 5(p). As to the survey and measurement of ships, including the ascertainment and certification of tonnage for registration purposes, see PARA 276.

23 Merchant Shipping (Registration of Ships) Regulations 1993, SI 1993/3138, Sch 4 para 5(q).

24 As to the meaning of 'maximum continuous engine power' see PARA 275 note 14.

25 As to the meaning of 'owner' for these purposes see PARA 255 note 13.

26 As to the meaning of 'registrar' see PARA 255 note 2.

27 As to the meaning of 'permanently de-rated engine power' see PARA 275 note 15.

28 Merchant Shipping (Registration of Ships) Regulations 1993, SI 1993/3138, Sch 4 para 5(r) (substituted by SI 1999/3206).

29 Merchant Shipping (Registration of Ships) Regulations 1993, SI 1993/3138, Sch 4 para 5(s).

30 Merchant Shipping (Registration of Ships) Regulations 1993, SI 1993/3138, Sch 4 para 5(t) (Sch 4 para 5(t)–(w) added by SI 1999/3206).

31 Merchant Shipping (Registration of Ships) Regulations 1993, SI 1993/3138, Sch 4 para 5(u) (as added: see note 30).

32 Merchant Shipping (Registration of Ships) Regulations 1993, SI 1993/3138, Sch 4 para 5(v) (as added: see note 30).

33 Merchant Shipping (Registration of Ships) Regulations 1993, SI 1993/3138, Sch 4 para 5(w) (as added: see note 30). As to the meaning of 'modification explanation' see PARA 275 note 15.

## 295. Particulars to be registered about bareboat charter ships.

In addition to the information otherwise to be registered[1] in respect of ships[2] registered or to be registered on Part I of the register[3] or in respect of fishing vessels registered or to be registered on Part II of the register[4], the following is to be registered in respect of bareboat charter ships[5]:

(1) the name and address of the owner[6];

(2) the name and address of the charterer[7];

(3) the name and address of any representative person[8];

(4) the unique number allocated to the ship for identification purposes by its primary register[9];

(5) its country of original registration[10];

(6) the commencement date of the charter period and its expiry date[11];

(7) the name by which the ship is known on the primary register (or a translation of that name)[12].

1 Ie the information in the Merchant Shipping (Registration of Ships) Regulations 1993, SI 1993/3138, reg 36(1), Sch 4 para 4 (as to which see PARA 293) or in Sch 4 para 5 (as to which see PARA 294): see Sch 4 para 6.

2 As to the meaning of 'ship' for these purposes see PARA 255 note 4.

3 As to the meaning of 'register' for these purposes see PARA 255 note 1. Part I of the register, as mentioned in the text, is for ships, owned by qualified persons, which are not fishing vessels or registered on that Part which is restricted to small ships: see the Merchant Shipping (Registration of Ships) Regulations 1993, SI 1993/3138, reg 2(1)(a); and PARA 255. As to the meaning of 'fishing vessel' for these purposes see PARA 255 note 7; and as to the meaning of 'small ship' for these purposes see PARA 255 note 6.

4 Part II of the register, as mentioned in the text, is reserved for fishing vessels: see the Merchant Shipping (Registration of Ships) Regulations 1993, SI 1993/3138, reg 2(1)(b); and PARA 255. As to the status of any Part II certificate under sea fisheries legislation see PARA 377.

5 Merchant Shipping (Registration of Ships) Regulations 1993, SI 1993/3138, Sch 4 para 6. As to the meaning of 'bareboat charter ship' see PARA 255 note 9.

6 Merchant Shipping (Registration of Ships) Regulations 1993, SI 1993/3138, Sch 4 para 6(a). As to the meaning of 'owner' for these purposes see PARA 255 note 13.

7 Merchant Shipping (Registration of Ships) Regulations 1993, SI 1993/3138, Sch 4 para 6(b).

8 Merchant Shipping (Registration of Ships) Regulations 1993, SI 1993/3138, Sch 4 para 6(c). As to the appointment of representative persons in relation to a ship see Pt V (regs 18, 19); and PARAS 267–268.

9 Merchant Shipping (Registration of Ships) Regulations 1993, SI 1993/3138, Sch 4 para 6(d) (substituted by SI 1999/3206). For these purposes, 'primary register' means the register on which the ship is registered at the time the application is made to register the ship as a bareboat charter ship: Merchant Shipping (Registration of Ships) Regulations 1993, SI 1993/3138, reg 1(2).

10 Merchant Shipping (Registration of Ships) Regulations 1993, SI 1993/3138, Sch 4 para 6(e).

11  Merchant Shipping (Registration of Ships) Regulations 1993, SI 1993/3138, Sch 4 para 6(f). As to the meaning of 'charter period' for these purposes under the Merchant Shipping Act 1995 see PARA 357 note 11.
12  Merchant Shipping (Registration of Ships) Regulations 1993, SI 1993/3138, Sch 4 para 6(g).

**296. Period of registration.** The registration of a ship[1] is valid, unless it is duly terminated[2], for a period of five years beginning with the date of registration specified in the certificate of registry[3] and expires at the end of that period unless it is duly[4] renewed[5].

1  As to the meaning of 'ship' for these purposes see PARA 255 note 4.
2  Ie unless it is terminated under the Merchant Shipping (Registration of Ships) Regulations 1993, SI 1993/3138: see reg 39 (amended by SI 1998/2976).
3  As to the meaning of 'certificate of registry' see PARA 255 note 17.
4  Ie unless it is renewed in accordance with the Merchant Shipping (Registration of Ships) Regulations 1993, SI 1993/3138, reg 42 (as to which see PARA 305): see reg 39 (as amended: see note 2).
5  Merchant Shipping (Registration of Ships) Regulations 1993, SI 1993/3138, reg 39 (as amended: see note 2). Regulation 39 is expressed to be subject to the transitional provisions contained in reg 116, whose effect has now lapsed: see reg 39 (as so amended). As to the surrender of a certificate on the termination or expiry of registration see PARA 375.

**297. Documents to be retained by the registrar.** On registering a ship[1], the registrar[2] must retain in his possession a copy of any builder's certificate[3] or bill of sale or other evidence of title produced on first registration, any certificate of measurement or survey[4] and all declarations of eligibility[5].

On a fishing vessel[6] changing from simple registration[7] to full registration[8], the registrar must retain in his possession a copy of the evidence adduced for that change[9].

On registering a fishing vessel which has had its engine power permanently de-rated[10], the registrar must retain in his possession the modification explanation[11] duly submitted to him[12].

All documents which have been produced to the registrar to establish title must be returned to the applicant once the ship has been registered[13]. The documents must be stamped by the registrar to indicate that they have been used for registration of a ship[14].

1  As to the meaning of 'ship' for these purposes see PARA 255 note 4.
2  As to the meaning of 'registrar' see PARA 255 note 2.
3  As to the meaning of 'builder's certificate' see PARA 275 note 5.
4  As to the survey and measurement of ships see PARA 276.
5  Merchant Shipping (Registration of Ships) Regulations 1993, SI 1993/3138, reg 40(1)(a). As to the meaning of 'declaration of eligibility' see PARA 272 note 2.
6  As to the meaning of 'fishing vessel' for these purposes see PARA 255 note 7.
7  As to the meaning of 'simple registration' see PARA 256.
8  As to the meaning of 'full registration' see PARA 256.
9  Merchant Shipping (Registration of Ships) Regulations 1993, SI 1993/3138, reg 40(1)(b) (amended by SI 1999/3206).
10  As to the meaning of 'permanently de-rated engine power' see PARA 275 note 15.
11  As to the meaning of 'modification explanation' see PARA 275 note 15.
12  Merchant Shipping (Registration of Ships) Regulations 1993, SI 1993/3138, reg 40(1)(c) (added by SI 1999/3206). The text refers to the modification explanation submitted to the registrar in accordance with the Merchant Shipping (Registration of Ships) Regulations 1993, SI 1993/3138, reg 29A(2) (see PARA 275): see reg 40(1)(c) (as so added).
13  Merchant Shipping (Registration of Ships) Regulations 1993, SI 1993/3138, reg 40(2).
14  Merchant Shipping (Registration of Ships) Regulations 1993, SI 1993/3138, reg 40(2).

G.    CERTIFICATES OF REGISTRY; TEMPORARY REGISTRATION DOCUMENTS FOR FISHING
                                        VESSELS

**298.   Issue of certificate of registry.** Upon registering a ship[1], the registrar[2] must issue and send to the owner[3] a certificate of registry[4] containing the prescribed particulars[5].

1   As to the meaning of 'ship' for these purposes see PARA 255 note 4.
2   As to the meaning of 'registrar' see PARA 255 note 2.
3   As to the meaning of 'owner' for these purposes see PARA 255 note 13.
4   As to the meaning of 'certificate of registry' see PARA 255 note 17.
5   Merchant Shipping (Registration of Ships) Regulations 1993, SI 1993/3138, reg 37. The particulars so prescribed are those set out in reg 37, Sch 5 (as to which see PARAS 209–301): see reg 37. The provisions of Sch 5 are applied also for the purposes of reg 82 (registration of a bareboat charter ship) (as to which see PARA 364). As to the issue of duplicate certificates of registry in certain circumstances see PARA 373.

**299.   Details contained in certificate of registry for a ship.** A certificate of registry[1] for a ship[2] registered or to be registered on Part I of the register[3] must contain[4]:

(1)    the full name and address of the owner[5] or owners[6];
(2)    the number of shares owned by each owner and, if any are jointly owned, with whom they are owned[7];
(3)    the following information about the ship[8]:
    (a)    name[9];
    (b)    either the IMO number[10] or the International Standards Organisation Hull Identification Number ('HIN'), as appropriate[11];
    (c)    radio call sign[12];
    (d)    port of choice[13];
    (e)    official number[14];
    (f)    year of build[15];
    (g)    method of propulsion, for example whether sail, steam, motor or dumb[16];
    (h)    length (metric units)[17];
    (i)    breadth (metric units)[18];
    (j)    depth (metric units)[19];
    (k)    type of ship, for example dry cargo, oil tanker, passenger, bulk carrier[20];
    (l)    such of the following tonnages as are specified in the certificate of survey: gross, net and registered[21];
    (m)    engine make and model[22];
    (n)    engine power in kilowatts[23];
(4)    the date of issue of the certificate[24];
(5)    the date the certificate expires[25].

1   As to the meaning of 'certificate of registry' see PARA 255 note 17.
2   As to the meaning of 'ship' for these purposes see PARA 255 note 4.
3   As to the meaning of 'register' for these purposes see PARA 255 note 1. Part I of the register, as mentioned in the text, is for ships, owned by qualified persons, which are not fishing vessels or registered on that Part which is restricted to small ships: see the Merchant Shipping (Registration of Ships) Regulations 1993, SI 1993/3138, reg 2(1)(a); and PARA 255. As to the meaning of 'fishing vessel' for these purposes see PARA 255 note 7; and as to the meaning of 'small ship' for these purposes see PARA 255 note 6.
4   Merchant Shipping (Registration of Ships) Regulations 1993, SI 1993/3138, reg 37, Sch 5 para 1.
5   As to the meaning of 'owner' for these purposes see PARA 255 note 13.
6   Merchant Shipping (Registration of Ships) Regulations 1993, SI 1993/3138, Sch 5 para 1(a).
7   Merchant Shipping (Registration of Ships) Regulations 1993, SI 1993/3138, Sch 5 para 1(b).
8   Merchant Shipping (Registration of Ships) Regulations 1993, SI 1993/3138, Sch 5 para 1(c).
9   Merchant Shipping (Registration of Ships) Regulations 1993, SI 1993/3138, Sch 5 para 1(c)(i). As to the proposal and approval of a ship's name see PARAS 277, 278.
10  As to the IMO number see PARA 293 note 4.

11 Merchant Shipping (Registration of Ships) Regulations 1993, SI 1993/3138, Sch 5 para 1(c)(ii) (substituted by SI 1998/2976).

12 Merchant Shipping (Registration of Ships) Regulations 1993, SI 1993/3138, Sch 5 para 1(c)(iii).

13 Merchant Shipping (Registration of Ships) Regulations 1993, SI 1993/3138, Sch 5 para 1(c)(iv). As to the meaning of 'port of choice' see PARA 278 note 12. As to the allocation of port of choice see PARA 279.

14 Merchant Shipping (Registration of Ships) Regulations 1993, SI 1993/3138, Sch 5 para 1(c)(v). As to the allocation of a ship's official number see PARA 279.

15 Merchant Shipping (Registration of Ships) Regulations 1993, SI 1993/3138, Sch 5 para 1(c)(vi).

16 Merchant Shipping (Registration of Ships) Regulations 1993, SI 1993/3138, Sch 5 para 1(c)(vii).

17 Merchant Shipping (Registration of Ships) Regulations 1993, SI 1993/3138, Sch 5 para 1(c)(viii).

18 Merchant Shipping (Registration of Ships) Regulations 1993, SI 1993/3138, Sch 5 para 1(c)(ix).

19 Merchant Shipping (Registration of Ships) Regulations 1993, SI 1993/3138, Sch 5 para 1(c)(x).

20 Merchant Shipping (Registration of Ships) Regulations 1993, SI 1993/3138, Sch 5 para 1(c)(xi).

21 Merchant Shipping (Registration of Ships) Regulations 1993, SI 1993/3138, Sch 5 para 1(c)(xii) (Sch 5 para 1(c)(xii) substituted for Sch 5 para 1(c)(xii)–(xiv) as originally enacted by SI 1998/2976). As to the survey and measurement of ships, including the ascertainment and certification of tonnage for registration purposes, see PARA 276.

22 Merchant Shipping (Registration of Ships) Regulations 1993, SI 1993/3138, Sch 5 para 1(c)(xv).

23 Merchant Shipping (Registration of Ships) Regulations 1993, SI 1993/3138, Sch 5 para 1(c)(xvi).

24 Merchant Shipping (Registration of Ships) Regulations 1993, SI 1993/3138, Sch 5 para 1(d).

25 Merchant Shipping (Registration of Ships) Regulations 1993, SI 1993/3138, Sch 5 para 1(e).

**300. Details contained in certificate of registry for a fishing vessel.** A certificate of registry[1] for a fishing vessel[2] registered or to be registered on Part II of the register[3] must contain[4]:

(1)      the name and address of each owner[5];

(2)      the name and address of any charterer[6];

(3)      the number of shares and, if any are jointly owned, with whom they are owned[7];

(4)      the following details about the vessel[8]:

       (a)     name[9];

       (b)     port of choice[10] and port number[11];

       (c)     official number[12];

       (d)     IMO number[13];

       (e)     radio call sign[14];

       (f)     registered length[15];

       (g)     overall length[16];

       (h)     breadth[17];

       (i)     depth[18];

       (j)     net tonnage[19];

       (k)     gross tonnage[20];

       (l)     engine make and model[21];

       (m)    maximum continuous engine power[22], in kilowatts, or if the owner notifies the registrar[23] of a modification, permanently de-rated engine power[24] in kilowatts[25];

       (n)     year of build[26];

       (o)     date of entry into service[27];

       (p)     modification explanation[28];

(5)      the date and time of the issue of the certificate[29];

(6)      the date of expiry of the certificate[30];

(7)      the kind of registration, that is, whether it is full[31] or simple registration[32].

1 As to the meaning of 'certificate of registry' see PARA 255 note 17.

2 As to the meaning of 'fishing vessel' for these purposes see PARA 255 note 7.

3 Part II of the register, as mentioned in the text, is reserved for fishing vessels: see the Merchant Shipping (Registration of Ships) Regulations 1993, SI 1993/3138, reg 2(1)(b); and PARA 255. As to the meaning of 'register' see PARA 255 note 1. As to the status of any Part II certificate under sea fisheries legislation see PARA 377.

4   Merchant Shipping (Registration of Ships) Regulations 1993, SI 1993/3138, reg 37, Sch 5 para 2.
5   Merchant Shipping (Registration of Ships) Regulations 1993, SI 1993/3138, Sch 5 para 2(a). As to the meaning of 'owner' for these purposes see PARA 255 note 13.
6   Merchant Shipping (Registration of Ships) Regulations 1993, SI 1993/3138, Sch 5 para 2(b).
7   Merchant Shipping (Registration of Ships) Regulations 1993, SI 1993/3138, Sch 5 para 2(c).
8   Merchant Shipping (Registration of Ships) Regulations 1993, SI 1993/3138, Sch 5 para 2(d).
9   Merchant Shipping (Registration of Ships) Regulations 1993, SI 1993/3138, Sch 5 para 2(d)(i). As to the proposal and approval of a ship's name see PARAS 277, 278.
10  As to the meaning of 'port of choice' see PARA 278 note 12. As to the allocation of port of choice see PARA 279.
11  Merchant Shipping (Registration of Ships) Regulations 1993, SI 1993/3138, Sch 5 para 2(d)(ii) (amended by SI 1999/3206). As to the meaning of 'port number' see PARA 279 note 8.
12  Merchant Shipping (Registration of Ships) Regulations 1993, SI 1993/3138, Sch 5 para 2(d)(iii). As to the allocation of a ship's official number see PARA 279.
13  Merchant Shipping (Registration of Ships) Regulations 1993, SI 1993/3138, Sch 5 para 2(d)(iv). As to the IMO number see PARA 293 note 4.
14  Merchant Shipping (Registration of Ships) Regulations 1993, SI 1993/3138, Sch 5 para 2(d)(v).
15  Merchant Shipping (Registration of Ships) Regulations 1993, SI 1993/3138, Sch 5 para 2(d)(vi).
16  Merchant Shipping (Registration of Ships) Regulations 1993, SI 1993/3138, Sch 5 para 2(d)(vii).
17  Merchant Shipping (Registration of Ships) Regulations 1993, SI 1993/3138, Sch 5 para 2(d)(viii).
18  Merchant Shipping (Registration of Ships) Regulations 1993, SI 1993/3138, Sch 5 para 2(d)(ix).
19  Merchant Shipping (Registration of Ships) Regulations 1993, SI 1993/3138, Sch 5 para 2(d)(x).
20  Merchant Shipping (Registration of Ships) Regulations 1993, SI 1993/3138, Sch 5 para 2(d)(xi).
21  Merchant Shipping (Registration of Ships) Regulations 1993, SI 1993/3138, Sch 5 para 2(d)(xii).
22  As to the meaning of 'maximum continuous engine power' see PARA 275 note 14.
23  As to the meaning of 'registrar' see PARA 255 note 2.
24  As to the meaning of 'permanently de-rated engine power' see PARA 275 note 15.
25  Merchant Shipping (Registration of Ships) Regulations 1993, SI 1993/3138, Sch 5 para 2(d)(xiii) (substituted by SI 1999/3206).
26  Merchant Shipping (Registration of Ships) Regulations 1993, SI 1993/3138, Sch 5 para 2(d)(xiv).
27  Merchant Shipping (Registration of Ships) Regulations 1993, SI 1993/3138, Sch 5 para 2(d)(xv).
28  Merchant Shipping (Registration of Ships) Regulations 1993, SI 1993/3138, Sch 5 para 2(d)(xvi) (added by SI 1999/3206). As to the meaning of 'modification explanation' see PARA 275 note 15.
29  Merchant Shipping (Registration of Ships) Regulations 1993, SI 1993/3138, Sch 5 para 2(e).
30  Merchant Shipping (Registration of Ships) Regulations 1993, SI 1993/3138, Sch 5 para 2(f).
31  As to the meaning of 'full registration' see PARA 256.
32  Merchant Shipping (Registration of Ships) Regulations 1993, SI 1993/3138, Sch 5 para 2(g) (added by SI 1998/2976). As to the meaning of 'simple registration' see PARA 256.

## 301. Details contained in certificate of registry for a bareboat charter ship.

A certificate of bareboat charter registry[1] for ships[2] registered or to be registered on Part IV of the register[3] must contain certain of the details prescribed for ships other than fishing vessels[4] or, as the case may be, those prescribed for fishing vessels[5], and the following[6]:

(1)    the name and address of the charterer[7];
(2)    the unique number allocated to the ship for identification purposes by its primary register[8];
(3)    the country of primary registration[9];
(4)    the original name (or a translation thereof) if different from its registered name[10].

1   As to the meanings of 'certificate of bareboat charter' and 'certificate of registry' see PARA 255 note 17.
2   As to the meaning of 'ship' for these purposes see PARA 255 note 4.
3   Part IV of the register is for ships which are bareboat charter ships: see the Merchant Shipping (Registration of Ships) Regulations 1993, SI 1993/3138, reg 2(1)(d); and PARA 255. As to the meaning of 'bareboat charter ship' see PARA 255 note 9; and as to the meaning of 'register' for these purposes see PARA 255 note 1.
4   Ie the details prescribed by the Merchant Shipping (Registration of Ships) Regulations 1993, SI 1993/3138, reg 37, Sch 5 para 1(a), (c)–(e) (as to which see PARA 299): see Sch 5 para 3 (amended by SI 1998/2976). As to the meaning of 'fishing vessel' for these purposes see PARA 255 note 7.

5  Ie the details prescribed by the Merchant Shipping (Registration of Ships) Regulations 1993, SI 1993/3138, Sch 5 para 2(a), (b), (d)–(f) (as to which see PARA 300): see Sch 5 para 3 (as amended: see note 4).
6  Merchant Shipping (Registration of Ships) Regulations 1993, SI 1993/3138, Sch 5 para 3 (as amended: see note 4).
7  Merchant Shipping (Registration of Ships) Regulations 1993, SI 1993/3138, Sch 5 para 3(a).
8  Merchant Shipping (Registration of Ships) Regulations 1993, SI 1993/3138, Sch 5 para 3(b) (substituted by SI 1999/3206). As to the meaning of 'primary register' see PARA 295 note 9.
9  Merchant Shipping (Registration of Ships) Regulations 1993, SI 1993/3138, Sch 5 para 3(c).
10 Merchant Shipping (Registration of Ships) Regulations 1993, SI 1993/3138, Sch 5 para 3(d) (amended by SI 1994/541).

**302. Status of certificate of registration.** The certificate of registration[1] of a British ship[2] may be used only for the lawful navigation of the ship and may not be subject to detention to secure any private right or claim[3].

1  As to certificates of registration see PARA 298 et seq.
2  As to the meaning of 'British ship' under the Merchant Shipping Act 1995 see PARA 230; and as to the meaning of 'ship' see PARA 229.
3  Merchant Shipping Act 1995 s 13.

**303. Temporary registration documents for fishing vessels.** The registrar[1] may, upon registering a fishing vessel[2], if the owner[3] so requests, issue to the owner through a local office[4] a temporary registration document[5]. The document must contain the registered particulars of the vessel and must specify the period, not exceeding two months, for which it is valid[6].

During the period of its validity, a temporary registration document has the effect of a certificate of registry[7].

1  As to the meaning of 'registrar' see PARA 255 note 2.
2  As to the meaning of 'fishing vessel' for these purposes see PARA 255 note 7.
3  As to the meaning of 'owner' for these purposes see PARA 255 note 13.
4  As to the meaning of 'local office' see PARA 269 note 5.
5  Merchant Shipping (Registration of Ships) Regulations 1993, SI 1993/3138, reg 38(1).
6  Merchant Shipping (Registration of Ships) Regulations 1993, SI 1993/3138, reg 38(1).
7  Merchant Shipping (Registration of Ships) Regulations 1993, SI 1993/3138, reg 38(2). As to the meaning of 'certificate of registry' see PARA 255 note 17.

### H.   RENEWAL OF REGISTRATION

**304. Renewal notices and time limit for renewal.** At least three months (but not more than six months) before the expiry of the registration period[1] for a ship[2], the registrar[3] must issue to the ship's owner[4] a renewal notice[5].

The owner may apply for renewal at any time between the date of issue of the renewal notice and the date of expiry of the current registration period[6]. Notwithstanding this, an application for renewal may be made prior to the last three months of the current registration (or issue of a renewal notice), for issue of a certificate of registry[7] commencing prior to the expiry of the current registration period[8]. Where such a certificate is issued, it is not valid for a period greater than five years commencing on that date of issue and the previous certificate then ceases to be valid[9].

1  As to the registration period see PARA 296.
2  As to the meaning of 'ship' for these purposes see PARA 255 note 4.
3  As to the meaning of 'registrar' see PARA 255 note 2.
4  As to the meaning of 'owner' for these purposes see PARA 255 note 13.
5  Merchant Shipping (Registration of Ships) Regulations 1993, SI 1993/3138, reg 41(1) (reg 41 substituted by SI 1998/2976).
6  Merchant Shipping (Registration of Ships) Regulations 1993, SI 1993/3138, reg 41(2) (as substituted: see note 5).
7  As to the meaning of 'certificate of registry' see PARA 255 note 17. As to the issue of duplicate certificates of registry in certain circumstances see PARA 373.

8 Merchant Shipping (Registration of Ships) Regulations 1993, SI 1993/3138, reg 41(3) (as substituted: see note 5).
9 Merchant Shipping (Registration of Ships) Regulations 1993, SI 1993/3138, reg 41(3) (as substituted: see note 5).

**305. Application for renewal of registration.** Application for renewal of a ship's registration[1] must be in a form approved by the Secretary of State[2] and must be accompanied by[3]:

(1)     a declaration of eligibility[4]; and

(2)     a declaration that there have been no changes to any registered details of the ship that have not been notified to the registrar[5].

In respect of certain fishing vessels[6], there must also be a declaration that the fishing vessel is correctly measured for tonnage under the tonnage regulations[7]; and, in the case of an application for renewal in respect of a fishing vessel, the application must in addition be accompanied by[8]:

(a)     where an engine has been permanently de-rated[9], a declaration describing the method by which the engine has been permanently de-rated[10]; or

(b)     in any other case, a declaration that the engine power recorded is the maximum continuous engine power[11].

Where no application for renewal is made, the registrar must notify each and every mortgagee of the expiration of the ship's registration[12].

1 As to the registration period see PARA 296; and as to the issue of a renewal notice see PARA 304. As to the meaning of 'ship' for these purposes see PARA 255 note 4.
2 As to the Secretary of State see PARA 36.
3 Merchant Shipping (Registration of Ships) Regulations 1993, SI 1993/3138, reg 42(1). As to the requirement to supply supplementary information or evidence where that provided on an application for registration is judged to be either not correct or insufficient see PARA 372.
4 Merchant Shipping (Registration of Ships) Regulations 1993, SI 1993/3138, reg 42(1)(a). As to the meaning of 'declaration of eligibility' see PARA 272 note 2. As to the power to dispense with declarations or other evidence otherwise required under the Merchant Shipping (Registration of Ships) Regulations 1993, SI 1993/3138, see PARA 371.
5 Merchant Shipping (Registration of Ships) Regulations 1993, SI 1993/3138, reg 42(1)(b). As to the meaning of 'registrar' see PARA 255 note 2. As to the requirement to remeasure tonnage in certain circumstances before a ship's registration can be renewed see PARA 380.
6 Ie in respect of all fishing vessels except those below 24 metres in length to which the Merchant Shipping (Tonnage) Regulations 1997, SI 1997/1510, Pt IIA (regs 12A–12E) (measurement of smaller fishing vessels) (see PARA 248) does not apply: see the Merchant Shipping (Registration of Ships) Regulations 1993, SI 1993/3138, reg 42(1)(c) (added by SI 1998/1915). 'Length' in the Merchant Shipping (Registration of Ships) Regulations 1993, SI 1993/3138, reg 42 has the same meaning as in the tonnage regulations: Merchant Shipping (Registration of Ships) Regulations 1993, SI 1993/3138, reg 1(2) (definition added by SI 1998/1915). As to the meaning of 'fishing vessel' for these purposes see PARA 255 note 7.
7 Merchant Shipping (Registration of Ships) Regulations 1993, SI 1993/3138, reg 42(1)(c) (as added: see note 6). As to the meaning of 'tonnage regulations' see PARA 276 note 2.
8 Merchant Shipping (Registration of Ships) Regulations 1993, SI 1993/3138, reg 42(1A) (added by SI 1999/3206).
9 As to the meaning of 'permanently de-rated engine power' see PARA 275 note 15.
10 Merchant Shipping (Registration of Ships) Regulations 1993, SI 1993/3138, reg 42(1A)(a) (as added: see note 8).
11 Merchant Shipping (Registration of Ships) Regulations 1993, SI 1993/3138, reg 42(1A)(b) (as added: see note 8). As to the meaning of 'maximum continuous engine power' see PARA 275 note 14.
12 Merchant Shipping (Registration of Ships) Regulations 1993, SI 1993/3138, reg 42(2).

I.     TRANSFERS ETC OF REGISTERED SHIPS

**306. In general.** Any transfer of a registered ship[1], or a share in such a ship, must be effected by a bill of sale satisfying the prescribed[2] requirements, unless the transfer will result in the ship ceasing to have a British connection[3]. Where any such ship or share has been so transferred, the transferee must not be registered as owner of the ship or share unless:

(1)      he has made the prescribed application to the registrar[4]; and

(2)      the registrar is satisfied that the ship retains a British connection and that he would not refuse to register the ship[5].

If such an application is granted by the registrar, the registrar must register the bill of sale in the prescribed manner[6]. Bills of sale must be registered in the order in which they are produced to the registrar for the purposes of registration[7].

Where a registered ship, or a share in a registered ship, is transmitted to any person by any lawful means other than a transfer by way of bill of sale[8] and the ship continues to have a British connection, that person may not be registered as owner of the ship or share unless[9]:

(a)      he has made the prescribed application to the registrar[10]; and

(b)      the registrar is satisfied that the ship retains a British connection and that he would not refuse to register the ship[11].

If such an application is granted by the registrar, the registrar must cause the applicant's name to be registered as owner of the ship or share[12].

Where the property in a registered ship or share in a registered ship is transmitted to any person by any lawful means other than a transfer by way of bill of sale[13], but as a result the ship no longer has a British connection, the High Court may, on application by or on behalf of that person, order a sale of the property so transmitted and direct that the proceeds of sale, after deducting the expenses of the sale, are to be paid to that person or otherwise as the court directs[14]. The court may require any evidence in support of the application it thinks requisite, and may make the order on any terms and conditions it thinks just, or may refuse to make the order, and generally may act in the case as the justice of the case requires[15]. Every such application must be made within the period of 28 days beginning with the date of the occurrence of the event on which the transmission has taken place, or within such further time, not exceeding one year, as the court may allow[16]. If such an application is not made within the time so allowed[17], or if the court refuses an order for sale[18], the ship or share transmitted is liable to forfeiture[19].

Where any court[20] orders the sale of any registered ship or share in a registered ship, the order of the court must contain a declaration vesting in some named person the right to transfer the ship or share[21]. The person so named is entitled to transfer the ship or share in the same manner and to the same extent as if he were the registered owner of the ship or share[22]. The registrar must deal with any application relating to the transfer of the ship or share made by the person so named as if that person were the registered owner[23].

The High Court may, if it thinks fit (without prejudice to the exercise of any other power), on the application of any interested person, make an order prohibiting for a specified time any dealing with a registered ship or share in a registered ship[24]. The court may make the order on any terms or conditions it thinks just, or may refuse to make the order, or may discharge the order when made, with or without costs, and generally may act in the case as the justice of the case requires[25]. The order, when a copy is served on the registrar, is binding on him, whether or not he was made a party to the proceedings[26].

Where the transfer of a vessel (whether British or not) is a sham, the original owner will retain beneficial ownership[27].

1    As to the meaning of 'ship' under the Merchant Shipping Act 1995 see PARA 229. As to the general private law powers of the registered owner of a ship see PARA 237.

2 For these purposes, 'prescribed' means prescribed in registration regulations: Merchant Shipping Act 1995 s 16(1), Sch 1 para 14. As to the meaning of 'registration regulations' see PARA 247.
3 Merchant Shipping Act 1995 Sch 1 para 2(1). As to the meaning of references to a ship's having a British connection see PARA 245 note 3. As to the form of the bill of sale see PARA 308; and as to the application of Sch 1 see PARA 252.
4 Merchant Shipping Act 1995 Sch 1 para 2(2)(a). As to the meaning of 'registrar' for these purposes see PARA 254 note 11.
5 Merchant Shipping Act 1995 Sch 1 para 2(2)(b).
6 Merchant Shipping Act 1995 Sch 1 para 2(3).
7 Merchant Shipping Act 1995 Sch 1 para 2(4).
8 Ie other than by a transfer under the Merchant Shipping Act 1995 Sch 1 para 2 (as to which see the text and notes 1–7): see Sch 1 para 3(1).
9 Merchant Shipping Act 1995 Sch 1 para 3(1).
10 Merchant Shipping Act 1995 Sch 1 para 3(1)(a).
11 Merchant Shipping Act 1995 Sch 1 para 3(1)(b).
12 Merchant Shipping Act 1995 Sch 1 para 3(2).
13 Ie other than by a transfer under the Merchant Shipping Act 1995 Sch 1 para 2 (as to which see the text and notes 1–7): see Sch 1 para 4(1).
14 Merchant Shipping Act 1995 Sch 1 para 4(1).
15 Merchant Shipping Act 1995 Sch 1 para 4(2).
16 Merchant Shipping Act 1995 Sch 1 para 4(3).
17 Merchant Shipping Act 1995 Sch 1 para 4(4)(a).
18 Merchant Shipping Act 1995 Sch 1 para 4(4)(b).
19 Merchant Shipping Act 1995 Sch 1 para 4(4).
20 Ie whether under the Merchant Shipping Act 1995 Sch 1 para 4 (as to which see the text and notes 13–19) or otherwise: see Sch 1 para 5(1).
21 Merchant Shipping Act 1995 Sch 1 para 5(1).
22 Merchant Shipping Act 1995 Sch 1 para 5(2).
23 Merchant Shipping Act 1995 Sch 1 para 5(3).
24 Merchant Shipping Act 1995 Sch 1 para 6(1).
25 Merchant Shipping Act 1995 Sch 1 para 6(2).
26 Merchant Shipping Act 1995 Sch 1 para 6(3).
27 *The Tjaskemolen (now named Visvliet)* [1997] 2 Lloyd's Rep 465.

**307. Evidence of title on registration of transfer of ship by way of bill of sale.** On application for registration[1] of a transfer of a registered ship[2] (or a share in a registered ship) by way of bill of sale, other than a fishing vessel[3] registered with simple registration[4], the bill of sale must be produced to the registrar[5].

When an application is made for the registration of a transfer of a fishing vessel which is registered with simple registration, evidence of the transfer satisfactory to the registrar must be produced to him[6].

1 Ie on an application under the Merchant Shipping Act 1995 s 16(1), Sch 1 para 2(1) (see PARA 306): see the Merchant Shipping (Registration of Ships) Regulations 1993, SI 1993/3138, reg 43(1); Interpretation Act 1978 s 17(2)(b). As to the meaning of 'application for registration' see PARA 269 note 1.
2 As to the meaning of 'ship' for these purposes see PARA 255 note 4.
3 As to the meaning of 'fishing vessel' for these purposes see PARA 255 note 7.
4 As to the meaning of 'simple registration' see PARA 256.
5 Merchant Shipping (Registration of Ships) Regulations 1993, SI 1993/3138, reg 43(1); Interpretation Act 1978 s 17(2)(b). As to the meaning of 'registrar' see PARA 255 note 2. As to the form of the bill of sale see PARA 308; and as to registration of a transfer see PARA 309.
6 Merchant Shipping (Registration of Ships) Regulations 1993, SI 1993/3138, reg 43(2).

**308. Form of bill of sale.** Every bill of sale effecting a transfer of a registered ship or a share in a ship[1] must be in the form approved by the Secretary of State[2] with appropriate attestation[3] and must contain a description of the ship sufficient to identify it[4].

1 Ie under the Merchant Shipping Act 1995 (see PARA 306) and the Merchant Shipping (Registration of Ships) Regulations 1993, SI 1993/3138: see reg 44. As to the meaning of 'ship' for these purposes see PARA 255 note 4.
2 As to the Secretary of State see PARA 36.

3   For these purposes, 'appropriate attestation' means attestation in a form approved by the Secretary of State: Merchant Shipping (Registration of Ships) Regulations 1993, SI 1993/3138, reg 1(2).
4   Merchant Shipping (Registration of Ships) Regulations 1993, SI 1993/3138, reg 44; Interpretation Act 1978 s 17(2)(b).

### 309. Registration of transfer of a ship by way of bill of sale.

If the application for the transfer of a ship[1] (or of shares in a ship) by way of bill of sale[2] is granted by the registrar[3], he must[4]:

(1)   register the bill of sale by entering the name of the new owner[5] in the register[6] as owner of the ship or share in question[7]; and

(2)   endorse on the bill of sale the fact that the entry has been made, together with the date and time when it was made[8].

If the registrar is satisfied with the evidence that the ship or share in the ship has been transferred[9], he must enter the name of the new owner in the register as the owner of the ship or share in question and issue a new certificate, which is valid for a period of five years[10].

1   For these purposes, 'transfer of a ship' includes, except where the context otherwise requires, transfer of a share in a ship: Merchant Shipping (Registration of Ships) Regulations 1993, SI 1993/3138, reg 1(2). As to the meaning of 'ship' for these purposes see PARA 255 note 4.
2   Ie under the Merchant Shipping Act 1995 s 16(1), Sch 1 para 2(2) (see PARA 306): see the Merchant Shipping (Registration of Ships) Regulations 1993, SI 1993/3138, reg 45(1); Interpretation Act 1978 s 17(2)(b). As to the bill of sale see PARA 308.
3   As to the meaning of 'registrar' see PARA 255 note 2.
4   Merchant Shipping (Registration of Ships) Regulations 1993, SI 1993/3138, reg 45(1); Interpretation Act 1978 s 17(2)(b).
5   As to the meaning of 'owner' for these purposes see PARA 255 note 13.
6   As to the meaning of 'register' see PARA 255 note 1.
7   Merchant Shipping (Registration of Ships) Regulations 1993, SI 1993/3138, reg 45(1)(a).
8   Merchant Shipping (Registration of Ships) Regulations 1993, SI 1993/3138, reg 45(1)(b).
9   Ie the evidence under the Merchant Shipping (Registration of Ships) Regulations 1993, SI 1993/3138, reg 43 (see PARA 307): see reg 45(2).
10  Merchant Shipping (Registration of Ships) Regulations 1993, SI 1993/3138, reg 45(2). As to the meaning of 'certificate of registry' see PARA 255 note 17. As to the issue of duplicate certificates of registry in certain circumstances see PARA 373.

### 310. Evidence of title on registration of ship transmitted other than by way of bill of sale.

An application for registration[1] of a transmission of a registered ship[2] (or a share in a registered ship) other than by way of bill of sale[3] must be made in the form approved by the Secretary of State[4].

The following evidence must be produced to the registrar[5] on an application for a transfer of a registered ship or share therein by way of transmission[6]:

(1)   if the transmission was consequent on death, the grant of representation[7] or an office copy thereof or of an extract therefrom[8];

(2)   if the transmission was consequent on bankruptcy, such evidence as is for the time being receivable in courts of justice as proof of title of persons claiming under bankruptcy[9];

(3)   if the transmission was consequent on an order of the court, a copy of the order or judgment of that court[10].

1   As to the meaning of 'application for registration' see PARA 269 note 1.
2   As to the meaning of 'ship' for these purposes see PARA 255 note 4.
3   Ie under the Merchant Shipping Act 1995 s 16(1), Sch 1 para 3(1) (see PARA 306): see the Merchant Shipping (Registration of Ships) Regulations 1993, SI 1993/3138, reg 46(1); Interpretation Act 1978 s 17(2)(b). As to the bill of sale see PARA 308.
4   Merchant Shipping (Registration of Ships) Regulations 1993, SI 1993/3138, reg 46(1); Interpretation Act 1978 s 17(2)(b). As to the Secretary of State see PARA 36.
5   As to the meaning of 'registrar' see PARA 255 note 2.
6   Merchant Shipping (Registration of Ships) Regulations 1993, SI 1993/3138, reg 46(2).
7   For these purposes, 'representation' means probate, administration, confirmation, or other instrument constituting a person the executor, administrator or other legal representative of a

deceased person, including a certificate of confirmation relating to a vessel: Merchant Shipping (Registration of Ships) Regulations 1993, SI 1993/3138, reg 1(2).

8 Merchant Shipping (Registration of Ships) Regulations 1993, SI 1993/3138, reg 46(2)(a).

9 Merchant Shipping (Registration of Ships) Regulations 1993, SI 1993/3138, reg 46(2)(b).

10 Merchant Shipping (Registration of Ships) Regulations 1993, SI 1993/3138, reg 46(2)(c).

**311. Declaration of eligibility on transfer or transmission.** Every application for the registration[1] of a transfer or transmission of a registered ship[2] must be accompanied by a declaration of eligibility[3] and, where the application is made on behalf of a body corporate, by the document or documents required for such applications[4].

1 As to the meaning of 'application for registration' see PARA 269 note 1.

2 As to an application for the transfer of a registered ship (or shares therein) see the Merchant Shipping Act 1995 s 16(1), Sch 1 para 2; and PARA 306. As to an application for the transmission of a registered ship (or shares therein) see Sch 1 para 3; and PARA 306. As to the meaning of 'ship' for these purposes see PARA 255 note 4.

3 As to the meaning of 'declaration of eligibility' see PARA 272 note 2. As to the power to dispense with declarations or other evidence otherwise required under the Merchant Shipping (Registration of Ships) Regulations 1993, SI 1993/3138, see PARA 371.

4 Merchant Shipping (Registration of Ships) Regulations 1993, SI 1993/3138, reg 47. The document (or documents) so required is (or are) that (or those) mentioned in reg 24 (see PARA 273) (applications by bodies corporate): see reg 47.

**312. Refusal of registration of transfer or transmission.** If, on an application for transfer or transmission of a ship (or shares) in a ship[1], the registrar[2] is not satisfied that the ship is eligible to be registered, then[3]:

(1) the registrar must serve a notice on the owner[4] of the ship[5] stating:

    (a) that the registrar is not satisfied that the vessel in question is eligible to be registered[6]; and

    (b) that the ship's registration will accordingly terminate at the end of the period mentioned in head (2) below[7]; and

(2) the ship's registration terminates at the end of the period of 14 days beginning with the date of the service of that notice[8].

1 As to an application for the transfer of a registered ship (or shares therein) see the Merchant Shipping Act 1995 s 16(1), Sch 1 para 2; and PARA 306. As to an application for the transmission of a registered ship (or shares therein) see Sch 1 para 3; and PARA 306. As to the meaning of 'ship' for these purposes see PARA 255 note 4.

2 As to the meaning of 'registrar' see PARA 255 note 2.

3 Merchant Shipping (Registration of Ships) Regulations 1993, SI 1993/3138, reg 48(1).

4 As to the meaning of 'owner' for these purposes see PARA 255 note 13.

5 Merchant Shipping (Registration of Ships) Regulations 1993, SI 1993/3138, reg 48(1)(a).

6 Merchant Shipping (Registration of Ships) Regulations 1993, SI 1993/3138, reg 48(1)(a), (2)(a).

7 Merchant Shipping (Registration of Ships) Regulations 1993, SI 1993/3138, reg 48(1)(a), (2)(b).

8 Merchant Shipping (Registration of Ships) Regulations 1993, SI 1993/3138, reg 48(1)(b).

### J. NOTIFICATION OF CHANGES

**313. Notification of changes of ownership etc.** If at any time there occurs, in relation to a registered ship[1]:

(1) any change affecting the eligibility of the ship to be registered, not being a change which affects the qualification or eligibility of the owner[2] or the British connection of a ship[3]; or

(2) in respect of a fishing vessel[4], any change, not affecting that eligibility, in the percentage of the property in the ship beneficially owned[5] by qualified persons or companies[6],

the owner of the ship must, as soon as practicable after the change occurs, notify the registrar[7]. Such notification must be made in writing, must be signed by the owner and must specify the nature of the change and the name and the official number of the ship[8]. Any person who contravenes the requirement to notify the registrar of such changes as are mentioned in heads (1) and (2) above is guilty of an offence[9].

Where there is any transfer or transmission of a registered ship or share in a registered ship[10]:

(a)     the person ceasing to own the ship or share (or in the event of his death, his legal personal representative) must notify the registrar and surrender the certificate of registry[11]; and

(b)     the registrar must cancel the certificate of registry and must freeze[12] the register pending the application for the registration of the transfer or transmission by the new owner or owners of the ship or share[13].

Where there is a transfer of a registered ship, the new owners must within 30 days of the transfer make application[14] for the transfer to be registered[15]. If the transfer is of all the shares in the ship, and application is not made within the 30 days, the registrar may cancel the registration of the ship and the certificate of registry[16]. If the transfer is of one or some of the shares in the ship, and application is not made within the 30 days, the registrar must serve a notice on the remaining registered owners notifying them that, unless an application to transfer the share or shares in question is made within 30 days of the date of the notice, the registration of the ship and the certificate of registry may be cancelled[17].

Where there is a transmission of a registered ship, the new owners must promptly make application[18] for the transmission to be registered[19]. If the transmission is all the shares in the ship, and application is not made within a reasonable time, the registrar may cancel the registration of the ship and the certificate of registry[20]. If the transmission is of one or some of the shares in the ship, and application is not made within a reasonable time, the registrar must serve a notice on the remaining registered owners notifying them that, unless an application to register the transmission of the share or shares in question is made within 30 days of the date of the notice, the registration of the ship and the certificate of registry may be cancelled[21].

Any person who fails to so notify the registrar, to so surrender the certificate of registry, or to make the required applications[22] in relation to the transfer or transmission of a registered ship (or share therein) is guilty of an offence[23].

Where such an application is made[24] to register a change of ownership of a registered fishing vessel (or share in such vessel)[25], the applicant must submit details of the maximum continuous engine power[26] and, where an engine is permanently de-rated[27], the modification explanation[28]. Any owner who contravenes this requirement is guilty of an offence[29].

1   Merchant Shipping (Registration of Ships) Regulations 1993, SI 1993/3138, reg 49(1). As to the meaning of 'ship' for these purposes see PARA 255 note 4.
2   Ie as prescribed in the Merchant Shipping (Registration of Ships) Regulations 1993, SI 1993/3138, reg 7 (qualification) (see PARA 258) and reg 12 (eligibility) (see PARA 262): see reg 49(1)(a) (amended by SI 1994/541). As to the meaning of 'owner' for these purposes see PARA 255 note 13.
3   Merchant Shipping (Registration of Ships) Regulations 1993, SI 1993/3138, reg 49(1)(a) (as amended: see note 2). The text refers to changes affecting the British connection of a ship as prescribed in reg 8 (British connection and majority interest in the ship) (see PARA 259) and reg 14 (British connection and representative persons for fishing vessels) (see PARA 263): see reg 49(1)(a) (as so amended). As to the meaning of references under the Merchant Shipping Act 1995 to a ship's having a British connection see PARA 245 note 3. As to the requirement to remeasure tonnage in certain circumstances where a ship's details have been changed see PARA 380.
4   As to the meaning of 'fishing vessel' for these purposes see PARA 255 note 7.
5   As to the meaning of 'beneficial ownership' for these purposes see PARA 262 note 15.
6   Merchant Shipping (Registration of Ships) Regulations 1993, SI 1993/3138, reg 49(1)(b).

7 Merchant Shipping (Registration of Ships) Regulations 1993, SI 1993/3138, reg 49(1). As to the meaning of 'registrar' see PARA 255 note 2.
8 Merchant Shipping (Registration of Ships) Regulations 1993, SI 1993/3138, reg 49(2). As to a ship's name see PARAS 277, 278; and as to the allocation of a ship's official number see PARA 279.
9 See the Merchant Shipping (Registration of Ships) Regulations 1993, SI 1993/3138, reg 49(3); and PARA 1068.
10 Merchant Shipping (Registration of Ships) Regulations 1993, SI 1993/3138, reg 50(1). As to an application for the transfer of a registered ship (or shares therein) see the Merchant Shipping Act 1995 s 16(1), Sch 1 para 2; and PARA 306. As to an application for the transmission of a registered ship (or shares therein) see Sch 1 para 3; and PARA 306.
11 Merchant Shipping (Registration of Ships) Regulations 1993, SI 1993/3138, reg 50(1)(a). As to the meaning of 'certificate of registry' see PARA 255 note 17.
12 For these purposes, 'freeze' means to prevent any entry, which includes a deletion of an entry, being made in the register: Merchant Shipping (Registration of Ships) Regulations 1993, SI 1993/3138, reg 1(2). As to the meaning of 'register' see PARA 255 note 1.
13 Merchant Shipping (Registration of Ships) Regulations 1993, SI 1993/3138, reg 50(1)(b).
14 Ie in accordance with the Merchant Shipping (Registration of Ships) Regulations 1993, SI 1993/3138: see reg 50(2)(a).
15 Merchant Shipping (Registration of Ships) Regulations 1993, SI 1993/3138, reg 50(2)(a).
16 Merchant Shipping (Registration of Ships) Regulations 1993, SI 1993/3138, reg 50(2)(b).
17 Merchant Shipping (Registration of Ships) Regulations 1993, SI 1993/3138, reg 50(2)(c).
18 Ie in accordance with the Merchant Shipping (Registration of Ships) Regulations 1993, SI 1993/3138: see reg 50(3)(a).
19 Merchant Shipping (Registration of Ships) Regulations 1993, SI 1993/3138, reg 50(3)(a).
20 Merchant Shipping (Registration of Ships) Regulations 1993, SI 1993/3138, reg 50(3)(b).
21 Merchant Shipping (Registration of Ships) Regulations 1993, SI 1993/3138, reg 50(3)(c).
22 Ie as required by the Merchant Shipping (Registration of Ships) Regulations 1993, SI 1993/3138, reg 50(1), (2) or (3) (see the text and notes 10–21): see reg 50(4); and PARA 1068.
23 See the Merchant Shipping (Registration of Ships) Regulations 1993, SI 1993/3138, reg 50(4); and PARA 1068.
24 Ie under the Merchant Shipping (Registration of Ships) Regulations 1993, SI 1993/3138, reg 50 (see the text and notes 10–21): see reg 29A(1)(c) (regs 29A, 29B added by SI 1999/3206).
25 Merchant Shipping (Registration of Ships) Regulations 1993, SI 1993/3138, reg 29A(1)(c) (as added: see note 24).
26 Merchant Shipping (Registration of Ships) Regulations 1993, SI 1993/3138, reg 29A(2)(a) (as added: see note 24). The text refers to details of the maximum continuous engine power, determined in accordance with Council Regulation (EC) 2930/86 of 22 September 1986 defining characteristics for fishing vessels (OJ L274, 25.9.1986, p 1) art 5: see the Merchant Shipping (Registration of Ships) Regulations 1993, SI 1993/3138, reg 29A(2)(a) (as so added). As to the meaning of 'maximum continuous engine power' see PARA 275 note 14. Where the registrar is not satisfied that the engine power details notified to him, or recorded, for any fishing vessel are correct, he may require the owner to have the engine power measured in accordance with Council Regulation (EC) 2930/86 of 22 September 1986 defining characteristics for fishing vessels (OJ L274, 25.9.1986, p 1) art 5: Merchant Shipping (Registration of Ships) Regulations 1993, SI 1993/3138, reg 29B (as so added).
27 As to the meaning of 'permanently de-rated engine power' see PARA 275 note 15.
28 Merchant Shipping (Registration of Ships) Regulations 1993, SI 1993/3138, reg 29A(2)(b) (as added: see note 24). As to the meaning of 'modification explanation' see PARA 275 note 15.
29 See the Merchant Shipping (Registration of Ships) Regulations 1993, SI 1993/3138, reg 29A(3); and PARA 1067.

**314. Change in registered particulars of ship.** Where there is a change:

(1)    in the registered particulars of a ship[1] (other than a change in the tonnage of the ship)[2]; or

(2)    in the name or address of an owner[3] entered in the register[4] (not being a change of ownership)[5],

application must be made as soon as practicable to the registrar[6] for the change to be recorded in the register[7]. Such application must be in writing and must be accompanied[8] by the certificate of registry[9] and such evidence as to the change as may be required by the registrar[10].

Where there is a change in the tonnage of a ship, it must be[11] resurveyed or remeasured[12]. Thereafter application in a form approved by the Secretary of

State[13] must be made as soon as practicable for the change to be recorded in the register[14]. The application must be accompanied by the certificate of survey or measurement and the certificate of registry[15].

On recording the change in the registered particulars, the registrar must cancel the existing certificate and issue to the owner a new certificate of registry expiring on the same date as the existing one[16].

Where such an application is made[17] to record a change in the length, breadth or engine power of a registered fishing vessel[18], the applicant must submit details of the maximum continuous engine power[19] and, where an engine is permanently de-rated[20], the modification explanation[21]. Any owner who contravenes this requirement is guilty of an offence[22].

1  As to the meaning of 'ship' for these purposes see PARA 255 note 4.
2  Merchant Shipping (Registration of Ships) Regulations 1993, SI 1993/3138, reg 51(1)(a).
3  As to the meaning of 'owner' for these purposes see PARA 255 note 13.
4  As to the meaning of 'register' see PARA 255 note 1.
5  Merchant Shipping (Registration of Ships) Regulations 1993, SI 1993/3138, reg 51(1)(b).
6  As to the meaning of 'registrar' see PARA 255 note 2.
7  Merchant Shipping (Registration of Ships) Regulations 1993, SI 1993/3138, reg 51(1). Any person who fails to make such an application is guilty of an offence: see reg 51(5); and PARA 1068.
8  Ie subject to the Merchant Shipping (Registration of Ships) Regulations 1993, SI 1993/3138, reg 111 (dispensing with production of certificate) (see PARA 376): see reg 51(2).
9  As to the meaning of 'certificate of registry' see PARA 255 note 17. As to the power to dispense with the production of a certificate in certain circumstances see PARA 376.
10  Merchant Shipping (Registration of Ships) Regulations 1993, SI 1993/3138, reg 51(2).
11  Ie in accordance with the Merchant Shipping (Registration of Ships) Regulations 1993, SI 1993/3138, reg 29 (see PARA 276): see reg 51(3). As to the requirement to remeasure tonnage in certain circumstances see PARA 380.
12  Merchant Shipping (Registration of Ships) Regulations 1993, SI 1993/3138, reg 51(3).
13  As to the Secretary of State see PARA 36.
14  Merchant Shipping (Registration of Ships) Regulations 1993, SI 1993/3138, reg 51(3). Any person who fails to make such an application is guilty of an offence: see reg 51(5); and PARA 1068.
15  Merchant Shipping (Registration of Ships) Regulations 1993, SI 1993/3138, reg 51(3). As to the survey and measurement of ships, including the ascertainment and certification of tonnage for registration purposes, see PARA 276.
16  Merchant Shipping (Registration of Ships) Regulations 1993, SI 1993/3138, reg 51(4).
17  Ie under the Merchant Shipping (Registration of Ships) Regulations 1993, SI 1993/3138, reg 51 (see the text and notes 1–16): see reg 29A(1)(b) (regs 29A, 29B added by SI 1999/3206).
18  Merchant Shipping (Registration of Ships) Regulations 1993, SI 1993/3138, reg 29A(1)(b) (as added: see note 17). As to the meaning of 'fishing vessel' for these purposes see PARA 255 note 7.
19  Merchant Shipping (Registration of Ships) Regulations 1993, SI 1993/3138, reg 29A(2)(a) (as added: see note 17). The text refers to details of the maximum continuous engine power, determined in accordance with Council Regulation (EC) 2930/86 of 22 September 1986 defining characteristics for fishing vessels (OJ L274, 25.9.1986, p 1) art 5: see the Merchant Shipping (Registration of Ships) Regulations 1993, SI 1993/3138, reg 29A(2)(a) (as so added). As to the meaning of 'maximum continuous engine power' see PARA 275 note 14. Where the registrar is not satisfied that the engine power details notified to him, or recorded, for any fishing vessel are correct, he may require the owner to have the engine power measured in accordance with Council Regulation (EC) 2930/86 of 22 September 1986 defining characteristics for fishing vessels (OJ L274, 25.9.1986, p 1) art 5: Merchant Shipping (Registration of Ships) Regulations 1993, SI 1993/3138, reg 29B (as so added).
20  As to the meaning of 'permanently de-rated engine power' see PARA 275 note 15.
21  Merchant Shipping (Registration of Ships) Regulations 1993, SI 1993/3138, reg 29A(2)(b) (as added: see note 17). As to the meaning of 'modification explanation' see PARA 275 note 15.
22  See the Merchant Shipping (Registration of Ships) Regulations 1993, SI 1993/3138, reg 29A(3); and PARA 1067.

K.   CHANGE OF NAME; TRANSFER OF PORT OF CHOICE

**315. Change of name.** An owner[1] of a registered ship[2] may apply to the registrar[3] to change the name of the ship[4]. The application must be made in a form approved by the Secretary of State[5] and must be accompanied[6] by the certificate of registry[7]. If it appears to the registrar that the name complies with the requirements relating to the approval of names[8], he must issue a marking note to the owner[9].

On receipt of the marking note, the owner must cause the ship to be marked with the new name and, in respect of ships over 24 metres and fishing vessels[10], must cause the marking to be duly[11] inspected[12]. The owner or inspector[13] must, if satisfied that the ship is marked in the prescribed manner[14], complete the marking note and return it to the registrar[15].

On receipt of the marking note duly completed, the registrar must re-register the ship with its new name and must cancel the existing certificate and must issue to the owner a new certificate of registry expiring on the same date as the existing one[16].

1　As to the meaning of 'owner' for these purposes see PARA 255 note 13.
2　As to the meaning of 'ship' for these purposes see PARA 255 note 4.
3　As to the meaning of 'registrar' see PARA 255 note 2.
4　Merchant Shipping (Registration of Ships) Regulations 1993, SI 1993/3138, reg 52(1).
5　As to the Secretary of State see PARA 36.
6　Ie subject to the Merchant Shipping (Registration of Ships) Regulations 1993, SI 1993/3138, reg 111 (dispensing with production of certificate) (see PARA 376): see reg 52(1).
7　Merchant Shipping (Registration of Ships) Regulations 1993, SI 1993/3138, reg 52(1). As to the meaning of 'certificate of registry' see PARA 255 note 17. As to the power to dispense with the production of a certificate in certain circumstances see PARA 376.
8　Ie the Merchant Shipping (Registration of Ships) Regulations 1993, SI 1993/3138, reg 52(2), Sch 1 (as to which see PARA 278): see reg 52(2).
9　Merchant Shipping (Registration of Ships) Regulations 1993, SI 1993/3138, reg 52(2).
10　As to the meaning of 'fishing vessel' for these purposes see PARA 255 note 7.
11　Ie inspected in accordance with the Merchant Shipping (Registration of Ships) Regulations 1993, SI 1993/3138, reg 33 (see PARA 286): see reg 54(1).
12　Merchant Shipping (Registration of Ships) Regulations 1993, SI 1993/3138, reg 54(1).
13　As to the meaning of 'inspector of marks' see PARA 280 note 8.
14　Ie in the manner required by the Merchant Shipping (Registration of Ships) Regulations 1993, SI 1993/3138, reg 54(2), Sch 3 (see PARA 281 et seq): see reg 54(2).
15　Merchant Shipping (Registration of Ships) Regulations 1993, SI 1993/3138, reg 54(2).
16　Merchant Shipping (Registration of Ships) Regulations 1993, SI 1993/3138, reg 55.

**316. Transfer of port of choice.** An owner[1] of a registered ship[2] may apply to the registrar[3] for the ship to change its port of choice[4] to another such port[5]. The application must be made in a form approved by the Secretary of State[6] and must be accompanied[7] by its certificate of registry[8].

On receipt of such an application in respect of a fishing vessel[9], the registrar must allocate to the vessel port letters[10] and numbers[11] for that port[12]. If it appears to the registrar that the requirements relating to the approval of names[13] are complied with, he must issue a marking note[14].

On receipt of the marking note, the owner must cause the ship to be marked with the new port of choice and, in respect of ships over 24 metres and fishing vessels, must cause the marking to be duly[15] inspected[16]. The owner or inspector[17] must, if satisfied that the ship is marked in the prescribed manner[18], complete the marking note and return it to the registrar[19].

On receipt of the marking note duly completed, the registrar must re-register the ship with its new port of choice and must cancel the existing certificate and must issue to the owner a new certificate of registry expiring on the same date as the existing one[20].

1　As to the meaning of 'owner' for these purposes see PARA 255 note 13.
2　As to the meaning of 'ship' for these purposes see PARA 255 note 4.
3　As to the meaning of 'registrar' see PARA 255 note 2.

4  As to the meaning of 'port of choice' see PARA 278 note 12. As to the allocation of port of choice see PARA 279.

5  Merchant Shipping (Registration of Ships) Regulations 1993, SI 1993/3138, reg 53(1).

6  As to the Secretary of State see PARA 36.

7  Ie subject to the Merchant Shipping (Registration of Ships) Regulations 1993, SI 1993/3138, reg 111 (dispensing with production of certificate) (see PARA 376): see reg 53(1).

8  Merchant Shipping (Registration of Ships) Regulations 1993, SI 1993/3138, reg 53(1). As to the meaning of 'certificate of registry' see PARA 255 note 17. As to the power to dispense with the production of a certificate in certain circumstances see PARA 376.

9  As to the meaning of 'fishing vessel' for these purposes see PARA 255 note 7.

10  As to the meaning of 'port letters' see PARA 279 note 3.

11  As to the meaning of 'port number' see PARA 279 note 8.

12  Merchant Shipping (Registration of Ships) Regulations 1993, SI 1993/3138, reg 53(2).

13  Ie the Merchant Shipping (Registration of Ships) Regulations 1993, SI 1993/3138, reg 52(2), Sch 1 (as to which see PARA 278): see reg 53(3).

14  Merchant Shipping (Registration of Ships) Regulations 1993, SI 1993/3138, reg 53(3).

15  Ie inspected in accordance with the Merchant Shipping (Registration of Ships) Regulations 1993, SI 1993/3138, reg 33 (see PARA 286): see reg 54(1).

16  Merchant Shipping (Registration of Ships) Regulations 1993, SI 1993/3138, reg 54(1).

17  As to the meaning of 'inspector of marks' see PARA 280 note 8.

18  Ie in the manner required by the Merchant Shipping (Registration of Ships) Regulations 1993, SI 1993/3138, reg 54(2), Sch 3 (see PARA 281 et seq): see reg 54(2).

19  Merchant Shipping (Registration of Ships) Regulations 1993, SI 1993/3138, reg 54(2).

20  Merchant Shipping (Registration of Ships) Regulations 1993, SI 1993/3138, reg 55.

## L.  TERMINATION OF SHIP'S REGISTRATION

**317. Removal from the register.** The registrar[1] may[2] terminate a ship's[3] registration in the following circumstances[4]:

(1)  on application by the owner[5];

(2)  if the registered owner has not notified the registrar that ownership of the ship has changed[6];

(3)  on the ship no longer being eligible to be registered[7];

(4)  on the ship being destroyed (which includes, but is not limited to, shipwreck, demolition, fire and sinking)[8];

(5)  if, taking into account any requirements of the Merchant Shipping Act 1995, including any instrument made thereunder, relating to the condition of the ship or its equipment so far as relevant to its safety or to any risk of pollution or to the safety, health and welfare of persons employed or engaged in any capacity on board the ship, he considers that it would be inappropriate for the ship to remain registered[9];

(6)  when a registered fishing vessel[10] which has been licensed to fish ceases to be so licensed for a continuous period of six months or more[11];

(7)  when a fishing vessel which requires a licence to fish but at the time of registration did not have such a licence and has not acquired such a licence within six months of the issue of its certificate of registry[12];

(8)  when any penalty imposed on the owner of a ship in respect of a contravention[13] of the Merchant Shipping Act 1995, or of any instrument in force thereunder, has remained unpaid for a period of more than three months, and no appeal against that penalty is pending[14];

(9)  when any summons for any such contravention has been duly served on the owner of a ship but the owner has failed to appear at the time and place appointed for the trial of the information or complaint in question and a period of not less than three months has elapsed since that time[15];

(10)  when the tonnage of certain fishing vessels[16] has not been duly measured[17] (or though so measured, that information has not been notified to the registrar)[18];

(11)    where the owner of a fishing vessel fails to respond to the registrar within 15 days of a request from him to supply information concerning details on the register[19] of a fishing vessel[20];

(12)    where the owner of a fishing vessel supplies information requested by the registrar, but that information is either false or incorrect, or is reasonably considered by the registrar to be insufficient[21];

(13)    where a fishing vessel certificate[22] has expired[23];

(14)    where[24] a person is required to notify the registrar of any transfer or transmission of a registered ship or share in a registered ship (or to make an application to do so) and has not done so[25]; or

(15)    where[26] a person is required to make an application for any change in the registered particulars of a ship or in the name or address of an owner to be recorded in the register, and has not done so[27].

Where it appears to the registrar that head (2) or head (3) above, or any of heads (5) to (15) above, applies, he may serve notice on the owner or managing owner[28], or on any charterer, manager or operator of the ship requiring him to produce, within 30 days, evidence (which may include a declaration of British connection[29]) sufficient to satisfy him that the ship is eligible to remain on the register[30]. If, at the expiry of that period of 30 days, the registrar is not so satisfied, he may either:

(a)     extend the notice and ask for further information or evidence[31]; or

(b)     serve a final notice which closes the ship's registration, such closure to take effect seven days after the service of that notice[32].

Where a ship's registration is so terminated, the registrar must issue a closure transcript[33] and the owner of the ship must forthwith surrender its certificate of registry[34].

Where the registrar terminates registration under head (1) or (4) above, he must forthwith issue a closure transcript to the owner of the ship and notify any mortgagees of the closure of the registration[35]. The registrar must issue a closure transcript also when he terminates registration under head (10) above[36]. On receipt of the closure transcript, the owner must immediately surrender the ship's certificate of registry to the registrar for cancellation[37].

Where the registration of a fishing vessel has been terminated by virtue of head (3) above, the ship may not again be registered[38] as a British ship[39] unless[40]:

(i)     the registrar consents to the vessel being so registered[41]; or

(ii)    the registrar is satisfied that the vessel has been disposed of by its former registered owner by means of a transaction at arm's length and that no person who for the time being is a relevant owner[42] of the vessel was a relevant owner of it at the time registration was terminated[43].

1   As to the meaning of 'registrar' see PARA 255 note 2.
2   Ie subject to the Merchant Shipping (Registration of Ships) Regulations 1993, SI 1993/3138, reg 101 (service of notices) (see the text and notes 28–34): see reg 56(1).
3   As to the meaning of 'ship' for these purposes see PARA 255 note 4.
4   Merchant Shipping (Registration of Ships) Regulations 1993, SI 1993/3138, reg 56(1).
5   Merchant Shipping (Registration of Ships) Regulations 1993, SI 1993/3138, reg 56(1)(a). As to the meaning of 'owner' for these purposes see PARA 255 note 13.
6   Merchant Shipping (Registration of Ships) Regulations 1993, SI 1993/3138, reg 56(1)(aa) (added by SI 1998/2976).
7   Merchant Shipping (Registration of Ships) Regulations 1993, SI 1993/3138, reg 56(1)(b).
8   Merchant Shipping (Registration of Ships) Regulations 1993, SI 1993/3138, reg 56(1)(c).
9   Merchant Shipping (Registration of Ships) Regulations 1993, SI 1993/3138, reg 56(1)(d); Interpretation Act 1978 s 17(2)(b).
10  As to the meaning of 'fishing vessel' for these purposes see PARA 255 note 7.
11  Merchant Shipping (Registration of Ships) Regulations 1993, SI 1993/3138, reg 56(1)(e).

12 Merchant Shipping (Registration of Ships) Regulations 1993, SI 1993/3138, reg 56(1)(f). As to the meaning of 'certificate of registry' see PARA 255 note 17.

13 As to the meaning of 'contravention' see PARA 51 note 3.

14 Merchant Shipping (Registration of Ships) Regulations 1993, SI 1993/3138, reg 56(1)(g); Interpretation Act 1978 s 17(2)(b).

15 Merchant Shipping (Registration of Ships) Regulations 1993, SI 1993/3138, reg 56(1)(h).

16 Ie except in the case of a fishing vessel below 24 metres in length to which the Merchant Shipping (Tonnage) Regulations 1997, SI 1997/1510, Pt IIA (regs 12A–12E) (measurement of smaller fishing vessels) (see PARA 248) does not apply: see the Merchant Shipping (Registration of Ships) Regulations 1993, SI 1993/3138, reg 56(1)(i) (added by SI 1998/1915). 'Length' in the Merchant Shipping (Registration of Ships) Regulations 1993, SI 1993/3138, reg 56, except in reg 56(4)(b) (see head (ii) in the text), has the same meaning as in the tonnage regulations: Merchant Shipping (Registration of Ships) Regulations 1993, SI 1993/3138, reg 1(2) (definition added by SI 1998/1915).

17 Ie not measured in accordance with the Merchant Shipping (Tonnage) Regulations 1997, SI 1997/1510 (see PARA 248): see the Merchant Shipping (Registration of Ships) Regulations 1993, SI 1993/3138, reg 56(1)(i) (as added: see note 16).

18 Merchant Shipping (Registration of Ships) Regulations 1993, SI 1993/3138, reg 56(1)(i) (as added: see note 16).

19 As to the meaning of 'register' see PARA 255 note 1.

20 Merchant Shipping (Registration of Ships) Regulations 1993, SI 1993/3138, reg 56(1)(j) (reg 56(1)(j)–(n) added by SI 1999/3206).

21 Merchant Shipping (Registration of Ships) Regulations 1993, SI 1993/3138, reg 56(1)(k) (as added: see note 20).

22 For these purposes, 'fishing vessel certificate' means a certificate of that name specified in the Merchant Shipping Act 1995 s 123 (as to which see PARA 609): Merchant Shipping (Registration of Ships) Regulations 1993, SI 1993/3138, reg 1(2) (definition added by SI 1999/3206).

23 Merchant Shipping (Registration of Ships) Regulations 1993, SI 1993/3138, reg 56(1)(l) (as added: see note 20).

24 Ie under the Merchant Shipping (Registration of Ships) Regulations 1993, SI 1993/3138, reg 50 (as to which see PARA 313): see reg 56(1)(m) (as added: see note 20).

25 Merchant Shipping (Registration of Ships) Regulations 1993, SI 1993/3138, reg 56(1)(m) (as added: see note 20).

26 Ie under the Merchant Shipping (Registration of Ships) Regulations 1993, SI 1993/3138, reg 51 (as to which see PARA 314): see reg 56(1)(n) (as added: see note 20).

27 Merchant Shipping (Registration of Ships) Regulations 1993, SI 1993/3138, reg 56(1)(n) (as added: see note 20).

28 Where the registrar serves a notice under the Merchant Shipping (Registration of Ships) Regulations 1993, SI 1993/3138, reg 101 on the owner of a vessel in respect of which a mortgage is registered, the registrar must send a copy of that notice to the mortgagee at the address recorded for him in the register: reg 102.

The term 'managing owner' is used in reg 23 (appointment of managing owner where ship has more than one owner) (as to which see PARA 271), as well as in reg 34, but it is not defined; however, see PARA 238.

29 As to the meaning of 'declaration of British connection' under the Merchant Shipping Act 1995 see PARA 245 note 3. As to the power to dispense with declarations or other evidence otherwise required under the Merchant Shipping (Registration of Ships) Regulations 1993, SI 1993/3138, see PARA 371.

30 Merchant Shipping (Registration of Ships) Regulations 1993, SI 1993/3138, reg 101(1) (amended by SI 1998/2976; SI 1999/3206).

31 Merchant Shipping (Registration of Ships) Regulations 1993, SI 1993/3138, reg 101(2)(a).

32 Merchant Shipping (Registration of Ships) Regulations 1993, SI 1993/3138, reg 101(2)(b).

33 For these purposes, 'closure transcript' means a certified extract from the register showing that the entry in the register in respect of a ship has been closed, the date of its closure, and the details about the ship and its ownership at the time of closure: Merchant Shipping (Registration of Ships) Regulations 1993, SI 1993/3138, reg 1(2).

34 Merchant Shipping (Registration of Ships) Regulations 1993, SI 1993/3138, reg 101(3).

35 Merchant Shipping (Registration of Ships) Regulations 1993, SI 1993/3138, reg 56(2).

36 Merchant Shipping (Registration of Ships) Regulations 1993, SI 1993/3138, reg 56(2A) (added by SI 1998/1915). In the case of fishing vessels of 24 metres or more in length, the closure transcript mentioned in the text has effect on or, as the case may be, after 1 January 1999; and, in the case of fishing vessels to which the Merchant Shipping (Tonnage) Regulations 1997, SI 1997/1510, Pt

IIA (see PARA 248) applies, it has effect on or, as the case may be, after the date on which Pt IIA applies to them: see the Merchant Shipping (Registration of Ships) Regulations 1993, SI 1993/3138, reg 56(2A) (as so added).

37 Merchant Shipping (Registration of Ships) Regulations 1993, SI 1993/3138, reg 56(3).

38 Ie without prejudice to the operation of any provision of the Merchant Shipping Act 1995 or the Merchant Shipping (Registration of Ships) Regulations 1993, SI 1993/3138: see reg 56(4); Interpretation Act 1978 s 17(2)(b).

39 As to the meaning of 'British ship' under the Merchant Shipping Act 1995 see PARA 230.

40 Merchant Shipping (Registration of Ships) Regulations 1993, SI 1993/3138, reg 56(4).

41 Merchant Shipping (Registration of Ships) Regulations 1993, SI 1993/3138, reg 56(4)(a).

42 For these purposes, a person is a relevant owner of a vessel at any time if at that time (Merchant Shipping (Registration of Ships) Regulations 1993, SI 1993/3138, reg 56(5)):
  (1)   the legal title to the vessel or any share in it is vested in that person (reg 56(5)(a)); or
  (2)   the vessel or any share in it is beneficially owned by that person (reg 56(5)(b)); or
  (3)   any share in a body corporate falling within head (1) or head (2) is legally or beneficially owned by that person (reg 56(5)(c)),
whether vested in or, as the case may be, owned by, that person alone or together with any other person or persons (reg 56(5)). As to the meaning of 'beneficial ownership' for these purposes see PARA 262 note 15.

43 Merchant Shipping (Registration of Ships) Regulations 1993, SI 1993/3138, reg 56(4)(b).

### (vii) Mortgages

#### A.   CREATION OF MORTGAGES

**318. Mortgages of registered ships.** A registered ship[1] (or share in a registered ship) may be made a security for the repayment of a loan or the discharge of any other obligation[2].

The instrument creating any such security (a 'mortgage') must be in the form prescribed by or approved under registration regulations[3]. Where a mortgage executed in this way is produced to the registrar[4], he must register the mortgage in the prescribed manner[5].

Mortgages must be registered in the order in which they are produced to the registrar for the purposes of registration[6].

1   As to the meaning of 'ship' see PARA 229. In connection with mortgages of unregistered ships see *The Shizelle* [1992] 2 Lloyd's Rep 444; in connection with mortgages of foreign-registered vessels see *Iraqi Ministry of Defence and others v Arcepey Shipping Co SA (Gillespie Brothers & Co Ltd intervening); The Angel Bell* [1980] 1 All ER 480; *Blue Sky One Ltd v Mahan Air; PK Airfinance US Inc v Blue Sky Two Ltd* [2010] EWHC 631 (Comm), [2010] All ER (D) 02 (Jun) (in particular at [151]–[155], per Beatson J).

2   Merchant Shipping Act 1995 s 16(1), Sch 1 para 7(1). As to the application of Sch 1 see PARA 252.

3   Merchant Shipping Act 1995 Sch 1 para 7(2). As to the meaning of 'registration regulations' see PARA 247. Accordingly, for the purposes of Sch 1, 'mortgage' must be construed in accordance with Sch 1 para 7(2): Sch 1 para 14. As to the prescribed form of mortgage see PARA 319. As to mortgaged vessels generally see MORTGAGE vol 77 (2016) PARA 101 et seq.

4   As to the meaning of 'registrar' for these purposes see PARA 254 note 11.

5   Merchant Shipping Act 1995 Sch 1 para 7(3). For these purposes, 'registered mortgage' means a mortgage registered under Sch 1 para 7(3): Sch 1 para 14. As to the prescribed manner of the registration of mortgages see PARA 320.

6   Merchant Shipping Act 1995 Sch 1 para 7(4). In addition, a charge on a ship or any share in a ship must be registered under the Companies Act 1985 s 396(1)(h) (prospectively repealed): see COMPANIES vol 15A (2016) PARA 1935. As to priority of registered mortgages see also PARAS 321–322.

**319. Form of mortgage.** A mortgage[1] produced for registration under the Merchant Shipping Act 1995[2], a transfer of a registered mortgage[3] and a discharge of a registered mortgage[4], must be in a form approved by the Secretary of State[5], in each case with appropriate attestation[6].

1   As to the meaning of 'mortgage' for the purposes of the Merchant Shipping Act 1995 see PARA 318 note 3.

2   Merchant Shipping (Registration of Ships) Regulations 1993, SI 1993/3138, reg 57(a); Interpretation Act 1978 s 17(2)(b). The text refers to the registration of mortgages of registered ships under the Merchant Shipping Act 1995 Sch 1 (as to which see PARA 318): see the Merchant Shipping (Registration of Ships) Regulations 1993, SI 1993/3138, reg 57(a); Interpretation Act 1978 s 17(2)(b).
3   Merchant Shipping (Registration of Ships) Regulations 1993, SI 1993/3138, reg 57(b). As to the meaning of 'registered mortgage' for the purposes of the Merchant Shipping Act 1995 see PARA 318 note 5.
4   Merchant Shipping (Registration of Ships) Regulations 1993, SI 1993/3138, reg 57(c).
5   As to the Secretary of State see PARA 36.
6   Merchant Shipping (Registration of Ships) Regulations 1993, SI 1993/3138, reg 57 (amended by SI 1994/541). As to the meaning of 'appropriate attestation' see PARA 308 note 3.

**320.  Registration of mortgage.** Where a mortgage on a ship[1] duly executed[2] is produced to the registrar[3] for registration, he must register the mortgage and endorse on it the date and time it was registered[4].

1   As to the meaning of 'mortgage' for the purposes of the Merchant Shipping Act 1995 see PARA 318 note 3. As to the meaning of 'ship' for these purposes see PARA 255 note 4.
2   Ie executed in accordance with the Merchant Shipping (Registration of Ships) Regulations 1993, SI 1993/3138, reg 57 (as to which see PARA 319): see reg 58.
3   As to the meaning of 'registrar' see PARA 255 note 2.
4   Merchant Shipping (Registration of Ships) Regulations 1993, SI 1993/3138, reg 58. In addition, a charge on a ship or any share in a ship must be registered under the Companies Act 1985 s 396(1)(h) (prospectively repealed): see COMPANIES vol 15A (2016) PARA 1935. As to priority of registered mortgages see also PARAS 321–322.

**321.  Priority of registered mortgages.** The rights of unregistered mortgagees are postponed to those of registered mortgagees, even though the date of the unregistered mortgage is antecedent to that of the registered mortgage[1], and even though the existence of the unregistered mortgage was known to the registered mortgagee when he took his mortgage[2]. The rights of the unregistered mortgagee are also postponed to those of a purchaser in good faith for value without notice from the legal owner[3], and to those of all persons with prior equities[4].

Where, under the Merchant Shipping Act 1995, two or more mortgages[5] are registered in respect of the same ship[6] or share, the priority of the mortgagees between themselves must be determined by the order in which the mortgages were registered, and not by reference to any other matter[7]. Where two or more mortgagees are registered in respect of the same ship or share, a subsequent mortgagee may not, except under an order of a court of competent jurisdiction, sell the ship without the concurrence of every prior mortgagee[8]. Registration regulations[9] may, however, provide for the giving to the registrar by intending mortgagees of 'priority notices' in a form prescribed by or approved under the regulations which, when recorded in the register[10], determine the priority of the interest to which the notice relates[11].

A mortgagee of a ship or share[12] has priority over the judgment creditors of the mortgagor[13], even though such creditors have a right in rem[14]. A registered mortgagee is entitled to the possession of the ship in priority to a subsequent purchaser without notice[15] and to a previous purchaser who has failed to register his title[16].

The rights of mortgagees are deferred to those of persons having either possessory[17] or maritime[18] liens.

1   *Coombes v Mansfield* (1855) 24 LJ Ch 513. As to the meaning of 'registered mortgage' for the purposes of the Merchant Shipping Act 1995 see PARA 318 note 5.
2   *Black v Williams* [1895] 1 Ch 408. Where a registered mortgagee has taken possession of ship and freight, he will be entitled to reimburse himself not only for his advances on the ship, but also for any advances he may have made on the freight without notice of other equitable charges: *Liverpool Marine Credit Co v Wilson* (1872) 7 Ch App 507, 1 Asp MLC 323.

3   See *Barclay & Co Ltd v Poole* [1907] 2 Ch 284, 10 Asp MLC 574. The rights of a legal mortgagee
    of a registered American ship who agreed with his mortgagor to conceal the mortgage in order to
    facilitate the sale of the ship in England were also postponed: *Hooper v Gumm* (1862) 2 John &
    H 602.
4   *Ward v Royal Exchange Shipping Co, ex p Harrison* (1887) 6 Asp MLC 239.
5   As to the meaning of 'mortgage' for the purposes of the Merchant Shipping Act 1995 see PARA 318
    note 3.
6   As to the meaning of 'ship' see PARA 229.
7   Merchant Shipping Act 1995 s 16(1), Sch 1 para 8(1). This provision is subject to Sch 1 para 8(2)
    (as to which see the text and notes 9–11): see Sch 1 para 8(1). As to the application of Sch 1 see
    PARA 252.
        In certain circumstances the priorities as between registered mortgages may not depend on the
    dates, and in such cases the statutory provisions do not apply. Thus, a first mortgagee whose
    mortgage is taken to cover future advances cannot claim over a second mortgagee the benefit of
    advances made after he has notice of the second mortgage: *The Benwell Tower* (1895) 8 Asp MLC
    13. A first registered mortgagee who enters into a subsequent mortgage agreement contained in a
    separate unregistered document will be postponed in respect of advances made under his
    unregistered mortgage to a second registered mortgagee, even though the latter had notice of the
    prior unregistered mortgage: *Parr v Applebee* (1855) 24 LJ Ch 767. Where a second mortgagee
    unsuccessfully disputes the claim of the first mortgagee, he will have to pay the costs of the dispute:
    *The Volant* (1864) Brown & Lush 321; *The Western Ocean* (1870) LR 3 A & E 38.
8   See the Merchant Shipping Act 1995 Sch 1 para 9(2); and PARA 333. This provision refers only
    to registered mortgagees; quaere whether unregistered mortgagees are within the principle. When
    a first mortgagee takes possession of the ship and freight, he may satisfy his own debt, and will then
    hold the balance for the benefit of subsequent mortgagees: *Tanner v Heard* (1857) 23 Beav 555;
    *The Benwell Tower* (1895) 8 Asp MLC 13. If there is such a balance, the first mortgagee becomes
    a trustee of the surplus proceeds and, if he retains them or converts them to his own use, the
    Limitation Act 1980 cannot be set up as a bar to a claim against him whether the trust is express
    or constructive: see s 21(1)(b); cf and *Banner v Berridge* (1881) 18 ChD 254, 4 Asp MLC 420
    (decided when such a bar could be set up in favour of a constructive trustee but not in favour of
    an express trustee).
9   As to the meaning of 'registration regulations' see PARA 247.
10  As to the meaning of 'register' for these purposes see PARA 254 note 2.
11  Merchant Shipping Act 1995 Sch 1 para 8(2). As to priority notices see PARA 322.
12  *The Harriet* (1868) 18 LT 804.
13  *Dickinson v Kitchen* (1858) 8 E & B 789. The rule applies even where garnishee orders have been
    obtained: *Japp v Campbell* (1887) 57 LJQB 79. See also *De Wolf v Pitcairn* (1869) 17 WR 914
    (creditor obtains debtor's rights subject to those of mortgagee); *Clydesdale Bank Ltd v Walker and
    Bain* 1926 SC 72. The creditors may arrest the ship in countries where the rights of mortgages,
    even though registered, are disregarded: *Liverpool Marine Credit Co v Hunter* (1868) 3 Ch
    App 479.
14  Ie as in the case of suppliers of goods and materials etc (*The Two Ellens* (1871) LR 3 A & E 345,
    1 Asp MLC 40; and see *Simpson v Fogo* (1860) 1 John & H 18; *Castrique v Behrens* (1861) 3 E
    & E 709; *The Pacific* (1864) Brown & Lush 243; *The Scio* (1867) LR 1 A & E 353). It is otherwise
    where the supplier has a possessory lien (*Williams v Allsup* (1861) 10 CBNS 417; *The Scio*). See
    also *The Zigurds (No 4)* [1932] P 113, 18 Asp MLC 324; and PARA 983. As to statutory rights
    in rem see PARA 973; and as to possessory lien see PARA 974. A mortgagee under a French
    *hypothèque*, although he has not the same right of property as under an English mortgage, has a
    right to arrest the ship in the hands of a subsequent owner. Since such a right resembles a maritime
    lien, the mortgagee is entitled under the *lex fori* to priority over suppliers of goods and materials
    etc: *The Colorado* [1923] P 102, 16 Asp MLC 145, CA.
15  *Cato v Irving* (1852) 5 De G & Sm 210.
16  *The Eastern Belle* (1875) 3 Asp MLC 19. Registered purchasers of shares are entitled, where they
    have contracted to do so, to apply the purchase money to paying off the ship's debts in priority to
    paying off an unregistered mortgage debt: *Barclay & Co Ltd v Poole* [1907] 2 Ch 284, 10 Asp
    MLC 574.
17  *Williams v Allsup* (1861) 10 CBNS 417; *The Scio* (1867) LR 1 A & E 353. Mortgagees, however,
    get their costs in priority to 'material men': *The Sherbro* (1883) 5 Asp MLC 88.
18  Ie as in the case of bottomry bond holders: *The Dowthorpe* (1843) 2 Wm Rob 73; and see *The
    Percy* (1837) 3 Hag Adm 402; *The Royal Arch* (1857) Sw 269. The principle applies even though
    the bond has been incurred in the course of a voyage taken in fraudulent breach of a contract
    existing between a mortgagor and mortgagee (*The Mary Ann* (1865) LR 1 A & E 8), or in the case
    of a master suing for wages or disbursements, even when appointed by the mortgagor (*The Mary
    Ann*; *The Feronia* (1868) LR 2 A & E 65; *The Ripon City* [1897] P 226, 8 Asp MLC 304). The

priority does not extend to any part of the mortgage debt personally guaranteed by the master: *The Bangor Castle* (1896) 8 Asp MLC 156. The master's right of priority does not extend to the recovery of the amount of a bond which he has been forced to enter into by reason of his own negligent navigation: *The Limerick* (1876) 1 PD 411, 3 Asp MLC 206, CA. As to bottomry bonds see PARA 435; as to crew's wages see *The Prince George* (1837) 3 Hag Adm 376 and PARA 484 et seq; and as to maritime liens see PARA 964 et seq.

**322. Notices by intending mortgagees; priority notices.** Where any person who is an intending mortgagee under a proposed mortgage of a registered ship[1] (or of a share in a registered ship)[2] notifies the registrar[3] of the interest which it is intended that he should have under the proposed mortgage, the registrar must record that interest[4]. The notice to the registrar for these purposes must be in a form approved by the Secretary of State and must contain the name[5] and official number of the ship[6], the name, address and signature of the intending mortgagor, the number of shares to be mortgaged, and the name and address of the intending mortgagee[7].

Where any person who is an intending mortgagee under a proposed mortgage of a ship which is not for the time being registered[8] (or of a share in any such ship)[9] notifies the registrar in writing of the interest which it is intended that he should have under the proposed mortgage[10], the registrar must record that interest in the register[11] and, if the ship is subsequently registered, must register the ship subject to that interest (or, if the mortgage has by then been duly executed[12] and produced to the registrar, subject to that mortgage)[13]. Such notice must be in a form approved by the Secretary of State and must contain the following information[14]:

(1)    the present name of the ship[15];
(2)    the intended name of the ship[16];
(3)    the approximate length of the ship[17];
(4)    where the ship is registered outside the United Kingdom[18], a copy of its certificate of registry[19] or other document evidencing its registration and giving its port of registration[20];
(5)    where the ship is a new ship, the builder's certificate[21] (or, if that is not available, the name and address of the builder and the ship's yard number)[22];
(6)    where the ship is neither a new ship nor a registered ship, details of any permanent marks on the ship which enable it to be clearly identified[23];
(7)    the name, address and signature of the intending mortgagor, the number of shares to be mortgaged, and the name and address of the intending mortgagee[24].

Any notification so given by a person[25], and anything done as a result of it, ceases to have effect[26]:

(a)    if the notification is withdrawn[27]; or
(b)    at the end of the period of 30 days beginning with the date of the notification, unless the notification is duly[28] renewed[29].

The person by whom any such notification is given may renew or further renew the notification on each occasion for a period of 30 days, by notice in writing given to the registrar before the end of the period mentioned in head (b) above[30] or before the end of a period of renewal[31], as the case may be[32].

In a case where the private law provisions relating to the priority of mortgages[33] operate to determine the priority between two or more mortgages[34] and where any of those mortgagees gave notification[35] with respect to his mortgage[36], those private law provisions have effect in relation to that mortgage as if it had been registered at the time when the relevant entry was made[37] in the register[38].

1   Merchant Shipping (Registration of Ships) Regulations 1993, SI 1993/3138, reg 59(1)(a). As to the meaning of 'ship' for these purposes see PARA 255 note 4.

2 Merchant Shipping (Registration of Ships) Regulations 1993, SI 1993/3138, reg 59(1)(b).

3 As to the meaning of 'registrar' see PARA 255 note 2. Any notice given under the Merchant Shipping (Registration of Ships) Regulations 1993, SI 1993/3138, reg 59 must be in a form approved by the Secretary of State: reg 59(8). As to the Secretary of State see PARA 36.

4 Merchant Shipping (Registration of Ships) Regulations 1993, SI 1993/3138, reg 59(1).

5 As to the proposal and approval of a ship's name see PARAS 277, 278.

6 As to the allocation of a ship's official number see PARA 279.

7 Merchant Shipping (Registration of Ships) Regulations 1993, SI 1993/3138, reg 59(2).

8 Merchant Shipping (Registration of Ships) Regulations 1993, SI 1993/3138, reg 59(3)(a).

9 Merchant Shipping (Registration of Ships) Regulations 1993, SI 1993/3138, reg 59(3)(b).

10 Merchant Shipping (Registration of Ships) Regulations 1993, SI 1993/3138, reg 59(3). As to notice given under reg 59 see note 3.

11 Merchant Shipping (Registration of Ships) Regulations 1993, SI 1993/3138, reg 59(3)(i). As to the meaning of 'register' see PARA 255 note 1.

12 Ie executed in accordance with the Merchant Shipping (Registration of Ships) Regulations 1993, SI 1993/3138, reg 57 (as to which see PARA 319): see reg 59(3)(ii).

13 Merchant Shipping (Registration of Ships) Regulations 1993, SI 1993/3138, reg 59(3)(ii).

14 Merchant Shipping (Registration of Ships) Regulations 1993, SI 1993/3138, reg 59(4).

15 Merchant Shipping (Registration of Ships) Regulations 1993, SI 1993/3138, reg 59(4)(a).

16 Merchant Shipping (Registration of Ships) Regulations 1993, SI 1993/3138, reg 59(4)(b).

17 Merchant Shipping (Registration of Ships) Regulations 1993, SI 1993/3138, reg 59(4)(c).

18 As to the meaning of 'United Kingdom' see PARA 16 note 3.

19 As to the meaning of 'certificate of registry' see PARA 255 note 17. As to the power to dispense with the production of a certificate in certain circumstances see PARA 376.

20 Merchant Shipping (Registration of Ships) Regulations 1993, SI 1993/3138, reg 59(4)(d).

21 As to the meaning of 'builder's certificate' see PARA 275 note 5.

22 Merchant Shipping (Registration of Ships) Regulations 1993, SI 1993/3138, reg 59(4)(e).

23 Merchant Shipping (Registration of Ships) Regulations 1993, SI 1993/3138, reg 59(4)(f).

24 Merchant Shipping (Registration of Ships) Regulations 1993, SI 1993/3138, reg 59(4)(g).

25 Ie under either the Merchant Shipping (Registration of Ships) Regulations 1993, SI 1993/3138, reg 59(1) (see the text and notes 1–4) or reg 59(3) (see the text and notes 8–13): see reg 59(6).

26 Merchant Shipping (Registration of Ships) Regulations 1993, SI 1993/3138, reg 59(6).

27 Merchant Shipping (Registration of Ships) Regulations 1993, SI 1993/3138, reg 59(6)(a).

28 Ie in accordance with the Merchant Shipping (Registration of Ships) Regulations 1993, SI 1993/3138, reg 59(7) (see the text and notes 30–32): see reg 59(6)(b).

29 Merchant Shipping (Registration of Ships) Regulations 1993, SI 1993/3138, reg 59(6)(b).

30 Merchant Shipping (Registration of Ships) Regulations 1993, SI 1993/3138, reg 59(7)(a). As to notice given under reg 59 see note 3.

31 Merchant Shipping (Registration of Ships) Regulations 1993, SI 1993/3138, reg 59(7)(b).

32 Merchant Shipping (Registration of Ships) Regulations 1993, SI 1993/3138, reg 59(7).

33 Ie the Merchant Shipping Act 1995 s 16(1), Sch 1 para 8 (as to which see PARA 321): see the Merchant Shipping (Registration of Ships) Regulations 1993, SI 1993/3138, reg 59(5)(a); Interpretation Act 1978 s 17(2)(b). As to the application of the Merchant Shipping Act 1995 Sch 1 see PARA 252.

34 Merchant Shipping (Registration of Ships) Regulations 1993, SI 1993/3138, reg 59(5)(a).

35 Ie under either the Merchant Shipping (Registration of Ships) Regulations 1993, SI 1993/3138, reg 59(1) (see the text and notes 1–4) or reg 59(3) (see the text and notes 8–13): see reg 59(5)(b).

36 Merchant Shipping (Registration of Ships) Regulations 1993, SI 1993/3138, reg 59(5)(b).

37 Ie under either the Merchant Shipping (Registration of Ships) Regulations 1993, SI 1993/3138, reg 59(1) (see the text and notes 1–4) or reg 59(3) (see the text and notes 8–13): see reg 59(5).

38 Merchant Shipping (Registration of Ships) Regulations 1993, SI 1993/3138, reg 59(5); Interpretation Act 1978 s 17(2)(b).

### B. TRANSFER AND TRANSMISSION OF REGISTERED MORTGAGES

**323. Transfer of registered mortgage.** A registered mortgage[1] may be transferred by an instrument made in the form prescribed[2] by or approved under registration regulations[3].

Where any such instrument is produced to the registrar[4], the registrar must register the transferee in the prescribed manner[5].

1 As to the meaning of 'mortgage' for the purposes of the Merchant Shipping Act 1995 see PARA 318 note 3; and as to the meaning of 'registered mortgage' for these purposes see PARA 318 note 5.

2  For these purposes, 'prescribed' means prescribed in registration regulations: Merchant Shipping
   Act 1995 s 16(1), Sch 1 para 14. As to the meaning of 'registration regulations' see PARA 247. As
   to the application of Sch 1 see PARA 252.
3  Merchant Shipping Act 1995 Sch 1 para 11(1).
4  As to the meaning of 'registrar' for these purposes see PARA 254 note 11.
5  Merchant Shipping Act 1995 Sch 1 para 11(2). As to registration of a transfer of mortgage see
   PARA 326.

### 324. Transmission of registered mortgage by operation of law. Where the
interest of a mortgagee in a registered mortgage[1] is transmitted to any person by
any lawful means other than by a transfer[2], the registrar[3] must, on production of
the prescribed[4] evidence, cause the name of that person to be entered in the
register[5] as mortgagee of the ship[6] or share in question[7].

1  As to the meaning of 'mortgage' for the purposes of the Merchant Shipping Act 1995 see PARA 318
   note 3; and as to the meaning of 'registered mortgage' for these purposes see PARA 318 note 5.
2  Ie other than by a transfer under the Merchant Shipping Act 1995 s 16(1), Sch 1 para 11 (see
   PARA 323): see Sch 1 para 12. As to the application of Sch 1 see PARA 252.
3  As to the meaning of 'registrar' for these purposes see PARA 254 note 11.
4  For these purposes, 'prescribed' means prescribed in registration regulations: Merchant Shipping
   Act 1995 Sch 1 para 14. As to the meaning of 'registration regulations' see PARA 247.
5  As to the meaning of 'register' for these purposes see PARA 254 note 2.
6  As to the meaning of 'ship' see PARA 229.
7  Merchant Shipping Act 1995 Sch 1 para 12. As to the evidence to be produced see PARA 325; and
   as to registration see PARA 326.

### 325. Evidence of transmission of mortgage. On the application for
registration[1] of a transmission of a registered mortgage[2], the evidence to be
produced to the registrar[3] is:
   (1)    a declaration of transmission of mortgage in a form approved by the
          Secretary of State[4]; and
   (2)    if the transmission was consequent on death, the grant of
          representation[5] (or any office copy thereof or an extract therefrom)[6]; or,
          if the transmission was consequent on bankruptcy, such evidence as is
          for the time being receivable in courts of justice as proof of title of
          persons claiming under bankruptcy[7]; or, if the transmission was
          consequent on an order of a court, a copy of the order of that court[8].

1  As to the meaning of 'application for registration' see PARA 269 note 1.
2  Ie as mentioned in the Merchant Shipping Act 1995 s 16(1), Sch 1 para 12 (see PARA 324): see the
   Merchant Shipping (Registration of Ships) Regulations 1993, SI 1993/3138, reg 60 (substituted by
   SI 1994/541); Interpretation Act 1978 s 17(2)(b).
3  As to the meaning of 'registrar' see PARA 255 note 2.
4  Merchant Shipping (Registration of Ships) Regulations 1993, SI 1993/3138, reg 60(a) (as
   substituted: see note 2). As to the Secretary of State see PARA 36. As to the power to dispense with
   declarations or other evidence otherwise required under the Merchant Shipping (Registration of
   Ships) Regulations 1993, SI 1993/3138, see PARA 371.
5  As to the meaning of 'representation' for these purposes see PARA 310 note 7.
6  Merchant Shipping (Registration of Ships) Regulations 1993, SI 1993/3138, reg 60(b)(i) (as
   substituted: see note 2).
7  Merchant Shipping (Registration of Ships) Regulations 1993, SI 1993/3138, reg 60(b)(ii) (as
   substituted: see note 2).
8  Merchant Shipping (Registration of Ships) Regulations 1993, SI 1993/3138, reg 60(b)(iii) (as
   substituted: see note 2).

### 326. Transfer or transmission of registered mortgage. Where a transfer of
a registered mortgage under the Merchant Shipping Act 1995[1], or evidence of a
transmission of a registered mortgage[2], is produced to the registrar[3], he must[4]:
   (1)    enter the name of the transferee (or the name of the person to whom the
          mortgage has been transmitted) in the register[5] as mortgagee of the ship[6]
          or share in question[7];

(2)  in respect of a transfer, endorse on the instrument of transfer the date and time the entry was made[8].

1  Ie under the Merchant Shipping Act 1995 s 16(1), Sch 1 para 11: see PARA 323. As to the meaning of 'mortgage' for the purposes of the Merchant Shipping Act 1995 see PARA 318 note 3; and as to the meaning of 'registered mortgage' for these purposes see PARA 318 note 5.
2  As to such evidence see PARA 325.
3  As to the meaning of 'registrar' see PARA 255 note 2.
4  Merchant Shipping (Registration of Ships) Regulations 1993, SI 1993/3138, reg 61 (substituted by SI 1994/541).
5  As to the meaning of 'register' see PARA 255 note 1.
6  As to the meaning of 'ship' for these purposes see PARA 255 note 4.
7  Merchant Shipping (Registration of Ships) Regulations 1993, SI 1993/3138, reg 61(a) (as substituted: see note 4).
8  Merchant Shipping (Registration of Ships) Regulations 1993, SI 1993/3138, reg 61(b) (as substituted: see note 4).

## C.  MORTGAGEE'S RIGHTS AND POWERS

**327.  In general.** The rights of mortgagees of ships are, so far as the special nature of the security permits, governed by the rules of law laid down in respect of the mortgages of other chattels[1]. However, as a ship differs in many respects from other forms of security[2], these rights have been the subject of special statutory enactments and numerous decisions[3].

1  *Thompson v Smith* (1815) 1 Madd 395; *The Benwell Tower* (1895) 8 Asp MLC 13; *Fletcher and Campbell v City Marine Finance Ltd* [1968] 2 Lloyd's Rep 520. As to rights of a mortgagee generally see MORTGAGE vol 77 (2016) PARA 395 et seq.
2  *Hooper v Gumm, McLellan v Gumm* (1867) 2 Ch App 282.
3  See PARA 328 et seq.

**328.  Protection of registered mortgagees.** Where a ship[1] or share is subject to a registered mortgage[2] then[3]:
(1)  except so far as may be necessary for making the ship or share available as a security for the mortgage debt, the mortgagee is not by reason of the mortgage to be treated as owner of the ship or share[4]; and
(2)  the mortgagor is to be treated as not having ceased to be owner of the ship or share[5].
The result is that, while as between the parties to the mortgage the property in the ship has passed[6], so far as regards third persons, the mortgagor remains in charge with regard to everything connected with the employment of the ship[7], and the mortgagee is protected from liabilities connected with her[8].

1  As to the meaning of 'ship' see PARA 229.
2  As to the meaning of 'mortgage' for the purposes of the Merchant Shipping Act 1995 see PARA 318 note 3; and as to the meaning of 'registered mortgage' for these purposes see PARA 318 note 5.
3  Merchant Shipping Act 1995 s 16(1), Sch 1 para 10. As to the application of Sch 1 see PARA 252.
4  Merchant Shipping Act 1995 Sch 1 para 10(a).
5  Merchant Shipping Act 1995 Sch 1 para 10(b).
6  *The Blanche* (1887) 6 Asp MLC 272.
7  *Keith v Burrows* (1877) 2 App Cas 636, 3 Asp MLC 481, HL; and see *Collins v Lamport* (1864) 4 De GJ & Sm 500.
8  *Dickinson v Kitchen* (1858) 8 E & B 789. As between himself and the mortgagor, the mortgagee may assume some of the liabilities of the owner of a ship: *Hudson and Humphrey v Swiftsure (Owners), The Swiftsure* (1900) 9 Asp MLC 65.

**329.  Injunction at suit of charterer against mortgagees out of possession.** An injunction may be granted at the suit of the charterers from a mortgagor of a ship to restrain registered mortgagees who are out of possession[1] from dealing with the ship in any manner which may interfere with the execution of the charterparty, provided that it is not shown that the charterparty is in any way prejudicial to the sufficiency of the mortgagees' security[2]. If, however, the charterparty impairs their security, the mortgagees are not bound by it[3].

1 As to the mortgagees' right to possession and their position when in possession see PARA 330 et seq.

2 *Collins v Lamport* (1864) 4 De GJ & Sm 500; *The Fanchon* (1880) 5 PD 173, 4 Asp MLC 272; *The Heather Bell* [1901] P 272, 9 Asp MLC 206, CA. See also the Merchant Shipping Act 1995 s 16(1), Sch 1 para 10 (cited in PARA 328); and CIVIL PROCEDURE vol 12 (2015) PARA 1152. Cf *The Lord Strathcona* [1925] P 143, 16 Asp MLC 536 (mortgagor unable to perform the charterparty; mortgagee granted order for sale); and see PARA 331 note 7.

3 *Law Guarantee and Trust Society v Russian Bank for Foreign Trade* [1905] 1 KB 815, 10 Asp MLC 41, CA. See also *The Heather Bell* [1901] P 272, 9 Asp MLC 206, CA; *The Manor* [1907] P 339, 10 Asp MLC 446, CA.

**330. Mortgagee's right to possession.** The chief right of a mortgagee of a ship[1], or of a majority of shares in a ship, is the right in proper circumstances to take possession. This he may do even before any part of the mortgage debt is due[2] if his security is being impaired[3] in some material way[4].

Possession may be either actual or constructive. Actual possession may be taken either by putting a person in possession without the assistance of the court, or by the arrest of the ship in a mortgagee's action[5]. To obtain constructive possession the mortgagee must clearly indicate his intention to assume the rights of ownership[6].

Where the mortgagee is justified in taking possession, and in so doing has been compelled to pay off claims for wages or disbursements, or to incur other expenses to avoid the exercise of a maritime lien[7] by third persons, he can recover the amount expended from the mortgagor[8].

1 *Japp v Campbell* (1887) 57 LJQB 79. As to the position of mortgagor and mortgagee generally see PARA 328.

2 In considering whether any part of the mortgage debt is due, the court will enforce all the equities between the parties: *The Cathcart* (1867) LR 1 A & E 314.

3 *The Blanche* (1887) 6 Asp MLC 272; *The Manor* [1907] P 339, 10 Asp MLC 446, CA. The security may be impaired by the action of the mortgagor himself, eg by the carriage of contraband (*Law Guarantee and Trust Society v Russian Bank for Foreign Trade* [1905] 1 KB 815, 10 Asp MLC 41, CA), or by so working the ship as to render her constantly liable to arrest (*The Manor*), or by the action of other persons, such as creditors, who may desire to seize the ship (*Dickinson v Kitchen* (1858) 8 E & B 789). See also *The Lord Strathcona* [1925] P 143, 16 Asp MLC 536; *Jackson v Vernon* (1789) 1 Hy Bl 114; *Baker v Buckle* (1822) 7 Moore CP 349; *Briggs v Wilkinson* (1827) 7 B & C 30; *The Celtic King* [1894] P 175, 7 Asp MLC 400; *The Myrto* [1977] 2 Lloyd's Rep 243 (on appeal [1978] 1 Lloyd's Rep 11, CA). In the following cases the security was held not to be impaired: *De Mattos v Gibson* (1858) 5 Jur NS 347; *Collins v Lamport* (1864) 4 De GJ & Sm 500; *The Innisfallen* (1866) LR 1 A & E 72; *The Cathcart* (1867) LR 1 A & E 314; *The Maxima* (1878) 4 Asp MLC 21; *Cory Bros & Co v Stewart* (1886) 2 TLR 508, CA; *The Blanche* (1887) 6 Asp MLC 272.

4 It is not enough merely to show that the enforcement of the security is about to be rendered difficult by the removal of the ship from the jurisdiction: *The Fanchon* (1880) 5 PD 173, 4 Asp MLC 272. Nor will the mortgagee be entitled to bail in such a case (*The Highlander* (1843) 2 Wm Rob 109); nor is it enough to show that the ship is not profitably employed (*Keith v Burrows* (1877) 2 App Cas 636, 3 Asp MLC 481, HL). As to failure to insure see *Laming & Co v Seater* (1889) 16 R 828; *The Heather Bell* [1901] P 272, 9 Asp MLC 206, CA; *Law Guarantee and Trust Society v Russian Bank for Foreign Trade* [1905] 1 KB 815, 10 Asp MLC 41, CA.

5 See PARA 161 et seq. Where the charterparty is not prejudicial to the security, a mortgagee of shares may not bring an action of restraint: *The Innisfallen* (1866) LR 1 A & E 72. As to costs see *The Kestrel* (1866) LR 1 A & E 78; applied in *Re Adelphi Hotel (Brighton) Ltd, District Bank Ltd v Adelphi Hotel (Brighton) Ltd* [1953] 2 All ER 498, [1953] 1 WLR 955. As to mortgagees' possession generally see MORTGAGE vol 77 (2016) PARA 419 et seq.

6 *The Benwell Tower* (1895) 8 Asp MLC 13. See also *Rusden v Pope* (1868) LR 3 Exch 269; *Beynon v Godden* (1878) 3 Ex D 263, 4 Asp MLC 10, CA.

7 As to maritime liens see PARA 964 et seq.

8 The mortgagee recovers on the principle that he has paid a debt for which another was liable by compulsion of law: *Johnson v Royal Mail Steam Packet Co* (1867) LR 3 CP 38; *The Orchis* (1890)

15 PD 38, 6 Asp MLC 501, CA; *The Heather Bell* [1901] P 272, 9 Asp MLC 206, CA. As to this principle generally see RESTITUTION vol 88 (2012) PARA 463 et seq. The principle appears to cover both the payment off of claims for wages and of those for disbursements: *The Blazer* (6 February 1911, unreported). It appears that the correct course for a mortgagee who has paid off liens or who desires to do so is to obtain leave from the court to stand in the shoes of the lien holder as against the mortgagor: *The Blazer*. To what extent the mortgagee may recover in rem money so paid in addition to the mortgage debt seems doubtful: *The Cornelia Henrietta* (1866) LR 1 A & E 51; *The St Lawrence* (1880) 5 PD 250; *The Tagus* [1903] P 44, 9 Asp MLC 371. Mortgagees of shares in a ship will not be held liable to contribute to the paying off of liens by other part owners, and will not be held impliedly to have authorised such payment merely from the fact that their property may have been thereby benefited: *The Ripon City* [1898] P 78, 8 Asp MLC 391.

### 331. General position of mortgagee in possession.
On taking possession[1], the mortgagee becomes entitled to enjoy any contractual rights relating to the employment of the ship into which the mortgagor may have entered[2]. The mortgagee, in addition to being liable for expenses incurred in the future working of the ship[3], is, however, bound[4] to perform contractual duties incurred by the mortgagor which are of a kind usually incurred by a person who has the apparent ownership and control of a vessel[5], provided that such engagements relate solely to the future[6] and are not of such a nature as to impair the security[7].

1  As to the mortgagee's right to take possession see PARA 330.
2  *Gumm v Tyrie* (1865) 6 B & S 298, Ex Ch; *Keith v Burrows* (1877) 2 App Cas 636, 3 Asp MLC 481, HL; *Stellar Chartering and Brokerage Inc v Efibanca-Ente Finanziario Interbancario SpA, The Span Terza (No 2)* [1984] 1 WLR 27, [1984] 1 Lloyd's Rep 119, HL (charterparty provided for delivery of bunkers to shipowners on delivery of vessel; mortgagees obtained order for sale of vessel; charterparty cancelled prematurely; term did not apply literally where premature cancellation, and no reason to imply it). As to the right to freight and the right to sell see PARAS 332, 333.
3  *Re Litherland, ex p Howden* (1842) 2 Mont D & De G 574.
4  *Collins v Lamport* (1864) 4 De GJ & Sm 500; *Cory Bros & Co v Stewart* (1886) 2 TLR 508, CA.
5  *Williams v Allsup* (1861) 10 CBNS 417; *Johnson v Royal Mail Steam Packet Co* (1867) LR 3 CP 38.
6  Neither the mortgagee nor the ship, when it has passed into his possession, is liable to the mortgagor's creditors unless such creditors are in a position to exercise a maritime lien: *The Troubadour* (1866) LR 1 A & E 302; *The El Argentino* [1909] P 236, 11 Asp MLC 280; *Clydesdale Bank Ltd v Walker and Bain* 1926 SC 72. As to maritime liens see PARA 964 et seq. Although not personally liable, the mortgagee may always come in and defend the ship when sued, but only such defences are open to him as would have been open to the mortgagor: *The Julindur* (1853) 1 Ecc & Ad 71; *The Chieftain* (1863) Brown & Lush 104.
7  *Law Guarantee and Trust Society v Russian Bank for Foreign Trade* [1905] 1 KB 815, 10 Asp MLC 41, CA. It appears that the mortgagee will not be bound, even though the contract was entered into before the mortgage came into existence, provided that he cannot be considered to have had notice or its equivalent (*The Celtic King* [1894] P 175, 7 Asp MLC 440); but see *Law Guarantee and Trust Society v Russian Bank for Foreign Trade*. If the mortgagee takes his mortgage with knowledge of a contract, he is bound: *De Mattos v Gibson* (1858) 5 Jur NS 347. Cf *The Lord Strathcona* [1925] P 143, 16 Asp MLC 536 (where the question whether a mortgagee is bound by a prior charterparty of which he had notice is discussed). As to impairment of the security see the cases cited in PARA 330 note 3.

### 332. Mortgagee's right to freight.
Until the mortgagee takes possession[1], the earnings of the ship, apart from special stipulation, remain the property of the mortgagor[2], but, directly the mortgagee takes possession, he becomes entitled to all the freight[3] not already due and payable[4]. When the freight has once come into the mortgagor's hands, the mortgagee, unless by some right other than that afforded by the mere mortgage[5], cannot recover it from him[6].

1  As to the mortgagee's right to take possession see PARA 330.
2  *Keith v Burrows* (1877) 2 App Cas 636, 3 Asp MLC 481, HL; and see *Rusden v Pope* (1868) LR 3 Exch 269; *Brown v Tanner* (1868) 3 Ch App 597; *Liverpool Marine Credit Co v Wilson* (1872) 7 Ch App 507, 1 Asp MLC 323, CA; *Wilson v Wilson* (1872) LR 14 Eq 32, 1 Asp MLC 265; *Anderson v Butler's Wharf Co Ltd* (1879) 48 LJ Ch 824; *The Benwell Tower* (1895) 8 Asp MLC 13. As to a separate mortgage of freight see MORTGAGE vol 77 (2016) PARA 213; and as to the position of the mortgagor and mortgagee generally see PARA 328.

3    The freight to which the mortgagee is entitled is the gross freight without any deduction of sums which may be due to the charterer from the mortgagor (*Tanner v Phillips* (1872) 42 LJ Ch 125, 1 Asp MLC 448), or of any expenditure not authorised by him incurred in the earning of the freight (*The El Argentino* [1909] P 236, 11 Asp MLC 280). As to the position of an assignee of freight see PARA 334; and as to the payment of freight generally see CARRIAGE AND CARRIERS vol 7 (2015) PARA 568 et seq.

4    If possession is taken before the voyage is concluded by the delivery or the cargo, the mortgagee is entitled to freight: *Cato v Irving* (1852) 5 De G & Sm 210; *Brown v Tanner* (1868) 3 Ch App 597. It is doubtful whether the mortgagee is entitled to the freight where the mortgagor has landed the goods retaining a lien for freight: *Belfast Harbour Comrs v Lawther and Marine Investment Society, The Edward Cardwell* (1865) 12 LT 677. The mortgagee is not entitled to freight, even though unpaid at the time of taking possession, if he has not taken possession until the cargo is delivered and the freight earned: *Shillito v Biggart* [1903] 1 KB 683, 9 Asp MLC 396. A mortgagee of shares is entitled to his proper share of freight earned and received after taking possession: *Alexander v Simms* (1854) 5 De GM & G 57; *Essarts v Whinney* (1903) 9 Asp MLC 363, CA. In certain cases the court may appoint a receiver: *Burn v Herlofson and Siemensen, The Faust* (1887) 6 Asp MLC 126, CA; and see RECEIVERS vol 88 (2012) PARA 13 et seq.

5    *Willis v Palmer* (1860) 7 CBNS 340.

6    *Gardner v Cazenove* (1856) 1 H & N 423.

**333. Registered mortgagee's power of sale.** A registered mortgagee[1] in possession has complete control over the ship[2].

Every registered mortgagee has power, if the mortgage money or any part of it is due, to sell the ship[3] or share in respect of which he is registered, and to give effectual receipts for the purchase money[4]. However, where two or more mortgagees are registered in respect of the same ship or share, a subsequent mortgagee may not, except under an order of a court of competent jurisdiction[5], sell the ship or share without the concurrence of every prior mortgagee[6].

A mortgagee may recover the expenses of the sale from the mortgagor[7].

1    As to the creation of mortgages see PARA 318 et seq.

2    *The Fairport* (1884) 10 PD 13, 5 Asp MLC 348 (dismissal of master). As to the mortgagee's right to take possession see PARA 330.

3    As to the meaning of 'ship' see PARA 229.

4    Merchant Shipping Act 1995 s 16(1), Sch 1 para 9(1). As to the application of Sch 1 see PARA 252.

5    As to the court's power of sale see PARA 241.

6    Merchant Shipping Act 1995 Sch 1 para 9(2). As to priorities of registered mortgages see PARA 321. The court may grant a sale to a mortgagee of shares: *The Fairlie* (1868) 37 LJ Adm 66. A mortgagee in possession is not bound to sell the ship, but may employ her in such a way as not to impair her value, and must not sell her disadvantageously: *European and Australian Royal Mail Co Ltd v Royal Mail Steam Packet Co* (1858) 4 K & J 676; *Marriott v Anchor Reversionary Co* (1861) 3 De GF & J 177; *Haviland Routh & Co v Thomson* (1864) 3 M 313. The mortgagee cannot be compelled by other persons interested to employ the ship instead of selling her: *Samuel v Jones* (1862) 7 LT 760. As between the mortgagor and mortgagee, the mortgagee may agree to terms limiting his powers of sale: *Brouard v Dumaresque* (1841) 3 Moo PCC 457; *Dickinson v Kitchen* (1858) 8 E & B 789.

7    *Wilkes v Saunion* (1877) 7 ChD 188.

**334. Position of assignee of freight.** An assignee of freight[1] has no rights as against a first mortgagee who has taken possession of freight by virtue of his mortgage[2], unless the assigned freight became due and payable before possession was taken[3]; but the assignee of freight has priority over a second mortgagee, even though he has taken the assignment with notice of the second mortgage[4]. Assignees of freight are entitled to the whole freight mentioned in the bill of lading, without deduction of amounts due from the assignor to the consignees[5].

1    As to a mortgagee's right to freight see PARA 332.

2    See *Liverpool Marine Credit Co v Wilson* (1872) 7 Ch App 507, 1 Asp MLC 323; *Wilson v Wilson* (1872) LR 14 Eq 32, 1 Asp MLC 265; *The Benwell Tower* (1895) 8 Asp MLC 13; *Black v Williams* [1895] 1 Ch 408. Assignments of freight, if legal, are governed by the Law of Property Act 1925 s 136(1) (see CHOSES IN ACTION vol 13 (2017) PARA 14 et seq) or, if equitable, by the rules of equity (see CHOSES IN ACTION vol 13 (2017) PARA 24 et seq).

3  *Shillito v Biggart* [1903] 1 KB 683, 9 Asp MLC 396. See also *Re The Pride of Wales and The Annie Lisle (Mortgagees)* (1867) 15 LT 606 (priority of trustee in bankruptcy); *Ward v Royal Exchange Shipping Co, ex p Harrison* (1887) 6 Asp MLC 239 (priority of debenture holders); *The Benwell Tower* (1895) 8 Asp MLC 13 (priority of second mortgagees); *Smith v Zigurds (Owners) and EA Casper, Edgar & Co Ltd* [1934] AC 209, 47 Ll L Rep 267, HL (priority of assignee). The usual rule as among persons with equitable charges is that he who is first has the strongest right: see EQUITABLE JURISDICTION vol 47 (2014) PARA 122.
4  *Liverpool Marine Credit Co v Wilson* (1872) 7 Ch App 507, 1 Asp MLC 323, CA.
5  *Weguelin v Cellier* (1873) LR 6 HL 286. As to the mortgage of freight see MORTGAGE vol 77 (2016) PARA 213.

D.   DISCHARGE OF REGISTERED MORTGAGES

**335. Discharge of mortgages.** Where a registered mortgage[1] has been discharged, the registrar[2] must, on production of the mortgage deed and with such evidence of the discharge as may be prescribed[3], cause an entry to be made in the register[4] to the effect that the mortgage has been discharged[5].

If for good reason the registered mortgage cannot be produced to the registrar, he may, on being satisfied that the mortgage has been properly discharged, record in the register that the mortgage has been discharged[6].

1  As to the meaning of 'mortgage' for the purposes of the Merchant Shipping Act 1995 see PARA 318 note 3; and as to the meaning of 'registered mortgage' for these purposes see PARA 318 note 5.
2  As to the meaning of 'registrar' for these purposes see PARA 254 note 11.
3  For these purposes, 'prescribed' means prescribed in registration regulations: Merchant Shipping Act 1995 s 16(1), Sch 1 para 14. As to the meaning of 'registration regulations' see PARA 247. As to the application of Sch 1 see PARA 252.
4  As to the meaning of 'register' see PARA 254 note 2.
5  Merchant Shipping Act 1995 Sch 1 para 13. Accordingly, where a registered mortgage has been discharged, the registrar must, on production of the mortgage deed and with such evidence of the discharge as satisfies him that the mortgage has been discharged, record in the register that the mortgage has been discharged: Merchant Shipping (Registration of Ships) Regulations 1993, SI 1993/3138, reg 62(1). As to the meaning of 'register' for these purposes see PARA 255 note 1; and as to the meaning of 'registrar' for these purposes see PARA 255 note 2.
6  Merchant Shipping (Registration of Ships) Regulations 1993, SI 1993/3138, reg 62(2).

**336. Effect of termination of registration on registered mortgage.** Where the registration of a ship[1] terminates[2], that termination does not affect any entry in the register[3] of any undischarged registered mortgage[4] of that ship or any share in it[5].

1  As to the meaning of 'ship' for these purposes see PARA 255 note 4.
2  Ie by virtue of the Merchant Shipping (Registration of Ships) Regulations 1993, SI 1993/3138: see reg 63. As to the termination of a ship's registration see PARA 317.
3  As to the meaning of 'register' for these purposes see PARA 255 note 1.
4  As to the meaning of 'mortgage' for the purposes of the Merchant Shipping Act 1995 see PARA 318 note 3; and as to the meaning of 'registered mortgage' for these purposes see PARA 318 note 5.
5  Merchant Shipping (Registration of Ships) Regulations 1993, SI 1993/3138, reg 63.

(viii)   Provisional Registration

**337. Provisional registration.** Where a ship[1] which the owner[2] intends should be registered on Part I or Part II of the register[3] is outside the British Islands[4], the owner may apply to the registrar[5] for provisional registration, or, if the ship is at a port outside the British Islands, the owner may alternatively apply to the appropriate person[6] for provisional registration of the ship[7].

1  As to the meaning of 'ship' for these purposes see PARA 255 note 4.
2  As to the meaning of 'owner' for these purposes see PARA 255 note 13.
3  As to the meaning of 'register' for these purposes see PARA 255 note 1. Part I of the register, as mentioned in the text, is for ships, owned by qualified persons, which are not fishing vessels or registered on that Part which is restricted to small ships: see the Merchant Shipping (Registration

of Ships) Regulations 1993, SI 1993/3138, reg 2(1)(a); and PARA 255. Part II of the register is for fishing vessels: see reg 2(1)(b); and PARA 255. As to the status of any Part II certificate under sea fisheries legislation see PARA 377. As to the meaning of 'fishing vessel' for these purposes see PARA 255 note 7; and as to the meaning of 'small ship' for these purposes see PARA 255 note 6.

4 As to the meaning of 'British Islands' see STATUTES AND LEGISLATIVE PROCESS vol 96 (2012) PARA 1208.

5 As to the meaning of 'registrar' for these purposes see PARA 255 note 2.

6 For these purposes, 'appropriate person' means (by virtue of the Merchant Shipping (Registration of Ships) Regulations 1993, SI 1993/3138, reg 1(2)), in relation to a port in a country outside the British Islands:

(1)  any British consular officer within whose consular district the port lies;

(2)  where Her Majesty's government in the United Kingdom is represented in that country by a High Commissioner, any member of the High Commissioner's official staff nominated by him for the purposes of the Merchant Shipping (Registration of Ships) Regulations 1993, SI 1993/3138; or

(3)  where that country is a colony, the governor of the colony or any person appointed by him for those purposes; and 'High Commissioner' includes an acting High Commissioner and 'governor' includes an acting governor.

As to the meaning of 'colony' see STATUTES AND LEGISLATIVE PROCESS vol 96 (2012) PARA 1208. As to British consular officers see INTERNATIONAL RELATIONS LAW vol 61 (2010) PARA 30.

7 Merchant Shipping (Registration of Ships) Regulations 1993, SI 1993/3138, reg 64. As to applications for provisional registration see PARA 338.

**338. Application for provisional registration.** An application for provisional registration[1] must be in a form approved by the Secretary of State[2] and must be accompanied by the prescribed particulars[3].

Where application is made to the appropriate person[4], he must forward those particulars to the registrar[5] who must, if he is satisfied that the ship[6] is eligible for registration, notify the appropriate person accordingly[7].

1  As to provisional registration see PARA 337.

2  As to the Secretary of State see PARA 36.

3  Merchant Shipping (Registration of Ships) Regulations 1993, SI 1993/3138, reg 65 (amended by SI 1994/541). The particulars so prescribed are those required by the Merchant Shipping (Registration of Ships) Regulations 1993, SI 1993/3138, reg 22(1) (applications for registration) (as to which see PARA 272) and reg 24 (applications by bodies corporate) (as to which see PARA 273): see reg 65 (as so amended). As to the requirement to supply supplementary information or evidence where that provided on an application for registration is judged to be either not correct or insufficient see PARA 372. Documents not in the English language which are produced in support of any application under the Merchant Shipping (Registration of Ships) Regulations 1993, SI 1993/3138 must be accompanied by a translation: see PARA 369.

4  As to the meaning of 'appropriate person' for these purposes see PARA 337 note 6.

5  As to the meaning of 'registrar' for these purposes see PARA 255 note 2.

6  As to the meaning of 'ship' for these purposes see PARA 255 note 4.

7  Merchant Shipping (Registration of Ships) Regulations 1993, SI 1993/3138, reg 66.

**339. Certification of provisional registration and its terms.** The registrar[1], on being satisfied that the ship[2] is eligible for provisional registration[3], or the appropriate person[4] on receipt of such notification[5] (but not otherwise), may proceed to register the ship provisionally for a period of three months[6].

The registrar or the appropriate person must issue to the owner[7] of the ship a certificate of provisional registration in a form approved by the Secretary of State[8]. The certificate has the effect of a certificate of registry[9] until[10]:

(1)  the expiration of three months from its date of issue[11]; or

(2)  the ship's arrival in the United Kingdom[12]; or

(3)  termination by the registrar on request from the owner[13],

whichever first occurs[14].

Where a ship has been provisionally registered once, it may not be provisionally registered again within one year of the date of the issue of the certificate of provisional registration, except with the consent of the registrar[15].

1  As to the meaning of 'registrar' for these purposes see PARA 255 note 2.
2  As to the meaning of 'ship' for these purposes see PARA 255 note 4.
3  As to provisional registration see PARA 337; and as to applications for provisional registration see PARA 338.
4  As to the meaning of 'appropriate person' for these purposes see PARA 337 note 6.
5  Ie notification made to the appropriate person by the registrar that he (the registrar) is satisfied that the ship is eligible for registration: see PARA 338.
6  Merchant Shipping (Registration of Ships) Regulations 1993, SI 1993/3138, reg 67.
7  As to the meaning of 'owner' for these purposes see PARA 255 note 13.
8  Merchant Shipping (Registration of Ships) Regulations 1993, SI 1993/3138, reg 68. As to the Secretary of State see PARA 36.
9  As to the meaning of 'certificate of registry' see PARA 255 note 17.
10  Merchant Shipping (Registration of Ships) Regulations 1993, SI 1993/3138, reg 68.
11  Merchant Shipping (Registration of Ships) Regulations 1993, SI 1993/3138, reg 68(a).
12  Merchant Shipping (Registration of Ships) Regulations 1993, SI 1993/3138, reg 68(b). As to the meaning of 'United Kingdom' see PARA 16 note 3.
13  Merchant Shipping (Registration of Ships) Regulations 1993, SI 1993/3138, reg 68(c).
14  Merchant Shipping (Registration of Ships) Regulations 1993, SI 1993/3138, reg 68.
15  Merchant Shipping (Registration of Ships) Regulations 1993, SI 1993/3138, reg 69.

**340. Condition of provisional registration for fishing vessels.** It is a condition of provisional registration for fishing vessels[1] that the vessel must not fish for profit while so registered[2]; and, if any provisionally registered vessel does fish for profit, its provisional registration immediately thereon terminates and the owner must as soon as practicable surrender the certificate of provisional registration[3] to the registrar[4].

1  As to the meaning of 'fishing vessel' for these purposes see PARA 255 note 7. As to provisional registration see PARA 337; as to applications for provisional registration see PARA 338; and as to the certification of provisional registration and its terms see PARA 339.
2  Merchant Shipping (Registration of Ships) Regulations 1993, SI 1993/3138, reg 70.
3  As to the certificate of provisional registration see PARA 339.
4  Merchant Shipping (Registration of Ships) Regulations 1993, SI 1993/3138, reg 70. As to the meaning of 'registrar' for these purposes see PARA 255 note 2.

## (ix) Transfers to, from or within the Register

**341. Transfer of registration to relevant British possession.** The registration of a ship[1] registered on Part I of the register[2] may be transferred from the register to the register of a port in a relevant British possession[3]. Where such an application is made for the transfer of a ship's registration, the registrar[4] must not proceed to deal with the application unless he is satisfied that registration of the ship at the intended port of registration is not precluded by either[5]:

(1)     any Order in Council in force under the Merchant Shipping Act 1995[6]; or
(2)     any provision of the law in force in the possession in question[7];

and any certificate purporting to be signed by the registrar of the intended port of registration and stating that any such provision is in force is conclusive evidence for the purposes of these provisions of the matters stated in it[8].

Where the registrar of the intended port of registration issues a certificate of registry[9] following any such application and on notification of the transfer by the registrar of the new port of registration, the registrar must terminate the registration of the ship[10].

Where the registration of a ship is transferred in this way[11], the certificate of registry must be surrendered to the registrar for cancellation[12].

1 As to the meaning of 'ship' for these purposes see PARA 255 note 4.
2 As to the meaning of 'register' for these purposes see PARA 255 note 1. Part I of the register, as mentioned in the text, is for ships, owned by qualified persons, which are not fishing vessels or registered on that Part which is restricted to small ships: see the Merchant Shipping (Registration of Ships) Regulations 1993, SI 1993/3138, reg 2(1)(a); and PARA 255. As to the meaning of 'fishing vessel' for these purposes see PARA 255 note 7; and as to the meaning of 'small ship' for these purposes see PARA 255 note 6.
3 Merchant Shipping (Registration of Ships) Regulations 1993, SI 1993/3138, reg 71(1). As to the meaning of 'relevant British possession' under the Merchant Shipping Act 1995 see PARA 16 note 3. As to the registrar's power, in certain circumstances, to transfer the registration of a ship from one Part of the register to a different Part see the Merchant Shipping (Registration of Ships) Regulations 1993, SI 1993/3138, reg 72A; and PARA 343.
4 As to the meaning of 'registrar' for these purposes see PARA 255 note 2.
5 Merchant Shipping (Registration of Ships) Regulations 1993, SI 1993/3138, reg 71(2).
6 Merchant Shipping (Registration of Ships) Regulations 1993, SI 1993/3138, reg 71(2)(a); Interpretation Act 1978 s 17(2)(b). The text refers to any Order in Council in force under the Merchant Shipping Act 1995 s 18 (as to which see PARA 246): see the Merchant Shipping (Registration of Ships) Regulations 1993, SI 1993/3138, reg 71(2)(a); Interpretation Act 1978 s 17(2)(b).
7 Merchant Shipping (Registration of Ships) Regulations 1993, SI 1993/3138, reg 71(2)(b).
8 Merchant Shipping (Registration of Ships) Regulations 1993, SI 1993/3138, reg 71(2). Documents not in the English language which are produced in support of any application under the Merchant Shipping (Registration of Ships) Regulations 1993, SI 1993/3138, must be accompanied by a translation: see PARA 369.
9 As to the meaning of 'certificate of registry' see PARA 255 note 17.
10 Merchant Shipping (Registration of Ships) Regulations 1993, SI 1993/3138, reg 71(3).
11 Ie under the Merchant Shipping (Registration of Ships) Regulations 1993, SI 1993/3138, reg 71: see reg 71(4).
12 Merchant Shipping (Registration of Ships) Regulations 1993, SI 1993/3138, reg 71(4).

**342. Transfer of registration from relevant British possession.** Where a ship[1], excluding a fishing vessel[2], is registered in a relevant British possession[3], the registration of that ship may be transferred to Part I of the register[4] if[5]:

(1)    an application to the registrar[6] of the existing port of registration has been made for that purpose by a declaration in writing by all the persons appearing on his register to be interested in the ship as owners[7]; and

(2)    the following documents have been transmitted to the registrar[8]:

    (a)    a copy of the application and declaration required by head (1) above transmitted by the registrar at the existing port of registration[9];

    (b)    a copy transmitted by him of all the registered particulars of the ship[10] and the names of all persons appearing on his register to be interested in the ship as owners and mortgagees[11]; and

    (c)    the ship's certificate of registry[12].

On making an application to transfer to the register, the applicant must specify one of the listed ports[13] which it is intended shall be the ship's port of choice[14].

Where the ship has not previously been required by the registrar of its existing port of registration to have its name approved by the registrar[15], the applicant must propose a name which the ship is to be called[16]. On being satisfied that the name complies with the statutory requirements[17], the registrar must issue a marking note[18]. On receipt of a marking note, the owner must proceed in accordance with the provisions[19] relating to re-marking of the ship[20].

On receipt of the required documents[21] and the completed marking note, the registrar must enter in the register all the particulars and names so transmitted and issue a new certificate of registry[22].

Where entitlement of a ship to be registered is[23] subject to any condition specified in that registration being satisfied, the registration of the ship may not be transferred to the register of British ships[24] in the United Kingdom[25] unless it appears to the registrar that that condition is satisfied[26].

A transfer of registration from a relevant British possession[27] does not affect the rights of any person mentioned in head (1) above[28].

Notwithstanding that a ship is otherwise entitled to be registered, the registrar may refuse to register it if, taking into account any requirement of the Merchant Shipping Act 1995, including any instrument made thereunder, relating to the condition of the ship or its equipment so far as it is relevant to its safety or to any risk of pollution or to the safety, health and welfare of persons employed or engaged in any capacity on board the ship, he considers that it would be inappropriate for the ship to be registered[29].

1 As to the meaning of 'ship' for these purposes see PARA 255 note 4.
2 As to the meaning of 'fishing vessel' for these purposes see PARA 255 note 7.
3 As to the meaning of 'relevant British possession' under the Merchant Shipping Act 1995 see PARA 16 note 3.
4 As to the meaning of 'register' for these purposes see PARA 255 note 1. Part I of the register, as mentioned in the text, is for ships, owned by qualified persons, which are not fishing vessels or registered on that Part which is restricted to small ships: see the Merchant Shipping (Registration of Ships) Regulations 1993, SI 1993/3138, reg 2(1)(a); and PARA 255. As to the meaning of 'small ship' for these purposes see PARA 255 note 6. As to the registrar's power, in certain circumstances, to transfer the registration of a ship from one Part of the register to a different Part see reg 72A; and PARA 343.
5 Merchant Shipping (Registration of Ships) Regulations 1993, SI 1993/3138, reg 72(1).
6 As to the meaning of 'registrar' for these purposes see PARA 255 note 2.
7 Merchant Shipping (Registration of Ships) Regulations 1993, SI 1993/3138, reg 72(1)(a). As to the meaning of 'owner' for these purposes see PARA 255 note 13. Documents not in the English language which are produced in support of any application under the Merchant Shipping (Registration of Ships) Regulations 1993, SI 1993/3138 must be accompanied by a translation: see PARA 369. As to the power to dispense with declarations or other evidence otherwise required under the Merchant Shipping (Registration of Ships) Regulations 1993, SI 1993/3138, see PARA 371.
8 Merchant Shipping (Registration of Ships) Regulations 1993, SI 1993/3138, reg 72(1)(b).
9 Merchant Shipping (Registration of Ships) Regulations 1993, SI 1993/3138, reg 72(1)(b)(i).
10 As to the requirements of registration under the Merchant Shipping Act 1995 see PARA 245 et seq.
11 Merchant Shipping (Registration of Ships) Regulations 1993, SI 1993/3138, reg 72(1)(b)(ii). As to mortgages of registered ships under the Merchant Shipping Act 1995 see PARA 318 et seq.
12 Merchant Shipping (Registration of Ships) Regulations 1993, SI 1993/3138, reg 72(1)(b)(iii). As to the meaning of 'certificate of registry' see PARA 255 note 17. As to the power to dispense with the production of a certificate in certain circumstances see PARA 376.
13 Ie one of the ports listed in the Merchant Shipping (Registration of Ships) Regulations 1993, SI 1993/3138, reg 72(2), Sch 2 Pt 1 (as to which see PARA 279 note 3): see reg 72(2).
14 Merchant Shipping (Registration of Ships) Regulations 1993, SI 1993/3138, reg 72(2). Any reference in any Act other than the Merchant Shipping Act 1995 or in any other instrument made under any such other Act to the port of registration of the ship or the port to which the ship belongs is to be construed as a reference to the port of choice required to be marked by reg 31 (see PARA 279), reg 53 (see PARA 316), reg 72 or reg 79 (see PARA 362): reg 122; Interpretation Act 1978 s 17(2)(b). As to the meaning of 'port of choice' see PARA 278 note 12.
15 Ie in accordance with the Merchant Shipping (Registration of Ships) Regulations 1993, SI 1993/3138, reg 72(3), Sch 1 (as to which see PARA 278): see reg 72(3).
16 Merchant Shipping (Registration of Ships) Regulations 1993, SI 1993/3138, reg 72(3).
17 Ie the requirements of the Merchant Shipping (Registration of Ships) Regulations 1993, SI 1993/3138, reg 72(3), Sch 1: see reg 72(4).
18 Merchant Shipping (Registration of Ships) Regulations 1993, SI 1993/3138, reg 72(4).
19 Ie in accordance with the Merchant Shipping (Registration of Ships) Regulations 1993, SI 1993/3138, reg 54 (as to which see PARA 315): see reg 72(5).
20 Merchant Shipping (Registration of Ships) Regulations 1993, SI 1993/3138, reg 72(5).
21 Ie on receipt of the documents specified in the Merchant Shipping (Registration of Ships) Regulations 1993, SI 1993/3138, reg 72(1) (see the text and notes 1–12): see reg 72(6).
22 Merchant Shipping (Registration of Ships) Regulations 1993, SI 1993/3138, reg 72(6).

23 Ie by virtue of the Merchant Shipping (Registration of Ships) Regulations 1993, SI 1993/3138, reg 8 (British connection and majority interest) (see PARA 259): see reg 72(7).
24 As to the meaning of 'British ship' under the Merchant Shipping Act 1995 see PARA 230.
25 As to the meaning of 'United Kingdom' see PARA 16 note 3.
26 Merchant Shipping (Registration of Ships) Regulations 1993, SI 1993/3138, reg 72(7).
27 Ie under the Merchant Shipping (Registration of Ships) Regulations 1993, SI 1993/3138, reg 72: see reg 72(8).
28 Merchant Shipping (Registration of Ships) Regulations 1993, SI 1993/3138, reg 72(8).
29 Merchant Shipping (Registration of Ships) Regulations 1993, SI 1993/3138, reg 72(9); Interpretation Act 1978 s 17(2)(b).

**343. Transfer within the register.** On application being made to him, the registrar[1] may, after provision of such information and evidence as he may require and if he is satisfied that the ship[2] is eligible to be registered in the new Part, transfer the registration of the ship to a different Part of the register[3]. All entries in the register relating to the ship (including any entries relating to mortgages[4]) will then be transferred[5].

1 As to the meaning of 'registrar' for these purposes see PARA 255 note 2.
2 As to the meaning of 'ship' for these purposes see PARA 255 note 4.
3 Merchant Shipping (Registration of Ships) Regulations 1993, SI 1993/3138, reg 72A (added by SI 1998/2976). As to the meaning of 'register' for these purposes see PARA 255 note 1. The register maintained by the registrar is divided into various parts depending on the type of ship to be registered: see PARA 255.
4 As to mortgages of registered ships under the Merchant Shipping Act 1995 see PARA 318 et seq.
5 Merchant Shipping (Registration of Ships) Regulations 1993, SI 1993/3138, reg 72A (as added: see note 3).

## (x) Registration of Small Ships

**344. Qualification and entitlement to be registered as a small ship on Part III of the register.** To be eligible to be registered on Part III of the register[1] a ship must be a small ship other than:
(1)    a fishing vessel[2]; or
(2)    a submersible vessel[3].

1 As to the meaning of 'register' for these purposes see PARA 255 note 1. Part III of the register, as mentioned in the text, is for small ships: see the Merchant Shipping (Registration of Ships) Regulations 1993, SI 1993/3138, reg 2(1)(c); and PARA 255. As to the meaning of 'ship' for these purposes see PARA 255 note 4; and as to the meaning of 'small ship' for these purposes see PARA 255 note 6.
2 Merchant Shipping (Registration of Ships) Regulations 1993, SI 1993/3138, reg 88(a). As to the meaning of 'fishing vessel' for these purposes see PARA 255 note 7.
3 Merchant Shipping (Registration of Ships) Regulations 1993, SI 1993/3138, reg 88(b). For these purposes, 'submersible vessel' means any vessel used or designed to be used under the surface of any waters: reg 1(2).

**345. Persons qualified to be the owners of a small ship to be registered on Part III of the register.** The following persons are entitled to be the owners[1] of a small ship[2] to be registered on Part III of the register[3]:
(1)    British citizens[4] or non-United Kingdom[5] nationals exercising their right of freedom of movement of workers or right of establishment[6];
(2)    British overseas territories citizens[7];
(3)    British Overseas citizens[8];
(4)    persons who under the British Nationality Act 1981 are British subjects[9];
(5)    persons who are British Nationals (Overseas)[10]; and
(6)    Commonwealth citizens[11] not falling within heads (1) to (5) above[12].

1 As to the meaning of 'owner' for these purposes see PARA 255 note 13.
2 As to the meaning of 'ship' for these purposes see PARA 255 note 4; and as to the meaning of 'small ship' for these purposes see PARA 255 note 6.

3 Merchant Shipping (Registration of Ships) Regulations 1993, SI 1993/3138, reg 89. As to the meaning of 'register' for these purposes see PARA 255 note 1. Part III of the register, as mentioned in the text, is for small ships: see reg 2(1)(c); and PARA 255.
4 Merchant Shipping (Registration of Ships) Regulations 1993, SI 1993/3138, reg 89(a)(i) (reg 89(a) substituted by SI 1998/2976). As to the meaning of 'British citizen' see BRITISH NATIONALITY vol 4 (2011) PARA 421 et seq.
5 As to the meaning of 'United Kingdom' see PARA 16 note 3.
6 Merchant Shipping (Registration of Ships) Regulations 1993, SI 1993/3138, reg 89(a)(ii) (as substituted: see note 4). As to the meaning of 'non-United Kingdom nationals exercising their right of freedom of movement of workers or right of establishment' see PARA 258 note 6.
7 Merchant Shipping (Registration of Ships) Regulations 1993, SI 1993/3138, reg 89(b) (amended by virtue of the British Overseas Territories Act 2002 s 2(3)). As to the meaning of 'British overseas territories citizen' see BRITISH NATIONALITY vol 4 (2011) PARAS 406, 445–458.
8 Merchant Shipping (Registration of Ships) Regulations 1993, SI 1993/3138, reg 89(c). As to the meaning of 'British Overseas citizen' see BRITISH NATIONALITY vol 4 (2011) PARA 459 et seq.
9 Merchant Shipping (Registration of Ships) Regulations 1993, SI 1993/3138, reg 89(d). As to British subjects under the British Nationality Act 1981 see BRITISH NATIONALITY vol 4 (2011) PARAS 407, 469–474.
10 Merchant Shipping (Registration of Ships) Regulations 1993, SI 1993/3138, reg 89(e); Interpretation Act 1978 s 17(2)(b). As to British Nationals (Overseas) within the meaning of the British Nationality Act 1981 see BRITISH NATIONALITY vol 4 (2011) PARAS 406, 465–467.
11 As to who are Commonwealth citizens see BRITISH NATIONALITY vol 4 (2011) PARA 409.
12 Merchant Shipping (Registration of Ships) Regulations 1993, SI 1993/3138, reg 89(f).

**346. British connection of small ships.** A small ship[1] is entitled[2] to be registered if it is owned by one or more persons who are ordinarily resident in the United Kingdom[3] and who are qualified[4] to be the owners of a small ship[5].

1 As to the meaning of 'ship' for these purposes see PARA 255 note 4; and as to the meaning of 'small ship' for these purposes see PARA 255 note 6.
2 Ie subject to the Merchant Shipping (Registration of Ships) Regulations 1993, SI 1993/3138, reg 93(2) (power to refuse registration) (see PARA 349): see reg 90.
3 As to the meaning of 'United Kingdom' see PARA 16 note 3. As to ordinary residence see CONFLICT OF LAWS vol 19 (2011) PARA 359; IMMIGRATION AND ASYLUM vol 57 (2012) PARA 140.
4 Ie by virtue of the Merchant Shipping (Registration of Ships) Regulations 1993, SI 1993/3138, reg 89 (see PARA 345): see reg 90.
5 Merchant Shipping (Registration of Ships) Regulations 1993, SI 1993/3138, reg 90.

**347. Disapplication of private law provisions to small ships.** The private law provisions for registered ships under the Merchant Shipping Act 1995[1] do not apply to small ships[2].

1 Ie the Merchant Shipping Act 1995 s 16(1), Sch 1 (as to which see PARAS 237, 306, 318, 321, 323, 324, 328, 333, 335): see the Merchant Shipping (Registration of Ships) Regulations 1993, SI 1993/3138, reg 91; Interpretation Act 1978 s 17(2)(b). As to the application of the Merchant Shipping Act 1995 Sch 1 see PARA 252.
2 Merchant Shipping (Registration of Ships) Regulations 1993, SI 1993/3138, reg 91; Interpretation Act 1978 s 17(2)(b). As to the meaning of 'ship' for these purposes see PARA 255 note 4; and as to the meaning of 'small ship' for these purposes see PARA 255 note 6.

**348. Applications for registration of small ships.** Applications for registration[1] of small ships[2] must be in a form approved by the Secretary of State[3] and must include[4]:

(1)  a description of the ship[5];
(2)  the overall length[6] of the ship[7];
(3)  the name of the ship[8];
(4)  the name and address of every owner[9] of the ship[10]; and
(5)  a declaration by every owner[11]: (a) that he is eligible[12] to be the owner of a small ship[13]; and (b) that the ship is entitled[14] to be registered on Part III of the register[15].

1 As to the meaning of 'application for registration' see PARA 269 note 1.

2　As to the meaning of 'ship' for these purposes see PARA 255 note 4; and as to the meaning of 'small ship' for these purposes see PARA 255 note 6.

3　As to the Secretary of State see PARA 36.

4　Merchant Shipping (Registration of Ships) Regulations 1993, SI 1993/3138, reg 92. As to the requirement to supply supplementary information or evidence where that provided on an application for registration is judged to be either not correct or insufficient see PARA 372. Documents not in the English language which are produced in support of any application under the Merchant Shipping (Registration of Ships) Regulations 1993, SI 1993/3138 must be accompanied by a translation: see PARA 369.

5　Merchant Shipping (Registration of Ships) Regulations 1993, SI 1993/3138, reg 92(a).

6　As to the meaning of 'overall length' see PARA 255 note 6.

7　Merchant Shipping (Registration of Ships) Regulations 1993, SI 1993/3138, reg 92(b).

8　Merchant Shipping (Registration of Ships) Regulations 1993, SI 1993/3138, reg 92(c).

9　As to the meaning of 'owner' for these purposes see PARA 255 note 13.

10　Merchant Shipping (Registration of Ships) Regulations 1993, SI 1993/3138, reg 92(d).

11　Merchant Shipping (Registration of Ships) Regulations 1993, SI 1993/3138, reg 92(e). As to the power to dispense with declarations or other evidence otherwise required under the Merchant Shipping (Registration of Ships) Regulations 1993, SI 1993/3138, see PARA 371.

12　Ie under the Merchant Shipping (Registration of Ships) Regulations 1993, SI 1993/3138, reg 89 (see PARA 345): see reg 92(e)(i).

13　Merchant Shipping (Registration of Ships) Regulations 1993, SI 1993/3138, reg 92(e)(i).

14　Ie in accordance with the Merchant Shipping (Registration of Ships) Regulations 1993, SI 1993/3138, reg 90 (see PARA 346): see reg 92(e)(ii).

15　Merchant Shipping (Registration of Ships) Regulations 1993, SI 1993/3138, reg 92(e)(ii). As to the meaning of 'register' for these purposes see PARA 255 note 1. Part III of the register, as mentioned in the text, is for small ships: see reg 2(1)(c); and PARA 255.

**349. Details to be registered in relation to small ships and refusal.** On receiving an application for registration[1] of a small ship[2] and being satisfied that the ship may properly be registered and that the name of the ship does not appear to him to be undesirable, the registrar[3] must register the ship and must record in the register[4] the following details[5]:

(1)　the registration number of the ship[6];

(2)　the date of registration[7];

(3)　the date of expiry of registration[8]; and

(4)　the details of the ship that are required to be included in any application for the registration of a small ship[9].

Where the registrar is not satisfied that the ship is eligible to be registered, he may[10] refuse to register the ship[11].

1　As to the meaning of 'application for registration' see PARA 269 note 1.

2　As to the meaning of 'ship' for these purposes see PARA 255 note 4; and as to the meaning of 'small ship' for these purposes see PARA 255 note 6. As to applications for the registration of small ships see PARA 348.

3　As to the meaning of 'registrar' see PARA 255 note 2.

4　As to the meaning of 'register' for these purposes see PARA 255 note 1. Part III of the register mentioned in the text is for small ships: see the Merchant Shipping (Registration of Ships) Regulations 1993, SI 1993/3138, reg 2(1)(c); and PARA 255.

5　Merchant Shipping (Registration of Ships) Regulations 1993, SI 1993/3138, reg 93(1).

6　Merchant Shipping (Registration of Ships) Regulations 1993, SI 1993/3138, reg 93(1)(a).

7　Merchant Shipping (Registration of Ships) Regulations 1993, SI 1993/3138, reg 93(1)(b).

8　Merchant Shipping (Registration of Ships) Regulations 1993, SI 1993/3138, reg 93(1)(c). The text refers to the date of expiry of registration in accordance with reg 96 (period of registration) (see PARA 352): see reg 93(1)(c).

9　Merchant Shipping (Registration of Ships) Regulations 1993, SI 1993/3138, reg 93(1)(d). The text refers to the details specified in reg 92(a)–(d) (see PARA 348): see reg 93(1)(d).

10　Ie subject to the Merchant Shipping (Registration of Ships) Regulations 1993, SI 1993/3138, reg 106 (requirement for supplementary information) (see PARA 372): see reg 93(2).

11　Merchant Shipping (Registration of Ships) Regulations 1993, SI 1993/3138, reg 93(2).

**350. Certificate of registry of a small ship.** On the registration of a small ship[1], the registrar[2] must issue a certificate which must contain the details recorded in the register[3], save for the address of any owner[4].

1  As to the meaning of 'ship' for these purposes see PARA 255 note 4; and as to the meaning of 'small ship' for these purposes see PARA 255 note 6. As to applications for the registration of small ships see PARA 348.
2  As to the meaning of 'registrar' see PARA 255 note 2.
3  Ie in accordance with the Merchant Shipping (Registration of Ships) Regulations 1993, SI 1993/3138, reg 93 (see PARA 349): see reg 94. As to the meaning of 'register' for these purposes see PARA 255 note 1. Part III of the register mentioned in the text is for small ships: see reg 2(1)(c); and PARA 255.
4  Merchant Shipping (Registration of Ships) Regulations 1993, SI 1993/3138, reg 94. As to the meaning of 'owner' for these purposes see PARA 255 note 13.

**351. Marking of a small ship.** The person registered as owner[1] of the small ship[2] must ensure that[3]:
(1)    within one month of the date on which the registration of the ship takes effect[4], there is clearly painted on or affixed to a visible external surface of the ship the number of its registration preceded by the letters SSR[5]; and
(2)    such marking is effectively maintained and renewed when necessary during the period of the registration of the ship[6].

1  As to the meaning of 'owner' for these purposes see PARA 255 note 13.
2  As to the meaning of 'ship' for these purposes see PARA 255 note 4; and as to the meaning of 'small ship' for these purposes see PARA 255 note 6. As to applications for the registration of small ships see PARA 348.
3  Merchant Shipping (Registration of Ships) Regulations 1993, SI 1993/3138, reg 95.
4  As to the period of registration of a small ship see PARA 352.
5  Merchant Shipping (Registration of Ships) Regulations 1993, SI 1993/3138, reg 95(a).
6  Merchant Shipping (Registration of Ships) Regulations 1993, SI 1993/3138, reg 95(b).

**352. Period of registration of a small ship.** The registration of a small ship[1] is valid, unless duly terminated[2], for a period of five years beginning with the date of registration specified in the certificate of registry[3] and expires at the end of that period unless it is duly renewed[4].

1  As to the meaning of 'ship' for these purposes see PARA 255 note 4; and as to the meaning of 'small ship' for these purposes see PARA 255 note 6. As to applications for the registration of small ships see PARA 348.
2  Ie under the Merchant Shipping (Registration of Ships) Regulations 1993, SI 1993/3138: see reg 96. As to termination of the registration of a small ship see PARA 356.
3  As to the certificate of registry of a small ship see PARA 350.
4  Merchant Shipping (Registration of Ships) Regulations 1993, SI 1993/3138, reg 96. The text refers to renewal under reg 97 (see PARA 353): see reg 96. As to the surrender of a certificate on the termination or expiry of registration see PARA 375.

**353. Renewal of registration of a small ship.** Application for renewal of registration of a small ship[1] may be made during the last three calendar months of the current registration period[2].
Application for renewal must be:
(1)    in writing[3]; and
(2)    accompanied by a declaration[4] by every owner[5]:
(a)    that he is eligible[6] to be the owner of a small ship[7]; and
(b)    that the ship is entitled[8] to be registered on Part III of the register[9].

1  As to the meaning of 'ship' for these purposes see PARA 255 note 4; and as to the meaning of 'small ship' for these purposes see PARA 255 note 6. As to applications for the registration of small ships see PARA 348.

2   Merchant Shipping (Registration of Ships) Regulations 1993, SI 1993/3138, reg 97(1). As to the period of registration of a small ship see PARA 352. As to the requirement to remeasure tonnage in certain circumstances before a ship's registration can be renewed see PARA 380.
3   Merchant Shipping (Registration of Ships) Regulations 1993, SI 1993/3138, reg 97(2).
4   Ie a declaration as required by the Merchant Shipping (Registration of Ships) Regulations 1993, SI 1993/3138, reg 92(e) (see PARA 348): see reg 97(2). As to the power to dispense with declarations or other evidence otherwise required under the Merchant Shipping (Registration of Ships) Regulations 1993, SI 1993/3138, see PARA 371.
5   As to the meaning of 'owner' for these purposes see PARA 255 note 13.
6   Ie under the Merchant Shipping (Registration of Ships) Regulations 1993, SI 1993/3138, reg 89 (see PARA 345): see regs 92(e)(i), 97(2).
7   Merchant Shipping (Registration of Ships) Regulations 1993, SI 1993/3138, regs 92(e)(i), 97(2).
8   Ie in accordance with the Merchant Shipping (Registration of Ships) Regulations 1993, SI 1993/3138, reg 90 (see PARA 346): see regs 92(e)(ii), 97(2).
9   Merchant Shipping (Registration of Ships) Regulations 1993, SI 1993/3138, regs 92(e)(ii), 97(2). As to the meaning of 'register' for these purposes see PARA 255 note 1. Part III of the register, as mentioned in the text, is for small ships: see reg 2(1)(c); and PARA 255.

### 354. Notification of changes of ownership etc of a registered small ship.

If at any time there occurs, in relation to a registered small ship[1]:

(1)     any change affecting the eligibility of the ship to be registered as a British ship[2]; or

(2)     any change in relation to the address of the registered owner of the ship[3]; or

(3)     any change in details relating to the ship[4],

the registered owner of the ship must, as soon as practicable after the change occurs, notify the registrar[5].

Notification so made must be in writing, must be signed by the registered owner and must specify the nature of the change and the name and the number of the ship[6].

1   Merchant Shipping (Registration of Ships) Regulations 1993, SI 1993/3138, reg 98(1). The text refers to a ship registered under Pt XI (regs 88–100) (see PARAS 344 et seq, 355 et seq): see reg 98(1). As to the meaning of 'ship' for these purposes see PARA 255 note 4; and as to the meaning of 'small ship' for these purposes see PARA 255 note 6. As to applications for the registration of small ships see PARA 348.
2   Merchant Shipping (Registration of Ships) Regulations 1993, SI 1993/3138, reg 98(1)(a). As to the meaning of 'British ship' under the Merchant Shipping Act 1995 see PARA 230.
3   Merchant Shipping (Registration of Ships) Regulations 1993, SI 1993/3138, reg 98(1)(b). As to the meaning of 'owner' for these purposes see PARA 255 note 13.
4   Merchant Shipping (Registration of Ships) Regulations 1993, SI 1993/3138, reg 98(1)(c) (amended by SI 1998/2976). As to the requirement to remeasure tonnage in certain circumstances where a ship's details have changed see PARA 380.
5   Merchant Shipping (Registration of Ships) Regulations 1993, SI 1993/3138, reg 98(1). As to the meaning of 'registrar' see PARA 255 note 2.
6   Merchant Shipping (Registration of Ships) Regulations 1993, SI 1993/3138, reg 98(2).

### 355. Supplementary evidence as to entitlement of small ship to registration.

Where it appears to the registrar[1] that there is any doubt as to the right of the small ship[2] to be registered on Part III of the register[3], he may require satisfactory evidence to be produced by the person registered as the owner[4] that the ship is entitled to be so registered[5]. Such evidence may include the production of the ship for inspection at a place and under such conditions as the registrar requires; and, if the necessary evidence is not provided within one month of being so required, he may terminate the registration of the ship[6].

1   As to the meaning of 'registrar' see PARA 255 note 2.
2   As to the meaning of 'ship' for these purposes see PARA 255 note 4; and as to the meaning of 'small ship' for these purposes see PARA 255 note 6.
3   As to the meaning of 'register' for these purposes see PARA 255 note 1. Part III of the register, as mentioned in the text, is for small ships: see the Merchant Shipping (Registration of Ships) Regulations 1993, SI 1993/3138, reg 2(1)(c); and PARA 255.

4  As to the meaning of 'owner' for these purposes see PARA 255 note 13.
5  Merchant Shipping (Registration of Ships) Regulations 1993, SI 1993/3138, reg 99(1).
6  Merchant Shipping (Registration of Ships) Regulations 1993, SI 1993/3138, reg 99(2) (amended by SI 1998/2976).

**356. Termination of registration of a small ship.** In the event of:
(1)      a ship[1] ceasing to be a small ship[2]; or
(2)      a change in the details recorded on the certificate of registry[3],
the registration of the ship terminates[4].

Where the registration of a ship is terminated, the certificate of registry ceases to have effect and must, within one month, be surrendered to the registrar[5] by the person registered prior to the termination as the owner[6] of the ship or, if he has died, by his legal personal representative[7].

1  As to the meaning of 'ship' for these purposes see PARA 255 note 4.
2  Merchant Shipping (Registration of Ships) Regulations 1993, SI 1993/3138, reg 100(1)(a). The text refers to a ship ceasing to be a ship to which Pt XI (regs 88–100) (see PARA 344 et seq) applies: see reg 100(1)(a). As to the meaning of 'small ship' for these purposes see PARA 255 note 6.
3  Merchant Shipping (Registration of Ships) Regulations 1993, SI 1993/3138, reg 100(1)(b). As to the certificate of registry of a small ship see PARA 350.
4  Merchant Shipping (Registration of Ships) Regulations 1993, SI 1993/3138, reg 100(1).
5  As to the meaning of 'registrar' see PARA 255 note 2.
6  As to the meaning of 'owner' for these purposes see PARA 255 note 13.
7  Merchant Shipping (Registration of Ships) Regulations 1993, SI 1993/3138, reg 100(2). As to the surrender of a certificate on the termination or expiry of registration see PARA 375.

### (xi)  Ships Bareboat Chartered-in

**357. Ships bareboat chartered-in by British charterers.** Any ship[1] which:
(1)      is registered under the law of a country other than the United Kingdom[2] (the 'country of original registration')[3];
(2)      is chartered on bareboat charter terms[4] to a charterer who is a person qualified to own British ships[5]; and
(3)      is so chartered in circumstances where the prescribed conditions of entitlement to registration[6], read with the requisite modifications[7], are satisfied as respects the charterer and the ship[8],
is entitled to be registered if an application for registration is duly made[9].

Such registration of a ship[10] remains in force, unless terminated earlier by virtue of registration regulations and subject to any suspension thereunder, until the end of the charter period[11] and then terminates by virtue of this provision[12].

The owner's obligation to take all reasonable steps to secure the termination of the ship's registration under the law of the country where it is already registered[13] does not apply to a ship registered by virtue of the provisions governing ships bareboat chartered-in by British charterers[14]; but registration regulations must include provision for securing that the authority responsible for the registration of ships in the country of original registration is notified of the registration of the ship and of the termination[15] of its registration[16].

Accordingly, throughout the period for which a ship is registered virtue of the provisions governing ships bareboat chartered-in by British charterers[17]:
(a)      the ship is entitled, as a British ship, to fly the British flag[18];
(b)      the Merchant Shipping Act 1995 applies to the ship as a British ship or as a registered ship as it applies to other British ships and to registered ships[19]; and
(c)      any other enactment applicable to British ships or ships registered under that Act applies[20] to the ship as a British ship or as a registered ship[21].

The private law provisions for registered ships[22] do not apply to a ship registered by virtue of the provisions governing ships bareboat chartered-in by British charterers[23]; and any matters or questions corresponding to those for which the private law provisions for registered ships make provision must be determined by reference to the law of the country of original registration[24].

Her Majesty may by Order in Council provide that any enactment falling within head (b) or (c) above[25]:

(i)     is not to have effect[26] in relation to a ship registered by virtue of the provisions governing ships bareboat chartered-in by British charterers[27]; or

(ii)    is so to have effect subject to such modifications, if any, as may be specified in the Order[28].

No provision may, however, be made by such an Order in Council which would have the effect of relaxing the relevant requirements of the Merchant Shipping Act 1995[29] in their application to a ship to which the provisions governing ships bareboat chartered-in by British charterers apply[30]. Such an Order in Council may make such transitional, incidental or supplementary provision as appears to Her Majesty to be necessary or expedient, including provision divesting or providing for the divestment of ownership in the ship[31].

1   As to the meaning of 'ship' see PARA 229.
2   As to the meaning of 'United Kingdom' see PARA 16 note 3.
3   Merchant Shipping Act 1995 s 17(1)(a).
4   For these purposes, 'bareboat charter terms', in relation to a ship, means the hiring of the ship for a stipulated period on terms which give the charterer possession and control of the ship, including the right to appoint the master and crew: Merchant Shipping Act 1995 s 17(11). As to the meaning of 'master' see PARA 444 note 1.
5   Merchant Shipping Act 1995 s 17(1)(b). As to the meaning of 'British ship' see PARA 230; and as to the meaning of 'qualified owners' see PARA 230 note 11.
6   Ie prescribed under the Merchant Shipping Act 1995 s 9(2)(b) (see PARA 245): see s 17(1)(c).
7   For these purposes, 'requisite modifications' of those conditions are the substitution for any requirement to be satisfied by or as respects the owner of a ship of a corresponding requirement to be satisfied by or as respects the charterer of the ship: Merchant Shipping Act 1995 s 17(2).
8   Merchant Shipping Act 1995 s 17(1)(c).
9   Merchant Shipping Act 1995 s 17(3). The registrar may, nevertheless, if registration regulations so provide, refuse to register or terminate the registration of a ship by virtue of s 17 if, having regard to any relevant requirements of the Merchant Shipping Act 1995, he considers it would be inappropriate for the ship to be or, as the case may be, to remain registered: s 9(3) (applied by s 17(3)). As to the meaning of 'registration regulations' see PARA 247.
10  Ie a ship registered by virtue of the Merchant Shipping Act 1995 s 17: see s 17(4).
11  For these purposes, 'charter period' means the period during which the ship is chartered on bareboat charter terms: Merchant Shipping Act 1995 s 17(11).
12  Merchant Shipping Act 1995 s 17(4).
13  Ie the obligation contained in the Merchant Shipping Act 1995 s 9(5) (as to which see PARA 245): see s 17(5).
14  Ie registered by virtue of the Merchant Shipping Act 1995 s 17: see s 17(5).
15  Ie whether by virtue of the Merchant Shipping Act 1995 s 17(4) (see the text and notes 10–12) or by virtue of the registration regulations: see s 17(5).
16  Merchant Shipping Act 1995 s 17(5).
17  Merchant Shipping Act 1995 s 17(6). The text refers to a ship which is registered by virtue of s 17: see s 17(6).
18  Merchant Shipping Act 1995 s 17(6)(a).
19  Merchant Shipping Act 1995 s 17(6)(b). The application of the Merchant Shipping Act 1995 set out in s 17(6)(b) is subject to s 17(7), (8) (see the text and notes 22–28): see s 17(6)(b).
20  Ie subject to the Merchant Shipping Act 1995 s 17(8) (see the text and note 25): see s 17(6)(c).
21  Merchant Shipping Act 1995 s 17(6)(c).
22  As to the meaning of 'the private law provisions for registered ships' see PARA 237 note 3.
23  Ie by virtue of the Merchant Shipping Act 1995 s 17: see s 17(7).
24  Merchant Shipping Act 1995 s 17(7).

25 Merchant Shipping Act 1995 s 17(8). At the date at which this volume states the law, no such Order in Council had been made but, by virtue of the Interpretation Act 1978 s 17(2)(b), the Merchant Shipping (Modification of Enactments) (Bareboat Charter Ships) Order 1994, SI 1994/774 (see PARAS 230, 255), has effect as if so made. As to the making of Orders in Council under the Merchant Shipping Act 1995 see PARA 39.

26 Ie in accordance with the Merchant Shipping Act 1995 s 17(6) (see the text and notes 17–21): see s 17(8)(a).

27 Merchant Shipping Act 1995 s 17(8)(a).

28 Merchant Shipping Act 1995 s 17(8)(b).

29 Ie as defined in the Merchant Shipping Act 1995 s 9(8) (see PARA 245 note 9): see s 17(9).

30 Merchant Shipping Act 1995 s 17(9).

31 Merchant Shipping Act 1995 s 17(10).

**358. Qualification and entitlement for registration of bareboat charter ships other than fishing vessels.** The persons qualified to be the owners of British ships[1] who charter a ship, other than a fishing vessel[2], on bareboat charter terms[3] are qualified to register under the Merchant Shipping Act 1995[4] a bareboat charter ship[5].

Where the charterer is not resident in the United Kingdom[6], he must appoint a representative person[7].

1 Ie by virtue of the Merchant Shipping (Registration of Ships) Regulations 1993, SI 1993/3138, reg 7(1) (see PARA 258): see reg 73. As to the meaning of 'owner' for these purposes see PARA 255 note 13; and as to the meaning of 'ship' for these purposes see PARA 255 note 4. As to the meaning of 'British ship' under the Merchant Shipping Act 1995 see PARA 230.

2 As to the meaning of 'fishing vessel' for these purposes see PARA 255 note 7.

3 As to the meaning of 'bareboat charter terms' under the Merchant Shipping Act 1995 see PARA 357 note 4.

4 Ie under the Merchant Shipping Act 1995 s 17 (see PARA 357): see the Merchant Shipping (Registration of Ships) Regulations 1993, SI 1993/3138, reg 73; Interpretation Act 1978 s 17(2)(b).

5 Merchant Shipping (Registration of Ships) Regulations 1993, SI 1993/3138, reg 73; Interpretation Act 1978 s 17(2)(b). As to the meaning of 'bareboat charter ship' see PARA 255 note 9.

6 As to the meaning of 'United Kingdom' see PARA 16 note 3. As to the rules of domicile and residence generally see CONFLICT OF LAWS vol 19 (2011) PARA 336 et seq.

7 Merchant Shipping (Registration of Ships) Regulations 1993, SI 1993/3138, reg 75. For these purposes, Pt V (regs 18, 19) (see PARAS 267–268) applies as if the charterer were the owner: see reg 75.

**359. Qualification and entitlement for registration of a fishing vessel as a bareboat charter ship.** The persons[1] who are qualified to be the owners[2] of fishing vessels[3] registered on Part II of the register[4] and who charter a fishing vessel on bareboat charter terms[5] are eligible to register it under the Merchant Shipping Act 1995[6] on Part IV of the register[7].

However, a fishing vessel may not be registered on Part IV of the register unless it is managed, and its operations controlled and directed, from within the United Kingdom[8]; and where the charterer is not resident in the United Kingdom he must appoint a representative person[9].

1 Ie the persons prescribed by the Merchant Shipping (Registration of Ships) Regulations 1993, SI 1993/3138, reg 12 (see PARA 262): see reg 74(1).

2 As to the meaning of 'owner' for these purposes see PARA 255 note 13.

3 As to the meaning of 'fishing vessel' for these purposes see PARA 255 note 7.

4 As to the meaning of 'register' for these purposes see PARA 255 note 1. Part II of the register, as mentioned in the text, is for fishing vessels: see the Merchant Shipping (Registration of Ships) Regulations 1993, SI 1993/3138, reg 2(1)(b); and PARA 255. As to the status of any Part II certificate under sea fisheries legislation see PARA 377.

5 As to the meaning of 'bareboat charter terms' under the Merchant Shipping Act 1995 see PARA 357 note 4.

6 Ie under the Merchant Shipping Act 1995 s 17 (see PARA 357): see the Merchant Shipping (Registration of Ships) Regulations 1993, SI 1993/3138, reg 74(1); Interpretation Act 1978 s 17(2)(b).

7   Merchant Shipping (Registration of Ships) Regulations 1993, SI 1993/3138, reg 74(1); Interpretation Act 1978 s 17(2)(b). Part IV of the register is for ships which are bareboat charter ships: see the Merchant Shipping (Registration of Ships) Regulations 1993, SI 1993/3138, reg 2(1)(d); and PARA 255. As to the meaning of 'ship' for these purposes see PARA 255 note 4; and as to the meaning of 'bareboat charter ship' see PARA 255 note 9.

     The charterers of fishing vessels which are, or are to be, registered as bareboat charter ships may apply for dispensation from the eligibility requirements in accordance with reg 15 (as to which see PARA 264): reg 76.

8   Merchant Shipping (Registration of Ships) Regulations 1993, SI 1993/3138, reg 74(2). As to the meaning of 'United Kingdom' see PARA 16 note 3.

9   Merchant Shipping (Registration of Ships) Regulations 1993, SI 1993/3138, reg 75. For these purposes, Pt V (regs 18, 19) (see PARAS 267–268) applies as if the charterer were the owner: see reg 75. As to the rules of domicile and residence generally see CONFLICT OF LAWS vol 19 (2011) PARA 336 et seq.

**360. Applications for registration of a bareboat charter ship.** Every application for registration[1] of a bareboat charter ship[2] must be made to the registrar[3] at the General Registry of Shipping and Seamen[4]. Every such application must be in a form approved by the Secretary of State[5] and must be accompanied by[6]:

(1)      a declaration of eligibility which must include[7]:

         (a)      a declaration by every charterer setting out his qualification to register a bareboat charter ship[8]; and

         (b)      in respect of fishing vessels[9], a declaration that the management, and direction and control, of the ship, will be carried out from within the United Kingdom[10];

(2)      a copy of the charterparty showing[11]:

         (a)      the name of the ship[12];

         (b)      the name of the charterer or charterers and the name of the owner or owners of the ship[13];

         (c)      the date of the charterparty[14];

         (d)      the duration of the charterparty[15];

(3)      the certificate of registry[16] (or other document) issued by the authority responsible for the registration of ships in the country of primary registration showing the ownership of the ship[17]; and

(4)      where the charterer is a body corporate, the document or documents required by the provisions[18] governing applications by such bodies[19].

The requirement that ships before registration must be surveyed and measured[20] applies to the registration of a bareboat charter ship[21].

The registrar may refuse to register any fishing vessel as a bareboat charter ship if he is not satisfied that there is in force in respect of the vessel any certificate required to be so in force by virtue of the Merchant Shipping Act 1995[22].

1   As to the meaning of 'application for registration' see PARA 269 note 1.
2   As to the meaning of 'bareboat charter ship' see PARA 255 note 9; and as to the meaning of 'ship' for these purposes see PARA 255 note 4.
3   As to the meaning of 'registrar' see PARA 255 note 2.
4   Merchant Shipping (Registration of Ships) Regulations 1993, SI 1993/3138, reg 77(1) (amended by SI 1999/3206). The Merchant Shipping (Registration of Ships) Regulations 1993, SI 1993/3138, reg 21 (the applicant) (see PARA 270) applies to Pt X (regs 73–87) (see PARAS 358 et seq, 361 et seq) as if the charterer were the owner: reg 77(2). As to the meaning of 'owner' for these purposes see PARA 255 note 13.
5   As to the Secretary of State see PARA 36.
6   Merchant Shipping (Registration of Ships) Regulations 1993, SI 1993/3138, reg 77(3). As to the requirement to supply supplementary information or evidence where that provided on an application for registration is judged to be either not correct or insufficient see PARA 372. Documents not in the English language which are produced in support of any application under the Merchant Shipping (Registration of Ships) Regulations 1993, SI 1993/3138 must be accompanied by a translation: see PARA 369.

7　Merchant Shipping (Registration of Ships) Regulations 1993, SI 1993/3138, reg 77(3)(a). As to the power to dispense with declarations or other evidence otherwise required under the Merchant Shipping (Registration of Ships) Regulations 1993, SI 1993/3138, see PARA 371.

8　Merchant Shipping (Registration of Ships) Regulations 1993, SI 1993/3138, reg 77(3)(a)(i). As to the qualification and entitlement to register bareboat charter ships other than fishing vessels see PARA 358.

9　As to the meaning of 'fishing vessel' for these purposes see PARA 255 note 7.

10　Merchant Shipping (Registration of Ships) Regulations 1993, SI 1993/3138, reg 77(3)(a)(ii). As to the meaning of 'United Kingdom' see PARA 16 note 3. As to the qualification and entitlement to register a fishing vessel as a bareboat charter ship see PARA 359.

11　Merchant Shipping (Registration of Ships) Regulations 1993, SI 1993/3138, reg 77(3)(b).

12　Merchant Shipping (Registration of Ships) Regulations 1993, SI 1993/3138, reg 77(3)(b)(i).

13　Merchant Shipping (Registration of Ships) Regulations 1993, SI 1993/3138, reg 77(3)(b)(ii).

14　Merchant Shipping (Registration of Ships) Regulations 1993, SI 1993/3138, reg 77(3)(b)(iii).

15　Merchant Shipping (Registration of Ships) Regulations 1993, SI 1993/3138, reg 77(3)(b)(iv).

16　As to the meaning of 'certificate of registry' see PARA 255 note 17.

17　Merchant Shipping (Registration of Ships) Regulations 1993, SI 1993/3138, reg 77(3)(c). As to the details contained in a certificate of registry for a bareboat charter ship generally see PARA 301. As to the power to dispense with the production of a certificate in certain circumstances see PARA 376.

18　Ie by the Merchant Shipping (Registration of Ships) Regulations 1993, SI 1993/3138, reg 24 (see PARA 273): see reg 77(3)(d).

19　Merchant Shipping (Registration of Ships) Regulations 1993, SI 1993/3138, reg 77(3)(d).

20　Ie the requirements of the Merchant Shipping (Registration of Ships) Regulations 1993, SI 1993/3138, reg 29 (see PARA 276): see reg 77(4).

21　Merchant Shipping (Registration of Ships) Regulations 1993, SI 1993/3138, reg 77(4). The text refers to the application of reg 29 to Pt X (see PARAS 358 et seq, 361 et seq) generally: see reg 77(4).

22　Merchant Shipping (Registration of Ships) Regulations 1993, SI 1993/3138, reg 77(5); Interpretation Act 1978 s 17(2)(b). The text refers to any certificate required to be so in force by virtue of the Merchant Shipping Act 1995 s 125 (see PARA 610): see the Merchant Shipping (Registration of Ships) Regulations 1993, SI 1993/3138, reg 77(5); Interpretation Act 1978 s 17(2)(b).

**361. Names of bareboat charter ship.** On making an application for registration[1] of a bareboat charter ship[2], the applicant[3] must propose a name which the ship is to be called while so registered[4].

If the registrar[5] is satisfied that the name complies with the requirements relating to the approval of names[6], he must approve the name[7].

1　As to the meaning of 'application for registration' see PARA 269 note 1.

2　As to the meaning of 'bareboat charter ship' see PARA 255 note 9; and as to the meaning of 'ship' for these purposes see PARA 255 note 4.

3　The Merchant Shipping (Registration of Ships) Regulations 1993, SI 1993/3138, reg 21 (the applicant) (see PARA 270) applies to Pt X (regs 73–87) (see PARAS 358 et seq, 362 et seq) as if the charterer were the owner: see reg 77(2); and PARA 360. As to the meaning of 'owner' for these purposes see PARA 255 note 13.

4　Merchant Shipping (Registration of Ships) Regulations 1993, SI 1993/3138, reg 78(1).

5　As to the meaning of 'registrar' see PARA 255 note 2.

6　Ie that the name is in compliance with the Merchant Shipping (Registration of Ships) Regulations 1993, SI 1993/3138, reg 78(2), Sch 1 (see PARA 278): see reg 78(2).

7　Merchant Shipping (Registration of Ships) Regulations 1993, SI 1993/3138, reg 78(2).

**362. Allocation of identifying number to bareboat charter ship; port of choice and port numbers.** On making application for registration[1] of a bareboat charter ship[2], the applicant[3] must specify one of the listed ports[4] which it is intended shall be the port of choice[5].

Where the application is made in respect of a fishing vessel[6] and the registrar[7] is satisfied that the vessel is eligible to be registered as a bareboat charter ship, he must[8]:

(1)　allocate a port number[9]; and

(2)　allocate an identifying number[10], whether or not the vessel already has a number allocated by its primary register[11].

In the case of any other ship, the registrar may allocate an identifying number, whether or not the ship already has a number allocated by its primary register[12].

1   As to the meaning of 'application for registration' see PARA 269 note 1.
2   As to the meaning of 'bareboat charter ship' see PARA 255 note 9; and as to the meaning of 'ship' for these purposes see PARA 255 note 4.
3   The Merchant Shipping (Registration of Ships) Regulations 1993, SI 1993/3138, reg 21 (the applicant) (see PARA 270) applies to Pt X (regs 73–87) (see PARAS 358 et seq, 363 et seq) as if the charterer were the owner: see reg 77(2); and PARA 360. As to the meaning of 'owner' for these purposes see PARA 255 note 13.
4   Ie one of the ports listed in the Merchant Shipping (Registration of Ships) Regulations 1993, SI 1993/3138, reg 79(1), Sch 2 Pt 1 or Pt 2 (see PARA 279), as is appropriate: see reg 79(1).
5   Merchant Shipping (Registration of Ships) Regulations 1993, SI 1993/3138, reg 79(1). As to the meaning of 'port of choice' see PARA 278 note 12. As to the allocation of port of choice see PARA 279. Any reference in any Act other than the Merchant Shipping Act 1995 or in any other instrument made under any such other Act to the port of registration of the ship or the port to which the ship belongs is to be construed as a reference to the port of choice required to be marked by the Merchant Shipping (Registration of Ships) Regulations 1993, SI 1993/3138, reg 31 (see PARA 279), reg 53 (see PARA 316), reg 72 (see PARA 342) or reg 79: reg 122; Interpretation Act 1978 s 17(2)(b).
6   As to the meaning of 'fishing vessel' for these purposes see PARA 255 note 7.
7   As to the meaning of 'registrar' see PARA 255 note 2.
8   Merchant Shipping (Registration of Ships) Regulations 1993, SI 1993/3138, reg 79(2) (reg 79(2), (3) substituted by SI 1999/3206).
9   Merchant Shipping (Registration of Ships) Regulations 1993, SI 1993/3138, reg 79(2)(a) (as substituted: see note 8). As to the meaning of 'port number' see PARA 279 note 8.
10  For these purposes, 'identifying number' means, where the registrar has allocated a bareboat charter ship a number under the Merchant Shipping (Registration of Ships) Regulations 1993, SI 1993/3138, reg 79(2)(b) (see head (2) in the text) or reg 79(3) (see the text and note 12), that number or, in any other case, the unique number allocated to a bareboat charter ship for identification purposes by its primary register: reg 1(2) (definition substituted by SI 1999/3206). As to the meaning of 'primary register' see PARA 295 note 9.
11  Merchant Shipping (Registration of Ships) Regulations 1993, SI 1993/3138, reg 79(2)(b) (as substituted: see note 8).
12  Merchant Shipping (Registration of Ships) Regulations 1993, SI 1993/3138, reg 79(3) (as substituted: see note 8).

**363. Marking of bareboat charter ship; inspection etc.** On being satisfied that the ship[1] is eligible for registration[2] and on production of any required certificate for survey[3], the registrar[4] must issue a carving and marking note[5].

On receipt of a carving and marking note, the charterer must[6]:

(1)     where the ship is not already so marked, cause it to be marked with its name[7], its port of choice[8], and (in respect of a fishing vessel[9]) its port number[10]; and

(2)     where the ship is not already so carved, cause it to be carved with its identifying number[11] and the number denoting its tonnage[12],

in accordance with the prescribed requirements for carving and marking[13].

The statutory provisions relating to inspection of marks[14] and to the cancellation of a carving and marking note[15] apply as if any reference in them to the owner[16] were a reference to the charterer[17].

1   Ie the bareboat charter ship. As to the meaning of 'bareboat charter ship' see PARA 255 note 9; and as to the meaning of 'ship' for these purposes see PARA 255 note 4.
2   As to the qualification and entitlement to register bareboat charter ships other than fishing vessels see PARA 358; and as to the qualification and entitlement to register a fishing vessel as a bareboat charter ship see PARA 359.
3   Ie any certificate for survey required under the Merchant Shipping (Registration of Ships) Regulations 1993, SI 1993/3138, reg 29 (survey and measurement of ship) (see PARA 276): see reg 80(1).
4   As to the meaning of 'registrar' see PARA 255 note 2.
5   Merchant Shipping (Registration of Ships) Regulations 1993, SI 1993/3138, reg 80(1).
6   Merchant Shipping (Registration of Ships) Regulations 1993, SI 1993/3138, reg 80(2).

7 Merchant Shipping (Registration of Ships) Regulations 1993, SI 1993/3138, reg 80(2)(a)(i).
8 Merchant Shipping (Registration of Ships) Regulations 1993, SI 1993/3138, reg 80(2)(a)(ii). As to the meaning of 'port of choice' see PARA 278 note 12. As to the allocation of port of choice see PARA 279; and see PARA 362 note 5.
9 As to the meaning of 'fishing vessel' for these purposes see PARA 255 note 7.
10 Merchant Shipping (Registration of Ships) Regulations 1993, SI 1993/3138, reg 80(2)(a)(iii) (amended by SI 1999/3206). As to the meaning of 'port number' see PARA 279 note 8.
11 As to the meaning of 'identifying number' see PARA 362 note 10.
12 Merchant Shipping (Registration of Ships) Regulations 1993, SI 1993/3138, reg 80(2)(b).
13 Merchant Shipping (Registration of Ships) Regulations 1993, SI 1993/3138, reg 80(2). The text refers to the requirements for carving and marking prescribed by reg 80(2), Sch 3 (as to which see PARA 281 et seq): see reg 80(2).
14 Ie the Merchant Shipping (Registration of Ships) Regulations 1993, SI 1993/3138, reg 33 (see PARA 286): see reg 81 (amended by SI 1994/541).
15 Ie the Merchant Shipping (Registration of Ships) Regulations 1993, SI 1993/3138, reg 35 (see PARA 288): see reg 81 (as amended: see note 14).
16 As to the meaning of 'owner' for these purposes see PARA 255 note 13.
17 Merchant Shipping (Registration of Ships) Regulations 1993, SI 1993/3138, reg 81 (as amended: see note 14).

**364. Registration of bareboat charter ship.** Where the registrar[1] is satisfied in respect of an application for registration[2] of a bareboat charter ship[3]:

(1)     that the ship has been duly carved and marked[4]; and

(2)     that, where required, the appropriate certificate of survey has been provided[5]; and

(3)     that the other requirements preliminary to registration have been complied with[6],

he must enter in the register[7] the details that are prescribed to be so entered[8].

Upon registering a ship, the registrar must:

(a)     issue and send to the charterer a certificate of bareboat charter registry[9] containing the required particulars[10]; and

(b)     retain in his possession a copy of the charter, a copy of any certificate of survey and all declarations of eligibility[11] and (if applicable) any declarations required under the provisions[12] relating to applications made by bodies corporate[13].

Notwithstanding that a ship is otherwise entitled to be registered, the registrar may refuse to register it if, taking into account any requirement of the Merchant Shipping Act 1995, including any instrument made thereunder, relating to the condition of the ship or its equipment so far as it is relevant to its safety or to any risk of pollution or to the safety, health and welfare of persons employed or engaged in any capacity on board the ship, he considers that it would be inappropriate for the ship to be registered[14].

1 As to the meaning of 'registrar' see PARA 255 note 2.
2 As to the meaning of 'application for registration' see PARA 269 note 1.
3 Merchant Shipping (Registration of Ships) Regulations 1993, SI 1993/3138, reg 82(1). As to the meaning of 'bareboat charter ship' see PARA 255 note 9; and as to the meaning of 'ship' for these purposes see PARA 255 note 4.
4 Merchant Shipping (Registration of Ships) Regulations 1993, SI 1993/3138, reg 82(1)(a). As to the carving and marking of bareboat charter ships see PARA 363.
5 Merchant Shipping (Registration of Ships) Regulations 1993, SI 1993/3138, reg 82(1)(b). As to the survey and measurement of ships, including the ascertainment and certification of tonnage for registration purposes, see PARA 276.
6 Merchant Shipping (Registration of Ships) Regulations 1993, SI 1993/3138, reg 82(1)(c).
7 As to the meaning of 'register' for these purposes see PARA 255 note 1. Part IV of the register is for ships which are bareboat charter ships: see the Merchant Shipping (Registration of Ships) Regulations 1993, SI 1993/3138, reg 2(1)(d); and PARA 255.
8 Merchant Shipping (Registration of Ships) Regulations 1993, SI 1993/3138, reg 82(1). The text refers to the details prescribed in reg 82(1), Sch 4 (see PARA 290 et seq): see reg 82(1).

9   As to the meanings of 'certificate of bareboat charter' and 'certificate of registry' see PARA 255 note 17. As to the issue of duplicate certificates of registry in certain circumstances see PARA 373.
10  Merchant Shipping (Registration of Ships) Regulations 1993, SI 1993/3138, reg 82(2) (amended by SI 1998/2976). The text refers to the particulars set out in the Merchant Shipping (Registration of Ships) Regulations 1993, SI 1993/3138, reg 82(2), Sch 5 (as to which see PARAS 299–301): see reg 82(2) (as so amended).
11  As to declarations of eligibility relating to applications for the registration of bareboat charter ships see PARA 360.
12  Ie the Merchant Shipping (Registration of Ships) Regulations 1993, SI 1993/3138, reg 24 (see PARA 273): see reg 82(3).
13  Merchant Shipping (Registration of Ships) Regulations 1993, SI 1993/3138, reg 82(3).
14  Merchant Shipping (Registration of Ships) Regulations 1993, SI 1993/3138, reg 82(4); Interpretation Act 1978 s 17(2)(b).

**365. Period of registration of bareboat charter ship; renewal.** The registration of a bareboat charter ship[1] expires[2]:

(1)    on the expiry of the charter period[3]; or
(2)    at the end of a period of five years beginning with the date of registration specified in the certificate of bareboat charter registry[4],

whichever is the earlier[5].

Three months before the expiry of the registration period, the registrar[6] must issue to the charterer of the ship a renewal notice[7].

Application for renewal of registration may be made during the last three calendar months of the current registration period[8].

Applications for renewal must be in a form approved by the Secretary of State[9] and must be accompanied by a declaration of eligibility[10] and by the certificate of bareboat charter registry[11].

1   As to the meaning of 'bareboat charter ship' see PARA 255 note 9; and as to the meaning of 'ship' for these purposes see PARA 255 note 4. As to the requirements for registration of a bareboat charter ship see PARA 357 et seq.
2   Merchant Shipping (Registration of Ships) Regulations 1993, SI 1993/3138, reg 83(1).
3   Merchant Shipping (Registration of Ships) Regulations 1993, SI 1993/3138, reg 83(1)(a). As to the meaning of 'charter period' for these purposes under the Merchant Shipping Act 1995 see PARA 357 note 11.
4   Merchant Shipping (Registration of Ships) Regulations 1993, SI 1993/3138, reg 83(1)(b) (amended by SI 1998/2976). As to the meanings of 'certificate of bareboat charter' and 'certificate of registry' see PARA 255 note 17.
5   Merchant Shipping (Registration of Ships) Regulations 1993, SI 1993/3138, reg 83(1). As to the surrender of a certificate on the termination or expiry of registration see PARA 375.
6   As to the meaning of 'registrar' see PARA 255 note 2.
7   Merchant Shipping (Registration of Ships) Regulations 1993, SI 1993/3138, reg 83(2).
8   Merchant Shipping (Registration of Ships) Regulations 1993, SI 1993/3138, reg 83(3). As to the requirement to remeasure tonnage in certain circumstances before a ship's registration can be renewed see PARA 380.
9   As to the Secretary of State see PARA 36.
10  As to declarations of eligibility relating to applications for the registration of bareboat charter ships see PARA 360. As to the power to dispense with declarations or other evidence otherwise required under the Merchant Shipping (Registration of Ships) Regulations 1993, SI 1993/3138, see PARA 371.
11  Merchant Shipping (Registration of Ships) Regulations 1993, SI 1993/3138, reg 83(4) (amended by SI 1998/2976).

**366. Notification of changes occurring in relation to bareboat charter ship.** If at any time there occurs, in relation to a bareboat charter ship[1], any change affecting the eligibility of the ship to be registered[2], the charterer of the ship must, as soon as practicable after the change occurs, notify the registrar[3]. Such notification must be made in writing, must be signed by the charterer and must specify the nature of the change and the name and the identifying number[4] of the ship[5]. Any person who contravenes the requirement to notify[6] is guilty of an offence[7].

The statutory provisions relating to change in the registered particulars of a ship[8], change of name[9], transfer to a port of choice[10] and re-marking of a ship[11] apply to bareboat charter ships[12] as if any reference in those provisions to the owner[13] were a reference to the charterer[14].

1   As to the meaning of 'bareboat charter ship' see PARA 255 note 9; and as to the meaning of 'ship' for these purposes see PARA 255 note 4.
2   As to the qualification and entitlement to register bareboat charter ships other than fishing vessels see PARA 358; and as to the qualification and entitlement to register a fishing vessel as a bareboat charter ship see PARA 359.
3   Merchant Shipping (Registration of Ships) Regulations 1993, SI 1993/3138, reg 84(1). As to the meaning of 'registrar' see PARA 255 note 2. As to the requirement to remeasure tonnage in certain circumstances where a ship's details have been changed see PARA 380.
4   As to the meaning of 'identifying number' see PARA 362 note 10.
5   Merchant Shipping (Registration of Ships) Regulations 1993, SI 1993/3138, reg 84(2).
6   Ie any person who contravenes the Merchant Shipping (Registration of Ships) Regulations 1993, SI 1993/3138, reg 84(1) (see the text and notes 1–3): see reg 84(3).
7   See the Merchant Shipping (Registration of Ships) Regulations 1993, SI 1993/3138, reg 84(3); and PARA 1068.
8   Ie the Merchant Shipping (Registration of Ships) Regulations 1993, SI 1993/3138, reg 51 (see PARA 314): see reg 85 (amended by SI 1994/541). As to offences relating to contraventions of reg 51 (including reg 51 as so applied) see PARA 1068.
9   Ie the Merchant Shipping (Registration of Ships) Regulations 1993, SI 1993/3138, reg 52 (see PARA 315): see reg 85 (as amended: see note 8).
10  Ie the Merchant Shipping (Registration of Ships) Regulations 1993, SI 1993/3138, reg 53 (see PARA 316): see reg 85 (as amended: see note 8).
11  Ie the Merchant Shipping (Registration of Ships) Regulations 1993, SI 1993/3138, reg 54 (see PARA 315): see reg 85 (as amended: see note 8).
12  Ie apply to the Merchant Shipping (Registration of Ships) Regulations 1993, SI 1993/3138, Pt X (regs 73–87) (see PARAS 358 et seq, 367 et seq): see reg 85 (as amended: see note 8).
13  As to the meaning of 'owner' for these purposes see PARA 255 note 13.
14  Merchant Shipping (Registration of Ships) Regulations 1993, SI 1993/3138, reg 85 (as amended: see note 8).

**367. Notification to foreign registries by the registrar.** The registrar[1] must notify the responsible authority for registration of ships[2] in the country of primary registration when[3]:
(1)   the ship has been registered as a bareboat charter ship[4] on the British register[5]; or
(2)   the ship's registration has closed by reason of the expiry of the certificate of registry[6]; or
(3)   the ship's registration has been closed by the registrar[7].

1   As to the meaning of 'registrar' see PARA 255 note 2.
2   As to the meaning of 'ship' for these purposes see PARA 255 note 4.
3   Merchant Shipping (Registration of Ships) Regulations 1993, SI 1993/3138, reg 86.
4   As to the meaning of 'bareboat charter ship' see PARA 255 note 9.
5   Merchant Shipping (Registration of Ships) Regulations 1993, SI 1993/3138, reg 86(a). As to the meaning of 'register' for these purposes see PARA 255 note 1.
6   Merchant Shipping (Registration of Ships) Regulations 1993, SI 1993/3138, reg 86(b). The text refers to closure under reg 83(1)(b) (see PARA 365): see reg 86(b). As to the meaning of 'certificate of registry' see PARA 255 note 17.
7   Merchant Shipping (Registration of Ships) Regulations 1993, SI 1993/3138, reg 86(c). The text refers to closure by reason of reg 87 (see PARA 368): see reg 86(c).

**368. Closure of bareboat charter ship's registration by the registrar.** The registrar[1] may[2] close the registration of a bareboat charter ship[3]:
(1)   on application by the charterer[4];
(2)   on the ship no longer being eligible to be registered[5];
(3)   on the ship being destroyed (which includes, but is not limited to, shipwreck, demolition, fire and sinking)[6];

(4)　　if, taking into account any requirement of the Merchant Shipping Act 1995, including any instrument made thereunder, relating to the condition of the ship or its equipment so far as relevant to its safety or to any risk of pollution or to the safety, health and welfare of persons employed or engaged in any capacity on board the ship, he considers that it would be inappropriate for the ship to remain registered[7];

(5)　　if the bareboat charter ship is a fishing vessel[8] which requires a licence to fish but at the time of registration did not have such a licence and has not acquired such a licence within six months of the issue of its certificate of bareboat charter registry[9];

(6)　　where the charterer of a fishing vessel fails to respond to the registrar within 15 days of a request from him to supply information concerning details on the register[10];

(7)　　where the charterer of a fishing vessel supplies information requested by the registrar, but that information is either false or incorrect or is reasonably considered by the registrar to be insufficient[11];

(8)　　where[12] the charterer is required to notify the registrar of any changes affecting the ship's eligibility to be registered, and has not done so[13];

(9)　　where[14] a person is required to make an application for any change in the registered particulars of a ship or in the name or address of a charterer to be recorded in the register, and has not done so[15]; or

(10)　　where a fishing vessel certificate[16] has expired[17].

On closure of a ship's registration under any of heads (1) to (10) above, the charterer must forthwith surrender to the registrar the certificate of bareboat charter registry for cancellation[18].

However, where it appears to the registrar that head (2) above, or any of heads (4) to (10) above, applies, he may serve notice on the owner or managing owner[19], or on any charterer, manager or operator of the ship requiring him to produce, within 30 days, evidence (which may include a declaration of British connection[20]) sufficient to satisfy him that the ship is eligible to remain on the register[21]. If, at the expiry of that period of 30 days, the registrar is not so satisfied, he may either:

(a)　　extend the notice and ask for further information or evidence[22]; or

(b)　　serve a final notice which closes the ship's registration, such closure to take effect seven days after the service of that notice[23].

Where a ship's registration is so terminated, the registrar must issue a closure transcript[24] and the owner of the ship must forthwith surrender its certificate of registry[25].

1　As to the meaning of 'registrar' see PARA 255 note 2.
2　Ie subject to the Merchant Shipping (Registration of Ships) Regulations 1993, SI 1993/3138, reg 101 (service of notices) (see the text and notes 19–25): see reg 87(1).
3　Merchant Shipping (Registration of Ships) Regulations 1993, SI 1993/3138, reg 87(1). As to the meaning of 'bareboat charter ship' see PARA 255 note 9; and as to the meaning of 'ship' for these purposes see PARA 255 note 4. As to the registration of a bareboat charter ship see PARA 357 et seq.
4　Merchant Shipping (Registration of Ships) Regulations 1993, SI 1993/3138, reg 87(1)(a).
5　Merchant Shipping (Registration of Ships) Regulations 1993, SI 1993/3138, reg 87(1)(b). As to the qualification and entitlement to register bareboat charter ships other than fishing vessels see PARA 358; and as to the qualification and entitlement to register a fishing vessel as a bareboat charter ship see PARA 359.
6　Merchant Shipping (Registration of Ships) Regulations 1993, SI 1993/3138, reg 87(1)(c).
7　Merchant Shipping (Registration of Ships) Regulations 1993, SI 1993/3138, reg 87(1)(d); Interpretation Act 1978 s 17(2)(b).
8　As to the meaning of 'fishing vessel' for these purposes see PARA 255 note 7.
9　Merchant Shipping (Registration of Ships) Regulations 1993, SI 1993/3138, reg 87(1)(e) (added by SI 1998/2976). As to the meanings of 'certificate of bareboat charter' and 'certificate of registry' see PARA 255 note 17.

10 Merchant Shipping (Registration of Ships) Regulations 1993, SI 1993/3138, reg 87(1)(f) (reg 87(1)(f)–(j) added by SI 1999/3206). As to the meaning of 'register' for these purposes see PARA 255 note 1.
11 Merchant Shipping (Registration of Ships) Regulations 1993, SI 1993/3138, reg 87(1)(g) (as added: see note 10).
12 Ie under the Merchant Shipping (Registration of Ships) Regulations 1993, SI 1993/3138, reg 84 (as to which see PARA 366): see reg 87(1)(h) (as added: see note 10).
13 Merchant Shipping (Registration of Ships) Regulations 1993, SI 1993/3138, reg 87(1)(h) (as added: see note 10).
14 Ie under the Merchant Shipping (Registration of Ships) Regulations 1993, SI 1993/3138, reg 51 (as to which see PARA 314), as applied by reg 85 (as to which see PARA 366): see reg 56(1)(i) (as added: see note 10).
15 Merchant Shipping (Registration of Ships) Regulations 1993, SI 1993/3138, reg 87(1)(i) (as added: see note 10).
16 As to the meaning of 'fishing vessel certificate' see PARA 317 note 22.
17 Merchant Shipping (Registration of Ships) Regulations 1993, SI 1993/3138, reg 87(1)(j) (as added: see note 10).
18 Merchant Shipping (Registration of Ships) Regulations 1993, SI 1993/3138, reg 87(2) (amended by SI 1998/2976).
19 As to the meaning of 'owner' for these purposes see PARA 255 note 13. The term 'managing owner' is used in the Merchant Shipping (Registration of Ships) Regulations 1993, SI 1993/3138, reg 23 (appointment of managing owner where ship has more than one owner) (as to which see PARA 271), as well as in reg 34, but it is not defined; however, see PARA 238.
   Where the registrar serves a notice under reg 101 on the owner of a vessel in respect of which a mortgage is registered, the registrar must send a copy of that notice to the mortgagee at the address recorded for him in the register: reg 102.
20 As to the meaning of 'declaration of British connection' under the Merchant Shipping Act 1995 see PARA 245 note 3. As to the power to dispense with declarations or other evidence otherwise required under the Merchant Shipping (Registration of Ships) Regulations 1993, SI 1993/3138, see PARA 371.
21 Merchant Shipping (Registration of Ships) Regulations 1993, SI 1993/3138, reg 101(1) (amended by SI 1998/2976; SI 1999/3206).
22 Merchant Shipping (Registration of Ships) Regulations 1993, SI 1993/3138, reg 101(2)(a).
23 Merchant Shipping (Registration of Ships) Regulations 1993, SI 1993/3138, reg 101(2)(b).
24 As to the meaning of 'closure transcript' see PARA 317 note 33.
25 Merchant Shipping (Registration of Ships) Regulations 1993, SI 1993/3138, reg 101(3).

## (xii) Miscellaneous Provisions relating to Registration

### A. DOCUMENTS ETC

**369. Documents not in the English language to be accompanied by a translation.** Any document which is not in the English language and is produced in support of any application for registration[1] of a ship[2] must be accompanied by a notarised translation of the document in the English language[3].

1 As to the meaning of 'application for registration' see PARA 269 note 1.
2 As to the meaning of 'ship' for these purposes see PARA 255 note 4.
3 Merchant Shipping (Registration of Ships) Regulations 1993, SI 1993/3138, reg 103.

**370. Witnessing of documents.** Where the signature on any document made pursuant to the provisions governing the registration of ships[1] is required to be witnessed, any witness to the signature must be a person of full age and must not be the spouse of the signatory[2].

1 Ie made under the Merchant Shipping (Registration of Ships) Regulations 1993, SI 1993/3138: see reg 104. As to the meaning of 'ship' for these purposes see PARA 255 note 4.
2 Merchant Shipping (Registration of Ships) Regulations 1993, SI 1993/3138, reg 104.

**371. Dispensing with declarations or evidence otherwise required.** Where, under the provisions governing the registration of ships[1]:

(1)　　any person is required to make a declaration on behalf of himself or any body corporate, but is unable to do so and can satisfy the registrar[2] that it is due to reasonable cause, the registrar may, on such terms as he thinks fit, dispense with the declaration[3]; or

(2)　　any evidence is required to be produced to the registrar, but such evidence is unable to be produced and the registrar is satisfied that it is due to reasonable cause, the registrar may, on production of such other evidence as he considers appropriate, dispense with the evidence[4].

1　Ie under the Merchant Shipping (Registration of Ships) Regulations 1993, SI 1993/3138: see reg 105. As to the meaning of 'ship' for these purposes see PARA 255 note 4.
2　As to the meaning of 'registrar' see PARA 255 note 2.
3　Merchant Shipping (Registration of Ships) Regulations 1993, SI 1993/3138, reg 105(a).
4　Merchant Shipping (Registration of Ships) Regulations 1993, SI 1993/3138, reg 105(b).

**372. Requirement for supplementary information.** Where the registrar[1] is not satisfied by the information provided on an application for registration[2] of a ship[3] that the ship is eligible for registration, or that any of the particulars or other information supplied is correct or sufficient, he may require such supplementary information or evidence as he considers appropriate[4].

1　As to the meaning of 'registrar' see PARA 255 note 2.
2　As to the meaning of 'application for registration' see PARA 269 note 1.
3　As to the meaning of 'ship' for these purposes see PARA 255 note 4.
4　Merchant Shipping (Registration of Ships) Regulations 1993, SI 1993/3138, reg 106 (substituted by SI 1999/3206).

B.　CERTIFICATES OF REGISTRY

**373. Duplicate certificates.** If it is shown to the satisfaction of the registrar[1] that the certificate of registry[2] for a ship[3] has been lost, stolen or destroyed or has become defaced or illegible (the 'event'), he may issue to the owner[4] a duplicate of that certificate, which must be marked as such, and is of the same effect as the original[5]. Where a duplicate certificate of registry is issued, the original, if then available or if subsequently found or recovered, must be forthwith surrendered to the registrar[6].

If:

(1)　　the port where the ship is at the time of the event or, as the case may be, where it first arrives after the event, is not in the United Kingdom[7]; and

(2)　　the master of the ship or some other person having knowledge of the facts of the case makes a declaration before the appropriate person[8] as to the loss, theft, destruction, defacement or illegibility of the certificate[9],

the appropriate person must notify the registrar[10]. On being notified of the event and being satisfied that the ship is entitled to be issued with a duplicate certificate, the registrar must[11]:

(a)　　fax to the appropriate person a copy of the duplicate certificate which the appropriate person must indorse with a statement of the circumstances under which it is granted[12]; or

(b)　　where there are no fax facilities, authorise the appropriate person to issue a provisional certificate so indorsed[13].

The faxed certificate or the provisional certificate must, within ten days of the ship arriving in a port in the United Kingdom, be surrendered to the registrar, and a duplicate certificate must be issued[14].

Any person who fails, without reasonable cause, to surrender a certificate of registry when required to do so by these provisions[15] commits an offence[16].

1　As to the meaning of 'registrar' see PARA 255 note 2.

2   As to the meaning of 'certificate of registry' see PARA 255 note 17.
3   As to the meaning of 'ship' for these purposes see PARA 255 note 4.
4   As to the meaning of 'owner' for these purposes see PARA 255 note 13.
5   Merchant Shipping (Registration of Ships) Regulations 1993, SI 1993/3138, reg 108(1). As to
    related offences see PARA 1070.
6   Merchant Shipping (Registration of Ships) Regulations 1993, SI 1993/3138, reg 108(2).
7   Merchant Shipping (Registration of Ships) Regulations 1993, SI 1993/3138, reg 108(3)(a). As to
    the meaning of 'United Kingdom' see PARA 16 note 3.
8   As to the meaning of 'appropriate person' for these purposes see PARA 337 note 6.
9   Merchant Shipping (Registration of Ships) Regulations 1993, SI 1993/3138, reg 108(3)(b).
10  Merchant Shipping (Registration of Ships) Regulations 1993, SI 1993/3138, reg 108(3).
11  Merchant Shipping (Registration of Ships) Regulations 1993, SI 1993/3138, reg 108(4).
12  Merchant Shipping (Registration of Ships) Regulations 1993, SI 1993/3138, reg 108(4)(a).
13  Merchant Shipping (Registration of Ships) Regulations 1993, SI 1993/3138, reg 108(4)(b)
    (amended by SI 1994/541).
14  Merchant Shipping (Registration of Ships) Regulations 1993, SI 1993/3138, reg 108(5).
15  Ie when required to do so by the Merchant Shipping (Registration of Ships) Regulations 1993, SI
    1993/3138, reg 108: see reg 114(4).
16  See the Merchant Shipping (Registration of Ships) Regulations 1993, SI 1993/3138, reg 114(4);
    and PARA 1071.

**374.  Custody of certificate.** A certificate of registry[1] must be used only for
lawful navigation of the ship[2] and is not subject to detention by reason only of any
title, lien, charge or interest whatever had or claimed by any owner[3], mortgagee
or other person to, on or in the ship[4].

If any person refuses, without reasonable cause, to surrender the certificate of
registry when in his possession or under his control to the person entitled to its
custody for the purposes of the lawful navigation of the ship, or to the registrar[5],
or an officer of revenue and customs[6] or any other person entitled by law to
demand such delivery, he is guilty of an offence[7].

1   As to the meaning of 'certificate of registry' see PARA 255 note 17.
2   As to the meaning of 'ship' for these purposes see PARA 255 note 4.
3   As to the meaning of 'owner' for these purposes see PARA 255 note 13.
4   Merchant Shipping (Registration of Ships) Regulations 1993, SI 1993/3138, reg 109(1).
5   As to the meaning of 'registrar' see PARA 255 note 2.
6   As to the appointment of officers of Revenue and Customs see INCOME TAXATION vol 58 (2014)
    PARA 33.
7   See the Merchant Shipping (Registration of Ships) Regulations 1993, SI 1993/3138, regs 109(2),
    114(4), (7); and PARA 1071.

**375.  Surrender of certificate on termination or expiry of registration.** On
the termination, whether by expiration of the registration period or otherwise, of
a ship's registration[1], the certificate of registry[2] must be returned by the owner[3] or
charterer to the registrar[4] for cancellation[5].

Any person who fails, without reasonable cause, to return a certificate of
registry when required to do so by these provisions[6] commits an offence[7].

1   As to the termination of a ship's registration see PARAS 317, 356, 368. As to the meaning of 'ship'
    for these purposes see PARA 255 note 4.
2   As to the meaning of 'certificate of registry' see PARA 255 note 17.
3   As to the meaning of 'owner' for these purposes see PARA 255 note 13.
4   As to the meaning of 'registrar' see PARA 255 note 2.
5   Merchant Shipping (Registration of Ships) Regulations 1993, SI 1993/3138, reg 110.
6   Ie when required to do so by the Merchant Shipping (Registration of Ships) Regulations 1993, SI
    1993/3138, reg 110: see reg 114(4).
7   See the Merchant Shipping (Registration of Ships) Regulations 1993, SI 1993/3138, reg 114(4);
    and PARA 1071.

**376.  Dispensing with production of certificate.** Where a certificate of
registry[1] is required[2] to accompany any application and it is shown to the
satisfaction of the registrar[3] that for any reasonable cause (which includes, but is

not limited to, the ship[4] being in a port outside the United Kingdom[5], or the certificate being needed for an imminent voyage, at the time the application was made) the certificate cannot be produced, the registrar may, subject to such conditions as he thinks fit, dispense with its production[6].

1 As to the meaning of 'certificate of registry' see PARA 255 note 17.
2 Ie required by the Merchant Shipping (Registration of Ships) Regulations 1993, SI 1993/3138: see reg 111.
3 As to the meaning of 'registrar' see PARA 255 note 2.
4 As to the meaning of 'ship' for these purposes see PARA 255 note 4.
5 As to the meaning of 'United Kingdom' see PARA 16 note 3.
6 Merchant Shipping (Registration of Ships) Regulations 1993, SI 1993/3138, reg 111.

**377. Status of a Part II certificate under sea fisheries legislation.** A certificate of registry[1] or a certificate of bareboat registry[2] of a fishing vessel[3] (including a valid temporary registration certificate) is to be a 'document relating to a boat' for the purposes of the Sea Fisheries Act 1968[4] and as such must at all times be carried on board the vessel[5].

1 As to the meaning of 'certificate of registry' see PARA 255 note 17.
2 As to the meaning of 'certificate of bareboat registry' see PARA 255 note 17.
3 As to the meaning of 'fishing vessel' for these purposes see PARA 255 note 7.
4 Ie for the purposes of the Sea Fisheries Act 1968 s 8(3)(b) (as to which see FISHERIES AND AQUACULTURE vol 51 (2013) PARA 276): see the Merchant Shipping (Registration of Ships) Regulations 1993, SI 1993/3138, reg 112 (amended by SI 1999/3206).
5 Merchant Shipping (Registration of Ships) Regulations 1993, SI 1993/3138, reg 112 (as amended: see note 4).

### C. REMOVAL OF MARKS

**378. Removal of marks on cessation of registration.** If a ship's registration is terminated[1], whether by expiration of the registration period[2] or otherwise, the prescribed marking[3] must be removed from the ship and written confirmation of that removal must be sent to the registrar[4].

1 As to registration see PARA 254 et seq; and as to the termination of a ship's registration see PARAS 317, 356, 368. As to the meaning of 'ship' for these purposes see PARA 255 note 4.
2 As to the registration period of a ship see PARAS 296, 352, 365.
3 Ie the marking prescribed under the Merchant Shipping (Registration of Ships) Regulations 1993, SI 1993/3138 (as to which specifically see PARAs 280 et seq, 351, 363): see reg 113.
4 Merchant Shipping (Registration of Ships) Regulations 1993, SI 1993/3138, reg 113. As to the meaning of 'registrar' see PARA 255 note 2.

### D. FEES PAYABLE TO REGISTRAR

**379. Fees prescribed in respect of any service or other transaction.** Where a fee is prescribed in respect of any service or other transaction to be carried out[1], the registrar[2] is not required to carry out the service or other transaction unless the appropriate fee has been paid[3].

1 Ie pursuant to the Merchant Shipping (Registration of Ships) Regulations 1993, SI 1993/3138: see reg 107.
2 As to the meaning of 'registrar' see PARA 255 note 2.
3 Merchant Shipping (Registration of Ships) Regulations 1993, SI 1993/3138, reg 107.

### E. RE-MEASUREMENT OF TONNAGE

**380. Re-measurement of tonnage required when changes in registration occur.** No transfer of ownership of a ship or shares in a ship[1], no renewal of registration[2], nor change of details of the ship or its owners[3] may be registered in respect of any ship which[4]:

(1) is required to have its tonnage measured in accordance with the International Convention on Tonnage Measurement of Ships 1969[5]; and

(2)     for which no such measurement has been undertaken and registered[6], until such re-measurement takes place and where necessary the certificate of survey has been lodged with the registrar[7] for amendment of the register[8]. However, this requirement does not apply where the transfer, or change of details, arises by reason of the death of an owner of a ship, or a share in a ship[9].

1   As to the meaning of 'ship' for these purposes see PARA 255 note 4. As to the transfer of ownership of a ship see PARA 306 et seq.
2   As to the renewal of registration of a ship see PARAS 304 et seq, 353, 365.
3   As to changes in the details of a ship or its owners see PARAS 313 et seq, 354, 366. As to the meaning of 'owner' for these purposes see PARA 255 note 13.
4   Merchant Shipping (Registration of Ships) Regulations 1993, SI 1993/3138, reg 113A(1) (reg 113A added by SI 1998/2976).
5   Merchant Shipping (Registration of Ships) Regulations 1993, SI 1993/3138, reg 113A(1)(a) (as added: see note 4). The International Convention on Tonnage Measurement of Ships (London, 23 June to 23 December 1969; TS 50 (1982); Cmnd 8716) is implemented by the Merchant Shipping (Tonnage) Regulations 1997, SI 1997/1510 (as to which see PARA 248 et seq): see PARA 7.
6   Merchant Shipping (Registration of Ships) Regulations 1993, SI 1993/3138, reg 113A(1)(b) (as added: see note 4).
7   As to the meaning of 'registrar' see PARA 255 note 2.
8   Merchant Shipping (Registration of Ships) Regulations 1993, SI 1993/3138, reg 113A(1) (as added: see note 4). As to the meaning of 'register' for these purposes see PARA 255 note 1.
9   Merchant Shipping (Registration of Ships) Regulations 1993, SI 1993/3138, reg 113A(2) (as added: see note 4).

# 4. HOVERCRAFT

## (1) HOVERCRAFT: IN GENERAL

**381. Meaning of 'hovercraft' for the purposes of the Hovercraft Act 1968.** For the purposes of the Hovercraft Act 1968, 'hovercraft' means a vehicle which is designed to be supported when in motion wholly or partly by air expelled from the vehicle to form a cushion of which the boundaries include the ground, water or other surface beneath the vehicle[1].

1 Hovercraft Act 1968 s 4(1). Except as otherwise provided by or under the Hovercraft Act 1968, or an enactment passed before 26 August 1968 (ie the date of the passing of the Hovercraft Act 1968), a hovercraft is not to be treated as being a ship, aircraft or motor vehicle for the purposes of any such enactment or any instrument having effect by virtue of any such enactment: s 4(3). For these purposes, 'enactment' includes an enactment contained in a local Act and an enactment contained in any Act passed after and in the same session as the Hovercraft Act 1968 (s 4(1)); and any reference in the Hovercraft Act 1968 to any enactment or instrument is a reference to it as amended, and includes a reference to it as applied, by or under any other enactment (s 4(2)).

**382. Power to make Orders in Council under the Hovercraft Act 1968.** Her Majesty may by Order in Council make such provision as she considers expedient[1]:

(1) with respect to the registration of hovercraft[2];

(2) for securing the safety of hovercraft and persons and property in hovercraft and at hoverports[3], and for preventing hovercraft from endangering other persons and property[4];

(3) for prohibiting or restricting the use of hovercraft unless the prescribed[5] certificates as to fitness are in force and the prescribed conditions as to maintenance and repair are satisfied with respect to them[6];

(4) for prohibiting persons from taking charge or otherwise acting as members of the crew of a hovercraft or from engaging in or being employed in connection with the maintenance or repair of hovercraft, in such capacities as may be prescribed, unless the prescribed conditions as to qualifications and other matters are satisfied with respect to those persons[7];

(5) with respect to the investigation of accidents involving hovercraft[8];

(6) for regulating the noise and vibration which may be caused by hovercraft[9];

(7) for providing that no action is to lie, and no proceedings in pursuance of Part III of the Environmental Protection Act 1990[10] are to be brought, in respect of nuisance by reason only of noise and vibration caused by hovercraft in respect of which the requirements imposed in pursuance of head (6) above are complied with[11];

(8) for applying in relation to hovercraft or to persons, things or places connected with hovercraft[12]:

(a) any enactment[13] or instrument[14] relating to ships, aircraft, motor vehicles or other means of transport or to persons, things, places connected therewith[15];

(b) any rules of law relating to ships or persons, things or places connected with ships (other than rules relating to maritime liens)[16];

(9) and, without prejudice to the generality of the above provisions, for providing that any enactment (other than an enactment mentioned above) is to have effect as if references in it, in whatever terms, to ships, aircraft or motor vehicles or activities connected therewith included references to hovercraft or activities connected with hovercraft[17];

(10) for applying the following enactments, and any instrument made under them, in relation to the following matters respectively[18], that is to say:

(a) in relation to the carriage by persons and their baggage by hovercraft, the Carriage by Air Act 1961[19] and the Carriage by Air (Supplementary Provisions) Act 1962[20];

(b) in relation to the carriage of property by hovercraft (except baggage in relation to which provisions of the Acts specified in head (9)(a) above are applied) the Carriage of Goods by Sea Act 1971[21] and certain provisions of the Merchant Shipping Act 1995[22] which limit liability, so far as those provisions relate to property on board a ship[23];

(c) in relation to loss of life or personal injury connected with a hovercraft which is caused to persons not carried by the hovercraft, in relation to the loss or damage connected with a hovercraft which is caused to property not carried by the hovercraft and in relation to infringements of rights through acts or omissions connected with a hovercraft, certain provisions of the Merchant Shipping Act 1995[24] which limit liability[25];

(11) for substituting references to hovercraft for references in any enactment or instrument to vehicles designed to be supported on a cushion of air[26];

(12) for repealing the provisions of any enactment or instrument[27], in so far as it appears to Her Majesty that those provisions are not required having regard to any provision made or proposed to be made by virtue of the power to make Orders in Council under the Hovercraft Act 1968[28];

(13) with respect to the application of the Order to the Crown and the extra-territorial operation of any provision made by or under the Order[29];

(14) for the extension of any provisions of the Order, with or without modifications[30], to Northern Ireland, any of the Channel Islands, the Isle of Man, any colony[31] and any country or place outside Her Majesty's dominions[32] in which for the time being Her Majesty has jurisdiction[33];

(15) for imposing penalties in respect of any contravention[34] of a provision made by or under the Order, not exceeding, in respect of any one contravention, a fine of £400 on summary conviction and imprisonment for 12 months and a fine on conviction on indictment[35];

(16) for detaining any hovercraft in order to secure compliance with any provision made by or under the Order or any hovercraft in respect of which such a contravention is suspected to have occurred[36]; and

(17) for requiring the payment of fees in respect of any matter relating to hovercraft which is specified in the Order and for determining with the approval of the Treasury the amount of any such fee or the manner in which that amount is to be determined[37].

Nothing in any of heads (1) to (16) above is to be construed as prejudicing the generality of any other of those heads; and in particular head (14) above does not prejudice head (8) above[38].

An Order in Council so made may[39]:

(i) make different provision for different circumstances or for hovercraft of different descriptions[40];

(ii) provide for exemptions from any of the provisions of the Order[41];

(iii) provide for the delegation of functions exercisable by virtue of the Order[42];

(iv) include such incidental, supplemental and consequential provisions as appear to Her Majesty to be expedient for the purposes of the Order[43];

(v)     authorise the making of regulations and other instruments for any of the above purposes, except the purposes of heads (7) to (11) above, and apply the Statutory Instruments Act 1946[44] to instruments made under the Order[45];

(vi)    provide that any enactment, instrument or rule of law applied by the Order shall have effect as so applied subject to such modifications as may be specified in the Order[46]; and

(vii)   be revoked or varied by a subsequent Order so made[47].

No recommendation may be made to Her Majesty in Council to make such an Order containing provisions authorised by heads (6) to (11) above unless a draft of the Order has been approved by a resolution of each House of Parliament[48]; and any other Order in Council under the above provisions, except an Order extending only to territory (other than Northern Ireland) which is mentioned in head (13) above, is subject to annulment in pursuance of a resolution of either House of Parliament[49].

1   Hovercraft Act 1968 s 1(1).
2   Hovercraft Act 1968 s 1(1)(a). As to the meaning of 'hovercraft' under the Hovercraft Act 1968 see PARA 381. In exercise of the power so conferred, Her Majesty has made the Hovercraft (General) Order 1972, SI 1972/674 (as to which see PARA 387 et seq).
3   For these purposes, 'hoverport' means any area, whether on land or elsewhere, which is designed, equipped, set apart or commonly used for affording facilities for the arrival and departure of hovercraft: Hovercraft Act 1968 s 4(1).
4   Hovercraft Act 1968 s 1(1)(b).
5   For these purposes, 'prescribed' means prescribed by an Order in Council under the Hovercraft Act 1968 s 1, or by an instrument made under such an Order: s 4(1).
6   Hovercraft Act 1968 s 1(1)(c).
7   Hovercraft Act 1968 s 1(1)(d).
8   Hovercraft Act 1968 s 1(1)(e).
9   Hovercraft Act 1968 s 1(1)(f).
10  Ie the Environmental Protection Act 1990 Pt III (ss 79–84) (as to which see NUISANCE vol 78 (2010) PARA 156 et seq) or corresponding Northern Ireland legislation: see the Hovercraft Act 1968 s 1(1)(g) (amended by the Control of Pollution Act 1974 s 108, Sch 3 para 26; the Environmental Protection Act 1990 s 162(1), Sch 15 para 9; the Environment Act 1995 s 120(3), Sch 24; prospectively further amended by the Clean Neighbourhoods and Environment Act (Northern Ireland) 2011 Sch 3 Pt 3).
11  Hovercraft Act 1968 s 1(1)(g) (as amended: see note 10).
12  Hovercraft Act 1968 s 1(1)(h).
13  As to the meaning of 'enactment' see PARA 381 note 1.
14  Ie other than an enactment or an instrument made under an enactment mentioned in the Hovercraft Act 1968 s 1(1)(i) (see head (9) in the text) or s 2(1) (see PARA 383) or an enactment contained in the Senior Courts Act 1981 ss 20–24 (Admiralty jurisdiction of the High Court) (see PARA 79 et seq): see the Hovercraft Act 1968 s 1(1)(h)(i) (amended by the Senior Courts Act 1981 s 152(1), Sch 5).
15  Hovercraft Act 1968 s 1(1)(h)(i) (as amended: see note 14).
16  Hovercraft Act 1968 s 1(1)(h)(ii). As to maritime liens see PARA 964 et seq.
17  Hovercraft Act 1968 s 1(1)(h). In exercise of the power so conferred, Her Majesty has made the Hovercraft (Civil Liability) Order 1986, SI 1986/1305: see PARA 386. The enactments and instruments with respect to which provision may be made by Order in Council under the Hovercraft Act 1968 s 1(1)(h) include the Merchant Shipping Act 1995, except Pt I (ss 1–7) (British ships) (see PARA 230 et seq) and Pt II (ss 8–23) (registration) (see PARA 245 et seq), and any instrument made thereunder (s 310); and the Prevention of Oil Pollution Act 1971 (see ENVIRONMENTAL QUALITY AND PUBLIC HEALTH vol 45 (2010) PARA 348) and any instrument made thereunder (s 31).
18  Hovercraft Act 1968 s 1(1)(i).
19  As to the Carriage by Air Act 1961 see CARRIAGE AND CARRIERS vol 7 (2015) PARA 121 et seq.
20  Hovercraft Act 1968 s 1(1)(i)(i). As to the Carriage by Air (Supplementary Provisions) Act 1962 see CARRIAGE AND CARRIERS vol 7 (2015) PARA 121.
21  As to the Carriage of Goods by Sea Act 1971 see CARRIAGE AND CARRIERS vol 7 (2015) PARA 368 et seq.

22  Ie the Merchant Shipping Act 1995 s 185 (as to which see PARA 992) and s 186 (as to which see PARA 1009): see the Hovercraft Act 1968 s 1(1)(i)(ii) (amended by the Merchant Shipping Act 1995 s 314(2), Sch 13 para 42; the Merchant Shipping and Maritime Security Act 1997 s 29(1), Sch 6 para 1).

23  Hovercraft Act 1968 s 1(1)(i)(ii) (as amended: see note 22); Carriage of Goods by Sea Act 1971 s 6(3).

24  Ie the Merchant Shipping Act 1995 s 185 (as to which see PARA 992) and s 186 (as to which see PARA 1009): see the Hovercraft Act 1968 s 1(1)(i)(iii) (amended by the Merchant Shipping Act 1995 Sch 13 para 42).

25  Hovercraft Act 1968 s 1(1)(i)(iii) (as amended: see note 24).

26  Hovercraft Act 1968 s 1(1)(j).

27  Ie including the provisions of the Hovercraft Act 1968 s 3, Schedule (as to which see PARA 384): see s 1(1)(k).

28  Hovercraft Act 1968 s 1(1)(k). The text refers to any provision made or proposed to be made by virtue of s 1: see s 1(1)(k).

29  Hovercraft Act 1968 s 1(1)(l).

30  For these purposes, 'modifications' includes additions, omissions and amendments: Hovercraft Act 1968 s 4(1).

31  As to the meaning of 'colony' see STATUTES AND LEGISLATIVE PROCESS vol 96 (2012) PARA 1208.

32  As to Her Majesty's dominions see COMMONWEALTH vol 13 (2017) PARA 605.

33  Hovercraft Act 1968 s 1(1)(m).

34  For these purposes, 'contravention' includes failure to comply: Hovercraft Act 1968 s 4(1).

35  Hovercraft Act 1968 s 1(1)(n).

36  Hovercraft Act 1968 s 1(1)(o).

37  Hovercraft Act 1968 s 1(1)(p). In exercise of the powers conferred on him by the Hovercraft (General) Order 1972, SI 1972/674, art 35 (see PARA 417), the Secretary of State made the Hovercraft (Fees) Regulations 1997, SI 1997/320 (see PARA 417). As to the Treasury see CONSTITUTIONAL AND ADMINISTRATIVE LAW vol 20 (2014) PARAS 262–265.

38  Hovercraft Act 1968 s 1(2).

39  Hovercraft Act 1968 s 1(3). The text refers to an order made under s 1: see s 1(3). In exercise of the power so conferred, Her Majesty has made the Hovercraft (Application of Enactments) Order 1972, SI 1972/971; and the Hovercraft (Application of Enactments) Order 1989, SI 1989/1350. See eg PARA 830 et seq.

40  Hovercraft Act 1968 s 1(3)(a).

41  Hovercraft Act 1968 s 1(3)(b).

42  Hovercraft Act 1968 s 1(3)(c).

43  Hovercraft Act 1968 s 1(3)(d).

44  As to the Statutory Instruments Act 1946 see STATUTES AND LEGISLATIVE PROCESS vol 96 (2012) PARA 1032 et seq.

45  Hovercraft Act 1968 s 1(3)(e).

46  Hovercraft Act 1968 s 1(3)(f).

47  Hovercraft Act 1968 s 1(3)(g). The text refers to a subsequent order made under s 1: see s 1(3)(g).

48  Hovercraft Act 1968 s 1(4).

49  Hovercraft Act 1968 s 1(4).

**383. Admiralty jurisdiction.** Hovercraft[1] are subject to the Admiralty jurisdiction of the High Court[2]. The law relating to maritime liens[3] applies[4] in relation to hovercraft and property connected with hovercraft as it applies in relation to ships and property connected with ships, notwithstanding that the hovercraft in question is on land at any relevant time[5].

Her Majesty may, however, by Order in Council[6] provide that the statutory provisions relating to Admiralty jurisdiction and the law relating to maritime liens[7] are not to apply in relation to hovercraft in such circumstances as may be specified in the Order, or are to have effect, in all circumstances involving hovercraft or such circumstances involving hovercraft as may be specified in the Order, subject to such modifications as may be so specified[8].

1   As to the meaning of 'hovercraft' under the Hovercraft Act 1968 see PARA 381.

2   Ie by virtue of the fact that, in the Senior Courts Act 1981 ss 20–24 (Admiralty jurisdiction of the High Court) (see PARA 79 et seq), 'ship' includes a hovercraft: see s 24(1); and PARA 85 note 7.

As to the jurisdiction of the High Court generally see COURTS AND TRIBUNALS vol 24 (2010) PARA 699 et seq; and as to county courts generally see COURTS AND TRIBUNALS vol 24 (2010) PARA 758 et seq.

3 As to maritime liens see PARA 964 et seq.

4 Ie subject to the Hovercraft Act 1968 s 2(3) (see the text and notes 6–8): see s 2(2).

5 Hovercraft Act 1968 s 2(2).

6 The provisions of the Hovercraft Act 1968 s 1(3) (Orders in Council) (see PARA 382) apply to an order under s 2(3) as they apply to an Order under s 1 but as if s 1(3)(c), (e), (f) (see PARA 382) was omitted: see s 2(3). No recommendation may be made to Her Majesty in Council to make an Order under s 2 unless a draft of the Order has been approved by a resolution of each House of Parliament: s 2(4).

7 Ie the Administration of Justice Act 1956 Pt V (ss 45–50), Sch 1 Pt I (which apply to Scotland only), and the County Courts Act 1984 ss 30, 31 (Hovercraft Act 1968 s 2(1) (amended by the Supreme Court Act 1981 Sch 5; the County Courts Act 1984 Sch 2 para 32; and the Crime and Courts Act 2013 Sch 9 para 141), and the law mentioned in the Hovercraft Act 1968 s 2(2) (see the text and notes 3–5) as extended: see s 2(3). Section 2(3) has effect as if the reference to the enactments mentioned in s 2(1) as extended by s 2(1) included a reference to the Senior Courts Act 1981 ss 20–24 (Admiralty jurisdiction of the High Court) (see PARA 79 et seq): Hovercraft Act 1968 s 2(3A) (added by the Senior Courts Act 1981 Sch 5).

8 Hovercraft Act 1968 s 2(3). At the date at which this volume states the law, no such Order in Council had been made.

## 384. Application of certain enactments to hovercraft.
Certain enactments[1] have effect subject to specified modifications[2] which provide for the application of those enactments in relation to hovercraft[3].

1 Ie the Dockyard Port Regulation Act 1865, the Explosives Act 1875, the Docking and Nicking of Horses Act 1949, the Prevention of Damage by Pests Act 1949, and the Pests Act 1954: see the Hovercraft Act 1968 s 3, Schedule (Schedule amended by the Immigration Act 1971 s 34(1), Sch 6; the Misuse of Drugs Act 1971 s 39(2), Sch 6; the British Nationality Act 1981 s 52(8), Sch 9 para 1(f); the Road Traffic Regulation Act 1984 s 146, Sch 14; and the Statute Law (Repeals) Act 1993).

2 Ie the modifications specified in the Hovercraft Act 1968 Schedule (see note 1): see s 3. As to the meaning of 'modifications' see PARA 382 note 30.

3 Hovercraft Act 1968 s 3. As to the meaning of 'hovercraft' under the Hovercraft Act 1968 see PARA 381. See also CUSTOMS AND EXCISE vol 31 (2012) PARA 918 (application of provisions to hovercraft), PARA 943 (control of movement of hovercraft), PARA 1070 (power to regulate small craft); MORTGAGE vol 77 (2016) PARA 214 (mortgages of aircraft and hovercraft); and PATENTS AND REGISTERED DESIGNS vol 79 (2014) PARA 514 (use of ships, aircraft, hovercraft and vehicles which would otherwise infringe a patent).

## 385. Financial provisions.
Any expenses incurred or sums received under the Hovercraft Act 1968 by any Minister of the Crown or government department must be defrayed out of moneys provided by Parliament or paid into the Consolidated Fund, as the case may be[1].

Any increase attributable to the Hovercraft Act 1968 in the sums which, under any other enactment, are payable out of or into the Consolidated Fund or the National Loans Fund or out of moneys provided by Parliament must be paid out of or into that Fund or out of moneys so provided, as the case may be[2].

1 Hovercraft Act 1968 s 6(1) (amended by the Post Office Act 1969 s 141, Sch 11 Pt II). As to the Consolidated Fund generally see CONSTITUTIONAL AND ADMINISTRATIVE LAW vol 20 (2014) PARA 480 et seq; PARLIAMENT vol 78 (2010) PARAS 1028–1031.

2 Hovercraft Act 1968 s 6(2). As to the National Loans Fund see CONSTITUTIONAL AND ADMINISTRATIVE LAW vol 20 (2014) PARA 500 et seq.

## (2) CIVIL LIABILITY

## 386. Application of general provisions relating to civil liability.
The statutory provisions relating to the carriage of passengers and baggage by air[1]

apply, with modifications[2], in relation to the carriage of passengers and their baggage by hovercraft[3] as they apply in relation to the carriage of passengers and their baggage by air[4].

The statutory provisions relating to goods on board or carried by ships[5] apply, with modifications[6], to the carriage of goods, other than passengers' baggage, by hovercraft as they apply in relation to goods on board or carried by ship[7].

The statutory provisions relating to the overall limitation of liability of shipowners[8] apply, with modifications[9], in relation to[10]:

(1)    loss of life or personal injury connected with a hovercraft which is caused to persons not carried by the hovercraft[11];

(2)    loss or damage connected with a hovercraft which is caused to property[12]; and

(3)    infringements of rights through acts or omissions connected with a hovercraft[13],

if and only if at the time of the incident causing the damage the hovercraft was on or over navigable water or on or over the foreshore, or was proceeding between navigable water and a hoverport, or was on or over a hoverport either preparing for or after such transit[14]; but this provision does not apply to claims in respect of loss or damage to passengers' baggage carried by the hovercraft or in respect of loss of or damage to crew's[15] property carried by the hovercraft[16].

The provisions relating to ships as to division of loss, damages for personal injuries, rights of contribution and apportionment of salvage[17] apply, with modifications[18], to hovercraft[19].

1   Ie the Carriage by Air Act 1961 and the Carriage by Air (Supplementary Provisions) Act 1962 (see CARRIAGE AND CARRIERS vol 7 (2015) PARA 121 et seq): see the Hovercraft (Civil Liability) Order 1986, SI 1986/1305, art 3.

2   Ie the modifications set out in the Hovercraft (Civil Liability) Order 1986, SI 1986/1305, art 3, Sch 1 (Sch 1 amended by SI 1987/1835): see the Hovercraft (Civil Liability) Order 1986, SI 1986/1305, art 3.

3   As to the meaning of 'hovercraft' under the Hovercraft Act 1968 see PARA 381.

4   Hovercraft (Civil Liability) Order 1986, SI 1986/1305, art 3. The enactments applied by the Hovercraft (Civil Liability) Order 1986, SI 1986/1305, apply with the further modifications that:

(1)    a vehicle and its contents are not to be treated as baggage (art 5(a)); and

(2)    subject thereto, any property of which the passenger takes charge himself is to be treated as baggage (art 5(b)).

For convenience of reference, the enactments applied by art 3, art 4 (see the text and notes 5–7) and art 6 (see the text and notes 8–16) are set out in art 10, Sch 4 (amended by SI 1987/1835; SI 1998/1257) with the modifications made in them by the Hovercraft (Civil Liability) Order 1986, SI 1986/1305: art 10.

5   Ie the Carriage of Goods by Sea Act 1971 (see CARRIAGE AND CARRIERS vol 7 (2015) PARAS 207, 368 et seq): see the Hovercraft (Civil Liability) Order 1986, SI 1986/1305, art 4.

6   Ie the modifications set out in the Hovercraft (Civil Liability) Order 1986, SI 1986/1305, art 4, Sch 2: see art 4.

7   Hovercraft (Civil Liability) Order 1986, SI 1986/1305, art4. See also note 4.

8   Ie the Merchant Shipping Act 1995 ss 185(1), (2), 186(1)–(3), (5), Sch 7 Pt II (paras 1–13) (see PARA 992 et seq): see the Hovercraft (Civil Liability) Order 1986, SI 1986/1305, art 6(1); Interpretation Act 1978 s 17(2)(b).

9   Ie the modifications set out in the Hovercraft (Civil Liability) Order 1986, SI 1986/1305, art 6(1), Sch 3 (amended by SI 1998/1257): see the Hovercraft (Civil Liability) Order 1986, SI 1986/1305, art 6(1). See also note 4. The provisions of art 6, Sch 3 apply in relation to Her Majesty's hovercraft as they apply in relation to other hovercraft (art 8(1)); and the Crown Proceedings Act 1947 ss 6, 30 (repealed) (see now the Merchant Shipping Act 1995 ss 190, 192(1); and PARAS 1013, 1015) apply in the case of hovercraft as they apply in the case of vessels (Hovercraft (Civil Liability) Order 1986, SI 1986/1305, art 8(2)).

10  Hovercraft (Civil Liability) Order 1986, SI 1986/1305, art6(1).

11  Hovercraft (Civil Liability) Order 1986, SI 1986/1305, art6(1)(a).

12  Hovercraft (Civil Liability) Order 1986, SI 1986/1305, art6(1)(b).

13  Hovercraft (Civil Liability) Order 1986, SI 1986/1305, art6(1)(c).

14 Hovercraft (Civil Liability) Order 1986, SI 1986/1305, art6(1).
15 For these purposes, 'crew' means a person who is on board a hovercraft or employed in connection with that hovercraft or with salvage operations, if he was so on board or employed under a contract of service governed by the law of any part of the United Kingdom; and 'salvage operations' has the same meaning as in the Merchant Shipping Act 1995 (see PARA 893) as modified by the Hovercraft (Civil Liability) Order 1986, SI 1986/1305: see art 6(2); Interpretation Act 1978 s 17(2)(b). As to the meaning of 'United Kingdom' see PARA 16 note 3.
16 Hovercraft (Civil Liability) Order 1986, SI 1986/1305, art6(2).
17 Ie the provisions of the Merchant Shipping Act 1995 ss 187–190 (see PARA 1010 et seq): see the Hovercraft (Civil Liability) Order 1986, SI 1986/1305, art 7; Interpretation Act 1978 s 17(2)(b).
18 Ie references to ships in the Merchant Shipping Act 1995 ss 187–190 (see PARA 1010 et seq) are to be read as if they included references to hovercraft: see the Hovercraft (Civil Liability) Order 1986, SI 1986/1305, art 7; Interpretation Act 1978 s 17(2)(b).
19 Hovercraft (Civil Liability) Order 1986, SI 1986/1305, art 7; Interpretation Act 1978 s 17(2)(b).

# (3) REGISTRATION ETC

## (i) Application of Provisions

**387. Application of general provisions to hovercraft.** The general provisions relating to the registration, certification, maintenance and operation of hovercraft[1] apply to hovercraft[2] which are used[3]:

(1) wholly or partly on or over the sea or navigable waters[4]; or

(2) on or over land to which the public has access or non-navigable waters to which the public has access[5]; or

(3) elsewhere for the carriage of passengers[6] for reward[7].

This is subject to the proviso that those same general provisions do not apply to hovertrains[8], nor do they prejudice the operation of the provisions of the Road Traffic Act 1988[9] which govern the application of road traffic legislation to hovercraft or hover vehicles[10].

1 Ie the Hovercraft (General) Order 1972, SI 1972/674 (see PARA 388 et seq): see art 2. As to the meaning of 'hovercraft' under the Hovercraft Act 1968 see PARA 381.
2 Ie subject to the proviso that the Hovercraft (General) Order 1972, SI 1972/674, Pt II (arts 7A–17) (certification and maintenance) (see PARA 396 et seq) and Pt III (arts 17A–24) (duties of operator and captain) (see PARA 402 et seq) do not apply to hovercraft to which the Merchant Shipping (High Speed Craft) Regulations 2004, SI 2004/302 (see PARA 617 et seq) apply: see the Hovercraft (General) Order 1972, SI 1972/674, art 7A (cited in PARA 396), art 17A (cited in PARA 402); Interpretation Act 1978 s 17(2)(b).
3 Hovercraft (General) Order 1972, SI 1972/674, art2.
4 Hovercraft (General) Order 1972, SI 1972/674, art 2(i). For these purposes, 'navigable water' means any water which is in fact navigable by ships or vessels, whether or not the tide ebbs and flows there, and whether or not there is a public right of navigation in that water: art 3(1).
5 Hovercraft (General) Order 1972, SI 1972/674, art2(ii).
6 For these purposes, 'passenger' means any person carried in a hovercraft, except a person employed or engaged in any capacity on board the hovercraft on the business of the hovercraft: Hovercraft (General) Order 1972, SI 1972/674, art 3(1).
7 Hovercraft (General) Order 1972, SI 1972/674, art2(iii).
8 Hovercraft (General) Order 1972, SI 1972/674, art 2(a). For these purposes, 'hovertrains' means hovercraft which are at all times guided by tracks, rails or guides fixed to the ground: art 3(1).
9 Ie the Road Traffic Act 1988 s 188 (application of the Road Traffic Regulation Act 1984 and the Road Traffic Act 1988 to hovercraft or hover vehicles) (as to which see ROAD TRAFFIC vol 89 (2011) PARA 18): see the Hovercraft (General) Order 1972, SI 1972/674, art 2(b); Interpretation Act 1978 s 17(2)(b).
10 Hovercraft (General) Order 1972, SI 1972/674, art 2(b); Interpretation Act 1978 s 17(2)(b).

**388. Crown application.** The general provisions relating to the registration, certification, maintenance and operation of hovercraft[1] apply to or in relation to hovercraft belonging to or exclusively employed in the service of Her Majesty as they apply to or in relation to other hovercraft; and, for the purposes of such application, the government department or other authority for the time being responsible on behalf of Her Majesty for the operational management of the hovercraft is deemed to be the operator[2] of the hovercraft and, in the case of a hovercraft belonging to Her Majesty, to be the owner of the interest of Her Majesty in the hovercraft[3].

Where a military hovercraft[4] is operated by a civilian and is not commanded by a person who is acting in the course of his duty as a member of any of Her Majesty's naval or military or air forces or as a member of a visiting force or international headquarters[5], that civilian is bound by the usual duties of a captain[6] on the occasion of that journey[7].

Nothing in the provisions governing Crown application[8] renders liable to any penalty[9] any department or other authority responsible on behalf of Her Majesty for the management of the hovercraft[10].

1  Ie the Hovercraft (General) Order 1972, SI 1972/674 (see PARAS 387, 389 et seq): see art 34(1). As to the meaning of 'hovercraft' under the Hovercraft Act 1968 see PARA 381.
2  For these purposes, 'operator', in relation to a hovercraft, means the person for the time being having the management of the hovercraft: Hovercraft (General) Order 1972, SI 1972/674, art 3(1).
3  Hovercraft (General) Order 1972, SI 1972/674, art34(1).
4  For these purposes, 'military hovercraft' means the naval, military or air force hovercraft of any country and includes (by virtue of the Hovercraft (General) Order 1972, SI 1972/674, art 3(1)):
    (1)      any hovercraft being constructed for the naval, military or air force of any country under a contract entered into by the Secretary of State; and
    (2)      any hovercraft in respect of which there is in force a certificate issued by the Secretary of State that the hovercraft is to be treated for the purposes of the Hovercraft (General) Order 1972, SI 1972/674, as a military hovercraft.
    As to the Secretary of State see PARA 36.
5  As to visiting forces see ARMED FORCES vol 3 (2011) PARA 405; and as to international headquarters see ARMED FORCES vol 3 (2011) PARA 420.
6  For these purposes, 'captain' means the person who is designated by the operator to be in charge of a hovercraft during any journey, or, failing such designation, the person who is for the time being lawfully in charge of the hovercraft: Hovercraft (General) Order 1972, SI 1972/674, art 3(1). As to the duties of a captain see PARA 405.
7  Hovercraft (General) Order 1972, SI 1972/674, art 34(3). Save as provided in art 34(3), nothing in the Hovercraft (General) Order 1972, SI 1972/674, applies to or in relation to any military hovercraft: art 34(2).
8  Ie nothing in the Hovercraft (General) Order 1972, SI 1972/674, art 34: see art 34(1) proviso.
9  As to penalties for contravention see PARA 1072.
10 Hovercraft (General) Order 1972, SI 1972/674, art34(1) proviso.

**389.  Extra-territorial effect.** Except where the context otherwise requires, the general provisions relating to the registration, certification, maintenance and operation of hovercraft[1] apply as follows[2]:
    (1)      in so far as they apply, whether by express reference or otherwise, to hovercraft registered in the United Kingdom[3], they apply to such hovercraft wherever they may be[4];
    (2)      in so far as they so apply to other hovercraft, they apply to such hovercraft when they are within the United Kingdom[5];
    (3)      in so far as they prohibit, require or regulate, whether by express reference or otherwise, the doing of anything by persons in, or by any of the crew of, any hovercraft registered in the United Kingdom, they apply to such persons and crew, wherever they may be[6]; and
    (4)      in so far as they prohibit, require or regulate, whether by express reference or otherwise, the doing of anything in relation to any hovercraft registered in the United Kingdom by other persons, they apply, where such persons are British subjects[7], to them wherever they may be[8].

However, nothing in the provisions governing the extra-territorial effect of the general hovercraft provisions[9] is to be construed as extending the criminal liability of certain persons who are not citizens of the United Kingdom and colonies[10] and whose liability is otherwise limited[11].

1 Ie the Hovercraft (General) Order 1972, SI 1972/674 (see PARAS 387, 388, 390 et seq): see art 36(1). As to the meaning of 'hovercraft' under the Hovercraft Act 1968 see PARA 381. As to the hovercraft to which the Hovercraft (General) Order 1972, SI 1972/674, applies see PARA 387; and as to Crown application see PARA 388.
2 Hovercraft (General) Order 1972, SI 1972/674, art36(1).
3 As to the registration of hovercraft in the United Kingdom see PARA 390 et seq. For these purposes, 'United Kingdom' includes the territorial waters adjacent to the United Kingdom: Hovercraft (General) Order 1972, SI 1972/674, art 3(1). As to the meaning of 'United Kingdom' see PARA 16 note 3. As to the extent of the territorial and non-territorial sea, the baselines used for delimitation, and associated rights see INTERNATIONAL RELATIONS LAW vol 61 (2010) PARA 121 et seq.
4 Hovercraft (General) Order 1972, SI 1972/674, art36(1)(a).
5 Hovercraft (General) Order 1972, SI 1972/674, art36(1)(b).
6 Hovercraft (General) Order 1972, SI 1972/674, art36(1)(c).
7 As to British subjects under the British Nationality Act 1981 see BRITISH NATIONALITY vol 4 (2011) PARAS 407, 469–474.
8 Hovercraft (General) Order 1972, SI 1972/674, art36(1)(d).
9 Ie nothing in the Hovercraft (General) Order 1972, SI 1972/674, art 36: see art 36(2).
10 As to citizenship of the United Kingdom and colonies see BRITISH NATIONALITY vol 4 (2011) PARAS 406, 414–419. As to the meaning of 'colony' see STATUTES AND LEGISLATIVE PROCESS vol 96 (2012) PARA 1208.
11 Hovercraft (General) Order 1972, SI 1972/674, art 36(2). The text refers to the provision that nothing in art 36 is to be construed as extending to make any person guilty of an offence in any case in which it is provided by the British Nationality Act 1948 s 3(1) (which limits the criminal liability of certain persons who are not citizens of the United Kingdom and Colonies) (see BRITISH NATIONALITY vol 4 (2011) PARA 488), that that person is to be guilty of an offence: see the Hovercraft (General) Order 1972, SI 1972/674, art 36(2). For the purposes of the British Nationality Act 1948, references to the colonies include references to the Channel Islands and the Isle of Man: see s 33(1).

## (ii) Registration

**390. Necessity for registration.** If used in the United Kingdom[1], a hovercraft[2] must be registered in the United Kingdom[3], unless[4]:

(1)     it is registered in some other country[5]; or
(2)     an unqualified person[6] holds a legal or beneficial interest in the hovercraft by way of ownership or share therein and the Secretary of State[7] consents to its use unregistered in the United Kingdom, subject to such conditions as he thinks fit[8].

A hovercraft may also be used unregistered in the United Kingdom if it has an unladen weight[9] of less than 1,000 kilograms and is not used for reward[10].

1 As to the meaning of 'United Kingdom' for these purposes see PARA 389 note 3.
2 As to the meaning of 'hovercraft' under the Hovercraft Act 1968 see PARA 381. As to the hovercraft to which the Hovercraft (General) Order 1972, SI 1972/674, applies see PARA 387; and as to Crown application see PARA 388.
3 Ie subject to the Hovercraft (General) Order 1972, SI 1972/674, art 7 (hovercraft registered outside the United Kingdom) (see PARA 395): see art 4.
4 Hovercraft (General) Order 1972, SI 1972/674, art4.
5 Hovercraft (General) Order 1972, SI 1972/674, art 4(a). As to hovercraft registered outside the United Kingdom see PARA 395; and as to penalties for contravention see PARA 1072.
6 For these purposes, 'unqualified person' means a person not qualified in accordance with the Hovercraft (General) Order 1972, SI 1972/674, art 5(3) (see PARA 391) to be the holder of a legal or beneficial interest by way of ownership in the hovercraft: art 3(1). 'Beneficial interest' includes interests arising under contract and other equitable interests: art 3(1).
7 As to the Secretary of State see PARA 36.
8 Hovercraft (General) Order 1972, SI 1972/674, art4(b).

9   For these purposes, 'unladen weight', in relation to a hovercraft, means the weight of a hovercraft ready for use, excluding the weight of usable fuel, occupants, baggage, cargo, stores, buoyant life-saving equipment, portable fire-fighting equipment, portable emergency equipment and non-permanent ballast: Hovercraft (General) Order 1972, SI 1972/674, art 3(1).

10  Hovercraft (General) Order 1972, SI 1972/674, art 4 proviso (amended by SI 1996/3173).

**391. Procedure for registration of hovercraft in the United Kingdom.** The Secretary of State[1] is the authority for registration of hovercraft[2] in the United Kingdom[3].

A hovercraft may not be registered or continue to be registered in the United Kingdom if it appears to the Secretary of State that[4]:

(1)   the hovercraft is registered outside the United Kingdom and that such registration does not cease by operation of law upon the hovercraft being registered in the United Kingdom[5]; or

(2)   an unqualified person[6] holds any legal or beneficial interest[7] in the hovercraft by way of ownership or any share therein[8].

Only the following persons and no others are qualified to be the holder of a legal or beneficial interest by way of ownership in a hovercraft registered in the United Kingdom or a share therein[9]:

(a)   the Crown in right of Her Majesty's government in the United Kingdom[10];

(b)   persons ordinarily resident in the United Kingdom[11];

(c)   bodies incorporated in the United Kingdom and having their principal place of business in the United Kingdom[12];

(d)   firms carrying on business in Scotland[13].

However, if an unqualified person holds a legal or beneficial interest by way of ownership in a hovercraft or a share in it, or is a charterer by demise of it, the Secretary of State may register the hovercraft in the United Kingdom subject to such conditions as he thinks fit[14]; and he may at any time cancel the registration of the hovercraft so registered[15].

1   As to the Secretary of State see PARA 36.

2   As to the meaning of 'hovercraft' under the Hovercraft Act 1968 see PARA 381. As to the hovercraft to which the Hovercraft (General) Order 1972, SI 1972/674, applies see PARA 387; and as to Crown application see PARA 388.

3   Hovercraft (General) Order 1972, SI 1972/674, art 5(1). As to the meaning of 'United Kingdom' for these purposes see PARA 389 note 3.

4   Hovercraft (General) Order 1972, SI 1972/674, art5(2).

5   Hovercraft (General) Order 1972, SI 1972/674, art 5(2)(a). As to hovercraft registered outside the United Kingdom see PARA 395; and as to penalties for contravention see PARA 1072.

6   As to the meaning of 'unqualified person' see PARA 390 note 6.

7   As to the meaning of 'beneficial interest' see PARA 390 note 6. For the purposes of the Hovercraft (General) Order 1972, SI 1972/674, art 5, references to an interest in a hovercraft do not include references to an interest in a hovercraft to which a person is entitled only by virtue of his membership of a hovercraft club: art 5(12).

8   Hovercraft (General) Order 1972, SI 1972/674, art5(2)(b).

9   Hovercraft (General) Order 1972, SI 1972/674, art5(3).

10  Hovercraft (General) Order 1972, SI 1972/674, art5(3)(a).

11  Hovercraft (General) Order 1972, SI 1972/674, art5(3)(b). As to ordinary residence see IMMIGRATION AND ASYLUM vol 57 (2012) PARA 140; CONFLICT OF LAWS vol 19 (2011) PARA 359.

12  Hovercraft (General) Order 1972, SI 1972/674, art 5(3)(c). As to a person's place of business see COMPANIES vol 14 (2016) PARA 117.

13  Hovercraft (General) Order 1972, SI 1972/674, art5(3)(d). For these purposes, 'firm' has the same meaning as in the Partnership Act 1890 (see PARTNERSHIP vol 79 (2014) PARA 1): see the Hovercraft (General) Order 1972, SI 1972/674, art 5(3).

14  Hovercraft (General) Order 1972, SI 1972/674, art5(4).

15  Hovercraft (General) Order 1972, SI 1972/674, art5(4).

**392. Application for the registration of a hovercraft in the United Kingdom.** Application for the registration of a hovercraft[1] in the United Kingdom[2] must be made in writing to the Secretary of State[3] and must include or be accompanied by such particulars and evidence relating to the hovercraft and the ownership and chartering of it as he may require to enable him to determine whether the hovercraft may properly be registered in the United Kingdom and to issue a certificate of registration[4].

Upon receiving an application for the registration of a hovercraft in the United Kingdom and being satisfied that the hovercraft may properly be so registered, the Secretary of State must (or, in the case of an application by an unqualified person[5], may) register the hovercraft, wherever it may be, and he must include in the register the following particulars[6]:

(1) the number of the certificate[7];

(2) the registration mark[8] assigned to the hovercraft by the Secretary of State[9];

(3) the name of the constructor of the hovercraft, its type and constructor's number[10];

(4) the name and address of every person who holds a legal interest[11] in the hovercraft by way of ownership or a share in it (or, in the case of a hire-purchase agreement[12], the name and address of the hirer)[13]; and

(5) in cases where the Secretary of State has allowed registration of a hovercraft in which an unqualified person holds a legal or beneficial interest[14] by way of ownership in a hovercraft or a share in it, or is a charterer by demise of it[15], an indication that it is so registered, and an indication as to whether the person in whose name it is registered is the owner or charterer by demise[16].

The Secretary of State must furnish to the person in whose name the hovercraft is registered (the 'registered owner') a certificate of registration which must include the above particulars and the date on which the certificate was issued[17].

If at any time after the hovercraft has been registered in the United Kingdom an unqualified person becomes the holder of a legal or beneficial interest in the hovercraft by way of ownership or a share in it, the registration of the hovercraft thereupon becomes void[18] and the certificate of registration must forthwith be returned by the registered owner to the Secretary of State for cancellation[19].

1 As to the meaning of 'hovercraft' under the Hovercraft Act 1968 see PARA 381. As to the hovercraft to which the Hovercraft (General) Order 1972, SI 1972/674, applies see PARA 387; and as to Crown application see PARA 388.

2 As to the meaning of 'United Kingdom' for these purposes see PARA 389 note 3. As to the procedure for registration of hovercraft in the United Kingdom see PARA 391.

3 As to the Secretary of State see PARA 36.

4 Hovercraft (General) Order 1972, SI 1972/974, art 5(5). The text refers to a certificate of registration issued as mentioned in art 5(7) (see the text and note 17): see art 5(5).

5 Ie an application under Hovercraft (General) Order 1972, SI 1972/674, art 5(4) (see PARA 391): see art 5(6). As to the meaning of 'unqualified person' see PARA 390 note 6.

6 Hovercraft (General) Order 1972, SI 1972/674, art5(6).

7 Hovercraft (General) Order 1972, SI 1972/674, art5(6)(a).

8 As to registration marks see PARA 394.

9 Hovercraft (General) Order 1972, SI 1972/674, art5(6)(b).

10 Hovercraft (General) Order 1972, SI 1972/674, art5(6)(c).

11 For the purposes of the Hovercraft (General) Order 1972, SI 1972/674, art 5, references to an interest in a hovercraft do not include references to an interest in a hovercraft to which a person is entitled only by virtue of his membership of a hovercraft club: art 5(12).

12 As to hire purchase agreements see CONSUMER CREDIT vol 21 (2016) PARAS 40, 64 et seq.

13 Hovercraft (General) Order 1972, SI 1972/674, art5(6)(d)(i).

14 As to the meaning of 'beneficial interest' see PARA 390 note 6.

15　Ie in the case of a hovercraft registered under Hovercraft (General) Order 1972, SI 1972/674, art 5(4) (see PARA 391): see art 5(6)(d)(ii).

16　Hovercraft (General) Order 1972, SI 1972/674, art5(6)(d)(ii).

17　Hovercraft (General) Order 1972, SI 1972/674, art5(7).

18　Ie subject to the Hovercraft (General) Order 1972, SI 1972/674, art 5(4) (see PARA 391): see art 5(8).

19　Hovercraft (General) Order 1972, SI 1972/674, art5(8). As to the cancellation of certificates see PARA 401.

### 393. Notification of changes in particulars furnished on application for registration.

Any person who is registered as the owner of a hovercraft[1] registered in the United Kingdom[2] must forthwith inform the Secretary of State[3] in writing of[4]:

(1)　any change in the particulars which were furnished to the Secretary of State upon application being made for the registration of the hovercraft[5];

(2)　the destruction of the hovercraft, or its permanent withdrawal from use[6];

(3)　in the case of a registered hovercraft in respect of which an unqualified person[7] is a charterer by demise[8], the termination of the demise charter[9].

Any person who becomes the owner of a hovercraft registered in the United Kingdom must immediately inform the Secretary of State in writing to that effect[10].

Whenever it appears to him necessary or appropriate to do so for certain purposes[11], the Secretary of State may amend the register, or, if he thinks fit, may cancel the registration of the hovercraft, and he must cancel that registration if he is satisfied that there has been a change in the ownership of the hovercraft[12].

1　As to the meaning of 'hovercraft' under the Hovercraft Act 1968 see PARA 381. As to the hovercraft to which the Hovercraft (General) Order 1972, SI 1972/674, applies see PARA 387; and as to Crown application see PARA 388. For the purposes of art 5(9), the reference to the registered owner of a hovercraft includes, in the case of a deceased person, his legal personal representative, and, in the case of a body corporate which has been dissolved, its successor: art 5(12).

2　As to the meaning of 'United Kingdom' for these purposes see PARA 389 note 3. As to the procedure for registration of hovercraft in the United Kingdom see PARAS 391, 392.

3　As to the Secretary of State see PARA 36.

4　Hovercraft (General) Order 1972, SI 1972/674, art5(9).

5　Hovercraft (General) Order 1972, SI 1972/674, art 5(9)(a). As to applications for registration of hovercraft in the United Kingdom see PARA 392.

6　Hovercraft (General) Order 1972, SI 1972/674, art5(9)(b).

7　As to the meaning of 'unqualified person' see PARA 390 note 6.

8　Ie in the case of demise chartered hovercraft registered in pursuance of the Hovercraft (General) Order 1972, SI 1972/674, art 5(4) (see PARA 391): see art 5(9)(c).

9　Hovercraft (General) Order 1972, SI 1972/674, art5(9)(c).

10　Hovercraft (General) Order 1972, SI 1972/674, art5(10).

11　Ie for the purposes of giving effect to the Hovercraft (General) Order 1972, SI 1972/674 (see PARAS 387 et seq, 394 et seq) or for bringing up to date or otherwise correcting the particulars entered on the register: see art 5(11).

12　Hovercraft (General) Order 1972, SI 1972/674, art5(11).

### 394. Nationality and registration marks.

A hovercraft[1] registered in the United Kingdom[2] must not be used unless[3]:

(1)　it bears prominently and clearly painted or affixed to the craft its nationality and registration marks[4]; and

(2)　the nationality and registration marks together with the name and address of the registered owner are engraved on a fire-proof metal plate affixed in a prominent position inside the hovercraft near an entrance[5].

The nationality mark of a hovercraft registered in the United Kingdom must be the capital letters 'GH' in Roman characters and the registration mark must be a group of four digits assigned by the Secretary of State[6] on the registration of the hovercraft[7]. The letters and digits must be without ornamentation and a hyphen must be placed between the nationality mark and the registration mark[8].

The nationality and registration marks of a hovercraft are to be used as the sole means of identification of the craft by radio[9].

1 As to the meaning of 'hovercraft' under the Hovercraft Act 1968 see PARA 381. As to the hovercraft to which the Hovercraft (General) Order 1972, SI 1972/674, applies see PARA 387; and as to Crown application see PARA 388.
2 As to the meaning of 'United Kingdom' for these purposes see PARA 389 note 3. As to the procedure for registration of hovercraft in the United Kingdom see PARA 391 et seq.
3 Hovercraft (General) Order 1972, SI 1972/674, art6(1). As to penalties for contravention see PARA 1072.
4 Hovercraft (General) Order 1972, SI 1972/674, art6(1)(i).
5 Hovercraft (General) Order 1972, SI 1972/674, art6(1)(ii).
6 As to the Secretary of State see PARA 36.
7 Hovercraft (General) Order 1972, SI 1972/674, art6(2).
8 Hovercraft (General) Order 1972, SI 1972/674, art6(2).
9 Hovercraft (General) Order 1972, SI 1972/674, art6(3).

**395. Hovercraft registered outside the United Kingdom.** A hovercraft[1] registered in a country other than the United Kingdom[2] must not be used for reward or in connection with a trade or business in or over the United Kingdom, except with the permission of the Secretary of State[3] to the operator[4] or charterer of the hovercraft and in accordance with any conditions to which such permission may be subject[5].

However, this requirement does not apply to the use of a hovercraft for passage through the territorial waters of the United Kingdom[6].

1 As to the meaning of 'hovercraft' under the Hovercraft Act 1968 see PARA 381. As to the hovercraft to which the Hovercraft (General) Order 1972, SI 1972/674, applies see PARA 387; and as to Crown application see PARA 388.
2 As to the meaning of 'United Kingdom' for these purposes see PARA 389 note 3. As to the procedure for registration of hovercraft in the United Kingdom see PARA 391 et seq.
3 Ie granted under the Hovercraft (General) Order 1972, SI 1972/674, art 7: see art 7(1). As to the Secretary of State see PARA 36.
4 As to the meaning of 'operator' see PARA 388 note 2.
5 Hovercraft (General) Order 1972, SI 1972/674, art7(1). As to penalties for contravention see PARA 1072.
6 Hovercraft (General) Order 1972, SI 1972/674, art 7(2). As to the extent of the territorial and non-territorial sea, the baselines used for delimitation, and associated rights see INTERNATIONAL RELATIONS LAW vol 61 (2010) PARA 121 et seq.

### (iii) Certification and Maintenance

**396. Application of provisions.** The provisions relating to certification and maintenance of a hovercraft[1] do not apply to hovercraft to which the Merchant Shipping (High-Speed Craft) Regulations 2004[2] apply[3].

1 Ie the Hovercraft (General) Order 1972, SI 1972/674, Pt II (arts 7A–17) (certification and maintenance) (see PARA 397 et seq): see art 7A (added by SI 1996/3173; amended by SI 2004/302). As to the meaning of 'hovercraft' under the Hovercraft Act 1968 see PARA 381. As to the hovercraft to which the Hovercraft (General) Order 1972, SI 1972/674, applies see PARA 387; and as to Crown application see PARA 388.
2 Ie the Merchant Shipping (High Speed Craft) Regulations 2004, SI 2004/302 (see PARA 617 et seq): see the Hovercraft (General) Order 1972, SI 1972/674, art 7A (as added and amended: see note 1).
3 Hovercraft (General) Order 1972, SI 1972/674, art 7A (as added and amended: see note 1).

**397. Safety certificate to be in force.** A hovercraft[1] registered in the United Kingdom[2] may not be used unless there is in force in respect of it a current safety certificate[3] and any conditions to which the certificate was issued are complied with[4]. This prohibition does not, however, apply, subject to the prior consent of the Secretary of State[5] and to any conditions subject to which that consent was given, to a hovercraft in respect of which a safety certificate has previously been in force, which is used solely for the purpose of enabling it[6]:

(1)　　to qualify for renewal of a safety certificate or a variation of a certificate after an application has been made for such renewal or variation[7];

(2)　　to proceed to or from a place at which any inspection or test of the hovercraft is to take place for the purpose of qualifying for renewal of a safety certificate or a variation of a certificate after an application has been made for such renewal or variation[8]; or

(3)　　to proceed to a place at which repairs can be effected[9].

1　As to the meaning of 'hovercraft' under the Hovercraft Act 1968 see PARA 381. As to the hovercraft to which the Hovercraft (General) Order 1972, SI 1972/674, applies see PARA 387; and as to Crown application see PARA 388. As to the application of art 8 see PARA 396.
2　As to the meaning of 'United Kingdom' for these purposes see PARA 389 note 3. As to the procedure for registration of hovercraft in the United Kingdom see PARA 391 et seq.
3　Ie issued in accordance with the Hovercraft (General) Order 1972, SI 1972/674: see art 8. As to the issue of safety certificates see PARA 398.
4　Hovercraft (General) Order 1972, SI 1972/674, art 8. As to penalties for contravention see PARA 1072.
5　As to the Secretary of State see PARA 36.
6　Hovercraft (General) Order 1972, SI 1972/674, art 8 proviso (b) (amended by SI 1996/3173).
7　Hovercraft (General) Order 1972, SI 1972/674, art 8 proviso (b)(i).
8　Hovercraft (General) Order 1972, SI 1972/674, art 8 proviso (b)(ii).
9　Hovercraft (General) Order 1972, SI 1972/674, art 8 proviso (b)(iii).

**398. Issue of safety certificates.** The Secretary of State[1] may issue a safety certificate in respect of a hovercraft[2] registered in the United Kingdom[3] upon being satisfied that it is fit to be used, having regard, in particular, to[4]:

(1)　　the results of such investigations of the hovercraft as the Secretary of State may require[5]; and

(2)　　the quality of the hovercraft's construction[6].

Every safety certificate may specify such categories[7] as have been applied for and are, in the Secretary of State's opinion, appropriate to the hovercraft, and the safety certificate must be issued subject to the condition that the hovercraft is to be used only for specified purposes[8] in relation to such categories[9]. Accordingly, the categories for which a safety certificate may be so issued are: passenger; cargo; and special[10]. In the passenger category, a hovercraft may be used for the purposes of the carriage of passengers[11] and their baggage, and any other purposes specified in the certificate[12]; in the cargo category, a hovercraft may be used for the purposes of the carriage of cargo generally, or for such cargo as may be specified in the certificate[13]; and, in the special category, a hovercraft may be used for any purpose specified in the certificate, but not including the carriage of passengers except as expressly permitted[14].

The Secretary of State may issue the safety certificate subject to such other conditions relating to the safety of the hovercraft as he thinks fit[15]; and he may, having regard to such investigations as he may require, vary[16] a safety certificate at the request of an applicant and such variation may be subject to such other conditions relating to the safety of hovercraft as he thinks fit[17].

A safety certificate remains in force[18] for such period not exceeding one year as may be specified in it, and may be renewed from time to time by the Secretary of State for such further period not exceeding one year as he thinks fit[19]. A safety certificate ceases to be valid in the event of the hovercraft ceasing to be registered in the United Kingdom[20].

1　As to the Secretary of State see PARA 36.

2 As to the meaning of 'hovercraft' under the Hovercraft Act 1968 see PARA 381. As to the hovercraft to which the Hovercraft (General) Order 1972, SI 1972/674, applies see PARA 387; and as to Crown application see PARA 388. As to the application of arts 11, 12 see PARA 396.
3 As to the meaning of 'United Kingdom' for these purposes see PARA 389 note 3. As to the procedure for registration of hovercraft in the United Kingdom see PARA 391 et seq.
4 Hovercraft (General) Order 1972, SI 1972/674, art 11(1) (amended by SI 1996/3173).
5 Hovercraft (General) Order 1972, SI 1972/674, art 11(1)(b) (amended by SI 1996/3173).
6 Hovercraft (General) Order 1972, SI 1972/674, art11(1)(c).
7 Ie the categories referred to in the Hovercraft (General) Order 1972, SI 1972/674, art 11(2)(b) (see the text and note 10): see art 11(2)(a) (amended by SI 1996/3173).
8 Ie the purposes indicated in the Hovercraft (General) Order 1972, SI 1972/674, art 11(2)(c) (see the text and notes 11–14): see art 11(2)(a) (as amended: see note 7).
9 Hovercraft (General) Order 1972, SI 1972/674, art 11(2)(a) (as amended: see note 7).
10 Hovercraft (General) Order 1972, SI 1972/674, art11(2)(b).
11 As to the meaning of 'passenger' see PARA 387 note 6.
12 Hovercraft (General) Order 1972, SI 1972/674, art11(2)(c).
13 Hovercraft (General) Order 1972, SI 1972/674, art11(2)(c).
14 Hovercraft (General) Order 1972, SI 1972/674, art11(2)(c).
15 Hovercraft (General) Order 1972, SI 1972/674, art 11(3) (amended by SI 1996/3173).
16 As to the variation of certificates see PARA 401.
17 Hovercraft (General) Order 1972, SI 1972/674, art 11(4) (amended by SI 1996/3173).
18 Ie subject to the provisions of the Hovercraft (General) Order 1972, SI 1972/674, art 11 and art 15 (revocation etc) (as to which see PARA 401): see art 12 (amended by SI 1996/3173).
19 Hovercraft (General) Order 1972, SI 1972/674, art12 (as amended: see note 18).
20 Hovercraft (General) Order 1972, SI 1972/674, art12 (as amended: see note 18).

**399. Certificates of compliance with international standards.** The Secretary of State[1] may issue in respect of a hovercraft[2] registered in the United Kingdom[3] such certificates as he deems appropriate, as a result of inspection and survey of the hovercraft by the Civil Aviation Authority[4], under the International Convention for the Safety of Life at Sea[5] and the International Convention on Load Lines 1966[6] for the purpose of complying with the law of a country other than the United Kingdom[7].

The Secretary of State may cancel or suspend[8] any certificate so issued where he has reason to believe[9]:

(1) that the certificate has been issued on the basis of inaccurate information[10]; or

(2) that since the issue of the certificate the hovercraft has sustained any material damage or that the condition of the hovercraft or of its equipment does not correspond substantially with the particulars of that certificate[11].

The Secretary of State may require any certificate so issued[12] which has expired or been cancelled or suspended to be delivered up as he directs[13].

1 As to the Secretary of State see PARA 36.
2 As to the meaning of 'hovercraft' under the Hovercraft Act 1968 see PARA 381. As to the hovercraft to which the Hovercraft (General) Order 1972, SI 1972/674, applies see PARA 387; and as to Crown application see PARA 388. As to the application of art 17 see PARA 396.
3 As to the meaning of 'United Kingdom' for these purposes see PARA 389 note 3. As to the procedure for registration of hovercraft in the United Kingdom see PARA 391 et seq.
4 As to the Civil Aviation Authority see AVIATION vol 2 (2017) PARA 752 et seq.
5 Ie the International Convention for the Safety of Life at Sea 1960 (London, 17 June 1966; TS 65 (1965); Cmnd 2812): see the Hovercraft (General) Order 1972, SI 1972/674, art 17(1). The current Convention is the International Convention for the Safety of Life at Sea 1974 ('SOLAS') (London, 1 November 1974 to 1 July 1975; TS 46 (1980); Cmnd 7874): see PARA 7.
6 Ie the International Convention on Load Lines (London, 5 April to 4 July 1966; TS 58 (1968); Cmnd 3708) (as to which see PARA 7) (implemented by the Merchant Shipping (Load Line) Regulations 1998, SI 1998/2241: see PARA 660 et seq): see the Hovercraft (General) Order 1972, SI 1972/674, art 17(1).
7 Hovercraft (General) Order 1972, SI 1972/674, art17(1).
8 As to the cancellation or suspension of certificates see PARA 401.

9　Hovercraft (General) Order 1972, SI 1972/674, art17(2).
10　Hovercraft (General) Order 1972, SI 1972/674, art17(2)(a).
11　Hovercraft (General) Order 1972, SI 1972/674, art17(2)(b).
12　Ie issued under the Hovercraft (General) Order 1972, SI 1972/674, art 17: see art 17(3).
13　Hovercraft (General) Order 1972, SI 1972/674, art17(3).

**400.　Inspection and maintenance of hovercraft.** The Secretary of State[1] may at any reasonable time inspect a hovercraft[2] or part of it or its equipment in respect of which a safety certificate[3]:

(1)　has been applied for[4]; or
(2)　has been issued and is still in force[5]; or
(3)　has been issued and has ceased within the preceding period of three months to be in force[6],

and he may, for that purpose, enter any premises where persons are employed in the design, construction, maintenance or storage of the hovercraft, or any hoverport[7].

A hovercraft in respect of which a safety certificate is in force[8] may not be used unless it is maintained in a condition satisfactory to the Secretary of State, and in accordance with arrangements approved by him[9].

For the purposes of the certification and maintenance of hovercraft[10], the Secretary of State may accept reports furnished to him by a person whom he may for the time being approve, either absolutely or subject to such conditions as he thinks fit, as qualified to furnish such reports[11].

1　As to the Secretary of State see PARA 36.
2　As to the meaning of 'hovercraft' under the Hovercraft Act 1968 see PARA 381. As to the hovercraft to which the Hovercraft (General) Order 1972, SI 1972/674, applies see PARA 387; and as to Crown application see PARA 388. As to the application of arts 13, 14, 16 see PARA 396.
3　Hovercraft (General) Order 1972, SI 1972/674, art 16 (amended by SI 1996/3173). As to safety certificates see PARAS 397, 398.
4　Hovercraft (General) Order 1972, SI 1972/674, art16(a).
5　Hovercraft (General) Order 1972, SI 1972/674, art16(b).
6　Hovercraft (General) Order 1972, SI 1972/674, art16(c).
7　Hovercraft (General) Order 1972, SI 1972/674, art 16. As to the meaning of 'hoverport' under the Hovercraft Act 1968 see PARA 382 note 3.
8　Ie in force under the Hovercraft (General) Order 1972, SI 1972/674 (see PARAS 387 et seq, 401 et seq): see art 13 (amended by SI 1996/3173).
9　Hovercraft (General) Order 1972, SI 1972/674, art 13 (as amended: see note 8). As to penalties for contravention see PARA 1072.
10　Ie for the purposes of the Hovercraft (General) Order 1972, SI 1972/674, Pt II (arts 7A–17) (certification and maintenance) (see PARAS 396 et seq, 401 et seq): see art 14 (amended by SI 1996/3173).
11　Hovercraft (General) Order 1972, SI 1972/674, art14 (as amended: see note 10).

**401.　Revocation, suspension, variation of certificates; power to prevent hovercraft being used.** The Secretary of State[1] may, if he thinks fit, provisionally suspend or vary any certificate[2], approval or other document issued, granted or having effect in relation to the certification and maintenance of hovercraft[3] pending inquiry into or consideration of the case; and he may[4], on sufficient ground being shown to his satisfaction after due inquiry, revoke, suspend or vary any such certificate, approval or other document[5].

The holder or any person having the possession or custody of any such certificate, approval or other document which has been duly revoked, suspended or varied[6] must surrender it to the Secretary of State within a reasonable time after being required to do so by him[7].

The breach of any condition subject to which any such certificate, approval or other document has been granted or issued renders the document invalid during the continuance of the breach[8].

If it appears likely to the Secretary of State that a hovercraft is intended or likely to be used[9]:

(1)      in such circumstances that any conditions on which the safety certificate[10] has been granted are breached[11];

(2)      whilst the approved maintenance arrangements are not adhered to[12];

(3)      whilst materially damaged[13]; or

(4)      in such circumstances that the Secretary of State has reason to believe that the hovercraft is or may be unsafe[14],

the Secretary of State may direct the operator[15] or the captain[16] of the hovercraft that he is not to permit the hovercraft to make the particular journey, or any other journey of such description as may be specified in the direction, until the direction has been revoked by the Secretary of State[17]; and the Secretary of State may take such steps as are necessary to detain the hovercraft for a period not exceeding seven days[18].

In the event of the Secretary of State provisionally suspending any certificate, approval or other document in this way[19], or so detaining a hovercraft[20], he must, within 48 hours, send to the holder of such certificate, approval or other document a statement in writing of his reasons[21].

Any document incorporated by reference in any certificate may be varied[22] on sufficient ground being shown to the satisfaction of the Secretary of State, whether or not after due inquiry[23].

1   As to the Secretary of State see PARA 36.
2   As to certificates generally see PARA 396 et seq.
3   Ie issued, granted or having effect under the Hovercraft (General) Order 1972, SI 1972/674, Pt II (arts 7A–17) (certification and maintenance) (see PARA 396 et seq): see art 15(1) (amended by SI 1996/3173). As to the meaning of 'hovercraft' under the Hovercraft Act 1968 see PARA 381. As to the hovercraft to which the Hovercraft (General) Order 1972, SI 1972/674, applies see PARA 387; and as to Crown application see PARA 388. As to the application of art 15 see PARA 396.
4   Ie without prejudice to the Hovercraft (General) Order 1972, SI 1972/674, art 11(4) (see PARA 398): see art 15(1) (as amended: see note 3).
5   Hovercraft (General) Order 1972, SI 1972/674, art 15(1) (as amended: see note 3). As to penalties for contravention see PARA 1072.
6   Ie revoked, suspended or varied under the Hovercraft (General) Order 1972, SI 1972/674, Pt II (arts 7A–17) (certification and maintenance) (see PARA 396 et seq): see art 15(2) (amended by SI 1996/3173).
7   Hovercraft (General) Order 1972, SI 1972/674, art15(2) (as amended: see note 6).
8   Hovercraft (General) Order 1972, SI 1972/674, art15(3).
9   Hovercraft (General) Order 1972, SI 1972/674, art 15(4) (amended by SI 1996/3173).
10   As to safety certificates see PARAS 397, 398.
11   Hovercraft (General) Order 1972, SI 1972/674, art15(4)(a).
12   Hovercraft (General) Order 1972, SI 1972/674, art15(4)(b).
13   Hovercraft (General) Order 1972, SI 1972/674, art15(4)(c).
14   Hovercraft (General) Order 1972, SI 1972/674, art 15(4)(d) (amended by SI 1996/3173).
15   As to the meaning of 'operator' see PARA 388 note 2.
16   As to the meaning of 'captain' see PARA 388 note 6.
17   Hovercraft (General) Order 1972, SI 1972/674, art15(4) (as amended: see note 9).
18   Hovercraft (General) Order 1972, SI 1972/674, art15(4) (as amended: see note 9).
19   Ie under the Hovercraft (General) Order 1972, SI 1972/674, art 15(1) (see the text and notes 1–5): see art 15(5) (amended by SI 1996/3173).
20   Ie under the Hovercraft (General) Order 1972, SI 1972/674, art 15(4) (see the text and notes 9–18): see art 15(5) (as amended: see note 19).
21   Hovercraft (General) Order 1972, SI 1972/674, art15(5) (as amended: see note 19).
22   Ie notwithstanding the Hovercraft (General) Order 1972, SI 1972/674, art 15(1) (see the text and notes 1–5): see art 15(6) (amended by SI 1996/3173).
23   Hovercraft (General) Order 1972, SI 1972/674, art15(6) (as amended: see note 22).

## (iv) Duties of Operator and Captain

**402. Application of provisions.** The provisions relating to the duties of the operator and the captain of a hovercraft[1] do not apply to hovercraft to which the Merchant Shipping (High-Speed Craft) Regulations 2004[2] apply[3].

1   Ie the Hovercraft (General) Order 1972, SI 1972/674, Pt III (arts 17A–24) (duties of operator and captain) (see PARA 403 et seq): see art 17A (added by SI 1996/3173). As to the meaning of 'hovercraft' under the Hovercraft Act 1968 see PARA 381. As to the hovercraft to which the Hovercraft (General) Order 1972, SI 1972/674, applies see PARA 387; and as to Crown application see PARA 388.
2   Ie the Merchant Shipping (High Speed Craft) Regulations 2004, SI 2004/302 (see PARA 617 et seq): see the Hovercraft (General) Order 1972, SI 1972/674, art 17A (as added: see note 1). The reference in the Hovercraft (General) Order 1972, SI 1972/674, art 17A, is to the Merchant Shipping (High Speed Craft) Regulations 1996, SI 1996/3188 (revoked), but it is submitted that the reference is now to the Merchant Shipping (High Speed Craft) Regulations 2004, SI 2004/302; cf the Hovercraft (General) Order 1972, SI 1972/674, art 7A (as to which see PARA 396).
3   Hovercraft (General) Order 1972, SI 1972/674, art17A (as added: see note 1).

**403. Operating permits.** Hovercraft[1] registered in the United Kingdom[2] must not be used for reward or in connection with a trade or business, otherwise than under and in accordance with a permit (an 'operating permit') granted to the operator[3] of the hovercraft[4]. Operating permits must be granted with a view to securing the safe operation of the hovercraft[5].

The Secretary of State[6] may grant or renew to any person applying therefor an operating permit for the operation of hovercraft of the types and in relation to the areas of operation specified in the operating permit for the purposes so specified[7]. The operating permit may be granted subject to such conditions as the Secretary of State thinks fit to impose with a view to securing the safe operation of hovercraft, remains in force for such time as may be specified in the operating permit or until suspended or revoked by the Secretary of State and may be renewed from time to time by him for such further period as he thinks fit[8]. The Secretary of State may vary an operating permit on application by the holder[9].

The conditions to which the operating permit may be subject may include[10] conditions in respect of the following matters[11]:

(1)   crew complement and qualifications[12];
(2)   type of hovercraft[13];
(3)   area of operation[14];
(4)   restrictions with regard to working hours and rest periods of crew[15];
(5)   safety arrangements at hoverports[16] or terminal areas[17];
(6)   the weather conditions in which the hovercraft may operate[18];
(7)   day or night operation[19];
(8)   life-saving equipment and procedures[20];
(9)   other equipment and procedures necessary for safety of operation[21];
(10)  radio and radar[22];
(11)  the keeping of records[23];
(12)  medical equipment to be carried[24].

1   As to the meaning of 'hovercraft' under the Hovercraft Act 1968 see PARA 381. As to the hovercraft to which the Hovercraft (General) Order 1972, SI 1972/674, applies see PARA 387; and as to Crown application see PARA 388. As to the application of art 18 see PARA 402.
2   As to the meaning of 'United Kingdom' for these purposes see PARA 389 note 3. As to the procedure for registration of hovercraft in the United Kingdom see PARA 391 et seq.
3   As to the meaning of 'operator' see PARA 388 note 2.
4   Hovercraft (General) Order 1972, SI 1972/674, art 18(1) (amended by SI 1996/3173). The permit referred to in the text is granted to the operator under the Hovercraft (General) Order 1972, SI 1972/674, art 18(2) (see the text and notes 6–9): see art 18(1) (as so amended). As to penalties for contravention see PARA 1072.

5 Hovercraft (General) Order 1972, SI 1972/674, art18(1) (as amended: see note 4).
6 As to the Secretary of State see PARA 36.
7 Hovercraft (General) Order 1972, SI 1972/674, art18(2). As to the variation of operating permits see PARA 401.
8 Hovercraft (General) Order 1972, SI 1972/674, art18(2).
9 Hovercraft (General) Order 1972, SI 1972/674, art18(2).
10 Ie without prejudice to the generality of the Hovercraft (General) Order 1972, SI 1972/674, art 18(2) (see the text and notes 6–9): see art 18(3).
11 Hovercraft (General) Order 1972, SI 1972/674, art18(3).
12 Hovercraft (General) Order 1972, SI 1972/674, art18(3)(a).
13 Hovercraft (General) Order 1972, SI 1972/674, art18(3)(b).
14 Hovercraft (General) Order 1972, SI 1972/674, art18(3)(c).
15 Hovercraft (General) Order 1972, SI 1972/674, art18(3)(d).
16 As to the meaning of 'hoverport' under the Hovercraft Act 1968 see PARA 382 note 3.
17 Hovercraft (General) Order 1972, SI 1972/674, art18(3)(e).
18 Hovercraft (General) Order 1972, SI 1972/674, art18(3)(f).
19 Hovercraft (General) Order 1972, SI 1972/674, art18(3)(g).
20 Hovercraft (General) Order 1972, SI 1972/674, art18(3)(h).
21 Hovercraft (General) Order 1972, SI 1972/674, art18(3)(i).
22 Hovercraft (General) Order 1972, SI 1972/674, art18(3)(j).
23 Hovercraft (General) Order 1972, SI 1972/674, art18(3)(k).
24 Hovercraft (General) Order 1972, SI 1972/674, art 18(3)(l) (added by SI 1989/1351).

**404. Duties of operator and owner.** The operator[1] of a hovercraft[2] registered in the United Kingdom[3] must not permit the hovercraft to be used without first[4]:

(1)    designating a member of the crew to be captain[5] on that journey[6];

(2)    ensuring that a minimum number of the crew corresponding to the complement necessary for the journey are adequately trained for their duties for that journey[7];

(3)    ensuring that the safety equipment required to be carried is in working order[8].

Without prejudice to his other statutory duties[9], an operator must at all times take all reasonable precautions at hoverports[10] and terminal areas so as to ensure the safety of persons and property in the hovercraft and on the ground[11].

An operator must not permit any hovercraft to be used if he has reason to believe or suspect it is in an unsafe condition[12].

1 As to the meaning of 'operator' see PARA 388 note 2.
2 As to the meaning of 'hovercraft' under the Hovercraft Act 1968 see PARA 381. As to the hovercraft to which the Hovercraft (General) Order 1972, SI 1972/674, applies see PARA 387; and as to Crown application see PARA 388. As to the application of art 19 see PARA 402.
3 As to the meaning of 'United Kingdom' for these purposes see PARA 389 note 3. As to the procedure for registration of hovercraft in the United Kingdom see PARA 391 et seq. The text also includes a reference to the operator of a hovercraft operating unregistered in the United Kingdom in accordance with the Hovercraft (General) Order 1972, SI 1972/674, art 4 proviso (i) (revoked): see art 19(1). Quaere whether the reference to art 4 proviso (i) was meant to have been deleted by the Hovercraft (General) (Amendment) Order 1996, SI 1996/3173: see eg art 14(a) (amending the Hovercraft (General) Order 1972, SI 1972/674, art 23(1) (see PARA 407)); and the Hovercraft (General) (Amendment) Order 1996, SI 1996/3173, art 15 (amending the Hovercraft (General) Order 1972, SI 1972/674, art 24(2) (see PARA 409)). Cf art 22; and PARA 408.
4 Hovercraft (General) Order 1972, SI 1972/674, art19(1).
5 As to the meaning of 'captain' see PARA 388 note 6.
6 Hovercraft (General) Order 1972, SI 1972/674, art19(1)(a). As to penalties for contravention see PARA 1072.
7 Hovercraft (General) Order 1972, SI 1972/674, art19(1)(b).
8 Hovercraft (General) Order 1972, SI 1972/674, art19(1)(c).
9 Ie his other duties under the Hovercraft (General) Order 1972, SI 1972/674 (see PARAS 387 et seq, 405 et seq): see art 19(2).
10 As to the meaning of 'hoverport' under the Hovercraft Act 1968 see PARA 382 note 3.
11 Hovercraft (General) Order 1972, SI 1972/674, art19(2).
12 Hovercraft (General) Order 1972, SI 1972/674, art19(3).

**405. Duties of captain.** The captain[1], before the departure of the hovercraft[2]:

(1)     must take reasonable steps to ensure[3]:
    (a)     that the craft is properly loaded and any cargo adequately secured in the craft[4];
    (b)     that there is an adequate supply of fuel[5]; and
    (c)     that the craft is in a fit state and that the safety equipment required to be carried is in a fit condition and ready to be used[6]; and

(2)     must satisfy himself that the journey can safely be made, taking into account the latest information available to him as to the route and weather[7].

1   As to the meaning of 'captain' see PARA 388 note 6.
2   Hovercraft (General) Order 1972, SI 1972/674, art 20. As to the meaning of 'hovercraft' under the Hovercraft Act 1968 see PARA 381. As to the hovercraft to which the Hovercraft (General) Order 1972, SI 1972/674, applies see PARA 387; and as to Crown application see PARA 388. As to the application of art 20 see PARA 402.
3   Hovercraft (General) Order 1972, SI 1972/674, art20(a). As to penalties for contravention see PARA 1072.
4   Hovercraft (General) Order 1972, SI 1972/674, art20(a)(i).
5   Hovercraft (General) Order 1972, SI 1972/674, art20(a)(ii).
6   Hovercraft (General) Order 1972, SI 1972/674, art20(a)(iii).
7   Hovercraft (General) Order 1972, SI 1972/674, art20(b).

**406. Duty of captain and operator to keep operational records.** The captain[1] of every hovercraft[2] registered in the United Kingdom[3] must ensure that records are kept of the following matters relating to any journey of the hovercraft[4]:

(1)     names of terminal and any intermediate points, and the times of departure from and arrival at such points[5];
(2)     weather conditions, such as wind, sea condition and visibility experienced[6];
(3)     any accidents[7] or unusual occurrences on the journey[8];
(4)     any births or deaths which occur on the journey[9];
(5)     a summary of all communications relating to distress, urgency and safety traffic[10].

The operator[11] of every hovercraft registered in the United Kingdom must keep records of crew emergency and distress drills (including names of persons present)[12], and the names of all crew aboard a hovercraft on any journey[13].

The captain or operator, as the case may be, must, within a reasonable time after being requested to do so by an authorised person[14], cause the records that are required to be kept by them[15] to be produced to that person[16]. Such records must be preserved by the operator for at least 12 months after any journey or drill to which they refer[17]; and the records to be kept by the captain[18] must be delivered to the operator of the hovercraft to which the records relate by the captain at the time he ceases to be the captain, or when the operator requires their delivery[19]. A person required to preserve any record by reason of his being the operator of a hovercraft must, if he ceases to be the operator of the hovercraft, continue to preserve the record as if he had not ceased to be the operator, and, in the event of his death, the duty to preserve the record falls upon his personal representative[20].

1   As to the meaning of 'captain' see PARA 388 note 6.
2   As to the meaning of 'hovercraft' under the Hovercraft Act 1968 see PARA 381. As to the hovercraft to which the Hovercraft (General) Order 1972, SI 1972/674, applies see PARA 387; and as to Crown application see PARA 388. As to the application of art 21 see PARA 402.
3   As to the meaning of 'United Kingdom' for these purposes see PARA 389 note 3. As to the procedure for registration of hovercraft in the United Kingdom see PARA 391 et seq.
4   Hovercraft (General) Order 1972, SI 1972/674, art21(1). As to penalties for contravention see PARA 1072.
5   Hovercraft (General) Order 1972, SI 1972/674, art21(1)(a).

6   Hovercraft (General) Order 1972, SI 1972/674, art21(1)(b).
7   As to accidents occurring on the journey see PARA 409.
8   Hovercraft (General) Order 1972, SI 1972/674, art21(1)(c).
9   Hovercraft (General) Order 1972, SI 1972/674, art 21(1)(d). As to the recording of births, deaths
    and missing persons by persons operating hovercraft registered in the United Kingdom see
    PARA 418 et seq.
10  Hovercraft (General) Order 1972, SI 1972/674, art21(1)(e).
11  As to the meaning of 'operator' see PARA 388 note 2.
12  Hovercraft (General) Order 1972, SI 1972/674, art21(2)(a).
13  Hovercraft (General) Order 1972, SI 1972/674, art21(2)(b).
14  For these purposes, 'authorised person' means any constable and any person authorised in writing
    by the Secretary of State either generally or in relation to a particular case or class of cases:
    Hovercraft (General) Order 1972, SI 1972/674, art 3(1). As to the Secretary of State see PARA 36.
15  Ie the records referred to in the Hovercraft (General) Order 1972, SI 1972/674, art 21(1), (2) (see
    the text and notes 1–13): see art 21(3).
16  Hovercraft (General) Order 1972, SI 1972/674, art21(3).
17  Hovercraft (General) Order 1972, SI 1972/674, art21(4)(a).
18  Ie the records referred to in the Hovercraft (General) Order 1972, SI 1972/674, art 21(1) (see the
    text and notes 1–10): see art 21(4)(b).
19  Hovercraft (General) Order 1972, SI 1972/674, art21(4)(b).
20  Hovercraft (General) Order 1972, SI 1972/674, art21(4)(c).

**407. Documents to be carried.** A hovercraft[1] registered in the United
Kingdom[2] must, when in operation, carry the following documents or true copies
of them[3]:
   (1)      its safety certificate[4];
   (2)      its certificate of registration, if any[5];
   (3)      any international certificate[6].
The safety certificate and international certificate or true copies of them must
be posted in some conspicuous place in the hovercraft[7].

1   As to the meaning of 'hovercraft' under the Hovercraft Act 1968 see PARA 381. As to the
    hovercraft to which the Hovercraft (General) Order 1972, SI 1972/674, applies see PARA 387; and
    as to Crown application see PARA 388. As to the application of art 23 see PARA 402.
2   As to the meaning of 'United Kingdom' for these purposes see PARA 389 note 3. As to the
    procedure for registration of hovercraft in the United Kingdom see PARA 391 et seq.
3   Hovercraft (General) Order 1972, SI 1972/674, art 23(1) (amended by SI 1996/3173). As to
    penalties for contravention see PARA 1072.
4   Hovercraft (General) Order 1972, SI 1972/674, art 23(1)(a) (amended by SI 1996/3173). As to
    safety certificates see PARAS 397, 398.
5   Hovercraft (General) Order 1972, SI 1972/674, art23(1)(b). As to the certificate of registration see
    PARA 392.
6   Hovercraft (General) Order 1972, SI 1972/674, art 23(1)(c). The text refers to any certificate
    issued to the hovercraft under art 17 (see PARA 399): see art 23(1)(c).
7   Hovercraft (General) Order 1972, SI 1972/674, art23(2).

**408. Medical equipment.** A hovercraft[1] registered in the United Kingdom[2]
must carry, when in use, first-aid equipment of good quality and sufficient in
quantity having regard to the number of persons on board and the circumstances
of the use of the hovercraft[3].

1   As to the meaning of 'hovercraft' under the Hovercraft Act 1968 see PARA 381. As to the
    hovercraft to which the Hovercraft (General) Order 1972, SI 1972/674, applies see PARA 387; and
    as to Crown application see PARA 388. As to the application of art 22 see PARA 402.
2   As to the meaning of 'United Kingdom' for these purposes see PARA 389 note 3. As to the
    procedure for registration of hovercraft in the United Kingdom see PARA 391 et seq. The text also
    includes a reference also to a hovercraft used unregistered in accordance with the Hovercraft
    (General) Order 1972, SI 1972/674, art 4 proviso (i) (revoked): see art 22 (amended by SI
    1989/1351). Quaere whether the reference to the Hovercraft (General) Order 1972, SI 1972/674,
    art 4 proviso (i) was meant to have been deleted by the Hovercraft (General) (Amendment) Order
    1996, SI 1996/3173: cf art 14(a) (amending the Hovercraft (General) Order 1972, SI 1972/674, art
    23(1) (see PARA 407)); and the Hovercraft (General) (Amendment) Order 1996, SI 1996/3173, art
    15 (amending the Hovercraft (General) Order 1972, SI 1972/674, art 24(2) (see PARA 409)). Cf
    art 19; and PARA 404.

3   Hovercraft (General) Order 1972, SI 1972/674, art 22 (as amended: see note 2). As to penalties for
    contravention see PARA 1072.

**409. Notification of casualties.** A hovercraft[1] casualty is deemed to occur[2]
when a hovercraft[3]:

   (1)   has sustained, caused or been involved in any accident occasioning loss
         of life or any serious injury to any person[4];
   (2)   becomes lost, abandoned, missing or stranded[5];
   (3)   suffers such damage as the result of any accident that its safety is
         impaired[6];
   (4)   becomes involved in a collision with another hovercraft or ship[7]; or
   (5)   causes any damage[8],

but only when the occurrence takes place:

   (a)   on or over the sea or other navigable water[9]; or
   (b)   between the time when any person goes on board the hovercraft for the
         purpose of making a journey which would involve crossing the sea or
         other navigable water and the time when it comes to rest at the end of
         such a journey[10]; or
   (c)   during the testing or maintenance of a hovercraft which normally makes
         journeys on or over the sea or other navigable water[11];

and also only if, at the time the occurrence takes place, the hovercraft was
registered in the United Kingdom[12] or was within the United Kingdom[13].

   Where a hovercraft casualty has occurred, the captain[14] (or, if the captain is
incapacitated, the operator[15]) of the hovercraft must[16]:

   (i)   by the quickest available means inform the Secretary of State[17] of the
         happening of the casualty, stating the registration number[18] or identity
         of the hovercraft[19] and the place where the casualty occurred or is
         believed to have occurred and, in the case of a hovercraft which is
         missing, the route it was on[20]; and
   (ii)  within 48 hours, or as soon thereafter as possible, transmit to the
         Secretary of State a report, signed by the captain or operator, of the
         casualty and of the probable occasion of it, stating the registration
         number or identity of the hovercraft and the place where the casualty
         occurred or is believed to have occurred[21].

1   As to the meaning of 'hovercraft' under the Hovercraft Act 1968 see PARA 381. As to the
    hovercraft to which the Hovercraft (General) Order 1972, SI 1972/674, applies see PARA 387; and
    as to Crown application see PARA 388. As to the application of art 24 generally see PARA 402.
2   Ie for the purposes of the Hovercraft (General) Order 1972, SI 1972/674, art 24: see art 24(2).
3   Hovercraft (General) Order 1972, SI 1972/674, art 24(2). The provisions of art 24 do not,
    however, apply to hovercraft which are less than 1,000 kilograms unladen weight and are not used
    for reward: art 24(1) proviso. As to the meaning of 'unladen weight' see PARA 390 note 9.
4   Hovercraft (General) Order 1972, SI 1972/674, art24(2)(a).
5   Hovercraft (General) Order 1972, SI 1972/674, art24(2)(b).
6   Hovercraft (General) Order 1972, SI 1972/674, art 24(2)(c) (amended by SI 1989/1351).
7   Hovercraft (General) Order 1972, SI 1972/674, art24(2)(d).
8   Hovercraft (General) Order 1972, SI 1972/674, art 24(2)(e) (added by SI 1989/1351).
9   Hovercraft (General) Order 1972, SI 1972/674, art 24(2)(i). As to the meaning of 'navigable water'
    see PARA 387 note 4.
10  Hovercraft (General) Order 1972, SI 1972/674, art24(2)(ii).
11  Hovercraft (General) Order 1972, SI 1972/674, art24(2)(iii).
12  As to the meaning of 'United Kingdom' for these purposes see PARA 389 note 3. As to the
    procedure for registration of hovercraft in the United Kingdom see PARA 391 et seq.
13  Hovercraft (General) Order 1972, SI 1972/674, art 24(2) (amended by SI 1996/3173).
14  As to the meaning of 'captain' see PARA 388 note 6.
15  As to the meaning of 'operator' see PARA 388 note 2.
16  Hovercraft (General) Order 1972, SI 1972/674, art24(1). As to penalties for contravention see
    PARA 1072.

17  As to the Secretary of State see PARA 36.
18  As to the registration number of a hovercraft see PARA 392.
19  As to the means of identification of hovercraft see PARA 394.
20  Hovercraft (General) Order 1972, SI 1972/674, art24(1)(a).
21  Hovercraft (General) Order 1972, SI 1972/674, art24(1)(b).

## (v)  Safety etc

**410.  Safety of persons and property.** A person must not wilfully or negligently[1]:

(1)  act in a manner likely to endanger a hovercraft[2], or any person in it[3]; or

(2)  go or attempt to go on a journey on a hovercraft without the consent of the captain[4] or other person authorised to give it[5].

A person must not:

(a)  enter a hovercraft when drunk or be drunk in a hovercraft[6]; or

(b)  smoke in a place in a hovercraft or at a hoverport[7] where and when smoking is prohibited by notice[8].

A person must not wilfully obstruct or impede any person acting in the exercise of his powers or the performance of his duties[9].

1  Hovercraft (General) Order 1972, SI 1972/674, art 26(1). As to penalties for contravention see PARA 1072.
2  As to the meaning of 'hovercraft' under the Hovercraft Act 1968 see PARA 381. As to the hovercraft to which the Hovercraft (General) Order 1972, SI 1972/674, applies see PARA 387; and as to Crown application see PARA 388.
3  Hovercraft (General) Order 1972, SI 1972/674, art26(1)(a).
4  As to the meaning of 'captain' see PARA 388 note 6.
5  Hovercraft (General) Order 1972, SI 1972/674, art26(1)(b).
6  Hovercraft (General) Order 1972, SI 1972/674, art26(2)(a).
7  As to the meaning of 'hoverport' under the Hovercraft Act 1968 see PARA 382 note 3.
8  Hovercraft (General) Order 1972, SI 1972/674, art26(2)(b).
9  Hovercraft (General) Order 1972, SI 1972/674, art 30. The text refers to a person acting in the exercise of his powers or the performance of his duties under the Hovercraft (General) Order 1972, SI 1972/674 (see PARAS 387 et seq, 411 et seq): see art 30.

**411.  Duty to obey captain.** Every person in a hovercraft[1] must obey all lawful commands which the captain[2] may give for the purpose of securing the safety of the hovercraft and of persons and property carried in it, or the safety, efficiency or regularity of navigation[3].

1  As to the meaning of 'hovercraft' under the Hovercraft Act 1968 see PARA 381. As to the hovercraft to which the Hovercraft (General) Order 1972, SI 1972/674, applies see PARA 387; and as to Crown application see PARA 388.
2  As to the meaning of 'captain' see PARA 388 note 6.
3  Hovercraft (General) Order 1972, SI 1972/674, art27. As to penalties for contravention see PARA 1072.

**412.  Right of access to hoverports.** The Secretary of State[1] and any authorised person[2] have the right of access at all reasonable times to any hoverport[3] and any place where a hovercraft[4] is for the purpose of inspecting any hovercraft or any document[5] which they have power to demand[6], and for the purpose of detaining any hovercraft[7].

1  As to the Secretary of State see PARA 36.
2  As to the meaning of 'authorised person' see PARA 406 note 14.
3  As to the meaning of 'hoverport' under the Hovercraft Act 1968 see PARA 382 note 3.
4  As to the meaning of 'hovercraft' under the Hovercraft Act 1968 see PARA 381. As to the hovercraft to which the Hovercraft (General) Order 1972, SI 1972/674, applies see PARA 387; and as to Crown application see PARA 388.
5  As to records to be kept and documents to be carried on board a hovercraft see PARA 406.
6  Ie under the provisions of the Hovercraft (General) Order 1972, SI 1972/674 (see PARAS 387 et seq, 413 et seq): see art 25.

7 Hovercraft (General) Order 1972, SI 1972/674, art 25. The text refers to the purpose of detaining any hovercraft under the provisions of the Hovercraft (General) Order 1972, SI 1972/674 (see PARAS 387 et seq, 413 et seq): see art 25.

**413. Power to prevent hovercraft from operating.** If it appears to the Secretary of State[1] or an authorised person[2] that any hovercraft[3] is intended or likely to be operated[4]:

(1)    in such circumstances that certain provisions as to the registration and operation of hovercraft[5] would be contravened in relation to the journey[6]; or

(2)    in such circumstances that the journey would be in contravention of any other general provision relating to hovercraft[7] and be a cause of danger to any person or property whether or not in the hovercraft[8]; or

(3)    while in a condition unfit for operation whether or not the journey would otherwise be in contravention of any of those provisions[9],

the Secretary of State or that authorised person may direct the operator[10] or the captain[11] of the hovercraft that he is not to permit the hovercraft to make the particular journey, or any other journey of such description as may be specified in the direction, until the direction has been revoked by the Secretary of State or by an authorised person; and the Secretary of State or that person may take such steps as are necessary to detain the hovercraft[12].

The Secretary of State or any authorised person may enter upon and inspect any hovercraft for these purposes[13].

1 As to the Secretary of State see PARA 36.
2 As to the meaning of 'authorised person' see PARA 406 note 14.
3 As to the meaning of 'hovercraft' under the Hovercraft Act 1968 see PARA 381. As to the hovercraft to which the Hovercraft (General) Order 1972, SI 1972/674, applies see PARA 387; and as to Crown application see PARA 388.
4 Hovercraft (General) Order 1972, SI 1972/674, art28(1). As to penalties for contravention see PARA 1072.
5 Ie any provision of the Hovercraft (General) Order 1972, SI 1972/674, art 4 (see PARA 390), art 6 (see PARA 394), art 7 (see PARA 395), art 8 (see PARA 397), art 13 (see PARA 400) or art 18 (see PARA 403): see art 28(1)(a).
6 Hovercraft (General) Order 1972, SI 1972/674, art28(1)(a).
7 Ie any other provision of the Hovercraft (General) Order 1972, SI 1972/674 (see PARAS 387 et seq, 414 et seq): see art 28(1)(b).
8 Hovercraft (General) Order 1972, SI 1972/674, art28(1)(b).
9 Hovercraft (General) Order 1972, SI 1972/674, art 28(1)(c). The text refers to any provision of the Hovercraft (General) Order 1972, SI 1972/674 (see PARAS 387 et seq, 414 et seq): see art 28(1)(c).
10 As to the meaning of 'operator' see PARA 388 note 2.
11 As to the meaning of 'captain' see PARA 388 note 6.
12 Hovercraft (General) Order 1972, SI 1972/674, art28(1). As to the enforcement of directions see PARA 415.
13 Hovercraft (General) Order 1972, SI 1972/674, art28(2).

**414. Revocation etc of certificates etc.** The Secretary of State[1] may, if he thinks fit, provisionally suspend any certificate, licence, approval, permission, exemption or other document issued, granted or having effect under the provisions relating to the registration and operation of hovercraft[2], pending inquiry into or investigation of the case, and may[3], on sufficient ground being shown to his satisfaction after due inquiry, revoke, suspend or vary any such certificate, licence, approval, permission, exemption or other document[4].

The holder or any person having the possession or custody of any certificate, licence, approval, permission, exemption or other document which has been revoked, suspended or varied under these provisions must surrender it to the Secretary of State within a reasonable time after being required to do so by him[5].

The breach of any condition subject to which any certificate, licence, approval, permission, exemption or other document has been granted or issued, or which has effect under the general provisions relating to hovercraft[6], renders the document invalid during the continuance of the breach[7].

1 As to the Secretary of State see PARA 36.
2 Ie the provisions of the Hovercraft (General) Order 1972, SI 1972/674 (see PARAS 387 et seq, 415 et seq), other than Pt II (arts 7A–17) (as to which see PARA 396 et seq): see art 29(1). As to the meaning of 'hovercraft' under the Hovercraft Act 1968 see PARA 381. As to the hovercraft to which the Hovercraft (General) Order 1972, SI 1972/674, applies see PARA 387; and as to Crown application see PARA 388.
3 Ie without prejudice to the Hovercraft (General) Order 1972, SI 1972/674, art 18(2) (see PARA 403): see art 29(1).
4 Hovercraft (General) Order 1972, SI 1972/674, art29(1). As to penalties for contravention see PARA 1072.
5 Hovercraft (General) Order 1972, SI 1972/674, art29(2).
6 Ie under the Hovercraft (General) Order 1972, SI 1972/674 (see PARAS 387 et seq, 415 et seq): see art29(3).
7 Hovercraft (General) Order 1972, SI 1972/674, art29(3).

**415. Enforcement of directions.** Any person who fails to comply with any direction given to him under any of the general hovercraft provisions[1] by the Secretary of State[2] or by any authorised person[3] is deemed to have contravened the provision under which the direction was given[4].

1 Ie under any provision of the Hovercraft (General) Order 1972, SI 1972/674 (see PARAS 387 et seq, 416, 417, 1072): see art 31. As to the meaning of 'hovercraft' under the Hovercraft Act 1968 see PARA 381. As to the hovercraft to which the Hovercraft (General) Order 1972, SI 1972/674, applies see PARA 387; and as to Crown application see PARA 388.
2 As to the Secretary of State see PARA 36.
3 As to the meaning of 'authorised person' see PARA 406 note 14.
4 Hovercraft (General) Order 1972, SI 1972/674, art31. As to penalties for contravention see PARA 1072.

**416. Exemptions.** The Secretary of State[1] may exempt from any of the general hovercraft provisions[2], or any regulations made thereunder, any hovercraft or persons or classes of hovercraft or persons, either absolutely or subject to such conditions as he thinks fit[3].

1 As to the Secretary of State see PARA 36.
2 Ie any of the provisions of the Hovercraft (General) Order 1972, SI 1972/674 (see PARAS 387 et seq, 417, 1072): see art 32. As to the meaning of 'hovercraft' under the Hovercraft (General) Order 1972, SI 1972/674, applies see PARA 387; and as to Crown application see PARA 388.
3 Hovercraft (General) Order 1972, SI 1972/674, art32.

### (vi) Fees

**417. Fees.** The Secretary of State[1] may, by regulations made by statutory instrument[2], require the payment of fees in respect of any specified matter relating to hovercraft[3]; and may prescribe, with the approval of the Treasury[4], the amount of any such fee or the manner in which it is to be determined[5].

1 As to the Secretary of State see PARA 36.
2 The Statutory Instruments Act 1946 ss 1–3 (as to which see STATUTES AND LEGISLATIVE PROCESS vol 96 (2012) PARA 1045 et seq) apply to the regulations: see the Hovercraft (General) Order 1972, SI 1972/674, art 35.
3 Ie any matter specified in the Hovercraft (General) Order 1972, SI 1972/674 (see PARAS 387 et seq, 1072): see art 35. As to the meaning of 'hovercraft' under the Hovercraft Act 1968 see PARA 381. As to the hovercraft to which the Hovercraft (General) Order 1972, SI 1972/674, applies see PARA 387; and as to Crown application see PARA 388.
4 As to the Treasury see CONSTITUTIONAL AND ADMINISTRATIVE LAW vol 20 (2014) PARAS 262–265.
5 Hovercraft (General) Order 1972, SI 1972/674, art 35. In exercise of the power so conferred, the Secretary of State has made the Hovercraft (Fees) Regulations 1997, SI 1997/320 (amended by SI 2004/1976, SI 2006/2053).

## (vii) Births, Deaths and Missing Persons

**418. Returns relating to births and deaths.** The operator of a hovercraft[1] registered in the United Kingdom[2] must, as soon as practicable but not later than three months after the occurrence in any part of the world of a birth or death in the hovercraft[3], transmit to the Secretary of State[4] a return of such birth or death in the prescribed form[5]. If, however, such particulars are not known to the operator of the hovercraft, he must so transmit so many of the particulars as he is reasonably able to ascertain having regard to the circumstances of the birth or death[6].

To facilitate the rendering of such returns, the person in command[7] of a hovercraft registered in the United Kingdom must make records available to the operator as soon as practicable of the occurrence in any part of the world of a birth or death in the hovercraft[8]. If, however, all such particulars are not known to the person in command of a hovercraft and cannot be readily ascertained by him, he must record and so make available so many of such particulars as are readily ascertainable[9].

1 As to the meaning of 'hovercraft' under the Hovercraft Act 1968 see PARA 381. Note, however, that the Hovercraft (Births, Deaths and Missing Persons) Regulations 1972, SI 1972/1513, were made under the Civil Aviation Act 1949 s 55 (repealed), but have effect as if made under the Civil Aviation Act 1982 s 83 (as to which see AVIATION vol 2 (2017) PARAS 1354, 1355).

2 As to the meaning of 'United Kingdom' for these purposes see PARA 389 note 3. As to the procedure for registration of hovercraft in the United Kingdom see PARA 391 et seq.

3 For these purposes, references to births or deaths in a hovercraft include references to births or deaths on a hovercraft's lifeboat or life-raft and, in the case of deaths, to being lost from a hovercraft or hovercraft's lifeboat of hovercraft's life-raft: Hovercraft (Births, Deaths and Missing Persons) Regulations 1972, SI 1972/1513, reg 2(1).

4 As to the Secretary of State see PARA 36.

5 Hovercraft (Births, Deaths and Missing Persons) Regulations 1972, SI 1972/1513, reg 3(1). The text refers to a return of such birth or death in the form, in accordance with the instructions for completion, and containing the particulars prescribed in reg 3(1), App A (in the case of a birth) or App B (in the case of a death) (reg 7 substituted, Apps A, B amended, by SI 2009/1892): see the Hovercraft (Births, Deaths and Missing Persons) Regulations 1972, SI 1972/1513, reg 3(1). In the case of the birth of an illegitimate child, the name of any person as father of such child is not to be entered in any return or record of particulars of the birth of that child unless the mother of the child and the father of the child have signed a completed form of return as informants: reg 7(1) (as so substituted). In the case of the birth of an illegitimate child, the name of any woman (other than the mother) as a parent of that child must not be entered in any return or record of particulars of the birth of that child unless the mother of the child and that woman have signed a completed form of return as informants: reg 7(2) (as so substituted). Regulation 7(2) only applies to a woman who is a parent of a child by virtue of the Human Fertilisation and Embryology Act 2008 s 43 (see CHILDREN AND YOUNG PERSONS vol 9 (2017) PARA 125) and who does not fall within the definition of second female parent: Hovercraft (Births, Deaths and Missing Persons) Regulations 1972, SI 1972/1513, reg 7(3) (as so substituted).

6 Hovercraft (Births, Deaths and Missing Persons) Regulations 1972, SI 1972/1513, reg3(1) proviso.

7 For these purposes, 'person in command' of a hovercraft means, in a case where a person other than the captain is in command of the hovercraft, that person and, in any other case, the captain: Hovercraft (Births, Deaths and Missing Persons) Regulations 1972, SI 1972/1513, reg 2(1).

8 Hovercraft (Births, Deaths and Missing Persons) Regulations 1972, SI 1972/1513, reg3(2).

9 Hovercraft (Births, Deaths and Missing Persons) Regulations 1972, SI 1972/1513, reg3(2) proviso.

**419. Records to be kept by the Secretary of State.** The Secretary of State[1] must keep in his department[2]:

(1) a separate record of births in the prescribed form[3] in which must be recorded the particulars transmitted to him of births occurring in any part of the world in hovercraft registered in the United Kingdom[4];

(2) a separate record of deaths in the prescribed form[5] in which must be recorded the particulars transmitted to him of deaths occurring in any part of the world in hovercraft registered in the United Kingdom[6];

(3)     a separate record in the prescribed form[7] of persons reported to him as missing persons[8].

1   As to the Secretary of State see PARA 36.
2   Hovercraft (Births, Deaths and Missing Persons) Regulations 1972, SI 1972/1513, reg4.
3   Ie in the form of the Hovercraft (Births, Deaths and Missing Persons) Regulations 1972, SI 1972/1513, reg 4(1), App C (amended by SI 2009/1892): see the Hovercraft (Births, Deaths and Missing Persons) Regulations 1972, SI 1972/1513, reg 4(1). As to recording the birth of an illegitimate child see reg 7; and PARA 418 note 5.
4   Hovercraft (Births, Deaths and Missing Persons) Regulations 1972, SI 1972/1513, reg 4(1). As to the meaning of 'United Kingdom' for these purposes see PARA 389 note 3. As to the procedure for registration of hovercraft in the United Kingdom see PARA 391 et seq.
5   Ie in the form of the Hovercraft (Births, Deaths and Missing Persons) Regulations 1972, SI 1972/1513, reg 4(2), App D: see reg 4(2).
6   Hovercraft (Births, Deaths and Missing Persons) Regulations 1972, SI 1972/1513, reg4(2).
7   Ie in the form of the Hovercraft (Births, Deaths and Missing Persons) Regulations 1972, SI 1972/1513, reg 4(3), App E: see reg 4(2).
8   Hovercraft (Births, Deaths and Missing Persons) Regulations 1972, SI 1972/1513, reg 4(3). For these purposes, 'missing persons' means persons with respect to whom there are reasonable grounds for believing that they have died on a hovercraft registered in the United Kingdom: reg 2(1).

**420. Transmission of copies of entries to the appropriate Registrar General.** The Secretary of State[1] must, within seven days of the completion of an entry in any record of births, deaths, or missing persons relating to hovercraft[2] registered in the United Kingdom[3] which is kept in his department[4], cause a certified copy of such entry to be transmitted to the appropriate Registrar General[5].

1   As to the Secretary of State see PARA 36.
2   As to the meaning of 'hovercraft' under the Hovercraft Act 1968 see PARA 381. Note, however, that the Hovercraft (Births, Deaths and Missing Persons) Regulations 1972, SI 1972/1513, were made under the Civil Aviation Act 1949 s 55 (repealed), but have effect as if made under the Civil Aviation Act 1982 s 83 (as to which see AVIATION vol 2 (2017) PARAS 1354, 1355).
3   As to the meaning of 'United Kingdom' for these purposes see PARA 389 note 3. As to the procedure for registration of hovercraft in the United Kingdom see PARA 391 et seq.
4   Ie any such record as is mentioned in the text kept pursuant to the Hovercraft (Births, Deaths and Missing Persons) Regulations 1972, SI 1972/1513 (see PARA 419): see reg 5.
5   Hovercraft (Births, Deaths and Missing Persons) Regulations 1972, SI 1972/1513, reg 5. Except where it appears to the Secretary of State that an entry in the relevant record has a connection to Scotland or Northern Ireland, a certified copy of an entry in the record of births, deaths, or missing persons, must be sent to the Registrar General of Births, Deaths and Marriages in England: see reg 6 (amended by SI 2009/1892). As to the Registrar General of Births, Deaths and Marriages in England see REGISTRATION CONCERNING THE INDIVIDUAL vol 88 (2012) PARA 334 et seq.

**421. Rectification of entries of births, deaths and missing persons.** If the Secretary of State[1] is satisfied that there is an error or omission in any entry made in the record of births, deaths, or missing persons relating to hovercraft[2] registered in the United Kingdom[3] which is kept in his department[4], he may, in accordance with evidence of the true facts relating to the entry, rectify it in such manner as may appear to him appropriate[5].

Within seven days after the correction of any such entry in his records, the Secretary of State must cause a certified copy of such corrected entry to be transmitted to the appropriate Registrar General[6].

1   As to the Secretary of State see PARA 36.
2   As to the meaning of 'hovercraft' under the Hovercraft Act 1968 see PARA 381. Note, however, that the Hovercraft (Births, Deaths and Missing Persons) Regulations 1972, SI 1972/1513, were made under the Civil Aviation Act 1949 s 55 (repealed), but have effect as if made under the Civil Aviation Act 1982 s 83 (as to which see AVIATION vol 2 (2017) PARAS 1354, 1355).
3   As to the meaning of 'United Kingdom' for these purposes see PARA 389 note 3. As to the procedure for registration of hovercraft in the United Kingdom see PARA 391 et seq.

4  As to such records as are mentioned in the text which must be kept by the Secretary of State pursuant to the Hovercraft (Births, Deaths and Missing Persons) Regulations 1972, SI 1972/1513, see PARA 419.
5  Hovercraft (Births, Deaths and Missing Persons) Regulations 1972, SI 1972/1513, reg8(1).
6  Hovercraft (Births, Deaths and Missing Persons) Regulations 1972, SI 1972/1513, reg 8(2). As to the appropriate Registrar General see reg 6; and PARA 420 note 5.

**422. Foreign and Commonwealth hovercraft.** The requirements for registration of births and deaths in a hovercraft[1] also apply in relation to any hovercraft not registered in the United Kingdom[2] which carry passengers to or from any port in the United Kingdom with respect to the registration of births and deaths of citizens of the United Kingdom and colonies[3] on board such hovercraft on a journey to or from any port in the United Kingdom[4].

1  Ie requirements of the provisions of the Hovercraft (Births, Deaths and Missing Persons) Regulations 1972, SI 1972/1513 (see PARAS 418–421): see reg 9. As to the meaning of 'hovercraft' under the Hovercraft Act 1968 see PARA 381. Note, however, that the Hovercraft (Births, Deaths and Missing Persons) Regulations 1972, SI 1972/1513, were made under the Civil Aviation Act 1949 s 55 (repealed), but have effect as if made under the Civil Aviation Act 1982 s 83 (as to which see AVIATION vol 2 (2017) PARAS 1354, 1355).
2  As to the meaning of 'United Kingdom' for these purposes see PARA 389 note 3. As to the procedure for registration of hovercraft in the United Kingdom see PARA 391 et seq.
3  As to citizenship of the United Kingdom and colonies see BRITISH NATIONALITY vol 4 (2011) PARAS 406, 414–419. As to the meaning of 'colony' see STATUTES AND LEGISLATIVE PROCESS vol 96 (2012) PARA 1208.
4  Hovercraft (Births, Deaths and Missing Persons) Regulations 1972, SI 1972/1513, reg9.

# 5. MASTERS AND CREWS

# (1) STATUTORY AND COMMON LAW FRAMEWORK

**423. The applicable provisions.** The employment, welfare etc of seafarers is largely governed by applicable provisions of the Maritime Labour Convention and associated legislation[1]. In this context 'seafarer' means any person, including the master of a ship[2], who is employed or engaged or works in any capacity on board a ship and whose normal place of work is on board a ship[3]. Subject to the exclusions set out below, the Convention framework[4] applies[5] to all sea-going United Kingdom ships[6] wherever they may be[7], and to non-United Kingdom sea-going ships in United Kingdom waters[8] whose crews are not otherwise protected by the applicable Convention provisions[9]. The matters dealt with are: minimum age[10]; recruitment and placement[11]; employment agreements and medical certification[12]; relief and repatriation[13]; crew accommodation[14]; and catering and medical care[15]. The Convention also makes limited provision relating to the payment of wages[16], although in the United Kingdom context this mostly continues to be a matter dealt with under the Merchant Shipping Act 1995[17], and makes provision in connection with working hours and time off for seafarers (though not for workers on inland waterways or aboard fishing vessels)[18].

The Convention framework does not, however, apply to fishing vessels[19], vessels which are not ordinarily engaged in commercial activities[20] or (other than in the context of working hours), ships of traditional build[21]. In respect of such vessels, matters within the scope of the Convention framework[22] are mainly dealt with under the Merchant Shipping Act 1995[23]. The Convention framework also does not apply to pleasure vessels[24] or to warships or naval auxiliaries[25]: no corresponding provision specifically relating to such vessels is made.

Matters outside the scope of the Convention framework, such as most matters concerning wages[26], the discharge of crews[27], competence, training and certification[28], and inquiries into the fitness and conduct of seamen and officers[29], are dealt with, in respect of all types of vessel, by the Merchant Shipping Act 1995 or by common law provisions. There is also a significant body of common law relating to the powers and duties of masters[30].

1   Ie the Maritime Labour Convention adopted by the General Conference of the International Labour Organisation on 23 February 2006 (Cm 7049). The applicable provisions of the Convention are implemented in United Kingdom law by the Merchant Shipping (Maritime Labour Convention) (Minimum Requirements for Seafarers etc) Regulations 2014, SI 2014/1613 (which also implement the corresponding parts of the Agreement set out in the Annex to Council Directive (EC) 2009/13 (OJ L124, 20.05.2009, p 30) implementing the Agreement concluded by the European Community Shipowners' Associations (ECSA) and the European Transport Workers' Federation (ETF) on the Maritime Labour Convention, and the Agreement set out in the Annex to Council Directive (EC) 1999/63 (OJ L167, 2.7.1999, p 33) concerning the Agreement on the organisation of working time of seafarers concluded by the European Community Shipowners' Association (ECSA) and the Federation of Transport Workers' Unions in the European Union (FST), cl 6, 11) (see PARAS 544–547); in the context of seafarers's working hours, by the Merchant Shipping (Hours of Work) Regulations 2002, SI 2002/2125 (which also implement applicable provisions of the European Agreement on the organisation of working time of seafarers dated 30 September 1998 and put into effect by Council Directive (EC) 1999/63 (OJ L167, 02.07.1999, p 33) concerning the Agreement on the organisation of working time of seafarers concluded by the European Community Shipowners' Association and the Federation of Transport Workers' Unions in the European Union; and Parliament and Council Directive (EC) 1999/95 (OJ L14, 20.01.2000, p 29) concerning the enforcement of provisions in respect of seafarers' hours of work on board ships calling at Community ports) (see PARAS 511–523); and in the context of the certification of vessels, by the Merchant Shipping (Maritime Labour Convention) (Survey and Certification) Regulations 2013, SI 2013/1785 (see PARA 604).

2   'Ship' includes hovercraft: Merchant Shipping (Hours of Work) Regulations 2002, SI 2002/2125, reg 1(1); Merchant Shipping (Working Time: Inland Waterways) Regulations 2003, SI 2003/3049,

reg 2(1); Merchant Shipping (Maritime Labour Convention) (Medical Certification) Regulations 2010, SI 2010/737, reg 2; Merchant Shipping (Maritime Labour Convention) (Minimum Requirements for Seafarers etc) Regulations 2014, SI 2014/1613, reg 2(1). In the application of the Merchant Shipping (Maritime Labour Convention) (Minimum Requirements for Seafarers etc) Regulations 2014, SI 2014/1613, to a hovercraft, a reference to the master of a ship includes a reference to the captain of that hovercraft: reg 2(2).

3    Merchant Shipping (Hours of Work) Regulations 2002, SI 2002/2125, reg 2(4)(a) (reg 2(4) added by SI 2014/308); Merchant Shipping (Maritime Labour Convention) (Medical Certification) Regulations 2010, SI 2010/737, reg 2 (amended by SI 2014/1614); Merchant Shipping (Maritime Labour Convention) (Minimum Requirements for Seafarers etc) Regulations 2014, SI 2014/1613, reg 2(1). In the application of the Merchant Shipping (Hours of Work) Regulations 2002, SI 2002/2125, to a seafarer 'engaged' means engaged under a contract, whether express or implied and (if it is express) whether oral or in writing, whereby the seafarer undertakes to do or perform personally any work or services for another party to the contract whose status is not by virtue of the contract that of a client or customer of any profession or business undertaking carried out by the seafarer (reg 2(4)(b) (as so added)); and for the purposes of those regulations 'employed seafarer' means a seafarer who is employed under a contract of employment or engaged (or, where the employment or engagement has ceased, was employed or engaged), 'employer' in relation to an employed seafarer means the person by whom the employed seafarer is or was employed or engaged, and 'employment' in relation to an employed seafarer is to be construed accordingly (reg 2(4)(c) (as so added)).

4    Ie the Merchant Shipping (Maritime Labour Convention) (Minimum Requirements for Seafarers etc) Regulations 2014, SI 2014/1613, Pts 2–10 (regs 4–53) and regs 54, 56, 58 (see PARAS 48–50, 51) (reg 3(1), (2)) and the Merchant Shipping (Hours of Work) Regulations 2002, SI 2002/2125, regs 4–14, 17A, 18–20 (see PARAS 511–523) (reg 3(1) (reg 3 substituted by SI 2014/308)). There are technical exclusions relating to non-United Kingdom ships with Convention Documentation: see the Merchant Shipping (Maritime Labour Convention) (Minimum Requirements for Seafarers etc) Regulations 2014, SI 2014/1613, regs 3(2), (4)(b) (which provide that regs 6, 15, 18, 28, 33, 41, 46, 55, 57, which are all concerned with the application of the regulations to non-United Kingdom ships with Convention Documentation (see PARAS 48, 50, 452, 482, 490, 492, 496, 448, 540), are not part of the Convention framework for the purposes of United Kingdom law). See also note 9.

5    Ie subject to the minor qualifications set out in the Merchant Shipping (Maritime Labour Convention) (Minimum Requirements for Seafarers etc) Regulations 2014, SI 2014/1613, reg 37(1) (see PARA 495) and reg 44(2) (see PARA 496).

6    For this purpose 'United Kingdom ship' means a ship which is a United Kingdom ship within the meaning of the Merchant Shipping Act 1995 s 85(2) (see PARA 230), a Government ship within the meaning of s 308(4) (see PARA 19) which is ordinarily engaged in commercial maritime operations, or a hovercraft registered under the Hovercraft Act 1968 (see PARA 381): Merchant Shipping (Hours of Work) Regulations 2002, SI 2002/2125, reg 2(1) (amended by SI 2014/308); Merchant Shipping (Maritime Labour Convention) (Medical Certification) Regulations 2010, SI 2010/737, reg 2; Merchant Shipping (Maritime Labour Convention) (Minimum Requirements for Seafarers etc) Regulations 2014, SI 2014/1613, reg 2(1). 'Sea-going', in relation to a United Kingdom ship, means (by virtue of the Merchant Shipping (Hours of Work) Regulations 2002, SI 2002/2125, reg 2(1) (as so amended); the Merchant Shipping (Maritime Labour Convention) (Medical Certification) Regulations 2010, SI 2010/737, reg 2 (definition substituted by SI 2014/1614); and the Merchant Shipping (Maritime Labour Convention) (Minimum Requirements for Seafarers etc) Regulations 2014, SI 2014/1613, reg 2(1)):

(1)    a ship which operates outside the waters specified as Category A, B, C and D waters in Merchant Shipping Notice 1837(M);

(2)    a ship to which the Merchant Shipping (Survey and Certification) Regulations 1995, SI 1995/1210 (see PARA 604) apply and in respect of which no exemption granted under reg 2(2) applies;

(3)    a ship to which the Merchant Shipping (Vessels in Commercial Use for Sport or Pleasure) Regulations 1998, SI 1998/2771, reg 4 (see PARA 613) applies and which falls within the description given in reg 4(3); or

(4)    a high speed craft in respect of which a permit to operate outside waters of Categories A, B, C or D has been issued in accordance with the Merchant Shipping (High Speed Craft) Regulations 2004, SI 2004/302, reg 8 (see PARA 623).

'Merchant Shipping Notice' means a notice described as such and issued by the MCA (ie the Maritime and Coastguard Agency, an executive agency of the Department for Transport), and any reference to a particular Merchant Shipping Notice includes a reference to a Merchant Shipping Notice amending or replacing that Notice which is considered by the Secretary of State to be relevant from time to time: Merchant Shipping (Hours of Work) Regulations 2002, SI 2002/2125, reg 2(1); Merchant Shipping (Working Time: Inland Waterways) Regulations 2003, SI 2003/3049, reg 2(1); Fishing Vessels (Working Time: Sea-fishermen) Regulations 2004, SI 2004/1713, reg 2(1); Merchant Shipping (Maritime Labour Convention) (Medical Certification) Regulations 2010, SI 2010/737, reg 2; Merchant Shipping (Maritime Labour Convention) (Minimum Requirements for Seafarers etc) Regulations 2014, SI 2014/1613, reg 2(1).

7 Merchant Shipping (Hours of Work) Regulations 2002, SI 2002/2125, reg 3(1); Merchant Shipping (Maritime Labour Convention) (Minimum Requirements for Seafarers etc) Regulations 2014, SI 2014/1613, reg 3(1)(a).

8 As to the meaning of 'United Kingdom waters' see the Merchant Shipping Act 1995 s 313(2); and PARA 48 (definition applied by the Merchant Shipping (Maritime Labour Convention) (Minimum Requirements for Seafarers etc) Regulations 2014, SI 2014/1613, reg 2(1)).

9 Ie (by virtue of the Merchant Shipping (Hours of Work) Regulations 2002, SI 2002/2125, reg 3(3) (as substituted: see note 4) and the Merchant Shipping (Maritime Labour Convention) (Minimum Requirements for Seafarers etc) Regulations 2014, SI 2014/1613, reg 3(1)(b)) sea-going ships which are not United Kingdom ships while they are in United Kingdom waters and:

(1) the Convention has not come into force for the state whose flag the ship is entitled to fly; or

(2) the Convention has come into force for the state whose flag the ship is entitled to fly, but the ship does not carry a Maritime Labour Certificate to which a Declaration of Maritime Labour Compliance is attached or an interim Maritime Labour Certificate.

Note that the Merchant Shipping (Hours of Work) Regulations 2002, SI 2002/2125, regs 14A, 17B, are excluded from being so applied: see reg 3(3) (as so substituted).

It is also provided that the Merchant Shipping (Hours of Work) Regulations 2002, SI 2002/2125, regs 4, 7, 9, 14A–16, 17B, 18 and the Merchant Shipping (Maritime Labour Convention) (Minimum Requirements for Seafarers etc) Regulations 2014, SI 2014/1613, regs 26, 49 and all of the provisions in Pt 3 (reg 8) and Pt 11 (regs 54–58) (other than reg 54), along with regs 6, 15, 18, 28, 33, 41, 46, 55, 57 (cited in note 4), apply to a sea-going ship which is not a United Kingdom ship while that ship is in United Kingdom waters if the Convention has come into force for the state whose flag the ship is entitled to fly and the ship carries a Maritime Labour Certificate to which a Declaration of Maritime Labour Compliance is attached or an interim Maritime Labour Certificate: Merchant Shipping (Hours of Work) Regulations 2002, SI 2002/2125, reg 3(2) (as so substituted); Merchant Shipping (Maritime Labour Convention) (Minimum Requirements for Seafarers etc) Regulations 2014, SI 2014/1613, reg 3(3), (4). This is subject to reg 3(5) (see the text and notes 19–21) and reg 46(4) (see PARA 496): reg 3(3).

'Maritime Labour Certificate' and 'interim Maritime Labour Certificate' mean, in relation to a ship, a certificate of that name issued in accordance with the Convention, in a form corresponding to the relevant model given in Appendix A5-II and having the contents, duration and validity specified in Regulation 5.1.3 and Standard A5.1.3; and 'Declaration of Maritime Labour Compliance' means, in relation to a ship, the Part 1 and Part 2 documents drawn up and issued in accordance with the Convention, in the forms corresponding to the relevant models given in Appendix A5-II and having the contents, duration and validity specified in Regulation 5.1.3 and Standard A5.1.3: Merchant Shipping (Hours of Work) Regulations 2002, SI 2002/2125, reg 2(1) (as so amended); Merchant Shipping (Maritime Labour Convention) (Minimum Requirements for Seafarers etc) Regulations 2014, SI 2014/1613, reg 2(1).

10 See the Merchant Shipping (Maritime Labour Convention) (Minimum Requirements for Seafarers etc) Regulations 2014, SI 2014/1613, Pt 2 (regs 4–7); and PARA 448.

11 See the Merchant Shipping (Maritime Labour Convention) (Minimum Requirements for Seafarers etc) Regulations 2014, SI 2014/1613, Pt 3 (reg 8); and PARA 456.

12 See the Merchant Shipping (Maritime Labour Convention) (Minimum Requirements for Seafarers etc) Regulations 2014, SI 2014/1613, Pt 4 (regs 9–15); the Merchant Shipping (Maritime Labour Convention) (Medical Certification) Regulations 2010, SI 2010/737; and PARAS 451–455, 464–467.

13 See the Merchant Shipping (Maritime Labour Convention) (Minimum Requirements for Seafarers etc) Regulations 2014, SI 2014/1613, Pt 6 (regs 19–28) and Pt 10 (regs 48–53); and PARAS 540–547.

14 In this context the Convention framework broadly applies the existing domestic provisions set out in the Merchant Shipping (Crew Accommodation) Regulations 1997, SI 1997/1508 (made under the Merchant Shipping Act 1995 s 43): see the Merchant Shipping (Maritime Labour Convention) (Minimum Requirements for Seafarers etc) Regulations 2014, SI 2014/1613, Pt 7 (regs 29–33); and PARAS 490–491.

15 See the Merchant Shipping (Maritime Labour Convention) (Minimum Requirements for Seafarers etc) Regulations 2014, SI 2014/1613, Pt 8 (regs 34–42) and Pt 9 (regs 43–47); and PARAS 492–497.

16 See the Merchant Shipping (Maritime Labour Convention) (Minimum Requirements for Seafarers etc) Regulations 2014, SI 2014/1613, Pt 5 (regs 16–18); and PARAS 482–483.

17 Other matters connected to wages are not within the scope of the Convention and are dealt with under the Merchant Shipping Act 1995: see note 28.

18 The general provisions which govern the organisation of working time for employees (ie the Working Time Regulations 1998, SI 1998/1833 (which implement Council Directive (EC) 93/104 (OJ L307, 13.12.93, p 18) concerning certain aspects of the organisation of working time (the Working Time Directive): see EMPLOYMENT vol 39 (2014) PARA 268 et seq) do not apply to the organisation of working time for seafarers (see instead the Merchant Shipping (Hours of Work) Regulations 2002, SI 2002/2125; and PARAS 511–514), for sea-fishermen (see the Fishing Vessels (Working Time: Sea-fishermen) Regulations 2004, SI 2004/1713; and PARAS 515–519) or for workers on inland waterways (see the Merchant Shipping (Working Time: Inland Waterways) Regulations 2003, SI 2003/3049; and PARAS 520–523). The Fishing Vessels (Working Time: Sea-fishermen) Regulations 2004, SI 2004/1713, apply to United Kingdom fishing vessels (ie sea-going fishing vessels registered in the United Kingdom) wherever they may be (regs 2(1), 3(1)), and regs 7, 16, 17 apply to fishing vessels registered in member states other than the United Kingdom when they are in United Kingdom waters (reg 3(2)). The Merchant Shipping (Working Time: Inland Waterways) Regulations 2003, SI 2003/3049, apply to any United Kingdom ship, wherever it may be, which operates, or ordinarily operates, under a certificate which does not allow the ship to go beyond the limits of waters of category A, B, C or D (as categorised in Merchant Shipping Notice No MSN 1776 (M)) or is not required to be certificated (reg 3(1)) and to any ship, other than a United Kingdom ship, which operates in the United Kingdom and does not go beyond the limits of waters of categories A, B, C and D, as categorised in Merchant Shipping Notice No MSN 1776 (M) (reg 3(2)).

19 Merchant Shipping (Hours of Work) Regulations 2002, SI 2002/2125, reg 3(4)(b); Merchant Shipping (Maritime Labour Convention) (Minimum Requirements for Seafarers etc) Regulations 2014, SI 2014/1613, reg 3(5)(b). As to the meaning of 'fishing vessel' in the context of the Convention see the Merchant Shipping Act 1995 s 313(1); and PARA 230 (definition applied by the Merchant Shipping (Maritime Labour Convention) (Minimum Requirements for Seafarers etc) Regulations 2014, SI 2014/1613, reg 2(1)). See further the material dealing with fishing vessels in note 25.

20 Merchant Shipping (Hours of Work) Regulations 2002, SI 2002/2125, reg 3(4)(d); Merchant Shipping (Maritime Labour Convention) (Minimum Requirements for Seafarers etc) Regulations 2014, SI 2014/1613, reg 3(5)(e).

21 Merchant Shipping (Maritime Labour Convention) (Minimum Requirements for Seafarers etc) Regulations 2014, SI 2014/1613, reg 3(5)(c). Only the shore leave provisions of the Merchant Shipping (Hours of Work) Regulations 2002, SI 2002/2125 (ie reg 12A: see PARA 512) are excluded in the context of ships of traditional build: see reg 3(5).

22 Ie the matters dealt with under the Merchant Shipping (Maritime Labour Convention) (Minimum Requirements for Seafarers etc) Regulations 2014, SI 2014/1613, Pts 2–10 (see the text and notes 10–17).

23 Ie under the Merchant Shipping Act 1995 Pt III (ss 24–84). The applicable provisions are:
   (1)      s 44 (complaints about provisions or water) (see PARA 500), s 45 (expenses or medical or other treatment) (see PARA 501), s 55 (young persons) (see PARA 449) and ss 73–75 (relief and repatriation) (see PARAS 548–550), which apply to sea-going United Kingdom ships and masters and seamen employed in them only if they are fishing vessels, ships of traditional build or vessels which are not ordinarily engaged in commercial activities (see s 24(2A) (added by SI 2014/1614); and the Merchant Shipping (Crew Agreements, Lists of Crew and Discharge of Seamen) Regulations 1991, SI 1991/2144, reg 3(2) (added by SI 2014/1614));
   (2)      the Merchant Shipping Act 1995 ss 25, 26 and the Merchant Shipping (Crew Agreements, Lists of Crew and Discharge of Seamen) Regulations 1991, SI 1991/2144, Pt 1 (regs 3–10) (crew agreements) (see PARAS 457–463), and the Merchant Shipping Act 1995 ss 30, 31, 33, 38(1) (certain provisions relating to wages for seamen employed under crew agreements) (see PARAS 470, 484, 485, 486), which apply to ships of traditional build and vessels which are not ordinarily engaged in commercial activities but not to fishing vessels (see the Merchant Shipping Act 1995 s 24(2A) and the Merchant Shipping (Crew Agreements, Lists of Crew and Discharge of Seamen) Regulations 1991, SI 1991/2144, reg 2 (definition of 'ship': see PARA 458 note 2); and
   (3)      the Merchant Shipping (Crew Agreements, Lists of Crew and Discharge of Seamen) Regulations 1991, SI 1991/2144, Pt 3 (regs 25–26) (discharge of crew: see PARA 468) and the Merchant Shipping (Seamen's Wages and Accounts) Regulations 1972, SI 1972/1700 (deductions from wages: see PARA 473), whose application is not restricted by the Merchant Shipping Act 1995 s 24(2A) to fishing vessels, ships of traditional build or vessels which are not ordinarily engaged in commercial activities, but which do not apply to fishing vessels (see the Merchant Shipping (Crew Agreements, Lists of Crew and

Discharge of Seamen) Regulations 1991, SI 1991/2144, reg 2 and the definitions of 'ship' and 'seaman' in the Merchant Shipping (Seamen's Wages and Accounts) Regulations 1972, SI 1972/1700, reg 1(2)).

Separate provision for fishing vessels is made by the Merchant Shipping (Crew Agreements, Lists of Crew and Discharge of Seamen) (Fishing Vessels) Regulations 1972, SI 1972/919: see FISHERIES AND AQUACULTURE vol 51 (2013) PARAS 312, 314, 316.

As a rule, the Merchant Shipping Act 1995 Pt III applies only to ships which are sea-going ships and masters and seamen employed in sea-going ships: s 24(1). However, no such restriction is applied to the application of s 43 (crew accommodation: see PARA 490), ss 46–52 (manning etc: see PARAS 502–507, 1083), s 54 (special certificates of competence: see PARA 503), s 55 (young persons: see PARA 449), s 58 (conduct endangering ships, structures or individuals: see PARA 1102), ss 61–68 (disciplinary matters) (see PARAS 508, 524–538, 1085) and s 69 (Scottish provisions): s 24(2). In its application to fishing vessels and persons serving in them, Pt III has effect subject to the modifications made by Pt V (ss 109–127); and in particular s 110 (payments of seaman's wages: see PARA 488) and s 112 (accounts of wages and catch: see PARA 489) apply to the exclusion of s 30 (payment of seaman's wages: see PARA 484) and s 31 (account of seaman's wages: see PARA 485): s 24(3).

The Secretary of State may grant exemptions from any requirements of Pt III or Pt V Ch I (ss 109–120) or of any regulations made thereunder:

(a)  with respect to any fishing vessel or to a fishing vessel of any description (s 120(a)); or

(b)  with respect to any person or a person of any description serving in a fishing vessel or in a fishing vessel of any description (s 120(b));

and nothing in any other provision of the provisions relating to masters and seamen or the provisions relating to the skipper and seamen of fishing vessels conferring a power to provide for or grant exemptions is to be taken to restrict the power conferred by these provisions (s 120).

As to the meaning of 'ship' see PARA 229. As to the meaning of 'master' see PARA 444 note 1. As to the meaning of 'seaman' see PARA 457 note 5. As to the meaning of 'fishing vessel' see PARA 230 note 9. As to the Secretary of State see PARA 36.

24 Merchant Shipping (Hours of Work) Regulations 2002, SI 2002/2125, reg 3(4)(a); Merchant Shipping (Maritime Labour Convention) (Minimum Requirements for Seafarers etc) Regulations 2014, SI 2014/1613, reg 3(5)(a). 'Pleasure vessel' means (by virtue of the Merchant Shipping (Crew Accommodation) Regulations 1997, SI 1997/1508, reg 2(1); the Merchant Shipping (Hours of Work) Regulations 2002, SI 2002/2125, reg 2(1) (amended by SI 2014/308); the Merchant Shipping (Maritime Labour Convention) (Medical Certification) Regulations 2010, SI 2010/737, reg 4(1)–(4); and the Merchant Shipping (Maritime Labour Convention) (Minimum Requirements for Seafarers etc) Regulations 2014, SI 2014/1613, reg 3(5)(a)):

(1)  any vessel which at the time it is being used is:

(a)  in the case of a vessel wholly owned by an individual or individuals, used only for the sport or pleasure of the owner or the immediate family or friends of the owner; or

(b)  in the case of a vessel owned by a body corporate, used only for sport or pleasure and on which the persons on board are employees or officers of the body corporate, or their immediate family or friends; and

on a voyage or excursion which is one for which the owner does not receive money for or in connection with operating the vessel or carrying any person, other than as a contribution to the direct expenses of the operation of the vessel incurred during the voyage or excursion; or

(2)  any vessel wholly owned by or on behalf of a members' club formed for the purpose of sport or pleasure which, at the time it is being used, is used only for the sport or pleasure of members of that club or their immediate family, and for the use of which any charges levied are paid into club funds and applied for the general use of the club,

where, in the case of any vessel referred to under head (1) or (2), no other payments are made by or on behalf of users of the vessel, other than by the owner. In the context of the Merchant Shipping (Hours of Work) Regulations 2002, SI 2002/2125; the Merchant Shipping (Maritime Labour Convention) (Medical Certification) Regulations 2010, SI 2010/737; and the Merchant Shipping (Maritime Labour Convention) (Minimum Requirements for Seafarers etc) Regulations 2014, SI 2014/1613, 'immediate family' means, in relation to an individual, the spouse or civil partner of the individual, and a relative of the individual or the individual's spouse or civil partner; and 'relative' means brother, sister, ancestor or lineal descendant: Merchant Shipping (Hours of Work) Regulations 2002, SI 2002/2125, reg 1(2) (as so amended); Merchant Shipping (Maritime Labour Convention) (Medical Certification) Regulations 2010, SI 2010/737, reg 4(5); Merchant Shipping (Maritime Labour Convention) (Minimum Requirements for Seafarers etc) Regulations 2014, SI 2014/1613, reg 2(1). In the Merchant Shipping (Maritime Labour Convention)

(Minimum Requirements for Seafarers etc) Regulations 2014, SI 2014/1613, 'employee' means an individual who is employed under a contract of employment: reg 2(1).

25	Merchant Shipping (Hours of Work) Regulations 2002, SI 2002/2125, reg 3(4)(c); Merchant Shipping (Maritime Labour Convention) (Minimum Requirements for Seafarers etc) Regulations 2014, SI 2014/1613, reg 3(5)(d).

26	In connection with entitlement to wages generally under the Merchant Shipping Act 1995 see PARAS 470–481; in connection with wages payable in respect of the operation of ships of traditional build and non-commercial vessels see PARAS 484–483; and in connection with fishing vessels only see PARAS 488–489. These provisions operate alongside the limited provision for wages made within the Convention framework (see PARAS 482–483).

27	In connection with the discharge of crews under the Merchant Shipping Act 1995 see PARAS 468–469.

28	In connection with competence, certification and training under the Merchant Shipping Act 1995 see PARAS 502–509.

29	In connection with the fitness and conduct of seamen and officers under the Merchant Shipping Act 1995 see PARAS 524–539.

30	See in particular PARAS 424–443.

# (2) MASTERS

## (i) Employment

**424. Contract of service.** The contract of service between an owner and a master is a matter of agreement[1]. However, by statute, in every contract of employment between the owner of a United Kingdom ship[2] and the master[3] of or any seaman[4] employed in the ship there is implied, notwithstanding any agreement to the contrary, an obligation on the owner of the ship that the owner, the master and every agent charged with the loading of the ship, the preparing of the ship for sea or the sending of the ship to sea must use all reasonable means to ensure the seaworthiness of the ship for the voyage at the time when the voyage commences, and to keep the ship in a seaworthy condition for the voyage during the voyage[5]. There is, however, no liability on the owner where, owing to special circumstances, the sending of the ship to sea in an unseaworthy state was reasonable and justifiable[6].

1	Reasonable notice of discharge must be given, having regard to the terms of the contract: *Creen v Wright* (1876) 1 CPD 591, 3 Asp MLC 245, DC. See also *Savage v British India Steam Navigation Co* (1930) 46 TLR 294. The law will presume that terms agreed upon with regard to a first voyage apply, in default of further stipulation, to a second voyage during which the master's services are retained: *The Gananoque* (1862) Lush 448. If wrongfully discharged, a master is entitled to damages equal to his wages up to the end of the voyage, or until he obtains other employment: *The Camilla* (1858) Sw 312. See also *The Royalist* (1863) Brown & Lush 46. An action in rem for wrongful dismissal may be brought in the High Court: *The Great Eastern* (1867) LR 1 A & E 384; *The Blessing* (1878) 3 PD 35, 3 Asp MLC 561.

2	As to the meaning of 'ship' under the Merchant Shipping Act 1995 see PARA 229; and as to the meaning of 'United Kingdom ship' see PARA 230.

3	As to the meaning of 'master' under the Merchant Shipping Act 1995 see PARA 444 note 1.

4	As to the meaning of 'seaman' under the Merchant Shipping Act 1995 see PARA 457 note 5.

5	See the Merchant Shipping Act 1995 s 42(1), (2); and PARA 603.

6	See the Merchant Shipping Act 1995 s 42(3); and PARA 603.

**425. Appointment and removal of master.** In the ordinary course the master is appointed or removed by the owners of the ship or by other persons having control over her, but he may be appointed or removed by persons who in cases of emergency are in a position to exercise authority[1]. Where the master dies at sea, his natural successor is the chief officer[2].

1	*The Alexander* (1812) 1 Dods 278 (consignees); *The Tartar* (1822) 1 Hag Adm 1 (bottomry bondholder); *The Zodiac* (1825) 1 Hag Adm 320 (consul); *Bowen v Fox* (1829) 10 B & C 41

(previous master); *The Kennersley Castle* (1833) 3 Hag Adm 1 (underwriters); *The Cynthia* (1852) 16 Jur 748 (consul); *The Segredo (otherwise The Eliza Cornish)* (1853) 1 Ecc & Ad 36 (naval officer).
2   See *The Favourite* (1799) 2 Ch Rob 232; *The Providence* (1825) 1 Hag Adm 391.

**426.  Change of master during voyage.** If a person ceases to be the master[1] of a United Kingdom ship[2] during a voyage of the ship, he must deliver to his successor the documents relating to the ship or its crew which are in his custody[3].

1   As to the meaning of 'master' under the Merchant Shipping Act 1995 see PARA 444 note 1.
2   As to the meaning of 'ship' under the Merchant Shipping Act 1995 see PARA 229; and as to the meaning of 'United Kingdom ship' see PARA 230.
3   See the Merchant Shipping Act 1995 s 81(1); and PARA 447.

### (ii)  Master's Authority and Liability

**427.  Master's general authority as owners' agent.** The master is the servant of the owners[1], and, in general, he will be their agent for those purposes for which he is employed, that is to say in all acts which are usual and necessary for the use and employment of the vessel[2]. Whether or not, in particular circumstances, the master has authority to bind shipowners to contractual obligations depends upon a number of considerations[3]. He may have express authority, derived from express instructions, written or oral[4]. His authority may be implied from those instructions, or from the fact of his employment as master[5], or it may be implied from the conduct of the owners[6]. In some cases, it may be conferred by the necessity of the circumstances[7]; and in others it may arise from subsequent ratification of an act which he was not authorised to perform but which he nevertheless purported to do as agent[8].

1   See *Hedley v Pinkney & Sons Steamship Co* [1892] 1 QB 58 at 62, 7 Asp MLC 135 at 137, CA, per Lord Esher MR; on appeal [1894] AC 222, 7 Asp MLC 483, HL (where the captain of a ship was held to be the owners' agent).
2   *Grant v Norway* (1851) 10 CB 665 at 687; *McLean and McLean and Hope v Fleming* (1871) LR 2 Sc & Div 128 at 130, 1 Asp MLC 160 at 161, HL, per Lord Chelmsford.
3   This was formerly a jury question: *Williamson v Page* (1844) 1 Car & Kir 581. As to the derivation or extent of the authority of an agent generally see AGENCY vol 1 (2008) PARA 29 et seq.
4   *Messageries Imperiales Co v Baines* (1863) 7 LT 763 (express authority to charter a ship).
5   As to the extent of the master's authority which can be implied from the fact of his employment as master see PARA 428.
6   *The Great Eastern* (1868) LR 2 A & E 88.
7   *Webster v Seekamp* (1821) 4 B & Ald 352; *Grant v Norway* (1851) 10 CB 665. See also PARA 432.
8   *Moore v 'City of Malines' and Purvis Shipping Co Ltd* (1947) 81 Ll L Rep 96 (where a master's promise to pay 'short hand money' was ratified subsequently).

**428.  Extent of master's implied authority as owners' agent.** The extent of the master's authority which may be implied from the fact of his employment as master varies according to the usages of trade and all the circumstances of the case, including the place where he is and the accessibility of the owners or other agents of the owners[1]. Thus, a master may have authority to bind his owners by charterparty when he is in a foreign port and his owners are not there, and there is difficulty in communicating with them[2]. He has, however, no implied authority to agree to the substitution of another voyage for one to which the owners have already bound themselves[3], or to vary the contract by substituting another and a more distant port of loading, or a different quality or description of cargo[4], although in minor matters he may vary the contract[5].

It is the master's duty to obey his owner's instructions, and his implied authority cannot extend to any act which is inconsistent with the law of the land because obedience to the law is implied in his instructions[6]. An owner may by express instructions to his master limit or extend what might otherwise be his implied authority[7], but third persons dealing with the master without notice of a limitation are not affected by it. If the matter is within the ordinary scope of a master's authority, the shipowners may be bound by his act[8].

1	*The Fanny, The Mathilda* (1883) 5 Asp MLC 75, CA. The scope of the master's authority has declined considerably during the last 100 years. This is due partly to the development of communications technology which makes it possible in many circumstances for masters to consult their owners to obtain express instructions before binding them to contractual obligations. In addition, many shipowners have appointed representatives at foreign ports who are authorised to act on their behalf for many purposes which formerly would have been part of the master's duties. Many of the authorities referred to subsequently must be read in the light of these developments and changing circumstances. As to the extent of the authority of an agent generally see AGENCY vol 1 (2008) PARA 30 et seq.
2	*The Fanny, The Mathilda* (1883) 5 Asp MLC 75 at 78, CA, per Brett LJ. Cf, however, *The Sir Henry Webb* (1849) 13 Jur 639 (charterparty made to secure a debt).
3	*Burgon v Sharpe* (1810) 2 Camp 529.
4	*Sickens v Irving* (1859) 7 CBNS 165. See also *Grant v Norway* (1851) 10 CB 665.
5	*Holman v Peruvian Nitrate Co* (1878) 5 R 657 (loading at a berth different from that named in charter so as to avoid delay).
6	*Earle v Rowcroft* (1806) 8 East 126 at 133 per Lord Ellenborough CJ; *Wilson v Rankin* (1865) 6 B & S 208. Where the owner decides to send a vessel on a voyage which might be dangerous because of quarrels between foreign countries, the master must not substitute another voyage instead of obeying his orders: *The Roebuck* (1874) 2 Asp MLC 387.
7	*Foreman & Co Proprietary Ltd v The Liddlesdale* [1900] AC 190, 9 Asp MLC 45, PC. When a person has notice of some limitation of the master's authority, he may still treat him as having the ordinary authority of a master in all matters not affected by the limitation: *Weston v Wright* (1841) 7 M & W 396.
8	*Manchester Trust v Furness* [1895] 2 QB 539, 8 Asp MLC 57, CA. As to ostensible authority and agency by estoppel see, however, AGENCY vol 1 (2008) PARA 25.

**429. Liability of master.** According to the principles of agency, a master will not be liable personally on a contract made in the course of the usual employment of the ship unless he has failed to disclose to the third person that he is an agent[1]. When a master purports to act as agent, he is deemed to warrant that he has authority to do so; if he has no such authority to bind his owners, he may be personally liable to third persons who have relied upon that warranty, and in consequence suffered loss or damage, for breach of his warranty of authority[2].

The master is personally responsible to his owners for any injury or loss to the ship or cargo by reason of his negligence or misconduct, or for acting without authority[3]. He is in the position of a trustee for his owners and is bound to account for all profits made by the ship while under his command[4].

1	See *Garnham v Bennett* (1728) 2 Stra 816; *Rich v Coe* (1777) 2 Cowp 636; and AGENCY vol 1 (2008) PARA 156 et seq.
2	See *Gordon v Hare* (1823) 1 LJOSKB 70. A master is liable upon bills of exchange drawn upon his owners if these are dishonoured upon presentation (*Watson and Parker v Gregory, The Cairo* [1908] WN 230, 11 Asp MLC 161); and he may be liable upon a bill of exchange drawn by him unless its terms relieve him of liability expressly or impliedly (*The Elmville* [1904] P 319, 9 Asp MLC 606).
3	*Fletcher v Braddick* (1806) 2 Bos & PNR 182; *Swainston v Garrick* (1833) 2 LJ Ex 255; *The Sir Charles Napier* (1880) 5 PD 73, 4 Asp MLC 231, CA; *Stumore, Weston & Co v Breen* (1886) 12 App Cas 698, HL. A master has no right to delegate his authority, and, except in the case of some higher authority (eg officers of the Royal Navy), he has no right to give up control except to one of his own officers: *The Bonvilston* (1914) 30 TLR 311 per Bargrave Deane J. The fact that a ship is being navigated in an area and in circumstances in which pilotage is compulsory for it does not affect any liability of the owner or master of the ship for any loss or damage caused by the ship or by the manner in which it is navigated: see the Pilotage Act 1987 s 16; and PARA 589. See also *The Prinses Juliana* [1936] P 139, [1936] 1 All ER 685; *The Hans Hoth* [1953] 1 All ER 218, [1952] 2 Lloyd's Rep 341; *Workington Harbour and Dock Board v Towerfield (Owners)* [1951] AC 112, [1950] 2 All ER 414, HL.
4	*Diplock v Blackburn* (1811) 3 Camp 43; *Shallcross v Oldham* (1862) 5 LT 824.

**430. Exoneration of master; ship's protests.** A ship's protest is a declaration by the master when damage has been caused to a ship or her cargo, and is made before a notary or British consul at the first port of call[1]. The object of a protest is to record promptly in an authentic form the circumstances in which loss or damage occurred so as to exonerate the master and his crew from blame[2]. Although protests are not compulsory or essential in England[3], they are often made in practice to support insurance claims by foreign cargo owners in countries where protests are required. In English courts they are not receivable in evidence, although they may be used in cross-examination[4].

1 An important branch of a notary's practice deals with the drawing up and noting of ships' protests: see LEGAL PROFESSIONS vol 66 (2015) PARA 1038. As to British consular officers see INTERNATIONAL RELATIONS LAW vol 61 (2010) PARA 30.

2 A 'note' of the protest is made in a book of the notary, stating the date, the name of the ship, the name of her master and the voyage, and protests against the perils of the seas causing damage: see LEGAL PROFESSIONS vol 66 (2015) PARA 1038. Thus, a protest would record details of an accident or heavy weather encountered on a voyage which might have caused loss of deck cargo or which might have prevented the ventilation of cargo or which might have delayed the voyage, or caused the vessel to put into a port of refuge.

3 *The Santa Anna* (1863) 32 LJPM & A 198. As to the meaning of 'England' see PARA 16 note 2.

4 *Senat v Porter* (1797) 7 Term Rep 158; *Appleton v Lord Braybrook* (1817) 6 M & S 34; *Black v Lord Braybrook* (1817) 6 M & S 39; *The Betsey Caines* (1826) 2 Hag Adm 28; *R v Scriveners' Co* (1830) 10 B & C 511; *Brown v Thornton* (1837) 6 Ad & El 185.

### (iii) Master's Authority to Make Contracts

**431. General instances of master's authority to contract.** The master of a ship has implied authority to contract to carry goods on board[1], to assign freight and to authorise the collection of freight[2], but he cannot bind his owners to carry freight free[3], or contract with the freighter to carry at a lower freight than that agreed upon with the owners[4], or authorise its payment in an unusual manner[5]. He may sign bills of lading for goods put on board[6], and acknowledge the weight, value and condition of such goods[7]. Shipowners are bound by statements by the master in the bill of lading as to the condition of goods[8] and as to whether freight is payable or not[9].

The master has implied authority to do whatever is necessary and prudent for the preservation of ship and cargo[10]. He has authority to contract for the services of a crew at an increased remuneration if the risks of war arise and to discharge the crew from their obligations under an existing contract of employment[11]. He has the authority to conclude contracts for salvage operations on behalf of the owner of the vessel and to conclude such contracts on behalf of the owner of the property on board the vessel[12]. If he is performing a charterparty which does not expressly bestow authority, he may deviate to save life, but not to save property[13]. The master has implied authority to bind the shipowner to pay for repairs, stores, provisions, disbursements paid and money advanced in circumstances necessary for the use and employment of the ship[14].

1 *Grant v Norway* (1851) 10 CB 665. See *The Rewia* [1991] 2 Lloyd's Rep 325 (where bills of lading are signed by or for the master, it is a matter of evidence whether authority comes from the owner or the charterer).

2 *HG Harper & Co v J Bland & Co Ltd* (1914) 84 LJKB 738, 13 Asp MLC 49.

3 *Dewell v Moxon* (1808) 1 Taunt 391; *Walshe v Provan* (1853) 8 Exch 843 at 850.

4 *Pickernell v Jauberry* (1862) 3 F & F 217; *Pearson v Göschen* (1864) 17 CBNS 352.

5 *Walshe v Provan* (1853) 8 Exch 843 (making freight payable at port of loading instead of port of discharge); *Reynolds v Jex* (1865) 7 B & S 86 (making freight payable to ship's agents so that they were able to set it off against a debt due in respect of another vessel of the owner).

6 The master has no authority to sue for freight (*Repetto v Millar's Karri and Jarrah Forests Ltd* [1901] 2 KB 306, 9 Asp MLC 215) or to begin an action on behalf of the owners of cargo laden on board his ship (*The Glenluce* (1930) 170 LT Jo 399). As to signing bills of lading see further CARRIAGE AND CARRIERS vol 7 (2015) PARA 329 et seq.

7 *Grant v Norway* (1851) 10 CB 665. A bill of lading representing goods to have been shipped or received for shipment, signed by the master and in the hands of the lawful holder acting in good faith, is conclusive evidence of such shipment or receipt as against the carrier: see the Carriage of Goods by Sea Act 1992 s 4; and CARRIAGE AND CARRIERS vol 7 (2015) PARAS 332, 344.

8 *Compania Naviera Vasconzada v Churchill and Sim* [1906] 1 KB 237, 10 Asp MLC 177.

9 See *Howard v Tucker* (1831) 1 B & Ad 712. See also ESTOPPEL vol 47 (2014) PARA 357. As to charterparties generally see CARRIAGE AND CARRIERS vol 7 (2015) PARA 208 et seq.

10 *Austin Friars Steamship Co Ltd v Spillers and Bakers Ltd* [1915] 1 KB 833; affd [1915] 3 KB 586, 13 Asp MLC 162, CA (a general average act). As to the master's authority to hypothecate a ship and freight see PARA 435; as to his authority to tranship and to jettison see PARAS 436, 437; and as to his authority to sell ship and cargo see PARA 438 et seq. Without authority the master may not insure the ship as this is not a matter of necessity: *The Serafina* (1864) Brown & Lush 277.

11 *Liston v Carpathian (Owners)* [1915] 2 KB 42, 13 Asp MLC 70.

12 See the International Convention on Salvage (London, 28 April 1989; Cm 1526) art 6(2); and PARA 853. As to the International Convention on Salvage 1989 generally see PARA 7; and as to its implementation by the Merchant Shipping (Salvage and Pollution) Act 1994 s 1(1), Sch 1 Pt I (repealed) (see now the Merchant Shipping Act 1995 Sch 11 Pt I) see PARA 851 et seq.

13 *Scaramanga v Stamp* (1880) 4 Asp MLC 295, CA.

14 As to necessaries see PARA 432.

## 432. Master's authority to contract for necessaries.

The master of a vessel has implied authority to contract as agent on behalf of the shipowner for such things as are necessary for the use and employment of the ship[1]. Thus, a shipowner is liable for necessary repairs done to a ship by the master's order[2]. The repairs must be such as are fit and proper for the vessel on her voyage[3] and such as a prudent owner himself, if present, would have ordered[4]. The master's authority may also extend to contracts for the supply of anchors, cables, rigging[5], fuel[6], provisions and clothing for the crew[7], copper sheathing[8], a screw propeller[9], or for the advance of money to pay for necessaries[10], or money to pay off a shipwright's lien for necessary repairs[11], or to pay towage and harbour charges[12] and such other things as a prudent owner would have authorised the master to order if he had been present at the time[13]. It must be shown not only that the money borrowed or goods supplied were reasonably necessary according to the ordinary course of prudent conduct, but also that it was reasonably necessary that the master should obtain or order them on the owner's credit[14]. The burden of proof lies upon the creditor who seeks to establish the shipowner's liability[15].

1 *Grant v Norway* (1851) 10 CB 665; *The Pontida* (1884) 9 PD 177, 5 Asp MLC 330, CA. The master has implied authority to sign all documents necessary for the proper performance of his duties: *Bahamas Oil Refining Co v Kristiansands Tankrederie A/S and Shell International Marine Ltd, The Polyduke* [1978] 1 Lloyd's Rep 211. As to the meaning of 'necessaries' see PARA 983 note 1.

2 *Webster v Seekamp* (1821) 4 B & Ald 352.

3 *Webster v Seekamp* (1821) 4 B & Ald 352.

4 *Webster v Seekamp* (1821) 4 B & Ald 352. See also *The Riga* (1872) LR 3 A & E 516, 1 Asp MLC 246.

5 *The Alexander* (1842) 1 Wm Rob 346; *The Sophie* (1842) 1 Wm Rob 368.

6 *The West Friesland* (1859) Sw 454; *The Comtesse de Fregeville* (1861) Lush 329; *The Mecca* [1895] P 95, 7 Asp MLC 529, CA.

7 *The NR Gosfabrick* (1858) Sw 344; *The William F Safford* (1860) Lush 69.

8 *The Perla* (1858) Sw 353; *The Turliani* (1875) 2 Asp MLC 603.

9 *The Flecha* (1854) 1 Ecc & Ad 438 at 441.

10 *Arthur v Barton* (1840) 6 M & W 138 at 144; *The Sophie* (1842) 1 Wm Rob 368; *The Albert Crosby* (1870) LR 3 A & E 37; *The Anna* (1876) 1 PD 253, 3 Asp MLC 237, CA; *The Onni* (1860) Lush 154. It is often to the advantage of the owner that the master should have cash to pay for necessaries for he may then get better terms: *Edwards v Havill* (1853) 14 CB 107 at 111. The lender may recover from the shipowner only the amount actually necessary for the purposes of the ship: see *Cary v White* (1710) 2 Eq Cas Abr 722, HL; *Mackintosh v Mitcheson* (1849) 4 Exch 175; *The Pontida* (1884) 9 PD 177, 5 Asp MLC 330, CA. The money advanced must be expressed to be for those purposes: *Thacker v Moates* (1831) 1 Mood & R 79.

11 *The Albert Crosby* (1870) LR 3 A & E 37.

12  *The St Lawrence* (1880) 5 PD 250. As to towage see PARA 597 et seq; and as to harbour charges
    see PORTS AND HARBOURS vol 85 (2012) PARA 68 et seq.
13  *Webster v Seekamp* (1821) 4 B & Ald 352; *The Riga* (1872) LR 3 A & E 516, 1 Asp MLC 246.
14  *Gunn v Roberts* (1874) LR 9 CP 331, 2 Asp MLC 250 per Brett J; see also *Gordon v Hare* (1823)
    1 LJOSKB 70: *Mitcheson v Oliver* (1855) 5 E & B 419, Ex Ch.
15  *Mackintosh v Mitcheson* (1849) 4 Exch 175; and see *The Alexander* (1842) 1 Wm Rob 346; *The
    Sophie* (1842) 1 Wm Rob 368.

### 433.  Master's lien and right of indemnity.

When a master acting within the
scope of his authority makes disbursements or accepts personal liabilities for the
benefit of the shipowners, he is entitled to be indemnified by them[1]. The master
has a statutory lien upon the ship for his remuneration, liabilities and
disbursements[2]. This lien only arises when the disbursements or liabilities were
made or incurred by the master acting as master and being entitled to pledge the
owner's credit[3]. The disbursement or liability must also have been necessary for
the protection of the owner's interest[4] in the circumstances where the master could
not communicate with the owner[5].

1  *Huntley v Sanderson* (1833) 1 Cr & M 467; *The James Seddon* (1866) LR 1 A & E 62. As to the
   master's authority and liability generally see PARA 427 et seq.
2  See the Merchant Shipping Act 1995 s 41; and PARA 480. Such a claim may be enforced by an
   action in rem: see the Senior Courts Act 1981 ss 20(2)(p), 21(3); and PARA 127.
3  *The Ripon City* [1897] P 226, 8 Asp MLC 304.
4  *Morgan v Castlegate Steamship Co, The Castlegate* [1893] AC 38, 7 Asp MLC 284, HL; *The
   Orienta* [1895] P 49, 7 Asp MLC 529, CA; *The Turgot* (1886) 11 PD 21.
5  *The Orienta* [1895] P 49, 7 Asp MLC 529, CA. As to liens on ships, freight and cargo see
   PARA 964 et seq.

### 434.  Owner's liability to third persons.

The owner is bound personally by
every contract made by the master when acting as his agent within the scope of his
authority[1], even if the vessel is subject to a time charterparty under which the
contract is expressed to be to the charterer's account[2] and even if the creditor
knew of the existence of the time charterparty[3]. This liability in personam remains
notwithstanding a change in the ownership of the ship[4].

The creditor may also be entitled to enforce his claim against the shipowner by
an action in rem[5] if the contract made by the master was in respect of goods or
materials supplied to a ship for her operation or maintenance or in respect of the
construction, repair or equipment of a ship or dock charges or dues[6]. Such a
claimant may institute proceedings in the High Court and, if necessary, arrest the
ship named in the action[7].

1  As to the scope of this authority see PARA 427 et seq.
2  *The Tolla* [1921] P 22.
3  *The Tolla* [1921] P 22.
4  *Trewhella v Rowe* (1809) 11 East 435; *Mackenzie v Pooley* (1856) 11 Exch 638.
5  As to the jurisdiction in rem in respect of such a claim see the Senior Courts Act 1981 s 21(4); and
   PARA 93.
6  See the Senior Courts Act 1981 s 20(2)(m), (n); and PARA 126.
7  As to the procedure for arresting property in a claim in rem see PARA 161 et seq.

### (iv)  Master's Authority to Hypothecate Ship and Freight

### 435.  Bottomry.

The master has authority in circumstances of unforeseen
necessity or distress to pledge the ship and freight to raise the necessary funds for
the voyage[1] by a contract called 'bottomry', the bottom or keel of the ship being
figuratively used to express the whole body of the ship[2].

There is no settled form for the bottomry contract. It has usually taken the form
of a bond[3] by which the master states the occasion for resorting to bottomry and
pledges himself the ship and freight, and sometimes the cargo, for the repayment

of the principal and interest on the safe arrival of the ship at the end of her voyage on such conditions as to risk as may be agreed upon. Where the cargo alone is hypothecated, the instrument is called a respondentia bond. Bottomry and respondentia are obsolete in practice[4].

1   *The Gratitudine* (1801) 3 Ch Rob 240; *The Jacob* (1802) 4 Ch Rob 245; *Smith v Bank of New South Wales, The Staffordshire* (1872) LR 4 PC 194, 1 Asp MLC 365. As to the mortgage of a ship and freight see MORTGAGE vol 77 (2016) PARAS 212–213; and as to pledges generally see BAILMENT AND PLEDGE vol 4 (2011) PARA 188 et seq.
2   In practice, such transactions are now obsolete, but see note 4.
3   See *Menetone v Gibbons* (1789) 3 Term Rep 267. Sometimes it takes the form of a bill of sale: see *Johnson v Shippen* (1704) 2 Ld Raym 982. Bills of exchange drawn by the master on the owner as security for money advanced to the master, even if accompanied by an oral agreement that the ship is to be pledged, are not instruments of bottomry: *Ex p Halkett* (1814) 3 Ves & B 135; *Miller & Co v Potter, Wilson & Co* (1875) 3 R 105. Bottomry bonds have been described as of 'a high and privileged nature', 'favoured instruments' to be liberally protected: *The Alexander* (1812) 1 Dods 278; *The Kennersley Castle* (1833) 3 Hag Adm 1 at 7; *The Reliance* (1833) 3 Hag Adm 66 at 74. See, however, *The Vibilia* (1838) 1 Wm Rob 1 at 5; *The Mary Ann* (1846) 4 Notes of Cases 376.
4   They are, however, still part of the jurisdiction in rem and in personam of the Admiralty court: see the Senior Courts Act 1981 s 20(1)(a), (2)(r); and PARA 134.

### (v) Master's Authority to Tranship or Jettison Cargo

**436.   Transhipment.** It is the master's duty to convey the cargo to the place of destination by any reasonable and practical method. Where the ship in the course of the voyage has suffered damage and cannot be repaired at all or not without very great loss of time or expense, the master is at liberty to tranship the cargo to another vessel to be forwarded to its original destination[1]. He is not bound to do this[2]; nor is he under an absolute obligation to the cargo owner to forward the cargo in the original vessel, although in his capacity of agent to the shipowner it is his duty to do so if he can[3].

1   See *Shipton v Thornton* (1838) 9 Ad & El 314; *Hansen v Dunn* (1906) 11 Com Cas 100.
2   *The Hamburg* (1864) Brown & Lush 253, PC.
3   *Benson v Chapman* (1849) 2 HL Cas 696; *The Bahia* (1864) Brown & Lush 292; *The Hamburg* (1864) Brown & Lush 253, PC; *Atwood v Sellar & Co* (1879) 4 QBD 342, 4 Asp MLC 153 (on appeal (1880) 5 QBD 286, 4 Asp MLC 283, CA). The master is under a duty, implied from the contract of affreightment, to do his best to protect the interests of the cargo owners if the voyage is interrupted by disaster: *Atwood v Sellar & Co.* As to transhipment see also CARRIAGE AND CARRIERS vol 7 (2015) PARA 497 et seq.

**437.   Jettison to remove danger.** In case of imminent danger to the ship or to the lives on board the ship, the master may jettison such amount of cargo as may be necessary to remove the danger. In extreme cases, he may jettison the whole of the cargo; and, when jettisoning, he may select what articles he pleases, and may determine what quantity[1].

If the master jettisons more cargo than is necessary to remedy the danger to the ship, the shipowner is liable to make good the full value to the cargo owner, and the shipowner is similarly liable when cargo has been rightly jettisoned in case of necessity, but at a time when there has been a deviation from the agreed voyage[2].

Whenever cargo is jettisoned from necessity, its owners are entitled to average contribution unless the cargo was carried on deck and there is no custom justifying such carriage[3].

1   *The Gratitudine* (1801) 3 Ch Rob 240 at 258. Jettison by the master in case of panic does not relieve the shipowner from liability to the cargo owner for the value of his goods: *Notara v Henderson* (1872) LR 7 QB 225 at 236, 1 Asp MLC 278 at 282, Ex Ch.
2   See *Notara v Henderson* (1872) LR 7 QB 225, 1 Asp MLC 278, Ex Ch. As to general responsibility for saving property cf CARRIAGE AND CARRIERS vol 7 (2015) PARA 515. See also *Leduc & Co*

*v Ward* (1888) 20 QBD 475, CA; *Glynn v Margetson & Co* [1893] AC 351, 7 Asp MLC 366, HL; *The Dunbeth* [1897] P 133, 8 Asp MLC 284; *Joseph Thorley Ltd v Orchis Steamship Co Ltd* [1907] 1 KB 660, 10 Asp MLC 431, CA.

3   *Wright v Marwood* (1881) 7 QBD 62, 4 Asp MLC 451, CA; *Apollinaris Co v Nord Deutsche Insurance Co* [1904] 1 KB 252 at 259, 9 Asp MLC 526 at 527. The fact that deck cargo is carried at merchant's risk does not relieve the shipowner from contributing in general average: *Burton v English* (1883) 12 QBD 218, 5 Asp MLC 187, CA. As to general average see also CARRIAGE AND CARRIERS vol 7 (2015) PARA 608; and INSURANCE vol 60 (2011) PARA 386 et seq.

## (vi) Master's Authority to Sell Ship or Cargo

**438.   Sale of ship.** By virtue of his employment, the master has not merely those powers which are necessary for the navigation of the ship and the conduct of the adventure to a safe termination, but also in case of extreme necessity[1], as when such termination becomes impossible and no prospect remains of bringing the vessel home, authority to do the best for all concerned, and, if necessary, to sell the ship[2]. Before resorting to a sale, he is bound, if money is what is required to enable the voyage to be completed, seriously and deliberately to try every other expedient to raise the necessary funds[3].

1   As to the meaning of 'necessity' see PARA 439.
2   *Robertson v Caruthers* (1819) 2 Stark 571; *Doyle v Dallas* (1831) 1 Mood & R 48; *Hunter v Parker* (1840) 7 M & W 322 at 342; *Knight v Faith* (1850) 15 QB 649; *Lindsay v Leathley* (1863) 11 LT 194; *Cobequid Marine Insurance Co v Barteaux* (1875) LR 6 PC 319, 2 Asp MLC 536; *Hall v Jupe* (1880) 4 Asp MLC 328. For examples where a sale was held not to be necessary see *East India Co v Ekines* (1718) 2 Bro Parl Cas 382; *Maeburn v Leckie* (1822) (cited in Abbott's Law of Merchant Ships and Seamen (14th Edn) 15, 16).
3   *Underwood v Robertson* (1815) 4 Camp 138.

**439.   Meaning of 'necessity'.** It is impossible to give an exact and concise definition of 'necessity', for it will depend upon all the circumstances of the case[1]. It must be impracticable for the master to communicate with the owners, and therefore modern means of communication make it a matter of extreme rarity for a master to act upon his authority to sell. The sale must be in good faith and for the benefit of all concerned, so that the prudent uninsured owner would have sold the ship; there must also be an urgent necessity for the sale[2]. The burden of proof that the sale was necessary lies on the person seeking to support the sale, on the purchaser as against the owner[3], and on the owner as against the insurers[4].

1   *The Victor* (1865) 13 LT 21.
2   *Green v Royal Exchange Assurance Co* (1815) 6 Taunt 68; *Somes v Sugrue* (1830) 4 C & P 276; *Domett v Young* (1842) Car & M 465; *The Margaret Mitchell* (1858) Sw 382 at 386; *Cobequid Marine Insurance Co v Barteaux* (1875) LR 6 PC 319, 2 Asp MLC 536; *The Uniao Vencedora (otherwise The Gipsy)* (1864) 11 LT 351.
3   *The Glasgow (otherwise The Ya Macraw)* (1856) Sw 145; *The Margaret Mitchell* (1858) Sw 382 at 386; *The Australia* (1859) Sw 480 at 484, PC.
4   *Domett v Young* (1842) Car & M 465.

**440.   Foreign judgment.** A judgment in rem of a foreign court, having jurisdiction in the matter, ordering the sale of the ship is binding even though all the facts were not before the court, provided that the judgment was not obtained by fraud[1]. If, however, in a foreign country the master, for the purpose of evading the effect of the restrictions on his powers of sale, either fraudulently procures the condemnation and sale of the ship as unfit for sea from some court or judge having jurisdiction in maritime matters, or without fraud procures such a condemnation from a court or judge not having jurisdiction, or from an official, these findings are not binding in the English courts, and the question of the necessity for sale may be inquired into and the sale declared void[2].

1   See CONFLICT OF LAWS vol 19 (2011) PARA 438.
2   *Hayman v Molton* (1803) 5 Esp 65; *Reid v Darby* (1808) 10 East 143; *Hunter v Prinsep* (1808) 10 East 378; *The Warrior* (1818) 2 Dods 288; *Morris v Robinson* (1824) 3 B & C 196; *The*

*Segredo (otherwise The Eliza Cornish)* (1853) 1 Ecc & Ad 36; *The Margaret Mitchell* (1858) Sw 382; *The Australia* (1859) Sw 480, PC. See also CONFLICT OF LAWS vol 19 (2011) PARA 438.

**441. Disputing the sale.** A master who is compelled to sell may receive the proceeds and give a good discharge[1]. If his owner wishes to impeach the sale, he must act promptly[2]. If he receives the purchase money knowing the circumstances in which the vessel was sold, and intending to appropriate the money to his own use, he is estopped from disputing the sale[3].

1  *Ireland v Thomson* (1847) 4 CB 149.
2  *The Australia* (1859) Sw 480, PC.
3  *Hunter v Parker* (1840) 7 M & W 322 at 342; *The Margaret Mitchell* (1858) Sw 382; *The Bonita* (1861) Lush 252.

**442. Sale of cargo.** A sale of cargo by the master is a matter which requires the utmost caution on his part, for the cargo has been entrusted to him for the express purpose of being carried to its destination[1]. When it becomes necessary to provide funds to enable the ship to reach her destination, and this can only be done by hypothecation of the cargo or a sale of a part of it, a sale is allowed, but it must be limited to a part of the cargo, for a sale of the whole would defeat the very purpose for which the master has been entrusted with the cargo, and this purpose he is bound to accomplish by every reasonable and practicable method[2].

1  As to the sale of cargo see CARRIAGE AND CARRIERS vol 7 (2015) PARA 509 et seq.
2  *Van Omeron v Dowick* (1809) 2 Camp 42. See also CARRIAGE AND CARRIERS vol 7 (2015) PARAS 510, 514.

**443. Rights of cargo owner.** Where cargo is improperly sold by the master, the cargo owner may sue the master or shipowner[1] or both[2]. Alternatively, he may recover the cargo from the purchaser, provided that the purchaser has not acquired a good title to it by the law of the place where he bought it[3], for, although the master's authority to sell is determined by the law of the country to which the vessel belongs[4], the purchaser's title is determined by the law of the country in which the sale is effected.

1  *Wilson v Dickson* (1818) 2 B & Ald 2; *Freeman v East India Co* (1822) 5 B & Ald 617; *Cannan v Meaburn* (1823) 1 Bing 243; *Morris v Robinson* (1824) 3 B & C 196 (where a purchaser under an order made without jurisdiction was liable in a case of failure to recover from the owner).
2  *Tronson v Dent* (1853) 8 Moo PCC 419; *Australasian Steam Navigation Co v Morse* (1872) LR 4 PC 222, 1 Asp MLC 407; *Hopper v Burness* (1876) 1 CPD 137, 3 Asp MLC 149. The cargo owner is entitled to the full amount received at the sale without deduction of pro rata freight, even though the goods realised more than if sold at the port of destination: *Hopper v Burness*.
3  *Cammell v Sewell* (1860) 5 H & N 728, Ex Ch. See also CONFLICT OF LAWS vol 19 (2011) PARA 439.
4  *Lloyd v Guibert* (1865) LR 1 QB 115, Ex Ch; *Droege v Suart, The Karnak* (1869) LR 2 PC 505; *The Gaetano and Maria* (1882) 7 PD 137, 4 Asp MLC 535, CA. See also CONFLICT OF LAWS vol 19 (2011) PARA 613.

### (vii) Powers exercisable in the interests of Safety, Good Order and Discipline

**444. Master's power to exclude drunken passengers from certain passenger ships.** The master[1] of any ship[2] may refuse to receive on board any person who by reason of drunkenness or otherwise is in such a state, or misconducts himself in such a manner, as to cause annoyance or injury to passengers on board, and, if any such person is on board, may put him on shore at any convenient place[3].

A person so refused admittance, or so put on shore, is not entitled to the return of any fare he has paid[4].

1  In the Merchant Shipping Act 1995, unless the context otherwise requires, 'master' includes every person (except a pilot) having command or charge of a ship and, in relation to a fishing vessel,

means the skipper: s 313(1). As to pilots and pilotage see PARA 574 et seq. As to the meaning of 'ship' under the Merchant Shipping Act 1995 see PARA 229. As to the meaning of 'fishing vessel' see PARA 230 note 9.

2   Ie any ship, whether or not a United Kingdom ship, carrying more than 12 passengers and employed in carrying passengers between places in the limited European trading area as for the time being defined in regulations made under the Merchant Shipping Act 1995 s 47 (see PARA 503) by the Secretary of State: see s 102(3). As to the meaning of 'United Kingdom ship' see PARA 230. As to the meaning of 'United Kingdom' see PARA 16 note 3. As to the Secretary of State see PARA 36.

3   Merchant Shipping Act 1995 s 102(1).

4   Merchant Shipping Act 1995 s 102(2).

**445. Master's power of arrest.** The master[1] of any United Kingdom ship[2] may cause any person on board the ship to be put under restraint if and for so long as it appears to him necessary or expedient in the interest of safety or for the preservation of good order or discipline on board the ship[3].

1   As to the meaning of 'master' see PARA 444 note 1.

2   As to the meaning of 'United Kingdom ship' see PARA 230. As to the meaning of 'ship' under the Merchant Shipping Act 1995 see PARA 229; and as to the meaning of 'United Kingdom' see PARA 16 note 3.

3   Merchant Shipping Act 1995 s 105. See *Hook v Cunard Steamship Co Ltd* [1953] 1 All ER 1021.

### (viii) Master's Duty to Assist Aircraft in Distress

**446. Duty to assist aircraft in distress.** The master of a ship[1], on receiving at sea a signal of distress from an aircraft[2] or information from any source that an aircraft is in distress, must proceed with all speed to the assistance of the persons in distress (informing them, if possible, that he is doing so), unless[3]:

(1)     he is unable, or in the special circumstances of the case considers it unreasonable or unnecessary to do so[4]; or

(2)     he is released from the duty by being informed by the persons in distress (or by the master of any ship that has reached the persons in distress) that assistance is no longer required[5].

If a master fails to comply with the duty to assist[6], he commits an offence[7].

Compliance by the master of a ship with the duty to assist[8] does not affect his right, or the right of any other person, to salvage[9].

1   The duties imposed on the master of a ship by the Merchant Shipping Act 1995 s 93(1) apply to the masters of United Kingdom ships and to the masters of foreign ships when in United Kingdom waters: s 93(3) (amended by SI 1998/1691). As to the meaning of 'master' see PARA 444 note 1; as to the meaning of 'ship' see PARA 229; and as to the meaning of 'foreign', in relation to a ship, see PARA 18 note 2. As to the meaning of 'United Kingdom ship' see PARA 230; and as to the meaning of 'United Kingdom waters' see PARA 48 note 10.

2   As to the duty to assist ships and hovercraft in distress see the International Convention for the Safety of Life at Sea 1974 (London, 1 November 1974 to 1 July 1975; TS 46 (1980); Cmnd 7874), with Protocol (London, 1 June 1978 to 1 March 1979; TS 40 (1981); Cmnd 8277) (see PARA 7), especially Ch V, to which effect is given by the Merchant Shipping (Safety of Navigation) Regulations 2002, SI 2002/1473 (as to which see PARA 634).

3   Merchant Shipping Act 1995 s 93(1) (amended by SI 1998/1691).

4   Merchant Shipping Act 1995 s 93(1) (as amended: see note 3).

5   Merchant Shipping Act 1995 s 93(1) (as amended: see note 3), Merchant Shipping Act 1995 s 93(5) (amended by SI 1998/1691).

6   Ie with the provisions of the Merchant Shipping Act 1995 s 93(1)–(5) (see the text and notes 1–5): see s 93(6).

7   See the Merchant Shipping Act 1995 s 93(6); and PARA 1135.

8   Ie compliance with the provisions of the Merchant Shipping Act 1995 s 93: see s 93(7).

9   Merchant Shipping Act 1995 s 93(7).

### (ix) Master's Duty where he ceases to be Master during Voyage

**447. Master's duty to deliver documents where he ceases to be master during voyage.** If a person ceases to be the master[1] of a United Kingdom ship[2] during a voyage of the ship, he must deliver to his successor the documents relating to the ship or its crew which are in his custody[3].

If without reasonable excuse the master of such a ship fails to comply with this requirement[4], he commits an offence[5].

1 As to the meaning of 'master' see PARA 444 note 1.
2 As to the meaning of 'United Kingdom ship' see PARA 230. As to the meaning of 'ship' under the Merchant Shipping Act 1995 see PARA 229; and as to the meaning of 'United Kingdom' see PARA 16 note 3.
3 Merchant Shipping Act 1995 s 81(1). As to the documents mentioned in the text see PARAS 254 et seq, 457 et seq. As to the application of s 81 see PARA 423.
4 Ie if he fails to comply with the Merchant Shipping Act 1995 s 81(1) (see the text and notes 1–3): see s 81(2).
5 See the Merchant Shipping Act 1995 s 81(2); and PARA 1101.

## (3) ENGAGEMENT AND EMPLOYMENT OF CREWS

### (i) Minimum Age of Seafarers

#### A.   UNITED KINGDOM SHIPS AND SHIPS IN UNITED KINGDOM WATERS

**448. Minimum ages.** A person under 16 years of age must not be employed[1], engaged[2] or work on board a United Kingdom ship[3] or a non-United Kingdom ship in United Kingdom waters[4]. Further, a seafarer under 18 years of age must not be employed, engaged or work on board such a ship at night[5] unless:

(1)     the effective training of the seafarer, in accordance with established programmes and schedules, would be impaired by such prohibition[6]; or

(2)     the specific nature of the duty or of a recognised training programme requires that the seafarer performs duties at night and the work to be carried out is specified[7] as not being detrimental to the health and well-being of seafarers under the age of 18[8].

A breach of either of these requirements is an offence by the shipowner, the master of the ship and the employer of the person under the age of 16 or, as the case may be, 18[9].

1 For these purposes 'employed' means employed under a contract of employment; and 'employer' means the person by whom a person under 16 years of age or, as the case may be, a seafarer under 18 years of age is employed or engaged (see note 2) in breach of the Merchant Shipping (Maritime Labour Convention) (Minimum Requirements for Seafarers etc) Regulations 2014, SI 2014/1613, reg 4, 5 or 6 (see the text and notes 2–9): reg 7. As to the meaning of 'seafarer' see PARA 423. As to the contract of employment generally see EMPLOYMENT vol 39 (2014) PARA 1 et seq.
2 For these purposes 'engaged' means engaged under a contract, whether express or implied and (if it is express) whether oral or in writing, whereby the person or seafarer so engaged undertakes to do or perform personally any work or services for the employer, or another party to the contract, whose status is not by virtue of the contract that of a client or customer of any profession or business undertaking carried out by the person or seafarer: Merchant Shipping (Maritime Labour Convention) (Minimum Requirements for Seafarers etc) Regulations 2014, SI 2014/1613, reg 7.
3 As to the meaning of 'ship' see PARA 423 note 2.
4 Merchant Shipping (Maritime Labour Convention) (Minimum Requirements for Seafarers etc) Regulations 2014, SI 2014/1613, reg 4(1). The reference to a United Kingdom ship and a non-United Kingdom ship in United Kingdom waters is a reference to a ship to which the Merchant Shipping (Maritime Labour Convention) (Minimum Requirements for Seafarers etc) Regulations 2014, SI 2014/1613 (which implements in United Kingdom law the Maritime Labour Convention (Cm 7049)), applies, that is, any such ship other than a fishing vessel, a ship of traditional build,

a pleasure vessel, a warship or naval auxiliary vessel or a vessel not ordinarily engaged in commercial activities: see further PARA 423. The provision of the Convention imposing minimum ages for seafarers is reg 1.1. The minimum age limit for employment on fishing vessels, ships of traditional build and non-commercial vessels is governed by the Merchant Shipping Act 1995: see s 55; the Merchant Shipping and Fishing Vessels (Health and Safety at Work) (Employment of Young Persons) Regulations 1998, SI 1998/2411; and PARAS 423, 449–450.

A sea-going non-United Kingdom ship in United Kingdom waters which is subject to the Maritime Labour Convention (see the Merchant Shipping (Maritime Labour Convention) (Minimum Requirements for Seafarers etc) Regulations 2014, SI 2014/1613, regs 3(3), (4)(b)(i); and PARA 423 note 9) must not be operated in breach of the prohibitions in paragraphs 1 and 2 of Standard A1.1 (minimum age) of the Convention, subject to any exceptions made by the state whose flag the ship is entitled to fly in accordance with paragraph 3 of that Standard: Merchant Shipping (Maritime Labour Convention) (Minimum Requirements for Seafarers etc) Regulations 2014, SI 2014/1613, reg 6(1). A breach of reg 6(1) is an offence by the shipowner, the master of the ship and the employer of a seafarer under the age prescribed in Regulation 1.1 of the Convention or, in the case of night work, the age prescribed in paragraph 2 of Standard A1.1 of the Convention: Merchant Shipping (Maritime Labour Convention) (Minimum Requirements for Seafarers etc) Regulations 2014, SI 2014/1613, reg 6(2). Such an offence is punishable on summary conviction by a fine: reg 59(1). In any proceedings for such an offence it is a defence for the person charged to show that all reasonable steps had been taken by that person to ensure compliance with the provision concerned: reg 60. As to the powers of magistrates' courts to issue fines on summary conviction see SENTENCING vol 92 (2015) PARA 176.

'Shipowner' means (by virtue of the Merchant Shipping (Hours of Work) Regulations 2002, SI 2002/2125, reg 2(1) (amended by SI 2014/308); and the Merchant Shipping (Maritime Labour Convention) (Minimum Requirements for Seafarers etc) Regulations 2014, SI 2014/1613, reg 2(1)):

(1)     in relation to a ship which has a valid Maritime Labour Certificate or interim Maritime Labour Certificate, the person identified as the shipowner on that Certificate; and

(2)     in relation to any other ship, the owner of the ship or, if different, any other organisation or person such as the manager, or the bareboat charterer, that has assumed the responsibility for the operation of the ship from the owner.

As to the meanings of 'Maritime Labour Certificate' and 'interim Maritime Labour Certificate' see PARA 423 note 9.

5   For this purpose 'night' means a period the duration of which is not less than nine consecutive hours and which starts no later than midnight and ends no earlier than 5 am (local time): Merchant Shipping (Maritime Labour Convention) (Minimum Requirements for Seafarers etc) Regulations 2014, SI 2014/1613, reg 5(3).

6   Merchant Shipping (Maritime Labour Convention) (Minimum Requirements for Seafarers etc) Regulations 2014, SI 2014/1613, reg 5(1), (2)(a).

7   Ie specified in Merchant Shipping Notice 1838(M): Merchant Shipping (Maritime Labour Convention) (Minimum Requirements for Seafarers etc) Regulations 2014, SI 2014/1613, reg 5(2)(b). As to the meaning of 'Merchant Shipping Notice' see PARA 423 note 6.

8   Merchant Shipping (Maritime Labour Convention) (Minimum Requirements for Seafarers etc) Regulations 2014, SI 2014/1613, reg 5(2)(b).

9   Merchant Shipping (Maritime Labour Convention) (Minimum Requirements for Seafarers etc) Regulations 2014, SI 2014/1613, regs 4(2), 5(4).

B.   FISHING VESSELS, SHIPS OF TRADITIONAL BUILD AND NON-COMMERCIAL VESSELS

**449.   Prohibition on employment of persons aged under 16.** A person under 16 years of age may not be employed in any sea-going[1] fishing vessel[2], ship of traditional build or non-commercial vessel which is a United Kingdom ship[3], and a person under school-leaving age[4] must not be employed in any such ship except as permitted by regulations[5]. If any person is employed in a ship in contravention of such provisions, or if any condition subject to which a person may be employed under regulations made for the purposes of these provisions is not complied with, the owner or master is liable on summary conviction to a fine[6].

1   'Sea going' is not defined for the purposes of the Merchant Shipping Act 1995; but cf the definition of 'sea going' in the Merchant Shipping (Maritime Labour Convention) (Minimum Requirements for Seafarers etc) Regulations 2014, SI 2014/1613, reg 2(1) (see PARA 423 note 6).

2   As to the meaning of 'fishing vessel' see the Merchant Shipping Act 1995 s 313(1); and PARA 230.

3   Merchant Shipping Act 1995 s 55(1A) (added by SI 2002/2125). The Merchant Shipping Act 1995 s 55 applies only to United Kingdom ships (to which the Merchant Shipping Act 1995 s 55(1A)

refers) which are fishing vessels, ships of traditional build and non-commercial vessels: see s 24(2A); and PARA 423 note 23. The minimum age limit for employment on other United Kingdom ships and non-United Kingdom ships in United Kingdom waters is governed by the Maritime Labour Convention (Cm 7049) and implemented by the Merchant Shipping (Maritime Labour Convention) (Minimum Requirements for Seafarers etc) Regulations 2014, SI 2014/1613: see regs 3–7; and PARAS 423, 448. As to the meaning of 'United Kingdom ship' see PARA 230.

4 For these purposes, a person employed in a ship is deemed to be over school-leaving age if he has, and under school-leaving age if he has not, attained the age which is the upper limit of compulsory school age under the enactments relating to education in the part of the United Kingdom in which he entered into the agreement under which he is so employed or, if he entered into that agreement outside the United Kingdom or is employed otherwise than under that agreement, under the enactments relating to education in England and Wales; and, if he is treated for the purposes of those enactments as not having attained that age, he is to be so treated also for the purposes of the Merchant Shipping Act 1995 s 55: s 55(5). As to the meaning of 'ship' see PARA 229. As to the meanings of 'England' and 'Wales' see PARA 16 note 2; and as to the meaning of 'United Kingdom' see PARA 16 note 3. As to compulsory school age see EDUCATION vol 35 (2015) PARA 19.

5 Merchant Shipping Act 1995 s 55(1) (amended by SI 2002/2125). The text refers to regulations made under the Merchant Shipping Act 1995 s 55: see s 55(1) (as so amended). Section 55(1) is subject to s 55(1A): see s 55(1) (as so amended); and the text and notes 1–3. For the regulations so made see the Merchant Shipping and Fishing Vessels (Health and Safety at Work) (Employment of Young Persons) Regulations 1998, SI 1998/2411 (made under the Merchant Shipping Act 1955 s 55(2), (3) (amended by SI 2002/2125) (see PARA 450). The Education Act 1996 s 560 (work experience in last year of compulsory schooling) does not permit the employment of any person contrary to the Merchant Shipping Act 1995 s 55(1): see the Education Act 1996 s 560(3); and CHILDREN AND YOUNG PERSONS vol 10 (2017) PARA 700.

As to the power of the Secretary of State to make subordinate legislation under the Merchant Shipping Act 1995, including his power to appoint committees for the purpose of advising him when considering the making or alteration of any regulations etc, see PARA 39; and as to the Secretary of State's power to make regulations prescribing fees to be charged in respect of the issue or recording of any certificate, licence or other document see PARA 63. As to the powers of inspectors appointed under s 256(6) (see PARA 46) to serve improvement notices or prohibition notices where s 55 and the provisions of any instrument of a legislative character having effect thereunder are being contravened, or where activities to which s 55 applies are carried on so as to involve serious personal injury or serious pollution, see PARA 51 et seq. As to the Secretary of State see PARA 36.

6 Merchant Shipping Act 1995 s 55(4). As to the powers of magistrates' courts to issue fines on summary conviction see SENTENCING vol 92 (2015) PARA 176.

### 450. Provisions regarding the employment of young persons on United Kingdom ships.

All of the provisions relating to the employment of young persons on United Kingdom ships[1] which are fishing vessels, ships of traditional build or non-commercial vessels[2] apply to all activities of young persons engaged as workers[3] on such ships[4]; and certain of those provisions[5] apply to all activities of young persons engaged as workers on such ships other than United Kingdom ships which are in United Kingdom waters[6]. However, in either case, the provisions do not apply to or in relation to:

(1)    the activities of a worker which are covered by the Management of Health and Safety at Work Regulations 1999[7];

(2)    any work[8] carried out in circumstances which are unusual and unforeseeable, beyond the employer's control or due to exceptional events[9], where:

(a)    that work is of a temporary nature and must be performed immediately[10];

(b)    adult workers are not available[11]; and

(c)    the young persons affected are allowed equivalent compensatory rest time within the following three weeks[12].

Except where a duty is imposed on any other person, it is the duty of every employer to comply with the provisions relating to the employment of young persons on ships[13]; and, where a person on whom a duty is imposed by any of those provisions does not have control of the matter to which the provision relates because he does not have responsibility for the operation of the ship, then any duty imposed by that provision also extends to any person who has control of that matter[14].

The provisions relating to the employment of young persons on United Kingdom ships which are fishing vessels, ships of traditional build or pleasure vessels also govern:

(i)     the appropriate measures to be taken by the employer to protect young persons at work[15];

(ii)    the specific minimum daily and weekly rest periods which must be provided by the employer[16];

(iii)   the requirement, except in specified circumstances, for young persons to be employed in any capacity on a ship only where an appropriate medical certificate certifies the young person to be fit to be engaged in that capacity[17];

(iv)    records to be kept of the young persons engaged as workers and the inclusion in every crew agreement of a short summary of the regulations governing the employment of young persons on such ships[18];

(v)     offences for the contravention of any duty[19], including provision made for corporate and partnership offences[20] and for the onus of proving what is reasonably practicable to fall on the defendant[21];

(vi)    the inspection and detention of ships[22] and non-United Kingdom ships[23], including provision made for the enforcement of detention[24]; and

(vii)   the application of provisions of the Merchant Shipping Act 1995 dealing with arbitration and compensation[25].

1   For these purposes, 'young person' means, in relation to employment on a sea-going United Kingdom ship, any person who is of the age of 16 or 17 or, in relation to employment on any other United Kingdom ship, any person who is under the age of 18 and, in Great Britain, is over school-leaving age for the purposes of the Merchant Shipping Act 1995 s 55 (as to which see PARA 449): Merchant Shipping and Fishing Vessels (Health and Safety at Work) (Employment of Young Persons) Regulations 1998, SI 1998/2411, reg 2(2) (definition substituted by SI 2002/2125). As to the meaning of 'Great Britain' see PARA 16 note 3. 'United Kingdom ship' means a ship which is a United Kingdom ship within the meaning of the Merchant Shipping Act 1995 s 85(2) (as to which see PARA 602 note 1) or which is a government ship within the meaning of s 308(4) (as to which see PARA 19) or which is a hovercraft registered under the Hovercraft Act 1968 (as to which see PARA 381 et seq): see the Merchant Shipping and Fishing Vessels (Health and Safety at Work) (Employment of Young Persons) Regulations 1998, SI 1998/2411, reg 2(2) (noting that these provisions now apply only in relation to fishing vessels, ships of traditional build or non-commercial vessels, pursuant to the Merchant Shipping Act 1995 s 24(2A): see PARA 423).

2   The Merchant Shipping and Fishing Vessels (Health and Safety at Work) (Employment of Young Persons) Regulations 1998, SI 1998/2411 (see the text and notes 3–25) apply only to United Kingdom ships which are fishing vessels, ships of traditional build and non-commercial vessels: see the Merchant Shipping Act 1995 s 24(2A); and PARAS 423 note 24, 449 note 3. The Merchant Shipping and Fishing Vessels (Health and Safety at Work) (Employment of Young Persons) Regulations 1998, SI 1998/2411, give effect as respects shipping activities in the United Kingdom both to Council Directive (EC) 94/33 (OJ L216, 20.8.1994, p 12) on the protection of young people at work and in part to the Merchant Shipping (Minimum Standards) Convention 1976 (International Labour Organisation Convention 147) (Cmnd 7183).

3   For these purposes, 'worker' means any person who is employed by an employer under a contract of employment, including trainees and apprentices, where the term 'trainees and apprentices' does not include trainees on a sail training vessel: Merchant Shipping and Fishing Vessels (Health and Safety at Work) (Employment of Young Persons) Regulations 1998, SI 1998/2411, reg 2(2). 'Employer' means a person by whom a worker is employed under a contract of employment; and 'contract of employment' means a contract of employment, whether express or implied, and if express, whether oral or in writing: reg 2(2). As to the contract of employment generally see EMPLOYMENT vol 39 (2014) PARA 1 et seq. 'Sail training vessel' means a vessel which is being used either to provide instruction in the principles of responsibility, resourcefulness, loyalty and team endeavour, and to advance education in the art of seamanship, or to provide instruction in navigation and seamanship for yachtsmen, and is operating under a statutory code, where

'statutory code' means the Code of Practice for the Safety of Small Commercial Sailing Vessels, the Code of Practice for the Safety of Small Commercial Motor Vessels, or the Code of Practice for the Safety of Large Commercial Sailing and Motor Vessels: see reg 2(2).

4  Merchant Shipping and Fishing Vessels (Health and Safety at Work) (Employment of Young Persons) Regulations 1998, SI 1998/2411, reg 3(1).

5  Ie the Merchant Shipping and Fishing Vessels (Health and Safety at Work) (Employment of Young Persons) Regulations 1998, SI 1998/2411, regs 1–3, 14–16 (as to which see heads (vi) and (vii) in the text): see reg 3(2).

6  Merchant Shipping and Fishing Vessels (Health and Safety at Work) (Employment of Young Persons) Regulations 1998, SI 1998/2411, reg 3(2).

7  Merchant Shipping and Fishing Vessels (Health and Safety at Work) (Employment of Young Persons) Regulations 1998, SI 1998/2411, reg 3(3)(a). The text refers to the Management of Health and Safety at Work Regulations 1999, SI 1999/3242 (as to which see HEALTH AND SAFETY AT WORK vol 52 (2014) PARA 392 et seq): see the Merchant Shipping and Fishing Vessels (Health and Safety at Work) (Employment of Young Persons) Regulations 1998, SI 1998/2411, reg 3(3)(a).

8  For these purposes, 'work' is to be construed by reference to the meaning of 'working time', which means any period during which the worker is working, at his employer's disposal and carrying out his activity or duties, and any additional period which is to be treated as working time for the purpose of the Merchant Shipping and Fishing Vessels (Health and Safety at Work) (Employment of Young Persons) Regulations 1998, SI 1998/2411, under a relevant agreement: reg 2(2). 'Relevant agreement', in relation to a worker, means a workforce agreement which applies to him, any provision of a collective agreement which forms part of a contract between him and his employer, or any other agreement in writing which is legally enforceable as between the worker and his employer: reg 2(2). 'Collective agreement' means a collective agreement within the meaning of the Trade Union and Labour Relations (Consolidation) Act 1992 s 178 (see EMPLOYMENT vol 41A (2014) PARAS 1093–1094), the trade union parties to which are independent trade unions within the meaning of s 5 (see EMPLOYMENT vol 41 (2014) PARA 904); and 'workforce agreement' means an agreement between an employer and workers employed by him or their representatives in respect of which the conditions set out in the Working Time Regulations 1998, SI 1998/1833, reg 2(1), Sch 1 (see EMPLOYMENT vol 39 (2014) PARA 272) are satisfied: Merchant Shipping and Fishing Vessels (Health and Safety at Work) (Employment of Young Persons) Regulations 1998, SI 1998/2411, reg 2(2).

9  Merchant Shipping and Fishing Vessels (Health and Safety at Work) (Employment of Young Persons) Regulations 1998, SI 1998/2411, reg 3(3)(b).

10  Merchant Shipping and Fishing Vessels (Health and Safety at Work) (Employment of Young Persons) Regulations 1998, SI 1998/2411, reg 3(3)(b)(i).

11  Merchant Shipping and Fishing Vessels (Health and Safety at Work) (Employment of Young Persons) Regulations 1998, SI 1998/2411, reg 3(3)(b)(ii).

12  Merchant Shipping and Fishing Vessels (Health and Safety at Work) (Employment of Young Persons) Regulations 1998, SI 1998/2411, reg 3(3)(b)(iii). For these purposes, 'week' means a period of seven days starting at midnight on Sunday: reg 2(2).

13  Merchant Shipping and Fishing Vessels (Health and Safety at Work) (Employment of Young Persons) Regulations 1998, SI 1998/2411, reg 4(1). The duty mentioned in the text is to comply with the provisions of the Merchant Shipping and Fishing Vessels (Health and Safety at Work) (Employment of Young Persons) Regulations 1998, SI 1998/2411: see reg 4(1).

14  Merchant Shipping and Fishing Vessels (Health and Safety at Work) (Employment of Young Persons) Regulations 1998, SI 1998/2411, reg 4(2).

15  See the Merchant Shipping and Fishing Vessels (Health and Safety at Work) (Employment of Young Persons) Regulations 1998, SI 1998/2411, reg 5, Schedule (amended by SI 2015/521). The text refers to measures to be taken in addition to the general duties required by the Merchant Shipping and Fishing Vessels (Health and Safety at Work) Regulations 1997, SI 1997/2962 (as to which see PARA 626): see the Merchant Shipping and Fishing Vessels (Health and Safety at Work) (Employment of Young Persons) Regulations 1998, SI 1998/2411, reg 5. Where the assessment of risk which is required under reg 5 shows the young person's safety or health is at risk (or where the young person will be regularly required to work at night) free health monitoring must be provided: see reg 7.

16  See the Merchant Shipping and Fishing Vessels (Health and Safety at Work) (Employment of Young Persons) Regulations 1998, SI 1998/2411, reg 6 (amended by SI 2002/2125). For these purposes, 'rest period' means any period which is not working time: Merchant Shipping and Fishing Vessels (Health and Safety at Work) (Employment of Young Persons) Regulations 1998, SI 1998/2411, reg 2(2). The Company (owner) is required to ensure that the employer meets the obligation set out in head (ii) in the text: see reg 6. 'Company', in relation to a ship to which the Merchant Shipping and Fishing Vessels (Health and Safety at Work) (Employment of Young

Persons) Regulations 1998, SI 1998/2411 apply, means the owner of the ship or any other organisation or person such as the manager, or bareboat charterer, who has assumed the responsibility for operation of the ship from the owner: reg 2(2).

17 See the Merchant Shipping and Fishing Vessels (Health and Safety at Work) (Employment of Young Persons) Regulations 1998, SI 1998/2411, reg 8 (amended by SI 2002/3135).

18 See the Merchant Shipping and Fishing Vessels (Health and Safety at Work) (Employment of Young Persons) Regulations 1998, SI 1998/2411, reg 9. For these purposes, 'crew agreement' means a crew agreement made under the Merchant Shipping Act 1995 s 25 (see PARA 457): Merchant Shipping and Fishing Vessels (Health and Safety at Work) (Employment of Young Persons) Regulations 1998, SI 1998/2411, reg 2(2).

19 See the Merchant Shipping and Fishing Vessels (Health and Safety at Work) (Employment of Young Persons) Regulations 1998, SI 1998/2411, reg 10; and PARA 1080.

20 See the Merchant Shipping and Fishing Vessels (Health and Safety at Work) (Employment of Young Persons) Regulations 1998, SI 1998/2411, reg 11; and PARA 1080.

21 See the Merchant Shipping and Fishing Vessels (Health and Safety at Work) (Employment of Young Persons) Regulations 1998, SI 1998/2411, reg 12; and PARA 1080.

22 See the Merchant Shipping and Fishing Vessels (Health and Safety at Work) (Employment of Young Persons) Regulations 1998, SI 1998/2411, reg 13. A relevant inspector may inspect any applicable United Kingdom ship and, if he is satisfied that there has been a failure to comply in relation to that ship with the requirements of the Merchant Shipping and Fishing Vessels (Health and Safety at Work) (Employment of Young Persons) Regulations 1998, SI 1998/2411, he may detain the ship until the health and safety of all young persons aboard the ship is secured; but he must not in the exercise of these powers detain or delay the ship unreasonably: see reg 13. For these purposes, 'relevant inspector' means a person mentioned in the Merchant Shipping Act 1995 s 258(1)(a), (b) or (c) (see PARA 48); and 'health and safety' includes the occupational health and safety of persons whilst on board the ship and whilst boarding or leaving the ship: Merchant Shipping and Fishing Vessels (Health and Safety at Work) (Employment of Young Persons) Regulations 1998, SI 1998/2411, reg 2(2).

23 See the Merchant Shipping and Fishing Vessels (Health and Safety at Work) (Employment of Young Persons) Regulations 1998, SI 1998/2411, reg 14. A relevant inspector may inspect any ship which is not a United Kingdom ship when the ship is in United Kingdom waters and, if satisfied that the ship does not conform to the standards required of United Kingdom ships by the Merchant Shipping and Fishing Vessels (Health and Safety at Work) (Employment of Young Persons) Regulations 1998, SI 1998/2411, he may send a report to the government of the country in which the ship is registered (and a copy thereof to the Director General of the International Labour Office) and, where conditions on board are clearly hazardous to health and safety, he may take such measures as are necessary to rectify those conditions or he may detain the ship: see reg 14(1). However, such measures (excluding the sending of reports) may be taken only when the ship has called at a United Kingdom port in the normal course of business for operational reasons (see reg 14(2)); and, if the inspector takes measures to rectify conditions or detain the ship, he must forthwith notify the nearest maritime, consular or diplomatic representative of the state whose flag the ship is entitled to fly (see reg 14(3)). The relevant inspector must not in exercise of his powers detain or delay the ship unreasonably: see reg 14(4).

24 See the Merchant Shipping and Fishing Vessels (Health and Safety at Work) (Employment of Young Persons) Regulations 1998, SI 1998/2411, reg 15.

25 See the Merchant Shipping and Fishing Vessels (Health and Safety at Work) (Employment of Young Persons) Regulations 1998, SI 1998/2411, reg 16.

## (ii) Seafarers' Employment Agreements and Crew Agreements

### A. UNITED KINGDOM SHIPS AND SHIPS IN UNITED KINGDOM WATERS

**451. Content of seafarers' employment agreement.** All seafarers' employment agreements relating to employment on United Kingdom ships[1] and non-United Kingdom ships in United Kingdom waters[2] must include provision[3] about:

(1)     the full name, birthplace and date of birth (or age at the time of entering into the agreement) of the seafarer[4];

(2)     the name and address of the shipowner[5];

(3)     the place where the agreement is entered into[6];

(4)     the date on which the agreement is entered into[7];

(5)      the capacity in which the seafarer is to work[8];
(6)      if the agreement has been made for a definite period, the termination date[9];
(7)      if the agreement has been made for an indefinite period, the period of notice of termination required and the circumstances in which such notice may be given[10];
(8)      if the agreement has been made for a particular voyage, the destination port and the period following arrival after which the agreement terminates[11];
(9)      the health and social security protection benefits to be provided to the seafarer under the agreement[12];
(10)     the maximum period of service on board following which the seafarer is entitled to repatriation (which must not exceed a period of 12 months less the number of days statutory paid leave to which the seafarer is entitled)[13];
(11)     the seafarer's entitlement to repatriation (including the mode of transport and destination of repatriation)[14];
(12)     the circumstances in which the seafarer is required to meet or reimburse the shipowner for the costs of repatriation[15];
(13)     the maximum sum which the shipowner will pay to the seafarer in respect of compensation for any loss of personal property arising from the loss or foundering of the ship[16]; and
(14)     details of any collective bargaining agreement which is incorporated (in whole or in part) into the agreement or is otherwise relevant to it[17].

If the seafarer is an employee[18] of the shipowner or of any other person the agreement must additionally[19] include provision about:

(a)      the wages (either the amount or the formula to be used in determining them)[20];
(b)      the manner in which wages must be paid[21];
(c)      the hours of work[22];
(d)      the paid leave (either the amount or the formula to be used in determining it)[23];
(e)      any pension arrangements, including any entitlement to participate in a pension scheme[24]; and
(f)      the grievance and disciplinary procedures[25],

and if the seafarer is not an employee, the agreement must additionally[26] include provision about:

(i)      the remuneration (either the amount or the formula to be used in determining it)[27]; and
(ii)     the manner in which the remuneration must be paid[28].

Where the agreement relates to training[29], the name and address of the approved training provider must be set out in the agreement[30].

A breach of these requirements is an offence by the shipowner[31].

1   As to the meaning of 'ship' see PARA 423 note 2.
2   The reference to United Kingdom ships and non-United Kingdom ships in United Kingdom waters is a reference to ships to which the Merchant Shipping (Maritime Labour Convention) (Minimum Requirements for Seafarers etc) Regulations 2014, SI 2014/1613 (which implements in United Kingdom law the Maritime Labour Convention (Cm 7049)), applies, that is, any such ship other than a fishing vessel, a ship of traditional build, a pleasure vessel, a warship or naval auxiliary vessel or a vessel not ordinarily engaged in commercial activities: see further PARA 423. The provision of the Convention making provision with respect to seafarers' employment agreements is reg 2.1. Corresponding provision with respect to employment on ships of traditional build and non-commercial vessels (ie crew agreements) is governed by the Merchant Shipping Act 1995: see, substantively, the Merchant Shipping (Crew Agreements, Lists of Crew and Discharge of Seamen) Regulations 1991, SI 1991/2144 (operative pursuant to the Merchant Shipping Act 1995 ss 25, 26); and PARAS 457–463. Corresponding provision in respect of employment on fishing vessels is

made by the Merchant Shipping (Crew Agreements, Lists of Crew and Discharge of Seamen) (Fishing Vessels) Regulations 1972, SI 1972/919; see FISHERIES AND AQUACULTURE vol 51 (2013) PARAS 312, 314, 316.

3 The required provision may be achieved by way of reference to another document which includes provision about the matters in question: Merchant Shipping (Maritime Labour Convention) (Minimum Requirements for Seafarers etc) Regulations 2014, SI 2014/1613, reg 10(2).

4 Merchant Shipping (Maritime Labour Convention) (Minimum Requirements for Seafarers etc) Regulations 2014, SI 2014/1613, reg 10(1), Sch 1 Pt 1 para 1. As to the meaning of 'seafarer' see PARA 423.

5 Merchant Shipping (Maritime Labour Convention) (Minimum Requirements for Seafarers etc) Regulations 2014, SI 2014/1613, Sch 1 Pt 1 para 2. As to the meaning of 'shipowner' see PARA 448 note 4.

6 Merchant Shipping (Maritime Labour Convention) (Minimum Requirements for Seafarers etc) Regulations 2014, SI 2014/1613, Sch 1 Pt 1 para 3.

7 Merchant Shipping (Maritime Labour Convention) (Minimum Requirements for Seafarers etc) Regulations 2014, SI 2014/1613, Sch 1 Pt 1 para 4.

8 Merchant Shipping (Maritime Labour Convention) (Minimum Requirements for Seafarers etc) Regulations 2014, SI 2014/1613, Sch 1 Pt 1 para 5.

9 Merchant Shipping (Maritime Labour Convention) (Minimum Requirements for Seafarers etc) Regulations 2014, SI 2014/1613, Sch 1 Pt 1 para 6.

10 Merchant Shipping (Maritime Labour Convention) (Minimum Requirements for Seafarers etc) Regulations 2014, SI 2014/1613, Sch 1 Pt 1 para 7. In connection with notices of termination see PARA 455.

11 Merchant Shipping (Maritime Labour Convention) (Minimum Requirements for Seafarers etc) Regulations 2014, SI 2014/1613, Sch 1 Pt 1 para 8.

12 Merchant Shipping (Maritime Labour Convention) (Minimum Requirements for Seafarers etc) Regulations 2014, SI 2014/1613, Sch 1 Pt 1 para 9. In connection with health and safety protection see PARAS 502–504; in connection with access to social security under the Maritime Labour Convention see reg 4.5.

13 Merchant Shipping (Maritime Labour Convention) (Minimum Requirements for Seafarers etc) Regulations 2014, SI 2014/1613, Sch 1 Pt 1 para 10. In connection with repatriation see PARAS 540–543.

14 Merchant Shipping (Maritime Labour Convention) (Minimum Requirements for Seafarers etc) Regulations 2014, SI 2014/1613, Sch 1 Pt 1 para 11.

15 Merchant Shipping (Maritime Labour Convention) (Minimum Requirements for Seafarers etc) Regulations 2014, SI 2014/1613, Sch 1 Pt 1 para 12.

16 Merchant Shipping (Maritime Labour Convention) (Minimum Requirements for Seafarers etc) Regulations 2014, SI 2014/1613, Sch 1 Pt 1 para 13.

17 Merchant Shipping (Maritime Labour Convention) (Minimum Requirements for Seafarers etc) Regulations 2014, SI 2014/1613, Sch 1 Pt 1 para 14.

18 'Employee' means an individual who is employed under a contract of employment: Merchant Shipping (Maritime Labour Convention) (Minimum Requirements for Seafarers etc) Regulations 2014, SI 2014/1613, reg 2(1). As to the contract of employment generally see EMPLOYMENT vol 39 (2014) PARA 1 et seq.

19 Ie in addition to the matters set out in heads (1)–(14) in the text.

20 Merchant Shipping (Maritime Labour Convention) (Minimum Requirements for Seafarers etc) Regulations 2014, SI 2014/1613, reg 10(1)(a), Sch 1 Pt 2 para 1. In connection with wages see PARA 470 et seq.

21 Merchant Shipping (Maritime Labour Convention) (Minimum Requirements for Seafarers etc) Regulations 2014, SI 2014/1613, Sch 1 Pt 2 para 2. This must include payment dates (the first of which must be no more than one month after the date on which the agreement is entered into, with all subsequent dates being no more than one month apart) and the circumstances (if any) in which wages may or must be paid in a different currency: Sch 1 Pt 2 para 2.

22 Merchant Shipping (Maritime Labour Convention) (Minimum Requirements for Seafarers etc) Regulations 2014, SI 2014/1613, Sch 1 Pt 2 para 3. In connection with working hours see the Maritime Labour Convention reg 2.3; and PARAS 511–523.

23 Merchant Shipping (Maritime Labour Convention) (Minimum Requirements for Seafarers etc) Regulations 2014, SI 2014/1613, Sch 1 Pt 2 para 4. In connection with leave see the Maritime Labour Convention reg 2.4.

24 Merchant Shipping (Maritime Labour Convention) (Minimum Requirements for Seafarers etc) Regulations 2014, SI 2014/1613, Sch 1 Pt 2 para 5.

25 Merchant Shipping (Maritime Labour Convention) (Minimum Requirements for Seafarers etc) Regulations 2014, SI 2014/1613, Sch 1 Pt 2 para 6.

26 See note 19.
27 Merchant Shipping (Maritime Labour Convention) (Minimum Requirements for Seafarers etc) Regulations 2014, SI 2014/1613, reg 10(1)(b), Sch 1 Pt 3 para 1.
28 Merchant Shipping (Maritime Labour Convention) (Minimum Requirements for Seafarers etc) Regulations 2014, SI 2014/1613, Sch 1 Pt 3 para 2. This must include payment dates (the first of which must be no more than one month after the date on which the agreement is entered into, with all subsequent dates being no more than one month apart) and the circumstances (if any) in which the remuneration may or must be paid in a different currency: Sch 1 Pt 3 para 2.
29 Ie where the agreement is one which falls within the Merchant Shipping (Maritime Labour Convention) (Minimum Requirements for Seafarers etc) Regulations 2014, SI 2014/1613, reg 9(4) (see PARA 452).
30 Merchant Shipping (Maritime Labour Convention) (Minimum Requirements for Seafarers etc) Regulations 2014, SI 2014/1613, reg 10(1).
31 Merchant Shipping (Maritime Labour Convention) (Minimum Requirements for Seafarers etc) Regulations 2014, SI 2014/1613, reg 10(3). Such an offence is punishable on summary conviction by a fine: reg 59(2)(a). In any proceedings for such an offence it is a defence for the person charged to show that all reasonable steps had been taken by that person to ensure compliance with the provision concerned: reg 60. As to the powers of magistrates' courts to issue fines on summary conviction see SENTENCING vol 92 (2015) PARA 176.

**452. Requirement for seafarers' employment agreement for employees.** If a seafarer[1] on board a United Kingdom ship[2] or a non-United Kingdom ship in United Kingdom waters[3] is an employee[4] but is not an employee of the shipowner[5], the employer[6] of the seafarer must be a party to the seafarer employment agreement[7] and, unless the seafarer is on board the ship for the principal purpose of receiving training from an approved training provider[8], the agreement must include provision under which the shipowner guarantees to the seafarer the performance of the employer's obligations under the agreement insofar as they relate to specified matters[9].

If such a seafarer is not an employee or is an employee of the shipowner, the shipowner must be a party to the seafarer employment agreement[10] (unless the seafarer is on board the ship for the principal purpose of receiving training from an approved training provider[11]).

A non-United Kingdom ship may not be operated unless it complies with the requirements as to seafarers' employment agreements[12]. A seafarer must have a seafarer employment agreement which complies with these provisions[13], a breach of which is an offence by the shipowner[14].

1  As to the meaning of 'seafarer' see PARA 423.
2  As to the meaning of 'ship' see PARA 423 note 2.
3  As to the vessels and seafarers to which these provisions apply see PARA 451 note 2.
4  As to the meaning of 'employee' see PARA 451 note 18.
5  As to the meaning of 'shipowner' see PARA 448 note 4.
6  For these purposes 'employer' means a person by whom the seafarer is employed under a contract of employment: Merchant Shipping (Maritime Labour Convention) (Minimum Requirements for Seafarers etc) Regulations 2014, SI 2014/1613, reg 9(6).
7  Merchant Shipping (Maritime Labour Convention) (Minimum Requirements for Seafarers etc) Regulations 2014, SI 2014/1613, reg 9(2)(a). As to the content of seafarer employment agreements see PARA 451.
8  The Merchant Shipping (Maritime Labour Convention) (Minimum Requirements for Seafarers etc) Regulations 2014, SI 2014/1613, reg 9(2)(b), (3) do not apply if the parties to a seafarer employment agreement are a seafarer who is on board the ship for the principal purpose of receiving training and an approved training provider: reg 9(4). 'Approved training provider' means a person who provides or secures the provision of seafarer training pursuant to an agreement with the Secretary of State: reg 9(6). As to the Secretary of State see PARA 36.
9  Merchant Shipping (Maritime Labour Convention) (Minimum Requirements for Seafarers etc) Regulations 2014, SI 2014/1613, reg 9(2)(b). The specified matters are those specified in Sch 1 Pt 1 paras 5–11 and Sch 1 Pt 2 (see PARA 451): reg 9(2)(b).
10 Merchant Shipping (Maritime Labour Convention) (Minimum Requirements for Seafarers etc) Regulations 2014, SI 2014/1613, reg 9(3).
11 See note 8.

12 Ie, a sea-going non-United Kingdom ship in United Kingdom waters which is subject to the Maritime Labour Convention (see the Merchant Shipping (Maritime Labour Convention) (Minimum Requirements for Seafarers etc) Regulations 2014, SI 2014/1613, regs 3(3), (4)(b)(ii); and PARA 423 note 9) must not be operated unless it complies with the requirements in paragraph 1 of Standard A2.1 (seafarers' employment agreements) of the Maritime Labour Convention (Merchant Shipping (Maritime Labour Convention) (Minimum Requirements for Seafarers etc) Regulations 2014, SI 2014/1613, reg 15(1)(a)) and paragraph 4 of Standard A2.1 of the Convention regarding the particulars to be contained in seafarers' employment agreements (Merchant Shipping (Maritime Labour Convention) (Minimum Requirements for Seafarers etc) Regulations 2014, SI 2014/1613, reg 15(1)(b)), whether or not the state whose flag the ship is entitled to fly has adopted any relevant laws or regulations (reg 15(1)). A breach of reg 15(1) is an offence by the shipowner unless it is a breach of the requirement in sub-paragraph 1(d) of Standard A2.1 of the Convention, in which event is an offence by the master of the ship: Merchant Shipping (Maritime Labour Convention) (Minimum Requirements for Seafarers etc) Regulations 2014, SI 2014/1613, reg 15(2), (3). An offence under reg 15(2) which consists of a breach of reg 15(1)(a) or (b) is punishable on summary conviction by a fine: reg 59(1), (2)(c). In any proceedings for such an offence it is a defence for the person charged to show that all reasonable steps had been taken by that person to ensure compliance with the provision concerned: reg 60. As to the powers of magistrates' courts to issue fines on summary conviction see SENTENCING vol 92 (2015) PARA 176.

13 Merchant Shipping (Maritime Labour Convention) (Minimum Requirements for Seafarers etc) Regulations 2014, SI 2014/1613, reg 9(1).

14 Merchant Shipping (Maritime Labour Convention) (Minimum Requirements for Seafarers etc) Regulations 2014, SI 2014/1613, reg 9(5). Such an offence is punishable on summary conviction by a fine: reg 59(1).

**453. Seafarer must understand employment agreement.** Prior to entering into a seafarer employment agreement[1] the shipowner[2] or[3] the approved training provider[4] must take reasonable steps to satisfy itself with regard to the following requirements:

(1)     the seafarer[5] must have had a sufficient opportunity to review and take advice on the terms and conditions of the agreement[6];

(2)     the seafarer must have received an explanation of his rights and responsibilities under the agreement[7]; and

(3)     the seafarer must be entering into the agreement freely[8].

Where a shipowner fails to take such reasonable steps or (in relevant cases) fails to take reasonable steps to ensure that the approved training provider has complied with his statutory duties[9], the shipowner commits an offence[10].

A seafarer employment agreement must contain a declaration by the shipowner and the seafarer or[11] by the approved training provider and the seafarer confirming that the requirements in heads (1) to (3) above have been met[12]. A breach this requirement is an offence by the shipowner[13].

1   As to the content of seafarer employment agreements see PARA 451; as to the requirement for seafarer employment agreement for employees see PARA 452.

2   As to the meaning of 'shipowner' see PARA 448 note 4.

3   Ie in the case of an agreement falling within the Merchant Shipping (Maritime Labour Convention) (Minimum Requirements for Seafarers etc) Regulations 2014, SI 2014/1613, reg 9(4) (see PARA 452).

4   As to the meaning of 'approved training provider' see PARA 452 note 8.

5   As to the meaning of 'seafarer' see PARA 423.

6   Merchant Shipping (Maritime Labour Convention) (Minimum Requirements for Seafarers etc) Regulations 2014, SI 2014/1613, reg 10(4)(a).

7   Merchant Shipping (Maritime Labour Convention) (Minimum Requirements for Seafarers etc) Regulations 2014, SI 2014/1613, reg 10(4)(b).

8   Merchant Shipping (Maritime Labour Convention) (Minimum Requirements for Seafarers etc) Regulations 2014, SI 2014/1613, reg 10(4)(c).

9   Ie the requirements of the Merchant Shipping (Maritime Labour Convention) (Minimum Requirements for Seafarers etc) Regulations 2014, SI 2014/1613, reg 9(4).

10  Merchant Shipping (Maritime Labour Convention) (Minimum Requirements for Seafarers etc) Regulations 2014, SI 2014/1613, reg 10(5). Such an offence is punishable on summary conviction by a fine: reg 59(1). In any proceedings for such an offence it is a defence for the person charged to show that all reasonable steps had been taken by that person to ensure compliance with the

provision concerned: reg 60. As to the powers of magistrates' courts to issue fines on summary conviction see SENTENCING vol 92 (2015) PARA 176.

11 See note 3.

12 Merchant Shipping (Maritime Labour Convention) (Minimum Requirements for Seafarers etc) Regulations 2014, SI 2014/1613, reg 10(6).

13 Merchant Shipping (Maritime Labour Convention) (Minimum Requirements for Seafarers etc) Regulations 2014, SI 2014/1613, reg 10(7). Such an offence is punishable on summary conviction by a fine: reg 59(2)(a).

**454. Documentation.** As soon as is practicable after entering into a seafarer employment agreement[1], the shipowner[2] must provide to the seafarer[3] an original of the agreement signed by each party and a copy of any document referred to in that agreement[4]. The shipowner must ensure that a copy of the seafarer employment agreement (and a copy of any document referred to in that agreement) for each seafarer on a ship[5] is held on board and allow each seafarer to see the copy of the seafarer employment agreement to which he is a party (and a copy of any document referred to in that agreement) on request[6]. As soon as is practicable after a seafarer's work on board a ship comes to an end, the shipowner must[7] provide to the seafarer a written record of his work on that ship[8].

A breach of any of these requirements is an offence by the shipowner[9].

1   As to the content of seafarer employment agreements see PARA 451; as to the requirement for seafarer employment agreement for employees see PARA 452.

2   As to the meaning of 'shipowner' see PARA 448 note 4.

3   As to the meaning of 'seafarer' see PARA 423.

4   Merchant Shipping (Maritime Labour Convention) (Minimum Requirements for Seafarers etc) Regulations 2014, SI 2014/1613, reg 12(1). Where a seafarer has a seafarer employment agreement which is not in the English language the shipowner must ensure that an English translation of the provisions of the agreement (including any provisions which are contained in another document referred to in the agreement) is held on board: reg 13(1), (2). A breach of this requirement is an offence by the shipowner (reg 13(3)) punishable on summary conviction by a fine (reg 59(3)(b)). In any proceedings for such an offence it is a defence for the person charged to show that all reasonable steps have been taken by that person to ensure compliance with the provision concerned: reg 60. As to the powers of magistrates' courts to issue fines on summary conviction see SENTENCING vol 92 (2015) PARA 176.

The master of a ship must produce to the Secretary of State, the Registrar-General of Shipping and Seamen or the Commissioners for Her Majesty's Revenue and Customs (or any person acting on their behalf) on demand copies of any documentation held on board pursuant to regs 12(3), 13(2): reg 14(1). A breach of reg 14(1) is an offence by the master of the ship (reg 14(2)) punishable on summary conviction by a fine (reg 59(1)). As to the Secretary of State see PARA 36. As to the appointment of officers of Revenue and Customs see INCOME TAXATION vol 58 (2014) PARA 33.

5   As to the meaning of 'ship' see PARA 423 note 2.

6   Merchant Shipping (Maritime Labour Convention) (Minimum Requirements for Seafarers etc) Regulations 2014, SI 2014/1613, reg 12(3). See reg 14; and note 4.

7   Ie, except where the Merchant Shipping (Crew Agreements, Lists of Crew and Discharge of Seamen) Regulations 1991, SI 1991/2144, reg 25 (see PARA 468) applies in respect of the seafarer: Merchant Shipping (Maritime Labour Convention) (Minimum Requirements for Seafarers etc) Regulations 2014, SI 2014/1613, reg 12(7).

8   Merchant Shipping (Maritime Labour Convention) (Minimum Requirements for Seafarers etc) Regulations 2014, SI 2014/1613, reg 12(5). For these purposes the record:
    (1)   must contain provision about the name, port of registry, gross or register tonnage and official number of the ship (Merchant Shipping (Maritime Labour Convention) (Minimum Requirements for Seafarers etc) Regulations 2014, SI 2014/1613, reg 12(6)(a), Sch 2 para 1); the description of the voyage (Sch 2 para 2); the capacity in which the seafarer worked on the ship (Sch 2 para 3); the date on which seafarer started work on the ship (Sch 2 para 4); and the date and location of seafarer's discharge from the ship (Sch 2 para 5);
    (2)   must not contain provision about the quality of the seafarer's work (reg 12(6)(b)); and
    (3)   must not contain provision about the seafarer's wages (reg 12(6)(c)).

9   Merchant Shipping (Maritime Labour Convention) (Minimum Requirements for Seafarers etc) Regulations 2014, SI 2014/1613, reg 12(2), (4), (8). A breach of the requirements of reg 12(1), (3), (5) or (6) is punishable on summary conviction by a fine: reg 59(1), (2)(b), (3)(a).

**455. Notice.** The minimum period of notice which must be given before terminating a seafarer employment agreement[1] is seven days or such longer period as may be specified in the agreement[2]. The minimum period of notice which must be given by a seafarer[3] before terminating a seafarer employment agreement must not be longer than the minimum period of notice which must be given by the shipowner[4] or, as the case may be, the approved training provider[5].

These provisions do not prevent the earlier termination of a seafarer employment agreement without penalty where this is requested by the seafarer on compassionate grounds or where the seafarer is dismissed for reasons of gross misconduct[6].

1   As to the content of seafarer employment agreements see PARA 451; as to the requirement for seafarer employment agreement for employees see PARA 452.
2   Merchant Shipping (Maritime Labour Convention) (Minimum Requirements for Seafarers etc) Regulations 2014, SI 2014/1613, reg 11(1).
3   As to the meaning of 'seafarer' see PARA 423.
4   As to the meaning of 'shipowner' see PARA 448 note 4.
5   Merchant Shipping (Maritime Labour Convention) (Minimum Requirements for Seafarers etc) Regulations 2014, SI 2014/1613, reg 11(2). As to the meaning of 'approved training provider' see PARA 452 note 8.
6   Merchant Shipping (Maritime Labour Convention) (Minimum Requirements for Seafarers etc) Regulations 2014, SI 2014/1613, reg 11(3).

**456. Shipowner's duty in respect of recruitment and placement services.** A shipowner[1] must not use a recruitment and placement service[2] to recruit a person as a seafarer to work on board a United Kingdom ship[3] or a non-United Kingdom ship in United Kingdom waters[4] unless it:

(1)     is based in the United Kingdom[5], in a country which has ratified the Maritime Labour Convention[6], or in a country to which another country's ratification of the Convention has been extended[7]; or

(2)     is based in another country and conforms to the Convention requirements relating to recruitment and placement services[8], whether or not those requirements are obligations under the law of the country in which it is based[9].

A breach of these requirements is an offence by the shipowner[10].

1   As to the meaning of 'shipowner' see PARA 448 note 4.
2   For these purposes 'recruitment and placement service' means any person or organisation which is engaged in recruiting seafarers on behalf of shipowners or placing seafarers with shipowners: Merchant Shipping (Maritime Labour Convention) (Minimum Requirements for Seafarers etc) Regulations 2014, SI 2014/1613, reg 8(4). As to the meaning of 'seafarer' see PARA 423.
3   As to the meaning of 'ship' see PARA 423 note 2.
4   The reference to a United Kingdom ship and a non-United Kingdom ship in United Kingdom waters is a reference to a ship to which the Merchant Shipping (Maritime Labour Convention) (Minimum Requirements for Seafarers etc) Regulations 2014, SI 2014/1613 (which implements in United Kingdom law the Maritime Labour Convention (Cm 7049)), applies, that is, any such ship other than a fishing vessel, a ship of traditional build, a pleasure vessel, a warship or naval auxiliary vessel or a vessel not ordinarily engaged in commercial activities: see further PARA 423. The provision of the Convention imposing duties on shipowners in this regard is reg 1.4. No corresponding provision is made in respect of the excluded types of vessel.
5   Merchant Shipping (Maritime Labour Convention) (Minimum Requirements for Seafarers etc) Regulations 2014, SI 2014/1613, reg 8(1), (2)(a)(i).
6   Merchant Shipping (Maritime Labour Convention) (Minimum Requirements for Seafarers etc) Regulations 2014, SI 2014/1613, reg 8(2)(a)(ii).
7   Merchant Shipping (Maritime Labour Convention) (Minimum Requirements for Seafarers etc) Regulations 2014, SI 2014/1613, reg 8(2)(a)(iii).
8   Ie the requirements referred to in paragraph 5 of Standard A1.4 of the Convention.
9   Merchant Shipping (Maritime Labour Convention) (Minimum Requirements for Seafarers etc) Regulations 2014, SI 2014/1613, reg 8(2)(b).
10   Merchant Shipping (Maritime Labour Convention) (Minimum Requirements for Seafarers etc) Regulations 2014, SI 2014/1613, reg 8(3). Such an offence is punishable on summary conviction

by a fine: reg 59(1). In any proceedings for such an offence it is a defence for the person charged to show that all reasonable steps had been taken by that person to ensure compliance with the provision concerned: reg 60. As to the powers of magistrates' courts to issue fines on summary conviction see SENTENCING vol 92 (2015) PARA 176.

B.    SHIPS OF TRADITIONAL BUILD AND NON-COMMERCIAL VESSELS

**457. General provision for crew agreements.** In relation to employment on a sea-going[1] United Kingdom ship[2] which is a ship of traditional build or a non-commercial vessel[3], an agreement in writing must[4] be made between each person employed as a seaman[5] and the person employing him, and must be signed both by him and by or on behalf of them[6].

The agreements so made with the several persons employed in such a ship must be contained in one document (a 'crew agreement')[7] except that in such cases as the Secretary of State[8] may approve[9]:

(1)     the agreements to be so made with the persons employed in such a ship may be contained in more than one crew agreement[10]; and

(2)     one crew agreement may relate to more than one ship[11].

The provisions and form of a crew agreement must be of a kind approved by the Secretary of State[12]; and different provisions and forms may be so approved for different circumstances[13].

Subject to any exemptions or variations which may be allowed and any liability for contraventions[14], a crew agreement must be carried in the ship to which it relates whenever the ship goes to sea[15].

Where, but for an exemption granted by the Secretary of State, a crew agreement would be required to be carried in a ship or a crew agreement carried in the ship would be required to contain an agreement with a person employed in a ship, the ship must carry such documents evidencing the exemption as the Secretary of State may direct[16].

If a ship goes to sea or attempts to go to sea in contravention of the requirements of the general provision for crew agreements, the master[18], or the person employing the crew, commits an offence[19]; and the ship, if in the United Kingdom, may be detained[20].

1    'Sea going' is not defined for the purposes of the Merchant Shipping Act 1995; but cf the definition of 'sea going' in the Merchant Shipping (Maritime Labour Convention) (Minimum Requirements for Seafarers etc) Regulations 2014, SI 2014/1613, reg 2(1) (see PARA 423 note 6).

2    As to the meaning of 'United Kingdom ship' see PARA 230.

3    The Merchant Shipping Act 1995 ss 25, 26 and the Merchant Shipping (Crew Agreements, Lists of Crew and Discharge of Seamen) Regulations 1991, SI 1991/2144 (see the text and notes 4–20; and PARAS 458–463) apply only to United Kingdom ships (to which the legislation refers) which are ships of traditional build and non-commercial vessels: see the Merchant Shipping Act 1995 s 24(2A); the Merchant Shipping (Crew Agreements, Lists of Crew and Discharge of Seamen) Regulations 1991, SI 1991/2144, reg 2 (definition 'ship': see PARA 458 note 2); and PARA 423 note 22. Corresponding provision relating to employment on other United Kingdom ships and non-United Kingdom ships in United Kingdom waters is governed by the Maritime Labour Convention (Cm 7049) and implemented by the Merchant Shipping (Maritime Labour Convention) (Minimum Requirements for Seafarers etc) Regulations 2014, SI 2014/1613: see regs 9–15; and PARAS 423, 451–455. Corresponding provision relating to employment on fishing vessels is made by the Merchant Shipping (Crew Agreements, Lists of Crew and Discharge of Seamen) (Fishing Vessels) Regulations 1972, SI 1972/919 (having effect as if made under the Merchant Shipping Act 1995 s 109) (see FISHERIES AND AQUACULTURE vol 51 (2013) PARAS 312, 314, 316). As to the meaning of 'fishing vessel' see PARA 230.

4    Ie except as provided under the Merchant Shipping Act 1995 s 25(5) (see PARA 458): see s 25(1).

5    In the Merchant Shipping Act 1995, unless the context otherwise requires, 'seaman' includes every person (except masters and pilots) employed or engaged in any capacity on board any ship: s 313(1). As to the meaning of 'master' see PARA 444 note 1. As to pilots and pilotage see PARA 574 et seq. As to the meaning of 'ship' see PARA 229. Persons have been regarded as seamen for the following purposes:

    (1)    wages: a woman employed as ship-keeper, steward and cook (*The Jane and Matilda*
            (1823) 1 Hag Adm 187); a crew engaged for a voyage in respect of which the ship had
            never left port (*Re Great Eastern Steamship Co, Williams' Claim* (1885) 5 Asp MLC
            511); a storekeeper who had not been actually engaged for a voyage (*Thomson v Hart*
            (1890) 28 SLR 28); a stevedore (*R v City of London Court Judge and SS Michigan
            (Owners)* (1890) 25 QBD 339); and
    (2)    regulations in respect of the accommodation of seamen: lascars (*Peninsular and Oriental
            Steam Navigation Co v R* [1901] 2 KB 686, 9 Asp MLC 228).

    Persons whose natural calling was the sea, but who were not at the time actually employed or
engaged as seamen, were held not to be seamen within the meaning of the Conspiracy and
Protection of Property Act 1875 s 16 (repealed): *R v Lynch and Jones* [1898] 1 QB 61, 8 Asp MLC
363, CCR. As to seamen's wages generally see PARA 470 et seq; and as to claims against seamen's
wages for maintenance of dependants in particular see PARA 481. As to social security
contributions for mariners see the Social Security Contributions and Benefits Act 1992 s 117; and
WELFARE BENEFITS AND STATE PENSIONS vol 104 (2014) PARA 30.

6   Merchant Shipping Act 1995 s 25(1). Crew agreements, lists of crews made under s 78 (see
    PARAS 553–558) and notices given under Pt III (ss 24–84) of additions to or changes in crew
    agreements and lists of crews, are admissible in evidence and, when in the custody of the Registrar
    General of Shipping and Seamen, are open to public inspection: see s 287(1)(c); and PARA 1058.
    As to the Registrar General of Shipping and Seamen see PARA 62. For a restriction on the statutory
    employment rights of persons employed as seamen see the Employment Rights Act 1996 s 199; and
    EMPLOYMENT vol 39 (2014) PARA 167.
7   In the Merchant Shipping Act 1995 Pt III (ss 24–84) 'crew agreement' has the meaning given to it
    by s 25(2): see s 84(1).
8   As to the Secretary of State see PARA 36.
9   Merchant Shipping Act 1995 s 25(2).
10  Merchant Shipping Act 1995 s 25(2)(a).
11  Merchant Shipping Act 1995 s 25(2)(b).
12  Merchant Shipping Act 1995 s 25(3).
13  Merchant Shipping Act 1995 s 25(3).
14  Ie subject to the Merchant Shipping Act 1995 s 25(5)–(8) (see the text and notes 15–21): s 25(4).
15  Merchant Shipping Act 1995 s 25(4). For the purposes of Pt III, references to going to sea include
    references to going to sea from any country outside the United Kingdom: s 84(2). As to offences
    relating to crew agreements see PARA 1073.
16  Merchant Shipping Act 1995 s 25(6). As to exemptions see PARA 458. As to the Secretary of State's
    power to give directions under the Merchant Shipping Act 1995 see PARA 39.
18  As to the meaning of 'contravention' see PARA 51 note 3.
19  As to the meaning of 'master' see PARA 444 note 1.
20  See the Merchant Shipping Act 1995 s 25(8); and PARA 1073.

## 458. Exemptions from general provision for crew agreements. The
requirements of the general statutory provisions relating to crew agreements for
sea-going United Kingdom ships which are ships of traditional build or
non-commercial vessels[1] do not apply to the following descriptions of ships[2] and
voyages[3]:
    (1)    a ship belonging to a general lighthouse authority[4];
    (2)    a ship of less than 80 register tons[5] engaged solely on coastal voyages[6];
    (3)    a pleasure yacht which is engaged on a coastal voyage, or a pleasure
          yacht which is engaged on any other voyage provided that not more
          than four members of the crew receive wages for their employment[7];
    (4)    a coastal voyage by any ship solely for the purpose of trials of the ship,
          its machinery or equipment[8].

Nor do the general provisions relating to crew agreements[9] apply to the
following descriptions of seamen[10]:
    (a)    a person employed in a ship solely in connection with the construction,
          alteration, repair or testing of the ship, its machinery or equipment, and
          not engaged in the navigation of the ship[11];
    (b)    a person solely employed in work directly related to:
          (i)    the exploration of the sea bed or subsoil or the exploitation of
              their natural resources[12];

(ii) the storage of gas in or under the sea bed or subsoil or the exploitation of their natural resources[13];

(iii) the laying, inspection, testing, repair, alteration, renewal or removal of any submarine telegraph cable[14];

(iv) pipeline works[15] including the assembling, inspection, testing, maintaining, adjusting, repairing, altering, renewing, changing the position of, or dismantling a pipeline or length of pipeline[16]; or

(v) the provision of goods, personal services or entertainment on board[17],

(c) and who is not employed by the owner[18] or the person employing the master of the ship and is not engaged in the navigation of the ship in the deck, engine room, radio, medical or catering department of that ship and who has been given a written statement by his employer specifying the nature of the employment, the remuneration, the intervals at which the remuneration is to be paid and the length of notice which he is required to give and entitled to receive to determine his employment and specifying any terms or conditions of his employment relating to sick pay, hours of work (including any terms and conditions relating to normal working hours), pensions and entitlement to holidays[19];

(d) a member of the naval, military or air forces of the Crown or of any service administered by the Defence Council[20], when acting as such a member[21].

1 Ie the Merchant Shipping Act 1995 s 25 (see PARA 457): see the Merchant Shipping (Crew Agreements, Lists of Crew and Discharge of Seamen) Regulations 1991, SI 1991/2144, reg 4(1) (partly having effect under the Merchant Shipping Act 1995 ss 25(5), (7), 26). As to the vessels and seamen to which these provisions apply see PARA 457 note 3. As to the meaning of 'United Kingdom ship' see PARA 230. As to the meaning of 'sea going' cf PARA 457 note 1. As to the meaning of 'crew agreement' under the Merchant Shipping Act 1995 see PARA 457. See also the Merchant Shipping (Crew Agreements, Lists of Crew and Discharge of Seamen) (Fishing Vessels) Regulations 1972, SI 1972/919; and FISHERIES AND AQUACULTURE vol 51 (2013) PARAS 312, 314, 316. Any power conferred by the Merchant Shipping Act 1995 Pt III to provide for or grant an exemption includes power to provide for or grant the exemption subject to conditions: s 84(5). As to the power of the Secretary of State to make subordinate legislation under the Merchant Shipping Act 1995 see PARA 39.

2 For these purposes, 'ship' means a ship registered in the United Kingdom but does not include a fishing vessel: Merchant Shipping (Crew Agreements, Lists of Crew and Discharge of Seamen) Regulations 1991, SI 1991/2144, reg 2. As to the meaning of 'United Kingdom' see PARA 16 note 3. As to the registration of ships in the United Kingdom see PARA 245 et seq.

3 Merchant Shipping (Crew Agreements, Lists of Crew and Discharge of Seamen) Regulations 1991, SI 1991/2144, reg 4(1).

4 Merchant Shipping (Crew Agreements, Lists of Crew and Discharge of Seamen) Regulations 1991, SI 1991/2144, reg 4(1)(a). As to General Lighthouse Authorities see PARA 1017.

5 For these purposes, references to the gross or to the register tonnage of a ship are, in the case of a ship having alternative gross or alternative register tonnages, references to the larger of its gross tonnages or to the larger of its register tonnages, as the case may be: Merchant Shipping (Crew Agreements, Lists of Crew and Discharge of Seamen) Regulations 1991, SI 1991/2144, reg 2.

6 Merchant Shipping (Crew Agreements, Lists of Crew and Discharge of Seamen) Regulations 1991, SI 1991/2144, reg 4(1)(b). For these purposes, 'coastal voyage' means a voyage between places in the British Islands, including the Republic of Ireland, or from and returning to such a place during which, in either case, no call is made at any place outside those islands: reg 2. As to the meaning of 'British Islands' see STATUTES AND LEGISLATIVE PROCESS vol 96 (2012) PARA 1208.

7 Merchant Shipping (Crew Agreements, Lists of Crew and Discharge of Seamen) Regulations 1991, SI 1991/2144, reg 4(1)(c).

8 Merchant Shipping (Crew Agreements, Lists of Crew and Discharge of Seamen) Regulations 1991, SI 1991/2144, reg 4(1)(d).

9 Ie the Merchant Shipping Act 1995 s 25 (see PARA 457): see the Merchant Shipping (Crew Agreements, Lists of Crew and Discharge of Seamen) Regulations 1991, SI 1991/2144, reg 4(2).

10 Merchant Shipping (Crew Agreements, Lists of Crew and Discharge of Seamen) Regulations 1991, SI 1991/2144, reg4(2).
11 Merchant Shipping (Crew Agreements, Lists of Crew and Discharge of Seamen) Regulations 1991, SI 1991/2144, reg4(2)(a).
12 Merchant Shipping (Crew Agreements, Lists of Crew and Discharge of Seamen) Regulations 1991, SI 1991/2144, reg4(2)(b)(i).
13 Merchant Shipping (Crew Agreements, Lists of Crew and Discharge of Seamen) Regulations 1991, SI 1991/2144, reg4(2)(b)(ii).
14 Merchant Shipping (Crew Agreements, Lists of Crew and Discharge of Seamen) Regulations 1991, SI 1991/2144, reg4(2)(b)(iii).
15 Ie as defined in the Offshore Safety Act 1992 s 1(4) (see ENERGY AND CLIMATE CHANGE vol 44 (2011) PARA 1078): see the Merchant Shipping (Crew Agreements, Lists of Crew and Discharge of Seamen) Regulations 1991, SI 1991/2144, reg 4(2)(b)(iv).
16 Merchant Shipping (Crew Agreements, Lists of Crew and Discharge of Seamen) Regulations 1991, SI 1991/2144, reg4(2)(b)(iv).
17 Merchant Shipping (Crew Agreements, Lists of Crew and Discharge of Seamen) Regulations 1991, SI 1991/2144, reg4(2)(b)(v).
18 In the Merchant Shipping Act 1995, and in any other enactment applicable to British ships or ships registered under that Act, any reference, however phrased, to the owner of a British ship, a United Kingdom ship or a ship registered in the United Kingdom, means, in relation to a bareboat charter ship, the person registered as the charterer: see the Merchant Shipping (Modification of Enactments) (Bareboat Charter Ships) Order 1994, SI 1994/774, art 2; and PARAS 230, 255, 357. For these purposes, 'bareboat charter ship' means a ship registered pursuant to the Merchant Shipping Act 1995 s 17(1)(a) (as to which see PARA 357): see the Merchant Shipping (Modification of Enactments) (Bareboat Charter Ships) Order 1994, SI 1994/774, art 1(2).
19 Merchant Shipping (Crew Agreements, Lists of Crew and Discharge of Seamen) Regulations 1991, SI 1991/2144, reg4(2)(b).
20 As to the Defence Council see CONSTITUTIONAL AND ADMINISTRATIVE LAW vol 20 (2014) PARA 562.
21 Merchant Shipping (Crew Agreements, Lists of Crew and Discharge of Seamen) Regulations 1991, SI 1991/2144, reg4(2)(c).

**459. Carrying of copy of crew agreement in ships.** A ship of traditional build or a non-commercial vessel[1] required[2] to carry a crew agreement[3] may, in the case of an agreement which relates to both that and to other ships and which is kept at an address ashore in the United Kingdom[4], comply with that requirement by carrying a copy of the agreement certified in the following manner[5], namely that such a copy so carried in a ship bears a certificate signed by the master certifying that it is a true copy of the crew agreement and specifying the address in the United Kingdom at which the crew agreement is kept and the name of the person by whom it is so kept[6].

1 As to the vessels and seamen to which these provisions apply see PARA 457 note 3. As to the meaning of 'ship' for these purposes see PARA 458 note 2.
2 Ie required under the Merchant Shipping Act 1995 s 25 (see PARA 457): see the Merchant Shipping (Crew Agreements, Lists of Crew and Discharge of Seamen) Regulations 1991, SI 1991/2144, reg 5(1).
3 As to the meaning of 'crew agreement' under the Merchant Shipping Act 1995 s 25 see PARA 457.
4 As to the meaning of 'United Kingdom' see PARA 16 note 3.
5 Merchant Shipping (Crew Agreements, Lists of Crew and Discharge of Seamen) Regulations 1991, SI 1991/2144, reg5(1).
6 Merchant Shipping (Crew Agreements, Lists of Crew and Discharge of Seamen) Regulations 1991, SI 1991/2144, reg5(2).

**460. Delivery of crew agreement.** An employer must, within three days of the date when the last person remaining employed under a crew agreement[1] ceases to be employed under that agreement, or, if it is not practicable within that period, as soon as practicable thereafter, deliver the crew agreement to a superintendent or proper officer[2] for the place where the ship[3] was when that person ceased to be so employed[4]. If the crew agreement covers an indefinite period, the employer must deliver the crew agreement within seven days of it being opened to a superintendent or proper officer for the place where the ship was when the agreement opened[5].

A person who fails to comply with such an obligation imposed on him[6] to deliver the crew agreement commits an offence[7].

1 As to the meaning of 'crew agreement' under the Merchant Shipping Act 1995 s 25 see PARA 457. As to the vessels and seamen to which these provisions apply see PARA 457 note 3.
2 For these purposes, 'appropriate superintendent or proper officer' means a superintendent or proper officer for the place at which a crew agreement, or an agreement with any person added to those contained in a crew agreement, is or is to be made: Merchant Shipping (Crew Agreements, Lists of Crew and Discharge of Seamen) Regulations 1991, SI 1991/2144, reg 3(1) (renumbered by SI 2014/1614).
3 As to the meaning of 'ship' for these purposes see PARA 458 note 2.
4 Merchant Shipping (Crew Agreements, Lists of Crew and Discharge of Seamen) Regulations 1991, SI 1991/2144, reg6.
5 Merchant Shipping (Crew Agreements, Lists of Crew and Discharge of Seamen) Regulations 1991, SI 1991/2144, reg6.
6 Ie imposed on him by the Merchant Shipping (Crew Agreements, Lists of Crew and Discharge of Seamen) Regulations 1991, SI 1991/2144, reg 6 (see the text and notes 1–5): see reg 10(1).
7 See the Merchant Shipping (Crew Agreements, Lists of Crew and Discharge of Seamen) Regulations 1991, SI 1991/2144, reg10(1); and PARA 1073.

**461. Display of crew agreement on ship.** The master of a ship of traditional build or a non-commercial vessel[1] must cause:

(1)     a copy of any crew agreement relating to the ship[2]; or

(2)     an extract containing the terms of that agreement applicable to all seamen employed under it and to each description of seamen so employed[3],

to be posted in some conspicuous place on board the ship where it can be read by the persons employed under the crew agreement[4]; and he must cause it to be kept so posted and legible so long as any seaman is employed in the ship under the crew agreement[5].

A master who fails to comply with such an obligation imposed on him[6] to display the crew agreement commits an offence[7].

1 As to the vessels and seamen to which these provisions apply see PARA 457 note 3. As to the meaning of 'ship' for these purposes see PARA 458 note 2.
2 Merchant Shipping (Crew Agreements, Lists of Crew and Discharge of Seamen) Regulations 1991, SI 1991/2144, reg 7(a). As to the meaning of 'crew agreement' under the Merchant Shipping Act 1995 s 25 see PARA 457.
3 Merchant Shipping (Crew Agreements, Lists of Crew and Discharge of Seamen) Regulations 1991, SI 1991/2144, reg7(b).
4 Merchant Shipping (Crew Agreements, Lists of Crew and Discharge of Seamen) Regulations 1991, SI 1991/2144, reg7.
5 Merchant Shipping (Crew Agreements, Lists of Crew and Discharge of Seamen) Regulations 1991, SI 1991/2144, reg7.
6 Ie imposed on him by the Merchant Shipping (Crew Agreements, Lists of Crew and Discharge of Seamen) Regulations 1991, SI 1991/2144, reg 7 (see the text and notes 1–5): see reg 10(2).
7 See the Merchant Shipping (Crew Agreements, Lists of Crew and Discharge of Seamen) Regulations 1991, SI 1991/2144, reg10(2); and PARA 1073.

**462. Supply and production of copy documents on demand by seamen.** Upon a seaman making a demand of his employer (or of the master), the employer (or the master, as the case may be) must, within a reasonable time[1]:

(1)     cause to be supplied to him a copy of the crew agreement under which he is employed[2] or such extracts therefrom as are necessary to show the terms on which he is employed[3]; and

(2)     cause to be made available to him a copy of any document referred to in the agreement[4].

A person or, as the case may be, a master who fails to comply with such an obligation imposed on him[5] to supply and produce on demand copy documents related to the crew agreement commits an offence[6].

1  Merchant Shipping (Crew Agreements, Lists of Crew and Discharge of Seamen) Regulations 1991, SI 1991/2144, reg 8.
2  As to the meaning of 'crew agreement' under the Merchant Shipping Act 1995 s 25 see PARA 457. As to the vessels and seamen to which these provisions apply see PARA 457 note 3.
3  Merchant Shipping (Crew Agreements, Lists of Crew and Discharge of Seamen) Regulations 1991, SI 1991/2144, reg8(a).
4  Merchant Shipping (Crew Agreements, Lists of Crew and Discharge of Seamen) Regulations 1991, SI 1991/2144, reg8(b).
5  Ie imposed on him by the Merchant Shipping (Crew Agreements, Lists of Crew and Discharge of Seamen) Regulations 1991, SI 1991/2144, reg 8 (see the text and notes 1–4): see reg 10(1), (2).
6  See the Merchant Shipping (Crew Agreements, Lists of Crew and Discharge of Seamen) Regulations 1991, SI 1991/2144, reg10(1), (2); and PARA 1073.

**463.  Production of documents on demand by officers.** The master must, on demand by an officer of revenue and customs[1], by any superintendent[2] or by the Registrar General of Shipping and Seamen[3] produce to him[4]:

(1)  any crew agreement[5], or the copy of any crew agreement[6]; and
(2)  any certificate evidencing an exemption granted by the Secretary of State[7] from the statutory requirements[8] with respect to the ship or to any person in it[9].

A master who fails to comply with such an obligation imposed on him[10] so to produce on demand any crew agreement (or an exemption) commits an offence[11].

1  As to the appointment of officers of Revenue and Customs see INCOME TAXATION vol 58 (2014) PARA 33.
2  As to the meaning of 'appropriate superintendent or proper officer' see PARA 460 note 2.
3  As to the Registrar General of Shipping and Seamen see PARA 62.
4  Merchant Shipping (Crew Agreements, Lists of Crew and Discharge of Seamen) Regulations 1991, SI 1991/2144, reg 9 (amended by virtue of the Commissioners for Revenue and Customs Act 2005 s 50(1), (2), (7)).
5  As to the meaning of 'crew agreement' under the Merchant Shipping Act 1995 s 25 see PARA 457. As to the vessels and seamen to which these provisions apply see PARA 457 note 3.
6  Merchant Shipping (Crew Agreements, Lists of Crew and Discharge of Seamen) Regulations 1991, SI 1991/2144, reg 9(a). The text refers to the copy of any crew agreement that may be carried in the ship in pursuance of reg 5 (see PARA 459): see reg 9(a).
7  As to the Secretary of State see PARA 36.
8  Ie from the Merchant Shipping Act 1995 s 25 (see PARA 457): see the Merchant Shipping (Crew Agreements, Lists of Crew and Discharge of Seamen) Regulations 1991, SI 1991/2144, reg 9(b).
9  Merchant Shipping (Crew Agreements, Lists of Crew and Discharge of Seamen) Regulations 1991, SI 1991/2144, reg9(b).
10  Ie imposed on him by the Merchant Shipping (Crew Agreements, Lists of Crew and Discharge of Seamen) Regulations 1991, SI 1991/2144, reg 9 (see the text and notes 1–9): see reg 10(2).
11  See the Merchant Shipping (Crew Agreements, Lists of Crew and Discharge of Seamen) Regulations 1991, SI 1991/2144, reg10(2); and PARA 1073.

### (iii)  Medical Fitness Certification for Workers Aboard United Kingdom Ships

**464.  Seafarers must hold medical fitness certificate.** No person may work as a seafarer[1] on board a United Kingdom ship[2], and no person may employ another person as a seafarer on such a ship, unless that seafarer has been issued with a medical fitness certificate[3] which is still valid and is not suspended[4] (although exceptions may be made in urgent cases[5]). Additionally, no person may work as a seafarer on a United Kingdom ship, and no person may employ a person as a seafarer on such a ship, either in a capacity of sea service or in a geographical area precluded by any restriction in that person's medical fitness certificate[6], or in breach of a condition of that person's medical fitness certificate[7].

Failure to comply with these restrictions and requirements is an offence[8].

1   As to the meaning of 'seafarer' see PARA 423.
2   As to the meaning of 'ship' see PARA 423 note 2. The reference to United Kingdom ships is a reference to ships to which the Merchant Shipping (Maritime Labour Convention) (Medical Certification) Regulations 2010, SI 2010/737, reg 1–19 (see the text and notes 3–8; and PARA 464 et seq) apply, that is, sea-going United Kingdom ships wherever they may be (see reg 5(1)(a)) other than pleasure vessels, fishing vessels, warships or naval auxiliaries and offshore installations whilst on their working stations (reg 5(2)). The regulations do not apply to (in the case of reg 7, do not apply as respects) any person whose work is not part of the routine business of the ship and whose principal place of work is ashore and any person who is subject to any requirement contained in the Working Time Regulations 1998, SI 1998/1833 (see EMPLOYMENT vol 39 (2014) PARA 268 et seq), the Merchant Shipping (Working Time: Inland Waterways) Regulations 2003, SI 2003/3049 (see PARA 520 et seq) or the Fishing Vessels (Working Time: Sea-fishermen) Regulations 2004, SI 2004/1713 (see PARAS 515, 516): Merchant Shipping (Maritime Labour Convention) (Medical Certification) Regulations 2010, SI 2010/737, reg 5(3). As to the meanings of 'sea-going' and 'United Kingdom ship' see PARA 423 note 6. As to the meaning of 'pleasure vessel' see PARA 423 note 24. 'Offshore installation' means any installation which is intended for underwater exploitation of mineral resources or exploration with a view to such exploitation: Merchant Shipping (Maritime Labour Convention) (Medical Certification) Regulations 2010, SI 2010/737, reg 2. The provision of the Maritime Labour Convention making provision with respect to medical certification is reg 1.2. See further PARA 423. Provision is made for the inspection of ships to ensure compliance with the Convention: see the Merchant Shipping (Maritime Labour Convention) (Medical Certification) Regulations 2010, SI 2010/737, regs 19, 20. Any person who obstructs a relevant inspector in the exercise of his powers under reg 20 or fails without reasonable excuse to comply with a requirement made under reg 20, is guilty of an offence and liable on summary conviction to a fine: reg 18(4). As to the powers of magistrates' courts to issue fines on summary conviction see SENTENCING vol 92 (2015) PARA 176. In any proceedings for an offence under the Merchant Shipping (Maritime Labour Convention) (Medical Certification) Regulations 2010, SI 2010/737, it is a defence for the person charged to show that all reasonable steps had been taken by that person to ensure compliance with the relevant provision: reg 18(5).
3   'Medical fitness certificate' means a certificate attesting to a person's fitness to perform the duties which that person will carry out at sea and which is issued under the Merchant Shipping (Maritime Labour Convention) (Medical Certification) Regulations 2010, SI 2010/737, reg 8 (see PARA 464) or reg 14 (see PARA 467) (whether or not subject to restriction or conditions): reg 2. Provision as to the issue, format and period of validity of medical fitness certificates is made by regs 8–11 (reg 8 amended by SI 2014/1614); replacement certificates may also be made available (see the Merchant Shipping (Maritime Labour Convention) (Medical Certification) Regulations 2010, SI 2010/737, reg 17). An employer who fails to comply with reg 8(3) is guilty of an offence and liable on summary conviction to a fine: reg 18(2).
4   Merchant Shipping (Maritime Labour Convention) (Medical Certification) Regulations 2010, SI 2010/737, regs 6(1), 7(1). A seafarer who has been issued with a medical fitness certificate must carry that certificate on board during the term of his employment on a ship to which these provisions apply: reg 6(2). A seafarer whose medical fitness certificate has expired during the course of a voyage may continue to work, and a person may continue to employ as a seafarer a person whose medical fitness certificate has expired during the course of a voyage, until the first port of call at which it is possible for the seafarer to make an application for a medical fitness certificate and be examined by a medical practitioner or the expiry of three months starting on the date of the expiry of the certificate, whichever is the sooner: regs 6(3), 7(2). 'Medical practitioner' means (by virtue of reg 2 (definition substituted by SI 2014/1614)):
    (1)    in the case of a practitioner ordinarily resident in the United Kingdom, a fully registered person who holds a licence to practise or meets the criteria specified in Merchant Shipping Notice 1839(M), being criteria which the Secretary of State considers appropriate having regard to the evidence of continuing professional development which such a practitioner must demonstrate in order to obtain a licence to practise; or
    (2)    in the case of a practitioner not ordinarily resident in the United Kingdom, a person who meets the criteria specified in Merchant Shipping Notice 1839(M), being criteria which the Secretary of State considers appropriate having regard to the qualifications and other credentials which must be demonstrated by a person falling within head (1) above.
    As to the Secretary of State see PARA 36. As to the meaning of 'Merchant Shipping Notice' see PARA 423 note 6. Records of medical examinations and reviews must be kept: see reg 16.
5   In urgent cases, with the Secretary of State's approval, if a seafarer does not hold a valid medical fitness certificate but has held a medical fitness certificate for a period of not less than 24 months (or in the case of a person under 18 years at the date of issue of the certificate, 12 months) and that certificate has expired no earlier than one month before the date on which that person joined a ship to which these provisions apply, that person may work as a seafarer, or another person may

employ that person as a seafarer, on that ship until the first port of call at which it is possible for an application for a medical fitness certificate as respects that seafarer to be made and for that seafarer to be examined by a medical practitioner, but in any case not for a period exceeding three months: regs 6(4), 7(3). 'Approval' means an approval given by the Secretary of State in writing and which specifies the date on which it takes effect, its duration and the conditions (if any) on which it is given, and 'approved' has a corresponding meaning: reg 2(1).

6   Merchant Shipping (Maritime Labour Convention) (Medical Certification) Regulations 2010, SI 2010/737, regs 6(5), 7(4).

7   Merchant Shipping (Maritime Labour Convention) (Medical Certification) Regulations 2010, SI 2010/737, regs 6(6), 7(5).

8   Any person who contravenes the Merchant Shipping (Maritime Labour Convention) (Medical Certification) Regulations 2010, SI 2010/737, reg 6 or 7 is guilty of an offence and is liable on summary conviction to a fine: reg 18(1).

**465. Reporting of medical conditions.** A person who is a seafarer[1] who holds a medical fitness certificate[2] and who is, or is likely to be, absent from work for a period of thirty days or more due to a medical condition[3] or develops a significant medical condition[4], must report that medical condition as soon as practicable[5]. If a seafarer must make such a report, the validity of that seafarer's medical fitness certificate or certificate of medical fitness is suspended from the date on which it first becomes practicable for that seafarer to make the report until the date (if any) on which a medical practitioner or the authority (as appropriate) has assessed, if necessary by conducting a medical examination of the seafarer, that the seafarer is[6] fit[7].

1   As to the meaning of 'seafarer' see PARA 423. As to the vessels and seafarers to which these provisions apply see PARA 464 note 2.

2   As to the meaning of 'medical fitness certificate' see PARA 464 note 3.

3   Merchant Shipping (Maritime Labour Convention) (Medical Certification) Regulations 2010, SI 2010/737, reg 12(1)(a).

4   Merchant Shipping (Maritime Labour Convention) (Medical Certification) Regulations 2010, SI 2010/737, reg 12(1)(b). For these purposes 'medical condition' includes both injury and illness, and a 'significant' medical condition is one which adversely affects or is reasonably likely adversely to affect the seafarer's ability to carry out his duties, including the seafarer's ability to undertake emergency duties: reg 12(4).

5   Merchant Shipping (Maritime Labour Convention) (Medical Certification) Regulations 2010, SI 2010/737, reg 12(1). Such report must be made:
   (1)   in the case of a person who has been issued with a certificate of medical fitness, to the authority which issued that certificate (reg 12(2)(a)); and
   (2)   in any other case, to a medical practitioner (reg 12(2)(b)).

6   Ie having regard to the medical standards specified by the Secretary of State in Merchant Shipping Notice 1839(M): Merchant Shipping (Maritime Labour Convention) (Medical Certification) Regulations 2010, SI 2010/737, reg 12(3) (amended by SI 2014/1614). As to the meaning of 'Merchant Shipping Notice' see PARA 423 note 6.

7   Merchant Shipping (Maritime Labour Convention) (Medical Certification) Regulations 2010, SI 2010/737, reg 12(3) (as amended: see note 6).

**466. Suspension and cancellation of certificates.** If a medical practitioner[1] has reasonable grounds for believing that:
   (1)   there has been a significant change in the medical fitness of a person[2] during the period of validity of that person's medical fitness certificate[3];
   (2)   a person is not complying with the terms of a condition to which his medical fitness certificate is subject[4];
   (3)   when a medical fitness certificate was issued to a person, had a medical practitioner been in possession of full details of that person's condition, the medical practitioner could not reasonably have considered that the person was[5] fit[6]; or
   (4)   a medical fitness certificate was unlawfully[7] issued to a person[8],
the medical practitioner may:
   (a)   suspend the validity of that certificate until the person to whom the certificate was issued has undergone further medical examination[9];

(b)	suspend the validity of the certificate for such period as the medical practitioner considers the person to whom the certificate was issued will remain unfit to perform the duties that person will carry out at sea[10]; or

(c)	cancel the certificate if the medical practitioner considers that the person to whom the certificate was issued is likely to remain permanently unfit to perform the duties that person will carry out at sea[11],

and must notify the person concerned accordingly[12].

1  As to the meaning of 'medical practitioner' see PARA 464 note 4.
2  For these purposes a 'significant change' in the medical fitness of a person is a condition which affects or would be reasonably likely to affect that person's ability to carry out their duties, including their ability to undertake emergency duties: Merchant Shipping (Maritime Labour Convention) (Medical Certification) Regulations 2010, SI 2010/737, reg 13(4).
3  Merchant Shipping (Maritime Labour Convention) (Medical Certification) Regulations 2010, SI 2010/737, reg 13(1)(a). As to the meaning of 'medical fitness certificate' see PARA 464 note 3.
4  Merchant Shipping (Maritime Labour Convention) (Medical Certification) Regulations 2010, SI 2010/737, reg 13(1)(b).
5  Ie having regard to the medical standards specified by the Secretary of State in Merchant Shipping Notice 1839(M): Merchant Shipping (Maritime Labour Convention) (Medical Certification) Regulations 2010, SI 2010/737, reg 13(1)(c) (amended by SI 2014/1614). As to the meaning of 'Merchant Shipping Notice' see PARA 423 note 6.
6  Merchant Shipping (Maritime Labour Convention) (Medical Certification) Regulations 2010, SI 2010/737, reg 13(1)(c) (as amended: see note 5).
7  Ie otherwise than in accordance with the Merchant Shipping (Maritime Labour Convention) (Medical Certification) Regulations 2010, SI 2010/737.
8  Merchant Shipping (Maritime Labour Convention) (Medical Certification) Regulations 2010, SI 2010/737, reg 13(1).
9  Merchant Shipping (Maritime Labour Convention) (Medical Certification) Regulations 2010, SI 2010/737, reg 13(2)(a). The medical practitioner may require that a person surrenders a medical fitness certificate which has been issued to that person and which has been suspended or cancelled pursuant to reg 13(2), as that practitioner directs: reg 13(3). A seafarer who fails without reasonable excuse to comply with a requirement made under reg 13(3) is guilty of an offence and liable on summary conviction to a fine: reg 18(3). In connection with offences see further PARA 464 note 2.
10  Merchant Shipping (Maritime Labour Convention) (Medical Certification) Regulations 2010, SI 2010/737, reg 13(2)(b). See note 9.
11  Merchant Shipping (Maritime Labour Convention) (Medical Certification) Regulations 2010, SI 2010/737, reg 13(2)(c). See note 9.
12  Merchant Shipping (Maritime Labour Convention) (Medical Certification) Regulations 2010, SI 2010/737, reg 13(2).

**467. Review of medical practitioner's decision.** A person who is aggrieved by the refusal of a medical practitioner[1] to issue[2] a medical fitness certificate[3], any restriction imposed on such a certificate[4] or the suspension for a period of more than three months or cancellation of such a certificate by[5] a medical practitioner[6], may apply to the Secretary of State[7] for the matter to be reviewed by a single medical referee appointed by the Secretary of State[8], and the Secretary of State must have the matter reviewed if the application was lodged with the Secretary of State within one month of the date on which the applicant was given notice of refusal, imposition of a restriction, suspension or cancellation[9], includes a consent for the medical practitioner responsible for the refusal, imposition of a restriction, suspension or cancellation to provide a report to the medical referee[10], and specifies the name and address of that practitioner[11]. In a refusal or suspension case[12], if the medical referee considers[13] that the applicant is fit to perform the duties he will carry out at sea, the medical referee must issue to the applicant[14] a medical fitness certificate or terminate the suspension of the applicant's medical fitness certificate, as the case may be[15]; in any case[16], if in the light of the medical evidence the medical referee considers that restrictions as to capacity of sea service or geographical areas should be imposed on a certificate issued to the applicant, or that any restriction so imposed by a medical practitioner should be deleted or varied, the medical referee must issue[17] to the applicant a medical fitness certificate which records any restrictions as so imposed or varied, and the former certificate ceases to have effect[18].

If[19] the medical referee considers that the applicant is unfit to perform the duties he will carry out at sea, the medical referee must notify the applicant of the period during which the medical referee considers that the applicant will remain unfit to go to sea[20].

1   As to the meaning of 'medical practitioner' see PARA 464 note 4.
2   Ie in accordance with the Merchant Shipping (Maritime Labour Convention) (Medical Certification) Regulations 2010, SI 2010/737, reg 8 (see PARA 464).
3   Merchant Shipping (Maritime Labour Convention) (Medical Certification) Regulations 2010, SI 2010/737, reg 14(1)(a).
4   Merchant Shipping (Maritime Labour Convention) (Medical Certification) Regulations 2010, SI 2010/737, reg 14(1)(b).
5   Ie pursuant to the Merchant Shipping (Maritime Labour Convention) (Medical Certification) Regulations 2010, SI 2010/737: see PARA 466.
6   Merchant Shipping (Maritime Labour Convention) (Medical Certification) Regulations 2010, SI 2010/737, reg 14(1)(c).
7   As to the Secretary of State see PARA 36. If the applicant fails to attend an appointment with the medical referee without giving adequate notice, then the Secretary of State may recover from the applicant as a civil debt the cost incurred by the Secretary of State of that appointment: Merchant Shipping (Maritime Labour Convention) (Medical Certification) Regulations 2010, SI 2010/737, reg 14(8).
8   Merchant Shipping (Maritime Labour Convention) (Medical Certification) Regulations 2010, SI 2010/737, reg 14(1).
9   Merchant Shipping (Maritime Labour Convention) (Medical Certification) Regulations 2010, SI 2010/737, reg 14(2)(a). If an application is made after the time prescribed in reg 14(2)(a), the Secretary of State, upon consideration of any reasons for the lateness of the application, may decide that the matter is nonetheless to be reviewed: reg 14(3).
10  Merchant Shipping (Maritime Labour Convention) (Medical Certification) Regulations 2010, SI 2010/737, reg 14(2)(b). If requested by the applicant, the medical practitioner must send to the applicant a copy of the report of the medical practitioner and any other evidence provided by the medical practitioner to the medical referee: reg 14(4).
11  Merchant Shipping (Maritime Labour Convention) (Medical Certification) Regulations 2010, SI 2010/737, reg 14(2)(c).
12  Ie in a case within the Merchant Shipping (Maritime Labour Convention) (Medical Certification) Regulations 2010, SI 2010/737, reg 14(1)(a) or (c).
13  Ie in the light of the medical evidence, and having regard to the medical standards specified by the Secretary of State in Merchant Shipping Notice 1839(M): Merchant Shipping (Maritime Labour Convention) (Medical Certification) Regulations 2010, SI 2010/737, reg 14(5) (reg 14(5)–(7) amended by SI 2014/1614). As to the meaning of 'Merchant Shipping Notice' see PARA 423 note 6.
14  Ie in the form specified in Merchant Shipping Notice 1839(M).
15  Merchant Shipping (Maritime Labour Convention) (Medical Certification) Regulations 2010, SI 2010/737, reg 14(5) (as amended: see note 13).
16  Ie in a case within the Merchant Shipping (Maritime Labour Convention) (Medical Certification) Regulations 2010, SI 2010/737, reg 14(1)(a), (b) or (c), and having regard to the medical standards specified by the Secretary of State in Merchant Shipping Notice 1839(M): Merchant Shipping (Maritime Labour Convention) (Medical Certification) Regulations 2010, SI 2010/737, reg 14(6) (as amended: see note 13).
17  See note 14.
18  Merchant Shipping (Maritime Labour Convention) (Medical Certification) Regulations 2010, SI 2010/737, reg 14(6) (as amended: see note 13).
19  Ie in the light of the medical evidence, and having regard to the medical standards specified by the Secretary of State in Merchant Shipping Notice 1839(M): Merchant Shipping (Maritime Labour Convention) (Medical Certification) Regulations 2010, SI 2010/737, reg 14(7) (as amended: see note 13).
20  Merchant Shipping (Maritime Labour Convention) (Medical Certification) Regulations 2010, SI 2010/737, reg 14(7) (as amended: see note 13).

## (iv) Discharge of Crews

**468. Procedure on discharge.** Where a seaman is present at the time of his discharge[1]:

(1)    the master, or one of the ship's[2] officers authorised by him in that behalf must, before the seaman is discharged[3]:

    (a)    if the seaman produces his discharge book[4] to him, record in it the name of the ship, its port of registry, gross or register tonnage and official number[5], the description of the voyage, the capacity in which the seaman has been employed in the ship, the date on which he began to be so employed and the date and place of his discharge[6]; or

    (b)    if the seaman does not produce his discharge book to him, give to the seaman a certificate of discharge containing the like particulars[7];

(2)    the master must ensure that the seaman is discharged in the presence of the master himself, or the seaman's employer or a person authorised in that behalf by the master or employer[8];

(3)    the person mentioned in head (2) above in whose presence the seaman is being discharged must[9]:

    (a)    make and sign an entry in the official log book[10] recording the place, date and time of the seaman's discharge[11]; and

    (b)    make and sign an entry in the crew agreement[12] or, if there is a list of crew separate from a crew agreement, in the list of crew, recording the place and date of, and the reason for, the seaman's discharge[13]; and

(4)    the seaman must sign the entry in the crew agreement and list of crew referred to in head (3)(b) above[14].

Any person, including a master:

(i)    who fails to comply with an obligation imposed on him by or under head (1) or head (3) above[15]; or

(ii)    who fails to comply with an obligation imposed on him by head (3)(b) above in relation to an entry in a crew agreement or in a list of crew[16],

commits an offence[17]; a master who fails to comply with an obligation imposed on him by head (2) above, or by head (3) above in circumstances where a seaman is not present at his own discharge[18], commits an offence[19]; and a seaman who fails to comply with an obligation imposed on him by head (4) above commits an offence[20].

If a seaman so requests, within a period of six months from the date of his discharge from or his leaving the ship, the master, or one of the ship's officers authorised by him in that behalf, must give to the seaman a certificate (which must be separate from any other document) either as to the quality of his work or indicating whether he has fully discharged his obligations under his contract of employment[21]. Any person, including a master, who fails to comply with this requirement commits an offence[22].

1    Merchant Shipping (Crew Agreements, Lists of Crew and Discharge of Seamen) Regulations 1991, SI 1991/2144, reg 25(1).

2    As to the meaning of 'ship' see PARA 458 note 2. The Merchant Shipping (Crew Agreements, Lists of Crew and Discharge of Seamen) Regulations 1991, SI 1991/2144, regs 25, 26 (partly having effect under the Merchant Shipping Act 1995 ss 27, 28) (see the text and notes 3–22) apply to all United Kingdom ships apart from fishing vessels. Being concerned with matters with which the Merchant Shipping (Maritime Labour Convention) (Minimum Requirements for Seafarers etc) Regulations 2014, SI 2014/1613 and the Maritime Labour Convention (Cm 7049)) are not concerned (see PARA 423), these provisions are not limited to the vessels excluded from the scope of the Convention (see further PARA 423 note 22). However, the Merchant Shipping (Crew Agreements, Lists of Crew and Discharge of Seamen) Regulations 1991, SI 1991/2144, do not

apply to fishing vessels: see reg 2 (definition 'ship': see PARA 458 note 2); and PARA 423 note 22. Corresponding provision relating to employment on fishing vessels is made by the Merchant Shipping (Crew Agreements, Lists of Crew and Discharge of Seamen) (Fishing Vessels) Regulations 1972, SI 1972/919 (having effect as if made under the Merchant Shipping Act 1995 s 109) (see FISHERIES AND AQUACULTURE vol 51 (2013) PARA 316). As to the meaning of 'fishing vessel' see PARA 230.

As to the power of the Secretary of State to make subordinate legislation under the Merchant Shipping Act 1995, including his power to appoint committees for the purpose of advising him when considering the making or alteration of any regulations etc, see PARA 39; and as to the Secretary of State's power to make regulations prescribing fees to be charged in respect of the issue or recording of any certificate, licence or other document see PARA 63.

For the purposes of the Merchant Shipping Act 1995 Pt III (ss 24–84), a seaman is discharged from a ship when his employment in that ship is terminated: s 84(3). As to the meaning of 'United Kingdom ship' see PARA 230. As to the meaning of 'United Kingdom' see PARA 16 note 3.

3   Merchant Shipping (Crew Agreements, Lists of Crew and Discharge of Seamen) Regulations 1991, SI 1991/2144, reg25(1)(a).
4   As to discharge books see PARAS 565–569.
5   As to a ship's name, its port of registry and official number etc see PARA 277 et seq. As to the meaning of references to the gross or to the register tonnage see PARA 458 note 5.
6   Merchant Shipping (Crew Agreements, Lists of Crew and Discharge of Seamen) Regulations 1991, SI 1991/2144, reg25(1)(a)(i).
7   Merchant Shipping (Crew Agreements, Lists of Crew and Discharge of Seamen) Regulations 1991, SI 1991/2144, reg25(1)(a)(ii).
8   Merchant Shipping (Crew Agreements, Lists of Crew and Discharge of Seamen) Regulations 1991, SI 1991/2144, reg25(1)(b).
9   Merchant Shipping (Crew Agreements, Lists of Crew and Discharge of Seamen) Regulations 1991, SI 1991/2144, reg 25(1)(c). Where a seaman is not present when he is discharged, the master, or a person authorised in that behalf by the master, must make the entries referred to in heads (3)(a) and (3)(b) in the text: reg 25(2).
10  As to the meaning official log book see PARAS 551–552. All entries in the official log book required under the Merchant Shipping (Crew Agreements, Lists of Crew and Discharge of Seamen) Regulations 1991, SI 1991/2144, reg 25(1), (2) must, in addition to being signed by the person making the entry, be signed also by a member of the crew: reg 25(3).
11  Merchant Shipping (Crew Agreements, Lists of Crew and Discharge of Seamen) Regulations 1991, SI 1991/2144, reg25(1)(c)(i).
12  As to crew agreements see PARAS 457–463.
13  Merchant Shipping (Crew Agreements, Lists of Crew and Discharge of Seamen) Regulations 1991, SI 1991/2144, reg25(1)(c)(ii).
14  Merchant Shipping (Crew Agreements, Lists of Crew and Discharge of Seamen) Regulations 1991, SI 1991/2144, reg25(1)(d).
15  See the Merchant Shipping (Crew Agreements, Lists of Crew and Discharge of Seamen) Regulations 1991, SI 1991/2144, reg26(1)(a); and PARA 1074.
16  See the Merchant Shipping (Crew Agreements, Lists of Crew and Discharge of Seamen) Regulations 1991, SI 1991/2144, reg26(1)(b); and PARA 1074.
17  See the Merchant Shipping (Crew Agreements, Lists of Crew and Discharge of Seamen) Regulations 1991, SI 1991/2144, reg26(1); and PARA 1074.
18  Ie an obligation imposed on him by the Merchant Shipping (Crew Agreements, Lists of Crew and Discharge of Seamen) Regulations 1991, SI 1991/2144, reg 25(2) (see note 9): see reg 26(2); and PARA 1074.
19  See the Merchant Shipping (Crew Agreements, Lists of Crew and Discharge of Seamen) Regulations 1991, SI 1991/2144, reg26(2); and PARA 1074.
20  See the Merchant Shipping (Crew Agreements, Lists of Crew and Discharge of Seamen) Regulations 1991, SI 1991/2144, reg26(3); and PARA 1074.
21  Merchant Shipping (Crew Agreements, Lists of Crew and Discharge of Seamen) Regulations 1991, SI 1991/2144, reg25(4).
22  See the Merchant Shipping (Crew Agreements, Lists of Crew and Discharge of Seamen) Regulations 1991, SI 1991/2144, reg26(1)(a), (2); and PARA 1074.

**469.   Discharge of seamen when ship ceases to be registered in the United Kingdom.** Where a United Kingdom ship[1] ceases to be registered[2], any seaman[3] employed in the ship is discharged from the ship[4] unless he consents in writing to continue his employment in the ship[5]; and the statutory provisions which relate to the payment and account of seamen's wages[6] apply in relation to his wages as if the ship had remained a United Kingdom ship[7].

1  As to the vessels and seamen to which these provisions apply see PARA 468 note 2. As to the meaning of 'ship' see PARA 229; and as to the meaning of 'United Kingdom ship' see PARA 230. As to the meaning of 'United Kingdom' see PARA 16 note 3.
2  As to the meaning of 'registered' under the Merchant Shipping Act 1995 see PARA 254 note 2.
3  As to the meaning of 'seaman' see PARA 457 note 5.
4  As to when a seaman is regarded as discharged from a ship see PARA 468 note 2.
5  Merchant Shipping Act 1995 s 29. A shipowner who discharges a seaman without obtaining the requisite consent is liable for the seaman's wages until the end of the voyage: *Hassan v Trader Navigation Co Ltd* [1965] 2 Lloyd's Rep 378.
6  Ie the Merchant Shipping Act 1995 ss 30–33 (see PARAS 484–486): see s 29. As to the meaning of 'wages' see PARA 470 note 4.
7  Merchant Shipping Act 1995 s 29. The provisions of the Merchant Shipping Act 1995 which relate to the relief and return of seamen etc left behind and shipwrecked (ie s 73) (see PARA 548) apply to a person left behind on being discharged in pursuance of s 29, whether or not at the time he is left behind the ship is still a United Kingdom ship: see s 73(7); and PARA 548.

## (v) Wages

A.   VESSELS AND SEAMEN GENERALLY

### (A)   Entitlement to Wages

**470. Right, or loss of right, to wages where ship is sold.** Where a United Kingdom ship[1] is sold while outside the United Kingdom or ceases to be a United Kingdom ship and a seaman's[2] employment in the ship is thereby terminated before the date contemplated in the agreement under which he is so employed, then, unless it is otherwise contemplated in the agreement, he is[3] entitled to wages[4] at the rate payable under the agreement at the date on which his employment is terminated for every day on which he is unemployed in the two months following that date[5]. A seaman is not, however, so entitled to wages for a day on which he was unemployed, if it is shown[6]:

(1)    that the unemployment was not due to the wreck or loss of the ship[7] or, as the case may be, the termination of his employment on the sale of the ship or its ceasing to be a United Kingdom ship[8]; or

(2)    that the seaman was able to obtain suitable employment for that day but unreasonably refused or failed to take it[9].

Wages continue to accrue after the institution of proceedings for recovery[10].

1  As to the meaning of 'ship' see PARA 229; and as to the meaning of 'United Kingdom ship' see PARA 230. As to the meaning of 'United Kingdom' see PARA 16 note 3. The Merchant Shipping Act 1995 ss 32, 34, 35–37, 38(2), (3), 39–41 (see the text and notes 2–10; and PARAS 473–481) apply to all United Kingdom ships: being concerned with matters with which the Merchant Shipping (Maritime Labour Convention) (Minimum Requirements for Seafarers etc) Regulations 2014, SI 2014/1613 and the Maritime Labour Convention (Cm 7049)) are not concerned (see PARA 423), these provisions are not limited to the vessels excluded from the scope of the Convention: see further PARA 423 note 22. However, s 38 does not apply to so much of the wages of a seaman employed in a fishing vessel as is in any manner related to the catch: s 114. As to the meaning of 'fishing vessel' see PARA 230.
2  As to the meaning of 'seaman' see PARA 457 note 5.
3  Ie subject to the Merchant Shipping Act 1995 s 38(3) (see the text and notes 6–9): see s 38(2).
4  For these purposes, 'wages' includes emoluments: Merchant Shipping Act 1995 s 313(1).
5  Merchant Shipping Act 1995 s 38(2).
6  Merchant Shipping Act 1995 s 38(3).
7  As to 'wreck' and 'loss' see PARA 483 notes 2, 3.
8  Merchant Shipping Act 1995 s 38(3)(a).
9  Merchant Shipping Act 1995 s 38(3)(b).
10  *Vogiatzis v SS Fairport, The Fairport* [1967] P 167, [1966] 2 All ER 1026, [1966] 2 Lloyd's Rep 7 (overruling *The Carolina* (1875) 34 LT 399, 3 Asp MLC 141).

**471. Extra wages.** As a general rule, seamen are not entitled to claim any additional wages in respect of services rendered in the course of the period of engagement, even though the master has agreed to pay them, the contract being considered void for absence of consideration as well as from public policy[1]. The fact that a vessel is about to sail short-handed is, however, a fact which will justify an agreement to pay additional remuneration[2]; and a seaman who is promoted during a voyage is entitled to be paid at an enhanced rate of payment[3], even though no alteration as to rate of pay is made in the ship's articles[4]. The owners may be bound by an agreement in reasonable terms made by the master to pay extra remuneration to the crew to bring a vessel home from a foreign port after war has broken out and the members of the crew have refused to sail, unless they are paid such extra remuneration in view of the war risks not contemplated by the members of the crew in their original agreement of wages for the voyage[5].

The crew may be bound by an agreement in reasonable terms to accept half wages in the event of certain contingencies[6].

1   *Harris v Watson* (1971) Peake 72; *Stilk v Myrick* (1809) 2 Camp 317; *Harris v Carter* (1854) 3 E & B 559; *Frazer v Hatton* (1857) 2 CBNS 512; *Hopkins v M'Bride* (1901) 50 WR 255; *Harrison v Dodd* (1914) 111 LT 47, 12 Asp MLC 503, DC. It is otherwise where a good consideration can be shown: *Clutterbuck v Coffin* (1842) 3 Man & G 842. In *Harrison v Dodd*, a chief engineer was held to have no authority to agree to pay overtime to a fireman. In connection with what amounts to consideration in this context see *Williams v Roffey Bros and Nicholls (Contractors) Ltd* [1991] 1 QB 1, [1990] 1 All ER 512; in connection with contractual entitlement to payments see *Attrill v Dresdner Kleinwort Ltd* [2012] EWHC 1189 (QB), [2012] IRLR 553.
2   *Hartley v Ponsonby* (1857) 7 E & B 872; *Turner v Owen* (1862) 3 F & F 176; *Moore v City of Malines (Owners) and Purvis Shipping Co Ltd* (1948) 81 Ll L Rep 96.
3   *Hanson v Royden* (1867) LR 3 CP 47.
4   *The Providence* (1825) 1 Hag Adm 391; *Hicks v Walker* (1856) 4 WR 511.
5   *Liston v The Carpathian (Owners)* [1915] 2 KB 42, 13 Asp MLC 70; cf *Pugh v Henville* [1957] 2 Lloyd's Rep 261 (where the members of the crew of a ship expecting a voyage to America were held to be rightly convicted for refusing to prepare the vessel for sea after the ship had been requisitioned and ordered to Cyprus, an area held not to be one of exceptional risk although the seamen honestly believed the Mediterranean to be dangerous because it was or might have become a war zone).
6   *The Hoghton* (1833) 3 Hag Adm 100.

**472. Compensation on wrongful dismissal.** In the absence of express agreement, the master of a vessel is entitled to reasonable notice of dismissal[1] and he may sue for damages for wrongful dismissal[2].

1   *Creen v Wright* (1876) 1 CPD 591, 3 Asp MLC 254, DC. The terms of the master's employment on one voyage continue to a succeeding voyage unless otherwise agreed: *The Gananoque* (1862) Lush 448. As to the measure of damages where a master was wrongfully dismissed abroad see *The Camilla* (1858) Sw 312.
2   *The Camilla* (1858) Sw 312; *Creen v Wright* (1876) 1 CPD 591, 3 Asp MLC 254, DC. An action for the recovery of wages by the master of the ship lies in rem and in personam: see PARA 477. As to the right of masters to interest if there is unreasonable delay in paying wages see the Merchant Shipping Act 1995 s 35; and PARA 475. The master may also have a right to wages during unemployment due to the wreck or loss of his ship by virtue of s 38(1): see PARA 482.

### (B)   Payment and Account of Wages

**473. Deductions from wages.** The following deductions are authorised to be made from the wages[1] due to a seaman (other than a person serving in a fishing vessel)[2] under a crew agreement[3] or seafarer employment agreement[4]:

(1)    deductions of any amount payable by the seaman to his employer in respect of canteen bills, goods supplied, radio or telephone calls, postage expenses, cash advances or allotments[5];

(2)    contributions by the seaman to a fund or in respect of membership of a body declared[6] to be a fund or body to which the provisions relating to restrictions on the assignment of and charge upon wages[7] apply[8];

(3)　　a deduction of an amount being the actual expense or pecuniary loss incurred or sustained by the employer in consequence of the seaman's absence or absences without leave, where the employer is satisfied on reasonable grounds that such absence is a breach of the seaman's obligations under the crew agreement or seafarer employment agreement[9];

(4)　　a deduction of an amount being the actual expense or pecuniary loss incurred or sustained by the employer, where the employer is satisfied on reasonable grounds that the expense or loss was caused by a breach or breaches of the seaman's obligations under the crew agreement or seafarer employment agreement not falling within head (3) above[10].

1　As to the meaning of 'wages' see PARA 470 note 4.

2　As to the vessels and seamen to which these provisions apply see PARA 470 note 1. As to the meaning of 'seaman' generally see PARA 457 note 5; in this context 'seaman' does not include a person serving in a fishing vessel: see the Merchant Shipping (Seamen's Wages and Accounts) Regulations 1972, SI 1972/1700, reg 1(2). As to the meaning of 'fishing vessel' see PARA 230. In connection with the wages of persons working on fishing vessels see PARAS 488–489; and FISHERIES AND AQUACULTURE vol 51 (2013) PARA 315.

3　As to the meaning of 'crew agreement' see PARA 457.

4　Merchant Shipping (Seamen's Wages and Accounts) Regulations 1972, SI 1972/1700, reg 4(1) (amended by SI 2014/1614) (having effect as if made under the Merchant Shipping Act 1995 s 32 (amended by SI 2014/1614)). In this context 'seafarer employment agreement' means an agreement required by the Merchant Shipping (Maritime Labour Convention) (Minimum Requirements for Seafarers etc) Regulations 2014, SI 2014/1613, reg 9 (see PARA 452) and a reference to a seafarer employment agreement in relation to a seafarer who works on a ship means the agreement of that description to which that seafarer is party in connection with that work: Merchant Shipping (Seamen's Wages and Accounts) Regulations 1972, SI 1972/1700, reg 1(2) (definition added by SI 2014/1614). 'Ship' means a ship registered in the United Kingdom but does not include a fishing vessel: Merchant Shipping (Seamen's Wages and Accounts) Regulations 1972, SI 1972/1700, reg 1(2). As to the meaning of 'ship' generally see PARA 229. As to the meaning of 'United Kingdom' see PARA 16 note 3.

　　The deductions authorised by these provisions:

　　(1)　　are without prejudice to any dispute relating to the amount payable to a seaman under the crew agreement or seafarer employment agreement and, subject to the provisions of the Merchant Shipping Act 1995, to the rights and obligations, whether of the employer or of the seaman, under the agreement or otherwise (reg 4(2)(a) (amended by SI 2014/1614)); and

　　(2)　　shall be in addition to any deduction authorised by any provision of the Merchant Shipping Act 1995 (except s 9) or of any other enactment (Merchant Shipping (Seamen's Wages and Accounts) Regulations 1972, SI 1972/1700, reg 4(2)(b)).

　　As to the power of the Secretary of State to make subordinate legislation under the Merchant Shipping Act 1995, including his power to appoint committees for the purpose of advising him when considering the making or alteration of any regulations etc, see PARA 39. As from a day to be appointed, the Secretary of State's general power to make regulations under s 32 includes power to provide that the amount of a deduction of a description specified in the regulations from wages in respect of employment in a fishing vessel is to be determined by a body established or approved by the Secretary of State in pursuance of regulations made under s 60 (see PARA 539): s 111. At the date at which this volume states the law s 111 had not been brought into force and no such order had been made.

5　Merchant Shipping (Seamen's Wages and Accounts) Regulations 1972, SI 1972/1700, reg 5(a).

6　Ie declared by regulations under the Merchant Shipping Act 1995 s 34(3) (see PARA 474).

7　Ie the Merchant Shipping Act 1995 s 34 (see PARA 474).

8　Merchant Shipping (Seamen's Wages and Accounts) Regulations 1972, SI 1972/1700, reg 5(b).

9　Merchant Shipping (Seamen's Wages and Accounts) Regulations 1972, SI 1972/1700, reg 5(c) (amended by SI 2014/1614).

　　The maximum amount which may be deducted from a seaman's wages in respect of any number of breaches of his obligations under the crew agreement:

　　(1)　　by virtue of the Merchant Shipping (Seamen's Wages and Accounts) Regulations 1972, SI 1972/1700, reg 5(c), is £100 (reg 6(a) (reg 6 substituted by SI 1994/791; Merchant Shipping (Seamen's Wages and Accounts) Regulations 1972, SI 1972/1700, reg 6(a) amended by SI 1999/3360)); and

(2) by virtue of the Merchant Shipping (Seamen's Wages and Accounts) Regulations 1972, SI 1972/1700, reg 5(d) (see the text and note 10) is £300 (reg 6(b) (as so substituted)).

No deduction may be made by virtue of reg 5(c) if the seaman satisfies the master that his absence was due to an accident or mistake or some other cause beyond his control and that he took all reasonable precautions to avoid being absent: reg 7.

Where it is possible for him to give a notice of deduction complying with the Merchant Shipping (Seamen's Wages and Accounts) Regulations 1972, SI 1972/170, reg 8(4) (see below) not less than 24 hours before the seaman's wages fall due to be paid, the seaman's employer or the master on his behalf must give to the seaman a notice of deduction complying with reg 8(4) and an opportunity to make representations about the deduction to the employer or to the master: reg 8(2). Where it is not possible for him to give a notice of deduction complying with reg 8(4) not less than 24 hours before the seaman's wages fall due to be paid, the seaman's employer or the master on his behalf must, if it is possible to do so before the seaman's wages fall due to be paid, give to the seaman a notice of deduction complying with reg 8(4) and an opportunity to make representations about the deduction to the employer or to the master, or, if the seaman has not been given such notice and opportunity, send to the seaman by registered post at his last known address a notice of deduction complying with reg 8(4): reg 8(3). A deduction may not be made by virtue of reg 5(c) or (d) unless either reg 8(2) or reg 8(3) has been complied with: reg 8(1) (amended by SI 2014/1614).

A notice of deduction must state that the employer is satisfied on reasonable grounds that there has been a breach or breaches, as the case may be, of the seaman's obligations under the crew agreement and that, subject to the provisions of regs 4–7, the deduction specified in the notice appears to the employer to be authorised to be made from the wages due to the seaman under the crew agreement or seafarer employment agreement; and such notice must also (reg 8(4) (amended by SI 2014/1614)):

(a) identify each provision of the crew agreement of which the employer is satisfied on reasonable grounds that there has been a breach and in respect of which he intends to make a deduction (Merchant Shipping (Seamen's Wages and Accounts) Regulations 1972, SI 1972/170,reg 8(4)(i));

(b) state the grounds upon which the employer is satisfied that each such breach has taken place (reg 8(4)(ii));

(c) specify, with sufficient particulars to show how it is calculated, the amount of the actual expense or pecuniary loss incurred or sustained by the employer in respect of each such breach or, if the total amount of such expense or loss in respect of which a deduction is made under reg 5(c) or (d) (or all or any of them as the case may be) exceeds the maximum which may be deducted under the appropriate paragraph or paragraphs, with sufficient particulars to show that such maximum is exceeded (reg 8(4)(iii) (amended by SI 1985/340; SI 2014/1614));

(d) specify the total amount of the deduction proposed to be made (Merchant Shipping (Seamen's Wages and Accounts) Regulations 1972, SI 1972/170, reg 8(4)(iv)).

10 Merchant Shipping (Seamen's Wages and Accounts) Regulations 1972, SI 1972/1700, reg 5(d) ) (amended by SI 2014/1614). See the Merchant Shipping (Seamen's Wages and Accounts) Regulations 1972, SI 1972/1700, regs 6, 8; and note 9: reg 5(d) is also subject to any additional limitations imposed by the crew agreement or seafarer employment agreement: reg 5(d) (as so amended).

**474. Restriction on assignment of and charge upon wages.** As respects the wages[1] due or accruing to a seaman[2] employed in a United Kingdom ship[3]:

(1) the wages are not subject to attachment[4];

(2) an assignment thereof before they have accrued does not bind the seaman and the payment of the wages to the seaman is valid notwithstanding any previous assignment or charge[5]; and

(3) a power of attorney or authority for the receipt of the wages is not irrevocable[6].

However, these restrictions do not affect the provisions with respect to allotment notes[7]; nor do they apply to any disposition relating to the application of wages[8]:

(a) in the payment of contributions to a fund declared by regulations made by the Secretary of State[9] to be a fund to which these provisions apply[10]; or

(b)    in the payment of contributions in respect of the membership of a body declared by regulations made by the Secretary of State to be a body to which these provisions apply[11];

or to anything done or to be done for giving effect to such a disposition[12].

1   As to the meaning of 'wages' see PARA 470 note 4.
2   As to the meaning of 'seaman' see PARA 457 note 5. As to the vessels and seamen to which these provisions apply see PARA 470 note 1. Nothing in the Merchant Shipping Act 1995 s 34 affects the operation of the Attachment of Earnings Act 1971 in relation to wages due to a person employed in a fishing vessel: see s 113. As to the meaning of 'fishing vessel' see PARA 230 note 9.
3   Merchant Shipping Act 1995 s 34(1). As to the meaning of 'ship' see PARA 229; and as to the meaning of 'United Kingdom ship' see PARA 230. As to the meaning of 'United Kingdom' see PARA 16 note 3.
4   Merchant Shipping Act 1995 s 34(1)(a). Head (1) in the text is subject, in relation to England and Wales, to the Attachment of Earnings Act 1971 (see MATRIMONIAL AND CIVIL PARTNERSHIP LAW vol 73 (2015) PARA 869 et seq) (Merchant Shipping Act 1995 s 34(4)) and is subject also to any provision made by or under the Child Support Act 1991 s 31 or s 33 (deductions from earnings orders) (see CHILDREN AND YOUNG PERSONS vol 9 (2017) PARA 642) (Merchant Shipping Act 1995 s 34(5)). As to the meanings of 'England' and 'Wales' see PARA 16 note 2. As to Scotland see s 34(1)(b).
5   Merchant Shipping Act 1995 s 34(1)(c).
6   Merchant Shipping Act 1995 s 34(1)(d).
7   Merchant Shipping Act 1995 s 34(2). The text refers to the provisions of Pt III (ss 24–84) with respect to allotment notes (as to which see PARA 476): see s 34(2).
8   Merchant Shipping Act 1995 s 34(3).
9   As to the Secretary of State see PARA 36; and as to the power of the Secretary of State to make subordinate legislation under the Merchant Shipping Act 1995, including his power to appoint committees for the purpose of advising him when considering the making or alteration of any regulations etc, see PARA 39.
10  Merchant Shipping Act 1995 s 34(3)(a). At the date at which this volumes states the law, no such regulations had been made but, by virtue of the Interpretation Act 1978 s 17(2)(b), the Merchant Shipping (Seamen's Wages) (Contributions) Regulations 1972, SI 1972/1699, have effect as if so made; and these regulations declare that the Merchant Shipping Act 1995 s 34 applies, in relation to contributions to a fund, to any pension fund and any charity: see the Merchant Shipping (Seamen's Wages) (Contributions) Regulations 1972, SI 1972/1699, regs 1, 2.
11  Merchant Shipping Act 1995 s 34(3)(b). Accordingly, s 34 applies, in relation to contributions in respect of membership of a body, to any trade union and any friendly society: see the Merchant Shipping (Seamen's Wages) (Contributions) Regulations 1972, SI 1972/1699, regs 1, 2. See also note 10.
12  Merchant Shipping Act 1995 s 34(3).

**475. Power of the court to award interest on wages due otherwise than under crew agreement.** In any proceedings by the master[1] of a ship[2] or a person employed in a ship otherwise than under a crew agreement[3] for the recovery of any sum due to him as wages[4], the court, unless it appears to the court that the delay in paying the sum was due to[5]:
(1)    a mistake[6];
(2)    a reasonable dispute as to liability[7];
(3)    the act or default of the person claiming the amount[8]; or
(4)    any other cause, not being the wrongful act or default of the persons liable to make the payment or their servants or agents[9],

may order them to pay, in addition to the sum due, interest on it at the rate of 20% per annum or such lower rate as the court may specify, for the period beginning seven days after the sum became due and ending when the sum is paid[10].

1   As to the meaning of 'master' see PARA 444 note 1.
2   As to the meaning of 'ship' see PARA 229. As to the vessels and seamen to which these provisions apply see PARA 470 note 1.
3   As to the meaning of 'crew agreement' see PARA 457.
4   As to the meaning of 'wages' see PARA 470 note 4.
5   Merchant Shipping Act 1995 s 35. As to the time limit for summary orders see PARA 1050.
6   Merchant Shipping Act 1995 s 35(a).

7   Merchant Shipping Act 1995 s 35(b).
8   Merchant Shipping Act 1995 s 35(c).
9   Merchant Shipping Act 1995 s 35(d).
10  Merchant Shipping Act 1995 s 35.

## (C)   Allotment of Wages

**476. Allotment notes.** A seaman[1] may[2], by means of an allotment note issued in accordance with regulations made by the Secretary of State[3], allot to any person or persons part of the wages[4] to which he is to become entitled in the course of his employment in a United Kingdom ship[5] or ships[6]. A seaman's right so to make an allotment is subject to such limitations as may[7] be imposed by regulations made by the Secretary of State[8].

Regulations made by the Secretary of State for these purposes may prescribe the form of allotment notes[9]; and:

(1)     may limit the circumstances in which allotments may be made[10];

(2)     may limit, whether by reference to an amount or by reference to a proportion, the part of the wages that may be allotted and the number of persons to whom it may be allotted and may prescribe the method by which that part is to be calculated[11];

(3)     may limit the persons to whom allotments may be made by a seaman to persons of such descriptions or persons standing to him in such relationships as may be prescribed by the regulations[12];

(4)     may prescribe the times and the intervals at which payments under allotment notes are to be made[13].

Regulations so made may make different provision in relation to different descriptions of seamen and different circumstances[14].

1   As to the meaning of 'seaman' see PARA 457 note 5. As to the vessels and seamen to which these provisions apply see PARA 470 note 1.
2   Ie subject to the Merchant Shipping Act 1995 s 36(2)–(4) (see the text and notes 7–14): see s 36(1).
3   As to the Secretary of State see PARA 36; and as to the power of the Secretary of State to make subordinate legislation under the Merchant Shipping Act 1995, including his power to appoint committees for the purpose of advising him when considering the making or alteration of any regulations etc, see PARA 39.
4   As to the meaning of 'wages' see PARA 470 note 4.
5   As to the meaning of 'ship' see PARA 229; and as to the meaning of 'United Kingdom ship' see PARA 230. As to the meaning of 'United Kingdom' see PARA 16 note 3.
6   Merchant Shipping Act 1995 s 36(1).
7   Ie by virtue of the Merchant Shipping Act 1995 s 36(3), (4) (see the text and notes 9–14): see s 36(2).
8   Merchant Shipping Act 1995 s 36(2).
9   Merchant Shipping Act 1995 s 36(3). At the date at which this volume states the law, no such regulations had been made but, by virtue of the Interpretation Act 1978 s 17(2)(b), the Merchant Shipping (Seamen's Allotments) Regulations 1972, SI 1972/1698 (amended by SI 2014/1613), have effect as if so made. Accordingly, as to the form prescribed for allotment notes see reg 5, Schedule.
10  Merchant Shipping Act 1995 s 36(3)(a). See the Merchant Shipping (Seamen's Allotments) Regulations 1972, SI 1972/1698, reg 2.
11  Merchant Shipping Act 1995 s 36(3)(b). See the Merchant Shipping (Seamen's Allotments) Regulations 1972, SI 1972/1698, reg 3(1)(a), (2).
12  Merchant Shipping Act 1995 s 36(3)(c). See the Merchant Shipping (Seamen's Allotments) Regulations 1972, SI 1972/1698, reg 3(1)(b).
13  Merchant Shipping Act 1995 s 36(3)(d). See the Merchant Shipping (Seamen's Allotments) Regulations 1972, SI 1972/1698, reg 4.
14  Merchant Shipping Act 1995 s 36(4).

**477. Right of person named in allotment to sue in own name.** A person to whom any part of a seaman's wages[1] has been allotted by an allotment note issued in accordance with the regulations[2] has the right to recover that part in his own name, and for that purpose has the same remedies as the seaman has for the recovery of his wages[3].

In any proceedings brought by a person named in such an allotment note as the person to whom any part of a seaman's wages has been allotted it is presumed, unless the contrary is shown, that the seaman is entitled to the wages specified in the note and that the allotment has not been varied or cancelled[4].

1   As to the meaning of 'seaman' see PARA 457 note 5; and as to the meaning of 'wages' see PARA 470 note 4. As to the vessels and seamen to which these provisions apply see PARA 470 note 1.
2   Ie regulations made under the Merchant Shipping Act 1995 s 36 (see PARA 476): see s 37(1). As to the Secretary of State see PARA 36; and as to his power to make subordinate legislation under the Merchant Shipping Act 1995 generally see PARA 39.
3   Merchant Shipping Act 1995 s 37(1).
4   Merchant Shipping Act 1995 s 37(2).

## (D)   Proceedings for Recovery of Wages

**478.   Admiralty jurisdiction relating to recovery proceedings.** A seaman has a maritime lien for wages[1] and cannot by any agreement forfeit it or be deprived of any remedy for the recovery of his wages to which, in the absence of the agreement, he would be entitled[2].

Seamen may sue in the Admiralty court either in rem or in personam and either separately or jointly on one claim under the Admiralty jurisdiction[3].

In the case of any such claim where the claim arises in connection with a ship and the person who would be liable on the claim in an action in personam (the 'relevant person') was, when the cause of action arose, the owner or charterer of, or in possession or in control of, the ship[4], an action in rem may, whether or not the claim gives rise to a maritime lien on that ship, be brought in the High Court against:

(1)     that ship, if at the time when the action is brought the relevant person is either the beneficial owner of that ship as respects all the shares in it or the charterer of it under a charter by demise[5]; or

(2)     any other ship of which, at the time when the action is brought, the relevant person is the beneficial owner as respects all the shares in it[6].

State-owned vessels are immune from arrest[7], but otherwise a ship against which an action in rem has been instituted may, if necessary, be arrested and sold by proper process to meet established claims for wages[8].

These provisions apply to all ships, whether British or not and whether registered or not and wherever the residence or domicile of their owners may be, but they do not extend the cases in which property or money is recoverable under the Merchant Shipping Act 1995[9]; and courts have a discretion to refuse to entertain an action in rem for wages by the master or member of the crew of a ship, not being a British ship, if the consul of the country to which the ship belongs on due notification of the action in rem protests against the action proceeding[10].

1   See *The Sydney Cove* (1815) 2 Dods 11; *The Neptune* (1824) 1 Hag Adm 227; and PARA 127. As to maritime liens see PARA 964 et seq. Employer pension contributions count as 'wages' in this context: see *The Halcyon Skies* [1976] 1 All ER 856, [1976] 1 Lloyd's Rep 461. See also *The Tacoma City* [1991] 1 Lloyd's Rep 330, CA.
2   See the Merchant Shipping Act 1995 s 39(1); and PARA 479. Any term in an agreement which is inconsistent (see *A-G v Fargrove Steam Navigation Co Ltd* (1906) 23 TLR 230) with the seaman's right to wages is void: see the Merchant Shipping Act 1995 s 39(1); and PARA 479. See also *Cil v Owners of the Turiddu (First National Bank Intervening)* [1999] 2 All ER (Comm) 161, CA (seamen who have directed part of their wages to be paid through an agency to persons nominated by them have a lien over any arrears of wages, which takes priority over a bank's mortgage in respect of the vessel).

3  See the Senior Courts Act 1981 s 20(1)(a), (2)(o) (cited in PARA 127 et seq), s 21(1), (3) (cited in PARA 93). As to claims in rem generally see PARA 92 et seq; and as to claims in personam ('other claims') generally see PARA 94 et seq. As to the Admiralty jurisdiction of the High Court of Justice generally see PARA 85 et seq.

4  See the Senior Courts Act 1981 s 20(1)(a), (2)(o) (cited in PARA 127 et seq), s 21(1), (4)(a), (b) (cited in PARA 93). As to the meaning of 'ship' for these purposes see PARA 85 note 7.

5  See the Senior Courts Act 1981 s 20(1)(a), (2)(o) (cited in PARA 127 et seq), s 21(1), (4)(i) (cited in PARA 93). As to the meaning of 'beneficial owner' for these purposes see PARA 93 note 32.

6  See the Senior Courts Act 1981 s 20(1)(a), (2)(o) (cited in PARA 127 et seq), s 21(1), (4)(ii) (cited in PARA 93). See also *Vogiatzis v SS Fairport, The Fairport* [1967] P 167, [1966] 2 All ER 1026, [1966] 2 Lloyd's Rep 7; *The Aventicum* [1978] 1 Lloyd's Rep 184.

7  See the Crown Proceedings Act 1947 s 29(1) (cited in PARA 179); and CROWN AND CROWN PROCEEDINGS vol 29 (2014) PARA 86.

8  See the Senior Courts Act 1981 s 21(6) (cited in PARA 93).

9  See the Senior Courts Act 1981 s 20(7)(a), proviso; and PARA 86.

10 *The Herzogin Marie* (1861) Lush 292; *The Octavie* (1863) Brown & Lush 215; *The Nina* (1868) LR 2 PC 38; *The Leon XIII, Wardrop v The Leon XIII* (1883) 8 PD 121, 5 Asp MLC 73, CA. As to the limitation of jurisdiction in the case of ships belonging to states specified by order under the Consular Relations Act 1968 s 4 see INTERNATIONAL RELATIONS LAW vol 61 (2010) PARA 303.

**479. Protection of certain rights and remedies.** A seaman's lien[1], his remedies for the recovery of his wages[2], his right to wages in case of the wreck or loss of his ship[3], and any right he may have or obtain in the nature of salvage[4] are not capable of being renounced by any agreement[5]. However, this does not affect such of the terms of any agreement made with the seamen belonging to a ship which, in accordance with the agreement, is to be employed on salvage service, as provide for the remuneration to be paid to them for salvage services rendered by that ship[6].

1  As to the meaning of 'seaman' see PARA 457 note 5. As to the vessels and seamen to which these provisions apply see PARA 484 note 3. As to maritime liens generally see PARA 964 et seq.

2  See PARA 478. As to the rights of the crew of a fishing vessel with regard to wages see PARA 488 et seq; and as to the master's rights see PARA 480. As to the meaning of 'wages' see PARA 470 note 4.

3  See PARA 470. As to the meaning of 'ship' see PARA 229.

4  As to salvage claims generally see PARA 849 et seq.

5  Merchant Shipping Act 1995 s 39(1).

6  Merchant Shipping Act 1995 s 39(2).

**480. Remedies of master for remuneration, disbursements and liabilities.** The master[1] of a ship[2] has the same lien[3] for his remuneration, and all disbursements or liabilities properly made or incurred by him on account of the ship[4], as a seaman[5] has for his wages[6].

1  As to the meaning of 'master' see PARA 444 note 1.

2  As to the meaning of 'ship' see PARA 229. As to the vessels and seamen to which these provisions apply see PARA 484 note 3.

3  As to maritime liens generally see PARA 964 et seq.

4  As to a master's employment, authority and liability see PARA 424 et seq.

5  As to the meaning of 'seaman' see PARA 457 note 5.

6  Merchant Shipping Act 1995 s 41. As to the meaning of 'wages' see PARA 470 note 4.

*(E)   Claims against Seamen's Wages for Maintenance etc of Dependants*

**481. In general.** Where, during a seaman's[1] employment in a ship[2], expenses are incurred by a responsible authority[3] for the benefit of any dependant of his and the expenses are of a kind specified in regulations[4] and such further conditions, if any, as may be so specified are satisfied, the authority may by notice in writing complying with the regulations require the persons employing the seaman[5]:

(1)   to retain for a period specified in the notice such proportion of his net wages as may be so specified[6]; and

(2)   to give to the responsible authority as soon as may be notice in writing of the seaman's discharge[7] from the ship[8];

and the persons employing the seaman must comply with the notice and give notice in writing of its contents to the seaman[9].

For these purposes;

(a)    the following persons, and no others, are to be taken to be a seaman's dependants, that is to say, his spouse and any other person under the age of 19 whom he is liable, for the purposes of any enactment in any part of the United Kingdom, to maintain or in respect of whom he is liable under any such enactment to make contributions to a local authority[10]; and

(b)    expenses incurred for the benefit of any person include, in addition to any payments made to him or on his behalf, expenses incurred for providing him with accommodation or care or for exercising supervision over him[11];

but no expenses may be specified in regulations made for these purposes[12] unless they are such that a magistrates' court has power under any enactment in force in any part of the United Kingdom to order the making of payments in respect thereof[13].

Not more than the following proportion of a seaman's wages[14] may be so retained, whether in pursuance of one or more notices[15]:

(i)    one-half (if the notice or notices relates or relate to one dependant only)[16];

(ii)    two-thirds (if the notice or notices relates or relate to two or more dependants)[17].

Where a responsible authority has so served a notice[18] on the persons employing a seaman, a magistrates' court may, on the application of the authority, make an order for the payment to the authority of such sum, not exceeding the proportion of the seaman's wages which those persons were required[19] to retain, having regard to the expenses incurred by the authority and the seaman's means, thinks fit[20].

Any sums paid out of a seaman's wages in pursuance of such an order are deemed to be paid to him in respect of his wages; and the service, on the persons who employed the seaman, of such an order or of an order dismissing an application for such an order terminates the period for which they were required to retain the wages[21].

An application for such an order[22] for the payment of any sum by the persons who employed the seaman is deemed, for the purposes of any proceedings, to be an application for an order against the seaman; but the order, when served on those persons, has effect as an order against them and may be enforced accordingly[23].

Any such notice or order[24] may be served by registered post or recorded delivery service[25].

Regulations have been made[26] specifying:

(A)    the expenses in respect of which a notice may be served by a responsible authority[27];

(B)    any conditions that must be satisfied if such a notice is to be served[28];

(C)    the period that may be specified in such a notice, being a period beginning with the service of the notice and ending a specified number of days after the seaman's discharge from his ship[29];

(D)    the form of such a notice and the information to be contained therein[30]; and

(E) the amounts to be deducted from a seaman's wages in computing his net wages for the purposes of these provisions[31].

1 As to the meaning of 'seaman' see PARA 457 note 5. As to the vessels and seamen to which these provisions apply see PARA 470 note 1.
2 As to the meaning of 'ship' see PARA 229.
3 For these purposes, 'responsible authority' means the Secretary of State or (except in Northern Ireland) any local authority: Merchant Shipping Act 1995 s 40(10). As to the Secretary of State see PARA 36. As to local authorities in England and Wales see LOCAL GOVERNMENT vol 69 (2009) PARA 22 et seq.
4 Ie specified in regulations made under the Merchant Shipping Act 1995 s 40 (see the text and notes 26–32): see s 40(1).
5 Merchant Shipping Act 1995 s 40(1). The Maintenance Orders Act 1950 Pt I (ss 4–15) (jurisdiction) and Pt III (ss 26–32) (general) (see CONFLICT OF LAWS vol 19 (2011) PARA 560 et seq) have effect as if an order under the Merchant Shipping Act 1995 s 40 were included among those referred to in the Maintenance Orders Act 1950 s 4(1), (2), s 9(1), (2) and s 12(1), (2); and any sum payable by any persons under an order made under the Merchant Shipping Act 1995 s 40 in any part of the United Kingdom may, in any other part of the United Kingdom, be recovered from them as a debt due to the authority on whose application the order was made: s 40(7). As to the meaning of 'United Kingdom' see PARA 16 note 3.
6 Merchant Shipping Act 1995 s 40(1)(a).
7 As to when a seaman is regarded as discharged from a ship see PARA 468 note 2.
8 Merchant Shipping Act 1995 s 40(1)(b).
9 Merchant Shipping Act 1995 s 40(1). This provision is subject to s 40(3) (see the text and notes 14–17): see s 40(1).
10 Merchant Shipping Act 1995 s 40(2)(a).
11 Merchant Shipping Act 1995 s 40(2)(b).
12 Ie specified in regulations made under the Merchant Shipping Act 1995 s 40 (see the text and notes 26–32): see s 40(2).
13 Merchant Shipping Act 1995 s 40(2).
14 As to the meaning of 'wages' see PARA 470 note 4.
15 Merchant Shipping Act 1995 s 40(3).
16 Merchant Shipping Act 1995 s 40(3)(a).
17 Merchant Shipping Act 1995 s 40(3)(b).
18 Ie under the Merchant Shipping Act 1995 s 40: see s 40(4).
19 Ie by virtue of the Merchant Shipping Act 1995 s 40: see s 40(4).
20 Merchant Shipping Act 1995 s 40(4).
21 Merchant Shipping Act 1995 s 40(5).
22 Ie under the Merchant Shipping Act 1995 s 40: see s 40(6).
23 Merchant Shipping Act 1995 s 40(6).
24 Ie under the Merchant Shipping Act 1995 s 40: see s 40(8).
25 Merchant Shipping Act 1995 s 40(8).
26 See the Merchant Shipping (Maintenance of Seamen's Dependants) Regulations 1972, SI 1972/1635 (amended by SI 1972/1875; SI 1988/479; SI 2009/462; SI 2014/107), having effect pursuant to the Merchant Shipping Act 1995 s 40(9).As to the power of the Secretary of State to make subordinate legislation under the Merchant Shipping Act 1995, including his power to appoint committees for the purpose of advising him when considering the making or alteration of any regulations etc, see PARA 39.
27 Merchant Shipping Act 1995 s 40(9)(a). See the Merchant Shipping (Maintenance of Seamen's Dependants) Regulations 1972, SI 1972/1635, reg 4 (amended by SI 1972/1875; SI 1988/479).
28 Merchant Shipping Act 1995 s 40(9)(b). See the Merchant Shipping (Maintenance of Seamen's Dependants) Regulations 1972, SI 1972/1635, reg 2.
29 Merchant Shipping Act 1995 s 40(9)(c). See the Merchant Shipping (Maintenance of Seamen's Dependants) Regulations 1972, SI 1972/1635, reg 3(1)(b).
30 Merchant Shipping Act 1995 s 40(9)(d). See the Merchant Shipping (Maintenance of Seamen's Dependants) Regulations 1972, SI 1972/1635, reg 3.
31 Merchant Shipping Act 1995 s 40(9)(e). The amounts specified under head (E) in the text may include amounts allotted by allotment notes issued under s 36 (see PARA 476): see s 40(9)(e). See the Merchant Shipping (Maintenance of Seamen's Dependants) Regulations 1972, SI 1972/1635, reg 5.

B.　ADDITIONAL PROVISIONS RELATING TO UNITED KINGDOM SHIPS AND SHIPS IN UNITED KINGDOM WATERS

**482.　Late payment.** If any amount in respect of wages or other remuneration payable to a seafarer[1] under a seafarer employment agreement[2] is not paid on the due date, interest must be paid on the unpaid amount at the rate of 20 per cent per annum from the date on which the amount was due until the date of payment[3]. This does not apply to the extent that the failure to make such payment on the required date was due to a mistake[4], a reasonable dispute as to liability[5], the act or default of the seafarer[6] or any other cause not being the wrongful act or default of the persons liable to make the payment or of their servants or agents[7].

1　As to the meaning of 'seafarer' see PARA 423.
2　As to seafarer employment agreements see PARAS 451–455. These provisions (ie the Merchant Shipping (Maritime Labour Convention) (Minimum Requirements for Seafarers etc) Regulations 2014, SI 2014/1613, Pt 2 (regs 16–18) apply to employment on ships to which the Merchant Shipping (Maritime Labour Convention) (Minimum Requirements for Seafarers etc) Regulations 2014, SI 2014/1613 (which implements in United Kingdom law the Maritime Labour Convention (Cm 7049)), applies, that is, all United Kingdom ships other than fishing vessels, ships of traditional build, pleasure vessels, warships or naval auxiliary vessels or vessels not ordinarily engaged in commercial activities, and all such non-United Kingdom ships in United Kingdom waters: see further PARA 423. The provision of the Convention making provision with respect to seafarers' wages is reg 2.2. Corresponding provision with respect to employment on fishing vessels, ships of traditional build and non-commercial vessels is governed by the Merchant Shipping Act 1995: see ss 30, 31, 33, 38(1); and PARAS 484, 485, 486, 483.
　　A sea-going non-United Kingdom ship in United Kingdom waters which is subject to the Maritime Labour Convention (see the Merchant Shipping (Maritime Labour Convention) (Minimum Requirements for Seafarers etc) Regulations 2014, SI 2014/1613, regs 3(3), (4)(b)(iii); and PARA 423 note 9) must not be operated unless the shipowner complies with the requirements in paragraph 2 of Standard A2.2 (wages) of the Convention: Merchant Shipping (Maritime Labour Convention) (Minimum Requirements for Seafarers etc) Regulations 2014, SI 2014/1613, reg 18(1). A breach of reg 18(1) is an offence by the shipowner: reg 18(2). As to the meaning of 'shipowner' see PARA 448 note 4. Such an offence is punishable on summary conviction by a fine: reg 59(4)(b). In any proceedings for such an offence it is a defence for the person charged to show that all reasonable steps had been taken by that person to ensure compliance with the provision concerned: reg 60. As to the powers of magistrates' courts to issue fines on summary conviction see SENTENCING vol 92 (2015) PARA 176.
3　Merchant Shipping (Maritime Labour Convention) (Minimum Requirements for Seafarers etc) Regulations 2014, SI 2014/1613, reg 16(1).
4　Merchant Shipping (Maritime Labour Convention) (Minimum Requirements for Seafarers etc) Regulations 2014, SI 2014/1613, reg 16(2)(a).
5　Merchant Shipping (Maritime Labour Convention) (Minimum Requirements for Seafarers etc) Regulations 2014, SI 2014/1613, reg 16(2)(b).
6　Merchant Shipping (Maritime Labour Convention) (Minimum Requirements for Seafarers etc) Regulations 2014, SI 2014/1613, reg 16(2)(c).
7　Merchant Shipping (Maritime Labour Convention) (Minimum Requirements for Seafarers etc) Regulations 2014, SI 2014/1613, reg 16(2)(d).

**483.　Accounts.** The shipowner[1] must ensure that an account of the seafarer's[2] wages or other remuneration under a seafarer employment agreement[3] is prepared and delivered to the seafarer:
　(1)　periodically during the term of the agreement, at intervals not exceeding one month[4]; and
　(2)　within one month of the agreement terminating[5].
Where the seafarer is an employee[6], such account must include:
　(a)　the name of the seafarer[7];
　(b)　the date of birth of the seafarer (if known)[8];
　(c)　the number of the seafarer's current discharge book (if any)[9];
　(d)　the capacity in which the seafarer worked on board the ship[10];
　(e)　the period covered by the account[11];
　(f)　the amounts payable for the period covered by the account[12]; and
　(g)　the type and amount of any deductions made during the period covered by the account[13];

and where the seafarer is not an employee, such account must include:

(i)     payments due[14];

(ii)    payments made (including any not falling within head (1) above)[15]; and

(iii)   any rates of exchange and any commissions paid which are relevant to those payments[16].

A breach of these requirements is an offence by the shipowner[17].

1  As to the meaning of 'shipowner' see PARA 448 note 4.

2  As to the meaning of 'seafarer' see PARA 423.

3  As to seafarer employment agreements see PARAS 451–455; as to the vessels and seafarers to which these provisions apply see PARA 482 note 2.

4  Merchant Shipping (Maritime Labour Convention) (Minimum Requirements for Seafarers etc) Regulations 2014, SI 2014/1613, reg 17(1)(a).

5  Merchant Shipping (Maritime Labour Convention) (Minimum Requirements for Seafarers etc) Regulations 2014, SI 2014/1613, reg 17(1)(b).

6  As to the meaning of 'employee' see PARA 451 note 18.

7  Merchant Shipping (Maritime Labour Convention) (Minimum Requirements for Seafarers etc) Regulations 2014, SI 2014/1613, reg 17(2)(a).

8  Merchant Shipping (Maritime Labour Convention) (Minimum Requirements for Seafarers etc) Regulations 2014, SI 2014/1613, reg 17(2)(b).

9  Merchant Shipping (Maritime Labour Convention) (Minimum Requirements for Seafarers etc) Regulations 2014, SI 2014/1613, reg 17(2)(c).

10 Merchant Shipping (Maritime Labour Convention) (Minimum Requirements for Seafarers etc) Regulations 2014, SI 2014/1613, reg 17(2)(d). As to the meaning of 'ship' see PARA 423 note 2.

11 Merchant Shipping (Maritime Labour Convention) (Minimum Requirements for Seafarers etc) Regulations 2014, SI 2014/1613, reg 17(2)(e).

12 Merchant Shipping (Maritime Labour Convention) (Minimum Requirements for Seafarers etc) Regulations 2014, SI 2014/1613, reg 17(2)(f). Where, pursuant to reg 17(2), the account includes information of amounts which have been determined by reference to a currency exchange rate, the account must include details of the relevant exchange rate and any commission paid: reg 17(4).

13 Merchant Shipping (Maritime Labour Convention) (Minimum Requirements for Seafarers etc) Regulations 2014, SI 2014/1613, reg 17(2)(g).

14 Merchant Shipping (Maritime Labour Convention) (Minimum Requirements for Seafarers etc) Regulations 2014, SI 2014/1613, reg 17(3)(a).

15 Merchant Shipping (Maritime Labour Convention) (Minimum Requirements for Seafarers etc) Regulations 2014, SI 2014/1613, reg 17(3)(b).

16 Merchant Shipping (Maritime Labour Convention) (Minimum Requirements for Seafarers etc) Regulations 2014, SI 2014/1613, reg 17(3)(c).

17 Merchant Shipping (Maritime Labour Convention) (Minimum Requirements for Seafarers etc) Regulations 2014, SI 2014/1613, reg 17(5). Such an offence is punishable on summary conviction by a fine: reg 59(4)(a). In any proceedings for such an offence it is a defence for the person charged to show that all reasonable steps had been taken by that person to ensure compliance with the provision concerned: reg 60. As to the powers of magistrates' courts to issue fines on summary conviction see SENTENCING vol 92 (2015) PARA 176.

C.   PROVISIONS APPLICABLE ONLY TO SHIPS OF TRADITIONAL BUILD AND NON-COMMERCIAL VESSELS

**484. Payment of seamen's wages on discharge.** Where a seaman[1] employed under a crew agreement[2] relating to a United Kingdom ship which is a ship of traditional build or a non-commercial vessel (and is not a fishing vessel)[3] leaves the ship on being discharged from it, then[4] the wages[5] due to the seaman under the agreement must either[6]:

(1)   be paid to him in full at the time when he so leaves the ship (the 'time of discharge')[7]; or

(2)   be paid to him within a pay cycle, in accordance with the provisions governing payment up-to-date at specified intervals[8].

If the amount shown in the account duly delivered to a seaman[9] as being the amount shown payable to him under head (1) above is replaced by an increased amount shown in a further account duly delivered to him[10], the balance must be paid to him within seven days of the time of discharge; and, if the amount so shown in the account so delivered to him exceeds £50 and it is not practicable to pay the whole of it at the time of discharge, not less than £50 nor less than one-quarter of the amount so shown must be paid to him at that time and the balance within seven days of that time[11].

If any amount which (except under head (2) above)[12] is payable to a seaman is not paid at the time at which it is so payable, the seaman is entitled to wages at the rate last payable under the crew agreement for every day on which it remains unpaid during the period of 56 days following the time of discharge; and, if any such amount or any amount so payable remains unpaid after the end of that period, it carries interest at the rate of 20 per cent per annum[13].

Where the crew agreement[14] provides for the seaman's basic wages to be payable up-to-date at specified intervals not exceeding one month, and for any additional amounts of wages to be payable within the pay cycle following that to which they relate, any amount of wages due to the seaman under the agreement must be paid to him not later than the date on which the next payment of his basic wages following the time of discharge would have fallen due if his employment under the agreement had continued[15]. If, however, it is not practicable, in the case of any amount due to the seaman by way of wages additional to his basic wages, to pay that amount by the required date[16], that amount must be paid to him not later than what would have been the last day of the pay cycle immediately following that date if his employment under the crew agreement had continued[17]. If any amount which is so payable[18] to a seaman is not paid at the time at which it is so payable, it carries interest at the rate of 20% per annum[19].

However, these provisions which govern the late payment of wages[20] do not apply if the failure to pay was due to[21]:

(a)  a mistake[22];

(b)  a reasonable dispute as to liability[23];

(c)  the act or default of the seaman[24]; or

(d)  any other cause, not being the wrongful act or default of the persons liable to pay his wages or of their servants or agents[25],

and so much of those provisions as relates to interest on the amount due does not apply if a court in proceedings for its recovery so directs[26].

Where a seaman is employed under a crew agreement relating to more than one ship, the provisions governing payment of his wages on discharge[27] have effect, in relation to wages due to him under the agreement, as if for any reference to the time of discharge there were substituted a reference to the termination of his employment under the crew agreement[28].

Where a seaman[29] is discharged from a ship outside the United Kingdom but returns to the United Kingdom under arrangements made by the persons who employed him, the provisions governing payment of his wages on discharge[30] have effect, in relation to the wages due to him under a crew agreement relating to the ship, as if for the references[31] to the time of discharge there were substituted references to the time of his return to the United Kingdom[32].

For these purposes, any amount of wages, if not paid to him in cash, is taken to have been paid to a seaman[33]:

(i)  on the date when a cheque, or a money or postal order issued by the Post Office company[34], for that amount was dispatched by the recorded delivery service to the seaman's last known address[35]; or

(ii)     on the date when any account kept by the seaman with a bank or other institution was credited with that amount[36].

1  As to the meaning of 'seaman' see PARA 457 note 5.
2  As to the meaning of 'crew agreement' see PARA 457.
3  The Merchant Shipping Act 1995 ss 30, 31, 33, 38(1) (see the text and notes 4–36; and PARAS 485–483) apply only to United Kingdom ships (to which the legislation refers) which are ships of traditional build and non-commercial vessels, and do not apply to fishing vessels: see the Merchant Shipping Act 1995 ss 24(2A), 25(2), 114; and PARA 423 note 22. Corresponding provision relating to employment on other United Kingdom ships and non-United Kingdom ships in United Kingdom waters is governed by the Maritime Labour Convention (Cm 7049) and implemented by the Merchant Shipping (Maritime Labour Convention) (Minimum Requirements for Seafarers etc) Regulations 2014, SI 2014/1613: see regs 16–18; and PARAS 482–483. Corresponding provision relating to employment on fishing vessels is made by the Merchant Shipping Act 1995 ss 110, 112 (which apply to the exclusion of ss 30, 31: see PARA 423 note 22) (see PARAS 488, 489), and by the Merchant Shipping (Crew Agreements, Lists of Crew and Discharge of Seamen) (Fishing Vessels) Regulations 1972, SI 1972/919 (having effect as if made under the Merchant Shipping Act 1995 s 109) (see FISHERIES AND AQUACULTURE vol 51 (2013) PARAS 312, 314, 316). As to the meaning of 'ship' see PARA 229; and as to the meaning of 'United Kingdom ship' see PARA 230. As to the meaning of 'United Kingdom' see PARA 16 note 3. As to the meaning of 'fishing vessel' see PARA 230.
4  Ie except as provided by or under the Merchant Shipping Act 1995 Pt III (ss 24–84) or any other enactment: see s 30(1).
5  As to the meaning of 'wages' see PARA 470 note 4.
6  Merchant Shipping Act 1995 s 30(1).
7  Merchant Shipping Act 1995 s 30(1)(a).
8  Merchant Shipping Act 1995 s 30(1)(b). The text refers to payment in accordance with s 30(4), (5) (see the text and notes 14–17): see s 30(1)(b).
9  Ie under the Merchant Shipping Act 1995 s 31(1) (see PARA 485): see s 30(2).
10  Ie under the Merchant Shipping Act 1995 s 31(3) (see PARA 485): see s 30(2).
11  Merchant Shipping Act 1995 s 30(2).
12  Ie any amount under the Merchant Shipping Act 1995 s 30(1)(a) (see head (1) in the text) or s 30(2) (see the text and notes 9–11) only: see s 30(3).
13  Merchant Shipping Act 1995 s 30(3).
14  Ie the crew agreement referred to in the Merchant Shipping Act 1995 s 30(1) (see the text and notes 1–8): see s 30(4).
15  Merchant Shipping Act 1995 s 30(4).
16  Ie the date mentioned in the Merchant Shipping Act 1995 s 30(4) (see the text and notes 14–15): see s 30(5).
17  Merchant Shipping Act 1995 s 30(5).
18  Ie under the Merchant Shipping Act 1995 s 30(4), (5) (see the text and notes 14–17): see s 30(6).
19  Merchant Shipping Act 1995 s 30(6).
20  Ie the Merchant Shipping Act 1995 s 30(3) (see the text and notes 12–13) or s 30(6) (see the text and notes 18–19): see s 30(7).
21  Merchant Shipping Act 1995 s 30(7).
22  Merchant Shipping Act 1995 s 30(7)(a).
23  Merchant Shipping Act 1995 s 30(7)(b).
24  Merchant Shipping Act 1995 s 30(7)(c).
25  Merchant Shipping Act 1995 s 30(7)(d).
26  Merchant Shipping Act 1995 s 30(7).
27  Ie the Merchant Shipping Act 1995 s 30(1)–(7) (see the text and notes 1–26): see s 30(8).
28  Merchant Shipping Act 1995 s 30(8).
29  Ie in pursuance of the Merchant Shipping Act 1995 s 29 (see PARA 469): see s 30(9).
30  Ie the Merchant Shipping Act 1995 s 30(1)–(7) (see the text and notes 1–26), s 30(8) being omitted: see s 30(9).
31  Ie in the Merchant Shipping Act 1995 s 30(1)–(4) (see the text and notes 1–15): see s 30(9).
32  Merchant Shipping Act 1995 s 30(9).
33  Merchant Shipping Act 1995 s 30(10).
34  Ie as defined by the Postal Services Act 2011 s 6 (see POSTAL SERVICES vol 85 (2012) PARA 223): see the Merchant Shipping Act 1995 s 30(10)(a) (amended by the Postal Services Act 2011 Sch 12 para 147).
35  Merchant Shipping Act 1995 s 30(10)(a) (as amended: see note 34).
36  Merchant Shipping Act 1995 s 30(10)(b).

**485. Account of seamen's wages.** The master[1] of every United Kingdom ship which is a ship of traditional build or a non-commercial vessel (and is not a fishing vessel)[2] must[3] deliver to every seaman[4] employed in the ship under a crew agreement[5] an account of the wages[6] due to him under that crew agreement and of the deductions subject to which the wages are payable[7]. The account must indicate that the amounts stated therein are subject to any later adjustment that may be found necessary and must be delivered not later than 24 hours before the time of discharge[8] or, if the seaman is discharged without notice or at less than 24 hours' notice, at the time of discharge[9]. If the amounts stated in the account require adjustment, the persons who employed the seaman must deliver to him a further account stating the adjusted amounts; and that account must be delivered not later than the time at which the balance of his wages is payable to the seaman[10].

Where certain of the provisions governing the late payment of wages customarily paid up-to-date at specified intervals[11] apply to the payment of any amount of wages due to a seaman under a crew agreement[12]:

(1)     the person who employed the seaman must deliver to him an account of the wages payable to him under those provisions[13] and of the deductions subject to which the wages are payable[14]; and

(2)     any such account must be so delivered at the time when the wages are paid to him[15]; and

(3)     the usual provisions as to delivery of an account[16] do not apply[17].

Where a seaman is employed under a crew agreement relating to more than one ship, any account which otherwise[18] would be required to be delivered to him by the master must instead be delivered to him by the persons employing him and must be so delivered on or before the termination of his employment under the crew agreement[19].

If a person fails without reasonable excuse to comply with the provisions which govern the accounting of seamen's wages[20], he commits an offence[21].

1 As to the meaning of 'master' see PARA 444 note 1.
2 As to the vessels and seamen to which these provisions apply see PARA 484 note 3. As to the meaning of 'ship' see PARA 229; and as to the meaning of 'United Kingdom ship' see PARA 230. As to the meaning of 'United Kingdom' see PARA 16 note 3.
3 Ie subject to the Merchant Shipping Act 1995 s 31(4), (5) (see the text and notes 11–19) and to regulations made under s 32 (regulations relating to wages and accounts) (see PARA 473) or s 73 (relief and return of seaman etc left behind and shipwrecked) (see PARA 548): see s 31(1).
4 As to the meaning of 'seaman' see PARA 457 note 5.
5 As to the meaning of 'crew agreement' see PARA 457.
6 As to the meaning of 'wages' see PARA 470 note 4.
7 Merchant Shipping Act 1995 s 31(1).
8 As to the meaning of 'time of discharge' see PARA 484.
9 Merchant Shipping Act 1995 s 31(2).
10 Merchant Shipping Act 1995 s 31(3).
11 Ie the Merchant Shipping Act 1995 s 30(4) or (5) (see PARA 484): see s 31(4).
12 Merchant Shipping Act 1995 s 31(4). The provisions which, for the purposes of s 30 (see PARA 484), govern when any amount of wages, if not paid to him in cash, is taken to have been paid to a seaman (see s 30(10); and PARA 484) apply for the purposes of s 31(4) as they apply for the purposes of s 30: see s 31(4).
13 Ie payable under the Merchant Shipping Act 1995 s 30(4) or (5) (see PARA 484), as the case may be: see s 31(4).
14 Merchant Shipping Act 1995 s 31(4)(a).
15 Merchant Shipping Act 1995 s 31(4)(b).
16 Ie the Merchant Shipping Act 1995 s 31(1)–(3) (see the text and notes 1–10): see s 31(4)(c).
17 Merchant Shipping Act 1995 s 31(4)(c).
18 Ie under the Merchant Shipping Act 1995 s 31(1)–(4) (see the text and notes 1–17): see s 31(5).
19 Merchant Shipping Act 1995 s 31(5).

20 Ie the Merchant Shipping Act 1995 s 31(1)–(5) (see the text and notes 1–19): see s 31(6).
21 See the Merchant Shipping Act 1995 s 31(6); and PARA 1075.

**486. Power of superintendent or proper officer to decide disputes about wages.** Any dispute relating to the amount payable to a seaman[1] employed under a crew agreement relating to a United Kingdom ship which is a ship of traditional build or a non-commercial vessel[2] may be submitted by the parties to a superintendent[3] or proper officer[4] for decision[5]. However, the superintendent or proper officer is not bound to accept the submission or, if he has accepted it, to decide the dispute, if he is of the opinion that the dispute, whether by reason of the amount involved or for any other reason, ought not to be decided by him[6].

The decision of a superintendent or proper officer on a dispute so submitted to him is final[7].

1 As to the meaning of 'seaman' see PARA 457 note 5.
2 As to the meaning of 'crew agreement' see PARA 457. As to the vessels and seamen to which these provisions apply see PARA 484 note 3. As to the meaning of 'ship' see PARA 229; and as to the meaning of 'United Kingdom ship' see PARA 230. As to the meaning of 'United Kingdom' see PARA 16 note 3.
3 As to the meaning of 'superintendent' see PARA 61 note 1. As to the appointment of superintendents see PARA 61.
4 As to the meaning of 'proper officer' see PARA 48 note 4.
5 Merchant Shipping Act 1995 s 33(1). Documents purporting to be submissions to or decisions by superintendents or proper officers under s 33 are admissible in evidence and, when in the custody of the Registrar General of Shipping and Seamen, are open to public inspection: see s 287(1)(a); and PARA 1058. As to the Registrar General of Shipping and Seamen see PARA 62.
6 Merchant Shipping Act 1995 s 33(1). See note 5.
7 Merchant Shipping Act 1995 s 33(2). See note 5.

**487. Right, or loss of right, to wages where ship is wrecked or lost.** Where a United Kingdom ship which is a ship of traditional build or a non-commercial vessel[1] is wrecked[2] or lost[3], a seaman[4] whose employment in the ship is thereby terminated before the date contemplated in the agreement under which he is so employed is[5] entitled to wages[6] at the rate payable under the agreement at the date of the wreck or loss for every day on which he is unemployed in the two months following that date[7].

1 As to the vessels and seamen to which these provisions apply see PARA 484 note 3. As to the meaning of 'ship' see PARA 229; and as to the meaning of 'United Kingdom ship' see PARA 230. As to the meaning of 'United Kingdom' see PARA 16 note 3.
2 A ship is a 'wreck' if she is so seriously damaged that she ceases to be a navigable ship: *The Olympic* [1913] P 92 at 101, 12 Asp MLC 318 at 321, CA, per Bargrave Deane J. A ship which collided with another on her first day out, and was so damaged that she was unable to continue her voyage, although she was able to regain her port of departure under her own steam, was, therefore, held to be a 'wreck': *The Olympic*. A ship is not necessarily deemed a 'wreck' because underwriters have abandoned her (*Lloyd v Sheen* (1905) 10 Asp MLC 75, DC (discovery of contraband cargo)); and in any case abandonment must be clearly proved (*The Warrior* (1862) Lush 476). The scuttling of a ship in port to put out a fire has been held to constitute 'wreck or loss': *The Woodhorn* (1891) 92 LT Jo 113. A seaman incapacitated by accident in the course of duty was formerly by maritime custom entitled to his wages for the whole voyage: *Chandler v Grieves* (1792) 2 Hy Bl 606n.
3 Destruction of a neutral ship, not shown to have been carrying contraband of war, by a belligerent state constitutes 'loss' (*Sievwright v Allen* [1906] 2 KB 81, 10 Asp MLC 251); but, where, unknown to the crew, the vessel is carrying contraband of war, the crew's right to wages does not cease with the capture of the ship (*Austin Friars Steam Shipping Co v Strack* [1905] 2 KB 315, 10 Asp MLC 70, DC; on appeal [1906] 2 KB 499, CA). See also *Horlock v Beal* [1916] 1 AC 486, 13 Asp MLC 250, HL (where a British ship was detained in an enemy port at the outbreak of war, and the crew interned; it was held that the detention of the ship did not constitute 'loss of the ship' within what is now the Merchant Shipping Act 1995 s 38, but that the further performance of the crew's contract of service had become impossible from the date of the detention of the ship, and that a seaman ceased to be entitled to his wages as soon as the further performance of the contract became impossible). The provision that is now embodied in the Merchant Shipping Act 1995 s

38(1) is not exhaustive: *Horlock v Beal*. Loss may also be caused by explosion: see *Collins v Simpson Steamship Co* (1907) 24 TLR 178, CA. The wreck or loss may be deemed to occur not when the vessel goes ashore but when the venture terminates: *The Terneuzen* [1938] P 109, [1938] 2 All ER 348, 60 Ll L Rep 368. As to wreck see the cases cited in note 2; and *Barras v Aberdeen Steam Trawling and Fishing Co Ltd* [1933] AC 402, 18 Asp MLC 384, HL (applying the meaning of 'wreck' in what is now the Merchant Shipping Act 1995 s 38(1)).

4  The Merchant Shipping Act 1995 s 38 applies to a master as it does to a seaman: s 38(4). As to the meanings of 'master' and 'seaman' see PARA 457 note 5.
5  Ie subject to the Merchant Shipping Act 1995 s 38(2)–(4) (see PARA 470): see s 38(1).
6  As to the meaning of 'wages' see PARA 470 note 4.
7  Merchant Shipping Act 1995 s 38(1). See also *Ellerman Lines Ltd v Murray* [1931] AC 126, 18 Asp MLC 184, HL (where a seaman's right to wages during the period of two months was held to be irrespective of the date on which, had the ship not been wrecked or lost, his service would, under his agreement, have terminated).

D.  PROVISIONS APPLICABLE ONLY TO FISHING VESSELS

**488. Payment of wages under crew agreement relating to a United Kingdom fishing vessel.** The wages[1] due to a seaman[2] under a crew agreement relating to a United Kingdom fishing vessel[3] must[4] be paid to him in full[5].

1  As to the meaning of 'wages' see PARA 470 note 4.
2  As to the meaning of 'seaman' see PARA 457 note 5.
3  As to the meaning of 'fishing vessel' see PARA 230 note 9; and as to the meaning of 'United Kingdom fishing vessel' see PARA 230. As to the meaning of 'United Kingdom' see PARA 16 note 3.
4  Ie except as provided by or under the Merchant Shipping Act 1995 Pt III (ss 24–84) or any other enactment: see s 110. As to the payment of wages due to a seaman see in particular PARA 470 et seq. Section 110 applies to the exclusion of s 30 (payment of seaman's wages) (see PARA 484); and s 112 (accounts of wages and catch) (see PARA 489) applies to the exclusion of s 31 (account of seaman's wages) (see PARA 485): see s 24(3); and PARA 423 note 22.
5  Merchant Shipping Act 1995 s 110.

**489. Accounts of wages and catch.** The persons employing any seaman[1] under a crew agreement relating to a United Kingdom fishing vessel[2] must[3] deliver to him at a time prescribed by regulations[4] an account of the wages[5] due to him under that crew agreement and of the deductions subject to which the wages are payable[6].

Where the wages of any person employed in a United Kingdom fishing vessel are in any manner related to the catch, the persons employing him must at a time prescribed by such regulations deliver to the master[7] an account (or, if the master is the person employing him, make out an account) showing how those wages (or any part of those wages related to the catch) are arrived at and must make the account available to the crew in such manner as may be prescribed by the regulations[8].

Where there is a partnership between the master and any members of the crew of a United Kingdom fishing vessel, the owner of the vessel must at a time prescribed by such regulations make out an account showing the sums due to each partner in respect of his share and must make the account available to the partners[9].

The Secretary of State may make regulations prescribing the time at which any such account[10] is to be delivered or made out, and the manner in which the account[11] is to be made available[12].

If a person fails without reasonable excuse to comply with the provisions governing the accounting of wages (and catch where wages are related to catch) in relation to a United Kingdom fishing vessel, he commits an offence[13].

1  As to the meaning of 'seaman' see PARA 457 note 5.

2   As to the meaning of 'fishing vessel' see PARA 230 note 9; and as to the meaning of 'United Kingdom fishing vessel' see PARA 230. As to the application of these provisions see PARA 488 note 4. As to the meaning of 'United Kingdom' see PARA 16 note 3.

3   Ie subject to regulations made under the Merchant Shipping Act 1995 s 32 (see PARA 473) or s 75 (see PARA 550): see s 112(1).

4   Ie prescribed by regulations made under the Merchant Shipping Act 1995 s 112: see s 112(1). As to the Secretary of State see PARA 36; and as to his power to make subordinate legislation under the Merchant Shipping Act 1995 generally see PARA 39.

5   As to the meaning of 'wages' see PARA 470 note 4.

6   Merchant Shipping Act 1995 s 112(1). Section 112 applies to the exclusion of s 30 (see PARA 484): see s 24(3); and PARA 423 note 22. At the date at which this volume states the law, no regulations under s 112 had been made and none have effect as if so made. However, by virtue of the Interpretation Act 1978 s 17(2)(b), the Merchant Shipping (Seamen's Wages and Accounts) (Fishing Vessels) Regulations 1972, SI 1972/1701 (as to which see FISHERIES AND AQUACULTURE vol 51 (2013) PARA 315) have effect as if made under the Merchant Shipping Act 1995 s 32.

7   As to the meaning of 'master' see PARA 444 note 1.

8   Merchant Shipping Act 1995 s 112(2).

9   Merchant Shipping Act 1995 s 112(3).

10  Ie any account required by the Merchant Shipping Act 1995 s 112: see s 112(4).

11  Ie the account required by the Merchant Shipping Act 1995 s 112(2), (3) (see the text and notes 7–9): see s 112(4).

12  Merchant Shipping Act 1995 s 112(4).

13  See the Merchant Shipping Act 1995 s 112(5); and PARA 1075.

### (vi) Crew Accommodation

**490. Requirements relating to crew accommodation.** The requirements relating to crew accommodation[1] to be complied with by United Kingdom[2] ships are stated to apply to every United Kingdom ship[3] apart from fishing vessels[4], pleasure vessels[5], ships belonging to a General Lighthouse Authority[6] and ships falling within the Convention framework[7]: however, ships falling within the Convention framework are expressed to be subject to such regulations[8] in addition to those imposed pursuant to the Convention[9]. The regulations cover:

(1)    divisions between the crew accommodation and other parts of the ship[10];

(2)    interior bulkheads[11];

(3)    overhead decks[12];

(4)    floor decks[13];

(5)    access and escape arrangements[14];

(6)    pipes in crew accommodation spaces[15];

(7)    awnings[16];

(8)    heating[17];

(9)    lighting[18];

(10)   ventilation[19];

(11)   sidescuttles and windows[20];

(12)   drainage[21];

(13)   interior finishes[22];

(14)   marking[23];

(15)   sleeping rooms[24];

(16)   beds[25];

(17)   furniture and fittings in sleeping rooms[26];

(18)   mess rooms[27];

(19)   furniture and fittings in mess rooms[28];

(20)   recreation spaces[29];

(21)   offices[30];

(22)   sanitary accommodation[31];

(23)   supply of drinking water and the supply of fresh water[32];

(24)    facilities for washing and drying clothes and for hanging oilskins and working clothes[33];
(25)    galleys[34];
(26)    dry provision store rooms[35];
(27)    cold store rooms and refrigerating equipment[36];
(28)    hospitals[37];
(29)    medical cabinet[38];
(30)    protection from mosquitoes[39];
(31)    maintenance and inspection of crew accommodation[40].

It is the duty of an owner of a ship to which these regulations apply[41] to ensure that:

(a)    the floor coverings in the decks as referred to in head (4) above and in every permanent hospital as referred to in head (28) above[42];
(b)    the sidescuttles or windows in a sleeping room, day room, mess room, recreation room or hospital ward as referred to in head (11) above[43];
(c)    the vacuum discharge pipe systems that are required to be connected to every water closet and the thermostatic mixing valves that required to be fitted to every shower as referred to in head (22) above[44]; and
(d)    plant used to produce drinking water and/or fresh water on board a ship as referred to in head (23) above[45], are of an approved type[46].

However, the Secretary of State may grant exemptions from all or any of the provisions relating to approved equipment[47], as may be specified in the exemption, on such terms (if any) as he may so specify and may, subject to giving reasonable notice, alter or cancel any such exemption[48]. Any owner who fails to ensure the supply of approved equipment as mentioned in heads (a) to (d) above commits an offence[49]; and the ship may be detained[50].

If the provisions of any of the regulations are contravened[51] in the case of a ship, the owner or master is liable on summary conviction to a fine[52] and the ship, if in the United Kingdom, may be detained[53].

1    Ie the Merchant Shipping (Crew Accommodation) Regulations 1997, SI 1997/1508 (made under the Merchant Shipping Act 1995 s 43). For these purposes, 'crew accommodation' includes sleeping rooms, mess rooms, sanitary accommodation, hospital accommodation, recreation accommodation, store rooms and catering accommodation provided for the use of seamen but does not include any accommodation which is also used by or provided for the use of passengers (Merchant Shipping Act 1995 s 43(7)); in the context of the Merchant Shipping (Maritime Labour Convention) (Minimum Requirements for Seafarers etc) Regulations 2014, SI 2014/1613, Pt 7 (regs 29–33) (as to the application of which see note 8) it means accommodation, including the construction, machinery, fittings and equipment of that accommodation, intended for or used by seafarers (reg 29(1)). As to the meaning of 'seaman' see PARA 457 note 5. As to the meaning of 'seafarer' see PARA 423. General provisions regarding crew accommodation requirements are also set out: see reg 4. As to the power of the Secretary of State to make subordinate legislation under the Merchant Shipping Act 1995, including his power to appoint committees for the purpose of advising him when considering the making or alteration of any regulations etc, see PARA 39.
2    As to the meaning of 'ship' see PARA 229; and as to the meaning of 'United Kingdom ship' see PARA 230. As to the meaning of 'United Kingdom' see PARA 16 note 3.
3    Merchant Shipping (Crew Accommodation) Regulations 1997, SI 1997/1508, reg 3(1). The regulations do not apply:
    (1)    to any ship the keel of which was laid or which was at a similar stage of construction before 1 July 1979, and which has not been substantially reconstructed or altered since that date, provided that it complies with the standards laid down in the Merchant Shipping (Crew Accommodation) Regulations 1978, SI 1978/795 (revoked), as if they had not been revoked (Merchant Shipping (Crew Accommodation) Regulations 1997, SI 1997/1508, reg 3(3)); and
    (2)    to ships to which the Merchant Shipping (Maritime Labour Convention) (Minimum Requirements for Seafarers etc) Regulations 2014, SI 2014/1613, apply (reg 3(2)(d) (added by SI 2014/1614)), although they are indirectly applied to such ships by the operation of reg 29(2) (see the text and notes 7–8).

See further PARA 423 notes 14, 22. The Merchant Shipping (Crew Accommodation) Regulations 1997, SI 1997/1508, also do not apply to certain vessels which have met the stated requirements set out in the Merchant Shipping (Vessels in Commercial Use for Sport or Pleasure) Regulations 1998, SI 1998/2771: see PARA 613. As to fishing vessels see the Fishing Vessels (Safety of 15–24 Metre Vessels) Regulations 2002, SI 2002/2201; the Merchant Shipping (Crew Accommodation) (Fishing Vessels) Regulations 1975, SI 1975/2220; and FISHERIES AND AQUACULTURE vol 51 (2013) PARA 310.

See also the Fishing Vessels (Safety of 15–24 Metre Vessels) Regulations 2002, SI 2002/2201 (see FISHERIES AND AQUACULTURE vol 51 (2013) PARAS 309, 310), which have to some extent been made under the Merchant Shipping Act 1995 s 43 and, by virtue of the Interpretation Act 1978 s 17(2)(b), and the Merchant Shipping (Crew Accommodation) (Fishing Vessels) Regulations 1975, SI 1975/2220 (as to which see FISHERIES AND AQUACULTURE vol 51 (2013) PARA 310), which also have effect as if so made.

4    Merchant Shipping (Crew Accommodation) Regulations 1997, SI 1997/1508, reg 3(2)(a). 'Fishing vessel' means a vessel for the time being used (or, in the context of an application for registration, intended to be used) for, or in connection with, fishing for seafish other than a vessel used (or intended to be used) for fishing otherwise than for profit and any vessel for the time being used (or intended to be used) wholly for the purpose of conveying persons wishing to fish for pleasure: reg 2(1).

5    Merchant Shipping (Crew Accommodation) Regulations 1997, SI 1997/1508, reg 3(2)(b). As to the meaning of 'pleasure vessel' see PARA 423 note 23.

6    Merchant Shipping (Crew Accommodation) Regulations 1997, SI 1997/1508, reg 3(2)(c). As to General Lighthouse Authorities see PARA 1017.

7    Ie ships to which the Merchant Shipping (Maritime Labour Convention) (Minimum Requirements for Seafarers etc) Regulations 2014, SI 2014/1613, apply: Merchant Shipping (Crew Accommodation) Regulations 1997, SI 1997/1508, reg 3(2)(d) (added by SI 2014/1614). The Merchant Shipping (Maritime Labour Convention) (Minimum Requirements for Seafarers etc) Regulations 2014, SI 2014/1613 apply to all sea-going United Kingdom ships wherever they may be, and to non-United Kingdom sea-going ships in United Kingdom waters whose crews are not otherwise protected by the applicable Convention provisions: see PARA 423. The provision of the Maritime Labour Convention dealing with accommodation and recreational facilities is reg 3.1.

8    See the Merchant Shipping (Maritime Labour Convention) (Minimum Requirements for Seafarers etc) Regulations 2014, SI 2014/1613, regs 29(2), 30(2), (3), read with Merchant Shipping Notice 1844 (M), para 1.3. Those provisions together provide that ships constructed, or substantially reconstructed or altered on or after July 1997, but before 7 August 2014 (ie the date on which the Merchant Shipping (Maritime Labour Convention) (Minimum Requirements for Seafarers etc) Regulations 2014, SI 2014/1613, were brought into force), must comply with the requirements relating to ship construction and equipment set out in the Merchant Shipping (Crew Accommodation) Regulations 1997, SI 1997/1508. For ships which were constructed before 11 July 1997, and not substantially reconstructed or altered after that, the requirements relating to ship construction and equipment that are set out in the Merchant Shipping (Crew Accommodation) Regulations 1978, SI 1978/795 (revoked and replaced by the Merchant Shipping (Crew Accommodation) Regulations 1997, SI 1997/1508) continue to apply: see the Merchant Shipping (Maritime Labour Convention) (Minimum Requirements for Seafarers etc) Regulations 2014, SI 2014/1613, reg 30(1), read with Merchant Shipping Notice 1844 (M), para 1.4. A breach of the Merchant Shipping (Maritime Labour Convention) (Minimum Requirements for Seafarers etc) Regulations 2014, SI 2014/1613, reg 29(2) or reg 30(1) or (2) is an offence by the shipowner, punishable on summary conviction by a fine: see regs 29(3), 30(4), 59(5)(a), (b). As to the powers of magistrates' courts to issue fines on summary conviction see SENTENCING vol 92 (2015) PARA 176. As to the meaning of 'shipowner' see PARA 448 note 4.

The Secretary of State may exempt a ship from some or all of the requirements of reg 29(2) where the exemption is expressly permitted by Standard A3.1 (accommodation and recreational facilities) of the Convention (reg 31(1)(a)) and the Secretary of State has fulfilled any obligation imposed on the competent authority by that Standard in respect of the exemption (reg 31(1)(b)). In reg 31(1)(a), the reference to an exemption which is expressly permitted includes anything permitted in accordance with paragraph 6(a) or (d) of Standard A3.1 of the Convention or allowed in accordance with paragraph 9(g) of that Standard: reg 31(1). An exemption under reg 31 must be given in writing, may be granted on such terms as the Secretary of State may specify and may be altered or cancelled by the Secretary of State giving written notice to the shipowner: reg 31(2). A breach of the terms of an exemption granted under reg 31(1) is an offence by the shipowner punishable on summary conviction by a fine: see regs 31(3), 59(5)(c).

In respect of a particular ship, or ships of a particular description, the Secretary of State may approve arrangements which, when taken together with the conditions to which the approval is subject, the Secretary of State considers are substantially equivalent to the requirements which are set out in Merchant Shipping Notice 1844(M): Merchant Shipping (Maritime Labour Convention) (Minimum Requirements for Seafarers etc) Regulations 2014, SI 2014/1613, reg 32(1). Such an approval must be given in writing; and must specify the date on which it takes effect and the conditions (if any) on which it is given: reg 32(2). Such an approval may be cancelled and the terms of an approval may be altered, in both cases by the Secretary of State giving written notice to the shipowner: reg 32(3). A breach of a condition on which such an approval is given is an offence by the shipowner punishable on summary conviction by a fine: see regs 32(4), 59(5)(d).

A sea-going non-United Kingdom ship in United Kingdom waters which is subject to the Maritime Labour Convention (see the Merchant Shipping (Maritime Labour Convention) (Minimum Requirements for Seafarers etc) Regulations 2014, SI 2014/1613, regs 3(3), (4)(b)(v); and PARA 423 note 9) must not be operated unless it complies with the minimum standards for on-board accommodation and recreational facilities set out in paragraphs 6 to 17 of Standard A3.1 (accommodation and recreational facilities) of the Convention: Merchant Shipping (Maritime Labour Convention) (Minimum Requirements for Seafarers etc) Regulations 2014, SI 2014/1613, reg 33(1). This is subject to the application provision in paragraph 2 of Regulation 3.1 of the Convention and any permissions, exemptions or variations which have been granted or allowed by the state whose flag the ship is entitled to fly and which are permitted by the Convention provisions referred to in reg 33(1): reg 33(2). A breach of reg 33(1) is an offence by the shipowner punishable on summary conviction by a fine: see regs 33(3), 59(5)(e).

9   As to these see PARA 491 et seq.
10  See the Merchant Shipping (Crew Accommodation) Regulations 1997, SI 1997/1508, reg 5.
11  See the Merchant Shipping (Crew Accommodation) Regulations 1997, SI 1997/1508, reg 6.
12  See the Merchant Shipping (Crew Accommodation) Regulations 1997, SI 1997/1508, reg 7.
13  See the Merchant Shipping (Crew Accommodation) Regulations 1997, SI 1997/1508, reg 8.
14  See the Merchant Shipping (Crew Accommodation) Regulations 1997, SI 1997/1508, reg 9.
15  See the Merchant Shipping (Crew Accommodation) Regulations 1997, SI 1997/1508, reg 10.
16  See the Merchant Shipping (Crew Accommodation) Regulations 1997, SI 1997/1508, reg 11.
17  See the Merchant Shipping (Crew Accommodation) Regulations 1997, SI 1997/1508, reg 12.
18  See the Merchant Shipping (Crew Accommodation) Regulations 1997, SI 1997/1508, reg 13, Schedule.
19  See the Merchant Shipping (Crew Accommodation) Regulations 1997, SI 1997/1508, reg 14.
20  See the Merchant Shipping (Crew Accommodation) Regulations 1997, SI 1997/1508, reg 15.
21  See the Merchant Shipping (Crew Accommodation) Regulations 1997, SI 1997/1508, reg 16.
22  See the Merchant Shipping (Crew Accommodation) Regulations 1997, SI 1997/1508, reg 17.
23  See the Merchant Shipping (Crew Accommodation) Regulations 1997, SI 1997/1508, reg 18.
24  See the Merchant Shipping (Crew Accommodation) Regulations 1997, SI 1997/1508, reg 19.
25  See the Merchant Shipping (Crew Accommodation) Regulations 1997, SI 1997/1508, reg 20.
26  See the Merchant Shipping (Crew Accommodation) Regulations 1997, SI 1997/1508, reg 21.
27  See the Merchant Shipping (Crew Accommodation) Regulations 1997, SI 1997/1508, reg 22.
28  See the Merchant Shipping (Crew Accommodation) Regulations 1997, SI 1997/1508, reg 23.
29  See the Merchant Shipping (Crew Accommodation) Regulations 1997, SI 1997/1508, reg 24.
30  See the Merchant Shipping (Crew Accommodation) Regulations 1997, SI 1997/1508, reg 25.
31  See the Merchant Shipping (Crew Accommodation) Regulations 1997, SI 1997/1508, reg 26.
32  See the Merchant Shipping (Crew Accommodation) Regulations 1997, SI 1997/1508, reg 27.
33  See the Merchant Shipping (Crew Accommodation) Regulations 1997, SI 1997/1508, reg 28.
34  See the Merchant Shipping (Crew Accommodation) Regulations 1997, SI 1997/1508, reg 29.
35  See the Merchant Shipping (Crew Accommodation) Regulations 1997, SI 1997/1508, reg 30.
36  See the Merchant Shipping (Crew Accommodation) Regulations 1997, SI 1997/1508, reg 31.
37  See the Merchant Shipping (Crew Accommodation) Regulations 1997, SI 1997/1508, reg 32.
38  See the Merchant Shipping (Crew Accommodation) Regulations 1997, SI 1997/1508, reg 33.
39  See the Merchant Shipping (Crew Accommodation) Regulations 1997, SI 1997/1508, reg 34.
40  See the Merchant Shipping (Crew Accommodation) Regulations 1997, SI 1997/1508, reg 35.
41  As to the application of the Merchant Shipping (Crew Accommodation) Regulations 1997, SI 1997/1508, see note 1.
42  See the Merchant Shipping (Crew Accommodation) Regulations 1997, SI 1997/1508, reg 36(1)(a).
43  See the Merchant Shipping (Crew Accommodation) Regulations 1997, SI 1997/1508, reg 36(1)(b).
44  See the Merchant Shipping (Crew Accommodation) Regulations 1997, SI 1997/1508, reg 36(1)(c), (d).
45  See the Merchant Shipping (Crew Accommodation) Regulations 1997, SI 1997/1508, reg 36(1)(e).
46  See the Merchant Shipping (Crew Accommodation) Regulations 1997, SI 1997/1508, reg 36(1). For these purposes, 'approved', in relation to an item of equipment, means approved under the

Merchant Shipping (Marine Equipment) Regulations 2016, SI 2016/1025 (see PARA 638): reg 36(2). As to the Secretary of State see PARA 36.

47 Ie the requirements of the Merchant Shipping (Crew Accommodation) Regulations 1997, SI 1997/1508, Pt III (regs 36–39): see reg 37.

48 Merchant Shipping (Crew Accommodation) Regulations 1997, SI 1997/1508, reg 37.

49 See the Merchant Shipping (Crew Accommodation) Regulations 1997, SI 1997/1508, reg 38; and PARA 1076.

50 See the Merchant Shipping (Crew Accommodation) Regulations 1997, SI 1997/1508, reg 39; and PARA 1076.

51 As to the meaning of 'contravention' see PARA 51 note 3.

52 As to the powers of magistrates' courts to issue fines on summary conviction see SENTENCING vol 92 (2015) PARA 176.

53 Merchant Shipping Act 1995 s 43(6). As to enforcing the detention of a ship under the Merchant Shipping Act 1995 see PARA 1190.

**491. Inspections and records.** In the context of a ship falling within the Convention framework[1], the master of the ship, or an officer appointed by the master for that purpose, must:

(1)     at intervals not exceeding seven days and accompanied by at least one member of the crew, inspect the crew accommodation[2] to ensure it is clean, decently habitable and maintained in a good state of repair[3]; and

(2)     record the findings of inspections so undertaken in the official log book of the ship[4].

A breach of either of these requirements is an offence by the master of the ship[5].

1 Ie a ship to which the Merchant Shipping (Maritime Labour Convention) (Minimum Requirements for Seafarers etc) Regulations 2014, SI 2014/1613, applies: see PARAS 423, 490. As to the meaning of 'ship' see PARA 423 note 2.

2 As to the meaning of 'crew accommodation' see PARA 490 note 1.

3 Merchant Shipping (Maritime Labour Convention) (Minimum Requirements for Seafarers etc) Regulations 2014, SI 2014/1613, reg 29(4).

4 Merchant Shipping (Maritime Labour Convention) (Minimum Requirements for Seafarers etc) Regulations 2014, SI 2014/1613, reg 29(6). The record must specify:

    (1)     the time and date of the inspection (reg 29(6)(a));

    (2)     the name and rank of each person making the inspection (reg 29(6)(b)); and

    (3)     particulars of any respect in which the crew accommodation was found by any of the persons making the inspection not to comply with the Merchant Shipping (Maritime Labour Convention) (Minimum Requirements for Seafarers etc) Regulations 2014, SI 2014/1613 (reg 29(6)(c)).

5 Merchant Shipping (Maritime Labour Convention) (Minimum Requirements for Seafarers etc) Regulations 2014, SI 2014/1613, reg 29(5), (7). The offence is punishable on summary conviction by a fine: see reg 59(3)(f), (4)(d). As to the powers of magistrates' courts to issue fines on summary conviction see SENTENCING vol 92 (2015) PARA 176. The master of a ship must comply with the requirements in paragraph 18 of Standard A3.1 of the Maritime Labour Convention with regard to frequent inspections and the recording of the results of such inspections and making those results available for review, whether or not the state whose flag the ship is entitled to fly has imposed those requirements in its national laws or otherwise: Merchant Shipping (Maritime Labour Convention) (Minimum Requirements for Seafarers etc) Regulations 2014, SI 2014/1613, reg 33(4). A breach of reg 33(4) is an offence by the master of the ship punishable on summary conviction by a fine: see regs 33(5), 59(1), (4)(e).

### (vii) Catering and Medical Care

A.     UNITED KINGDOM SHIPS AND SHIPS IN UNITED KINGDOM WATERS

**492. Requirement to provide food and drinking water.** The shipowner[1] and the master of a ship which is a United Kingdom ship or a non-United Kingdom ship in United Kingdom waters[2] must ensure that food and drinking water are provided on board the ship which:

(1)    are suitable in respect of quantity, quality and, in relation to food, nutritional value and variety, taking account of the number of seafarers[3] on board and the character, nature and duration of the voyage and the different religious requirements and cultural practices in relation to food of the seafarers on board[4];

(2)    do not contain anything which is likely to cause sickness or injury to health or which renders any food or drinking water unpalatable[5]; and

(3)    are otherwise fit for consumption[6].

The shipowner and master of a ship must ensure that food and drinking water provided in accordance with the above are provided free of charge to all seafarers while they are on board[7].

A breach of either of these requirements is an offence by the shipowner and the master of the ship[8].

1    As to the meaning of 'shipowner' see PARA 448 note 4.

2    The reference to a United Kingdom ship and a non-United Kingdom ship in United Kingdom waters is a reference to a ship to which the Merchant Shipping (Maritime Labour Convention) (Minimum Requirements for Seafarers etc) Regulations 2014, SI 2014/1613 (which implements in United Kingdom law the Maritime Labour Convention (Cm 7049)), applies, that is, any such ship other than a fishing vessel, a ship of traditional build, a pleasure vessel, a warship or naval auxiliary vessel or a vessel not ordinarily engaged in commercial activities: see further PARA 423. As to the meaning of 'ship' see PARA 423 note 2. The provision of the Convention concerned with catering and medical care are regs 3.2, 4.1. Corresponding provision relating to other types of vessel continues to be made under the Merchant Shipping (Provisions and Water) Regulations 1989, SI 1989/102; in connection with employment on fishing vessels, ships of traditional build and non-commercial vessels see the Merchant Shipping Act 1995: see ss 44, 45; and PARAS 500–501.

    A sea-going non-United Kingdom ship in United Kingdom waters which is subject to the Maritime Labour Convention (see the Merchant Shipping (Maritime Labour Convention) (Minimum Requirements for Seafarers etc) Regulations 2014, SI 2014/1613, regs 3(3), (4)(b)(vi); and PARA 423 note 9) must not be operated unless it complies with paragraphs 1 and 2 of Regulation 3.2 (food and catering) of the Maritime Labour Convention: Merchant Shipping (Maritime Labour Convention) (Minimum Requirements for Seafarers etc) Regulations 2014, SI 2014/1613, reg 41(1). The master of a ship must comply with the requirements in paragraph 7 of Standard A3.2 of the Convention with regard to frequent inspections and the documenting of such inspections, whether or not the State whose flag the ship is entitled to fly has imposed those requirements in its national laws or otherwise: Merchant Shipping (Maritime Labour Convention) (Minimum Requirements for Seafarers etc) Regulations 2014, SI 2014/1613, reg 41(3). A ship must not be operated unless it meets the minimum standards set out in sub-paragraph 2(b) of Standard A3.2 of the Convention (Merchant Shipping (Maritime Labour Convention) (Minimum Requirements for Seafarers etc) Regulations 2014, SI 2014/1613, reg 41(5)(a)) and sub-paragraph 2(c) of that Standard (Merchant Shipping (Maritime Labour Convention) (Minimum Requirements for Seafarers etc) Regulations 2014, SI 2014/1613, reg 41(5)(b)). Subject to any dispensation issued by the state whose flag the ship is entitled to fly in accordance with paragraph 6 of standard A3.2 of the Convention, a shipowner must comply with the requirements in paragraphs 3 and 4 of Standard A3.2 of the Convention: Merchant Shipping (Maritime Labour Convention) (Minimum Requirements for Seafarers etc) Regulations 2014, SI 2014/1613, reg 41(8). A breach of reg 41(1) or (5)(a) is an offence by the shipowner and the master of the ship; a breach of reg 41(3) is an offence by the master of the ship; and a breach of reg 41(5)(b) or (8) is an offence by the shipowner: reg 41(2). (4), (6), (7), (9). The offence is punishable by a fine: see reg 59(1), (3)(i), (5)(g). As to the powers of magistrates' courts to issue fines on summary conviction see SENTENCING vol 92 (2015) PARA 176.

3    As to the meaning of 'seafarer' see PARA 423.

4    Merchant Shipping (Maritime Labour Convention) (Minimum Requirements for Seafarers etc) Regulations 2014, SI 2014/1613, reg 34(1)(a).

5    Merchant Shipping (Maritime Labour Convention) (Minimum Requirements for Seafarers etc) Regulations 2014, SI 2014/1613, reg 34(1)(b).

6    Merchant Shipping (Maritime Labour Convention) (Minimum Requirements for Seafarers etc) Regulations 2014, SI 2014/1613, reg 34(1)(c).

7    Merchant Shipping (Maritime Labour Convention) (Minimum Requirements for Seafarers etc) Regulations 2014, SI 2014/1613, reg 34(2).

8    Merchant Shipping (Maritime Labour Convention) (Minimum Requirements for Seafarers etc) Regulations 2014, SI 2014/1613, reg 34(3). The offence is punishable by a fine: see reg 59(1).

**493. Organisation and inspection of food and catering facilities.** The shipowner[1] and the master of a ship which is a United Kingdom ship or a non-United Kingdom ship in United Kingdom waters[2] must ensure that food and drinking water which are provided for seafarers[3] are stored and handled, and the catering department[4] is organised and equipped, in accordance with the regulatory[5] requirements[6]. The master of such a ship must also ensure that, not less than once a week the supplies of food and drinking water on board are[7] inspected[8] and the catering department and its equipment are[9] inspected[10]. Such an inspection must be carried out by the master of the ship or a person authorised by the master, together with a member of the catering staff[11]. The master of the ship must ensure that the results of any such inspection are recorded in the official logbook of the ship[12].

A breach of any of these requirements is an offence by the master of the ship[13].

1 As to the meaning of 'shipowner' see PARA 448 note 4.
2 As to the ships to which these provisions apply see PARA 492 note 2.
3 As to the meaning of 'seafarer' see PARA 423.
4 'Catering department' means the galley, mess rooms and any other areas on board intended or used for the storage or preparation of food for seafarers or the service of meals to seafarers: Merchant Shipping (Maritime Labour Convention) (Minimum Requirements for Seafarers etc) Regulations 2014, SI 2014/1613, reg 42.
5 Ie the requirements set out in Merchant Shipping Notice 1845(M).
6 Merchant Shipping (Maritime Labour Convention) (Minimum Requirements for Seafarers etc) Regulations 2014, SI 2014/1613, reg 35(1).
7 Ie to check compliance with the Merchant Shipping (Maritime Labour Convention) (Minimum Requirements for Seafarers etc) Regulations 2014, SI 2014/1613, reg 34 (see PARA 492) and reg 35 (see the text and notes 1–6).
8 Merchant Shipping (Maritime Labour Convention) (Minimum Requirements for Seafarers etc) Regulations 2014, SI 2014/1613, reg 36(1)(a).
9 Ie to check compliance with the Merchant Shipping (Maritime Labour Convention) (Minimum Requirements for Seafarers etc) Regulations 2014, SI 2014/1613, reg 35.
10 Merchant Shipping (Maritime Labour Convention) (Minimum Requirements for Seafarers etc) Regulations 2014, SI 2014/1613, reg 36(1)(b).
11 Merchant Shipping (Maritime Labour Convention) (Minimum Requirements for Seafarers etc) Regulations 2014, SI 2014/1613, reg 36(2). 'Catering staff' means seafarers whose normal duties include the preparation and storage of food, the service of meals to seafarers on board the ship or other work in the galley or in areas where food is stored or handled: reg 42.
12 Merchant Shipping (Maritime Labour Convention) (Minimum Requirements for Seafarers etc) Regulations 2014, SI 2014/1613, reg 36(4).
13 Merchant Shipping (Maritime Labour Convention) (Minimum Requirements for Seafarers etc) Regulations 2014, SI 2014/1613, regs 35(2), 36(3), (5). The offence is punishable on summary conviction by a fine: see reg 59(1), (2)(d), (3)(h).

**494. Certification of ship's cooks and training of catering staff.** On receipt of an application for a certificate of competency as a ship's cook and the appropriate fee (if any), the Secretary of State[1] must, on being satisfied that the applicant is an eligible person[2], issue a certificate of competency to the applicant[3]. Before the issue of any such certificate, the Secretary of State may require the applicant to produce such certificates of discharge and such other documentary evidence as may be necessary to establish to the satisfaction of the Secretary of State that the applicant is an eligible person[4]. Provision is made for the issue of duplicate certificates[5] and for the recognition of existing certificates[6].

The shipowner[7] must ensure that every member of catering staff is properly trained or instructed[8] for their position[9] and that any person processing food in the galley is properly trained or instructed[10] in areas including food and personal hygiene and handling[11]. A breach of these requirements is an offence by the shipowner[12].

1 As to the Secretary of State see PARA 36.
2 'Eligible person' means a seafarer who is 18 years of age or over and has completed training in accordance with the requirements in Merchant Shipping Notice 1846(M), and has served for not

less than one month at sea: Merchant Shipping (Maritime Labour Convention) (Minimum Requirements for Seafarers etc) Regulations 2014, SI 2014/1613, reg 42.

3 Merchant Shipping (Maritime Labour Convention) (Minimum Requirements for Seafarers etc) Regulations 2014, SI 2014/1613, reg 38(1). A record of all certificates of competency issued under these provisions and of the suspension, cancellation or alteration of, and any other matters affecting, any such certificate must be kept, in such manner as the Secretary of State may require, by the Registrar General of Shipping and Seamen or by such other person as the Secretary of State may direct: reg 38(8).

The provisions of the Merchant Shipping Act 1995 ss 62–69 (disqualification of seamen and inquiries) apply in respect of a certificate of competency issued under the Merchant Shipping (Maritime Labour Convention) (Minimum Requirements for Seafarers etc) Regulations 2014, SI 2014/1613, reg 38(1) as if such a certificate were a certificate to which those provisions apply (reg 38(3)); and for the purposes of any inquiry under the Merchant Shipping Act 1995 s 63 and of any re-hearing of an inquiry under s 64 in relation to a certificate of competency issued under the Merchant Shipping (Maritime Labour Convention) (Minimum Requirements for Seafarers etc) Regulations 2014, SI 2014/1613, reg 38(1), the Merchant Shipping (Section 63 Inquiries) Rules 1997, SI 1997/347 (see PARA 531 et seq) apply as if the definition of 'certificate holder' in r 2(1) included a reference to the holder of a certificate of competency issued under the Merchant Shipping (Maritime Labour Convention) (Minimum Requirements for Seafarers etc) Regulations 2014, SI 2014/1613, reg 38(1) (reg 38(5)).The provisions prescribed in the Merchant Shipping (Disqualification of Holder of Seaman's Certificates) Regulations 1997, SI 1997/346 (see PARA 509) apply in respect of a certificate of competency issued under the Merchant Shipping (Maritime Labour Convention) (Minimum Requirements for Seafarers etc) Regulations 2014, SI 2014/1613, reg 38(1) as if the Merchant Shipping (Disqualification of Holder of Seaman's Certificates) Regulations 1997, SI 1997/346, reg 2 included a reference to such a certificate (Merchant Shipping (Maritime Labour Convention) (Minimum Requirements for Seafarers etc) Regulations 2014, SI 2014/1613, reg 38(4)).

4 Merchant Shipping (Maritime Labour Convention) (Minimum Requirements for Seafarers etc) Regulations 2014, SI 2014/1613, reg 38(2).

5 If an eligible person satisfies the Secretary of State that a certificate already issued to that person has been lost, destroyed or stolen and pays the appropriate fee (if any), the Secretary of State must issue a copy of the certificate to that person: Merchant Shipping (Maritime Labour Convention) (Minimum Requirements for Seafarers etc) Regulations 2014, SI 2014/1613, reg 38(6). Any such copy must, before it is so issued, be certified as such by the Registrar General of Shipping and Seamen or, as the case may be, by such person as the Secretary of State may have directed to keep the record referred to in reg 38(8): reg 38(7).

6 A certificate of competency issued under the Merchant Shipping (Certification of Ships' Cooks) Regulations 1981, SI 1981/1076 (revoked) treated as equivalent under reg 8, or deemed under reg 9 to be issued pursuant to the Merchant Shipping Act 1970 s 43 (repealed), which is in force and not suspended on 7 August 2014 (ie the date on which the Merchant Shipping (Maritime Labour Convention) (Minimum Requirements for Seafarers etc) Regulations 2014, SI 2014/1613, came into force), has effect as if it were a certificate of competency as a ship's cook issued under reg 38: reg 39(1). A certificate to which reg 39(1) applies remains valid for a period of 5 years beginning on 7 August 2014 unless it is suspended or cancelled in accordance with the Merchant Shipping Act 1995 s 62 (see PARA 508): Merchant Shipping (Maritime Labour Convention) (Minimum Requirements for Seafarers etc) Regulations 2014, SI 2014/1613, reg 39(2).

7 As to the ships to which these provisions apply see PARA 492 note 2.

8 Ie in accordance with the relevant requirements set out in Merchant Shipping Notice 1846(M).

9 Merchant Shipping (Maritime Labour Convention) (Minimum Requirements for Seafarers etc) Regulations 2014, SI 2014/1613, reg 40(1)(a).

10 See note 8.

11 Merchant Shipping (Maritime Labour Convention) (Minimum Requirements for Seafarers etc) Regulations 2014, SI 2014/1613, reg 40(1)(b).

12 Merchant Shipping (Maritime Labour Convention) (Minimum Requirements for Seafarers etc) Regulations 2014, SI 2014/1613, reg 40(2). The offence is punishable by a fine: see reg 59(1). As to the powers of magistrates' courts to issue fines on summary conviction see SENTENCING vol 92 (2015) PARA 176.

## 495. Requirement that a ship's cook is on board.

A ship which is a United Kingdom ship or a non-United Kingdom ship in United Kingdom waters[1] must not be operated unless a qualified ship's cook[2] is on board[3]. In circumstances of exceptional necessity the Secretary of State[4] may grant an exemption from this requirement until the next port of call or for a period not exceeding one month, but only if there is a person on board the ship who is trained or instructed[5] in areas including food and personal hygiene and safe handling and storage of food[6]. The Secretary of State may also approve as respects a particular ship, or as respects ships of a particular description, arrangements which, when taken together with the conditions to which the approval is subject, the Secretary of State considers are substantially equivalent to the statutory requirement[7] that a ship's cook be aboard[8]. A breach of these requirements[9] is an offence by the shipowner and the master of the ship[10].

1   As to the ships to which these provisions apply see PARA 492 note 2. The Merchant Shipping (Maritime Labour Convention) (Minimum Requirements for Seafarers etc) Regulations 2014, SI 2014/1613, reg 37 (see the text and notes 2–10) does not apply to a ship which ordinarily operates with fewer than 10 seafarers on board a ship which operates only within 60 miles of a safe haven and which does not operate to or from, or call at, a port in a country other than the United Kingdom: reg 37(1). 'Safe haven' means a harbour or shelter of any kind which affords entry and protection from the weather: reg 37(1). As to the meaning of 'seafarer' see PARA 423. As to the meaning of 'ship' see PARA 423 note 2. As to the meaning of 'United Kingdom' see PARA 16 note 3.
2   'Qualified ship's cook' means a person who has been issued with a ship's cook certificate which has not expired or been cancelled and which is not suspended; 'ship's cook certificate' means a certificate of competency as a ship's cook which has been issued under the Merchant Shipping (Maritime Labour Convention) (Minimum Requirements for Seafarers etc) Regulations 2014, SI 2014/1613, reg 38 (see PARA 494); a certificate which under reg 39 (see PARA 494) which has effect as if it were a certificate of competency as a ship's cook issued under reg 38; or a certificate which the Secretary of State has specified in Merchant Shipping Notice 1846(M) is equivalent to a certificate of competency as a ship's cook issued under reg 38: reg 42.
3   Merchant Shipping (Maritime Labour Convention) (Minimum Requirements for Seafarers etc) Regulations 2014, SI 2014/1613, reg 37(2).
4   As to the Secretary of State see PARA 36.
5   Ie in accordance with the relevant requirements in Merchant Shipping Notice 1846(M).
6   Merchant Shipping (Maritime Labour Convention) (Minimum Requirements for Seafarers etc) Regulations 2014, SI 2014/1613, reg 37(3). Such an exemption must be given in writing, may be granted on such terms as the Secretary of State may specify and may be altered or cancelled by the Secretary of State giving written notice to the shipowner: reg 37(4).
7   Ie the requirement in the Merchant Shipping (Maritime Labour Convention) (Minimum Requirements for Seafarers etc) Regulations 2014, SI 2014/1613, reg 37(2) (see the text and notes 1–3).
8   Merchant Shipping (Maritime Labour Convention) (Minimum Requirements for Seafarers etc) Regulations 2014, SI 2014/1613, reg 37(5). Such an approval must be given in writing and must specify the date on which it takes effect and the conditions (if any) on which it is given: reg 37(6). Such an approval may be cancelled and the terms of an approval may be altered, in both cases by the Secretary of State giving written notice to the shipowner: reg 37(7).
9   Ie a breach of the Merchant Shipping (Maritime Labour Convention) (Minimum Requirements for Seafarers etc) Regulations 2014, SI 2014/1613, reg 37(2), of the terms of an exemption granted under reg 37(3) (see the text and notes 4–6) or of a condition on which an approval is given under reg 37(5) (see the text and notes 7–8).
10  Merchant Shipping (Maritime Labour Convention) (Minimum Requirements for Seafarers etc) Regulations 2014, SI 2014/1613, reg 37(8). The offence is punishable by a fine: see reg 59(5)(f). As to the powers of magistrates' courts to issue fines on summary conviction see SENTENCING vol 92 (2015) PARA 176.

**496. Duty to carry medical practitioner and right to medical care.** A ship with 100 or more persons on board engaged on an international voyage lasting more than 72 hours[1] must not be operated unless a medical practitioner[2] is carried on board the ship[3] and it carries a qualified medical doctor[4] who is responsible for providing medical care[5]. Where a United Kingdom ship[6] does not carry a registered medical practitioner among the seamen[7] employed in it, the master[8] must make arrangements for securing that any medical attention on board the ship is given either by him or under his supervision by a person appointed by him for the purpose[9].

When a ship[10] is in a port of call, the shipowner[11] must permit a seafarer[12] to go ashore for medical attention of a kind which is not available on board the ship, where this is reasonably practicable[13]. In the case of a sea-going non-United Kingdom ship in United Kingdom waters which is subject to the Maritime Labour Convention[14], a seafarer must:

(1)     be given access to prompt and adequate medical care whilst working on board the ship at no cost to the seafarer[15]; and

(2)     be permitted to visit a qualified medical doctor or dentist without delay in ports of call, where practicable[16].

A breach of any of these requirements is an offence by the shipowner[17].

1   The Merchant Shipping (Maritime Labour Convention) (Minimum Requirements for Seafarers etc) Regulations 2014, SI 2014/1613, regs 44, 46(3) do not apply to a ship unless it has more than 100 persons on board and it is engaged on an international voyage lasting more than 72 hours: regs 44(2), 46(4). As to the ships and seafarers to which regs 44, 46 apply see PARA 492 note 2.

2   In this context 'medical practitioner' means (by virtue of the Merchant Shipping (Maritime Labour Convention) (Minimum Requirements for Seafarers etc) Regulations 2014, SI 2014/1613, reg 47):

(1)     in the case of a practitioner ordinarily resident in the United Kingdom, a fully registered person who holds a licence to practise or meets the criteria specified in Merchant Shipping Notice 1841(M), being criteria which the Secretary of State considers appropriate having regard to the evidence of continuing professional development which such a practitioner must demonstrate in order to obtain a licence to practise; or

(2)     in the case of a practitioner not ordinarily resident in the United Kingdom, a person who meets the criteria specified in Merchant Shipping Notice 1841(M), being criteria which the Secretary of State considers appropriate having regard to the qualifications and other credentials which must be demonstrated by a person falling within head (1) above.

As to the meanings of 'fully registered person' and 'licence to practice; see the Medical Act 1983 s 55(1); and MEDICAL PROFESSIONS vol 74 (2011) PARAS 176, 197 (definitions applied by the Merchant Shipping (Maritime Labour Convention) (Minimum Requirements for Seafarers etc) Regulations 2014, SI 2014/1613, reg 47).

3   Merchant Shipping (Maritime Labour Convention) (Minimum Requirements for Seafarers etc) Regulations 2014, SI 2014/1613, reg 44(1).

4   In this context 'qualified medical doctor' means a person who is recognised as such by, and who (for the purposes of sub-paragraph 4(b) of Standard A4.1 (medical care on board ship and ashore) of the Convention) has the qualifications required by, the state whose flag the ship is entitled to fly: Merchant Shipping (Maritime Labour Convention) (Minimum Requirements for Seafarers etc) Regulations 2014, SI 2014/1613, reg 46(6).

5   Merchant Shipping (Maritime Labour Convention) (Minimum Requirements for Seafarers etc) Regulations 2014, SI 2014/1613, reg 46(3).

6   As to the meaning of 'United Kingdom ship' in this context (these not being provisions deriving from the Merchant Shipping (Maritime Labour Convention) (Minimum Requirements for Seafarers etc) Regulations 2014, SI 2014/1613) see PARA 230. As to the meaning of 'ship' under the Merchant Shipping Act 1995 see PARA 229; and as to the meaning of 'United Kingdom' see PARA 16 note 3.

7   As to the meaning of seaman' see PARA 457 note 5.

8   As to the meaning of 'master' see PARA 444 note 1.

9   Merchant Shipping Act 1995 s 53. As to the application of s 53 see PARA 423.

As to the powers of inspectors appointed under s 256(6) (see PARA 46) to serve improvement notices or prohibition notices where s 53 and the provisions of any instrument of a legislative character having effect thereunder are being contravened, or where activities to which s 53 applies are carried on so as to involve serious personal injury or serious pollution, see PARA 51 et seq.

10  As to the ships and seafarers to which the Merchant Shipping (Maritime Labour Convention) (Minimum Requirements for Seafarers etc) Regulations 2014, SI 2014/1613, regs 45, 46(1), (2) apply see PARA 492 note 2.

11  As to the meaning of 'shipowner' see PARA 448 note 4.

12  As to the meaning of 'seafarer' see PARA 423.

13  Merchant Shipping (Maritime Labour Convention) (Minimum Requirements for Seafarers etc) Regulations 2014, SI 2014/1613, reg 45(1).

14  See the Merchant Shipping (Maritime Labour Convention) (Minimum Requirements for Seafarers etc) Regulations 2014, SI 2014/1613, regs 3(3), (4)(b)(vii); and PARA 423 note 9.

15  Merchant Shipping (Maritime Labour Convention) (Minimum Requirements for Seafarers etc) Regulations 2014, SI 2014/1613, reg 46(1)(a).

16  Merchant Shipping (Maritime Labour Convention) (Minimum Requirements for Seafarers etc) Regulations 2014, SI 2014/1613, reg 46(1)(b).

17 Merchant Shipping (Maritime Labour Convention) (Minimum Requirements for Seafarers etc) Regulations 2014, SI 2014/1613, regs 44(3), 45(2), 46(2), (5). The offence is punishable by a fine: see reg 59(1), (2)(e), (f). As to the powers of magistrates' courts to issue fines on summary conviction see SENTENCING vol 92 (2015) PARA 176.

**497. Medical expenses.** Where a seafarer[1] suffers sickness or injury which:

(1) first occurs during a period which starts on the date on which that seafarer's seafarer employment agreement[2] commences and ends on the next date on which the shipowner's[3] duty to make provision for the repatriation of that seafarer[4] ends[5], or which starts after such a period but is caused by circumstances or events arising during that period[6]; and

(2) does not first occur during a period of leave, other than shore leave[7],

the shipowner must ensure that the seafarer is provided with medical care on board, so far as is practicable[8], and meet any applicable expenses[9] which are reasonably incurred in connection with the seafarer's sickness or injury[10]. A breach of this requirement is an offence by the shipowner[11].

1 As to the meaning of 'seafarer' see PARA 423. As to the ships and seafarers to which these provisions apply see PARA 492 note 3.
2 As to seafarer employment agreements see PARAS 451–455.
3 As to the meaning of 'shipowner' see PARA 448 note 4.
4 Ie under the Merchant Shipping (Maritime Labour Convention) (Minimum Requirements for Seafarers etc) Regulations 2014, SI 2014/1613, reg 19 (see PARA 540).
5 Ie under the Merchant Shipping (Maritime Labour Convention) (Minimum Requirements for Seafarers etc) Regulations 2014, SI 2014/1613, reg 21 (see PARA 540).
6 Merchant Shipping (Maritime Labour Convention) (Minimum Requirements for Seafarers etc) Regulations 2014, SI 2014/1613, reg 43(1), (2)(a).
7 Merchant Shipping (Maritime Labour Convention) (Minimum Requirements for Seafarers etc) Regulations 2014, SI 2014/1613, reg 43(2)(b).
8 Merchant Shipping (Maritime Labour Convention) (Minimum Requirements for Seafarers etc) Regulations 2014, SI 2014/1613, reg 43(3)(a).
9 Ie expenses of surgical, medical, dental or optical treatment (including the supply, repair or replacement of any appliance) and expenses for board and lodging: Merchant Shipping (Maritime Labour Convention) (Minimum Requirements for Seafarers etc) Regulations 2014, SI 2014/1613, reg 43(4).
10 Merchant Shipping (Maritime Labour Convention) (Minimum Requirements for Seafarers etc) Regulations 2014, SI 2014/1613, reg 43(3)(b). The duty to meet expenses referred to in reg 43(3)(b) does not apply to expenses which are met by a public authority and does not affect any duty on the shipowner under reg 22 (see PARA 541) and does not apply in respect of any expenses met by the shipowner in accordance with that duty: reg 43(5).The duty to meet expenses referred to in reg 43(3)(b) is limited to expenses incurred during whichever of the following periods is the shorter:
    (1) a period of 16 weeks beginning on the day on which the sickness or injury first occurs (reg 43(6)(a)); or
    (2) a period beginning on the day on which the sickness or injury first occurs and ending on the day on which a person authorised to issue seafarer medical certificates notifies the seafarer of a decision that the seafarer is not fit to carry out the duties which that seafarer is required to carry out under the terms of that seafarer's seafarer employment agreement and the seafarer is unlikely to be fit to carry out duties of that nature in the future (reg 43(6)(b)).
    'Person authorised to issue seafarer medical certificates' means a person who has been authorised by or on behalf of the Secretary of State or another national maritime administration to issue medical certificates to seafarers for the purposes of the Maritime Labour Convention reg 1.2 (medical certificate: see PARAS 464–467) or the International Convention on Standards of Training, Certification and Watchkeeping for Seafarers 1978 (London, 1 December 1978 to 30 November 1979; TS 50 (1984); Cmnd 9266) ('the STCW Convention': see PARA 7) reg I/9: Merchant Shipping (Maritime Labour Convention) (Minimum Requirements for Seafarers etc) Regulations 2014, SI 2014/1613, reg 47. As to the Secretary of State see PARA 36. As to the Maritime Labour Convention see PARA 423. If a person authorised to issue seafarer medical certificates has notified a seafarer of a decision in the terms described in reg 43(6)(b) and that or another such person subsequently notifies the seafarer that such a decision no longer applies in both or either respects, the duty to meet expenses referred to in reg 43(3)(b) is limited to expenses incurred during the period set out in reg 43(6)(a): reg 43(7). The shipowner may recover from the seafarer as a civil debt any expenses it has met under the duty to meet expenses referred to in reg

43(3)(b) in connection with injury suffered otherwise than in the service of the ship, injury or sickness arising from the wilful misconduct of the seafarer who is injured or sick, or injury or sickness intentionally concealed by the seafarer prior to entering into the seafarer employment agreement: reg 43(8). If any expenses are incurred by a seafarer to which the duty in reg 43(3) applies, the seafarer may (other than in the circumstances referred to in reg 43(8)) recover those expenses from the shipowner as a civil debt: reg 43(9).

11 Merchant Shipping (Maritime Labour Convention) (Minimum Requirements for Seafarers etc) Regulations 2014, SI 2014/1613, reg 43(10). The offence is punishable by a fine: see reg 59(1). As to the powers of magistrates' courts to issue fines on summary conviction see SENTENCING vol 92 (2015) PARA 176.

**498. Requirement to carry on board prescribed medical stores.** Every United Kingdom ship and government ship (other than a ship employed in inland navigation, a pleasure vessel used for non-commercial purposes and not manned by a professional crew, or a tug[1] operating in harbour areas)[2] must carry on board prescribed medical stores[3].

All medical stores required to be so kept on board a vessel:

(1)     must conform to the standards and requirements of the British National Formulary, the British Pharmacopoeia, the European Pharmacopoeia or the United States Pharmacopoeia[4];

(2)     must be properly packaged and labelled[5], stored[6] and replenished[7].

Every such ship must carry guides as to the use of medical stores required to be so carried on board it appropriate to their categories, including in particular specified instructions for the use of antidotes[8].

The owner[9] of such a ship must ensure that the medical stores are inspected by a competent person or authority at least once a year to ensure that:

(a)     the ship is carrying the medical stores which it is so required to carry[10];

(b)     such medical stores are correctly stored[11];

(c)     any perishable medicines have been duly replaced[12].

Contravention of the above requirements is an offence[13]; and the ship may be detained until the above requirements are met if, after inspection, an inspector is satisfied that there has been a failure so to comply, in relation to that ship[14].

1   For these purposes, 'tug' means a vessel constructed solely for the purpose of, and normally used for, providing external motive power for floating objects or vessels: Merchant Shipping and Fishing Vessels (Medical Stores) Regulations 1995, SI 1995/1802, reg 1(3). The Merchant Shipping and Fishing Vessels (Medical Stores) Regulations 1995, SI 1995/1802, do not apply to a small commercial vessel which has been examined, and in respect of which a certificate has been issued, in accordance with the applicable Code of Practice, or to a vessel which is operating under the phase-in arrangements of the Code of Practice: see PARA 614.

2   See the Merchant Shipping and Fishing Vessels (Medical Stores) Regulations 1995, SI 1995/1802, reg 3. For these purposes, 'harbour area' means any harbour in the United Kingdom in respect of which a harbour authority, within the meaning of the Harbours Act 1964 (see PORTS AND HARBOURS vol 85 (2012) PARA 20), has statutory powers or duties of improvement, maintenance or management: Merchant Shipping and Fishing Vessels (Medical Stores) Regulations 1995, SI 1995/1802, reg 1(3).

3   See the Merchant Shipping and Fishing Vessels (Medical Stores) Regulations 1995, SI 1995/1802, reg 4. For these purposes, 'medical stores' includes medicines, medical equipment and antidotes: reg 1(3). The medical stores mentioned in the text are those specified in the Merchant Shipping and Fishing Vessels (Medical Stores) Regulations 1995, SI 1995/1802, reg 4(1), Table (Table amended by SI 1996/2821): see the Merchant Shipping and Fishing Vessels (Medical Stores) Regulations 1995, SI 1995/1802, reg 4.

4   See the Merchant Shipping and Fishing Vessels (Medical Stores) Regulations 1995, SI 1995/1802, reg 6.

5   Ie in accordance with the requirements of the Merchant Shipping and Fishing Vessels (Medical Stores) Regulations 1995, SI 1995/1802, reg 7 (packaging and labelling of containers).

6   Ie in accordance with the Merchant Shipping and Fishing Vessels (Medical Stores) Regulations 1995, SI 1995/1802, reg 8 (storage of medicines).

7   Ie in accordance with the Merchant Shipping and Fishing Vessels (Medical Stores) Regulations 1995, SI 1995/1802, reg 9 (replenishment of dated medicines).

8   See the Merchant Shipping and Fishing Vessels (Medical Stores) Regulations 1995, SI 1995/1802, reg 10.
9   For these purposes, 'owner', in relation to a ship, means the registered owner of the ship unless the ship has been chartered by demise or is managed, either wholly or in part, by a person other than the registered owner under the terms of a management agreement; in that case 'owner' includes the demise charterer or the person managing the ship, as the case may be: Merchant Shipping and Fishing Vessels (Medical Stores) Regulations 1995, SI 1995/1802, reg 1(3).
10  Merchant Shipping and Fishing Vessels (Medical Stores) Regulations 1995, SI 1995/1802, reg 11(a). The text refers to the medical stores required to be carried by reg 4 (see the text and notes 1–3): see reg 11(a).
11  Merchant Shipping and Fishing Vessels (Medical Stores) Regulations 1995, SI 1995/1802, reg 11(b).
12  Merchant Shipping and Fishing Vessels (Medical Stores) Regulations 1995, SI 1995/1802, reg 11(c). The text refers to perishable medicines replaced in accordance with the requirements of reg 9 (see note 7): see reg 11(c).
13  See the Merchant Shipping and Fishing Vessels (Medical Stores) Regulations 1995, SI 1995/1802, regs 12, 13. See also PARA 1117.
14  See the Merchant Shipping and Fishing Vessels (Medical Stores) Regulations 1995, SI 1995/1802, reg 14. Those provisions of the Merchant Shipping Act 1995 which deal with the enforcement of detention (ie s 284 (see PARA 1253)) are applied with modifications for these purposes: see the Merchant Shipping and Fishing Vessels (Medical Stores) Regulations 1995, SI 1995/1802, reg 15; Interpretation Act 1978 s 17(2)(b).

**499. Transfer from night duties on medical grounds.** If a medical practitioner[1] or medical referee has certified that a seafarer[2] engaged on watchkeeping duties is suffering from health problems which the practitioner considers to be due to the fact that the seafarer performs work during the night[3], and it is possible for the seafarer's employer to transfer the seafarer to work to which the seafarer is suited and which is to be undertaken during periods such that the seafarer will cease to perform work during the night, the employer must transfer the seafarer accordingly[4].

1   As to the meaning of 'medical practitioner' see PARA 464 note 4.
2   As to the meaning of 'seafarer' see PARA 423. As to the vessels and seafarers to which these provisions apply see PARA 464 note 2.
3   in this context 'night' means a period the duration of which is not less than nine consecutive hours and which includes the period between midnight and 5 am (local time): Merchant Shipping (Maritime Labour Convention) (Medical Certification) Regulations 2010, SI 2010/737, reg 15(2).
4   Merchant Shipping (Maritime Labour Convention) (Medical Certification) Regulations 2010, SI 2010/737, reg 15(1). An employer who fails to comply with reg 15(1) is guilty of an offence and liable on summary conviction to a fine: reg 18(2). In connection with offences see further PARA 464 note 2.

B.    FISHING VESSELS, SHIPS OF TRADITIONAL BUILD AND NON-COMMERCIAL VESSELS

**500. Complaints about provisions or water.** If three or more seamen[1] employed in a sea-going United Kingdom ship which is a fishing vessel, a ship of traditional build or a non-commercial vessel[2] consider that the provisions or water provided for the seamen employed in that ship are not in accordance with safety regulations[3] containing requirements as to the provisions and water to be provided on ships, whether of bad quality, unfitness for use or deficiency in quantity, they may complain to the master[4], who must investigate the complaint[5].

If the seamen are dissatisfied with the action taken by the master as a result of his investigation or by his failure to take any action, they may state their dissatisfaction to him and may claim to complain to a superintendent[6] or proper officer[7]; and thereupon the master must make adequate arrangements to enable the seamen to do so as soon as the service of the ship permits[8]. The superintendent or proper officer to whom a complaint has been so made must investigate the complaint and may examine the provisions or water or cause them to be examined[9].

If the master fails without reasonable excuse to comply with the procedure governing complaints so made to a superintendent or proper officer[10], he commits an offence[11]; and, if the master has been notified in writing by the person duly making an examination of the provisions or water[12] that any provisions or water are found to be unfit for use or not of the quality required by the safety regulations, then:

(1)	if they are not replaced within a reasonable time, the master or owner commits an offence unless he proves that the failure to replace them was not due to his neglect or default[13]; or

(2)	if the master without reasonable excuse permits them to be used, he commits an offence[14].

1	As to the meaning of 'seaman' see PARA 457 note 5.
2	The Merchant Shipping Act 1995 ss 44, 45 (see the text and notes 5–14; and PARA 501) apply only to United Kingdom ships (to which the legislation refers) which are fishing vessels, ships of traditional build or non-commercial vessels: see the Merchant Shipping Act 1995 s 24(2A); and PARA 423 note 22. As to the meaning of 'fishing vessel' see the Merchant Shipping Act 1995 s 313(1); and PARA 230. Corresponding provision relating to catering and medical care on other United Kingdom ships and non-United Kingdom ships in United Kingdom waters is governed by the Maritime Labour Convention (Cm 7049) and implemented by the Merchant Shipping (Maritime Labour Convention) (Minimum Requirements for Seafarers etc) Regulations 2014, SI 2014/1613: see regs 34–47; and PARA 492 et seq. As to the meaning of 'fishing vessel' see PARA 230. As to the meaning of 'ship' see PARA 229; and as to the meaning of 'United Kingdom ship' see PARA 230. As to the meaning of 'United Kingdom' see PARA 16 note 3.
3	As to the meaning of 'safety regulations' see PARA 602 note 1.
4	As to the meaning of 'master' see PARA 444 note 1.
5	Merchant Shipping Act 1995 s 44(1). As to the powers of inspectors appointed under s 256(6) (see PARA 46) to serve improvement notices or prohibition notices where s 44 and the provisions of any instrument of a legislative character having effect thereunder are being contravened, or where activities to which s 44 applies are carried on so as to involve serious personal injury or serious pollution, see PARA 51 et seq.
6	As to the meaning of 'superintendent' see PARA 61 note 1. As to the appointment of superintendents see PARA 61.
7	As to the meaning of 'proper officer' see PARA 48 note 4.
8	Merchant Shipping Act 1995 s 44(2).
9	Merchant Shipping Act 1995 s 44(3).
10	Ie the provisions of the Merchant Shipping Act 1995 s 44(2) (see the text and notes 6–8): see s 44(4).
11	See the Merchant Shipping Act 1995 s 44(4); and PARA 1077.
12	Ie under the Merchant Shipping Act 1995 s 44(3) (see the text and note 9): see s 44(4).
13	See the Merchant Shipping Act 1995 s 44(4)(a); and PARA 1077.
14	See the Merchant Shipping Act 1995 s 44(4)(b); and PARA 1077.

## 501. Expenses of medical and other treatment during voyage.

If a person, while employed in a sea-going United Kingdom ship which is a ship of traditional build or a non-commercial vessel[1], receives outside the United Kingdom any surgical or medical treatment or such dental or optical treatment, including the repair or replacement of any appliance, as cannot be postponed without impairing efficiency, the reasonable expenses thereof must be borne by the persons employing him[2].

If a person dies while employed in a United Kingdom ship[3] and is buried or cremated outside the United Kingdom, the expenses of his burial or cremation must also be borne by those persons[4].

1	As to the vessels and seamen to which these provisions apply see PARA 500 note 2. As to the meaning of 'ship' see PARA 229; and as to the meaning of 'United Kingdom ship' see PARA 230. As to the meaning of 'United Kingdom' see PARA 16 note 3.
2	Merchant Shipping Act 1995 s 45(1).

3	For these purposes, the reference to dying in a ship includes a reference to dying in a ship's boat: Merchant Shipping Act 1995 s 45(3); and, for the purposes of Pt III (ss 24–84), 'ship's boat' includes a life-raft: s 84(1).
4	Merchant Shipping Act 1995 s 45(2).

### (viii) Training, Certification and Manning

**502. Ships and voyages to which the training, certification and manning provisions apply.** The provisions governing manning, qualifications, training etc as they relate to masters[1] and seamen[2] apply to every United Kingdom ship[3], and also to any ship registered under the law of a country outside the United Kingdom which carries passengers[4] either:

(1)	between places in the United Kingdom or between the United Kingdom and the Isle of Man or any of the Channel Islands[5]; or

(2)	on a voyage which begins and ends at the same place in the United Kingdom and on which the ship calls at no place outside the United Kingdom[6].

1	As to the meaning of 'master' see PARA 444 note 1.
2	Ie the Merchant Shipping Act 1995 ss 47–51 (see PARAS 503–507): see s 46. As to the meaning of 'seaman' see PARA 457 note 5.
3	The Merchant Shipping Act 1995 ss 46–48, 50, 51 (and, by extension, s 62) and associated subordinate legislation (see the text and notes 4–6; and PARAS 503–509) apply to all United Kingdom ships: being concerned with matters with which the Merchant Shipping (Maritime Labour Convention) (Minimum Requirements for Seafarers etc) Regulations 2014, SI 2014/1613 and the Maritime Labour Convention (Cm 7049)) are not concerned (see PARA 423), these provisions are not limited to the vessels excluded from the scope of the Convention (see further PARA 423 note 22). As to the meaning of 'ship' see PARA 229; and as to the meaning of 'United Kingdom ship' see PARa 230. As to the meaning of 'United Kingdom' see PARA 16 note 3. The Merchant Shipping Act 1995 ss 47–50, 52 also extend to certain non-United Kingdom ships operating in inland and certain coastal waters: see the Merchant Shipping (Boatmasters' Qualifications, Crew and Hours of Work) Regulations 2015, SI 2015/410, reg 5. In connection with career development under the Maritime Labour Convention see reg 2.8.
4	Merchant Shipping Act 1995 s 46. As to the powers of inspectors appointed under s 256(6) (see PARA 46) to serve improvement notices or prohibition notices where s 46 and the provisions of any instrument of a legislative character having effect thereunder are being contravened, or where activities to which s 46 applies are carried on so as to involve serious personal injury or serious pollution, see PARA 51 et seq.
5	Merchant Shipping Act 1995 s 46(a).
6	Merchant Shipping Act 1995 s 46(b).

**503. Mandatory standards of competence and training.** Provision is made[1] specifying mandatory standards of competence and training and certification requirements which must be met by seafarers serving aboard sea-going ships and hovercraft registered in the United Kingdom[2]. Such provisions do not apply to a fishing vessel[3], a pleasure vessel[4] which is less than 80 GT[5] or under 24 metres in length[6], or a wooden ship of primitive build[7]. Certificates of competency or proficiency are prescribed, and their holding required, for ship's officers and security officers[8], seafarers performing engine-room and navigational watch duties[9], radiocommunication personel[10], electro-technical and rescue ratings and seafarers[11] and able seafarers[12]; and training is prescribed for seafarers generally[13], seafarers assigned specific safety roles[14], and seafarers on oil, gas and chemical tankers[15]. Provision is also made for the application, issuing, recognition, validity, cancellation, replacement and registration of certificates[16] and for ensuring the quality of training[17] and certification[18]. If these provisions are contravened a ship may be detained[19]; certain contraventions are also offences[20].

Any person serving or engaged to serve in any United Kingdom ship and holding any certificate or other document which is evidence that he is duly qualified[21] must on demand produce it to any superintendent[22], surveyor of ships[23]

or proper officer[24] and, if he is not himself the master[25], to the master of the ship[26]. If without reasonable excuse a person fails to comply with this requirement[27], he commits an offence[28].

1   Ie by the Merchant Shipping (Standards of Training, Certification and Watchkeeping) Regulations 2015, SI 2015/782, Pt 2 (regs 4–41) and Pt 3 (regs 42–44). The regulations are made under the Merchant Shipping Act 1995 s 47, Sch 14 para 4 (s 47 amended by the Marine Navigation Act 2013 s 10). As to the ships to which the training, certification and manning provisions apply see PARA 502; and as to the statutory framework relating to crews etc generally see PARA 423. As to the power of the Secretary of State to make subordinate legislation under the Merchant Shipping Act 1995, including his power to appoint committees for the purpose of advising him when considering the making or alteration of any regulations etc, see PARA 39.

    The Secretary of State may issue and record documents certifying the attainment of any standard of competence relating to ships or their operation, notwithstanding that the standard is not among those prescribed or otherwise specified pursuant to s 47, and may, in relation thereto, make regulations for purposes corresponding thereto: see s 54(1). At the date at which this volume states the law no such regulations had been made. As to the Secretary of State see PARA 36. If a person makes a statement which he knows to be false or recklessly makes a statement which is false in a material particular for the purpose of obtaining for himself or another person a document which may be issued under s 54, he commits an offence: see s 54(2); and PARA 1084. As to the powers of inspectors appointed under s 256(6) (see PARA 46) to serve improvement notices or prohibition notices where s 54 and the provisions of any instrument of a legislative character having effect thereunder are being contravened, or where activities to which s 54 applies are carried on so as to involve serious personal injury or serious pollution, see PARA 51 et seq.

    Provision is also made, pursuant to s 47, in connection with the qualifications to be held by the boatmasters and crew of United Kingdom and non-United Kingdom ships operating in inland and certain coastal United Kingdom waters: see the Merchant Shipping (Boatmasters' Qualifications, Crew and Hours of Work) Regulations 2015, SI 2015/410, Pts 2–7 (regs 6–54). See also the Merchant Shipping Act 1995 Sch 14 para 3 (certificates of competency and recognition of certificates granted overseas), under which no regulations relating to the issue of certificates currently have effect, although provision for recognition continues to be made under the following Orders in Council: the Merchant Shipping (Certificates of Competency as AB) (New Zealand) Order 1956, SI 1956/1895; the Merchant Shipping (Certificates of Competency as AB) (Barbados) Order 1957, SI 1957/1371; the Merchant Shipping (Certificates of Competency as AB) (Canada) Order 1959, SI 1959/2213; the Merchant Shipping (Certificates of Competency as AB) (Mauritius) Order 1960, SI 1960/1662; the Merchant Shipping (Certificates of Competency as AB) (Trinidad and Tobago) Order 1960, SI 1960/1663; the Merchant Shipping (Certificates of Competency as AB) (Ghana) Order 1963, SI 1963/1316; the Merchant Shipping (Certificates of Competency as AB) (Nigeria) Order 1964, SI 1964/700; the Merchant Shipping (Certificates of Competency as AB) (Gilbert and Ellice Islands Colony) Order 1972, SI 1972/1105; the Merchant Shipping (Certificates of Competency as AB) (Malta) Order 1975, SI 1975/1045; and the Merchant Shipping (Certificates of Competency as AB) (Isle of Man) Order 1986, SI 1986/2220.

2   See the Merchant Shipping (Standards of Training, Certification and Watchkeeping) Regulations 2015, SI 2015/782, regs 4, 42. As to the meaning of 'ship' see PARA 229; and as to the meaning of 'United Kingdom ship' see PARA 230. As to the meaning of 'United Kingdom' see PARA 16 note 3. For the provisions of the Maritime Labour Convention (Cm 7049)) dealing with training and qualifications see reg 1.3; in connection with health and safety and accident prevention see reg 4.3' in connection with access to shore-based welfare facilities see reg 4.4.

3   Merchant Shipping (Standards of Training, Certification and Watchkeeping) Regulations 2015, SI 2015/782, reg 4(a). 'Fishing vessel' means a vessel used for catching fish or other living resources of the sea: reg 3(1).

    As from a day to be appointed the Secretary of State may make regulations for securing that the skipper of and every seaman employed or engaged in a United Kingdom fishing vessel is trained in safety matters: Merchant Shipping Act 1995 s 127(1). Section 127 does not have effect until the Secretary of State by order appoints a day for it to come into force: see s 314(3), Sch 14 para 5(1), (2); and PARA 15 note 1. At the date at which this volume states the law, no such order had been made. Regulations under s 127 may provide that, if a person goes to sea on a fishing vessel in contravention of a requirement of the regulations he, and the skipper and each owner of the vessel, commits an offence and is liable on summary conviction to a fine: s 127(2). Regulations under s 127 may make different provision for different cases, or descriptions of case, including different provisions for different descriptions of vessel or according to the circumstances of operation of a vessel: s 127(3). At the date at which this volume states the law, no such regulations had been made under s 127 and none have effect as if so made. As to the meaning of 'seaman' see PARA 457 note

5. As to the meaning of 'fishing vessel' see PARA 230 note 9; and as to the meaning of 'United Kingdom fishing vessel' see PARA 230. As to the meaning of 'United Kingdom' see PARA 16 note 3.

4   As to the meaning of 'pleasure vessel' see the Merchant Shipping (Vessels in Commercial Use for Sport or Pleasure) Regulations 1998, SI 1998/2771, reg 2(1); and PARA 612 (definition applied by the Merchant Shipping (Standards of Training, Certification and Watchkeeping) Regulations 2015, SI 2015/782, reg 3(1)).

5   'GT' means gross tonnage as determined under the Merchant Shipping (Tonnage) Regulations 1997, SI 1997/1510 (see PARa 248): Merchant Shipping (Standards of Training, Certification and Watchkeeping) Regulations 2015, SI 2015/782, reg 3(1).

6   Merchant Shipping (Standards of Training, Certification and Watchkeeping) Regulations 2015, SI 2015/782, reg4(b).

7   Merchant Shipping (Standards of Training, Certification and Watchkeeping) Regulations 2015, SI 2015/782, reg4(c).

8   See the Merchant Shipping (Standards of Training, Certification and Watchkeeping) Regulations 2015, SI 2015/782, regs 6, 21.

9   See the Merchant Shipping (Standards of Training, Certification and Watchkeeping) Regulations 2015, SI 2015/782, regs 7, 14, 15.

10  See the Merchant Shipping (Standards of Training, Certification and Watchkeeping) Regulations 2015, SI 2015/782, reg 8.

11  See the Merchant Shipping (Standards of Training, Certification and Watchkeeping) Regulations 2015, SI 2015/782, regs 18–20.

12  See the Merchant Shipping (Standards of Training, Certification and Watchkeeping) Regulations 2015, SI 2015/782, regs 16, 17.

13  See the Merchant Shipping (Standards of Training, Certification and Watchkeeping) Regulations 2015, SI 2015/782, regs 22, 23.

14  See the Merchant Shipping (Standards of Training, Certification and Watchkeeping) Regulations 2015, SI 2015/782, regs 24–27.

15  See the Merchant Shipping (Standards of Training, Certification and Watchkeeping) Regulations 2015, SI 2015/782, regs 9–13.

16  See the Merchant Shipping (Standards of Training, Certification and Watchkeeping) Regulations 2015, SI 2015/782, regs 28–40, 44.

17  See the Merchant Shipping (Standards of Training, Certification and Watchkeeping) Regulations 2015, SI 2015/782, reg 41.

18  See the Merchant Shipping (Standards of Training, Certification and Watchkeeping) Regulations 2015, SI 2015/782, regs 51, 52.

19  See the Merchant Shipping (Standards of Training, Certification and Watchkeeping) Regulations 2015, SI 2015/782, reg 54.

20  Ie contraventions of reg 42(2), 51(2), (4) or (6) and 52: see the Merchant Shipping (Standards of Training, Certification and Watchkeeping) Regulations 2015, SI 2015/782, reg 55(1)–(4), (6), (7).

21  Ie qualified for the purposes of the Merchant Shipping Act 1995 s 47 (see the text and notes 1–20): see s 50(1). Corresponding provision relating to fishing vessels is made by s 116.

22  As to the meaning of 'superintendent' see PARA 61 note 1. As to the appointment of superintendents see PARA 61.

23  As to the meaning of 'surveyor of ships' see PARA 46 note 13. As to the appointment of surveyors see PARA 46.

24  As to the meaning of 'proper officer' see PARA 48 note 4.

25  As to the meaning of 'master' see PARA 444 note 1.

26  Merchant Shipping Act 1995 s 50(1).

27  Ie fails to comply with the Merchant Shipping Act 1995 s 50(1) (see the text and notes 1–7): see s 50(2). As to the powers of inspectors appointed under s 256(6) (see PARA 46) to serve improvement notices or prohibition notices where s 50 and the provisions of any instrument of a legislative character having effect thereunder are being contravened, or where activities to which s 50 applies are carried on so as to involve serious personal injury or serious pollution, see PARA 51 et seq.

28  See the Merchant Shipping Act 1995 s 50(2); and PARA 1081.

**504. Safe manning and watchkeeping arrangements.** In relation to sea-going ships and hovercraft which are United Kingdom ships and hovercraft[1] wherever they are and other ships and hovercraft when in United Kingdom waters (other than fishing vessels[2], pleasure vessels[3] or certain small commercial vessels[4]), provision is made[5] for:

    (1)     the issuing of a safe manning document in respect of the vessel and the manning of the vessel in accordance with such document[6]; and

(2)    ensuring the adequate provision of watchkeeping arrangements[7].

If these provisions are contravened a ship may be detained[8]; certain contraventions are also offences[9].

1    As to the meaning of 'ship' see PARA 229; and as to the meaning of 'United Kingdom ship' see PARa 230. As to the meaning of 'United Kingdom' see PARA 16 note 3. As to the ships to which the training, certification and manning provisions apply see PARA 502; and as to the statutory framework relating to crews etc generally see PARA 423.
2    As to the meaning of 'fishing vessel' see PARA 503 note 3.
3    As to the meaning of 'pleasure vessel' see PARA 503 note 4.
4    Ie a vessel referred to in the Merchant Shipping (Vessels in Commercial Use for Sport or Pleasure) Regulations 1998, SI 1998/2771, reg 5(3) (see PARA 614).
5    Ie by the Merchant Shipping (Standards of Training, Certification and Watchkeeping) Regulations 2015, SI 2015/782, Pt 4 (regs 45–50): reg 45. See also reg 53 (inspection of non-United Kingdom ships). The Secretary of State may grant, on such terms, if any, as may be specified, exemptions from all or any of the provisions of Pt 4 for classes of case or individual cases, and may amend or cancel any exemptions so granted: reg 50. As to the Secretary of State see PARA 36.
6    See the Merchant Shipping (Standards of Training, Certification and Watchkeeping) Regulations 2015, SI 2015/782, reg 46. In connection with safe manning levels under the Maritime Labour Convention (Cm 7049)) see reg 2.7.
7    See the Merchant Shipping (Standards of Training, Certification and Watchkeeping) Regulations 2015, SI 2015/782, regs 47–49.
8    See the Merchant Shipping (Standards of Training, Certification and Watchkeeping) Regulations 2015, SI 2015/782, reg 54.
9    Ie contraventions of regs 46(1), (2), 47(1), (2) or (3), 48 and 49: see the Merchant Shipping (Standards of Training, Certification and Watchkeeping) Regulations 2015, SI 2015/782, reg 55(2), (3), (5)–(7).

**505. Power to exempt from manning requirements.** The Secretary of State[1] may exempt any United Kingdom ship[2] or description of ship from any requirements of regulations relating to manning requirements made by him[3]. An exemption so given may be confined to a particular period or to one or more particular voyages[4].

1    As to the Secretary of State see PARA 36.
2    As to the ships to which the training, certification and manning provisions apply see PARA 502; and as to the statutory framework relating to crews etc generally see PARA 423. As to the meaning of 'ship' see PARA 229; and as to the meaning of 'United Kingdom ship' see PARa 230. As to the meaning of 'United Kingdom' see PARA 16 note 3.
3    Merchant Shipping Act 1995 s 48(1). The text refers to regulations made under s 47 (see PARA 503): see s 48(1). The fee for the granting by the Secretary of State of an exemption, pursuant to s 48, from the requirements in the Merchant Shipping (Officer Nationality) Regulations 1995, SI 1995/1427, reg 3 (see PARA 507) relating to a strategic ship is £160: Merchant Shipping (Fees) Regulations 2006, SI 2006/2055, reg 3, Sch 1 Pt 15.
     As to the powers of inspectors appointed under the Merchant Shipping Act 1995 s 256(6) (see PARA 46) to serve improvement notices or prohibition notices where s 48 and the provisions of any instrument of a legislative character having effect thereunder are being contravened, or where activities to which s 48 applies are carried on so as to involve serious personal injury or serious pollution, see PARA 51 et seq.
4    Merchant Shipping Act 1995 s 48(2).

**506. Requirements as to crew's knowledge of English.** Where, in the opinion of a superintendent[1] or proper officer[2], the crew of a United Kingdom ship[3] consists of or includes persons who may not understand orders given to them in the course of their duty because of their insufficient knowledge of English and the absence of adequate arrangements for transmitting the orders in a language of which they have sufficient knowledge[4], then:

(1)    if the superintendent or proper officer has informed the master[5] of that opinion, the ship must not go to sea[6]; and
(2)    if the ship is in the United Kingdom, it may be detained[7].

If a ship goes to sea or attempts to go to sea in contravention of these restrictions[8], the owner or master is liable on summary conviction to a fine[9].

1   As to the meaning of 'superintendent' see PARA 61 note 1. As to the appointment of superintendents see PARA 61.
2   As to the meaning of 'proper officer' see PARA 48 note 4.
3   Ie any ship to which the Merchant Shipping Act 1995 s 51 applies: see s 51(1). As to the meaning of 'ship' see PARA 229. As to the ships which these provisions apply see PARA 502; and as to the statutory framework relating to crews etc generally see PARA 423.
4   Merchant Shipping Act 1995 s 51(1). As to the powers of inspectors appointed under s 256(6) (see PARA 46) to serve improvement notices or prohibition notices where s 51 and the provisions of any instrument of a legislative character having effect thereunder are being contravened, or where activities to which s 51 applies are carried on so as to involve serious personal injury or serious pollution, see PARA 51 et seq.
5   As to the meaning of 'master' see PARA 444 note 1.
6   Merchant Shipping Act 1995 s 51(1)(a). As to the meaning of 'going to sea' for these purposes see PARA 457 note 15.
7   Merchant Shipping Act 1995 s 51(1)(b). As to enforcing the detention of a ship under the Merchant Shipping Act 1995 see PARA 1190.
8   Ie in contravention of the Merchant Shipping Act 1995 s 51(1) (see the text and notes 1–7): see s 51(2); and PARA 1082.
9   See the Merchant Shipping Act 1995 s 51(2); and PARA 1082.

### 507. Officer nationality requirements for masters of strategic ships. The master of every strategic ship, that is to say:

(1)     a British registered fishing vessel[1] of 24 metres or more in length[2]; or
(2)     a United Kingdom ship[3] of 500 tons[4] or more which is a cruise ship[5], a product tanker[6] or a ro-ro ship[7],

must be:

(a)     a Commonwealth citizen[8]; or
(b)     an EEA[9] national[10]; or
(c)     a national of a state, other than an EEA state, which is a member of the North Atlantic Treaty Organisation[11].

1   For these purposes, 'British registered fishing vessel' means a fishing vessel registered in the register of British ships established under the Merchant Shipping Act 1995 s 8 (see PARA 254): Merchant Shipping (Officer Nationality) Regulations 1995, SI 1995/1427, reg 2 (having effect under the Merchant Shipping Act 1995 s 47: see PARA 503).
2   For these purposes, 'length', in relation to a British registered fishing vessel, means the register length shown on the vessel's certificate of registry: Merchant Shipping (Officer Nationality) Regulations 1995, SI 1995/1427, reg 2. As to certificates of registry see PARA 298 et seq.
3   For these purposes, 'United Kingdom ship' has the same meaning as in the Merchant Shipping Act 1995 s 85(2) (see PARA 230): Merchant Shipping (Officer Nationality) Regulations 1995, SI 1995/1427, reg 2. Since these provisions have effect under the Merchant Shipping Act 1995 s 47 (see note 1), the ships and voyages to which these provisions apply are limited to those to which s 47 applies, as to which see PARA 502.
4   For these purposes, 'tons' means gross tons: see the Merchant Shipping (Officer Nationality) Regulations 1995, SI 1995/1427, reg 2.
5   For these purposes, 'cruise ship' means a passenger ship of Class I, within the meaning of the Merchant Shipping (Passenger Ship Construction: Ships of Classes I, II and II(A)) Regulations 1998, SI 1998/2514 (see PARA 602 note 3), certified to carry more than 200 passengers: Merchant Shipping (Officer Nationality) Regulations 1995, SI 1995/1427, reg 2.
6   For these purposes, 'product tanker' means either an oil tanker constructed for the carriage of petroleum products in bulk or a chemical tanker constructed for the carriage in bulk of any liquid chemical listed in the 'International Code for the Construction and Equipment of Ships carrying Dangerous Chemicals in Bulk (IBC Code)' (1990 Edition), published by the International Maritime Organisation: Merchant Shipping (Officer Nationality) Regulations 1995, SI 1995/1427, reg 2. As to the International Maritime Organisation see PARA 12.
7   For these purposes, 'ro-ro ship' means a ship provided with cargo or vehicle spaces in which cargo or vehicles can be loaded and unloaded in a horizontal direction: Merchant Shipping (Officer Nationality) Regulations 1995, SI 1995/1427, reg 2.
8   Merchant Shipping (Officer Nationality) Regulations 1995, SI 1995/1427, reg 3(a). As to who are Commonwealth citizens see BRITISH NATIONALITY vol 4 (2011) PARA 409.

9    The European Economic Area ('EEA') is formed under the Agreement on the European Economic
     Area (Oporto, 2 May 1992; EC 7 (1992); Cm 2183) as adjusted by the Protocol (Brussels, 17
     March 1993; EC 2 (1993); Cm 2183).
10   Merchant Shipping (Officer Nationality) Regulations 1995, SI 1995/1427, reg 3(b).
11   Merchant Shipping (Officer Nationality) Regulations 1995, SI 1995/1427, reg 3(c). The fee for the
     granting by the Secretary of State of an exemption, pursuant to the Merchant Shipping Act 1995
     s 48 (power to exempt from manning requirements) (see PARA 505), from the requirements in the
     Merchant Shipping (Officer Nationality) Regulations 1995, SI 1995/1427, reg 3 relating to a
     strategic ship is £160: Merchant Shipping (Fees) Regulations 2006, SI 2006/2055, reg 3, Sch 1 Pt
     15. As to the North Atlantic Treaty Organisation see INTERNATIONAL RELATIONS LAW 61
     (2010) PARA 518.

**508.  Disqualification of holder of seaman's certificate other than an officer.** Where it appears to the Secretary of State[1] that a person who is the holder of a certificate of competence[2] or any certificate issued under the provisions relating to manning[3], other than one certifying that a person is qualified as an officer[4], is unfit to be the holder of such a certificate, whether by reason of incompetence or misconduct or for any other reason, the Secretary of State may give him notice in writing that he is considering the suspension or cancellation of the certificate[5]. The notice must state the reasons why it appears to the Secretary of State that that person is unfit to be the holder of such a certificate and must state that, within a period specified in the notice, or such longer period as the Secretary of State may allow, he may make written representations to the Secretary of State or claim to make oral representations to the Secretary of State[6]. After considering any representations so made, the Secretary of State must decide whether or not to suspend or cancel the certificate and must give the holder of it written notice of his decision[7].

Where the decision is to suspend or cancel the certificate, the notice must state the date from which the cancellation is to take effect, or the date from which and the period for which the suspension is to take effect, and must require the holder to deliver the certificate to the Secretary of State not later than the date so specified unless before that date the holder has required the case to be dealt with by a statutory inquiry[8]. Where, before the date specified in the notice, he requires the case to be dealt with by such an inquiry, then, unless he withdraws the requirement, the suspension or cancellation does not take effect except as ordered in pursuance of the inquiry[9].

The Secretary of State may make regulations[10] prescribing the procedure to be followed with respect to the making and consideration of such representations[11], the form of any notice to be given and the period to be specified in any such notice as the period within which any steps are to be taken[12].

Where a seaman's certificate has been cancelled or suspended[13], the Secretary of State, if of the opinion that the justice of the case requires it, may reissue the certificate or, as the case may be, reduce the period of suspension and return the certificate, or may grant a new certificate of the same or a lower grade in place of the cancelled or suspended certificate[14].

1    As to the Secretary of State see PARA 36.
2    Ie a certificate issued under the Merchant Shipping Act 1995 s 54 (see PARA 503): s 62(7). As to
     the application of s 62 see PARA 502; and as to the statutory framework relating to crews etc
     generally see PARA 423.
3    Ie any certificate issued under the Merchant Shipping Act 1995 s 47 (see PARAS 503, 507): s 62(7).
4    See the Merchant Shipping Act 1995 s 62(1), (7). As to qualification as an officer see PARA 507.
5    Merchant Shipping Act 1995 s 62(1).
6    Merchant Shipping Act 1995 s 62(2).
7    Merchant Shipping Act 1995 s 62(3).
8    Merchant Shipping Act 1995 s 62(4). The text refers to an inquiry under s 63 (see PARA 530): see
     s 62(4). If a person fails to deliver a cancelled or suspended seaman's certificate as required by s
     62 he commits an offence: see s 66; and PARA 1085.

9 Merchant Shipping Act 1995 s 62(5).

10 As to the power of the Secretary of State to make subordinate legislation under the Merchant Shipping Act 1995, including his power to appoint committees for the purpose of advising him when considering the making or alteration of any regulations etc, see PARA 39.

11 Ie in pursuance of the Merchant Shipping Act 1995 s 62: s 62(6).

12 Merchant Shipping Act 1995 s 62(6). In exercise of the power so conferred, the Secretary of State made the Merchant Shipping (Disqualification of Holder of Seaman's Certificates) Regulations 1997, SI 1997/346 (as to which see PARA 509).

13 Ie under the Merchant Shipping Act 1995 s 62 (see the text and notes 1–12), s 61 (see PARA 524), s 63 or s 64 (see PARA 537): see s 67.

14 Merchant Shipping Act 1995 s 67.

**509. Suspension or cancellation of seaman's certificate.** A notice served[1] by the Secretary of State[2] stating that he is considering the suspension or cancellation of a certificate of competence[3] or any certificate or other document issued under the provisions relating to manning[4], other than one certifying that a person is qualified as an officer[5], must be given to the holder of the certificate in the prescribed form[6]. Service of such notice must be effected either by serving the holder of the certificate concerned personally or by sending it to him at his last known address by registered post or by the recorded delivery service[7].

Within six weeks of the receipt of such notice, or such longer period as the Secretary of State may allow, the holder of the certificate may inform the Secretary of State of his intention to make written representations or claim to make oral representations to the Secretary of State[8]. In the case of a claim to make oral representations, the Secretary of State must seek to agree with the holder of the certificate a suitable date and place for the oral representations to be heard and, if no such agreement is reached, they must be heard at the prescribed address[9] on the last working day of the period for representations so allowed[10]. If oral representations are to be made, the holder of the certificate may be accompanied by a friend who may advise him or speak on his behalf[11]. Representations, whether written or oral, must be made within ten weeks of receipt of the notice[12].

The Secretary of State must give the holder notice of his decision in the prescribed form[13]; and service of that notice must be effected either by serving the holder of the certificate concerned personally or by delivering it to his last known address or by sending it by post to his last known address[14].

1 Ie pursuant to the Merchant Shipping Act 1995 s 62(1) (see PARA 508): see the Merchant Shipping (Disqualification of Holder of Seaman's Certificates) Regulations 1997, SI 1997/346, reg 3(1).

2 As to the Secretary of State see PARA 36.

3 Ie a certificate issued under the Merchant Shipping Act 1995 s 54 (see PARA 503): see the Merchant Shipping (Disqualification of Holder of Seaman's Certificates) Regulations 1997, SI 1997/346, regs 1(2), 2, 3(1).

4 Ie any certificate or other document issued under the Merchant Shipping Act 1995 s 47 (see PARAS 503, 507): see the Merchant Shipping (Disqualification of Holder of Seaman's Certificates) Regulations 1997, SI 1997/346, regs 1(2), 2, 3(1).

5 See the Merchant Shipping (Disqualification of Holder of Seaman's Certificates) Regulations 1997, SI 1997/346, regs 2, 3(1). As to qualification as an officer see PARA 507.

6 Merchant Shipping (Disqualification of Holder of Seaman's Certificates) Regulations 1997, SI 1997/346, regs 1(2), 3(1). For the prescribed form of certificate see reg 3(1), Sch 1 (Notice of Intention to suspend or cancel certificate).

7 Merchant Shipping (Disqualification of Holder of Seaman's Certificates) Regulations 1997, SI 1997/346, reg 3(2).

8 Merchant Shipping (Disqualification of Holder of Seaman's Certificates) Regulations 1997, SI 1997/346, reg 4(1).

9 Ie the address given in the Merchant Shipping (Disqualification of Holder of Seaman's Certificates) Regulations 1997, SI 1997/346, Sch 1 (see note 6): see reg 4(2).

10 Merchant Shipping (Disqualification of Holder of Seaman's Certificates) Regulations 1997, SI 1997/346, reg 4(2).

11 Merchant Shipping (Disqualification of Holder of Seaman's Certificates) Regulations 1997, SI 1997/346, reg 4(3).

12  Merchant Shipping (Disqualification of Holder of Seaman's Certificates) Regulations 1997, SI 1997/346, reg 4(4).
13  Merchant Shipping (Disqualification of Holder of Seaman's Certificates) Regulations 1997, SI 1997/346, reg 5(1). For the prescribed form of notice see reg 5(1), Sch 2 (Notice of Decision concerning suspension or cancellation of certificate).
14  Merchant Shipping (Disqualification of Holder of Seaman's Certificates) Regulations 1997, SI 1997/346, reg 5(2).

**510. Performance of seafaring duties by crew.** A seaman is not bound to perform any services other than those specified in his contract of service[1]. However, he is required to perform duties which, although not specifically stipulated, are reasonably incidental to a seafaring life. Thus, the seaman must navigate the ship in all sorts of weather and perils unless the contract of service is duly dissolved[2]; he must conduct himself in a properly respectful manner towards his superiors[3]; and he must assist with the working of the cargo in ports of call[4].

1  Thus a seaman who has agreed to serve on an ordinary voyage is not bound to continue to serve when the voyage has become extraordinary, eg:
   (1)  as when the risk ceases to be a commercial risk by reason of the carriage of contraband (*Burton v Pinkerton* (1867) LR 2 Exch 340; *O'Neil v Armstrong, Mitchell & Co* [1895] 2 QB 418, 8 Asp MLC 63, CA; *Lloyd v Sheen* (1905) 10 Asp MLC 75, DC; *Austin Friars Steam Shipping Co v Strack* [1905] 2 KB 315, 10 Asp MLC 70, DC (on appeal [1906] 2 KB 499, CA); *Palace Shipping Co Ltd v Caine* [1907] AC 386, 10 Asp MLC 529, HL; *Collins v Simpson Steamship Co* (1907) 24 TLR 178, CA); or
   (2)  where the voyage is to a war zone (*Robson v Sykes* [1938] 2 All ER 612, 61 Ll L Rep 16, DC); or
   (3)  where war breaks out and the ship is in danger of being captured or sunk (*Liston v The Carpathian (Owners)* [1915] 2 KB 42, 13 Asp MLC 70); or
   (4)  where the voyage is extended beyond the time and scope agreed upon (*The Eliza* (1823) 1 Hag Adm 182; *The Countess of Harcourt* (1824) 1 Hag Adm 248; *The Minerva* (1825) 1 Hag Adm 347; *The George Home* (1825) 1 Hag Adm 370; *The Westmorland* (1841) 1 Wm Rob 216; *Donkin v Hastie* (1897) 61 JP 568, DC); or
   (5)  where there is a shortage of provisions (*The Castilia* (1822) 1 Hag Adm 59).
   As to when a voyage will be deemed to be terminated see *Haylett v Thompson* [1911] 1 KB 311, 11 Asp MLC 512, DC. The voyage to be considered is the 'voyage of the ship', not the voyage of the cargo: *The Scarsdale* [1906] P 103, 10 Asp MLC 235, CA (affd sub nom *Board of Trade v Baxter, The Scarsdale* [1907] AC 373, 10 Asp MLC 525, HL).
2  *The Neptune* (1824) 1 Hag Adm 227; *The Florence* (1852) 16 Jur 572; *The Sappho* (1871) LR 3 PC 690, 1 Asp MLC 65; *The Albionic* [1941] P 99, 70 Ll L Rep 257 (affd (1942) P 81, 72 Ll L Rep 91, CA). Dissolution of the contract may be by:
   (1)  the act of the master if he discharges the seaman (see PARAS 468–469); or
   (2)  the legitimate abandonment of the vessel at sea to save life, and with the authority of the master; or
   (3)  the hostile capture of the vessel (see PARA 1147 et seq).
3  *The Lowther Castle* (1825) 1 Hag Adm 384.
4  *The Cambridge* (1829) 2 Hag Adm 243.

### (ix)  Working Hours and Leave

#### A.    SEA-GOING SHIPS

**511. Minimum hours of rest and permitted exceptions.** The minimum hours of rest for a seafarer[1] may not be less than:
   (1)  ten hours in any 24-hour period[2]; and
   (2)  77 hours in any seven-day period[3],
and it is the duty of a shipowner[4], a master of a ship[5] or, in the case of an employed seafarer, any employer of the employed seafarer[6], to ensure that a seafarer is provided with at least those minimum hours of rest[7]. Hours of rest may be divided into no more than two periods, one of which must be at least six hours in length, and the interval between consecutive such periods must not exceed 14 hours[8]. However, the Maritime and Coastguard Agency may authorise a collective

agreement[9] or workforce agreement[10] permitting exceptions to these limits[11], and the master of a ship may require a seafarer to work any hours of work necessary for the immediate safety of the ship, persons on board ship or cargo or for the purpose of giving assistance to another ship or to a person in distress at sea[12]. Failure to comply with these requirements is an offence[13].

Statutory and contractual rights to hours of rest and paid leave[14] may not be exercised separately[15].

1   As to the meaning of 'seafarer' see PARA 423 note 3. As to the vessels and seafarers to which these provisions apply see PARA 423 (in particular note 18). The provision of the Maritime Labour Convention (see PARA 423 note 1) regulating hours of work and hours of rest is reg 2.3. Nothing in these provisions (ie the Merchant Shipping (Hours of Work) Regulations 2002, SI 2002/2125, reg 5) restricts the operation of the Merchant Shipping and Fishing Vessels (Health and Safety at Work) (Employment of Young Persons) Regulations 1998, SI 1998/2411, reg 6 (see PARA 450): Merchant Shipping (Hours of Work) Regulations 2002, SI 2002/2125, reg 5(5).

2   Merchant Shipping (Hours of Work) Regulations 2002, SI 2002/2125, reg 5(1)(a). These minimum hours are subject to reg 6 (see the text and notes 9–11): reg 5(1), (2).

3   Merchant Shipping (Hours of Work) Regulations 2002, SI 2002/2125, reg 5(1)(b). See note 2.

4   Merchant Shipping (Hours of Work) Regulations 2002, SI 2002/2125, reg 4(a) (reg 4 substituted by SI 2014/308). As to the meaning of 'shipowner' see PARA 448 note 4.

5   Merchant Shipping (Hours of Work) Regulations 2002, SI 2002/2125, reg 4(b) (as substituted: see note 4). As to the meaning of 'ship' see PARA 423 note 2. 'Master', in the application of the Merchant Shipping (Hours of Work) Regulations 2002, SI 2002/2125, to hovercraft, includes the captain of a hovercraft: reg 1(2).

6   Merchant Shipping (Hours of Work) Regulations 2002, SI 2002/2125, reg 4(c) (as substituted: see note 4). As to the meanings of 'employed seafarer' and 'employer' see PARA 423 note 3.

7   Merchant Shipping (Hours of Work) Regulations 2002, SI 2002/2125, reg 4 (as substituted: see note 4). Tables of scheduled hours of rest must be posted aboard the ship, and records of rest hours taken must be maintained: regs 7, 9 (amended by SI 2014/308). A seafarer who is on call on board ship must have an adequate compensatory rest period if his normal period of rest is disturbed by call-outs to work: Merchant Shipping (Hours of Work) Regulations 2002, SI 2002/2125, reg 5(4).

8   Merchant Shipping (Hours of Work) Regulations 2002, SI 2002/2125, reg 5(2). See note 2. A shipowner must provide the Maritime and Coastguard Agency with such information as the Agency may specify on watchkeepers and other seafarers working at night: reg 11 (amended by SI 2014/308). As to the Maritime and Coastguard Agency see PARA 423 note 6.

9   'Collective agreement' means a collective agreement within the meaning of the Trade Union and Labour Relations (Consolidation) Act 1992 s 178 (see EMPLOYMENT vol 41A (2014) PARAS 1093–1094), the trade union parties to which are independent trade unions within the meaning of s 5 (see EMPLOYMENT vol 41 (2014) PARA 904): Merchant Shipping (Hours of Work) Regulations 2002, SI 2002/2125, reg 2(1).

10  'Workforce agreement' means an agreement between an employer and his employees or their representatives in respect of which the conditions set out in the Merchant Shipping (Hours of Work) Regulations 2002, SI 2002/2125, Sch 1 are satisfied: reg 2(1).

11  Merchant Shipping (Hours of Work) Regulations 2002, SI 2002/2125, reg 6(1). Such exceptions may take account of more frequent or longer leave periods, or the granting of compensatory leave for watchkeeping seafarers or seafarers working on board ship on short voyages: reg 6(2).

12  Merchant Shipping (Hours of Work) Regulations 2002, SI 2002/2125, reg 8(1). For these purposes the master may suspend the hours of rest scheduled in the table under reg 7 (see note 7) and require a seafarer to perform any hours of work necessary until the normal situation has been restored: reg 8(2). As soon as practicable after the normal situation has been restored the master must ensure that any seafarer who has performed work in hours of rest scheduled in the table under reg 7 is provided with an adequate rest period: reg 8(3).

13  Any contravention by the master of a ship of the Merchant Shipping (Hours of Work) Regulations 2002, SI 2002/2125, reg 4, 7(1), 8(3), 9(1), (4) or (5), by an employer of reg 4, by a person authorised by the master of a ship of reg 7(1) or 9(1) or (4), or by a shipowner of reg 4, 9(5) or 11, is an offence punishable on summary conviction by a fine (reg 20(1)(a)–(d) (reg 20(1)(a), (d) amended by SI 2014/308)); and where there is a contravention of the Merchant Shipping (Hours of Work) Regulations 2002, SI 2002/2125, reg 5(3) or (4), the master of the ship is guilty of an offence punishable on summary conviction by a fine (reg 20(2)). As to the powers of magistrates' courts to issue fines on summary conviction see SENTENCING vol 92 (2015) PARA 176. In any proceedings for an offence under the Merchant Shipping (Hours of Work) Regulations 2002, SI 2002/2125, it is a defence for the defendant to show that all reasonable steps had been taken by him to ensure compliance with the Regulations: reg 20(5).

14 As to the right to paid leave see PARA 512.
15 Where during any period a seafarer is entitled to hours of rest or paid leave both under the Merchant Shipping (Hours of Work) Regulations 2002, SI 2002/2125, and under a separate provision (including a provision of his contract), he may not exercise the two rights separately, but may, in taking hours of rest or paid leave during that period, take advantage of whichever right is, in any particular respect, the more favourable: reg 13 (amended by SI 2014/308).

**512.   Entitlement to annual leave and shore leave.** An employed seafarer[1] is entitled to:

(1)   paid annual leave that is to be calculated on the basis of two and a half days for each month of employment in the leave year and pro rata for incomplete months[2]; and

(2)   additional paid leave of eight days in each leave year and pro rata for incomplete years[3].

An employed seafarer may present a complaint to an employment tribunal[4] that the seafarer's employer has refused to permit the exercise of these[5] rights[6] or has failed to pay the seafarer the whole or any part of any amount due[7] to the seafarer[8], and the tribunal may make an award of compensation[9] or order the employer to pay the amounts owed[10], as applicable.

The shipowner[11] and the master[12] must ensure that shore leave is granted to seafarers to benefit their health and well-being where consistent with the operational requirements of their positions[13].

Failure to comply with these requirements is an offence[14].

Statutory and contractual rights to hours of rest[15] and paid leave may not be exercised separately[16].

1   As to the meanings of 'seafarer', 'employed seafarer', 'employer' and 'employment' see PARA 423 note 3. As to the vessels and seafarers to which these provisions apply see PARA 423 (in particular note 18).
2   Merchant Shipping (Hours of Work) Regulations 2002, SI 2002/2125, reg 12(1) (reg 12 substituted by SI 2014/308). Leave to which a seafarer is so entitled may be taken in instalments (Merchant Shipping (Hours of Work) Regulations 2002, SI 2002/2125, reg 12(3)(a) (as so substituted) and may not be replaced by a payment in lieu, except where the seafarer's employment is terminated (reg 12(3)(b) (as so substituted)).
      Justified absences from work are not considered as annual leave for these purposes: reg 12(4) (as so substituted). For these purposes 'justified absences from work' include an absence authorised by any enactment, contract between the seafarer's employer and the seafarer, collective agreement or workplace agreement or by custom and practice: reg 12(4) (as so substituted). As to the meanings of 'collective agreement' and 'workplace agreement' see PARA 511 notes 9, 10.
3   Merchant Shipping (Hours of Work) Regulations 2002, SI 2002/2125, reg 12(2) (as substituted: see note 2). See note 2.
4   An employment tribunal may not consider a complaint under these provisions unless it is presented:
      (1)   before the end of the period of three months beginning with the date on which it is alleged that the exercise of the right should have been permitted (or in the case of a period of annual leave or additional leave extending over more than one day, the date on which it should have been permitted to begin) or, as the case may be, the payment should have been made (Merchant Shipping (Hours of Work) Regulations 2002, SI 2002/2125, reg 22(2)(a) (regs 22, 22A added by SI 2014/308)); or
      (2)   within such further period as the tribunal considers reasonable in a case where it is satisfied that it was not reasonably practicable for the complaint to be presented before the end of that period of three months (Merchant Shipping (Hours of Work) Regulations 2002, SI 2002/2125, reg 22(2)(b) (as so added)).
      In working out when the time limit set by reg 22(2)(a) expires the period beginning with the day after the day on which the seafarer concerned complies with the requirement in the Employment Tribunals Act 1996 s 18A(1) (requirement to contact ACAS before instituting proceedings: see EMPLOYMENT vol 39 (2014) PARA 152) in relation to the matter in respect of which the proceedings are brought ('Day A') and ending with the day on which the seafarer concerned receives or, if earlier, is treated as receiving (by virtue of regulations made under s 18A(11)) the certificate issued under s 18A(4) ('Day B') is not to be counted: Merchant Shipping (Hours of Work) Regulations 2002, SI 2002/2125, regs 22(2A), 22A(1), (2) (as so added). If the

time limit set by reg 22(2)(a) would (if not extended by reg 22A(3)) expire during the period beginning with Day A and ending one month after Day B, the time limit expires instead at the end of that period: reg 22A(3) (as so added). The power conferred on the employment tribunal by reg 22(2)(b) to extend the time limit set by reg 22(2)(a) is exercisable in relation to that time limit as extended by reg 22A: reg 22A(4) (as so added).

5 Ie any right that the seafarer has under the Merchant Shipping (Hours of Work) Regulations 2002, SI 2002/2125, reg 12(1) or (2) (see the text and notes 1–3).

6 Merchant Shipping (Hours of Work) Regulations 2002, SI 2002/2125, reg 22(1)(a) (as added: see note 4).

7 Ie under the Merchant Shipping (Hours of Work) Regulations 2002, SI 2002/2125, reg 12(1) or (2) (see the text and notes 1–3).

8 Merchant Shipping (Hours of Work) Regulations 2002, SI 2002/2125, reg 22(1)(b) (as added: see note 4).

9 Where an employment tribunal finds a complaint under the Merchant Shipping (Hours of Work) Regulations 2002, SI 2002/2125, reg 22(1)(a) (see the text and notes 4–6) well-founded, it must make a declaration to that effect and may make an award of compensation to be paid by the employer to the seafarer: reg 22(3) (as added: see note 4). The amount of the compensation must be such as the tribunal considers just and equitable in all the circumstances having regard to the employer's default in refusing to permit the seafarer to exercise the seafarer's right and any loss sustained by the seafarer which is attributable to the matters complained of: reg 22(4) (as so added).

10 Where on a complaint under the Merchant Shipping (Hours of Work) Regulations 2002, SI 2002/2125, reg 22(1)(b) (see the text and notes 7–8) an employment tribunal finds that an employer has failed to pay a seafarer in accordance with reg 12(1) or (2), it must order the employer to pay to the seafarer the amount which it finds to be due to the seafarer: reg 22(5) (as added: see note 4).

11 As to the meaning of 'shipowner' see PARA 448 note 4.

12 As to the meaning of 'master' see PARA 511 note 5.

13 Merchant Shipping (Hours of Work) Regulations 2002, SI 2002/2125, reg 12A (added by SI 2014/308).

14 Any contravention by the master of a ship or a shipowner of the Merchant Shipping (Hours of Work) Regulations 2002, SI 2002/2125, reg 12A, is an offence punishable on summary conviction by a fine (reg 20(1)(a), (d) (amended by SI 2014/308)); and where there is a contravention of the Merchant Shipping (Hours of Work) Regulations 2002, SI 2002/2125, reg 12(1), (2), the employer of the seafarer is guilty of an offence punishable on summary conviction by a fine (reg 20(4) (amended by SI 2014/308)). As to offences and proceedings see further PARA 512 note 13.

15 As to the right to hours of rest see PARA 511.

16 See PARA 511 note 15.

**513. Restriction on contracting out.** Any provision in an agreement (whether a contract of employment or not) is void in so far as it purports to exclude or limit the operation of the statutory requirements[1] as to hours of rest and annual and shore leave[2] or to preclude a person from bringing proceedings[3] before an employment tribunal[4]. This prohibition does not apply to:

(1) any agreement to refrain from instituting or continuing proceedings where a conciliation officer has taken[5] conciliation action[6]; or

(2) any agreement to refrain from instituting or continuing proceedings[7] if the conditions regulating settlement agreements[8] are satisfied in relation to the agreement[9].

1 Ie any provision of the Merchant Shipping (Hours of Work) Regulations 2002, SI 2002/2125 (see PARAS 511, 512), save in so far as provided for under reg 6 (exceptions in collective agreements: see PARA 511): reg 23(1)(a) (reg 23 added by SI 2014/308).

2 Merchant Shipping (Hours of Work) Regulations 2002, SI 2002/2125, reg 23(1)(a) (as added: see note 1).

3 Ie proceedings under the Merchant Shipping (Hours of Work) Regulations 2002, SI 2002/2125.

4 Merchant Shipping (Hours of Work) Regulations 2002, SI 2002/2125, reg 23(1)(b) (as added: see note 1).

5 Ie under any of the Employment Tribunals Act 1996 ss 18A–18C (see EMPLOYMENT vol 39 (2014) PARAS 152–153).

6 Merchant Shipping (Hours of Work) Regulations 2002, SI 2002/2125, reg 23(2)(a) (as added (see note 1); amended by SI 2014/386).

7   Ie within the Employment Tribunals Act 1996 s 18(1)(n) (proceedings under the Merchant
    Shipping (Hours of Work) Regulations 2002, SI 2002/2125, where conciliation is available: see
    EMPLOYMENT vol 39 (2014) PARA 152).
8   For these purposes of the conditions regulating settlement agreements under the Merchant
    Shipping (Hours of Work) Regulations 2002, SI 2002/2125, are that:
    (1)    the agreement must be in writing (reg 23(3)(a) (as added: see note 1));
    (2)    the agreement must relate to the particular complaint (reg 23(3)(b) (as so added));
    (3)    the seafarer must have received advice from a relevant independent adviser as to the
           terms and effect of the proposed agreement and, in particular, its effect on his ability to
           pursue his rights before an employment tribunal (reg 23(3)(c) (as so added));
    (4)    there must be in force, when the adviser gives the advice, a contract of insurance, or an
           indemnity provided for members of a profession or a professional body, covering the
           risk of a claim by the seafarer in respect of loss arising in consequence of the advice (reg
           23(3)(d) (as so added));
    (5)    the agreement must identify the adviser (reg 23(3)(e) (as so added)); and
    (6)    the agreement must state that the conditions regulating settlement agreements under the
           Merchant Shipping (Hours of Work) Regulations 2002, SI 2002/2125, are satisfied (reg
           23(3)(f) (as so added)).
    As to the meaning of 'seafarer' see PARA 423 note 3. A person is a relevant independent adviser
    for the purposes of reg 23(3)(c):
    (a)    if he is a qualified lawyer (reg 23(4)(a) (as so added));
    (b)    if he is an officer, official, employee or member of an independent trade union who has
           been certified in writing by the trade union as competent to give advice and as authorised
           to do so on behalf of the trade union (reg 23(4)(b) (as so added)); or
    (c)    if he works at an advice centre (whether as an employee or as a volunteer) and has been
           certified in writing by the centre as competent to give advice and as authorised to do so
           on behalf of the centre (reg 23(4)(c) (as so added)),
    but a person is not a relevant independent adviser for those purposes:
    (i)    if he is, is employed by or is acting in the matter for the employer or an associated
           employer (reg 23(5)(a) (as so added));
    (ii)   in the case of a person within reg 23(4)(b), if the trade union is the employer or an
           associated employer (reg 23(5)(b) (as so added)); or
    (iii)  in the case of a person within reg 23(4)(c), if the seafarer makes a payment for the advice
           received from him (reg 23(5)(d) (as so added)).
    In reg 23(4)(a) 'qualified lawyer' means a person who, for the purposes of the Legal Services
    Act 2007, is an authorised person in relation to an activity which constitutes the exercise of a right
    of audience or the conduct of litigation (within the meaning of that Act: see ss 1(4), 12(1)(a), (b);
    and LEGAL PROFESSIONS vol 65 (2015) PARAS 202, 352) (Merchant Shipping (Hours of Work)
    Regulations 2002, SI 2002/2125, reg 23(6)(a)); and for the purposes of reg 23(5) any two
    employers are treated as associated if one is a company of which the other (directly or indirectly)
    has control or both are companies of which a third person (directly or indirectly) has control; and
    'associated employer' is construed accordingly.
9   Merchant Shipping (Hours of Work) Regulations 2002, SI 2002/2125, reg 23(2)(b) (as added (see
    note 1); amended by SI 2014/431).

## 514. Compliance and inspection.

Provision is made for the inspection of
United Kingdom and non-United Kingdom ships[1] to ensure compliance with the
statutory requirements[2] as to hours of rest and annual and shore leave[3]; ships
found to be in breach of those requirements may also be detained on safety
grounds or on grounds of persistent breach[4].

1   As to the meaning of 'ship' see PARA 423 note 2; as to the meaning of 'United Kingdom ship' see
    PARA 423 note 18.
2   Ie the Merchant Shipping (Hours of Work) Regulations 2002, SI 2002/2125 (see PARAS 511, 512).
3   See the Merchant Shipping (Hours of Work) Regulations 2002, SI 2002/2125, reg 14 (substituted
    by SI 2014/308) (inspection of United Kingdom ships and certain other ships); the Merchant
    Shipping (Hours of Work) Regulations 2002, SI 2002/2125, reg 14A (added by SI 2014/308;
    amended by SI 2014/1614) (inspection of non-United Kingdom ships with Maritime Labour
    Convention documentation); and the Merchant Shipping (Hours of Work) Regulations 2002, SI
    2002/2125, regs 15, 16, 19 (amended by SI 2014/1614; SI 2014/308) (inspection of ships other
    than United Kingdom ships and rectification of deficiencies).
4   See the Merchant Shipping (Hours of Work) Regulations 2002, SI 2002/2125, regs 17A, 17B
    (added by SI 2014/308) (detention of United Kingdom ships and other ships with and without

Maritime Labour Convention documentation). See also the Merchant Shipping (Hours of Work) Regulations 2002, SI 2002/2125, reg 18 (added by SI 2014/308) (arbitration and compensation following detention).

### B.   FISHING VESSELS

**515.  Maximum weekly working time.** In the case of a fishing vessel[1] a worker's[2] working time[3], including overtime, in any reference period which is applicable in his case[4] may not exceed an average of 48 hours for each seven days[5], and an employer must take all reasonable steps, in keeping with the need to protect the health and safety of workers, to ensure that such limit is complied with in the case of each worker employed by him in relation to whom it applies[6]. Failure to comply with this requirement is an offence[7].

The Secretary of State[8] may grant an exception from the maximum weekly working time requirement[9] for objective or technical reasons or reasons concerning the organisation of work[10], and workers may be required to work additional hours in an emergency[11].

1   As to the vessels to which these provisions apply see PARA 423 note 18. As to the meaning of 'fishing vessel' see the Merchant Shipping Act 1995 s 313(1); and PARA 230.
2   'Worker' means a person employed (or, where the employment has ceased, who was employed) on board a fishing vessel; 'employer', in relation to a worker, means the person by whom the worker is (or, where the employment has ceased, was) employed; 'employment', in relation to a worker, means employment under his contract, and 'employed' is construed accordingly: Fishing Vessels (Working Time: Sea-fishermen) Regulations 2004, SI 2004/1713, reg 2(1). Subject to reg 2(1), words and expressions used in the Fishing Vessels (Working Time: Sea-fishermen) Regulations 2004, SI 2004/1713, have the same meaning as in Council Directive (EC) 93/104 (OJ L307, 13.12.93, p 18) concerning certain aspects of the organisation of working time (the Working Time Directive): see EMPLOYMENT vol 39 (2014) PARA 268 et seq): Merchant Shipping (Working Time: Inland Waterways) Regulations 2003, SI 2003/3049, reg 2(2).
3   'Working time', in relation to a worker, means (by virtue of the Fishing Vessels (Working Time: Sea-fishermen) Regulations 2004, SI 2004/1713, reg 2(1)):
    (1)     any period during which he is working, at his employer's disposal and carrying out his activity or duties; and
    (2)     any period during which he is receiving relevant training,
    and 'work' is construed accordingly. 'Relevant training' means work experience provided pursuant to a training course or programme, training for employment, or both, other than work experience or training the immediate provider of which is an educational institution or a person whose main business is the provision of training and which is provided on a course run by that institution or person; 'relevant agreement', in relation to a worker, means a workforce agreement which applies to him, any provision of a collective agreement which forms part of a contract between him and his employer, or any other agreement in writing which is legally enforceable as between the worker and his employer; 'collective agreement' means a collective agreement within the meaning of the Trade Union and Labour Relations (Consolidation) Act 1992 s 178 (see EMPLOYMENT vol 41A (2014) PARAS 1093–1094), the trade union parties to which are independent trade unions within the meaning of s 5 (see EMPLOYMENT vol 41 (2014) PARA 904); and 'workforce agreement' means an agreement between an employer and workers employed by him or their representatives in respect of which the conditions set out in the Fishing Vessels (Working Time: Sea-fishermen) Regulations 2004, SI 2004/1713, Sch 1 are satisfied: reg 2(1).
4   The reference period which applies in the case of a worker is any period of 52 weeks in the course of his employment (Fishing Vessels (Working Time: Sea-fishermen) Regulations 2004, SI 2004/1713, reg 6(3)), except where a worker has worked for his employer for less than 52 weeks, when it is the period that has elapsed since he started work for his employer (reg 6(4)).
5   Fishing Vessels (Working Time: Sea-fishermen) Regulations 2004, SI 2004/1713, reg 6(1). Provision for determining a worker's average working time for each seven days is made by reg 6(5), (6). Records are required to be kept to show that the limit imposed under reg 6(1) is being complied with: see reg 10. An employer who fails to comply with reg 10 is guilty of an offence, punishable on summary conviction by a fine: reg 18(2). As to the powers of magistrates' courts to issue fines on summary conviction see SENTENCING vol 92 (2015) PARA 176. In any proceedings for an offence under the Fishing Vessels (Working Time: Sea-fishermen) Regulations 2004, SI 2004/1713, it is a defence for the defendant to show that all reasonable steps had been taken by him to ensure compliance with the regulations: reg 18(3).
6   Fishing Vessels (Working Time: Sea-fishermen) Regulations 2004, SI 2004/1713, reg 6(2).

7    Subject to reg 14 (emergencies: see the text and note 11), an employer who fails to comply with reg 6(2) is guilty of an offence, punishable on summary conviction by a fine: reg 18(1). See note 5.

8    As to the Secretary of State see PARA 36.

9    Ie the requirements of the Fishing Vessels (Working Time: Sea-fishermen) Regulations 2004, SI 2004/1713, reg 6(1) (see the text and notes 1–5).

10   Fishing Vessels (Working Time: Sea-fishermen) Regulations 2004, SI 2004/1713, regs 5, 13(1). The Secretary of State may grant an exception from the limit in reg 6(1) or the requirements of reg 7(3), (4) (see PARA 516) only if he has first (so far as is possible) consulted representatives of the employers and workers concerned (reg 13(1)(a)) and the exception is subject to such conditions and limitations as will protect the health and safety of workers (reg 13(1)(b)). The Secretary of State may, on giving reasonable notice and after consulting such persons (if any) as he considers may be affected, alter or cancel any exception so granted: reg 13(2). An exception granted in accordance with reg 13(1) must be limited to the extent necessary for the reasons mentioned therein (reg 13(3)(a)) and may take account of the granting of compensatory leave periods to workers in place of the limit in reg 6(1) and the rest periods required by reg 7(3), (4): reg 13(3). An exception under reg 13(1) may relate to classes of cases (a 'class exception') or to individual cases (an 'individual exception'): reg 13(4). An individual exception granted under reg 13(1), and an alteration or cancellation of such an exception under reg 13(2), must be given in writing (reg 13(5)(a)), specify the date on which it takes effect (reg 13(5)(b)), and in the case of the grant of an exemption, specify the conditions and limitations subject to which it is granted in accordance with reg 13(1)(b) (reg 13(5)(c)). A class exception granted under reg 13(1), and an alteration or cancellation of such an exception under reg 13(2) may relate to particular types of fishing vessel and methods of fishing (reg 13(6)(a)) and must be specified by the Secretary of State in a Merchant Shipping Notice which is considered by him to be relevant from time to time (reg 13(6)(b)). As to the meaning of 'Merchant Shipping Notice' see PARA 423 note 6.

11   Nothing in the Fishing Vessels (Working Time: Sea-fishermen) Regulations 2004, SI 2004/1713, prevents the master of a fishing vessel from requiring a worker to work any hours of work necessary for the immediate safety of the vessel, persons on board the vessel or cargo or for the purpose of giving assistance to another ship or to a person in distress at sea: reg 14(1). For these purposes the word 'vessel' includes her fishing gear and the word 'cargo' includes the catch of a fishing vessel: reg 14(2).

**516. Rest periods and annual leave.** A worker on a fishing vessel[1] is entitled to 'adequate rest'[2], his minimum rest periods must be not be less than 10 hours in any 24-hour period[3] and 77 hours for each seven-day period[4]. Such a worker is also entitled to at least four weeks' annual leave and to be paid in respect of any such leave at the rate of a week's pay in respect of each week of leave[5]. A worker may present a complaint to an employment tribunal[6] that his employer has refused to permit the exercise of these[7] rights[8] or has failed to pay him the whole or any part of any amount due[9] to him[10], and the tribunal may make an award of compensation[11] or order the employer to pay the amounts owed[12], as applicable. The Secretary of State[13] may grant an exception from the requirements as to minimum rest periods[14] for objective or technical reasons or reasons concerning the organisation of work[15], and workers may be required to work additional hours in an emergency[16].

Where the pattern according to which an employer organises work is such as to put the health and safety of a worker employed by him at risk, in particular because the work is monotonous or the work-rate is predetermined, the employer must ensure that the worker is given reasonable rest breaks[17]. Failure to comply with this requirement is an offence[18].

Statutory and contractual rights to rest periods and annual leave may not be exercised separately[19].

1    As to the vessels to which these provisions apply see PARA 423 note 18. As to the meaning of 'worker' see PARA 515 note 2. As to the meaning of 'fishing vessel' see the Merchant Shipping Act 1995 s 313(1); and PARA 230.

2    Fishing Vessels (Working Time: Sea-fishermen) Regulations 2004, SI 2004/1713, reg 7(1). 'Adequate rest' means that a worker has regular rest periods, the duration of which are expressed in units of time and which are sufficiently long and continuous to ensure that, as a result of fatigue or other irregular working patterns, he does not cause injury to himself, to fellow workers or to

others and that he does not damage his health, either in the short term or in the longer term: reg 7(2). Records of rest periods must be kept: see reg 10. An employer who fails to comply with reg 10 is guilty of an offence: see PARA 515 note 5.

3 Fishing Vessels (Working Time: Sea-fishermen) Regulations 2004, SI 2004/1713, reg 7(3)(a). These rest periods may be divided into no more than two periods, one of which must be at least six hours in length; and the interval between consecutive rest periods must not exceed 14 hours: reg 7(4).

4 Fishing Vessels (Working Time: Sea-fishermen) Regulations 2004, SI 2004/1713, reg 7(3)(b).

5 Fishing Vessels (Working Time: Sea-fishermen) Regulations 2004, SI 2004/1713, reg 11(1). In respect of a period of employment of less than one year, a worker is entitled to annual leave of a proportion of four weeks equal to the proportion the period of employment in question bears to one year; the proportion to be determined in days and any fraction of a day to be treated as a whole day: reg 11(2). Leave to which a worker is entitled under reg 11 may be taken in instalments (reg 11(3)(a)) and may not be replaced by a payment in lieu, except where the worker's employment is terminated (reg 11(3)(b)). Provision for calculating the amount of a week's pay for this purpose is made by reg 11(4), (5).

A right to such payment does not affect any right of a worker to remuneration under his contract ('contractual remuneration'): reg 11(6). Any contractual remuneration paid to a worker in respect of a period of leave goes towards discharging any liability of the employer to make payments under reg 11 in respect of that period; and, conversely, any payment of remuneration under reg 11 in respect of a period goes towards discharging any liability of the employer to pay contractual remuneration in respect of that period: reg 11(7).

6 An employment tribunal may not consider a complaint under these provisions unless it is presented:

   (1) before the end of the period of three months beginning with the date on which it is alleged that the exercise of the right should have been permitted (or in the case of a rest period or leave extending over more than one day, the date on which it should have been permitted to begin) or, as the case may be, the payment should have been made (Fishing Vessels (Working Time: Sea-fishermen) Regulations 2004, SI 2004/1713, reg 19(2)(a)); or

   (2) within such further period as the tribunal considers reasonable in a case where it is satisfied that it was not reasonably practicable for the complaint to be presented before the end of that period of three months (reg 19(2)(b)).

   In working out when the time limit set by reg 19(2)(a) expires the period beginning with the day after the day on which the worker concerned complies with the requirement in the Employment Tribunals Act 1996 s 18A(1) (requirement to contact ACAS before instituting proceedings: see EMPLOYMENT vol 39 (2014) PARA 152) in relation to the matter in respect of which the proceedings are brought ('Day A') and ending with the day on which the worker concerned receives or, if earlier, is treated as receiving (by virtue of regulations made under s 18A(11)) the certificate issued under s 18A(4) ('Day B') is not to be counted: Fishing Vessels (Working Time: Sea-fishermen) Regulations 2004, SI 2004/1713, regs 19(2A), 19A(1), (2) (regs 19(2A), 19A added by SI 2014/386). If the time limit set by the Fishing Vessels (Working Time: Sea-fishermen) Regulations 2004, SI 2004/1713, reg 19(2)(a) would (if not extended by reg 19A(3)) expire during the period beginning with Day A and ending one month after Day B, the time limit expires instead at the end of that period: reg 19A(3) (as so added). The power conferred on the employment tribunal by reg 19(2)(b) to extend the time limit set by reg 19(2)(a) is exercisable in relation to that time limit as extended by reg 19A: reg 19A(4) (as so added).

7 Ie any right that the worker has under the Fishing Vessels (Working Time: Sea-fishermen) Regulations 2004, SI 2004/1713, reg 7(1), (3) or (4) or 11(1) (see the text and notes 1–6).

8 Fishing Vessels (Working Time: Sea-fishermen) Regulations 2004, SI 2004/1713, reg 19(1)(a).

9 Ie under the Fishing Vessels (Working Time: Sea-fishermen) Regulations 2004, SI 2004/1713, reg 11(1).

10 Fishing Vessels (Working Time: Sea-fishermen) Regulations 2004, SI 2004/1713, reg 19(1)(b).

11 Where an employment tribunal finds a complaint under the Fishing Vessels (Working Time: Sea-fishermen) Regulations 2004, SI 2004/1713, reg 19(1)(a) (see the text and notes 6–8) well-founded, it must make a declaration to that effect and may make an award of compensation to be paid by the employer to the worker: reg 19(3). The amount of the compensation must be such as the tribunal considers just and equitable in all the circumstances having regard to the employer's default in refusing to permit the worker to exercise his right and any loss sustained by the worker which is attributable to the matters complained of: reg 19(4).

12 Where on a complaint under the Fishing Vessels (Working Time: Sea-fishermen) Regulations 2004, SI 2004/1713, reg 19(1)(b) (see the text and notes 9–10) an employment tribunal finds that an employer has failed to pay a worker in accordance with reg 11(1), it must order the employer to pay to the worker the amount which it finds to be due to the seafarer: reg 19(5).

13 As to the Secretary of State see PARA 36.

14 Ie the requirements of the Fishing Vessels (Working Time: Sea-fishermen) Regulations 2004, SI 2004/1713, reg 7(3), (4) (see the text and notes 3, 4).
15 Fishing Vessels (Working Time: Sea-fishermen) Regulations 2004, SI 2004/1713, regs 5, 13(1). In connection with such exceptions see further reg 13 (2)–(6); and PARA 515 note 10.
16 See PARA 515 note 11.
17 Fishing Vessels (Working Time: Sea fishermen) Regulations 2004, SI 2004/1713, reg 9.
18 Fishing Vessels (Working Time: Sea-fishermen) Regulations 2004, SI 2004/1713, reg 18(1). In connection with offences see further PARA 515 note 5.
19 Where during any period a worker is entitled to a rest period or annual leave both under a provision of the Fishing Vessels (Working Time: Sea-fishermen) Regulations 2004, SI 2004/1713, and under a separate provision (including a provision of his contract), he may not exercise the two rights separately, but may, in taking a rest period or annual leave during that period, take advantage of whichever right is, in any particular respect, the more favourable: reg 12.

**517. Restriction on contracting out.** Any provision in an agreement (whether a contract of employment or not) is void in so far as it purports to exclude or limit the operation of the statutory requirements[1] as to hours of rest and leave for workers aboard fishing vessels[2] or to preclude a person from bringing proceedings[3] before an employment tribunal[4]. This prohibition does not apply to:

(1)      any agreement to refrain from instituting or continuing proceedings where a conciliation officer has taken[5] conciliation action[6]; or

(2)      any agreement to refrain from instituting or continuing proceedings[7] if the conditions regulating settlement agreements[8] are satisfied in relation to the agreement[9].

1 Ie any provision of the Fishing Vessels (Working Time: Sea-fishermen) Regulations 2004, SI 2004/1713 (see PARAS 515–516), save in so far as those regulations provide for such an agreement to have effect: reg 20(1)(a). As to the meaning of 'worker' see PARA 515 note 2. As to the meaning of 'fishing vessel' see the Merchant Shipping Act 1995 s 313(1); and PARA 230. As to the vessels to which these provisions apply see PARA 423 note 18.
2 Fishing Vessels (Working Time: Sea-fishermen) Regulations 2004, SI 2004/1713, reg 20(1)(a).
3 Ie proceedings under the Fishing Vessels (Working Time: Sea-fishermen) Regulations 2004, SI 2004/1713.
4 Fishing Vessels (Working Time: Sea-fishermen) Regulations 2004, SI 2004/1713, reg 20(1)(b).
5 Ie under any of the Employment Tribunals Act 1996 ss 18A–18C (see EMPLOYMENT vol 39 (2014) PARAS 152–153).
6 Fishing Vessels (Working Time: Sea-fishermen) Regulations 2004, SI 2004/1713, reg 20(2)(a) (amended by SI 2014/486).
7 Ie within the Employment Tribunals Act 1996 s 18(1)(r) (Fishing Vessels (Working Time: Sea-fishermen) Regulations 2004, SI 2004/1713, where conciliation is available: see EMPLOYMENT vol 39 (2014) PARA 152).
8 For these purposes of the conditions regulating settlement agreements under the M Fishing Vessels (Working Time: Sea-fishermen) Regulations 2004, SI 2004/1713, are that:
    (1)      the agreement must be in writing (reg 20(3)(a) (reg 20(3) amended by SI 2013/1956));
    (2)      the agreement must relate to the particular complaint (Fishing Vessels (Working Time: Sea-fishermen) Regulations 2004, SI 2004/1713, reg 20(3)(b));
    (3)      the worker must have received advice from a relevant independent adviser as to the terms and effect of the proposed agreement and, in particular, its effect on his ability to pursue his rights before an employment tribunal (reg 20(3)(c));
    (4)      there must be in force, when the adviser gives the advice, a contract of insurance, or an indemnity provided for members of a profession or a professional body, covering the risk of a claim by the worker in respect of loss arising in consequence of the advice (reg 20(3)(d));
    (5)      the agreement must identify the adviser (reg 20(3)(e)); and
    (6)      the agreement must state that the conditions regulating settlement agreements under the Fishing Vessels (Working Time: Sea-fishermen) Regulations 2004, SI 2004/1713, are satisfied (reg 20(3)(f) (amended by SI 2013/1956)).
    As to the meaning of 'worker' see PARA 515 note 2. A person is a relevant independent adviser for the purposes of the Fishing Vessels (Working Time: Sea-fishermen) Regulations 2004, SI 2004/1713, reg 20(3)(c):
    (a)      if he is a qualified lawyer (reg 20(4)(a));

(b)    if he is an officer, official, employee or member of an independent trade union who has been certified in writing by the trade union as competent to give advice and as authorised to do so on behalf of the trade union (reg 20(4)(b)); or

(c)    if he works at an advice centre (whether as an employee or as a volunteer) and has been certified in writing by the centre as competent to give advice and as authorised to do so on behalf of the centre (reg 20(4)(c)),

but a person is not a relevant independent adviser for those purposes:

(i)    if he is, is employed by or is acting in the matter for the employer or an associated employer (reg 20(5)(a));

(ii)   in the case of a person within reg 20(4)(b), if the trade union is the employer or an associated employer (reg 20(5)(b)); or

(iii)  in the case of a person within reg 20(4)(c), if the worker makes a payment for the advice received from him (reg 20(5)(d)).

In reg 20(4)(a) 'qualified lawyer' means a person who, for the purposes of the Legal Services Act 2007, is an authorised person in relation to an activity which constitutes the exercise of a right of audience or the conduct of litigation (within the meaning of that Act: see ss 1(4), 12(1)(a), (b); and LEGAL PROFESSIONS vol 65 (2015) PARAS 202, 352) (Fishing Vessels (Working Time: Sea-fishermen) Regulations 2004, SI 2004/1713, reg 20(6)(a) (amended by SI 2009/3348)); and for the purposes of the Fishing Vessels (Working Time: Sea-fishermen) Regulations 2004, SI 2004/1713, reg 20(5) any two employers are treated as associated if one is a company of which the other (directly or indirectly) has control or both are companies of which a third person (directly or indirectly) has control; and 'associated employer' is construed accordingly (reg 20(6)(b)).

9    Fishing Vessels (Working Time: Sea-fishermen) Regulations 2004, SI 2004/1713, reg 20(2)(b) (amended by SI 2013/1956; SI 2014/431).

## 518. Compliance and inspection.

Where a relevant inspector[1] is of the opinion that the statutory requirements as to hours of rest[2] have not been complied with in respect of any worker on a fishing vessel[3], and a hazard to the health or safety of any worker is thereby created[4], the vessel may be detained until the worker has had sufficient rest to resume his duties without creating a hazard to the health or safety of any worker[5]. This power of detention may not be exercised unreasonably[6]. Provision is made in connection with the enforcement of detention under these provisions[7], and for arbitration and compensation[8].

1    For these purposes 'relevant inspector' means a person mentioned in the Merchant Shipping Act 1995 s 258(1)(a), (b) or (c) (see PARA 48): Fishing Vessels (Working Time: Sea-fishermen) Regulations 2004, SI 2004/1713, reg 2(1).

2    Ie the Fishing Vessels (Working Time: Sea-fishermen) Regulations 2004, SI 2004/1713, reg 7 (see PARA 516).

3    Fishing Vessels (Working Time: Sea-fishermen) Regulations 2004, SI 2004/1713, reg 16(1)(a). As to the meaning of 'worker' see PARA 515 note 2. As to the meaning of 'fishing vessel' see the Merchant Shipping Act 1995 s 313(1); and PARA 230. As to the vessels to which these provisions apply see PARA 423 note 18.

4    Fishing Vessels (Working Time: Sea-fishermen) Regulations 2004, SI 2004/1713, reg 16(1)(b).

5    Fishing Vessels (Working Time: Sea-fishermen) Regulations 2004, SI 2004/1713, reg 16(1).

6    Fishing Vessels (Working Time: Sea-fishermen) Regulations 2004, SI 2004/1713, reg 16(2).

7    See the Fishing Vessels (Working Time: Sea-fishermen) Regulations 2004, SI 2004/1713, reg 16(3), (4) (applying the Merchant Shipping Act 1995 s 284: see PARA 1190).

8    See the Fishing Vessels (Working Time: Sea-fishermen) Regulations 2004, SI 2004/1713, reg 17 (applying the Merchant Shipping Act 1995 ss 96, 97: see PARAS 1142–1143).

## 519. Night work.

An employer:

(1)    must not assign a worker on a fishing vessel[1] to work which is to be undertaken during periods such that the worker will become a night worker[2] unless the worker has accessed a free[3] health assessment[4];

(2)    must ensure that each night worker employed by him has the opportunity of a free health assessment at regular intervals of whatever duration may be appropriate in his case[5].

Where a registered medical practitioner has advised an employer that a worker employed by the employer is suffering from health problems which the practitioner considers to be connected with the fact that the worker performs night work[6], and it is possible for the employer to transfer the worker to work to which the worker is suited and which is to be undertaken during periods such that the worker will cease to be a night worker, the employer must transfer the worker accordingly[7].

Failure to comply with these requirements is an offence[8], although workers on fishing vessels may be required to work additional hours in an emergency[9].

1   Ie a worker to whom the Fishing Vessels (Working Time: Sea-fishermen) Regulations 2004, SI 2004/1713, applies: reg 8(1). As to the meanings of 'worker' and 'employer' see PARA 515 note 2; as to the vessels and workers to which these provisions apply see PARA 423 note 18. Records of compliance with these requirements must be kept: see reg 10. Failure to comply with the record-keeping requirements is an offence punishable by a fine: see reg 18(2). In connection with offences see further PARA 515 note 5.

2   'Night worker' means (by virtue of the Fishing Vessels (Working Time: Sea-fishermen) Regulations 2004, SI 2004/1713, reg 2(1)) a worker:
    (1)     who, as a normal course, works at least three hours of his daily working time during night time, or
    (2)     who is likely, during night time, to work at least such proportion of his annual working time as may be specified for the purposes of the Fishing Vessels (Working Time: Sea-fishermen) Regulations 2004, SI 2004/1713, in a collective agreement or a workforce agreement,
    and, for the purpose of head (1) above, a person works hours as a normal course (without prejudice to the generality of that expression) if he works such hours on the majority of days on which he works. 'Night time' means (by virtue of reg 2(1)) a period the duration of which is not less than seven hours and which includes the period between midnight and 5 am (local time), which is determined for the purposes of the Fishing Vessels (Working Time: Sea-fishermen) Regulations 2004, SI 2004/1713, by a relevant agreement, or, in default of such a determination, the period between 11pm and 6am (local time). As to the meanings of 'collective agreement', 'workforce agreement' and 'relevant agreement' see PARA 515 note 3 (fishing vessels).
        An employer must, by sending it to the Maritime and Coastguard Agency, provide the Secretary of State with such information on night workers as the Secretary of State may specify in writing: see the Fishing Vessels (Working Time: Sea-fishermen) Regulations 2004, SI 2004/1713, reg 15. As to the Secretary of State see PARA 36. Failure to comply with this requirement is an offence punishable by a fine: see reg 18(2).

3   An assessment is 'free' if it is at no cost to the worker to whom it relates: Fishing Vessels (Working Time: Sea-fishermen) Regulations 2004, SI 2004/1713, reg 8(2). No person may disclose an assessment made for these purposes to any person other than the worker to whom it relates, unless:
    (1)     the worker makes the disclosure (reg 8(3)(a));
    (2)     the worker has given his consent to it in writing (reg 8(3)(a)); or
    (3)     the disclosure is confined to a statement that the assessment shows the worker to be fit either to take up (in a case where reg 8(1)(a)(i) (see note 4) applies) or continue to undertake (in a case where reg 8(1)(b) (see note 4) applies) an assignment (reg 8(3)(b)).

4   Ie unless:
    (1)     the employer has ensured that the worker will have the opportunity of a free health assessment before he takes up the assignment (Fishing Vessels (Working Time: Sea-fishermen) Regulations 2004, SI 2004/1713, reg 8(1)(a)(i)); or
    (2)     the worker had a health assessment before being assigned to work to be undertaken during such periods on an earlier occasion, and the employer has no reason to believe that that assessment is no longer valid (reg 8(1)(a)(ii)).

5   Fishing Vessels (Working Time: Sea-fishermen) Regulations 2004, SI 2004/1713, reg 8(1)(b).
6   Fishing Vessels (Working Time: Sea-fishermen) Regulations 2004, SI 2004/1713, reg 8(4)(a). 'Night work' means work during night time: reg 2(1).
7   Fishing Vessels (Working Time: Sea-fishermen) Regulations 2004, SI 2004/1713, reg 8(4)(b).
8   Subject to the Fishing Vessels (Working Time: Sea-fishermen) Regulations 2004, SI 2004/1713, reg 14 (see the text and note 9), an employer who fails to comply with reg 8(1) or (4) is guilty of an offence, punishable on summary conviction by a fine: reg 18(1).
9   See the Fishing Vessels (Working Time: Sea-fishermen) Regulations 2004, SI 2004/1713, reg 14; and PARA 515 note 11.

C.   SHIPS OPERATING ON INLAND WATERWAYS

520. **Maximum weekly working time.** Where a vessel operates only or mainly on inland waterways[1] a worker's[2] working time[3], including overtime, in

any reference period which is applicable in his case[4] may not exceed an average of 48 hours for each seven days[5], and an employer must take reasonable steps, in keeping with the need to protect the health and safety of workers, to ensure that such limit is complied with in the case of each worker employed by him in relation to whom it applies[6]. Failure to comply with this requirement is an offence[7].

These provisions[8] do not apply in relation to a worker where, on account of the specific characteristics of the activity in which he is engaged, the duration of his working time is not measured or pre-determined or can be determined by the worker himself, as may be the case for managing executives or other persons with autonomous decision-taking powers[9] or family workers[10]. Where part of the working time of a worker is measured or pre-determined or cannot be determined by the worker himself but the specific characteristics of the activity are such that, without being required to do so by the employer, the worker may also do work the duration of which is not measured or pre-determined or can be determined by the worker himself, these provisions apply only to so much of his work as is measured or pre-determined or cannot be determined by the worker himself[11].

1    As to the vessels to which these provisions apply see PARA 423 note 18.
2    'Worker' means a person employed (or, where the employment has ceased, who was employed) as a member of the travelling personnel of a ship to which the Merchant Shipping (Working Time: Inland Waterways) Regulations 2003, SI 2003/3049, apply by an undertaking which operates services for passengers or goods, but does not include persons who are training in a sail training vessel or persons who are not engaged in the navigation of, or have no emergency safety responsibilities on, such a vessel; 'employer', in relation to a worker, means the person by whom the worker is (or, where the employment has ceased, was) employed; 'employment', in relation to a worker, means employment under his contract, and 'employed' is construed accordingly: reg 2(1). Subject to reg 2(1), words and expressions used in the Merchant Shipping (Working Time: Inland Waterways) Regulations 2003, SI 2003/3049, have the same meaning as in Council Directive (EC) 93/104 (OJ L307, 13.12.93, p 18) concerning certain aspects of the organisation of working time (the Working Time Directive): see EMPLOYMENT vol 39 (2014) PARA 268 et seq): Merchant Shipping (Working Time: Inland Waterways) Regulations 2003, SI 2003/3049, reg 2(2).
    'Sail training vessel' means a sailing vessel which is being used either to provide instruction in the principles of responsibility, resourcefulness, loyalty and team endeavour and to advance education in the art of seamanship, or to provide instruction in navigation and seamanship for yachtsmen; and to which either the Code of Practice for the Safety of Small Commercial Sailing Vessels, the Code of Practice for Safety of Large Commercial Sailing and Motor Vessels, the Code of Practice for the Safety of Small Commercial Motor Vessels, or the Code of Practice for the Safety of Small Vessels in Commercial Use for Sport or Pleasure Operating from a Nominated Departure Point applies: Merchant Shipping (Working Time: Inland Waterways) Regulations 2003, SI 2003/3049, reg 2(1).
3    'Working time', in relation to a worker, means (by virtue of the Merchant Shipping (Working Time: Inland Waterways) Regulations 2003, SI 2003/3049, reg 2(1)):
    (1)    any period during which he is working, at his employer's disposal and carrying out his activity or duties;
    (2)    any period during which he is receiving relevant training; and
    (3)    any additional period which is to be treated as working time for the purpose of the Merchant Shipping (Working Time: Inland Waterways) Regulations 2003, SI 2003/3049, under a relevant agreement,
and 'work' is construed accordingly. 'Relevant training' means work experience provided pursuant to a training course or programme, training for employment, or both, other than work experience or training the immediate provider of which is an educational institution or a person whose main business is the provision of training and which is provided on a course run by that institution or person; 'relevant agreement', in relation to a worker, means a workforce agreement which applies to him, any provision of a collective agreement which forms part of a contract between him and his employer, or any other agreement in writing which is legally enforceable as between the worker and his employer; 'collective agreement' means a collective agreement within the meaning of the Trade Union and Labour Relations (Consolidation) Act 1992 s 178 (see EMPLOYMENT vol 41A (2014) PARAS 1093–1094), the trade union parties to which are independent trade unions within the meaning of s 5 (see EMPLOYMENT vol 41 (2014) PARA 904); and 'workforce agreement' means an agreement between an employer and workers employed by him or their representatives

in respect of which the conditions set out in the Merchant Shipping (Working Time: Inland Waterways) Regulations 2003, SI 2003/3049, Sch 1 are satisfied: reg 2(1).

4    The reference periods which apply in the case of a worker are:

    (1)    where a relevant agreement provides for the application of the Merchant Shipping (Working Time: Inland Waterways) Regulations 2003, SI 2003/3049, in relation to successive periods of 17 weeks, each such period (reg 6(3)(a)); or

    (2)    in any other case, any period of 17 weeks in the course of his employment (reg 6(3)(b)).

This is subject to the following special cases:

    (a)    where a worker has worked for his employer for less than 17 weeks, the reference period applicable in his case is the period that has elapsed since he started work for his employer (reg 6(3), (4)); and

    (b)    where either:

        (i)    the worker is engaged in security and surveillance activities requiring a permanent presence in order to protect property and persons, as may be the case for security guards and caretakers (regs 5, 6(5), 14(a));

        (ii)    the worker's activities involve the need for continuity of service or production, as may be the case in relation to work at docks, industries in which work cannot be interrupted on technical grounds, or the carriage of passengers on regular urban transport services (reg 14(b));

        (iii)    there is a foreseeable surge of activity, as may be the case in relation to tourism (reg 14(c)); or

        (iv)    the worker's activities are affected by an occurrence due to unusual and unforeseeable circumstances, beyond the control of the worker's employer, exceptional events, the consequences of which could not have been avoided despite the exercise of all due care by the employer, or an accident or the imminent risk of an accident (reg 14(d)),

the reference periods which apply in the case of that worker are calculated (ie in the context of either heads (1) or (2) or head (a) above) in relation to periods of 26 weeks instead of 17 weeks.

Additionally, a collective agreement or workforce agreement may for objective or technical reasons or reasons concerning the organisation of work, modify the application of reg 6(3), (4) in relation to particular workers or groups of workers by the substitution, for each reference to 17 weeks, of a different period (being a period not exceeding 52 weeks): regs 6(3), 15.

5    Merchant Shipping (Working Time: Inland Waterways) Regulations 2003, SI 2003/3049, reg 6(1). Provision for determining a worker's average working time for each seven days is made by reg 6(6), (7). Records are required to be kept to show that the limit imposed under reg 6(1) is being complied with: see reg 9.

6    Merchant Shipping (Working Time: Inland Waterways) Regulations 2003, SI 2003/3049, reg 6(2).

7    An employer who fails to comply with the Merchant Shipping (Working Time: Inland Waterways) Regulations 2003, SI 2003/3049, reg 6(2), is guilty of an offence punishable on summary conviction by a fine: reg 17(1). As to the powers of magistrates' courts to issue fines on summary conviction see SENTENCING vol 92 (2015) PARA 176. In any proceedings for an offence under the Merchant Shipping (Working Time: Inland Waterways) Regulations 2003, SI 2003/3049, it is a defence for the defendant to show that all reasonable steps had been taken by him to ensure compliance with the regulations: reg 17(2).

8    Ie the Merchant Shipping (Working Time: Inland Waterways) Regulations 2003, SI 2003/3049, reg 6(1), (2) (see the text and notes 1–6).

9    Merchant Shipping (Working Time: Inland Waterways) Regulations 2003, SI 2003/3049, reg 13(1)(a).

10    Merchant Shipping (Working Time: Inland Waterways) Regulations 2003, SI 2003/3049, reg 13(1)(b).

11    Merchant Shipping (Working Time: Inland Waterways) Regulations 2003, SI 2003/3049, reg 13(2).

**521.   Rest periods and annual paid leave.** A worker on an inland waterway[1] is entitled to 'adequate rest'[2], and during any reference period applicable to a worker the total number of hours comprised in his rest periods[3] must not be less than 77 hours for each seven days[4]. These provisions do no apply where the worker's activities are affected by:

    (1)    an occurrence due to unusual and unforeseeable circumstances, beyond the control of the worker's employer[5];

    (2)    exceptional events, the consequences of which could not have been avoided despite the exercise of all due care by the employer[6]; or

(3)　　an accident or the imminent risk of an accident[7].

Such a worker is also entitled to four weeks' annual leave and to be paid in respect of any such leave at the rate of a week's pay in respect of each week of leave[8]. A worker may present a complaint to an employment tribunal[9] that his employer has refused to permit the exercise of these[10] rights[11] or has failed to pay the worker the whole or any part of any amount due[12] to him[13], and the tribunal may make an award of compensation[14] or order the employer to pay the amounts owed[15], as applicable.

Where the pattern according to which an employer organises work is such as to put the health and safety of a worker employed by him at risk, in particular because the work is monotonous or the work-rate is predetermined, the employer must ensure that the worker is given reasonable rest breaks[16]. Failure to comply with this requirement is an offence[17].

Statutory and contractual rights to rest periods and annual leave may not be exercised separately[18].

1　As to the meaning of 'worker' see PARA 520 note 2; as to the vessels to which these provisions apply see PARA 423 note 18.

2　Merchant Shipping (Working Time: Inland Waterways) Regulations 2003, SI 2003/3049, reg 10(1). 'Adequate rest' means that a worker has regular rest periods, the duration of which are expressed in units of time and which are sufficiently long and continuous to ensure that, as a result of fatigue or other irregular working patterns, he does not cause injury to himself, to fellow workers or to others and that he does not damage his health, either in the short term or in the longer term: reg 10(2).

3　Ie the periods referred to in note 2.

4　Merchant Shipping (Working Time: Inland Waterways) Regulations 2003, SI 2003/3049, reg 10(3).

5　Merchant Shipping (Working Time: Inland Waterways) Regulations 2003, SI 2003/3049, regs 10(4), 14(d)(i). As to the meaning of 'employer' and cognate expressions see PARA 520 note 2.

6　Merchant Shipping (Working Time: Inland Waterways) Regulations 2003, SI 2003/3049, reg 14(d)(ii).

7　Merchant Shipping (Working Time: Inland Waterways) Regulations 2003, SI 2003/3049, reg 14(d)(iii).

8　Merchant Shipping (Working Time: Inland Waterways) Regulations 2003, SI 2003/3049, reg 11(1). In respect of a period of employment of less than one year, a worker is entitled to annual leave of a proportion of four weeks equal to the proportion the period of employment in question bears to one year; the proportion to be determined in days and any fraction of a day to be treated as a whole day: reg 11(2). Leave to which a worker is entitled under reg 11 may be taken in instalments (reg 11(3)(a)) and may not be replaced by a payment in lieu, except where the worker's employment is terminated (reg 11(3)(b)). Provision for calculating the amount of a week's pay for this purpose is made by reg 11(4), (5).

　　A right to such payment does not affect any right of a worker to remuneration under his contract ('contractual remuneration'): reg 11(6). Any contractual remuneration paid to a worker in respect of a period of leave goes towards discharging any liability of the employer to make payments under reg 11 in respect of that period; and, conversely, any payment of remuneration under reg 11 in respect of a period goes towards discharging any liability of the employer to pay contractual remuneration in respect of that period: reg 11(7).

9　An employment tribunal may not consider a complaint under these provisions unless it is presented:

(1)　before the end of the period of three months beginning with the date on which it is alleged that the exercise of the right should have been permitted (or in the case of a rest period or leave extending over more than one day, the date on which it should have been permitted to begin) or, as the case may be, the payment should have been made (Merchant Shipping (Working Time: Inland Waterways) Regulations 2003, SI 2003/3049, reg 18(2)(a)); or

(2)　within such further period as the tribunal considers reasonable in a case where it is satisfied that it was not reasonably practicable for the complaint to be presented before the end of that period of three months (reg 18(2)(b)).

　　In working out when the time limit set by reg 18(2)(a) expires the period beginning with the day after the day on which the worker concerned complies with the requirement in the

Employment Tribunals Act 1996 s 18A(1) (requirement to contact ACAS before instituting proceedings: see EMPLOYMENT vol 39 (2014) PARA 152) in relation to the matter in respect of which the proceedings are brought ('Day A') and ending with the day on which the worker concerned receives or, if earlier, is treated as receiving (by virtue of regulations made under s 18A(11)) the certificate issued under s 18A(4) ('Day B') is not to be counted: Merchant Shipping (Working Time: Inland Waterways) Regulations 2003, SI 2003/3049, regs 18(2A), 18A(1), (2) (regs 18(2A), 18A added by SI 2014/386). If the time limit set by the Merchant Shipping (Working Time: Inland Waterways) Regulations 2003, SI 2003/3049, reg 18(2)(a) would (if not extended by reg 18A(3)) expire during the period beginning with Day A and ending one month after Day B, the time limit expires instead at the end of that period: reg 18A(3) (as so added). The power conferred on the employment tribunal by reg 18(2)(b) to extend the time limit set by reg 18(2)(a) is exercisable in relation to that time limit as extended by reg 18A: reg 18A(4) (as so added).

10  Ie any right that the worker has under the Merchant Shipping (Working Time: Inland Waterways) Regulations 2003, SI 2003/3049, reg 10(1) or (3) or 11(1) (see the text and notes 1–8).

11  Merchant Shipping (Working Time: Inland Waterways) Regulations 2003, SI 2003/3049, reg 18(1)(a).

12  Ie under the Merchant Shipping (Working Time: Inland Waterways) Regulations 2003, SI 2003/3049, reg 11(1).

13  Merchant Shipping (Working Time: Inland Waterways) Regulations 2003, SI 2003/3049, reg 18(1)(b).

14  Where an employment tribunal finds a complaint under the Merchant Shipping (Working Time: Inland Waterways) Regulations 2003, SI 2003/3049, reg 18(1)(a) (see the text and notes 9–11) well-founded, it must make a declaration to that effect and may make an award of compensation to be paid by the employer to the worker: reg 18(3). The amount of the compensation must be such as the tribunal considers just and equitable in all the circumstances having regard to the employer's default in refusing to permit the worker to exercise his right and any loss sustained by the worker which is attributable to the matters complained of: reg 18(4).

15  Where on a complaint under the Merchant Shipping (Working Time: Inland Waterways) Regulations 2003, SI 2003/3049, reg 18(1)(b) (see the text and notes 12–13) an employment tribunal finds that an employer has failed to pay a worker in accordance with reg 11(1), it must order the employer to pay to the worker the amount which it finds to be due to the seafarer: reg 18(5).

16  Merchant Shipping (Working Time: Inland Waterways) Regulations 2003, SI 2003/3049, reg 8.

17  An employer who fails to comply with the Merchant Shipping (Working Time: Inland Waterways) Regulations 2003, SI 2003/3049, reg 8 is guilty of an offence, punishable on summary conviction by a fine: reg 17(1). As to offences see further PARA 520 note 7.

18  Where during any period a worker is entitled to a rest period or annual leave both under a provision of the Merchant Shipping (Working Time: Inland Waterways) Regulations 2003, SI 2003/3049, and under a separate provision (including a provision of his contract), he may not exercise the two rights separately, but may, in taking a rest period or annual leave during that period, take advantage of whichever right is, in any particular respect, the more favourable: reg 12.

**522. Restriction on contracting out.** Any provision in an agreement (whether a contract of employment or not) is void in so far as it purports to exclude or limit the operation of the statutory requirements[1] as to hours of rest and leave for workers on inland waterways[2] or to preclude a person from bringing proceedings[3] before an employment tribunal[4]. This prohibition does not apply to:

(1)     any agreement to refrain from instituting or continuing proceedings where a conciliation officer has taken[5] conciliation action[6]; or

(2)     any agreement to refrain from instituting or continuing proceedings[7] if the conditions regulating settlement agreements[8] are satisfied in relation to the agreement[9].

1   Ie any provision of the Merchant Shipping (Working Time: Inland Waterways) Regulations 2003, SI 2003/3049 (see PARAS 520–521), save in so far as those regulations provide for such an agreement to have effect: reg 19(1)(a). As to the vessels to which these provisions apply see PARA 423 note 18.

2   Merchant Shipping (Working Time: Inland Waterways) Regulations 2003, SI 2003/3049, reg 19(1)(a).

3   Ie proceedings under the Merchant Shipping (Working Time: Inland Waterways) Regulations 2003, SI 2003/3049.

4   Merchant Shipping (Working Time: Inland Waterways) Regulations 2003, SI 2003/3049, reg 19(1)(b).

5   Ie under any of the Employment Tribunals Act 1996 ss 18A–18C (see EMPLOYMENT vol 39
    (2014) PARAS 152–153).
6   Merchant Shipping (Working Time: Inland Waterways) Regulations 2003, SI 2003/3049, reg
    19(2)(a) (amended by SI 2014/486).
7   Ie within the Employment Tribunals Act 1996 s 18(1)(p) (proceedings under the Merchant
    Shipping (Working Time: Inland Waterways) Regulations 2003, SI 2003/3049, where conciliation
    is available: see EMPLOYMENT vol 39 (2014) PARA 152).
8   For these purposes of the conditions regulating settlement agreements under the Merchant
    Shipping (Working Time: Inland Waterways) Regulations 2003, SI 2003/3049, are that:
    (1)    the agreement must be in writing (reg 19(3)(a) (reg 19(3) amended by SI 2013/1956));
    (2)    the agreement must relate to the particular complaint (Merchant Shipping (Working
           Time: Inland Waterways) Regulations 2003, SI 2003/3049, reg 19(3)(b));
    (3)    the worker must have received advice from a relevant independent adviser as to the
           terms and effect of the proposed agreement and, in particular, its effect on his ability to
           pursue his rights before an employment tribunal (reg 19(3)(c));
    (4)    there must be in force, when the adviser gives the advice, a contract of insurance, or an
           indemnity provided for members of a profession or a professional body, covering the
           risk of a claim by the worker in respect of loss arising in consequence of the advice (reg
           19(3)(d));
    (5)    the agreement must identify the adviser (reg 19(3)(e)); and
    (6)    the agreement must state that the conditions regulating settlement agreements under the
           Merchant Shipping (Working Time: Inland Waterways) Regulations 2003, SI
           2003/3049, are satisfied (reg 19(3)(f) (amended by SI 2013/1956)).
    As to the meaning of 'worker' see PARA 520 note 2. A person is a relevant independent adviser
    for the purposes of the Merchant Shipping (Working Time: Inland Waterways) Regulations 2003,
    SI 2003/3049, reg 19(3)(c):
    (a)    if he is a qualified lawyer (reg 19(4)(a));
    (b)    if he is an officer, official, employee or member of an independent trade union who has
           been certified in writing by the trade union as competent to give advice and as authorised
           to do so on behalf of the trade union (reg 19(4)(b)); or
    (c)    if he works at an advice centre (whether as an employee or as a volunteer) and has been
           certified in writing by the centre as competent to give advice and as authorised to do so
           on behalf of the centre (reg 19(4)(c)),
    but a person is not a relevant independent adviser for those purposes:
    (i)    if he is, is employed by or is acting in the matter for the employer or an associated
           employer (reg 19(5)(a));
    (ii)   in the case of a person within reg 19(4)(b) or (c), if the trade union or advice centre is
           the employer or an associated employer (reg 19(5)(b)); or
    (iii)  in the case of a person within reg 19(4)(c), if the worker makes a payment for the advice
           received from him (reg 19(5)(d)).
    In reg 19(4)(a) 'qualified lawyer' means a person who, for the purposes of the Legal Services
    Act 2007, is an authorised person in relation to an activity which constitutes the exercise of a right
    of audience or the conduct of litigation (within the meaning of that Act: see ss 1(4), 12(1)(a), (b);
    and LEGAL PROFESSIONS vol 65 (2015) PARAS 202, 352) (Merchant Shipping (Working Time:
    Inland Waterways) Regulations 2003, SI 2003/3049, reg 19(6)(a) (amended by SI 2009/3348));
    and for the purposes of the Merchant Shipping (Working Time: Inland Waterways) Regulations
    2003, SI 2003/3049, reg 19(5) any two employers are treated as associated if one is a company of
    which the other (directly or indirectly) has control or both are companies of which a third person
    (directly or indirectly) has control; and 'associated employer' is construed accordingly (reg
    19(6)(b)).
9   Merchant Shipping (Working Time: Inland Waterways) Regulations 2003, SI 2003/3049, reg
    19(2)(b) (amended by SI 2013/1956; SI 2014/431).

## 523.  Night work. An employer:

(1)    must not assign a worker on an inland waterway[1] to work which is to
       be undertaken during periods such that the worker will become a night
       worker[2] unless the worker has accessed a free[3] health assessment[4];

(2)    must ensure that each night worker employed by him has the
       opportunity of a free health assessment at regular intervals of whatever
       duration may be appropriate in his case[5].

Where a registered medical practitioner has advised an employer that a worker
employed by the employer is suffering from health problems which the
practitioner considers to be connected with the fact that the worker performs

night work[6], and it is possible for the employer to transfer the worker to work to which the worker is suited and which is to be undertaken during periods such that the worker will cease to be a night worker, the employer must transfer the worker accordingly[7].

Failure to comply with these requirements is an offence[8].

1 Ie a worker to whom the Merchant Shipping (Working Time: Inland Waterways) Regulations 2003, SI 2003/3049 applies: reg 7(1). As to the meanings of 'worker' and 'employer' see PARA 520 note 2; as to the vessels and workers to which these provisions apply see PARA 423 note 18. Records of compliance with these requirements must be kept: see reg 9. Failure to comply with the record-keeping requirements is an offence punishable by a fine: see reg 17(1). In connection with offences see further PARA 520 note 7.

2 'Night worker' means (by virtue of the Merchant Shipping (Working Time: Inland Waterways) Regulations 2003, SI 2003/3049, reg 2(1)) a worker:
   (1)    who, as a normal course, works at least three hours of his daily working time during night time; or
   (2)    who is likely, during night time, to work at least such proportion of his annual working time as may be specified for the purposes of the Merchant Shipping (Working Time: Inland Waterways) Regulations 2003, SI 2003/3049, in a collective agreement or a workforce agreement,
and, for the purpose of head (1) above, a person works hours as a normal course (without prejudice to the generality of that expression) if he works such hours on the majority of days on which he works. 'Night time' means (by virtue of reg 2(1)) a period the duration of which is not less than seven hours and which includes the period between midnight and 5 am (local time), which is determined for the purposes of the Merchant Shipping (Working Time: Inland Waterways) Regulations 2003, SI 2003/3049, by a relevant agreement, or, in default of such a determination, the period between 11pm and 6am (local time). As to the meanings of 'collective agreement', 'workforce agreement' and 'relevant agreement' see PARA 520 note 3.
   An employer must, by sending it to the Maritime and Coastguard Agency, provide the Secretary of State with such information on night workers as the Secretary of State may specify in writing: see reg 16. As to the Secretary of State see PARA 36. Failure to comply with this requirement is an offence punishable by a fine: see reg 17(1).

3 An assessment is 'free' if it is at no cost to the worker to whom it relates: Merchant Shipping (Working Time: Inland Waterways) Regulations 2003, SI 2003/3049, reg 7(2). No person may disclose an assessment made for these purposes to any person other than the worker to whom it relates, unless:
   (1)    the worker has given his consent to it in writing (reg 7(3)(a)); or
   (2)    the disclosure is confined to a statement that the assessment shows the worker to be fit either to take up (in a case where reg 7(1)(a)(i) (see note 4) applies) or continue to undertake (in a case where reg 7(1)(b) (see note 4) applies) an assignment (reg 7(3)(b)).

4 Ie unless:
   (1)    the employer has ensured that the worker will have the opportunity of a free health assessment before he takes up the assignment (Merchant Shipping (Working Time: Inland Waterways) Regulations 2003, SI 2003/3049, reg 7(1)(a)(i)); or
   (2)    the worker had a health assessment before being assigned to work to be undertaken during such periods on an earlier occasion, and the employer has no reason to believe that that assessment is no longer valid (reg 7(1)(a)(ii)).

5 Merchant Shipping (Working Time: Inland Waterways) Regulations 2003, SI 2003/3049, reg 7(1)(b).

6 Merchant Shipping (Working Time: Inland Waterways) Regulations 2003, SI 2003/3049, reg 7(4)(a). 'Night work' means work during night time: reg 2(1).

7 Merchant Shipping (Working Time: Inland Waterways) Regulations 2003, SI 2003/3049, reg 7(4)(b).

8 An employer who fails to comply with the Merchant Shipping (Working Time: Inland Waterways) Regulations 2003, SI 2003/3049, reg 8(1) or (4) is guilty of an offence, punishable on summary conviction by a fine: reg 17(1).

## (x) Inquiries into Fitness or Conduct of Officers and Seamen

### A. OFFICERS

**524. Inquiry into fitness or conduct of officer.** If it appears to the Secretary of State[1] that an officer[2]:

(1) is unfit to discharge his duties, whether by reason of incompetence or misconduct or for any other reason[3]; or

(2) has been seriously negligent in the discharge of his duties[4]; or

(3) has failed to comply with his duty to assist another ship[5] in case of collision[6],

the Secretary of State may cause an inquiry to be held by one or more persons appointed by him and, if he does so, may, if he thinks fit, suspend, pending the outcome of the inquiry, any certificate issued to the officer under the manning provisions[7] and require the officer to deliver it to him[8]. Where a certificate issued to an officer has been suspended in this way[9], the suspension may, on the application of the officer, be terminated by the High Court, and the decision of the court on such an application is final[10].

Any such inquiry[11] must be conducted in accordance with the inquiry rules[12]; and those rules must require the persons holding the inquiry to hold it with the assistance of one or more assessors[13].

The persons holding such an inquiry[14] into the fitness or conduct of an officer[15]:

(a) may, if satisfied of any of the matters mentioned in heads (1) to (3) above, cancel or suspend any certificate issued to him[16] or censure him[17];

(b) may make such order with regard to costs of the inquiry as they think just[18]; and

(c) must make a report on the case to the Secretary of State[19];

and, if the certificate is cancelled or suspended, the officer, unless he has delivered it to the Secretary of State[20], must deliver it forthwith to the persons holding the inquiry or to the Secretary of State[21]. Provision is made for the reissue and restoration of cancelled or suspended certificates[22].

1 As to the Secretary of State see PARA 36.
2 Merchant Shipping Act 1995 s 61(1). As to qualification as an officer see PARA 495 et seq. The Merchant Shipping Act 1995 ss 60–68, the Merchant Shipping (Section 52 Inquiries) Rules 1982, SI 1982/1752, and the Merchant Shipping (Section 63 Inquiries) Rules 1997, SI 1997/347 (see the text and notes 2–22; and PARAS 525–529) apply in relation to all United Kingdom ships apart from fishing vessels: being concerned with matters with which the Merchant Shipping (Maritime Labour Convention) (Minimum Requirements for Seafarers etc) Regulations 2014, SI 2014/1613 and the Maritime Labour Convention (Cm 7049)) are not concerned (see PARA 423), these provisions are not limited to the vessels excluded from the scope of the Convention (see further PARA 423 note 22). As to the meaning of 'fishing vessel' see PARA 230.
3 Merchant Shipping Act 1995 s 61(1)(a).
4 Merchant Shipping Act 1995 s 61(1)(b).
5 As to the meaning of 'ship' see PARA 229.
6 Merchant Shipping Act 1995 s 61(1)(c). Head (3) in the text refers to a failure to comply with the provisions of s 92 (see PARA 727): see s 61(1)(c).
7 Ie in pursuance of the Merchant Shipping Act 1995 s 47 (see PARA 503): s 61(1).
8 Merchant Shipping Act 1995 s 61(1). If a person fails to deliver a cancelled or suspended seaman's certificate as required by s 61 he commits an offence: see s 66; and PARA 1085.
9 Ie under the Merchant Shipping Act 1995 s 61(1) (see the text and notes 1–8): see s 61(2).
10 Merchant Shipping Act 1995 s 61(2).
11 Ie any inquiry under the Merchant Shipping Act 1995 s 61: see s 61(3).
12 Ie rules made under the Merchant Shipping Act 1995 s 65(1) (see PARAS 525–529): see s 61(3).
13 Merchant Shipping Act 1995 s 61(3). As to the role of nautical assessors generally see PARA 205.
14 Ie an inquiry under the Merchant Shipping Act 1995 s 61: see s 61(4).
15 Merchant Shipping Act 1995 s 61(4).
16 Ie issued to him under the Merchant Shipping Act 1995 s 47: s 61(4)(a).
17 Merchant Shipping Act 1995 s 61(4)(a).

18 Merchant Shipping Act 1995 s 61(4)(b). Any costs which a person is ordered to pay under s 61(4)(b) may be recovered from him by the Secretary of State: s 61(5).
19 Merchant Shipping Act 1995 s 61(4)(c).
20 Ie in pursuance of the Merchant Shipping Act 1995 s 61(1) (see the text and notes 1–8): see s 61(4).
21 Merchant Shipping Act 1995 s 61(4). See note 8.
22 See the Merchant Shipping Act 1995 s 67; and PARA 508.

**525. Notice of inquiry into fitness or conduct of officer.** When the Secretary of State[1] causes an inquiry into the fitness or conduct of an officer[2] to be held, he must cause a notice (a 'notice of inquiry') to be served on the officer concerned, who must be made a party to the inquiry[3]. Service of such a notice must be effected at least 30 days[4] before the date fixed for the inquiry either by serving the officer concerned personally or by sending the notice to his last known address by registered post or by the recorded delivery service[5].

The notice of inquiry must state:

(1)    the facts giving rise to the inquiry[6];
(2)    the allegation[7] made against the officer to whom the notice is addressed and the grounds therefor[8];
(3)    the time and date when and the place where the inquiry is to be held[9];
(4)    the officer's rights[10] at the inquiry[11].

1   As to the Secretary of State see PARA 36.
2   Ie an inquiry under the Merchant Shipping Act 1995 s 61 (see PARA 524): see the Merchant Shipping (Section 52 Inquiries) Rules 1982, SI 1982/1752, rr 2(1), 4(1) (having effect under the Merchant Shipping Act 1995 s 65). For these purposes, 'officer' means an officer qualified for the purposes of s 47 (see PARA 507) and includes a master, skipper, mate, second hand, deck officer, marine engineer officer, radio officer and doctor: Merchant Shipping (Section 52 Inquiries) Rules 1982, SI 1982/1752, r 2(1). As to the context in which these provisions apply see PARA 524 note 2.
3   Merchant Shipping (Section 52 Inquiries) Rules 1982, SI 1982/1752, r 4(1).
4   For these purposes, any period of time specified by reference to days is exclusive of the first day and inclusive of the last day unless the last day falls on a Saturday, Sunday, Christmas Day, Good Friday or any day appointed by law to be a bank holiday in that part of the United Kingdom where the inquiry is to be held, in which case the time is to be reckoned exclusively of that day also: Merchant Shipping (Section 52 Inquiries) Rules 1982, SI 1982/1752, r 2(2). As to the meaning of 'United Kingdom' see PARA 16 note 3.
5   Merchant Shipping (Section 52 Inquiries) Rules 1982, SI 1982/1752, r 4(1).
6   Merchant Shipping (Section 52 Inquiries) Rules 1982, SI 1982/1752, r 4(2)(a).
7   For these purposes, 'allegation' means an allegation by the Secretary of State that an officer's fitness or conduct falls within the Merchant Shipping Act 1995 s 61(1)(a)–(c) (see PARA 524): Merchant Shipping (Section 52 Inquiries) Rules 1982, SI 1982/1752, r 2(1).
8   Merchant Shipping (Section 52 Inquiries) Rules 1982, SI 1982/1752, r 4(2)(b).
9   Merchant Shipping (Section 52 Inquiries) Rules 1982, SI 1982/1752, r 4(2)(c).
10  Ie his rights as set out in the Merchant Shipping (Section 52 Inquiries) Rules 1982, SI 1982/1752, r 7(2), (3) (see PARA 528): see r 4(2).
11  Merchant Shipping (Section 52 Inquiries) Rules 1982, SI 1982/1752, r 4(2).

**526. Appointment of court of inquiry into fitness or conduct of officer.** The person appointed[1] to hold an inquiry into the fitness or conduct of an officer[2] must conduct it with the assistance of one or more assessors who must be appointed by the Lord Chancellor[3].

Wherever possible, at least one of the assessors appointed must have had experience in the same capacity and in the same type of ship as the officer concerned[4]. However, a person may not be appointed after the day on which he attains the age of 70 to assist with such an inquiry as an assessor[5].

1   For these purposes, 'person appointed' means the person or persons appointed by the Secretary of State to hold an inquiry under the Merchant Shipping Act 1995 s 61 (see PARA 524): Merchant Shipping (Section 52 Inquiries) Rules 1982, SI 1982/1752, r 2(1).

2　Ie an inquiry under the Merchant Shipping Act 1995 s 61 (see PARA 524): see the Merchant Shipping (Section 52 Inquiries) Rules 1982, SI 1982/1752, rr 2(1), 5(1). As to the meaning of 'officer' for these purposes see PARA 525 note 2. As to the context in which these provisions apply see PARA 524 note 2.

3　Merchant Shipping (Section 52 Inquiries) Rules 1982, SI 1982/1752, r 5(1). As to the role of nautical assessors generally see PARA 205. As to the Lord Chancellor see CONSTITUTIONAL AND ADMINISTRATIVE LAW vol 20 (2014) PARAS 255–261.

4　Merchant Shipping (Section 52 Inquiries) Rules 1982, SI 1982/1752, r 5(3).

5　Merchant Shipping (Section 52 Inquiries) Rules 1982, SI 1982/1752, r 5(4) (added by the Judicial Pensions and Retirement Act 1993 s 26(10), Sch 6 para 62).

**527. Holding of inquiry into fitness or conduct of officer.** At the time and the place appointed for holding an inquiry into the fitness or conduct of an officer[1], the person appointed[2] may proceed with the inquiry whether the party upon whom the notice of inquiry[3] was served, any other party, any person who has applied to become a party, or any of them, are present or not; but, where the officer concerned has been served with the notice of inquiry by post, the person appointed must not proceed with the inquiry in his absence unless satisfied that the officer has been duly served[4].

Any other person, not being the officer concerned, may, with the leave of the person appointed, become a party to the inquiry[5].

The inquiry must be held in public save to the extent to which the person appointed is properly satisfied that in the interests of justice, or for other good and sufficient reason in the public interest, any part of the evidence or any argument relating thereto should be heard in private[6].

1　Ie an inquiry under the Merchant Shipping Act 1995 s 61 (see PARA 524): see the Merchant Shipping (Section 52 Inquiries) Rules 1982, SI 1982/1752, r 2(1). As to the meaning of 'officer' for these purposes see PARA 525 note 2. As to the context in which these provisions apply see PARA 524 note 2.

2　As to the meaning of 'person appointed' see PARA 526 note 1.

3　As to the meaning of 'notice of inquiry' see PARA 525.

4　Merchant Shipping (Section 52 Inquiries) Rules 1982, SI 1982/1752, r 6(1). The text refers to an officer who has been served in accordance with the requirements of r 4(1) (see PARA 525): see r 6(1).

5　Merchant Shipping (Section 52 Inquiries) Rules 1982, SI 1982/1752, r 6(2).

6　Merchant Shipping (Section 52 Inquiries) Rules 1982, SI 1982/1752, r 6(3).

**528. Procedure at inquiry into fitness or conduct of officer.** The proceedings at an inquiry into the fitness or conduct of an officer[1] must commence with the presentation of behalf of the Secretary of State[2] of the case against the officer concerned[3].

The officer concerned has the right:

(1)　to defend himself against the allegation[4], in person or otherwise[5];

(2)　to admit, before or at any time after the commencement of the inquiry, the allegation or any part of it made against him[6].

Where more than one allegation is made against an officer, his admission of an allegation or any part of it pursuant to head (2) above is without prejudice to his right to defend himself against any other allegation which he does not admit[7].

Any party to the inquiry has the right in person or by a representative to make an opening statement, call witnesses[8], cross-examine witnesses called by other parties, tender evidence other than oral evidence and address the person appointed in such order as the person appointed[9] may direct[10]. If a party does not appear in person at the inquiry and is not represented by another person, he may make representations in writing to the person appointed and such written representations must be read out at the inquiry by or on behalf of the person appointed[11].

Without prejudice to the admission of documents as secondary evidence allowed by statute or otherwise, affidavits, depositions, statutory declarations and other written evidence must, unless the person appointed considers it unjust, be accepted as evidence at the inquiry[12].

The person appointed may postpone or adjourn the hearing of the inquiry for such period as he thinks fit either of his own motion or upon the application of any party[13].

1  Ie an inquiry under the Merchant Shipping Act 1995 s 61 (see PARA 524): see the Merchant Shipping (Section 52 Inquiries) Rules 1982, SI 1982/1752, r 2(1). As to the meaning of 'officer' for these purposes see PARA 525 note 2. As to the context in which these provisions apply see PARA 524 note 2.
2  As to the Secretary of State see PARA 36.
3  Merchant Shipping (Section 52 Inquiries) Rules 1982, SI 1982/1752, r 7(1).
4  As to the meaning of 'allegation' see PARA 525 note 7.
5  Merchant Shipping (Section 52 Inquiries) Rules 1982, SI 1982/1752, r 7(2)(a)(i).
6  Merchant Shipping (Section 52 Inquiries) Rules 1982, SI 1982/1752, r 7(2)(a)(ii).
7  Merchant Shipping (Section 52 Inquiries) Rules 1982, SI 1982/1752, r 7(2)(b).
8  As to the power of the person holding an inquiry to summon witnesses see PARA 536.
9  As to the meaning of 'person appointed' see PARA 526 note 1.
10 Merchant Shipping (Section 52 Inquiries) Rules 1982, SI 1982/1752, r 7(3).
11 Merchant Shipping (Section 52 Inquiries) Rules 1982, SI 1982/1752, r 7(3).
12 Merchant Shipping (Section 52 Inquiries) Rules 1982, SI 1982/1752, r 7(4).
13 Merchant Shipping (Section 52 Inquiries) Rules 1982, SI 1982/1752, r 7(5).

**529. Decision of inquiry into fitness or conduct of officer.** The person appointed[1] must, at the conclusion of an inquiry into the fitness or conduct of an officer[2] or as soon as possible thereafter, announce his decision in public and make a report on the case[3] to the Secretary of State[4]. Each assessor[5] must either sign the report with or without reservations, or state in writing his dissent therefrom and his reasons for such dissent; and such reservations or dissent and reasons, if any, must be forwarded to the Secretary of State with the report[6].

The Secretary of State must inform the officer concerned, in writing, of the decision of the person appointed if the officer was not in court when that decision was announced and must make a copy of the report available to him[7].

A copy of the report must be made available to any party to the inquiry upon request to the Secretary of State[8].

1  As to the meaning of 'person appointed' see PARA 526 note 1.
2  Ie an inquiry under the Merchant Shipping Act 1995 s 61 (see PARA 524): see the Merchant Shipping (Section 52 Inquiries) Rules 1982, SI 1982/1752, r 2(1). As to the meaning of 'officer' for these purposes see PARA 525 note 2. As to the context in which these provisions apply see PARA 524 note 2.
3  Ie pursuant to the Merchant Shipping Act 1995 s 61(4)(c) (see PARA 524): see the Merchant Shipping (Section 52 Inquiries) Rules 1982, SI 1982/1752, r 8. As to the Secretary of State see PARA 36.
4  Merchant Shipping (Section 52 Inquiries) Rules 1982, SI 1982/1752, r 8.
5  As to the appointment of assessors to inquiries as to fitness or conduct see PARA 526. As to the role of nautical assessors generally see PARA 205.
6  Merchant Shipping (Section 52 Inquiries) Rules 1982, SI 1982/1752, r 8.
7  Merchant Shipping (Section 52 Inquiries) Rules 1982, SI 1982/1752, r 8.
8  Merchant Shipping (Section 52 Inquiries) Rules 1982, SI 1982/1752, r 8.

B.    SEAMEN OTHER THAN OFFICERS

**530. Inquiry into fitness or conduct of seaman other than officer.** Where a person has, before the due date[1], required his case to be dealt with by an inquiry into the fitness or conduct of a seaman[2] other than an officer[3], the Secretary of State[4] must cause an inquiry to be held by one or more persons appointed by him[5].

Any such inquiry must be conducted in accordance with inquiry rules made by the Secretary of State[6]; and those rules must require the persons holding the inquiry to hold it with the assistance of one or more assessors[7].

The persons holding any such inquiry:

(1) may confirm the decision of the Secretary of State and cancel or suspend the certificate accordingly[8];

(2) may, where the decision was to cancel the certificate, suspend it instead[9];

(3) may, where the decision was to suspend the certificate, suspend it for a different period[10];

(4) may, instead of confirming the decision of the Secretary of State, censure the holder of the certificate or take no further action[11];

(5) may make such order with regard to the costs of the inquiry as they think just[12]; and

(6) must make a report on the case to the Secretary of State[13];

and, if the certificate is cancelled or suspended, it must be delivered forthwith to the persons holding the inquiry or to the Secretary of State[14]. Provision is made for the reissue and restoration of cancelled or suspended certificates[15].

1 Ie before the date mentioned in the Merchant Shipping Act 1995 s 62(4) (see PARA 508), being the date from which the cancellation of a certificate issued under s 54 (see PARA 503), or of any certificate issued under s 47 (see PARAS 503, 507), is to take effect, or the date from which and the period for which the suspension of such a certificate is to take effect: see s 63(1).
2 As to the meaning of 'seaman' see PARA 457 note 5. As to the context in which these provisions apply see PARA 524 note 2.
3 Ie an inquiry under the Merchant Shipping Act 1995 s 63 (see PARA 530): s 63(1).
4 As to the Secretary of State see PARA 36.
5 Merchant Shipping Act 1995 s 63(1).
6 Ie in accordance with rules made under the Merchant Shipping Act 1995 s 65(1) (see PARAS 531–535): see s 63(2).
7 Merchant Shipping Act 1995 s 63(2). As to the role of nautical assessors generally see PARA 205.
8 Merchant Shipping Act 1995 s 63(3)(a).
9 Merchant Shipping Act 1995 s 63(3)(b).
10 Merchant Shipping Act 1995 s 63(3)(c).
11 Merchant Shipping Act 1995 s 63(3)(d).
12 Merchant Shipping Act 1995 s 63(3)(e). Any costs which a person is ordered to pay under s 63(3)(e) may be recovered from him by the Secretary of State: s 63(4).
13 Merchant Shipping Act 1995 s 63(3)(f).
14 Merchant Shipping Act 1995 s 63(3). If a person fails to deliver a cancelled or suspended seaman's certificate as required by s 63 he commits an offence: see s 66; and PARA 1085.
15 See the Merchant Shipping Act 1995 s 67; and PARA 508.

**531. Notice of inquiry into the fitness or conduct of a seaman other than an officer.** Where the Secretary of State[1] causes an inquiry into the fitness or conduct of a seaman other than an officer[2] to be held, he must cause a notice (a 'notice of inquiry') to be served in writing on the certificate holder[3] concerned who must be made a party to the inquiry[4]. Service of such a notice must be effected at least 30 days[5] before the date fixed for the inquiry either by serving the certificate holder concerned personally or by sending the notice to his last known address by registered post or by the recorded delivery service[6].

The notice of inquiry must state:

(1) the facts giving rise to the inquiry[7];

(2) the allegation[8] made against the certificate holder to whom the notice is addressed and the grounds therefor[9];

(3) the time and date when, and the place where, the inquiry is to be held[10];

(4) the certificate holder's rights[11] at the inquiry[12].

1 As to the Secretary of State see PARA 36.

2 For these purposes, 'inquiry' means any inquiry, and any rehearing of such an inquiry, to which the Merchant Shipping (Section 63 Inquiries) Rules 1997, SI 1997/347, apply (r 2(1)); and the Merchant Shipping (Section 63 Inquiries) Rules 1997, SI 1997/347, apply to any inquiry under the Merchant Shipping Act 1995 s 63 (see PARA 530), and to any rehearing of such an inquiry under s 64 (see PARA 537) which is not held by the High Court (Merchant Shipping (Section 63 Inquiries) Rules 1997, SI 1997/347, r 3). The Merchant Shipping (Section 63 Inquiries) Rules 1997, SI 1997/347, are made under the Merchant Shipping Act 1995 s 65).
3 For these purposes, 'certificate holder' means the holder of a certificate of competency issued under either the Merchant Shipping Act 1995 s 47 (see PARAS 503, 507) (other than one certifying that a person is qualified as an officer) or s 54 (see PARA 503): Merchant Shipping (Section 63 Inquiries) Rules 1997, SI 1997/347, r 2(1). As to the context in which these provisions apply see PARA 524 note 2.
4 Merchant Shipping (Section 63 Inquiries) Rules 1997, SI 1997/347, r 4(1).
5 Any period specified in the Merchant Shipping (Section 63 Inquiries) Rules 1997, SI 1997/347, by reference to days is exclusive of the first day and inclusive of the last day unless the last day falls on a Saturday, Sunday, Christmas Day, Good Friday or any day appointed by law to be a bank holiday in the part of the United Kingdom where the inquiry is to be held, in which case the time must be reckoned exclusively of that day also: r 2(2). As to the meaning of 'United Kingdom' see PARA 16 note 3.
6 Merchant Shipping (Section 63 Inquiries) Rules 1997, SI 1997/347, r 4(2).
7 Merchant Shipping (Section 63 Inquiries) Rules 1997, SI 1997/347, r 4(3)(a).
8 For these purposes, 'allegation' means an allegation by the Secretary of State that a certificate holder is unfit to be the holder of such a certificate, whether by reason of incompetence or misconduct or for any other reason, within the meaning of the Merchant Shipping Act 1995 s 62(1) (see PARA 508); Merchant Shipping (Section 63 Inquiries) Rules 1997, SI 1997/347, r 2(1).
9 Merchant Shipping (Section 63 Inquiries) Rules 1997, SI 1997/347, r 4(3)(b).
10 Merchant Shipping (Section 63 Inquiries) Rules 1997, SI 1997/347, r 4(3)(c).
11 Ie the rights as set out in the Merchant Shipping (Section 63 Inquiries) Rules 1997, SI 1997/347, r 7(2), (3) (see PARA 534): see r 4(3)(d).
12 Merchant Shipping (Section 63 Inquiries) Rules 1997, SI 1997/347, r 4(3)(d).

**532. Appointment of court of inquiry into the fitness or conduct of a seaman other than an officer.** The person appointed[1] to hold an inquiry[2] into the fitness or conduct of a seaman other than an officer must conduct it with the assistance of one or more assessors who must be appointed by the Lord Chancellor[3]. An assessor must be suitably qualified to assess the competence of a seaman to discharge the duties and responsibilities commensurate with his certificate[4].

1 For these purposes, 'person appointed' means the person or persons appointed by the Secretary of State to hold an inquiry under the Merchant Shipping Act 1995 s 63 (see PARA 530): Merchant Shipping (Section 63 Inquiries) Rules 1997, SI 1997/347, r 2(1). As to the Secretary of State see PARA 36.
2 As to the meaning of 'inquiry' for these purposes see PARA 531 note 2. As to the context in which these provisions apply see PARA 524 note 2.
3 Merchant Shipping (Section 63 Inquiries) Rules 1997, SI 1997/347, r 5(1). As to the role of nautical assessors generally see PARA 205. As to the Lord Chancellor see CONSTITUTIONAL AND ADMINISTRATIVE LAW vol 20 (2014) PARAS 255–261.
4 Merchant Shipping (Section 63 Inquiries) Rules 1997, SI 1997/347, r 5(2).

**533. Holding of inquiry into the fitness or conduct of a seaman other than an officer.** At the time and place appointed for holding an inquiry[1] into the fitness or conduct of a seaman other than an officer, the person appointed[2] may proceed with the inquiry in the absence of the certificate holder[3] upon whom the notice of inquiry[4] was served, any other party, or any person who has applied to become a party, or any of them[5]. Where, however, the certificate holder concerned has been served with the notice of inquiry by post, the person appointed must not proceed with the inquiry in his absence unless satisfied that the certificate holder has been duly served[6].

Any other person, not being the certificate holder concerned, may, with the leave of the person appointed, become a party to the inquiry[7].

The inquiry must be held in public except to the extent to which the person appointed is satisfied that in the interests of justice, or for other good and sufficient reason in the public interest, any part of the evidence or any argument relating thereto should be heard in private[8].

1 As to the meaning of 'inquiry' for these purposes see PARA 531 note 2. As to the context in which these provisions apply see PARA 524 note 2.
2 As to the meaning of 'person appointed' see PARA 532 note 1.
3 As to the meaning of 'certificate holder' for these purposes see PARA 531 note 3.
4 As to the meaning of 'notice of inquiry' see PARA 531.
5 Merchant Shipping (Section 63 Inquiries) Rules 1997, SI 1997/347, r 6(1).
6 Merchant Shipping (Section 63 Inquiries) Rules 1997, SI 1997/347, r 6(1) proviso. The text refers to a certificate holder who has been served in accordance with the requirements of r 4(1), (2) (see PARA 531): see r 6(1) proviso.
7 Merchant Shipping (Section 63 Inquiries) Rules 1997, SI 1997/347, r 6(2).
8 Merchant Shipping (Section 63 Inquiries) Rules 1997, SI 1997/347, r 6(3).

**534. Procedure at inquiry into the fitness or conduct of a seaman other than an officer; decision.** The proceedings at an inquiry[1] into the fitness or conduct of a seaman other than an officer must commence with the presentation on behalf of the Secretary of State[2] of the case against the certificate holder[3] concerned[4].

The certificate holder has the right:

(1) to defend himself against the allegation[5], in person or otherwise[6];
(2) to admit before or at any time after the commencement of the inquiry the allegation or any part of it[7].

Where more than one allegation is made against a certificate holder, his admission of an allegation or any part of it pursuant to head (2) above is without prejudice to his right to defend himself against any other allegation which he does not admit[8].

Any party to the inquiry has the right in person or by a representative to make an opening statement, call witnesses[9], cross-examine witnesses called by other parties or on behalf of the Secretary of State, tender evidence other than oral evidence and address the person appointed[10] in such order as the person appointed may direct[11].

If a party does not appear in person at the inquiry and is not represented by another person, he may make representations in writing to the person appointed and such written representations must be read out at the inquiry by or on behalf of the person appointed[12].

Without prejudice to the admission of documents as secondary evidence allowed by statute or otherwise, affidavits, depositions, statutory declarations and other written evidence must, unless the person appointed considers it unjust, be accepted as evidence at the inquiry[13].

The person appointed may postpone or adjourn the hearing of the inquiry for such period as he thinks fit either of his own motion or upon the application of any party[14].

1 As to the meaning of 'inquiry' for these purposes see PARA 531 note 2. As to the context in which these provisions apply see PARA 524 note 2.
2 As to the Secretary of State see PARA 36.
3 As to the meaning of 'certificate holder' for these purposes see PARA 531 note 3.
4 Merchant Shipping (Section 63 Inquiries) Rules 1997, SI 1997/347, r 7(1).
5 As to the meaning of 'allegation' see PARA 531 note 8.
6 Merchant Shipping (Section 63 Inquiries) Rules 1997, SI 1997/347, r 7(2)(a)(i).
7 Merchant Shipping (Section 63 Inquiries) Rules 1997, SI 1997/347, r 7(2)(a)(ii).
8 Merchant Shipping (Section 63 Inquiries) Rules 1997, SI 1997/347, r 7(2)(b).
9 As to the power to summon witnesses see PARA 536.

10  As to the meaning of 'person appointed' see PARA 532 note 1.
11  Merchant Shipping (Section 63 Inquiries) Rules 1997, SI 1997/347, r 7(3).
12  Merchant Shipping (Section 63 Inquiries) Rules 1997, SI 1997/347, reg 7(4).
13  Merchant Shipping (Section 63 Inquiries) Rules 1997, SI 1997/347, reg 7(5).
14  Merchant Shipping (Section 63 Inquiries) Rules 1997, SI 1997/347, reg 7(6).

**535.  Decision of inquiry into the fitness or conduct of a seaman other than an officer.** The person appointed[1] must, at the conclusion of an inquiry[2] into the fitness or conduct of a seaman other than an officer, or as soon as possible thereafter, announce his decision in public[3].

Each assessor[4] must either sign the report with or without reservations, or state in writing his dissent therefrom and his reasons for such dissent, and any such reservations or dissent and reasons must be forwarded to the Secretary of State[5] with the report[6].

The Secretary of State must inform the certificate holder[7] concerned, in writing, of the decision of the person appointed if the certificate holder was not present when that decision was announced and make a copy of the report available to him[8].

A copy of the report must be made available to any party to the inquiry upon request to the Secretary of State[9].

1   As to the meaning of 'person appointed' see PARA 532 note 1.
2   As to the meaning of 'inquiry' for these purposes see PARA 531 note 2. As to the context in which these provisions apply see PARA 524 note 2.
3   Merchant Shipping (Section 63 Inquiries) Rules 1997, SI 1997/347, reg 8(1).
4   As to the appointment of assessors for these purposes see PARA 532.
5   As to the Secretary of State see PARA 36.
6   Merchant Shipping (Section 63 Inquiries) Rules 1997, SI 1997/347, reg 8(2).
7   As to the meaning of 'certificate holder' for these purposes see PARA 531 note 3.
8   Merchant Shipping (Section 63 Inquiries) Rules 1997, SI 1997/347, reg 8(3).
9   Merchant Shipping (Section 63 Inquiries) Rules 1997, SI 1997/347, reg 8(4).

C.   HEARINGS AND APPEALS

**536.  Power to summon witnesses before inquiries into fitness or conduct.** The persons holding an inquiry into the fitness or conduct of an officer[1], or of a seaman other than an officer[2], may[3]:

(1)     by summons require any person to attend, at a time and place stated in the summons, to give evidence or to produce any documents in his custody or under his control which relate to any matter in question at the inquiry[4]; and

(2)     take evidence on oath (and for that purpose administer oaths) or, instead of administering an oath, require the person examined to make a solemn affirmation[5].

If, on the failure of a person to attend such an inquiry in answer to such a summons[6]:

(a)     the persons holding the inquiry are satisfied by evidence on oath that the person in question is likely to be able to give material evidence or produce any document which relates to any matter in question at the inquiry, that he has been duly served with the summons and that a reasonable sum has been paid or tendered to him for costs and expenses[7]; and

(b)     it appears to them that there is no just excuse for the failure[8],

they may issue a warrant to arrest him and bring him before the inquiry at a time and place specified in the warrant[9].

If any person attending or brought before such an inquiry refuses without just excuse to be sworn or give evidence, or to produce any document, the persons holding the inquiry may[10]:

(i) commit him to custody until the end of such period not exceeding one month as may be specified in the warrant or until he gives evidence or produces the document, whichever occurs first[11]; or

(ii) impose on him a fine not exceeding £1,000[12],

or both[13].

1 Ie under the Merchant Shipping Act 1995 s 61 (see PARA 524): s 68(1). As to qualification as an officer see PARA 507. As to the context in which these provisions apply see PARA 524 note 2.
2 Ie under the Merchant Shipping Act 1995 s 63 (see PARA 530): s 68(1). As to the meaning of 'seaman' see PARA 457 note 5.
3 Merchant Shipping Act 1995 s 68(1).
4 Merchant Shipping Act 1995 s 68(1)(a).
5 Merchant Shipping Act 1995 s 68(1)(b).
6 Merchant Shipping Act 1995 s 68(2).
7 Merchant Shipping Act 1995 s 68(2)(a).
8 Merchant Shipping Act 1995 s 68(2)(b).
9 Merchant Shipping Act 1995 s 68(2).
10 Merchant Shipping Act 1995 s 68(3).
11 Merchant Shipping Act 1995 s 68(3)(a).
12 Merchant Shipping Act 1995 s 68(3)(b). A fine imposed under s 68(3)(b) is to be treated for the purpose of its collection, enforcement and remission as having been imposed by the magistrates' court for the area in which the inquiry in question was held; and the persons holding the inquiry must, as soon as practicable after imposing the fine, give particulars of it to the proper officer of that court: s 68(4) (amended by the Access to Justice Act 1999 s 90(1), Sch 13 para 174(1), (2)). For this purpose, 'proper officer' means, in relation to a magistrates' court in England and Wales, the designated officer for the court: see the Merchant Shipping Act 1995 s 68(4A) (added by the Access to Justice Act 1999 Sch 13 para 174(1), (3); amended by the Courts Act 2003 s 109(1), Sch 8 para 366). As to the meanings of 'England' and 'Wales' see PARA 16 note 2.
13 Merchant Shipping Act 1995 s 68(3).

## 537. Rehearing of and appeal from inquiries into fitness or conduct.

Where an inquiry has been held into the fitness or conduct either of officers[1], or of seamen other than officers[2], the Secretary of State[3] may order the whole or part of the case to be reheard[4]; and he must do so:

(1) if new and important evidence which could not be produced at the inquiry has been discovered[5]; or

(2) if there appear to the Secretary of State to be other grounds for suspecting that a miscarriage of justice may have occurred[6].

Such an order may provide for the rehearing to be by the persons who held it, by a wreck commissioner[7] or by the High Court[8].

Any rehearing which is not held by the High Court must be conducted in accordance with the statutory rules[9].

Where the persons holding the inquiry have decided to cancel or suspend the certificate of any person or have found any person at fault, then, if no application for an order[10] has been made, or if such an application has been refused, that person or any other person who, having an interest in the inquiry, has appeared at the hearing and is affected by the decision or finding may appeal to the High Court[11]. Provision is made for the reissue and restoration of cancelled or suspended certificates[12].

1 Ie under the Merchant Shipping Act 1995 s 61 (see PARA 524): s 64(1). As to qualification as an officer see PARA 507. As to the context in which these provisions apply see PARA 524 note 2.
2 Ie under the Merchant Shipping Act 1995 s 63 (see PARA 530): s 64(1). As to the meaning of 'seaman' see PARA 457 note 5.
3 As to the Secretary of State see PARA 36.
4 Merchant Shipping Act 1995 s 64(1).

5  Merchant Shipping Act 1995 s 64(1)(a).
6  Merchant Shipping Act 1995 s 64(1)(b).
7  As to the appointment of wreck commissioners see PARA 59.
8  Merchant Shipping Act 1995 s 64(2).
9  Merchant Shipping Act 1995 s 64(3). The text refers to rules made under s 65(1) (see PARA 509): scc s 64(3).
10  Ie under the Merchant Shipping Act 1995 s 64(1) (see the text and notes 1–6): see s 64(4).
11  Merchant Shipping Act 1995 s 64(4).
12  See the Merchant Shipping Act 1995 s 67; and PARA 508.

**538. Procedure on rehearing of inquiry into fitness or conduct.** Any rehearing of an inquiry into fitness or conduct of an officer[1] which is not held by the High Court must be conducted in accordance with the relevant statutory rules that are applied for the purpose[2].

Any rehearing of an inquiry into fitness or conduct of a seaman other than an officer[3] which is not held by the High Court must be conducted in accordance with the relevant statutory rules that apply for that purpose[4].

1  Ie an inquiry under the Merchant Shipping Act 1995 s 61 (see PARA 524): see the Merchant Shipping (Section 52 Inquiries) Rules 1982, SI 1982/1752, r 9. As to the context in which these provisions apply see PARA 524 note 2.
2  Merchant Shipping (Section 52 Inquiries) Rules 1982, SI 1982/1752, r 9. The text refers to the provisions of the Merchant Shipping (Section 52 Inquiries) Rules 1982, SI 1982/1752, rr 4–8 (see PARAS 525–529): see r 9.
3  Ie under the Merchant Shipping Act 1995 s 63 (see PARA 530): see the Merchant Shipping (Section 63 Inquiries) Rules 1997, SI 1997/347, r 3.
4  Merchant Shipping (Section 63 Inquiries) Rules 1997, SI 1997/347, r 3. The text refers to the provisions of the Merchant Shipping (Section 63 Inquiries) Rules 1997, SI 1997/347 (see PARAS 531–535): see r 3. See also PARA 531 note 2.

D.  CODES OF CONDUCT

**539. Codes of conduct.** As from a day to be appointed, the following provisions have effect[1].

The Secretary of State may make regulations[2] for the purpose of maintaining discipline on board United Kingdom ships[3].

Regulations may provide for the hearing on shore in the United Kingdom, by a disciplinary body[4], of a complaint by the master[5] or owner of a United Kingdom ship (other than a fishing vessel[6]) against a seaman[7] alleging that during his employment on board the ship the seaman contravened[8] a provision of a code of conduct approved by the Secretary of State[9]. The alleged contravention may be one on or off the ship and in the United Kingdom or elsewhere[10].

Regulations may enable a disciplinary body:

(1)  to dismiss the complaint if it finds the allegation not proved[11];

(2)  if it finds the allegation proved, to warn the seaman, to reprimand the seaman or to recommend to the Secretary of State that the seaman is, either for a period specified in the recommendation or permanently, to cease to be entitled to a discharge book[12] and is to be required to surrender any such book which has been issued to him[13].

Regulations may:

(a)  enable the seaman to appeal against such a recommendation to another disciplinary body (an 'appellate body')[14];

(b)  enable an appellate body to confirm the recommendation, to cancel the recommendation or, in the case of a recommendation that the seaman is to cease to be entitled to a discharge book permanently or for a particular period, to substitute for it a recommendation that he is to cease to be so entitled, instead of permanently, for a period specified in the substituted recommendation or, instead of for the particular period, for a shorter period so specified[15].

Regulations may make provision:

(i) for securing that a recommendation that the seaman is to permanently cease to be entitled to a discharge book is not submitted to the Secretary of State unless it has been confirmed, either on appeal or otherwise, by an appellate body[16];

(ii) for the establishment or approval for these purposes of such number of bodies as the Secretary of State thinks fit and with respect to the composition, jurisdiction and procedure of any such body[17];

(iii) for the payment, out of money provided by Parliament, of such remuneration and allowances as the Secretary of State may, with the consent of the Treasury[18], determine to any member of such a body[19].

Regulations also may[20] include provision for any proceedings to take place notwithstanding the absence of the seaman to whom they relate[21].

However, nothing in the regulations or done in pursuance of the regulations is to be construed as affecting any power to institute, prosecute, entertain or determine proceedings, including criminal proceedings, under any other enactment or at common law[22].

In relation to United Kingdom fishing vessels[23], the provisions relating to breaches by seamen of codes of conduct[24] have effect with modification[25].

1 The Merchant Shipping Act 1995 s 60 does not have effect until the Secretary of State by order appoints a day for s 60 to come into force: s 314(3), Sch 14 para 5(1), (2); and PARA 15 note 1. At the date at which this volume states the law, no such day had been appointed. As to the Secretary of State see PARA 36. As to the context in which these provisions apply see PARA 524 note 2.

2 Ie under the Merchant Shipping Act 1995 s 60(2)–(10) (see the text and notes 4–22): see s 60(1). Regulations may make different provision for different circumstances and may contain such incidental and supplemental provisions as the Secretary of State considers appropriate: s 60(8). See note 1. At the date at which this volume states the law, no such regulations had been made under s 60 and none had effect as if so made. As to the power of the Secretary of State to make subordinate legislation under the Merchant Shipping Act 1995, including his power to appoint committees for the purpose of advising him when considering the making or alteration of any regulations etc, see PARA 39.

3 Merchant Shipping Act 1995 s 60(1). See note 1. As to the meaning of 'United Kingdom ship' see PARA 230. As to the meaning of 'ship' see PARA 229; and as to the meaning of 'United Kingdom' see PARA 16 note 3.

4 For the purposes of the Merchant Shipping Act 1995 s 60, 'disciplinary body' means a body established or approved by the Secretary of State under s 60(6) (see head (ii) in the text): see s 60(1). As from a day to be appointed, the power to make regulations under s 32 includes power to provide for the determination of certain deductions from wages in respect of employment in fishing vessels by a body established or approved under s 32: see s 111 (not yet in force); and PARA 473.

5 As to the meaning of 'master' see PARA 444 note 1.

6 As to the meaning of 'fishing vessel' see PARA 230 note 9. As to the application of the Merchant Shipping Act 1995 s 60 to fishing vessels see further the text and notes 23–25.

7 As to the meaning of 'seaman' see PARA 457 note 5.

8 As to the meaning of 'contravention' see PARA 51 note 3.

9 Merchant Shipping Act 1995 s 60(2). The text refers to a code of conduct approved by the Secretary of State for the purposes of s 60: see s 60(2). See note 1.

10 Merchant Shipping Act 1995 s 60(2). See note 1.

11 Merchant Shipping Act 1995 s 60(3)(a). See note 1.

12 Ie in pursuance of the Merchant Shipping Act 1995 s 80 (see PARA 565): see s 60(3)(b).

13 Merchant Shipping Act 1995 s 60(3)(b). See note 1.

14 Merchant Shipping Act 1995 s 60(4)(a). See note 1.

15 Merchant Shipping Act 1995 s 60(4)(b). See note 1.

16 Merchant Shipping Act 1995 s 60(5). See note 1.

17 Merchant Shipping Act 1995 s 60(6). See note 1.

18 As to the Treasury see CONSTITUTIONAL AND ADMINISTRATIVE LAW vol 20 (2014) PARAS 262–265.

19 Merchant Shipping Act 1995 s 60(7). See note 1.

20 Ie without prejudice to the generality of the Merchant Shipping Act 1995 s 60(1)–(8) (see the text and notes 1–19): see s 60(9).

21 Merchant Shipping Act 1995 s 60(9). See note 1.

22 Merchant Shipping Act 1995 s 60(10). See note 1.

23 As to the meaning of 'United Kingdom fishing vessel' see PARA 230.

24 Ie the Merchant Shipping Act 1995 s 60 (see the text and notes 1–22): see s 119(2).

25 See the Merchant Shipping Act 1995 s 119(2). The modification is that s 60 has effect with the substitution for s 60(2) (see the text and notes 4–10) of the following: regulations may provide for the hearing on shore in the United Kingdom, by a disciplinary body, of a complaint by the master or owner of such a fishing vessel against a seaman alleging that during his employment in the vessel, the seaman contravened a local industrial agreement relating to his employment on the vessel and for requiring the disciplinary body to have regard to the agreement in determining whether the allegation is proved: see s 60(2) (substituted by s 119(2)). The alleged contravention may be one on or off the ship and in the United Kingdom or elsewhere: see s 60(2) (as so substituted). Regulations under s 60 (see the text and notes 1–22) may include provision authorising persons to determine, for the purposes of s 60 in its application to United Kingdom fishing vessels, what agreements are or were local industrial agreements and which local industrial agreement relates or related to a person's employment in a particular vessel: s 119(3).

The provisions of s 119(2) and s 119(3) do not have effect until the Secretary of State by order appoints a day for s 119(2), (3) to come into force: s 314(3), Sch 14 para 5(1), (2); and PARA 15 note 1. At the date at which this volume states the law, no such order had been made.

## (xi) Relief and Repatriation of Seamen

### A. UNITED KINGDOM SHIPS AND SHIPS IN UNITED KINGDOM WATERS

#### (A) Repatriation

**540. Duty to repatriate.** A shipowner[1] must[2] make such provision as is necessary for repatriation of a seafarer[3] as soon as is practicable:

(1)  where the seafarer employment agreement expires[4];

(2)  where the seafarer employment agreement is terminated by the shipowner[5];

(3)  where the seafarer employment agreement is terminated by the seafarer in accordance with the terms of the agreement[6];

(4)  where the seafarer is no longer able to carry out the seafarer's duties under the seafarer's employment agreement or cannot be expected to carry them out in the specific[7] circumstances[8];

(5)  where the seafarer has completed the maximum period of service on board following which the seafarer is entitled to repatriation in accordance with the seafarer employment agreement[9]; and

(6)  where the seafarer employment agreement is terminated pursuant to an order of a court or tribunal[10].

A breach of these requirements is an offence by the shipowner[11]. However, where there is a duty on a shipowner to provide for the repatriation of a seafarer under these provisions, that duty ends when:

(a)  the seafarer is[12] repatriated[13];

(b)  the shipowner makes reasonable arrangements for repatriation which are unsuccessful because of the seafarer's unreasonable conduct[14];

(c)  the shipowner has used reasonable endeavours to contact the seafarer for a period of three months or more, but has been unable to make such contact[15];

(d) the seafarer confirms in writing to the shipowner that repatriation is not required[16]; or

(e) the seafarer is dead[17].

In the case of a sea-going non-United Kingdom ship in United Kingdom waters which is subject to the Maritime Labour Convention[18], a shipowner must make such provision as is necessary for the repatriation of a seafarer as soon as is practicable[19], subject to any national provisions which have been adopted by the state[20] whose flag the ship is entitled to fly[21]. A breach of these requirements[22] is an offence by the shipowner[23].

If a shipowner of a United Kingdom ship fails to make provision for repatriation[24], the Secretary of State[25] must (or, in the case of a non-United Kingdom ship[26], may) make the required provision (or secure that it is made) and may recover costs incurred from the shipowner as a civil debt[27]. If a shipowner of a United Kingdom ship fails to make such provision and the seafarer incurs costs in making the required provision or securing that it is made, the seafarer may recover such costs from the shipowner as a civil debt[28].

1 As to the meaning of 'shipowner' see PARA 448 note 4. These provisions (ie the Merchant Shipping (Maritime Labour Convention) (Minimum Requirements for Seafarers etc) Regulations 2014, SI 2014/1613, Pt 6 (regs 19–28) and Pt 10 (reg 48–53) (see the text and notes 2–28; and PARAS 541–547) apply in relation to any ship to which the Merchant Shipping (Maritime Labour Convention) (Minimum Requirements for Seafarers etc) Regulations 2014, SI 2014/1613 (which implements in United Kingdom law the Maritime Labour Convention (Cm 7049)), applies, that is, any United Kingdom ship or non-United Kingdom ship in United Kingdom waters other than a fishing vessel, a ship of traditional build, a pleasure vessel, a warship or naval auxiliary vessel or a vessel not ordinarily engaged in commercial activities: see further PARA 423. The provision of the Convention imposing minimum ages for seafarers is reg 2.5. Provision for repatriation relating to fishing vessels, ships of traditional build and non-commercial vessels is governed by the Merchant Shipping Act 1995: see ss 73–75; the Merchant Shipping (Repatriation) Regulations 1979, SI 1979/97; and PARAS 423, 548–550.
   A shipowner must ensure that a copy of the Merchant Shipping (Maritime Labour Convention) (Minimum Requirements for Seafarers etc) Regulations 2014, SI 2014/1613, Pt 6 and Marine Guidance Note 479(M) are held on board the ship and are available to seafarers: Merchant Shipping (Maritime Labour Convention) (Minimum Requirements for Seafarers etc) Regulations 2014, SI 2014/1613, reg 25(1), (4). Unless the shipowner reasonably considers that all of the seafarers on board the ship understand English sufficiently to understand the documents referred to in reg 25(1), the duty in reg 25(1) includes the duty to hold on board the ship and make available to seafarers such translated versions of those documents as are sufficient to ensure that all of the seafarers on board the ship can understand at least one version: reg 25(2). There are also financial security requirements: see reg 26(1). A breach of reg 25 or reg 26(1) is an offence by the shipowner: regs 25(3), 26(2). Such an offence is punishable on summary conviction by a fine: reg 59(1), (3)(d). In any proceedings for such an offence it is a defence for the person charged to show that all reasonable steps had been taken by that person to ensure compliance with the provision concerned: reg 60. As to the powers of magistrates' courts to issue fines on summary conviction see SENTENCING vol 92 (2015) PARA 176.
2 Ie subject to the Merchant Shipping (Maritime Labour Convention) (Minimum Requirements for Seafarers etc) Regulations 2014, SI 2014/1613, reg 21 (see the text and notes 12–17).
3 As to the meaning of 'seafarer' see PARA 423. Where there is a duty on a shipowner to provide for the repatriation of a seafarer under these provisions, a seafarer is entitled to repatriation to the destination provided for in the seafarer employment agreement, or such other place as may subsequently be agreed with the shipowner: Merchant Shipping (Maritime Labour Convention) (Minimum Requirements for Seafarers etc) Regulations 2014, SI 2014/1613, reg 20(1). As to seafarer employment agreements see PARAS 451–455. If the seafarer employment agreement does not identify a destination, and there has been no agreement between the seafarer and the shipowner as to the destination, the seafarer is entitled to repatriation to the seafarer's choice of the following destinations the place at which the seafarer entered into the seafarer's employment agreement or the seafarer's country of residence: reg 20(2).
4 Merchant Shipping (Maritime Labour Convention) (Minimum Requirements for Seafarers etc) Regulations 2014, SI 2014/1613, reg 19(1)(a).
5 Merchant Shipping (Maritime Labour Convention) (Minimum Requirements for Seafarers etc) Regulations 2014, SI 2014/1613, reg 19(1)(b).

6   Merchant Shipping (Maritime Labour Convention) (Minimum Requirements for Seafarers etc)
    Regulations 2014, SI 2014/1613, reg 19(1)(c).
7   Ie including in the following circumstances:
    (1)     the seafarer has an illness, injury or medical condition which requires their repatriation
            when found medically fit to travel (Merchant Shipping (Maritime Labour Convention)
            (Minimum Requirements for Seafarers etc) Regulations 2014, SI 2014/1613, reg
            19(1)(d)(i));
    (2)     shipwreck (reg 19(1)(d)(ii));
    (3)     the shipowner is not able to fulfil its legal or contractual obligations to the seafarer
            following insolvency, the sale of the ship or a change in the ship's registration (reg
            19(1)(d)(iii)); or
    (4)     the ship is bound for a war zone to which the seafarer does not consent to go (reg
            19(1)(d)(iv)).
8   Merchant Shipping (Maritime Labour Convention) (Minimum Requirements for Seafarers etc)
    Regulations 2014, SI 2014/1613, reg 19(1)(d).
9   Merchant Shipping (Maritime Labour Convention) (Minimum Requirements for Seafarers etc)
    Regulations 2014, SI 2014/1613, reg 19(1)(e).
10  Merchant Shipping (Maritime Labour Convention) (Minimum Requirements for Seafarers etc)
    Regulations 2014, SI 2014/1613, reg 19(1)(f).
11  Merchant Shipping (Maritime Labour Convention) (Minimum Requirements for Seafarers etc)
    Regulations 2014, SI 2014/1613, reg 19(2). Such an offence is punishable on summary conviction
    by a fine: reg 59(1).
12  Ie in accordance with the Merchant Shipping (Maritime Labour Convention) (Minimum
    Requirements for Seafarers etc) Regulations 2014, SI 2014/1613, reg 20 (see note 3).
13  Merchant Shipping (Maritime Labour Convention) (Minimum Requirements for Seafarers etc)
    Regulations 2014, SI 2014/1613, reg 21(a).
14  Merchant Shipping (Maritime Labour Convention) (Minimum Requirements for Seafarers etc)
    Regulations 2014, SI 2014/1613, reg 21(b).
15  Merchant Shipping (Maritime Labour Convention) (Minimum Requirements for Seafarers etc)
    Regulations 2014, SI 2014/1613, reg 21(c).
16  Merchant Shipping (Maritime Labour Convention) (Minimum Requirements for Seafarers etc)
    Regulations 2014, SI 2014/1613, reg 21(d).
17  Merchant Shipping (Maritime Labour Convention) (Minimum Requirements for Seafarers etc)
    Regulations 2014, SI 2014/1613, reg 21(e).
18  See the Merchant Shipping (Maritime Labour Convention) (Minimum Requirements for Seafarers
    etc) Regulations 2014, SI 2014/1613, regs 3(3), (4)(b)(ix); and PARA 423 note 9.
19  Ie in the circumstances described in paragraph 1 of Standard A2.5 of the Convention.
20  Ie pursuant to paragraph 2 of Standard A2.5 of the Convention.
21  Merchant Shipping (Maritime Labour Convention) (Minimum Requirements for Seafarers etc)
    Regulations 2014, SI 2014/1613, reg 28(1). A shipowner must comply with the prohibitions in
    paragraph 3 of Standard A2.5 of the Convention, whether or not those prohibitions apply in the
    state whose flag the ship is entitled to fly (Merchant Shipping (Maritime Labour Convention)
    (Minimum Requirements for Seafarers etc) Regulations 2014, SI 2014/1613, reg 28(3)(a)), and the
    requirement in paragraph 9 of Standard A2.5 of the Convention, whether or not the state whose
    flag the ship is entitled to fly has imposed that requirement in its national laws or otherwise
    (Merchant Shipping (Maritime Labour Convention) (Minimum Requirements for Seafarers etc)
    Regulations 2014, SI 2014/1613, reg 28(3)(b)).
22  Ie a breach of the Merchant Shipping (Maritime Labour Convention) (Minimum Requirements for
    Seafarers etc) Regulations 2014, SI 2014/1613, reg 28(1) or (3).
23  Merchant Shipping (Maritime Labour Convention) (Minimum Requirements for Seafarers etc)
    Regulations 2014, SI 2014/1613, reg 28(2), (4). Such an offence is punishable on summary
    conviction by a fine: reg 59(1), (3)(e).
24  Ie the provision required under the Merchant Shipping (Maritime Labour Convention) (Minimum
    Requirements for Seafarers etc) Regulations 2014, SI 2014/1613, reg 19 (see the text and notes
    1–17) or reg 22 (see PARA 541).
25  As to the Secretary of State see PARA 36.
26  As to the meaning of 'United Kingdom ship' see PARA 423 note 6.
27  Merchant Shipping (Maritime Labour Convention) (Minimum Requirements for Seafarers etc)
    Regulations 2014, SI 2014/1613, reg 27(1), (2). The costs which the Secretary of State may so
    recover include costs incurred by the Secretary of State in making the required provision (or
    securing that it is made) and costs incurred by the Secretary of State in reimbursing another person
    (including a State which has made provision pursuant to paragraph 5 of Standard A2.5
    (repatriation) of the Convention) for having made the required provision (or having secured its

provision), whether or not the Secretary of State has requested or required them to do so: Merchant Shipping (Maritime Labour Convention) (Minimum Requirements for Seafarers etc) Regulations 2014, SI 2014/1613, reg 27(3). Regulation 27(3) is subject to reg 27(5) (see note 22).

28 Merchant Shipping (Maritime Labour Convention) (Minimum Requirements for Seafarers etc) Regulations 2014, SI 2014/1613, reg 27(4). This is subject to reg 27(5), which provides that the costs incurred by the seafarer which are referred to in reg 27(4) (see the text and note 22) may not be recovered by the seafarer under reg 27(4) if they have been recovered by the Secretary of State under reg 27(1) and may not be recovered by the Secretary of State under reg 27(1) if they have been recovered by the seafarer under reg 27(4).

**541. Duty pending repatriation.** A shipowner[1] to which a repatriation duty[2] applies must make such provision as is necessary for the seafarer's[3] relief and maintenance pending repatriation[4] and must have regard to the seafarer's personal circumstances and requirements when determining what provision is so required[5]. Without prejudice to the generality of these requirements the provision for relief and maintenance must include:

(1)     food[6];
(2)     clothing[7];
(3)     accommodation[8];
(4)     toiletries and other personal necessaries[9];
(5)     surgical, medical, dental or optical treatment (including the repair or replacement of any appliance) for any condition requiring immediate care[10]; and
(6)     in cases where legal aid is unavailable or insufficient, reasonable costs for the defence of the seafarer in any criminal proceedings in respect of any act or omission within the scope of the seafarer's employment, being proceedings where neither the shipowner nor an agent of the shipowner is the complainant[11].

A breach of these requirements is an offence by the shipowner[12]. Provision is made for the recovery of costs by the Secretary of State or the seafarer when the shipowner fails to comply with these requirements[13].

1   As to the meaning of 'shipowner' see PARA 448 note 4. As to the vessels and seamen to which these provisions apply see PARA 540 note 1.
2   Ie a duty under the Merchant Shipping (Maritime Labour Convention) (Minimum Requirements for Seafarers etc) Regulations 2014, SI 2014/1613, reg 19 (see PARA 540). The duty under these provisions ends when the duty in reg 19 ends: reg 22(4).
3   As to the meaning of 'seafarer' see PARA 423.
4   Merchant Shipping (Maritime Labour Convention) (Minimum Requirements for Seafarers etc) Regulations 2014, SI 2014/1613, reg 22(1).
5   Merchant Shipping (Maritime Labour Convention) (Minimum Requirements for Seafarers etc) Regulations 2014, SI 2014/1613, reg 22(2).
6   Merchant Shipping (Maritime Labour Convention) (Minimum Requirements for Seafarers etc) Regulations 2014, SI 2014/1613, reg 22(3)(a).
7   Merchant Shipping (Maritime Labour Convention) (Minimum Requirements for Seafarers etc) Regulations 2014, SI 2014/1613, reg 22(3)(b).
8   Merchant Shipping (Maritime Labour Convention) (Minimum Requirements for Seafarers etc) Regulations 2014, SI 2014/1613, reg 22(3)(c).
9   Merchant Shipping (Maritime Labour Convention) (Minimum Requirements for Seafarers etc) Regulations 2014, SI 2014/1613, reg 22(3)(d).
10  Merchant Shipping (Maritime Labour Convention) (Minimum Requirements for Seafarers etc) Regulations 2014, SI 2014/1613, reg 22(3)(e).
11  Merchant Shipping (Maritime Labour Convention) (Minimum Requirements for Seafarers etc) Regulations 2014, SI 2014/1613, reg 22(3)(f).
12  Merchant Shipping (Maritime Labour Convention) (Minimum Requirements for Seafarers etc) Regulations 2014, SI 2014/1613, reg 22(5). Such an offence is punishable on summary conviction by a fine: reg 59(1). In any proceedings for such an offence it is a defence for the person charged to show that all reasonable steps had been taken by that person to ensure compliance with the provision concerned: reg 60. As to the powers of magistrates' courts to issue fines on summary conviction see SENTENCING vol 92 (2015) PARA 176.

13 See the Merchant Shipping (Maritime Labour Convention) (Minimum Requirements for Seafarers etc) Regulations 2014, SI 2014/1613, reg 27; and PARA 540.

**542. Prohibition on recovering costs from seafarer.** A shipowner[1] must not[2] enter into an agreement with a seafarer[3] under which the seafarer must make payment in respect of either repatriation costs[4] or relief and maintenance costs[5], although a seafarer employment agreement[6] may provide that the seafarer must reimburse repatriation costs where the agreement is terminated because of the seafarer's serious misconduct[7]. If a seafarer employment agreement does not contain such provision, the shipowner may only recover the repatriation, relief or maintenance costs[8] (or damages in respect of such costs) where the agreement is terminated because of the seafarer's serious misconduct[9].

A breach of these requirements is an offence by the shipowner[10].

1 As to the meaning of 'shipowner' see PARA 448 note 4. As to the vessels and seamen to which these provisions apply see PARA 540 note 1.
2 Ie subject to the Merchant Shipping (Maritime Labour Convention) (Minimum Requirements for Seafarers etc) Regulations 2014, SI 2014/1613, reg 23(2) (see the text and notes 6–7).
3 As to the meaning of 'seafarer' see PARA 423. An agreement is void to the extent it provides that a seafarer must make a payment to the shipowner in respect of either repatriation costs or relief and maintenance costs in breach of these provisions: Merchant Shipping (Maritime Labour Convention) (Minimum Requirements for Seafarers etc) Regulations 2014, SI 2014/1613, reg 23(6).
4 Merchant Shipping (Maritime Labour Convention) (Minimum Requirements for Seafarers etc) Regulations 2014, SI 2014/1613, reg 23(1)(a).
5 Merchant Shipping (Maritime Labour Convention) (Minimum Requirements for Seafarers etc) Regulations 2014, SI 2014/1613, reg 23(1)(b).
6 As to seafarer employment agreements see PARAS 451–455.
7 Merchant Shipping (Maritime Labour Convention) (Minimum Requirements for Seafarers etc) Regulations 2014, SI 2014/1613, reg 23(2). If a seafarer employment agreement contains provision described in reg 23(2) and that obligation arises, a deduction equivalent to those costs may be made from the wages due to the seafarer under that agreement: reg 23(3).
8 Ie costs described in the Merchant Shipping (Maritime Labour Convention) (Minimum Requirements for Seafarers etc) Regulations 2014, SI 2014/1613, reg 23(1) (see the text and notes 1–5).
9 Merchant Shipping (Maritime Labour Convention) (Minimum Requirements for Seafarers etc) Regulations 2014, SI 2014/1613, reg 23(4).
10 Merchant Shipping (Maritime Labour Convention) (Minimum Requirements for Seafarers etc) Regulations 2014, SI 2014/1613, reg 23(5). Such an offence is punishable on summary conviction by a fine: reg 59(1). In any proceedings for such an offence it is a defence for the person charged to show that all reasonable steps had been taken by that person to ensure compliance with the provision concerned: reg 60. As to the powers of magistrates' courts to issue fines on summary conviction see SENTENCING vol 92 (2015) PARA 176.

**543. Seafarer property.** Where a shipowner[1] is under a repatriation duty[2] in respect of a seafarer[3] and property belonging to that seafarer has been left behind on board a ship[4], the master of the ship must take charge of that property and enter a description of each item in the official log book[5]. The master of the ship may at any time sell any part of the property which is of a perishable or deteriorating nature[6] and destroy or otherwise dispose of any part of the property considered a potential risk to the health or safety of any person[7]: subject to this, the master of the ship and the shipowner must ensure that reasonable care is taken of the property pending its delivery[8] to the seafarer or to the seafarer's next of kin[9].

A breach of these requirements is an offence[10].

1 As to the meaning of 'shipowner' see PARA 448 note 4. As to the vessels and seamen to which these provisions apply see PARA 540 note 1.
2 Ie a duty under the Merchant Shipping (Maritime Labour Convention) (Minimum Requirements for Seafarers etc) Regulations 2014, SI 2014/1613, reg 19 (see PARA 540).
3 Merchant Shipping (Maritime Labour Convention) (Minimum Requirements for Seafarers etc) Regulations 2014, SI 2014/1613, reg 24(1)(a). As to the meaning of 'seafarer' see PARA 423.
4 Merchant Shipping (Maritime Labour Convention) (Minimum Requirements for Seafarers etc) Regulations 2014, SI 2014/1613, reg 24(1)(b).

5   Merchant Shipping (Maritime Labour Convention) (Minimum Requirements for Seafarers etc)
    Regulations 2014, SI 2014/1613, reg 24(2).
6   Merchant Shipping (Maritime Labour Convention) (Minimum Requirements for Seafarers etc)
    Regulations 2014, SI 2014/1613, reg 24(6)(a). The proceeds of any sale under reg 24(6)(a) are the
    property of the seafarer and the master of the ship must ensure that details of the sale are entered
    in the official log book: reg 24(7).
7   Merchant Shipping (Maritime Labour Convention) (Minimum Requirements for Seafarers etc)
    Regulations 2014, SI 2014/1613, reg 24(6)(b). The master of the ship must ensure that details of
    any destruction or disposal under reg 24(6)(b) are entered in the official log book: reg 24(8).
8   Ie delivery in accordance with the Merchant Shipping (Maritime Labour Convention) (Minimum
    Requirements for Seafarers etc) Regulations 2014, SI 2014/1613, reg 24(10), which provides that
    the shipowner must cause the property and a document containing the information entered in the
    log book pursuant to reg 24(7), (8) to be delivered to the seafarer or to the seafarer's next of kin.
    This is subject to reg 24(11), which provides that the duty in reg 24(10) is discharged if the
    shipowner causes the delivery to be made to the last known address of the seafarer or the next of
    kin, as the case may be.
9   Merchant Shipping (Maritime Labour Convention) (Minimum Requirements for Seafarers etc)
    Regulations 2014, SI 2014/1613, reg 24(4). The seafarer or the next of kin, as the case may be,
    must reimburse the shipowner for the reasonable delivery costs if demanded: reg 24(13).
10  A breach of the Merchant Shipping (Maritime Labour Convention) (Minimum Requirements for
    Seafarers etc) Regulations 2014, SI 2014/1613, reg 24(2), (7), or (8) is an offence by the master of
    the ship; a breach of reg 24(4) is an offence by the master of the ship and the shipowner; and a
    breach of reg 24(10) is an offence by the shipowner: reg 24(3), (5), (9), (12). Such an offence is
    punishable on summary conviction by a fine: reg 59(1), (3)(c), (4)(c). In any proceedings for such
    an offence it is a defence for the person charged to show that all reasonable steps had been taken
    by that person to ensure compliance with the provision concerned: reg 60. As to the powers of
    magistrates' courts to issue fines on summary conviction see SENTENCING vol 92 (2015)
    PARA 176.

## (B)   Compensation, Sick Pay, Disposal of Remains

**544. Ships must be insured against having to make compensation payments to seafarers.** A United Kingdom ship, or a non-United Kingdom ship in United Kingdom waters[1] must not be operated unless there is in force in relation to the ship a contract of insurance (or other form of security) which provides financial assurance of an amount which the shipowner[2] reasonably considers adequate to ensure that he will be able to meet any liabilities he may have, including liabilities under seafarer employment agreements[3], to provide compensation in the event of death or long term disability to seafarers[4] arising from occupational injury, illness or hazard[5].

A breach of this requirement is an offence by the shipowner[6].

1   As to the vessels and seamen to which these provisions apply see PARA 540 note 1.
2   As to the meaning of 'shipowner' see PARA 448 note 4.
3   As to seafarer employment agreements see PARAS 451–455.
4   As to the meaning of 'seafarer' see PARA 423.
5   Merchant Shipping (Maritime Labour Convention) (Minimum Requirements for Seafarers etc)
    Regulations 2014, SI 2014/1613, reg 49(1), (2).
6   Merchant Shipping (Maritime Labour Convention) (Minimum Requirements for Seafarers etc)
    Regulations 2014, SI 2014/1613, reg 49(3). Such an offence is punishable on summary conviction
    by a fine: reg 59(5)(h). In any proceedings for such an offence it is a defence for the person charged
    to show that all reasonable steps had been taken by that person to ensure compliance with the
    provision concerned: reg 60. As to the powers of magistrates' courts to issue fines on summary
    conviction see SENTENCING vol 92 (2015) PARA 176.

**545. Compensation of seafarers where ship is lost.** Where a United Kingdom ship, or a non-United Kingdom ship in United Kingdom waters[1], which on which a seafarer[2] is working founders or is lost, and the loss or foundering causes the seafarer to become unemployed or to suffer injury or loss, the shipowner[3] must pay to the seafarer:

(1)     in the case of unemployment, an amount equivalent to the wages[4] which would otherwise have been payable under the seafarer employment agreement[5] for every day on which the seafarer is unemployed in the two month period commencing on the day following the day on which the loss or foundering occurred[6]; and

(2)     in the case of injury or loss[7], compensation[8].

A seafarer may recover any sum so due from the shipowner as a civil debt[9].

1   As to the vessels and seamen to which these provisions apply see PARA 540 note 1.
2   As to the meaning of 'seafarer' see PARA 423.
3   As to the meaning of 'shipowner' see PARA 448 note 4.
4   'Wages; means the pay, however composed, for the seafarer's normal hours of work including overtime, allowances, paid leave and other remuneration (but excluding bonuses): Merchant Shipping (Maritime Labour Convention) (Minimum Requirements for Seafarers etc) Regulations 2014, SI 2014/1613, reg 53.
5   As to seafarer employment agreements see PARAS 451–455.
6   Merchant Shipping (Maritime Labour Convention) (Minimum Requirements for Seafarers etc) Regulations 2014, SI 2014/1613, reg 48(1), (2). For the provisions of the Maritime Labour Convention (Cm 7049)) dealing with seafarer compensation for a ship's loss or foundering see reg 2.6.
7   Ie other than the loss of wages referred to in the Merchant Shipping (Maritime Labour Convention) (Minimum Requirements for Seafarers etc) Regulations 2014, SI 2014/1613, reg 48(2) (see the text and notes 1–6).
8   Merchant Shipping (Maritime Labour Convention) (Minimum Requirements for Seafarers etc) Regulations 2014, SI 2014/1613, reg 48(3). In relation to loss other than personal injury or death, the duty in reg 48(3) is limited to the amount specified (if any) in the seafarer employment agreement: reg 48(4).
9   Merchant Shipping (Maritime Labour Convention) (Minimum Requirements for Seafarers etc) Regulations 2014, SI 2014/1613, reg 48(5).

**546.   Sick pay.** A shipowner[1] must make good the wages[2] (and, where relevant, take care of and return the property[3]) of:

(1)     any seafarer[4] who suffers sickness or injury during his period of employment[5] which results in his incapacity for work[6] and who does not receive the wages payable under the seafarer employment agreement in respect of the period[7] of sickness of injury[8]; and

(2)     any seafarer who suffers sickness or injury resulting in his incapacity for work during his period of employment[9], or during a period which starts after such period[10] but caused by circumstances or events arising during that period[11], and who is incapable of work during the repatriation period[12] but does not receive the basic wages[13] payable under the seafarer employment agreement for the incapacity period[14].

The sums so payable must be paid in the same manner and at the same frequency as wages are (or, as the case may be, were) payable under the seafarer employment agreement[15]. The seafarer may recover any sum due from the shipowner under these provisions as a civil debt[16].

These provisions not apply to a seafarer where:

(a)     the injury[17] was sustained while the seafarer was not at work[18];

(b)     the injury or sickness[19] was sustained or arose due to the seafarer's wilful misconduct[20]; or

(c)     the sickness or incapacity for work existed at the time when the seafarer entered the seafarer employment agreement, and the seafarer deliberately concealed the sickness or incapacity from the shipowner[21].

1   As to the meaning of 'shipowner' see PARA 448 note 4. As to the vessels and seamen to which these provisions apply see PARA 540 note 1.
2   As to the meaning of 'wages' see PARA 545 note 4.
3   To the extent it would not otherwise apply, the Merchant Shipping (Maritime Labour Convention) (Minimum Requirements for Seafarers etc) Regulations 2014, SI 2014/1613, reg 24(2), (4),

(6)–(8), (10), (11), (13) (seafarer property: see PARA 543) applies in respect of property left behind on board the ship by a seafarer falling within these provisions: reg 51.

4    As to the meaning of 'seafarer' see PARA 423.

5    Ie sickness or injury which first occurs during a period which starts on the date on which the seafarer's seafarer employment agreement commences and ends on the next date on which the shipowner's duty to make provision for the repatriation of that seafarer under the Merchant Shipping (Maritime Labour Convention) (Minimum Requirements for Seafarers etc) Regulations 2014, SI 2014/1613, reg 19 or 21 (see PARA 540) (reg 50(1)(a)(i)) and does not first occur during a period of leave, other than shore leave (reg 50(1)(b)). As to seafarer employment agreements see PARAS 451–455. In connection with sick pay under the Maritime Labour Convention (Cm 7049)) see reg 4.2.

6    Merchant Shipping (Maritime Labour Convention) (Minimum Requirements for Seafarers etc) Regulations 2014, SI 2014/1613, reg 50(1)(c).

7    Ie the period starting on the date of the injury or the first day of the sickness and ending on the date on which the duty to repatriate the seafarer under the Merchant Shipping (Maritime Labour Convention) (Minimum Requirements for Seafarers etc) Regulations 2014, SI 2014/1613, reg 19 ends under reg 21 (or, if such a duty does not arise, the date on which the seafarer leaves the ship): reg 50(3).

8    Merchant Shipping (Maritime Labour Convention) (Minimum Requirements for Seafarers etc) Regulations 2014, SI 2014/1613, reg 50(2). In this context the requirement to 'make good' the seafarer's wages is a requirement that the shipowner must pay to the seafarer a sum equal to the difference between any sums received by the seafarer in respect of wages for the period referred to in note 7 under the seafarer employment agreement and the wages which would have been payable to the seafarer under that agreement if the seafarer had remained fit for work throughout that period, and (where the agreement would otherwise have terminated during that period) if the agreement had continued on the same terms throughout that period: reg 50(2).

9    Ie the period referred to in note 5.

10   Ie after the period referred to in the Merchant Shipping (Maritime Labour Convention) (Minimum Requirements for Seafarers etc) Regulations 2014, SI 2014/1613, reg 50(1)(a)(i) (see note 2).

11   Merchant Shipping (Maritime Labour Convention) (Minimum Requirements for Seafarers etc) Regulations 2014, SI 2014/1613, reg 50(1)(a)(ii).

12   Ie after the date on which the duty to repatriate the seafarer under the Merchant Shipping (Maritime Labour Convention) (Minimum Requirements for Seafarers etc) Regulations 2014, SI 2014/1613, reg 19 ends under reg 21 (or if such a duty does not arise, the date on which the seafarer leaves the ship).

13   'Basic wages' means the pay, however composed, for the seafarer's normal hours of work excluding overtime, bonuses, allowances, paid leave and other remuneration: Maritime Labour Convention) (Minimum Requirements for Seafarers etc) Regulations 2014, SI 2014/1613, reg 53.

14   Merchant Shipping (Maritime Labour Convention) (Minimum Requirements for Seafarers etc) Regulations 2014, SI 2014/1613, reg 50(4). The 'incapacity period' is the period starting on the date on which the duty to repatriate the seafarer under reg 19 ends under reg 21 (or if such a duty does not arise, the date on which the seafarer leaves the ship) and ending on the date on which the seafarer is again fit for work: reg 50(4). In this context the requirement to 'make good' the seafarer's wages is a requirement that the shipowner must pay to the seafarer a sum equal to the difference between any sums received by the seafarer in respect of basic wages for the period referred to in reg 50(4) under that agreement, and the basic wages which would have been payable to the seafarer under that agreement if the seafarer had remained fit for work throughout that period, and (where the agreement would otherwise have terminated during that period) if the agreement had continued on the same terms throughout that period: reg 50(4). The duty in reg 50(4) ends on the expiry of the period of 16 weeks commencing on the day following the date of the injury or the first day of the sickness referred to in reg 50(1) (reg 50(5)), and is conditional upon the seafarer applying for all relevant social security benefits payable in consequence of the seafarer's incapacity for work and the sickness or injury which resulted in the incapacity for work, under the laws of the United Kingdom or the laws or arrangements in the country to which the seafarer is repatriated (reg 50(6)). If the seafarer receives social security benefits of the kind described in reg 50(6) in respect of the period referred to in reg 50(5) or any part of that period, the amount which the shipowner must pay to the seafarer under reg 50(4) is to be reduced by that amount and the shipowner may recover as a civil debt any payments already made to the seafarer to the extent that they exceed such reduced amounts: reg 50(7). The seafarer must on request provide information to the shipowner as to the amounts received by the seafarer in social security benefits during the period referred to in reg 50(5): reg 50(8).

15   Merchant Shipping (Maritime Labour Convention) (Minimum Requirements for Seafarers etc) Regulations 2014, SI 2014/1613, reg 50(9).

16 Merchant Shipping (Maritime Labour Convention) (Minimum Requirements for Seafarers etc) Regulations 2014, SI 2014/1613, reg 50(10).

17 Ie the injury referred to in the Merchant Shipping (Maritime Labour Convention) (Minimum Requirements for Seafarers etc) Regulations 2014, SI 2014/1613, reg 50(1) (see the text and notes 1–14).

18 Merchant Shipping (Maritime Labour Convention) (Minimum Requirements for Seafarers etc) Regulations 2014, SI 2014/1613, reg 50(11)(a).

19 Ie the injury or sickness referred to in the Merchant Shipping (Maritime Labour Convention) (Minimum Requirements for Seafarers etc) Regulations 2014, SI 2014/1613, reg 50(1) (see the text and notes 1–14).

20 Merchant Shipping (Maritime Labour Convention) (Minimum Requirements for Seafarers etc) Regulations 2014, SI 2014/1613, reg 50(11)(b).

21 Merchant Shipping (Maritime Labour Convention) (Minimum Requirements for Seafarers etc) Regulations 2014, SI 2014/1613, reg 50(11)(c).

**547. Burial or cremation of seafarer.** If a seafarer[1] dies while on board a ship[2] on which the seafarer works or on shore leave in a country other than the seafarer's country of residence, the shipowner[3] must meet any expenses reasonably incurred in connection with the seafarer's burial or cremation[4]. Where the seafarer's personal representatives incur costs in meeting expenses which should be met by the shipowner under these provisions, whether by incurring such costs directly or by reimbursing another person who has incurred those costs, those representatives may recover those costs from the shipowner as a civil debt[5].

1 As to the meaning of 'seafarer' see PARA 423. As to the vessels and seamen to which these provisions apply see PARA 540 note 1.
2 As to the meaning of 'ship' see PARA 423 note 2.
3 As to the meaning of 'shipowner' see PARA 448 note 4.
4 Merchant Shipping (Maritime Labour Convention) (Minimum Requirements for Seafarers etc) Regulations 2014, SI 2014/1613, reg 51(1). This duty does not apply to expenses which are met by a public authority: reg 51(2).
5 Merchant Shipping (Maritime Labour Convention) (Minimum Requirements for Seafarers etc) Regulations 2014, SI 2014/1613, reg 51(3).

B. FISHING VESSELS, SHIPS OF TRADITIONAL BUILD AND NON-COMMERCIAL VESSELS

**548. Relief and return of seaman etc left behind and shipwrecked.** Where:

(1) a person employed as a seaman[1] in a sea-going[2] United Kingdom ship which is a fishing vessel[3], ship of traditional build or non-commercial vessel[4] is left behind in any country outside the United Kingdom or is taken to such a country on being shipwrecked[4]; or

(2) a person who became so employed under an agreement entered into outside the United Kingdom is left behind in the United Kingdom or is taken to the United Kingdom on being shipwrecked[5],

the persons who last employed him as a seaman must make such provision for his return and for his relief and maintenance[6] until his return[7]. Provision is made[8] in connection with:

(a) the return and relief of seamen left behind or shipwrecked[9];
(b) other matters relating to seamen left behind and shipwrecked seamen[10];
(c) the place for return[11];
(d) a seaman's return, relief and maintenance by superintendents and proper officers[12];
(e) conveyance orders and directions[13];
(f) wages of seamen employed in fishing vessels who are left behind[14];
(g) other records and accounts[15];
(h) the property of seamen left behind and of shipwrecked seamen[16]; and
(i) official log book entries[17].

1 As to the meaning of 'seaman' see PARA 457 note 5.

2   The Merchant Shipping Act 1995 ss 73–75 (see the text and notes 3–17; and PARAS 549–550) apply only to sea-going United Kingdom ships (to which the legislation refers) which are fishing vessels, ships of traditional build or non-commercial vessels: see the Merchant Shipping Act 1995 s 24(2A); and PARA 423 note 22. Corresponding provision relating to other United Kingdom ships and non-United Kingdom ships in United Kingdom waters is governed by the Maritime Labour Convention (Cm 7049) and implemented by the Merchant Shipping (Maritime Labour Convention) (Minimum Requirements for Seafarers etc) Regulations 2014, SI 2014/1613: see regs 19–28, 48–53; and PARAS 540–547. As to the meaning of 'fishing vessel' see PARA 230. As to the meaning of 'sea going' see PARA 449 note 1. As to the meaning of 'ship' see PARA 229; and as to the meaning of 'United Kingdom ship' see PARA 230. As to the meaning of 'United Kingdom' see PARA 16 note 3.

3   For the purposes of the Merchant Shipping Act 1995 Pt III (ss 24–84), a seaman discharged from a ship in any country and left there is deemed to be left behind in that country notwithstanding that the ship also remains there (s 84(4)); and a seaman is discharged from a ship when his employment in that ship is terminated (s 84(3)). Section 73 applies:

    (1)   to a person left behind on being discharged in pursuance of s 29 (see PARA 469) (ie when a ship ceases to be registered in the United Kingdom) whether or not at the time he is left behind the ship is still a United Kingdom ship (s 73(7)); and

    (2)   to the master of a ship as it applies to a seaman; and s 74 (limit of employer's liability under s 73) (see PARA 549) and s 75 (recovery of expenses incurred for relief and return etc) (see PARA 550) have effect accordingly (s 73(8)).

    As to the meaning of 'master' see PARA 444 note 1.

4   Merchant Shipping Act 1995 s 73(1)(a).

4   Merchant Shipping Act 1995 s 73(1)(a).

5   Merchant Shipping Act 1995 s 73(1)(b). See note 3.

6   For these purposes, 'relief and maintenance' includes the provision of surgical or medical treatment and such dental and optical treatment, including the repair or replacement of any appliance, as cannot be postponed without impairing efficiency: Merchant Shipping Act 1995 s 84(1).

7   Merchant Shipping Act 1995 s 73(1).

8   Ie by regulations made by the Secretary of State having effect under the Merchant Shipping Act 1995 s 73(1)–(5). As to the Secretary of State see PARA 36. As to the power of the Secretary of State to make subordinate legislation under the Merchant Shipping Act 1995, including his power to appoint committees for the purpose of advising him when considering the making or alteration of any regulations etc, see PARA 39. As to the application of the regulations see the Merchant Shipping (Repatriation) Regulations 1979, SI 1979/97, reg 2 (amended by SI 2014/1614).

9   See the Merchant Shipping (Repatriation) Regulations 1979, SI 1979/97, reg 3 (amended by SI 1979/1519).

10  See the Merchant Shipping (Repatriation) Regulations 1979, SI 1979/97, regs 4, 5 (both amended by SI 1979/1519).

11  See the Merchant Shipping (Repatriation) Regulations 1979, SI 1979/97, reg 6.

12  See the Merchant Shipping (Repatriation) Regulations 1979, SI 1979/97, reg 7.

13  See the Merchant Shipping (Repatriation) Regulations 1979, SI 1979/97, regs 8–10 (regs 8, 9 amended by SI 1979/1519).

14  See the Merchant Shipping (Repatriation) Regulations 1979, SI 1979/97, regs 12–14 (reg 12 amended by SI 1979/1519). The provisions of the Merchant Shipping (Repatriation) Regulations 1979, SI 1979/97, regs 12–14 also apply to any seaman who became employed in a ship registered in the United Kingdom under an agreement entered into in the United Kingdom and who leaves his ship in the United Kingdom, otherwise than on being discharged therefrom: see reg 2(2).

15  See the Merchant Shipping (Repatriation) Regulations 1979, SI 1979/97, reg 15 (amended by SI 1979/1519).

16  See the Merchant Shipping (Repatriation) Regulations 1979, SI 1979/97, reg 16 (amended by SI 1979/1519).

17  See the Merchant Shipping (Repatriation) Regulations 1979, SI 1979/97, reg 17.

### 549. Limit of employer's liability with regard to seaman etc left behind and shipwrecked.

Where a person left behind in or taken to any country[1] remains there after the end of a period of three months, the persons who last employed him as a seaman[2] are not liable[3] to make provision for his return or for any matter arising after the end of that period, unless they have before the end of that period been under an obligation imposed on them by regulations made by the Secretary of State[4] to make provision with respect to him[5].

1   Ie as mentioned in the Merchant Shipping Act 1995 s 73(1) (see PARA 548): see s 74.

2   As to the meaning of 'seaman' see PARA 457 note 5. As to the vessels and seamen to which these
    provisions apply see PARA 548 note 2. The Merchant Shipping Act 1995 s 73 (see PARA 548)
    applies to the master of a ship as it applies to a seaman and s 74 has effect accordingly: s 73(8).
    As to the meaning of 'master' see PARA 444 note 1.
3   Ie under the Merchant Shipping Act 1995 s 73: see s 74.
4   Ie regulations made under the Merchant Shipping Act 1995 s 73: see s 74. As to the Secretary of
    State see PARA 36.
5   Merchant Shipping Act 1995 s 74.

## 550. Recovery of expenses incurred for relief and return of seaman etc left behind and shipwrecked.

Where any expenses are incurred in respect of any matter for which the employers of a seaman[1] left behind and shipwrecked are required to make provision[2], then:

(1)    if the expenses are incurred by the Secretary of State[3] (or are incurred by the government of any country outside the United Kingdom[4] and repaid to them on behalf of the Crown) the Secretary of State may recover them from the employers[5];

(2)    if the expenses are incurred by the seaman, he may recover them from the employers unless they prove either that under the terms of his employment they were to be borne by him or that he would not have been left behind but for his own wrongful act or neglect[6].

Where, in the case of any seaman, expenses are incurred by the Secretary of State or are incurred by the government of any country outside the United Kingdom and repaid to them on behalf of the Crown:

(a)    in respect of any matter for which[7] the seaman's last employers would otherwise[8] have been required to make provision[9]; or

(b)    in respect of any matter for which provision is required to be made[10] with respect to persons who are British citizens[11], British overseas territories citizens[12] or British Overseas citizens[13] and are found in distress in any country outside the United Kingdom after being employed in ships registered in, or belonging to the government of, such a country[14],

the Secretary of State may recover them from the seaman, or, if he has died, from his personal representatives[15].

1   As to the meaning of 'seaman' see PARA 457 note 5. As to the vessels and seamen to which these
    provisions apply see PARA 548 note 2.
2   Ie under the Merchant Shipping Act 1995 s 73 (see PARA 548): see s 75(1). Section 73 applies to
    the master of a ship as it applies to a seaman and s 75 has effect accordingly: s 73(8). As to the
    meaning of 'master' see PARA 444 note 1.
3   As to the Secretary of State see PARA 36.
4   As to the meaning of 'United Kingdom' see PARA 16 note 3.
5   Merchant Shipping Act 1995 s 75(1)(a).
6   Merchant Shipping Act 1995 s 75(1)(b).
7   Ie but for the Merchant Shipping Act 1995 s 74 (limit of employer's liability under s 73) (see
    PARA 549): see s 75(2)(a).
8   Ie under the Merchant Shipping Act 1995 s 73: see s 75(2)(a).
9   Merchant Shipping Act 1995 s 75(2)(a).
10  Ie under the Merchant Shipping Act 1995 s 73(4)(b) (see PARA 527): see s 75(2)(b).
11  As to the meaning of 'British citizen' see BRITISH NATIONALITY vol 4 (2011) PARA 23 et seq.
12  As to the meaning of 'British overseas territories citizen' see BRITISH NATIONALITY vol 4 (2011)
    PARAS 406, 445–458.
13  As to the meaning of 'British Overseas citizen' see BRITISH NATIONALITY vol 4 (2011) PARA 459
    et seq.
14  Merchant Shipping Act 1995 s 75(2)(b).
15  Merchant Shipping Act 1995 s 75(2).

## (xii) Required Documentation

### A. OFFICIAL LOG BOOKS

**551. Keeping official log books.** An official log book in a form approved by the Secretary of State[1] must[2] be kept in every United Kingdom ship[3].

If a person intentionally destroys or mutilates or renders illegible any entry in an official log book, he commits an offence[4].

1 As to the Secretary of State see PARA 36.
2 Ie except as provided by regulations under the Merchant Shipping Act 1995 s 77 (see PARA 552): see s 77(1).
3 Merchant Shipping Act 1995 s 77(1). The Merchant Shipping Act 1995 ss 77–80; the Merchant Shipping (Official Log Books) Regulations 1981, SI 1981/569; the Merchant Shipping (Crew Agreements, Lists of Crew and Discharge of Seamen) Regulations 1991, SI 1991/2144; and the Merchant Shipping (Seamen's Documents) Regulations 1987, SI 1987/408 (see the text and note 4; and PARAS 552–573) apply in relation to all United Kingdom ships: being concerned with matters with which the Merchant Shipping (Maritime Labour Convention) (Minimum Requirements for Seafarers etc) Regulations 2014, SI 2014/1613 and the Maritime Labour Convention (Cm 7049)) are not concerned (see PARA 423), these provisions are not limited to the vessels excluded from the scope of the Convention (see further PARA 423 note 22). As to the meaning of 'ship' see PARA 229. As to the meaning of 'United Kingdom ship' see PARA 230. As to the meaning of 'United Kingdom' see PARA 16 note 3.
     The official log book of any ship kept under the Merchant Shipping Act 1995 s 77 and, without prejudice to s 288(2) (see PARA 1059), any document purporting to be a copy of an entry therein and to be certified as a true copy by the master of the ship, are admissible in evidence and, when in the custody of the Registrar General of Shipping and Seamen, are open to public inspection: see s 287(1)(b); and PARA 1058. As to the Registrar General of Shipping and Seamen see PARA 62.
4 See the Merchant Shipping Act 1995 s 77(6); and PARA 1086.

**552. Entries in official log books.** The following provision is made[1] in relation to the maintenance of official log books[2]:

(1)     exemptions from the statutory requirements to keep official log books[3];
(2)     entries to be made in official log books[4];
(3)     making, signing and witnessing entries[5];
(4)     annexes to official log books[6];
(5)     making false, inaccurate or incomplete entries[7];
(6)     the time for making entries[8];
(7)     the amendment and cancellation of entries[9];
(8)     production on demand of the official log book[10];
(9)     delivery of the official log book[11]; and
(10)    offences[12].

1 Ie by the Merchant Shipping (Official Log Books) Regulations 1981, SI 1981/569, which, by virtue of the Interpretation Act 1978 s 17(2)(b), have effect as if made under the Merchant Shipping Act 1995 s 77(2)–(5).
2 As to official log books see PARA 551. As to the vessels and seamen to which these provisions apply see PARA 551 note 3.
3 See the Merchant Shipping (Official Log Books) Regulations 1981, SI 1981/569, reg 2.
4 See the Merchant Shipping (Official Log Books) Regulations 1981, SI 1981/569, reg 3 (added by SI 1991/2145), the Merchant Shipping (Official Log Books) Regulations 1981, SI 1981/569, Schedule (amended by SI 1991/2145; SI 1997/1511; SI 2002/1473).
5 See the Merchant Shipping (Official Log Books) Regulations 1981, SI 1981/569, regs 4, 5, Schedule (Schedule as amended: see note 4).
6 See the Merchant Shipping (Official Log Books) Regulations 1981, SI 1981/569, reg 6.
7 See the Merchant Shipping (Official Log Books) Regulations 1981, SI 1981/569, reg 6A (added by SI 1991/2145).
8 See the Merchant Shipping (Official Log Books) Regulations 1981, SI 1981/569, reg 7.
9 See the Merchant Shipping (Official Log Books) Regulations 1981, SI 1981/569, reg 8.
10 See the Merchant Shipping (Official Log Books) Regulations 1981, SI 1981/569, reg 9 (amended by SI 1991/2145; SI 1997/2971).
11 See the Merchant Shipping (Official Log Books) Regulations 1981, SI 1981/569, reg 10 (amended by SI 1991/2145).

12 See the Merchant Shipping (Official Log Books) Regulations 1981, SI 1981/569, reg 11 (amended by SI 1991/2145).

B.   LISTS OF CREW

**553. List of crew to be maintained.** The master[1] of every United Kingdom ship[2] must[3] make and maintain a list of the crew containing such particulars as may be required by regulations[4]. This duty does not apply in relation to a pleasure yacht which is[5] engaged on a coastal or any other voyage, provided that not more than four members of the crew receive wages for their employment[6].

A list of crew remains in force until all of the persons employed on the ship whose particulars are contained on the list have been discharged[7].

1   As to the meaning of 'master' see PARA 444 note 1.
2   As to the meaning of 'United Kingdom ship' see PARA 230. As to the meaning of 'ship' under the Merchant Shipping Act 1995 see PARA 229; and as to the meaning of 'United Kingdom' see PARA 16 note 3. As to the vessels and seamen to which these provisions apply see PARA 551 note 3.
3   Ie except as provided by regulations under the Merchant Shipping Act 1995 s 78 (see the text and note 4): see s 78(1).
4   Merchant Shipping Act 1995 s 78(1). As to the regulations see the Merchant Shipping (Crew Agreements, Lists of Crew and Discharge of Seamen) Regulations 1991, SI 1991/2144 (made under the Merchant Shipping Act 1995 s 78(2)–(5)); and PARAS 554–558. Lists of crews made under s 78 and notices given under Pt III (ss 24–84) of additions to or changes in lists of crews, are admissible in evidence and, when in the custody of the Registrar General of Shipping and Seamen, are open to public inspection: see s 287(1)(c); and PARA 1058. As to the Registrar General of Shipping and Seamen see PARA 62.
5   Merchant Shipping (Crew Agreements, Lists of Crew and Discharge of Seamen) Regulations 1991, SI 1991/2144, reg 12 (made under the Merchant Shipping Act 1995 s 78(2)–(5)).
6   Merchant Shipping (Crew Agreements, Lists of Crew and Discharge of Seamen) Regulations 1991, SI 1991/2144, reg 12. As to the meaning of 'coastal voyage' for these purposes see PARA 458 note 6. In Pt II (regs 11–22), except where the context otherwise requires, references to the employment of a seaman in a ship include references to engagement; and 'seaman' includes the master of a ship: reg 11. As to the meaning of 'ship' for these purposes see PARA 458 note 2.
7   Merchant Shipping (Crew Agreements, Lists of Crew and Discharge of Seamen) Regulations 1991, SI 1991/2144, reg 19 (substituted by SI 2014/1614).

**554. Particulars to be specified in list of crew.** A list of crew must[1] contain the following particulars[2]:
(1)   the name of the ship[3], its port of registry and official number[4];
(2)   the name of the owner of the ship and his address and of any other person registered as manager or ship's husband[5];
(3)   with respect to every seaman[6] from time to time on board the ship[8]:
  (a)   his name[9];
  (b)   his address[10];
  (c)   the number of his current discharge book[11], if any, or the date and place of his birth[12];
  (d)   the name of the ship in which he was last employed, and, if he was discharged[13] from that ship more than 12 months before he became employed in the ship to which the crew list relates, the year in which he was so discharged[14];
  (e)   the capacity in which he is employed in the ship[15];
  (f)   the grade, including any command, service or other endorsement[16], and number of any certificate of competency or of service held by him[17];
  (g)   the date on which he went on board the ship to commence his employment in it[18];
  (h)   the date on and place at which he left the ship and, if he left on discharge, the reason for his discharge[19];

    (i)     if he is left behind otherwise than on discharge, the date and place of and the reason, if known to the master, for this being done[20]; and

    (j)     the name and relationship of his next of kin and the address of his next of kin, if different from that of the seaman[21].

A list of crew which relates to a ship belonging to a general lighthouse authority[22] need contain only the particulars referred to in heads (1), (3)(a), (3)(b), (3)(g) and (3)(h) above[23].

With respect to a member of the naval, military or air forces of the Crown or of any service administered by the Defence Council[24] when acting as such a member, a list of crew need contain only the particulars referred to in heads (3)(a), (3)(b), (3)(g) and (3)(h) above[25].

1  Ie subject to the Merchant Shipping (Crew Agreements, Lists of Crew and Discharge of Seamen) Regulations 1991, SI 1991/2144, reg 14(2), (3) (see the text and notes 22–23): see reg 14(1). As to the requirement to keep a list of the crew see PARA 553. As to the vessels and seamen to which these provisions apply see PARA 551 note 3.

2  Merchant Shipping (Crew Agreements, Lists of Crew and Discharge of Seamen) Regulations 1991, SI 1991/2144, reg14(1).

3  As to the meaning of 'ship' for these purposes see PARA 458 note 2. As to a ship's name for registration purposes see PARA 277 et seq.

4  Merchant Shipping (Crew Agreements, Lists of Crew and Discharge of Seamen) Regulations 1991, SI 1991/2144, reg 14(1)(a)(i). As to the registration of ships under the Merchant Shipping Act 1995 see PARA 245 et seq; and as to the allocation of an official number see PARA 279 et seq.

5  Merchant Shipping (Crew Agreements, Lists of Crew and Discharge of Seamen) Regulations 1991, SI 1991/2144, reg14(1)(a)(ii).

6  Ie subject to the Merchant Shipping (Crew Agreements, Lists of Crew and Discharge of Seamen) Regulations 1991, SI 1991/2144, reg 14(4) (see the text and notes 28–29): see reg 14(1)(b). As to the meaning of 'seaman' for these purposes see PARA 536 note 4.

8  Merchant Shipping (Crew Agreements, Lists of Crew and Discharge of Seamen) Regulations 1991, SI 1991/2144, reg 14(1)(b) (amended by SI 2014/1614).

9  Merchant Shipping (Crew Agreements, Lists of Crew and Discharge of Seamen) Regulations 1991, SI 1991/2144, reg14(1)(b)(i).

10  Merchant Shipping (Crew Agreements, Lists of Crew and Discharge of Seamen) Regulations 1991, SI 1991/2144, reg14(1)(b)(ii).

11  As to discharge books see PARA 565 et seq.

12  Merchant Shipping (Crew Agreements, Lists of Crew and Discharge of Seamen) Regulations 1991, SI 1991/2144, reg14(1)(b)(iii).

13  For these purposes, except where the context otherwise requires, references to discharge include references to termination of engagement: Merchant Shipping (Crew Agreements, Lists of Crew and Discharge of Seamen) Regulations 1991, SI 1991/2144, reg 11.

14  Merchant Shipping (Crew Agreements, Lists of Crew and Discharge of Seamen) Regulations 1991, SI 1991/2144, reg14(1)(b)(iv).

15  Merchant Shipping (Crew Agreements, Lists of Crew and Discharge of Seamen) Regulations 1991, SI 1991/2144, reg14(1)(b)(v).

16  For these purposes, 'endorsement', in relation to a certificate of competency or of service means an endorsement in respect of a trading area, type of ship or dangerous cargo: Merchant Shipping (Crew Agreements, Lists of Crew and Discharge of Seamen) Regulations 1991, SI 1991/2144, reg 11.

17  Merchant Shipping (Crew Agreements, Lists of Crew and Discharge of Seamen) Regulations 1991, SI 1991/2144, reg14(1)(b)(vi).

18  Merchant Shipping (Crew Agreements, Lists of Crew and Discharge of Seamen) Regulations 1991, SI 1991/2144, reg14(1)(b)(vii).

19  Merchant Shipping (Crew Agreements, Lists of Crew and Discharge of Seamen) Regulations 1991, SI 1991/2144, reg14(1)(b)(viii).

20  Merchant Shipping (Crew Agreements, Lists of Crew and Discharge of Seamen) Regulations 1991, SI 1991/2144, reg14(1)(b)(ix).

21  Merchant Shipping (Crew Agreements, Lists of Crew and Discharge of Seamen) Regulations 1991, SI 1991/2144, reg14(1)(b)(x).

22  As to General Lighthouse Authorities see PARA 1017.

23 Merchant Shipping (Crew Agreements, Lists of Crew and Discharge of Seamen) Regulations 1991, SI 1991/2144, reg14(2).
24 As to the Defence Council see CONSTITUTIONAL AND ADMINISTRATIVE LAW vol 20 (2014) PARA 562 et seq.
25 Merchant Shipping (Crew Agreements, Lists of Crew and Discharge of Seamen) Regulations 1991, SI 1991/2144, reg14(4).

**555. Duties with regard to copies of list of crew.** A copy of every list of crew[1], including all changes in it notified to the owner[2], must be maintained by the owner of the ship at an address in the United Kingdom[3]; and a person who fails to do so commits an offence[4].

The master must, as soon as practicable and in any event within three days of any change being made in the list of crew, notify the change to the owner of the ship[5]; and a master who fails to do so commits an offence[6].

When any person having in his possession the copy of a list of crew[7] has reason to believe that the ship to which it relates has been lost or abandoned, he must immediately deliver the copy of the list to the Secretary of State[8]. A person who fails to do so commits an offence[9].

A person having in his possession a copy of a list of crew[10] must produce it on demand to the Secretary of State[11]; and a person who fails to do so commits an offence[12].

1 As to the requirement to keep a list of the crew see PARA 553. As to the vessels and seamen to which these provisions apply see PARA 551 note 3.
2 For these purposes, 'owner of the ship' means either the person registered as managing owner, ship's husband or manager, or (if there is no such person) the owner of the ship: Merchant Shipping (Crew Agreements, Lists of Crew and Discharge of Seamen) Regulations 1991, SI 1991/2144, reg 15(3). As to the meaning of 'ship' for these purposes see PARA 458 note 2.
3 Merchant Shipping (Crew Agreements, Lists of Crew and Discharge of Seamen) Regulations 1991, SI 1991/2144, reg 15(1). As to the meaning of 'United Kingdom' see PARA 16 note 3.
4 See the Merchant Shipping (Crew Agreements, Lists of Crew and Discharge of Seamen) Regulations 1991, SI 1991/2144, reg22(2); and PARA 1087.
5 Merchant Shipping (Crew Agreements, Lists of Crew and Discharge of Seamen) Regulations 1991, SI 1991/2144, reg15(2).
6 See the Merchant Shipping (Crew Agreements, Lists of Crew and Discharge of Seamen) Regulations 1991, SI 1991/2144, reg22(1); and PARA 1087.
7 Ie which is required to be maintained under the Merchant Shipping (Crew Agreements, Lists of Crew and Discharge of Seamen) Regulations 1991, SI 1991/2144, reg 15 (see the text and notes 1–3, 5).
8 Merchant Shipping (Crew Agreements, Lists of Crew and Discharge of Seamen) Regulations 1991, SI 1991/2144, reg 16 (amended by SI 2014/1614). As to the Secretary of State see PARA 36.
9 See the Merchant Shipping (Crew Agreements, Lists of Crew and Discharge of Seamen) Regulations 1991, SI 1991/2144, reg22(2); and PARA 1087.
10 Ie which is required to be maintained under the Merchant Shipping (Crew Agreements, Lists of Crew and Discharge of Seamen) Regulations 1991, SI 1991/2144, reg 15 (see the text and notes 1–3, 5).
11 Merchant Shipping (Crew Agreements, Lists of Crew and Discharge of Seamen) Regulations 1991, SI 1991/2144, reg 17 (amended by SI 2014/1614).
12 See the Merchant Shipping (Crew Agreements, Lists of Crew and Discharge of Seamen) Regulations 1991, SI 1991/2144, reg22(2); and PARA 1087.

**556. Delivery on demand of list of crew to Registrar General.** The owner[1] must, on demand, deliver to the Registrar General of Shipping and Seamen[2] within 28 days of such demand being made a list of the crew on board the ship at a date specified by the Registrar General of Shipping and Seamen[3].

A person who fails to comply with such an obligation commits an offence[4].

1 As to the meaning of 'owner of the ship' for these purposes see PARA 555 note 2; and as to the meaning of 'ship' see PARA 458 note 2. As to the vessels and seamen to which these provisions apply see PARA 551 note 3.
2 As to the Registrar General of Shipping and Seamen see PARA 62.

3   Merchant Shipping (Crew Agreements, Lists of Crew and Discharge of Seamen) Regulations 1991,
    SI 1991/2144, reg 18. As to the requirement to keep a list of the crew see PARA 553.
4   See the Merchant Shipping (Crew Agreements, Lists of Crew and Discharge of Seamen)
    Regulations 1991, SI 1991/2144, reg22(2); and PARA 1088.

**557.   Delivery of list of crew.** The master must, within three days after a list of
crew (other than one relating to a ship[1] of less than 25 gross tons[2] or to a ship
belonging to a general lighthouse authority[3]) has ceased to be in force (or, if it is
not practicable within that period, as soon as practicable thereafter), deliver the
list to a superintendent or proper officer for the place where the ship is when the
list of crew ceases to be in force[4]. A master who fails so to comply commits an
offence[5].

The shipowner must deliver a list of crew to the Registrar-General of Shipping
and Seamen[6] within seven days of the expiry of each period of six months after the
date on which it is made, for so long as it remains in force[7]. A person who fails
so to comply commits an offence.

1   As to the meaning of 'ship' for these purposes see PARA 458 note 2. As to the requirement to keep
    a list of the crew see PARA 553. As to the vessels and seamen to which these provisions apply see
    PARA 551 note 3.
2   As to the meaning of references to the gross tonnage of a ship see PARA 458 note 5.
3   As to General Lighthouse Authorities see PARA 1017.
4   Merchant Shipping (Crew Agreements, Lists of Crew and Discharge of Seamen) Regulations 1991,
    SI 1991/2144, reg20(1).
5   See the Merchant Shipping (Crew Agreements, Lists of Crew and Discharge of Seamen)
    Regulations 1991, SI 1991/2144, reg22(1); and PARA 1089.
6   As to the Registrar General of Shipping and Seamen see PARA 62.
7   Merchant Shipping (Crew Agreements, Lists of Crew and Discharge of Seamen) Regulations 1991,
    SI 1991/2144, reg 20(2) (substituted by SI 2014/1614).

**558.   Production of lists of crew on demand to officials.** A master must, on
demand, produce to the Registrar General of Shipping and Seamen[1], a proper
officer, a surveyor of ships in the course of any inspection of the ship[2] or an officer
of revenue and customs[3] the list of crew required to be maintained in the ship[4].
A master who fails so to comply commits an offence[5].

1   As to the Registrar General of Shipping and Seamen see PARA 62.
2   Ie in pursuance of his functions under the Merchant Shipping Act 1995 s 256 (see PARA 46) or
    under s 258 (see PARA 48): see the Merchant Shipping (Crew Agreements, Lists of Crew and
    Discharge of Seamen) Regulations 1991, SI 1991/2144, reg 21 (amended by SI 2014/1614).
3   As to the appointment of officers of Revenue and Customs see INCOME TAXATION vol 58 (2014)
    PARA 33.
4   Merchant Shipping (Crew Agreements, Lists of Crew and Discharge of Seamen) Regulations 1991,
    SI 1991/2144, reg 21 (amended by virtue of the Commissioners for Revenue and Customs Act
    2005 s 50(1), (2), (7)). As to the meaning of 'ship' for these purposes see PARA 458 note 2. As to
    the requirement to keep a list of the crew see PARA 553. As to the vessels and seamen to which
    these provisions apply see PARA 551 note 3.
5   See the Merchant Shipping (Crew Agreements, Lists of Crew and Discharge of Seamen)
    Regulations 1991, SI 1991/2144, reg22(1); and PARA 1090.

C.   BRITISH SEAMEN'S CARDS AND DISCHARGE BOOKS

*(A)   British Seamen's Cards*

**559.   Application for British seaman's card.** A person who satisfies the
conditions specified in heads (1) and (2) below, whether or not he has previously
held a British seaman's card or a British seaman's identity card[1], may apply for a
British seaman's card[2]. The conditions so specified are that the person[3]:
(1)      is a British seaman who is employed or ordinarily employed in a ship
         otherwise than in an employment[4], being:
         (a)      employment in a fishing vessel[5];

(b)  employment in a ship belonging to a general lighthouse authority[6];

(c)  except in the case of a person who is a cadet, employment on terms under which he receives no wages or only nominal wages[7]; and

(d)  in the case of a person who is not a citizen of the United Kingdom[8] and colonies[9] or a British protected person[10], employment in a ship registered otherwise than in the United Kingdom, the Channel Islands, the Isle of Man or any colony, protectorate[11] or protected state[12],

(e)  [13]; and

(2)  is not the holder[14] of a British seaman's card duly issued to him[15] by the Secretary of State[16] or duly indorsed[17].

The provisions which govern entitlement to apply for a British seaman's card[18] do not apply to:

(i)  a person who is not a British citizen[19], a British overseas territories citizen[20] or a British Overseas citizen[21], a British protected person[22], or a British subject[23] without citizenship[24], and who holds a seaman's identity document which has been issued to him by or under the authority of the government of a specified Commonwealth country[25] or of any territory or trust territory[26] under the protection of or administered by such government or of the Republic of Ireland, and of which he has not ceased to be regarded as the holder by that government[27];

(ii)  a person who holds a seaman's identity document which has been issued to him by the government of any colony, protectorate or protected state[28] and of which he has not ceased to be regarded as the holder by that government[29];

(iii)  a person in the employment of the Crown who is employed, but not ordinarily employed, as a master or seaman[30]; and

(iv)  a member of the naval, military or air forces of the Crown or of any service administered by the Defence Council[31].

A person applying for a British seaman's card must make an application in accordance with the statutory provisions[32] and, unless it has been lost or destroyed, must surrender to the Registrar General of Shipping and Seamen[33] or a superintendent any British seaman's card or British seaman's identity card previously held by him[34].

1  For these purposes, 'British seaman's identity card' means a British seaman's identity card issued under the British Seamen's Identity Cards Order 1942, SR & O 1942/2682 (revoked): see the Merchant Shipping (Seamen's Documents) Regulations 1987, SI 1987/408, reg 1(2)(b) (having effect under the Merchant Shipping Act 1995 s 79(1), (2)). 'British seamen' means persons who are not aliens within the meaning of the British Nationality Act 1981 (see BRITISH NATIONALITY vol 4 (2011) PARA 411) and are employed, or ordinarily employed, as masters or seamen: Merchant Shipping Act 1995 s 79(3). As to the meaning of 'seaman' see PARA 457 note 5; and as to the meaning of 'master' see PARA 444 note 1. As to the vessels and seamen to which these provisions apply see PARA 551 note 3.

2  Merchant Shipping (Seamen's Documents) Regulations 1987, SI 1987/408, reg 2(1). This provision is subject to reg 3 (see the text and notes 4–13, 18–31): see reg 2(1). If a person makes a statement which he knows to be false or recklessly makes a statement which is false in a material particular for the purpose of obtaining for himself or another person a British seaman's card, he is liable on summary conviction to a fine: Merchant Shipping Act 1995 s 79(4). As to the powers of magistrates' courts to issue fines on summary conviction see SENTENCING vol 92 (2015) PARA 176.

3  Merchant Shipping (Seamen's Documents) Regulations 1987, SI 1987/408, reg 2(2).

4  Merchant Shipping (Seamen's Documents) Regulations 1987, SI 1987/408, regs 2(2)(a), 3(1)(a).

5   Merchant Shipping (Seamen's Documents) Regulations 1987, SI 1987/408, reg 3(2)(a).
6   Merchant Shipping (Seamen's Documents) Regulations 1987, SI 1987/408, reg 3(2)(b). As to General Lighthouse Authorities see PARA 1017.
7   Merchant Shipping (Seamen's Documents) Regulations 1987, SI 1987/408, reg 3(2)(c).
8   As to the meaning of 'United Kingdom' see PARA 16 note 3. See also BRITISH NATIONALITY vol 4 (2011) PARA 405.
9   For these purposes, 'colony' has the same meaning as it has in and for the purposes of the British Nationality Act 1981 (see BRITISH NATIONALITY vol 4 (2011) PARA 415): Merchant Shipping (Seamen's Documents) Regulations 1987, SI 1987/408, reg 1(2)(a).
10  For these purposes, 'British protected person' has the same meaning as it has in and for the purposes of the British Nationality Act 1981 (see BRITISH NATIONALITY vol 4 (2011) PARAS 408, 476 et seq): Merchant Shipping (Seamen's Documents) Regulations 1987, SI 1987/408, reg 1(2)(a).
11  For these purposes 'protectorate' has the same meaning as it has in and for the purposes of the British Nationality Act 1981 (see BRITISH NATIONALITY vol 4 (2011) PARA 415): Merchant Shipping (Seamen's Documents) Regulations 1987, SI 1987/408, reg 1(2)(a).
12  Merchant Shipping (Seamen's Documents) Regulations 1987, SI 1987/408, reg 3(2)(d). For these purposes, 'protected state' has the same meaning as it has in and for the purposes of the British Nationality Act 1981 (see BRITISH NATIONALITY vol 4 (2011) PARA 415): Merchant Shipping (Seamen's Documents) Regulations 1987, SI 1987/408, reg 1(2)(a).
13  Merchant Shipping (Seamen's Documents) Regulations 1987, SI 1987/408, regs 2(2)(a), 3(1)(b).
14  For these purposes, a person to whom a British seaman's card or a discharge book has been issued is referred to as the holder of it: Merchant Shipping (Seamen's Documents) Regulations 1987, SI 1987/408, reg 1(2)(d).
15  Ie under the Merchant Shipping (Seamen's Documents) Regulations 1987, SI 1987/408, reg 5 (see PARA 560): see reg 2(2)(b).
16  As to the Secretary of State see PARA 36.
17  Merchant Shipping (Seamen's Documents) Regulations 1987, SI 1987/408, reg 2(2)(b). The text refers to a British seaman's card indorsed under reg 8 (see PARA 561): see reg 2(2)(b).
18  Ie the Merchant Shipping (Seamen's Documents) Regulations 1987, SI 1987/408, reg 2 (see the text and notes 1–17): see reg 3(3).
19  For these purposes, 'British citizen' has the same meaning as it has in and for the purposes of the British Nationality Act 1981 (see BRITISH NATIONALITY vol 4 (2011) PARA 421 et seq): Merchant Shipping (Seamen's Documents) Regulations 1987, SI 1987/408, reg 1(2)(a).
20  For these purposes, 'British overseas territories citizen' has the same meaning as it has in and for the purposes of the British Nationality Act 1981 (see BRITISH NATIONALITY vol 4 (2011) PARA 406, 455–458): Merchant Shipping (Seamen's Documents) Regulations 1987, SI 1987/408, reg 1(2)(a) (definition substituted by virtue of the British Overseas Territories Act 2002 s 2(3)).
21  Merchant Shipping (Seamen's Documents) Regulations 1987, SI 1987/408, reg 3(3)(a)(i). (amended by virtue of the British Overseas Territories Act 2002 s 2(3)). For these purposes, 'British Overseas citizen' has the same meaning as it has in and for the purposes of the British Nationality Act 1981 (see BRITISH NATIONALITY vol 4 (2011) PARA 459 et seq): Merchant Shipping (Seamen's Documents) Regulations 1987, SI 1987/408, reg 1(2)(a).
22  Merchant Shipping (Seamen's Documents) Regulations 1987, SI 1987/408, reg 3(3)(a)(ii).
23  As to British subjects under the British Nationality Act 1981 see BRITISH NATIONALITY vol 4 (2011) PARAS 407, 469–474.
24  Merchant Shipping (Seamen's Documents) Regulations 1987, SI 1987/408, reg 3(3)(a)(iii).
25  Ie a country specified in the British Nationality Act 1981 s 37, Sch 3 (see BRITISH NATIONALITY vol 4 (2011) PARA 409): see the Merchant Shipping (Seamen's Documents) Regulations 1987, SI 1987/408, reg 3(3)(a).
26  As to the meaning of 'United Kingdom trust territory' under the British Nationality Act 1948 s 32(1) (now repealed) see BRITISH NATIONALITY vol 4 (2011) PARA 415.
27  Merchant Shipping (Seamen's Documents) Regulations 1987, SI 1987/408, reg 3(3)(a).
28  Merchant Shipping (Seamen's Documents) Regulations 1987, SI 1987/408, reg 3(3)(b)(i).
29  Merchant Shipping (Seamen's Documents) Regulations 1987, SI 1987/408, reg 3(3)(b)(ii).
30  Merchant Shipping (Seamen's Documents) Regulations 1987, SI 1987/408, reg 3(3)(c).
31  Merchant Shipping (Seamen's Documents) Regulations 1987, SI 1987/408, reg 3(3)(d). As to the Defence Council see CONSTITUTIONAL AND ADMINISTRATIVE LAW vol 20 (2014) PARA 562 et seq.
32  Ie in accordance with the Merchant Shipping (Seamen's Documents) Regulations 1987, SI 1987/408, reg 29 (see PARA 573): see reg 4.
33  As to the Registrar General of Shipping and Seamen see PARA 62.
34  Merchant Shipping (Seamen's Documents) Regulations 1987, SI 1987/408, reg 4.

**560. Issue etc of British seaman's card.** If a person applying for a British seaman's card satisfies the specified conditions[1] and has paid the fee, if any, prescribed, then, in the case of a person having the right of abode[2], the Secretary of State[3] must, and in any other case, may issue a British seaman's card to him[4].

A British seaman's card must be in book form and must provide for there to be recorded in it from time to time in relation to its holder[5] statements of the following particulars[6]:

(1)     a statement that the document is a seafarer's identity document for the purposes of the International Labour Organisation Convention Concerning Seafarers' National Identity Documents[7];

(2)     full name of the holder[8];

(3)     height[9];

(4)     colour of eyes[10];

(5)     date and place of birth[11];

(6)     distinguishing marks, if any[12];

(7)     discharge book number, if any[13];

(8)     nationality[14];

(9)     home address[15];

(10)    national insurance number[16];

(11)    photograph of holder[17];

(12)    signature of holder[18];

(13)    a statement of the period of validity[19].

When his British seaman's card is lost, destroyed, defaced or required to be surrendered, a person ceases to be regarded as the holder of a British seaman's card[20].

1   Ie the conditions set out in the Merchant Shipping (Seamen's Documents) Regulations 1987, SI 1987/408, reg 2(2) (see PARA 559): see reg 5. As to the vessels and seamen to which these provisions apply see PARA 551 note 3.

2   For these purposes, a person is treated as having the right of abode if he has the right of abode in the United Kingdom under the Immigration Act 1971 s 2 (as to which see BRITISH NATIONALITY vol 4 (2011) PARA 412): Merchant Shipping (Seamen's Documents) Regulations 1987, SI 1987/408, reg 1(3). As to the meaning of 'United Kingdom' see PARA 16 note 3.

3   As to the Secretary of State see PARA 36.

4   Merchant Shipping (Seamen's Documents) Regulations 1987, SI 1987/408, reg 5. As to related offences concerning improper alterations made in seamen's documents see PARAS 572, 1100.

5   As to the meaning of references to 'holder' for these purposes see PARA 559 note 14.

6   Merchant Shipping (Seamen's Documents) Regulations 1987, SI 1987/408, reg 6. The particulars are those specified in Sch 2 (see heads (1) to (13) in the text): see reg 6.

7   Merchant Shipping (Seamen's Documents) Regulations 1987, SI 1987/408, Sch 2 para 1. The Convention referred to in head (1) in the text is the Convention Concerning Seafarers' National Identity Documents (ILO No 108) (13 May 1958): see the Merchant Shipping (Seamen's Documents) Regulations 1987, SI 1987/408, Sch 2 para 1.

8   Merchant Shipping (Seamen's Documents) Regulations 1987, SI 1987/408, Sch 2 para 2.

9   Merchant Shipping (Seamen's Documents) Regulations 1987, SI 1987/408, Sch 2 para 3.

10  Merchant Shipping (Seamen's Documents) Regulations 1987, SI 1987/408, Sch 2 para 4.

11  Merchant Shipping (Seamen's Documents) Regulations 1987, SI 1987/408, Sch 2 para 5.

12  Merchant Shipping (Seamen's Documents) Regulations 1987, SI 1987/408, Sch 2 para 6.

13  Merchant Shipping (Seamen's Documents) Regulations 1987, SI 1987/408, Sch 2 para 7.

14  Merchant Shipping (Seamen's Documents) Regulations 1987, SI 1987/408, Sch 2 para 8.

15  Merchant Shipping (Seamen's Documents) Regulations 1987, SI 1987/408, Sch 2 para 9.

16  Merchant Shipping (Seamen's Documents) Regulations 1987, SI 1987/408, Sch 2 para 10.

17  Merchant Shipping (Seamen's Documents) Regulations 1987, SI 1987/408, Sch 2 para 11.

18  Merchant Shipping (Seamen's Documents) Regulations 1987, SI 1987/408, Sch 2 para 12.

19  Merchant Shipping (Seamen's Documents) Regulations 1987, SI 1987/408, Sch 2 para 13.

20  Merchant Shipping (Seamen's Documents) Regulations 1987, SI 1987/408, reg 9.

**561. Validity of British seaman's card.** A British seaman's card issued after 8 April 1987[1] is valid until the end of the period of ten years from the date of issue, provided that, if at the end of such period the holder[2] is not present in the United Kingdom[3], his British seaman's card remains valid until he first returns to the United Kingdom or the expiry of a further 12 months from the date of expiry, whichever is the sooner[4].

1 Ie the date of the coming into operation of the Merchant Shipping (Seamen's Documents) Regulations 1987, SI 1987/408: see reg 1(1). As to the vessels and seamen to which these provisions apply see PARA 551 note 3.
2 As to the meaning of references to 'holder' for these purposes see PARA 559 note 14.
3 As to the meaning of 'United Kingdom' see PARA 16 note 3.
4 Merchant Shipping (Seamen's Documents) Regulations 1987, SI 1987/408, reg 7. As to British seamen's cards issued pursuant to previous legislation see the Merchant Shipping (Seamen's Documents) Regulations 1987, SI 1987/408, regs 8, 13, 14. As to related offences concerning improper alterations made in seamen's documents see PARAS 572, 1100.

**562. Requirement to produce British seaman's card.** The holder[1] of a British seaman's card must produce it to the Registrar General of Shipping and Seamen[2] or a superintendent, a proper officer, his employer or the master of his ship, on demand or within such period as the person requiring its production may allow[3].

A person who fails to produce his British seaman's card in pursuance of such a requirement[4] commits an offence[5]; but it is a defence for a person so charged to prove that he took all reasonable precautions to avoid the commission of the offence[6].

1 As to the meaning of references to 'holder' for these purposes see PARA 559 note 14. As to the vessels and seamen to which these provisions apply see PARA 551 note 3.
2 As to the Registrar General of Shipping and Seamen see PARA 62.
3 Merchant Shipping (Seamen's Documents) Regulations 1987, SI 1987/408, reg 10(1).
4 Ie in pursuance of a requirement made under the Merchant Shipping (Seamen's Documents) Regulations 1987, SI 1987/408, reg 10 (see the text and notes 1–3): see reg 10(2).
5 See the Merchant Shipping (Seamen's Documents) Regulations 1987, SI 1987/408, reg 10(2); and PARA 1091.
6 See the Merchant Shipping (Seamen's Documents) Regulations 1987, SI 1987/408, reg 30(2); and PARA 1091.

**563. Requirement to surrender British seaman's card.** The holder[1] of a British seaman's card[2] must surrender it to the Registrar General of Shipping and Seamen[3] or a superintendent[4], either:

(1)     forthwith, upon his ceasing to be a British seaman or upon the card being defaced[5]; or

(2)     on demand, after he has ceased to have the right of abode[6].

A person who fails to comply with such a requirement[7] commits an offence[8]; but it is a defence for a person so charged to prove that he took all reasonable precautions to avoid the commission of the offence[9].

1 As to the meaning of references to 'holder' for these purposes see PARA 559 note 14. As to the vessels and seamen to which these provisions apply see PARA 551 note 3.
2 As to British seamen's cards see PARA 559 et seq.
3 As to the Registrar General of Shipping and Seamen see PARA 62.
4 Merchant Shipping (Seamen's Documents) Regulations 1987, SI 1987/408, reg 11(1).
5 Merchant Shipping (Seamen's Documents) Regulations 1987, SI 1987/408, reg 11(1)(a).
6 Merchant Shipping (Seamen's Documents) Regulations 1987, SI 1987/408, reg 11(1)(b). As to the meaning of 'right of abode' for these purposes see PARA 560 note 2.
7 Ie the requirements of the Merchant Shipping (Seamen's Documents) Regulations 1987, SI 1987/408, reg 11 (see the text and notes 1–6): see reg 11(2); and PARA 1092.
8 See the Merchant Shipping (Seamen's Documents) Regulations 1987, SI 1987/408, reg 11(2); and PARA 1092.
9 See the Merchant Shipping (Seamen's Documents) Regulations 1987, SI 1987/408, reg 30(2); and PARA 1092.

**564. Requirement to deliver British seaman's card.** Any person who comes into possession of a British seaman's card[1] of which he is not the holder[2] must forthwith deliver it to the Registrar General of Shipping and Seamen[3] or to a superintendent[4]. A person who fails so to deliver a British seaman's card[5] commits an offence[6]; but it is a defence for a person so charged to prove that he took all reasonable precautions to avoid the commission of the offence[7].

1 As to British seamen's cards see PARA 559 et seq. As to the vessels and seamen to which these provisions apply see PARA 551 note 3.
2 As to the meaning of references to 'holder' for these purposes see PARA 559 note 14.
3 As to the Registrar General of Shipping and Seamen see PARA 62.
4 Merchant Shipping (Seamen's Documents) Regulations 1987, SI 1987/408, reg 12(1).
5 Ie who fails to comply with the Merchant Shipping (Seamen's Documents) Regulations 1987, SI 1987/408, reg 12 (see the text and notes 1–4): see reg 12(2); and PARA 1093.
6 See the Merchant Shipping (Seamen's Documents) Regulations 1987, SI 1987/408, reg 12(2); and PARA 1093.
7 See the Merchant Shipping (Seamen's Documents) Regulations 1987, SI 1987/408, reg 30(2); and PARA 1093.

## (B) Discharge Books

**565. Application for discharge book.** A person who satisfies the following conditions[1], that is to say:
(1)    that he is not exempted from the statutory requirements relating to crew agreements[2] by regulations made thereunder[3]; and
(2)    that he is either:
    (a)    employed as a seaman in a ship registered in the United Kingdom[4] otherwise than in an employment which is to be disregarded for these purposes[5]; or
    (b)    being a citizen of the United Kingdom[6] and colonies[7], has been discharged abroad after being so employed and has arrived in the United Kingdom within six months of being discharged, unless, at the time he arrived in the United Kingdom, he did not intend to take such employment[8]; and
(3)    that he is not the holder[9] of a discharge book duly issued[10]; and
(4)    that he has not been required by the Secretary of State[11] to surrender a discharge book duly issued[12],
must apply for a discharge book within seven days of satisfying those conditions[13].

The provisions which govern entitlement to apply for a discharge book[14] do not apply to a person[15]:
(i)    if he holds a document:
    (A)    containing substantially the same information as a discharge book[16];
    (B)    which has been issued to him by or under the authority of the government of a specified country[17]; and
    (C)    of which he has not ceased to be regarded as the holder by that government[18];
(ii)    if he is in the employment of the Crown and is not ordinarily employed as a master or seaman[19].

A person applying for a discharge book must make an application in accordance with the statutory provisions[20] and, unless it has been lost or destroyed, produce to the Registrar General of Shipping and Seamen[21] or a superintendent the latest discharge book or seaman's record book[22], if any, previously held by him[23].

Any person required[24] to apply for a discharge book who fails to make an application for a discharge book in accordance with the statutory provisions[25] commits an offence[26]; but it is a defence for a person so charged to prove that he took all reasonable precautions to avoid the commission of the offence[27].

1 Ie the conditions specified in the Merchant Shipping (Seamen's Documents) Regulations 1987, SI 1987/408, reg 15(2) (see heads (1) to (4) in the text) (having effect under the Merchant Shipping Act 1995 s 80(1)–(3) (amended by the Merchant Shipping and Maritime Security Act 1997 s 18(1), (2))). As to the vessels and seamen to which these provisions apply see PARA 551 note 3.

2 Ie the requirements of the Merchant Shipping Act 1995 s 25 (see PARA 457): see the Merchant Shipping (Seamen's Documents) Regulations 1987, SI 1987/408, reg 15(2)(a).

3 Merchant Shipping (Seamen's Documents) Regulations 1987, SI 1987/408, reg 15(2)(a). The text refers to exemption by virtue of regulations made under the Merchant Shipping Act 1995 s 25(5)(b) (ie with respect to exemptions expressed in terms of descriptions of seamen) (see PARA 457): see the Merchant Shipping (Seamen's Documents) Regulations 1987, SI 1987/408, reg 15(2)(a).

4 As to the meaning of 'United Kingdom' see PARA 16 note 3. As to the registration of ships in the United Kingdom see PARA 245 et seq.

5 Merchant Shipping (Seamen's Documents) Regulations 1987, SI 1987/408, reg 15(2)(b)(i). For these purposes, no regard is to be had to employment in a fishing vessel or in a ship exempted from the requirements of the Merchant Shipping Act 1995 s 25 by virtue of regulations made under s 25(5)(a) (ie with respect to exemptions expressed in terms of descriptions of certain ships or voyages) (see PARA 457): Merchant Shipping (Seamen's Documents) Regulations 1987, SI 1987/408, reg 16(3).

6 See BRITISH NATIONALITY vol 4 (2011) PARA 405.

7 For these purposes, 'colony' has the same meaning as it has in and for the purposes of the British Nationality Act 1981 (see BRITISH NATIONALITY vol 4 (2011) PARA 415): Merchant Shipping (Seamen's Documents) Regulations 1987, SI 1987/408, reg 1(2)(a).

8 Merchant Shipping (Seamen's Documents) Regulations 1987, SI 1987/408, reg 15(2)(b)(ii).

9 As to the meaning of references to 'holder' for these purposes see PARA 559 note 14.

10 Merchant Shipping (Seamen's Documents) Regulations 1987, SI 1987/408, reg 15(2)(c). The text refers to a discharge book issued in accordance with the Merchant Shipping (Seamen's Documents) Regulations 1987, SI 1987/408: see reg 15(2)(c). As to the issue, form and content of a discharge book see PARA 566.

11 Ie under the Merchant Shipping (Seamen's Documents) Regulations 1987, SI 1987/408, reg 27(1) (see PARA 571): see reg 15(2)(d). As to the Secretary of State see PARA 36.

12 Merchant Shipping (Seamen's Documents) Regulations 1987, SI 1987/408, reg 15(2)(d). The text refers to a discharge book issued in accordance with the Merchant Shipping (Seamen's Documents) Regulations 1987, SI 1987/408: see reg 15(2)(d).

13 Merchant Shipping (Seamen's Documents) Regulations 1987, SI 1987/408, reg 15(1). In computing any of the periods of seven days referred to in reg 15(1), any period during which the person concerned is not present in the United Kingdom must be disregarded: reg 1(4).

14 Ie the Merchant Shipping (Seamen's Documents) Regulations 1987, SI 1987/408, reg 15 (see the text and notes 1–13): see reg 16(1). As from a day to be appointed a person who, in the United Kingdom or elsewhere, obtains employment as a seaman on board a United Kingdom ship and does so when he is disentitled to a discharge book, or employs as such a seaman a person who he knows or has reason to suspect is so disentitled, commits an offence: see the Merchant Shipping Act 1995 s 80(4) (not yet in force); and PARA 1094. As to the meaning of 'seaman' see PARA 457 note 5.

15 Merchant Shipping (Seamen's Documents) Regulations 1987, SI 1987/408, reg 16(1).

16 Merchant Shipping (Seamen's Documents) Regulations 1987, SI 1987/408, reg 16(1)(a).

17 Merchant Shipping (Seamen's Documents) Regulations 1987, SI 1987/408, reg 16(1)(b). The countries referred to in the text are specified in Sch 4 (substituted by SI 1999/3281) and, accordingly, comprise: Bangladesh; Barbados; Canada; Falkland Islands; Fiji; Ghana; Guyana; Hong Kong; India; Republic of Ireland; Isle of Man; Jamaica; Kenya; Kiribati; Malaysia; Malta; Mauritius; Nigeria; Pakistan; Papua New Guinea; St Lucia; Seychelles; Sierra Leone; Singapore; South Africa; Sri Lanka; Tanzania; Tonga; Trinidad and Tobago; Tuvalu; Western Samoa; and Zambia.

18 Merchant Shipping (Seamen's Documents) Regulations 1987, SI 1987/408, reg 16(1)(c).

19 Merchant Shipping (Seamen's Documents) Regulations 1987, SI 1987/408, reg 16(2).

20 Ie in accordance with the Merchant Shipping (Seamen's Documents) Regulations 1987, SI 1987/408, reg 29 (see PARA 573): see reg 17(1).

21 As to the Registrar General of Shipping and Seamen see PARA 62.

22 For these purposes, 'seaman's record book' means a seaman's record book and certificates of discharge issued to a seaman by the Secretary of State: see the Merchant Shipping (Seamen's Documents) Regulations 1987, SI 1987/408, reg 1(2)(e).

23 Merchant Shipping (Seamen's Documents) Regulations 1987, SI 1987/408, reg 17(1).

24 Ie under the provisions of the Merchant Shipping (Seamen's Documents) Regulations 1987, SI 1987/408, reg 15(1) (see the text and notes 1–13): see reg 17(2); and PARA 1095.

25 Ie in accordance with the Merchant Shipping (Seamen's Documents) Regulations 1987, SI 1987/408 (see the text and notes 20–23): see reg 17(2); and PARA 1095.

26 See the Merchant Shipping (Seamen's Documents) Regulations 1987, SI 1987/408, reg 17(2); and PARA 1095.

27 See the Merchant Shipping (Seamen's Documents) Regulations 1987, SI 1987/408, reg 30(2); and PARA 1095.

**566. Issue, form and content of discharge book.** If a person applying for a discharge book is required[1] to apply for a discharge book and has paid the fee, if any, prescribed, the Secretary of State[2] must issue to him a discharge book containing the following particulars[3]:

(1)     the name of the person applying for the document[4];
(2)     his home address[5];
(3)     the date and place of his birth[6];
(4)     any previous names (including, in the case of a woman who is or has been married, her maiden surname)[7];
(5)     his nationality[8];
(6)     the colour of his eyes[9];
(7)     his distinguishing marks, if any[10];
(8)     his height[11];
(9)     the number of his discharge book, if any[12];
(10)    the grade, number and date of issue of any certificate of competency held by him[13];
(11)    the name, relationship and address of his next of kin[14];
(12)    his Merchant Navy Officer's Pension Fund ('MNOPF')/Merchant Navy Ratings Pension Fund ('MNRPF') number[15];
(13)    union membership number, if any[16].

If a person applying for a discharge book:

(a)     is not required[17] to apply for a discharge book[18];
(b)     is, or has been, employed in a ship registered in the United Kingdom[19] or (if the person is a British citizen[20]) in a ship registered outside the United Kingdom[21];
(c)     in respect of employment in a ship registered outside the United Kingdom, is otherwise unable, for whatever reason, to obtain a document containing substantially the same information as a discharge book from or acceptable to the ship's flag state[22]; and
(d)     has paid the fee, if any, prescribed[23],

the Secretary of State may issue to him a discharge book containing the particulars specified in heads (1) to (13) above[24].

A discharge book must be in book form and must provide for there to be recorded in it from time to time, in relation to the holder[25], statements of the following particulars[26]:

(i)     those specified in heads (1) to (3) and (5) to (13) above[27];
(ii)    the name of each ship registered in the United Kingdom in which he is employed, its port of registry, official number[28] and gross or register tonnage, the capacity in which he is employed in the ship, the date on which and the place at which he begins to be so employed, and the description of each voyage and the date and place of his discharge; and like details in respect of employment in any other vessel[29];

(iii) dates of any Merchant Navy Training Board training courses he attends for instruction in survival at sea and the certificates or other qualifications, if any, obtained; and the dates and nature of any other training courses (including pre-sea training courses) he attends and the certificates or other qualifications, if any, obtained[30];

(iv) his income tax code, the year to which it applies and the date on which it becomes effective[31];

(v) his inoculation and vaccination certificates[32];

(vi) records of tests of his eyesight except where these formed part of a statutory medical examination[33]; and

(vii) a record of certificates issued under the Merchant Shipping (Medical Examination) Regulations 2002[34].

Only specified persons may make entries in a discharge book[35]. A superintendent, a proper officer or the Registrar General of Shipping and Seamen[36] may at any time correct any entry in a discharge book[37].

1  Ie under the Merchant Shipping (Seamen's Documents) Regulations 1987, SI 1987/408, reg 15(1) (see PARA 565): see reg 18(1). As to the vessels and seamen to which these provisions apply see PARA 551 note 3.
2  As to the Secretary of State see PARA 36.
3  Merchant Shipping (Seamen's Documents) Regulations 1987, SI 1987/408, reg 18(1). The particulars referred to in the text are specified in Sch 3 (amended by SI 1995/1900) (see heads (1) to (13) in the text): see the Merchant Shipping (Seamen's Documents) Regulations 1987, SI 1987/408, reg 18(1). However, the information in heads (10) to (13) in the text is not required for application for a British seamen's card: Sch 3.
4  Merchant Shipping (Seamen's Documents) Regulations 1987, SI 1987/408, Sch 3 para 1.
5  Merchant Shipping (Seamen's Documents) Regulations 1987, SI 1987/408, Sch 3 para 2.
6  Merchant Shipping (Seamen's Documents) Regulations 1987, SI 1987/408, Sch 3 para 3.
7  Merchant Shipping (Seamen's Documents) Regulations 1987, SI 1987/408, Sch 3 para 4.
8  Merchant Shipping (Seamen's Documents) Regulations 1987, SI 1987/408, Sch 3 para 5.
9  Merchant Shipping (Seamen's Documents) Regulations 1987, SI 1987/408, Sch 3 para 6.
10 Merchant Shipping (Seamen's Documents) Regulations 1987, SI 1987/408, Sch 3 para 7.
11 Merchant Shipping (Seamen's Documents) Regulations 1987, SI 1987/408, Sch 3 para 8.
12 Merchant Shipping (Seamen's Documents) Regulations 1987, SI 1987/408, Sch 3 para 9.
13 Merchant Shipping (Seamen's Documents) Regulations 1987, SI 1987/408, Sch 3 para 10.
14 Merchant Shipping (Seamen's Documents) Regulations 1987, SI 1987/408, Sch 3 para 12.
15 Merchant Shipping (Seamen's Documents) Regulations 1987, SI 1987/408, Sch 3 para 13.
16 Merchant Shipping (Seamen's Documents) Regulations 1987, SI 1987/408, Sch 3 para 14.
17 Ie under the provisions of the Merchant Shipping (Seamen's Documents) Regulations 1987, SI 1987/408, reg 15(1) (see PARA 565): see reg 18(2)(a).
18 Merchant Shipping (Seamen's Documents) Regulations 1987, SI 1987/408, reg 18(2)(a).
19 As to the meaning of 'United Kingdom' see PARA 16 note 3. As to the registration of ships in the United Kingdom see PARA 245 et seq.
20 For these purposes, 'British citizen' has the same meaning as it has in and for the purposes of the British Nationality Act 1981 (see BRITISH NATIONALITY vol 4 (2011) PARA 421 et seq): Merchant Shipping (Seamen's Documents) Regulations 1987, SI 1987/408, reg 1(2)(a).
21 Merchant Shipping (Seamen's Documents) Regulations 1987, SI 1987/408, reg 18(2)(b) (reg 18(2)(b) substituted, reg 18(2)(bb) added, by SI 1999/3281).
22 Merchant Shipping (Seamen's Documents) Regulations 1987, SI 1987/408, reg 18(2)(bb) (as added: see note 21).
23 Merchant Shipping (Seamen's Documents) Regulations 1987, SI 1987/408, reg 18(2)(c).
24 Merchant Shipping (Seamen's Documents) Regulations 1987, SI 1987/408, reg 18(2). As to related offences concerning improper alterations made in seamen's documents see PARAS 572, 1100.
25 As to the meaning of references to 'holder' for these purposes see PARA 559 note 14.
26 Merchant Shipping (Seamen's Documents) Regulations 1987, SI 1987/408, reg 19.
27 Merchant Shipping (Seamen's Documents) Regulations 1987, SI 1987/408, reg 19(a).
28 As to a ship's port of registry and official number etc see PARA 279 et seq.
29 Merchant Shipping (Seamen's Documents) Regulations 1987, SI 1987/408, reg 19(b).
30 Merchant Shipping (Seamen's Documents) Regulations 1987, SI 1987/408, reg 19(c).
31 Merchant Shipping (Seamen's Documents) Regulations 1987, SI 1987/408, reg 19(d).

32 Merchant Shipping (Seamen's Documents) Regulations 1987, SI 1987/408, reg 19(e).
33 Merchant Shipping (Seamen's Documents) Regulations 1987, SI 1987/408, reg 19(f).
34 Merchant Shipping (Seamen's Documents) Regulations 1987, SI 1987/408, reg 19(g). The text refers to certificates issued under the Merchant Shipping (Medical Examination) Regulations 2002, SI 2002/2055: see the Merchant Shipping (Seamen's Documents) Regulations 1987, SI 1987/408, reg 19(g).
35 See the Merchant Shipping (Seamen's Documents) Regulations 1987, SI 1987/408, reg 20(1), (2) (reg 20(1) amended by SI 1999/3281).
36 As to the Registrar General of Shipping and Seamen see PARA 62.
37 Merchant Shipping (Seamen's Documents) Regulations 1987, SI 1987/408, reg 21.

**567. Requirement to produce discharge book.** The holder[1] of a discharge book[2] must produce it on demand at any time[3]:

(1)    to a superintendent, a proper officer, or the Registrar General of Shipping and Seamen[4];

(2)    to his employer and to the master of the ship in which the holder is employed[5]; and

(3)    to any other person authorised[6] to make an entry in it, for the purpose of making that entry[7].

The holder of a discharge book who fails to produce it when required to do so[8] commits an offence[9]; but it is a defence for a person so charged to prove that he took all reasonable precautions to avoid the commission of the offence[10].

A person to whom a discharge book is produced must return it to the holder as soon as is practical after the entry has been made or any inspection of it[11].

1  As to the meaning of references to 'holder' for these purposes see PARA 559 note 14. As to the vessels and seamen to which these provisions apply see PARA 551 note 3.
2  As to discharge books see PARA 565 et seq.
3  Merchant Shipping (Seamen's Documents) Regulations 1987, SI 1987/408, reg 22(1).
4  Merchant Shipping (Seamen's Documents) Regulations 1987, SI 1987/408, reg 22(1)(a) (amended by SI 1999/3281). As to the Registrar General of Shipping and Seamen see PARA 62.
5  Merchant Shipping (Seamen's Documents) Regulations 1987, SI 1987/408, reg 22(1)(b).
6  Ie authorised under the Merchant Shipping (Seamen's Documents) Regulations 1987, SI 1987/408, reg 20 (see PARA 566): see reg 22(1)(c).
7  Merchant Shipping (Seamen's Documents) Regulations 1987, SI 1987/408, reg 22(1)(c).
8  Ie in accordance with the Merchant Shipping (Seamen's Documents) Regulations 1987, SI 1987/408, reg 22 (see the text and notes 1–5): see reg 22(2); and PARA 1096.
9  See the Merchant Shipping (Seamen's Documents) Regulations 1987, SI 1987/408, reg 22(2); and PARA 1096.
10 See the Merchant Shipping (Seamen's Documents) Regulations 1987, SI 1987/408, reg 30(2); and PARA 1096.
11 Merchant Shipping (Seamen's Documents) Regulations 1987, SI 1987/408, reg 22(3).

**568. Requirement to deliver discharge book.** Any person having possession of a discharge book[1] must, after he becomes aware that the holder[2] has died, has been discharged from any ship[3], or has been left behind in any country[4], deliver it to a superintendent or proper officer or to the Registrar General of Shipping and Seamen[5] as soon as practicable[6].

A person who fails to comply with the requirement so to deliver a discharge book[7] commits an offence[8]; but it is a defence for a person so charged to prove that he took all reasonable precautions to avoid the commission of the offence[9].

1  As to discharge books see PARA 565 et seq.
2  As to the meaning of references to 'holder' for these purposes see PARA 559 note 14. As to the vessels and seamen to which these provisions apply see PARA 551 note 3.
3  As to the discharge of seamen generally see PARA 468 et seq; and see the Merchant Shipping Act 1995 s 60 (breaches by seamen of codes of conduct) (cited in PARA 539).
4  See the Merchant Shipping Act 1995 s 28 (seamen left behind abroad otherwise than on discharge); and PARA 468.
5  As to the Registrar General of Shipping and Seamen see PARA 62.
6  Merchant Shipping (Seamen's Documents) Regulations 1987, SI 1987/408, reg 23(1).

7   Ie where any person fails to comply with requirements of the Merchant Shipping (Seamen's
    Documents) Regulations 1987, SI 1987/408, reg 23 (see the text and notes 1–6): see reg 23(2); and
    PARA 1097.
8   See the Merchant Shipping (Seamen's Documents) Regulations 1987, SI 1987/408, reg 23(2); and
    PARA 1097.
9   See the Merchant Shipping (Seamen's Documents) Regulations 1987, SI 1987/408, reg 30(2); and
    PARA 1097.

**569.  Effect of loss, destruction, defacement or filling up of discharge books.** When his discharge book[1] is lost, destroyed or defaced, or when the space provided in it for entries of any particulars[2] is filled up, a person ceases to be regarded as the holder[3] of a discharge book and must, within seven days of satisfying the statutory conditions[4], apply for a new discharge book[5].

1   As to discharge books see PARA 565 et seq.
2   Ie except those referred to in the Merchant Shipping (Seamen's Documents) Regulations 1987, SI
    1987/408, reg 18(1), Sch 3 (see PARA 566): see reg 24.
3   As to the meaning of references to 'holder' for these purposes see PARA 559 note 14. As to the
    vessels and seamen to which these provisions apply see PARA 551 note 3.
4   Ie the conditions specified in the Merchant Shipping (Seamen's Documents) Regulations 1987, SI
    1987/408, reg 15(2) (see PARA 565): see reg 24.
5   Merchant Shipping (Seamen's Documents) Regulations 1987, SI 1987/408, reg 24. As to
    applications for a discharge book see PARA 565.

*(C)   Provisions relating to British Seamen's Cards and to Discharge Books*

**570.  Notification of errors in seamen's documents.** If it appears to the holder[1] thereof that any entry in a seaman's document[2] is not correct, he must forthwith inform the Registrar General of Shipping and Seamen[3] or a superintendent[4].

Any person who fails to comply with the requirement so to notify[5] commits an offence[6]; but it is a defence for a person so charged to prove that he took all reasonable precautions to avoid the commission of the offence[7].

1   For the purposes of the Merchant Shipping (Seamen's Documents) Regulations 1987, SI 1987/408,
    Pt III (regs 25–30), references to the holder of a seaman's document are to be construed in
    accordance with the definition of 'seaman's document' (see note 2): see reg 25. As to the vessels and
    seamen to which these provisions apply see PARA 551 note 3.
2   For these purposes, 'seaman's document' means a British seaman's card or a discharge book: see
    the Merchant Shipping (Seamen's Documents) Regulations 1987, SI 1987/408, reg 25. As to
    British seamen's cards see PARA 553 et seq; and as to discharge books see PARA 565 et seq.
3   As to the Registrar General of Shipping and Seamen see PARA 62.
4   Merchant Shipping (Seamen's Documents) Regulations 1987, SI 1987/408, reg 26(1).
5   Ie where any person fails to comply with requirements of the Merchant Shipping (Seamen's
    Documents) Regulations 1987, SI 1987/408, reg 26 (see the text and notes 1–4): see reg 26(2); and
    PARA 1098.
6   See the Merchant Shipping (Seamen's Documents) Regulations 1987, SI 1987/408, reg 26(2); and
    PARA 1098.
7   See the Merchant Shipping (Seamen's Documents) Regulations 1987, SI 1987/408, reg 30(2); and
    PARA 1098.

**571.  Surrender of seamen's documents.** If it appears to a superintendent, a proper officer, a police officer or the Registrar General of Shipping and Seamen[1]:

(1)     that the holder[2] of a seaman's document[3] was not entitled to apply for
        it at the time it was issued to him[4]; or

(2)     that the person having possession of a seaman's document is not the
        holder thereof[5],

the person, including the holder, having possession of that document must, on demand made by a superintendent, a proper officer, a police officer or the Registrar General of Shipping and Seaman, as the case may be, surrender it to him[6].

Upon the recommendation of a shore-based disciplinary committee[7] that the holder of a discharge book[8] who was employed under a crew agreement, approved by the Secretary of State, to which the National Maritime Board agreement on disciplinary procedures applied and which required him to comply with the Code of Conduct, is no longer entitled to be the holder, consequent upon the commission by him of one of the breaches of the Code specified therein[9], the holder must, on demand made by the Secretary of State, surrender the discharge book to him for a temporary period or permanently according to his demand[10].

Any person who fails to comply with the requirement[11] so to surrender a seaman's document commits an offence[12]; but it is a defence for a person so charged to prove that he took all reasonable precautions to avoid the commission of the offence[13].

1 Merchant Shipping (Seamen's Documents) Regulations 1987, SI 1987/408, reg 27(1). As to the Registrar General of Shipping and Seamen see PARA 62.
2 As to the meaning of 'holder' for these purposes see PARA 570 note 1. As to the vessels and seamen to which these provisions apply see PARA 551 note 3.
3 As to the meaning of 'seaman's document' for these purposes see PARA 570 note 2.
4 Merchant Shipping (Seamen's Documents) Regulations 1987, SI 1987/408, reg 27(1)(a).
5 Merchant Shipping (Seamen's Documents) Regulations 1987, SI 1987/408, reg 27(1)(b).
6 Merchant Shipping (Seamen's Documents) Regulations 1987, SI 1987/408, reg 27(1).
7 For these purposes, 'shore-based disciplinary committee' means a committee established on shore by the National Maritime Board to review the future sea-going employment of seamen employed under a crew agreement, approved by the Secretary of State, to which the National Maritime Board agreement on disciplinary procedures applies and which requires seamen to comply with the Code of Conduct, in respect of whom the master is satisfied that they have committed any of the breaches of the Code specified in para 9 of the Code: Merchant Shipping (Seamen's Documents) Regulations 1987, SI 1987/408, reg 1(2)(f). 'Code of Conduct' means the publication entitled 'Code of Conduct for the Merchant Navy' published in 1978 by the National Maritime Board (revised June 2001): Merchant Shipping (Seamen's Documents) Regulations 1987, SI 1987/408, reg 1(2)(g). As to the Secretary of State see PARA 36.
8 As to discharge books see PARA 565 et seq.
9 Ie one of the breaches of the Code of Conduct specified in para 9 (see note 7): see the Merchant Shipping (Seamen's Documents) Regulations 1987, SI 1987/408, reg 27(2).
10 Merchant Shipping (Seamen's Documents) Regulations 1987, SI 1987/408, reg 27(2).
11 Ie the requirements of the Merchant Shipping (Seamen's Documents) Regulations 1987, SI 1987/408, reg 27 (see the text and notes 1–10): see reg 27(3); and PARA 1099.
12 See the Merchant Shipping (Seamen's Documents) Regulations 1987, SI 1987/408, reg 27(3); and PARA 1099.
13 See the Merchant Shipping (Seamen's Documents) Regulations 1987, SI 1987/408, reg 30(2); and PARA 1099.

**572. Alterations in seamen's documents.** No person other than a person duly authorised[1] and duly acting[2] may make any mark or entry upon, or erase, cancel or alter any mark or entry made upon or otherwise deface or destroy a seaman's document[3].

Any person who contravenes this requirement[4] commits an offence[5]; but it is a defence for a person so charged to prove that he took all reasonable precautions to avoid the commission of the offence[6].

1 Ie authorised by the Merchant Shipping (Seamen's Documents) Regulations 1987, SI 1987/408, reg 5 (issue of British seamen's cards) (see PARA 560), reg 8 (validity of previously-issued British seamen's cards) (see PARA 561), reg 18 (issue of discharge books) (see PARA 566), reg 20 (entries in discharge books) (see PARA 566) or reg 21 (correction of entries in discharge books) (see PARA 566), as the case may be: see reg 28(1).
2 Ie acting in accordance with the Merchant Shipping (Seamen's Documents) Regulations 1987, SI 1987/408, reg 5, 8, 18, 20 or 21, as the case may be: see reg 28(1).
3 Merchant Shipping (Seamen's Documents) Regulations 1987, SI 1987/408, reg 28(1). As to the meaning of 'seaman's document' for these purposes see PARA 570 note 2. As to the vessels and seamen to which these provisions apply see PARA 551 note 3.

4 Ie any person who contravenes the provisions of the Merchant Shipping (Seamen's Documents) Regulations 1987, SI 1987/408, reg 28 (see the text and notes 1–3): see reg 28(2); and PARA 1100.
5 See the Merchant Shipping (Seamen's Documents) Regulations 1987, SI 1987/408, reg 28(2); and PARA 1100.
6 See the Merchant Shipping (Seamen's Documents) Regulations 1987, SI 1987/408, reg 30(2); and PARA 1100.

**573. Applications relating to seamen's documents.** An application for the issue of a seaman's document[1] or for the endorsement of a British seaman's card[2] must be made in writing to the Registrar General of Shipping and Seamen[3] or a superintendent[4], and:

(1)     where:

    (a)     in the case of an application for a British seaman's card, the applicant surrenders to the Registrar General of Shipping and Seamen or a superintendent a British seaman's card[5]; or

    (b)     in the case of an application for a discharge book, the applicant produces to the Registrar General of Shipping and Seamen or a superintendent a discharge book or a seaman's record book held by him[6]; or

    (c)     in the case of an application for a British seamen's card or for a discharge book, it appears to the Registrar General of Shipping and Seamen or a superintendent that the applicant has lost his latest British seaman's card or discharge book, as the case may be, and that the Secretary of State[7] has in his possession particulars of any of the matters that are required to furnished in such applications[8],

(2)     must state the applicant's name and particulars of such of the other required matters[9] as are not correctly stated in the document (if any) which has been surrendered or produced in accordance with head (a) or head (b) above, or in the particulars referred to in head (c) above[10]; and

(3)     in any other case, must state particulars of the matters that are required to furnished in such applications[11];

and the applicant must furnish to the Registrar General of Shipping and Seamen or a superintendent such documents[12] and such other evidence as he may require for the proper consideration of the application[13].

1 Ie a British seaman's card or a discharge book: see the Merchant Shipping (Seamen's Documents) Regulations 1987, SI 1987/408, reg 25; and PARA 570 note 2. As to applications for the issue of a British seamen's card see PARA 553 et seq; and as to applications for the issue of a discharge book see PARA 565 et seq. As to the vessels and seamen to which these provisions apply see PARA 551 note 3.
2 Ie under the Merchant Shipping (Seamen's Documents) Regulations 1987, SI 1987/408, reg 8 (validity of previously-issued British seamen's cards) (see PARA 561): see reg 29.
3 As to the Registrar General of Shipping and Seamen see PARA 62.
4 Merchant Shipping (Seamen's Documents) Regulations 1987, SI 1987/408, reg 29.
5 Merchant Shipping (Seamen's Documents) Regulations 1987, SI 1987/408, reg 29(a)(i).
6 Merchant Shipping (Seamen's Documents) Regulations 1987, SI 1987/408, reg 29(a)(ii).
7 As to the Secretary of State see PARA 36.
8 Merchant Shipping (Seamen's Documents) Regulations 1987, SI 1987/408, reg 29(a)(iii). The text refers to particulars of any of the matters set out in reg 18(1), Sch 3 (see PARA 566): see reg 29(a)(iii).
9 Ie the matters set out in the Merchant Shipping (Seamen's Documents) Regulations 1987, SI 1987/408, Sch 3: see reg 29(a).
10 Merchant Shipping (Seamen's Documents) Regulations 1987, SI 1987/408, reg 29(a).
11 Merchant Shipping (Seamen's Documents) Regulations 1987, SI 1987/408, reg 29(b). The text refers to particulars of the matters required for the application set out in Sch 3: see reg 29(b).
12 Ie including, in the case of an application for both a British seaman's card and a discharge book, four copies, and in any other case, two copies, of a recent head and shoulders photograph of

himself measuring 50 millimetres by 50 millimetres (two inches by two inches): see the Merchant Shipping (Seamen's Documents) Regulations 1987, SI 1987/408, reg 29.

13  Merchant Shipping (Seamen's Documents) Regulations 1987, SI 1987/408, reg 29.

# 6. PILOTAGE AND TOWAGE

## (1) PILOTAGE

### (i) Pilotage Functions of Competent Harbour Authorities

#### A. IN GENERAL

**574. Meanings of 'pilot' and 'authorised pilot' for the purposes of the Pilotage Act 1987.** In the Pilotage Act 1987, except where the context otherwise requires, 'pilot' means any person not belonging to a ship[1] who has the conduct thereof; and 'pilotage' is to be construed accordingly[2]. 'Authorised pilot', in relation to any area, means a person authorised[3] for that area and, in relation to any ship, a person so authorised in respect of ships of that description[4].

1 For these purposes, 'ship' has the same meaning as in the Harbours Act 1964 (see PORTS AND HARBOURS vol 85 (2012) PARA 9) and includes both British ships and foreign ships: Pilotage Act 1987 s 31(1).
2 Pilotage Act 1987 s 31(1) (definition amended by the Merchant Shipping Act 1995 Sch 13 para 80(b)). See also *The Andoni* [1918] P 14 at 18, 14 Asp MLC 326 at 328 (where it was held that 'pilot' means prima facie a person taken on board at a particular place for the purpose of conducting a ship through a river, road or channel or from or into a port).
3 Ie under the Pilotage Act 1987 s 3 (see PARA 577): see s 31(1).
4 See the Pilotage Act 1987 s 31(1).

**575. Meanings of 'competent harbour authority' and 'harbour' under the Pilotage Act 1987.** 'Competent harbour authority' means any harbour authority[1]:

(1)  which has statutory powers[2] in relation to the regulation of shipping movements and the safety of navigation within its harbour[3]; and

(2)  whose harbour falls wholly or partly within an active former pilotage district[4];

and references to a harbour authority's harbour are to the area or areas inside the limits of which its statutory powers and duties[5] as a harbour authority are exercisable but, where there are two or more separate such areas, include only those areas which fall wholly or partly within an active former pilotage district[6].

If the Secretary of State[7] considers that in the interests of efficiency and safety of navigation a competent harbour authority should exercise pilotage functions both as respects its harbour and another area, he may by order[8] provide:

(a)  that the Pilotage Act 1987 is to apply to that authority as if its harbour included that other area[9]; and

(b)  in a case where the other area is or falls within the harbour of another competent harbour authority, that that other authority is not to be a competent harbour authority for the purposes of the 1987 Act[10].

A harbour authority in England or Wales is not a competent harbour authority for these purposes while it is specified in an order of the Secretary of State[12]. A harbour authority which is not a competent harbour authority may apply to the Secretary of State to be treated for the purpose of the 1987 Act as such an authority; and on such an application the Secretary of State may by order provide that the applicant is to be a competent harbour authority for the purposes of the 1987 Act[12].

The Secretary of State must maintain a list of the authorities which are for the time being competent harbour authorities for these purposes[13].

1  In the Pilotage Act 1987, except where the context otherwise requires, 'competent harbour authority' has the meaning given in s 1; and 'harbour authority' has the same meaning as in the Harbours Act 1964 (see PORTS AND HARBOURS vol 85 (2012) PARA 20): Pilotage Act 1987 s 31(1). However, for the purposes of s 1(1), 'harbour authority' does not include:
    (1)  any authority excluded by virtue of the Harbours Act 1964 s 58 (see PORTS AND HARBOURS vol 85 (2012) PARA 20) from being taken as a harbour authority for the purposes of the Harbours Act 1964 (Pilotage Act 1987 s 1(9)(a));
    (2)  a Queen's harbour master (s 1(9)(b)); or
    (3)  any own account operator (s 1(9)(c)).
    For this purpose, 'own account operator' means a statutory harbour undertaker within the meaning of the Harbours Act 1964 s 42 (see PORTS AND HARBOURS vol 85 (2012) PARA 85) whose activities in the harbour in question relate wholly or mainly to ships resorting to the harbour wholly or mainly for the purpose of bringing or receiving goods which:
    (a)  have been manufactured or produced by the statutory harbour undertaker or any connected person (Pilotage Act 1987 s 1(11)(a)); or
    (b)  are to be used by him or any connected person for the manufacture or production of goods or electricity (s 1(11)(b));
    and, for these purposes, a person is connected with a statutory harbour undertaker if he is a holding company or subsidiary of the undertaker or a member of a consortium the members of which between them own, directly or indirectly, more than half of the issued share capital of the undertaker (s 1(11)). As to the meaning of 'ship' see PARA 574 note 1. As to Queen's harbour masters see PORTS AND HARBOURS vol 85 (2012) PARA 94.
2  For these purposes, 'statutory powers' has the same meaning as in the Harbours Act 1964 (see PORTS AND HARBOURS vol 85 (2012) PARA 19): Pilotage Act 1987 s 31(1).
3  Pilotage Act 1987 s 1(1)(a). For these purposes, powers exercisable by the harbour master for a harbour are to be taken to be exercisable by the harbour authority which appointed him: s 1(10). 'Harbour', in relation to a competent harbour authority, has the meaning given in s 1 (see the text and notes 5–6): see s 31(1).
4  Pilotage Act 1987 s 1(1)(b). For these purposes, any reference to a former pilotage district is to a district which was a pilotage district within the meaning of the Pilotage Act 1983 (repealed) immediately before 1 October 1988 (Pilotage Act 1987 ss 1(2), 31(1)); and, for the purposes of s 1(1), such a district is an active district if:
    (1)  at least one act of pilotage was performed there in 1984, 1985, 1986 or 1987 in respect of which information was given by the pilotage authority for the district in a return made by it under the Pilotage Act 1983 s 19 (repealed) (see the Pilotage Act 1987 s 1(2)(a)); or
    (2)  a certificate granted under the Pilotage Act 1983 s 20 (repealed) (masters' and first mates' pilotage certificates) was in force in respect of the district at any time in any of those years in respect of which information was so given (see the Pilotage Act 1987 s 1(2)(b)).
    As to the meaning of 'pilotage' see PARA 574.
5  For these purposes, 'statutory duties' has the same meaning as in the Harbours Act 1964 (see PORTS AND HARBOURS vol 85 (2012) PARA 19): Pilotage Act 1987 s 31(1).
6  Pilotage Act 1987 s 1(1).
7  As to the Secretary of State see PARA 36.
8  An order under the Pilotage Act 1987 s 1 may include transitional, consequential, incidental or supplemental provision (s 1(8B) (s 1(4A), (8AA), (8B) added, s 1(5) substituted, s 1(7) amended, by the Marine Navigation Act 2013 s 1)) and may be amended or revoked by further order (Pilotage Act 1987 s 1(5) (as so substituted). Before making an order under s 1(3) or (4), the Secretary of State must inform the persons he considers may be affected by the order of the terms of the proposed order and that they may, within such reasonable period as he may specify, object to the making of the order by giving him notice in writing: s 1(7) (as so amended). Where any person has duly objected under s 1(7) to the making of a proposed order and has not withdrawn his objection, then, if the Secretary of State makes an order in that form, or a substantially similar form, it is subject to special parliamentary procedure, and the Statutory Orders (Special Procedure) Act 1945 (see STATUTES AND LEGISLATIVE PROCESS vol 96 (2012) PARA 856 et seq) has effect accordingly but as if ss 2, 10(2) (preliminary proceedings) were omitted: Pilotage Act 1987 s 1(8). As orders under the Pilotage Act 1987 s 1 are local in nature, they are not noted in this work.
9  Pilotage Act 1987 s 1(3)(a).
10 Pilotage Act 1987 s 1(3)(b).
12 Pilotage Act 1987 s 1(4).

12 Pilotage Act 1987 s 1(4).
13 Pilotage Act 1987 s 1(6).

### B. PROVISION OF PILOTAGE SERVICES

**576. General duties as to provision of pilotage services.** Each competent harbour authority[1] must keep under consideration:

   (1)    whether any and, if so, what pilotage[2] services need to be provided to secure the safety of ships[3] navigating[4] in or in the approaches to its harbour[5]; and

   (2)    whether in the interests of safety pilotage should be compulsory for ships navigating in any part of that harbour or its approaches and, if so, for which ships and in which circumstances and what pilotage services need to be provided for those ships[6].

Each competent harbour authority must, in performing these functions[7], have regard in particular[8] to the hazards involved in the carriage of dangerous goods or harmful substances by ship[9].

Each competent harbour authority must provide such pilotage services as it considers need to be provided as mentioned in heads (1) and (2) above[10].

1 As to the meaning of 'competent harbour authority' see PARA 575.
2 As to the meaning of 'pilotage' see PARA 574.
3 As to the meaning of 'ship' see PARA 574 note 1.
4 In the Pilotage Act 1987, references to a ship navigating or being navigated include references to its moving or being moved within a harbour for the purpose of changing from one mooring to another or of being taken into or out of any dock: s 31(2). As to the meaning of 'harbour' see PARA 575.
5 Pilotage Act 1987 s 2(1)(a).
6 Pilotage Act 1987 s 2(1)(b).
7 Ie its functions under the Pilotage Act 1987 s 2(1) (see the text and notes 1–6): see s 2(2).
8 Ie without prejudice to the generality of the Pilotage Act 1987 s 2(1): see s 2(2).
9 Pilotage Act 1987 s 2(2).
10 Pilotage Act 1987 s 2(3). The purpose of s 2 is not to impose duties on competent harbour authorities to pilot ships but to require them to supply properly authorised pilots for ships: *Oceangas (Gibraltar) Ltd v Port of London Authority, The Cavendish* [1993] 2 Lloyd's Rep 292 (Port of London Authority not vicariously liable in tort for the negligence of the pilot on board), applying *Fowles v Eastern and Australian SS Co Ltd* [1916] 2 AC 556, PC.

**577. Authorisation of pilots.** A competent harbour authority[1] may authorise[2] such persons to act as pilots[3] in or in any part of the area in relation to which its statutory duty to provide pilotage services[4] is exercisable as it considers are suitably qualified to do so[5]; and such an authorisation must specify the area within which it has effect and may specify that it only has effect in relation to ships[6] of a particular description[7].

The authority may determine the qualifications in respect of physical fitness, time of service, local knowledge, skill, character and otherwise to be required from persons applying for authorisation and provide for the examination of such persons[8].

A competent harbour authority may suspend or revoke such an authorisation granted by it[9] if it appears to it:

   (1)    that the authorised person has been guilty of any incompetence or misconduct affecting his capability as a pilot[10];

   (2)    that the authorised person has ceased to have the qualifications required from persons applying for authorisation[11] or has failed to provide evidence that he continues to have those qualifications[12];

   (3)    that the number of persons for the time being so authorised by it[13] exceeds the number required to be authorised[14]; or

(4)    that it is appropriate to do so by virtue of the termination of any contract or other arrangement under which the services of pilots are provided within its harbour[15].

Before suspending or revoking an authorisation under head (1) or head (2) above, a competent harbour authority must give written notice of its intention to do so to the authorised person, stating the reasons for which it proposes to act, and must give him a reasonable opportunity of making representations[16]. Where a competent harbour authority suspends or revokes an authorisation of any person by virtue of head (3) or head (4) above, it must give him notice in writing stating that the suspension or revocation was by virtue of head (3) or head (4) above and specifying the duration of the authorisation in question and any previous authorisations granted to that person by the authority[17].

If any person who is not an authorised pilot[18] for an area describes himself while he is in that area as being such a pilot or so holds himself out as to indicate or be reasonably understood to indicate that he is such a pilot, he is guilty of an offence[19].

A person who is an authorised pilot for a harbour for which the competent harbour authority is a local authority[20] is not by reason of his holding any office or employment as a pilot disqualified for being a member of any committee of that local authority with any functions in respect of which knowledge or experience relevant to pilotage is material or for being a representative of the local authority on a joint committee of the authority and another authority with such functions[21]. Similarly, a person who is an authorised pilot for a harbour for which the competent harbour authority is a local authority which is operating executive arrangements[22] is not by reason of his holding any office or employment as a pilot disqualified[23]:

(a)    for being a member of the executive of the local authority where that executive is to any extent responsible for any function in respect of which knowledge or experience relevant to pilotage is material[24]; or

(b)    for being a member of a committee of the executive of the local authority with any functions in respect of which knowledge or experience relevant to pilotage is material[25].

1    As to the meaning of 'competent harbour authority' see PARA 575.
2    Ie subject to the Pilotage Act 1987 s 3(1A) (see note 5), s 3(3) (see note 8) and s 4 (see PARA 578): see s 3(1) (amended by SI 2003/1230).
3    As to the meaning of 'pilot' see PARA 574.
4    Ie under the Pilotage Act 1987 s 2(1) (see PARA 576): see s 3(1) (as amended: see note 2). As to the meaning of 'pilotage' see PARA 574.
5    Pilotage Act 1987 s 3(1) (as amended: see note 2). In considering whether a person is suitably qualified either to be authorised under s 3(1) to act as a pilot in inland waters only, or in inland waters and other waters, or to continue to be so authorised, a competent harbour authority must act in accordance with Sch A1 (added by SI 2003/1230): Pilotage Act 1987 s 3(1A) (added by SI 2003/1230). The Pilotage Act 1987 Sch A1 (as so added) applies:
    (1)    where a competent harbour authority requires particular formal qualifications from persons applying for authorisation, and a person applying for authorisation is a national of an EEA state other than the United Kingdom, and does not hold the required qualifications, but holds formal qualifications obtained in an EEA state other than the United Kingdom (see Sch A1 paras 2, 4 (as so added));
    (2)    where a competent harbour authority requires persons applying for authorisation to have knowledge of, and to demonstrate that they apply, specific national rules in force, and a person applying for authorisation is a national of an EEA State other than the United Kingdom and envisages acting as a pilot in a self-employed capacity or as a manager of an undertaking (see Sch A1 paras 3, 4 (as so added)); and

(3)   where a competent harbour authority requires general commercial or professional knowledge and ability from persons applying for authorisation, and such an applicant has appropriate experience gained in an EEA state other than the United Kingdom (see Sch A1 paras 5, 6 (as so added)).

As to the proof required of various matters in relation to applications made under heads (1) to (3) see Sch A1 paras 7–11 (as so added). For these purposes, 'EEA state' means any state which is a contracting party to the Agreement on the European Economic Area (Oporto, 2 May 1992; EC 7 (1992); Cm 2183) as adjusted by the Protocol (Brussels, 17 March 1993; EC 2 (1993); Cm 2183): see the Pilotage Act 1987 Sch A1 para 1(2) (as so added). As to the meaning of 'United Kingdom' see PARA 16 note 3.

6   As to the meaning of 'ship' see PARA 574 note 1.

7   Pilotage Act 1987 s 3(1) (as amended: see note 2).

8   Pilotage Act 1987 s 3(2) (amended by SI 2006/1031). However, nothing in any determination made by a competent harbour authority under the Pilotage Act 1987 s 3(2) permits the authority to act in such a way as to contravene Sch A1 (see note 5), which makes provision about persons with qualifications obtained in EEA states other than the United Kingdom: s 3(2A) (added by SI 2003/1230). Transitional provision was made as to the qualifications required for authorisation under the Pilotage Act 1987 s 3 in relation to persons who immediately before 1 October 1988 were the holders of licences under the Pilotage Act 1983 s 12 (repealed), time-expired apprentice pilots or recognised assistant pilots (see the Pilotage Act 1987 s 3(2) (as so amended)); and in relation to persons who were not immediately before that date holders of full licences (see s 3(3), (4)). For these purposes, 'recognised assistant pilot' means a person who acts as an assistant to pilots in a pilotage district and is recognised as such an assistant by the pilotage authority for the district but is not the holder of such a licence; and 'time-expired apprentice pilot' means a person who has served the full term of his apprenticeship as a pilot but is not the holder of a licence under the Pilotage Act 1983 s 12 (repealed): Pilotage Act 1987 s 3(10).

9   Ie under the Pilotage Act 1987 s 3 (see the text and notes 1–7): see s 3(5).

10   Pilotage Act 1987 s 3(5)(a).

11   Ie authorisation by the competent harbour authority under the Pilotage Act 1987 s 3 (see the text and notes 1–7): see s 3(5)(b).

12   Pilotage Act 1987 s 3(5)(b).

13   Ie authorised by the competent harbour authority under the Pilotage Act 1987 s 3 (see the text and notes 1–7): see s 3(5)(c).

14   Pilotage Act 1987 s 3(5)(c). Transitional provision was made in relation to revocation by an authority by virtue of head (3) in the text in cases where a person provided his services as a pilot under a contract for services: see s 3(5).

15   Pilotage Act 1987 s 3(5)(d). As to the meaning of 'harbour' see PARA 575. See *Hutchison v Clydeport Operations Ltd* 1998 SC 336, 1998 SLT 765, Ct of Sess (scope of the Pilotage Act 1987 s 3(5)(d) is not limited to self-employed persons but applies to any person providing the services of a pilot or pilots under a contract or arrangement).

16   Pilotage Act 1987 s 3(6).

17   Pilotage Act 1987 s 3(7).

18   As to the meaning of 'authorised pilot' see PARA 574.

19   See the Pilotage Act 1987 s 3(8); and PARA 1168.

20   For these purposes, 'local authority' means, in England and Wales, a local authority within the meaning of the Local Government Act 1972 (see LOCAL GOVERNMENT vol 69 (2009) PARA 22 et seq): Pilotage Act 1987 s 3(10). As to the meanings of 'England' and 'Wales' see PARA 16 note 2.

21   Pilotage Act 1987 s 3(9).

22   For these purposes, 'executive' and 'executive arrangements' have the same meaning as in the Local Government Act 2000 Pt II (ss 10–48) (see LOCAL GOVERNMENT vol 69 (2009) PARA 303): Pilotage Act 1987 s 3(10) (definitions added in relation to England by SI 2001/2237; and in relation to Wales by SI 2002/808).

23   Pilotage Act 1987 s 3(9A) (added in relation to England by SI 2001/2237; and in relation to Wales by SI 2002/808).

24   Pilotage Act 1987 s 3(9A)(a) (as added: see note 23).

25   Pilotage Act 1987 s 3(9A)(b) (as added: see note 23).

**578. Employment etc of authorised pilots.** A competent harbour authority[1] may make such arrangements as it considers appropriate for the provision of the services of authorised pilots[2] in the area in relation to which its statutory duty to provide pilotage services[3] is exercisable, whether under a contract of employment or a contract for services[4].

A competent harbour authority may refuse to authorise any person who is not willing to provide his services as a pilot in accordance with the arrangements made for the provision of such services in its area[5].

A competent harbour authority may pay into any pilots' benefit fund[6] such contributions as may be required by the rules governing that fund in respect of any authorised pilot providing his services under such arrangements as mentioned above[7].

1  As to the meaning of 'competent harbour authority' see PARA 575.
2  As to the meanings of 'authorised pilot' and 'pilot' see PARA 574.
3  Ie under the Pilotage Act 1987 s 2(1) (see PARA 576): see s 4(1). As to the meaning of 'pilotage' see PARA 574. There is no vicarious liability even where pilotage is not compulsory: see *Oceanic Crest Shipping Co v Pilbara Harbour Services Pty Ltd* (1986) 160 CLR 626; *Esso Petroleum Co Ltd v Hall Russell & Co Ltd (Shetland Islands Council, third party); The Esso Bernicia* [1989] AC 643, [1989] 1 All ER 37; and *Oceangas (Gibraltar) Ltd v Port of London Authority, The Cavendish* [1993] 2 Lloyd's Rep 292.
4  Pilotage Act 1987 s 4(1). Transitional provision was made for a competent harbour authority, should it be so required, to offer contracts of employment to persons authorised under s 3 (see PARA 577) who were not, around the time of commencement of the Pilotage Act 1987 (ie 1 October 1988) employed by it under such a contract: see s 4(2), (3).
5  Pilotage Act 1987 s 4(4).
6  Ie established under the Pilotage Act 1983 s 15(1) (repealed): see the Pilotage Act 1987 s 4(5). Any pilots' benefit fund established under the Pilotage Act 1983 s 15(1)(i) (repealed) continued in existence notwithstanding the repeal of s 15 by the Pilotage Act 1987; and the Secretary of State had power by order to make such provision as he considered appropriate as to:
   (1)  the operation after the repeal of the Pilotage Act 1983 s 15 (repealed) of the byelaws under which any such fund was established (Pilotage Act 1987 s 32(3), Sch 1 para 4(1)(a));
   (2)  the appointment of the managers of any such fund and any powers to be exercisable as respects the management of the fund by the persons who were to appoint those managers (Sch 1 para 4(1)(b)); and
   (3)  the powers of any such managers to amend or revoke the byelaws or any other provision governing the fund (Sch 1 para 4(1)(c)).
   Before making such an order in respect of any fund, the Secretary of State had to consult such persons or organisations as appeared to him to be representative of competent harbour authorities and such persons as appeared to him to be representative of the persons who might benefit from the fund: Sch 1 para 4(2). In exercise of the power so conferred the Secretary of State made (inter alia) the Pilotage Act 1987 (Pilots' National Pension Fund) Order 1987, SI 1987/2139. As to the Secretary of State see PARA 36.
7  Pilotage Act 1987 s 4(5). The text refers to such arrangements as mentioned in s 4(1) (see the text and notes 1–4): see s 4(5).

**579. Pilot boats.** Ships[1] regularly employed in pilotage[2] services provided by or on behalf of any competent harbour authority[3] ('pilot boats') must:
   (1)    if they are operated by the authority, be approved by the authority[4]; and
   (2)    otherwise be licensed by it[5];
and the authority must not so approve or license any ship unless it is satisfied that it is suitable for use as a pilot boat[6].

A competent harbour authority must make such other provision as it considers necessary for the operation of pilot boats[7].

1  As to the meaning of 'ship' see PARA 574 note 1.
2  As to the meaning of 'pilotage' see PARA 574.
3  As to the meaning of 'competent harbour authority' see PARA 575.
4  Pilotage Act 1987 s 6(1)(a).
5  Pilotage Act 1987 s 6(1)(b).
6  Pilotage Act 1987 s 6(1). In the Pilotage Act 1987, except where the context otherwise requires, 'pilot boat' has the meaning given in s 6: s 31(1).
7  Pilotage Act 1987 s 6(2).

## C. COMPULSORY PILOTAGE

**580. Pilotage directions.** If a competent harbour authority[1] considers that in the interests of safety it should do so, it must direct that pilotage[2] is compulsory for ships[3] navigating[4] in any area or part of an area in relation to which its statutory duty to provide pilotage services[5] is exercisable[6]. Such a direction is called a 'pilotage direction'[7].

A pilotage direction:

(1)     may[8] apply to all ships or all ships of a description specified in the direction, subject to any exceptions there specified[9];

(2)     must specify the area and circumstances in which it applies[10];

(3)     may specify the circumstances in which an authorised pilot[11] in charge of a ship to which it applies is to be accompanied by an assistant who is also an authorised pilot[12]; and

(4)     may contain such supplementary provisions as the authority considers appropriate[13].

A pilotage direction does not apply to ships of less than 20 metres in length or to fishing boats of which the registered length is less than 47.5 metres[14].

Before giving a pilotage direction, a competent harbour authority must consult:

(a)     the owners of ships which customarily navigate in the area to which the proposed direction would apply[15]; and

(b)     any other persons who carry on harbour operations[16] within the harbour[17] of the authority[18];

or, in either case, such persons as it considers to be representative of them[19].

If a competent harbour authority considers that pilotage should be compulsory for ships navigating in any area outside its harbour, it must apply for a harbour revision order to be made[20] to extend the limits within which the authority has jurisdiction for the purposes of pilotage to include that area; and a pilotage direction given by it does not apply to that area until the limits have been so extended[21].

A competent harbour authority must arrange for any pilotage direction given by it to be published in such manner as to bring it to the notice of those persons likely to be interested[22].

1   As to the meaning of 'competent harbour authority' see PARA 575.
2   As to the meaning of 'pilotage' see PARA 574.
3   As to the meaning of 'ship' see PARA 574 note 1.
4   As to the meaning of references to a ship navigating or being navigated see PARA 576 note 4.
5   Ie under the Pilotage Act 1987 s 2(1) (see PARA 576): see s 7(1).
6   Pilotage Act 1987 s 7(1). This provision is subject to s 7(2)–(6) (see the text and notes 8–22): see s 7(1).
7   See the Pilotage Act 1987 ss 7(1), 31(1).
8   Ie subject to the Pilotage Act 1987 s 7(3) (see the text and note 14): see s 7(2)(a).
9   Pilotage Act 1987 s 7(2)(a).
10  Pilotage Act 1987 s 7(2)(b).
11  As to the meaning of 'authorised pilot' see PARA 574.
12  Pilotage Act 1987 s 7(2)(c).
13  Pilotage Act 1987 s 7(2)(d).
14  Pilotage Act 1987 s 7(3).
15  Pilotage Act 1987 s 7(4)(a).
16  For these purposes, 'harbour operations' has the same meaning as in the Harbours Act 1964 (see PORTS AND HARBOURS vol 85 (2012) PARA 19): Pilotage Act 1987 s 31(1).
17  As to the meaning of 'harbour' see PARA 575.
18  Pilotage Act 1987 s 7(4)(b).
19  Pilotage Act 1987 s 7(4).
20  Ie under the Harbours Act 1964 s 14 (see PORTS AND HARBOURS vol 85 (2012) PARA 27 et seq): see the Pilotage Act 1987 s 7(5).

21 Pilotage Act 1987 s 7(5). Transitional provision was made in relation to circumstances where a competent harbour authority, which proposed on or after 1 October 1988 to direct that pilotage should be compulsory for ships navigating in an area outside its harbour, applied before that day for the making of the harbour revision order which would be required by virtue of s 7(5) and that area was an area in which pilotage was compulsory by virtue of an order under the Pilotage Act 1983 s 9(1)(i) (repealed): see the Pilotage Act 1987 s 32(3), Sch 1 para 3.

22 Pilotage Act 1987 s 7(6).

**581. Pilotage exemption certificates.** A competent harbour authority[1] which has given a pilotage direction[2] must, on application by any person who is bona fide a deck officer[3] of any ship[4], grant a certificate (a 'pilotage exemption certificate')[5] to him if it is satisfied (by examination or by reference to such other requirements as it may reasonably impose)[6]:

(1)     that his skill, experience and local knowledge are sufficient for him to be capable of piloting the ship of which he is a deck officer (or that and any other ships specified in the certificate) within its harbour[7] or such part of its harbour as may be so specified[8]; and

(2)     in any case where it appears to the authority to be necessary in the interests of safety, that his knowledge of English is sufficient for that purpose[9].

The requirements so imposed[10]:

(a)     must not be unduly onerous having regard to the difficulties and danger of navigation in the harbour in question[11]; and

(b)     must not be more onerous than those required to be met by a person[12] applying to the authority[13] for authorisation[14].

If the Secretary of State[15] is satisfied, on application by a competent harbour authority, that it is appropriate to do so by reason of the unusual hazards involved in shipping movements within its harbour, he may direct that during such period, not exceeding three years, as he may specify, notwithstanding that the authority is satisfied as to the matters mentioned in heads (1) and (2) above[16], it may refuse to grant[17] pilotage exemption certificates[18]. Where a direction is so given[19] in respect of a competent harbour authority, any pilotage exemption certificate granted by the authority ceases to have effect and the authority must notify the holders of such certificates of that fact[20].

A pilotage exemption certificate does not remain in force for more than three years from the date on which it is granted[21]; but:

(i)     if the holder continues to be a deck officer of a ship, may be renewed annually by the competent harbour authority on application by the holder if the authority continues to be satisfied as to the matters mentioned in heads (1) and (2) above[22]; and

(ii)    on the application of the holder may be altered so as to refer to different ships from those to which it previously referred if the authority is so satisfied as respects those ships[23].

A competent harbour authority may by written notice suspend or revoke a person's pilotage exemption certificate on specified grounds[24], for a maximum period of 28 days[25].

Before refusing an application by any person[26] for the grant, renewal or alteration of a certificate or suspending or revoking a certificate held by any person, a competent harbour authority must give him written notice of its intention to do so, stating the reasons for which it proposes to act, and must give him a reasonable opportunity of making representations[27].

A competent harbour authority may charge such fees in respect of any examination so required to be taken[28] or the grant, renewal or alteration of any pilotage exemption certificate as the authority considers reasonable for the purposes of meeting its administrative costs in connection therewith[29].

1   As to the meaning of 'competent harbour authority' see PARA 575.
2   As to the meaning of 'pilotage direction' see PARA 580.
3   'Deck officer', in relation to a ship, includes the master and first mate: Pilotage Act 1987 s 31(1) (ss 8(1), (5)(a), 31(1) amended, ss 8A, 8B added, by the Marine Navigation Act 2013 ss 2(1), (2), (4), 3). For these purposes, 'master' has the same meaning as in the Merchant Shipping Act 1995 (see PARA 444 note 1): Pilotage Act 1987 s 31(1) (definition amended by the Merchant Shipping Act 1995 Sch 13 para 80(b)).
4   As to the meaning of 'ship' see PARA 574 note 1.
5   In the Pilotage Act 1987, except where the context otherwise requires, 'pilotage exemption certificate' means a certificate granted under s 8: s 31(1). Transitional provision was made in relation to any pilotage certificate which immediately before 1 October 1988 was in force under the Pilotage Act 1983 s 20 (repealed): see the Pilotage Act 1987 s 32(3), Sch 1 para 5.
6   Pilotage Act 1987 s 8(1) (as amended: see note 3). This provision is subject to s 8(3) (see the text and notes 15–18): see s 8(1).
7   As to the meaning of 'harbour' see PARA 575.
8   Pilotage Act 1987 s 8(1)(a).
9   Pilotage Act 1987 s 8(1)(b).
10  Ie under the Pilotage Act 1987 s 8(1) (see the text and notes 1–9): see s 8(2).
11  Pilotage Act 1987 s 8(2)(a).
12  Ie other than a person who immediately before 1 October 1988 was the holder of a licence under the Pilotage Act 1983 s 12 (repealed) or a time-expired apprentice pilot or recognised assistant pilot within the meaning of the Pilotage Act 1987 s 3 (see PARA 577 note 8): see s 8(2)(b).
13  Ie under the Pilotage Act 1987 s 3 (see PARA 577): see s 8(2)(b).
14  Pilotage Act 1987 s 8(2)(b).
15  As to the Secretary of State see PARA 36.
16  Ie notwithstanding that the authority is satisfied as mentioned in the Pilotage Act 1987 s 8(1) (see the text and notes 1–9): see s 8(3).
17  Ie under the Pilotage Act 1987 s 8(1) (see the text and notes 1–9): see s 8(3).
18  Pilotage Act 1987 s 8(3).
19  Ie under the Pilotage Act 1987 s 8(3) (see the text and notes 15–18): see s 8(4).
20  Pilotage Act 1987 s 8(4).
21  Pilotage Act 1987 s 8(5).
22  Pilotage Act 1987 s 8(5)(a) (as amended: see note 3). The text refers to the authority continuing to be satisfied as mentioned in s 8(1) (see the text and notes 1–9): see s 8(5)(a).
23  Pilotage Act 1987 s 8(5)(b).
24  Pilotage Act 1987 s 8A(1) (as added: see note 3). An authority may suspend or revoke a person's pilotage exemption certificate in the following cases:
    (1)   ('Case 1'): where an event has occurred as a result of which the authority is no longer satisfied of the matters specified in s 8(1)(a) (see the text and notes 1–8) (Pilotage Act 1987 s 8A(2) (as so added));
    (2)   ('Case 2'): where the authority thinks that the person has provided false information to the authority as to any of those matters (s 8A(3) (as so added));
    (3)   ('Case 3'): where the authority thinks that the person has been guilty of professional misconduct while piloting a ship (s 8A(4) (as so added)); and
    (4)   ('Case 4'): where pilotage notification was given under s 15(4)(b) (see PARA 1169) in reliance on the person's certificate and in the event, the pilotage was carried out by a person who was neither an authorised pilot nor acting in accordance with a pilotage exemption certificate (s 8A(5) (as so added)).
25  Pilotage Act 1987 s 8B(1) (as added: see note 24). However if a harbour authority has suspended a person's certificate and is considering whether to revoke it, the authority may by written notice extend the suspension for a single period of up to 28 days: s 8B(2) (as so added). A suspended certificate may be revoked (on the same or different grounds): s 8B(3) (as so added). Before revoking a person's certificate a harbour authority must give the person written warning, stating the reasons for the proposed revocation and allow the person a reasonable opportunity to make representations: s 8B(4) (as so added). A competent harbour authority which has suspended or revoked a certificate may pay compensation to any person who has suffered, or is likely to suffer, loss as a result: s 8B(5) (as so added).
26  Ie under the Pilotage Act 1987 s 8 (see the text and notes 1–9): see s 8(7).
27  Pilotage Act 1987 s 8(7).

28 Ie for the purposes of the Pilotage Act 1987 s 8 (see the text and notes 1–27): see s 8(8).
29 Pilotage Act 1987 s 8(8).

## 582. Prevention of discrimination in favour of authority's ships.

A competent harbour authority[1] must secure that any ship[2] owned or operated by it and used by it in the exercise of its functions otherwise than under the Pilotage Act 1987 is subject to the same obligations as respects pilotage[3] whilst navigating[4] within its harbour[5] as any other ship[6].

1  As to the meaning of 'competent harbour authority' see PARA 575.
2  As to the meaning of 'ship' see PARA 574 note 1.
3  As to the meaning of 'pilotage' see PARA 574.
4  As to the meaning of references to a ship navigating or being navigated see PARA 576 note 4.
5  As to the meaning of 'harbour' see PARA 575.
6  Pilotage Act 1987 s 9.

### D.  CHARGING BY AUTHORITIES

## 583. Pilotage charges.

A competent harbour authority[1] may make reasonable charges in respect of the pilotage services provided by it[2]. The charges to be so made may include[3]:

(1)    charges for the services of a pilot[4] authorised by the authority[5];
(2)    charges in respect of any expenses reasonably incurred by such a pilot in connection with the provision of his services as a pilot[6];
(3)    charges by way of penalties payable in cases where the estimated time of arrival or departure of a ship[7] is not notified as required by the authority or the ship does not arrive or depart at the notified time[8];
(4)    charges in respect of the cost of providing, maintaining and operating pilot boats[9] for the area[10]; and
(5)    charges in respect of any other costs involved in providing and maintaining the pilotage organisation provided by the authority[11].

A competent harbour authority which has given a pilotage direction[12] may also make reasonable charges in respect of any ship navigating[13] within the area to which the direction applies under the pilotage of a deck officer[14] who is the holder of a pilotage exemption certificate[15] in respect of the area and ship in question[16].

Different charges may be made[17] in different circumstances[18].

A competent harbour authority must arrange for the charges to be made by it[19] to be published in such manner as to bring them to the notice of those persons likely to be interested[20].

Charges so imposed by a competent harbour authority[21] are recoverable as a civil debt or in any other manner in which ship, passenger and goods dues[22] are recoverable by the authority[23]. There is also a right of arrest[24].

1  As to the meaning of 'competent harbour authority' see PARA 575.
2  Pilotage Act 1987 s 10(1). As to the meaning of 'pilotage' see PARA 574.
3  Pilotage Act 1987 s 10(2). Section 10(2) is without prejudice to the generality of s 10(1) (see the text and notes 1–2): see s 10(2).
4  As to the meaning of 'pilot' see PARA 574.
5  Pilotage Act 1987 s 10(2)(a).
6  Pilotage Act 1987 s 10(2)(b).
7  As to the meaning of 'ship' see PARA 574 note 1.
8  Pilotage Act 1987 s 10(2)(c).
9  As to the meaning of 'pilot boat' see PARA 579.
10 Pilotage Act 1987 s 10(2)(d).
11 Pilotage Act 1987 s 10(2)(e).
12 As to the meaning of 'pilotage direction' see PARA 580.
13 As to the meaning of references to a ship navigating or being navigated see PARA 576 note 4.
14 As to the meaning of 'deck officer' see PARA 581 note 3.
15 As to the meaning of 'pilotage exemption certificate' see PARA 581.
16 Pilotage Act 1987 s 10(3) (amended by the Marine Navigation Act 2013 s 2(3)).

17 Ie under the Pilotage Act 1987 s 10: see s 10(4).

18 Pilotage Act 1987 s 10(4).

19 Ie under the Pilotage Act 1987 s 10: see s 10(5).

20 Pilotage Act 1987 s 10(5).

21 Ie under the Pilotage Act 1987 s 10: see s 10(7).

22 For these purposes, 'ship, passenger and goods dues' has the same meaning as in the Harbours Act 1964 (see PORTS AND HARBOURS vol 85 (2012) PARA 27): Pilotage Act 1987 s 10(8).

23 Pilotage Act 1987 s 10(7). The Harbours Act 1964 s 31(2)–(12) (right of objection to ship, passenger and goods dues) (see PORTS AND HARBOURS vol 85 (2012) PARA 72) applies as respects charges imposed by an authority by virtue of the Pilotage Act 1987 s 10 as it applies as respects charges to which the Harbours Act 1964 s 31 applies, but with the substitution for the references to the persons mentioned in s 31(2)(a), (b), (3)(b) of references to the owners of ships which customarily navigate in the harbour in question, to any persons who carry on harbour operations within that harbour, and to any other harbour authority to whose harbour ships obtain access through that harbour (or, in any of those cases, persons representative of them) and with the omission of s 31(2)(i), (iii): Pilotage Act 1987 s 10(6). As to the meaning of 'harbour operations' see PARA 580 note 16.

24 See the Senior Courts Act 1981 s 21(4); and PARA 94.

## E. AGENTS AND JOINT ARRANGEMENTS

**584. Use of agents; joint arrangements.** A competent harbour authority[1] may arrange for its functions in relation to the provision of pilotage services, with exceptions[2], to be exercised on its behalf by such other persons as it thinks fit and may establish such companies as it thinks fit to exercise those functions on its behalf[3].

A competent harbour authority may arrange for all or any of its functions relating to pilotage[4], other than its statutory duty to provide pilotage services[5], to be exercised on its behalf by another competent harbour authority[6].

Two or more competent harbour authorities may arrange to discharge any of their functions relating to pilotage jointly; and such arrangements may provide for the discharge of such functions by a joint committee or any other body established by the authorities for that purpose[7].

An authority which has so entered into such arrangements with another authority[8] may withdraw from the arrangements on giving reasonable notice to the other authority[9].

1 As to the meaning of 'competent harbour authority' see PARA 575.

2 Ie other than its functions under the Pilotage Act 1987 s 2(1) (see PARA 576), s 3(1) (see PARA 577), s 4(2) (see PARA 578), s 6(1)(b) (see PARA 579), s 7(1) (see PARA 580), s 8(1) (see PARA 581) or s 28 (repealed) or its function of determining the qualifications to be required from persons applying for authorisation under s 3(2) (see PARA 577) or any charge to be imposed under s 10(1) or (3) (see PARA 583): see s 11(1).

3 Pilotage Act 1987 s 11(1).

4 As to the meaning of 'pilotage' see PARA 574.

5 Ie other than its duty under the Pilotage Act 1987 s 2(1) (see PARA 576): see s 11(2).

6 Pilotage Act 1987 s 11(2).

7 Pilotage Act 1987 s 11(3).

8 Ie under the Pilotage Act 1987 s 11(2) or (3) (see the text and notes 4–7): see s 11(4).

9 Pilotage Act 1987 s 11(4).

**585. Information and directions as to joint arrangements.** Where:

(1)     the harbours[1] of two or more competent harbour authorities[2] fall wholly or partly within a single former pilotage district[3];

(2)     access for ships[4] to the harbour of a competent harbour authority is customarily available through the harbour of another competent harbour authority[5];

(3)     there is any person other than the competent harbour authority who carries on harbour operations[6] within the harbour of a competent harbour authority[7];

(4)     there is any person who carries on harbour operations in a harbour[8] which is not the harbour of a competent harbour authority and access to which is customarily available through the harbour of a competent harbour authority[9]; or

(5)     the harbour of a competent harbour authority and a dockyard port[10] for which a Queen's harbour master has been appointed[11] fall wholly or partly within a single former pilotage district[12],

the Secretary of State[13] may require any of the authorities (or, in the case of heads (3), (4) or (5) above, the authority) concerned to provide him with such information as he may require concerning the arrangements made or proposed by the authorities (or authority) in question for the provision of pilotage services and that information must be provided in such form as the Secretary of State may require[14].

If the Secretary of State considers that any arrangements of which particulars are so provided[15] are not satisfactory, he may direct that they are to have effect subject to such modifications as he may specify in the direction[16] or he may direct the authorities (or authority) concerned to make different arrangements[17].

If the statement so provided[18] is to the effect that no arrangements have been made or proposed by the authorities (or authority) in question for the provision of pilotage services in the area concerned and the Secretary of State considers that such arrangements should be made, he must direct the authorities (or authority) in question to make appropriate arrangements[19].

1   As to the meaning of 'harbour' see PARA 575.
2   As to the meaning of 'competent harbour authority' see PARA 575.
3   Pilotage Act 1987 s 12(1)(a). As to the meaning of 'former pilotage district' see PARA 575 note 4.
4   As to the meaning of 'ship' see PARA 574 note 1.
5   Pilotage Act 1987 s 12(1)(b).
6   As to the meaning of 'harbour operations' see PARA 580 note 16.
7   Pilotage Act 1987 s 12(1)(c).
8   Ie within the meaning of the Harbours Act 1964 (see PORTS AND HARBOURS vol 85 (2012) PARA 9): see the Pilotage Act 1987 s 12(1)(d).
9   Pilotage Act 1987 s 12(1)(d).
10  Ie within the meaning of the Dockyard Ports Regulation Act 1865 (see PORTS AND HARBOURS vol 85 (2012) PARA 11): see the Pilotage Act 1987 s 12(1)(e).
11  Ie under the Dockyard Ports Regulation Act 1865 (see PORTS AND HARBOURS vol 85 (2012) PARA 94): see the Pilotage Act 1987 s 12(1)(e).
12  Pilotage Act 1987 s 12(1)(e).
13  As to the Secretary of State see PARA 36.
14  Pilotage Act 1987 s 12(1). As to the resolution of disputes between authorities concerning arrangements or statements about arrangements see PARA 586.
15  Ie under the Pilotage Act 1987 s 12(1) (see the text and notes 1–14): see s 12(2).
16  Pilotage Act 1987 s 12(2)(a). Section 11(4) (see PARA 584) does not apply to any arrangements made or modified by virtue of a direction under s 12: s 12(4).
17  Pilotage Act 1987 s 12(2)(b).
18  Ie under the Pilotage Act 1987 s 12(1) (see the text and notes 1–14): see s 12(3).
19  Pilotage Act 1987 s 12(3).

**586. Resolution of disputes between authorities concerning arrangements.** Where any dispute arises between two or more competent harbour authorities[1] concerning:

(1)     arrangements for the provision of pilotage[2] services made by one authority which affects navigation in another authority's harbour[3];

(2)     arrangements made by two or more authorities for the discharge of their functions in relation to pilotage jointly[4]; or

(3)     arrangements that are required to be made or any statement that is required to be prepared about arrangements made or proposed for the provision of pilotage services[5],

or between a competent harbour authority and:

(a)  any person other than the competent harbour authority who carries on harbour operations[6] within the harbour of a competent harbour authority[7];

(b)  any person who carries on harbour operations in a harbour[8] which is not the harbour of a competent harbour authority and access to which is customarily available through the harbour of a competent harbour authority[9]; or

(c)  a Queen's harbour master who has been appointed[10] for the harbour of a competent harbour authority and a dockyard port[11] falling wholly or partly within a single former pilotage district[12],

(d)  concerning arrangements for the provision of pilotage services made by the authority which affect navigation in the harbour of the competent harbour authority or such a statement or arrangement[13],

any party to the dispute may appeal to the Secretary of State[14].

On such an appeal, the Secretary of State must settle the dispute in such manner as he considers appropriate[15]; and he may in particular direct:

(i)  that such arrangements[16] are not to have effect or are to have effect subject to such modifications as he may specify[17]; or

(ii)  in the case of a dispute between two competent harbour authorities, that one authority only may exercise functions under the Pilotage Act 1987 in relation to any area in respect of which there is a dispute[18].

1  As to the meaning of 'competent harbour authority' see PARA 575.
2  As to the meaning of 'pilotage' see PARA 574.
3  Pilotage Act 1987 s 13(1)(a). As to the meaning of 'harbour' see PARA 575. The arrangements mentioned in s 13(1) include arrangements concerning which a previous dispute has been settled under s 13(2) (see the text and notes 15–18) and arrangements made or modified by virtue of s 13(2): s 13(3).
4  Pilotage Act 1987 s 13(1)(b). See note 3.
5  Pilotage Act 1987 s 13(1)(c). The text refers to any statement required to be prepared or arrangements required to be made under s 12 (see PARA 585): see s 13(1)(c). See note 3.
6  As to the meaning of 'harbour operations' see PARA 580 note 16.
7  Ie such a person as is mentioned in the Pilotage Act 1987 s 12(1)(c) (see PARA 585): see s 13(1).
8  Ie within the meaning of the Harbours Act 1964 (see PORTS AND HARBOURS vol 85 (2012) PARA 9): see the Pilotage Act 1987 s 12(1)(d).
9  Ie such a person as is mentioned in the Pilotage Act 1987 s 12(1)(d) (see PARA 575): see s 13(1).
10  Ie under the Dockyard Ports Regulation Act 1865 (see PORTS AND HARBOURS vol 85 (2012) PARA 94): see the Pilotage Act 1987 s 12(1)(e).
11  Ie within the meaning of the Dockyard Ports Regulation Act 1865 (see PORTS AND HARBOURS vol 85 (2012) PARA 11): see the Pilotage Act 1987 s 12(1)(e).
12  Ie such a person as is mentioned in the Pilotage Act 1987 s 12(1)(e) (see PARA 585): see s 13(1).
13  Pilotage Act 1987s 13(1). See note 3.
14  Pilotage Act 1987s 13(1). As to the Secretary of State see PARA 36.
15  Pilotage Act 1987 s 13(2).
16  Ie such arrangements as are mentioned in the Pilotage Act 1987 s 13(1) (see the text and notes 1–14): see s 13(2).
17  Pilotage Act 1987 s 13(2)(a).
18  Pilotage Act 1987 s 13(2)(b).

F.  ACCOUNTS OF COMPETENT HARBOUR AUTHORITY

**587. Authority's obligations to provide statement of accounts.** Regulations under the Harbours Act 1964[1] may require any authority[2] which is a competent harbour authority[3] to make available for inspection by the public any statement of accounts required to be prepared by it which relate to the activities of the authority, or any agent of the authority, in relation to pilotage[4].

Where any such activities of a competent harbour authority are carried out on its behalf by any agent, the agent must furnish the authority with all such information concerning those activities as the authority may reasonably require to fulfil its obligations in relation to any such statement of accounts[5].

1 Ie under the Harbours Act 1964 s 42 (see PORTS AND HARBOURS vol 85 (2012) PARA 85): see the Pilotage Act 1987 s 14(1).
2 Ie any authority to which the Harbours Act 1964 s 42 applies: see the Pilotage Act 1987 s 14(1).
3 As to the meaning of 'competent harbour authority' see PARA 575.
4 Pilotage Act 1987 s 14(1). As to the meaning of 'pilotage' see PARA 574. For the relevant requirements see the Statutory Harbour Undertakings (Pilotage Accounts) Regulations 1988, SI 1988/2216, which make provision in relation to the authorities and activities to which the regulations apply (see reg 3); pilotage accounts (see reg 4); and the publication of pilotage accounts (see reg 5).
5 Pilotage Act 1987 s 14(3).

## (ii) General Provisions concerning Pilotage

### A. COMPULSORY PILOTAGE

**588. Requirements where compulsory pilotage in force.** A ship[1] which is being navigated[2] in an area and in circumstances in which pilotage[3] is compulsory for it by virtue of a pilotage direction[4] must be:

(1) under the pilotage of an authorised pilot[5] accompanied by such an assistant, if any, as is required by virtue of the direction[6]; or

(2) under the pilotage of a deck officer[7] possessing a pilotage exemption certificate[8] in respect of that area and ship[9].

If any ship is not under pilotage as so required[10] after an authorised pilot has offered to take charge of the ship, or the ship is navigated in an area in which a pilotage direction applies to it and pilotage notification has not been given, the master of the ship is guilty of an offence[11].

1 As to the meaning of 'ship' see PARA 574 note 1.
2 As to the meaning of references to a ship navigating or being navigated see PARA 576 note 4.
3 As to the meaning of 'pilotage' see PARA 574.
4 As to the meaning of 'pilotage direction' see PARA 580.
5 As to the meaning of 'authorised pilot' see PARA 574. As to the rights of authorised pilots see PARA 590 et seq.
6 Pilotage Act 1987 s 15(1)(a).
7 As to the meaning of 'deck officer' see PARA 581 note 3.
8 As to the meaning of 'pilotage exemption certificate' see PARA 581.
9 Pilotage Act 1987 s 15(1)(b) (amended by the Marine Navigation Act 2013 s 2(3)).
10 Ie as required by the Pilotage Act 1987 s 15(1) (see the text and notes 1–9): see s 15(2); and PARA 1169.
11 See the Pilotage Act 1987 s 15(2), (3); and PARA 1169.

**589. Liability for ships under compulsory pilotage.** The fact that a ship[1] is being navigated[2] in an area and in circumstances in which pilotage[3] is compulsory[4] for it does not affect any liability of the owner or master[5] of the ship for any loss or damage caused by the ship or by the manner in which it is navigated[6].

1 As to the meaning of 'ship' see PARA 574 note 1.
2 As to the meaning of references to a ship navigating or being navigated see PARA 576 note 4.
3 As to the meaning of 'pilotage' see PARA 574.
4 As to compulsory pilotage see PARA 588.
5 As to the meaning of 'master' see PARA 581 note 3.
6 Pilotage Act 1987 s 16. Section 16 creates the relationship of master and servant between the compulsory pilot and the shipowner so as to make the shipowner liable to third parties: *Oceangas (Gibraltar) Ltd v Port of London Authority, The Cavendish* [1993] 2 Lloyd's Rep 292 (Port of London Authority held not to be vicariously liable in tort for the negligence of the pilot on board). See also *Esso Petroleum Co Ltd v Hall Russell & Co Ltd, The Esso Bernicia* [1989] AC 643, [1989] 1 All ER 37, HL (decided under the Pilotage Act 1983 s 15(1) (repealed)).

**590. Rights of authorised pilot to supersede unauthorised pilot.** An authorised pilot[1] may, within the harbour[2] in relation to which or a part of which he is authorised, supersede as the pilot[3] of a ship[4] any unauthorised person who has been employed to pilot it[5].

If:

(1)      the master of any ship navigates it in any part of a harbour under the pilotage[6] of an unauthorised person without first notifying the competent harbour authority that he proposes to do so, he is guilty of an offence[7];

(2)      an unauthorised person pilots a ship within a harbour knowing that an authorised pilot has offered to pilot it, he is guilty of an offence[8];

(3)      the master of a ship navigating within a harbour knowingly employs or continues to employ an unauthorised person to pilot the ship after an authorised pilot has offered to pilot it[9],

he is guilty of an offence[10].

1    As to the meaning of 'authorised pilot' see PARA 574.
2    As to the meaning of 'harbour' see PARA 575.
3    As to the meaning of 'pilot' see PARA 574.
4    As to the meaning of 'ship' see PARA 574 note 1.
5    Pilotage Act 1987 s 17(1). For these purposes, a person is an unauthorised person if he is neither an authorised pilot nor the holder of a pilotage exemption certificate in respect of the ship and the area in question; and any person, other than the master or one of the crew of a ship, who is on the bridge of the ship or in any other position from which the ship is navigated, whether on board or elsewhere, is deemed to be piloting the ship unless he proves otherwise: s 17(5). As to the meaning of 'master' see PARA 581 note 3; and as to the meaning of 'pilotage exemption certificate' see PARA 581. As to the meaning of references to a ship navigating or being navigated see PARA 576 note 4.
        Section 17(1) and s 17(2)–(4) (see the text and notes 6–10) do not apply:
        (1)    to a ship which a person is piloting or ordered to pilot in a dockyard port, within the meaning of the Dockyard Ports Regulation Act 1865 (see PORTS AND HARBOURS vol 85 (2012) PARA 11), in the course of his duties as a servant of the Crown (Pilotage Act 1987 s 17(7)(a)); or
        (2)    if the competent harbour authority has directed that the provisions of s 17(1)–(4) are not to apply to movements in its harbour or a specified part of its harbour for the purpose of changing a ship or a ship of a specified description from one mooring to another or of taking it into or out of any dock, to a ship or a ship of that description being moved in that harbour or that part for that purpose (s 17(7)(b));
        but nothing in s 17(7)(a) (see head (1)) is to be construed as derogating from any immunity which affects such a ship as there mentioned apart from head (1) (s 17(7)). A competent harbour authority must not give a direction under s 17(7)(b) (see head (2)) unless the area in relation to which it will apply is either:
        (a)    an area in relation to which a byelaw under the Pilotage Act 1983 s 38 (repealed) (exemptions from compulsory pilotage for ships moving within harbours, docks etc) was in force immediately before 1 October 1988 (Pilotage Act 1987 s 17(8)(a)); or
        (b)    a closed dock, lock or other closed work which is not in a former pilotage district (s 17(8)(b)).
        As to the meaning of 'competent harbour authority' see PARA 575; and as to the meaning of 'former pilotage district' see PARA 575 note 4.
6    As to the meaning of 'pilotage' see PARA 574.
7    See the Pilotage Act 1987 s 17(2); and PARA 1170. See also note 5.
8    See the Pilotage Act 1987 s 17(3); and PARA 1170. See also note 5.
9    See the Pilotage Act 1987 s 17(4); and PARA 1170. See also note 5.
10   See PARA 1170.

**591. Declaration as to draught etc of ship.** A pilot[1] may require the master[2] of any ship[3] which he is piloting to declare its draught of water, length and beam, and to provide him with such other information relating to the ship or its cargo as the pilot specifies and is necessary to enable him to carry out his duties as the pilot of the ship[4].

The master of a ship must bring to the notice of any person who pilots the ship any defects in, and any matter peculiar to, the ship and its machinery and equipment of which the master knows and which might materially affect the navigation of the ship[5].

Any master of a ship who:

(1)    refuses to comply with such a request[6]; or

(2)    makes a statement which is false in a material particular in answer to such a request, knowing it to be false or being reckless as to whether it is false, or fails without reasonable excuse to correct such a statement made by another person in answer to such a request, although himself knowing it to be false[7]; or

(3)    without reasonable excuse fails to bring to the notice of any person who pilots the ship any defects in, and any matter peculiar to, the ship and its machinery and equipment of which the master knows and which might materially affect the navigation of the ship[8],

is guilty of an offence[9].

1    As to the meaning of 'pilot' see PARA 574.
2    As to the meaning of 'master' see PARA 581 note 3.
3    As to the meaning of 'ship' see PARA 574 note 1.
4    Pilotage Act 1987 s 18(1).
5    Pilotage Act 1987 s 18(2).
6    See the Pilotage Act 1987 s 18(3)(a); and PARA 1171. The text refers to a request made to the master of a ship in pursuance of s 18(1) (see the text and notes 1–4): see s 18(3)(a); and PARA 1171.
7    See the Pilotage Act 1987 s 18(3)(b); and PARA 1171.
8    See the Pilotage Act 1987 s 18(3)(c); and PARA 1171. The text refers to any person who without reasonable excuse contravenes s 18(2) (see the text and note 5): see s 18(3)(c); and PARA 1171.
9    See the Pilotage Act 1987 s 18(3); and PARA 1171.

**592. Authorised pilot not to be taken out of his area.** A master[1] of a ship[2] must not without reasonable excuse take an unauthorised pilot[3] without his consent beyond the point up to which he has been engaged to pilot the ship[4].

A person who contravenes this prohibition[5] is guilty of an offence[6].

1    As to the meaning of 'master' see PARA 581 note 3.
2    As to the meaning of 'ship' see PARA 574 note 1.
3    As to the meaning of 'authorised pilot' see PARA 574.
4    Pilotage Act 1987 s 19(1).
5    Ie a person who contravenes the Pilotage Act 1987 s 19(1) (see the text and notes 1–4): see s 19(2); and PARA 1172.
6    See the Pilotage Act 1987 s 19(2); and PARA 1172.

**593. Facilities to be given for pilot boarding or leaving ship.** Where:

(1)    the master[1] of a ship[2], which is navigating[3] in an area in circumstances in which pilotage[4] is compulsory[5] for it but is not under the pilotage of an authorised pilot[6] or deck officer[7] possessing a pilotage exemption certificate[8] in respect of the ship and the area, is offered the services of an authorised pilot[9]; or

(2)    the master of a ship accepts the services of an authorised pilot in any other circumstances[10],

he must facilitate the pilot boarding and subsequently leaving the ship[11].

If the master of any ship without reasonable excuse contravenes these requirements[12], he is guilty of an offence[13].

1    As to the meaning of 'master' see PARA 581 note 3.
2    As to the meaning of 'ship' see PARA 574 note 1.
3    As to the meaning of references to a ship navigating or being navigated see PARA 576 note 4.
4    As to the meaning of 'pilotage' see PARA 574.
5    As to compulsory pilotage see PARA 588.

6 As to the meaning of 'authorised pilot' see PARA 574.
7 As to the meaning of 'deck officer' see PARA 581 note 3.
8 As to the meaning of 'pilotage exemption certificate' see PARA 581.
9 Pilotage Act 1987 s 20(1)(a) (amended by the Marine Navigation Act 2013 s 2(3)).
10 Pilotage Act 1987 s 20(1)(b).
11 Pilotage Act 1987 s 20(1).
12 Ie if any person contravenes the Pilotage Act 1987 s 20(1) (see the text and notes 1–11): see s 20(2); and PARA 1173.
13 See the Pilotage Act 1987 s 20(2); and PARA 1173.

### C. LIMITATION OF LIABILITY

**594. Limitation of liability in respect of pilots.** The liability of an authorised pilot[1] for any loss or damage caused by any act or omission of his while acting as such a pilot must not exceed £1,000 and the amount of the pilotage charges[2] in respect of the voyage during which the liability arose[3]. For these purposes, a person is deemed to be an authorised pilot notwithstanding that he is acting as a pilot of a ship[4] navigating[5] outside the area in relation to which he is authorised if:

(1) he is piloting the ship to that area from a place where pilots authorised for that harbour[6] regularly board ships navigating to it[7]; or

(2) he is piloting the ship from that harbour to a place where such pilots regularly leave ships navigating from it[8]; and

(3) in either case, the ship is one in respect of which he is authorised[9].

Where, without any personal act or omission by a competent harbour authority[10], any loss or damage to any ship, to any property on board any ship or to any property or rights of any kind is caused by an authorised pilot employed by it, the authority is not liable to damages beyond the amount of £1,000 multiplied by the number of authorised pilots employed by it at the date when the loss or damage occurs[11]. Where, without any such personal act or omission by a person providing pilotage services on behalf of a competent harbour authority (the 'agent'), any such loss or damage is caused by an authorised pilot employed by him, the agent is not liable to damages beyond the amount of £1,000 multiplied by the number of authorised pilots employed by him providing pilotage services for that authority at the date when the loss or damage occurs[12].

The limit of liability under these provisions[13] applies to the whole of any losses and damages which may arise upon any one distinct occasion although such losses and damages may be sustained by more than one person[14].

Where any proceedings are taken against any person (the 'defendant') for any act or omission in respect of which liability is limited as so provided[15] and other claims are or appear likely to be made in respect of the same act or omission, the court[16] in which the proceedings are taken may:

(a) determine the amount of the liability[17];

(b) upon payment by the defendant of that amount into court, distribute that amount rateably among the claimants[18];

(c) stay any proceedings pending in any other court in relation to the same matter[19];

(d) proceed in such manner and subject to such requirements as the court thinks just[20]:

    (i) as to making interested persons parties to the proceedings[21];

    (ii) as to the exclusion of any claimants whose claims are not made within a certain time[22];

    (iii) as to requiring security from the defendant[23]; and

    (iv) as to payment of any costs[24].

A competent harbour authority is not liable for any loss or damage caused by any act or omission of a pilot authorised by it[25] by virtue only of that authorisation[26].

1  As to the meaning of 'authorised pilot' see PARA 574.
2  As to pilotage charges see PARA 583. As to the meaning of 'pilotage' see PARA 574.
3  Pilotage Act 1987 s 22(1).
4  As to the meaning of 'ship' see PARA 574 note 1.
5  As to the meaning of references to a ship navigating or being navigated see PARA 576 note 4.
6  As to the meaning of 'harbour' see PARA 575.
7  Pilotage Act 1987 s 22(2)(a).
8  Pilotage Act 1987 s 22(2)(b).
9  Pilotage Act 1987 s 22(2)(c).
10  Ie any such personal act or omission as is mentioned in the Convention on Limitation of Liability for Maritime Claims (London, 1 to 19 November 1976; Cmnd 7035) art 4 (see PARA 996), implemented by the Merchant Shipping Act 1995 Sch 7 Pt I: see the Pilotage Act 1987 s 22(3) (amended by the Merchant Shipping Act 1995 Sch 13 para 80(a)). As to the meaning of 'competent harbour authority' see PARA 575.
11  Pilotage Act 1987 s 22(3) (as amended: see note 10). Nothing in s 22(3) or s 22(4) (see the text and note 12) affects any liability which may be limited under the Merchant Shipping Act 1995 s 185 (see PARA 992) or is excluded under s 186 (see PARA 1009): Pilotage Act 1987 s 22(7) (amended by the Merchant Shipping Act 1995 Sch 13 para 80(a)).
12  Pilotage Act 1987 s 22(4). See note 11.
13  Ie under the Pilotage Act 1987 s 22: see s 22(5).
14  Pilotage Act 1987 s 22(5).
15  Ie as provided by the Pilotage Act 1987 s 22: see s 22(6).
16  For these purposes, 'court' means the High Court: Pilotage Act 1987 s 22(9)(a).
17  Pilotage Act 1987 s 22(6)(a).
18  Pilotage Act 1987 s 22(6)(b).
19  Pilotage Act 1987 s 22(6)(c).
20  Pilotage Act 1987 s 22(6)(d).
21  Pilotage Act 1987 s 22(6)(d)(i).
22  Pilotage Act 1987 s 22(6)(d)(ii).
23  Pilotage Act 1987 s 22(6)(d)(iii).
24  Pilotage Act 1987 s 22(6)(d)(iv).
25  Ie under the Pilotage Act 1987 s 3 (see PARA 577): see s 22(8).
26  Pilotage Act 1987 s 22(8).

### D.  DEEP SEA PILOTAGE

**595. Deep sea pilotage certificates.** The Secretary of State[1] may authorise any body appearing to him to be competent to do so to grant certificates ('deep sea pilotage certificates') in respect of such part of the sea falling outside the harbour[2] of any competent harbour authority[3] as he may specify[4].

Any body for the time being so authorised by the Secretary of State[5] may grant a deep sea pilotage certificate to any person on application by him if it is satisfied (by examination or by reference to such criteria as it may reasonably impose) that he is qualified to act as a pilot[6] of a ship[7] for the area in respect of which the body is so authorised by the Secretary of State[8].

1  As to the Secretary of State see PARA 36.
2  As to the meaning of 'harbour' see PARA 575.
3  As to the meaning of 'competent harbour authority' see PARA 575.
4  Pilotage Act 1987 s 23(1). Transitional provision was made in relation to any body which immediately before 1 October 1988 was authorised under the Pilotage Act 1983 (repealed) to grant deep sea pilotage certificates and in relation to any deep sea pilotage certificates which immediately before 1 October 1988 were granted under the Pilotage Act 1983: see the Pilotage Act 1987 Sch 1 para 6.
5  Ie authorised under the Pilotage Act 1987 s 23: see s 23(2).
6  As to the meaning of 'pilot' see PARA 574.
7  As to the meaning of 'ship' see PARA 574 note 1.
8  Pilotage Act 1987 s 23(2).

**596. Pilotage of vessels by deep-sea pilots in the North Sea and English Channel.** Member states which have coasts bordering the North Sea and the English Channel must take all necessary and appropriate measures to ensure that vessels availing themselves of the services of a deep-sea pilot for pilotage in those waters are provided with adequately qualified deep-sea pilots in possession of a certificate delivered by a competent authority of one of those member states certifying that such pilots are qualified to pilot vessels in those waters[1]. Furthermore, each member state must take all necessary and appropriate measures to encourage vessels flying its national flag to avail themselves in those waters of the services of only those deep-sea pilots who are in possession of such a certificate or of an equivalent certificate delivered by another North Sea coastal state, when seeking the assistance of deep-sea pilots[2].

1  Council Directive (EC) 79/115 (OJ L33, 08.02.1979, p 32) art 1(1). As to deep sea pilotage
   certificates issued under the Pilotage Act 1987 see PARA 595.
2  Council Directive (EC) 79/115 (OJ L33, 08.02.1979, p 32) art 1(2).

## (2) TOWAGE

**597. Ordinary obligations as to efficiency of tug.** In an ordinary contract of towage[1], the owner of the tug contracts that the tug is to be efficient for the purpose for which she is employed, and that her crew, tackle and equipment are to be equal to the work to be accomplished, in the weather and in the circumstances reasonably to be expected[2]. There is a warranty implied in such a contract that at the outset the crew, tackle and equipment are equal to the work to be accomplished in circumstances reasonably to be expected[3], and there is an implied obligation that competent skill and best endeavours are to be used in doing the work[4]. The grounding of a vessel in tow may in some circumstances constitute prima facie evidence either of the insufficient power of the tug, or of the inefficiency of her crew, tackle or equipment[5].

There is no implied warranty that the tug is to be able to accomplish the work in all circumstances and at all hazards, and, if the contract is rendered impossible by force majeur, the obligation of the tug is discharged, but the occurrence of unforeseen difficulties does not in itself discharge the tug from her contract; but such difficulties may be of a nature to entitle the tug to salvage remuneration instead of mere towage remuneration[6].

Where the contract is for the service of a specified tug, there is no implied warranty that she is fit for the purpose for which she was supplied[7].

1  As to special conditions relieving the tug owner see PARA 600.
2  *The West Cock* [1911] P 208, 12 Asp MLC 57, CA (following *The Minnehaha* (1861) Lush 335
   at 347, PC); *The Robert Dixon* (1879) 5 PD 54, 4 Asp MLC 246, CA; *The Undaunted* (1886) 11
   PD 46, 5 Asp MLC 580. In a contract providing for different towage rates, the words 'not normal'
   in 'towage of steamers not normal' was held to refer to steamers and not to the towage: *The
   Princesa* [1946] P 79, [1945] 2 All ER 429n, CA. As to the position of the parties to a contract of
   towage where one or both vessels are involved in a collision see PARAS 774, 783. As to the
   jurisdiction of the Admiralty Court in actions for towage see the Senior Courts Act 1981 s 20(1)(a),
   (2)(k); and PARA 125.
3  *The Maréchal Suchet* [1911] P 1 at 12, 11 Asp MLC 553 at 556. See also PARA 783.
4  *The West Cock* [1911] P 208, 12 Asp MLC 57, CA (following *Steel v State Line Steamship Co*
   (1877) 3 App Cas 72 at 76, 86, 3 Asp MLC 516 at 517, 519, HL). See also *The Refrigerant* [1925]
   P 130, 16 Asp MLC 559 (cited in PARA 600 note 8).
5  *Preston Corpn v Biornstad, The Ratata* [1898] AC 513 at 517, 8 Asp MLC 427 at 429; *The
   Maréchal Suchet* [1911] P 1, 11 Asp MLC 553.
6  *The Minnehaha* (1861) Lush 335, PC; and see *The Hjemmett* (1880) 5 PD 227, 4 Asp MLC 274.
   See also *The Leon Blum* [1915] P 290, 13 Asp MLC 273, CA. As to salvage of a towed vessel see
   PARA 871; and as to impossibility of performance of contract see *The Salvador* (1909) 26 TLR
   149; and CONTRACT vol 22 (2012) PARA 468 et seq.

7　*Robertson v Amazon Tug and Lighterage Co Ltd* (1881) 7 QBD 598, 4 Asp MLC 496, CA; but
　see *Fraser and White Ltd v Vernon* [1951] 2 Lloyd's Rep 175. See also *Point Anne Quarries Ltd
　v The MF Whalen* (1922) 39 TLR 37, 13 Ll L Rep 40, PC.

## 598. Ordinary mutual obligation to use due care.

Where an ordinary contract of towage[1] has been made, there is an implied agreement that each vessel will perform her duty in accomplishing it, that proper skill and diligence will be used on board of each, and that neither vessel will by neglect or misconduct create unnecessary risk to the other or increase any risk which may be incidental to the service undertaken[2]. Where the breach by either vessel of this duty causes damage to the other, the vessel committing the breach will be liable to the other unless the sufferer has by misconduct or lack of skill on her own part contributed to the accident[3], in which case the loss is divided in proportion to the degrees of fault[4]. This obligation continues until the work undertaken to be done is carried out to its conclusion[5] or the contract is otherwise determined.

Where, in the course of carrying out such a contract, a tug fails to fulfil her obligations, and in consequence of the failure the services become of a salvage nature, the tug is not permitted to recover as for salvage[6].

1　As to special conditions relieving the tug owner see PARA 600.
2　*The Julia* (1860) Lush 224 at 231, PC; cf *Smith v St Lawrence Tow-Boat Co* (1873) LR 5 PC 308
　at 314, 2 Asp MLC 41 at 44; *Spaight v Tedcastle* (1881) 6 App Cas 217 at 220, 4 Asp MLC 406
　at 407, HL; *The Altair* [1897] P 105, 8 Asp MLC 224; *The Valsesia* [1927] P 115, 17 Asp MLC
　207; and see PARA 600. As to collision between tug and tow see PARA 783.
3　See the cases cited in note 2.
4　See PARA 771 et seq.
5　*Preston Corpn v Biornstad, The Ratata* [1898] AC 513 at 516, 8 Asp MLC 427 at 428, HL; *The
　Vigilant* [1921] P 312, 15 Asp MLC 337.
6　*The Minnehaha* (1861) Lush 335, PC; *The Robert Dixon* (1879) 5 PD 54, 4 Asp MLC 246, CA;
　*The Maréchal Suchet* [1911] P 1, 11 Asp MLC 553; and see *The Madras* [1898] P 90, 8 Asp MLC
　397. Cf *The Leon Blum* [1915] P 290, 13 Asp MLC 273, CA (where the cargo owners were not
　exempted by a clause in the towage agreement of 'no salvage charges'); and PARA 871.

## 599. Tug ordinarily under control of tow.

In an ordinary contract of towage[1], the tug is under the control of the tow, and must obey the directions given to her by those in charge of the tow[2]. In such a case the tug is not liable if, by reason of these directions, the tow gets into a position of danger[3], but, if without good cause these directions are disobeyed by the tug, and damage ensues to the tow, the tug is liable for any resulting damage and may forfeit her towage remuneration[4]. A tug is not obliged, however, to obey these directions if to do so would threaten the destruction of the vessel towed and endanger lives and property[5]. Although in general the tow should give directions to the tug, the question as to the relation between them is one of fact[6]. The tow is not bound on all occasions to give detailed directions to the tug[7], and, where no directions are given by the tow, it is the duty of the tug to direct the course[8]. It is also always the duty of the tug, although she is controlled by the tow, to look out both for herself and the tow[9].

1　As to special conditions relieving the tug owner see PARA 600.
2　*The Gipsey King* (1847) 5 Notes of Cases 282 at 288; *The Christina* (1848) 3 Wm Rob 27 (affd
　sub nom *Petley v Catto, The Christina* 6 Moo PCC 371); *The Energy* (1870) LR 3 A & E 48; *The
　Robert Dixon* (1879) 5 PD 54, 4 Asp MLC 246, CA; *The Isca* (1886) 12 PD 34, 6 Asp MLC 63;
　*The Niobe* (1888) 13 PD 55, 6 Asp MLC 300. See also *Maridive VII v Key Singapore, The Key
　Singapore* [2004] EWHC 2227 (Comm), [2005] 1 All ER (Comm) 99, [2005] 1 Lloyd's Rep 91,
　where the court held that a review of past decisions emphasised the fact sensitive nature of any
　analysis of the relative responsibilities of tug and tow.
3　*The Robert Dixon* (1879) 5 PD 54, 4 Asp MLC 246, CA.
4　*The Christina* (1848) 3 Wm Rob 27 (affd sub nom *Petley v Catto, The Christina* 6 Moo PCC 371);
　*Spaight v Tedcastle* (1881) 6 App Cas 217, 4 Asp MLC 406, HL.
5　*The Christina* (1848) 3 Wm Rob 27; affd sub nom *Petley v Catto, The Christina* 6 Moo PCC 371.
6　*Devonshire (Owners) v Barge Leslie (Owners)* [1912] AC 634, 12 Asp MLC 210, HL.

7  *The Sinquasi* (1880) 5 PD 241, 4 Asp MLC 383; *The Isca* (1886) 12 PD 34, 6 Asp MLC 63; *Trishna (Owners, Master and Crew) v Panther and Ericbank (Owners), The Panther and The Ericbank* [1957] P 143, [1957] 1 All ER 641, [1957] 1 Lloyd's Rep 57. See further PARA 742.

8  *Smith v St Lawrence Tow-Boat Co* (1873) LR 5 PC 308, 2 Asp MLC 41.

9  *The Jane Bacon* (1878) 27 WR 35, CA.

## 600. Special conditions relieving the tug.

It is competent for a tug by her contract[1] to relieve herself, during the period of towage[2], from any of the ordinary obligations[3] incident to the contract of towage[4]. Where, however, there is any ambiguity in the terms of such relieving conditions, they are strictly construed against the party relying upon them[5]. Moreover, a tug owner may be precluded from relying on an exception clause by his own breach of the contract[6]. Where the cause of the damage complained of is the negligence of himself or his employees, the tug owner cannot rely upon conditions exempting him from liability, if negligence is not expressly excepted[7], and the conditions exempting from liability must be read, unless clear words indicate the contrary intention, as applying only when the tug owner has fulfilled his duty as to the fitness of the tug when the towage service begins[8]. Although, as between the owner of the tug and the owner of the tow, the owner of the tug may by his contract be freed from liability for damage done by a vessel in tow, such a contract does not amount to an indemnity by the owner of the tow against any damages for which the tug has been held liable[9].

1  As to ordinary obligations under a contract of towage see PARAS 597–599.

2  As to the commencement of towage under conditions agreed see *The Clan Colquhoun* [1936] P 153, 54 Ll L Rep 221, sub nom *Port of London Authority v SS Clan Colquhoun (Owners)* [1936] 1 All ER 429 (towage deemed to commence when row rope passed to each of two tugs). As to the meaning of 'when tug in a position to receive orders' in the United Kingdom Standard Towage Conditions see *The Uranienborg* [1936] P 21, 53 Ll L Rep 165 (merely being within hailing distance held insufficient); *Glen Line Ltd v WJ Guy & Sons, The Glenaffric* [1948] P 159, sub nom *WJ Guy & Son (a firm) v Glen Line Ltd* [1948] 1 All ER 245, CA (not necessary for ship to be ready to give orders); *Partafelagid Farmur v Grangemouth and Forth Towing Co Ltd* [1953] 2 Lloyd's Rep 699; *Blenheim (Owners) v Impetus (Owners), The Impetus* [1959] P 111, [1959] 2 All ER 354, [1959] 1 Lloyd's Rep 269 (not necessary for tug to be in position to carry out orders); *The Apollon, British Transport Docks Board v Apollon (Owners)* [1971] 2 All ER 1223, [1971] 1 Lloyd's Rep 476. As to liability under those conditions see *Great Western Rly Co v Royal Norwegian Government* [1945] 1 All ER 324, 78 Ll L Rep 152 (hirer liable for loss of life whilst towing); *Taylor v Geelong Harbour Trust Comrs and Howard Smith Ltd* [1962] 1 Lloyd's Rep 143 (Vict); *Knapp v Port of London Authority and Cory Bros Shipping Ltd* [1977] 1 Lloyd's Rep 662, DC. As to the commencement of 'hiring', and as to when a tug is in 'attendance for purpose of making fast', see *The Ramsden* [1943] P 46, 75 Ll L Rep 86. As to the meaning of 'towage or assistance services' see *The Baltyk* [1948] P 1, [1947] 2 All ER 560, 80 Ll L Rep 668.

3  Liability for death or personal injury resulting from negligence cannot be excluded or restricted in a contract of marine towage: see the Unfair Contract Terms Act 1977 ss 1(2), 2(1), Sch 1 para 2(a); and CONTRACT vol 22 (2012) PARA 416.

4  *The United Service* (1883) 9 PD 3, 5 Asp MLC 170, CA; *The Tasmania* (1888) 13 PD 110, 6 Asp MLC 305; *The Richmond* (1902) 19 TLR 29, DC; and see *The Luna* [1920] P 22, 15 Asp MLC 152 (contract of towage containing an indemnity clause held binding although the master of the tow could not read English). See also *The President Van Buren* (1924) 16 Asp MLC 444; *The Kite* [1933] P 154, 46 Ll L Rep 83. See also *A Turtle Offshore SA v Superior Trading Inc* [2008] EWHC 3034 (Admlty), [2009] 1 Lloyd's Rep 177, [2008] All ER (D) 147 (Dec).

5  *The Forfarshire* [1908] P 339, 11 Asp MLC 158; *The West Cock* [1911] P 208, 12 Asp MLC 57, CA, following *Waikato (Cargo Owners) v New Zealand Shipping Co* [1899] 1 QB 56 at 58, 8 Asp MLC 442, CA; *Rathbone Bros & Co v D MacIver Sons & Co* [1903] 2 KB 378 at 384, 9 Asp MLC 467 at 469, CA; *Elderslie Steamship Co v Borthwick* [1905] AC 93 at 96, 10 Asp MLC 24 at 26, HL; *Nelson Line (Liverpool) Ltd v James Nelson & Sons Ltd* [1908] AC 16 at 19, 20, 10 Asp MLC 581 at 583, HL. If tug owners desire to put upon the tow the liability for damage to the tug, they must do so in clear and unambiguous language: see *Emily Charlotte v Newona* (1920) 4 Ll L Rep 156 at 158 per Hill J.

6   See *The Albion, France, Fenwick and Tyne and Wear Co Ltd v Swan Hunter and Wigham Richardson Ltd* [1953] 2 All ER 679, sub nom *Swan Hunter and Wigham Richardson Ltd v France, Fenwick Tyne & Wear Co Ltd, The Albion* [1953] 1 WLR 1026, [1953] 2 Lloyd's Rep 82, CA.

7   *The Forfarshire* [1908] P 339, 11 Asp MLC 158.

8   *The Undaunted* (1886) 11 PD 46, 5 Asp MLC 580; *The West Cock* [1911] P 208, 12 Asp MLC 57, CA; and see the cases cited in note 5. See also *The Millwall* [1905] P 155, 10 Asp MLC 110, 113, CA; *The Adriatic* (1915) 85 LJP 12; *The Cap Palos* [1921] P 458, 15 Asp MLC 403, CA (where a clause giving the tug owner exemption from liability for negligence etc covered only default during the actual performance of the duties of the contract, and not an unjustified handing over of those obligations to someone else for performance). This principle was applied in *The Refrigerant* [1925] P 130, 16 Asp MLC 559 (where the master of the tug gave up trying to perform the contract in the way contemplated by the parties).

9   *The Richmond* (1902) 19 TLR 29, DC; and see *The Devonshire and The St Winifred* [1913] P 13, 12 Asp MLC 314. See also *The Carlton* [1931] P 186, 18 Asp MLC 240 (where an indemnity clause was held only to affect third party claims), approved in *The Lindenhall* [1945] P 8, CA; *Det Forenede Dampskibs Selskab v Barry Rly Co* (1919) 1 Ll L Rep 658 (where an indemnity clause was held not to cover damage done to the tug owner's property through the negligence of the tug).

   As to collision, and as to the requirements to avoid it, when under tow see PARAS 713–714, 742–743, 783–784; and as to the application of a contract of indemnity where several craft were in tow, and as to costs, see *The Riverman* [1928] P 33, 17 Asp MLC 344.

# INDEX

# Shipping and Maritime Law

**References are to paragraph numbers; superior figures refer to notes**

**References are to paragraph numbers; superior figures refer to notes**

**References are to paragraph numbers; superior figures refer to notes**

**References are to paragraph numbers; superior figures refer to notes**

**References are to paragraph numbers; superior figures refer to notes**

**References are to paragraph numbers; superior figures refer to notes**

**References are to paragraph numbers; superior figures refer to notes**

**References are to paragraph numbers; superior figures refer to notes**

PILOTAGE—*continued*
services, provision of 576
PIRACY
cooperation required as to 33
offence, as maritime 1186
PLEASURE VESSEL
provisions for 612
safety—
code of practice—
equivalent provisions outside
regulations and code 615
large vessels 613
small vessels 614
equivalent provisions outside
regulations and code 615
general regulations 35
offences 616
power to detain 616
provisions for 612
PORT STATE CONTROL
anomalies, duty to report 682
complaints 683
detention—
deficiencies, in case of 680
prohibition against entering UK
ports if repairs needed 681
EU ports, shipping using—
application of provisions 678
detention—
deficiencies, in case of 680
inspection—
*meaning* 679
deficiencies, rectification and
detention in case of 680
prohibition against entering UK ports
if repairs needed 681
PROHIBITION NOTICE
contents and effect of 53
generally 52
invalid notice, compensation for 55
offence, contravention as 1178
references of notices to arbitration 54
RECEIVER OF WRECK
appointment of 929
claims of owners to wrecks in
possession of 949
duty to notify receiver, failure as
to 1160
notification of wreck, duties and
powers on 936
ownership of items, investigations as
to 60
power of entry 940
sale of wreck, powers as to 956

RECEIVER OF WRECK—*continued*
salvage powers of—
apportionment of reward 902
receiver of wreck, powers of 919
sale of detained property, as to 920
valuation of property, as to 887
taking possession of wreck, duty to
give notice on 937
unclaimed—
Crown's right to 950
disposal after one year of 952
notice to persons entitled to 951
RECREATIONAL CRAFT
safety regulations as to 35
REGISTRAR GENERAL OF SHIPPING
AND SEAMEN
*meaning* 62
appointment and removal of 62
crew list, failure as to delivery of 556,
1088
registration of merchant ship—
documents to be retained 297
fees payable to registrar 379
supplementary information required
by registrar 372
SAFETY
recreational craft, safety regulations as
to 35
terrorism, prevention of 34
SALVAGE (MARITIME)
*meaning* 849
arbitral awards—
publication of 922
reward, as to 918
claims—
aircraft, in respect of 114
jurisdiction, extent of 113
limitation period 154
contract—
application of Salvage
Convention 853
Lloyd's Open Form: meaning 853
Crown—
claims against 854
rights of 854
humanitarian cargoes, prohibition
against seizure of 921
jurisdiction 113, 852
life. *See* LIFE SALVAGE
Lloyd's Open Form: meaning 853
operations—
*meaning* 850
co-operation, obligations as to 859
duty to render assistance 858
master, duties of 856

**References are to paragraph numbers; superior figures refer to notes**

**References are to paragraph numbers; superior figures refer to notes**

**References are to paragraph numbers; superior figures refer to notes**

**References are to paragraph numbers; superior figures refer to notes**